The Ultimate Idaho
Atlas and Travel Encyclopedia

First Edition

Written and compiled by
Kristin E. Hill

Graphics, Maps, and Layout by
Elizabeth Dougherty

Ultimate Press

RIVERBEND
PUBLISHING

an *Ultimate*® Guide Book

Copyright © 2005 Michael Dougherty

Published by Riverbend Publishing, Helena, Montana

ISBN 10: 1-931832-82-X

ISBN 13: 978-1-931832-82-3

Printed in the U.S.A.

1 2 3 4 5 6 7 8 9 MG 15 14 13 12 11 10 09 08 07

Written, designed and produced by:

Ultimate Press

an imprint of Champions Publishing, Inc.

301 Evergreen, Suite 201D
Bozeman, Montana 59715
Phone: 406-585-0237
Website: www.ultimateidaho.com

For advertising inquiries and editorial comments, please contact Ultimate Press at the address above.

For book sales, please contact:

RIVERBEND PUBLISHING

PO Box 5833
Helena, MT 59604
Phone toll-free: 1-866-787-2363
Fax: 1-406-449-0330
Email: info@riverbendpublishing.com
Website: www.RiverbendPublishing.com

Cover Photos:

Fishing photo courtesy of Mile High Outfitters, Challis
Whitewater photo courtesy of Idaho Adventures, Salmon
All other photos by Michael Dougherty

CONTENTS

ACKNOWLEDGMENT

We offer a sincere thank you to all of the sponsors who, without their financial support, this book would not have been possible. Throughout the book, you'll see their names in bold. Stop in and see them when you're in their area. They would like to hear from you.

DISCLAIMER

This guide focuses on recreational activities including traveling to some sites that are off the more frequently traveled roads. As all such activities contain elements of risk, the publisher, author, affiliated individuals and companies included in this guide disclaim any responsibility for any injury, harm, or illness that may occur to anyone through, or by use of, the information in this book. Although the author and publisher have made every effort to ensure that the information was correct at the time of going to press, the author and publisher do not assume and hereby disclaim any liability to any party for any loss or damage to person or property caused by errors, omissions, or any potential travel disruption due to labor or financial difficulty, whether such errors or omissions result from negligence, accident, or any other cause.

Throughout this book, public domain documents of government agencies (National Park Service, U.S.D.A. Forest Service, Bureau of Land Management, and Idaho State Wildlife, Fish and Parks) were reprinted. Also, brochures published by local area chambers of commerce and from the various attractions were reprinted in part or in their entirety. Permissions were obtained where required.

IDAHO
THE GEM STATE

Welcome to Idaho

THE GEM STATE

Idaho – a state rich with history, phenomenal scenery, and legendary hospitality! Flanked by the lush Pacific Northwest and the rugged western slopes of the Rocky Mountains, Idaho is situated halfway between the Equator and the North Pole. Over 83,000 square miles of wildly diverse terrain allows Idaho to produce some of the world's most precious stones, a fact that granted the state its nickname. For some, the epithet comes as a shock. After all, Idaho's license plates advertise the state's historically bumper crops of spuds. So the state's nickname isn't "The Potato State"? Thank goodness, no. Are the potatoes still famous? Overwhelmingly, yes. Is that all Idaho has to offer? Definitely not!

Those traveling through America's fourteenth largest state will quickly discover that Idaho's most precious commodity is the landscape itself. Bordered by Montana and Wyoming on the east, Utah and Nevada to the south, Oregon and Washington on the west, and Canada's British Columbia to the north, every region of the state offers its own natural wonders. Thundering waterfalls, towering mountains, pristine lakes, raging rivers, shadowy forests, velvety plains, rolling farmland, geothermal phenomena, desert plateaus, and volcanic craters paint one of America's most awe-inspiring masterpieces.

Although Idaho often stands in the shadow of its popular neighboring states, the Gem State demands just as much respect for its natural treasures. Between hosting the continental U.S.' largest unspoiled backcountry area in the 2.3 million-acre Frank Church-River of No Return Wilderness and North America's deepest river gorge at Hells Canyon, Idaho is also home to the continent's tallest single structured sand dune and the largest population of nesting raptors. Land lovers will find that Idaho is the most mountainous of all Rocky Mountain States as over eighty recognized

ranges pierce the crisp azure skies and soar to a maximum height of 12,662 feet. At the lower end of the elevation spectrum, the Owyhee Canyonlands and Craters of the Moon provide respective glimpses into the isolated nature of silent deserts and twisted volcanic remains. Water worshippers are greeted with 3,100 winding river miles (the nation's most!) and the ever-present Snake River, while the legendary Salmon River is distinguished as America's longest free-flowing tributary beginning and ending within a single state. As an added bonus, Idaho's 2,000+ blue water jewels allow the state to claim the American West's greatest concentration of lakes.

It's no wonder, then, that the forty-third state to enter the union is a place that beckons new discovery. Nearly every geological formation known on Earth can be found in Idaho, and recreation abounds year-round. Extraordinary? Yes, but that's to be expected in a state that widened early explorers' eyes with pure reverence. For those willing to join the ranks of adventurous voyagers and look beyond Idaho's agricultural fame, the Gem State offers a treasure trove of uncrowded expanses and unparalleled beauty worth its weight in gold. Discover Idaho for yourself, and unearth the gem that it really is!

NATURAL HISTORY

Drawing its name from the Native American word "idahow" meaning "gem of the mountains" or "sun coming down the mountains," Idaho and its mountains and distinctive landscape have spanned the millennia. Sediment layers on the state's rocky bluffs provide testimony to minerals and rocks deposited across hundreds of thousands of years, and fossils scattered throughout both northern and southern Idaho clearly indicate that the land was once a tropical paradise. In fact, Idaho is home to some of America's finest preserved fossil

remains of ancient leaves, insects, fish, and mammals, including Bald Cypress, Chinese Pine, Fir, Redwood, zebras, and camels.

In more recent geological terms, Idaho has been the subject of dramatic upheaval and catastrophic natural events that shaped the state into its present form. Between 15,000 and 20,000 years ago, North America's once largest lake encompassed over 20,000 square miles of Idaho and Utah territory. Formed in a basin in the state's southeastern corner, Lake Bonneville cradled massive amounts of water within its bowl while the natural rock dam at Red Rock Pass ensured that no water escaped to the Pacific Ocean. As the earth's plates beneath Idaho's crust began to shift, volcanic eruptions and violent magma explosions forced the lake over its dam and created the world's second largest known flood. In this massive draining process, Idaho's Snake River channel was carved, and the hanging valleys characteristic of southeastern Idaho took shape.

As the volcanoes continued to erupt and magma snaked across the land to create cinder cones, craters, and twisted lava formations, North America's glaciers were also sculpting Idaho's terrain. As recently as 10,000 years ago, glaciers chiseled the mountains, carved U-shaped valleys and hundreds of alpine cirques, and deposited fields of boulders in their wake. Earthquakes aided the glacial

IDAHO AT A GLANCE

Population (2000): 1,321,006

Entered union: July 3, 1890

Capital: Boise

Nickname: Gem State

Motto: "Esto perpetua" (Let it be Perpetual)

Bird: Mountain Bluebird

Flower: Syringa

Song: "Here We Have Idaho"

Stones: Idaho Star Garnet

Tree: Western White Pine

Animal: Apaloosa Horse

Fish: Cutthroat Trout

Fossil: Hagerman Horse Fossil

Land area: 83,574 square miles

Size ranking: 14th

Geographic center: Custer County on the Yankee Fork River, southwest of Challis

Length: 630 miles

Width: 280 miles

Highest point: 12,662 feet (Borah Peak)

Lowest point: 710 feet (Snake River)

Highest temperature: 118 deg. on July 28, 1934, at Orofino

Lowest temperature: -60 deg. on Jan. 16, 1943, at Island Park Dam

COWBOY WAVE

Idaho features many rural areas, and like rural areas in other states, Idaho is pretty friendly to most who care to be friendly back. When you're traveling the back roads, particularly the gravel roads, you'll encounter a variety of waves from passing pickups and motorists.

The most common is the one finger wave, accomplished by simply raising the first finger (not the middle finger as is common in other states) from the steering wheel. If the driver is otherwise occupied with his hands or if it is a fairly rough road, you may get a light head nod. Occasionally, you may get a two finger wave which often appears as a modified peace sign if the passerby is having a particularly good day. On rare occasions, you may get an all out wave.

The most important things is that whatever wave you get, be sure and wave back.

Breadloaves Rock is just one of the unique features found in the City of Rocks.

activity, lowering the elevation of valley floors and forcing jagged mountain peaks to thrust even higher.

Today, geologists rush to study Idaho's granite batholith complex situated in the center of the state. The massive rock creation formed during a series of volcanic events, and the "veins" in the rock contain vast deposits of gold, silver, lead, zinc, copper, cobalt, star garnets, topaz, jasper, and other precious minerals and stones that give Idaho its appropriate nickname.

Although the state's geological formations appear stable and relatively static to the untrained eye, Idaho's terrain continuously provides evidence of the planet's powerful capabilities. Magma oozed from the Earth's core at Craters of the Moon just 2,000 years ago, and Idaho is often recognized as one of America's most geologically active regions. Such changes may seem invisible today, but Idaho's landscape is constantly in motion and will continue to erode, evolve, and take new shape until the end of time.

IDAHO'S LAND & CLIMATE

Topographic Features

Measuring 479 miles long and 305 miles wide, Idaho spans seven latitudinal and six longitudinal degrees that provide the state with a complex and spectacular topography. Although the state's mean elevation is 5,000 feet, the highest elevation climbs to 12,662 feet at Mount Borah while Lewiston's famous Snake River seaport rests at a mere 710 feet above sea level. More than 40% of the state's 82,751 square land miles is forested (distinguishing it as the Rocky Mountain's most heavily forested state), and Idaho boasts fifty mountain peaks that climb over 10,000 feet. Amid the 823 square miles of Idaho cloaked in water, individuals will find 16,000 miles of streams, 2,000+ lakes, and nearly 239,000 acres of reservoirs. Due to Idaho's size and location, the state is divided into two time zones. Those traveling through the northern panhandle are treated to Pacific Standard Time while the rest of the state sets its clocks to Mountain Standard Time.

With such varied elevations, each region of Idaho offers its own topographic wonders. Idaho's northern panhandle is instantly recognized for its legendary lakes, velvet green valleys, and pristine forests reminiscent of its lush Pacific Northwest neighbors. The Coeur d'Alene, Selkirk, Cabinet, and Purcell Mountain Ranges are also residents

here. Rising above the Idaho Panhandle National Forest and peeking their heads into the clouds, these mountains frame the region's lakes in a stunning palette of swirling blues and greens.

Slightly south of the panhandle, north-central Idaho blooms in blue on the Camas Prairie, while the rolling Palouse hills and fertile farmland stand in stark contrast to the Seven Devils Mountains' granite spires and the Hells Canyon Wilderness Area. Farther east, additional backcountry awaits in the Selway-Bitterroot and Gospel Hump Wilderness Areas. Placid rivers and churning whitewater zigzag across the region, and the Snake, Salmon, Clearwater, Lochsa, Selway, and Potlatch Rivers combine to provide north-central Idaho with the state's greatest concentration of exhilarating rapids.

Southwestern Idaho is perhaps one of the most diverse regions in the entire state. From its pastoral valleys to high desert plateaus to alpine lakes, this section of Idaho offers something for everyone. Running through the region's heart and dividing the area into two distinct topographic zones, the Snake River welcomes the convergence of the Payette and Boise Rivers. South of the river, the Snake River Plain is dotted with irrigated farmland and famous fruit orchards ripe with color and regional flavor. Heading towards the Nevada border, the Owyhee, Jarbidge, and Bruneau Rivers whittle impressive canyons through the isolated desert terrain as sand dunes rise 470 feet on the horizon. North of the Snake River, agricultural valleys gradually meld into the Payette and Boise National Forests. Lakes rest in bowls of snow-capped mountains, and elevations rise the closer one moves towards central Idaho.

Regarded as one of Mother Nature's most dramatic creations, the high country of central Idaho is marked with mountain grandeur. The craggy peaks of the White Cloud and Boulder Mountains ascend majestically amid the Sawtooth National Forest, and the jagged teeth of the Sawtooth Mountains dominate the 756,000-acre Sawtooth National Recreation Area. To the northeast, mountains continue to reign supreme as Idaho's highest elevation rests at the summit of Mount Borah in the Lost River Range. Nearby, the Lemhi Range and Beaverhead Mountains cradle a portion of the Challis and Salmon National Forests. North-central Idaho is more than just extreme mountain

splendor, though. As with other regions in the state, natural hot springs boil and bubble, and the Salmon River curls and crashes. Further south, the uninhabited lava flows, craters, and cinder cones of Craters of the Moon shroud the landscape in a veil of oddity.

The lava flows of Craters of the Moon continue into south-central Idaho. North of the Snake River, hardened basalt gray of yesteryear's volcanic activity intermingles with red dirt and sagebrush prairie to form an eerie reminder of Idaho's violent geological history. Ice caves, lava tubes, and the rugged remains of cooled magma eventually transform into spring-lined canyons and majestic waterfalls as the Snake River provides irrigation to the Magic Valley. The flat area lying directly south of the Snake River is home to some of America's richest farmland, and a cornucopia of crops are annually produced. Standing in juxtaposition with this fertility are high desert plateaus and the intriguing City of Rocks strewn with boulders.

Eastern Idaho welcomes visitors with the quieter side of the Grand Teton Mountains, and the Targhee National Forest shades the Idaho/Wyoming stateline with a border of towering trees and drastic elevation changes. The region also features a volcanic caldera, thundering waterfalls, and remote alpine lakes. Flowing throughout the region, the Henry's Fork and the main branch of the Snake River wind freely near fields of potatoes and sugar beets.

Mounds of potato blossoms extend into southeastern Idaho, and the Snake River makes its presence known once again as it flows towards the Snake River Plain. 47,000 acres of waving prairie grass highlight the region's Curlew National Grassland, while the neighboring Caribou and Cache-Wasatch National Forests provide stunning scenery, lush valley floors, and timbered peaks. Water abounds in the region, from the Malad, Portneuf, and Bear Rivers to Bear Lake, Blackfoot Reservoir, and American Falls Reservoir. A welcome sight to Oregon Trail pioneers, the region's naturally warm, carbonated springs spark intrigue to this day.

Flora and Fauna

With its extremes in both elevation and topography, the Gem State is home to widely divergent vegetation and wildlife. Northern Idaho's moist,

cool climate is ideal for supporting large stands of grand fir, western red cedar, western hemlock, western white pine, and the Pacific yew. Many of Idaho's largest and oldest trees can be found here. At the state's highest elevations, Engelmann spruce, subalpine fir, mountain hemlock, quaking aspen, lodgepole pine, subalpine larch, whitebark pine, and limber pine flourish. Douglas fir and ponderosa pine line several of Idaho's highways, while cottonwoods and weeping willows stand guard along the state's many riverbanks. At the lowest elevations, sagebrush, bitterbrush, and a variety of juniper species intermingle with box elder, bigtooth maple trees, and chokecherry and serviceberry bushes.

Idaho's wildlife is just as diverse as the flora that blankets the state's landscape with color and texture. Woodland caribou, grizzly bears, and wolves are among Idaho's most endangered species. Mountain lions, black bears, bobcats, and Canadian lynx are known to roam throughout Idaho's mountains, and a host of raptors, including bald eagles, cast their shadow against Idaho's sunset splendor. Harboring a less aggressive nature, mountain goats, wild horses, bighorn sheep, white-tailed deer, elk, mule deer, and moose are joined by beavers, marmots, pikas, and river otters. With its many rivers, Idaho also possesses an abundant fish population that includes salmon, an array of trout species, sturgeon, and several varieties of warm-water fish.

Weather

Idaho enjoys a four-season climate, but weather patterns across the state vary drastically from region to region. Idaho is fortunate enough to escape the path of destructive hurricanes, and tornadoes are extremely rare. Hail damage during summer storms is also often insignificant, and on average, the entire state receives an abundant amount of sunshiny days each year with relatively low humidity.

Although the highest temperature recorded in the state was a scorching 118 degrees Fahrenheit in 1934 and the lowest a teeth-chattering, bone-biting minus 60 degrees in 1943, the state's temperatures generally avoid such extremes. On average, the state's monthly temperatures range from a maximum high of 90.6 degrees to a low of 15.1 degrees Fahrenheit. During all seasons, however, the state's weather patterns can change suddenly. Travelers should be prepared at all times for a variety of conditions, especially in the state's higher elevations and backcountry areas.

Pacific weather patterns moderate temperature extremes in Idaho's panhandle, and as expected, the region enjoys a typical Pacific Northwest climate. Summers are usually clear and dry with daytime highs reaching just 80 degrees. Mild, wet storms flowing off the Pacific Ocean bring a mixture of clouds, rain, and snow during winter. In some years, the area receives more than sixty inches of annual rainfall.

North-central Idaho's numerous river canyons and lower elevations provide the region with the state's warmest temperatures. Towns situated in the canyon floors receive very little wind, and summer temperatures frequently soar over 100 degrees Fahrenheit. Although such heat might sound unappealing, the region receives the perk of over 200 growing season days per year, winter temperatures that rarely, if ever, dip below freezing, and the arrival of an early spring. Those towns situated at a higher elevation on north central Idaho's prairie also enjoy fairly warm winters, but summer temperatures tend to hover in the 80 degree range.

Southwestern Idaho's elevations range from just 2,000 feet above sea level at the Snake River to more than 5,000 feet in the mountainous region encompassing McCall and Cascade. The low-lying valleys surrounding the region's main rivers often receive their fair share of hot summer days with fairly mild winters. Boise and its neighboring cities report below freezing temperatures only during December and January. In fact, the Snake River Plain south of Boise historically records an average annual mean temperature of 55 degrees Fahrenheit. Father north, the region's residents are treated to four distinct seasons. Higher elevations create cooler temperatures year-round in McCall, and the area also records the state's highest average snowfall.

Much of the mountainous region comprising central Idaho's high country boasts elevations well above 6,000 feet. Such high elevations translate into nearly perfect summer days, but winters are long and filled with plenty of days where the mercury dips below freezing. Stanley, in fact, boasts the state's lowest average temperature, reading in at just over 35 degrees Fahrenheit! Spring comes late, summers are generally dry, and winters provide hundreds of inches of powder. Outside the scenic mecca of Salmon, Stanley, and Sun Valley, the region's eastern side experiences much warmer temperatures and near desert conditions with virtually no precipitation.

South-central Idaho's landscape averages extremely warm summer temperatures with daytime highs in the low 90s. Winter temperatures tend to hover between 20 and 40 degrees. Freezing temperatures generally occur just between December and February, and the area's heaviest precipitation comes in the form of May showers.

Henry's Lake

Situated farthest away from the Pacific moisture affecting the rest of the state, eastern Idaho receives the remnants of storms pushing out from the west, cold fronts moving south from Canada, and weather flows extending north from the Gulf of Mexico. As the hub of such forces, eastern Idaho's weather is the exact opposite of that in the panhandle and lower western elevations. The region experiences the widest variation in seasonal temperatures, spring and summer pack along afternoon thunderstorms and drenching rainstorms, and winters generally produce the state's finest and lightest powder due to extremely cold temperatures.

Southeastern Idaho's climate nearly mimics that of eastern Idaho. Spring and summer visitors should pack along an umbrella in preparation for some of the state's most spectacular displays of lightning, thunder, and refreshing rain.

THE HISTORY OF IDAHO'S PEOPLE

Ancient Inhabitants
Long before the arrival of mountain men, westward expansionists, miners, and farmers, Idaho housed indigenous tribes who thrived upon the region's diverse topography and wildlife populations. Archaeological findings in south-central Idaho indicate that nomadic hunters wandered the state's expansive terrain as early as 13,000 B.C. Arrowheads, spears, rock shelters lined with petroglyphs, and remnants of long-extinct horse, camel, and sloth species have been carbon-dated to 12,500 B.C. Based upon such findings, many archaeologists believe America's first residents resided in Idaho and passed their bloodline onto the region's Native American inhabitants.

Native Americans
The total combined population of Idaho's Native American inhabitants has never been significantly large, but Idaho's history remains interwoven with the tribes who were dependent upon the region for survival. Prior to the arrival of horses in 1700, most of Idaho's Native American tribes maintained a solitary life. As a result, conflict was kept at bay, and encounters between different tribes were purposeful intertribal powwows, social gatherings, and religious ceremonies.

The Kootenai, a distant relation of the eastern Algonquin tribe, migrated through British Columbia and the Pacific Northwest before planting roots in Idaho's panhandle. The abundant rivers in the region supplied the Kootenai with salmon and sturgeon while the tribe's hunters preyed upon caribou, deer, and elk. The lush forests and valleys of this Idaho region further supplied the tribe with an array of berries and wild vegetables and roots.

Residing slightly south of their Kootenai neighbors, the Nez Perce tribe claimed Idaho's Clearwater Valley as its beloved home. The river contained abundant salmon, and the valley was home to a plethora of bears, bighorn sheep, deer, elk, and moose that provided nearly all of the tribe's food and shelter requirements. In addition, the area featured numerous camas bulbs critical in supplying the tribe with ingredients for traditional tribal recipes.

The remote deserts and canyons now found within southwestern Idaho's Owyhee Canyonlands served as home territory for the Shoshone and Paiute tribes. These small nomadic tribes were known for their peaceful nature as they scoured the land in pursuit of deer, antelope, rabbits, squirrels, prairie dogs, and upland birds. On rare occasions, the tribes were lucky enough to add seeds, berries, and pine nuts to their traditionally meaty diet.

The Shoshone people also lived in harmony among south-central and southeastern Idaho's Bannock tribes. Despite maintaining different languages, the hunting lifestyle of both tribes and similar home turf bonded the groups together in peace.

The territory of all Idaho tribes expanded greatly with the introduction of horses. The pack animal provided Idaho's Native Americans with mobility they had never experienced and opened up travel to annual buffalo hunts in present-day Montana and Wyoming. This increased mobility and greed for horses came with a price, however. Conflicts over Native American hunting grounds became more frequent, and tribal warfare over stolen horses occasionally occurred. The 1800s introduction of guns to the traditional Native American lifestyle further complicated tribal relations.

At the same time power struggles were escalating between tribes, the painful tale of Native American encounters with America's expansionist legacy began to take its toll on Idaho's tribes. Although just four percent of Oregon Trail emigrant deaths in Idaho were the result of Indian skirmishes, the region's tribes were painted as violent heathens who deserved justice at the hands of the U.S. military. After the 1854 Ward Massacre and 1860 Otter-Van Orman Massacre where Idaho's tribes revolted against dwindling food supplies and desecration of traditional hunting grounds and sacred places, the U.S. government intervened. The military carried out one of the American West's most horrendous and senseless slaughters of Native Americans in southeastern Idaho's 1863 Battle of Bear River. The bloodbath only fueled the growing Native American/white conflict, resulting in further negative encounters with white pioneers and eventually instigating the unprecedented Nez Perce War of 1877.

After years of treaty talks, the American government ordered all Nez Perce onto Idaho's Lapwai Reservation by June 1877. Outraged at the demand and angered by a history of Native American abuse at the hands of whites, the non-treaty bands of Chief Joseph, White Bird, and Looking Glass fled the region with 750 men, women, and children in tow. During their 1,700-mile retreat toward an attempted safe haven in Canada, the Nez Perce fought over 2,000 U.S. soldiers and proved themselves as brave and skillful fighters. Environmental conditions, however, eventually took their toll on the young and old. Just forty miles shy of the Canadian border at Bear's Paw, Chief Joseph analyzed the dire situation of his cold, starving people and surrendered on October 6, 1877. Looking Glass was killed when he attempted to escape to Canada, but White Bird and a small band managed to evade the U.S. troops in the shadow of night and successfully crossed the border.

As a result of the conflict, Chief Joseph and his followers were sent to Washington's Colville Reservation, and the tribal members of Chief Looking Glass and White Bird were relegated back to Idaho's Lapwai Reservation. Although Joseph continually petitioned the U.S. government for permission to return to his beloved Wallowa Valley homeland, Congress denied every request. He was forced to remain brokenhearted on the reservation until his September 21, 1904 death.

The tragedy of the Nez Perce War, however, extended far deeper than the U.S. taxpayer cost of $1,873,410.43 and the destiny of the Nez Perce tribe. The conflict also reinforced the American government's belief in the necessity of reservation lands. As in other western states, Idaho's first inhabitants were forced onto reservations where boundaries were continually decreased to make room for American homesteading policies.

Today, the Coeur d'Alene Reservation rests on the southern shores of Lake Coeur d'Alene; the Fort Hall Reservation near Pocatello is home to the Shoshone-Bannock tribe; the Shoshone-Paiute tribes were forced onto the Idaho/Nevada Duck Valley Reservation; and the Nez Perce Reservation remains in the heart of north-central Idaho. The only tribe not forced onto its own reservation was

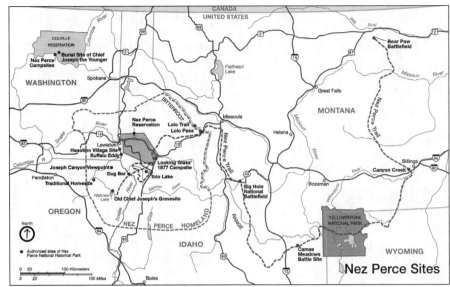
Nez Perce Sites

the Kootenai. Despite governmental promises to provide all tribes with substantial economic aid, such pledges were never honored. In addition to minimal federal funding, Idaho's current tribal members rely upon the gaming industry to fight the reservations' widespread poverty.

Lewis and Clark Discover Idaho

Designated by President Thomas Jefferson and receiving U.S. governmental funds for their duties, twenty-six-year-old, Meriwether Lewis, and thirty-year-old, William Clark, were selected in 1803 to find a route linking the Missouri River to the Pacific Ocean. After spending the winter of 1803-1804 gathering supplies and a team of forty knowledgeable members, Lewis and Clark set out in May 1804 on what would become one of America's most legendary journeys.

Recognized and revered as the Corp of Discovery, the group of men left their St. Louis headquarters and headed west into previously uncharted territory. The Corp moved upstream, traveling up to a maximum of twenty-five miles per day when wind speeds allowed and favorable weather conditions permitted. The group of explorers faced many trials and tribulations as they wandered through present-day Nebraska, Iowa, South Dakota, North Dakota, and Montana, but the Corp persevered.

Finally, over a year after the journey's onset, the Corp of Discovery crossed the Continental Divide at Lemhi Pass on August 12, 1805 and became the first white Americans to set foot in present-day Idaho. Upon crossing over the Divide, the group continued west with the navigational and translational aid of native Idahoan, Sacajawea. The area Native Americans embraced the explorers and provided useful tips as the Corp planned its next route west. Although the group had planned to navigate the Lemhi and Salmon Rivers, they discovered upon scouting that the rivers were simply impassable. Instead, the group was forced to cross the Continental Divide two more times as they crested Lost Trail Pass into present-day Montana and then crossed over Lolo Pass back into Idaho.

The group's next encounter with Idaho's Native Americans resulted in the same warm hospitality they received upon their initial entry into the region. The group relied upon the support and well wishes of the Nez Perce, and Lewis and Clark established hunting camps near present day Orofino and Ahsaka. Naming one of these camps

"Canoe Camp," the men pooled their time, resources, and work ethic to fashion sturdy canoes that would transport them to the Pacific Ocean. On October 6, 1805, the group's canoes were finished, and they set sail on the final leg of their great American journey. After enduring months of stormy winter weather, meager provisions, and scarce hunting prospects, the explorers finally made it to their destination. On November 18, 1805, Lewis and Clark's Corp of Discovery set eyes on the convergence of the Columbia River with the Pacific Ocean. The group had successfully fulfilled its mission, complete with extensive journals, maps, and tales that would satisfy even the most discriminating audience.

The group wintered along the shores of the Pacific Ocean and began their return journey on March 23, 1806. Following a nearly identical route east, the Corp proceeded back through Idaho, relying upon the help of their Native American friends to navigate Idaho's treacherous mountain ranges. Six months later, on September 23, 1806, the explorers finally concluded their adventure in St. Louis much to the shock and great relief of their supporters.

Today, the route the explorers first followed over Lemhi Pass into Idaho is maintained as the Lewis and Clark National Backcountry Byway. The Corp's routes over Lost Trail Pass and Lolo Pass are marked with Visitor Centers at the respective Idaho/Montana borders on U.S. Highway 93 and U.S. Highway 12.

The Arrival of Fur Trappers, Traders, and Mountain Men

Upon the successful completion of Lewis and Clark's westward journey, British and American fur companies jumped on the exploration bandwagon and headed west to survey potential ground for their expanding businesses. David Thompson, working for Britain's Hudson's Bay Company, entered Idaho from Canada in 1808 along with his wife and children. Working as a geographer, Thompson surveyed the surrounding region before finally settling in Idaho's panhandle. In September 1809, Thompson constructed a regional trade center at the Kullyspell House near present-day Hope. He successfully traded with the Flathead, Nez Perce, and Blackfeet Indians, sold numerous beaver pelts to London's fashion elite, and used his log trading post as the base for further Pacific Northwest exploration before migrating to Canada in 1812.

Jaded at the thought of an Englishman making such successful waves in the industry, the Missouri Fur Company ordered company partner, Andrew Henry, to stake an American claim in a region that was growing quite lucrative. Henry followed orders, and in autumn of 1810, he and a small group of comrades began their journey. After crossing over the Continental Divide, Henry discovered a scenic lake (a lake now bearing his name) in present-day eastern Idaho and designated it as an ideal winter camp. Henry, however, was not prepared for the region's harsh winters, and a lack of prey further complicated the group's situation. Forced to either starve to death or eat their transportation, Henry and his men chose to cook up their horses one by one in a desperate attempt to survive the 1810-1811 winter. Once spring arrived, Henry abandoned his company's fur trading dreams and returned to civilized life in St. Louis.

Andrew Henry's ill fortune in Idaho, however, did not deter others from enthusiastically heading

Couer d'Alene

IDAHO MOVIES

Although Idaho is far-removed from the drama of Hollywood, the state has a long history of film appearances. Idaho's striking scenery and diverse landscape have provided the state with a starring role in a wide range of movies, television shows, and commercials, and renowned directors and actors frequently look to the region for inspiration. Whether you've actually set foot in Idaho, you've no doubt already discovered its unique terrain while watching the following movies that were filmed here:

2004: *Napoleon Dynamite* (Preston)

2003: *Peluca* (Preston)

2001: *Hemmingway: The Hunter of Death* (Ketchum); *Shredder* (Kellogg); *Tattoo: A Love Story* (Boise); *Town & Country* (Sun Valley)

1999: *Breakfast of Champions* (Twin Falls)

1998: *Smoke Signals* (Coeur d'Alene Indian Reservation); *Wild Wild West* (Pierce)

1997: *Dante's Peak* (Wallace); *Vanishing Pond* (Riddle)

1995: *White Wolves II: Legend of the Wild* (Island Park/Henry's Fork of the Snake River/Targhee National Forest)

1992: *Dark Horse* (Wood River Valley)

1991: *Talent for the Game* (Genessee)

1990: *Ghost Dad* (Boise)

1988: *Moving* (Boise)

1985: *Pale Rider* (Sawtooth National Recreation Area)

1980: *Bronco Billy* (Boise/Garden City/Meridian/Nampa); *Heaven's Gate* (Wallace); *Powder Heads* (Sun Valley)

1976: *Breakheart Pass* (Lewiston)

1973: *Idaho Transfer* (Arco/Craters of the Moon)

1965: *Ski Party* (Sun Valley)

1957: *Luci-Desi Comedy Hour Episode "Lucy Goes to Sun Valley"* (Sun Valley; aired April 14, 1958)

1956: *Bus Stop* (near Ketchum)

1955: *Miracle of Todd-AO* (Sun Valley)

1947: *The Unconquered* (Falls River/North Fork of the Snake River)

1941: *A Woman's Face* (Sun Valley); *Sun Valley Serenade* (Ketchum/Sun Valley)

1940: *Northwest Passage* (McCall/Sandpoint/Payette Lake); *The Mortal Storm* (Sun Valley)

1937: *I Met Him in Paris* (Sun Valley)

1931: *Believe It or Not* (Coeur d'Alene)

1926: *Snowed In* (McCall)

1925: *The Tornado* (St. Maries)

1923: *The Grub Stake* (Coolin); *Little Dramas of Big Places* (Priest Lake)

1922: *Miss Lewiston* (Lewiston)

1919: *Told in the Hills* (Priest Lake)

1915: *The Cowpuncher* (Idaho Falls)

---

to the region. In October 1811, Wilson Price Hunt led an expedition of John Jacob Astor's Pacific Fur Company across the Grand Tetons to Henry's abandoned lakefront fort. The men then decided to speed along their journey with a river passage. Although the group had little problem navigating the Snake River's Idaho Falls and American Falls, the river took a swift turn as the men discovered the turbulent waters of Milner Reach and Caldron Linn. After losing party members and valuable supplies, the Wilson Price Hunt expedition took to dry ground, bypassed the rest of Idaho on foot, and arrived at the Columbia River's headwaters in February 1812.

Drawing upon his experience with the Wilson Price Hunt party, native Scotsman, Donald Mackenzie, traveled back to Idaho for more adventure. Mackenzie worked as a successful Snake River guide, and on many of his trips, he received company from Hawaii islanders shipped to the Northwest as laborers. Referred to as "Owyhees," the laborers were highly regarded for their strong work ethic, and Mackenzie decided to capitalize on this characteristic on a fateful 1818 expedition. At Mackenzie's command, three of the Owyhee laborers set out to trap on an unexplored river in present day southwestern Idaho. When the laborers failed to return, Mackenzie and the

rest of his party left them behind, assuming that the men had either become lost or were killed by indigenous tribes. In honor of these men, Mackenzie dubbed the river, "Owyhee River."

Next to hit the growing Idaho fur-trading scene was Scottish immigrant, Finan McDonald. As a Hudson's Bay Company employee, McDonald led a party of trappers and explorers from Spokane to Montana in 1823. Deciding to follow the trail of Lewis and Clark, McDonald and his men began their return to Washington via Idaho's Lemhi Pass. Although the group's journey had been marked with few hardships up to that point, McDonald and his men were surprised with a Blackfeet ambush on the Lemhi River's upper stretches. Miraculously, the men defeated the notoriously fierce and brutal Blackfeet, losing just six expedition members while killing sixty-eight of the seventy-five Blackfeet warriors. After the battle's conclusion, McDonald and his men set aside fur-trading thoughts and hightailed it back to Washington. Although McDonald adamantly refused to return to the Idaho region, his bravery and well-led expedition ultimately opened additional trapping corridors in the region.

Despite their employee's harrowing experience in the wilds of Idaho, the Hudson's Bay Company continued its grand plans for British domination of the Pacific Northwest and Rocky Mountain fur trade. In 1824, Peter Skene Ogden became the Snake River operations leader. His demand for perfection and thoroughness from trappers further heightened the growing competition between British and American fur trading companies. Ogden led several prosperous trips through Snake River country and trapped thousands of beaver, his success began to dwindle in 1830 with the arrival of independent fur-trappers.

Known as mountain men, these freelance adventurers were well aware of the dangers associated with trapping amid rugged country that warring Native Americans occasionally inhabited. Their keen sense of the land's topography, weather conditions, and general beaver trapping knowl-

Craters of the Moon National Monument

6

edge gave these rugged frontiersmen the upper edge against company-employed trappers accustomed to foreign countries and posh living conditions. Jedediah Smith, Jim Bridger, and Jeremiah Johnston were just a few of the successful mountain men who scoured Idaho and the American West in search of trapping treasure.

Despite the good fortune of these trapping entrepreneurs and their highly successful seasonal trading rendezvous, American and British companies continued pouring money into their own fur trapping exploration in the Idaho region. The Hudson's Bay Company established Fort Boise on the Snake River in 1834 as a permanent fur-trading fort. The fort's arrival was quickly followed by the initiation of Fort Hall. Located near present-day Blackfoot, Fort Hall celebrated its grand opening on August 5, 1834 under the management of Boston entrepreneur, Nathaniel Wyeth. Competition was fierce between the two trade forts, and Wyeth's initial excitement soon faded. Upon losing a large amount of money, Wyeth abandoned his fort in 1836, and the Hudson's Bay Company took over operations until the fort's 1856 closure.

As quickly as the rush for beaver pelts came, the fur trapping and trading business dwindled overnight when modern fashion in London declared beaver skin hats and decorative pelts a fashion faux pas. At the same time, the Rocky Mountain beaver population had become nearly extinct, and both company fur trappers and freelance mountain men were soon in search of new professions. Utilizing the routes established during the chaotic fur trapping days, many of these men assumed roles as pioneer wagon guides to the next wave of Idaho inhabitants – devoted missionaries on the prowl for converts and pioneers greedy for a piece of unspoiled Idaho mountain grandeur!

Early Missionaries & Native Americans

As Idaho's fur trapping era began to fizzle, plans were already being made for the next invasion of easterners upon the once isolated life of Idaho's Native Americans. In 1831, several Nez Perce tribal members who had assisted the Corp of Discovery at the dawn of the nineteenth century traveled to St. Louis to visit William Clark. The Nez Perce knew that Clark had been designated the Head of U.S. Indian Affairs upon the conclusion of the famous western expedition, and they decided to petition him to send reading, writing, and agricultural instructors to aid their tribe.

Clark was quite responsive to the Nez Perce request, but somehow, the petition was misinterpreted as a call for education about the white man's god. U.S. Easterners were humbled at the long journey the Nez Perce had undertaken in an effort to embrace Christianity and denounce their heathen ways. Within no time, preachers across America were calling for missionaries to answer the Nez Perce request and spread the word of God to all indigenous tribes inhabiting the Rocky Mountain region.

Although the preachers' pleas fell on many deaf ears and made cowards out of hundreds of individuals too scared to enter the untamed western frontier, the Spaldings and Whitmans courageously accepted the call as their religious duty. In 1836, the two young Presbyterian couples loaded their wagons, left St. Louis, and relied on their faith to carry them to an unknown land. On July 4, the missionaries arrived in Idaho, dedicated to fulfilling the Nez Perce plea that had mistakenly been made to Clark five years earlier.

As the Whitmans continued their journey to establish a Washington mission among the Cayuse

Under the watch of the Grand Tetons, haybales dot the landscape surrounding Highway 33.

Indians, Henry and Eliza Spalding stayed in Nez Perce country and developed the Lapwai Mission near Idaho's Clearwater River. The Spaldings' mission was highly effective in its early years. Eliza learned the Nez Perce language and began teaching the Native Americans English while Henry spent his time proselytizing and educating the Nez Perce about farming. Despite the mission's early success, the Nez Perce gradually became weary of Henry's harsh discipline and began losing interest in farming. When word reached the Spaldings that the Whitmans had been massacred, the Spaldings abandoned the Lapwai Mission and headed west for the Willamette Valley. Henry's heart, however, never left the mission, and he returned to Lapwai in 1863 where he remained until his 1874 death.

The Spaldings and the Whitmans were not alone in their efforts to convert Idaho's indigenous tribes. In 1841, Father Pierre Jean de Smet arrived in Coeur d'Alene and began making plans for the Catholic Mission of the Sacred Heart. In 1847, Father Antonio Ravalli finished de Smet's mission on a hilltop overlooking the Coeur d'Alene River and began spreading Catholicism to all open ears. Additional Catholic missions spread like wildfire across Idaho's panhandle and extended into north-central Idaho. Today, many of the region's Native Americans retain the Catholic heritage that their ancestors acquired from Father de Smet, Father Ravalli, and the era's other dedicated nuns and priests.

Arriving on the heels of the Protestants and Catholics were twenty-seven young Mormon men commissioned by Brigham Young to enter central Idaho's Lemhi Valley in 1855. Located at an ideal site near present-day Tendoy where the fervent missionaries could spread Mormon teachings to Shoshone, Bannock, and Nez Perce tribal members, the mission was successful in its infancy. The missionaries established favorable relationships with all three tribes, but the tribes ultimately began to resent one another. Out of jealousy and rage of one another, the Indians turned on the missionaries, stole the mission's horses and supplies, and forced the Mormon men to head back to Utah in spring of 1858. Despite this setback for

the Mormon Church, Brigham Young stared down discouragement, and many more Mormons were eventually ordered to migrate north towards Idaho on the heels of other pioneers.

Pioneers and Mormons

When Narcissa Whitman and Eliza Spalding became the first white women to safely cross the Continental Divide into the vast Rocky Mountain region, they unknowingly paved the way for thousands of pioneer emigrants. Prior to their crossing, the American West was viewed negatively as a rugged land where women and children were incapable of survival. Narcissa and Eliza, however, dispelled the myth, and adventure-seeking easterners began viewing the west as a place where dreams came true and families could live peacefully away from the east's overcrowded cities. In 1842, the first wagon train of families from Missouri, Kentucky, Illinois, and Iowa crossed the Continental Divide into Idaho. From there, the wagons continued to Oregon's verdant Willamette Valley, carving out the Oregon Trail route that was soon embraced by thousands of other migrating families.

Between 1842 and 1847, just over 5,000 people made the average five-month long journey west. Word continued to spread about the region's abundant land and livable terrain. Despite growing incidences of Indian attacks, thousands more cast aside their fears and left behind the comforts of established homes to create a new family destiny. Between 1849 and 1860, 42,000 pioneers headed to Oregon, while over 200,000 more took the trail to California. By the end of the great westward migration, 500,000 pioneers had safely completed the journey, an innumerable amount had lost their lives to disease, and the American West was transformed from a land of mystery into a land of promise and freedom where all were welcome.

Embracing the west's new image and realizing the potential to escape religious persecution, Mormon church officials christened Utah Territory as the new base for the religion's faith. Between 1846 and 1869, Prophet Brigham Young and 70,000 other Mormon believers moved the church's former Nauvoo, Illinois headquarters to the Great

FAMOUS IDAHO NATIVES AND TRANSPLANTS

Joe Albertson: Founder of Albertson's grocery store chain

Ezra Taft Benson: LDS Church Prophet and former U.S. Secretary of Agriculture

Gutzon Borglum: Sculptor of Mount Rushmore

Carol R. Brink: Author of "Caddie Woodlawn" and 1936 Newberry Medal Winner

Edgar Rice Burroughs: Author of "Tarzan" stories

Frank F. Church: U.S. Senator; namesake of Idaho's Frank Church Wilderness

Ty Cobb: Baseball player

Christin Cooper: 1984 Olympic skiing silver medalist

Lillian Disney: Wife of Walt Disney

Lou Dobbs: Anchor/managing editor of CNN's "Moneyline"

Fred Dubois: U.S. Senator

Wyatt Earp: Western gunfighter

Larry EchoHawk: Elected Idaho Attorney General in 1991; he represents the first Native American to hold this post in any U.S. state

Bill Fagerbakke: Actor

Philo Farnsworth: Television inventor

Vardis Fisher: Author

Dick Fosbury: Inventor of high jumping technique known as "Fosbury Flop"

Gretchen Fraser: 1948 Olympic skiing gold medalist

Joseph Garry: Elected in 1956 as the first Native American in Idaho's legislature; twice named Outstanding Indian in North America

Mary Hallock Foote: Author

Gene Harris: Jazz musician

Ernest Hemingway: Author

Larry Jackson: St. Louis Cardinals and Chicago Cubs pitcher

Bill Johnson: 1984 Olympic skiing champion

Walter "Big Train" Johnson: Baseball pitcher

Chief Joseph: Nez Perce Indian Chief

Harmon Killebrew: Minnesota Twins baseball player

Jerry Kramer: Green Bay Packers' offensive lineman and kicker

Vernon Law: Pittsburg Pirates pitcher

Patrick McManus: Author

Barbara Morgan: NASA Teacher in Space

Dan O'Brien: Decathlete; 1996 Olympic gold medal and World Record Holder

Gracie Bowers Pfost: Idaho's first woman in the U.S. senate (served five terms)

Jake Plummer: NFL quarterback

Ezra Pound: Poet

Edward Pulaski: Inventor of fire-fighting tool, the Pulaski

Malcolm Refrew: Inventor/Chemist

Paul Revere: Musician of "Paul Revere and the Raiders"

Marjorie Reynolds: Actress

Sacajawea: Shoshone Indian woman who served as Lewis and Clark's translator

Edward Scott: Revolutionized skiing with the Scott Ski Pole

Nell Shipman: Silent screen film director and actress

J.R. Simplot: Business executive and industrialist; creator of frozen French fry

Robert E. Smylie: Political leader

Henry Spalding: Lapwai Valley missionary

Picabo Street: 1994 Olympic skiing silver medalist; 1995 and 1996 World Champion Downhill Racer.

Lana Turner: Actress

Roger Williams: Musician

Salt Lake region in Utah. Within no time, Brigham Young sent settlers north into Wyoming and the outer reaches of Utah Territory to tame the deviant ways of those with no religious background. On one such occasion in April 1860, a group of Utah Mormons headed north, established a farming community, developed an irrigation system, and spread their religion throughout the region. Although the pioneers believed their small town of Franklin was situated in Utah, an official 1872 government survey proved otherwise. As luck would have it, Brigham Young's Mormon followers had successfully founded Idaho's first permanent white settlement. Within a matter of years, the church's procreation emphasis allowed the Mormon faith to spread widely across southeastern Idaho and throughout the Cache Valley. A dense Mormon population in eastern Idaho is evident to this day.

Fortune Hunters

While visions of a free religious society occupied the thoughts of Mormon officials, many pioneers migrating through Idaho had a much different agenda on their minds. The "Golden State" of California and its lucrative gold mines left men all across the globe lusting after strike-it-rich dreams. Sparked by the 1849 discovery of California gold, thousands of treasure hunters surged westward in search of their own mother lode.

Since most of these men felt no attachment to California, many were just as happy to wander around the American West in search of any available lucky strike. Miners flocked to Montana, Colorado, Wyoming, and finally in 1860, to Idaho. Hearing stories of rich lodes in Idaho's Nez Perce Country, E. D. Pierce and ten of his associates snuck onto the Nez Perce Reservation and began digging for gold on the Clearwater River banks. Although the men failed to receive permission from the Native Americans, the Indians begrudgingly allowed the men to stay. When Pierce's associate, Wilbur Bassett, found a strike of "oro fino" (Spanish for "fine gold"), Idaho became the new future of gold mining.

Despite Nez Perce Reservation boundaries that technically prohibited white settlement, nothing would stand in the way of a new wave of determined treasure seekers. The towns of Pierce City and Orofino sprang up overnight, and by spring 1862, more than 10,000 white people and Chinese immigrants illegally inhabited the Nez Perce tribal land. Over the course of its operation, the Orofino Mining District shipped out $3 million in gold dust. At the same time, a new strike was in full swing in the Boise Basin and Owyhee

Boats at rest in McCall.

Mountains. Idaho City, Placerville, Centerville, Rocky Bar, Atlanta, Murray, Eagle City, and Silver City became the new "best" places in Idaho to unearth a fortune. Although the availability of gold eventually dwindled and lost its allure, Idaho's rich mining history was far from over.

In 1879, Wood River Valley miners discovered Idaho's first deposits of silver, lead, and zinc, and a new mining boom was under way with the establishment of mining camps at Ketchum, Hailey, and Bellevue. Six years later, Noah Kellogg made his lucky silver strike on the South Fork of the Coeur d'Alene River near present day Wardner. Word spread overnight of Kellogg's find, and the area was immediately christened "Silver Valley." Most of Idaho's mining boomtowns have since become mere echoes of their past, but mines in the state's panhandle remain a profitable testimony to this rich aspect of Idaho's economic history and future. The region continues to be recognized as one of the world's most profitable mining districts.

The Arrival of the Railroad

Although the Oregon Trail and mining gold rush contributed significantly to the settlement of Idaho, the arrival of the railroad was responsible for creating several new communities and spurring the state's economic development during the late 1800s and early 1900s. Idaho's first railroad line arrived on May 2, 1874 when the Utah Northern Railroad made its way from Ogden, Utah to Franklin. With the line's arrival, Franklin became a major freight center. Ten years later, the Utah and Northern Railway Company decided to make a profit off this Idaho shipping center and extended a line from Franklin to the Northern Pacific Railroad Line in Garrison, Montana. In its wake, the line initiated the establishment of several southeastern Idaho towns, including Rexburg, Rigby, and Victor.

Prior to the arrival of the Utah Northern in southeastern Idaho, Union Pacific Railroad officials had long had their eye on the booming Idaho region. Scouts surveyed the area around Pocatello as early as 1867, but construction was not initiated until 1881. Serving as an affiliate of the Union Pacific, the Oregon Short Line Railroad made its way through Montpelier, Pocatello, Shoshone, and the Wood River Valley mines before arriving at its final destination of Huntington, Oregon for the first time on November 17, 1884.

1882 saw the arrival of a Northern Pacific Railway line running through Sandpoint on its journey from Montana to Washington. Over the course of the next two decades, the Great Northern Railway and the Chicago, Milwaukee, St. Paul, and Pacific Railroad pushed additional lines through northern Idaho. The railroads accelerated the region's booming silver mine activity, and Idaho was finally connected to the rest of the world with modern transportation.

Railroad officials continued to bisect Idaho with new lines throughout the remainder of the 1800s and into the early twentieth century. As a result, America began to shrink, the American West became an even more hospitable place, and Idaho was well on its way to attracting new residents and businesses.

The Timber, Agricultural, and Energy Boom

When the railroad industry chugged and steamed its way across Idaho's plains, forests, and mountains, it brought with it new economic prosperity and diversified job opportunities. With the expansion of the railroad into western territories, timber barons who had previously made a fortune clear-

The Mormon Temple behind the falls of Idaho Falls.

cutting the U.S.' eastern forests began looking for new horizons. These individuals' quick scan of railroad accessible land drew them to the Idaho panhandle where they discovered endless stands of great white pines. As the twentieth century dawned across Idaho's pristine northern forests, the region's miners were forced to make room for another industry dependent upon the state's natural resources.

Droves of loggers enveloped the northern panhandle, and the timber industry teamed up with the railroads in a lucrative business of clear-cutting and shipping. Although the industry contributed greatly to Idaho's economy and the budding development of new construction in the Pacific Northwest, the activity came with a price. A few workers lost their lives or were injured in the profession, and unscrupulous cutting restrictions resulted in the desecration of what once encompassed some of Idaho's most scenic territory. Today, the logging industry remains a visible presence in Idaho but on a much smaller-scale with more stringent and responsible business practices.

While loggers migrated to northern Idaho, a mass exodus of farmers from across the nation was making its way to other regions in Idaho. Dry farmers first settled on north-central Idaho's Palouse Hills. The rolling green hills were transformed into acres of profitable crops and orchards that supplied the food needs of the ever-expanding Idaho and Pacific Northwest population. Although the Palouse region's dry farming continues to this day, many farmers were eventually lured to the Snake River country in southwestern and south-central Idaho with the 1894 Carey Act. Farmers rushed to buy their own piece of the area's irrigated farmland, and both private and Bureau of Reclamation dam projects ensured that irrigation would be available for years to come. Today, the once dry, desert terrain of south-central Idaho has been reconfigured into an irrigated green oasis boasting some of America's richest farmland. Several other irrigated farms can be found throughout Idaho, and sugar beets, potatoes, and wheat remain the state's most bountiful crops.

As hydroelectric projects grew across the state in response to increasing farming demands, the

U.S. government began making its own energy-related plans. The Atomic Energy Commission constructed the National Reactor Testing Station in southeastern Idaho in 1949 and immediately set to work experimenting with atomic energy. On December 20, 1951, the site's Experimental Breeder Reactor-1 became the world's first nuclear reactor to produce usable amounts of electricity. This unprecedented feat led to the July 17, 1955 accomplishment where scientists created a chain reaction lighting the nearby town of Arco with over two million watts of atomically powered electric service. The testing site is now known as the Idaho National Engineering and Environmental Laboratory (INEEL), and experiments with atomic energy presently employ hundreds of Idaho residents.

THE NATIONAL TRAILS SYSTEM

"I should compare the (South) pass to the ascent of the capitol hill from the avenue at Washington." – John Fremont, 1843, describing the ease of using South Pass to cross the Rocky Mountains

In 1800, America's western border reached only as far as the Mississippi River. Following the Louisiana Purchase in 1803, the country nearly doubled in size, pushing the nation's western edge past the Rocky Mountains.

Yet the wilderness known as Oregon Country (which included present-day Oregon, Washington, and part of Idaho) still belonged to the British, a fact that made many Americans eager to settle the region and claim it for the United States.

American Indians had traversed this country for many years, but for whites, it was unknown territory. Lewis and Clark's secretly funded expedition in 1803 was part of a U.S. Government plan to open Oregon Country to settlement. However,

Idaho Trivia

In Idaho, it is illegal to give another person a box of candy weighing more than 50 pounds.

Snake River near Bruneau

the hazardous route blazed by this party was not feasible for families traveling by wagon. An easier trail was needed.

Robert Stewart of the Astorians (a group of fur traders who established Fort Astoria in western Oregon's Columbia River) became the first white to use what later became known as the Oregon Trail. Stewart's 2,000-mile journey from Fort Astoria to St. Louis in 1810 took 10 months to complete; still, it was a much less rugged trail than Lewis and Clark's route.

It wasn't until 1836 that the first wagons were used on the trek from Missouri to Oregon. A missionary party headed by Marcus Whitman and his wife Narcissa bravely set out to reach the Willamette Valley. Though the Whitmans were forced to abandon their wagons 200 miles short of Oregon, they proved that families could go west by wheeled travel.

In the spring of 1843, a wagon train of nearly 1,000 people organized at Independence, Missouri

Idaho Trivia

Only the state of Texas, with 129 million acres under cultivation, has more farmland than Idaho with 58.6 million acres. Approximately 63 percent of Idaho land is involved in farming or ranching. Only Kansas and North Dakota harvest more wheat annually than Idaho, and only North Dakota harvests more barley. Idaho exports almost 70 percent of its wheat to foreign countries. There are about 24,000 ranchers in Idaho at an average age of 60. 5.9 percent of Idaho's work force is involved in farming versus 1.9 percent nationwide. While wheat, barley, and hay provide the most total economic benefit, potatoes, sugar beets, and dry beans bring the most money per acre. Farming is the only economic sector in Idaho where wages are above the national average.

with plans to reach Oregon Country. Amidst an overwhelming chorus of naysayers who doubted their success, the so-called "Great Migration" made it safely to Oregon. Crucial to their success was the use of South Pass, a 12-mile wide valley that was virtually the sole place between the plains and Oregon where wagons could cross the formidable Rocky Mountains.

By 1846, thousands of emigrants who were drawn west by cheap land, patriotism, or the promise of a better life found their way to Oregon Country. With so many Americans settling the region, it became obvious to the British that Oregon was no longer theirs. They ceded Oregon Country to the United States that year.

"When you start over these wide plains, let no one leave dependent on his best friend for anything; for if you do, you will certainly have a blow-out before you get far." – John Shivley, 1846

Before railroads or automobiles, people in America had to travel by foot, horse, boat, or wagon. Some of these routes from our nation's early days still remain today as reminders of our historic past. A National Historic Trail (NHT) such as the Oregon NHT is an extended trail that follows original routes of travel of national historical significance.

In 1995, the National Park Service established the National Trails System Office in Salt Lake City, Utah. The Salt Lake City Trails Office administers the Oregon, the California, the Mormon Pioneer, and the Pony Express NHTs.

The National Trails System does not manage trail resources on a day-to-day basis. The responsibility for managing trail resources remains in the hands of the current trail managers at the federal, state, local, and private levels.

The Office was established to improve interstate and interregional coordination. Specific responsibilities of this trails office include coordinating and supporting the protection of trail resources, marking and interpreting the trails, designating and marking an auto-tour route, and identifying and certifying high-potential sites.

In 1968, Congress enacted the National Trails System Act, and in 1978, National Historic Trail designations were added. The National Historic Trails System commemorates these historic routes

and promotes their preservation, interpretation, and appreciation.

National Historic Trails recognize diverse facets of history such as prominent past routes of exploration, migration, trade, communication, and military action. The historic trails generally consist of remnant sites and trail segments, and thus are not necessarily contiguous. Although National Historic Trails are administered by federal agencies, land ownership may be in public or private hands. Of the 11 National Historic Trails, nine are administered by the National Park Service, one by the U.S.DA Forest Service, and one by the Bureau of Land Management.

If Americans today were to undertake a four-month, 2,000-mile journey on foot without the aid of modern conveniences, many would be in for a harsh jolt. Despite the lingering romance with which many view the emigrant tide on the Oregon Trail, the journey was tough.

Emigrants traveled under the dual yoke of fear and withering physical requirements. Rumors of hostile Indians coupled with unforgiving country, disease, and dangerous work made life difficult. Yet thousands did make it to Oregon. What was their journey like on a day-to-day basis?

First of all, timing was important to the emigrants' success in reaching Oregon. The most favorable time to depart from Missouri was in April or May. This would put them on schedule to make the high mountain passes when winter snows would not be a threat.

Mistakes were often made before the journey even began. In preparing for the trip, many emigrants overloaded their wagons with supplies. As a result, not long after leaving Missouri, dumping excess items was a common sight along the trail. Tools, guns, and food were considered vital – heirlooms were not.

The relatively gentle first leg of the route along the Platte River was a time for the emigrants to settle into travel mode. This meant getting used to hitching and unhitching the oxen, cattle, and mules whenever a stop was made – hard and dangerous work. It also meant constant wagon maintenance, foraging for firewood and clean water, cooking over open fires, and learning how to break and set camp every day.

When emigrants reached Chimney Rock and Scotts Bluff, their journey was one-third over. But more challenging terrain lay ahead as water, firewood, and supply depots became more scarce. Buffalo herds that initially were a dependable food source for the emigrants also thinned out due to excessive killing.

The challenge of crossing many rivers and the Continental Divide created other severe tests for the emigrants. Summer temperatures, miles of shadeless trail, and choking dust compounded to make life decidedly unenjoyable. Though confrontations with Indians were rare, the fear of attack was a constant worry.

The last leg of the trail was the most difficult. But thoughts of approaching winter snows kept emigrants motivated to move as quickly as possible. The Blue Mountains in eastern Oregon and the Cascade Ranger in the west presented barriers that slowed progress.

Upon reaching Oregon City, the emigrants were faced with either taking their chances on the dangerous Columbia River, or, starting in 1846, taking the safer but longer Barlow Road. Sam Barlow's toll road became the preferred route for the emigrants. Finally, if money, animals, wagons, supplies, and morale held out, the emigrants reached the Willamette Valley.

Reprinted from a National Park Service brochure

Grand Targhee in full fall foliage.

THE OREGON TRAIL

Onto Oregon! It all began with a crude network of rutted traces across the land from the Missouri River to the Willamette River that was used by nearly 400,000 people. Today, the 2,170-mile Oregon Trail still evokes an instant image, a ready recollection of the settlement of this continent, of the differences between American Indians and white settlers, and of new horizons. In 1840, only three states existed west of the Mississippi River. Maine's boundary with Canada was undefined. The western boundaries of the Nation lay roughly along the Continental Divide. Within 10 years, the United States and Great Britain had drawn a boundary that stretched from the Atlantic to the Pacific. The western boundary moved from the Rocky Mountains to the Pacific Ocean. In another 40 years, successive waves of emigrants completely eliminated any sense of frontier, changed the way of life of the American Indians, and ravaged many wild animal species, especially the herds of buffalo. Plows and barbed wire subdued the prairies. Transcontinental railroads knitted the great distances together.

The first Europeans to see the trans-Mississippi West were the mountain men, trappers, and maritime explorers along the west coast. In Canada, the Hudson's Bay Company fur frontier was approaching the Columbia River basin. In 1812, John Jacob Astor established Astoria at the mouth of the Columbia in a countermove and sent Robert Stuart overland to carry dispatches east. Stuart found South Pass by following a Crow Indian trail. Only 7,000 feet above sea level with easy gradients, South pass has an attractive geographic proximity to the upper reaches of the Platte River. Both were determining factors in the routing of the Oregon Trail. The early frontiersman found the passes, crossed the great rivers, and defined the vast reaches of the western interior. From the beginning these explorers contributed to a growing campaign to make the Oregon Country a part of either the United States or Great Britain, according to their own sometimes confused loyalties.

Economic depressions in 1837 and 1841 frustrated farmers and businessmen alike. The collapse of the international fur trade in 1839 intensified the hard times, and concerns of British domination of the Northwest grew. At the same time, eastern churches saw the American Indians of the Oregon Country as ready candidates for European ideas of civilization. Churches formed ardent missionary societies to create an active appetite for Christianity. In 1836, Marcus Whitman and his new wife, Narcissa, along with Henry and Eliza Spalding, headed for Oregon as missionaries. The letters they sent home publicized the opportunities and advantages of Oregon. Many people for many reasons had become interested in Oregon, but it was not until 1841 that the first group with serious intent to emigrate left the banks of the Missouri River and headed west. In 1843, nearly 1,000 completed the trip – an omen of the multitudes to follow.

The Oregon Trail was never a clearly defined track. In places the wagons passed in columns that might be hundreds of yards apart; those traces shifted with the effects of weather and use. In the course of time, nature obliterated many of the fainter traces. Road builders followed the deeper, more permanent traces because they marked the best route. The Oregon Trail was quickly being forgotten. In 1906, 76-year-old Ezra Meeker, Oregon settler in 1852 and a tireless champion of the trail, set out in a covered wagon to retrace the route from west to east. Among his goals: to create a general interest in marking the route, to raise public awareness of the trail's history and heritage, and to point out the loss and damage resulting from careless disregard. Meeker met with Presidents Theodore Roosevelt and Calvin Coolidge, testified before Congress, and made several other publicity trips over the trail before his death in 1928. Today, the National Park Service, in concert with the Bureau of Land Management, the Forest Service, and the states of Missouri, Kansas, Nebraska, Wyoming, Idaho, Oregon, and Washington strive to protect this legacy.

Reprinted from a National Park Service brochure

Across the Plains

Guidebooks

In book or pamphlet form, guidebooks were soon available for emigrants. Some provided good, solid, reliable information. Others contributed to the Oregon Fever that swept the country in the 1840s describing the land in almost Biblical terms.

Each part of the journey had its difficulties. For the first third of the way, the emigrants got used to the routine and work of travel. They learned to hitch and unhitch their livestock, to keep the wagons in good running order, and to make sure that their animals got the water and food they needed to survive. They learned to get along with their fellow emigrants, to agree on rules they would all follow on the journey, and to set up and break camp every night and morning. They learned to spread out in several columns so that they raised less dust and fewer of them had to breathe the choking air. They rotated positions in the line in a spirit of fairness. They learned to travel six out of seven days as experienced voices told them that some of the most difficult sections to travel would come at the end, when they would have to cross mountains before the winter snows. Fortunately, the landscape was relatively gentle as they traveled through the Platte River Valley heading for the High Plains. Starting in the spring, too, provided them with abundant grass for the livestock. Water was also plentiful, and if they were early enough in the year, campsites and waterholes would not be overgrazed or fouled. Cholera, whose cause was then unknown (but we now know can be traced to contaminated water) killed more travelers than anything else. How many emigrants died along the trail can never be known. The number of deaths varied from year to year. Most likely, the death rate was little different from that for those who resisted the lure of the trail with all its potential disasters.

Loading the Wagon

Wagons usually measured 4 feet wide by 12 feet long. Into those 48 square feet were put supplies for traveling the trail and the wherewithal for beginning a new life. The emphasis was on tools and food, but a few family treasures and heirlooms were also carried. Using the wagon as shelter was almost an afterthought.

Over the Continental Divide

Excitement abounded when the emigrants passed the landmarks of Chimney Rock and Scotts Bluff, about one-third of the way on the trail. It meant they were making progress. By this time, too, they would have an idea if their money would hold out. Tolls at ferries and bridges had to be paid. Supplies and food were bought at trading posts along the way or from other emigrants. A week's journey beyond Scotts Bluff brought them to Fort Laramie, the great supply depot and resting place. Here they could replenish dwindling stocks of food and other staples – for a price. Wheels could be repaired and wagon boxes tightened before they set out on the steepening ascent to the Continental Divide. Water and grass for livestock became more scarce. The drier air caused wooden wheels to shrink and the iron tires that held the wheels together loosened or rolled off. Buffalo herds on which the emigrants had depended for fresh meat to supplement their staples became increasingly hard to find the farther west they went. Cooking fuel, whether wood or buffalo chips, was also harder to find. To lighten their wagons, the emigrants left treasured pieces of furniture and other personal belongings by the wayside. Surviving the trip had become of paramount importance; food and tools were vital, heirlooms were not. From Fort Laramie to Fort Bridger, on the western edge of present-day Wyoming, the Mormon Trail flowed with the Oregon and California Trails. At Fort Bridger, the emigrants parted ways as those bound for Oregon turned northwest toward the Snake River Valley. Alternate routes included Sublette's Cutoff and the Lander Cutoff. Beginning just west of South Pass, Sublette's Cutoff crossed a barren, arid stretch of country where for 50 miles there was no water and little grass. Those who chose the grueling route and survived had saved 85 miles and a week of travel.

Emigrant and Indian

Early emigrants generally found the Indians they encountered to be cordial and helpful. Some never even saw any Indians. As emigrant numbers multiplied, however, the friendly relationships became strained. Hostilities and casualties occurred often enough after 1860 to keep both sides nervous when emigrant wagons crossed Indian lands. Wise members of both groups made an effort to avoid trouble, and they usually succeeded. Rather than fight, Indians often assisted emigrant parties on the way west. Countless instances of assistance in the form of extra wagon teams, food, and medical help were provided by Indians, who served as trail guides and pilots at dangerous crossings. Indian life was affected radically by the emigrants, who brought disease and killed the wild game. And despite popular fiction, emigrants circled their wagons to corral their livestock rather than to ward off Indian attacks.

Trail's End

Footsore, weary, and exhausted, traveler and beast alike faced the final third and the most difficult part of the trail. Yet speed was of the essence, for winter snows could close mountain passes or trap unprepared and tired groups of emigrants as they crossed both the Blue Mountains in eastern Oregon and the Cascades to the west. In the early years, before the Barlow Road across the Cascades was opened as a toll road in 1846, emigrants had no choice but to go down the Columbia from The Dalles on a raft or abandon their wagons and build boats. The Columbia was full of rapids and dangerous currents; many emigrants lost their lives, almost within sight of their goal. Once the settlers arrived in the Willamette Valley, they spread out to establish farms and small towns. Initially, few emigrants settled north of the Columbia, but once the United States and Great Britain agreed on an international boundary and the Hudson's Bay Company moved its post at Fort Vancouver to Vancouver Island, Americans settled in present-day Washington as well. The 1850 census showed that 12,093 people lived in Oregon. Ten years later, when Oregon had been a state for one year, 52,495 were counted. Small towns were on the verge of becoming cities. Frame houses replaced log cabins. Orchards grew to maturity. The land was acquiring the look of civilization that the emigrants had left behind.

Reprinted from a National Park Service brochure

THE CALIFORNIA TRAIL

Manifest Destiny – Paradise

"Ho for California!" Free land. Gold. Adventure. Between 1841 and 1869, more than a quarter million people answered this call and crossed the plains and mountains to the "El Dorado" of the West. By 1849, the lure of instant wealth and tales of gold beckoned at the end of the 2,000-mile California Trail. The story of the men, women, and children who traveled overland to the West coast has become an American epic.

Since the late 1700s, the West had held out the promise of boundless opportunity. After Lewis and Clark found a way to the Pacific in 1805, fur traders followed Indian trails up western river valleys and across mountain passes, filling in the blank spaces on early maps that represented unknown country. By the late 1830s, mountain men had explored most of the routes that became overland trails. In 1837, an economic panic swept the United States and gave people already itching to move an additional reason to go west.

Throughout the 1840s, promoters and trail guides worked hard to create an idyllic picture of the prospects for greater fortune and better health open to Americans who made the journey to California. One young emigrant reported that a pamphlet describing a lush California with its ideal climate and flowers that bloomed all winter "made me just crazy to move out there, for I thought such a country must be a paradise."

Why Go West?

Watching "one continual stream" of honest-looking, open-hearted people "going west in 1846, mountain man James Clyman asked why "so many of all kinds and classes of people should sell out comfortable homes in Missouri and elsewhere, pack up and start across such an immense barren waste to settle in some new place of which they have at most so uncertain information." Clyman's answer? – "this is the character of my countrymen."

What was the character of Americans in the 1840s? Many embraced Manifest Destiny, a phrase penned by journalist John O'Sullivan in July 1845 to explain the U.S. government's thirst for expansion. It was a new term but not a new idea. Since the beginning of the republic, leaders had aggressively claimed land for the United States. Manifest Destiny crystallized the idea that it was God's will and the rightful destiny of Americans to take over the continent. It became a rallying cry for overlanders to head west.

Personal motives of the emigrants varied. Some planned to build permanent homes or farms, but many hoped to make their fortunes and return east. One 1846 traveler noted that his companions all "agreed in the one general object, that of bettering their condition," but individual hopes and dreams "were as various as can well be imagined." Dreams spurred a diversity of emigrants too: Americans, African Americans, Indians, Canadians, Europeans – people of all ages and backgrounds crossed the plains.

Beginnings

The Bidwell-Bartleson party, the first emigrants to go to California, left Missouri in May 1841 with 69 people. At Soda Springs, Idaho, some continued on to Oregon. The others, knowing only "that California lay to the west," struggled across the north end of the Great Salt Lake Desert. They

A lone group of trees stands out against the St. Anthony Sand Dunes.

abandoned their wagons before reaching the Humboldt River, packed their livestock with necessities, and in November, 39 travelers reached California.

In 1844, the Stephens-Townsend-Murphy party, traveling the Truckee route, reached the Sierra Nevada in November. Stalled by snow, they left some wagons at Donner Lake and packed onward. In the spring, they retrieved their wagons, becoming the first emigrants to take wagons all the way to Sutter's Fort, California. In 1845, John C. Fremont explored a new route across the Great Basin. The next summer, promoter Lansford W. Hastings convinced about 80 wagons of late-starting emigrants to try this new cutoff across the Great Salt Lake Desert. The last of them was the ill-fated Donner-Reed party.

In 1846, a party from the Willamette Valley opened a southern route to Oregon, now known as the Applegate Trail. Peter Lassen branched south from this route in 1848 to reach his ranch in northern California. Not all early traffic on the California Trail headed west. After marching across the Southwest during the war with Mexico, Mormon Battalion veterans left Sutter's Fort in 1848 for the Valley of the Great Salt Lake. They opened a wagon road over Carson Pass, south of Lake Tahoe, that became the preferred route for wagon travel during the gold rush.

Gold Rush
James W. Marshall discovered gold on January 24, 1848, at John Sutter's sawmill on the South Fork of the American River, about 40 miles east of Sutter's Fort. Fortune hunters from California, Oregon, and Sonora, Mexico, flooded the goldfields by June, but the news spread more slowly across the continent. In December 1848, President James Polk confirmed the discovery in a report to Congress, thus setting the stage for the largest voluntary migration in American history.

By the spring of 1849 gold fever was an epidemic. Single men headed west to find wealth and adventure. Married men left families and jobs, hoping to return home in a year or so with enough money to last a lifetime. Thousands of travelers clogged the trail to California. The size of the rush created a host of problems. Almost every blade of grass vanished before the enormous trail herds. Overcrowded campsites and unsanitary conditions contributed to the spread of cholera. Desperation created tension as Indians saw the plants and animals they depended on for food disappear.

The gold rush added new trails to California. Mountain man Jim Beckwourth and surveyor William Nobles opened routes across the Sierra Nevada, while thousands traveled to the goldfields across Mexico and the Southwest. Cherokee Indians from Arkansas and present-day Oklahoma opened a route through the Rockies, the first that did not use South Pass.

Cutoffs and Variants
The California Trail eventually offered many ways to get to the West Coast. The network of cutoffs and variants became what is often described as a rope with frayed ends. Most emigrants set out from towns on the Missouri River and followed the Oregon Trail along the Platte and North Platte Rivers. The trails became a single cord (more or less) between Fort Kearny and South Pass in present-day Wyoming. At Parting of the Ways, the strands unwound again. The western end of the rope fanned out at the Humboldt Sink into routes leading to California and the goldfields.

South Pass marked the halfway point on the trail and the end of the long ascent up the Continental Divide. West of South Pass, travelers could go several ways: to Idaho and the Raft River area, where the main branch of the California Trail separated from the Oregon Trail; or to Utah and the settlements of the Latter-day Saints, Mormons, which were popular way stations. After visiting Salt Lake City, most emigrants followed the Salt Lake Cutoff back to the main trail at City of Rocks in present-day Idaho. For wagons, the Humboldt River Valley provided the best practical wagon road through the basin-and-range country, but overlanders continually sought easier ways to cross the formidable Sierra Nevada.

By 1860, freight and mail companies, military expeditions, new settlements and trading stations, and thousands of travelers going in both directions transformed the California Trail into a road.

Seeing the Elephant
Every great human migration seems to have its own catchphrase, and the forty-niners were no exception. "Seeing the elephant" characterized emigrant encounters with vast plains and barren deserts and the difficulty of surviving the harrowing trek across the western landscape. The expression predated the gold rush and was based on the thrill of seeing these exotic beasts in circuses. For overlanders, the elephant symbolized a challenging trip, the adventure of a lifetime.

If you had "seen the elephant," you had seen about all there was to see! People had never encountered anything like these prairies, canyons, deserts, and rugged mountains. The deserts of the Great Basin and the barrier of the Sierra Nevada made the California Trail the most difficult of all overland trails. Almost every emigrant recalled seeing the elephant somewhere along this arduous stretch. For many the encounter came on the Humboldt River – the Humbug, as some called it in disgust – a stream that got more sluggish and alkaline as it bent west and south until it finally disappeared into a shallow lake.

Others met the beast on the Fortymile Desert east of today's Reno, Nevada. The travelers lucky enough to escape the deserts of the Great Basin with animals and outfit intact were almost certain to see the elephant among the steep passes of the Sierra Nevada. Those who turned back often claimed to have seen the elephant's tail. One emigrant, who turned back after only 700 miles said "he had seen the Elephant and eaten its ears."

Wagons and Waybills
Going west was an expensive proposition. Emigrants needed supplies (food, utensils, stoves, bedding, lanterns, and more), hardware (axes, wagon parts, shovels, rope, other tools), livestock, and money to last for many months. Most travelers used light farm wagons that came to be called prairie schooners because their canvas tops reminded emigrants of sails on a ship. Schooners could carry about a ton of food and supplies, and often travelers packed their belongings into every bit of space. Treasures such as china, heirlooms, and furniture were jettisoned when it became obvious that the load was too heavy.

Overlanders preferred oxen to pull their wagons. They were slower than horses but cheaper, more reliable and powerful, and harder to steal. Oxen also fared better on prairie grass than did horses and mules, and important consideration because emigrants' lives could depend on the health of their livestock.

Getting started was one thing – getting safely to California was another. Guidebooks, or "waybills," became available almost as soon as the trail opened. Most waybills offered practical advice

IDAHO LICENSE PLATE NUMBERS

Throughout the history of Idaho's Motor Vehicle Department, Idaho's license plates have featured nearly every color of the rainbow along with a wide range of artistic designs. Coupled with the plates' changing artwork was a once frequently evolving numbering system used to identify different regions throughout the state. Prior to 1932, Idaho's license plates featured a simple numerical system. After several other numbering systems were tested and applied to Idaho's license plates, the state finally adopted its current county prefix designation system in 1945.

1A: Ada County
2A: Adams County
1B: Bannock County
2B: Bear Lake County
3B: Benewah County
4B: Bingham County
5B: Blaine County
6B: Boise County
7B: Bonner County
8B: Bonneville County
9B: Boundary County
10B: Butte County
1C: Camas County
2C: Canyon County
3C: Caribou County
4C: Cassia County
5C: Clark County
6C: Clearwater County
7C: Custer County
E: Elmore County
1F: Franklin County
2F: Fremont County
1G: Gem County
2G: Gooding County
I: Idaho County
1J: Jefferson County
2J: Jerome County
K: Kootenai County
1L: Latah County
2L: Lemhi County
3L: Lewis County
4L: Lincoln County
1M: Madison County
2M: Minidoka County
N: Nez Perce County
1O: Oneida County
2O: Owyhee County
1P: Payette County
2P: Power County
S: Shoshone County
1T: Teton County
2T: Twin Falls County
V: Valley County
W: Washington County

Introduction

about routes, landmarks, distances, and what equipment and supplies to take. Some, such as "The Emigrants Guide to Oregon and California, 1845" by promoter and guide Lansford W. Hastings, described California in almost heavenly terms and helped fuel what became "California fever."

Women and Families

Although single men made up the majority of early emigrants and forty-niners, women and families played an important role on the trail.

The first major wagon train, the Bidwell-Bartleson party, set out in 1841 with five women and about 10 children. At age 19, Nancy Kelsey (carrying her baby over the Sierra Nevada after the party abandoned its wagons) became the first covered-wagon woman to reach California. Iowans Catherine Haun and her husband caught gold fever in 1849. The Hauns, and about 25 of their neighbors in the wagon party, longed to go west, pick up gold off the ground, and return home to pay off their debts.

Catherine wrote in her journal that women and children on the trail "exerted a good influence, as the men did not take such risks, were more alert about the teams and seldom had accidents, [and] more attention was paid to cleanliness and sanitation." Even "the meals were more regular and better cooked thus preventing much sickness." Births on the trail were as common as deaths. As one girl recalled, "Three days after my little sister died…we stopped for a few hours, and my sister Olivia was born."

By 1852, about a third of all those crossing the plains were women. Five years later, it was common to find wagon parties made up largely of women and children. These women, as did all emigrants, left familiar homes and endured hardships to find a better life.

Indians and Emigrants

The quiet land along the California Trail may have seemed empty but Indian nations had lived there for more than 10,000 years. Unlike Hollywood stereotypes, Indians were more of a help than a danger to emigrants. In the 1840s fatal confrontations were rare. Travelers entrusted their wagons and families to Indians who guided them across swift rivers and through unfamiliar country.

In 1844, Paiute Chief Truckee guided emigrants along the route and the river that they named after him. Stories of Indian massacres far outnumbered actual hostile encounters. "We are continually hearing of the depredations of the Indians," wrote Caroline Richardson in 1852, "but we have not seen any one yet." Conflict increased in the 1850s and 1860s as thousands of emigrants and their livestock destroyed Indian food sources. Some Indians tried to collect payment for passage across tribal lands. A few emigrants paid, but most felt little sympathy for Indian claims to the land. Relations deteriorated: Indians killed travelers, and emigrants killed Indians.

The violence attracted attention, but it was not the reason most emigrants perished. Thousands died from drownings, accidents, and disease, especially cholera. Many incidents were the work of criminals called "white Indians," who were notorious for their brutality. One 1850 traveler concluded that "the savage Indians" were "afraid to come near the road" and "near all the stealing and killing is done by the Whites following the Trains."

An Enduring Legacy

Travel to California in days, not months! In 1869, the Union Pacific from the east and the Central Pacific from the west connected their rail tracks at Utah's Promontory Summit. A golden spike tapped symbolically to celebrate the union hailed a new, exciting way to travel the continent, and it signaled the demise of the wagon trails to the West.

Although dust from the wagons settled nearly 150 years ago, the California Trail's heritage lives on with the people who love its history and in the railroads, interstate highways, and powerlines that follow the routes of the old emigrant trails. Today, public lands preserve much of the original landscape. Surviving ruts offer silent testimony of the California Trail, but no one tells this epic better than the people who traveled it.

Westward travelers shared similar experiences: the drudgery of walking more than 2,000 miles, the struggle to cross forbidding landscapes, extremes of temperature and weather, shortages of food and water, fear of Indians, accidents, sickness, and death. These emigrants, who saw the elephant and more, remembered the trip west as their life's greatest adventure. Their experiences – often recorded eloquently in journals, drawings, and letters – inspired American popular culture and influenced art, literature, and the movies. Their stories are part of the legacy of the American West.

Reprinted from a National Park Service brochure

POPULATION

Since entering the union as the forty-third state on July 3, 1890, Idaho and its population has grown in leaps and bounds. Between 1900 and 1910, the state's population more than doubled and sparked a population trend that continues to this day. Idaho was recognized as one of the fastest growing states in America between 1990 and 2000 and is presently home to over 1,300,000 permanent residents as the U.S.' thirty-ninth most populous state.

As more and more people flock to the Gem State in search of wide-open spaces, outdoor recreation, low crime rates, and family-friendly communities, native Idahoans have both welcomed and disparaged the development of their beloved home. The state's population growth has brought new economic opportunities, jumpstarted the state's arts and cultural scene, and has provided homeowners in many parts of Idaho with increased property values. At the same time, urban sprawl has left some residents complaining about desecration of wildlife habitat, increased traffic, commuter woes, and overcrowded cities further congested by shrinking availability of uninhabited land.

Despite the widely debated pros and cons of Idaho's growth pattern, the expanding population has given Idaho a new sense of life and vigor with the complexity of people now residing in the state. Metropolitan areas in Coeur d'Alene and Boise (which by most standards are simply mid-sized American cities) weave their livelihoods amid isolated farmland, forests, and rural towns where Main Street represents the community's only paved avenue. Native American groups mix with Caucasians and people of Hispanic origin, and a significant Basque population inhabits southwestern Idaho. Variety not only consumes Idaho's topography, but it is also the name of the game when it comes to the state's numerous towns and cities.

Even though some of Idaho's small towns may still be waiting the arrival of their first movie theater and hushed starry nights may have forever faded from the city skyscape, Idaho's widely divergent residents are still linked with a common

appreciation for the gem they've discovered. Like the state's earliest residents, today's population is drawn to the diversity that encapsulates the Gem State, the opportunities Idaho affords, and a landscape still open to new exploration and individual dreams!

ECONOMY

Reflective of the state's diverse habitation and natural resources, Idaho's economy has long been multifaceted. The state's founding financial fathers embraced the mining, timber, and agricultural industries, and this economic heritage remains widespread throughout Idaho. Although no longer the state's primary source of income, the valuable mining industry produces silver, gold, lead, zinc, antimony, phosphates, copper, garnets, diamonds, clay, molybdenum, and a host of other precious minerals. On the agricultural front, Idaho's famous potatoes lead the way, followed closely by crops of sugar beats, wheat, hay, alfalfa, beans, peas, hops, mint, and bluegrass seed. Beef cattle, dairy goods, sheep, and wool also contribute to the farm and ranch sector. Timber companies, although on the decline, rely upon Idaho's numerous forests and increasingly stringent business practices to supply the nation with building materials and paper products.

At the dawn of the twenty-first century, Idaho's financial picture began to change with a future shifting away from traditional economic mainstays. For the first time in state history, manufacturing and service industries outpaced agriculture and mining as the leaders of Idaho's economy. Technologically advanced industries, such as computer component manufacturers, have found a new home in Idaho's more metropolitan areas, and Boise is consistently ranked as one of America's top cities for hosting technology-based businesses. The addition of large construction firms, food processing plants, and wholesale and retail trade has also established Idaho's presence in the global market.

The newest addition to Idaho's economic pie is a developing tourism sector. Although Idaho was once ranked the least visited state in America, state officials, corporate enterprises, and local business owners have joined forces to climb out of this economically ruinous pit. As a result, people across the world are now standing up and taking notice of the awe-inspiring and unspoiled nature encompassing much of Idaho's terrain. Sun Valley, America's first destination ski-resort, has developed itself into a highly regarded year-round vacation destination, while Coeur d'Alene plays upon its lakeside location to drive in visitors. Smaller communities have followed suit, with Kellogg developing a ski hill and McCall actively promoting its year-round scenic treasures. As more Idaho towns embrace the reality of Idaho's attractiveness to vacationers, the tourism industry will become an even more viable source of state revenue and an economic platform for Idaho's future.

ARTS AND CULTURE

Home to both past and present creative geniuses, Idaho features an arts and culture scene brimming with vibrancy. Literary legends, including Ernest Hemingway and Ezra Pound, trace a portion of their wandering roots to Idaho, and many actors, musicians, and artists have found their inspirational beginnings here as well. As a proud reflection of this heritage, both small towns and larger cities in Idaho offer diverse cultural opportunities for residents and visitors.

Shakespeare comes alive every summer in Idaho's parks, ballerinas twirl to the famous *Nutcracker Suite*, and operas, symphonies, and community bands take the spotlight in community performance centers and open-air theaters. For those craving fine art, Idaho art galleries are abundant, and local art walks occur year-round. In addition, many rural retailers specialize in selling local creative wares, from handmade pottery to log furniture to blown glass. Idaho's cultural scene is further enhanced with dramatic performances ranging from comedic hilarities to heart-wrenching dramas.

For those who venture off the main highways to glimpse a bit of local color, a thriving arts scene is just around the corner. Dig just a little, and you'll be rewarded with some of the nation's most talented artisans, musicians, and stage performers!

RECREATION

While the rest of the country is hibernating during winter or staying indoors to avoid another summer scorcher, Idaho is buzzing with activity. Placid blue lakes, thundering whitewater torrents, rivers filled with trophy trout, forests covered with trails, and mountain slopes frosted with fluffy flakes combine to create one of America's most spectacular destinations.

In Idaho, public land and pristine nature are so prevalent that it is hard to avoid at least some form of recreation. Idaho is often nicknamed the whitewater capital of the world, and kayakers and rafters tempt fate each summer as they crazily crash down the Salmon, Snake, Lochsa, Payette, Clearwater, Owhyee, Bruneau, Jarbidge, and Selway Rivers. Hikers, equestrians, and mountain bike enthusiasts will find trails of all skill levels within the state's spectacular forests and mountain ranges, and hunters flock to the state each fall in search of elk, antelope, deer, bears, mountain lions, moose, and upland birds. Winter enthusiasts are greeted with local and destination downhill ski areas, miles of groomed Nordic ski trails under Idaho's Park and Ski System, and glassy lakes frozen into popular ice skating rinks. Fishing maintains a loyal fan club year-round, and Idaho caters to anglers with hundreds of fishing access areas. Fishing licenses are reasonably priced and may be obtained by calling the Idaho Department of Fish and Game at (208) 334-3700. Natural hot springs also bubble and steam in both undeveloped and commercial sites, and many are available for soaking year-round.

Take a ride on the wild side and turn your vacation into an adventure you'll always remember. Directions to and descriptions of hot springs, river adventures, mountain bike rides, downhill ski resorts, cross-country skiing areas, hiking trails, lake recreation, and popular fishing spots line the pages of this book. As an added bonus, the back of each regional section includes a complete list of the area's outfitters and guides who are happy to assist you on the Idaho adventure of your choice.

IDAHO'S STATE PARK SYSTEM

In addition to boasting contiguous America's largest backcountry area and recreational opportunities located within easy walking or driving distance of several communities, Idaho preserves thirty unique state parks. The Idaho Department of Parks and Recreation represents the great variety and beauty of Idaho and develops and maintains trails while managing an array of outdoor

Strollers shop the farmer's market in downtown Boise.

recreation programs and facilities.

Idaho State Parks are scattered throughout the state and afford a diversity of visitor facilities, from showers and concessions to primitive camping sites. Further information is available from the Idaho State Parks and Recreation Office in Boise, on the Internet at www.idahoparks.org, or by calling (208) 334-4199.

When visiting any of Idaho's State Parks, please note the following fee schedule and rules in an effort to sustain the parks for the enjoyment of future generations.

Fees:
There is a charge for camping, with or without hookups. Camping is permitted only in designated areas, and reservations for campsites, cabins, and yurts can be made up to ninety days in advance online or by telephone. The fees collected by the Idaho Department of Parks and Recreation go right back into the operation and maintenance of parks and recreation programs. The following fees are subject to change pending legislative action. Idaho's six percent sales tax applies to campsites. Camping fees include the right to use designated campgrounds and facilities. Utilities and facilities may be restricted by weather or other factors.

- Primitive Campsite (may include a table, grill, camp-spur, vault toilet, no water): $7 per day

- Basic Campsite (may include a table, grill, camp-spur, vault toilet, central water): $9 per day

- Developed Campsite (may include a table, grill, camp-spur, flush toilets, central water): $12 per day

- Deluxe Campsite (designed to accommodate higher occupancy limits of up to 12 persons): $22 per day

- Electric hookups at site, where available: Additional $4 per day

- Sewer hookups at site, where available: Additional $2 per day

Length of Stay
Length of stay is limited to 15 days in any 30-day period.

Motorized Vehicle Entrance Fee
The Motorized Vehicle Entrance Fee (MVEF) is a daily charge for motorized vehicles. The $4 MVEF is charged when a vehicle enters a designated state park area. The fee is the same regardless of how many people are in the vehicle. Visitors entering an Idaho State Park without a motorized vehicle do not pay. The MVEF does not permit use of campsites.

Annual State Park Passport
The $25 passport allows you to bring your vehicle into any of Idaho's state parks as many times as you wish during the calendar year without paying the MVEF. A passport for a second vehicle is $5 at any time. The second vehicle passport must be purchased at the same location as the first passport. A vehicle registration in the same owner's name is required. The Annual Passport does not apply to camping.

Camping in Boats, Moorage
Overnight moorage for persons who have paid a campsite fee is $5 for any length of vessel. The charge for overnight moorage while camping on a vessel is $8 per night for vessels under 26 feet and $11 per night for vessels 26 feet and over. Priest Lake, Heyburn, and Coeur d'Alene Parkway allow camping on your boat. You may also boat in, camp in the campground, and moor your boat overnight at Heyburn and Priest Lake. The charge for any length of vessel moored at a buoy overnight is $5.

Quiet Hours
The hours between 10 PM and 7 AM are quiet hours, unless otherwise posted. No generators or other motorized equipment emitting sound and exhaust may be operated during quiet hours.

Campsite Parking
All boats, trailers, rigs, and motorized vehicles must fit entirely within the campsite parking spur. All equipment which does not fit entirely within the campsite parking spur must be parked outside

Sunbathers worship the pristine waters of Redfish Lake.

the campground in an area designated by the park manager. If no outside parking is available, a second campsite must be purchased. All camping equipment and personal belongings must be maintained within the assigned campsite. One extra vehicle is allowed per campsite, if it fits. If it does not, a second site must be purchased.

Check Out
Check out time is 1 PM.

Visitors
Visitors are welcome during day-use hours. They must park outside the campground, except with permission of the park manager. Visitors must pay the Motorized Vehicle Entrance Fee if they bring a vehicle into the park.

Prohibited Camping
No camping is permitted on beaches, parking lots, or day-use facilities.

Campfires and Fireworks
Fires are allowed only in designated areas. Fireworks are not permitted.

Motorized Vehicle Use
Motor vehicles, including motorbikes and ATVs, must stay on established roadways and in parking lots.

Pets
Pets are welcome in most parks, but you must keep them on a leash no longer than six feet, or confined to your camper. Do not leave pets unattended in a closed vehicle during the heat of the day. At night, they must be kept inside a vehicle or tent. Some parks have established pet exercise areas. Please ask. Pets are not allowed on beaches. They are not allowed at Eagle Island State Park or at the Sandy Point Unit of Lucky Peak State Park. Pets are allowed only in the parking lot at Harriman State Park.

Resource Protection
Wildlife and vegetation are protected in all Idaho State Parks.

Swimming
Swimming is authorized only in plainly marked areas. There are no lifeguards on duty. Glass containers are not allowed on beaches or at swim areas.

Group Facilities
There are many opportunities for small or large groups to use the facilities of the Idaho Department of Parks and Recreation. Scout groups, family reunions, company picnics, Samborees – they all come under the heading of group use.

Groups of 25 or more, or any group needing special considerations, will need a permit. Permits are required to assure that, if needed, arrangements have been made for sanitation, park population density limitations, safety, and regulation of traffic.

Additional Information
For information about a specific park or facility, contact the park manager. The minimum non-refundable reservation fee is $25. Additional fees may be charged depending on the cost of services provided. Most parks can accommodate group activities of 25 to 100 people, and some parks have special accommodations for groups.

Fees and rules information reprinted from the Idaho State Parks and Recreation Department website

FOREST SERVICE CABINS

One of the best-kept secrets in Idaho is the availability of cabins and lookout stations that the U.S. Forest Service makes available to the public at a nominal fee. At the end of each section, a list of available cabins along with detailed information on each has been provided. Following is some general information about reserving and using the cabins.

Making Reservations
The recreational cabins in the National Forests of Idaho are available for use on a first-come, first-served basis, but reservations are required. Reservations may be made in person, by mail, or by phone by contacting the specific Ranger District listed. Reservations for some cabins may also be made through the National Recreation Reservation Service at 1-877-444-6777.

Facilities
The cabins available through the rental program are rustic and primitive. These facilities were once used as guard stations and fire lookouts by Forest Rangers. Most cabins are located in remote areas, generally accessible via narrow, winding, dirt or gravel roads. With the exception of a few cabins, there are no modern conveniences or the safeguards of modern society – no telephones, traffic jams, neighbors, and no emergency services.

When making reservations, inquire about what is or is not furnished with the cabin or lookout. The facilities are generally equipped with the bare basics, including a table, chairs, wood stove, and bunks (most with mattresses, some without). Bedding is not furnished. Cooking utensils are available at some cabins, but not all. Electricity and piped-in water are generally not available. It may be necessary to bring in safe drinking water, or be prepared to chemically treat or boil water for consumption. At some cabins, you will need to find and cut your own firewood. Expect to use outdoor privies.

Potential Risks
Travel on the National Forests and use of rustic cabins or lookouts involves a degree of risk. Recreationists must assume responsibility of obtaining the knowledge and skills necessary to protect themselves from injury and illness. Weather, road conditions, personal preparation, and other factors can influence travel time and difficulty. Weather changes rapidly in the backcountry. Visitors may encounter sudden storms, including lightning, as well as cold, unexpected temperatures. Responsible preparation is essential. Before the trip, contact the local Ranger District for current conditions of facilities and accessibility.

Cleanup
Before leaving, all users are requested to: make certain all fires are out; pack out all garbage, including empty bottles or cans; clean the cabin; and leave a supply of firewood.

Partially reprinted from a U.S. Forest Service brochure

WIDE OPEN SPACE

Unlike many of its Rocky Mountain counterparts where most land is privately owned, Idaho fortunately claims over 37 million acres of public land. This natural outdoor playground is brimming with campgrounds, trails, and backcountry roads that invite discovery. Many of these pristine, wide-open spaces are under the active management of the U.S. Forest Service, the Bureau of Land Management, and other federal and state land management agencies.

Intermingled with Idaho's stunning and well-maintained public land, however, are occasional plots of private land. While some private landowners are more than willing to share their piece of this marvelous state with others, some are not, and "No Trespassing" signs should be taken seriously. In all instances, exercise common courtesy and always receive permission from the property owner before entering or wandering across these privately maintained open spaces.

In some instances, public land access may also be restricted. Federal and state agencies will occasionally close public roads to protect animal mating environments or preserve fragile forest and rangeland ecosystems. All recreational users are asked to respect such closures and should at all times practice "leave no trace" outdoor ethics. Detailed information and maps regarding public land access are available from regional land and forest managers.

THE ROADS

Gravel roads intermingle with interstates and state highways in this part of the country. Although most of Idaho's paved roads are well-maintained, some mountain roads are narrow and windy with little or no shoulder. Speed limits are posted on most roads and are vigorously enforced for the safety of all travelers.

During wet or wintry weather, beware of black ice! This is a virtually invisible layer of ice that forms on road surfaces after fog. Be particularly careful on stretches of road that parallel rivers and creeks. The early morning fog rising off the water can settle on the road, freezing instantly if temperatures are just right. If you feel yourself sliding, tap your brakes gently. If you slam on the brakes, it is all but over. Gently steer into the direction of your skid (if your back end is going right – steer right).

GUMBO

We gave this subject a separate headline, and it is very important that you read it – and heed it. While Idaho isn't the only state that has gumbo, it has its fair share. If you become a resident, it is one of the first things for which you develop a healthy respect. Grizzlies and rattlesnakes might be the hazards you're warned about, but gumbo is the one that will get you.

You'll find gumbo in various parts of the state, predominantly in more rural areas where backcountry roads frequently criss-cross the terrain. It lies in wait on what in dry weather appears to be an ordinary rock hard dirt road. Your first clue is the occasional sign that reads Road Impassable When Wet. This is a clear understatement. When these roads become even mildly wet, they turn into a monster that swallows all sizes of vehicles – and yes, even 4-wheel drive SUVs. Think you'll get a tow? Forget it. No tow truck operator with a higher IQ than dirt will venture onto it until it dries. If you walk on it, you will grow six inches taller and gain 25 pounds all on the bottom of your shoes. It can coat your tires until they won't turn anymore. Of course, this is if it doesn't swallow you whole first like an unsuspecting native in a Tarzan movie who steps into quicksand.

Bottom line, heed the signs. If it looks like rain, head for the nearest paved road. When it comes to swallowing things whole, the Bermuda Triangle is an amateur compared to Idaho gumbo.

PRECAUTIONS

Water Sports
Beware of high river waters in the spring due to melting snow. Before venturing out on a river adventure, contact knowledgeable local businesses or state recreation officials for the latest water conditions.

Animal Caution
Grizzly bears are scattered throughout Idaho's mountains, forests, and wilderness areas. Grizzlies are vicious when provoked, and it doesn't take much to rile them. Check with local rangers for bear updates and guidelines before heading into bear country. Never hike alone, and make noise along the trail to warn bears of your presence. If you camp, do not sleep near strong smells (toiletries) or food. Cook meals and hang all food from branches at least 100 yards from your tent. Also be alert for mountain lions and moose. Mountain lions are rarely spotted, but are violent predators when provoked. Moose, especially those

with offspring, have been known to charge if individuals get too close or the animal feels threatened.

Rattlesnake Warning
Rattlesnakes are common, especially in the desert terrain of southern Idaho. A bite from the snake can be fatal if not properly treated. These snakes are not aggressive and will usually retreat unless threatened. It is recommended that you wear strong and high top boots when hiking, and be mindful of your step. Be especially careful near rocky areas; snakes often sun themselves on exposed rocks. If you hear a rattle, stop and slowly back away. If bitten, immobilize the area and seek medical care immediately.

Weather
Extremes are commonplace in Idaho without a moment's notice. In high temperatures, drink plenty of water. Idaho's humidity is relatively low, which aids dehydration in warm weather. Nights can be cold even during summer, so pack extra clothes if your plans include the outdoors. Sudden storms can blow in; be prepared with rain and wind gear.

Winter weather is the greatest concern. While roads can be treacherous when snow covered, melting snow and ice can also leave small and invisible patches of ice on the road. In addition, wildlife commonly descend from the mountains and forests in search of food; be aware of deer, elk, and moose on the road, particularly at dusk, sunset, or at night when visibility is limited. If you travel by automobile during Idaho's winter, have plenty of blankets or a sleeping bag, warm clothing, flashlight, and food and water on hand.

HOW TO USE THIS BOOK

In accordance with Idaho's tourism department, we have divided the state into seven sections. Each section has a common personality and at least one major city or town (by Idaho standards). The material in each section is loosely ordered along the highway routes through the section and organized by locator numbers.

Locator Numbers
These are the numbers on the map in white on a black circle (❶). All information relating to the area on the map marked by that number is presented together in the section. The sections of the book are ordered from north to south, then west to east. The numbers allow you to follow the routes mile by mile and quickly find information along your path relating to your location on the path. In a nutshell, find the number on the map, then find that number heading in the section, and listed under that number is everything there is to see or do at that location on the map. If you know where you are on the map, you will know about everything there is around you.

Category Classification
Each item listed is classified under one of eight categories. The classification key is the shaded letter immediately preceding the item listed. This makes it very simple to find the type of information you're looking for immediately. If you're hungry, look for any items preceded by an F. Looking for something to do? Look for a T or V. Want to buy something to take home with you? Look for an S. Here is a key for the categories:

H Historic Marker
We have taken the text from over hundreds of historical and interpretive markers throughout the state and reprinted them here. They're fun read-

ing, and in total, provide an excellent background on the history, growth, and features of Idaho. The state wouldn't have placed them if they weren't of some significance. Since it would take you weeks, if not months, to travel the state and view them all personally, we have provided the legends from each and entered them where they are located. Even though we've presented the text of these markers here, take time to stop at everyone you can. The text we've included is only a label for the actual site or event they speak of, and the experience is only complete if you are able to view the area to which they refer.

T Attraction
This category includes just about anything worth stopping for. It might be a museum, a ghost town, a park, or just some quirky thing on the side of the road that makes traveling through Idaho so interesting. Whatever it is, we've tried to provide enough information to let you decide whether you want to plan a stop or not.

V Adventure
This category encompasses just about anything in which you would get out of your car and actively participate, including a fishing or whitewater rafting trip, horseback ride, hike, etc.

F Food
We didn't discriminate. If there is prepared food available, we list it. We've listed everything ranging from the finest restaurants in the state (and there are a lot of them), to fast food and hot dog stands. Bottom line, if they'll fix it for you, they're listed here. While we don't rate any of the establishments, we highly encourage you to try the mom and pop eateries and the locally owned fine dining spots. Dayton Duncan, in his excellent book Out West: American Journey Along the Lewis and Clark Trail (1987, Penguin Books) gave the best advice we've heard:

"Franchises are not for the traveler bent on discovery. Forsaking franchises, like forsaking interstates, means that you're willing to chance the ups and downs, the starts and the stops of gastronomy as well as motoring. It means sometimes finishing a supper so good that you order the piece of pie you hadn't realized you wanted and you're sure you don't need—and spending the night in town just so you can have breakfast in the same place."

In Idaho, you're pretty safe. Just consider the logic. Many towns are so small that any place not serving up good grub isn't going to last long anyway. Accountability. While much of America has forgotten that concept, it is still a harsh and unforgiving rule in Idaho.

As for fine dining, we'd put scores of Idaho's best against the best anywhere outside of the state. Some of the most talented culinary artists in the world have settled here for the lifestyle and share their talents with residents and visitors alike.

L Lodging
If they'll put a roof over your head and a mattress under your back, they're listed here. Again, we don't discriminate. Truth is, it's hard to find a bad motel in this state. The same concept that applies to Idaho eateries applies to the state's lodging facilities. If business owners don't put up a good product, they don't last long.

C Camping
These are private campgrounds that wished to be included in the main portion of each section. Otherwise, all private campgrounds are listed at the back of each section.

S Shopping

Do we need to explain this one? Obviously, we don't list every place in the state you can buy something. Only those who wanted to be in here are listed. And yes, they paid for the opportunity. It would be impractical to list every place in the state you can buy something. And you probably wouldn't want to wade through all of them to get to the ones that count. So we left it up to the merchants to decide whether or not they might offer something of interest to you and to choose whether or not to include themselves in this book.

M Misc. Services

This would be just about anything that doesn't fall into one of the other categories above, including realtors, chambers of commerce, etc.

Maps

We've included a map for just about anything that requires your use of a map. At the beginning of each section is a detailed map of the section. We've also included a map of any town too big to see everything on Main Street standing in one spot—fifty-three in all. In addition, section maps are marked with campground locations, and we've also included a number of maps of special locations.

Campgrounds

Public campgrounds are marked on the map with a tent symbol. These symbols give an idea of where camping is available. At the end of each section is a chart listing each campground along with pertinent information about that site. We listed every maintained campground, public and private, we could find. If you find any we missed, please let us know. Please note, there are countless primitive campgrounds in the state that are not maintained and have no facilities. You'll find almost all of Idaho's public campgrounds to be uncrowded. It's not unusual, even at the peak of tourist season,

to be the only campers at a site. Most public campgrounds charge a small fee to cover the cost of maintenance.

We especially wish to thank the Idaho RV Campgrounds Association/IRVCA for graciously allowing us to use their RV park/campground information. Visit IRVCA on the web at www.rvidaho.org.

Fishing Sites

Idaho's fisheries and trout-filled waters are famous across the world, and we've taken that fact into account. Throughout the pages of this book, you'll find access information and descriptions of both popular and hidden fishing destinations, including rivers, streams, lakes, and reservoirs. Each listing also includes the species anglers are likely to find when wetting their line in a particular fishing hole.

Scenic Drives

We have tried to offer some scenic or interesting side trips wherever possible. Some take you on backroads while others simply take you to a scenic overlook. Some require just an hour to complete and others are longer day trips. We feel the book itself offers one long scenic trip, but if you want to travel off the beaten path, these drives offer some choices. Heed the warnings about gumbo and other backroad hazards mentioned earlier in this book.

Hikes

We have offered you a number of hikes at the end of every section. Directions for accessing each hike are provided along with a general description of the hike's mileage, difficulty, and scenic highlights.

Information Please

Here we give you phone numbers for just about anything we missed earlier in the section that may be of interest to you.

Dining and Lodging Quick Reference Guides

These charts, which are located at the end of each section, allow you to take a quick scan of all of the region's dining and lodging facilities in a manner that allows you to find and compare information quickly. Map locator numbers and addresses are listed with each entry to help you find the facility's location. Businesses in bold print paid to include additional information under the appropriate map locator number in the body of the section.

Notes

We've provided you ample room at the back of each section to make notes or record additional information about your trip. This is a good place to store reservation confirmation numbers or schedule information.

We've made every effort to make this book a tool for you to get the most from your visit to Idaho. If you already live here, we hope it awakens you to the endless things there are to do and see in this magnificent chunk of America.

AND FINALLY...

In instances where we have included information from other well-researched, well-written materials, we have attempted to credit every source as accurately as possible. It was our goal to provide you, the reader, the maximum amount of information possible to make your explorations of Idaho enjoyable while providing all the resources you need in one book. Hopefully we accomplished that goal. If there is anything we've overlooked, we would certainly like to hear from you so that we can include it in future editions.

Happy Trails!

NOTES:

IDAHO ZIP CODES

By Town

Aberdeen	83210
Acequia	83350
Ahsahka	83520
Albion	83311
Almo	83312
American Falls	83211
Arbon	83212
Arcs	83213
Arimo	83214
Ashton	83420
Ashton	83447
Athol	83801
Atlanta	83601
Atomic City	83215
Avery	83802
Bancrott	83217
Banks	83602
Basalt	83218
Bayview	83803
Bellevue	83313
Bern	83220
Blackfoot	83221
Blanchard	83804
Bliss	83314
Bloomington	83223
Boise	83701
Boise	83702
Boise	83703
Boise	83704
Boise	83705
Boise	83706
Boise	83707
Boise	83708
Boise	83709
Boise	83711
Boise	83712
Boise	83713
Boise	83714
Boise	83715
Boise	83716
Boise	83717
Boise	83788
Boise	83799
Bonners Ferry	83805
Bovill	83806
Bruneau	83604
Buhl	83316
Burley	83318
Calder	83808
Caldwell	83605
Caldwell	83606
Caldwell	83607
Cambridge	83610
Carey	83320
Careywood	83809
Carmen	83462
Cascade	83611
Castleford	83321
Cataldo	83810
Centervllle	83631
Challis	83226
Challis	83229
Cheater	83421
Chubbuck	83202
Clark Fork	83811
Clarkia	83812
Clayton	83227
Clearwater	83539
Clifton	83228
Cobalt	83229
Cocolalla	83813
Coeur d'Alene	83814
Coeur d'Alene	83815
Coeur d'Alene	83816
Colburn	83865
Conda	83230
Coolin	83821
Corral	83322
Cottonwood	83522
Cottonwood	83533
Cottonwood	83538
Council	83612
Craigmont	83523
Culdesac	83524
Culdesac	83548
Dalton Gardens	83815
Darlington	83255
Dayton	83232
Deary	83823
Declo	83323
Desmet	83824
Dietrlch	83324
Dingle	83233
Dixie	83525
Donnelly	83615
Dover	83825
Downey	83234
Driggs	83422
Dubois	83423
Dubois	83446
Eagle	83616
Eastport	83826
Eden	83325
Elba	83342
Elk City	83525
Elk Horn	83354
Elk River	83827
Ellis	83235
Emmett	83617
Fairfield	83322
Fairfield	83327
Felt	83424
Fenn	83531
Ferdinand	83526
Fernwood	83830
Filer	83328
Firth	83236
Fish Haven	83287
Fort Hall	83203
Franklin	83237
Fruitland	83619
Fruitvale	83620
Garden Valley	83622
Geneses	83832
Geneva	83238
Georgetown	83239
Gibbonsville	83463
Glenns Ferry	83623
Gooding	83330
Grace	83241
Grace	83283
Grand View	83624
Grangeville	83530
Grangeville	83531
Grasmere	83604
Greencreek	83533
Greenleaf	83626
Hagerman	83332
Hailey	83333
Hamer	83425
Hammett	83627
Hansen	83334
Harrison	83833
Harvard	83834
Hayden	83835
Hayden Lake	83835
Hazelton	83335
Headquarters	83546
Heyburn	83336
Hidden Springs	83703
Hill City	83337
Holbrook	83243
Homedale	83628
Hope	83836
Horseshoe Bend	83629
Howe	83244
Huston	83630
Idaho City	83631
Idaho Falls	83401
Idaho Falls	83402
Idaho Falls	83403
Idaho Falls	83404
Idaho Falls	83405
Idaho Falls	83406
Indian Valley	83632
Inkom	83245
Iona	83427
Irwin	83428
Island Park	83429
Island Park	83433
Jerome	83338
Juilaetta	83535
Kamiah	83536
Kellogg	83837
Kendrick	83537
Ketchum	83340
Keuterville	83522
Keuterville	83538
Kimberly	83341
King Hill	83633
Kingston	83839
Kooskia	83539
Kootenal	83840
Kuna	83634
Laciede	83841
Lake Fork	83635
Lapwai	83540
Lava Hot Springs	83246
Leadore	83464
Lemhi	83465
Lenore	83541
Laths	83636
Lewiston	83501
Lewlavfile	83431
Lowman	83637
Luclle	83542
Mackay	83251
Hacks Inn	83433
Malad City	83252
Malad City	83280
Malta	83342
Marsing	83639
May	83253
McCall	83635
McCall	83638
McCommon	83250
Medimont	83842
Melba	83641
Marian	83434
Meridian	83642
Meridian	83680
Mesa	83643
Middleton	83644
Midvale	83645
Minidoka	83343
Monteview	83435
Montour	83617
Montpelier	83254
Moore	83255
Moreland	83256
Moscow	83843
Mountain Home	83647
Mountain Home AFB	83648
Moyle Springs	83845
Muilan	83846
Murphy	83650
Murray	83874
Murtaugh	83344
Nat	83342
Nampa	83651
Nampa	83652
Nampa	83653
Nampa	83686
Nampa	83687
Naples	83847
New Centerville	83631
New Meadows	83654
New Plymouth	83655
Newdale	83436
Nez Perceperce	83543
Nordman	83848
North Fork	83466
North Fork	83469
Notus	83656
Oakley	83346
Obsidian	83340
Ola	83657
Oldtown	83822
Onaway	83855
Oreana	83650
Orofino	83544
Osburn	83849
Ovid	83254
Palisades	83428
Paris	83261
Paris	83287
Parker	83438
Parma	83660
Patterson	83253
Paul	83347
Payette	83661
Peck	83545
Picabo	83348
Pierce	83546
Pinehurst	83850
Pingree	83262
Pioneerville	83631
Placerville	83666
Plummer	83851
Pocatello	83201
Pocatello	83202
Pocatello	83204
Pocatello	83205
Pocatello	83206
Pocatello	83203
Pollock	83547
Ponderay	83852
Porthill	83853
Post Falls	83854
Post Falls	83877
Potlatch	83855
Preston	83263
Priest Riverer	83856
Princeton	83857
Rathdrum	83858
Reubens	83548
Rexburg	83440
Richfield	83349
Riddle	83604
Rigby	83442
Riggins	83549
RIrle	83443
Roberts	83444
Rockiand	83271
Rogerson	83302
Rupert	83343
Rupert	83350
Sagle	83860
Salmon	83467
Samuels	83862
Sandpoint	83809
Sandpoint	83840
Sandpoint	83862
Sandpoint	83864
Sandpoint	83865
Santa	83866
Shelley	83274
Shoshone	83324
Shoshone	83352
Shoup	83469
Silverton	83867
Smelterville	83868
Soda Springs	83230
Soda Springs	83276
Soda Springs	83285
Spalding	83551
Spencer	83446
Spirit Lake	83869
Springfield	83277
Squirrel	83447
St Anthony	83445
St Charles	83272
St Maries	83861
Stanley	83278
Star	83669
Star Ranch	83631
Sterling	83210
Stiles	83552
Stone	83280
Sugar City	83448
Sun Valley	83353
Sun Valley	83354
Swan Valley	83449
Swanlake	83281
Sweet	83670
Tendoy	83468
Tensed	83870
Terreton	83450
Telon	83451
Tetonia	83424
Tetonia	83452
Thatcher	83283
Troy	83871
Twin Falls	83301
Twin Falls	83302
Twin Falls	83303
Twin Lakes	83858
Ucon	83454
Victor	83455
Viola	83872
Wallace	83873
Wallace	83874
Warren	83671
Wayan	83285
Weippe	83553
Weiser	83672
Wendell	83355
Weston	83286
White Bird	83554
Wilder	83676
Winchester	83555
Worley	83876
Yellow Pine	83677

By Zip Code

Zip	City	Zip	City	Zip	City	Zip	City	Zip	City
83201	Pocatello	83303	Twin Falls	83446	Dubois	83622	Garden Valley	83806	Bovill
83202	Chubbuck	83311	Albion	83446	Spencer	83623	Glenns Ferry	83808	Calder
83202	Pocatello	83312	Almo	83447	Ashton	83624	Grand View	83809	Careywood
83203	Fort Hall	83313	Bellevue	83447	Squirrel	83626	Greenleaf	83809	Sandpoint
83203	Pocatello	83314	Bliss	83448	Sugar City	83627	Hammett	83810	Cataldo
83204	Pocatello	83316	Buhl	83449	Swan Valley	83628	Homedale	83811	Clark Fork
83205	Pocatello	83318	Burley	83450	Terreton	83629	Horseshoe Bend	83812	Clarkia
83206	Pocatello	83320	Carey	83451	Telon	83630	Huston	83813	Cocolalla
83210	Aberdeen	83321	Castleford	83452	Tetonia	83631	Centervllle	83814	Coeur d'Alene
83210	Sterling	83322	Corral	83454	Ucon	83631	Idaho City	83815	Coeur d'Alene
83211	American Falls	83322	Fairfield	83455	Victor	83631	New Centerville	83815	Dalton Gardens
83212	Arbon	83323	Declo	83462	Carmen	83631	Pioneerville	83816	Coeur d'Alene
83213	Arcs	83324	Dietrlch	83463	Gibbonsville	83631	Star Ranch	83821	Coolin
83214	Arimo	83324	Shoshone	83464	Leadore	83632	Indian Valley	83822	Oldtown
83215	Atomic City	83325	Eden	83465	Lemhi	83633	King Hill	83823	Deary
83217	Bancrott	83327	Fairfield	83466	North Fork	83634	Kuna	83824	Desmet
83218	Basalt	83328	Filer	83467	Salmon	83635	Lake Fork	83825	Dover
83220	Bern	83330	Gooding	83468	Tendoy	83635	McCall	83826	Eastport
83221	Blackfoot	83332	Hagerman	83469	North Fork	83636	Laths	83827	Elk River
83223	Bloomington	83333	Hailey	83469	Shoup	83637	Lowman	83830	Fernwood
83226	Challis	83334	Hansen	83501	Lewiston	83638	McCall	83832	Geneses
83227	Clayton	83335	Hazelton	83520	Ahsahka	83639	Marsing	83833	Harrison
83228	Clifton	83336	Heyburn	83522	Cottonwood	83641	Melba	83834	Harvard
83229	Challis	83337	Hill City	83522	Keuterville	83642	Meridian	83835	Hayden
83229	Cobalt	83338	Jerome	83523	Craigmont	83643	Mesa	83835	Hayden Lake
83230	Conda	83340	Ketchum	83524	Culdesac	83644	Middleton	83836	Hope
83230	Soda Springs	83340	Obsidian	83525	Dixie	83645	Midvale	83837	Kellogg
83232	Dayton	83341	Kimberly	83525	Elk City	83647	Mountain Home	83839	Kingston
83233	Dingle	83342	Elba	83526	Ferdinand	83648	Mountain Home AFB	83840	Kootenal
83234	Downey	83342	Malta	83530	Grangeville	83650	Murphy	83840	Sandpoint
83235	Ellis	83342	Nat	83531	Fenn	83650	Oreana	83841	Laciede
83236	Firth	83343	Minidoka	83531	Grangeville	83651	Nampa	83842	Medimont
83237	Franklin	83343	Rupert	83533	Cottonwood	83652	Nampa	83843	Moscow
83238	Geneva	83344	Murtaugh	83533	Greencreek	83653	Nampa	83845	Moyle Springs
83239	Georgetown	83346	Oakley	83535	Juilaetta	83654	New Meadows	83846	Muilan
83241	Grace	83347	Paul	83536	Kamiah	83655	New Plymouth	83847	Naples
83243	Holbrook	83348	Picabo	83537	Kendrick	83656	Notus	83848	Nordman
83244	Howe	83349	Richfield	83538	Cottonwood	83657	Ola	83849	Osburn
83245	Inkom	83350	Acequia	83538	Keuterville	83660	Parma	83850	Pinehurst
83246	Lava Hot Springs	83350	Rupert	83539	Clearwater	83661	Payette	83851	Plummer
83250	Mc Common	83352	Shoshone	83539	Kooskia	83666	Placerville	83852	Ponderay
83251	Mackay	83353	Sun Valley	83540	Lapwai	83669	Star	83853	Porthill
83252	Malad City	83354	Elk Horn	83541	Lenore	83670	Sweet	83854	Post Falls
83253	May	83354	Sun Valley	83542	Lucile	83671	Warren	83855	Onaway
83253	Patterson	83355	Wendell	83543	Nezperce	83672	Weiser	83855	Potlatch
83254	Montpelier	83401	Idaho Falls	83544	Orofino	83676	Wilder	83856	Priest Riverer
83254	Ovid	83402	Idaho Falls	83545	Peck	83677	Yellow Pine	83857	Princeton
83255	Darlington	83403	Idaho Falls	83546	Headquarters	83680	Meridian	83858	Rathdrum
83255	Moore	83404	Idaho Falls	83546	Pierce	83686	Nampa	83858	Twin Lakes
83256	Moreland	83405	Idaho Falls	83547	Pollock	83687	Nampa	83860	Sagle
83261	Paris	83406	Idaho Falls	83548	Culdesac	83701	Boise	83861	St Maries
83262	Pingree	83420	Ashton	83548	Reubens	83702	Boise	83862	Samuels
83263	Preston	83421	Cheater	83549	Riggins	83703	Boise	83862	Sandpoint
83271	Rockiand	83422	Driggs	83551	Spalding	83703	Hidden Springs	83864	Sandpoint
83272	St Charles	83423	Dubois	83552	Stiles	83704	Boise	83865	Colburn
83274	Shelley	83424	Felt	83553	Weippe	83705	Boise	83865	Sandpoint
83276	Soda Springs	83424	Tetonia	83554	White Bird	83706	Boise	83866	Santa
83277	Springfield	83425	Hamer	83555	Winchester	83707	Boise	83867	Silverton
83278	Stanley	83427	Iona	83601	Atlanta	83708	Boise	83868	Smelterville
83280	Malad City	83428	Irwin	83602	Banks	83709	Boise	83869	Spirit Lake
83280	Stone	83428	Palisades	83604	Bruneau	83711	Boise	83870	Tensed
83281	Swanlake	83429	Island Park	83604	Grasmere	83712	Boise	83871	Troy
83283	Grace	83431	Lewlavfile	83604	Riddle	83713	Boise	83872	Viola
83283	Thatcher	83433	Island Park	83605	Caldwell	83714	Boise	83873	Wallace
83285	Soda Springs	83433	Hacks Inn	83606	Caldwell	83715	Boise	83874	Murray
83285	Wayan	83434	Marian	83607	Caldwell	83716	Boise	83874	Wallace
83286	Weston	83435	Monteview	83610	Cambridge	83717	Boise	83876	Worley
83287	Fish Haven	83436	Newdale	83611	Cascade	83788	Boise	83877	Post Falls
83287	Paris	83438	Parker	83612	Council	83799	Boise	83619	Fruitland
83301	Twin Falls	83440	Rexburg	83615	Donnelly	83801	Athol		
83302	Rogerson	83442	Rigby	83616	Eagle	83802	Avery		
83302	Twin Falls	83443	Rlrle	83617	Emmett	83803	Bayview		
		83444	Roberts	83617	Montour	83804	Blanchard		
		83445	St Anthony	83620	Fruitvale	83805	Bonners Ferry		

IDAHO COUNTIES

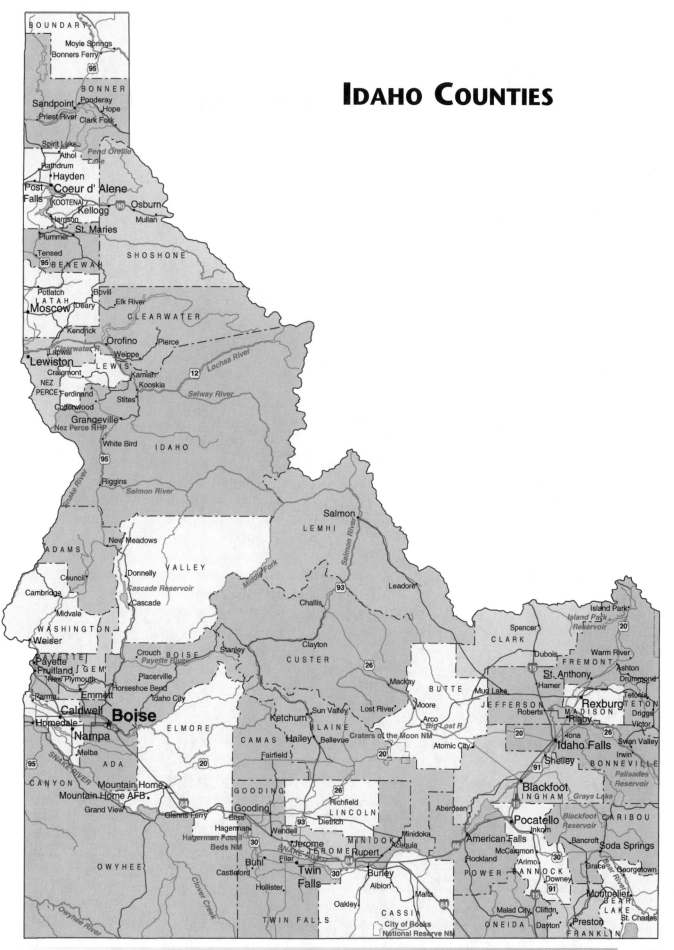

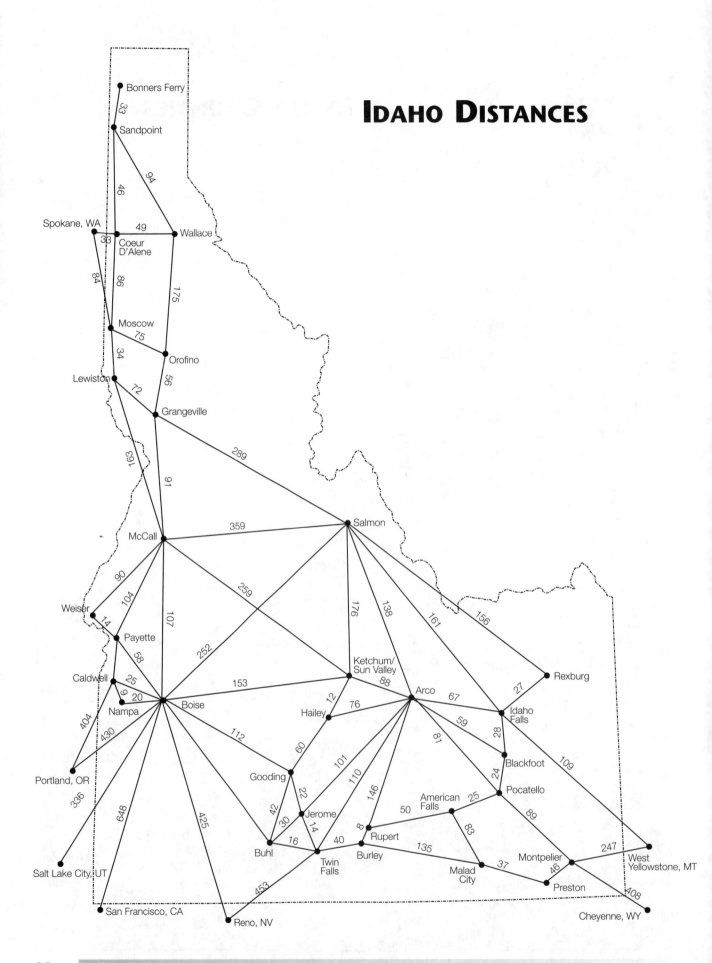

IDAHO DISTANCES

Bonners Ferry

33

Sandpoint

46 · 94

Spokane, WA · 49 · Wallace

33 · Coeur D'Alene

84 · 86 · 175

Moscow

75

34 · Orofino

Lewiston · 72 · 56

163 · Grangeville

91 · 289

McCall · 359 · Salmon

90 · 259

104 · 176 · 138 · 161 · 156

Weiser · 107

14 · 252 · Ketchum/Sun Valley · Rexburg

Payette · 153 · 88 · Arco · 67 · 27

58 · 12 · 76

Caldwell · 25 · 59 · Idaho Falls

9 · 20 · Boise · Hailey · 81 · 28

Nampa · 112 · 24 · Blackfoot · 109

404 · 60 · 101 · Pocatello

430 · Gooding · 110 · 146 · American Falls · 25 · 89

Portland, OR · 22 · 50

336 · 42 · Jerome · 83 · 247

849 · 30 · 14 · 8 · Rupert · Montpelier · West Yellowstone, MT

425 · Buhl · 16 · 40 · Burley · 135 · Malad City · 37 · 46

Twin Falls · Preston · 408

Salt Lake City, UT · 453

San Francisco, CA · Reno, NV · Cheyenne, WY

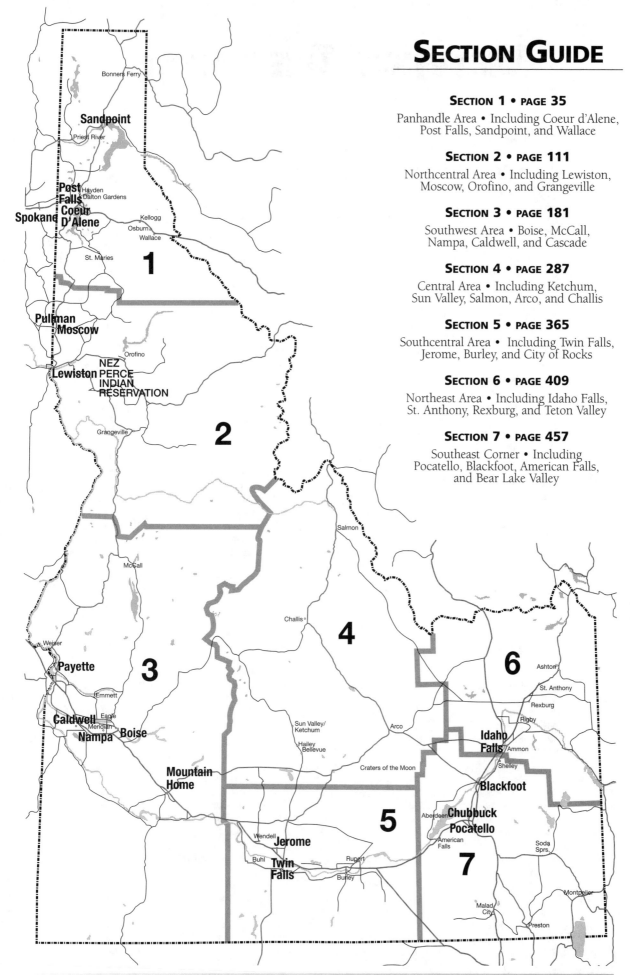

Introduction

DRIVING DISTANCE

American Falls to
Arco	102
Blackfoot	45
Boise	210
Bonners Ferry	582
Buhl	109
Burley	53
Butte, MT	278
Caldwell	235
Cheyenne, WY	531
Coeur d'Alene	535
Gooding	116
Grangeville	408
Hailey	151
Idaho Falls	72
Jerome	95
Lewiston	480
McCall	317
Malad City	83
Montpelier	114
Moscow	513
Nampa	226
Orofino	464
Payette	268
Pocatello	25
Portland, OR	638
Preston	93
Reno, NV	542
Rexburg	99
Rupert	50
Salmon	231
Salt Lake City, UT	167
Sandpoint	556
San Francisco, CA	765
Spokane, WA	572
Sun Valley/Ketchum	163
Twin Falls	93
Wallace	487
Weiser	282
W. Yellowstone, MT	181

Arco to
American Falls	102
Blackfoot	59
Boise	189
Bonners Ferry	489
Buhl	126
Burley	144
Butte, MT	235
Caldwell	214
Cheyenne, WY	587
Coeur d'Alene	446
Gooding	100
Grangeville	388
Hailey	76
Idaho Falls	67
Jerome	101
Lewiston	460
McCall	297
Malad City	138
Montpelier	169
Moscow	493
Nampa	205

Orofino	443
Payette	248
Pocatello	81
Portland, OR	618
Preston	148
Reno, NV	563
Rexburg	87
Rupert	146
Salmon	138
Salt Lake City, UT	241
Sandpoint	463
San Francisco, CA	786
Spokane, WA	475
Sun Valley/Ketchum	88
Twin Falls	110
Wallace	394
Weiser	261
W. Yellowstone, MT	169

Blackfoot to
American Falls	45
Arco	59
Boise	248
Bonners Ferry	539
Buhl	153
Burley	97
Butte, MT	234
Caldwell	273
Cheyenne, WY	529
Coeur d'Alene	492
Gooding	158
Grangeville	446
Hailey	135
Idaho Falls	28
Jerome	139
Lewiston	518
McCall	355
Malad City	80
Montpelier	111
Moscow	551
Nampa	264
Orofino	502
Payette	306
Pocatello	24
Portland, OR	677
Preston	91
Reno, NV	585
Rexburg	55
Rupert	94
Salmon	187
Salt Lake City, UT	184
Sandpoint	512
San Francisco, CA	808
Spokane, WA	528
Sun Valley/Ketchum	147
Twin Falls	137
Wallace	443
Weiser	320
W. Yellowstone, MT	147

Boise to
American Falls	210
Arco	189

Blackfoot	248
Bonners Ferry	465
Buhl	119
Burley	163
Butte, MT	425
Caldwell	25
Cheyenne, WY	741
Coeur d'Alene	389
Gooding	102
Grangeville	198
Hailey	141
Idaho Falls	257
Jerome	112
Lewiston	270
McCall	107
Malad City	292
Montpelier	323
Moscow	303
Nampa	20
Orofino	254
Payette	58
Pocatello	234
Portland, OR	430
Preston	302
Reno, NV	425
Rexburg	276
Rupert	165
Salmon	252
Salt Lake City, UT	336
Sandpoint	434
San Francisco, CA	648
Spokane, WA	379
Sun Valley/Ketchum	153
Twin Falls	128
Wallace	413
Weiser	72
W. Yellowstone, MT	358

Bonners Ferry to
American Falls	582
Arco	489
Blackfoot	539
Boise	465
Buhl	584
Burley	628
Butte, MT	330
Caldwell	471
Cheyenne, WY	980
Coeur d'Alene	79
Gooding	567
Grangeville	267
Hailey	545
Idaho Falls	512
Jerome	577
Lewiston	196
McCall	358
Malad City	618
Montpelier	649
Moscow	162
Nampa	480
Orofino	237
Payette	437
Pocatello	561

Portland, OR	461
Preston	628
Reno, NV	862
Rexburg	507
Rupert	630
Salmon	351
Salt Lake City, UT	729
Sandpoint	33
San Francisco, CA	972
Spokane, WA	109
Sun Valley/Ketchum	528
Twin Falls	594
Wallace	127
Weiser	424
W. Yellowstone, MT	481

Buhl to
American Falls	109
Arco	126
Blackfoot	153
Boise	163
Bonners Ferry	628
Burley	56
Butte, MT	360
Caldwell	149
Cheyenne, WY	636
Coeur d'Alene	507
Gooding	42
Grangeville	317
Hailey	85
Idaho Falls	180
Jerome	30
Lewiston	389
McCall	226
Malad City	170
Montpelier	217
Moscow	422
Nampa	140
Orofino	372
Payette	177
Pocatello	133
Portland, OR	546
Preston	201
Reno, NV	459
Rexburg	207
Rupert	63
Salmon	264
Salt Lake City, UT	238
Sandpoint	551
San Francisco, CA	682
Spokane, WA	502
Sun Valley/Ketchum	97
Twin Falls	16
Wallace	519
Weiser	191
W. Yellowstone, MT	289

Burley to
American Falls	53
Arco	144
Blackfoot	97
Boise	163
Bonners Ferry	628

Buhl	56
Butte, MT	331
Caldwell	188
Cheyenne, WY	585
Coeur d'Alene	552
Gooding	69
Grangeville	361
Hailey	100
Idaho Falls	124
Jerome	48
Lewiston	433
McCall	270
Malad City	135
Montpelier	166
Moscow	466
Nampa	179
Orofino	416
Payette	221
Pocatello	77
Portland, OR	588
Preston	146
Reno, NV	491
Rexburg	151
Rupert	8
Salmon	282
Salt Lake City, UT	177
Sandpoint	596
San Francisco, CA	714
Spokane, WA	533
Sun Valley/Ketchum	16
Twin Falls	40
Wallace	537
Weiser	235
W. Yellowstone, MT	233

Butte, MT to
American Falls	278
Arco	235
Blackfoot	234
Boise	425
Bonners Ferry	330
Buhl	360
Burley	331
Caldwell	448
Cheyenne, WY	650
Coeur d'Alene	285
Gooding	335
Grangeville	290
Hailey	312
Idaho Falls	208
Jerome	336
Lewiston	335
McCall	381
Malad City	313
Montpelier	344
Moscow	359
Nampa	440
Orofino	294
Payette	460
Pocatello	257
Portland, OR	654
Preston	324
Reno, NV	798

Rexburg 203
Rupert 327
Salmon 146
Salt Lake City, UT 413
Sandpoint 303
San Francisco, CA 1002
Spokane, WA 314
Sun Valley/Ketchum 324
Twin Falls 346
Wallace 238
Weiser 446
W. Yellowstone, MT 148

Caldwell to
American Falls 235
Arco 214
Blackfoot 273
Boise 25
Bonners Ferry 471
Buhl 149
Burley 188
Butte, MT 448
Cheyenne, WY 765
Coeur d'Alene 394
Gooding 127
Grangeville 204
Hailey 162
Idaho Falls 282
Jerome 141
Lewiston 276
McCall 123
Malad City 317
Montpelier 348
Moscow 309
Nampa 9
Orofino 259
Payette 34
Pocatello 259
Portland, OR 404
Preston 327
Reno, NV 408
Rexburg 301
Rupert 189
Salmon 277
Salt Lake City, UT 362
Sandpoint 438
San Francisco, CA 631
Spokane, WA 386
Sun Valley/Ketchum 174
Twin Falls 153
Wallace 418
Weiser 47
W. Yellowstone, MT 383

Cheyenne, WY to
American Falls 531
Arco 587
Blackfoot 529
Boise 741
Bonners Ferry 980
Buhl 636
Burley 585
Butte, MT 650
Caldwell 765
Coeur d'Alene 935
Gooding 647
Grangeville 939
Hailey 663
Idaho Falls 520

Jerome 626
Lewiston 985
McCall 848
Malad City 501
Montpelier 408
Moscow 1009
Nampa 757
Orofino 944
Payette 797
Pocatello 507
Portland, OR 1168
Preston 454
Reno, NV 946
Rexburg 511
Rupert 581
Salmon 667
Salt Lake City, UT 428
Sandpoint 953
San Francisco, CA 1169
Spokane, WA 964
Sun Valley/Ketchum 676
Twin Falls 620
Wallace 886
Weiser 810
W. Yellowstone, MT 500

Coeur d'Alene to
American Falls 535
Arco 446
Blackfoot 492
Boise 389
Bonners Ferry 79
Buhl 507
Burley 552
Butte, MT 285
Caldwell 394
Cheyenne, WY 935
Gooding 491
Grangeville 191
Hailey 193
Idaho Falls 465
Jerome 501
Lewiston 119
McCall 282
Malad City 571
Montpelier 602
Moscow 86
Nampa 403
Orofino 160
Payette 365
Pocatello 514
Portland, OR 384
Preston 581
Reno, NV 785
Rexburg 460
Rupert 553
Salmon 304
Salt Lake City, UT 687
Sandpoint 46
San Francisco, CA 897
Spokane, WA 33
Sun Valley/Ketchum 481
Twin Falls 517
Wallace 49
Weiser 347
W. Yellowstone, MT 433

Gooding to
American Falls 116

Arco 100
Blackfoot 158
Boise 102
Bonners Ferry 567
Buhl 42
Burley 69
Butte, MT 335
Caldwell 127
Cheyenne, WY 647
Coeur d'Alene 491
Grangeville 300
Hailey 60
Idaho Falls 167
Jerome 22
Lewiston 372
McCall 210
Malad City 182
Montpelier 240
Moscow 405
Nampa 118
Orofino 356
Payette 160
Pocatello 140
Portland, OR 531
Preston 208
Reno, NV 489
Rexburg 180
Rupert 71
Salmon 238
Salt Lake City, UT 249
Sandpoint 535
San Francisco, CA 712
Spokane, WA 486
Sun Valley/Ketchum 72
Twin Falls 35
Wallace 493
Weiser 174
W. Yellowstone, MT 262

Grangeville to
American Falls 408
Arco 388
Blackfoot 446
Boise 198
Bonners Ferry 267
Buhl 317
Burley 361
Butte, MT 290
Caldwell 204
Cheyenne, WY 939
Coeur d'Alene 191
Gooding 300
Hailey 344
Idaho Falls 450
Jerome 310
Lewiston 72
McCall 91
Malad City 490
Montpelier 521
Moscow 105
Nampa 211
Orofino 56
Payette 170
Pocatello 432
Portland, OR 426
Preston 500
Reno, NV 599
Rexburg 445
Rupert 363

Salmon 289
Salt Lake City, UT 533
Sandpoint 234
San Francisco, CA 822
Spokane, WA 182
Sun Valley/Ketchum 352
Twin Falls 327
Wallace 215
Weiser 157
W. Yellowstone, MT 436

Hailey to
American Falls 151
Arco 76
Blackfoot 135
Boise 141
Bonners Ferry 545
Buhl 85
Burley 100
Butte, MT 312
Caldwell 162
Cheyenne, WY 663
Coeur d'Alene 193
Gooding 60
Grangeville 344
Idaho Falls 144
Jerome 61
Lewiston 412
McCall 247
Malad City 222
Montpelier 256
Moscow 444
Nampa 157
Orofino 395
Payette 200
Pocatello 158
Portland, OR 572
Preston 225
Reno, NV 524
Rexburg 163
Rupert 106
Salmon 186
Salt Lake City, UT 283
Sandpoint 513
San Francisco, CA 747
Spokane, WA 521
Sun Valley/Ketchum 12
Twin Falls 70
Wallace 447
Weiser 212
W. Yellowstone, MT 245

Idaho Falls to
American Falls 72
Arco 67
Blackfoot 28
Boise 257
Bonners Ferry 512
Buhl 180
Burley 124
Butte, MT 208
Caldwell 282
Cheyenne, WY 520
Coeur d'Alene 465
Gooding 167
Grangeville 344
Hailey 144
Jerome 169
Lewiston 496

McCall 364
Malad City 107
Montpelier 138
Moscow 529
Nampa 273
Orofino 454
Payette 315
Pocatello 51
Portland, OR 680
Preston 118
Reno, NV 611
Rexburg 27
Rupert 121
Salmon 161
Salt Lake City, UT 210
Sandpoint 486
San Francisco, CA 834
Spokane, WA 502
Sun Valley/Ketchum 156
Twin Falls 164
Wallace 417
Weiser 329
W. Yellowstone, MT 109

Jerome to
American Falls 95
Arco 101
Blackfoot 139
Boise 112
Bonners Ferry 577
Buhl 30
Burley 48
Butte, MT 336
Caldwell 141
Cheyenne, WY 626
Coeur d'Alene 501
Gooding 22
Grangeville 310
Hailey 61
Idaho Falls 169
Lewiston 382
McCall 219
Malad City 177
Montpelier 208
Moscow 415
Nampa 128
Orofino 366
Payette 171
Pocatello 119
Portland, OR 544
Preston 188
Reno, NV 468
Rexburg 188
Rupert 50
Salmon 240
Salt Lake City, UT 220
Sandpoint 547
San Francisco, CA 691
Spokane, WA 495
Sun Valley/Ketchum 74
Twin Falls 14
Wallace 495
Weiser 184
W. Yellowstone, MT 270

Lewiston to
American Falls 480
Arco 460
Blackfoot 518

Boise	270
Bonners Ferry	196
Buhl	389
Burley	433
Butte, MT	335
Caldwell	276
Cheyenne, WY	985
Coeur d'Alene	119
Gooding	372
Grangeville	72
Hailey	412
Idaho Falls	496
Jerome	382
McCall	163
Malad City	562
Montpelier	593
Moscow	34
Nampa	283
Orofino	42
Payette	242
Pocatello	504
Portland, OR	353
Preston	573
Reno, NV	670
Rexburg	491
Rupert	435
Salmon	335
Salt Lake City, UT	606
Sandpoint	163
San Francisco, CA	861
Spokane, WA	109
Sun Valley/Ketchum	424
Twin Falls	399
Wallace	158
Weiser	229
W. Yellowstone, MT	481

McCall to

American Falls	317
Arco	297
Blackfoot	355
Boise	107
Bonners Ferry	358
Buhl	226
Burley	270
Butte, MT	381
Caldwell	123
Cheyenne, WY	848
Coeur d'Alene	282
Gooding	210
Grangeville	91
Hailey	247
Idaho Falls	364
Jerome	219
Lewiston	163
Malad City	383
Montpelier	441
Moscow	196
Nampa	120
Orofino	147
Payette	104
Pocatello	341
Portland, OR	490
Preston	409
Reno, NV	525
Rexburg	383
Rupert	272
Salmon	359
Salt Lake City, UT	450

Sandpoint	325
San Francisco, CA	748
Spokane, WA	276
Sun Valley/Ketchum	259
Twin Falls	236
Wallace	306
Weiser	90
W. Yellowstone, MT	465

Malad City to

American Falls	83
Arco	138
Blackfoot	80
Boise	292
Bonners Ferry	618
Buhl	170
Burley	135
Butte, MT	313
Caldwell	317
Cheyenne, WY	501
Coeur d'Alene	571
Gooding	182
Grangeville	490
Hailey	222
Idaho Falls	107
Jerome	208
Lewiston	593
McCall	441
Montpelier	94
Moscow	595
Nampa	308
Orofino	546
Payette	350
Pocatello	58
Portland, OR	709
Preston	37
Reno, NV	608
Rexburg	134
Rupert	132
Salmon	267
Salt Lake City, UT	100
Sandpoint	591
San Francisco, CA	831
Spokane, WA	599
Sun Valley/Ketchum	234
Twin Falls	175
Wallace	522
Weiser	364
W. Yellowstone, MT	216

Montpelier to

American Falls	114
Arco	169
Blackfoot	111
Boise	323
Bonners Ferry	649
Buhl	217
Burley	166
Butte, MT	344
Caldwell	348
Cheyenne, WY	408
Coeur d'Alene	602
Gooding	240
Grangeville	521
Hailey	256
Idaho Falls	138
Jerome	415
Lewiston	34
McCall	196

Malad City	94
Moscow	626
Nampa	339
Orofino	577
Payette	381
Pocatello	89
Portland, OR	750
Preston	46
Reno, NV	654
Rexburg	165
Rupert	163
Salmon	298
Salt Lake City, UT	150
Sandpoint	622
San Francisco, CA	877
Spokane, WA	630
Sun Valley/Ketchum	268
Twin Falls	206
Wallace	553
Weiser	395
W. Yellowstone, MT	247

Moscow to

American Falls	513
Arco	493
Blackfoot	551
Boise	303
Bonners Ferry	162
Buhl	422
Burley	466
Butte, MT	359
Caldwell	309
Cheyenne, WY	1009
Coeur d'Alene	86
Gooding	405
Grangeville	105
Hailey	444
Idaho Falls	529
Jerome	128
Lewiston	283
McCall	120
Malad City	595
Montpelier	626
Nampa	316
Orofino	75
Payette	275
Pocatello	537
Portland, OR	386
Preston	605
Reno, NV	700
Rexburg	524
Rupert	468
Salmon	368
Salt Lake City, UT	639
Sandpoint	129
San Francisco, CA	891
Spokane, WA	84
Sun Valley/Ketchum	457
Twin Falls	432
Wallace	127
Weiser	262
W. Yellowstone, MT	514

Nampa to

American Falls	226
Arco	205
Blackfoot	264
Boise	20
Bonners Ferry	480

Buhl	140
Burley	179
Butte, MT	440
Caldwell	9
Cheyenne, WY	757
Coeur d'Alene	403
Gooding	118
Grangeville	211
Hailey	157
Idaho Falls	273
Jerome	128
Lewiston	283
McCall	120
Malad City	308
Montpelier	339
Moscow	316
Orofino	266
Payette	42
Pocatello	250
Portland, OR	412
Preston	318
Reno, NV	405
Rexburg	292
Rupert	180
Salmon	268
Salt Lake City, UT	354
Sandpoint	445
San Francisco, CA	628
Spokane, WA	393
Sun Valley/Ketchum	169
Twin Falls	144
Wallace	425
Weiser	56
W. Yellowstone, MT	374

Orofino to

American Falls	464
Arco	443
Blackfoot	502
Boise	254
Bonners Ferry	237
Buhl	372
Burley	416
Butte, MT	294
Caldwell	259
Cheyenne, WY	944
Coeur d'Alene	160
Gooding	356
Grangeville	56
Hailey	395
Idaho Falls	454
Jerome	366
Lewiston	42
McCall	147
Malad City	546
Montpelier	577
Moscow	75
Nampa	266
Payette	226
Pocatello	488
Portland, OR	374
Preston	540
Reno, NV	654
Rexburg	449
Rupert	418
Salmon	293
Salt Lake City, UT	597
Sandpoint	213
San Francisco, CA	878

Spokane, WA	151
Sun Valley/Ketchum	407
Twin Falls	366
Wallace	175
Weiser	212
W. Yellowstone, MT	444

Payette to

American Falls	268
Arco	248
Blackfoot	306
Boise	58
Bonners Ferry	437
Buhl	177
Burley	221
Butte, MT	460
Caldwell	34
Cheyenne, WY	797
Coeur d'Alene	365
Gooding	160
Grangeville	170
Hailey	200
Idaho Falls	315
Jerome	171
Lewiston	242
McCall	104
Malad City	350
Montpelier	381
Moscow	275
Nampa	42
Orofino	266
Pocatello	292
Portland, OR	376
Preston	361
Reno, NV	429
Rexburg	335
Rupert	223
Salmon	310
Salt Lake City, UT	391
Sandpoint	405
San Francisco, CA	652
Spokane, WA	354
Sun Valley/Ketchum	212
Twin Falls	187
Wallace	385
Weiser	14
W. Yellowstone, MT	417

Pocatello to

American Falls	25
Arco	81
Blackfoot	24
Boise	234
Bonners Ferry	561
Buhl	133
Burley	77
Butte, MT	257
Caldwell	259
Cheyenne, WY	507
Coeur d'Alene	514
Gooding	140
Grangeville	432
Hailey	158
Idaho Falls	51
Jerome	119
Lewiston	504
McCall	341
Malad City	58
Montpelier	89

Ultimate Idaho Atlas and Travel Encyclopedia

Moscow ... 537
Nampa ... 250
Orofino ... 488
Payette ... 292
Portland, OR ... 662
Preston ... 68
Reno, NV ... 566
Rexburg ... 77
Rupert ... 74
Salmon ... 210
Salt Lake City, UT ... 161
Sandpoint ... 535
San Francisco, CA ... 789
Spokane, WA ... 504
Sun Valley/Ketchum ... 170
Twin Falls ... 117
Wallace ... 465
Weiser ... 306
W. Yellowstone, MT ... 159

Portland, OR to
American Falls ... 638
Arco ... 618
Blackfoot ... 677
Boise ... 430
Bonners Ferry ... 461
Buhl ... 546
Burley ... 588
Butte, MT ... 654
Caldwell ... 404
Cheyenne, WY ... 1168
Coeur d'Alene ... 384
Gooding ... 531
Grangeville ... 426
Hailey ... 572
Idaho Falls ... 680
Jerome ... 544
Lewiston ... 353
McCall ... 490
Malad City ... 709
Montpelier ... 750
Moscow ... 386
Nampa ... 412
Orofino ... 374
Payette ... 376
Pocatello ... 662
Preston ... 732
Reno, NV ... 588
Rexburg ... 705
Rupert ... 594
Salmon ... 592
Salt Lake City, UT ... 770
Sandpoint ... 428
San Francisco, CA ... 641
Spokane, WA ... 340
Sun Valley/Ketchum ... 580
Twin Falls ... 556
Wallace ... 434
Weiser ... 400
W. Yellowstone, MT ... 784

Preston to
American Falls ... 93
Arco ... 148
Blackfoot ... 91
Boise ... 302
Bonners Ferry ... 628
Buhl ... 201
Burley ... 146
Butte, MT ... 324
Caldwell ... 327
Cheyenne, WY ... 454
Coeur d'Alene ... 581
Gooding ... 208
Grangeville ... 500
Hailey ... 225
Idaho Falls ... 118
Jerome ... 188
Lewiston ... 573
McCall ... 409
Malad City ... 37
Montpelier ... 46
Moscow ... 605
Nampa ... 318
Orofino ... 540
Payette ... 361
Pocatello ... 68
Portland, OR ... 732
Reno, NV ... 624
Rexburg ... 144
Rupert ... 142
Salmon ... 277
Salt Lake City, UT ... 106
Sandpoint ... 602
San Francisco, CA ... 847
Spokane, WA ... 614
Sun Valley/Ketchum ... 237
Twin Falls ... 185
Wallace ... 532
Weiser ... 374
W. Yellowstone, MT ... 226

Reno, NV to
American Falls ... 542
Arco ... 563
Blackfoot ... 585
Boise ... 425
Bonners Ferry ... 862
Buhl ... 459
Burley ... 491
Butte, MT ... 798
Caldwell ... 408
Cheyenne, WY ... 946
Coeur d'Alene ... 785
Gooding ... 489
Grangeville ... 599
Hailey ... 524
Idaho Falls ... 611
Jerome ... 468
Lewiston ... 670
McCall ... 525
Malad City ... 608
Montpelier ... 654
Moscow ... 700
Nampa ... 405
Orofino ... 654
Payette ... 429
Pocatello ... 566
Portland, OR ... 588
Preston ... 624
Rexburg ... 639
Rupert ... 497
Salmon ... 702
Salt Lake City, UT ... 518
Sandpoint ... 830
San Francisco, CA ... 223
Spokane, WA ... 784
Sun Valley/Ketchum ... 535
Twin Falls ... 453
Wallace ... 813
Weiser ... 442
W. Yellowstone, MT ... 720

Rexburg to
American Falls ... 99
Arco ... 87
Blackfoot ... 55
Boise ... 276
Bonners Ferry ... 507
Buhl ... 207
Burley ... 151
Butte, MT ... 203
Caldwell ... 301
Cheyenne, WY ... 511
Coeur d'Alene ... 460
Gooding ... 180
Grangeville ... 445
Hailey ... 163
Idaho Falls ... 27
Jerome ... 188
Lewiston ... 491
McCall ... 383
Malad City ... 134
Montpelier ... 165
Moscow ... 524
Nampa ... 292
Orofino ... 449
Payette ... 335
Pocatello ... 77
Portland, OR ... 705
Preston ... 144
Reno, NV ... 639
Rupert ... 148
Salmon ... 156
Salt Lake City, UT ... 236
Sandpoint ... 481
San Francisco, CA ... 862
Spokane, WA ... 497
Sun Valley/Ketchum ... 175
Twin Falls ... 191
Wallace ... 412
Weiser ... 348
W. Yellowstone, MT ... 82

Rupert to
American Falls ... 50
Arco ... 146
Blackfoot ... 94
Boise ... 165
Bonners Ferry ... 630
Buhl ... 63
Burley ... 8
Butte, MT ... 327
Caldwell ... 189
Cheyenne, WY ... 581
Coeur d'Alene ... 553
Gooding ... 71
Grangeville ... 363
Hailey ... 106
Idaho Falls ... 121
Jerome ... 50
Lewiston ... 435
McCall ... 272
Malad City ... 132
Montpelier ... 163
Moscow ... 468
Nampa ... 180
Orofino ... 418
Payette ... 223
Pocatello ... 74
Portland, OR ... 594
Preston ... 142
Reno, NV ... 497
Rexburg ... 148
Salmon ... 284
Salt Lake City, UT ... 175
Sandpoint ... 598
San Francisco, CA ... 720
Spokane, WA ... 544
Sun Valley/Ketchum ... 118
Twin Falls ... 47
Wallace ... 539
Weiser ... 237
W. Yellowstone, MT ... 230

Salmon to
American Falls ... 231
Arco ... 138
Blackfoot ... 187
Boise ... 252
Bonners Ferry ... 351
Buhl ... 264
Burley ... 282
Butte, MT ... 146
Caldwell ... 277
Cheyenne, WY ... 667
Coeur d'Alene ... 304
Gooding ... 238
Grangeville ... 289
Hailey ... 186
Idaho Falls ... 161
Jerome ... 240
Lewiston ... 335
McCall ... 359
Malad City ... 267
Montpelier ... 298
Moscow ... 368
Nampa ... 268
Orofino ... 293
Payette ... 310
Pocatello ... 210
Portland, OR ... 592
Preston ... 277
Reno, NV ... 702
Rexburg ... 156
Rupert ... 284
Salt Lake City, UT ... 379
Sandpoint ... 324
San Francisco, CA ... 925
Spokane, WA ... 330
Sun Valley/Ketchum ... 176
Twin Falls ... 248
Wallace ... 255
Weiser ... 324
W. Yellowstone, MT ... 238

Salt Lake City, UT to
American Falls ... 167
Arco ... 241
Blackfoot ... 184
Boise ... 336
Bonners Ferry ... 729
Buhl ... 238
Burley ... 177
Butte, MT ... 413
Caldwell ... 362
Cheyenne, WY ... 428
Coeur d'Alene ... 687
Gooding ... 249
Grangeville ... 533
Hailey ... 283
Idaho Falls ... 210
Jerome ... 220
Lewiston ... 606
McCall ... 450
Malad City ... 100
Montpelier ... 150
Moscow ... 639
Nampa ... 354
Orofino ... 597
Payette ... 391
Pocatello ... 161
Portland, OR ... 770
Preston ... 106
Reno, NV ... 518
Rexburg ... 236
Rupert ... 175
Salmon ... 379
Sandpoint ... 689
San Francisco, CA ... 741
Spokane, WA ... 700
Sun Valley/Ketchum ... 296
Twin Falls ... 222
Wallace ... 622
Weiser ... 412
W. Yellowstone, MT ... 315

Sandpoint to
American Falls ... 556
Arco ... 463
Blackfoot ... 512
Boise ... 434
Bonners Ferry ... 33
Buhl ... 551
Burley ... 596
Butte, MT ... 303
Caldwell ... 438
Cheyenne, WY ... 953
Coeur d'Alene ... 46
Gooding ... 535
Grangeville ... 234
Hailey ... 513
Idaho Falls ... 486
Jerome ... 547
Lewiston ... 163
McCall ... 325
Malad City ... 591
Montpelier ... 622
Moscow ... 129
Nampa ... 445
Orofino ... 213
Payette ... 405
Pocatello ... 535
Portland, OR ... 428
Preston ... 602
Reno, NV ... 830
Rexburg ... 481
Rupert ... 598
Salmon ... 324
Salt Lake City, UT ... 689
San Francisco, CA ... 940
Spokane, WA ... 72
Sun Valley/Ketchum ... 501
Twin Falls ... 562
Wallace ... 94

Weiser	.391
W. Yellowstone, MT	.450

San Francisco, CA to

American Falls	.765
Arco	.786
Blackfoot	.808
Boise	.648
Bonners Ferry	.972
Buhl	.682
Burley	.714
Butte, MT	1002
Caldwell	.631
Cheyenne, WY	1169
Coeur d'Alene	.897
Gooding	.712
Grangeville	.822
Hailey	.747
Idaho Falls	.834
Jerome	.691
Lewiston	.861
McCall	.748
Malad City	.831
Montpelier	.877
Moscow	.891
Nampa	.628
Orofino	.878
Payette	.652
Pocatello	.789
Portland, OR	.641
Preston	.847
Reno, NV	.223
Rexburg	.862
Rupert	.720
Salmon	.925
Salt Lake City, UT	.741
Sandpoint	.940
Spokane, WA	.868
Sun Valley/Ketchum	.759
Twin Falls	.676
Wallace	.946
Weiser	.665
W. Yellowstone, MT	.943

Spokane, WA to

American Falls	.572
Arco	.475
Blackfoot	.528
Boise	.379
Bonners Ferry	.109
Buhl	.502
Burley	.533
Butte, MT	.314
Caldwell	.386
Cheyenne, WY	.964
Coeur d'Alene	.33
Gooding	.486
Grangeville	.182
Hailey	.521
Idaho Falls	.502
Jerome	.495
Lewiston	.109
McCall	.276
Malad City	.599
Montpelier	.630
Moscow	.84
Nampa	.393
Orofino	.151
Payette	.354
Pocatello	.504
Portland, OR	.340
Preston	.614
Reno, NV	.784
Rexburg	.497
Rupert	.544
Salmon	.330
Salt Lake City, UT	.700
Sandpoint	.72
San Francisco, CA	.868
Sun Valley/Ketchum	.511
Twin Falls	.507
Wallace	.83
Weiser	.342
W. Yellowstone, MT	.464

Sun Valley/Ketchum to

American Falls	.163
Arco	.88
Blackfoot	.147
Boise	.153
Bonners Ferry	.528
Buhl	.97
Burley	.116
Butte, MT	.324
Caldwell	.174
Cheyenne, WY	.676
Coeur d'Alene	.481
Gooding	.72
Grangeville	.352
Hailey	.12
Idaho Falls	.156
Jerome	.74
Lewiston	.424
McCall	.259
Malad City	.234
Montpelier	.268
Moscow	.457
Nampa	.169
Orofino	.407
Payette	.212
Pocatello	.170
Portland, OR	.580
Preston	.237
Reno, NV	.535
Rexburg	.175
Rupert	.118
Salmon	.176
Salt Lake City, UT	.296
Sandpoint	.501
San Francisco, CA	.759
Spokane, WA	.511
Twin Falls	.82
Wallace	.432
Weiser	.225
W. Yellowstone, MT	.257

Twin Falls to

American Falls	.93
Arco	.110
Blackfoot	.137
Boise	.128
Bonners Ferry	.594
Buhl	.16
Burley	.40
Butte, MT	.346
Caldwell	.153
Cheyenne, WY	.620
Coeur d'Alene	.517
Gooding	.35
Grangeville	.327
Hailey	.70
Idaho Falls	.164
Jerome	.14
Lewiston	.399
McCall	.236
Malad City	.175
Montpelier	.206
Moscow	.432
Nampa	.144
Orofino	.366
Payette	.187
Pocatello	.117
Portland, OR	.556
Preston	.185
Reno, NV	.453
Rexburg	.191
Rupert	.47
Salmon	.248
Salt Lake City, UT	.222
Sandpoint	.562
San Francisco, CA	.676
Spokane, WA	.507
Sun Valley/Ketchum	.82
Wallace	.503
Weiser	.200
W. Yellowstone, MT	.273

Wallace to

American Falls	.487
Arco	.394
Blackfoot	.443
Boise	.413
Bonners Ferry	.127
Buhl	.519
Burley	.537
Butte, MT	.238
Caldwell	.418
Cheyenne, WY	.886
Coeur d'Alene	.49
Gooding	.493
Grangeville	.215
Hailey	.447
Idaho Falls	.417
Jerome	.495
Lewiston	.158
McCall	.306
Malad City	.522
Montpelier	.553
Moscow	.127
Nampa	.425
Orofino	.175
Payette	.385
Pocatello	.465
Portland, OR	.434
Preston	.532
Reno, NV	.813
Rexburg	.412
Rupert	.539
Salmon	.255
Salt Lake City, UT	.622
Sandpoint	.94
San Francisco, CA	.946
Spokane, WA	.83
Sun Valley/Ketchum	.432
Twin Falls	.503
Weiser	.371
W. Yellowstone, MT	.385

Weiser to

American Falls	.282
Arco	.261
Blackfoot	.320
Boise	.72
Bonners Ferry	.424
Buhl	.191
Burley	.235
Butte, MT	.446
Caldwell	.47
Cheyenne, WY	.810
Coeur d'Alene	.347
Gooding	.174
Grangeville	.157
Hailey	.212
Idaho Falls	.329
Jerome	.184
Lewiston	.229
McCall	.90
Malad City	.364
Montpelier	.395
Moscow	.262
Nampa	.56
Orofino	.212
Payette	.14
Pocatello	.306
Portland, OR	.400
Preston	.374
Reno, NV	.442
Rexburg	.348
Rupert	.237
Salmon	.324
Salt Lake City, UT	.412
Sandpoint	.391
San Francisco, CA	.665
Spokane, WA	.342
Sun Valley/Ketchum	.225
Twin Falls	.200
Wallace	.371
W. Yellowstone, MT	.430

W. Yellowstone, MT to

American Falls	.181
Arco	.169
Blackfoot	.147
Boise	.358
Bonners Ferry	.481
Buhl	.289
Burley	.233
Butte, MT	.148
Caldwell	.383
Cheyenne, WY	.500
Coeur d'Alene	.433
Gooding	.262
Grangeville	.436
Hailey	.245
Idaho Falls	.109
Jerome	.270
Lewiston	.481
McCall	.465
Malad City	.216
Montpelier	.247
Moscow	.514
Nampa	.374
Orofino	.444
Payette	.417
Pocatello	.159
Portland, OR	.784
Preston	.226
Reno, NV	.720
Rexburg	.82
Rupert	.230
Salmon	.238
Salt Lake City, UT	.315
Sandpoint	.450
San Francisco, CA	.943
Spokane, WA	.464
Sun Valley/Ketchum	.257
Twin Falls	.273
Wallace	.385
Weiser	.430

Notes:

_____

_____

_____

_____

CITY/TOWN LOCATOR

Town	Section
Aberdeen	7
Acequia	5
Ahsahka	2
Albion	5
Almo	5
Alta	6
American Falls	7
Ammon	6
Arbon	7
Arco	4
Arimo	7
Ashton	6
Athol	1
Atlanta	3
Atomic City	4
Avery	1
Baker	4
Bancroft	7
Banida	7
Banks	3
Basalt	7
Bayview	1
Bellevue	4
Bennington	7
Bern	7
Blackfoot	7
Blanchard	1
Bliss	5
Bloomington	7
Boise	3
Bone	6
Bonners Ferry	1
Border	7
Bovill	2
Bowmont	3
Bruneau	3
Buhl	5
Burke	1
Burley	5
Butte City	4
Cabinet	1
Calder	1
Caldwell	3
Cambridge	3
Carey	4
Careywood	1
Carmen	4
Cascade	3
Castleford	5
Cataldo	1
Cavendish	2
Challis	4
Chester	6
Chubbuck	7
Clark Fork	1
Clarkia	1
Clayton	4
Clearwater	2
Clifton	7
Cocolalla	1
Coeur d'Alene	1
Colburn	1
Conda	7
Coolin	1
Corral	4
Cottonwood	2
Council	3
Craigmont	2
Crouch	3
Culdesac	2

Town	Section
Dalton Gardens	1
Darlington	4
Dayton	7
Deary	2
Declo	5
DeSmet	1
Dietrich	5
Dingle	7
Dixie	2
Donnelly	3
Dover	1
Downey	7
Driggs	6
Drummond	6
Dubois	6
Eagle	3
East Hope	1
Eastport	1
Eden	5
Egin	6
Elk City	2
Elk River	2
Elmira	1
Emida	1
Emmett	3
Enaville	1
Fairfield	4
Felt	6
Fenn	2
Ferdinand	2
Fernan Lake	1
Fernwood	1
Filer	5
Firth	7
Fish Haven	7
Fort Hall	7
Franklin	7
Fruitland	3
Fruitvale	3
Gannett	4
Garden City	3
Garden City (Ghost Town)	4
Garden Valley	3
Gardena	3
Garfield Bay	1
Gem	1
Genesee	2
Geneva	7
Georgetown	7
Gibbonsville	4
Gilmore	4
Glenns Ferry	3
Golden	2
Gooding	5
Grace	7
Grand View	3
Grangemont	2
Grangeville	2
Greencreek	2
Greenleaf	3
Greer	2
Hagerman	5
Hailey	4
Hamer	6
Hammett	3
Hansen	5
Harrison	1
Harvard	2
Hauser	1
Hayden	1
Hayden Lake	1

Town	Section
Hazelton	5
Headquarters	2
Heise	6
Helmer	2
Henry	7
Heyburn	5
Hill City	4
Holbrook	7
Hollister	5
Homedale	3
Hope	1
Horseshoe Bend	3
Howe	4
Huetter	1
Idaho City	3
Idaho Falls	6
Indian Valley	3
Inkom	7
Iona	6
Irwin	6
Island Park	6
Jerome	5
Juliaetta	2
Kamiah	2
Kellogg	1
Kendrick	2
Ketchum	4
Keuterville	2
Kilgore	6
Kimberly	5
King Hill	3
Kooskia	2
Kootenai	1
Kuna	3
Laclede	1
Lake Fork	3
Lakeview	1
Lamb Creek	1
Lane	1
Lapwai	2
Lava Hot Springs	7
Leadore	4
Lenore	2
Letha	3
Lewiston	2
Lewisville	6
Lincoln	7
Lorenzo	6
Lost River	4
Lowell	2
Lowman	3
Lucile	2
Mackay	4
Macks Inn	6
Malad City	7
Malta	5
Marsing	3
Marysville	6
May	4
Mayfield	3
McCall	3
McCammon	7
Meadows	3
Medimont	1
Melba	3
Menan	6
Meridian	3
Middleton	3
Midvale	3
Minidoka	5
Mink Creek	7

Town	Section
Monteview	6
Montpelier	7
Moore	4
Moreland	7
Moscow	2
Mount Idaho	2
Mountain Home	3
Moyie Springs	1
Mud Lake	6
Mullan	1
Murphy	3
Murray	1
Murtaugh	5
Myrtle	2
Nampa	3
Naples	1
New Meadows	3
New Plymouth	3
Newdale	6
Nezperce	2
Nordman	1
North Fork	4
Notus	3
Oakley	5
Ola	3
Oldtown	1
Onaway	2
Orofino	2
Orogrande	2
Osburn	1
Ovid	7
Oxford	7
Paris	7
Parker	6
Parkline	1
Parma	3
Patterson	4
Paul	5
Pauline	7
Payette	3
Peck	2
Pegram	7
Picabo	4
Pierce	2
Pine	3
Pinehurst	1
Pingree	7
Pioneerville	3
Placerville	3
Plummer	1
Pocatello	7
Pollock	2
Ponderay	1
Porthill	1
Post Falls	1
Potlatch	2
Preston	7
Prichard	1
Priest Riverer	1
Princeton	2
Rathdrum	1
Raymond	7
Reubens	2
Rexburg	6
Reynolds	3
Richfield	5
Riddle	3
Rigby	6
Riggins	2
Ririe	6
Riverside	7

Town	Section
Roberts	6
Rockford	7
Rockford Bay	1
Rockland	7
Rogerson	5
Rose Lake	1
Rupert	5
Sagle	1
Salmon	4
Samaria	7
Samuels	1
Sandpoint	1
Santa	1
Shelley	7
Shoshone	5
Silverton	1
Smelterville	1
Smiths Ferry	3
Soda Springs	7
Southwick	2
Spalding	2
Spencer	6
Spirit Lake	1
Springfield	7
St. Anthony	6
St. Charles	7
St. Joe	1
St. Maries	1
Stanley	4
Stateline	1
Sterling	7
Stites	2
Stone	7
Sugar City	6
Sun Valley	4
Sunbeam	4
Swan Valley	6
Swanlake	7
Sweet	3
Tendoy	4
Tensed	1
Teton	6
Tetonia	6
Thatcher	7
Thornton	6
Troy	2
Twin Falls	5
Ucon	6
Victor	6
Viola	2
Virginia	7
Waha	2
Wallace	1
Wardner	1
Warm Lake	3
Warm River	6
Warren	2
Wayan	7
Weippe	2
Weiser	3
Wendell	5
Westmond	1
Weston	7
White Bird	2
Wilder	3
Winchester	2
Woodland	2
Worley	1
Yellow Pine	3

All Idaho Area Codes are 208

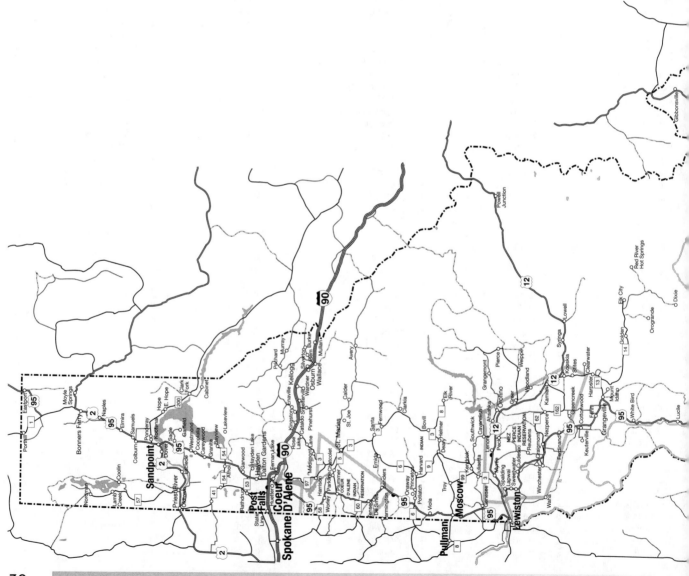

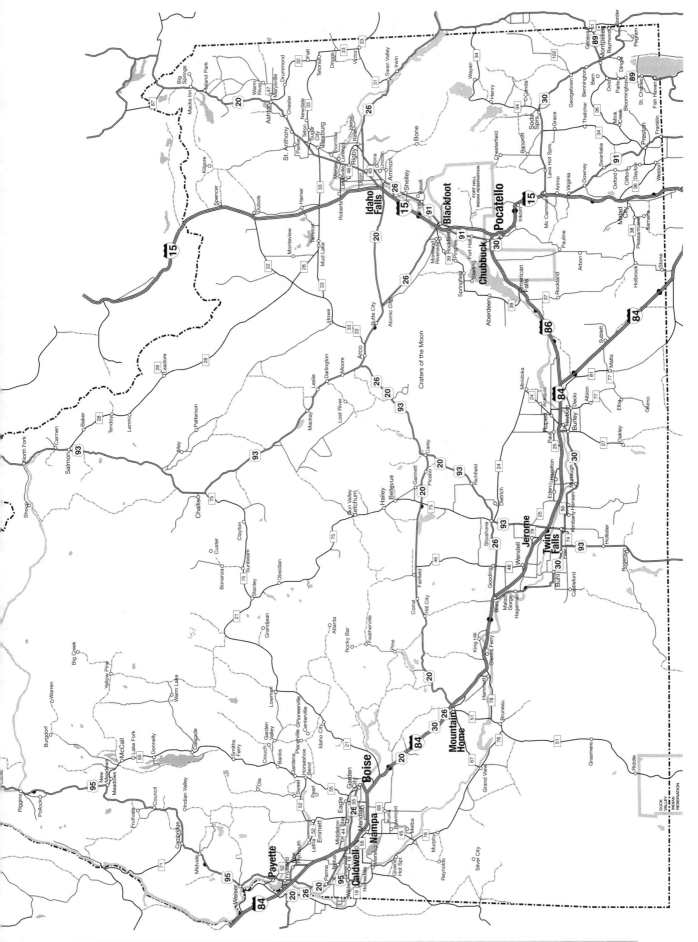

Introduction

All Idaho Area Codes are 208

Alphabetical

Aberdeen 397	Boise 391	Boise 988	Dubois 374	Idahofalls 709	Meridian 846	Pocatello 223
Albeni 437	Boise 392	Boiseriver 653	Elba 638	Idahofalls 881	Meridian 855	Pocatello 213
Albion 673	Boise 393	Bonners Ferry 267	Elk Bend 894	Indian Valley 256	Meridian 870	Pocatello 220
Almo 824	Boise 395	Bonners Ferry 295	Elk City 842	Irwin 270	Meridian 871	Pocatello 221
Alpine 564	Boise 396	Bovill 826	Emmett 365	Irwin 483	Meridian 884	Pocatello 226
Arbon 335	Boise 407	Bruneau 845	Emmett 369	Island Park 558	Meridian 887	Pocatello 232
Arco 527	Boise 409	Burley 203	Emmett 398	Julietta 276	Meridian 888	Pocatello 233
Arco 554	Boise 422	Burley 219	Emmett 477	Kamiah 935	Meridian 893	Pocatello 234
Arco 767	Boise 424	Burley 312	Emmett 963	Kellogg 512	Meridian 895	Pocatello 235
Ashton 652	Boise 426	Burley 586	Evergreen 268	Kellogg 682	Meridian 898	Pocatello 236
Atlanta 864	Boise 429	Burley 647	Fairfield 764	Kellogg 783	Meridian 922	Pocatello 237
Bayview 561	Boise 433	Burley 650	Filer 326	Kellogg 784	Meridian 955	Pocatello 238
Bayview 683	Boise 439	Burley 654	Freedom 873	Kellogg 786	Midvale 355	Pocatello 239
Blackfoot 604	Boise 440	Burley 670	Fruitland 452	Kendrick 289	Minidoka 531	Pocatello 240
Blackfoot 643	Boise 441	Burley 677	Garden Valley 462	Ketchum 205	Monteview 657	Pocatello 241
Blackfoot 680	Boise 445	Burley 678	Genesee 285	Ketchum 309	Moscow 301	Pocatello 242
Blackfoot 681	Boise 447	Burley 679	Grand View 834	Ketchum 450	Moscow 310	Pocatello 244
Blackfoot 684	Boise 460	Burley 808	Grangeville 451	Ketchum 471	Moscow 596	Pocatello 251
Blackfoot 690	Boise 472	Burley 878	Grangeville 507	Ketchum 481	Moscow 669	Pocatello 252
Blackfoot 782	Boise 474	Caldwell 402	Grangeville 981	Ketchum 578	Moscow 874	Pocatello 254
Blackfoot 785	Boise 484	Caldwell 453	Grangeville 982	Ketchum 594	Moscow 882	Pocatello 269
Blackfoot 789	Boise 485	Caldwell 454	Grangeville 983	Ketchum 622	Moscow 883	Pocatello 282
Bluebell 274	Boise 489	Caldwell 455	Grasmerddl 759	Ketchum 720	Moscow 885	Pocatello 317
Boise 202	Boise 494	Caldwell 459	Hamer 662	Ketchum 721	Moscow 892	Pocatello 339
Boise 229	Boise 514	Caldwell 649	Harrison 214	Ketchum 725	Mt Home 366	Pocatello 380
Boise 246	Boise 545	Caldwell 779	Harrison 689	Ketchum 726	Mt Home 580	Pocatello 406
Boise 247	Boise 555	Caldwell 795	Hayden Lake 209	Ketchum 727	Mt Home 587	Pocatello 417
Boise 248	Boise 562	Cambridge 257	Hayden Lake 635	Ketchum 788	Mt Home 590	Pocatello 425
Boise 272	Boise 567	Carey 823	Hayden Lake 762	Ketchum 806	Mt Home 591	Pocatello 427
Boise 275	Boise 571	Cascade 382	Hayden Lake 772	Kilgore 778	Mt Home 598	Pocatello 478
Boise 279	Boise 573	Challis 879	Holbrook 698	Kooskia 926	Mt Home 599	Pocatello 530
Boise 283	Boise 575	Clark Fork 266	Homedale 337	Lakeview 222	Mt Home 696	Pocatello 540
Boise 284	Boise 577	Clayton 838	Hope 264	Lapwai 621	Mt Home 828	Pocatello 547
Boise 287	Boise 581	Coeur d'Alene 277	Horsebend 781	Lapwai 843	Mt Home 832	Pocatello 565
Boise 319	Boise 602	Coeur d'Alene 292	Horsebend 793	Leadore 768	Mullan 744	Pocatello 589
Boise 321	Boise 608	Coeur d'Alene 297	Howster 655	Lenore 836	Murtaugh 432	Pocatello 637
Boise 322	Boise 629	Coeur d'Alene 415	Idaho Falls 200	Leon 224	Nampa 249	Pocatello 646
Boise 323	Boise 639	Coeur d'Alene 416	Idaho Falls 201	Lewiston 298	Nampa 250	Pocatello 648
Boise 327	Boise 658	Coeur d'Alene 444	Idaho Falls 204	Lewiston 299	Nampa 318	Pocatello 705
Boise 330	Boise 672	Coeur d'Alene 446	Idaho Falls 206	Lewiston 305	Nampa 442	Pocatello 747
Boise 331	Boise 685	Coeur d'Alene 449	Idaho Falls 227	Lewiston 413	Nampa 461	Pocatello 760
Boise 332	Boise 692	Coeur d'Alene 620	Idaho Falls 243	Lewiston 503	Nampa 463	Pocatello 775
Boise 333	Boise 693	Coeur d'Alene 625	Idaho Falls 346	Lewiston 553	Nampa 465	Pocatello 776
Boise 334	Boise 694	Coeur d'Alene 640	Idaho Falls 351	Lewiston 717	Nampa 466	Pocatello 833
Boise 336	Boise 703	Coeur d'Alene 641	Idaho Falls 356	Lewiston 743	Nampa 467	Pocatello 840
Boise 338	Boise 713	Coeur d'Alene 651	Idaho Falls 357	Lewiston 746	Nampa 475	Pocatello 847
Boise 340	Boise 723	Coeur d'Alene 659	Idaho Falls 359	Lewiston 748	Nampa 498	Pocatello 851
Boise 341	Boise 724	Coeur d'Alene 660	Idaho Falls 360	Lewiston 750	Nampa 697	Pocatello 852
Boise 342	Boise 728	Coeur d'Alene 661	Idaho Falls 390	Lewiston 790	Nampa 880	Pocatello 897
Boise 343	Boise 730	Coeur d'Alene 664	Idaho Falls 403	Lewiston 791	Nampa 899	Pocatello 904
Boise 344	Boise 761	Coeur d'Alene 665	Idaho Falls 419	Lewiston 792	New Plymouth 278	Pocatello 915
Boise 345	Boise 794	Coeur d'Alene 666	Idaho Falls 496	Lewiston 798	New Meadows 347	Post Falls 262
Boise 348	Boise 830	Coeur d'Alene 667	Idaho Falls 520	Lewiston 799	Nezperce 937	Post Falls 457
Boise 353	Boise 841	Coeur d'Alene 676	Idaho Falls 521	Lewiston 816	Norland 532	Post Falls 618
Boise 361	Boise 850	Coeur d'Alene 691	Idaho Falls 522	Lewiston 848	Nu Acres 566	Post Falls 619
Boise 362	Boise 853	Coeur d'Alene 699	Idaho Falls 523	Mackay 588	Nu Acres 570	Post Falls 773
Boise 363	Boise 854	Coeur d'Alene 704	Idaho Falls 524	Malad 294	Nu Acres 674	Post Falls 777
Boise 364	Boise 859	Coeur d'Alene 714	Idaho Falls 525	Malad 766	Nu Acres 707	Potlatch 875
Boise 367	Boise 860	Coeur d'Alene 755	Idaho Falls 526	Malta 645	Oakley 862	Powell 942
Boise 368	Boise 861	Coeur d'Alene 763	Idaho Falls 528	Marsing 896	Orofino 476	Prairie 868
Boise 371	Boise 863	Coeur d'Alene 765	Idaho Falls 529	May 876	Orofino 827	Priest River 306
Boise 373	Boise 866	Coeur d'Alene 769	Idaho Falls 533	McCall 271	Paris 945	Priest River 428
Boise 375	Boise 867	Coeur d'Alene 771	Idaho Falls 534	McCall 315	Parma 722	Priest River 448
Boise 376	Boise 869	Coeur d'Alene 797	Idaho Falls 535	McCall 630	Paul 438	Priestlake 443
Boise 377	Boise 890	Coeur d'Alene 818	Idaho Falls 538	McCall 634	Payette 207	Raft River 349
Boise 378	Boise 891	Coeur d'Alene 929	Idaho Falls 542	Melba 495	Payette 230	Rathdrum 687
Boise 379	Boise 914	Coeur d'Alene 964	Idaho Falls 557	Meridian 286	Payette 291	Rathdrum 712
Boise 381	Boise 919	Cola 668	Idaho Falls 592	Meridian 288	Payette 405	Richfield 487
Boise 383	Boise 921	Cottonwood 962	Idaho Falls 612	Meridian 350	Payette 563	Rigby 228
Boise 384	Boise 938	Council 253	Idaho Falls 656	Meridian 401	Payette 642	Rigby 745
Boise 385	Boise 939	Craigmont 924	Idaho Falls 716	Meridian 412	Payette 739	Rigby 754
Boise 386	Boise 941	Cuprum 258	Idaho Falls 757	Meridian 493	Payette 740	Riggins 628
Boise 387	Boise 947	Deary 877	Idaho Falls 821	Meridian 585	Payette 741	Rock Creek 273
Boise 388	Boise 975	Donnelly 325	Idaho Falls 932	Meridian 631	Peck 486	Rockland 548
Boise 389	Boise 977	Driggs 354	Idahofalls 313	Meridian 695	Pierce 464	Rupert 259
	Boise 978	Driggs 456	Idahofalls 552	Meridian 706	Plumerwrly 686	Rupert 260
	Boise 979	Driggs 787	Idahofalls 569	Meridian 822		Rupert 300

762 . .Hayden Lake	786 . . . . . .Kellogg	825 . . . .Twin Falls	850 . . . . . . .Boise	874 . . . . .Moscow	897 . . . .Pocatello	942 . . . . . .Powell
763 .Coeur d'Alene	787 . . . . . . .Driggs	826 . . . . . .Bovill	851 . . . .Pocatello	875 . . .Potlatch	898 . . . .Meridian	944 . . .Twin Falls
764 . . . .Fairfield	788 . . . .Ketchum	827 . . . . .Orofino	852 . . . .Pocatello	876 . . . . . . .May	899 . . . . . .Nampa	945 . . . . . . .Paris
765 .Coeur d'Alene	789 . . . .Blackfoot	828 . . . .Mt Home	853 . . . . . . .Boise	877 . . . . . .Deary	904 . . . .Pocatello	946 . . . Sandpoint
766 . . . . . .Malad	790 . . . .Lewiston	829 . . . .Twin Falls	854 . . . . . . .Boise	878 . . . . . .Burley	914 . . . . . .Boise	947 . . . . . . .Boise
767 . . . . . . .Arco	791 . . . .Lewiston	830 . . . . . . .Boise	855 . . . .Meridian	879 . . . . .Challis	915 . . . .Pocatello	948 . . .Twin Falls
768 . . . . .Leadore	792 . . . .Lewiston	832 . . . .Mt Home	857 . .Three Creek	880 . . . . .Nampa	919 . . . . . .Boise	955 . . . .Meridian
769 .Coeur d'Alene	793 . . .Horsebend	833 . . . .Pocatello	858 . . . .Wellesley	881 . .Idaho Falls	921 . . . . . .Boise	961 . . . .Twin Falls
771 .Coeur d'Alene	794 . . . . . . .Boise	834 . . .Grand View	859 . . . . . . .Boise	882 . . . . .Moscow	922 . . . .Meridian	962 . .Cottonwood
772 . .Hayden Lake	795 . . . .Caldwell	835 . . . . . . .Troy	860 . . . . . . .Boise	883 . . . . .Moscow	924 . . .Craigmont	963 . . . . .Emmett
773 . . .Post Falls	796 . . . .Tipanuk	836 . . . . . .Lenore	861 . . . . . . .Boise	884 . . . .Meridian	926 . . . .Kooskia	964 .Coeur d'Alene
774 . . . . .Stanley	797 .Coeur d'Alene	837 . . . .Twin Falls	862 . . . . .Oakley	885 . . . . .Moscow	929 .Coeur d'Alene	969 . . . .Twin Falls
775 . . . .Pocatello	798 . . . .Lewiston	838 . . . . .Clayton	863 . . . . . . .Boise	886 . . .Twin Falls	931 . . . . . .Rupert	975 . . . . . . .Boise
776 . . . .Pocatello	799 . . . .Lewiston	839 . .White Bird	864 . . . . .Atlanta	887 . . . .Meridian	932 . . .Idaho Falls	977 . . . . . . .Boise
777 . . .Post Falls	806 . . . .Ketchum	840 . . . .Pocatello	865 . . . . .Salmon	888 . . . .Meridian	933 . . .Twin Falls	978 . . . . . . .Boise
778 . . . .Kilgore	808 . . . . . .Burley	841 . . . . . . .Boise	866 . . . . . . .Boise	890 . . . . . .Boise	934 . . .Twin Falls	979 . . . . . . .Boise
779 . . . .Caldwell	816 . . . .Lewiston	842 . . . .Elk City	867 . . . . . . .Boise	891 . . . . . .Boise	935 . . . . .Kamiah	981 . . .Grangeville
781 . . .Horsebend	818 .Coeur d'Alene	843 . . . . . .Lapwai	868 . . . . .Prairie	892 . . . . .Moscow	937 . . .Nezperce	982 . . .Grangeville
782 . . . .Blackfoot	821 . . .Idaho Falls	845 . . . .Bruneau	869 . . . . . . .Boise	893 . . . .Meridian	938 . . . . . .Boise	983 . . .Grangeville
783 . . . . .Kellogg	822 . . . .Meridian	846 . . . .Meridian	870 . . . .Meridian	894 . . . .Elk Bend	939 . . . . . .Boise	988 . . . . . . .Boise
784 . . . . .Kellogg	823 . . . . . .Carey	847 . . . .Pocatello	871 . . . .Meridian	895 . . . .Meridian	940 . . . . .Salmon	989 . . . . . .Nampa
785 . . . .Blackfoot	824 . . . . . . .Almo	848 . . . .Lewiston	873 . . . .Freedom	896 . . . . .Marsing	941 . . . . . .Boise	

NOTES:

SECTION 1

PANHANDLE AREA

INCLUDING COEUR D'ALENE, POST FALLS, SANDPOINT, AND WALLACE

Lake Coeur d'Alene is surrounded by lush forest, providing ample recreational opportunities.

1

Eastport
Pop. 125

Esablished in 1910, the Eastport Post Office marked the development of this small community. The town, which marks the boundary between Idaho and Canada, was named because it is the easterly of Idaho's two border stations.

Porthill
Pop. 65

Previously known as Ockanook, Porthill was founded in 1893 as one of Idaho's two Canadian border stations. Some claim the name recognizes former postmaster, Charles Hill. Others believe James Barnes named the town because it was a "port-on-a-hill" and the port of entry. While mining played the leading economic role from 1915 to the 1950s, the current economy rests on the production of hops. Farms in the area raise thousands of acres of hops each year for use in Anheuser-Busch beers.

T Kootenai River
Boundary County

Idaho's Kootenai River is unique in that it flows not only through different states, but also in two different countries. Located in the northern end of Idaho's panhandle, the river originates in southeastern British Columbia. It then flows through Montana, heads sixty-six miles through Idaho, and then returns to Canada. On its path through Idaho, the river represents the state's only drainage possessing native ling (burbot). Once home to a thriving white sturgeon population that is now slowly being rebuilt, the Kootenai and its tributaries possess redband rainbow trout, hatchery rainbow trout, eastern brook trout, westslope cutthroat trout, bull trout, mountain whitefish, and a few remaining kokanee salmon.

Predominantly a recreational river today, the Kootenai played an important historic role in the gold rush. Ferryboats navigated the waters to carry gold prospectors back and forth to British Columbia's Wild Horse Creek.

2 *Food, Lodging*

Bonners Ferry
Pop. 2,515

The settlement of Bonners Ferry dates back to 1864 when Edwin L. Bonner, a local ferry operator, went to business along the Kootenai River. He charged $.50 for any person on foot and $1.50 for loaded pack animals. Bonner's location was a popular crossing point for travelers going to British Columbia to cash in on the gold discovered on Wild Horse Creek. E.L. Bonner operated his ferry until 1902 when the county bought it for $500. In 1906 the Spokane International Railroad built a bridge over the Kootenai River, making the ferry obsolete. What had simply started as an ideal ferry location grew into a thriving settlement. The community was granted an official title in 1894 and was named Boundary County seat in 1915. Today, Bonners Ferry's economy centers upon timber, agriculture, and tourism. Although E.L. Bonner left Idaho and pursued a powerful political and merchant life in Missoula, Montana, the name of his famous ferry remained as a testimony to the community's origins.

Moyie Springs
Pop. 656

Once basing its economy on the logging industry, Moyie Springs is now most commonly recognized as a small resort town located at the mouth of the Moyie River. The forested site of the community's settlement was discussed in the 1811 journal of explorer David Thompson and served as a trappers' camp from 1832 until 1850. The town's name comes from British Columbia and is a type of quartz. A post office has operated here since 1920.

H Wild Horse Trail
Milepost 503.7 on U.S. Hwy. 95

Thousands of eager miners came by here in an 1864-65 gold rush to Wild Horse, British Columbia. Parts of their pack trail can still be seen. An extension of N. America's earlier gold excitements, Wild Horse was served by pack trains that hauled supplies from Columbia River steamboats and wagon roads that connected with this trail. Some packers used camel trains that made an odd sight in this forested wilderness.

H Glacial Lakes
Milepost 503.7 on U.S. Hwy. 95

Moving from the north down this valley, the edge of the continental ice sheet blocked rivers and formed glacial lakes. As the ice gradually melted, a lake rose here behind the receding ice dam and extended up Kootenai Valley into Canada. Until the ice disappeared about 10,000 years ago, this lake drained through the valley to the south. Then, the Kootenai River cut down the lake bottom, exposing the small tree-covered granite hill in the valley before you. Lakes Coeur d'Alene and Pend Oreille, to the south, are remnants of this glacial action.

H Bonner's Ferry
Milepost 507.8 on U.S. Hwy. 95

Gold miner's rushing to Wild Horse in British Columbia in 1863 were paddled across this

Bonners Ferry	Jan	Feb	March	April	May	June	July	Aug	Sep	Oct	Nov	Dec	Annual
Average Max. Temperature (F)	32.1	38.7	48.2	59.8	68.8	75.2	83.6	82.8	72.3	57.0	41.6	34.1	57.9
Average Min. Temperature (F)	18.8	22.6	27.4	33.9	40.5	46.7	50.0	48.7	41.9	34.1	27.8	22.4	34.6
Average Total Precipitation (in.)	2.95	1.85	1.57	1.30	1.68	1.66	0.93	0.95	1.31	1.91	3.02	3.08	22.20
Average Total Snowfall (in.)	21.1	11.3	4.9	0.5	0.1	0.0	0.0	0.0	0.0	0.4	8.4	18.8	65.4
Average Snow Depth (in.)	7	6	2	0	0	0	0	0	0	0	1	4	2

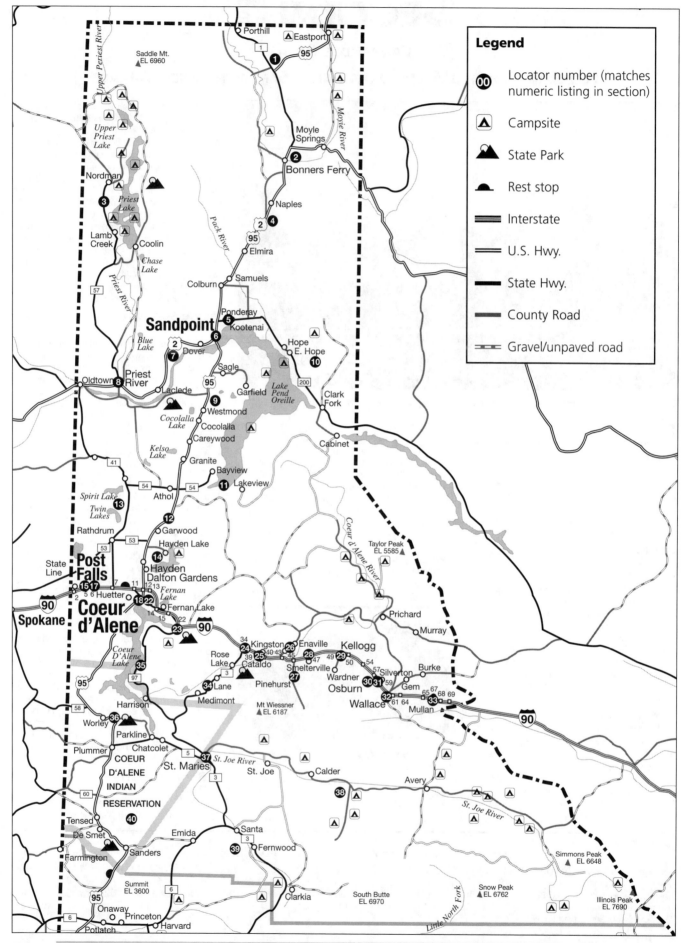

Legend

00 Locator number (matches numeric listing in section)

🔺 Campsite

🏔 State Park

⬤ Rest stop

Interstate

U.S. Hwy.

State Hwy.

County Road

Gravel/unpaved road

Porthill

Eastport

1

95

Saddle Mt.
EL 6960

1

Moyle
Springs

2

Bonners Ferry

Nordman

Upper
Priest
Lake

3

Priest
Lake

Lamb
Creek

Coolin

Chase
Lake

Naples

2 4

95

Elmira

57

Priest River

Colburn

Samuels

Ponderay

5

Sandpoint

6

Kootenai

Hope

E. Hope

10

Blue
Lake

2

Dover

7

Sagle

Garfield

Lake
Pend
Oreille

200

Clark
Fork

Oldtown

8

Priest
River

Laclede

95

9

Westmond

Cocolalla
Lake

Cocolalla

Careywood

Cabinet

Kelso
Lake

Granite

Bayview

Taylor Peak
EL 5585

Coeur d'Alene River

41

54

54

Athol

Spirit Lake

13

Twin
Lakes

Lakeview

11

Rathdrum

12

Garwood

53

53

Hayden Lake

14

Prichard

State
Line

**Post
Falls**

Hayden

Dalton Gardens

Murray

90

**Coeur
d'Alene**

15 17

7 11

12 13

Fernan
Lake

5 6

Huetter

18 22

2

14

Fernan Lake

15

22

Spokane

23

90

34

Kingston

26

Enaville

Kellogg

Rose
Lake

24

40 43

25

45

28

47

49

29

50

54

57

Silverton

Burke

Coeur
D'Alene
Lake

35

97

Cataldo

Smelterville

Pinehurst

27

Wardner

Osburn

39

30 31

59

Gem

65 67

68 69

95

34

Lane

Medimont

Mt Wiessner
EL 6187

32

61 64

33

Wallace

Mullan

58

Harrison

36

90

Worley

Parkline

Chatcolet

Plummer

**COEUR
D'ALENE**

5

37

St. Joe River

INDIAN

St. Maries

3

St. Joe

Calder

Avery

RESERVATION

60

38

Tensed

40

De Smet

Emida

Santa

St. Joe River

Farmington

Sanders

3

Fernwood

39

Summit
EL 3600

6

Simmons Peak
EL 6648

95

Onaway

Princeton

Clarkia

South Butte
EL 6970

Snow Peak
EL 6762

Little North Fork

Illinois Peak
EL 7690

6

Harvard

Potlatch

river by Indians. In 1864, E.L. Bonner established a proper ferry here. The ferry and its trading store served the Wild Horse pack trains for many years. Steamers – the first tiny one dragged in overland – came to the river in the 1880s and the Great Northern Railway arrived in 1892. A thriving town soon sprang up where once the ferryman and his family had been the only white people.

H David Thompson
Milepost 509.7 on U.S. Hwy. 95

Coming from Canada, the famous map maker and trader for the Northwest Company explored this area and river in 1808. On May 8 somewhere near here, Thompson's famished party, all sick from eating "much tainted" antelope, met 10 lodges of Indians who could give them only a "few dried carp (of last year's catch!) and some moss bread...but acceptable to the hungry." Leaving here, he found the route which U.S. 95 follows north. Next year, he returned to establish Idaho's initial fur trading post on Lake Pend Oreille.

T Elk Mountain Farms
From Bonner's Ferry, drive north on U.S. Hwy. 95 to the junction with State Hwy. 1. Bear left on Copeland Road and proceed to W.side Rd. Here, travel south to access farm overviews.

Under the direction of Busch Agricultural Resources, Inc., Elk Mountain Farms was established in 1987. Situated in the lush Kootenai River Valley, the farm boasts 1,800 acres and grows only traditional German hops – Saaz, Hallertau/Mittefrau, and Tettnang. Each of the 889 hops plants per acre are taken from rootstock originating in Europe and grown to perfection on an impressive system of poles and trellises. Harvest of the 20-foot tall vines begins in late August and continues through early September. From the overlook area, visitors have access to the world's largest aroma hop farm that contributes its sizeable yield towards production of the acclaimed Anheuser-Busch beer.

T Kootenai National Wildlife Refuge
HCR 60, Bonners Ferry. 267-5570. http://kootenai.fws.gov Drive 5 miles west from downtown Bonners Ferry on Riverside Road to the refuge entrance.

Established in 1965 just twenty miles south of the Canadian border, this 2,774-acre wildlife refuge was created by the Bureau of Sport Fisheries and Wildlife to provide a resting place for migrating waterfowl. Lined with wetlands, meadows, riparian forests, and agricultural fields, the refuge provides a habitat that can support a variety of species. Not only is the area scenic, but it is also a wildlife enthusiast's dream come true.

Since its inception, more than 230 species of birds, forty-five species of mammals, and twenty-two species of fish have been observed at the refuge. Thousands of migrating ducks, swans, and geese travel to the refuge each fall. During the summer, bald eagles, ospreys, and herons are just some of the birds calling the Kootenai Refuge home. Black bears, moose, white-tailed deer, mountain lions, and elk also make an occasional appearance.

The refuge is open daily year-round during daylight hours. However, some roads are closed for public safety in autumn during waterfowl hunting season. Best hours for observing wildlife are early morning and early evening, but there is always some species wandering about no matter what time of day. Visitors can opt to take the 4.5-mile auto tour that winds past the main ponds

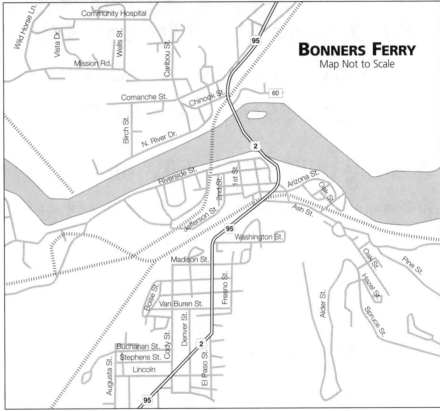

BONNERS FERRY
Map Not to Scale

and provides numerous observation opportunities. For those interested in up-close views or better photo ops, check out the refuge's system of foot trails. Camping, fires, swimming, wading, horseback riding, fruit picking, and firewood gathering are all strictly prohibited. An on-site refuge office is open 8 AM to 4:30 PM Monday through Friday to provide visitors with additional information. All visitors are encouraged to bring binoculars or a spotting scope to safely observe wildlife at a distance.

Idaho Trivia
The community of Bonners Ferry offers more than a small town atmosphere. It also is apparently home to some of the state's nicest people. Idaho State's Governor recently crowned the town "Most Friendly Town in Idaho." The title was conferred after the results were tallied from a poll of tourists who had visited each county in the state.

T Mirror Lake Golf Course
South of Bonners Ferry on U.S. Hwy. 95. 267-5314.

Built in 1974, this 9-hole golf course offers everything from water hazards to expansive fairways. Rated at a par 36, the course features two sets of tees per hole and will test every golfer's abilities. The course measures 2,885 yards on the front nine and 3,050 yards on the back. Tee times are appreciated, and the course is open from April 1 to November 1 depending on weather conditions.

T Kootenai Tribal Sturgeon Hatchery
3 miles west of Bonners Ferry on Kootenai Tribal property. 267-7082.

The Kootenai Tribe and white sturgeon have long populated the land and waters of northern Idaho. So when the sturgeon became an endangered species, the Kootenai Tribe stepped in and developed a hatchery in spring 1991. The hatchery breeds one and two year old sturgeon with funding from the Bonneville Power Administration. Hatchery personnel are proud of their well-main-

tained facility, and visitors can take a peek at the spawning process from April to June as well as thousands of sturgeon swimming in fifteen foot long steel tanks. Sturgeon of all ages are available for viewing as it normally takes fifteen months before the fish are stocked into the best possible natural environment. The facility is open Monday through Friday from 8 AM to 4 PM, and visitors are encouraged to stop by or schedule a personal tour.

T Boundary County Historical Society and Museum
7229 Main St., Bonners Ferry. 267-7720.

Visitors can catch a glimpse of Boundary County's heritage in this small museum. Housing numerous historical photos, exhibits, and artifacts, the museum is open Monday through Friday from May to August. Admission is free, but donations are gladly accepted.

T Kootenai Tribal Mission
Northwest of Bonners Ferry on the Kootenai Indian Reservation

Jesuit missionaries arrived in Idaho in the mid 1800s, and their first outreaches were commonly aimed at local Native Americans. Inhabiting northern Idaho, the Kutenai (name has been changed over the years to "Kootenai") Indians are a distant Algonquin tribe possessing no affiliation with any other western tribe. When Jesuit missionaries arrived in the 1880s, several of the Kootenai abandoned any past religious beliefs and converted to Catholicism. In 1888, a log mission church was erected on Mission Hill. The church was later replaced with a frame building and was eventually moved to the center of town where government housing was available. Today, the church has been christened "St. Michael's" and still stands with regular attendance.

T Moyie River Dam
Near Moyie Springs Bridge 11 miles northeast of Bonners Ferry on U.S. Hwy. 2

The Moyie River Dam has provided Bonners Ferry residents with hydroelectric power for nearly a century. In 1921, residents constructed the first dam over the Moyie River, which was later replaced with the current dam in 1949. The dam rises 212 feet to the sky and continually provides Idaho's northern panhandle residents with some of the state's cheapest electric rates.

T Moyie River Overlook and Bridge
0.5 miles east of Moyie Springs on U.S. Hwy. 2

View Idaho's second-highest bridge while capturing spectacular vistas of the Moyie River Canyon 450 feet below. Completed in 1964, the steel truss bridge cost $1.4 million and took two years to complete. Since the bridge's design is fairly narrow, a $2.3 million project is planned to replace the existing bridge with a wider and safer concrete structure. View Moyie Falls and the Moyie River Dam from a pullout at the bridge's southeast corner.

T Katherine Haynes Art Gallery
Bonners Ferry. 267-2007. From Bonners Ferry, drive north on U.S. Hwy. 95. After crossing the bridge, turn at the first right onto County Road 60. Continue 3.5 miles to the gallery located at HCR 85.

Since she was a child, Katherine Haynes has always had the urge to paint. Born and educated in Alberta, Canada, Katherine took every opportunity to advance her artistic knowledge and ability to paint. With an art major and a degree in the field of education from the University of Alberta, and courses at the Banff School of Fine Arts, as well as the famous artist course from Westport, Connecticut, she continued to improve her mastery of painting in oil, acrylic, and watercolors.

In 1978, she took the first of many workshops with the internationally known watercolorist, Zoltan Szabo. It was at this point that she decided to devote her time exclusively to watercolors.

Katherine's paintings are always fresh and vibrant, refuting the idea that watercolors are weak and washed out. Her subjects are the great outdoors, from silent ponds to old buildings to wild roses and the northern lights. Most of her work is in the U.S. and in Canada, but many paintings have found there way to other countries around the world.

For 30 years, Katherine has lived in the beautiful Kootenai Valley near Bonners Ferry. The area provides constant inspiration for her paintings. In addition to showing her work in area galleries, she has a gallery in her home where she hosts an annual open house in the spring. The gallery is open to the public free of charge.

Reprinted from a Katherine Haynes Art Gallery brochure

T Spokane International Railroad Bridge
Historic Downtown, Bonners Ferry. Contact the Bonners Ferry Chamber of Commerce at 267-5922.

When D. C. Corbin founded the Spokane International Railroad, his line ran through present day Bonners Ferry. A railroad bridge constructed for the line in 1906 still stands in the community's historic downtown. The bridge represents one of Idaho's few remaining wood truss railroad bridges.

TV Gamlin Lake
Near Bonners Ferry

In addition to providing a sanctuary for wetland vegetation and wildlife, Gamlin Lake is also a popular recreation spot. Located in the panhandle's lush forests, Gamlin Lake is open year round to canoes, hikers, fishermen, and wildlife observers.

TV Ball Creek Ranch Preserve
In Bonners Ferry, bear left on Riverside Ave. Proceed on this road as it passes the Kootenai Wildlife Refuge and becomes W. Side Rd. Continue driving 5 miles on W. Side R.d, and cross the Ball Creek Bridge to locate a parking area on the road's left side.

Among its many attractions, the Kootenai River Valley is home to the 2,300-acre Ball Creek Ranch Preserve. Encompassing four miles along the Kootenai River, the preserve includes a wetland pond and natural wildlife habitat. In addition to bird and wildlife watching, the preserve offers visitors the opportunity to hike, hunt, canoe, kayak, fly-fish, cross-country ski, and snowshoe.

TV Robinson Lake Day Use Area
Bonners Ferry Ranger District, Bonners Ferry. 267-5561. Located 19 miles north of Bonners Ferry via Forest Rd. 449 off U.S. Hwy. 95.

Overview
Enjoy your visit to Robinson Lake Day Use Area. Two shaded picnic tables with fire rings, two vault

toilets, an interpretive trail, fishing access to Robinson Lake, and a boat dock help make Robinson Lake a pleasant place to spend your day.

Robinson Lake Habitat
What kind of home do you live in? Is it a two-story, a ranch style, a duplex, a trailer, or something else? Just as we like certain kinds of homes, animals need certain kinds of homes or habitats for their activities.

A diverse forest provides habitats for many kinds of wildlife. Some birds prefer to nest only in deciduous trees, others nest only in conifers. Tall trees are used as perches and nesting sites for eagles and hawks. Hummingbirds nest on limbs over the water. Shrubs and low tree limbs are the nesting choices of still other birds.

Once a tree starts to die, it attracts even more wildlife. Insects in dead or dying trees (snags) are food for thrushes, woodpeckers, nuthatches, shrews, and many other animals. Holes in dead trees are used by over 20 kinds of birds for nesting. Squirrels, owls, bluebirds, raccoons, wood ducks, and wrens are just a few of the animals that use old woodpecker holes for nesting or shelter.

As a tree weakens and falls over, it is used as cover for mice, rabbits, fawns, weasels, snakes, and countless other wildlife. Logs at the water's edge are home to salamanders, toads and frogs, or lookout perches for herons, mink, and other fish-eating animals. Larger hollow logs, brush piles, or cavities in rock outcroppings may be dens for bobcats, lynx, or pine martens.

The "Water, Woods, and Wildlife Interpretive Trail" will take you through many forest areas. You will see a variety of plant species, which provide habitats for much wildlife.

Wildlife Viewing Tips
Most recreationists and wildlife viewers share a genuine concern for and appreciation of wildlife. As "guest" in the homes or habitats of animals, we need to follow some guidelines to benefit both wildlife and viewers.
- Use binoculars for that "close-up" view. This will minimize disturbance to animals and their activities. Watch for signs of distress.
- Use slow, quiet movements to avoid scaring wildlife. A car or boat makes a great blind.
- Keep far from nests and dens; the young and the adults are sensitive to disturbance.
- Avoid chasing or feeding animals or allowing pets to harass wildlife. Obey posted rules.
- Walk on trails to lessen impact to sensitive plant and habitat areas. Respect seasonal trail closures to allow animals to raise their young. Observing good wildlife viewer etiquette will allow wildlife to continue using the habitat areas and allow all of us to continue watching wildlife.

Reprinted from U.S. Forest Service brochure

V Snow Creek Cross Country Trails
14 miles west of Bonners Ferry. Contact the Kaniksu National Forest at 245-2531. South of Bonners Ferry, bear west off U.S. Hwy. 95 just before reaching the golf course. Continue until reaching Snow Creek Road 402. Bear right and continue 2 miles to the trail system's parking area. Drivers should note that Snow Creek Road is steep and often requires chains.

Once maintained under Idaho's Park N' Ski Program, Snow Creek is now a free public site for cross-country skiing. Although the trails are not groomed, intermediate to experienced Nordic skiers will find a series of loop trails covering thirteen miles of terrain. Skiers should use caution on weekends when the area becomes a popular snowmobiling site.

V Rafting the Moyie River
Northeast of Bonners Ferry. Contact the Bonners Ferry Chamber of Commerce at 267-5922.

Situated in Idaho's panhandle, the Moyie River provides intermediate to experienced boaters with a one-day recreational outlet. Stretching over eighteen miles, the route traverses consistent and fast-flowing Class II and III whitewater rapids in May and June. On its path, the route winds through a cedar forest and spectacular rock formations. Canoeists, kayakers, and rafters should note that the river becomes too low to float after June.

FL Bear Creek Lodge
5952 Main St., Hwy 95 S., Bonners Ferry. 267-7268 or 877-267-7268. www.creek-lodge.com

Located near the Kootenai River and offering easy access to year-round recreation, Bear Creek Lodge is one of the Northwest's finest log inns. Cozy, non-smoking rooms feature cable TV, refrigerators, microwaves, and coffeemakers, free local calls, and comfortable queen size beds. Pets are allowed, children under 12 stay free, and on-site laundry facilities and an outdoor hot tub add to the standard amenities. For dinner, enjoy the convenient and delicious on-site restaurant, Kodiaks Steak and Pasta. Sample savory steaks, pasta dishes, grilled chicken selections, and homemade soups and salads, or select from the children's menu. On your next trip, enjoy nature, the service you desire, and overnight lodging that exceeds your expectations. After all, Bear Creek Lodge isn't simply a vacation lodge. It's a home away from home!

S Boardwalk Boutique
7160 Main St., Bonners Ferry. 267-3313.

In the quaint riverside downtown of Bonners Ferry, you'll find a truly wonderful shopping experience at Boardwalk Boutique. Established in 1982, the Boardwalk offers an eclectic mix of contemporary fashion, accessories, and jewelry for women age 25 and up. Always unique and constantly evolving to fit the northwest woman's lifestyle, the Boardwalk carries clothing from major shows throughout the west, including French Dressing Jeanswear, Tribal, and Tianello, and one-of-a-kind designer jewelry. Women from Canada, Spokane, and surrounding areas shop here, and the boutique's friendly staff is happy to help customers locate the perfect selection for everyday or elegant evening attire. Recognized

throughout the region for its personal touch, Boardwalk Boutique assures shoppers quality and enduring style in clothing that can be worn in Idaho and across the world.

M Shelman Realty
6737 Cody St., Bonners Ferry. 267-5515 or (800) 788-5515. www.shelmanrealty.com

M Jan Keener, Century 21
1836 Northwest Blvd., Bonners Ferry. 664-6984 or (800) 664-6984. www.idahowaterfront.com

M Bonners Ferry Chamber of Commerce
7198 Hwy. 95, Bonners Ferry. 267-5922. www.bonnersferrychamber.com

3

Coolin
Pop. 100

This tiny resort town was named after Andrew Coolin, one of the area's first settlers. Although the town's name was changed to "Williams" while a gentleman named Walt Williams served as postmaster, the name later reverted back to Coolin. The first post office was established here in 1893.

Lamb Creek
Pop. 0

Situated near the shores of Priest Lake, Lamb Creek was named in 1894 after early homesteader, Harvey T. Lamb.

Nordman
Pop. 50

Situated near the border of Washington near the shores of Priest Lake, Nordman serves as both a logging and recreational area. Early settler, John Nordman, is honored with this small community's name, and a post office was established here in 1915.

T Priest Lake Museum and Visitor's Center
Directly north of Hill's Resort on Luby Bay, Coolin. 443-2676.

In 1935, the Civilian Conservation Corps constructed a log cabin to serve as a headquarters for the Kaniksu National Forest Ranger Station. Today, this well-preserved cabin serves as a museum and visitor center for the Priest Lake area. Numerous articles and exhibits illustrate the region's rich heritage. The history of Native Americans, missionaries, trappers, homesteaders, loggers, and miners is presented, and the cabin's living room and kitchen

TIMBER TERMINOLOGY

Priest River experienced its glory days from the 1920s to the 1950s when the timber industry was the community's economic staple. Hundreds of men worked the annual log drives down the Priest River to the Pend Oreille River. The hardworking, adventurous men who worked the log drives soon acquired the nickname "River Pigs." River Pigs were responsible for floating the river beside the logs in unique flat-bottomed boats. These men worked to ensure proper flow of the logs on their course to the mill and broke up any log jams. Due to the job's dangerous nature, several men were injured or killed during each year's timber harvest.

have been furnished with 1930s décor typically found in area homes at that time. For those more interested in wildlife and the region's vegetation, the center also offers exhibits on numerous animals and rare plant species populating the region. The museum is open 10 AM to 4 PM Tuesday through Sunday from June to Labor Day.

T Priest Lake Golf Club
152 Fairway Dr., Priest Lake. 443-2525.
www.priestlakegolfcourse.com

Located at Lamb Creek, the Priest Lake Golf Course was recently expanded to 18 holes and opened in 2002. Offering 6,500 yards, the challenging course is situated amid the lush forests and wetlands characterizing the Priest Lake area. A driving range, lessons, and club and cart rentals are available with green fees beginning at $15.

T Vinther – Nelson National Historical Site Walking Tour
Eightmile Island on Priest Lake outside Nordman. Contact the Priest Lake Ranger District at 443-2512.

The following is a walking tour of important sites at the Vinther – Nelson National Historical Site.

1) U.S. Forest Service Historical Marker
In 1989, the U.S. Forest Service erected this marker to provide visitors a brief history of the Vinther – Nelson Historic Cabin. One year later, a windstorm caused a large tree to fall, landing dead center on the structure. Fortunately, the metal plaque popped off the mounting and was unharmed. The support structure was destroyed and had to be rebuilt.

The cabin sits on Federal Forest Service land and in 1967, it was determined by the U.S. Department of Agriculture that all cabins situated on U.S. Government owned islands in Priest Lake must be torn down. In 1982, after many years of negotiations and effort on the part of the Vinther and Nelson families, an agreement was reached that the cabin would remain as a historic site and was declared such by its acceptance on the National Register of Historic Places.

The cabin was then donated to the U.S. Government by the Vinther and Nelson families and the families now serve as permanent caretakers and curators of the cabin.

2) The Cabin
The Crenshaw brothers were remarkable log cabin builders. The logs of the cabin are the original logs, as are the purlins that support the shakes of the roof. Note how each log has been cut flat on the sides, both inside and outside to give the appearance of a flat wall. Small strips of wood were used to fill the cracks below ceiling level and a mud mixture above. Each log was cut from the wealth of trees on the island that existed at that time. Each log was cut by hand and shaped to fit snugly together using a broad axe.

3) Initials From the Past
Trappers, miners, and hunters often visited the Vinther-Nelson cabin, leaving their initials on the corners of the logs. If you look closely, you can see the initials that were formed by hammering spent bullet casings into the wood.

4) Transportation
Travel from the city was an arduous task, requiring three days: first day by train, then a horse drawn buckboard, and finally a boat trip. The first night was spent at a halfway house located between Priest River and Priest Lake.

The second night was spent at the Northern Hotel in Coolin (built in 1904 and destroyed by

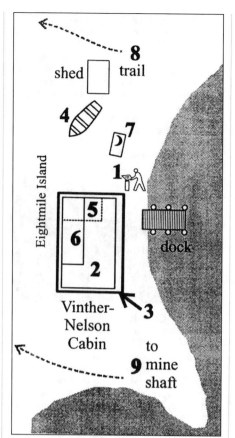

fire in 1938). The trip on the lake was either by rowing or by hitching a ride on the steamer that carried supplies up the lake from Coolin to the miner's campsites.

Rowing eight miles in all kinds of weather required strength and endurance. Note the rowboat has double oarlocks. Usually two men would row together, carrying their families and often towing a second boat full of supplies.

5) Kitchen
The original kitchen extended completely across the back of the cabin. In the early 1930s, however, as both the Vinther family and the Nelson family grew in numbers and in generations, "too many wives in the kitchen" brought a decision to divide the kitchen in half. This provided a "Vinther Kitchen" and a "Nelson Kitchen." Each family had its own table in the main living area.

Finally, in the 1940s, the whole cabin was divided by a wall, giving each family its own privacy. All this was done without any outward conflict between them. The wall was removed in 1983, restoring the cabin back to its original structure.

The restoration of the kitchen was the Nelson side and represents what it looked like in the early days.

6) Museum
A collection of many articles has been placed in the cabin museum. Displays include a series of pictures dating back to the 1920s and 1930s. Fashionable swimsuits for both males and females can be found.

A displayed bearskin represents a major contribution made by one of the wildlife that inhabited the island. A family member shot it when it attempted to break into the cabin.

The featured marimba was handmade by Revered Cecil T. Axworthy, a Spokane minister, who vacationed with the families one summer. Each piece was hand carved to the exact tone and the tubes were fashioned from paper rolls.

7) Old Outhouse Door
Many visitors to the Vinther and Nelson cabin also made use of the modern two-holer. Signing their names and date was part of the ceremony. The door itself was the original door on the first Vinther and Nelson outhouse. If you look closely you will find the signature of steamboat Captain W. E. Slee, dated '08.

8) Trial to Island Top
A beautiful clearing exists at the top of Eightmile Island, the remains of a farmer's attempt to make the land productive. In 1898, one year after the Crenshaws built the cabin, W. J. Anders and his family purchased the cabin and attempted farming.

Clearing the land, bringing in cattle, and planting crops proved too much for a family with young children. So in 1900, the sale was made to two cousins, Sam Vinther and Nels Nelson, who were anxious to make their fortune working the mine started four years earlier. No minerals of value were to be found, so they were unable to obtain a patent for their mining claim.

The hike to the top still reveals a clearing started in 1898. It is a favorite grazing area for deer, rabbits, and sometimes moose and elk. An easy trail will take you around the top and back to your starting point in approximately one hour.

9) Trail to Old Mine
Long since producing anything of value, the "Deer Trail Lode" mine can be seen only as an indentation in the bank of the island. On a short walk along the water's edge on the island's east side, one can find tailings brought from the mine, which has long since caved in. With only your imagination, visualize two men working 14-16 hour days, digging deep into the island side and in their spare time building the beautiful structure now known as the Vinther and Nelson Historic Cabin.

Walking Tour Hours
The walking tour is available Wednesday through Sunday during the summer from 10 AM to 3 PM. Admission is free.

Reprinted from U.S. Forest Service brochure

T Vinther-Nelson Cabin
Eightmile Island on Priest Lake near Nordman. Contact the Priest Lake Ranger District at 443-2512.

In 1897, two brothers named Crenshaw moved to Eightmile Island in search of riches. Mining for silver and building a soundly constructed log home at the same time, the brothers labored up to sixteen hours every day. Despite their hard work, they found no riches. In 1898, the Crenshaws transferred the property to W. J. Anders and his family who attempted to farm the land. Tired of failing, Anders sold the property to two cousins, Sam Vinther and Nels Nelson, just two years later.

When the Vinther-Nelson families arrived, they intended to restore mining activity on the island. But as the Crenshaw brothers had previously discovered, hope of finding riches on the island was nothing more than an unrealistic dream. Unlike the island's other residents, the Vinther-Nelson families decided to stay on the island and received visitors in their log home ranging from fur trappers to miners.

Although nearly demolished in 1967 in a U.S. Department of Agriculture Order, the historic cabin where the two families lived was preserved at the request of family descendents. Today, the home is listed on the National Register of Historic Sites, and tours are offered free of charge during the summer from 10 AM to 3 PM Wednesday through Sunday.

T Roosevelt Grove of Ancient Cedars Scenic Area
From Nordman, drive 14 miles north to the scenic area on Forest Rd. 2512. Contact the Priest Lake Ranger District Office in Priest River at 443-2512.

About the Groves
Fourteen miles north of Nordman, Idaho, there's a unique area of old-growth cedar named for President Theodore Roosevelt. Since the early 1900s, this area was noted for its beauty. On April 15, 1943, the grove was officially designated as a Scenic Area.

A fire in 1926 destroyed nearly seventy-five percent of the original grove and left two small remnants. The Lower Grover, approximately two acres, has four picnic sites available under the towering trees. The Upper Grove, approximately twenty acres accessible via a trail system following an old logging road, has been left undeveloped. Feel free to explore this grove on foot.

Estimating the age of these giants, which range from four to twelve feet in diameter and reach heights of 150 feet, is difficult due to heart rot which hollows out the center of the tree; therefore, an accurate count of the rings cannot be made. Through cutting windfalls and increment borings of healthy trees, the average age has been estimated at 800 years, with a few hearty survivors achieving the 2,000 to 3,000 year old status.

Stagger Inn Trailhead History
The trailhead was named after a fire camp that was used in 1926. At that time, the road extended only as far north as Nordman. Firefighters weary from hiking and battling blazes more or less staggered into the camp and someone appropriately named it "Stagger Inn." A log smoke chaser cabin was constructed on the site in about 1928, and later, the Forest Service developed recreation facilities. Four picnic sites, parking, and toilet facilities are available at the trailhead.

Vegetation
Two trails are maintained from the trailhead area to the groves. While hiking, you may find Beargrass, Lily of the Valley, Bedstraw, Spring Beauty, Bracken Fern, Stinging Nettle, Devil's Club, Trilliums, Foamflower Violets, Huckleberries, Wild Giner, and Yew.

Reprinted from U.S. Forest Service brochure

T Hanna Flats Cedar Grove
Located directly south of the Ranger District Office in Nordman. Contact the Priest Lake Ranger District Office in Priest River at 443-2512.

Spared by a 1926 80,000-acre wildfire and dismissed by early loggers, Hanna Flats Cedar Grove now offers a rare glimpse of several old-growth cedars.

Festival of Sandpoint
Sandpoint is known as one of the most eclectic, artsy communities in all of Idaho, and it proudly displays this heritage at the annual Festival of Sandpoint held each summer. The non-profit festival was started in 1983 and annually features internationally renowned performers, including the Spokane Symphony Orchestra. Situated near the river's edge at Memorial Field, the festival's summer weekly music concert series is held underneath the stars and is audience friendly. Food and beverage vendors are on-site, but attendees can also pack their own picnic.

Sandpoint Winter Carnival
The Sandpoint Winter Carnival provides a respite from the long winter days and cabin fever. Held annually each January since 1974, the weeklong event features plenty of fun for the whole family. The carnival features ski competitions, a parade of lights, scrumptious food, snow sculpting contests, bonfires on the beach, fireworks, pie walks, pizza eating contests, music, and much, much more. Contact the Sandpoint Chamber of Commerce for more information.

Coeur d'Alene Tribe Pow Wow
Idaho's Coeur d'Alene tribe hosts the Northwest's largest pow wow each July. The pow wow celebrates the Native American tribal tradition and includes an Indian horse parade, art auction, and all the grand pageantry of tribal dancing. Spectators are welcome at the three-day event.

Dickens Festival
Kellogg returns to the Victorian era in its annual Dickens Festival. Held during a December weekend prior to Christmas, the whimsical event features residents dressed in period costume, carolers throughout town, plays, skits, puppet shows, high Victorian tea parties, and a parade.

Polar Bear Plunge
Join in the icy fun during Coeur d'Alene's Annual Polar Bear Plunge. Following a traditional New Year's Race, event participants jump into the frigid Lake Coeur d'Alene for an icy romp sure to set your teeth a-chattering!

Priest River Timber Days
Every July, residents and tourists alike gather for Priest River's Chamber of Commerce sponsored "Timber Days Celebration." The weekend celebration kicks off with a car show and continues with a parade, fun run, huckleberry pancake breakfast, arts and crafts booths, food vendors, children's games, and various logging competitions.

Fred Murphy Days
Every spring, Coeur d'Alene honors one of its earliest entrepreneurs and settlers with Fred Murphy Days. Fred Murphy was a legendary tugboat captain, and the event held in his honor boasts an assortment of fun fare for the entire family. The weekend event includes a parade, street dances, a variety of contests, and a plethora of food and drink concessionaires.

North Idaho Fair & Rodeo
In August, the Kootenai County Fairgrounds comes alive with the annual North Idaho Fair and Rodeo. The weeklong event features a large selection of family oriented fare sure to please the pickiest crowd. Nationally ranked cowboys turn out in groves for the PRCA Rodeo, a demolition derby and motocross sports makes fans' hearts race, and a draft horse show and animal petting farm are always popular with the kids. On top of it all, daily live entertainment includes musical acts, magicians, and hypnotists while a carnival and concessions catering to every salt and sugar craving round out the standard fair activities.

Harrison Old Time Picnic
Harrison remembers its glory days and the life of early settlers and lumberjacks in its annual summer "Old Time Picnic." The weekend event features standard old-fashioned picnic fare along with a parade on Lake Coeur d'Alene's southeastern shore and live entertainment.

Depot Days
In 1986, curious locals gathered together to watch as the Northern Pacific Railroad Depot was moved from its historic setting to its present-day location. What started out as mere interest in a one-time event has since developed into an annual extravaganza. Held each May, Wallace's Depot Days features a full day of arts, crafts, and food vendors, kids' activities, live entertainment, and a classic car show featuring nearly 300 historic beauties.

The U.S. Forest Service created this sixteen-acre area in 1955 and has since preserved the remaining trees, some of which date back more than 200 years. The area features a short interpretive trail, and best times for viewing are during the summer as the site receives nearly ninety inches of snow each year!

The grove's name honors the legacy of one of the area's first settlers. During early settlement days, a gentleman named "Gumpp" built a small cabin near the cedars. When Gumpp moved away for the winter, Jim Hanna and his family arrived. They found the abandoned cabin, and assuming the owner had either moved or was dead, the Hanna family took over the residence. Later that spring/summer when he returned home, Gumpp was amazed to find the Hanna family in his cabin. The two resolved the issue peacefully, and Gumpp left the area in search of his new home.

T Hanna Flats Cedar Grove Interpretive Trail
Located directly south of the Ranger District Office in Nordman. Contact the Priest Lake Ranger District Office in Priest River at 443-2512.

Among these giant trees lies a story of survival. Etched deeply here are evidences of the struggle that left Hanna Flats a stand unbowed.

1) These same trees that tower over you also swayed over Jim Hanna's family as they searched for a home site in the spring of 1921. The grove had no open space for cattle, and the ground was too moist and spongy to support a cabin so they moved on. The family came upon an abandoned homestead nine miles northwest of here, a place carved out of the wild by a man named Gumpp. Gumpp had moved that winter so his children could be near a school. When he returned in the

spring, the Hannas had already settled into his home, so Gumpp simply moved on.

2) In the first years that the Hannas lived here, the area changed little from the early explorer's descriptions. The western white pine grew in abundance on the hillsides while the flats were covered with western red cedar and western hemlock. Unlike white pine, cedar and hemlock were considered trash by the early loggers – not even worth cutting down, much less hauling out. Cutting timber was a difficult job, so the early loggers took only the best trees near log-floating creeks. They didn't give a second thought to places like Hanna Flats.

3) This is the tree that the first loggers were after, the western white pine – massive, straight trunks of knotless lumber. In the mid-twenties, about the time Hanna received his homestead deed, loggers had moved this far north and had begun cutting as many of the giant trees as they could float to the mills at Priest River. The logging activity was not to pass without influencing the future of Hanna Flats.

4) The forest that once protected this cedar grove from wind is now gone. Blow-downs now bring an early demise to trees that may have lived for centuries before succumbing to disease. As these old ones die, the new forest begins. Eventually, the forest succession will reach its climax with a cedar and hemlock stand similar to Hanna Flats. Take a stroll up the viewpoint trail, which leaves the main trail just ahead. You'll have a beautiful view of the sixteen-acre grove waving 100 feet above the neighboring trees.

5) It was July 11, 1926. The rising sun brought another hot, dry day. When clouds began to gather, folks hoped to have an end to the drought. Lightning flashed, hopes were crushed, the parched forest and the logging slash roared into flame. Firefighters watched helplessly as the fire engulfed 125 square miles on forestland. When the smoke cleared in mid-August, Hanna Flats emerged unscathed. The moist soil and lack of underbrush forced the fire to seek an easier route along the dry, pine-covered hillsides. Loggers salvaged what trees they could, but the Depression dealt them a final blow. The mills closed, and logging came to a standstill.

6) The Depression ended and our nation slowly regained its economic feet. When hemlock was in demand, the loggers of the forties now looked with interest at what loggers of the twenties had disdained. Fortunately, the Forest Service saw beyond lumber to the recreational and scientific values of virgin stands. In 1955, Hanna Flats Cedar Grove was preserved as a natural area for future generations to enjoy.

7) Many years and many modifying forces have left Hanna Flats Grove a survivor. Homesteading, logging, wind, and fire – Hanna Flats has withstood them all and has remained a stand unbowed.

Vegetation
The following are some of the trees, shrubs, and plants found in and around the Hanna Flats Cedar Grove.

Trees: Western red cedar, western white pine, grand fir, western hemlock, western larch, Engelmann spruce, black cottonwood, and cascara.

Shrubs: Snowberry, serviceberry, redberry elder, blueberry elder, red osier dogwood, devil's club, wild rose, thimbleberry, black mountain huckleberry, and mountain lover.

Plants: Queens cup, bullthistle, cinquifoil, salsify, yarrow, and goldenrod.

Reprinted from U.S. Forest Service brochure

T Kalispell Bay
Traveling north from Priest River on State Hwy. 57, continue past Priest Lake State Park and bear east on Forest Rd. 1338. Drive 1 mile to the bay.

Peaceful Kalispell Bay provides easy boat access to Kalispell Island and its five sheltered campgrounds. In addition to the recreational possibilities it offers, Kalispell Bay also houses historic Indian pictographs. At the shoreline road's end, the granite rock face features a pictograph of unknown meaning captured approximately six feet above the water. The symbol, which is only eight inches wide, is nearly four feet long.

T Shoe Tree
Near Roosevelt Grove outside Priest Lake. Contact the Priest Lake Chamber of Commerce at 443-3191. From Nordman, travel north on State Hwy. 57 as it becomes Forest Road 302. Locate the tree south of Granite Falls at the short spur leading to Trails 261 and 264 on the road's west side.

Although nobody appears to know where the tradition started or how long it has existed, the Priest Lake region is home to a unique "Shoe Tree." Decades worth of shoes hang from the old tree's limbs, a reminder of unknown visitors who have happened upon the region and the funny tree.

TV Priest Lake State Park
314 Indian Creek Park Rd., Coolin. 443-6710.

Priest Lake State Park is often referred to as Idaho's "crown jewel." More than 523,000 forested acres of public land surround the beautiful 23,000-acre lake, and recreational opportunities abound. Seventy-two miles of white sand beaches beckon adults and children alike during the summer, and the crystal blue water provides trophy fishing, swimming, boating, and waterskiing. But the recreation potential extends far beyond just the lake. Miles of hiking trails let visitors explore northern Idaho, its vegetation, and wildlife, and huckleberry picking is becoming increasingly popular. During the winter, 400 miles of groomed snowmobile trails await visitors, as well as nordic skiing and several powder snow bowls. In addition to these activities, Priest Lake State Park also features local history and natural-history interpretive sites. For additional information, visitors should contact the park headquarters at the Indian Creek Unit located on East Shore Road eleven miles north of Coolin.

The park's history is dotted with several interesting anecdotes. In the 1940s, the park headquarters served as a logging camp for the Diamond Match Company. Logs were floated up to three miles away on Indian Creek. Today, the headquarters features a portion of the old flume used in the logging operation. Further down the road is the Lionhead Park Unit, site of a famous Hollywood venture. From 1923 to 1926, actress and filmmaker, Nell Shipman, set up a movie camp to direct wildlife films. With a movie crew of thirty other individuals, Shipman managed more than seventy animals and produced several short films in the area. Unfortunately, when Shipman's head director suffered gangrene on his frostbitten toes, the company began to fail. As the creditors poured in, Shipman's director experienced a mental breakdown, the rapidly deteriorating animals were taken to the San Diego Zoo, and Shipman returned to Los Angeles. Today, all that remains of the venture is Priest Lake's beautiful surroundings.

TV Chimney Rock
Located on the east side of Priest Lake State Park To access, drive on Forest Road (FR) 24 for 4 miles and merge onto FR 2. Proceed on FR 2 until its end. After parking, hike one to two hours to the rock's base.

Idaho is famous for its wide selection of perfect rock climbing peaks, and the formidable monument called Chimney Rock is a favorite of both locals and tourists. Rising above beautiful Priest Lake in the Selkirk Mountains, Chimney Rock climbs a completely vertical 350 feet to the skyline. The granite mass is characterized with flakes and cracks and offers rock climbers over thirty-five possible routes varying in difficulty.

For those with no interest in rock climbing, the noted landmark can also be seen from the main road in the park.

V Upper Priest Lake
North of Priest Lake

A narrow, two-mile long channel connects Upper Priest Lake with the larger, lower lake comprising Priest Lake State Park. While the lower lake is open to a host of recreational vehicles, Upper Priest Lake was designated a Wilderness Area in 1986 and is therefore roadless. Owned by the State of Idaho and the U.S. Forest Service, Upper Priest Lake provides visitors with solitude, beauty, and serenity. Canoes are allowed on the lake, but visitors must hike to the area from the lower lake. Campers are reminded that bears populate the area, so regulations should be followed at all times in regards to proper food and trash storage.

V Beaver Creek Recreation Site
Located at Priest Lake. Contact the Priest Lake Ranger District in Priest River at 443-2512.

General Information
The scenic Beaver Creek Recreation Site at the north end of Priest Lake was once used as a Forest Service Ranger Station from the 1920s through the 1950s. The Beaver Creek Ranger Station served as a staging facility for forest management and fire protection operations in the Upper Priest River drainage. A fireplace is the only reminder of this earlier use of the area.

Today, the Beaver Creek Recreation Site serves forest visitors as the gateway to the Upper Priest Lake Scenic Area. Upper Priest Lake was classified as a Scenic Area by the Forest Service in 1968. It is managed in cooperation with the State of Idaho's Department of Public Lands for its roadless, pristine recreation opportunities.

Facilities
41 Unit Family Campground: Each unit includes a parking spur, table, grate, and tent pad. Drinking water, vault toilets, and trash containers at central locations.
35 Person Group Camping Area: Includes four tables, grills, tent pads, and large central fire rings. Drinking water and sanitation available adjacent to the site. Parking area provided. Reservations for the group site must be made through the National Forest Campground Reservation System at 877-444-6777.

Swimming Area

This protected area is provided in conjunction with the family campground. There is no fee for this area. Swimmers should be aware of "Swimmer's Itch" parasite that is frequently found in the water. A brochure is available from the campground host. A cold water shower is available to rinse off after swimming.

Trailhead Parking

Trailhead parking provides access to Navigation and Plowboy Campgrounds and portage trails. Toilets are on site.

Hikers/Backpackers

Popular hiking and backpacking areas are easily accessed from the Beaver Creek Recreation Site. The Navigation Trail (#291) starts at the Upper Trailhead parking area and leads to the scenic Upper Priest River country. The Lakeshore Trail (#294) begins near the access trail to the swimming area. This trail accesses viewpoints, sandy beaches, and excellent secluded camping areas along the shoreline of Priest Lake. Plowboy Mountain Trail begins 2-1/2 miles up Road #1341 from the entrance to Beaver Creek.

Canoeists/Boaters/Campers

The Beaver Creek Recreation site is a popular starting point for canoeists and campers heading for the unroaded Upper Priest Lake region. Canoers can access the thoroughfare to the Upper Lake either from the Upper Trailhead parking area where a 1,000-foot portage takes you to the thoroughfare itself or by putting directly into Priest Lake at the access parking area. There are several other locations on the lake south of Beaver Creek. Boat launching is also available at Priest Lake State Park (Lionhead Unit) on the east side of Priest Lake. Please remember there is no water skiing allowed in the thoroughfare or on the Upper Priest Lake. There is a 5 MPH – no wake speed restriction in the thoroughfare.

Reprinted from U.S. Forest Service brochure

V Cavanaugh Bay
From State Hwy. 57, bear right at the Dickensheet Junction, crossing the Priest River and continuing towards Coolin. The bay is located immediately north of Coolin.

In the 1940s and 1950s, Diamond Match Company log drives drove hundreds of hardworking men to Cavanaugh Bay. Today, this industrious past has nearly been forgotten, as year-round recreation draws locals and tourists alike to Cavanaugh Bay. Nestled on the eastern edge of Priest Lake State Park, the bay is a popular bank-fishing destination during the summer. In winter months, gentle snowy hills and flats welcome Nordic skiers. Cross-country skiers should use caution at all times, however, as the bay is an increasingly popular snowmobiling area.

M Coolin/Priest Lake Chamber of Commerce
PO Box 174, Coolin. 443-3191 or (888) 774-3785. www.priestlake.org/; plcc@povn.com

4 *Food, Lodging*

Colburn
Pop. 100

Originally named "Coburn" after an early settler, the name was later changed to Colburn when the Great Northern Railroad established area service. At one time, the town contributed to Idaho's timber industry with H.E. Brown founding a timber company and sawmill here in 1908.

Elmira
Pop. 20

This tiny town was originally known as Halfway. It was later renamed after Elmira Peak, which rises about one mile northeast of town. The post office ran from 1892 to 1917, and the town draws activity simply from its location on a Great Northern Railroad line.

Naples
Pop. 130

Naples' economy is based upon farming, cattle, and logging. Italian construction workers on the Great Northern Railroad named the settlement during the winter of 1892 in honor of Naples, Italy. The workers were so proficient, they sometimes laid four miles of iron in a single day! Located in the shadow of the forested Selkirk Mountains, this quiet town is most recognized for its beautiful, peaceful landscape.

Samuels
Pop. 10

Originally called Iola, this small community was later renamed to honor Henry F. Samuels, a ranch owner in 1913. He was responsible for establishing the post office in 1914.

5 *Food, Lodging*

Kootenai
Pop. 441

This small community was laid out in 1895 along with the establishment of a post office. The town's name is a Kootenai tribal word meaning "water people," reflecting the presence of Native Americans who occupied the land until white pioneers migrated west. Once recognized as buffalo hunters, the remote Kutenai people left the plains and settled in this region's forested areas to escape conflicts with homesteaders.

In 1899, the Northern Pacific Railroad came through and bolstered the town's economy as a lumbering center. Today, the town is most widely known for the 2,700-acre Kootenai Wildlife Refuge. 215 varieties of birds have been sighted at this refuge.

Ponderay
Pop. 638

Located near Sandpoint, this town was established in 1907 with the arrival of a post office. The town's name evolved from the moniker, "Pend Oreille," which graces regional geographical sites with its presence.

H Lake Pend Oreille
Milepost 44.3 on State Hwy. 200

When the last of the continental ice sheets blocked this valley, a great lake extended over 200 miles into Montana.

Ice as high as the mountain ridges held back water as deep as 800 to 1,000 feet at Missoula, 10,000 to 20,000 years ago. At times this lake cut through the ice dam and came back. Finally, the climate turned warm and the great ice sheet melted. Lake Pend Oreille is a small remnant of that glacial action.

L Monarch Mountain Lodge
363 Bonner Mall Way, Ponderay. 263-1222 or (800) 543-8193.

Offering a warm at-home atmosphere, Monarch Mountain Lodge is centrally located near year-round recreation, including skiing, fishing, boating, and golfing. In addition to free cable, guest laundry, low long distance rates, free local calls, 24-hour coffee, fax/mail services, non-smoking rooms, and microwaves and refrigerators, Monarch Mountain also features two indoor hot tubs, a dry sauna, and a complimentary continental breakfast including homemade sourdough waffles. Looking for luxury? Reserve one of the Jacuzzi Tub suites. As a bonus, Silverwood Amusement Park tickets are available on-site, while guests can pick up discounted golf passes and Schweitzer Mountain lift tickets. Of course, don't forget your pets and kids. Dogs are welcome, and children 12 and under are free. So visit Monarch Mountain Lodge. It's where comfort and recreation are wrapped together in one convenient location.

6 *Food, Lodging*

Sandpoint
Pop. 6,835

David Thompson, the Canadian explorer and trapper, mentions in his 1809 journals a point of sand along the shores of Lake Pend Oreille. It is this point of sand from which Sandpoint derives its name. Robert Weeks opened a general store at this location in 1880. Between that year and 1906, three different railroads laid tracks in the region and drove potential settlers through the site. In 1898, when L.D. Farmin subdivided his Sand Creek homestead, the town was surveyed and platted. Just two years later, the growing city was incorporated with an economy based upon logging and milling. By the time the major sawmill closed in 1931, over two million board feet of lumber had been produced. At one time, the city also served as the American West's largest cedar pole shipping point.

In 1910, the area's population boomed when land prices dropped as low as $1.25 per acre. The settlers and would-be farmers cleared the timber-filled land with horses, chains, and dynamite. However, the homesteaders quickly realized that land that readily grew trees wouldn't necessarily

Sandpoint	Jan	Feb	March	April	May	June	July	Aug	Sep	Oct	Nov	Dec	Annual
Average Max. Temperature (F)	32.3	38.0	46.3	57.2	66.3	73.2	81.9	81.0	70.5	57.0	41.5	34.1	56.6
Average Min. Temperature (F)	20.3	22.8	27.6	33.9	40.2	45.9	48.5	47.0	41.0	34.0	28.3	23.1	34.4
Average Total Precipitation (in.)	4.06	3.16	2.74	2.08	2.33	2.26	0.99	1.19	1.69	2.63	4.28	4.57	31.99
Average Total Snowfall (in.)	22.8	13.3	6.3	0.8	0.0	0.0	0.0	0.0	0.0	0.5	6.6	20.2	70.7
Average Snow Depth (in.)	9	8	3	0	0	0	0	0	0	0	1	4	2

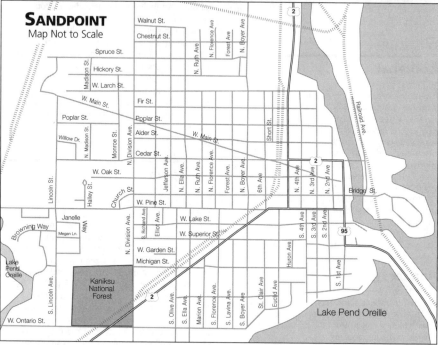

SANDPOINT
Map Not to Scale

grow good crops. Area mining was also a disappointment, and when three fires tore through the downtown district, the city suffered economic and population losses.

Despite these downtimes, the town resurrected itself. The 1970s brought in numerous artists. Soon after, outdoor recreation, hunting, skiing, and fishing drew attention to the area. Today, Sandpoint's residents are a culturally diverse mix of loggers, outdoor lovers, and writers and artists. The town also relies on its outstanding scenic splendor and Lake Pend Oreille to attract hundreds of tourists each year.

T Sandpoint Elks Golf Course
1 mile north of Sandpoint on State Hwy. 200.
263-4321.

The user-friendly, public Sandpoint Elks Golf Course offers golfers of all expertise a 9-hole, par-

36 game. Measuring 2,900 yards on the front side and 2,700 yards on the back, the course features separate tees for those who wish to play the same holes twice. Golfers should call to schedule a tee time for this nicely groomed course.

T Hidden Lakes Golf Resort
151 Clubhouse Way, Sandpoint. 263-1642 or (888) 806-6673. Drive 7 miles east on State Hwy. 200 from Sandpoint, bearing left towards the course directly past milepost 37.

Recognized as one of the most scenic golf courses in the northwest, the par-71 championship Hidden Lakes course surrounds golfers with panoramic beauty. The course is nestled between the shores of Lake Pend Oreille and the Selkirk Mountains, and the bluegrass manicured fairways are home to a variety of wildlife. At last count, eleven moose call Hidden Lakes home, deer and

elk peer behind the trees, and bald eagles and osprey circle above the action. With strategically placed bunkers, bentgrass greens, and water hazards on 17 of the 18 holes, Hidden Lakes also provides a variety of tees to accommodate all skill levels. Guests are treated to the finest amenities, including a traveling beverage cart that roams the course, and a new clubhouse, restaurant, lounge, golf shop, and locker facilities. *Golf Digest* gives Hidden Lakes four stars, and it is open April 1 to November 15 with green fees starting at $59.

T The Panida
300 N. 1st St., Sandpoint. 255-7801.

The Panida Theater is Sandpoint's community owned cultural center for cinema, theatre, and musical performances. Opened in 1927 as a premier vaudeville and movie house under the direction of F.C. Weskil, the Panida drew its name from its mission: to provide audiences in the panhandle of Idaho with cultural enrichment.

On its opening night, patrons were amazed at the beautiful Spanish Mission styling and artistic interior rivaling some of the finest architectural structures in the Pacific Northwest. Today, the Panida is listed on the National Register of Historic Places and has received special notice from the Idaho Heritage Trust, the U.S. Department of Interior, the Idaho Commission of the Arts, and the Idaho Centennial Commission.

The Panida operated until 1980, and in 1985, a group of local volunteers set out to rescue the abandoned building. After making several major repairs to bring the building up to date, the Panida reopened and has become a cornerstone of cultural activity in the region. Hundreds of performers share their talents each year. Bonnie Raitt, Arlo Guthrie, George Winston, Wynton Marsalis, the Paris Chamber Ensemble, the Cavini String Quartet, the Spokane Symphony, and the San Francisco Opera are just some of the many fine performers in a long list of outstanding productions presented at the Panida. Each year, thousands of individuals experience a range of performances in the Panida's acoustically perfect theater house.

Seating 550, the Panida boasts more than 150 performances annually. Ticket prices vary, but reservations are highly recommended.

T McArthur Wildlife Management Area
17 miles north of Sandpoint off U.S. Hwy. 95 on County Road A4

A variety of wildlife abounds in Idaho's panhandle, and individuals can see both small and big game at the McArthur Wildlife Management Area. Waterfowl, coyotes, white-tailed deer, moose, elk, Canadian geese, and bald eagles have all been sighted. The area is open year-round, and visitors are reminded to safely observe the animals from a distance.

T Sandpoint Long Bridge
U.S. Hwy. 95 N. entering Sandpoint

Bridges have long characterized Sandpoint's landscape – no matter what direction residents or tourists enter town, one will always find themselves crossing a bridge. The most notable bridge by far, though, is known simply as Long Bridge.

Leading to Lake Pend Oreille's northwestern shore and offering breathtaking views of the surrounding Selkirk Mountains, Long Bridge has a long history. As the town continued to attract new residents, it was clear that a reliable highway to and from Sandpoint was desperately needed. In 1910, the original long bridge was constructed. Built entirely from wood and stacked on 1,540 cedar pilings, the bridge was nearly two miles long at its completion, making it the world's longest wooden bridge at the time. Since then, the bridge has been replaced numerous times and has lost its distinguished world title, but it remains a Sandpoint landmark.

Today, the bridge hosts the annual Long Bridge Swim. The prmier open-water swimming event is held annually each summer, and the bridge marks the starting and stopping point. Long Bridge is also the perfect spot to soak up Sandpoint's beauty while taking a leisurely stroll year-round on the adjacent pedestrian bridge.

T Vintage Wheel Museum
218 Cedar St., Sandpoint. 263-7173.

Visitors are taken on a nostalgic journey into the history of American transportation at the Vintage Wheel Museum. The museum includes more than fifty authentic and intriguing displays, all exploring the development of transportation systems throughout the U.S.. Exhibits include well-restored antique cars, such as a 1913 Cadillac and 1932 Ford Roadster, horse drawn vehicles, steam engines, and much more. The museum is open from 9:30 AM to 5:30 PM Monday through Saturday and 11 AM to 5 PM on Sundays year-round.

T Bonner County Historical Museum
611 S. Ella St., Sandpoint. 263-2344.

Located in Lakeview Park, the Bonner County Historical Museum is dedicated to preserving the history and development of Bonner County. Featuring four exhibit rooms, the museum outlines the region's history with such topics as the Kootenai and Kalispell Indians, fur traders and steamboats, and the timber and railroad industries. With an extensive collection of old photos, newspapers, and other important regional documents, the museum has a research team available on Tuesdays and Thursdays from 11 AM to 2 PM to assist with the public's research requests. The museum is open year-round from 10 AM to 4 PM on Tuesdays through Saturdays. Admission is adults $2, family $5, students ages 6-18 $1, and under 6 are free.

T Pend d'Oreille Winery
220 Cedar St., Sandpoint. 265-8545 From U.S. Hwy. 95, exit into Sandpoint, and merge onto First Ave. Proceed along First Ave., which turns into Cedar Street. Locate the winery on the right corner of Cedar St. and Third Ave. in the old Pend Oreille Brewing Company building.

Named Idaho Winery of the Year for 2003, Pend d'Oreille (pronounced pond der ray) is the most northern winery in the Pacific Northwest. After perfecting their craft in both France and America, Julie and Stephen Meyer pride themselves on producing distinctive, award winning wines. Each wine contains hand-harvested grapes and is slowly aged in French oak barrels to ensure a unique balance of fruit and oak flavors. With years of experi-

ence, the Meyers' wine production now includes Chardonnay, Pinot Noir, Merlot, Cabernet Sauvignon, Cabernet Franc, and reserve wines available only at the winery. The winery is open daily for guided tours and boasts a new tasting room and art gallery.

T America's Largest Paper Birch
105 Gooby Rd., Sandpoint. Contact the Sandpoint Chamber of Commerce at 263-0887.

The lush climate of Sandpoint is perfect for growing a variety of vegetation, and more than fifty different species of trees have been noted in the area. In addition, the community is home to the nation's largest inland Westernpaper birch and has received "National Champion" status. The tree measures nearly fourteen feet in circumference with swaying branches shooting up more than seventy-five feet into the air. The tree's most impressive feature is its thick trunk that has quickly split into several side branches. As a result, the tree's crown features an impressive sixty-foot width.

Sandpoint is also home to the lower forty-eight's largest Rocky Mountain Maple tree. The tree was discovered in 1989 and measures in at more than eighty feet tall with a fifty-three inch circumference. Although not easily accessible, the maple can be found on a wooded hillside above Sandpoint's Bottle Bay.

T Jeff Jones Town Square
3rd & Main Streets, Sandpoint. Contact the Sandpoint Chamber of Commerce at 263-0887.

Dedicated in November 2003, Sandpoint's Jeff Jones Town Square is the result of a community revitalization project. Once strewn with weeds and concrete barriers, the area was known as the "bullpen" and was a local eyesore. Under the direction of City Planning Director, Jeff Jones, the area received a much-needed facelift. Today, the town square honors the now deceased Jones and includes benches, tables, information kiosks, and an interactive water fountain. The site is also home to Sandpoint's annual Christmas tree lighting ceremony.

T North Idaho Native Plant Arboretum Lakeview Park,
611 S. Ella Avenue, Sandpoint. Contact the Sandpoint Chamber of Commerce at (800) 800-2106.

Since the Arboretum's founding in 1999, the Kinnikinnick Chapter of the Idaho Native Plant Society volunteers have gradually converted the southwest corner of Lakeview Park into a series of native plant exhibits, seven of which represent different native plant habitats one might find in the Idaho Panhandle.

Dry Forest Habitat
Dry forests are most often characterized by somewhat shallow, rocky soils and are usually dominated by ponderosa pine, Douglas fir, or grand fir trees. The understory consists of such grasses as Idaho fescue, bluebunch wheatgrass, and pinegrass; perennial forbs including lupines; and such shrubs as serviceberry, ninebark, oceanspray, and common chokecherry. Kinnikinnick is a common low shrub. This habitat occurs on ridges and slopes at lower to middle elevations, usually on southerly to westerly aspects.

Dry Rock Habitat
Usually surrounded by forested habitats, dry rock habitats occur when plants establish themselves in soil deposited between rocks. Many plants found

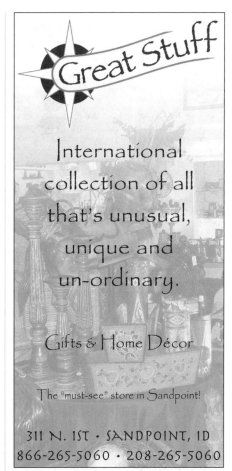

here are also found in dry forest and even moist forest habitats; however, some plants occur only when a dry rock habitat receives ample moisture in the spring before drying up in summer. Scarlet gilia, blanket flower, kittentails, pearhip rose, ninebark, oceanspray, smooth sumac, wild yarrow, and kinnikinnick are often found here.

Interior Rain Forest/Rare Plant Habitat
Unique in north Idaho – and a result of warm, Pacific maritime weather patterns – interior rain forests support the wettest forest habitats in the state. An overstory of western red cedar and western hemlock towers over devil's club, lady fern, maidenhair fern, and oak fern. Many rare species occur in rainland forests, including some you can see here in the Arboretum: beadruby, maidenhair spleenwort, northern beechfern, deerfern, purple meadowrue, and white shooting star.

Meadow Habitat
Dry to moist meadow habitats in north Idaho support Idaho fescue, blue wildrye, Junegrass, sticky geranium, lupines, goldenrod, and other grasses and perennial forbs. Such shrubs as common chokecherry may occasionally occur.

Moist Forest Habitat
In moist forests, a mixed overstory of various conifers provides shade to an understory of forbs, such as wild ginger, queencup, twinflower, pioneer violet, and bunchberry dogwood. Sword fern may also be found here. Such habitats occur in ephemeral draws and swales and on mountain slopes at lower to middle elevations.

Riparian Habitat
These streamside habitats are found along perennial streams and large rivers, but may also occur on the margins of such wetlands as ponds, fens,

Continued on page 47

IDAHO'S FAMOUS LADIES OF THE NIGHT

In the 1800s American West, harsh living conditions and male-oriented occupations scared many women away from the frontier. When Easterners heard of the mining boom in the western territories, most wives simply refused to give up the refineries of life and wished their men the best of luck. As a result, the earliest frontier communities were rough and tumble places full of vigilante justice, hardcore drinking, very few women, and a mass of lonely men. In some places, women were so scarce that men outnumbered them 200 to 1!

For bold women who could take care of themselves on the frontier, this situation presented lucrative opportunities to make a fortune. Capitalizing on the needs of single miners, cowboys, and soldiers, thousands of women prostituted themselves in saloons, cribs, shacks, dance halls, and brothels.

While many women chose this life as a means of supporting their children, greedy husbands or slave traders tragically forced others into the profession. In the mid 1800s and continuing into the 1920s, Chinese girls as young as eleven were illegally brought to America and forced into a slave life. Upon arrival in Oregon and California, these women were paraded, purchased, taken to booming mine towns, and prostituted. Since they were purchased for their passage price, these women became the slaves of saloonkeepers, pimps, and brothel owners and were forced into prostitution to recoup their owner's money. They earned nothing for their work, and due to strict rules regarding "sick days," it was virtually impossible to win one's freedom. Often, these women were forced into tiny shacks, made to catcall their customers, and were lucky to live past their early twenties. Although the petite frames and dark hair of the Chinese girls intrigued young white miners, these features were also the source for discrimination. Few were lucky to escape and marry a white man. At the same time, Chinese men generally wanted nothing to do with these girls as a Chinese woman who slept with a white man was the ultimate disgrace. Living under these harsh conditions, a single Chinese prostitute who could no longer provide a profit to her owner was frequently forced to choose between committing suicide or being murdered.

Although virtuous women on the frontier surely snubbed these ladies of the night, most miners and cowboys respected the brothel prostitutes and held them in the highest esteem for their kind hearts. Many of the prostitutes willingly shut up shop to serve as nurses whenever a man fell sick, and if a miner could not afford a meal or lodging, a prostitute would rush to his aid and offer financial assistance. It is no surprise, then, that when a brothel prostitute died, every business in town generally closed in honor of the dead woman. In mining towns, it was fairly common for a carnival to follow the prostitute's funeral in celebration of the life she led.

In addition to their daily activities, prostitutes were frequently found providing testimony to frontier lawmen in the courtroom. Because of their continual contact with men, these women often knew every detail of local barroom brawls and could testify whether a man partook out of self-defense. The women also provided credible alibis for thousands of men falsely charged, thus helping save the innocent from hefty fines or untimely deaths.

Filled with both virtue and scandal, the lives of these enterprising women intrigued their contemporaries as well as today's historians. Through historical records, diaries, and photographs, the lives of these women have been preserved, including many of Idaho's own famous ladies of the night.

Molly b'Dam

Molly b'Dam is perhaps Idaho's most famous and well-loved lady of the night. Born in Dublin, Ireland in 1853, Molly b'Dam was originally known as Maggie Hall. As a child, Maggie was raised in a strict Catholic family, was well-educated, and had several friends. Although Maggie loved her family tremendously, Ireland could not reign in her love for adventure. Much to her parents' dismay, Maggie immigrated alone to the U.S. at age twenty in 1873, sure that she would be well-received and instantly find a job. New York City's streets were flooded with immigrants, though, and as her money dwindled, Maggie was forced to take the only job she could find. Working as a barmaid in a popular New York saloon, Maggie's striking looks caught the eye of many men, including one wealthy gentleman named Burdan. After just three meetings, Burdan proposed to Maggie. Maggie had always dreamed of a large Catholic wedding, but Burdan insisted that a justice of the peace marry them in the middle of the night. In addition, Maggie was forced to change her name to the more formal "Molly" and keep her marriage a secret. Burdan told Maggie that if his parents learned of the marriage, all monetary assistance would be cut off, forcing both she and he to live on the streets.

Molly followed her husband's wishes, and although she longed to continue working at the saloon, Burdan strictly forbade it. It wasn't long before Burdan's parents, however, found out about the secret marriage, and the couple stopped receiving assistance. Destitute and unwilling to find a job for himself, Burdan brought home a friend and begged Molly to sleep with him for a profit. As a strong Catholic girl who loved her husband, Molly was heartbroken at the thought but finally agreed to her husband's pleas. Unfortunately, Burdan continued to bring home frequent male guests, and as his pleas turned into orders, Molly lost all love for her husband. She also lost the love and support from her church. Learning of her deeds, Molly's parish priest excommunicated her for following her husband's immoral commands. At age twenty-four, Molly left Burdan and New York City and headed west.

Excommunicated from the church and destined for hell in her own eyes, Molly arrived in Thompson Falls, MT, and bought a passage to take her to Murray, Idaho where she planned to open a brothel. The route to Idaho over Thompson Pass was dangerous, and the harsh 1884 winter made the journey even more treacherous. Noting that a mother and her small child were struggling, Molly told the rest of the party to travel ahead. She would stay behind and rest for the night with the young mother and continue to Idaho the next day. That night, a fierce blizzard hit. The party who had by now arrived in Murray was sure that the three would never be seen alive again. But Molly persevered, and when she and the mother and child galloped into Murray the next day, a host of cheers greeted them. At that moment, Molly knew she had found her new home.

When she arrived and stated her name as Molly Burdan, her heavy Irish brogue caused one miner to misunderstand her. She was known as Molly b'Dam from that moment on. With an engaging personality and a refinery uncommon among most frontier ladies, Molly opened a saloon and brothel to serve every man's need in Murray. Her favorite pastime was the widely publicized public bath she held behind her brothel. Bringing out a tub full of water, the miners knew that when the bottom of the tub was covered with gold, Molly would undress and slip into the tub. For the right price, miners could take turns washing the "Irish Queen's" back.

Molly's schemes, however, were quickly abandoned when a smallpox outbreak hit Murray. When many residents hid in fear in their cabins, Molly organized the town's efforts, established a makeshift hospital in one of Murray's hotels, and tended to the sick and dying around the clock. Molly never contracted smallpox, but the strenuous pace of nursing hundreds of sick residents took its toll. Shortly after the outbreak subsided, Molly became very ill and developed consumption. With no known cure available, Murray's most beloved lady died on January 17, 1888. She is buried in the Murray cemetery, and her gravestone reads, "Maggie Hall – Sacred to the Memory of Molly-B-Dam."

Anna King

As a dance-hall girl, Anna King never earned the same respect and esteem that the brothel ladies enjoyed. Nevertheless, she became a notorious figure in Idaho's history. Bonanza, Idaho's dance-hall girls were known as greedy swindlers only interested in taking a man's hard-earned money, and Anna was one of these girls. Despite the girls' reputations, men from Bonanza frequented the facility for the stunning good looks of most of the dancers. As was common on the early frontier, a brawl broke out one evening at the hall. Amidst the chaos, Anna was mysteriously murdered, and no one was ever charged with her death.

Since she lived and worked in Bonanza, it was natural that she be buried in the local cemetery. But Bonanza's residents protested, citing Anna's uncomely behavior as a reason. Learning of the situation, a committee of miners from Custer rode to Bonanza, picked up Anna's lifeless body, and took her to the outskirts of Custer where she was buried in a beautiful spot lined with pine trees. Ironically, while few cared for Anna during life, the U.S. Department of Forestry later became responsible for tending her grave and its surrounding trees.

Mother Mac

When some miners moved west in search of riches, a few were lucky enough to have wives that agreed to accompany them. Mother Mac was one of these wives. Known as a model wife who proudly took care of her husband, never drank, and never swore, Mother Mac possessed the finest moral character. But when her husband died in a tragic mining accident, Mother Mac was devastated. Turning to whiskey for comfort, she refused to bathe for weeks, didn't comb her hair, and eventually drank herself into a coma. When she awoke, a new Mother Mac was born, and she packed her belongings for Silver City.

Upon arriving in Silver City, Mother Mac opened the best brothel in the red-light district and was reported to have some of Idaho's finest prostitutes. Although it is known that Mother Mac never drank again, there is speculation surrounding her other activities. While some claim she offered herself up for services, others adamantly state that Mother Mac continued to pine for her one true love – her husband – and simply provided a place for other women to showcase their profession.

Emma and Alvie Davis
In 1882, Emma and Alvie Davis traveled from Salt Lake City to Bellevue, Idaho and for just a few short months, opened a highly successful brothel. That fall, when the sisters returned to Salt Lake City, they had $3,000 in their pockets and used the money to open an even more successful parlor house in the city's extensive red-light district.

Peg-Leg-Annie and Dutch Em
Annie Morrow arrived in Atlanta on her father's back at age four and never left the surrounding area. While her father worked as a miner, Annie grew up to be a wild woman who saw the potential money she could earn if she serviced the many lonely miners' needs. Teaming up with emigrant and friend, Dutch Em (Emma van Losch), Annie and Emma made a good living for themselves and looked forward to paydays when they would travel to nearby Rocky Bar for their own entertainment. In May 1898, this usual outing took a tragic turn.

Starting out on a Friday night, Annie and Dutch Em were caught in a freak blizzard that dumped nearly four feet of snow in the area. Continuing on to Bald Mountain and Black Warrior Canyon, the women took shelter on Saturday night next to a rock. While Annie took off her warm underclothes and put them on her friend to protect her from the frigid conditions, Annie's Newfoundland dog cuddled next to her and the three waited out the night. The weather was too much for Dutch Em, and by Sunday morning, her dead body was frozen stiff. Annie set out in search of help, and she soon met up with mail carrier, Bill Tate. With his assistance, Annie was taken to a cabin near Atlanta to rest, eat, and gather her strength while a party of men was dispatched to locate Dutch Em's body. Dutch Em was later buried on a hillside near the edge of Atlanta.

Annie survived the ordeal but not without a price. After examining her condition at the cabin, Tate sent word to Rocky Bar that Doc Newkirk was needed immediately. Two days later, the doctor arrived with a jack knife and meat saw. As Annie guzzled whiskey, the doctor amputated her feet above the ankle and she acquired her legendary nickname, Peg-Leg-Annie.

Moving to Rocky Bar, Peg-Leg-Annie eventually found a steady beau, and together, they raised five children. She made a new living as a boardinghouse keeper and would sell whiskey to anyone with money. Although Peg-Leg-Annie was well-liked in the community, no one dreamed of challenging her as she always packed a pistol and was known to be a good shot. Peg-Leg-Annie died in the 1930s and is buried in Boise's Morris Hill Cemetery.

China Annie
Similar to the fate of many other young Chinese girls born into destitute families, China Annie was illegally shipped to America and forced into the world of prostitution where she earned as little as $0.25 or $0.50 per customer. After a member of the Yeong Wo Company purchased her, China Annie was taken to Idaho City where the Chinese prostitute trade was thriving.

During her ordeal, China Annie fell in love with a man named Ah Guan, a Chinaman who did not scorn her even though she had slept with white men. After much planning, China Annie escaped from her owner and traveled to Boise where she married her lover. Her owner was livid when he discovered China Annie's absence, and he filed a larceny charge against her for stealing herself. Four weeks after her disappearance, China Annie was apprehended and returned to Idaho City for a court appearance. Miraculously, the judge looked favorably upon China Annie's plight, dismissed the case, and allowed China Annie to return to Boise and her new husband.

Polly Bemis
Born Lalu Nathoy on September 11, 1853 near Beijing, China, Polly Bemis is the most famous Chinese woman in Idaho's frontier history. As a child, Lalu's family lived in poverty. When a man approached them and offered them $2,500 and two bags of seeds for Lalu, her parents sold her in order to save themselves and the rest of the starving family. Not knowing her fate, Lalu boarded the ship to America and arrived in Portland two months later. Lalu was immediately sold to Big Jim, a saloonkeeper and domineering leader of Warren's Chinese colony, and was renamed Polly.

After spending time in Idaho City, Big Jim brought Polly downriver to Warren where she continued to work as a prostitute. Although one legend states that Polly won her freedom in a poker game, this is simply a case of mistaken identity. The poker bride was actually a Native American woman by the name of Molly, and Polly won her freedom from Big Jim when he died.

As a free woman, Polly worked as a housekeeper and ran a boardinghouse for the unfriendly Charley Bemis down at Bemis Point, just a few miles outside Warren. Though Bemis was known as a strange man who was always armed, he treated Polly well and taught her to speak English fluently. In return, Polly nursed Bemis back to health in 1890 after he was shot in a dispute over a card game and took care of him as though she were his wife.

In 1894, when Polly was faced with deportation, Bemis made Polly his official wife and they continued to live at Bemis Point near the Salmon River that Polly dearly loved. When Polly's husband died in 1923, friends tried to persuade Polly to move to Boise and experience the luxuries of life she had never known. The city scared Polly, though, and she returned to Bemis Point and lived alone the last ten years of her life, often nursing other neighbors back to health during that time. When Polly died on November 6, 1933, members of the Grangeville City Council served as pallbearers for this beloved woman who had risen above her tragic frontier beginnings.

and marshes. They may be forested with evergreens or with a mixture of evergreens and hardwoods (such as coyote willow, water birch, Sitka alder, thinleaf alder, or the rare dwarf birch). Wet meadow habitats support tufted hairgrass and common camas (the latter having been an important traditional food for local Native Americans).

Subalpine Habitat
These habitats occur at middle to higher elevations, on mountain slopes, ridges, and in draws. They also can be found at lower elevations in cold air drainages (often found in the Priest River area). Subalpine fir and Engelmann spruce often dominate forested habitats, with huckleberry, menziesia, and mountain ash or alpine bluegrass and alpine timothy in the understory. The rare Sitka mistmaiden occurs on wet cliffs and ledges.

Wild Medicinals is a Unique Exhibit
Located on the east side of the log cabin that serves as Arboretum headquarters, Wild Medicinals is the only exhibit not limited to native plants. The reason is that many medicinal plants we think of as being "natives" are not truly native, but were brought here by traders, colonists, soldiers, and native peoples. As these plants have naturalized in the wild over the past few hundred years, many people think of them as being native to north Idaho. Because of this history and the fact that many of these herbs are still used medicinally, some of these naturalized plants are included in this exhibit; however, to separate them from the truly native plants, they are identified by a red dot on the label.

Reprinted from a Kinnikinnick Chapter of the Idaho Native Plant Society brochure

⊤ Sandpoint Railroad Depot
East end of Cedar St., Sandpoint. Contact the Sandpoint Chamber of Commerce at 263-0887.

Sandpoint's Burlington Northern Railroad office represents Idaho's only Gothic-inspired railroad depot. Constructed in 1916 for the Northern Pacific Railroad, the building features stone finial topped gables and open porches. The building's elaborate architectural style transports visitors back in time to the day when railroads were a community's life support system.

⊤ Purcell Trench
North of Sandpoint on U.S. Hwy. 95

As U.S. Highway 95 winds north from Sandpoint, the route flattens into an area dubbed Purcell Trench. At an elevation of less than 2,600 feet, the area was covered by a lake 30 million years ago. As regional faults became active, the landscape of the area changed. Approximately 32,000 to 80,000 years ago, Canadian glaciers flowed south, carving a trough in their wake. Today, the Selkirk Mountain Range to the west and the Cabinet Mountains to the east border the trench.

⊤ Pack River
10.6 miles north of Sandpoint on U.S. Hwy. 95

Flowing under U.S. Highway 95, Idaho's Pack River is most famous for hosting a small herd of mountain caribou. Among the country's rarest animals, Idaho's caribou are speculated to be the only natural band living in the U.S. mainland.

Although belonging to the deer family, caribou possess many unique characteristics. Both male and female caribou grow antlers, and while larger than deer, they are generally smaller than elk. Northern Idaho's landscape and climate are well-suited to the distinguished animals. During summer, caribou enjoy alpine habitats, while winter finds them residing in moister basins.

T Sandpoint Art Walk
Downtown Sandpoint. Contact the Sandpoint
Chamber of Commerce at 263-0887.

Sandpoint is known for its dense population of
artisans, and the downtown area reflects this characteristic with its many diverse art galleries. Most
of the area galleries participate in the community
Art Walk, a free self-guided tour of the various art
shops and creations available throughout town.
brochures are available at any of the galleries or at
the Sandpoint Chamber of Commerce.

TS Cedar Street Bridge
Corner of Cedar St. & First Ave., Sandpoint.
263-2265.

Sandpoint's Cedar Street Bridge is a community
landmark. Remodeled into a shopping mall in the
mid 1970s, the site represents the only U.S. marketplace situated on a bridge. Massive tamarack
logs and incredible views of Sand Creek from the
passive solar windows are architectural highlights.
Within the marketplace, visitors will find a variety
of shops, including the company headquarters for
clothing giant, Coldwater Creek. The marketplace
is open 9 AM to 9 PM on weekdays and 10 AM to
7 PM on weekends.

TV Schweitzer Mountain Resort
10000 Schweitzer Mountain Rd., Sandpoint.
263-9555 or (800) 831-8810.

Nestled in the beautiful Selkirk Mountains,
Schweitzer Mountain Resort offers adventure and
family fun year-round. There's so many activities
going on, Schweitzer's visitors often have a hard
time deciding whether they prefer the winter or
summer season more!

For the winter lover, Schweitzer offers wide-
open, underused terrain, and *Snow Country* has
rated it as one of the nation's top forty ski resorts.
The resort features 2,500 acres and 59 designated
trails catering to all skill levels. 20% of the trails
are rated for beginners, 40% are intermediate,
35% are for advanced skiers, and 5% are for
experts only. With more than 300 average inches
of snow per year, Schweitzer is a winter enthusiast's dream. In addition to downhill skiing, the
resort also features a snowboarding terrain park,
30 kilometers of groomed nordic trails, snowshoeing trails, snowmobile touring, a snowskate park,
and special day care and learn-to-ski programs for
children ages three months to twelve years. Open
from 9 AM to 4 PM November through April,
Schweitzer also operates two lighted runs starting
in mid-December on Friday and Saturday
evenings until 8 PM. Lift tickets start at $44 for
adults 18 and over, but plenty of stay and ski
packages are available.

Schweitzer offers a variety of summer options
as well. Visitors can take a 2,000-foot vertical ride
to the top of the mountain on the Great Escape
Quad. On top, scenic views and access to hundreds of mountain biking and hiking trails are
offered. In addition, invigorating games of sand
volleyball, huckleberry picking in August and
September, disc golf, summer concerts, paint ball,
and a special climbing wall and bungee area are
offered. With so many different activities, the area
provides something for everyone. An added perk
is the Mountain Activity Center. Hosting weekend
crafts, guided hikes, and movies, the center also
rents out the latest equipment and gear and can
help arrange golf days, kayak tours, chartered fly-
fishing tours, whitewater rafting trips, and guided
horseback rides.

TV Lake Pend Oreille
Sandpoint. Contact the Sandpoint Chamber of
Commerce at 263-0887.

Hugging the Sandpoint community, Lake Pend
Oreille is Idaho's largest lake and was formed during
the Pleistocene Era sometime within the last million
years. Measuring more than forty-three miles long
and six miles wide with depths up to 1,200 feet,
the lake's brilliant blue waters showcase huge cliffs
to the southeast and the rugged Selkirk Mountain
peaks to the northwest. For years, the lake has
been home to a variety of recreationists. During
the summer, swimmers, boaters, and water skiers
flock to the lake as anglers search for fourteen
species of game fish residing in the lake's deep
waters. Don't expect the number of visitors to
dwindle during cooler months, as winter finds the
waters populated with ice skaters and ice fishermen.

TV Sandpoint City Beach
Located in downtown Sandpoint at the base of
Bridge Street off U.S. Hwy. 95

The Sandpoint City Beach is a community and
tourist favorite located on a small strip of land
extending into Lake Pend Oreille. Besides opportunities for swimming and soaking up the warm
summer rays on shore, the beach features its own
recreation area. The site includes picnic areas, basketball and volleyball courts, and a playground.

V Floating the Pack River
Contact the Sandpoint Chamber of Commerce at
263-0887. From Sandpoint, travel 3 miles east of
U.S. Hwy. 95 to the bridge on Colburn-Culver Rd.
Continue 1.5 miles further east to the put-in point
at the bridge on Rapid Lightning Rd.

The Pack River is known for its gentle meanderings outside Sandpoint between U.S. Hwy. 95 and
State Hwy. 200. Although this section of river can
be floated in its entirety, the trip would take a full
day if not two days to complete. One of the best
stretches to float for a half-day trip lies between
the Rapid Lightning Bridge and the take-out point
at the State Hwy. 200 Bridge. The winding route
lazily twists through valleys, past hillsides covered
with drooping cottonwood trees, and near the
Hidden Lakes Golf Resort. Occasional wildlife can
be spotted, and river traffic is minimal on this
approximately four-hour route.

F Di Luna's Cafe
207 Cedar St., Sandpoint. 263-0846.

Enjoy breakfast, lunch, and dinner in the beautiful
and relaxing décor of Di Luna's Café. Featuring
local hormone-free meats cut to order, usual and
unique specialties include smoked salmon and
cream cheese scramble, huevos rancheros, sweet
potato hash browns and fries, fresh fish, Greek

and vegetarian entrees, lemon-roasted chicken,
rack of lamb, and ground sirloin burgers rumored
to be the town's best! In addition, semi-monthly
weekend dinner concerts feature a variety of live
music and artists. Sip your favorite wine, sample a
homemade dessert, or simply relax while listening
to the strains of blues, jazz, bluegrass, and folk
music. Wine dinners, featuring special fare paired
to blend with a visiting winemaker's wares, are
also extremely popular. Make reservations today to
enjoy wines from around the world and delectable
food!

F Bangkok Cuisine
202 2nd Ave., Sandpoint. 265-4149.

Treat yourself to unique chef specials and freshly
prepared, authentic Thai food at Bangkok Cuisine.
Begin your lunch or dinner with an appetizer
soup followed by one of several entrees.
Specialties include Thai curry varieties, boneless
crispy duck with garlic sauce, pineapple fried rice,
chicken peanut sauce over spinach, seafood com-
binations, salads and noodle dishes, lamb, and
vegetarian entrees. Meat dishes can be substituted
with vegetables, and some dishes can be specially
prepared for those with food allergies. Finish your
meal with Thai iced coffee or one of the delicious
homemade desserts, including fried ice cream,
fried bananas, and coconut and ginger ice creams.
Bangkok Cuisine is open Monday through Friday
from 11:30 AM to 2:30 PM for lunch and Monday
through Saturday from 5 to 9 PM for dinner.

F Café Trinity
116 N. 1st, Sandpoint. 255-7558.

Named after a southern cooking term referring to
the combination of bell pepper, onion, and celery
used in the base of southern cooking, Café Trinity
offers an upbeat atmosphere and friendly, courteous staff. Chef Gabriel Cruz trained with Jan
Birnbaum, a well-known Louisiana chef, and takes
special pride in preparing every dish individually.
Select from S.ern-inspired American foods including gumbo, etouffee, fresh seafood, steaks, juicy
burgers, the café's famous spunky crawfish chow-
der, and decadent desserts like Banana Foster.

Catch the beat of live music on Friday and Saturday nights, and overlook Sand Creek during the summer on one of Sandpoint's few outdoor dining decks. Every dish is made to order. So sit back and enjoy Sandpoint's only exhibition kitchen as Chef Cruz and staff entertain with culinary delights.

F Ivano's Ristorante Italiano
102 S. First Ave., Sandpoint. 263-0211.

Located on the corner of First and Pine, Ivano's Ristorante Italiano has been serving the Sandpoint community and visitors fine food and excellent service for over twenty years. Italian dining, classic wines, and a gracious atmosphere combine to make this restaurant a long-standing favorite. For lunch, the restaurant's excellent bakery features organic fair trade coffee, fresh pastries, and deli-style offerings Monday through Friday starting at 11 AM. Dinner is served seven nights a week beginning at 4:30 PM featuring delectable entrees including pasta, fresh seafood, buffalo, beef, veal, chicken, and vegetarian specialties. Patio seating is offered during the summer, and offsite catering is available for weddings, family get-togethers, and other large gatherings. Make reservations today to dine at First and Pine, and discover a community legacy offering the finest in Italian dining!

LC Country Inn & RV Park
470700 Hwy. 95, Sandpoint. 263-3333 or 866-835-3361.

Nestled in the Selkirk Mountains, Country Inn & RV Park offers great accommodations at low rates. The inn's rooms and king and queen suites include cable TV, HBO, refrigerators, microwaves, and free local calls. Continental breakfast is standard, and an outdoor hot tub beckons guests to relax. Staying awhile? Reserve the one-bedroom cabin for a week or month complete with a living room and fully stocked kitchen. For campers, the RV park offers ten full hookup RV sites and a tent area. Picnic tables and barbeques are free, and a playground area offers children hours of fun. As a bonus, guests may request a free bike to explore the area's numerous scenic bike trails. No matter your lodging preference, Country Inn & RV Park can accommodate all your vacation needs!

L Church Street House Bed and Breakfast
401 Church St., Sandpoint. 255-7094.
www.churchstreethouse.com

Featuring an Arts and Crafts Bungalow style, Church Street House Bed and Breakfast was

built in 1915 and offers a comfortable year-round respite. Fully renovated in 2001, there are two guest rooms, with private bath and a pillow-top queen size brass bed. Period furnishings and antiques complement the interior Douglas-fir woodwork, and central air conditioning adds a touch of modernity. In the morning, wake up to coffee, tea, and a delicious breakfast while watching Sandpoint come to life through the dining room's beautiful bay window. Cozy up by the fire in the winter, sip wine in the garden during the summer, or take a short walk to downtown Sandpoint's lakefront beach, shops, and restaurants. Make reservations today at this Nationally Registered Historic Place, and experience comfort, convenience, and old-world charm around every corner.

L The Coit House Bed & Breakfast and K2 Inn
502 N. 4th Ave., Sandpoint. 263-3441 or (866) 265-2648. www.coithouse.com or www.k2inn.com

Explore beautiful Sandpoint with the convenient Downtown accommodations found at The Coit House Bed and Breakfast and neighboring K2 Inn. Walk inside The Coit House to discover the charm of a beautifully restored 1907 Victorian Manor. Every room is equipped with private baths. Other amenities include clawfoot tubs, queen pillow top beds, and telephones and cable television. For larger accommodations, reserve the family suite complete with kitchen facilities. Gourmet hot breakfast is included with all rooms. For a standard hotel experience, stay at the affordable K2 Inn and relax in the guest hot tub. Cleanliness is prized, and virtually any room combination guests may need is available. Rooms include queen beds, refrigerators, microwaves, cable/HBO, complimentary coffee, and a few offer full kitchens. Experience Sandpoint with these affordable select lodgings on your next vacation or business trip!

S Great Stuff
311 N. 1st, Sandpoint. 265-5060 or 866-265-5060.

Great Stuff offers an international collection of wonderful gifts and home décor. Add style indoors with distinctive wicker selections, or let the soothing sound of bamboo wind chimes fill

your yard. Stunning pottery, large leather animals, beautiful baskets, and nautical items lend a worldly accent to any décor. Reproduction balance toys delight all ages, and kids can't resist the hand-carved rocking horse, motorcycle, airplane, or train. B.C. Bones dinosaur and other educational puzzles also make great gifts. Carved in Bali, a collection of wooden animals with jointed legs and arms offers something for everyone - from giraffes and zebras to roosters and pigs. Need something sweet? Great Stuff's selection of chocolate goodies and fabulous homemade fudges makes it your one-stop source for distinctive gifts and décor.

M Lana Kay Realty
105 Pine St., Ste. 103, Sandpoint. 263-9546 or (800) 726-9546. www.lanakayrealty.com

With over 41 years of real estate experience, Lana Kay Realty provides unparalleled service and professionalism. Selling real estate in northern Idaho since 1964, Lana Kay Hanson founded her own real estate firm in 1980 in scenic Sandpoint. Lana's sons, Matt and Mark, joined her in 1984, at which time the business adopted a family/team approach. Today, Lana Kay Realty prides itself on handling all types of northern Idaho and western Montana real estate, including residential, commercial, recreational, and bare acreage listings. They are familiar with creative financing options and innovative marketing approaches, and they strive to help each customer find the results they deserve. For knowledge and experience you can count on when selling or buying a home, see the professionals at Lana Kay Realty.

M Sandpoint Chamber of Commerce
900 N. 5th Ave., Sandpoint. 263-2161 or (800) 800-2106. www.sandpointchamber.org; info@sandpointchamber.com

7 Food

Dover
Pop. 342

Dover was named after stockholders in the Dover Lumber Company. It is unknown if these men originated from Dover, Ohio or Dover, England. Originally named Welty in honor of the lumber company's president, the town acquired postal services in 1912.

Laclede
Pop. 200

As the Great Northern Railroad was being built in 1891, this small town was founded and named after a French engineer on the railroad. The train carried supplies and mail to the area's new settlers, and a large sawmill provided the bulk of the town's employment and a stable economy.

H Seneacquoteen
8 miles east of Priest River on U.S. Hwy. 2 at the mouth of Hoodoo Creek

Once one of Idaho's most recognized settlements, Seneacquoteen (a Kalispell or Pend Oreille Indian word) flourished from 1810 until

1910. Surrounded by lush meadows, the area was first home to Native Americans quickly followed by explorers from the North West Company. As more and more travelers and surveyors began using Seneacquoteen for their base of operations, construction began on permanent buildings. In 1860, Thomas Forde erected the first log building and created a ferry system. When gold fever hit Idaho, miners rushed to and through the town, allowing a productive trading post to be established here.

Seneacquoteen continued to grow in popularity throughout the late 1800s. The Territorial Legislature designated the town as the first county seat for Kootenai County, and the county's first school opened here and operated for more than fifty years. As with many other frontier communities, though, the newly established Northern Pacific and Great Northern Railroads bypassed the community, initiating the town's collapse. The community's doomed fate was sealed in 1910 when a wagon bridge was established in nearby Sandpoint. Today, a small cemetery is all that remains of one of Idaho's earliest settlements.

H Seneacquoteen
Milepost 15 at Laclede on U.S. Hwy. 2

Long before white men discovered this river, Indians used to camp here at this important early crossing.

Fur traders, surveyors, and miners followed the old Indian trail that forded the river here at Seneacquoteen – a Kalispell word meaning "crossing." During the Kootenay gold rush of 1864, a wagon road came from Walla Walla to a ferry here. The Wild Horse Trail – a pack route – ran on north to the Kootenay mines in British Columbia.

V Laclede Rocks
2 miles west of Laclede on U.S. Hwy. 2

Situated adjacent to the highway, Laclede Rocks is a popular and conveniently accessed rock-climbing destination. The area contains a few easy routes, but most are rated in the 5.8-5.12 range and require previous experience.

8 *Food, Lodging*

Priest River
Pop. 1,754

This community was first settled in 1888, but the town site was forced to move a mile east to its present location because of regular flooding from the nearby Priest River. Drawing its name from the river, the town experienced a population boost thanks to the arrival of the Great Northern Railroad. As the line moved west from Montana in 1891 and 1892, several Italian immigrants responded to the advertisements calling for large quantities of laborers. When the line was completed, many of the former line workers stayed in the region, filed for homesteads, and eventually saved enough money to send for their wives and children still living in the homeland.

From 1901 to 1931, thousands of white pine, ponderosa and cedar logs were cut in the Priest River area and floated downriver to Pend Oreille Lake and Newport, Washington. The area's economic dependence upon the timber industry has since declined, but a celebration of logging activities is held every July to commemorate the town's history.

Oldtown
Pop. 190

Established in 1893 on the Pend Oreille River under the name "Newport," this town's river port attracted several settlers to the region. Within no time, "Newport" was a booming community home to a ferry, general store, dry goods store, hotel, numerous saloons, a post office, and a line of the Great Northern Railroad running along the Idaho/Washington border. In its infancy, the railroad depot was housed in a boxcar. Unfortunately, the boxcar burned in 1894, and this event changed the area's history. Instead of rebuilding a depot on the Idaho border, railroad officials built on the Washington side. Next, railroad employee Charles Talmadge purchased 40 acres of land and platted out a city site adjacent to the Washington depot. Slowly, residents of Newport, Idaho began moving over to the Washington side where more business opportunities and services were becoming available in "new" Newport. As residents crossed over the border, the old town site quickly became a place of chaos. The once thriving area became known as the old part of town and was home to several saloons, houses of ill-repute, and illegal gambling. While the Idaho area became unincorporated, Newport, Washington was thriving.

In 1946, when Idaho's liquor laws became more stringent, the village of Oldtown was incorporated. Oldtown retained its status as a village for 21 years. In 1967, however, the Idaho Legislature mandated that no villages could technically be part of the state. Thus, Oldtown finally attained official city status. Today, Oldtown has its own mayor and city council, but shares a Chamber of Commerce with its border neighbor, Newport. Together, these two cities with the same founding history share panoramic views of the surrounding area's natural beauty.

T Priest River Ranch Club
Directly west of Priest River on U.S. Hwy. 2. 448-1731.

Popular among the locals, the Priest River Ranch Club offers golfers 2,530 yards of play. This nine-hole course is rated a par 33 for men and par 36 for women.

WOOL LOVERS

While driving around Sandpoint, visitors may notice a curious looking animal atypical of the area's average wildlife. The strange, three-foot tall creature is none other than the alpaca. Native to South America's Peru, Bolivia, and Chile, the alpaca is similar to the llama but is prized in North America for its dense, thick wool. The alpaca's wool features more than twenty-two distinct colors and is reputed to be five times warmer than sheep's wool and of higher quality than cashmere. Due to growing demand for the prized wool, the Sandpoint area is littered with alpaca ranches, and alpaca are frequently seen grazing in Sandpoint's outlying fields.

T Albeni Falls Dam
Near Oldtown on U.S. Hwy. 2. 437-3133.

French-Canadian, Albeni Poirier (pronounced "Albany") arrived in Idaho on the first Northern Pacific train, and with his brother, operated a cattle ranch until 1892. At that time, Poirier decided to move, and his wife and thirteen children joined him on his new land near Albeni Falls.

The dam, which made the actual waterfall disappear, draws its name from this early Idaho settler. In cooperation with the National Defense Program, the project was authorized in 1951. At a price of $34 million, the U.S. Army Corps of Engineers began building the dam in 1951, completing it four years later. With a spillway measuring 400 feet long, the dam backs up the Pend Oreille River, and water release is maintained in conjunction with other dams on the nearby Columbia River.

The dam's primary purpose is to produce electricity while eliminating potential floods. On average, more than 200 million kilowatts of energy are generated each year at the dam, which is then distributed to customers all across the Pacific Northwest. It is estimated that annually, this saves America from purchasing 4.9 million imported barrels of oil.

Visitors can learn more about the dam by stopping in at the visitor center or taking a guided tour of the powerhouse's inner workings. A scenic vista of the area is also found on Highway 2 where visitors can walk along a paved trail for an overview of the spillway.

T Keyser House Museum
301 Montgomery St., Priest River. 448-2721.

Built in the late 1800s, the now restored Keyser House Museum is reputed to be the first timber frame home constructed in Priest River. Today, the house is home to the Priest River Chamber of Commerce as well as an interesting museum dedicated to preserving and celebrating the area's long relationship with the logging industry. Exhibits include pioneer antiques, historical artifacts from the town's early logging days, pictures and videos illustrating life as a logger, and a timber educational center. The museum also displays a Diamond Match Company boat once used to haul workers on log drives down the Priest and Pond Oreille Rivers. Exhibits change quarterly, and the museum is open 8 AM to 4 PM Monday through Friday during the summer with varying weekend hours.

T Priest River Experimental Forest

Contact the Priest River Experimental Forest Supervisor at 448-1793.

In 1911, the Priest River Forest became one of America's first experimental forests dedicated as a forestry research center. Originally serving as the headquarters for the experimental forest, the forest was incorporated into the Northern Rocky Mountain Forest in 1930. Today, Idaho's Rocky Mountain Research Station administers the forest.

During its nearly 100 years of operation, the forest has been the site for groundbreaking studies. Famous researchers have continually visited the area, and the forestry principles developed here are still used today in forests across the Pacific Northwest and in the Rocky Mountains.

Visitors can arrange a personal visit to the forest, and depending on the season, the lookout tower may be open offering panoramic views of the surrounding area. The site also features huckleberry and mushroom picking and plenty of wildlife. Past species spotted have included mule and whitetail deer, elk, moose, cougars, coyotes, and various types of birds.

Advance visiting arrangements are necessary.

T Priest River Historic District Walking Tour

Contact the Priest River Chamber of Commerce at 448-2721.

From the late 1800s to 1924, Priest River experienced a building boom and the downtown area was soon home to a variety of new stores. Although many of the original buildings have long since passed with the closing of historic businesses, a few remain that offer visitors a glimpse into Priest River's glory days.

Chamber of Commerce/Priest River Museum
301 Montgomery Street
Once the impressive Keyser home, this building was constructed in 1895. It was built entirely with square nails and represents the town's first balloon stick structure.

Presta Building
117-225 Main Street
The Presta Building was completed in 1914 and was home to the Rex Theater, a billiard parlor, a restaurant, and a stageline. Today, the building houses Mercer's Memories.

Kaniksu Mercantile
207-209 Main Street
This building was constructed in 1913 and served as one of the community's first grocery stores.

City Market
205 Main Street
Listed for its architectural style, the City Market Building is now home to a used furniture dealership.

309 High Street
One of the last projects completed during the historic downtown development phase, this building was completed in 1920 and was home to the community's first real estate office.

Hotel Charbonneau
207 Wisconsin Street
During the 1900s, several hotels were established in downtown Priest River. None, however, achieved the prestigious status that graced the Hotel Charbonneau. Built in 1912, the hotel was considered the community's most elite, and it was a popular destination for business travelers and the wealthy. The hotel operated continuously until 1989 when it was abandoned. The structure was

added to the National Register of Historic Places in 1991, and efforts have been made to restore the historic treasure.

Henley's Union 76 Gas Station & Service Garage
Corner of Wisconsin & High Street
This building has been continuously occupied since its 1923 construction date.

Paul Mears Store
120 Wisconsin Street
One of Priest River's earliest and most recognized businessmen, Paul Mears opened a general mercantile store in this building in 1914. Although now non-existent, Mears' store was a major supply point for residents and travelers in its glory days.

The Beardmore Block
109-119 Main Street & 302-310 High Street
Still recognized as one of Priest River's founding business fathers, Charles Beardmore played an influential role in the town's development. While Charles was one of the town's most successful businessmen, his wife represented the area in Idaho's State Legislature. With his business successes, Beardmore established the impressive Beardmore Block. The district was home to a grand ballroom, hardware store, butcher shop, mercantile, theater, Diamond Match Company offices, and Beardmore's own lumber and sawmill company. The block retains its historic imposing character.

Young Residence
101 Main Street
This building served as a social center for the growing Priest River community in the early 1900s. It was constructed between 1902-1906.

River Pigs Inn
114 Main Street
Charles Naccarato and his sons constructed this brick facility in the early 1920s. The building was home to a store and pool hall and later became Priest River's most notorious house of ill-repute. In 1989, the building was remodeled with two new additions added to the original structure.

Citizen's State Bank
218 High Street
Citizen's State Bank was one of Priest River's first financial institutions. Despite a plague of robbers in its early days, the bank retains its original safe. Interestingly, the bank operated without restroom facilities until 1997 when it was remodeled to include more modern facilities.

Interstate Telephone Company
212 High Street
Interstate Telephone Company was responsible for providing Priest River with its first communication services. Today, the building is home to various business offices.

Runck's Garage
208 High Street
This car garage was constructed in 1920 and was originally the town's Dodge dealership. For more than seventy-five consecutive years, this building has been servicing Priest River's car maintenance needs.

C & C Café
215 High Street
C & C Café has been a staple of Priest River dining since the early 1930s. In the 1980s, the original business bought out a historic, neighboring 1910 building and expanded the café to better serve customer's needs. The 1910 structure was originally a local butcher shop's smokehouse, and the café's current dining room was once the town's popular gambling hall.

MOUNTAIN BIKING IN NORTHERN IDAHO

Mountain biking trails abound in the cities and forested areas comprising Idaho's Panhandle region. While locals and visitors are encouraged to take advantage of this recreational opportunity to view amazing scenery, all riders are asked to follow a common set of etiquette guidelines. By following these suggestions and packing the right equipment, bikers can be assured of a safe and memorable trip.

Trail Etiquette
- Be courteous to all users; if the path you're on allows joggers and skaters, watch out for these users and yield to pedestrians
- Slower traffic always has the right of way; follow this guideline to avoid accidents
- Do not block the path; if you must stop, pull off to the trail's edge so that other users can pass by
- Do not attempt more than two riders abreast
- Be aware of trail conditions and keep a safe speed
- Signal at all times when approaching from the rear
- Keep right on the trail except to pass
- If you bring pets along on your ride, control them so they don't become a distraction and/or hazard to other riders; also, be courteous and pack out your animal's excrement
- Follow the standard guideline of packing out what you pack in; this will ensure that future generations of recreational lovers will be able to enjoy the trail

Useful Equipment
When mountain biking or enjoying any of northern Idaho's scenic trails, always be prepared for whatever situation may arise.

- Make sure to pack in and drink plenty of water
- Bring a daypack to hold all your trip's necessities
- Snack on high-energy food and pack extra in your daypack
- Always be prepared with a portable first-aid kit that includes gauze, bandages, and antiseptic wipes
- Know where you're going at all times with a trail map or brochure and make sure someone else knows your route in case of an emergency; trail maps are generally available at U.S. Forest Service Ranger Stations
- Protect your eyes and skin with sunglasses and sunscreen.
- Northern Idaho scenery is breathtaking, so be sure to pack along a camera and film

General Safety Tips
- Mountain bikers should always wear helmets to protect their heads in case of an accident
- If you must ride at night, always use a light
- Some trails do have road crossings; obey all road crossing signs for the safety of yourself and others
- When riding in forested areas, be aware of the area's wildlife habitats and know what to do should you encounter wildlife

T Kaniksu National Forest
10 miles north of Priest River on State Hwy. 57

In 1897, President Cleveland established the 650,000-acre Priest River Forest Reserve. From this reserve, the Kaniksu National Forest was created in 1908. The forest, part of which is included in the Idaho Panhandle National Forest, encompasses areas in Idaho, Washington, and Montana while neighboring Canada for fifty miles. In addition, the forest is home to the world's largest known larch tree. The tree is visible on Highway 57's west side after traveling approximately ten miles north of Priest River.

TV Mudhole Recreation Area
At the intersection of Pend Oreille and Priest Rivers in Priest River. Contact the Priest River Chamber of Commerce at 448-2721.

Despite its misleading name, the community's Mudhole Recreation Area is one of many scenic recreation sites situated beside Priest River. The site includes picnicking, camping, swimming, and a boat launch area.

V Priest River
Priest River. Contact the Priest River Chamber of Commerce at 448-2721.

Flowing just north of town, the Priest River provides this small community with its namesake as well as year-round recreational adventures. Visitors can enjoy whitewater rafting, tubing, canoeing, fishing, and swimming. Rafters should keep in mind that Class III rapids frequently occur on the river during spring, but by late summer, most of the river is less than three feet deep. Don't be surprised when the local wildlife appears as spectators!

V Riley Creek Recreation Area
2376 E. Hwy. 2, Oldtown. 437-3133. From Laclede, travel west on U.S. Hwy. 2. At Riley Creek Rd., turn south, and travel 1 mile to the recreation area.

Riley Creek Recreation Area is one of the most popular recreational sites in northern Idaho. Established under the Albeni Falls Project, the area was built by the Corps of Engineers on the banks of the Pend Oreille River. Individuals of all ages can enjoy the boat ramp, boat basin, playground, bicycle and hiking trails, picnic shelters, horseshoe pits, and the swimming beach. In addition, the area features a special trail where animal owners can walk their pets. The recreation area is open from 7 AM to 10 PM May to October.

V Pend Oreille River
South of Priest River community. Contact the Priest River Chamber of Commerce at 448-2721.

The Pend Oreille River drains over 24,000 square miles of land in northern Idaho and western Montana with several major tributaries. In Idaho, the Priest and Pack Rivers, Priest and Upper Priest Lakes, and Pend Oreille Lake are linked to the Pend Oreille River, while Montana's Clark Fork, Flathead, Bitterroot, Blackfoot, and St. Regis Rivers are tributaries. Flowing across thousands of acres of land, the river offers numerous recreational possibilities. A thirty-eight mile stretch of boatable water can be found between Albeni Falls Dam and Sandpoint, and swimming, waterskiing, camping, picnicking, and duck hunting are all favorite pastimes.

Anglers on the Pend Oreille River and its tributaries are rewarded with a variety of possible fresh catches. The waters are home to westslope cutthroat trout, brook trout, brown trout, bull trout, eastern brook trout, lake trout, pygymy whitefish, mountain whitefish, largemouth and smallmouth bass, northern pike, tiger muskie, yellow perch, black crappie, pumpkinseed, bluegill, bullhead, and channel catfish.

M John L. Scott Real Estate
910 Albeni Hwy., Priest River. 448-1003 or (877) 524-7253. www.johnlscott.com

John L. Scott Real Estate has served as the Northwest's industry leader for over seventy years. Under the management of Broker/Owner, Mary Ann Jones, the Priest River office provides professional agents dedicated to customer service. Offices are conveniently located in Priest River and Priest Lake, Idaho with the corporate office in Newport, Washington. The office is a member of the Spokane, Coeur d'Alene, and Bonner County Multiple Listing Services, ensuring access to the largest selection of properties. Technologically advanced agents are experienced in virtual tours, and several agents are licensed in both Washington and Idaho. Whether you're buying or selling, John L. Scott has the tools and professionals to ensure a smooth transaction. Find out for yourself today why this office continually garners rave customer reviews!

M Priest River Chamber of Commerce
301 Montgomery St., Priest River. 448-2721. www.priestriver.org/chamber; prchamber@povn.com

---

9 *Food, Lodging*

Careywood
Pop. 10

First known as "King's Spur," this tiny village was renamed "Severance" in 1907 when the first post office was established here. The community received its current title shortly thereafter when a man named Carey purchased several acres in the area and proceeded to name the settlement after himself.

Cocolalla
Pop. 25

"Cocolalla" is a Coeur d'Alene tribal word describing water that is "very cold." The name was first attributed to the nearby lake then given to the town upon its establishment in 1903. The small community remains nestled on Cocolalla Lake's southern shore.

Garfield Bay
Pop. 0

Lying near Lake Pend Oreille's shores, Garfield Bay was originally a school district that became a Mormon Church ward in 1908. The site was named after President James A. Garfield and today serves as a remote recreation area.

Sagle
Pop. 100

When the post office arrived here in 1900, the town's first resident, Mr. Powell, applied for the name of Eagle. The moniker was rejected as there was already an Idaho town by that name. Lacking the gumption to completely change the name, Powell simply substitued an "S" for the "E" to form Sagle. The post office agreed with his suggestion, and the town became an essential access point to the Glengary Ferry.

Westmond
Westmond is nestled near Cocolalla Lake in Idaho's upper panhandle. Once relying heavily

---

IDAHO CENTENNIAL TRAIL

Extending over 1,200 miles from the Idaho borders with Nevada and Canada, the Idaho Centennial Trail was officially designated on June 1, 1990 as part of the state's Centennial Celebration. The idea for the route was conceived when two Idaho residents, Roger Williams and Syd Tate, hiked a similar path in 1986. With the help of these two recreationists, the Idaho Centennial Trail became a reality.

Passing through eleven national forests, the trail traverses every ecological zone in Idaho, including clear glacial lakes, old growth cedars, sagebrush desert, rugged peaks, granite spires, wildflower-filled alpine meadows, raging rivers, and six major canyons. More specifically, on its path from the Idaho/Nevada border to the Canadian border, the trail crosses through the Owyhee Uplands, the Sawtooth National Forest and Recreation Area, the Challis, Boise, Payette, Clearwater, and Nez Perce National Forests, the Frank Church-River of No Return Wilderness, and the Idaho Panhandle National Forests. In addition, the trail crosses the historic Oregon Trail near the Snake River as well as the route of Lewis and Clark along the Clearwater-Lochsa divide.

Natural hot springs, caves, and other geological formations provide interesting highlights along the trail's path, and adventurers may encounter wildlife, including bighorn sheep, mountain goats, deer, elk, moose, antelope, bears, mountain lions, pheasants, grouse, and several other upland game birds. Although undoubtedly passing through some of Idaho's most unique and scenic areas, the trail is more than just an outdoor adventure. It also provides a look back at what Idaho was like more than a century ago. Along the way, abandoned homesteads and cabins, ghost towns, old mines, and logging camps are visual reminders of the state's founding fathers and the sacrifices that were made to live out the American Dream in the Rocky Mountain West.

Trail elevations range from 1,900 feet up to 9,200 feet, and the route is open for horseback riding, hiking, cross-country skiing, snowmobiling, mountain biking, and motorized trail riding. All users should first contact the Idaho Department of Parks and Recreation for current weather and route conditions along the trail. Users are also encouraged to bring along maps as portions of the trail are not yet designated with official route signs.

upon the timber industry, the settlement was named after George Westmond and the Westmond Lumber Company that established a sawmill in town.

TV Round Lake State Park and Lake Cocolalla

Sagle. 263-3489. From Cocolalla, drive 4 miles north on U.S. Hwy. 95 before bearing west on Dufort Rd. Continue 2 miles to the park's entrance.

Carved by glaciers millions of years ago, the 142-acre Round Lake State Park offers year-round recreation opportunities. During the summer, fifty-three wooded campsites await visitors near the lake's shores, and the two-mile "Trappers Trail" meanders under a forested canopy of vegetation. Fishing is also a popular pastime in both summer and winter as brook and rainbow trout, bass, perch, bullhead, crappie, and sunfish populate the clean water. During the winter, the lake becomes a natural skating rink, and snowshoers, sledders, and cross-country skiers arrive in droves to enjoy the area's pristine beauty.

The 800-acre Cocolalla Lake is situated between the communities of Westmond and Cocolalla. Besides fine scenery, visitors will also find numerous fishermen searching for trout, catfish, crappie, perch, and bass year-round. Small boats are also welcome on this lake, and a launch ramp is located at the lake's northeastern shore.

TV Mineral Point Recreation Area

Sandpoint Ranger District, Sandpoint. 263-5111. Drive 5 miles south of Sandpoint on U.S. Hwy. 95 bearing east onto Sagle Rd. Proceed 9 miles, staying right at the road's fork, and continue past Garfield Bay. At the next road fork, turn left and drive to the sign for Trail #82. Bear right onto Forest Road (FR) 532, and proceed 4 miles to Mineral Point. At the fork with FR 2672, stay to the left, and at the junction with FR 532, keep right.

Mineral Point has a short interpretive trail that lets visitors discover and investigate the forest around them. The area also features a picnic area overlooking beautiful Lake Pend Oreille and a toilet facility. All the facilities and a portion of the interpretive trail are accessible to disabled individuals. There are no grills, fire rings, or potable water.

The interpretive hike should take one-half hour to an hour, depending on how much time you take at each stop. Although there is a bit of a climb on the return trip, the trail is not too difficult for hikers of all ages. Users are reminded to watch their step in places where there may be loose rock or where the trail is damp.

Reprinted from U.S. Forest Service brochure

V Green Bay

Near Sandpoint. Contact the Sandpoint Chamber of Commerce at 263-0887. From Sandpoint, merge off U.S. Hwy. 95 and head east on Sagle Rd. At Garfield Bay Rd., bear right and continue to Garfield Bay Cut-off Rd.. Here, drive to the bay on Forest Rd. (FR) 532.

A secluded alcove, Green Bay is located on the shores of Lake Pend Oreille and offers outstanding views of the surrounding countryside. The bay features a cobblestone beach and is a popular summer access point for swimmers. In addition, the bay is renowned for its small cliffs, and adventurous cliff divers can often be found in the area on hot July and August afternoons. The bay is located approximately thirty minutes from downtown Sandpoint.

Cabinet
Pop. 10

The tiny village of Cabinet is located on the Idaho-Montana border and dates back as early as 1868. The community is most renowned for the narrow, z-shaped Cabinet Gorge and nearby dam.

Clark Fork
Pop. 448

The Clark Fork River is named in honor of William Clark of the 1805 Corp of Discovery Expedition. The town, which is situated near the Idaho/Montana border, was then christened after the river. Trappers appear to have used the townsite as early as 1809, and lead and silver mines were active in the region from 1913 to 1943. Twenty-four million pounds of lead and one million ounces of silver resulted in profits over $2.5 million during that time.

Hope
Pop. 79

When the Northern Pacific Railroad announced plans to build a line through the region in 1882, work began on the establishment of Hope. The small town draws its name from veterinarian, Dr. Hope, who treated the railroad's hardworking horses.

Although a post office began operating in the town in 1887, it wasn't until 1896 that the town was platted, and it waited until 1903 before being officially incorporated. The town has boasted a relatively stable population of just a handful of residents and is best known for David Thompson's Kullyspell House. Thompson founded the site on Hope Peninsula as Idaho's first trading post in 1809, and a memorial outside town commemorates his numerous accomplishments.

East Hope
Pop. 200

This community is situated on the Pend Oreille Scenic Byway on Lake Pend Oreille's shores. Starting out as an extension of the neighboring town, Hope, East Hope is now a community of its own with lush scenery found around every corner.

H Kullyspell House
Milepost 48.2 on State Hwy. 200 Idaho's fur trade began in the fall of 1809 when David Thompson built a trading post two-and-a-half miles southwest of here.

Kullyspell House (Thompson spelled "Kalispell" that way) was the earliest fur trade post in the American Pacific Northwest. A geographer and surveyor of rare skill, Thompson explored and mapped vast fur regions for the North West Company of Montreal. Reaching south from present day British Columbia, he added what is now North Idaho to the Canadian fur empire. It was David Thompson who discovered the route this highway now follows.

T Cabinet Gorge Dam
15 miles from the Idaho/Montana border on the Pend Oreille Scenic Byway (State Hwy. 200)

Constructed by the Morrison Knudsen Corporation and sponsored by the Defense Program, the Cabinet Gorge Dam is an engineering wonder. Although the Defense Program estimated at least two to three years building time, construction on the dam began in 1951 and ended just one year later in April 1952.

At a cost of $47 million, the dam features a true arch structure measuring 208 feet high and 600 feet long. Behind the dam's uniform 40-foot thick walls rests the 24 mile long Clark Fork Reservoir. More than 500,000 cubic yards of rock were removed during the construction process, and the dam's strength lies in the force that the arched dam places on the canyon walls. From the dam, visitors have outstanding views of the gorge's sheer walls that floods carved out more than 20,000 years ago.

T David Thompson Game Preserve
On the Hope Peninsula off State Hwy. 200

Named after early explorer and mapmaker extraordinaire, this game preserve honors the memory and contributions of David Thompson. Visitors can peek at herds of whitetail deer grazing the countryside, gaggles of Canadian geese flying overhead, and captivating bald eagles soaring along Idaho's skyline. Wildlife photo opportunities abound at this site for the animal lover.

SPOKANE FLOOD:
THE GREATEST DOCUMENTED FLOOD IN THE HISTORY OF MAN

The now quiet landscape of Idaho's Clark Fork community and State Hwy. 200 was once the site of massive flood destruction not since experienced by man. Approximately 100,000 years ago, glaciers from British Columbia heaved southward, creating massive valleys in their wake throughout Montana, Idaho, and Washington. As the Purcell ice lobe moved southwest towards present day Spokane, the Clark Fork River flow was altered. A wall of ice rising nearly 2,000 feet high dammed the mouth of the Clark Fork River, forming the glacial Lake Missoula.

As glacier melts continued to pour into Lake Missoula, the lake expanded to over 3,000 square miles with depths extending nearly 1,000 feet. Eventually, the lake had no option but to overflow its banks. As the ice dam crumbled approximately 18,000 to 20,000 years ago, a wall of water raced across Pend Oreille and Coeur d'Alene Lakes, washed over Idaho's Rathdrum Prairie, and surged towards the Spokane River valley. Geologists estimate that the flood flowed at 386 million cubic feet per second, more than ten times the combined flow for all the world's rivers.

In its path of destruction, the world's largest documented flood eroded lava flows, sculpted eastern Washington's channeled landscape, and deposited boulders and gravels in great dunes and long ridges. Despite the flood's magnificent force, geologists speculate that the flood lasted just two days with normal river flows and lake levels restored within a month. The flood occured 8 miles east of Hope.

Section 1

PANHANDLE AREA • INCLUDING COEUR D'ALENE, POST FALLS, SANDPOINT, AND WALLACE

WATERFALLS

Moyie Falls

Take U.S. Hwy. 2, exiting just west of the Moyie River Bridge at Moyie Springs; proceed for 0.5 mile until turning left on a residential road flanking a lumberyard; continue on this street for 0.5 mile where you will find numerous parking pull-outs providing picture-perfect views of the falls.

With awe-inspiring scenery and easy vehicle accessibility, Moyie Falls is undoubtedly one of Idaho's great natural attractions. Crashing through a rocky canyon, the Moyie River descends in tiered form. While the upper portion plummets 60 to 100 feet under an obsolete bridge connecting the gorge, the lower portion tumbles 20 to 40 feet.

Smith Falls

For easy access, take U.S. Hwy. 95 north of Bonners Ferry for 15 miles; next, turn north onto Scenic Rd. 1 and proceed 1 mile before turning west (left) onto an unmarked, paved road; continue for 5 miles, crossing the Kootenai River during your drive; at W. Side Rd. #417, bear north (right) to locate a marked viewing area of the falls in approximately 8 miles.

Plunging 60 feet along Smith Creek, Smith Falls offers visitors of all ages vehicle accessible views. Sightseers, however, are advised to follow all posted regulations as the falls and viewing area are located on private property.

Falls Creek Falls

Exit Scenic Route 3 approximately 0.5 mile northeast of St. Maries; turn east onto St. Joe River Rd. and proceed 10.5 miles; note Shadowy St. Joe Camp and continue forward 4.5 miles until reaching a parking area near Falls Creek Bridge where the falls can be seen.

Descending as a wide stream from the broad St. Joe River, Falls Creek Falls drops 20 to 30 feet on private property. Enclosed by St. Maries Ranger District in the St. Joe National Forest, Falls Creek Falls is situated at 1,980 feet and is easily accessible.

Torrelle Falls

At Priest River, ID, depart U.S. Hwy. 2 onto Scenic Route 57; continue 8.5 miles north to locate the falls on the west side of the road.

Descending from a narrow stream into a pool below, Torrelle Falls is easily accessible by vehicle. At the bottom of the cataract's 10 to 15 foot descent, visitors will find a unique restaurant extending across the W. Branch Priest River.

Mission Falls

Take Scenic Route 57 19 miles north of Priest River, ID.

After visiting Torrelle Falls, continue north to locate Mission Falls descending 5 to 10 feet along the Upper West Branch Priest River in the Idaho Panhandle National Forest, Priest Lake Ranger District. For close-up access, park across the river on the northeast side of the bridge and using a jeep trail, walk for 0.2 mile to a road junction. After taking a right fork at this junction, continue down the path for 1.5 miles more, turning right at all following junctions. As you approach the river, follow the well-used trail a few hundred yards to the falls.

Snow Creek Falls

Take U.S. Hwy. 2/95 south of Bonners Ferry for 2.5 miles; at the golf course, bear right onto Moravia Rd. for 3 miles; next, turn right on W. Side Rd. #417 and continue for approximately 2 miles; at the junction of Rd. #417 and Snow Creek Rd. #402, turn left (west) and proceed 1.5 miles where a restricted view of the 75 to 125 foot falls is offered.

Found in Bonners Ferry Ranger District of the Idaho Panhandle National Forest, Snow Creek Falls is easy to access but offers visitors limited viewing potential.

Rapid Lightning Falls

Turn east onto Scenic Route 200 from U.S. Hwy. 2/95 and proceed 6 miles; after turning north (left) on Colburn-Culver Rd., drive 2.9 miles and bear right at the schoolhouse onto Rapid Lightning Creek Rd. #629; continue 3.4 miles, stopping at an unmarked turnout.

Descending beside Rapid Lightning Creek for 20 to 30 feet, Rapid Lightning Falls are easily accessible. From the turnout point, follow one of the short, well-worn trails to the falls. (Advisory: Rapid Lightning Falls may be located on private property).

Lower Snow Creek Falls

Take U.S. Hwy. 2/95 south past Bonner's Ferry for 2.5 miles; bearing right at the golf course onto Moravia Rd., continue for 3 miles; at W. Side Rd. #417, turn right, and proceed 2 miles to a parking turnout.

Located in the largely undeveloped Bonner's Ferry Ranger District of the Idaho Panhandle National Forest, these falls descend 50 to 75 feet in multiple threads as Snow Creek divides. From the turnout, locate the north side of Snow Creek and follow the short, nameless trail to the falls. Avoid taking the named trail on Snow Creek's south side as this follows a ridge and affords no access to the waterfall.

Granite Falls and LaSota Falls

Requiring a fairly easy hike, access Granite Falls by first taking Scenic Route (SR) 57 north for 37 miles from Priest River to Nordman; continue along SR 57 for 13 more miles (2 miles past Nordman, SR 57 converts to Granite Creek Rd. #30) until you reach the entrance for Stagger Inn Camp and Granite Falls; turning at this entrance, locate the falls' trailhead at the camp's southern end.

Actually situated just inside Washington's border, Granite Falls descends vertically within 50 to 75 feet of the Priest Lake Ranger District of the Idaho Panhandle National Forest. However, easiest entry to these falls is through the northwest tip of Idaho. After reaching the trailhead, note that the sign is misguiding. Instead of following the arrow suggesting that visitors cross a log over the stream, disregard the direction and hike directly past the sign. Walk approximately one hundred yards to reach the cascade. Continue walking upstream to locate LaSota Falls.

Grouse Creek Falls

Exit east at Colburn off U.S. 2/95 and merge onto Colburn-Culver Rd.; proceed 4.5 miles east, making a left turn onto the unpaved Rd. #280; winding along Grouse Creek Valley, drive 6 miles to a parking turnout on your right near a dirt road.

Cascading 15 to 20 feet over bedrock in a series of steps, Grouse Creek Falls is found in the Idaho Panhandle National Forest's Sandpoint Ranger District. After parking at the turnout, visitors will need to take a fairly easy hike. Follow the dirt road for 0.3 mile until it becomes a trail, and then continue onward to reach the falls in another 0.2 mile.

Wellington Creek Falls

To reach the falls, turn east off U.S 2/95 onto Scenic Route 200 and drive 12.2 miles to Trestle Creek Rd. #275 where you will turn east (left) and continue for 13 miles to Lightning Creek Rd. #419; turn south (right) and proceed along Lightning Creek Rd. past Char Falls for 4.2 miles until you arrive at Augor Rd. #489; bearing west (right), go across Lightning Creek to a bumpy road on your left; further vehicle access does require 4-wheel drive, but visitors can choose to hike the road.

Wellington Creek Falls promises visitors a sight worth seeing as these falls tumble 50 to 75 feet amidst abundant foliage. Located in the Sandpoint Ranger District of the Idaho Panhandle's National Forest, the falls require a moderate hike as well as caution when nearing the fall's unfenced ledge. After parking your vehicle, walk 0.4 mile and turn right at the fork. Proceed along the road's last 0.4 mile. Listening for the falls, hike upstream toward Wellington Creek where overviews of the falls can be found.

Copper Falls

Rd. #2517 affords visitors with the most direct route to the falls; sightseers can choose to turn off U.S. Hwy. 95 onto Rd. #2517 14 miles northeast of the Scenic Rd. 1 junction or 0.7 mile south of the Eastport border crossing; travel 2 miles on this rough gravel road until you reach Copper Falls Trail #20.

At an elevation of 3,400 feet in the Idaho Panhandle National Forest's Bonners Ferry Ranger District, Copper Creek plunges 160 feet from a cliff to form Copper Falls. Visitors should be prepared for a short, moderately steep 0.3-mile hike to the falls.

Willow Creek Falls

To locate, take Exit 68 off I-90 at Mullan and proceed east through town; this route heads right and becomes Willow Creek Rd. in 1.5 miles; drive 1.5 miles more until the road ends at an unused set of railroad tracks near Willow Creek Trail #8008 following this trail, hike 2 miles to the falls' viewing area.

Accessible from late summer to early autumn, Willow Creek Falls are located near the Bitterroot Divide separating Idaho and Montana. Parking at the road's end, visitors should take Trail #8088 and make a modest, 2-mile hike to reach the E. Fork Willow Creek's 10 to 20 foot cascade.

Stevens Lake Falls

Taking Exit 68 off I-90, drive through Mullan and proceed east; in 1.5 miles, this street turns right and converts into Willow Creek Rd.; passing under I-90, follow this road to its end at a set of old railroad tracks (approximately another 1.5 miles).

Stevens Lake Falls are situated near the Bitterroot Divide in the Wallace Ranger District of St. Joe National Forest. Accessible late summer until early fall, this tiered waterfall requires visitors to engage in a fairly difficult day hike. For those enjoying a challenge, close-up views of the falls' 30 to 50 foot descents in both upper and lower tiers awaits. After parking at the road's end, hike 2 miles on Willow Creek Trail #8008 past Willow Creek Falls. The trail becomes much steeper, but continue 0.2 mile to reach the lower tier or 0.4 mile for a view of the upper falls.

Myrtle Creek Falls

Drive west on Riverside Rd. from U.S. Hwy. 2/95 in Bonners Ferry; this road parallels the south shore of the Kootenai River, and once it leaves Bonners Ferry it turns into County Rd. #18; proceed approximately 5 miles, driving past the Kootenai National Wildlife Refuge; the road will soon make a sharp left bend, and in 2 miles the Wildlife Refuge office will become visible; locate the Myrtle Creek Falls trailhead across from the Refuge office on Auto Trail Rd..

Visitors are urged to bring bug repellent while viewing this waterfall in the Idaho Panhandle National Forest. From the trailhead, hike the very steep trail 0.2 mile until reaching a viewing area of the large cascade halfway up the falls.

Jeru Creek Falls

Turning northwest at Samuels off U.S. Hwy. 2/95, merge onto Pack River Rd., and proceed 9 miles to Jeru Creek's north side where an unmarked parking area is located.

At an elevation of 3,060 feet, Jeru Creek rushes down 100 to 150 feet on land that is likely private property. Although offering a spectacular scene, this destination requires a moderate hike on an undeveloped trail. All visitors are urged to wear sturdy hiking boots, and the site is not recommended for young children or those with any physical limitations. Leaving the parking area, hike for 1 mile along a rarely used four-wheel drive road that soon becomes a primitive trail. When it seems that the trail has ended, keep walking as the descent to the falls will shortly appear.

Char Falls

To access, turn east off U.S. Hwy. 2/95 onto Scenic Route 200 and proceed for 12.2 miles to Trestle Creek Rd. #275; turn east (left) and continue for 13 miles until you reach Lightning Creek Rd. #419; here, turn south (right), driving 0.6 mile to an unpaved road on the left where parking is available.

Situated within the Idaho Panhandle National Forest's Sandpoint Ranger District, Char Falls is the result of Lightning Creek crushing 50 to 75 foot descent down a bedrock surface. Requiring a fairly difficult hike, Char Falls provides visitors with outstanding scenery as the falls are bordered with coniferous trees. After parking, hike 0.5 mile along a rock-strewn road until it ends at a broad trail. Proceeding on this trail for 20 yards, notice a faint path appear on the right, and take this path for approximately 100 yards to the fall's precipice. Be careful in this area as the overlook is unfenced.

Upper Priest Falls

Take Scenic Route (SR) 57 for 37 miles from Priest River, ID to Nordman, ID; passing through Nordman, continue on SR 57 (which turns into Granite Creek Rd. #30 2 miles past Nordman) for 13 more miles and take the entrance road to Stagger Inn Camp; here, proceed north on Rd. #302 for 1.7 miles and then turn right on Rd. #1013, which later becomes Rd. #637; drive approximately 11.5 miles and park at the Upper Priest River Trailhead #308.

Located within the solitude of Idaho's northwestern tip, the Upper Priest River tumbles 100 to 125 feet to form Upper Priest Falls. Also known as American Falls to differentiate it from Canadian Falls located upstream, these falls are easiest to visit during early summer through late fall. From Trailhead #308, visitors should be prepared to take a difficult day hike along a 9-mile trail that winds along Upper Priest River and ends at the falls. Alternatively, if your four-wheel drive vehicle has high clearance, continue driving for another 11 miles along Rd. #637 until you reach Continental Trail #28. Hike north on Trail #28 for 0.7 mile, turning right on Trail #308 for the final 1.5 miles to the falls.

The following Idaho waterfalls are also located in this section with limited directions/access available:

Rambiker Falls, Fern Falls, and Shadow Falls

All three of these relatively unknown waterfalls lie within Idaho's Shoshone County in the Idaho Panhandle National Forest. Little information exists in reference to Rambiker Falls, but it appears on topographic maps that a road passes by the falls while hiking towards St. Joe Lake near the Bitterroot Divide. Directions to Fern Falls and Shadow Falls are vague, but it is known that both are located in Shoshone County north of Kellogg near Prichard. To reach Fern Falls, situated at an elevation of 3,280 feet, as well as the 25-foot cascade of Shadow Falls, follow Yellow Dog Trail paralleling Yellow Dog Creek. Hiking for approximately 100 to 300 yards, visitors can readily reach the falls for best viewing in spring and early summer.

Cooper Gulch Falls

While Cooper Gulch Falls is actually situated within Montana, northeastern Idaho provides easiest admittance to the falls. It appears that crossing Thompson Pass on the Bitterroot Divide east of Murray and Prichard, ID may provide visitors with some access.

McAbee Falls

McAbee Falls, contained within Bonner County near the Priest Lake Ranger District, offers visitors minimal access as few directions to the falls exist. Viewing of topographic maps, however, suggests that a bridge crosses Priest River near the falls.

Johnson Creek Falls

Situated within the Sandpoint Ranger District of the Idaho Panhandle National Forest, Johnson Creek Falls is near Lake Pend Oreille at Clark Fork, ID on U.S. Hwy. 200. An unmarked road passing near the falls in Bonner County is shown on topographic maps.

Hellroaring Creek Falls

Located in the Idaho Panhandle National Forest's Sandpoint Ranger District, Hellroaring Creek Falls are found off U.S. Hwy. 2/95 near Colburn, ID, but are remote and inaccessible to visitors.

Chute Creek Falls, Kalispell Falls, and LaSota Falls

Found near the Idaho Panhandle National Forest's Priest Lake Ranger District, these remote falls are actually contained within Washington's borders. However, no roads or trails are found leading to either Chute Creek Falls or Kalispell Falls.

Caribou Falls

Caribou Falls may be the most remote waterfall within the Idaho Panhandle National Forest. Situated in Boundary County, topographic maps illustrate no roads or trails leading to the falls.

T David Thompson's Kullyspell House & Memorial
Outside of Hope on the community frontage road

Relatively unmentioned in the annals of history, David Thompson was undoubtedly one of the finest geographers in American and Canadian history. Although his life started and ended in poverty, the discoveries and exploratory trips he made during his mid-life shaped the western world and further opened up the American West to settlement.

Thompson was born in England to impoverished Welsh parents. Unable to provide for themselves, let alone a growing boy, Thompson's parents bound him to the Hudson Bay Company when he was just fourteen years old. His first assignment during his seven-year apprenticeship arrived in 1784 when he was sent to the Churchill Factory on Hudson Bay. A quick study, Thompson proved himself as an intelligent and resourceful wilderness man capable of trapping, trading, and surveying. His skills brought him several Canadian exploration assignments, all of which he successfully completed. When his apprenticeship concluded, Thompson had gained the valuable skills he needed to join with Montreal's North West Company.

Confident in Thompson's skills, the North West Company sent Thomson on numerous important mapping assignments. During his explorations and fur trapping, Thompson nearly identified the Mississippi River's source, surveyed the shores of Lake Superior and the foothills of the Rockies, and headed west to the Continental Divide in 1806. In 1808, Thompson arrived in Idaho along with his wife and children for the first time and began opening trade with the Flathead, Nez Perce, and Blackfeet Indians. He would travel east one more time before returning to Idaho's northern panhandle in September 1809. Upon his second arrival, Thompson and his crew built the first permanent white structure in Idaho near the present town of Hope. Naming the log house "Kullyspell House" after the region's Kalispel Indians, Thompson quickly succeeded in opening a trade center with the region's tribes. During his few years at Kullyspell House, Thompson sent numerous beaver pelts to London where beaver hats were the height of fashion. He also used the trading post as a base for further exploration and mapping of the panhandle and Pacific Northwest.

In 1812, Thompson and his family settled in Montreal where he continued surveying for ten years. As Thompson aged, however, he became ill and was forced to pawn all his scientific instruments. The only mementos he kept of his exploration days were his journals and maps. An 1880s geologist working for the Canadian Geological Survey later discovered these important documents. Finally, in 1916, Thompson's detailed, accurate maps and journal were published, and the world had their first glimpse of one of the west's most important explorers.

Through his explorations and the establishment of Kullyspell House in what would eventually become Idaho, Thompson set the stage for friendly relationships with the area Indians and for further white exploration of Idaho's panhandle. Although the Kullyspell House has long since crumbled, historians estimate that the post was situated near Hope Peninsula now on private land. To honor Thompson's contributions, a granite memorial was dedicated in 1928 on a frontage road outside Hope.

T Hope Peninsula
Outside Clark Fork 8 miles east of Hope on State Hwy. 200

Also commonly referred to as Memaloose Point, Hope Peninsula stretches into Lake Pend Oreille outside Clark Fork. The peninsula is known for its abundant population of Canadian geese and grazing whitetail deer. The promontory also supports several Indian petroglyphs of unknown origin and meaning. On the end of the peninsula, visitors will locate an area eighteen feet in length covered with twenty-eight sketches. The pictures appear to represent bear's claws, arrowheads, a mountain goat, and numerous sets of circles. Just offshore, Memaloose Island and Cottage Island sport similar petroglyphs.

T Cabinet Gorge
State Hwy. 200 between Hope and the Idaho/Montana state border

Running beside State Highway 200 near the Idaho/Montana state border, Cabinet Gorge was formed during ancient times as the Clark Fork River eroded the area's sedimentary rocks. French trappers christened the area after noticing large recesses in the rock walls lining the river.

M Clark Fork Chamber of Commerce
PO Box 159, Clark Fork. 266-1551.

11 *Food, Lodging*

Bayview
Pop. 200

Bayview was founded in 1894 with the advent of northern Idaho's timber industry. As time passed, the community's economic dependence upon lumber shifted to the area's large limestone deposits. The stone, which is the remains of ancient fossilized invertebrates, was quarried, and in 1911, an extension of the Spokane International Railroad arrived in Bayview. This development futher enhanced the economic vitality of the industrial community as the limestone was directly hauled to Spokane markets. Over time, the limestone quality deteriorated, and the quarries were forced to abandon their pursuits in the early 1930s. In 1936, the railroad that had promised a future for Bayview responded by shutting down the line.

Today, this community nestled along Lake Pend Oreille's shores is a summer resort and quiet fishing getaway. For those still living in Bayview year-round, a mail boat transports packages on a daily water route. The town is also recognized as home to the Naval Surface Warfare Center, a site where the Navy researches and tests submarine technology.

Lakeview
Pop. 25

On the south shore of Lake Pend Oreille lies Lakeview, named for its beautiful view. It was first settled in 1888 and was known as "Chloride" due to the prominent local mining industry. Limestone deposits formed from the remains of fossil invertebrates are still visible near Lakeview, with some deposits as thick as 200 feet. In the early 1900s, carbonate was also quarried from area adits and shipped to Hope, Idaho for use by the Washington Brick and Lime Company. Eventually the standards for the lime were raised, the Lakeview quality diminished, and the quarries were forced to close in the 1930s. The post office operated from 1892 to 1965. Today, Lakeview is a resort town boasting all the recreation and beauty of the lake.

H Pend Oreille City
Milepost 8.4 on State Hwy. 54

A gold rush to Montana brought steamboat service to Lake Pend Oreille City, two miles south of here on Buttonhook Bay.

Traffic to British Columbia's Wild Horse mines also was attracted to this route, which provided a comfortable lake excursion for miners and freighters tired of packing over a long, rough trail. At its height, Pend Oreille City had two grocery stores, a billiard saloon, a hotel, and a stable.

H Bayview Limekilns
Milepost 14.7 on State Hwy. 54

Large kilns that produced lime from 1904 to 1932 still can be visited in Bayview, about two miles from here.

Production of lime for nearby mines and Spokane buildings commenced in this area as soon as rail transportation and markets became available. For 14 years after 1887, steamboats hauled lime to a Northern Pacific Railway dock at Hope. When an interurban rail connection reached here in 1911, lime for cement products was exported from Bayview until an economic depression destroyed regional demand for concrete.

M Bayview Chamber of Commerce
PO Box 121, Bayview. 683-2963.
www.bayviewidaho.org; bviewchmbr@hotmail.com

12 *Food, Lodging*

Athol
Pop. 676

Established during the late 1800s and supposedly named after a Native American chief who once inhabited the area, Athol was incorporated in 1895 with the arrival of the first post office. By 1903, the settlement had grown to include a large steam-powered sawmill; however, when the structure was decimated in a 1912 fire, the town nearly disappeared. Upon the construction of the Farragut Naval Training Center in 1942, the town revitalized itself and thrived as the host to over 55,000 military personnel. No longer a ghost town, Athol actually became the state's largest "city." The training center, however, closed after World War II and was recreated into Farragut State Park in 1964. Today, the small town attracts park tourists and those visiting nearby Silverwood Theme Park, the Pacific Northwest's largest amusement park.

H Farragut State Park
Milepost 12.4 on State Hwy. 54

In 1942, a large United States naval training station, with facilities for 40,000 sailors, opened here. From 1946 to 1949, it became Farragut College.

When postwar college enrollments slacked off, Farragut State Park was developed here, with accommodations adequate for an International Boy Scout Jamboree in 1967, as well as for national Boy Scout and Girl Scout camping experiences. Idaho's largest state park offers an attractive lakeshore setting for thousands of visitors each year.

T Rimrock Golf Course
21794 N. Wishful Trail, Athol. 762-5054.. Travel 12 miles north of Coeur d'Alene on U.S. Hwy. 95.

The Rimrock Golf Course's claim to fame is a 225-yard shot on one of the 9 holes. Boasting a driving range and no required tee times, the course's green fee is a mere $13.

T Cocolalla Winery
U.S. Hwy. 95 N., Milepost 463, Athol. 263-3774.

Known as the "House of Fine Champagnes," the Cocolalla Winery is famous for aging its traditional champagnes four years in the old Silver Star Mine. Relying heavily on Pinot Noir and Chardonnay grapes, the winery has an inventory of over 12,000 bottles and produces an average of 800 cases each year. The facility is now under the new ownership of Mike Wagoner and interested individuals should call to schedule a private appointment.

T Pend Oreille City
Near Buttonhook Bay in Farragut State Park

In 1865, Pend Oreille City was one of the earliest settlements in the Idaho panhandle. Established on the northwestern edge of Buttonhook Bay, the community was founded by Zenas Leonard and quickly grew to include a hotel, general store, pool hall, and five houses. The community not only served as an overnight stop for freighters on Pend Oreille Lake, but also served as the lake's first steamboat port. In 1866, Mr. Moody launched his 108-foot long *Mary Moody* steamboat capable of carrying fifty passengers, 10,000 pounds of freight, and eighty-five mules. The business and community flourished until 1876 when Missouri merchants beefed up their fleet of drift boats traveling to Fort Benton. The competition destroyed Mr. Moody's business, and Pend Oreille City was soon just a fading memory.

T Silverwood Theme Park
26225 N. U.S. Hwy. 95, Athol. 683-3400.

Silverwood Theme Park is recognized as the Northwest's largest theme park, showcasing more than sixty rides and attractions. The 700-acre park features plenty of rollercoasters, some topping out at fifty-five miles per hour, as well as waterslides sure to ease the summer heat. The park is open daily from May through October with a general admission fee charged per person.

TV Farragut State Park
13400 E. Ranger Rd., Athol. 683-2425. Located 20 miles north of Coeur d'Alene and 4 miles east of the junction of U.S. Hwy. 95 and State Hwy. 54.

Welcome to Farragut State Park, nestled at the foot of the Coeur d'Alene and Bitterroot Mountain Ranges. This four-season vacationer's paradise awaits you with scenic mountains, pristine forests, abundant wildlife and the crystal clear, azure blue waters of the largest lake in Idaho, Pend Oreille (Pond Oray). Lake Pend Oreille, with its 1,150-foot depths, is spectacular! Whether you come in

---

FARRAGUT NAVAL TRAINING CENTER TRIVIA

Selected in 1942 as one of the largest American naval training centers, Farragut Naval Training Center reportedly owes its location on the Pend Oreille lakeshore to Eleanor Roosevelt. Rumor has it that on a flight from Washington, D.C. to Seattle, Mrs. Roosevelt noticed the beautiful lake below. Knowing her husband, President Franklin D. Roosevelt, was searching for a secure site for a new naval training center, Mrs. Roosevelt mentioned the area upon her return to D.C. President Roosevelt then made a secret trip to Idaho to inspect the site, and the rest is history.

search of world record fishing, national class sailing, wide-open water skiing, or a suntan while floating on your inner tube, Pend Oreille offers something for everyone.

An intriguing biological community exists in this scenic forested setting of lodgepole pine, ponderosa pine, white pine, Douglas fir, western red cedar, and western larch and tamarack. These forests are homes for the whitetail deer, badger, black bear, coyote, bobcat, and occasional elk, along with the robin, owl, humming bird, kingfisher, bald eagle, a wide variety of water fowl, and Idaho's State bird, the Mountain Bluebird. The park offers excellent feeding for the Columbian Ground Squirrel, which in turn is a good food source for such aerial hunters as the red-tailed hawk. Grab your camera, binoculars, and a picnic lunch, and come explore this beautiful and diverse sanctuary. Spend an hour, a day, or your entire vacation. You'll see why Farragut State Park and N. Idaho is a great getaway!

History
Because of the mountainous northern location, the Farragut area served only as a seasonal shop for the early Indian and pioneer miner migrations. In the late 1800s, Buttonhook Bay became a vital link in the Pony Express route between Walla Walla, Washington and Missoula, Montana. Bayview became a lumber, fishing, mining, and railroad center. By 1941, the U.S. Navy Department had acquired much of the area, transforming it into the second largest naval training center in the world. After a series of ownership changes, the area became Farragut State Park in 1965. In 1965, Farragut was selected for the National Girl Scout Roundup and since that time has been host to the 1967 World Boy Scout Jamborees. Over 130,000 scouts have experienced the beauty and serenity offered by Farragut State Park since its establishment.

Farragut Naval Training Station
With World War II in progress, the first construction started on April 10, 1942 with 22,000 men working on the vast project. The first contingent of Naval personnel, in the capacity of "Ship's Company," arrived to man the new training station on August 9, 1942.

Six training camps opened within six months. They were: Camp Bennion – September 15, 1942; Camp Ward – October 1, 1942; Camp Waldron – November 8, 1942; Camp Hill – December 2, 1942; Camp Scott – December 19, 1942; and Camp Peterson – March 25, 1943.

Each of the self-contained "camps" was designed to house, feed, and train some 5,000 men at a time. Each camp was laid out in the form of an oval with the huge drill field or "grinder" in the center. Along one side was the gigantic drill hall, large enough to accommodate six basketball courts with a swimming pool, 75 foot square, attached to one end. Each camp had its own mess hall, 22 double deck barracks, two medical dispensaries, a recreation and ship's store building, indoor rifle range, regimental headquarters, Chief Petty Officers' quarters, and service buildings.

Basic training was given to 293,381 sailors at Farragut in 15 months. In June 1946, Farragut was formally decommissioned. A portion of the former Service School area of Camp Peterson reopened in October 1946 as the Farragut College and Technical Institute where many servicemen received educational training under the GI Bill of Rights.

About the Park
• Established in 1965
• 4,000 acres – borders Lake Pend Oreille

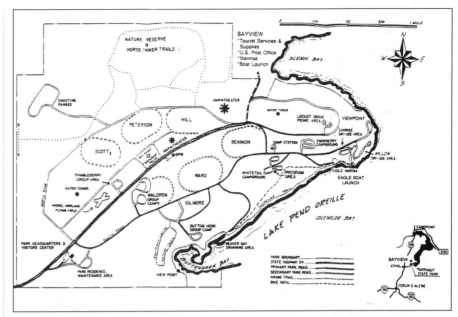

• Elevation 2,054 feet to 2,450 feet
• Open for year-round use
• Motor vehicle entrance fee required
• Campgrounds for tents and trailers; a fee is charged
• Modern restroom facilities with showers
• Visitor Center and Park Museum
• Group camping and activity areas
• Picnic areas
• Swimming area – a lifeguard is on duty
• Model airplane/glider flying field
• Hiking trails
• Bicycle routes
• Photography
• Boat launch and docks
• Fish cleaning facilities
• Fishing
• Horseback riding trails
• Cross-country skiing on groomed trails
• Snowmobiling
• Sledding
• Snowshoeing

Reservation Information
The following park sites are available for reservation:
• Campground spaces – both hookup and non-hookup
• Group camping facilities
• Sunrise day-use area; two shelters are available here
• Shooting ranges
• Locust Grove picnic shelter
• Large group special events

Visitors interested in learning more or making a reservation should contact the Farragut State Park Ranger Office.

Reprinted from Idaho State Parks and Recreation brochure

M Rathdrum Area Chamber of Commerce
8184 W. Main St., Rathdrum. 687-2866.

13 Food

Blanchard
Pop. 120

Situated near Blanchard Lake, this town and its surrounding natural features were named in 1908 after an early pioneer in the area who successfully homesteaded on Blanchard Creek. Originally, however, the town was named White, and its post office was established in 1900. Today, the area serves as a popular resort town on the Idaho/Washington border.

Rathdrum
Pop. 4,816

Cradled in a glacial plain, Rathdrum was settled as a fertile farming area in the 1870s. It was formerly called Westwood after mail carrier, Charles Wesley Wood, but the post office rejected the name in 1881 on grounds that too many other regional towns bore the Westwood title. Thus, the birthplace of an elderly Irish immigrant was selected.

In July of 1881, the Northern Pacific Railroad came through town, and Frederick Post (1871 founder of Post Falls) boosted the area's growing economy when he established a sawmill and flourmill. Today, the town serves as an agricultural and peaceful escape from the growing nearby cities of Post Falls and Coeur d'Alene.

Spirit Lake
Pop. 1,376

Although the Spirit Lake area historically attracted Native Americans with white settlers arriving as early as 1884, the official establishment of this community dates to Frank Blackwell's 1902 arrival in Idaho. He purchased 100,000 acres of timbered land here and proceeded to form a lumber company with a few prominent Pennsylvania associates. After four years, the company was sold for a sum of $6 million. Blackwell then purchased 100,000 more acres along the nearby lakeshore, and the Panhandle Lumber Company and Spirit Lake Land Company were organized. When the company's large sawmill was completed, Blackwell's land company platted a town site from 1907 to 1908

SPOKANE INTERNATIONAL RAILROAD

As the 20th Century arrived in Idaho, so did the Northern Pacific and Great Northern Railroads. As the only railroads serving northern Idaho, these two lines enjoyed a market monopoly and were known for charging high freight rates. Disgusted with the railroads' practices, a group of Spokane businessmen decided to take action and create a competing line catering to farmers and miners. In close cooperation with the Canadian Pacific Railroad, the Spokane International Railway Company was incorporated in 1905 under the direction of D. C. Corbin.

Work began in February 1906 to construct the 140-mile line leading across northern Idaho to Spokane, Washington. In November 1906, the line was completed at a cost of $3,634,000 and opened with eleven locomotives, 200 freight cars, and twelve passenger cars furnished with silk plush and gold accents. In no time, business was booming for the Spokane International that prided itself on offering fair freight and passenger rates. Under Corbin's management, the line later extended to Lake Pend Oreille and Lake Coeur d'Alene, taking advantage of tourist and travel dollars. Satisfied with the line he created, Corbin sold the Spokane International Railway to the Canadian Pacific Railroad in 1916.

The Spokane International operated under Canadian Pacific's control until the Depression when the line reorganized into an independent company. However, larger railroad companies were unhappy with the line's independent status. Responding to the larger companies' complaints, the Interstate Commerce Commission endorsed a merger of the Spokane International with the Union Pacific Railroad in 1956.

and began selling lots. Blackwell provided residents with water and sewage systems along with cement sidewalks free of charge. Within a year, Blackwell's company town boomed to over 1,000 residents, and over 100 homes had been constructed. Blackwell didn't stop there, though. Before his death in 1922, Blackwell went on to construct the Idaho and Washington Northern Railroad from Rathdrum, Idaho through Spirit Lake to Metaline Falls, Washington.

Although the lumber industry was responsible for this town's creation, Spirit Lake now attracts visitors and residents with its resort-like atmosphere and scenic wonders. As for the town's namesake, Blackwell adopted the same title as a nearby lake. The lake's name reportedly originated with the Indian word Tesemini, meaning "Lake of the Spirits." Legend states that Chief Hyas-Tyee-Skokum-Tum-Tum of a local Indian tribe bore a daughter who deeply loved one of the tribe's young warriors. Another area leader, Chief Pu-Pu-Mox-Mox, threatened war if the girl were not given to him as his bride. Desiring peace, the girl's father reluctantly agreed to the other chief's arrangement, but the deal would never materialize. Before the chief's daughter was to be married, she and her true love securely tied their hands together and jumped into the lake. The Indians

believe that Tesemini, the water spirit, claimed the pair in anger and retaliation. From then on, the lake was known as Tesemini, "lake of the spirits," which was translated and gradually changed to Spirit Lake.

T Stoneridge Golf Course
355 Stoneridge Rd., Blanchard. 437-4653. Drive 35 miles northwest of Coeur d'Alene to locate the course directly off State Hwy. 41

Thick conifer forests and blue mountain lakes surround golfers on this championship 6,684-yard, par 71 course. Recently renovated for $2.5 million, the course features 19 holes, several water hazards, and sand bunkers playable to both seasoned and occasional golfer. Open from April 1 to October 31, Stoneridge also offers a driving range. Green fees, which include a cart and range balls, are $33 on weekdays and $39 on weekends.

T Twin Lakes Village Golf Course
5500 W. Village Blvd., Rathdrum. 687-1311.

Designed by Kim Krause and built in 1973, the Twin Lakes Village Golf Course boasts bluegrass fairways lined with trees. This relatively flat 18-hole, par 71 course includes water hazards on eleven holes and provides a challenge to a variety of handicaps. Measuring 6,178 yards, the course and driving range are open from April 1 to October 31. Green fees are $25, and advance tee times are required.

T St. Stanislaus Catholic Church
Corner of McCartney & 3rd Sts., Rathdrum.

This Gothic Revival style church represents Idaho's oldest brick church. When Catholic and Jesuit missionaries arrived in Idaho, they established the St. Stanislaus Kostka Mission in 1900. One year later, the St. Stanislaus Church was completed under the direction of Bishop Alphonosus Glorieux. Complete with a wooden tower, the church has been serving northern Idaho Catholics for over a century. The building was added to the National Register of Historic Places in 1977.

T Rathdrum Prairie
State Hwy. 41 outside Rathdrum

The fertile Rathdrum Prairie borders the small town of Rathdrum and is regarded by geologists as one of America's best examples of a glacial plain. Situated on the western fork of the Purcell Trench, the prairie was carved when massive glaciers moved south from Canada 30,000 to 80,000 years ago. In their wake, the glaciers left behind piles of gravel, clay, silt, and sand measuring several hundred feet deep. Today, the plain and the gravel deposits act as the Spokane River aquifer. The prairie is also home to a major Kentucky bluegrass seed growing operation.

TV Spirit Lake
10 miles north of Rathdrum on State Hwy. 41

Views of the majestic Selkirk Mountains form the northwestern backdrop of tranquil Spirit Lake.

SALOON DAYS

While some of Idaho's residents shun liquor, others have continued the tradition started by rugged, hard working early settlers. Spirit Lake's White Horse Saloon is just one of the community's many old buildings and claims to be the oldest continuously operating saloon in the state.

One of just two lakes in the entire world featuring a sealed bottom, Spirit Lake measures four and a half miles long by one mile across and is 100 feet at its deepest. Although Spirit Lake is actually one of Idaho's smallest lakes, it boasts year-round recreation. Fishing, swimming, and boating are favorites during the summer, while ice-skating and ice fishing round out the winter activities.

TV Twin Lakes
Outside Rathdrum on State Hwy. 41

Neighboring the Rathdrum community, Twin Lakes were originally dubbed "Sturgeon Lakes." Today, the lakes are home to excellent bass fishing and are a popular summer camping site for locals and tourists alike.

14 *Food, Lodging*

Hayden
Pop. 9,159

Hayden serves as a suburb to Coeur d'Alene.

Hayden Lake
Pop. 494

This pristine community compliments its neighbor, Coeur d'Alene, as a resort town. In its origination days, it was a fishing and trapping village. Matt Heyden won the right to name the lake, and subsequently the town, in an 1878 card game of seven-up. The name was later misspelled when the post office arrived in 1907.

Dalton Gardens
Pop. 2,278

This suburb community is located directly north of Coeur d'Alene and is nestled in Kootenai County in the northern panhandle. Agriculture, forestry, aluminum, the railroad, and tourism represent the community's economic mainstays.

T Avondale Golf and Tennis Club
10745 Avondale Loop Rd., Hayden Lake. 772-5963. www.avondalegolfcourse.com

The Avondale Golf and Tennis Club offers golfers an 18-hole, 6,573-yard PGA rated course north of Coeur d'Alene. Including a driving range, the course does have a strict dress code to which all golfers must adhere. Current green fees are $40 daily for all 18-holes with lessons beginning at $35.

T The Sunflower Farm
16438 N. Rimrock Rd., Hayden Lake. 772-4597.

The Sunflower Farm provides families with a unique and upclose experience with several tame farm animals. See "Trooper" the dog who does acrobatic tricks, fainting goats, lambs, and llamas at this down-home setting. The farm also offers seasonal hayrides, wagon rides, and sleigh rides by reservation. The Sunflower Farm is open to the public June through September on weekends.

TV Hayden Lake

Bordering the communities of Hayden and Hayden Lake.

Encompassing 4,000 acres and featuring more than forty miles of shoreline, Hayden Lake is situated just north of Lake Coeur d'Alene and offers summer recreation for everyone. Visitors can enjoy boating, waterskiing, and fishing on the lake's calm waters while taking in beautiful views of the neighboring forested hills rising in every direction. On the lake's shores, the Honeysuckle Recreation Area provides a sandy beach, a roped swimming area, a boat dock, and public restrooms.

V English Point

Near Hayden Lake. Contact the Hayden Lake Chamber of Commerce at 762-1185. From Hayden Lake, bear east onto Lancaster Rd. from U.S. Hwy. 95 and proceed 3.5 miles to English Point Rd.

Nestled against the northern shores of scenic Hayden Lake, English Point represents a well-preserved section of national forest land. English Point's trail system caters to hikers during the summer and cross-country ski enthusiasts.

M Hayden Chamber of Commerce

157 W. Hayden Ave., Ste. 103, Hayden. 762-1185. www.haydenchamber.org; join@haydenchamber.org

15 *Food, Lodging*

Hauser

Pop. 668

Centered in a logging district north of Stateline, this small town hosted several names between the years 1864 and 1881 before adopting its present one. Those names were: Antoine Plantes Ferry, Cowleys Ferry, and Spokane Bridge. In 1886, the name Hauser was suggested in honor of S.T. Hauser, an owner of the Coeur d'Alene Railway and Navigation Company. The post office operated from 1888 to 1907.

Stateline

Pop. 38

Nestled outside Post Falls, the village of Stateline borders Washington between the economic centers of Couer D'Alene and Spokane, Washington. Stateline's stadium speedway has become a popular outing for area residents.

H Purcell Trench

Milepost 0.4 on State Hwy. 53 at the Washington State Line

A long, glaciated valley, extending from British Columbia this far into Idaho, brought part of a continental ice sheet past here thousands of years ago.
Rocks and boulders transported here by glacial ice backed up Lake Coeur d'Alene. Then a gradually warming climate let an outlet from Lake Pend Oreille discharge past here – sometimes with catastrophic results. As ice receded, the Kootenai River also flowed past here before lower channels in British Columbia no longer were blocked by a glacial barrier. In those days, this was the Columbia River's main channel.

T Corbin Park

Corbin Park Rd., Post Falls. 773-0539. Merge off I-90 at Exit 2 and drive south on Pleasant View Avenue to Riverbend Avenue. Bear left onto Riverbend Avenue and then right on Corbin Park Rd. Continue 1 mile to the park.

D.C. Corbin, early Idaho railroad developer, serves as the namesake for this 28-acre park. Situated beside the rushing Spokane River, the park provides river access for rafting and fishing, as well as a

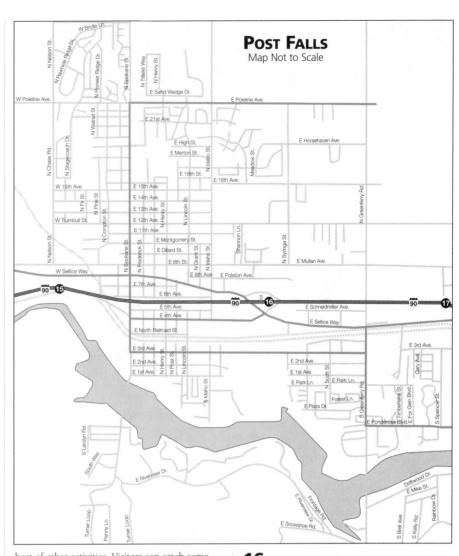

POST FALLS
Map Not to Scale

host of other activities. Visitors can catch some action on the Corbin Park Wave during late spring and summer, but this activity is recommended only to experienced surfers. For land lovers, Corbin Park offers a disc golf course, volleyball court, softball diamond, and numerous picnic areas.

T Coeur d'Alene Greyhound Park

5100 Riverbend Ave., Post Falls. 773-0545 or (800) 828-4880. Merge off I-90 at Exit 2 near the Idaho/Washington border.

Although once a hot spot for greyhound racers and the target of animal-rights activists, Coeur d'Alene Greyhound Park discontinued its live races in 1995. Today, the site is a popular destination to view simulcast premier horse and dog races from around the world, as well as play an exciting round of bingo. The park is open year-round with free admission.

TV Hauser Lake Park

State Hwy. 53 near the Idaho/Washington border. Contact the Idaho Department of Parks and Recreation at 334-4199.

Situated slightly northwest of Coeur d'Alene, Hauser Lake Park juts up against the Idaho/Washington border and is a recreational site for the entire family. The park includes a boat dock and boat launching area, a swimming beach, picnic facilities and barbeque grills, playground equipment, and a basketball court.

16 *Food, Lodging*

Post Falls

Pop. 17,247

A German emigrant who migrated from Illinois, Frederick Post constructed a lumber mill at this location along the Spokane River in 1871 on land he purchased from Andrew Seltice, Chief of the Coeur d'Alene tribe. Seltice and Post had an agreement for the land purchase, which was depicted as a pictograph on a granite stone near the town's railroad tracks.

Post's building site for the saw and grist mill was located beside a waterfall (later known as Spokane Falls). In the building process, he dammed all three Spokane River channels in the area and raised the natural height of the nearby waterfall. Despite all intentions to operate the mill himself, Post offered the property to the U.S. Army for just $2,000 when construction on nearby Fort Sherman began. The military refused Post's offer and built its own mill. As a result, Post went on in 1900 to sell his mill and most of the water rights to R. K. Neill for a whopping $25,000. Afterwards, Post created a three-story, fifty-four room wooden hotel in Post Falls in hope of Coeur d'Alene Lake steamboats traveling downriver to his landing. The plan never materialized, however. Post's hotel burnt to the ground shortly after its establishment, and the enterprising gentleman died in 1908. Along with his name, Post left behind a beloved wife and six daughters.

H Treaty Rock
Exit 5 on I-90, Post Falls Business Loop at Treaty Rock Park

On June 1, 1871, Frederick Post made a deal with Seltice – a prominent Coeur d'Alene Indian leader – to obtain more than 200 acres of land to start a mill near here.

Post noted his land cession on this prominent rock, incising his name and treaty date above some old Indian rock art that still can be seen there. He operated his sawmill for many years at a major hydroelectric site now used for a large power plant.

T The Highlands Golf and Country Club
N. 701 Inverness Dr., Post Falls. 773-3673.

While playing a round, golfers have access to incredible scenery while overlooking the Spokane River and the Rathdrum Prairie. Built in 1990, this 18-hole course is hilly, the fairway is tree-lined, and water hazards come into play on ten holes. The course is best known for its eleventh hole where golfers will play a 109-yard, par 3, 250-foot drop to a canyon green. Measuring 6,369 total yards, the course was rated Idaho's seventh best public course by *Golf Digest* in 1996. A driving range and practice area add to this golf course's many fine features. Green fees are $23 during the week and $25 on weekends.

T Prairie Falls Golf Course
3200 N. Spokane St., Post Falls. 457-0210.

Opened in the summer of 1998, this 18-hole course measure 6,200 yards and is rated at a par-70. Golfers will find a driving range, a three-tiered grass tee, and a full-service pro shop along with reasonable green fees.

T The Links Golf Club
6400 N. Chase Rd., Post Falls. 777-7611.

The Links Golf Club is one of the newest courses to hit the Idaho fairway. Opened on May 6, 2000, the course boasts Scottish style links with the only par- 6 hole in the entire northwest region. Wide-open fairways, long holes, and wind await golfers

on this 18-hole course. Green fees range from $16.50 to $24.50, and golfers should call ahead for a tee time.

T Q'Emlin Riverside Park
Located on Park Way Dr., Post Falls. 773-0539. Merge off I-90 at Exit 5, and drive south on Spokane Street. Proceed across the river, bearing right onto Park Way Dr.

Meaning "throat of the river," this 78.5-acre park was first home to a Coeur d'Alene Indian village. Situated on the shores of the Spokane River, Q'Emlin (pronounced ka-mee-lin) offers miles of hiking along fourteen different posted trails. The paths wind next to peaceful streams, lead through rocky canyons, travel past waterfalls, and offer scenic vistas at every turn. The park also features abundant wildlife, a swimming beach, seasonal boat launching area, picnic shelters, barbeque pits, horseshoe playing area, and user-friendly playgrounds. While the park's attractions are free, there is a small parking charge from Memorial Day to Labor Day.

T Millenium Skate Park
Greensferry and 3rd Ave., Post Falls. 773-0539.

Built and opened in 2002, the Millenium Skate Park is a dream for skateboarders and in-line skaters. Situated on 1.25 acres, the skate park features 10,000 square feet of free style terrain. Users are reminded to wear helmets and protective clothing at all times.

T Treaty Rock Park
609 Compton St., Post Falls. 773-0539.

This 4-acre park offers visitors scenery along numerous short trails and at the designated picnic area. But unlike other parks in town, Treaty Rock Park also features an interesting component of Post Fall's history.

Originating from Germany, Frederick Post moved to Idaho from Illinois in 1871 and quickly became an important businessman in the area. Upon his arrival, Post's heart and mind were immediately set on purchasing a parcel of land next to the Spokane River Falls. Learning that the land belonged to Coeur d'Alene tribal leader,

Andrew Seltice, Post went forth to strike an agreement. When the two men met, a contract was devised on a granite outcropping. This 1871 historical contract features Post's signature and date and a Native American pictograph of a red horseback rider with a coyote escorting a family. This contract stood without issue for nearly 20 years as Post established numerous businesses in his fledgling community. However, in 1889, the U.S. government questioned the legitimacy of the informal agreement. Chief Seltice signed a sworn statement regarding the contract, and President Cleveland and Congress then recognized the agreement. Today, the contract is still faintly visible on the rock now deemed "Treaty Rock."

T Falls Park
4th St., Post Falls. Merge off I-90 and drive south on Spokane Street; bear right onto 4th Street to locate the park.

Post Falls boasts numerous well-maintained parks, and the 22-acre Falls Park is a perfect spot for a stroll or leisurely lunch. Within the park, visitors can view the waterfall that has made this community famous and the scenic Spokane River gorge. Also on site are several picnic tables, handicapped accessible playground equipment, a small fishpond, and interpretive historical signs describing important events and individuals in Post Falls' development.

T Post Falls Dam
Spokane St., Post Falls. Contact the Post Falls Chamber of Commerce at 773-5016. To access the dam, merge off I-90 at Exit 5 and proceed south on Spokane Street.

In 1902, the Washington Water Power Company (WWP) signed contracts with six Coeur d'Alene mining companies, agreeing to provide power to the district. Construction began immediately on a dam near Post Falls on the Spokane River that included a 100-mile, 60,000-volt transmission line. Work was done mostly during the night so as to provide power during the day and the first turbine at Post Falls began operating in 1906. Today, the dam helps control water flow to Lake Coeur d'Alene.

V Centennial Trail
Post Falls. Access from Falls Park on 4th St. Contact the Post Falls Chamber of Commerce at 773-5016.

The paved Centennial Trail winds next to the Spokane River. Bicyclists, joggers, walkers, skaters, and cross-country skiers can opt for a twenty-four mile trip from Post Falls to Higgins Point on Lake Coeur d'Alene or instead can cross over the Idaho/Washington border and travel thirty-nine miles to Spokane. The trail is accessible year-round with interpretive signs highlighting several interesting points along the way.

F Three Sisters Coffee House
621 N. Spokane St., Post Falls. 457-1691.

Conveniently located off I-90, Three Sisters Coffee House will satisfy your coffee, tea, and hunger cravings. Enjoy locally roasted drip coffees and espresso beverages, teas, blended drinks and smoothies, and freshly baked bagels, muffins, scones, cookies, and more. For those with larger appetites, sample a delicious sandwich or order a steaming bowl of soup. A private meeting room accommodating 10-12 people is open to reservations or walk-ins. Computer and free wireless Internet access is available to all customers. With comfortable seating and an inviting and unique atmosphere, Three Sisters Coffee House is perfect for catching up on some work or simply relaxing. The coffeehouse is open 6:30 AM-7:30 PM Monday through Thursday, 6:30 AM-9 PM Fridays and Saturdays, and 7 AM-6 PM on Sundays.

L Red Lion Templin's Hotel on the River
414 E. 1st Ave., Post Falls. 773-1611 or (800) 283-6754. www.redlion.com

Nestled among mountains in historic Post Falls, Red Lion Templin's Hotel neighbors the Spokane River bank and is a AAA-approved resort. Enjoy spectacular river views and breakfast, lunch, and dinner at Mallard's Restaurant and Lounge. Recreate at the private sandy beach and picnic area, wade in the river, or take a seasonal river cruise departing daily from the hotel. At night, relax in one of 167 guest rooms and suites featuring dataports, king and queen beds, coffeemakers, irons, and hairdryers. The hotel also provides a fitness center, tennis and volleyball courts, full-service marina, indoor swimming pool, 11,000 square feet of river view meeting space accommodating groups up to 750, airport transportation, complimentary parking, and special corporate and leisure packages. Come work or play with us!

M Post Falls Area Chamber of Commerce
510 E. 6th Ave., Post Falls. 773-5016 or (800) 292-2553. www.postfallschamber.com

17 Food

Huetter
Pop. 96

Huetter is a small suburb located outside Coeur d'Alene near Post Falls.

T Spokane River
East of Post Falls

Surrounded by cliffs, the Spokane River runs westerly beside the south side of I-90 on its path to Lake Coeur d'Alene. The river winds more than 225 miles and is responsible for draining 4,300 square miles of northern Idaho.

18 Food, Lodging

T The Coeur d'Alene Golf Club
2201 S. Fairway Dr., Coeur d'Alene. 765-0218.

For those Coeur d'Alene golfers looking for a more laid-back atmosphere in comparison to the famed resort course, check out the Coeur d'Alene Golf Club. This 18-hole, 6,274-yard course is situated on the western edge of town and is filled with trees. At a par-72, the course includes a driving range, and green fees are a humble $18 to $24 a round.

T Idaho Panhandle National Forest Nursery
3600 Nursery Rd., Coeur d'Alene. 765-7375. From Coeur d'Alene, drive north on U.S. Hwy. 95, merging west onto the Forest Service Nursery Rd. The nursery is located approximately 3 miles northwest of Coeur d'Alene.

The Idaho Panhandle National Forest Nursery was established in 1960 and represents the only Forest Service tree nursery in all of Idaho, Washington, Oregon, Montana, Wyoming, Colorado, and Utah. Encompassing 220-acres of agriculturally rich soil, the site is one of just thirteen Forest Service nurseries in the nation. The nursery works hard to provide quality seedlings for national forests in northern Idaho, Montana, and North Dakota.

On-site, the Forest Service manages 130 acres of irrigated seedbeds and fifteen controlled environment greenhouses. Production takes place year-round with 16,000,000 seedlings produced annually in the seedbeds and 4,000,000 grown in the greenhouses. Primary seedlings grown include Douglas fir, western white pine, ponderosa pine, Engelmann spruce, western larch, lodgepole pine, western red cedar, and western hemlock.

In addition to providing seedlings to cooperative federal and state agencies, the nursery conducts genetic research on various tree species. The valuable findings are presented to companies and universities with whom the nursery is associated.

To learn more about reforestation practices, visitors are invited to take a free tour of the nursery. The nursery is open Monday through Friday from 7:30 AM to 4:00 PM. Drop-ins are welcome, but large tour groups are requested to make arrangements prior to arriving.

TV Cougar Bay Preserve
Coeur d'Alene. 676-8176. Drive 2 miles south from Coeur d'Alene on U.S. Hwy. 95 and loca,te the entrance on the road's east side. To paddle the bay, proceed 0.75 miles north of the entrance and locate the put-in on the highway's left side.

Protected under the Nature Conservancy, Idaho's 88-acre Cougar Bay Preserve is a wildlife haven on Lake Coeur d'Alene's shores. More than 146 species of migrating and nesting birds have been seen in the area, and moose, beaver, otter, and deer revel in the coniferous forests and meadows bordering the preserve. The Nature Conservancy hopes to protect the area from commercial development but does encourage visitors to experience the preserve's beauty. Recreationists will find more than five miles of hiking trails, canoeing and kayaking, educational programs, and an information kiosk on-site.

TV Idaho Panhandle National Forest
Forest Supervisor's Office, 3815 Schreiber Way, Coeur d'Alene. 765-7223.

The Idaho Panhandle National Forest comprises 2.5 million acres of public land in northern Idaho and is a product of the Coeur d'Alene and portions of the Kaniksu and St. Joe National Forests. Situated between the Cascade Mountains to the west and the Bitterroot Mountains to the east, the forest lies in the east-central part of the Columbia Plateau and is a scenic wonder. Rugged mountaintops thrust toward the sky as waterfalls drop into clear blue lakes and rivers. During the summer, the scent of wild huckleberry wafts through stands of white pine, western red cedar, Douglas fir, and ponderosa pine.

With such diversity and so much land, it's no wonder that the Idaho Panhandle National Forest is a favorite destination for a variety of recreation lovers. Whitewater rafting, canoeing, sailing, fishing, hiking, camping, mountain biking, ATV riding,

and picnicking are individual and family favorites during the summer. Come winter, recreationists turn to cross-country skiing, downhill skiing, snowshoeing, sledding, and snowmobiling. Cabin and lookout rentals are popular year-round, as well as wildlife watching. Whitetail deer, black bear, grizzly bear, woodland caribou, eagles, osprey, and waterfowl are known to frequent the area.

To learn more about the Idaho Panhandle National Forest, contact the Forest Supervisor.

L Best WesternCoeur d'Alene Inn & Conference Center
414 W. Appleway, Coeur d'Alene. 765-3200 or (800) 251-7829. www.cdainn.com

Conveniently located near area attractions, the Best Western Coeur d'Alene Inn & Conference Center is northern Idaho's newest affordable resort. Experience deluxe accommodations with access to nearby Coeur d'Alene Resort's facilities. Rooms include desks, free wireless Internet, free local calls, free parking, coffeemakers, irons, morning newspapers, in-room movies, satellite cable TV, and room service. Microwaves, refrigerators, and suites are also available. Eight conference rooms and a ballroom offer 8,000 square feet of meeting space, and a multilingual staff, dry cleaning, fitness center, golf and ski packages, and indoor and outdoor pools ensure a full-service, quality stay. Dine on signature breakfast, lunch, and dinner items at Mulligan's Grille and Sports Bar featuring the area's first rotisserie spit. For business or pleasure, stay, work, and play with us at the heart of the Northwest playground!

M Hope Realty
1410 Lincoln Way, Coeur d'Alene. 765-3641 or (800) 765-3641. www.hoperealtyidaho.com

Founded in 1975, Hope Realty is a top-producing real-estate firm in northern Idaho. From resorts to vacant land, commercial to waterfront properties, and dream homes to vacation retreats, Hope Realty specializes in all listing types. Thousands of properties and access to the MLS database are available at the company website, www.hoperealtyidaho.com, and a large staff of experienced, friendly agents is eager to help 24 hours a day. If you're selling your home, request a free market analysis of its current value. For those moving to Coeur d'Alene, Hope Realty is pleased to send out relocation packages acquainting you with your new community. With a proven track record and commitment to integrity, Hope Realty is dedicated to offering the service you deserve for all your real-estate needs.

19 *Food, Lodging*

M Coeur d'Alene Visitor & Convention Bureau
1621 N. 3rd St., Ste. 100, Coeur d'Alene. 664-3194 or (877) 782-9232. www.coeurdalene.org; info@coeurdalene.org

20 *Food*

21 *Lodging*

H Lake Steamers
Exit 15 on I-90, on Centennial Trail off of Coeur d'Alene Lake Dr.

Built by the Army in 1880 to carry hay and supplies for Fort Coeur d'Alene, the "Amelia Wheaton" was the first of a long list of steamers on this lake.

Commercial steamboating began in 1884 with the mining rush. In later years, fleets of tall-funneled boats hauled freight, towed logs, and carried passengers and excursionists. Steamers served the lake and river communities until highways changed the transportation pattern.

T Fernan Lake
Pop. 186

Fernan Lake was named for an early settler in about 1888 and lies just outside the Coeur d'Alene city limits. The area is a resort-type village recognized for its less metropolitan atmosphere.

T Coeur d'Alene Resort Golf Course
900 Floating Green Dr., Coeur d'Alene. 667-4653. Merge off I-90 at Exit 15

Designer Scott Miller created this one-of-a-kind course to ensure sport enthusiasts a pure golf experience free from interruptions. Named by *Golf Digest* as America's most beautiful resort golf course, the immaculate green is surrounded by an expansive lakeshore, forested ridges, rolling woodlands, and Fernan Creek. The course is most renowned for possessing the only floating green in the world, the 14th hole. Golfers come from all over the world to test their skills on this challenging 18-hole, par 71 course. Measuring 6,309 yards, the pristine course offers golfers the experience of a lifetime. A forecaddie accompanies every group, and each golf cart is equipped with on-board ball washers and waste receptacles. Visitors be advised, though – a dress code is required, and if you're not a guest at the resort, green fees run well over $150.

Idaho Trivia
In 1990, *Ski Magazine* named Coeur d'Alene America's Top Ski Town due to its relative proximity to two major ski hills: Schweitzer Mountain and Silver Mountain. Just one year later, the American Civic League named Coeur d'Alene an All-American City. Since then, the city has continued to receive praise from dozens of national travel and recreation magazines.

T Ponderosa Springs Golf Course
2814 Galena Dr., Coeur d'Alene. 664-1101.

This locally popular, 9-hole course measures 1,160 yards and is rated at par-27. Tee times are not required, there is no dress code, and green fees are just $15.

TV Fernan Lake
East of Coeur d'Alene near I-90

Neighboring the village of Fernan Lake, Fernan Lake is a favorite local site for a quieter atmosphere away from Lake Coeur d'Alene's famous shores. The lake offers a dock and launching area for boating and water skiing, as well as abundant populations of cutthroat and rainbow trout, largemouth bass, crappie, perch, and catfish for anglers.

22 *Food, Lodging*

Coeur d'Alene
Pop. 34,514

The location of this beautiful city was originally part of the aboriginal Coeur d'Alene's four million acres. Jesuit missionary, Father Pierre De Smet, visited these Native Americans here as early as 1842 and received a warm welcome. In later years Christianity, would have a major effect on the history of their tribe.

Named after this aboriginal tribe, the city of Coeur d'Alene originated in 1879 with a U.S. Army Fort. Roughly, the name translates into "heart like an awl," and awl can also be interpreted as "pointed," "sharp-hearted," or "needle-hearted." This was representative of the shrewd trading abilities of the Indians. Later, the fort was renamed Fort Sherman, in honor of General William Tecumseh Sherman, who originally scouted the location of the fort. The town that had grown around it remained Coeur d'Alene. In 1898, the entire army that occupied Fort Sherman was sent to fight in the Spanish-American War. In 1901 the Fort was officially abandoned. Today, North Idaho College is built on the old fort location.

The first road through the area, the Mullan Rd., was constructed in 1862. This 624-mile long road served for military use, as a settlers' route, and as a supply route for the Northern Pacific Railroad. It also eventually provided access to the Coeur d'Alene Mining District.

Rumors of the existence of gold in the area circulated as early as the 1860s. From 1883 to 1885, miners flocked to the area to get their share of gold, silver, zinc, and lead, which had been recently discovered in abundance in nearby Wallace. Over $5 billion worth of precious metals were extracted from the Coeur d'Alene Mining District. The District also boasts the deepest mine, Star-Morning Mine at Burke, at 7,000 feet; the richest mine, Sunshine Mine on Big Creek, as having produced over 300 million ounces of silver; and

the biggest mine, Bunker Hill, which featured over 180 miles of underground workings.

The town was officially incorporated in 1887, the same year the post office was established. Steamboats were built to ferry people and fresh produce back and forth across Lake Coeur d'Alene. At the turn of the century, the steamboats became a popular tourist attraction for locals and not-so-locals. Folks from Spokane, Washington and other areas came to Coeur d'Alene to escape the city and enjoy the recreation of the lake.

In 1910, the Great Idaho Fire swept through the region, consuming several hundred thousand acres of land and timber and destroying homes, jobs, and lives in its path. Later that year, the Chicago, Milwaukee, and St. Paul Railroad established tracks connecting Spokane to Coeur d'Alene. By 1915, Coeur d'Alene had shipping facilities on five transcontinental railroads. In addition to that, the city supported an electric railroad that provided transportation between it and Spokane, WA, on an hourly basis.

The city that used to thrive around steamboats and railroad cars now hosts scads of tourists and recreation lovers alike.

T Coeur d'Alene Summer Theatre & Carrousel Players
1000 W. Garden (Northern Idaho College Auditorium), Coeur d'Alene. 769-7780 or (800) 423-2849.

Specializing in Broadway musical productions, The Carrousel Players is Idaho's oldest performing arts troupe. Casts are composed of nationally recruited individuals who have gone on to pursue fulfilling careers on Broadway and in film. Boasting thirty-six performances annually in June, July, and August, the Coeur d'Alene Summer Theatre is a growing attraction for locals and tourists alike in the Inland Northwest. Showcased with state of the art sound and lighting systems, The Carrousel Players' productions are renowned. Ticket prices are $29 for adults, $27 for seniors over 60, and $19 for youth ages 12 and under. Group rates are available upon request.

T Opera Plus
Coeur d'Alene. 664-2827. www.operaplus.org

Organized in spring 2000 in association with the North Idaho Friends of the Opera and the Arts, Opera Plus is dedicated to providing cultural enrichment and educational opportunities across Idaho. Opera Plus provides quality performances at a wide array of northern Idaho events. Past venues have included microbrew and wine tastings, free musical picnics in the park, performances at the annual city celebration "Arts from the Heart," and special opera/dining events. While ticket prices vary, quality performances are always assured.

T Lake City Playhouse
1320 E. Garden Ave., Coeur d'Alene. 667-1323.

Coeur d'Alene is home to a myriad of performing arts and cultural opportunities, and the Lake City Playhouse is among them. Tucked inside a quaint, historic setting, the playhouse features musicals, classic, contemporary, and original plays. Talented performers from the region and across the U.S. provide audiences with a close-up theatrical experience. As an added feature, the playhouse offers insight programs after the final show of each production. Audience members have an opportunity to meet the cast, crew, and director, learn about the play and its special effects, and take a backstage tour. Reservations are recommended for all performances, and ticket prices vary.

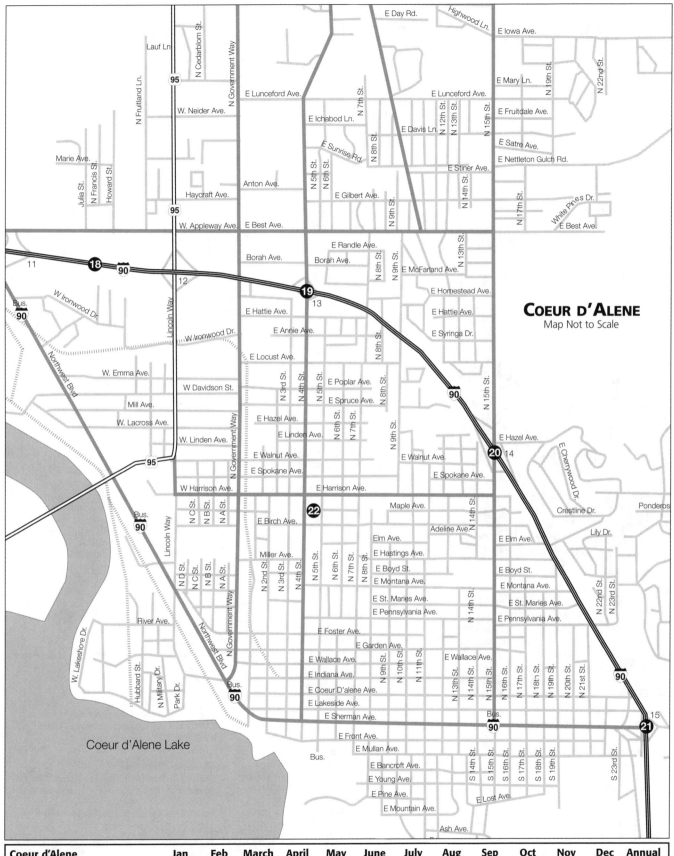

COEUR D'ALENE
Map Not to Scale

Coeur d'Alene	Jan	Feb	March	April	May	June	July	Aug	Sep	Oct	Nov	Dec	Annual
Average Max. Temperature (F)	34.5	40.4	48.4	58.4	68.0	75.1	85.0	84.8	73.9	60.3	44.2	36.6	59.1
Average Min. Temperature (F)	21.8	24.3	28.6	34.3	41.6	48.2	52.9	52.0	44.7	37.2	30.0	25.4	36.8
Average Total Precipitation (in.)	3.37	2.48	2.28	1.74	2.00	1.80	0.71	0.92	1.28	1.95	3.09	3.63	25.26
Average Total Snowfall (in.)	16.1	9.0	3.6	0.5	0.0	0.0	0.0	0.0	0.0	0.2	4.3	12.7	46.4
Average Snow Depth (in.)	5	3	1	0	0	0	0	0	0	0	0	2	1

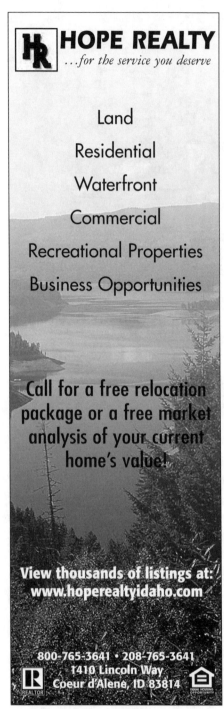
T The Coeur d'Alene Symphony Orchestra
Coeur d'Alene. 765-3833.

The Coeur d'Alene Symphony Orchestra is proud to offer superior musical entertainment to residents and visitors in Idaho's panhandle.

Established in 1981, the orchestra is a non-profit organization supported by the time and talents of dedicated volunteers. The orchestra averages between 65 and 72 members annually, and many of the members travel up to 50 miles to share their special musical talents with the community. Ticket holders will experience a variety of performances, including classical family concerts, Christmas showcases, regional talent extravaganzas, and musical picnics in downtown Coeur d'Alene. Ticket prices are $12 for adults, $7 for seniors, and $5 for students.

T Historical Walking Tour of Downtown
Coeur d'Alene

Founded in the late 1800s, downtown Coeur d'Alene abounds with history. City streets are lined with impressive architectural structures, and each of the historic buildings tells a story of individuals or industry that helped shape Coeur d'Alene into what it is today. On your next visit to Idaho, plan to spend some time exploring the following historic sights.

Coeur d'Alene-Spokane Electric Interurban Railway Booster Substation
Mullan Road and Northwest Boulevard
An electric railroad serviced Coeur d'Alene from 1903 to the mid 1930s. This substation, designed by Coeur d'Alene architect, George Williams, was built in 1904 near Independence Point. The station was important for the city's tourism as it launched passengers aboard steamboats for various outings on Lake Coeur d'Alene or the St. Joe River. Today, the substation is part of the National Register of Historic Places.

Fort Sherman Officer's Quarters
917 W. Garden
Constructed in 1878, the Fort Sherman Officer's Quarters was one of the first buildings erected at the Army post. The facility remained in government use until 1900 when the fort was closed. Today, North Idaho College owns and maintains the structure that is listed on the National Register of Historic Places. It serves as home to several college faculty offices and a renowned history center.

Fort Sherman Chapel
332 Hubbard
This site listed on the National Register of Historic Places was built in 1880. Constructed out of simple clapboard material, the chapel served both Fort Sherman's men and Coeur d'Alene's early residents. Not only was the chapel the first church in Coeur d'Alene, but the building also served as the town's first school and library. In 1926, a belfry was added, and today, the Museum of Northern Idaho manages the site. It is still frequently used for special church services and is host to several weddings each year.

Fort Sherman Powder Magazine
North Idaho College Campus
This gabled, red brick building was erected in 1885 for the necessary purpose of storing Fort Sherman supplies. During the post's heyday, the building was well-stocked with a variety of ammunition and spare weapons. Today, the building is home to the Fort Sherman museum and is listed on the National Register of Historic Places.

The Dike
Rosenberry Drive
Named after the self-designated Skeetsho Indian tribe (referred to by white men as the Coeur d'Alene Indians), Lake Coeur d'Alene was formed with glacial deposits and a natural moraine dam. Although both residents and tourists love the lake, this scenic body of water proved potentially hazardous on Christmas 1933. Rising thirteen feet above normal, the water threatened nearby residents with possible flooding. But with some quick thinking and hard work, city volunteers gathered and sandbagged the shore to protect Coeur d'Alene's growing population. To prevent similar future occurrences, the dike was built in 1934.

701 W. Lakeshore Drive
This early Coeur d'Alene home was built out of virgin pine in 1914. The house was moved to its present location in 1955.

600 block of Lakeshore Drive
Lakeshore Drive is lined with historic houses once home to Coeur d'Alene's earliest and most intriguing residents. 613 W. Lakeshore was built in 1907. In 1908, 615 W. Lakeshore was erected as the Tendall House. Finally, in 1910, 607 W. Lakeshore arrived on the block.

205 Park Drive
Originally built on the Fort Sherman military complex, this building was constructed between 1908 and 1909.

303 Park Drive
Early Coeur d'Alene residents, Harry and Orene Knight, built their dream home together in 1907. Shortly after its completion, these two soul mates died just fourteen hours apart. The house was later remodeled by owners in 1952, 1980, and most recently in 1995.

Coeur d'Alene City Park
Park Drive
One of the most popular spots in this friendly community is the downtown city park. It, too, has historic beginnings. In early 1905, the park was established as part of the Fort Sherman post. Hoping to draw larger crowds to the area and provide passengers with a worthwhile spot to relax, the Coeur d'Alene and Spokane Railway Company acquired the lot in late 1905 and began making plans for a new and improved park. $6,000 later, the Coeur d'Alene City Park was complete and included a brand new dance pavilion. Today, tourists and residents flock to the well-maintained park at the heart of downtown to enjoy the public swimming beach, large shade trees, and a 6,000 square foot wooden play structure.

Roosevelt School
105 Wallace Avenue
Renowned Coeur d'Alene architect, George Williams (1859-1929), designed this Queen Anne/Romanesque building constructed in 1905. During the first years of its operation, the Roosevelt School was the only educational building in the city to have a bell. Based on this design, Williams distinguished himself as a master of school architecture. Since the building's construction, the bell tower has been reconstructed, the original two floors have been turned into three, and the school was revamped into the Roosevelt Inn Bed and Breakfast in 1994. The site is listed on the National Register of Historic Places.

Kootenai County Courthouse
501 Government Way
The Kootenai County Courthouse was fashioned in a Georgian-Revival architectural style by Spokane, Washington architect, Julius Zittle. Palladian arched windows distinguish the building, and it is embellished with terra cotta accents. The site has served as the Kootenai County Courthouse since its construction in 1928. In 1977, the building was added to the National Register of Historic Places.

627 Government Way
Spokane architect, Kirkland Cutter, not only left his mark in Washington, but also in Coeur d'Alene. This private residence was built in 1915 from a neo-classical, Cutter design.

424 Foster
Small bungalows were an ideal home choice for Coeur d'Alene's early residents. This well-crafted house, built in 1913, is an excellent example of the popular and economic style.

501 Foster Avenue
This beautiful home has changed ownership several times since its origination in 1893. Built as

housing for the Fort Sherman postmaster, the postal carrier remained in the house even after the post's closure, living there from 1893 until 1917. In 1927, the home was remodeled and updated to suit the next owner's needs. In 1959, ownership was transferred to the Johnstone-Spaulding family. In 1985, the owners turned a portion of the house into the Colonial Wedding House. The wedding business thrives to this day and offers couples a popular and unique wedding ceremony location steeped in history.

515 and 521 Foster Avenue
During the Great Depression, the once popular bungalow style home was abandoned in favor of the more cost-effective Cotswold/Cape Cod Cottage design. These two residences, built in 1933, illustrate this shift in the city's architectural history.

601 Foster Avenue
A gentleman known as Mr. Landt constructed this Classic Revival/Italian style home in 1905. The residence was built specifically for one of Coeur d'Alene's most prominent citizens, Robert E. McFarland. Traveling with his new bride, McFarland arrived off the Coeur d'Alene River in 1885 to take his position as registrar of the U.S. Land Office. McFarland enjoyed a reputable career in Idaho government and his fine house remains as a legacy to him.

Giles Home
618 Foster Avenue
In 1904, one of Coeur d'Alene's earliest plumbers built this fashionable house. But after only two years, he sold it to Roy Giles, co-owner of the Red Collar Steam Lines. Giles and his company were so powerful they once controlled all of Lake Coeur d'Alene's available water transportation services. The home remained in the Giles' family line until 1989 when Giles' son, Gordon, died and the home transferred ownership.

701 Foster Avenue
This half-timbered home constructed in 1929 is an excellent illustration of Tudor Revival architectural style.

712 Foster Avenue
The first home built in this block of town, this building was constructed in 1895 by Dr. Young. Young served as a veterinarian for Fort Sherman and was wary of the rowdy soldiers' behavior. In response to his concern, Young built this home to shelter his young daughter from any inappropriate soldier advances. In 1935, Ms. Young sold the home to the Scott family. Amazingly, the exterior paint color is original.

720 Foster Avenue
Heine Glindeman built this stunning Victorian home in 1907. Glindeman later was elected as Coeur d'Alene's mayor and served from 1917 to 1921. Although the home has changed ownership over the years, it has been lovingly preserved. In 1984, Steven Handlen began a comprehensive restoration project. As part of his plan, Handlen hand-cut 2,100 shingles and created a local and nationally acclaimed diamond design roof.

The Salt Box
801 Foster Avenue
Affectionately known to locals as "The Salt Box," this home was built in 1913 for O.W. Edmonds by his father, Arthur Edmonds. Nicknamed "Foxy," O.W. Edmonds went on to serve many terms as Coeur d'Alene's mayor.

818 Foster Avenue
This home constructed in 1914 serves as another example of a bungalow style residence.

906 Foster Avenue
Built in 1907, this home is a rare and impressive three-story historic beauty.

916 Foster Avenue
This house constructed in 1906 has a mysterious past. T.C. Cannon built the home in 1906, but in the 1970s, the owners were shocked. After 50 plus years of being sealed off, a small room was found hiding upstairs.

917 Foster Avenue
Coeur d'Alene received a bit of international flair when this home was developed in 1939. "Blue mud" stucco from S.ern California was used to the build the 6,000 square foot house. With eleven-inch thick walls, this hefty home is situated on nearly one acre of land.

Old Central School
602 Garden Avenue
Built in 1904, the school originally had just one floor. A growing town, however, called for a growing school. In 1908, the second and third stories were added to accommodate increasing student populations. Despite suffering a devastating fire in 1933, the school was restored and now functions as a pre-school.

Homes of Garden Avenue
At 514 Garden Avenue, passerby will have a chance to see a Dutch Colonial style home built in 1910. Nearby is 501 Garden Avenue, another impressive home constructed in the same year.

St. Luke's Episcopal Church
501 Wallace Avenue
After years of planning and building, this Queen Anne style church was completed in 1892. At a cost of $1,500, G.H. Connors built the church completely from native woods.

Greenbriar Inn
315 Wallace Avenue
Renowned Coeur d'Alene architect, George Williams, designed this impressive American Colonial Revival style building. In 1908, contractor Harvey Davey acquired the building plans and constructed the inn as an advertising method to sell his skills as a professional and competent brick layer and laborer. His plan worked, and this ten-bedroom beauty is now listed on the National Register of Historic Places.

Northern Pacific Railroad Depot
201 N. 3rd Street
Prior to the arrival of this building, Coeur d'Alene was home to two previous wooden railroad depots. When fire destroyed both of those depots, Northern Pacific Railroad officials decided to build a more fire-resistant depot in 1910. The depot was used for waiting passengers, and the railroad tracks were located on 3rd street. The railroad played an instrumental role in transporting ore from the Coeur d'Alene mining district.

Montgomery Ward Building
117 N. 4th Street
Wealthy Coeur d'Alene businessman, J.W. Wiggett, financed this building in 1929 that served as the town's Montgomery Ward Department Store. Now home to the Wiggett Antiques Mall, the building is accented with a French plaque on its façade.

Federal Building
4th Street and Lakeside Avenue
This Adamesque style building was constructed in 1927 and still serves as the launching point for one of the U.S.' few water mail routes. The building has been added to the National Register of Historic Places.

First Presbyterian Church
521 Lakeside Avenue
In 1890, Coeur d'Alene became home to a First Presbyterian Church, and it remained in its original state until a first remodeling project occurred in 1910. In 1959, the Hunter Memorial Addition was created, and in 1989, the entire facility was remodeled again. Despite the addition and restoration projects, the church retains its original structure and ornate stained glass windows.

M.D. Wright House
703 Lakeside Avenue
In 1914, M.D. Wright built this as a personal residence. Twenty-four years later, his home became the Coeur d'Alene Community Hospital for a short period of time. In 1945, the Ralph Nelson family donated the building to the city, upon which it was renovated into a community library. The public enjoyed this library until 1986 when an insurance company purchased the historic site.

P.W. Johnson House
622 Coeur d'Alene Avenue
Utilizing shipyard laborers, P.W. Johnson built this home in 1911. Upon completion, the home was a community masterpiece. It was so modern that it even included an elevator in which wood could be carried throughout the home during winter.

United Methodist Church
618 Wallace Avenue
Built between 1906 and 1909, this Tudor-Gothic style church is unique among Idaho churches for its stepped, gabled façade. Made from pressed bricks, it is one of few churches that renowned architect, George Williams, designed. Embellished with stained-glass windows, the church was one of the finest structures in northern Idaho during its prime. Today, the beautiful church is listed on the National Register of Historic Places.

The Redemptorist Mission House
919 Indiana Avenue
In hopes of ministering to residents in E.ern Washington, Idaho, and Montana, the Missouri Redemptorist Order needed a home mission base. In 1913, the order assumed ownership of the city's proposed St. Thomas Catholic Church and its building debt. Upon completion of the church, the order added an Early American Colonial mission house in 1928. This monastery was initially connected to the church with a sheltered breezeway, and the order continues to serve the church parish to this day.

St. Thomas Catholic Church
919 Indiana Avenue
Spokane architects, Rooney and Stritesky, designed this Romanesque style brick church. With a painted galvanized iron spire and a gold-flaked cross, the building's architectural design is unique in Idaho's landscape. Inside, the church features a Greek-Ionic motif and a one-of-a-kind altar found nowhere else in America. Complete with leaded glass windows, the church was built by E.M. Kreig for $46,000. This historic beauty is recognized on the National Register of Historic Places.

Idaho Trivia

To accommodate the growing number of residents inhabiting Lake Coeur d'Alene's shores, the U.S. Postal Service established a water mail route in the area in 1914. The service continued through 1937 and is believed to be America's first postal water route.

The Blackwell House
820 Sherman Ave.
Frederick Blackwell built this Victorian style showpiece as a present for his son, Russell, and new daughter-in-law. The senior Blackwell was famous around Coeur d'Alene as a shrewd businessman. In 1901, he invested in several mills. Two years later, he co-founded the Electric Interurban Railway Company, which he then used as a platform to promote area tourism.

Southwest Corner of 4th St. and Sherman Ave.
This building was constructed in 1901 as one of Coeur d'Alene's first community banks.

Northeast Corner of 4th St. and Sherman Ave.
The First National Bank was built here in 1904.

Southeast Corner of 4th St. and Sherman Ave.
Shopping was a popular pastime in Coeur d'Alene's early days. In 1891, this building was constructed as a department store.

5th Street and Sherman Ave.
The Coeur d'Alene City Hall was established here in 1908.

515 Sherman Ave.
To meet the growing need for media and current news, the Coeur d'Alene Journal was established in the 1890s and occupied this building.

307 Sherman Avenue
All of Coeur d'Alene's elite were pleased when Clarks Jewelry Store opened its doors here in 1908.

Wiggett Building
325 Sherman Ave.
Constructed sometime around 1890, Dr. Merriam financed this building project. Subsequently, the surrounding block was dubbed "Merriam Block" in his honor. In 1898, Merriam sold the two-story building to one of Coeur d'Alene's richest men, J.W. Wiggett. In 1912, Wiggett added the third floor.

Hudson's Hamburgers
207 Sherman Ave.
Hudson Hamburgers has seen a lot of customers since Harley Hudson opened up shop in 1907. Now a downtown staple, the business made famous by the "Huddy Burger" is still family-operated on the same city block.

T Lake Coeur d'Alene & City Beach
Downtown Coeur d'Alene

National Geographic has honored Lake Coeur d'Alene as one of the five most beautiful lakes in America, and it is easy to see why. Covering more than 25 miles with 135 miles of user-friendly shoreline and forested coves, Lake Coeur d'Alene was formed with a glacial moraine deposit millions of years ago. Today, the lake is a scenic wonder and a recreational paradise. Downtown, residents and tourists populate the free city beach, fishermen search for the lake's abundant kokanee salmon, and waterskiers rush across the blue water. Numerous short boat tours and dinner cruises are available for those who want to explore farther than the shoreline, and kayaking, rafting, and parasailing are also popular pursuits.

In addition to serving as a recreational mecca, Lake Coeur d'Alene is a focal point for community celebration and tradition. Every Fourth of July, a spectacular showcase of fireworks lights up the night sky, casting colorful reflections on the lake's surface. On Labor Day weekend, look above the lake for the traditional hot air balloon festival. Winter illuminates the lake with the annual Fantasy in Lights and Laser Extravaganza. Boasting the Pacific Northwest's largest light display, the lake glows with nearly one million lights and ushers in the Christmas holiday spirit. No matter what season, beautiful Lake Coeur d'Alene remains at the heart of this community.

T Lake Coeur d'Alene Boardwalk
115 S. 2nd St. at the Coeur d'Alene Resort

Coeur d'Alene is not only home to beautiful scenery, but also the world's longest floating boardwalk. Measuring 3,300 feet long, the boardwalk is situated at the Coeur d'Alene Resort and is a perfect spot to take a leisurely stroll while capturing outstanding vistas of Lake Coeur d'Alene. The boardwalk is free to the public year-round, and also serves as the site of the popular annual wooden boat festival held each August.

T Museum of North Idaho
115 Northwest Blvd., Coeur d'Alene.
664-3448. www.museumni.org

The Museum of North Idaho preserves the fascinating history of Kootenai County and the surrounding region. Opened in 1973, the museum features displays exploring sawmills, steamboats, railroads, communities, recreation, the logging and mining industries, Fort Sherman, the Cataldo Mission, the role of the Forest Service in the area, and the Coeur d'Alene Indians. In addition, the museum has an archive of over 20,000 photographs of neighboring counties and towns. Visit the museum from 11 AM to 5 PM Tuesday through Saturday from April 1 to October 31. Admission is $5 for a family, $2 for adults, and $1 for children.

T Fort Sherman Museum
North Idaho College, 1000 W. Garden Ave., Coeur d'Alene. 769-3300.

In 1877, General William Tecumseh Sherman came west and established an army fort that would become one of the Northwest's major military institutions. Pioneers quickly settled around the fort, and in 1892, troops were sent from the fort to the Silver Valley to stop one of Idaho's most notable mining disputes. At the outbreak of the Spanish American War, however, troops were dispatched again and the fort was abandoned in 1900. Today, a few structures remain amid North Idaho College's modern buildings, and a walking tour to the preserved buildings is available. Visitors will also find displays about the passenger boat known as Miss Spokane, a model of what Fort Sherman looked like in its prime, outdoor exhibits of logging equipment, and a 1924 smoke-jumper's cabin. The museum is open from 1 PM to 4:45 PM Tuesday through Saturday from May 1 to September 30.

T Tubbs Hill
Downtown Coeur d'Alene. Contact the Coeur d'Alene Visitor & Convention Bureau at 877-782-9232.

Coeur d'Alene's Tubbs Hill reflects the community's value for beauty over invasive development. As the city of Coeur d'Alene grew, developers in the 1960s proposed constructing numerous hotels and condominiums on the hill overlooking the scenic lake. Appalled at the thought of losing the beautiful open space, residents raised money to purchase the hill's thirty-four acres of open space with the intention of developing the land as a community park.

Today, Tubbs Hill is a city highlight featuring groves of Douglas fir and old-growth ponderosa pine trees as well as spectacular overviews of the lake and city. The area is only open to foot-traffic, and various nature trails lead to hidden natural treasures including beaches, coves, and forests. The park honors the memory of Coeur d'Alene's first justice of the peace, Tony Tubbs. Tubbs was also one of the area's first homesteaders and was instrumental in supporting the Bunker Hill Mine.

TV Coeur d'Alene City Park
Downtown Coeur d'Alene

Tucked against the shores of Lake Coeur d'Alene, the community's City Park is a child's dream. The park includes a 6,000 square foot wooden play structure, a public swimming beach, and plenty of room for summer family picnics. Skaters, frisbee players, and joggers also frequently stop at the park to enjoy the area's outstanding scenery.

V Canfield Mountain
U.S.FS Fernan Ranger Station, 2502 E. Sherman Ave., Coeur d'Alene. 769-3000.

The thirty-two mile Canfield Mountain Trail System uses a web of logging roads and was designed for use without having to travel on any roads open to cars or trucks. Featuring single and double track paths, the trail system is open to mountain bikes, horsemen, hikers, and motorcycles. A complete map of the trails and numerous access points is available at the Fernan Ranger Station.

V Buried History
Lake Coeur d'Alene. Contact the Coeur d'Alene Visitor & Convention Bureau at (877) 782-9232.

In early settlement days, steamers loaded with passengers and cargo lined the breathtaking blue waters of Lake Coeur d'Alene. Today, two of the lake's most recognizable icons are buried beneath their old stomping grounds. The "Georgie Oaks" was a famous sternwheeler that operated until 1917. With a 100-ton capacity, several passengers made their way to Coeur d'Alene on this famous boat. The second boat, known as "Idaho," featured twin side wheels and could carry a maximum of 1,000 passengers and their freight on each trip. For those curious in further exploration of the site, local divers lead guided trips to the steamer wreckage.

L The McFarland Inn
601 E. Foster Ave., Coeur d'Alene. 667-1232 or (800) 335-1232. www.mcfarlandinn.com

Welcome to one of the most elegant, historic homes in Coeur d'Alene, Idaho. Built in 1905, the McFarland Inn is located on a quiet, tree lined street within walking distance of the lake, park, and downtown attractions. For its 100th birthday, the home was completely renovated to add 21st century amenities while maintaining its original charm. Each of the five guest rooms has a private bath, TVs with DVD/VCRs, and wireless internet access. Your stay includes a full gourmet breakfast in our beautiful sunroom, "get-to-know-you" hour with hors d'ouvres, and wine tasting. Their guest lounge offers a complimentary snack bar, refrigerator, computer work station, games, TV with DVD and video library. Peak season room rates are $135-$175. Children over 12 years of age are welcome. Special wedding and honeymoon packages are available.

L The State Motel
1314 E. Sherman Ave., Coeur d'Alene. 664-8239. www.thestatemotel.com

Situated near downtown Coeur d'Alene, the State Motel features front door parking and easy access to area attractions. Shopping, restaurants, and City Beach are within walking distance, and a convenient 24-hour grocery store is across the street. Each cozy one or two bedroom suite features a knotty pine décor and includes a table with chairs, refrigerator, microwave, tub/shower combination, cable TV and HBO, high speed Internet connection, free local calls with no long distance access charge on phone cards, and voice mail. The most unique feature is the massaging "magic fingers" built into

each bed. For just a quarter, ease away the aches and pains of your road-weary body. On your next trip, discover the State Motel where half of all room reservations are previous customers.

S Devin Galleries
507 Sherman Ave., Coeur d'Alene. 667-2898. www.devingalleries.com

Situated in beautiful downtown Coeur d'Alene, Devin Galleries is one of the Northwest's largest galleries with nearly 7,000 square feet of museum quality art. Works from both emerging and established artists are featured including original paintings, bronze and stone sculpture, hand-blown contemporary art glass, limited edition prints, jewelry and much more. Devin Galleries' diverse offerings range from realism to impressionism and contemporary to abstract with artwork for every taste, style, and budget. Additionally, Devin Galleries' professional staff provide in-home and in-business art consulting services, and the custom framing department can handle the most demanding framing projects. The gallery is available for group tours, private showings, and other events by appointment. Whether you're touring on Art Walk night or simply browsing on your own, be sure to visit one of America's premier fine art galleries!

M Keller Williams Realty®
1044 Northwest Blvd. Suite F, Coeur d'Alene. 667-2399. www.kwcda.com

Keller Williams Realty® is America's newest, most innovative, and fastest growing national real estate company, and the Coeur d'Alene office bolsters this reputation with its exceptional northern Idaho property listings. At Keller Williams Realty® Coeur d'Alene, buyers and sellers receive personal attention where customer service and satisfaction always come first. Honesty, teamwork, communication, integrity, and creativity are high priorities for Keller Williams' agents as they strive to create win-win scenarios based on trusting relationships. With a belief that no transaction is worth their reputation, each agent grows personally through education and looks forward to helping buyers and sellers achieve their real-estate goals. Although the Keller Williams Realty® network may be national, the support and service that every customer receives is personal and local! Check out their listings online, or call for a free customized search.

T Wolf Lodge Bay

BLM Coeur d'Alene District Office. 769-5000. Merge off I-90 at Wolf Lodge Exit 22 (8 miles east of Coeur d'Alene). Bear right and proceed on State Hwy. 97 to the bay.

For the last thirty-years, Bureau of Land Management officials have watched and recorded in awe as record numbers of bald eagles swoop down on Idaho's Wolf Lodge Bay during annual migration season. Arriving at the bay on Lake Coeur d'Alene's shores during November, the bald eagles' population peaks at the end of December. During the last week of December and into early January, visitors will likely see an average of thirty to sixty bald eagles feasting on kokanee salmon. The area has become so popular that BLM officials now sponsor an annual "Eagle Watch Week" starting immediately after Christmas.

T Veteran's Centennial Memorial Bridge

East of Coeur d'Alene on I-90

As part of a $20 million project to finish I-90 east of Coeur d'Alene to the Pacific Northwest, the U.S. Hwy. Department completed the Bennett Bay Centennial Bridge in 1991. Designed by Howard Needles Tannem and Bergendoff (HNTB), the bridge was renamed the Veteran's Centennial Memorial Bridge by the Idaho Legislature in 1992 to honor the state's military veterans. The 1,730 foot long bridge was designed under a strict environmental code so as to minimize any negative visual effects on the surrounding landscape. The four-lane bridge has received several engineering achievement awards and towers 300 feet above Lake Coeur d'Alene.

T Thompson Lake Wildlife Viewing Area

Travel 6 miles east of Coeur d'Alene on I-90, merging south onto State Hwy. 97 at the Wolf Lodge Exit. Proceed 25 miles before bearing left on Thompson Lake Rd. The viewing blind is located in approximately 1.3 miles.

Introduction

This location offers wildlife watchers, photographers, and artists the opportunity to view birds and mammals without disturbing them. A viewing structure screens viewers, allowing them to see wildlife species up close and undisturbed.

General Information

Thompson Lake is a natural location for the viewing site since the marsh and the adjoining lake have wildlife present nearly year round. Wetlands are natural magnets for many species of wildlife. The abundance of water and plant life provides rich habitat for animals of all sizes; dragonfly to white-tailed deer. It is also an important resting area for birds, especially waterfowl. Many species of these birds use the lake on their migration routes.

The viewing blind is on Thompson Lake Road just two miles north of Harrison. A short trail leads from the four-vehicle parking lot to a rock outcropping that supports the blind. The blind is a six-sided structure made of cedar. It has a cement floor and walls of angled slats to permit visitors to view wildlife without being seen. The blind is handicap accessible.

Viewing Tips

Important equipment is a pair of binoculars. Also a spotting telescope may be useful for distance viewing. Good viewing times typically are early morning and late afternoon hours. For bird migrations, large numbers can be seen during spring and fall seasons.

Responsible Viewing

Unintentional actions may harm wildlife through direct disturbance, feeding the animals, littering, or disobeying laws.

• Minimize disturbance
• Watch for subtle signs of distress
• Make quiet, slow movements to avoid scaring wildlife
• Keep far from nests and dens
• Don't harass wildlife
• Don't pick up wildlife that appear sick or orphaned
• Never feed wildlife
• Keep pets leashed
• Never litter or deface property
• Respect the rights of others already present at the site

Wildlife Species You May See

• Swallow
• Painted Turtle
• E.ern Kingbird
• Chipmunk
• Pine Squirrel
• Garter Snake
• Common Loon
• Black Tern
• Wood Duck
• Muskrat
• Beaver
• Elk
• Bald Eagle
• Coyote
• Mallard Duck
• Tundra Swan
• Columbian Ground Squirrel
• Canada Goose
• Great Blue Heron
• White-tailed Deer
• American Kestrel
• Red-tailed Hawk
• Belted Kingfisher

Reprinted from U.S. Forest Service and Idaho Dept. of Fish & Game brochure

TV Mineral Ridge Recreation Area & Trails

East of Coeur d'Alene on State Hwy. 97 2 miles south of the intersection with I-90. Contact the BLM Coeur d'Alene District Office at 769-5000.

The Bureau of Land Management has overseen the operation of this scenic 152-acre reserve since its establishment in 1963. Three miles of loop trails lead to spectacular overviews of Beauty Bay and Wolf Lodge Bay on Lake Coeur d'Alene, and picnicking and camping are also available.

TV Beauty Bay Recreation Area

4 miles south of I-90 on State Hwy. 97. Contact the BLM Coeur d'Alene District Office at 769-5000.

Located southeast of Coeur d'Alene, the Beauty Bay Recreation Area offers a scenic, forested resting stop. Seven individual picnic spots are available, and an easy half-mile trail leads to a breathtaking view of Lake Coeur d'Alene. Also on site is a paved path leading to an observation deck of Beauty Bay. Beauty Bay is the most photographed area on the entire Lake Coeur d'Alene, and wildlife abounds in the region.

H Saint Joseph Indian Mission

Milepost 92.4 on State Hwy. 3

On November 4, 1842, Father Nicholas Point began a Jesuit mission that settled here after a winter at Coeur d'Alene.

Eagerly sought by the Coeur d'Alene Indians, the black-robed missionaries supervised the building of a log cabin and in the spring began to teach "the mysteries of plowing and planting." Soon, two-thirds of the tribe was baptized. But floods gave trouble here and in 1846, the mission moved north to Cataldo.

H The Mullan Road

Milepost 95.7 on State Hwy. 3 south of Cataldo

Designed to connect the Missouri and the Columbia Rivers, this military wagon road was constructed past here in 1859.

Swamps in the St. Joe Valley had to be corduroyed with logs, and 70 men spent a week digging out sidehills south of here and chopping through three miles of forest. But after all that work, spring floods made this route impassable. Two years later, Mullan had to survey and build a new section of his road around the north of Coeur d'Alene Lake.

T Mullan Tree

3 miles west of Fourth of July Summit on I-90 (near Exit 28) locate a gravel road on the interstate's northern edge. Proceed 75 yards along this road to a white marble statue.

Lieutenant John Mullan gained fame and notoriety in the 1850s and 1860s when U.S. Army officer, Isaac Stevens, assigned him to create a wagon route connecting Fort Benton, Montana and Fort Walla Walla, Washington. A highly regarded topographical engineer, Mullan accepted the assignment with enthusiasm and set off to work.

Although unexpected problems, bad weather, and a lack of skilled workers plagued the road's construction process, Mullan carried forth with orders, including one handed down by the Secretary of War. In the process of creating the wagon road, Mullan was ordered to mark the route with the road's initials (M. R. for Mullan Road) and the date on which the inscription was made. Mullan routinely obeyed this order, often carving the inscription into trees lining the route.

One such tree and historical engraving remains. At the base of the marble statue representing Lt. John Mullan, a flight of stairs leads down to a fenced, twelve-foot tree stump marked "Y 4" at the base. The tree, estimated at 325 years old when a fierce wind blew most of it down in 1962, showcases a tiny remnant of Mullan's handicraft.

In 1861, Mullan and his men stopped working on their road to briefly celebrate Fourth of July in this Idaho canyon. During that celebration,

---

SNOWMOBILE PARADISE

The Idaho panhandle, and particularly the Silver Valley, is regarded as a snowmobiler's paradise. Hundreds of inches of snow each year combined with a variety of terrain and thousands of miles of groomed snowmobile trails provide a winter full of fun. The trails are so extensive that the Silver Valley is reputed to hold the world's largest developed trail system for snowmobiles, mountain bikes, and ATVs. Most trails run at elevations exceeding 7,000 feet and provide outstanding views of the surrounding area. For more information on trails, rentals, and regulations, contact the Historic Silver Valley Chamber of Commerce at 784-0821.

Mullan took a moment to carve "M. R. July 4, 1861" into the famous tree. Today, the "Y 4" remains for all visitors to see. Gazing east and west from the tree, visitors can view remnants of Mullan's wagon road.

V Fourth of July Pass Cross Country Ski Trails

18 miles east of Coeur d'Alene. Contact the Idaho Department of Parks and Recreation at 666-6711. From Coeur d'Alene, drive 18 miles east on I-90, merging off at the 4th of July Summit Exit (Exit 28). Bear south on Forest Road 614 and continue 0.25 miles to the signed entrance.

Cross-country skiing is a favorite northern Idaho pastime, and Fourth of July Pass offers a series of beginner level trails. Winding through thick stands of trees with distant mountain views, the groomed trails make three different loops and cover nearly twelve miles. The area is part of Idaho's Park N' Ski system, and permits are required. Permits may be obtained at the nearest Ranger Station, and fees are as follows: $25 annual permit (good at all Idaho Park N' Ski areas), $7.50 3-day permit, and $2 day use permit.

25 Food

H Old Mission of the Sacred Heart

Exit 39 on I-90 at the Cataldo Mission; bear right on Frontage Rd.

Opened for services in 1853, this is the oldest building in Idaho.

Black-robed Jesuits founded the mission in 1842, but moved here from their St. Joe River site in 1846 and raised this imposing building in a complete wilderness. Old outbuildings are now gone, and their mission moved to Desmet in 1877. But this National Historic Landmark is preserved as a state park.

T Cataldo

Pop. 100

Cataldo is one of the oldest settlements in the Idaho panhandle, boasting the Coeur d'Alene Mission of the Sacred Heart, or "Old Mission." Father Antonio Ravalli of Italy built the mission in 1848. Father Joseph Cataldo, for whom the town is named, lead the Catholic parishioners in 1865 and eventually founded the Lapwai and Lewiston missions. Cataldo is known for its missionary work among Native Americans, a pursuit that Father Cataldo carried out until he was ninety years old.

T Old Mission State Park

Exit 40 off I-90, Cataldo. 682-3814.

A living landmark, Old Mission stands serenely on a hilltop 24 miles east of Coeur d'Alene along I-90.

THE MULLAN ROAD

In 1853, Isaac Stevens, a U.S. Army officer, was made Governor of Washington Territory. At that time, the territory included northern Idaho. That same year, Congress obtained permission to survey possible routes for the Northern Pacific Railroad – the first of the proposed transcontinental routes. General Stevens was to choose the survey party. Most of the surveying was easy. The real trouble was where to cross the Rocky Mountains. John Mullan, a topographical engineer, was chosen to lead the investigating party and they set out to find a wagon route between Fort Benton, Montana, and Fort Walla Walla, Washington. The road was initially built as a military undertaking, but was expected to serve as an alternate route for westbound emigrants and as a right-of-way for the proposed railroad.

In 1854, Congress approved $30,000 for the project. Mullan gathered the necessary information and ended up crossing the Continental Divide six times. The Indian War of 1858 delayed work on the road; during that year, Mullan got involved in the war, commanding a party of Nez Perce scouts and helping Col. Wright end the hostilities. In the spring of 1859, construction began progressing east from Walla Walla. The seventy-man crew worked quickly and soon was at Coeur d'Alene Lake. They constructed a forty-foot ferry on which to cross the St. Joe River and made it past the Cataldo Mission before their troubles really began. The forest was incredibly thick along the Coeur d'Alene river, and the twenty soldiers, who were part of the crew, refused to cut any more trees down. With the crew down to fifty men, the trees and fallen timber stretching out before them seemed nearly impossible to conquer. The forest, coupled with several river crossings, made for a long summer, but by fall, the men had reached the Montana side of the Bitterroots. They wintered at that location and then began surveying the road's route to Fort Benton.

That year, 1860, spring flood waters convinced Mullan he had chosen the wrong route around Coeur d'Alene Lake. In 1861, Congress approved an additional $100,000 to reroute that portion of the road. All summer long, the men constructed a new route, once again through dense forest. On July Fourth, the men celebrated in a canyon that now bears the name "Fourth of July Canyon." Only a short distance was yet to be covered before they arrived at the Cataldo Mission, which they reached a month later. Sixty river crossings had to be built just on the Coeur d'Alene River alone in the course of their construction of the road. The St. Regis River required almost as many.

The year 1862 brought hardship for the men. The winter was the worst to hit the area in many decades and the men – lucky to have survived – had to eat their horses. Many workers quit that spring and Mullan was unable to make improvements to the 624-mile eastern portion of the road. Then, in the spring of 1862, the spring floodwaters destroyed substantial stretches of the road. Construction repairs were necessary, but no monetary provisions were made for them. During the short course of its life, the Mullan Road was only used by a handful of emigrants and some packers. The railroad never did use the route; instead they chose a more productive route to the north. The road was reclaimed by nature but found itself the center of attention a century later when the U.S. Interstate 90 route was being considered. The route chosen matched Mullan's route across northern Idaho.

Today, a white marble statue of John Mullan stands near Interstate 90, just east of Fourth of July Summit and not far from a twelve-foot tree stump. This tree is known as the Mullan Tree, and has the phrase "M.R. July 4, 1861" carved into it. The initials stand for "military road," and were ordered, by the Secretary of War, to be used as markers along the road at frequent intervals. The Mullan Tree, a white pine, is estimated to have been 325 years old at the time it was reduced to just its trunk in a 1962 wind storm. Traces of the old Mullan wagon road can be seen to the east and west of the tree, evidence of a short-lived legacy.

The Mission Church is unique in its architecture, venerably in its year, romantic in its history, beckoning to all who pass. Constructed in 1850-53 by members of the Coeur d'Alene Indian Tribe and Catholic Missionaries, the church stands today as Idaho's oldest standing building. It was designed by a true Renaissance man, Father Anthony Ravalli. In Italy, Ravalli studied theology, philosophy, mathematics, natural science, medicine, art, and architecture.

The church's stone foundation had to be dug in the mountains half a mile away. The Indians dragged in timbers and rafters, then dressed and put them into place all by hand. Willow saplings were fastened to the uprights, woven with grass, and plastered with mud and clay. Around the building designed in the Greek Revival style stood many other structures of a self-sufficient village.

The Mission served as the site for council after conflict with Colonel Steptoe and as headquarters for Captain John Mullan when building his road. In 1887, because of pressure from encroaching white population, the fact that the mission did not center within the reservation's boundaries, and the development of agricultural deficiencies, the mission was relocated to its present day site at DeSmet, Idaho.

The Mission has been many different things for many different people and will always have a place in history. Now, the church remains only as a monument to the past, probably the most remarkable building in Idaho.

Old Mission State Park's natural beauty and historic significance combine to make the site a perfect setting for celebrations and special events that connect the present generation with the past. Three major events are: 1) The Historic Skills Fair scheduled for the second Sunday of each July at which men, women, and children dressed in historic costume demonstrate pioneer crafts while Old Time fiddlers play music. 2) The annual Feast of Assumption Pilgrimage of the Coeur d'Alene Indians takes place each August 15. 3) The third weekend in August the park hosts the Annual Mountain Men Rendezvous.

Reprinted from Idaho State Parks & Recreation brochure

SILVER VALLEY'S HISTORIC BUNKER HILL MINE

In the late 1870s, miners from across the country rushed to the North Fork of the Coeur d'Alene in hopes of striking it rich with gold. Although gold was discovered in 1878, the claims played out by 1885, and many locals were left without work.

Deciding to venture out on his own expedition, sixty-year-old carpenter, Noah Kellogg, acquired economic backing and headed to the South Fork of the Coeur d'Alene with his jackass in tow in 1885. He soon returned to Murray, declaring that his first venture was unsuccessful. Gaining new backing, he returned to the South Fork and made a move that would distinguish the entire area as Silver Valley.

Historians speculate that Kellogg actually did find galena ore on his first trip (while looking for his lost jackass) but was unhappy with the financial backing of his first investors. Thus, with a more prosperous financial backing, Kellogg returned to the same site and laid claim to what would become one of the most profitable silver mines in the world.

Upon his find, Kellogg and his investors founded the Bunker Hill and Sullivan Mine. As other large mining companies moved to the area, Bunker Hill and Sullivan were constantly involved in claim litigations, and early development of their lode was slowed by the need to find an outlet for the ore. The first diggings were sent by wagon to Kingston, transported on a steamer to Coeur d'Alene, and then transported by wagon to Rathdrum and the Northern Pacific Railroad depot. This roundabout means of shipping the mine's ore was certainly frustrating. But just one year later, a railroad was completed from Cataldo to Wardner Junction, and in 1887, a route running all the way to Wallace was finished. These railroad improvements greatly enhanced the mine's production ability, and by 1892, Bunker Hill and Sullivan ore was shipped to a smelter in Helena, MT. The mine would later acquire its own smelter in Tacoma, Washington.

Under the early management of Simon Gannett Reed, Bunker Hill and Sullivan attempted to reduce hourly wages, to which the miners responded with the formation of the Wardner Miner's Union. Although the company withdrew its plan, the battle between the company and union workers had begun. After just a short period of time, Reed sold the company in 1892 to a California mine inspector and several San Francisco bankers. Under new management, the company's success grew. By 1899, Bunker Hill and Sullivan employed nearly 400 miners. But not everything was rosy in the mining scene.

Bunker Hill and Sullivan employees received less than the region's standard $3.50 per ten-hour-day wage, and any former or current union members were blacklisted from the company. Angered at the management's policies and unfair treatment of their non-union cohorts, the Wardner Local of the WesternFederation of Miners decided to take action in spring 1899. They demanded that the union be recognized, a request that Bunker Hill and Sullivan firmly denied. In response, the company mandated that any employee who joined a union be fired, and armed guards were added to secure the facility.

The company's refusal of their request, however, didn't stop the Wardner Union. On April 29, 1899, 300-armed men overtook the Northern Pacific train in Wallace and picked up hundreds of men along the way to Bunker Hill. When the union men arrived at the concentrator, they blew the mill to shambles. Within hours, troops were on-site to secure the area, and martial law went into effect on May 3. The involved men were herded into a bullpen, and authorities and mine officials were determined to wipe out unionism. As Bunker Hill rebuilt its concentrator, martial law remained in place until March 1901.

Within a few years, the Bunker Hill and Sullivan Mine was back on its feet. But despite increased productivity, wages remained at an all-time low. In 1956, the company name was changed to Bunker Hill Corporation, but in 1962, the head office closed. Six years later, the company was under the operation of Gulf Resources and Chemical Corporation. Bunker Hill was so profitable that it contributed more than 66% of its operating company's profits. Despite these early gains, the U.S. economic recession eventually forced the mine to close in August 1981.

Despite its closure, the mine has still been in the forefront of area news. Several lawsuits were filed in the early 1980s alleging that the company was knowingly responsible for permanent brain and physical damage to area children due to increased lead emissions. Although the company was aware that its emitted smelter gasses were several times higher in lead than permissible levels, company officials disregarded the safety controls and carried on with operations. A settlement was reached in 1981. Even today, environmentalists are still concerned about Silver Valley's lead levels.

When he first discovered his lode, Noah Kellogg likely didn't fathom the historic legacy his discovery would leave behind. However, his lucky strike led to one of the most productive and notorious silver mines in American and world mining history.

the 1880s. The community honors the memory of Princess Ena, Queen Victoria's daughter who later held the Queen of Spain title. Today, the small town's most recognizeable attraction is its "resort." Previously known as the Snake Pit, Josie's, and the Clark Hotel, the building served as a saloon, depot, hotel, and house of ill-repute before achieving its current use as a family restaurant.

Kingston
8 miles west of Kellogg in Shoshone County

Located on the Mullan Road, Kingston was once known as the liveliest settlement in the Coeur d'Alene Mining District. Established in the early 1880s, Kingston had a population of several hundred during its heyday, but the town was short-lived. In 1890, a flood destroyed Kingston and the town was never rebuilt. Today, the Coeur d'Alene River flows over the original townsite.

T Magee Historic Ranger Station

Contact the U.S.FS Coeur d'Alene River Ranger District-Silverton Office at 752-1221. Merge off I-90 at Exit 43 near Kingston, and proceed 24 miles north on Forest Rd. (FR) 9 to the Prichard junction. Here, merge onto FR 208 and continue 28 miles to FR 6310. Travel 7 miles on the narrow, gravel FR 6310 to the Magee Administrative site and Ranger Cabin.

The Ranger Station's History

The Magee Ranger Station was the site of a local Forest Service Administrative Headquarters from 1908 until 1973.

The first recorded settlement in the Trail Creek-Tepee Creek drainage was a 160-acre homestead claim made by Charles "Charley" Magee in the early 1900s.

In June 1908, the site, including part of Charley Magee's original homestead, was reserved as a Forest Service administration site. Seven men originally manned the headquarters (a log cabin constructed by Charley Magee sometime between 1905 and 1908).

The Forest Service employees at the Magee site performed such seasonal work as constructing and maintaining trails, fighting fires, manning fire lookouts, supervising timber harvests, planting trees, constructing roads with horse-drawn plows, and blister rust control.

Most of the existing buildings at the Magee site were constructed between 1922 and 1935. The Ranger Station was decommissioned in 1973 when the District was divided up and reassigned to the Wallace and Fernan Ranger Districts. In its most active period, about 50 people were seasonally employed at Magee.

The Magee area was also the focus of activities of the Army Corps of Engineers in the early 1940s and the Civilian Conservation Corps in the 1930s. The site was placed on the National Register of Historic Places in 1981.

The Ranger's House

This six-room structure was built of hand-hewn logs with dovetailed corners in 1925. A broad axe was used to square the wall logs. A general renovation by the Civilian Conservation Corps in the 1930s included covering the hewn log walls with simulated round-log siding.

Reprinted from U.S. Forest Service brochure

Idaho Trivia

Although tiny in size, Wallace has left a huge mark on the world. The town is famous as the "Silver Capital of the World." Since mining began in 1884, the area has produced over 1.1 billion ounces of silver.

26 *Lodging*

Enaville
Pop. 50

Originally established as a lumber community on the Union Pacific Railroad, Enaville became a supply center for local miners and sportsmen during

27

Pinehurst
Pop. 1,661

Pinehurst, named after the forest in which it is located, was once a very prosperous and busy mining town founded in the 1880s. Situated along the South Fork of the Coeur d'Alene River, the area once was dotted with huge cottonwoods and cedar trees growing along its banks.

H Kellogg's Jackass
Exit 49 on I-90, Kellogg Business Loop at the Kellogg Information Center

With a grubstake of one jackass and $18.75 worth of flour, bacon, and beans, Noah Kellogg came here prospecting in 1885.

Not far from here, his jackass strayed away. Kellogg finally found his wandering burro grazing on a tremendous outcropping of galena on the hillside above Wardner, about two miles south of here. Such was the discovery of the world-famous Bunker Hill mine, which has produced more than 28 million tons of lead, silver, and zinc – and the end is not yet in sight.

C By the Way RV Campground
907 N. Division, Pinehurst. 682-4855 or (800) 473-2143.

M West Valley Insurance & Realty
Fairway Shopping Center, Pinehurst. 682-2142 or toll-free (800) 473-2143. www.westvalleyrealty.com

28 Food

Smelterville
Pop. 651

Smelterville was considered part of Kellogg in its infancy, but as the Bunker Hill mining operations grew, so did the settlement around that particular location. The new community obtained its own stores and lead and zinc smelters, and soon established itself as a separate settlement when postal services were granted.

29 Food, Lodging

Kellogg
Pop. 2,395

Originally called Jackass after Noah Kellogg's famous donkey who discovered the area's first gold vein, this northern Idaho community was established in 1886. When Robert and Jonathan Ingall platted the town near Milo Creek, they logically christened the fledgling mining community, "Milo." Just one year later, residents decided to change the town's name one last time in honor of Bunker Hill mine discoverer, Noah Kellogg. Developed around the mine, this small town and its economy was devastated when the local smelter and refinery suddenly closed in the early 1980s. In an attempt to recoup its losses and establish a new reputation, Kellogg developed the local ski hill into a major attraction with the world's longest gondola. Lifting skiers nearly 3,400 vertical feet over 3.1 miles, the Silver Mountain gondola is popular year-round for the stunning views it provides of the valley below.

Wardner
Pop. 215

Following Noah Kellogg's famed discovery on Bunker Hill, miners rushed to the Silver Valley and founded Wardner in October 1885. Situated on Milo Creek, early residents first named their town "Kentuck" after the successful owners of the nearby Golden Chest mine. However, when the community applied for postal services, the U.S. Postal Department rejected the town name. After much discussion, community residents finally came up with a new name. James Wardner, although a conman with several get-rich-quick schemes, was quite popular in the area and had done well since engaging in mining activities in

the Silver Valley. To honor Wardner's contributions and promotion of the Bunker Hill and Sullivan mines, residents christened the settlement after him.

H Sunshine Mine Disaster
Exit 54 on I-90; Milepost 3.7 on Old U.S. Hwy. 10 at the Sunshine Mine Memorial

On May 2, 1972, fire broke out in the mine. Carbon monoxide, heat, smoke, and gas spread quickly through the tunnels, severely hampering rescue efforts.

One hundred seventy-six miners were working at various levels. Eighty-five made it out to safety. Seven days later, two miners were found alive. On May 13, the last of the 91 victims were brought out. This was the country's worst hardrock mine disaster since 1917. The Sunshine Silver Mine is a mile deep and has 100 miles of tunnels.

T The Sunshine Mine
Sunshine Mine Memorial located east of Kellogg off I-90 at Exit 54

In September 1884, Dennis and True Blake located the Yankee Boy silver vein a few miles from Kellogg. Although the vein was just six inches wide, it became a top producer just six years later. Along with one other employee, the brothers worked the vein for twenty-five years, shipping out ore every two months that was worth $75 to $400 per ton. After True Blake died, his wife Hattie moved to California and sold the Yankee Boy claims. For the next thirteen years, a line of lessees worked the mine until they faced bankruptcy. Then, in 1921, the Spokane based Sunshine Mining Company purchased the claim, and with help from eastern investors, the mine was up and running again in 1927. New veins were discovered, and soon, the Sunshine Mine reached peak production in 1937. Still in operation, the Sunshine Mine is now renowned as the world's largest all-time silver producer.

But in the mine's great history of success also comes a story of great tragedy. On the morning of May 2, 1972, the normal day shift of 173 men arrived at the Sunshine Mine, ready to go down below the surface and partake in the regular activities of their jobs. After enjoying lunch, however, two electricians walked out into the 3,700-foot level and smelled smoke around 11:40 AM. After a twenty-minute search, smoke began pouring into the search area. At 12:03 PM, the Number 10 shaft foreman told the maintenance foreman to engage the stench-warning system, and at 12:10 PM, hoisting evacuation of men from the 5,600-foot level to the 3,100-foot level began, twelve men at a time. This evacuation continued until the hoistman died at 1:02 PM, leaving several miners trapped below. Despite heroic rescue attempts, a total of only eighty men had made it to the surface by 1:30 PM when it was deemed too dangerous to go back in the mine.

By 2:00 PM, miners' families and rescue teams from U.S. and Canadian mines arrived on the scene, and the fire was assumed to be located between the 3,100 and 3,700 foot levels. At 4:30 PM, five miners were brought to the surface. Poor ventilation in the mine, however, slowed rescue efforts. On May 9, two lucky survivors were found, the last to live through the ordeal. Finally, on May 13, the rest of the miners' bodies were recovered. All had been victims of carbon monoxide poisoning and smoke inhalation.

Known as one of the worst mining disasters in U.S. history, a report on the tragedy revealed that the stench-warning system had never been tested

and was operating at just twenty percent of its capacity. Investigators also discovered that the emergency escape ladders were inadequate, and the twenty-minute delay to search for the fire's source likely cost more lives. After its reconstruction and with new safety measures in place, the Sunshine Mine reopened on December 8, 1972.

In honor of the victims, a twelve-foot steel statue designed by Ken Lonn was erected and depicts a miner at work. Dedicated two years to the date of the tragedy, the memorial is inscribed with the following poem by Phil Batt who would later serve as Idaho's governor:

We Were Miners Then
Our Tongues have not Tasted the Bitter Dust,
The Roar of the Drills has never reached our Ears.
Unfelt to us is the Darkness of the Shafts.
Yet We Are Idahoans
And We Were Miners Then.
We are Farmers.
We Run the Water from Melted Snows
Onto Parched Desert Soil
The Planted Seeds Take Root and Grow
The Harvest Fills our Granaries
The Pits are Strange to Us
But We Are Idahoans
And We Were Miners Then.
We are Loggers.
We are your Neighbors,
We Share the High Country with you.
But We Sing our Song
To the Buzzing of the Chainsaws
And do our Dance on Spinning Logs
There is no Room in the Mine
For our Trees to Fall.
But We Are Idahoans
And We Were Miners Then.
We are Cattlemen, Innkeepers, Merchants,
Men of the Law and Men of the Cloth
Ours are a Thousand Trades.
But only you go into the Bowels of the Earth
To do your Daily Chores.
Yet We Are Idahoans
And We Were Miners Then.
Yes We Were Miners:
We Waited in Spirit at
The Mouth of the Pit
Asked in Unison at the News of the Dead
Joined in the Jubilation
At the Rescue of the Living
Marveled at the Poise of
the Tiny Community
And We Became Strong:
The Flux of the Widow's Tears
Welded your Strength to Our Bodies
And We Were All Idahoans
And We Were All Miners
And We Were All Proud.

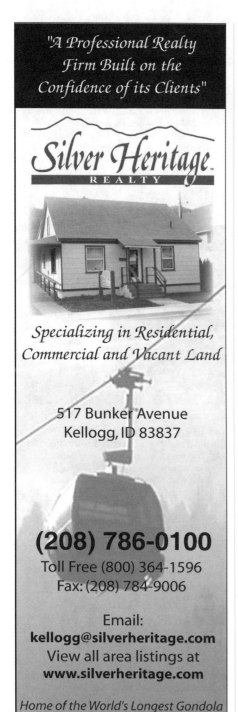
T Crystal Gold Mine Tour

Silver Valley Rd., Kellogg. 783-4653. Take Exit 54 off I-90, and proceed to the Miner's Memorial. Bear west (left) onto Silver Valley Rd., and drive 2 miles to the mine.

This tour provides visitors with the opportunity to view an authentic 1880s gold mine. In 1879, early gold prospector, Tom Irwin, discovered a gold vein here and mined it for three years. Before leaving his mine and cabin, Irwin blasted the hillside down to cover the min, but left all his tools and mine car inside. It appears that Irwin had every intention of returning to the Kellogg area, but he never did, and his whereabouts remain unknown. For the next 100 years, Irwin's mine remained hidden. In 1991, the owner noticed water trickling from the hillside, and he partially uncovered the mine's entrance. However, it was not until 1996 that the mine was sold to the current owner

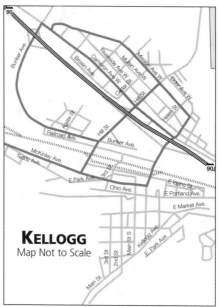

KELLOGG
Map Not to Scale

and transformed into a unique and informative tour about Idaho's rich mining legacy.

Transported back in time, visitors will walk through a 550 foot drift while following a gold-bearing quartz vein and learning about the mine's history. During the mine's 100 year closure, smith-sonite crystals formed on the walls, and displays of high-grade gold and silver are highlighted. Visitors are also privy to hand-steeling demonstrations on this easy walking tour. Recommended by AAA and *Horizon Air Magazine*, the Crystal Gold Mine Tour provides educational fun for the entire family. The mine is open daily year round with ticket prices as follows: adults $10, senior citizens $8.50, and youth under 17 $7.50, with special discounts for school tour groups. The mine is open 10 AM to 4 PM November 1 to April 1 and 9 AM to 6 PM April 2 to October 31. Visitors are encouraged to bring cameras and a light jacket as the average mine temperature is 48 degrees Fahrenheit.

T Shoshone Golf Club

Merge off I-90 at the Big Creek Exit (Exit 54) between Kellogg and Wallace

Situated atop Gold Mountain, this 9-hole course offers outstanding views of the Silver Valley lying below. Covering hilly terrain, the course includes two sets of tees on each hole and encompasses 6,405 yards. The course is rated as a par 72 for men and par 74 for women.

T Pinehurst Golf Course

11 Country Club Ln., Kellogg. 682-2013.

The Pinehurst Golf Course is nestled in Idaho's beautiful Silver Valley and is open to the public. Rated at a par 72, this 18-hole course includes a small stream that cuts in and out of play, providing a challenge to golfers of all abilities. Tee times are unnecessary on weekdays, but are recommended for weekends. Range fees are $18 for 18 holes and $12 for 9 holes.

T Staff House Museum

820 McKinley Avenue, Kellogg. 786-4141.

Locally referred to as the Shoshone County Mining and Smelting Museum, the Staff House Museum is full of interesting tidbits regarding the mining boom at Bunker Hill. The building housing the museum is also historic. The Bunker Hill and Sullivan Mining Company built the two-story home in 1906 as a wedding present for Manager Stanley Easton and his new bride. Although the

family lived quite comfortably in this residence, they moved to Couer d'Alene in 1920, and the home was converted into a residence for single Bunker Hill staff members (whereby the museum draws its name). In 1940, the residence was moved to its current location, and in 1986, the Staff House Museum opened its doors.

Thirteen exhibit rooms house numerous historical photos, rock and mineral displays, mining history and old mining equipment, impressive facts regarding Bunker Hill's 96 years of operation, a 3D model of the underground mine, and an art gallery. The museum is open 10 AM to 5 PM daily May through September. Admission is $4 for adults ages 19-54, $3 for seniors, $1 for youth ages 6-18, free for those under 6, $6 per family, plus special group rates.

T Silver Valley

Contact the Historic Silver Valley Chamber of Commerce at 784-0821.

Cradled between the Coeur d'Alene and Bitterroot Mountain Ranges, the Silver Valley prides itself on a rich history and stunning scenery. Although hopes of striking it rich with gold initially drew miners to present-day Idaho, northern Idaho's treasure would soon prove to be silver.

After the gold rush panned out in nearby Murray, Noah Kellogg set off to the South Fork of the Coeur d'Alene where he discovered high-grade galena ore. Returning a second time with the support of new partners, Kellogg verified his claim and his Bunker Hill and Sullivan Mine soon became one of the richest silver mines in the world. Silver riches made the Coeur d'Alene Mining District famous, and miners from all across North America flocked to the "Silver Valley."

Today, mining activity in historic Silver Valley has decreased, but it nonetheless remains an important economic mainstay. A more recent find are the recreational treasures awaiting valley residents and tourists. Amid breathtaking scenery, the Silver Valley offers hiking, mountain biking, cross-country and downhill skiing, hunting, ATV riding, camping, picnicking, and abundant wildlife viewing.

For early settlers, Silver Valley was a dream come true, and this heritage carries through to this day.

T Wardner Museum

652 Main St., Wardner. 786-2641.

Situated in downtown Wardner, this community museum features a plethora of area history. The museum houses a collection of photos and regional memorabilia highlighting early settlers' lives and the town's mining heritage.

T Wardner Cemetery

East off Division St., Wardner. Contact the Historic Silver Valley Chamber of Commerce at 784-0821.

Amid the many miners' graves who helped work the Silver Valley and turn it into one of the most profitable mining districts in the world is the burial site for Noah Kellogg. Kellogg was responsible for discovering the Bunker Hill lode in 1885. His find paved the way for silver mining activities, and his grave is marked with a fence and monument.

TV Silver Mountain

610 Bunker Ave. (Exit 49 off I-90), Kellogg. 783-1111 or (800) 204-6428. www.silvermt.com

Skiing has been a popular pastime in the Silver Valley and on Wardner Peaks since the late 1960s. After dropping the name Jackass and Silverhorn, the ski area adopted its present name of Silver Mountain. Despite the popularity of skiing, a major problem existed in the 1980s that drove potential skiers away – navigation of the steep road leading to the mountain's base. In response, Kellogg city councilman, Wayne Ross, proposed that a gondola be built to carry skiers from town to the mountaintop.

With the help of Von Roll Tramways of Switzerland, the world's longest single stage person gondola was completed in just a year and opened on June 30th, 1990. The resort itself also received a makeover in time for the 1990 season opening, and the area is now known as a year-round outdoor playground.

Dubbed one of skiing's biggest secrets by *Ski Magazine*, Silver Mountain offers 1,500 acres with both intermediate and expert runs. But the resort's activity doesn't die down at the end of ski season. During the summer months, visitors can buy day or season passes for the scenic 3.1-mile gondola ride or chairlift passes taking them to an incredible world of outdoor beauty and fun. Mountain biking and bike rentals are offered atop the mountain, as well as a paintball course, disc golf, hiking trails, a fire tower lookout, living history performances, and a popular summer concert series held in the resort's open-air amphitheater. The resort is open Wednesday through Sunday, and pre-season ski passes are offered at a discounted rate.

VS Excelsior Cycle
21 Railroad Ave., Kellogg. 786-3751.

L Super 8 -Kellogg
601 Bunker Ave., Kellogg. 783-1234 or (800) 784-5443. www.super8kellogg.com

Access year-round entertainment and outdoor recreation from the Super 8 Motel in Kellogg. Consistently receiving outstanding ratings and dubbed "the Souped Up Super 8" by Horizon magazine, the quiet hotel offers first class accommodations at economy prices. Exceptionally clean rooms feature an inviting atmosphere, cable TV, and free local calls, and children under 12 stay free. In addition, free coffee and an indoor pool and hot tub are available 24 hours. Guests also enjoy ski/bike storage, laundry services, and a continental breakfast including fruit, English muffins, bagels, toast, cereal, numerous condiments, and juice and coffee. Situated two blocks off I-90, the Kellogg Super 8 is on the Trail of the

Coeur d'Alene and across the street from the Silver Mountain Gondola. Make yourself at home and experience superior service and genuine hospitality!

L The Trail Motel
206 W. Cameron, Kellogg. 784-1161.

Centrally located and easily accessible off I-90 at Exit 50, The Trail Motel prides itself on offering clean, comfortable accommodations at affordable rates. Each quiet room features cable television, private telephones, refrigerators, and air-conditioning. The motel also offers convenient access to area attractions and shopping. Silver Mountain Ski Resort is just one-half mile away, offering year-round recreation and the opportunity to ride the world's longest gondola. Winding next to the hotel on its scenic journey from Mullan to Plummer is northern Idaho's 72-mile "Trails of the Coeur d'Alene" bike path, while one of the nation's most renowned car dealerships is just one block away. On your next visit to Kellogg, stay at the reasonably priced Trail Motel and discover all that this town offers.

M Silver Heritage Realty
517 Bunker Ave., Kellogg. 786-0100 or toll-free (800) 364-1596.
www.silverheritagerealty.com

Silver Heritage Realty is conveniently located next to the Kellogg Super 8 and across from the world's longest gondola base. With years of regional experience, these real estate professionals have received excellence awards from area realty associations and possess extensive knowledge about a variety of real estate transactions. The friendly staff is proud to serve the communities of northern Idaho, including Kellogg, Wardner, Smelterville, Page, Pinehurst, Kingston, Cataldo, Rose Lake, N. Fork, Osburn, Silverton, Wallace, and Mullan. A member of the Kellogg Area Chamber of Commerce, Silver Heritage Realty guarantees the special care and attention each customer deserves in locating the perfect residential, commercial, or recreational property.

M Tomlinson Black Realty
501 Bunker Ave., Kellogg. 783-1121 or (800) 858-5582. & 518 Bank St., Wallace. 556-0223. www.tomlinsonblack.com

Tomlinson Black has been ranked number one in sales in the inland northwest for the past four years and plans to uphold this tradition. Committed for twenty-eight years to the communities it serves, Tomlinson Black Silver Valley provides offices in both Kellogg and Wallace with twelve professional agents ready to help you discover Silver Valley and its numerous attractions. Whether you're interested in a vacation home or permanent residence, every agent is prepared to assist you in obtaining the right property in the shortest time possible at a price that fits your budget. Affiliated with RELO, the largest and most successful network of real estate agents, Tomlinson Black Silver Valley is your full-service realty agency offering the education, dedication, and affordable mortgages you need to make your real estate dreams a reality.

M Coeur d'Alene Area B & B Association
683-0572. www.bb-cda.com

M Kellogg-Historic Silver Salley Chamber of Commerce
10 Station Ave., Kellogg. 784-0821.
www.historicsilvervalleychamberofcommerce.com

30 *Food*

Osburn
Pop. 1,545

This town site was originally a construction camp for the Mullan Rd. After construction was complete, the town was abandoned. When the Union Pacific Railroad built a line through the area, railroad officials platted out a town on the former construction camp and named it "Georgetown." The name was chosen in honor of Lee George, one of the townsite's owners. However, when residents applied for a post office, the postal department decided that too many Georgetowns already existed in Idaho Territory and across the nation. In response, residents renamed their town after Bill Osborne, the first postmaster and owner of the town's first store. The postal department misspelled the application request, and the name has been Osburn since 1877.

31

Silverton
Pop. 800

Originally named West Wallace for its proximity to the community of Wallace, the name was changed in 1941 to reflect the large amounts of silver ore mined here. The town's most notable building is a brick structure visible from the highway. Erected between 1916 and 1917, the $2 mil-

Kellogg	Jan	Feb	March	April	May	June	July	Aug	Sep	Oct	Nov	Dec	Annual
Average Max. Temperature (F)	34.9	40.9	48.8	58.7	68.0	75.3	85.2	84.1	73.7	60.0	44.0	35.9	59.1
Average Min. Temperature (F)	20.3	23.4	28.3	33.7	40.2	46.3	49.8	48.0	41.9	34.8	28.7	23.0	34.9
Average Total Precipitation (in.)	3.78	2.83	2.91	2.35	2.57	2.20	1.02	1.14	1.71	2.66	3.78	3.89	30.83
Average Total Snowfall (in.)	18.7	10.0	5.6	0.7	0.0	0.0	0.0	0.0	0.0	0.3	5.0	13.9	54.2
Average Snow Depth (in.)	6	4	1	0	0	0	0	0	0	0	0	2	1

lion building is highlighted with several dormer windows and was initially operated as a county hospital. Although the structure still stands, the hospital it once held is long gone.

V Floating the Upper Coeur d'Alene River

Coeur d'Alene River Ranger District, Silverton. 752-1221.

The River

Imagine yourself as part of the last log drive on this river in 1933…or you're bringing up a pack string loaded with supplies; or just take pleasure in the present with a scenic float trip down the Coeur d'Alene River.

The river meanders 55 miles between Senator Creek and the town of Cataldo on I-90. Mountain scenery, various rock formations, wildlife, and fish are among the sights waiting for you.

Floaters should check water levels before setting out on a float trip, since navigation can be greatly affected by a relatively small change in stream flow. In the late spring, the river is swift and high with the snowmelt from the mountains. As the warm summer months arrive, the water gradually slows and the river depth drops.

Canoes and rafts may float most of the river until late July. At this time, due to water depth, floating is best from Shoshone Creek downstream. Low water spots may still be encountered in this river stretch. Inner-tubing and some rafting may still be done on the upper section of the river. Life jackets should be worn by everyone floating the river.

Access Areas

The following areas are frequent access points to the Upper Coeur d'Alene River. Average canoe paddling times are provided.

1) Stoney Creek-Swift Creek Bridge: Undeveloped roadside parking. (1 – 1 1/2 hours)
2) Big Hank Bridge: Access is available from the meadow across from Big Hank Campground. (1 hour)
3) Long Pool Bridge: Undeveloped camping and parking. (1 hour)
4) Jupiter Creek Landing: Undeveloped parking. (2 hours)

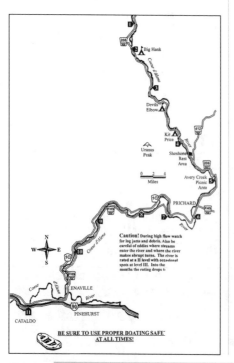

5) Avery Creek Picnic Area: Developed picnic area and parking. (2 hours)
6) Prichard Bridge: Undeveloped parking. (1 – 1 1/2 hours)
7) Bridge at Roads 9 & 530 Junction: Undeveloped roadside parking. (4 hours)
8) Graham Meadow: Undeveloped roadside parking. (1 1/2 hours)
9) Spring Creek Access Point: 2 hours
10) Bumblebee Bridge Access Point: Undeveloped parking area. (5 hours)
11) Cataldo Access Point: Undeveloped roadside parking. (5 hours)

During high flow, watch for log jams and debris. Also be careful of eddies where streams enter the river and where the river makes abrupt turns. The river is rated at a II level with occasional spots at level III. Into the summer months, the rating drops to I.

Rules & Regulations

Campsites: Camp only on Federal or State land unless you have received prior permission from the private landowner! Select unused campsites; avoid heavily used areas. Use only dead wood for your camp needs. Use camp stoves or charcoal, if possible.

Fire: Select a site on level ground, sheltered from high wind and away from heavy brush, logs, tree trunks, and overhanging branches. Clear the ground to mineral soil. Keep your fire small; use a circle of small stones to contain it. Never leave your fire unattended. Put the fire dead out. Take care while smoking on shore.

Pack In – Pack Out: Keep the river clean. Pack out everything in a litter bag. Use burnable containers, if possible. Remove all evidence of any temporary structure when you leave. Leave the river scene undisturbed. Stay well back from the river when cleaning camp utensils. Keep soap and detergent out of the river. Dump wash and waste away from camp and the river. Dispose of wet organic garbage and fish parts the same as human waste. Clean fish away from the river in water you have carried for the purpose.

Human Waste: Select a screened spot at least 100 feet from the river or camp. Dig a hole no deeper than eight inches. After use, replace the soil and tramp in the sod. Nature will do the rest.

Water: Surface or spring water along the river should be considered unfit for human consumption. Boil it vigorously for 3 to 5 minutes, or bring water from home.

Difficulty Level: At the peak run-off period (April to June), you may encounter some class III rapids. Always scout ahead. Snags and deadheads are common.

International Scale for Grading the Difficulty of River Routes

Overview: Grade I is easy enough for the beginners who know the basics of boat handling technique for white water. It is preferable for a beginner to ride in a two-man boat with an experienced partner on Grade II water. Additionally, during high water the river grades increase, usually one grade.

I Easy (Practiced Beginner): Sand banks, bends without difficulty, occasional small rapids with waves regular and low. Correct course easy to find, but care is needed with minor obstacles like pebble banks, fallen trees, etc., especially on narrow rivers. River speed is less than hard back-paddling speed.

II Medium (Intermediate): Fairly frequent but unobstructed rapids, usually with regular waves, easy eddies, and easy bends. Course generally easy to recognize. River speeds occasionally exceed hard back-paddling speed.

III Difficult (Experienced): Maneuvering in rapids necessary. Small falls, large regular waves covering boat, numerous rapids. Main current may swing under bushes, branches, or overhangs. Course not always easily recognizable. Current speed is usually less than fast-forward paddling speed.

IV Very Difficult (Experienced): Long, rocky rapids with difficult and turbulent passages requiring precise maneuvering. Scouting from shore is necessary and rescue is difficult. Not for open canoes or kayaks.

Reprinted from U.S. Forest Service brochure

32 Food, Lodging

Wallace
Pop. 960

Stepping into this town cradled in the bottom of a narrow valley and surrounded with forested hills brings visitors into one of the most interesting towns in Idaho's mining history. Situated near the convergence of Canyon, Placer, and Ninemile Creeks with the South Fork of the Coeur d'Alene River, Wallace was initially called Cedar Swamp after the cedar groves surrounding the area. In 1884, the name was changed to Placer Center after lucrative placer mining began. When Colonel W.R. Wallace, site owner and member of the city council, applied for postal services in 1888, the settlement's name changed a final time to Wallace. Shortly thereafter, Wallace became the first incorporated Idaho town in Shoshone County, and business boomed. As a mining supply center, seven freight trains passed through town each day. Soon, the town reached 2,000 inhabitants and supported a variety of economic activity: five doctors, one teacher, one preacher, a power company supplying electric lighting to residents for just $1.50 a month, a renowned printing press powered by Printers Creek, twenty-eight saloon owners, ten lawyers, and one judge who always allowed criminals one drink at a saloon before heading to jail. As hard as Wallace's miners and business owners worked, they also played hard and took advantage of several entertaining events. Drilling contests, prize fights, horse races, hot air balloon festivals, community dances, hunting, fishing, trips to Coeur d'Alene Lake, and local baseball games were favorite pastimes. By early 1890, Wallace was the third largest town in Idaho.

Despite its stellar beginnings, Wallace was hit with disaster. During summer 1890, a devastating fire destroyed the entire business district valued at $500,000. Persevering, business owners bounced back, only to have one-third of the town destroyed again during the Great Idaho Fire of 1910. After this fire, the town's water supply was so limited that the mayor ordered all saloonkeepers to serve free beer in an effort to hydrate residents and ward off a typhoid outbreak.

Today, Wallace has quieted down from its rowdy days as a lively mining town. Still, the town remains much the same architecturally with many well-preserved 19th-century buildings found throughout Wallace and its surrounding foothills. Serving as Shoshone County's county seat, the entire town is listed on the National Historic Register, and several museums can be found detailing Wallace's fascinating past.

Murray
Pop. 100

Although now just a sleepy little town located on Prichard Creek, Murray once boasted a population of 25,000 western thrill-seekers and fortune hunters! The gold rush spurred this town into existence in 1884 along with the help of Civil War vetern, Andrew J. Prichard. Desiring to start a free-thinking religious mountain colony, Prichard traveled to Idaho and Montana in 1878. While searching for a suitable colony location in 1881, Prichard discovered lead placers valued near $42 a pan. He tried to keep his discovery a secret, but he was forced to share the wealth and stake his claim when other prospectors arrived. By early 1884, prospect advertisements from the Northern Pacific Railroad led hundreds of miners to the area, including George Murray.

As thousands of would-be miners settled in the area, the town of "Curry" sprang to life. When George Murray became part-owner of one of the town's building claims, the settlement's name changed to Murraysville. The name was changed one last time in 1885 when the post office shortened the name. That same year, the town received the honor of becoming Shoshone County seat.

Pan mining continued in the area for several years, with dredge mining beginning around 1918. Although the dredge produced over $1 million in profits, it tore apart the land, and evidence of its activity is still visible. The area's gold and silver mines prospered until 1924 before finally shuddering out of profitable business and shooing residents out of town in search of more prosperous claims.

Gem
Pop. 100

Now considered a near ghost town, Gem was named after the area's first mine, the Gem of the Mountain. This small mining settlement was established in 1886 after silver was discovered in its hills. In addition to a having a saloon that was run by the mayor of town, Gem also hosted one of the more famous labor disputes.

In 1892, the price of silver dropped greatly. Many mines around Coeur d'Alene were closed until prices increased. The railroads and smelters agreed to lower their fees and the companies offered to reopen their mines if miners would accept lower wages. However, union miners

balked at the plan and refused to accept the terms. In response, some mining companies hired immigrants to work the mines and protected them with company guards. On July 11, 1892, union miners from the surrounding areas gathered in Gem and began marching toward the mine and mill. They were greeted by armed guards, and shots on both sides broke out. During the exchange, the mill burnt to the ground. Remarkably, only one man was killed with just seven others were injured. The union workers then surrounded the surrendered guards and non-union workers and placed them under careful watch at Gem's Union Hall. Later, as the day and night shift took place, a non-union man crossing the Canyon Creek Bridge was shot down. The mine's guards had had enough. As women and children were escorted to Wallace, an intense gun battle between the guards and union workers took place. Finally, the county sheriff and U.S. marshals arrived, and a conference was held between the union men and the mine manager, A.L. Gross. The non-union men were outnumbered, and union miners gave Gross an ultimatum: surrender the mine or lose it. Since Gross refused to surrender the mine, he lost it. As a result, all non-union workers lost their jobs, were forced to surrender their weapons, and received orders to leave town.

Although the non-union workers complied with the decree, mine owners convinced Governor Wiley to declare martial law. When troops arrived on July 13, the union men were forced to surrender their position. On July 25, twenty-five prisoners were taken to Boise for trial. The men all pleaded not guilty to the charges, but ten were eventually found guilty of contempt of court and sentenced to a short stay in jail. Other prisoners were taken to Coeur d'Alene for a twenty-three day trial where four men were found guilty. All the other prisoners were eventually acquitted.

Despite rounding up several of the union workers, martial law remained in effect in Gem for four months, and the mine was not allowed to reopen until the following year. Although a tense truce was reached in 1892, it was broken in the 1899 Bunker Hill mining incident spurred by the activity of the Western Federation of Miners. As it turns out, the jail sentences for the Gem union workers gave them plenty of opportunity to develop a new and improved union organization, a group that just so happened to call itself the Western Federation of Miners.

Burke
Pop. 80

Situated on Canyon Creek and founded in 1883 with the discovery of silver, Burke was named by its thirty miner residents in 1885. Although Onealville (meaning "one for all") was suggested, the miners decided to honor local miner and politician J. M. Burke. When the U.S. Postal Department tried to change the name to "Bayard," the residents scoffed at the plan, and the post office allowed Burke to remain as the community's official title. Due to the town's very cramped setting, Burke is often recognized as the Idaho community that has been featured on "Ripley's Believe It or Not" twice!

This tiny mining town is only three air miles from its neighbor, Mullan, Idaho, but by road it's 13 miles! In the early years (1884) the town situated in the narrow canyon barely held the miners that came seeking silver in the Tiger and Poorman mines. The Tiger and Poorman mines had to close in 1908 after exhausting their ores. Production of ore now occurs in the Star-Morning mine, which dates back to 1889. A 2,000 foot adit travels south for over two miles from the surface plant at Burke, and the production itself occurs over 8,100 feet

below ground. This makes it the deepest lead-zinc ore body mined in the world. Production is estimated at about 1,000 tones of ore in a single day.

Prichard
Pop. 25

This tiny settlement north of Wallace was named for Andrew J. Prichard, the first prospector to discover gold along the nearby stream in 1881. A post office operated here from 1910 until approximately 1934.

H Frisco Mill
Milepost 5.1 on State Hwy. 4 between Wallace and Burke

During a gun war that broke out between company and union miners here, several boxes of dynamite were exploded, shattering a four-story mill, July 11, 1892.

Northern Pacific Depot Railroad Museum

Overwhelmed by union miners, company managers surrendered. Six fatalities – half from each side – preceded four months of martial law and military occupation by 1,000 soldiers. A long series of battles followed. Resumed in N. Idaho in 1899, this conflict continued in Colorado, Montana, Nevada, and Arizona.

H Burke
Milepost 7.1 on State Hwy. 4

Lead-silver discoveries in 1884 attracted a railroad to Burke by 1887. Hundreds of miners lived there in a canyon so narrow that they scarcely had room for streets.

So in 1888, S. S. Glidden's Tiger Hotel had to be built over, rather than beside, Canyon Creek. Railroad tracks and Burke's only highway also had to run through his hotel. When a second railroad arrived in 1890, its tracks had to be laid in Burke's only street. No other hotel had two railroads, a street, and a stream running through it.

H Wallace
Exit 61 on I-90, Wallace Business Loop at Magnuson Centennial Park

Founded as a mining town in 1884, Wallace became a railroad center in 1887 and Shoshone County seat in 1889.

Rebuilt after a disastrous fire in 1890, Wallace has preserved its pioneer mining heritage. North Idaho's two million-acre forest fire was

stopped here in 1910, and business buildings of that era survive in an impressive historic district. A museum in Wallace's restored 1901 Northern Pacific Depot, on Sixth St., interprets the region's railway history.

H Lead-Silver Mines
Exit 61 on I-90, Wallace Business Loop at Magnuson Centennial Park

In more than a century after rich lodes were discovered in 1884, this valley has become North and South America's largest producer of silver.

More than $5 billion worth of lead, silver, and zinc – including more than a billion ounces of silver – have come from these camps. Old mines and towns at Burke, Kellogg, Murray, Mullan, Osburn, and Wardner can be reached from Wallace. First, visit the Coeur d'Alene Mining Museum at 509 Bank Street in Wallace to review the region's mining development.

H Murray Gold Fields
Exit 61 on I-90, Wallace Business Loop at Magnuson Centennial Park

After prospecting north of here from 1878 to 1882, A.J. Prichard showed a few fortune hunters where to find gold. More than a year later, a horde of miners rushed there to start Eagle City.

A permanent camp followed at Murray, January 22, 1884. As Shoshone County seat (1885-98) and this area's gold center, Murray flourished for more than a decade. Important buildings – a courthouse, Masonic Hall, and other landmarks – have been preserved there to reflect life in a gold rush camp a century ago.

T Eagle City
I-90 to Ninemile Canyon Rd.; follow this paved road to Murray, and continue 3.5 miles northwest of Murray.

Miners came in droves to Eagle City (Eagle) and founded the "capital of the Couer d' Alenes" in 1883. While some historians say the town was named after an empty eagle's nest in a nearby tree, others argue that eagles nested in the trees lining Eagle Creek and the town was dubbed after the creek.

Whichever interpretation is more accurate, it is known that Eagle City prospered in 1884. Complete with two newspapers and thousands of hopeful miners, the town also drew famous his-

torical characters. In 1884, Courtney Meek, the son of famous trapper and guide, Joe Meek, was listed on the town's election ballots. Wyatt, James, and Warren Earp also briefly settled in Eagle City. On April 26, 1884 the brothers bought the White Elephant Saloon for $132 and ran the popular establishment in a tent. By the end of 1884, however, the brothers had left and several other disillusioned miners abandoned Eagle City for more prosperous settlements nearby. The town finally died in 1893 as the remaining businesses moved to Murray.

T Sierra Silver Mine Tour
420 5th St., Wallace. 752-5151. www.silverminetour.org

On this tour, view the underground world of hard-rock mining in one of the world's richest silver districts. Established in 1900, the Sierra Silver Mine's ore was never continuously mined as it wasn't rich enough to warrant such activity. In 1982, the mine received its current role as a travel destination and is now one of the most popular tours in the Northwest.

Leaving from the ticket office, spectators will board a vintage trolley and travel through historic downtown Wallace to the mine's entrance. Hardhats are issued at the historic mine's portal, and a retired miner serves as guide while visitors walk through the mine's main drift. Inside, visitors are privy to the work, daily experiences, and risks associated with the mining lifestyle, and active equipment displays illustrate both historic and modern techniques used to mine silver, lead, zinc, copper, and gold. Visitors are encouraged to bring cameras as well as a light jacket since the mine's average temperature is 48 degrees Fahrenheit! Tours begin at 9 AM and depart from the ticket office every 30 minutes. In May, June, and September, the last tour leaves at 4 PM, and in July and August, at 6 PM. Ticket prices for the one-hour fifteen-minute tour are $9 for adults, $8 for seniors over 60, and $7.50 for youth ages 4-16. For safety reasons, no children under age 4 are permitted on the tour.

T Sixth Street Theater and Melodrama
212 Sixth St., Wallace. 752-8871 or 1-877-SIXTHST. www.sixthstreetmelodrama.com

Lively year-round theater is found in Wallace's oldest standing wood frame structure. Providing entertainment for more than twenty years, the local thespian troupe performs spirited comedies, old-fashioned Westernmelodramas, and musicals that the whole family will enjoy. Booing and hissing are part of the fun as the audience is involved in the action. Ticket prices are $10 to $12 with special family rates available for all shows. The box office opens two hours before performances, and audience members are asked to pick up their tickets at least one hour prior to curtain call. Call or check them out online for the latest schedule of upcoming performances.

T Sprag Pole Museum
Main St. in the town center, Murray. 682-3901.

The near ghost town of Murray is filled with a colorful past, and this heritage is captured in the many unique collections and exhibits found at the Sprag Pole Museum. The building was named after the supporting poles needed to hold up the wooden walls during winter when the facility was first constructed as an inn and saloon. Today, five connected buildings with a combined 10,000 square feet of space offer some of the most interesting relics and history in Idaho's panhandle.

Memorabilia includes mining machinery, a vintage barbershop and doctor's office, an old fashioned school room and post office, a replica of the bedroom of Murray's most famous madam, Maggie "Mollie B'Damm" Hall, thousands of historic photos, Native American artifacts, and the plow that began Lookout Pass in 1921. In addition, over 100 collectible exhibits are on display, covering such topics as radios, phonographs, phones, rocks, bullets, and saloon jugs. Admission is always free, but visitors should call for museum hours.

T Wallace District Mining Museum
509 Bank St., Wallace. 556-1592.

The beautiful mountains and valleys surrounding Wallace are home to one of the world's richest silver mining regions. With production exceeding one billion ounces of silver, the region's heritage is based largely upon a mining tradition. This rich heritage is captured and preserved for both residents and tourists in the Wallace District Mining Museum. Artifacts, historical photographs, commissioned paintings, and videos illustrate the hard life endured by hundreds of miners and their families in the Silver Valley. Unique exhibits include the world's largest silver dollar, measuring 3 feet in diameter and weighing 150 pounds. The museum is open 8 AM to 8 PM daily in July and August and 8 AM to 6 PM daily May, June, and September. During the rest of the year, museum hours are 9 AM to 4 PM weekdays and 10 AM to 3 PM on Saturdays. Admission is $2 for adults ages 16-54, $1.50 for seniors, $.50 for youth ages 6-15, and free for children under 6. A special $5 rate for a school bus (up to grade 12) and $20 rate for tour busses is offered.

T Oasis Bordello Museum
605 Cedar St., Wallace. 753-0801.

The history of early mining towns is often filled with the lives of men who both worked hard and played hard, and Wallace is no exception. In this richest silver mining district in the world, it wasn't long before men outnumbered women 200 to 1, and several enterprising women decided to develop the town's first red light district. In 1895, Wallace's Bi Metallic Building was a popular hotel and saloon. At some undetermined date, however, the saloon became the Oasis Rooms, just one of the town's five popular brothels. The Oasis Rooms quickly became a favorite local stop, and eventually, the Oasis was the only brothel continuing to offer its one-of-a-kind service. Although the ladies changed, the popularity of the Oasis Rooms remained the same as the business operated until 1988, fifteen years after Idaho's governor criminalized prostitution.

Mysteriously, when the final ladies departed in January 1988, they left nearly everything behind, including clothes, makeup, personal items, and even dirty dishes in the sink. This atmosphere has been preserved, and today, visitors can take an accurate guided tour of the establishment. Information gleaned from the ladies themselves,

previous clients, local police officers, the women's hairstylists, and former maids and bouncers is tastefully presented, and the tour has been praised from past clients to church groups. In the basement, visitors can also view a still and old wine press left from the town's early days. Tours are offered on the half hour from 9:30 AM to 6:30 PM Monday through Saturday and 10 AM to 5 PM on Sundays. Admission is $5 for person, but the main floor gift shop and Robert Thomas Murals are free.

T Northern Pacific Depot Railroad Museum
219 6th St., Wallace. 752-0111.

Railroads have played an important role in this region dating back to 1887. When the railroad announced its plans in 1901 to arrive in Wallace, a beautiful chateau-style building was constructed. The building has its own unique story as the bricks imported from China were originally destined for an upscale hotel in Tacoma, Washington. When those plans didn't materialize, the bricks were transported to Wallace. In 1976, the building was named to the National Register of Historic Places, and the depot operated until 1980 as a stop for the Northern Pacific's Yellowstone Park Line. When the trains no longer came, the building became home to the renowned Northern Pacific Depot Railroad Museum.

Stepping inside, visitors are transported back in time when the railroad was the finest transportation available. Exhibits explore the major role the railroad had in developing the Silver Valley Mining District, old railroad artifacts, and numerous historic photos. In May, residents and tourists alike participate in the annual Depot Day that celebrates railroad nostalgia. Activities include live music, children's activities, various ethnic and traditional food booths, melodramas, model train exhibits, and an opportunity to send a Morse code telegram from the depot's restored telegraph office. The museum is open from 10 AM to 3 PM Monday through Saturday in April; 9 AM to 5 PM daily in May; 9 AM to 7 PM daily June through September; and 10 AM to 3 PM Monday through Saturday from October 1 to October 15. Admission prices are $2 for adults, $1.50 for adults over 60, $1 for youth ages 6-16, and free for those children under 6. Special group and family rates are available.

T Settler's Grove of Ancient Cedars
From Prichard, drive east up Prichard Creek to the junction of Prichard and Eagle Creeks. Turn onto Forest Road (FR) 152, and at the junction with FR 805, go left 5 miles up the west fork of FR 805 to the grove. The grove is marked with a large sign.

Comparable in size and beauty to California's Redwoods, the Settler's Grove of Ancient Cedars escaped the horrific 1910 Idaho fire and was set aside in 1970 as a natural botanical area by the Idaho Panhandle National Forest Supervisor. The dense, relatively undisturbed ecosystem features western red cedars measuring up to thirty feet in diameter with life spans hundreds of years old. The 180-acre grove also features western white pine, Engelmann spruce, grand fir, and hemlock. A short trail winds underneath a canopy of leaves through the grove.

T Bedroom Goldmine
Downtown Murray. 682-4394.

The hunger for gold apparently lingered in Murray long after the 1800s gold rush. In the mid 1950s, a man decided he wanted a placer mine of

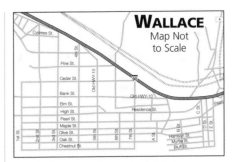

WALLACE
Map Not to Scale

his own, but since it was cold outside, he came up with a unique idea. In order to stay warm, the man used a vacant bedroom in his home and dug through his floor thirty-six feet down to bedrock. After tunneling around the bedrock, the man's dreams came true. He located a sizeable eleven-ounce nugget of gold. Today, a bar marks the spot of the unusual discovery with pictures of the find available on-site.

T Mining Heritage Exhibition
I-90 Exit 61, Wallace. Contact the Wallace Chamber of Commerce at 753-7151.

The Historic Wallace Visitor Center offers individuals an inside look at the region's rich mining history. The free outdoor exhibit includes machinery and artifacts used throughout the past to mine the area's abundant silver.

T John Mullan Park
5th St., Wallace. Contact the Wallace Chamber of Commerce at 753-7151.

Wallace's John Mullan Park honors the legacy of Captain John Mullan. Undertaking an engineering feat, Mullan created the "Mullan Wagon Road" between 1859 and 1862 as a military route later used by a few westward bound emigrants. The park is a peaceful spot to enjoy an afternoon picnic and includes a statue of the early Silver Valley developer.

T Mount Pulaski
1.5 miles southwest of Wallace

Located just outside Wallace, Mount Pulaski juts 5,480 feet into the Earth's atmosphere and towers over the historic mining community. The peak honors Edward Pulaski, longtime Burke Canyon resident, first ranger of the Wallace Ranger District, hero of the 1910 fire, and inventor of the Pulaski tool.

T Historic Wallace Downtown District Walking Tour
Contact the Wallace Chamber of Commerce at 753-7151.

With dozens of buildings dating back to the turn of the century, it's no surprise that the entire town of Wallace is listed on the National Register of Historic Places. Although nearly all of Wallace's original buildings (save two) were destroyed in an early 1890s fire, residents immediately reconstructed their village. Today, the town reflects the efforts of these first settlers, and most buildings retain much of their original architectural accents and character.

Northern Pacific Railroad Depot & Museum
219 6th Street
In 1902, Wallace's elegant brick depot was completed in a chateau style. The elaborate structure is fashioned out of bricks imported from China and has long been considered one of the Pacific Northwest's finest depots. Before being moved in 1986, the building originally stood on the river's north side.

EDWARD PULASKI: HERO & INVENTOR

Born in 1870, Edward "Big Ed" Pulaski had a pioneering, ingenious spirit from the day of his birth. As he matured, Edward settled in Idaho and Montana and began life as a prospector. But it wasn't long before his true passion arose and he found his calling with the U.S. Forest Service. In 1894, Edward joined the U.S. Forest Service and became a well-respected ranger known for his excellent judgment and concern for the Coeur d'Alene National Forest.

As a ranger, Edward assumed administrative tasks as well as firefighting duties. It wasn't long before he grew weary of lugging the standard forest service firefighting tools into the backcountry – rakes, axes, hoes, and shovels. Edward not only found the system draining of firefighter's strength, but also completely inefficient in most effectively fighting and containing fires. He knew that there must be a better way to fight fires.

Edward's invention ideas, however, were interrupted with the arrival of the Great Idaho Fire of 1910. Supervising a crew of 150 men in Placer Creek outside Wallace, Edward soon realized that his crew was in the danger zone. Although residents of Wallace had lit a fire in an attempt to save their town with a back burn, they inadvertently trapped Edward and his crew between two walls of encroaching flames. On August 21, Edward rounded up forty-five of the closest men, forcing them at gunpoint into the long War Eagle mineshaft. To avoid suffocating on the fire gasses, smoke, and ashes, Edward ordered his men to lie face down. Most passed out as Edward guarded the entrance and attempted to put out the approaching flames with his bare hands and water from the mine. Eventually, he too collapsed.

When the men awoke the next morning, they discovered that just five crewmembers had died. Badly injured, the men followed Edward through burning logs and smoking ashes back to Wallace. Edward then bought dinner for his men at the town's only surviving restaurant, escorted the injured to the hospital (where he also was briefly treated), and returned home to his wife and child who believed he had surely died in the disaster.

As the flames of the 1910 fire sunk into the earth, it became apparent that the devastation was beyond anything anyone had ever seen. Unlike many rangers of the day who left the Forest Service in search of new careers, Edward served out the rest of his career in the Wallace, Idaho Ranger District. With his help, the Wallace community was rebuilt and the surrounding forests were replanted.

Edward also had time to return to his great invention. Naturally possessing a few blacksmithing skills, Edward experimented with the standard issue firefighting tools. Eventually, a brilliant idea came to him. Edward took a double-bladed axe and rotated one blade sideways. He had just created a single hand tool with an axe-head and hoe that would soon become known worldwide as the "Pulaski." Although Edward died in 1931, his genius lives on.

The Pulaski hand tool is now the tool of choice for firefighters and trailblazers across the world. A basic firefighting resource, the Pulaski features a thirty-six inch handle with the versatility to chop or dig. For firefighters, the tool represents the leadership of its creator and a giant step forward in managing forests and backcountry firefighting.

The Jameson Hotel
304 6th Street
This pair of concrete block three-story buildings was built for Theodore Jameson in 1907 to replace the original Jameson Hotel destroyed in the 1890 fire. The buildings are missing their original matching cornices, but the interior has been restored with period furnishings throughout. A ghost named Maggie reportedly haunts the hotel.

Sweets Hotel
308 Sixth Street
The three-story Sweets Hotel was completed in 1907 and includes its original molded window beams. Constructed from concrete blocks, the hotel features simple lines with historic photos of the area displayed inside.

Camia Building
521 Sixth Street
Joseph Turner completed the three-story red brick Camia Building in October 1890. Featuring overhanging metal cornices, the building's second and third floor window frames are accented with terra cotta squares. A chimney fire here is believed to be the culprit of the disastrous fire that destroyed Wallace's downtown area in the 1890s.

Kelly Building
212 Sixth Street
This two-story, flat-roofed building was completed in 1891 and is thought to be the business district's oldest wood-frame structure. Throughout its history, the Kelly Building has served as a hotel and hardware store, and at one time, rented upstairs rooms to ladies of the night. Today, the building is home to the Sixth Street Melodrama.

Wallace Carnegie Library
River & Fifth Streets
The Wallace Carnegie Library features a Renaissance Neoclassic architectural design and was constructed between 1910 and 1911. With a low-pitched roof, the building features three-inch thick doors accented with reproduced leaded glass. The building served as a template for several other small-town libraries across America and was restored in 1999.

Elks Temple
419 Cedar Street
Spokane, Washington architect, Charles I. Carpenter, designed this 1924 building in a Second Renaissance Real style. The temple was dedicated on June 6, 1925, and civic organizations have been allowed to use the building since 1927.

Day Building
500 Cedar Street
Situated on the corner of Cedar and Fifth Streets, this 1905 building was originally constructed to house the "Hope Hospital." But when the Day brothers acquired the building in 1916, they located their mining business on the upper floor, and a grocery store soon occupied the building's west end. In 1992, the Day Building was refashioned into the Brooks Hotel.

Furst Building
517 Cedar Street
In 1900, Norwegian John G. Furst constructed this three-story brick building featuring cast iron cornices and decorative window moldings. The first floor housed a soda fountain, ice cream parlor, eight glass card rooms, a dance floor, and a sandwich bar while the second and third stories were home to over forty hotel rooms and suites.

Eagles Building
515 Cedar
Spokane architects, Galbraith and Hall, designed the ornate Eagles Lodge completed in 1905. The building features local concrete and distinctive silver and gold accents from area mines.

Follett Building
518 Cedar Street
The one-story brick Follett Building was completed in 1898 and was first home to Fonks General Store before being used as a butcher shop and theater. The building, once owned by an entrepreneur named Funklerudd, retains much of its vintage character despite two remodeling projects to the façade.

Holohan-McKinlay Building
Cedar & Sixth Streets
Constructed between 1900 and 1901, this building is sometimes called the O'Neil-Samuels Building. Despite a discrepancy in its naming, it is known that this building once housed five separate stores on the first floor at the same time! Throughout the years, professional offices have occupied the second floor with private apartments on the third floor.

Wallace Corner/Hotel
525 Cedar Street
This brick structure represents Wallace's oldest hotel and was erected almost immediately after the disastrous 1890s fire. The Wallace Corner/Hotel was home to the community's first male and female bowling alley, and a sports gym was located in the building's basement in the 1920s and 1930s.

Arment Building
601 Cedar Street
Completed in 1911, this is the third Arment Building to occupy the same land. While the first Arment Building was destroyed in the 1890s fire, the second wooden frame structure was later demolished to make way for the current brick building. Throughout its long history, the Arment Building has housed jewelry, clothing, and thrift stores while the second floor was home to a popular house of ill-repute from 1920 to 1980.

Civic (Tabor) Building
602 Cedar Street
Jesse Tabor constructed the first building on this lot in the 1890s, and when a fire destroyed the wooden structure in 1933, the present two-story brick building was established. G.A. Pherson of Spokane designed the Art Deco building that includes detailed terra cotta trim rated among Idaho's finest. Tabor's store continues business under its original name and celebrated its centennial in 1991. The building's north side became known as the Civic Entrance when federal offices began occupying the space.

The Bi-Metallic Building
605 Cedar Street
Since its construction in 1895, the two-story Bi-Metallic Building features much of its original cast-iron details and was primarily used as a hotel and saloon. The Oasis Bordello, now a museum,

occupied the second floor until its ladies suddenly left in 1988. Today, a gift shop operates on the first floor.

Ryan Hotel
608 Cedar Street
The Ryan Hotel, completed in 1903, is rumored to be Wallace's continuously operated reputable hotel that was never home to any ladies of the night. In fact, its slogan has always been, "Bring Your Own Woman." The multi-colored brick building was restored in 1983 with original hardware.

Barnard Studio
614 Cedar Street
A Wyoming native, T. N. Barnard arrived in Wallace intent on recording life in Idaho's gold fields. Barnard and his assistant, Nellie Stockbridge, are primarily responsible for most of the photographs documenting the area's history.

Wallace City Hall & Fire Department
703 Cedar Street
The bricked City Hall and Fire Department was constructed in 1924 as a replacement for an earlier wooden structure prone to fire concerns. The building includes three large bays and two narrow bays.

Former Site of Samuels Hotel
Cedar & Seventh Streets
When it was completed and opened in 1906, the bricked Samuels Hotel was known to offer the Pacific Northwest's finest Victorian accommodations. However, its massive size and increasing maintenance costs forced the owners to level the building in 1974.

Gyde-Taylor Building
414 Seventh Street
The Gyde-Taylor Building dates back to 1917 and has been used by the renowned, highly productive Hecla Mining Company since the 1960s.

Shoshone County Courthouse
700 Bank Street
This Neoclassical Revival style building was built in 1905 with locally made concrete blocks now covered with stucco. The three-story courthouse is the design of Spokane architects, Stritesky and Sweatt, and includes many distinct features. Detailed cornices, fluted pilasters, and two-story arched windows provide the courthouse with a stately, dignified character.

Hale Building
621 Bank Street
The two-story red brick Hale Building was constructed in 1905 and is one of Wallace's most well-preserved historical structures. Most of its original character and embellishments have been retained, including second floor terra cotta details. In 1996, Universal Studios film crews used the Hale Building as a tavern in the movie, "Dante's Peak."

Otterson Building
622 Bank Street
The brick Otterson Building, constructed in 1890, is located on what most townspeople agree is the oldest block in downtown Wallace. Complete with arched windows and cast iron details, the building was first used as a dry goods store.

Coeur d'Alene Hardware Building
612 Bank Street
Holley, Mason, Marks, and Company owned the original wood structure on this lot in the late 1800s, but in 1890, this architecturally sound and fire-resistant brick building replaced its forerunner. While the exterior features arched windows with brick cornices, the interior was used as a hardware outlet and manufacturing plant for mining machinery. The business eventually grew into the largest non-mining business in the region and shipped products across the world. In the 1980s, Coeur d'Alene Hardware left Wallace, shortened its name to Coeur d'Alenes Company, and relocated to Spokane.

Heller Building
608 Bank Street
Built between 1891 and 1896, the two-story Heller Building features two storefronts connected inside. The brick structure includes arched windows and its original cast iron accents.

Stevens Building
607 Bank Street
A resident of downtown since 1906, the two-story brick Stevens Building features its original window arrangement and keystone accents. Despite the absence of its original brick cornices, this structure retains much of its early character.

Masonic Hall & Temple
605 Bank Street
Spokane architect, G. I. Hubbell, designed this building constructed in 1917. Featuring extensive terra cotta accents and granite trim, this distinguished building is further accented with an arched entryway. This building serves as the second home to Wallace's Masons. The original building was destroyed by fire in 1915.

Howes and King Building
606 Bank Street
Early Wallace merchants, Henry E. Howes and Horace G. King, opened a store on this site in 1884 but replaced the original building with the current structure in 1890. The bricks used to construct the structure were manufactured in nearby Silverton, and the building features an original zinc/tin ceiling under its current false ceiling. The men operated a grocery business and general store for several years.

Manheim Building
604 Bank Street
The two-story brick Manheim Building was erected in 1894 and has seen numerous changes over its long life. With a string of owners, the building's doorway positioning has changed and windows have been covered up and then exposed again. Today, the building retains its original tin ceiling, cast iron details on the first floor, and the second floor's brick cornices. Among its various functions, the building has served as a U.S. Forest Service office, pool hall, and bar.

Rossi Insurance Building
602 Bank Street
In 1890, this structure was built to house the Bank of Wallace. When the bank failed, a second bank moved in, but it soon failed as well. Two years after its completion date, the building became home to the First National Bank of Wallace, which operated here until 1916. In 1917, Herman Rossi bought the building for an insurance office, and it has retained this function ever since. The building features double doors, leaded glass, and a pressed metal turret that was added in 1895.

First National Bank Building
419 Sixth Street
Featuring a Renaissance Revival style complete with white terra cotta accents, arched windows, and columns, this building was constructed in 1917 for the growing First National Bank of

Rossi Insurance Building

Wallace. The bank was first located at 602 Bank Street and was the region's first nationally chartered bank.

The Idaho Building
413 Sixth Street
Built for Mrs. Otterson and O.D. "Deke" Jones, this two-story brick building was constructed in 1917. It includes original terra cotta trim and mezzanine windows and has housed one of Idaho's most prominent brokerage firms since 1925.

Gearon Building
414 Sixth Street
David Graham and Sons from Missoula, Montana were awarded a $45,000 contract to construct the two-story Gearon Building in 1924. In its planning stages, the building was to include two mercantile stores, a doctor's office, a barbershop, a beauty parlor, and an apartment on the second floor. The building was best known for its long-time resident, Gaebe's Jewelry, and its distinctive sidewalk clock.

DeLashmutt Building
424 Sixth Street
After the disastrous 1890s fire, this spared building erected in 1890 was temporarily home to the post office and county courthouse until the present courthouse was established in 1905. On the second floor, female boarders lived in the "courting rooms" and operated business by night.

White & Bender Building
524 Bank Street
Constructed in 1890, this site represents one of the finest Queen Anne commercial buildings in all of Wallace. After expanding business from nearby Murray, White and Bender Company operated a retail/wholesale mercantile store here into the 1930s. The building was the first to feature electric lights in Wallace.

Aulbach Building
520 Bank Street
Editor-in-Chief of the Wallace Free Press, Adam Aulbach, constructed this building in 1890 to house his print shop. Printer's Creek, which powered the printing press, was routed under the building.

Finch Building
516 Bank Street
Featuring a common façade with two internally connected buildings, the Finch Building is named after early resident, John Finch. Finch was one of the first

THE GREAT IDAHO FIRE OF 1910

Forest fires have plagued the drought-stricken western U.S. over the past several years, spreading smoke plumes thousands of miles while consuming millions of forested acres and mountain properties. Despite the disastrous aftermath of recent western forest fires, the fire of 1910 remains the largest forest fire in American history. Spanning day and night on August 20 and 21, 1910, a sequence of fires ravaged across northern Idaho and western Montana, scorching three million acres of prime timberland and charring towns and buildings in its path. While some claimed that the fire was actually comprised of 1,736 smaller fires, others insist that nearly 3,000 fires were burning on those fateful August days. In either case, the event's magnitude remains unmatched and earned the nicknames, "The Big Burn" and "The Great Idaho Fire."

In the Fire's Path
In 1910, Idaho found itself facing a predicament. With the driest year on record and summer temperatures soaring, the landscape was ripe for disaster. Throughout the summer, thunderstorms and lightening strikes sparked fires across the panhandle. By August 19, most fires seemed under control.

But the fire situation was far from contained. On August 20, hurricane force winds whipped through Idaho and Montana, stirring up smoking ashes and igniting new blazes in the Coeur d'Alene National Forest. In just a matter of hours, the fire situation was far worse than anything Idaho firefighters and residents had ever seen. Towers of smoke eclipsed the sun by mid-afternoon as fireballs rolled across mountain ridges upwards of seventy miles an hour. The destruction was so extensive that by August 21, America and neighboring countries lay in a shroud of smoke. Daylight ceased around noon as far north as Saskatchewan, Canada and as far east as Watertown, New York. At night, the smoky atmosphere blocked out the stars' radiant light nearly 500 miles off America's western coast.

Supply shortages and a scarcity of firefighters further exacerbated the situation's gravity. Hand shovels, axes, crosscut saws, and grub hoes were limited. In addition, lack of adequate roads to the fire's core forced men to lose time as they painstakingly carved out a path to the fires they had been ordered to extinguish. Men from all walks of life united to save what they could of Idaho's and Montana's forests and the boomtowns cradled within. U.S. Infantry, Idaho loggers, Montana miners, and bums from Spokane joined together in a line of 10,000 men to fight the fires. For their efforts, the men were paid twenty-five cents per hour and received a bedroll, pancakes, coffee, and canned tomatoes. Finally, when the men thought they could fight no more, a rain and snowstorm washed over the area. The fire was now under control.

The Big Burn's Aftermath
In just two days, the fire's searing flames had encompassed three million forested acres and destroyed enough timber to load a 2,400-mile long freight train. Wildlife ran for their lives, but no estimate has ever been applied to the number of animals who perished in the fire or afterwards when food sources were scarce. One ranger reported watching helplessly as a frightened black bear, trapped in his fate, clung to life in a burning pine as bright orange flames viciously licked the tree's base.

Humans also became tragic victims of the fire. Prosperous towns burned to the ground, and eighty-six people lost their lives in what many thought was the world's end. Among the victims were twenty-nine men on the fire lines who tried to outrun the fire near Storm Creek. They unfortunately lost the battle, and U.S. Infantry buried the men in a sixty-foot long trench. Tales also recount frightened individuals scared of waiting out a sure death. Men jumped to their deaths from burning trains, others shot themselves in the face of approaching fires, and still others walked into the flames instead of waiting in fear for the fire to reach them.

Despite the death count, hundreds survived, a few of whom owe their lives to Forest Ranger, Edward Pulaski. Supervising fire crews approximately five miles south of Wallace, Pulaski realized that his men were in the danger zone on August 21. He gathered forty-five of the nearest men and ushered them into the old War Eagle Mine shaft where he ordered them at gunpoint to lie face down to avoid suffocation. As the flames raged outside, the men prayed for their lives as Pulaski stood near the entrance with rags dampened from water in the mine. Eventually, most of the men fell unconscious. When they awoke the next morning, the canyon outside was no longer a furnace but a pile of smoking debris. They stumbled across burning logs, burning the shoes off their feet, and eventually made it back to Wallace where they were treated at the local hospital. Thanks to Pulaski, only five men died instead of the whole crew. Pulaski's heroism has lived on since that day, and members of his crew wrote to the Wallace Ranger District as late as 1961 in praise of the brave ranger.

In the end, it took years for the Forest Service and Civil Conservation Corp to clear dead timber from the area. Just ten percent of the timber killed was ever salvaged, and logs jammed streams and canyon bottoms. Throughout the following years, erosion became a major problem, and bark beetles invaded newly planted forests. Until 1940, Idaho's northern panhandle experienced a sequence of fires with nearly forty percent of the land burned in the 1910 fire going up in flames in subsequent fires.

Exploring the Causes of the 1910 Fire
Despite its magnificent size and its effect on Idaho forests and residents, the exact cause of the 1910 fire remains a mystery to researchers. No official cause for the fire has ever been identified, yet speculations abound. Researchers suggest that lack of precipitation throughout the previous year created a drought unlike anything since experienced in Idaho. As snows melted early and raging rivers became trickling streams, nearby forests dried up and became a perfect fuel source for lightning strikes.

In addition to natural causes, campers, homesteaders, and loggers accidentally ignited several fires earlier in summer 1910. As the new Chicago, Milwaukee, and Puget Sound Railway passed through the densely forested Bitterroot Mountains, another potential fire hazard was created. Coal powered these locomotives, and red-hot ashes often scattered down to the forested floor. Although the railroad industry was aware of this problem and actually hired individuals to walk the rails behind the train and extinguish any small fires, their efforts were not enough. The red-hot ashes combined with the aforementioned factors created an environment perfect for hosting a fire disaster.

Today, much of the land charred in the Great Idaho Fire is now painted green with new growth, and fire-resistant brick buildings are the norm. Despite its memorial as a monster of mass devastation, the 1910 fire helped create modern-day fire suppression philosophy, sparing future American generations from similar horrors.

---

operators at the Standard Mammoth Mine along with Amos B. Campbell. In 1996, "Dante's Peak" film crews used this building as its headquarters.

The Herrington Hotel
512 Bank Street
Herman Rossi constructed this two-story brick building in 1898. It retains its original second story façade and is now used as an apartment building.

Elks Lodge Hall
506 and 508 Bank Street
Utilizing the design of Spokane architects, Pruesse and Zittle, this two-story brick building was built in 1905 and was the first home of the Wallace Elks Lodge. Elk footprints in the sidewalk denote the building's original capacity, and the second floor retains its original windows. At one time, the building contained three bays.

Wallace District Mining Museum
509 Bank Street
Before housing the Wallace District Mining Museum, this building was home to Rice Bakery. Mr. Rice was renowned for his baked goods, operating the bakery until the early 1970s.

Shoshone Building
416 and 420 Fifth Street
This two-story building was built in 1916 and features much of its original character. Rounded arched windows and a cast stone entry distinguish the building that is now home to a variety of offices.

North Idaho Telephone Company
517 and 517 1/2 Bank Street
This architecturally distinct brick building was established in 1893. It features its original storefront and is distinguished with double-recessed doors and brick dentils.

T Walking Tour of Wallace's Historic Residential District
Contact the Wallace Chamber of Commerce at 753-7151.

Just as impressive as the historical downtown district, Wallace's residential district is lined with notable architectural masterpieces. These homes and churches, most featuring a Queen Anne style, were constructed at the turn of the century and maintain much of their original decorative accents.

St. Alphonsus Catholic Church
Beginning in 1888, the first Catholic priest arrived in the area, and this property site was purchased in 1890. In 1895, church members had raised enough funds to build a wood-frame structure, which was then replaced in 1926 with the present building. The church, shaped in the form of a cross, features a Tudor Gothic architectural style and was designed by Virgil Kirkemo of Missoula,

Montana. It is accented with red bricks, white terra cotta trim, three pointed arches, and a copper roof that was added in 1984.

101 Pine
The 1888 elected Wallace Marshall, Angus Sutherland, built this one and one-half story home in 1906. The bungalow style building was originally intended for use as a retirement home but has become a private residence.

221 Pine
This two-story framed home was once occupied by the Hutton family, who were associated with the Hercules Mine. The home features an inset porch, gabled extensions, and a hip roof. In need of care, the home was restored in 2001.

United Methodist Church
Joshua Pannebaker served as general contractor overseeing construction of Wallace's United Methodist Church in 1900. The framed Gothic Revival style church features a wooden belfry, a multi-sided tower, and stained glass windows that were added in 1915.

Holy Trinity Episcopal Church
Constructed in 1910, the current Holy Trinity Episcopal Church was built to replace the original 1889 house of worship. Kirland K. Cutter designed the English Country style church featuring buttressed corners, terra cotta trim, and large stained glass windows. The addition behind the church was added in 1915 as a Sunday School wing.

United Church of Christ Congregational
Dating back to 1898, members of the United Church of Christ Congregational have resided in Wallace for over a hundred years. The first church on this lot was built in 1903 but was replaced with the present structure in 1958. The church's east end features its original stained glass windows.

301 Cedar
This stately home was built in 1893 for business owner, Henry White, who was the region's major grocery retailer in Wallace's early days. Featuring two and one-half stories, the home is embellished with a wraparound porch, Roman Doric columns, an octagonal tower, and gables.

304 Cedar
Completed in 1901, this home features an American Colonial Revival architectural style complete with gabled dormers, Tuscan columns, and a wraparound porch. August Paulsen, associated with the nearby Hercules Mine, bought the home in 1903, and May Hutton (also associated with the Hercules Mine) is believed to have served tea here in 1903 to President Roosevelt.

224 Cedar
This Queen Anne style home was built in 1890 and is one of Wallace's oldest standing homes. The frame house includes two and one-half stories accented with diamond shingles, a two-story bay window, a wraparound porch, and a cross-gabled roof.

221 Cedar
Herman Rossi, insurance agent and Wallace's mayor in 1897, 1904, 1927, and 1935, built this bungalow style home in 1907 out of locally made concrete blocks. Over its one and one-half stories, the home features a wide wraparound porch, timber and stucco gables, and gabled details on the home's east and west end.

211 Cedar
This 1892 home features both Queen Anne and American Colonial Revival architectural accents.

Prominent town mayor, Walter Hanson, purchased the home from previous occupants, and Hanson's daughter remained in the home until 1993. The house includes one and one-half stories and is distinguished by its gabled front.

218 Cedar
An early Wallace architect's plans served as the inspiration for this Queen Anne style home. Enlarged from plans drafted by R. H. Wallas, the one and one-half story residence was built in 1892 and is adorned with gabled walls, dormers, and bay windows.

114 Cedar
This 1890 home features both Queen Anne and American Colonial Revival architectural accents and originally included a hipped roof and gabled walls. Harry L. Day, discoverer of the Hercules Mine, was the original owner of this one and one-half story home. Throughout its history, the home has undergone significant remodeling along with an addition added to the home's east side.

125 Cedar
Eugene Day, co-founder of the Hercules mine, was the first occupant of this Victorian style home. The house was constructed in 1896.

121 Cedar
In 1910, this one and one-half story red brick house was constructed. The home includes a gabled front along with elements of the Queen Anne bungalow style.

107 Cedar
This stately, three-story American Colonial Revival home was completed in autumn 1904. The home includes dormers, a hipped roof, Palladian windows in the library, and original wood floors on the first floor. The home is often referred to as the C. W. Beale House, a mining attorney who was the first occupant along with his family.

102 and 106 Cedar
These reverse bungalow homes were completed in 1914 for brothers, Walter H. and Dr. Leonard E. Hanson. Complete with hipped roofs and gables, the homes were unique as they featured telephone outlets in each room, woodwork made from Tennessee gum, and built-in vacuum systems. The brothers were Wallace legends, as Leonard was known for his fair medical practices, and Walter served as Wallace's mayor and later an Idaho Legislator.

406 First
This American Colonial Revival home dates back to 1912. Amid its hipped roof, bay windows, large front porch, and half dormers, the two and one-half story home retains its original siding, leaded glass, and wood flooring.

504 First
Featuring a basic L-shaped plan, this one and one-half story frame house was constructed in 1910. The home is characterized with bungalow details such as an open front deck and screened two-story porch.

21 Bank
This home, constructed in 1916 for a former Wallace mayor (Herman Rossi), is the second largest historical home in Wallace. With two and one-half stories, the home features a gable front and dormers and once included a two-story porch. The home was donated in 1958 to Our Lady of Lourdes Academy, and since then, has often been referred to as the nunnery.

411 Third Street
This large home was constructed in 1910 for prominent businessman, John Callahan, and his family. The home retains its original cast iron

fence and jerkin-head roof. It is also continuously recognized for its magnificent garden.

T South Hill Stairways Walking Tour
Wallace. Contact the Wallace Chamber of Commerce at 753-7151.

On the south side of town, a series of ten wooden stairways encompassing 663 steps leads up tree-lined streets through several residential neighborhoods. The historic public stairways were established as the mining town boomed and homes were constructed on the South Hill overlooking town. Residents used the stairways to travel back and forth to work and downtown shopping while children traversed the pathways on their way to school. Visitors to the stairway system will discover a historic district of homes in various stages of remodeling, remnants of old stairways long since abandoned, and incredible overviews of the Silver Valley. The self-guided tour is free and available year-round.

T Geologic Pressure Folds
Eastern outskirts of Wallace. Contact the Wallace Chamber of Commerce at 753-7151. In downtown Wallace, proceed east 0.3 miles on Bank St., crossing the railroad tracks and merging onto a paved road that parallels the railroad. Continue 0.3 miles to locate the pressure folds on the road's left side.

Lying beside the Osburn fault line, the Coeur d'Alene Mining District and surrounding regions in the Silver Valley were once part of a shallow sea. This sea, dating back 2.5 billion years, slowly eroded and turned the nearby mountains into fine sand deposits. As the sea sunk and erosion continued over the course of millions of years, the sand layers were compressed into a nearly five mile thick wall of argillite and quartzite rock. Known as the "Belt Series," the rocks are estimated at 1.4 to 1.6 billion years old, and only a fraction of the belt is visible. As younger rocks began covering the belt, tectonic forces twisted the layered rocks sideways, compressing and folding the rock into intricate wrinkles. These ancient geologic folds are still evident today.

T Historical Tour of Downtown Murray
Although now just a shadow of its prosperous past, Murray is home to a small collection of historical buildings dating back to the turn of the century.

Masonic Lodge
South side of Main Street
Murray's Masonic Lodge was built in 1890 and continues to be used today. The two-story impres-

sive frame structure features a false front complete with bracket corners.

Sprag Pole Inn
One block east of the Masonic Lodge on Main Street's north side

The Sprag Pole Inn, now an eclectic museum of Idaho's panhandle, originally functioned as a hotel and saloon. Amid its many curiosities, the building features the original gravestone of famous, Maggie Burdan. Maggie (aka Mollie B'Damm) was Murray's most famous lady of the night.

Shoshone County Courthouse
East of the Sprag Pole Inn on Main Street's north side

The second courthouse in Shoshone County, this building has fallen into disrepair but still contains an interesting historical story within its walls. In 1887, Noah Kellogg was on trial for a murder that occurred in a local saloon. The incident occurred when Kellogg was sharing drinks with the judge and the trial's prosecutor and was slapped in the face with a pint of beer. Angry at the incident, Kellogg turned around to confront his Irish assailant and shot him for being rude.

The trial concluded with a controversial acquittal. Outraged that Kellogg was not punished for his crime, the Wallace Free Press backlashed against Murray's court system and its employees. They labeled the court "lawless," the judge "stupid," and the lawyers "unscrupulous." Although it was presumed that the jury was handpicked and that witnesses were intimidated, nothing more was made of the case and Kellogg carried on with his normal routine.

F The Brooks Hotel Restaurant
500 Cedar St, Wallace. 556-1571 or (800) 752-0469.

L The Brooks Hotel
500 Cedar St., Wallace. 556-1571 or (800) 752-0469

M Historic Wallace Chamber of Commerce
10 River St., Wallace. 753-7151 or (800) 434-4204. www.wallaceidahochamber.com; director@wallaceidahochamber.com

33 *Food, Lodging*

Mullan
Pop. 840

Platted in 1888, Mullan was named after a W. Point graduate, Lt. John Mullan, who created a military wagon route between Fort Benton, Montana and Fort Walla Walla, Washington. In the town's first days, horse-drawn stages hauled travelers between Mullan and nearby Wallace for a $2.50 round-trip ticket. The arrival of the Northern Pacific Railroad drastically improved the town's transportation and supply situation, resulting in increasing populations. Although railroad officials tried to rename the settlement "Ryan" after a key railroad figure, town residents refused and kept the original town name instead. The town's growth and current economic livelihood is based upon the neighboring gold, silver, and lead mines.

H Willow Creek Slide
Milepost 71.4, E.bound on I-90, at Lookout Pass Scenic Overlook

A spectacular avalanche on February 10, 1903, swept away part of a trestle – 300 feet high – that let Northern Pacific Railway trains descend from this pass since 1890.

An engine that plunged 80 feet was buried in 30 feet of snow; a passenger car dangled over open space; and a caboose with eight people dropped into a deep snowbank.

Miraculously, everyone aboard survived that terror-stricken trip. But a new, less-hazardous grade replaced that trestle route.

H 1910 Fire
Milepost 72.7, W.bound on I-90, at Lookout Pass Scenic Overlook

More than two million acres of timber in this area burned during an exceptionally dry summer in 1910. A gigantic firestorm on August 20 did unprecedented damage.

Skies in Montreal and London were blackened by its smoke, which interfered with North Atlantic navigation. Strenuous efforts saved most of Wallace from its flames, but 85 firefighters were lost, mostly in other areas. Edward Pulaski's heroic measures to save his crew in a nearby mine tunnel have become a forest legend recounted in Wallace's mining museum at 509 Bank Street.

T Captain John Mullan Museum
229 Earle St., Mullan. 744-1461.

Captain John Mullan arrived in this Idaho region in the 1850s and began constructing the famous Mullan Road now paralleling I-90. Mullan's road was a turning point for the Pacific Northwest as it opened up the west for growth and further exploration. In his honor, this small community and its local museum have adopted his name. Inside the museum, visitors will find regional memorabilia and artifacts dating as far back as 1880. Displays include historical furnishings, vintage clothing, photos, newspapers, and mining relics. The museum is open 12 PM to 4 PM Monday through Saturday from June 1 to September 1.

T Lucky Friday Mine
1 mile east of Mullan on the north side of I-90

The Lucky Friday Mine is another historic mine in Idaho's Silver Valley. Tracing its roots back to six claims staked between 1899 and 1906, the area was patented in 1926. However, discouraged by a lack of shallow underground workings, the area was abandoned until 1938 when the Lucky Friday Mine stepped in.

Immediately, the company began deeper explorations and found remarkable lead, silver, and zinc veins. In January 1942, the first ore shipment was sent out, and in just forty years, the mine profits exceeded $310 million. After expanding its operation, the Lucky Friday Silver-Lead Mines Company merged in 1964 with the Hecla Mining Company. Throughout subsequent years, Hecla/Lucky Friday has become America's leading producer of newly-mined silver. The surface plant, hoist, and mill are visible to the roadside.

TV Lookout Pass
I-90 at the Idaho/Montana Border

Nestled at an elevation of 4,725 feet in the Bitterroot Mountains, Lookout Pass straddles the scenic Idaho/Montana border. Besides boasting a downhill ski area, Lookout Pass is a year-round departure site for recreational pursuers. Snowmobilers, anglers, equestrians, mountain bikers, and hikers all head to the hills here for world-class adventure.

V Trail of the Coeur d'Alenes
Mullan to Plummer

On June 5th, 2004, one of the most spectacular trails for biking, walking, and in-line skating in the Pacific Northwest was completed. Extending from the small mining community of Mullan to the Idaho/Washington border at Plummer, this seventy-three mile paved trail is managed by the

Idaho Department of Parks and Recreation and the Coeur d'Alene tribe. Users will travel along high mountain ridges, through the historic Silver Valley, into the famous bass and northern pike fishing area surrounding the chain lakes, beside Lake Coeur d'Alene's shores, and into Heyburn State Park before arriving at the Coeur d'Alene Indian Reservation. Evergreen trees line the path as users pass in and out of pine and cedar canyons with numerous opportunities to view herons, moose, deer, elk, and geese along the way. The trail is equipped with twenty parking lots/access points, thirteen restrooms, forty tables and benches providing perfect picnic spots, and several interpretive sites.

V Lookout Pass Ski Area
On the Idaho/Montana border east of Mullan (Exit 0 off I-90). 744-1301. www.skilookout.com

Opened in 1935, Lookout Pass Ski and Recreation Area is Idaho's second-oldest ski area. Although small with only 150 acres of slopes, Lookout Pass has prided itself on faithfully serving Silver Valley residents and tourists with a warm, friendly atmosphere for seventy years. With a free ski school for children and reasonable rates, Lookout Pass is a popular and affordable family destination.

The ski area offers 14+ downhill runs and cross-country trails for beginners to experts, a brand new chairlift, and terrain parks for snowboarders. After a fun day on the slopes, the cozy day lodge offers a relaxing atmosphere highlighted with lively local conversation. Lookout Pass receives nearly 390 inches of snow each year, and ski season is from mid-November through early April. The area is open Thursdays through Mondays, and operating hours are 9 AM to 4 PM on weekdays and 8:30 AM to 4 PM on weekends. During the summer, be sure to check out the incredible views from Lookout Pass as well as the outstanding mountain-biking terrain.

V The Route of the Hiawatha
Lookout Pass Ski and Recreation Area east of Mullan (Exit 0 off I-90). 744-1301. www.ridethehiawatha.com

The Route of the Hiawatha has been called one of the most scenic stretches of rail trail in America and has an incredible history. Facing competition with other railroad companies, the Chicago, Milwaukee, and St. Paul Railroad Company decided to venture into the Pacific Northwest and take advantage of new settlements and mining activity. With construction beginning in 1906, hundreds of Norwegian, Swedish, Irish, Spanish, Canadian, French, Japanese, Hungarian, Belgian, Austrian, Montenegrin, Serb, and Italian laborers worked together continuously to make the railroad's dream a reality. In 1911, after spending $260 million, the Milwaukee Railroad extension was complete and open for business. Notably, the line was equipped with electric locomotives and it represented the first use of electrification over an extended distance (440 miles). Carrying both freight and passengers through the rugged Bitterroot Mountains, the line went bankrupt in 1977, and the last train to travel west of Butte, Montana occurred in 1980.

For seventeen years, the historic line remained abandoned amidst Idaho and Montana's breathtaking mountain scenery. But in 1997, with the aid of government funding and private donations, construction of a new biking/hiking trail following the line began. Rails were removed, and on May 29th, 1998, the Idaho portion of the route was opened to the public.

The 13-mile Idaho stretch travels between

Roland and Pearson and wanders through eleven large tunnels and over nine sky-high trestles offering panoramic views along the way. In 2000, the renowned Taft Tunnel (St. Paul Pass) was completed. Burrowing 1.7 miles under the Bitterroot Mountains, the tunnel connects Idaho and Montana and allowed for an additional 33 miles to be constructed along the historic line in Montana. Today, bicyclists and hikers can travel the entire 46-mile Route of the Hiawatha between Pearson, Idaho and St. Regis, Montana and learn more about the rich history of the railroad, area mining, and early practices of the Forest Service through interpretive signs along the way.

All bikes must be equipped with lights for traveling through the dark tunnels, and bikers must wear safety helmets at all times. In order to maintain the trail, users must purchase a day pass or season pass. A day pass for adults is $8, and children ages 3-13 are $4. An adult must accompany all children, and tickets can be purchased on the trail or at Lookout Pass Ski Area. Depending on the weather, the trail is open June to October from 8:30 AM to 5:00 PM with extended hours in July and August. A shuttle is available between the Roland and Pearson trailheads, but visitors should call ahead for transportation schedules.

34

Rose Lake
Pop. 100

Located on the shores of a small lake bearing the same name, the community of Rose Lake is actually a misspelling. The settlement's original title was "Rowe's Lake," named after an early homesteader. The post office distorted the name when it arrived in 1905.

Medimont
Pop. 30

This small town is named after nearby Medicine Mountain. It serves as a supply center for the surrounding farmers, ranchers, and sportsmen and has boasted a post office since 1891.

Lane

Lane was originally established as a lumber town along the Coeur d'Alene River in the 1880s. It apparently draws its name from a logger who settled in the area during its golden days. The town's post office operated from 1891 to 1930.

35 Food

Harrison
Pop. 267

Harrison lies along the southeast shore of Coeur d'Alene Lake and was part of the area's Indian Reservation until 1889. At that point, regional timber companies requested that President Benjamin Harrison extract a mile-wide strip of shoreline from the reservation and deem it public use so that a sawmill and community could be established on the site. The President obliged them, and in return, the tim-

ber companies bestowed the honor of Harrison's name on this small town.

The railroad arrived in 1890, boosting mining traffic significantly. By the turn of the century, Harrison was home to nearly 2,000 people and boasted eleven lumber mills, four shingle mills, over a dozen saloons, and a substantial red-light district full of several houses of ill-repute. But, the party ended in 1917 when a huge fire destroyed the town. Soon after, the steamboats were declared unnecessary due to the railroad's presence, and the lumber industry died out. Today, Harrison is mostly a tourist town where fishing, boating, and sunsets on the lake beckon people to stay awhile. Interestingly, the first house built in town (1891) still stands and houses the Crane Historical Society Museum. Additionally, the Osprey Inn, constructed in 1915 as a lumberjack boardinghouse, still stands, now hosting tourists instead of laborers.

H Submerged Valley
Milepost 67.3 on State Hwy. 97

Glacial activity about 9,000 to 12,000 years ago created this lake out of what previously had been the valley of a river.

The ice sheet occupied major valleys north of here. As the glacier receded, melt waters flooded across the outlet of this valley, beyond modern Coeur d'Alene. Rock, sand, and gravel deposited there by those floods raised the level of the land and blocked the old river channel. This backed up the river, submerged the valley before you, and produced one of Idaho's lovely views.

H Coeur d'Alene Lake
Milepost 97 on State Hwy. 97

Look to the north: blocking the northward passage of the rivers which form this lake, a great

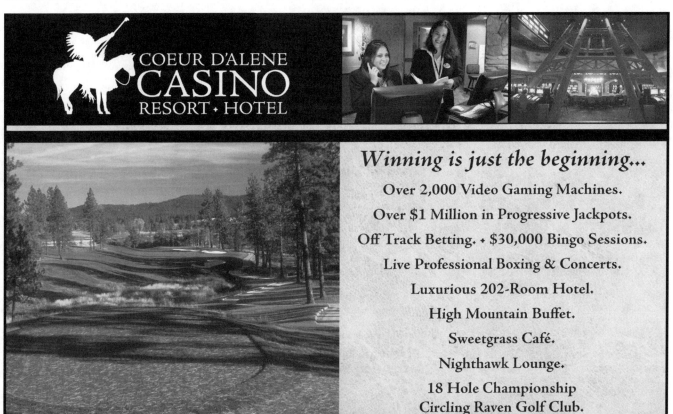

continental ice sheet once towered above the horizon as far as the eye can see.

When the glacier melted, it left a wide moraine – a plain of rocks and sand – that extended to Rathdrum and formed this lake. This is as far south as any continental ice sheet ever reached into Idaho. Lake Facts: Area – 50 square miles; Length – 32 miles; Elevation – 2,124 feet.

T Chain Lakes
Contact the Coeur d'Alene Visitor & Convention Bureau at (877) 782-9232.

Beginning near Harrison near Lake Coeur d'Alene's eastern shore, the Chain Lakes is a thirteen-mile expanse of lakes, wetlands, and marshes. The area abounds with wildlife, including beavers, muskrats, wood ducks, great blue herons, and the American kestrel. In addition, thousands of birds make a pit-stop here during spring and fall migration. Ducks, Canadian geese, osprey, and white tundra swans are all frequently reported. Wildlife viewing is available along the entire stretch, and visitors are encouraged to bring binoculars.

T Crane Historical Society Museum
Main St., Harrison. 689-3111.

When Addison Crane arrived in Harrison during the late 19th century, he quickly began selling lots in the growing community, and with his profits, built the town's first house in 1891. Today, Crane's house is a museum operated by the town's historical society. Inside, visitors will find relics from the late 1800s and early 1900s depicting local history. Visitors can also see the town's 1920 jail that was recently moved to the museum site. The museum is open 12 PM to 4 PM on weekends and holidays from Memorial Day to Labor Day with other visitation times available by appointment.

36 *Food, Lodging*

Plummer
Pop. 990

Plummer lies in the heart of the Coeur d'Alene Indian Reservation and was founded in 1911 when government surveyors mapped out the Reservation boundaries. Many different tales exist regarding Plummer's namesake. Some argue that the town was named after outlaw Henry Plummer who maintained a hideout near the townsite.

However, others insist the name honors a member of the original survey crew, while still many more claim the town memorializes Mrs. Plummer and her purchase of the town's first residential lot. The latter reason is widely disputed because the town's name appears on a 1909 map, long before area lots were even up for sale. Lumber used to be the basis of employment in the area, but when the large stands of ponderosa, fir, cedar, and tamarack trees were exhausted around World War I, the timber boom ended. Today, the sleepy town serves as a supply center for regional farmers and miners.

Rockford Bay
Pop. 50

Also known as Rockford Bay, this settlement is situated on the western side of Lake Coeur d'Alene and served as an Indian village from 1837 to 1852. In 1911, a post office was established and named after the Washington State's Rockford community.

Worley
Pop. 223

Rolling farmland surrounds this small town situated in the northern part of the Coeur d'Alene Indian Reservation. The town, named after an early reservation superintendent, was plotted in 1909 with postal services beginning in 1911. Worley comes alive each July as the Coeur d'Alene Indians hold their annual tribal festival.

Parkline
Pop. 65

Parkline is one of the newest towns to hit the Idaho scene. When the old town of Chatcolet disincorporated itself from the state on December 13, 1994, some residents were displeased. Formed from part of Chatcolet, Parkline was incorporated on the very same day.

H Logging Railroads
Milepost 444.6 on U.S. Hwy. 95

A network of Pacific Northwest logging railroads hauled timber from rough mountain country to local sawmills for several decades prior to 1940.

Owned by timber companies, these lines used small, powerful locomotives that could climb 10% grades and negotiate very sharp curves. An Ohio Match Company engine that used to operate near here is now included in a Potlatch Company display in Lewiston.

T Chatq'ele' Interpretive Center
7 miles east of Plummer near Heyburn State Park's main entrance

Situated within Heyburn State Park, the Pacific Northwest's oldest state park, the Chatq'ele' Interpretive Center is a treasure of information about the surrounding area. Visitors will find several exhibits about the Civilian Conservation Corp, art and artifacts of the Coeur d'Alene Tribe that once inhabited the area, and displays about local history and wildlife. Contact the Idaho State Parks and Recreation Department at (208) 334-4199 for additional information.

TV Blackwell Island Recreation Site
Contact the BLM Coeur d'Alene District Office at 769-5000. From Coeur d'Alene, travel south on U.S. Hwy. 95. Turn at the first right after the river crossing.

The Blackwell Island Recreation Site opened in 2003 and is quickly becoming a favorite local and visitor destination. Located along the Spokane River near Lake Coeur d'Alene's outlet, the recre-

ation area features a group picnic shelter, fourteen individual picnic units, a four lane boat launching ramp, and a one-quarter mile elevated boardwalk trail complete with wildlife viewing decks. The area is open from mid-May through mid-October.

TV Heyburn State Park
6 miles east of Plummer on State Hwy. 5. 686-1308.

The Coeur d'Alene Indians were the first settlers in this Idaho area now distinguished as Heyburn State Park. Like the Indians that came before them, early white homesteaders found the area an ideal encampment complete with plenty of food sources and natural beauty.

Idaho Senator Weldon Heyburn also appreciated this parcel of land, and despite being a fierce foe of federal activities in Idaho, sought to turn the area into a national park. Much to Heyburn's displeasure, the park never received the national status for which he had hoped. Instead, President William Howard Taft in an act of Congress on April 20, 1908 conferred state park status to the area. The territory was gleaned from the Coeur d'Alene Indian Reservation, and with 5,505 acres of land and 2,333 acres of water, it became Idaho's first and largest state park. To this day, the park also remains the oldest state park in the Pacific Northwest.

The park features the once separate Chatcolet, Round, and Benewah Lakes that were merged in a 1906 damming of the Spokane River. The most intriguing feature is the St. Joe River flowing through the lakes. Before the Post Falls Dam was constructed, the river flowed though the area's lowlands between tree-lined levees. The dam, however, raised water levels, and most of the river is now under water. Visitors today can distinguish the river's previous course, as the levees now appear as tiny strips of land separating the river from the lakes.

Year-round recreation is a popular drawing point of Heyburn. Camping, hiking, swimming, sailing, water-skiing, kayaking, and canoeing are all favorite park sports. Wildlife viewing is also popular as the park is home to one of North America's largest nesting osprey populations, elk, deer, bears, and wild turkeys.

FLM Coeur d'Alene Casino Resort Hotel
27068 S. Hwy 95, Worley. 686-0248 or (800) 523-2464. www.cdacasino.com

Discover a unique northern Idaho experience situated near major regional attractions at the Coeur d'Alene Casino Resort Hotel. The deluxe hotel features in-room high speed Internet, a 24-hour pool, spa, and fitness center, and over 30,000 square feet of conference and event facilities with state of the art audio/visual accommodating groups from 5 to 2,000. Custom affordable stay packages are standard with free shuttles to the Spokane International Airport, Coeur d'Alene, and Post Falls. A variety of award-winning cuisine awaits in the on-site restaurants, and the spacious casino features more than 2,000 Vegas-style gaming machines. For golfers, Golf Magazine rated the resort's 18-hole championship Circling Raven Golf Club a #1 must play. Whether you're planning a family vacation or business conference, the Coeur d'Alene Resort Hotel welcomes you to unforgettable fun and excitement!

M Harrison Chamber of Commerce
107 S. Coeur d'Alene Ave., Harrison. 689-3669.

37 *Food, Lodging*

St. Maries
Pop. 2,652

In 1842, Father Pierre-Jean DeSmet arrived at the convergence of the St. Joe and St. Maries Rivers and developed a mission to convert area Coeur d'Alene Indians to Catholicism. Feeling extremely blessed in his endeavors, Father DeSmet named his mission St. Maries (pronounced St. Mary's) and the name remained as other settlers moved into the area. By 1889, the site was no longer a hub of religious activity as the timber industry began to boom. Joe Fisher and his two brothers filed a claim and built the area's first sawmill, and their prosperity greatly improved as the railroad carrying passengers and freight arrived in town. Soon, the town was a thriving economic center. In 1902, St. Maries was incorporated, and in 1915, became the county seat for Benewah County.

Despite its humble and holy beginnings, however, the town's economic activity also brought with it considerable notoriety. Murders, bar brawls, and encounters with famed prostitutes were common occurrences in the town's early days. Fortunately, this reputation was short-lived. Today, after surviving several great floods, St. Maries' economy still thrives on the timber industry, and the area is popular for boating and floating.

H John Mullan
Milepost 17.8 on State Hwy. 5 at John Mullan Park in St. Maries

John Mullan was the Army officer who in 1859-62 surveyed and built the Mullan Road from Walla Walla, Washington to Fort Benton, Montana.

The road was to connect the Missouri and the Columbia Rivers. Congress approved it in 1855. Indian troubles and lack of funds delayed the job, but the road was completed in 1862. The first route in 1859 had passed about six miles west of here, but floods forced a change, and the final road passed north of Coeur d'Alene Lake. I-90 follows Mullan's final route.

Idaho Trivia
Throughout its long history, the Clark Fork River has seen its fair share of names. Once known as Silverbow, Missoula, Hell Gate, Deer Lodge, and Bitterroot, the river received its final and current title in 1921. The Board on Geographic Names unanimously voted to eliminate all other names in favor of "Clark Fork."

T Historic Hughes House Museum
606 Main Ave., St. Maries. 245-1501.

In 1902, this log house was built as the St. Maries Men's Club, but the organization proved short-lived. In 1906, the building was turned into a doctor's office and remained in operation until the early 1920s when the business was foreclosed. Noting that the building was rapidly deteriorating, Raleigh Hughes purchased the house in 1926 and lovingly restored it. The home remained in private possession until 1989 when the Centennial Committee purchased the home and opened it as the Historic Hughes House Museum on June 18, 1990. Inside, visitors will catch a glimpse of St. Maries' younger days. Several photos, antiques, and artifacts depict early life in St. Maries and Northern Idaho. Please call for additional information concerning hours of operation.

T St. Maries Golf Course
1 mile east of St. Maries on State Hwy 3. 245-3842.

Although only 9 holes and just a par 35, the 2,729-yard St. Maries Golf Course provides plenty of challenges along its well-maintained fairways. Cart rentals are available, and green fees are $16 on weekdays and $18 on weekends.

T Garnet Digging at the Emerald Creek Garnet Area
St. Joe Ranger District, St. Maries. 245-2531. From St. Maries, drive 24 miles south on State Hwy. 3 to

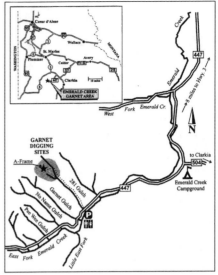

Forest Rd. (FR) 447. Continue 8 miles southwest on FR 447 to the parking area. From there, walk 0.5 miles up 281 Gulch Rd. where you'll find permits, information, and digging areas.

Star Garnets: The Idaho State Gemstone
Idaho and India are the only two places in the world where Star Garnets are found. The twelve-sided (dodecahedron) crystals range in size from sand particles to golf balls or larger and often have four or six-ray stars. Gem quality faceting material is also found.

Garnet digging is wet, muddy work! You'll have to dig from one to ten feet deep to find them, generally in alluvial deposits of gravel and sand just above bedrock or in mica schist parent material.

How Do I Get a Permit?
Permits are available at the A-frame building at the digging site. The cost is $10.00 for adults, $5.00 for children age 14 or under, and is valid for one

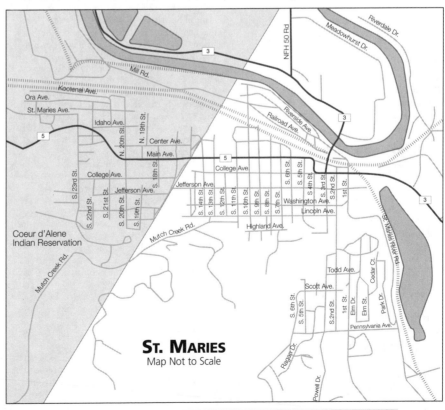

ST. MARIES
Map Not to Scale

day. A permit is required for anyone digging, screening, or washing gravels. A permit allows you to dig in designated areas only!

You may take up to five pounds of garnets with your daily permit. If you want to remove more garnet during the same day, you can buy another permit for each additional five pounds or fraction thereof that is removed. You are limited to six permits or 30 pounds of garnets per year.

How Long Does it Take?
We recommend you allow at least four hours at the site. Many families like to bring their lunch and make it an all-day outing at the Garnet Area. Some rockhounds like to return several days in a row.

What Equipment Do I Need to Bring?
• Rubber boots, waders, or old tennis shoes
• Drinking water
• Snacks or lunch
• Change of clothes
• Standard shovel
• Bucket for bailing water
• Container for garnets
• Screen box for washing gravel
• Rental tools are available

What Facilities are Avcailable?
At parking lot: Information sign, directions, and restroom

At administration building: Permit sales, displays, assistance to garnet diggers, restroom and rental equipment

Forest Service personnel are available to provide: Visitor information, permit sales, and enforcement of regulations.

What Acoomodations are Available?
• Emerald Creek Campground
• Cedar Creek Campground
• Clarkia Work Center Guest Bunkhouse Rental
• Food, gas, and other supplies are available in Clarkia, Fernwood, and Emida
• The nearest safe drinking water is in the Emerald Creek Campground

Guidelines
• Pets are allowed when restrained by a leash
• Motorized equipment is not allowed in digging areas

Hours of Operation
The Emerald Creek Garnet Area is open Memorial Day Weekend through Labor Day from 9 AM to 5 PM Fridays through Tuesdays.

Reprinted from U.S. Forest Service brochure

T Hobo Cedar Grove Botanical Area
St. Joe Ranger District, St. Maries. 245-2531. From Clarkia, drive 10 miles northeast on Forest Rd. (FR) 321. After crossing Hobo Pass, turn right onto FR 3357, and locate a parking area for the grove in approximately 2 miles.

Christened after an early homesteader named "Hobart," the 240-acre Hobo Cedar Grove Botanical Area has been a National Natural Landmark since 1969. The site features 500-year-old western red cedars, as well as stands of grand fir, western larch, Pacific yew, and Engelmann spruce. A short interpretive trail winds under the shady canopy of these magnificent trees that have miraculously escaped forest fires and the logging industry.

TV St. Maries River
South of the St. Maries community near State Hwy. 3

Rising in the southwest corner of Idaho's Shoshone County, the fifty mile long St. Maries

River distinguishes itself as the St. Joe River's main tributary. Once used for extensive log drives, the placid river is surrounded by pine forests and is a recreational retreat for canoeists, kayakers, and rafters. Placid waters ensure a smooth boating trip, while waterfowl viewing in the spring and magnificent autumn colors further enhance the river experience. Although the river is stocked with fish between Clarkia and Santa, fishing is forbidden in the Alder Creek area.

TV St. Maries Wildlife Management Area
On State Hwy. 3 between St. Maries and Santa, bear west onto Flat Creek Rd. The road leads directly to the management area.

Situated just five miles south of St. Maries, the St. Maries Wildlife Management Area is located near the lower end of the St. Maries River drainage in diverse terrain composed of forest and mountain meadows. The area is an important wintering location for approximately 150 to 200 white-tailed and mule deer along with nearly thirty elk. In addition, the area boasts a large population of moose, black bear, mountain lion, ruffled grouse, and blue grouse.

The area is open year-round to recreational use, including hunting, hiking, wildlife viewing, snowmobiling, horseback riding, picnicking, and camping. The site is a popular angling area as westslope cutthroat trout, mountain whitefish, rainbow trout, brook trout, kokanee salmon, and smallmouth bass inhabit the river and nearby streams.

M St. Maries Chamber of Commerce
906 Main Ave., St. Maries. 245-3563. www.stmarieschamber.org; info@stmarieschamber.org

38 *Food, Lodging*

Avery
Pop. 430

Avery was originally founded in 1886 when Sam "49" Williams homesteaded in the area. When some of his friends joined him a few years later, the men worked as trappers and joined in the Idaho timber industry by floating logs down to Harrison. By 1906, Williams' site was unofficially designated "Pinchot" after important forest service employee, Gifford Pinchot. When the Chicago, Milwaukee, & St. Paul Railroad built a line to the area in 1908, the small settlement was renamed Avery after Avery Rockefeller, the grandson of railroad director, William Rockefeller. The town finally incorporated in 1910 with the arrival of the area's first post office.

Although the settlement was nearly destroyed in the Great Idaho Fire of 1910, Avery was spared and grew to include a three-story hotel, several homes, and eventually a school. By 1917, Avery boasted 1,100 residents, including several Japanese, many of whom were employed by the railroad. When the line went bankrupt in the 1970s, the Potlatch Company purchased a portion of the rails in 1980 while the rest were torn apart during construction of the popular "Route of the Hiawatha" mountain-biking trail.

Today, Avery serves as just one of the Panhandle's many recreation launching regions.

Calder
Pop. 130

Before Calder received its "official" name, it was called Elk River by John Rice, an early settler, then Gordon in 1891, and then Remington in 1906. A railroad construction crew was stationed here in

the early 1900s soon after a homesteader opened a small store at the location. The town's present name actually honors one of the railroad crew men. The railroad, miners, and loggers kept the area economically busy, and the townsite barely escaped the great fire of 1910. Many men from Calder lost their lives fighting the blaze that summer. Profiting from such a tragedy, the Milwaukee Land Company salvaged the burnt logs north of town, and later the Mica Creek logging company joined in. A sawmill was built in 1942.

Clarkia
Pop. 190

Established as a flourishing lumber camp, Clarkia draws its name from famous explorer, William Clark. Unbeknownst to Clarkia's earliest residents, however, was that the town used to rest at the bottom of an ancient lake. Although the lake bottom is dated over twenty million years old, its intriguing history wasn't discovered until the early 1970s. Today, Clarkia is home to a variety of prehistoric animal and plant fossils that have attracted national geological and tourist attention.

St. Joe
Pop. 50

The Milwaukee Railroad and Milwaukee Land Company played instrumental roles in establishing St. Joe in the late 1880s. When the nearby town of Ferrell refused to cooperate with the railroad's building requests, railroad surveyors simply changed their plan and laid the railroad upriver from Ferrell. At the same time, the Milwaukee Land Company purchased several acres near the railroad and began selling lots. Lured by the Timber and Stone Act of 1878 and the Forest Homestead Act of 1906 that made land affordable, new residents arrived in droves to purchase and develop the heavily timbered area. The area prospered, and soon, a sawmill, hospital, school, and post office were built to serve the needs of area loggers and their families. However, when the Rose Lake Lumber Company ceased operations in 1926 and the sawmill burned, St. Joe's prosperity

ST. JOE DISCOVERY TOUR

St. Joe Ranger District, St. Maries. 245-2531.

Welcome to N. Idaho and the opportunity to enjoy part of America's great outdoors!

1) Heyburn State Park
In 1908, Heyburn became the first state park in the Northwest. With over 5,500 acres of land and 2,300 acres of water, it includes the St. Joe River, which flows between the lakes. Part of the original Mullan Military Rd. passes through the Park.

2) St. Maries
The St. Maries and St. Joe Rivers merge here. Resting place of 1910 firefighters who lost their lives. Home of a historic logging steam donkey.

3) Emerald Creek Garnet Area
The Idaho Star Garnet is treasured by collectors. The digging area is open Memorial Day through Labor Day.

4) Hobo Cedar Grove
Take a walk along an easy 1/2-mile trail in a 240-acre botanical area. Enjoy large cedar trees in a quiet setting.

5) Historical Logging
A hike down the Hobo Historical Trail takes you to the remnants of a splash dam, logging camp, and steam donkey.

6) Marble Creek Splash Dam
Stop to look at the remnants of an early 1900s logging splash dam.

7) Marble Creek Interpretive Site
View displays of logging history from the early 1900s to the present. Picnic alongside Marble Creek.

8) Avery
Originally a railroad community where steam engines and electric trains met. Visit the community museum and historic ranger station.

9) St. Joe River
Sixty miles of the St. Joe River above Avery has been classified as a part of the National Wild and Scenic Rivers System. The river road leads you along the lower part of the classified portion of the river. The upper twenty-nine miles is accessible only by trail.

10) Montana Trail
The Montana Trail from the Palouse Prairie to Montana crossed at Conrad Crossing. The trail was one the Indians used for an east-west travel route.

11) Red Ives Ranger Station
Originally built in the 1930s, the station is now on the National Historic Register.

12) Mullan
See mining and Mullan Rd. artifacts, or visit Shoshone Park and the community's fish hatchery.

13) Wallace
Visit the Mining Museum, the 1910 Fire Memorial in Placer Creek, the Sierra Mine Tour, and the Historic Northern Pacific Depot Railroad Museum.

14) Big Creek Sunshine Memorial
Near Kellogg, Exit 54. Memorial to miners who lost their lives in a mining disaster.

15) Old Mission State Park
Idaho's oldest building was constructed by the Coeur d'Alene Indians between 1850 and 1853 under the guidance of Jesuit missionaries.

16) Mullan Rd.
Walk along a remnant of the first road built through the area in the 1870s under the command of Captain John Mullan.

Reprinted from a U.S. Forest Service brochure

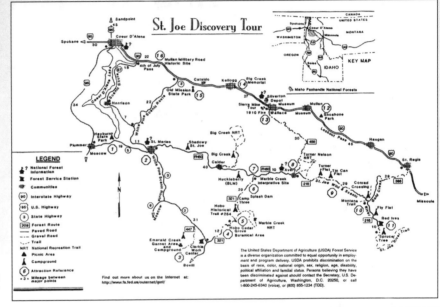

dwindled and the post office closed in 1927. Today, this tiny community's economy is still tied to its history in the logging/timber industry.

Ferrell
12.5 miles east from St. Maries up the St. Joe River

Realizing the potential economic value of a settlement located near the St. Joe River, William Ferrell moved to the meadowland from Coeur d'Alene in 1883. As other homesteaders expressed interested in the Upper St. Joe River region, Ferrell platted a community in his name, built a hotel, established a general store, and began selling business and residence lots.

Before long, business was booming in Ferrell with the arrival of excursion steamers. By 1907, two more hotels lined the streets along with a bank, drugstore, telephone company, and ten saloons. The town boomed so quickly that railroad surveyors were interested in developing a possible route through Ferrell. William Ferrell, however, decided to play hardball with the surveyors, hoping to receive $100,000 for a right-of-way through his community. Balking at his request, the Milwaukee and Puget Sound Railroad simply bypassed Ferrell, created a bridge to the river's south side, and began selling acreage for the new town-site, St. Joe City.

Ferrell could not compete with the trade and economic center established at nearby St. Joe City, and in just four years, most of Ferrell's residents had left. William Ferrell eventually moved to St. Joe City, relocating upriver a few years later to Avery. A schoolhouse operated in Ferrell until 1925, but today, only a quiet prairie remains at the old town-site.

▼ Avery Community Museum
Downtown Avery

Like many other small Idaho communities, Avery owes its existence to the Chicago, Milwaukee, and St. Paul Railroad. Avery served as an important transfer point until the railroad went bankrupt in the 1970s. Today, the line's old depot serves as a museum detailing the area's history.

▼ Avery Historic Ranger Station
St. Joe Ranger District, Avery. 245-4517.
Located outside Avery on Forest Rd. 50.

When the Chicago, Milwaukee, St. Paul, and Pacific Railway decided to build a railroad along the St. Joe River, the Forest Service decided it was time to build a Ranger Station to serve the area.

Since its construction in 1909, the Station has undergone several renovations and name changes.

Originally, the station was a two-story, four-room office building named Pinchot Ranger Station after the first Chief of the Forest Service. During this time, the Ranger Station became an important point for distributing supplies and outfitting packtrains for travel into the Forest.

The ranger station was called N. Fork Ranger Station for awhile, but as the town of Avery grew, the local people began referring to the station as the "Avery Ranger Station." Over the years, the name became "official."

Like the name, the station and the land around the station have changed several times. In 1923 and 1924, two dwellings and a cookhouse were added to the site and in 1928, a bunkhouse was built. All of these buildings were made of logs that are dovetailed and flattened at the corners. During the 1930s, a large barn and a number of other smaller buildings were built. The barn was later destroyed by fire and several of the other buildings were removed. The new log bunkhouses at the north end of the station were added in 1979.

The station would go through several more remodeling jobs, until 1967 when the decision was made to move the Ranger District Headquarters downriver to Hoyt Flat where there was more room. The old Avery Ranger Station has been used as a work center since this time.

The old Avery Ranger Station was added to the National Register of Historic Places in 1974.

Reprinted from U.S. Forest Service brochure

T Fall Creek
3.5 miles upriver from St. Joe

Fall Creek is often considered the dividing point between the rushing rapids of the upper St. Joe River and the calmer, slower pace of the lower St. Joe. Historically, the Fall Creek bridge area is rich. Although calm and quiet now, the site was once home to Thomas "Honey" Jones. After homesteading the meadow near Fall Creek in 1907 at age 71, Jones' entrepreneurial spirit kicked in. He developed secluded picnic sites along the river catering to residents and passerby, charging one dollar per site. He then began raising bees, supplementing his picnic site income by selling honey. Jones was known for his long beard that he kept tucked underneath his shirt, and continued working the Fall Creek area until his death in 1927 at age 91. Today, a grave on the hill overlooking the creek remembers the area's first resident and the meadow's interesting history.

T Fitzgerald Creek
Approximately 5.5 miles upriver from St. Joe City

Located on the north side of the St. Joe River, Fitzgerald Creek represents a historic site from the area's rich logging days in the 1920s and 1930s. A lengthy log flume was constructed in Fitzgerald Creek allowing loggers to reach more remote stands of white pine. The flume on Fitzgerald Creek eventually carried these logs to the St. Joe River.

Above Fitzgerald Creek, portions of the old "Goat Road" established in 1907 and 1908 are still visible. Teams and wagons used the road to travel the St. Joe River corridor, hauling supplies and mail to Milwaukee Railroad construction crews.

T Mica Creek
Approximately 27.7 miles east of St. Maries on the St. Joe River Rd

When the U.S. government signed into law the Timber and Stone Act, homesteaders arrived in droves at Mica Creek. In 1916, a sawmill was established to cut timber for a large flume constructed here in 1917. The large, impressively built flume transported area logs down the St. Joe River, and St. Maries Lumber Company used the area timber until 1920. Rose Lake Lumber Company also operated in the Mica Creek area in the early 1900s, establishing a narrow-gauge railroad to help transport materials. Today, all that remains of the once booming logging site are traces of the heavily used flume.

T Big Creek and Herrick Flat
30 miles east of St. Maries on the St. Joe River Rd

The Big Creek drainage and Herrick Flat possess a varied history of activity and residents. Fred Herrick, a Wisconsin native, is presumed to be the area's first white resident, settling near Big Creek in 1909. After establishing the Milwaukee Lumber Company, Herrick began constructing a railroad up Big Creek for transporting timber. His hard work, however, was decimated in the Great Idaho Fire of 1910. Along with Herrick's property, ten firefighters met their fate in America's historically largest forest fire.

After the fire cooled, Herrick immediately went back to work. He reconstructed sixteen miles of his railroad line and began salvaging area timber. Herrick continued in this line of work for several years and was known for treating all his employees fairly while never selling out to larger companies. Herrick's scruples paid off as his company soon became the largest independent lumber contractor in the Northwest.

When Herrick stepped down from his business, the Civilian Conservation Corp moved into the Big Creek area. In the 1930s, nine CCC camps were established beside the St. Joe River, one of which was based at Herrick Flat. The men of these CCC camps were instrumental in flood and fire control and helped build a road from St. Joe City to Avery.

When the CCC camps were abandoned at the onset of World War II, only a few individuals remained to inhabit Herrick Flat, including the Herrick Bar owners. But when these owners were murdered in 1945, the event was enough to drive away any remaining inhabitants. Today, Herrick Flat remains the quiet space of land it has been for the past sixty years.

Idaho Trivia
Mark Twain's adventurous Huck Finn character is reportedly modeled after one of Idaho's earliest settlers. During Murray's gold mining days, a gentleman named "Captain Toncray" arrived in town. Credited with providing inspiration for Twain's character, Toncray is buried in a historic cemetery just one mile south of Murray.

T Tank Creek
35 miles east of St. Maries on the St. Joe River Rd.

Situated near Marble Creek, Tank Creek was the site where steam locomotives passing through the St. Joe River Valley were rewatered. Tank Creek is also known for its winding path under a natural arch near its confluence with the St. Joe River.

T Fishhook Creek
2 miles west of Avery

Fishhook Creek was the site of substantial logging in the 1920s and draws its name from early resident, Fishhook Graham. Graham, accompanied by his African-American friend, Brown Gravy Sam, was originally from the south but migrated west in hopes of realizing new dreams. Together, Graham and Sam operated a restaurant near the creek. The restaurant was quite popular with residents and tourists but closed when the railroad interrupted business. Today, the area is recognized for the 400-foot tunnel that the CCC constructed four miles up the creek in 1939.

TV St. Joe River
Idaho Panhandle National Forest. 765-7223.

Beginning on the Continental Divide, the St. Joe River flows 120 miles through the St. Joe and Clearwater Mountains into Coeur d'Alene Lake. Pierre-Jean DeSmet, an early Catholic priest in the area, dubbed the river "St. Joseph," which was shortened through the years to St. Joe. Situated at 2,128 feet above sea level, it is the world's highest navigable river, running between seven lakes and three rivers on its winding course.

While some of the river is classified as wild and scenic and should only be run by experienced kayakers, other portions of the river are far gentler. Rafters and kayakers will undoubtedly have no problem finding a river section suited to their individual ability level. In addition to boating, the river offers anglers the opportunity for trout fishing.

TV Snow Peak Wildlife Management Area
From Avery, travel 20 miles east on Forest Road (FR) 50 to FR 509 (Bluff Creek Road). Bear east, driving 9 miles before turning left onto FR 201. Continue 4 miles to the wildlife management area.

Managed by the U.S. Forest service and the Idaho Department of Game and Fish, the 32,000 acre Snow Peak Wildlife Management Area displays a thriving variety of wildlife. Elk, deer, pileated woodpeckers, northern goshawks, and pine martens are among the most prevalent species. In addition, the area boasts a large mountain goat herd, so large in fact that offspring are routinely transplanted throughout the western U.S. to bolster other mountain goat herds.

Representing one of Idaho's largest roadless areas, this predominantly backcountry management site ranges in elevation from 2,300 to 7,000 feet and features old growth forests and steep terrain. The area is open year-round and is a popular destination for backpackers, hikers, anglers, wildlife photographers, and hunters.

V St. Joe River Float Trips
St. Joe Ranger District, Avery. 245-4517.

Background

The St. Joe River contains over 120 miles of free-flowing river which offers a challenging adventure to canoers, kayakers, and rafters. All types of water can be encountered, from raging white water suitable only for teams of expert kayakers, to placid meanderings for the beginning canoeist.

The following information will help you select a river trip on the St. Joe which is suited to your abilities and desires. The difficulty rating assigned to each trip is based on average July and August water levels. During spring runoff from March through June, the difficulty of running the St. Joe increases at least one full grade.

The Trips

1) Heller Creek to Spruce Tree Campground
A 17-mile wilderness canyon run that contains rapids in Classes II through V. It is recommended that you plan two days for this trip. There are no campgrounds or roads; however, a trail does follow the right bank. It should also be noted that snow blocks the road to Heller Creek until July, and water flow sufficient for boating lasts only until mid-July.

This trip should be attempted only by highly skilled and experienced paddlers in slalom kayaks. Log jams which are nearly impossible to avoid, maneuvering in large waves with abrupt bends, violent eddies, and falls up to four feet cause this to be a very dangerous run.

2) Spruce Tree Campground to Gold Creek
Twelve miles of Class II and III rapids that can be run in about 6 hours. It should only be attempted by experienced paddlers in canoes, rafts, or kayaks. In the spring, large waves necessitate covered boats.

During low water the boulder strewn portions of the river require careful rock dodging. Generally, the water on this section of the river is too low for boating by mid-July, but for those who don't mind

Idaho Trivia
Just because Avery is small in size doesn't mean that nationally recognized figures have overlooked the community. On the contrary, Avery has had the privilege of hosting President Taft, President Harding, and President Truman in the course of its history.

a few scratches, the course can be run into August. Developed campgrounds are available.

3) Gold Creek to Bluff Creek Bridge
Seven miles of floating through this scenic canyon with sheer moss-covered cliffs and deep pools takes 3 to 5 hours. Because the canyon is narrow, the water is usually deep enough to run through July. In August, though, this run may mean a well-scarred boat. Several undeveloped campgrounds are available.

The roughest rapids on the St. Joe River are on this section. Tumble Down Falls, a 6-foot drop located about 0.2 miles above Tumble Down Creek, is preceded by 200 yards of Class IV rapids. Several violent eddies and souse holes, plus other long difficult rapids, dictate that this run be attempted only by experts in white water kayaks and rafts.

4) Bluff Creek to Turner Flats Campground
Sixteen miles of Class II rapids make this a delightful one-day trip for intermediate boaters. In the summer, it is run by rafts, open canoes, and kayaks. In the spring, the large waves demand a cover on all crafts. This run provides a leisurely cruise through fast water with no difficult hazards. Good swimming and fishing spots abound, and there are plenty of rapids to give intermediate canoers a chance to practice.

All boaters are cautioned to land boats at the Turner Flats Campground, and in no case proceed past Tourist Creek. Several hundred yards after Tourist Creek, the river enters Skookum Canyon. A thousand yards of violent Class III and IV rapids limit this section of the river to highly skilled experts who have first thoroughly scouted this section. Each year, this canyon claims several boats.

5) Packsaddle Campground to St. Joe City
Thirty-eight miles of grade I and II rapids require two or more days to travel. All summer, this trip can be made with anything from air mattresses and inner-tubes to canoes and kayaks. The river offers good fishing, swimming, and paddling as well as the availability of several undeveloped campgrounds.

The toughest rapids are at the beginning of the trip. These rapids may be inspected from the road, and if they appear too difficult, they may be avoided by beginning the float trip below Avery at Fishhook Creek or at the bridge at Hoyt Flats.

6) St. Joe City to Coeur d'Alene Lake
Thirty-one miles of deep, slow-moving water pokes along at about one-half mile per hour, requiring at least two days of paddling to travel the entire distance. The only serious obstacles are the waves kicked up by the passing motorboats. Developed campgrounds are available at the Forest Service's "Shadowy St. Joe" two miles below St. Joe City and Heyburn State Park on Chatcolet Lake.

This is known as the world's highest navigable river. At an elevation of 2,128 feet, tugboats can be seen towing large brails of logs to the mills at Coeur d'Alene. The scenery is outstanding, mostly in a primitive state, even though the river flows through somewhat populated areas. These tranquil waters, lined with cottonwood trees, give rise to the river's nickname, "The Shadowy St. Joe." The lower six miles are on the "River through the Lakes," a unique phenomenon where the St. Joe River with its natural tree-lined levees meanders through Benewah, Round, Chatcolet, and Coeur d'Alene Lakes. These levees are the summer home for the largest colony of osprey in N. America. There are several good take-out points on Lake Chatcolet.

Reprinted from U.S. Forest Service brochure

39 *Food, Lodging*

Emida
Pop. 100

This settlement originated in 1896 with the arrival of the E., Miller, and Dawson families. The ingenious homesteaders combined letters from all three family names for an original town name. An unknown word trickster also suggested that the little town didn't have much to offer and wasn't worth "a dime." Spell "a dime" backwards, and suddenly you have Emida. Despite this play on words, Emida is recognized for its down-home bar and cafe where tourists and strangers are treated with the hospitality and kindness of a neighbor.

Fernwood
Pop. 315

When a man named Mr. Fenn applied to have this settlement named Fennwood in 1901, the postal authorities misread the name and spelled it as Fernwood instead. The name was never corrected. Ironically, the nearby creek, named for Mr. Fenn as well, today appears on maps as Finn Creek. According to stories, Saturday nights in Fernwood between 1913 and 1930 were very wild. Lumberjacks from the many local camps would flock to town to drink, gamble, and be entertained by the local women. Today, the town's boisterous past has long since quieted.

Santa
Pop. 100

Santa was named after Santa Anna Creek, which was later shortened to Santa Creek. Jesuit settlers are recognized for naming this area near St. Maries and establishing a post office here in 1887.

T Marble Creek Historic Area
From Clarkia, drive up Marble Creek Road (Forest Road 321) toward Hobo Pass.

In the late 1800s and early 1900s, the U.S. Government passed several bills in hopes of encouraging westernsettlement. When homesteaders arrived in Idaho's Marble Creek Area, they not only saw a chance to build a home, but also the possibility of making some money.

In its early years, Marble Creek was lined with groves of old-growth trees. When settlers arrived, they began building houses and then decided to cut down the trees. But transporting the trees into town where the material could be turned into quick cash was not as easy as they thought it would be. Instead, many original homesteaders sold out their claims to logging companies and by 1915, more than three-fourths of the Marble Creek drainage was owned by timber companies.

During their reign in Marble Creek, the logging companies developed a system of sending harvested trees down Marble Creek and eventually into the St. Joe River. Splash dams, flumes, and chutes were erected to aid in the process, and many men lost their lives during the operation. By 1930, the once vegetated area was completely stripped of virgin timber and the stream's once abundant fish population was basically non-existent. Instead of allowing the timber companies to proceed, the government intervened and bought back the logged-out lands.

Today, several remains of Marble Creek's violent logging history can still be found. Railroad trestles, old logging camps, splash dams, chutes, and steam donkeys are all visible, and two short interpretive trails lead to particularly historic sites.

T Miocene Lake & Fossil Bowl
Clarkia. 245-3608.

Approximately 20 million years ago, Clarkia was buried under a giant lake. Over time, thousands of plants and insects floated to the lake's bottom and were buried in the sand and sediment. Today, the lake's bottom is now home to Clarkia and the famous Fossil Bowl. Clarkia offers some of the country's best fossil remains of ancient leaves, insects, and fish, including Bald cypress, Chinese Pine, fir, and Dawn Redwood. Visitors are encouraged to bring butter knives to dig at the site and newspaper in which to collect and preserve fossil finds. The site is open daily during the summer from 8 AM to 7 PM.

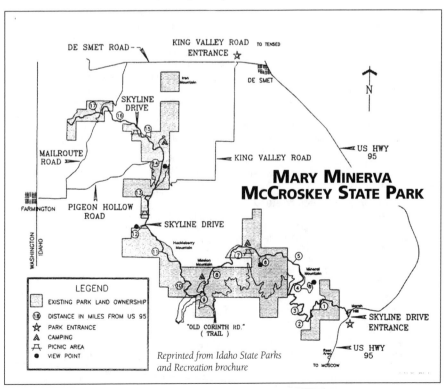

Reprinted from Idaho State Parks and Recreation brochure

H McCroskey Park
Milepost 371.7 on U.S. Hwy 95
at McCroskey State Park

Dedicated in memory of pioneer women, Mary Minerva McCroskey State Park has a forested skyline drive that offers spectacular views of forests, farms, and distant mountains.

Virgil T. McCroskey devoted his life to preserving trees and scenery. Here he purchased 4,500 acres of cedar, pine, and fir. He donated and endowed this magnificent state park in 1954 and maintained and enlarged it for 16 more years until his death at age 94.

H DeSmet Mission
Milepost 381.2 on U.S. Hwy. 95

When their annual Montana plains buffalo hunt proved futile in 1876, north Idaho's Coeur d'Alene Indians needed to move from Cataldo to a better farming area.

So in 1877, their Jesuit mission was located there. After their community grew large enough, a three-story school building – still preserved by Coeur d'Alene Tribal Council authorities – was built in 1900. It serves as a community cultural center for DeSmet.

T DeSmet
Pop. 85

DeSmet is named in honor of Father Pierre Jean DeSmet, a Belgian Jesuit missionary who arrived in Idaho in 1842. The Catholic missionary's third site of his historic Sacred Heart Mission was established here upon his arrival, and the missionaries worked closely with the three bands of Coeur d'Alene Indians living near the mission on the St. Joe River. In 1881, construction began on the Cathedral of the Sacred Heart. The large, elaborate building served as a house of worship until it tragically burned down in 1939. Today, the Coeur d'Alene tribal grammar school is still located in the small community.

T Tensed
Pop. 126

Settled during the era of Father Pierre-Jean DeSmet's Sacred Heart Mission in the St. Joe River Valley, Tensed was initially dubbed DeSmet in honor of this now historical figure. As the town grew, area residents applied for postal services. However, since another Idaho community was already named DeSmet, postal authorities rejected the request. Trying again, the residents reversed the spelling of their town's name and submitted a request for a post office in "Temsed." Authorities approved the post office in 1914, but an error occurred during processing, changing the name to its final state as Tensed.

TV Mary Minerva McCroskey State Park
Near Tensed. Contact Idaho State Parks and Recreation at 666-6711. 1 mile south of Tensed, merge of U.S. Hwy. 95 at the DeSmet turnoff, and drive approximately 6 miles. Bear left on King Valley Rd. that eventually leads to Skyline Dr. Proceed along the narrow, gravel road to the park.

About the Park
McCroskey State Park was given to the people of Idaho in 1955 by Virgil Talmage McCroskey in honor of his mother, Mary Minerva McCroskey and all the pioneer women of the Northwest, whom he believed had a more difficult life on the frontier than men.

These 5,000+ acres comprise the third largest and second oldest state park in Idaho. The park is a lasting tribute to the conservation vision and tireless efforts of one man who dedicated his life to caring for nature so that its power and tranquility could be passed along as a source of enjoyment from one generation to the next.

Mostly timberland with spectacular wildflowers in the western portion, the park is comprised of a mosaic of different forest and grassland vegetation. ponderosa pines dominate most sites, with Douglas fir comprising about a third of the area. Grand fir and Cedar occur on some northern slopes and in lower drainages. Head high mountain maple and alders line many of the vegetation transition zones.

The park has three picnicking and primitive camping areas with vault toilets, and four additional roadside areas. Skyline Drive is marked by signs denoting "Where the Mountains Meet the Sun" and is over 17 miles long. It provides access to more than 30 miles of multipurpose trails, including mountain biking and hiking.

Park History
Mary Minerva McCroskey was born in 1841 in Tennessee, and at the age of eighteen she married Joshua McCroskey. In 1879 following the post Civil War Depression, she moved with her family (now having ten children) by buggy, train, steamship, and finally by wagon with a team of horses that had been discarded by the army to their new home near Steptoe, Washington. She accomplished this on a limited budget and with very little food. Mary died in 1891, due to the extreme hardship of frontier life.

While growing up, Virgil Talmage McCroskey could see the Skyline Ridge that now is McCroskey State Park from his home at the base of Steptoe Butte. Graduating from college in 1899, he owned and worked a drugstore in Colfax, Washington until inheriting the family farm on the passing of his father. He labored on the family land until World War II, planting trees, shrubs, and flowers. Realizing that his efforts may be in vain depending upon the next owner, he sold the land to generate funds to purchase the Skyline Ridge in Idaho and Steptoe Butte in Washington. Steptoe Butte was given to the State of Washington in 1946. It took two attempts for Virgil to convince the Idaho Legislature to accept his State Park gift of 4,400 acres. Then it was with the stipulation that he provide $500 annually for the first fifteen years and maintain the park himself. Virgil kept his promise and labored endlessly in the park until his death at age 93 in 1970.

Additional Information
McCroskey State Park remains much as it was when it was dedicated in 1955. There is no drinking water available and there is no garbage collection. Please take out what you bring in and tread lightly so Virgil McCroskey's dream of providing a park "for all the people, forever and ever" will continue. Also, large travel units or trailer towing over 25 feet is not recommended on Skyline Drive.

Reprinted from Idaho State Parks and Recreation brochure

SCENIC DRIVES

White Pine Scenic Byway
The White Pine Scenic Byway begins on Idaho 3 at Interstate 90 near Cataldo, home to Old Mission of the Sacred Heart. Built in the mid-

1800s, the mission itself is the oldest building still standing in Idaho; travelers can also visit the nearby Parish House and two historic cemeteries on the grounds, and enjoy the visitor center, walking trails, and picnic areas.

From Cataldo, the White Pine Scenic Byway passes through the lush forests of Idaho's timber country and the numerous lakes and marshlands of the lower Coeur d'Alene River to the town of St. Maries, the Hughes House Museum, and other attractions. The byway then crosses the picturesque St. Maries and St. Joe rivers, the latter of which is the highest navigable river in the world.

The route continues on Idaho 6, meandering south through the town of Emida, and the St. Joe National Forest which boasts the largest stand of White Pine in the country. The byway winds through rolling hills of the Palouse region to the historic town of Potlatch, once site of the largest white pine lumber mill in the world, and U.S. 95.

Idaho 3 and Idaho 6 are both two-lane roads with no passing lanes. The byway is open year-round, and travelers should allow at least 2 hours for this 82.8-mile trip.

Reprinted from Idaho Department of Transportation brochure

Lake Coeur d'Alene Scenic Byway
The Lake Coeur d'Alene (c⁻ør-da-lane) Scenic Byway travels an area where the lakes, mountains, and beautiful summer weather have made it one of the most famous summer playgrounds and resort destinations in the Pacific Northwest. It's also home to a variety of wildlife, including moose, deer, elk, bear, and several bird species, still roaming the pristine forests of northern Idaho.

Beginning at the junction of Interstate 90 and Idaho 97, the route travels south along the eastern shoreline of Lake Coeur d'Alene, home to bald eagles and the largest population of nesting osprey in the Western states. Take a break and stretch your legs on the Mineral Ridge Trail, which offers panoramic views of the lake, as well as several learning stations describing the area's botany and animal life.

The route continues through gentle hills and dense forests to the charming town of Harrison. This byway ends at Idaho 3, where it meets the White Pine Scenic Byway and its southern route to the Palouse.

Idaho 97 is a two-lane, winding road with few passing lanes. The byway can be seen year-round, but eagle watching is great in December and January between Wolf Lodge bay and Beauty Bay. Travelers should allow at least 1.5 hours for the 35.8-mile trip.

Reprinted from Idaho Department of Transportation brochure

Pend Oreille National Scenic Byway
The Pend Oreille (pon-der-ray) Scenic Byway offers travelers some of Idaho's most spectacular water views. Beginning at the intersection with U.S. 95, Idaho 200 meanders eastward to the Montana state line across farmlands, through river deltas, and along the rocky northern shores of Lake Pend Oreille, all sculpted by the massive force of glaciers and the floodwaters of Glacial Lake Missoula. Pullouts along the byway allow visitors to stop and enjoy breathtaking vistas of mountainous horizons framing miles of open water.

Four-season recreational opportunities begin along the shores of the lake and reach across the vast regions of national forest overlooking the Pend

Oreille Scenic Byway. Whether you are inclined to swim or fish, boat or golf, hunt or hike mountain trails, alpine ski or snowmobile, water ski or bird watch – each of our distinctive four seasons offers an outstanding recreational opportunity for almost every person who enjoys the outdoors. Anglers will find more than 14 different species of game fish, and 111 miles of beautiful shoreline.

Visitors can find varying accommodations from unimproved mountain campsites to maintained shoreline campgrounds to recreational vehicle parks along the water or choose from lakefront resorts or motels.

Idaho 200 is a two-lane road with no passing lanes, but numerous scenic turnouts. Winter driving conditions require drivers to pay attention. The byway can be seen year-round. Winter scenes can be magnificent, spring and fall colors are dramatic. Travelers should allow at least 1.5 hours to enjoy the scenery and interpretive information on this 33.4-mile trip.

Reprinted from Idaho Department of Transportation brochure

Wild Horse Trail Scenic Byway

The Wild Horse Trail Scenic Byway, part of the International Selkirk Loop, starts on the northwestern shores of Lake Pend Oreille in the resort community of Sandpoint. Heading north along the eastern side of the Selkirk Mountains, the roadway follows the Kootenai Tribe's historic path to fishing grounds at Lake Pend Oreille. In 1808, the first white explorer David Thompson also utilized this trail. The "Wild Horse Trail" became more than a path in 1863 when gold was discovered in "Wild Horse Creek," 120 miles to the north of Bonners Ferry, Idaho in British Columbia. There was a large movement of men and pack animals along the "Wild Horse Trail" until the gold rush ceased circa 1880. Upon arrival of the Northern Pacific Railroad to this region, David Thompson's old route became a main freight line for the railroad.

Just south of Bonners Ferry a stunning wide glacial valley comes into view. The rich soil deposits left behind as the glaciers receded formed fertile lands which even today support a wide variety of agriculture throughout the Kootenai Valley.

In 1864 Edwin Bonner created a ferry crossing the Kootenai River to accommodate gold seekers as they made their way north, leading to the formal establishment of Bonners Ferry in 1893. Historic buildings in the downtown district remain today, reminding visitors of bygone eras.

The byway begins on U.S. 95 in downtown Sandpoint and follows it north through Bonners Ferry to the junction of U.S. 95 and Idaho 1, then proceeds north on Idaho 1 to the Canadian border at Porthill. U.S. 95 is predominantly a two-lane road with four lanes starting two miles north of Sandpoint for five miles. There are a few passing lanes. The byway can be seen year-round, and activities and events are available each month. Fall colors are especially dramatic. Travelers should allow at least 1.5 hours for the 48.2 mile trip from Sandpoint to the junction of U.S. 95/Idaho 1 and the 11 mile trip to the International Border at Porthill.

Reprinted from Idaho Department of Transportation brochure

HIKES

For information on additional area trails, please contact the Forest Service Ranger Districts listed at the back of this section.

Athol Area
Farragut State Park Lakeshore
Distance: 5 miles roundtrip
Climb: flat
Difficulty: easy
Usage: heavy
Location: Inside Farragut State Park, locate the lakeside trailheads from either the swimming beach or the Willow Day Use Area

Several easy trails wind through Idaho's Farragut State Park, but the trails leading to the lakeshore offer some of the best scenery in the area. Best months for hiking are late spring through late fall.

Clarkia Area
Hobo Cedar Grove
Distance: 1 mile roundtrip
Climb: flat
Difficulty: easy
Usage: heavy
Location: From Clarkia, travel 10 miles northeast on State Highway 3. Merge onto Merry Creek Road and travel to the trailhead for the Hobo Cedar Grove Nature Trail.

Providing visitors of all ages with an easy hiking opportunity, this short trail winds through a forest lined with old-growth cedars as well as lady ferns. The trail is part of the Hobo Cedar Grove Botanical Area.

Coeur d'Alene Area
Tubbs Hill
Distance: 2.5 miles roundtrip
Climb: flat
Difficulty: easy
Usage: heavy
Location: Next to downtown Coeur d'Alene starting between McEuen Park and the Coeur d'Alene Resort

Situated just outside the city, the Tubbs Hill trail is very popular as it affords quick access to the surrounding wilderness. Several hikers enjoy hunting for secluded swimming areas, and wildflowers flourish in the area during spring. This trail can be accessed nearly year round.

Caribou Ridge Trail
Distance: 4.6 miles roundtrip
Climb: moderate
Difficulty: moderately difficult
Location: Exit State Highway 97 (Lake Coeur d'Alene Scenic Byway onto Forest Road (FR)439 to locate the trailhead

Climbing in elevation from 2,200 feet to 4,000 feet and including four switchbacks, the Caribou Ridge Trail highlights Beauty Creek and Mt. Coeur d'Alene. Hikers will find outstanding vistas of the surrounding mountain peaks and lakes, but little wildlife viewing opportunities exist. Although the trail is named after the caribou, these animals have since migrated farther north into the Idaho Panhandle. Best months for hiking are June through September.

Independence Creek Trail System
Distance: 34 miles roundtrip
Climb: moderate
Difficulty: moderate to difficult
Location: At Kingston, exit north of Interstate 90 and merge onto Forest Road (FR) 209. Traveling past Lake Pend Oreille, locate FR 258 directly before reaching Honeysuckle Campground and follow it to FR 904. FR 904 leads to the Independence Creek Trailhead.

Partially winding along an early 20th century wagon road, the Independence Creek Trail is situated east of Hayden Lake and was once used to link the Lake Pend Oreille and Lakeview mines with the Independence Creek Valley. Although a 1910 forest fire devastated the area, little evidence remains of this event and the backcountry is filled with a variety of foliage. Trail users will locate several waterfalls and likely view numerous water ousels. All of the trails are open to hikers and horses. Best months for hiking are June through September.

Mullan Area
Stateline Trail
Distance: 18 miles roundtrip
Climb: moderate to steep in places
Difficulty: moderate to difficult
Location: Found within the Wallace Ranger District. Exit off Interstate 90 at Mullan to locate the trailhead.

This trail designed for experienced backpackers traverses across several high mountain ridges and follows a portion of the Centennial Trail.

Priest River/Nordman Area
Upper Priest River
Distance: 13 miles roundtrip
Climb: gentle
Difficulty: easy
Usage: moderate
Location: From the town of Priest River, drive north 36 miles to Nordman on State Highway 57. Highway 57 officially ends here, but continue on the same paved road 2 miles until it turns into the gravel Forest Road (FR) 302. Drive on FR 302 for 10 miles to the three-way junction at Granite Pass, then proceed on the middle road, FR 1013. 12 miles from the junction for FR 1013, find the Trail 308 trailhead.

This trail immediately enters into a rare northwestern rainforest lined with towering firs and red cedars, and occasionally, mountain caribou and grizzlies can be spotted. After walking 5.5 miles along the canyon floor, hikers will reach the junction for Trail 28. Although many hikers turn around at this point, those who continue on Trail 28 will face a steep 1-mile descent to Upper Priest Falls tumbling near the U.S./Canadian border. Best months for hiking are mid-June through October.

Roosevelt Grove of Ancient Cedars
Distance: 4.5 miles roundtrip
Climb: moderate to steep in places
Difficulty: difficult
Location: Take Scenic Route (SR) 57 north for 37 miles from Priest River to Nordman. Continue along SR 57 for 13 more miles (2 miles past Nordman, SR 57 converts to Granite Creek Road) leading to the Stagger Inn Picnic Area. Across the main road (#302), locate the trailhead for Roosevelt Trail 266.

Located in the Priest Lake Ranger District, Roosevelt Trail climbs numerous switchbacks before ending in a large area of old-growth cedar trees. This trail also provides access to panoramic views of the surrounding area from Little Grass Mountain, Boulder Mountain, and Zero Creek. Best months for hiking are mid-June through September.

Grassy Top Mountain
Distance: 16 miles roundtrip
Climb: steep
Difficulty: difficult
Location: From the town of Priest River, follow Scenic Route (SR) 57 north for 37 miles to Nordman. Continue on SR 57 for 13 more miles (2 miles past Nordman, SR 57 turns into Granite Creek Road) until you reach the entrance for Stagger Inn Picnic Area. Proceed south another .75 mile and locate the trailhead for Trail 379.

For experienced hikers ready for a challenging climb, Grassy Top Trail ascends to the top of Grassy Top Mountain. Outstanding views of the surrounding area wait at the mountaintop. Best months for hiking are mid-June through September.

Navigation Trail

Distance: 10 miles one-way
Climb: moderate
Difficulty: moderate
Location: From Nordman, drive 12 miles north on Forest Road (FR) 2512 to Beaver Creek Campground on Priest Lake's northern shore. The trail begins at the campground.

Passing through both meadows and forests, this trail affords panoramic views of Upper Priest Lake. The trail also passes by beaver ponds and a historical trapper's cabin before its end at FR 1013. Best months for hiking are June through September.

Beach Trail and Lakeshore National Recreation Trail

Distance: Beach Trail – 9 miles; Lakeshore National Recreation Trail – 15.2 miles roundtrip
Climb: Flat
Difficulty: Easy
Usage: Heavy
Location: Beach Trail begins at Priest Lake's south end near Outlet Bay and continues to Kalispell Bay. To locate the Lakeshore Trail, proceed to Nordman and merge onto Forest Road (FR) 1339. Follow FR 1339 to the trailhead at Beaver Creek. The Lakeshore Trail proceeds south.

Both trails gently wind along the popular Priest Lake's western shores. The area provides beautiful scenery, but expect to have company along the way.

Sandpoint Area

Beehive Lake

Distance: 9 miles roundtrip
Climb: moderate
Difficulty: moderate
Location: From Sandpoint, proceed 10.5 miles north on U.S. Highway 95. After crossing the Pack River Bridge, bear left onto Forest Road (FR) 231 (also called Pack River Road). Continue 17 miles to a sign for Beehive Lakes, park, and follow the footbridge to Trail 279.

After hiking along a fairly rough trail, hikers will discover a lake surrounded with numerous rock ridges and slabs. Moose have often been spotted wading in the lake, and Beehive is renowned for its population of cutthroat trout. Best months for hiking are June through September.

Selkirk Mountains Area

Harrison Lake

Distance: 8 miles roundtrip
Climb: gentle to moderately steep in places
Difficulty: moderate
Location: From downtown Bonners Ferry, locate Riverside Street and proceed west to the Kootenai Wildlife Refuge headquarters. Continue 1.5 miles and turn on Forest Road (FR) 663 leading through Myrtle Creek Canyon. After driving 10.5 miles, the road is renumbered to FR 633A. Proceed 2 more miles past the Two Mouths Trailhead where the road number changes to FR 661. Follow FR 661 1.5 miles and then turn right onto FR 2409. Continue 1.5 miles along FR 2409 to its dead end at the trailhead marked Harrison Lake 4, Trail No. 6.

Climbing 950 feet over the Myrtle Creek-Pack River Divide, hikers will make their way through continuous patches of huckleberry, currant, gooseberry, serviceberry, elderberry, and mountain sumac before reaching Harrison Lake. Surrounded by large slabs of white granite, Harrison Lake is situated in a cirque basin at an elevation of 6,182 feet. From the lake, hikers can view the hatchet-shaped Harrison Peak rising 7,292 feet in the Selkirk Mountain Range. While several campsites surround the lake's east side, most are closed for revegetation. Hikers should also watch for bears, particularly in August when the huckleberries ripen. Best months for hiking are July through September.

Hidden Lake and Red Top Mountain

Distance: 6.5 miles roundtrip
Climb: gentle
Difficulty: moderate
Location: At Bonners Ferry, drive north on U.S. Highway 95 to the junction of State Highway 1. Exiting onto Highway 1, proceed 1 mile, then bear left onto the paved side road. After reaching the Kootenai Valley floor, turn left and cross the Kootenai River. Continue west to the foot of the Selkirk Mountains and locate a T intersection in the road. Turn right onto Westside Road and follow for 9 miles to Smith Creek Road. Smith Creek Road climbs through Smith Creek Canyon and is paved for 6 miles. Once the road turns to gravel, it is renamed Forest Road (FR) 281. Proceed along FR 281 3 miles, then bear left and follow FR 665 for 2 miles. Next, drive up Beaver Creek Canyon on FR 2545 and continue 3 miles to the trailhead.

This non-motorized trail begins with a set of gentle switchbacks up a cirque wall, then passes through subalpine fir and spruce before reaching Hidden Lake in just one mile. Characterized by numerous huckleberry bushes and a tree-lined shore, Hidden Lake rests at the shoulder of Joe Peak and is rumored to hold abundant trout. Just prior to reaching the lake, the trail divides. While the right trail dead-ends at the shoreline, the left trail (Trail 102) continues eastward, crossing two streams and passing through a campsite. To reach Red Mountain, proceed uphill from the campground to your left on Trail 102. At the junction with Trail 21, continue left on Trail 102 through thick forests. Although the trail becomes faint, it is well cleared and leads directly to Red Top Mountain, named for the abundant red ripe huckleberry bushes dominating the landscape. At the summit, find impressive views of Joe Peak, the clear-cut border between the U.S. and Canada, and numerous other peaks to the south at Smith Creek. From this point, hikers can turn around or continue 3 miles forward on Trail 102 that descends 2,400 feet to the upper portion of Smith Creek. Best months for hiking are late August to mid-September when there are few insects and foliage is in full bloom.

Optional Hikes: Instead of continuing on Trail 102 at the junction for Trail 21, proceed right along Trail 21. After following the trail 2 miles downhill, hikers will reach West Fork Cabin. Take Trail 347 at West Fork Cabin for a longer hike, ending at West Fork Smith Creek and West Fork Lake.

Long Canyon

Distance: 30 mile near loop
Climb: steep
Difficulty: very difficult
Usage: light
Location: Drive north from Bonners Ferry on U.S. Highway 95, exiting onto State Highway 1. Proceed 1 mile on Highway 1, and then turn left onto a paved side road leading to the Kootenai Valley floor. From the floor, bear left, cross the Kootenai River, and proceed west to the base of the Selkirk Mountains. At the foot of the mountains, locate a T intersection in the road and turn right onto Westside Road. Continue 6.5 miles, crossing Parker and Long Canyon Creeks. In another 0.5 mile, locate a marked side road leading to Long Canyon Creek Trailhead/Trail 16.

For experienced hikers interested in a multi-day backpacking trip, Long Canyon provides exceptional wildlife viewing opportunities (including grizzly bears and woodland caribou), a rainforest, waterfalls, a trail flanked by two of Idaho's tallest mountain peaks (Smith and Parker), and a ridge walk. However, backpackers should also be prepared for three difficult creek crossings, faint areas in the trail, limited water sources during the first and last five miles, and steep descents. After proceeding along Trail 16 for 12.5 miles, the trail fades out and Trail 7 begins, leading hikers across a creek and out of Long Canyon. Trail 7 climbs 2,400 feet in 4 miles to Pyramid Pass, but 0.5 mile below the pass, turn onto Trail 221. Trail 221 climbs to Long Mountain's ridge, then follows the ridgeline to the hike's end at Westside Road. As hikers descend from Long Mountain and reach the trip's 20-mile mark, some may opt to veer left on a side trail that dead-ends in 500 feet at Parker Lake. Another side hike is found at mile mark 21.5 where backpackers can climb Parker Peak, the highest peak in the Selkirk Mountains. Best months for hiking are July through late September.

Salmo-Priest Divide Loop

Distance: 16 mile loop
Climb: moderate to steep in places
Difficulty: moderate
Usage: moderate
Location: From Metaline Falls, Washington, drive north on Washington Highway 6 for 1.5 miles. Bear right onto Pend Oreille County Road 9345 and continue to Forest Road (FR) 22. Turn left on FR 22 and drive to the junction with FR 2220. Bear left on FR 2220, which climbs up Deemer Creek to Salmo Pass. At the pass, turn right to reach the trailhead for Trail 506.

Beginning in Washington's Salmo-Priest Wilderness, this hike climbs through old-growth rain forest crosses over into Idaho after the first 5.5 miles. Hikers should note that Crutch Creek (just before crossing into Idaho) provides the last reliable water source before reaching the head of the South Salmo River. After entering Idaho, hikers will climb to Snowy Top Pass. Many hikers choose to take a three-hour side trip to climb Snowy Top for its views of the Selkirk Mountains in Idaho, Washington, and Canada. For those less adventurous, continue south along the trail that is now numbered Trail 512 and cross over the Shedroof Divide. After reaching Hughes Saddle, proceed 2.5 miles to the junction of Trail 535 that takes hikers back to the trailhead. Best months for hiking are mid-July through late September, and hikers should watch for black bears and grizzlies during August when huckleberries are ripe in the area.

Optional Hikes: After crossing over the Snowy Top Pass on Trail 512, Trail 349 veers to the left 0.4 miles past the slopes of Little Snowy Top Mountain. This 4.5-mile trail descends 3,400 feet to the upper Priest River and includes 70 switchbacks. Another side hike occurs at the junction for Trail 512 and Trail 535. Instead of immediately returning to the trailhead on Trail 535, explore

Shedroof Divide by heading south on Trail 512 past Shedroof Mountain.

Two Mouths Lakes
Distance: 8 miles roundtrip
Climb: moderate
Difficulty: moderate
Usage: heavy
Location: Locate Riverside Street in downtown Bonners Ferry and continue west to the Kootenai Wildlife Refuge office. Passing the refuge's headquarters, proceed 1.5 miles to Forest Road (FR) 663 leading into Myrtle Creek Canyon. In approximately 10.5 miles the road is renumbered FR 633A. Continue 2 miles to the Two Mouths Trailhead for Trail 268.

Hikers start out on an overgrown logging road and soon reach Peak Creek. As the trail heads along Peak Creek, it splits, and hikers should stay on the left trail. Winding along a granite mountainside, hikers climb to the top of Slide Creek and reach Selkirk Crest above Two Mouths Lakes. From the crest, views of glacier peaks surrounding Slide Creek are abundant, and a short descent leads to the lakes. While the left fork in the trail leads to the east lake, the right fork leads to the west lake following a spring-fed creek through a meadow lined with granite boulders. Best months for hiking are July through September.

INFORMATION PLEASE

All Idaho area codes are 208.

Road Information

ID Road & Weather Conditions	
888-432-7623 or local 884-7000	
Idaho State Police	736-3090

Tourism Information

Idaho Travel Council 800-VISIT-ID outside Idaho
334-2470 in Idaho
www.visitid.org
North Idaho Tourism Alliance   888-333-3737
www.visitnorthidaho.com

Airports

Bonners Ferry	267-3711
Hayden	772-7838
Kellogg	786-5381
Sandpoint	263-9102
St. Maries	245-4619

Government Offices

Idaho Bureau of Reclamation	334-1466
www.usbr.gov	
Idaho Department of Commerce	
(800) 847-4843 or 334-2470	
www.visitid.org or http://cl.idaho.gov/	
Idaho Department of Fish and Game	
(800) ASK-FISH or 334-3700	
http://fishandgame.idaho.gov	
Idaho Department of Parks and Recreation	
334-4199	
www.idahoparks.org	
State BLM Office	373-3889 or 373-4000
www.id.blm.gov	
Bureau of Land Management Coeur d'Alene Office	
769-5000	
Idaho Panhandle National Forests	765-7223

Hospitals

Boundary Community	
Bonners Ferry	267-3141
Kootenai Medical Center	
Coeur d'Alene	666-2000
Shoshone Medical Center • Kellogg	784-1221
Northwest Specialty Hospital	
Post Falls	457-9205
Benewah Community • Saint Maries	245-5551
Bonner General Hospital • Sandpoint	263-1441

Golf Courses

Rimrock Golf Course • Athol	762-5054
Stoneridge Country Club • Blanchard	437-4653
Mirror Lake Golf • Bonners Ferry	267-5314
North Idaho Resorts • Bonners Ferry	267-7625
Coeur D'alene Public Golf Club	
Coeur D Alene	765-0218
Ponderosa Springs Par 3	
Coeur d'Alene	664-1101
Avondale Gold • Hayden Lake	772-5963
Shoshone Golf • Kellogg	784-0161
Shoshone Golf • Osburn	784-0161
Pinehurst Golf Course • Pinehurst	682-2013
Coeur D'Alene Public Golf Club	
Post Falls	667-5286
Highlands Country Club • Post Falls	773-3673
Links Golf Club • Post Falls	777-7611
Prairie Falls Golf Club • Post Falls	457-0210
Priest Lake Golf Course • Priest Lake	443-2525
Ranch Club Golf Course • Priest River	448-1731
Twin Lake Village • Rathdrum	687-1311
Elks Golf Club • Sandpoint	263-4024
Hidden Lakes • Sandpoint	263-1642
St Maries Golf • St. Maries	245-3842

Bed & Breakfasts

Coeur d'Alene B&B Association	
www.bb-cda.com	
Coit House B&B • Sandpoint	265-4035
Church Street House • Sandpoint	255-7094
McFarland Inn • Coeur d'Alene	667-1232
Baragar House • Coeur d'Alene	664-9125
Cougar Crest Lodge • Coeur d'Alene	769-7991
The Hideaway • Coeur d'Alene	666-8846
The Roosevelt • Coeur d'Alene	765-5200
Cedar Mountain Farm • Athol	683-0572
Country Lane Inn • Kingston	682-2698
Katie's Wild Rose Inn • Coeur d'Alene	765-9474
Heaven On Earth • Post Falls	457-9519
Cedar Springs • Rathdrum	687-9333
Dromore Manor • Bayview	683-9311
The Ponderosa • Athol	683-2251
St. Joe Riverfront Bed & Breakfast	
St. Maries	245-8687
Coeur d'Alene B&B • Coeur d'Alene	667-7527
Log Spirit Bed & Breakfast • Athol	683-4722
The Rivercove B&B • Post Falls	773-9190
Wolf Lodge Creek B&B	
Coeur d'Alene	667-5902
Monte's Mountain Ranch & Lodge	
Athol	683-7216
Berry Patch Inn B&B	
Coeur d'Alene	765-4994
Hideaway on Rockford Bay	
Coeur d'Alene	666-8846
International Inn B&B	
Coeur d'Alene	664-6666
O'Neill B&B • Coeur d'Alene	664-5356
Someday House B&B	
Coeur d'Alene	664-6666
Driftwood B&B • Harrison	800-451-1795
Pegis Bed and Breakfast Place	
Harrison	689-9502
Ranch B&B • Kingston	682-4862
Heyburn Farms • Plummer	686-7005
Whispering Waters B&B	
Priest River	443-3229
Midas Inn B&B • Sagle	263-6074

GHOST TOWNS

Mace
Interstate 90 approximately 13 miles north of Mullan
Devastation swept through this small mining community in 1910 when a snowslide swept down Burke Canyon and killed forty miners and one mine superintendent. Although the town persevered, it suffered its share of unpleasant natural phenomena, including winter temperatures averaging thirty below zero, twenty-foot snowpacks, and floods along Canyon Creek from spring runoff.

In August 1923, the town was hit again with disaster. While passing through town, a Union Pacific train threw sparks that set fire to several house roofs. The fire quickly spread through the canyon, and while residents evacuated, several miners were trapped below a burning surface above them. Today, metal buildings located near these tracks represent the mining endeavors of Hecla Mining Company.

Delta
Interstate 90 approximately 10 miles north of Wallace
Found along the Ninemile Canyon Road, Delta is a mere shadow of its past on Beaver Creek. Historians speculate that the town, at one point boasting a population of 1,000, was named after its position at the mouth of Trail Creek.

Storm Creek
Near Avery
Located near Avery, Storm Creek marks a devastating point in Idaho history. Four miles up the creek is the site of a tragedy forever burned into the minds of Idaho residents. During the summer of 1910, the "Big Burn" swept across Montana and Idaho's northern panhandle with a fury unrivaled by any other American forest fire. In its path, towns were scorched and brave men lost their lives in an attempt to save their families and communities.

Twenty-eight of these brave men met their fate on Storm Creek. The men, miners from Butte, Montana who volunteered to help fight the blaze, chose to disregard the Forest Service's instruction to leave their post and return to Avery. Little did they know that the fire would soon sweep over them. With no hope of escape, most of the men were burned beyond recognition with watches, stopped by the intense heat, recording their time of death. One man attempted to run for his life up the canyon, but his efforts only gave him seven more minutes of life. The men were initially buried in a trench on Storm Creek and were later moved to the St. Maries' cemetery.

Granite
Situated near Lake Pend Oreille in Bonner County, Granite served as a way station when gold was discovered in the area in 1874. The community has long since passed away, but the name remains as a testament to the numerous granite outcroppings scattered throughout the county.

Waterhouse • Sandpoint 265-9112
Fort Hemenway Manor B&B
St Maries 245-7979

Guest Ranches & Resorts

Bear Creek Lodge • Bonners Ferry 267-7268
Monarch Mountain Lodge
Ponderay 263-1222
Kelso Lake Resort • Athol 683-2297
Monte's Mountain Ranch & Lodge
Athol 683-7216
Boileau's Resort & Marina • Bayview 683-2213
Macdonald's Hudson Bay Resort
Bayview 683-2211
Stoneridge Resort & Loft Restaurant
Blanchard 437-2451
Bonners Ferry Resort/The Lantern
Bonners Ferry 267-2422
Gold Bar Ranch Resort Lodge
Bonners Ferry 267-3526
Shiloh Christian Guest Ranch
Calder 245-3600
Diamond T Guest Ranch
Clark Fork 970-663-4183
River Delta Resort • Clark Fork 266-1335
Arrow Point Resort • Coeur d'Alene 664-1593
Coeur d'Alene KOA, RV, Tent & Cabin Resort
Coeur d'Alene 664-4471
Coeur d'Alene Resort on the Lake
Coeur d'Alene 765-4000
Rider Ranch • Coeur d'Alene 667-3373
Cavanaugh Bay Resort • Coolin 443-2095
Inn at Priest Lake Resort & Conference Center
Coolin 443-4066
Eagle Ridge Ranch • Hamer 558-0900
Carlin Bay Resort • Harrison 689-3295
Hidden Creek Ranch • Harrison 689-3209
Lakeview Lodge • Harrison 689-3318
Squaw Bay Resort & Marina
Harrison 664-6782
Holiday Shores Resort & Marin
Hope 264-5515
Idaho Country Resorts • Hope 264-5505
Pend Oreille Shores Resort • Hope 264-5828
Red Fir Resort • Hope 264-5287
Silver Mountain Resort • Kellogg 783-1111
Hemlocks Resort • Moyie Springs 267-9822,
Elkins Resort on Priest Lake
Nordman 443-2432
Kaniksu Resort, RV Park & Marina
Nordman 443-2609
Low's Resort • Nordman 443-2631
Grandview Lodge & Resort
Priest Lake 443-2433
Hill's Resort • Priest Lake 443-2551
Beyond Hope Resort • Priest River 264-5251
Bottle Bay Resort & Marina • Sagle 263-5916
Hidden Lakes Golf Resort • Sandpoint 255-4500
West Shore Lodge • Sandpoint 487-3636
Western Pleasure Guest Ranch
Sandpoint 263-9066
Silver Beach Resort • Spirit Lake 623-4842

Vacation Homes & Cabins

Gold Creek Lodge • Bayview 222-7669
Hudson Bay Resort Inc • Bayview 683-2211
Macdonald's On the Bay • Bayview 683-2211
Aunt Jeans Cabin • Hayden Lake 772-2284
Cabin On the Green • Sandpoint 263-1642
Caribou Mountain Lodge • Sandpoint 255-2333

Forest Service Cabins

Idaho Panhandle National Forest
Deer Ridge (40í Lookout Tower)
26 mi. NE of Bonners Ferry 267-5561
Capacity: 4 Nightly Fee: $25
Available: 6/15-9/30

Acc. By forest road; last mile rough, narrow, caution
adv. Discourage bringing children

Snyder Guard Station
22 mi. NE of Bonners Ferry 267-5561
Cap: 6 Nightly Fee: $35 night/$175/week
Available: 5/15-9/30
1 bldg., electric heat, hot shower, kitchen, horse
corral; .25 mi.from plowed road in winter.
Provisions may be made to accommodate more

Shorty Peak (Lookout Cabin)
23 mi. SW from Bonners Ferry 267-5561
Cap: 4 Nightly Fee: $25
Available: 6/15-9/30
Access by Forest Rd 408.

Arid Peak Lookout
23 mi. S of Wallace 245-4517
Cap: 8 Nightly Fee: $50
Available: 6/15-9/30 (max. 5 nights)
Access via 2-lane gravel road, moderate 3 mile
hike. Tables and Chairs, 2 single beds, outhouse,
woodstove, propane cook stove and lantern. Not
recommended for small children.

Red Ives Cabin
86 mi. SE of St. Maries, along St. Joe W&S River
245-4517
Cap: 8 Nightly Fee: $50
Available: Memorial Day weekend to 9/30 (max. 3
days)
Access by FR 218. Bring drinking water. 2 bedroom, kitchen, living room and bathroom, propane
cook stove and refrigerator, hot water, flush toilet
and shower, heat and lights via generator. No pets.

Magee Cabin
64 mi NW of Wallace 664-2318
Cap: 6 Nightly Fee: $50
Available: Memorial Day weekend to 9/30 (max. 5
days)
Accessible via paved hwy. And paved/gravel Forest
roads. 3 bedrooms, kitchen, living room, propane
cook stove, refrigerator, heater, hot water, drinking
water. No elec.

Little Guard Peak Lookout Cabin
49 mi. N of Wallace 664-2318
Cap: 4 Nightly Fee: $30
Available: 7/1-9/30
Access by paved/gravel road, last 2 mi. rough/nar-
row road. Two-level lookout. No tower. Lookout
plus downstairs kitchen w/propane stove. Single
hole outhouse.

Lunch Peak 25í Lookout Tower
25 mi. NE of Sandpoint 263-5111
Cap: 4 Nightly Fee: $25
Available: 8/1-9/30
Access roads 275 and 1091 not drivable until
mid-July, depending on weather

Surveyors Lookout
106 mi. SE of St. Maries, near Mallard-Larkins
Pioneer Area 245-4517
Cap: 4 Nightly Fee: $35
Available 7/15-9/30 dep. On snow levels (max. 5
nights)
Access via paved Forest Service road and rugged
one land road w/pullouts. Not recommended for
low clearance vehicles. 6000 elevation. Propane
lights, cook stove and heater, 1 bed, table and
chairs.

Clarkia Bunkhouse
30 mi. S of St. Maries on State Hwy. 3 245-2531
Cap: 15 Nightly Fee: $30-45 per room,
$200/night for entire bunkhouse
Avail: All year
Communal bathroom, showers, laundry and
kitchen. 2-,3-,4-person rooms. Ideal for groups,
families or individuals

Car Rental

Bonners Ferry Towing • Bonners Ferry 267-3100
Riverside • Bonners Ferry 267-3181
Avis • Coeur d'Alene 665-7797
Budget • Coeur d'Alene 667-5940
Dollar • Coeur d'Alene 664-0682
Enterprise • Coeur d'Alene 765-1070
Thrifty • Coeur d'Alene 765-2277
Tom Addis Dodge Inc
Coeur d'Alene 664-4000
Autorental of Coeur d'Alene
Coeur d'Alene 667-4905
Oldtown Auto • Oldtown 437-4011
Budget • Ponderay 263-0314
Enterprise • Ponderay 255-1553
Budget • Post Falls 777-9067
Enterprise • Sandpoint 255-1553
Taylor-Parker Motor Co. • Sandpoint 263-2138
Thrifty Car Rental • Sandpoint 255-7909

Outfitters & Guides

F=Fishing H=Hunting
R=River Guides
E=Horseback Rides
G=General Guide Services

Id Outfitters & Guides Association
800-49-IDAHO
Outfitters & Guides Licensing Board 327-7380
C d/A River Big Game Outfitters HE 683-2154
Russell Point Outfitter HEG 245-2458
Clark Fork Outfitters FH 266-1910
River Odysseys West FHER 765-0841
Northwest Outfitters F 772-1497
Hidden Creek Ranch FHEG 689-3209
A-W Outfitters FHEG 772-2831
Buckshot Outfitting H 267-3885
Granite Outfitters H 777-2145
All About Adventures, Inc FRG 263-6959
Buckshot Outfitting H 263-1512
Bitterroot Mountain Outfitters H 927-7069
Russell Pond Outfitters H 245-2458
St. Joe Outfitters & Guides FHERG 245-4002

Cross-Country Ski Centers

Silver Mountain • Kellogg 783-1111
Schweitzer Mountain Resort
Sandpoint 263-9555
Lookout Pass Ski Area • Wallace 774-1301

Downhill Ski Areas

North Sough Ski Bowl • Emida 245-4222
Silver Mountain • Kellogg 783-1111
Schweitzer Mountain • Sandpoint 263-9555
Look out Pass • Wallace 744-1301

Snowmobile Rentals

H20 and Snow • Coeur d'Alene 424-3093
Sun Rental Center • Coeur d'Alene 664-0457
Vacation Sports Rentals
Coeur d'Alene 665-0686
Cascade Lodge • Post Falls 773-3469
Red Line Rentals • Post Falls 777-9405
Cavanaugh Bay Resort • Priest Lake 443-2095
Grandview Lodge • Priest Lake 443-2433
Hills Resort • Priest Lake 443-2551
Highmountain Adventures • Wallace 556-2442
Idaho Magic • Wallace 556-2442

Bike Rentals

Excelsior Cycle & Sport Shop
Kellogg 786-3751
Island Rentals • Coeur d'Alene 666-1626
Pedal Pushers • Harrison 689-3436
Outdoor Experience • Sandpoint 263-6028
Hughes Ace Hardware • St. Maries 245-6545

Campground Quick Reference

Campground Name				Phone
Public/Commercial	Unit Price	#Spaces	Max. Length	Seasons
Directions				
Amenities/Activities				

Campground Name				Phone
Public/Commercial	Unit Price	#Spaces	Max. Length	Seasons
Directions				
Amenities/Activities				

Athol

Kelso Lake Resort   683-2297
C $12-16   18   All Year
Hwy. 95, 25 mi. N. of Coeur d'Alene
Hookups, Limited Access, Mini-Mart, Pets OK, Showers, Waterfront, Handicap Access

Farragut State Park   683-2425
P $7-22   108   31'   All Year
Hwy 95, E. 4 mi. on Hwy. 54 to park entrance
Boating Facilities, Camping Cabins, Credit Cards OK, Drinking Water, Dump Station, Hookups, Pets OK, Playground, Pull-thru Sites, Reservations, Showers, Tenters Welcome, Vault Toilets

Avery

Swiftwater Motel & RV Park   245-2845
C $15   12   All Year
See web site for directions
Cable TV Hookups, Credit Cards OK, Drinking Water, Dump Station, Fire Rings, Hookups, Pets OK, Reservations, Tenters Welcome, Waterfront

Big Creek   245-4517
P   8   30'   Summer, Fall
5 mi. E. on Northside Rd., 3 mi. NW on Forest Rd. 537 (Big Creek Rd.)
Vault Toilets

Conrad Crossing   245-4517
P $8   8   16'   Summer, Fall
28 mi. E. on Forest Rd. 50
Drinking Water, Vault Toilets

Fly Flat   245-4517
P $6   14   32'   Summer, Fall
29 mi. E. on Forest Rd. 50, then 4 mi. on Forest Rd. 218
Drinking Water, Swimming Pool, Vault Toilets

Line Creek (Horse Camp)   245-4517
P   9   35'   Summer, Fall
29 mi. E. on Forest Rd. 50, then 11 mi. on Forest Rd. 218
Drinking Water, Pull-thru Sites, Vault Toilets

Spruce Tree   245-4517
P   9   35'   Summer, Fall
29 mi. E. on Forest Rd. 50, then 12 mi. S. on Forest Rd. 218
Drinking Water, Pull-thru Sites, Vault Toilets

Tin Can Flat   245-4517
P $6   11   32'   Summer, Fall
10 mi. E. on Forest Rd. 50
Drinking Water, Vault Toilets

Turner Flat   245-4517
P $6   11   32'   Summer, Fall
8 mi. E. on Forest Rd. 50
Drinking Water, Vault Toilets

Packsaddle   245-4517
P   None   2   June-October
5 miles E of Avery on Forest Highway 50
Primitive Camping, Restrooms, Biking, Non-Motorized Boating, Whitewater Rafting, Fishing, Horseback Riding, Off Highway Vehicles

Squaw Creek   245-4517
P   None   5   May-October
6 miles N of Avery on FR 456, then south 1 mile on Moon Pass Rd
Primitive Camping, Restrooms, Biking, Fishing, Hiking/Backpacking, Off Highway Vehicles

Mammoth Springs   245-4517
P   None   8   June-October
22 miles E of Avery on Forest Highway 50, then 14 miles S on FR 509, then 2.5 miles S on FR 201
Developed Campground, Drinking Water, Restrooms, Hiking/Backpacking

Heller Creek   245-4517
P   None   4   June-October
29 miles E of Avery on Forest Highway 50, then 10 miles S on FR 218, then 13 miles E of the Red Ives Information Center on FR 320. The road is not suitable for cars.
Primitive Camping, Restrooms, Cultural/Historic Sites, Biking, Fishing, Hiking/Backpacking

Bayview

MacDonald's Hudson Bay Resort, Inc.   683-2211
C $18-26   14   All Year
.75 mi. E. of Bayview on Hudson Bay Rd.
Cable TV Hookups, Dump Station, Hookups, Mini-Mart, Reservations, Showers, Handicap Access

Bayview Scenic Motel & RV Park   683-2215
C $20-25   10   All Year
25 mi. N. of Coeur d'Alene, Hwy. 54 to end of road
Cable TV Hookups, Dump Station, Hookups, Pets OK

Scenic Bay Marina, Motel, Mobile Home Park, RV & Campsites 683-2243
C $15-25   10   All Year
Hwy. 95, 25 mi. N. of Coeur d'Alene
Credit Cards OK, Hookups, Pets OK, Showers, Waterfront

Lakeland RV Park   683-4108
C $24   25   Summer, Fall, Spring
Hwy. 95 to Hwy. 54, E. 4 mi. to Farragut State Park, then 4 mi. to Bayview. Bear left on Main St. to Perimeter Rd.
Cable TV Hookups, Hookups, Pull-thru Sites, Showers, Handicap Access

Bonners Ferry

Loewenshaw Vineyards Retreat & RV Park 267-2029
C $15-26   40   Summer, Fall, Spring
8 mi. S. of Bonners Ferry
Dump Station, Hookups, Pets OK, Pull-thru Sites, Reservations, Showers, Tenters Welcome, Handicap Access

Bonners Ferry Resort   267-2422
C $14-60   61   All Year

Handicap Access

Idyl Acres RV Park   267-3629
C $20   10   40'   Summer
Hwy. 95, 4 mi. S. of the Canadian border
Hookups, Pets OK, Pull-thru Sites, Reservations, Showers

Carriage House Inn & RV Park   267-7915
C $20   20   All Year
Hwy. 95, 6506 Main St.
Credit Cards OK, Drinking Water, Dump Station, Hookups, Mini-Mart, Pets OK, Playground, Pull-thru Sites, Reservations, Showers, Tenters Welcome, Handicap Access

Copper Creek   267-5561
P $6   16   32'   Summer, Fall
30 mi. N. on Hwy. 95
Drinking Water, Pets OK, Tenters Welcome, Vault Toilets

Meadow Creek Campground   267-5561
P $6   22   22'   Summer, Fall
Hwy 2, 12 mi. N. on Meadow Creek Rd.
Drinking Water, Pets OK, Tenters Welcome, Vault Toilets, Waterfront

Robinson Lake   267-5561
P $8   10   32'   Summer, Fall
25 mi. N. on Hwy. 95
Drinking Water, Pets OK, Swimming Pool, Tenters Welcome, Vault Toilets

Smith Lake   267-5561
P   7   22'   Summer, Fall
5 mi. N. on Hwy. 95, 2 mi. on Forest Rd. 1005
Drinking Water, Swimming Pool, Vault Toilets

Campground Quick Reference-continued

Deer Ridge Lookout Tower 267-5561/877-444-6777
P $25/2 night min. 4 people 7/1-9/30
5 miles NE of Bonners Ferry on Hwy. 2, then 10 miles NE on FR 229, then 7 miles E on FR 2540
Restrooms, Biking, Hiking/Backpacking

Cataldo

Kahnderosa River Campground 682-4613
C 21 70' All Year
I-90, exit 40
Dump Station, Hookups, Pets OK, Pull-thru Sites, Reservations, Showers, Tenters Welcome, Waterfront

Clark Fork

River Delta Resort 266-1335
C $18 56 Summer, Fall, Spring
Hwy. 200, 5 mi. E. of Clark Fork
Dump Station, Hookups, LP Gas, Pets OK, Showers, Laundry

River Lake RV Park 266-1115
C $18 31 40' Summer, Fall, Spring
2.5 mi. SE of Clark Fork
Drinking Water, Dump Station, Hookups, Pets OK, Pull-thru Sites, Showers, Tenters Welcome, Waterfront

Clark Fork Lodge 266-1716
C $15 14 All Year
Hwy. 200 from Sandpoint
Hookups, Modem Hookups, Pets OK, Pull-thru Sites, Reservations, Showers, Laundry, Handicap Access

Porcupine Lake 263-5111
P None 5 June-September
9 miles N of Clark Fork on Lightning Creek Rd. (FR 419), then 6 miles W on Porcupine Creek Rd. (FR 632)
Primitive Camping, Restrooms, Boat Ramp, Biking, Non-Motorized Boating, Fishing, Hiking/Backpacking, Off-Highway Vehicles

Clarkia

Cedar Creek 245-4517
P None 3 June-October
3 miles N of Clarkia on Hwy. 3
Primitive Camping, Restrooms, Non-Motorized Boating, Fishing

Cocolalla

Sandy Beach Resort 263-4328
C $16-22.95 90 All Year
Hwy. 95, 10 mi. S. of Sandpoint, 2 mi. W. on Cocolalla Loop Rd.
Credit Cards OK, Dump Station, Hookups, Limited Access, LP Gas, Mini-Mart, Pets OK, Pull-thru Sites, Showers, Handicap Access

Coeur d'Alene

Coeur d'Alene KOA RV, Tent & Cabin Resort 664-4471/800-562-2609
C $22-159 68 All Year
I-90, exit 22, .3 mi. S. on Hwy. 97
Boating Facilities, Camping Cabins, Credit Cards OK, Drinking Water, Dump Station, Fire Rings, Game Room, Hookups, LP Gas, Mini-Mart, Modem Hookups, Pets OK, Playground, Pull-thru Sites, Reservations, Showers, Swimming Pool, Yurts/Teepees, Tenters Welcome, Waterfront, Laundry, Handicap Access

Monte Vista Motel & RV Park 765-2369
C $15-75 12 All Year

Credit Cards OK, Hookups, Pets OK, Playground, Showers, Tenters Welcome, Laundry

River Walk RV Park 765-5943/888-567-8700
C $10-24 42 36' All Year
I-90, exit 11, S. on Northwest Blvd. .5mi., right on Mill Ave.
Cable TV Hookups, Hookups, Modem Hookups, Pets OK, Pull-thru Sites, Reservations, Showers, Handicap Access

Black Rock Marina 676-8696
C $25 20 All Year
Hwy. 95, 14 mi. S. of Coeur d'Alene, at Rockford Bay
Cable TV Hookups, Drinking Water, Dump Station, Hookups, Mini-Mart, Pets OK, Pull-thru Sites, Reservations, Showers, Tenters Welcome, Waterfront, Handicap Access

Shady Acres RV Park & Campground 664-3087/877-212-0523
C $13-16 32 All Year
I-90, exit 12, Hwy. 95 N., 3 blks., right on Kathleen, right on Government Way
Cable TV Hookups, Hookups, Pets OK, Pull-thru Sites, Reservations, Showers, Handicap Access

Silverwood RV Park 340-0139
C $28 127 All Year
Hwy. 95, 15 mi. N. of Coeur d'Alene
Credit Cards OK, Hookups, LP Gas, Mini-Mart, Modem Hookups, Pets OK, Showers, Laundry

Alpine Country Store & RV Park 772-4305
C $20-23 25 Summer, Fall, Spring
Hwy. 95, 10 mi. N. of Coeur d'Alene, 7 mi S. of Silverwood Theme Park
Credit Cards OK, Hookups, Mini-Mart, Modem Hookups, Pets OK, Pull-thru Sites, Reservations, Showers, Laundry, Handicap Access

Boulevard Motel & RV Park 664-4978/877-611-7275
C $14-20 38 All Year
I-90, exit 11, S. side of freeway
Cable TV Hookups, Dump Station, Hookups, Pets OK, Playground, Pull-thru Sites

Bambi RV Park 664-6527/877-381-5534
C 28 All Year
.25 mi. N. of Appleway, on W. side of Government Way w/ White Vinyl Fence, .2 mi. from lake
Cable TV Hookups, Drinking Water, Dump Station, Hookups, Modem Hookups, Pets OK, Pull-thru Sites, Reservations, Showers, Tenters Welcome, Laundry

Blackwell Island RV Park 665-1300/888-571-2900
C $24-38 182 All Year
1.5 mi. from downtown, 1 mi. S. on Hwy. 95
Boating Facilities, Cable TV Hookups, Credit Cards OK, Drinking Water, Hookups, LP Gas, Playground, Pull-thru Sites, Reservations, Showers, Waterfront, Laundry

Cedar Motel & RV Park 664-2278
C $15-18 39 Summer, Fall, Spring
I-90, exit 15 (Sherman Ave.) 2 blks. S. on Coeur d'Alene Lake Dr.
Cable TV Hookups, Credit Cards OK, Dump Station, Hookups, Pull-thru Sites, Showers, Swimming Pool, Tenters Welcome, Laundry

Wolf Lodge Campground 664-2812/866-664-2812
C $18-28 55 Summer, Fall, Spring
I-90, 8 mi. E. of Coeur d'Alene, exit 22, 1.5 mi. to campground
Hookups, Mini-Mart, Modem Hookups, Pets OK, Playground, Pull-thru Sites, Showers, Laundry, Handicap Access

Beauty Creek 765-7223
P 15 32' Summer, Fall
7 mi. E. on I-90, exit 22, 3 mi. W. on Hwy. 97, 1 mi. SE on Forest Rd. 438
Drinking Water, Vault Toilets

Bumblebee 769-3000
P 25 16' Summer, Fall
I-90, 28 mi. E. to exit 43, 6 mi. N. on Forest Rd. 9, 3 mi. W. on Forest Rd. 209
Drinking Water, Vault Toilets

Honeysuckle 769-3000
P 8 16' Summer, Fall
11 mi. NE on Forest Rd. 268, 11 mi. E. on Forest Rd. 612
Drinking Water, Vault Toilets

Killarney Lake 769-5030
P 24' Summer, Fall
I-90 E., Hwy. 3 exit, 5 mi. S. to Killarney Lake Rd., 3.5 mi.
Pets OK, Vault Toilets

All Idaho Area Codes are 208

Section 1

Ultimate Idaho Atlas and Travel Encyclopedia

Campground Quick Reference-continued

Campground Name				Phone	
Public/Commercial	Unit Price	#Spaces	Max. Length	Seasons	
Directions					
Amenities/Activities					

Kit Price
P   52   22'   769-3000   Summer, Fall
11 mi. NW on Forest Rd. 208
Drinking Water, Reservations, Vault Toilets

Mokins Bay
P   16   22'   769-3000   Summer, Fall
N. 6 mi., E. on Lancaster Rd. 5 mi., then 11 mi. around Hayden Lake
Drinking Water, LP Gas, Vault Toilets

Garfield

Green Bay
P   None   3   263-5111   May-October
2 miles east of Garfield on FR 532, or accessible by boat from Lake Pend Oreille
Developed Campground, Restrooms, Exhibits Boat Ramp, Motorized and Non-Motorized Boating, Swimming Beach, Fishing, Hiking/Backpacking, Winter Sports

Harrison

Carlin Bay Resort
C $27   24   689-3295   All Year
Hwy. 97, 10 mi. N. of Harrison
Credit Cards OK, Drinking Water, Dump Station, Hookups, LP Gas, Mini-Mart, Modem Hookups, Pets OK, Pull-thru Sites, Reservations, Showers, Waterfront

Squaw Bay Lake Front Resort
C $18-30   50   664-6782   Summer, Fall, Spring
I-90 to Hwy. 97, 7 mi. S.
Boating Facilities, Camping Cabins, Credit Cards OK, Drinking Water, Dump Station, Fire Rings, Hookups, LP Gas, Mini-Mart, Playground, Pull-thru Sites, Reservations, Showers, Yurts/Teepees, Tenters Welcome, Waterfront, Laundry, Handicap Access

Harrison City RV Park
C $9-17   21   689-3212   Summer, Fall, Spring
Hwy. 97, 37 mi. SE of Coeur d'Alene
Drinking Water, Dump Station, Hookups, Reservations, Showers, Tenters Welcome, Waterfront

Bell Bay
P   26   22'   769-3000   Summer, Fall, Spring
3 mi. N. on Hwy. 97, 3 mi. W. on Cty. Rd. 314

Hauser

Westside Resort
C $10-12   7   773-4968   Summer, Fall, Spring
7 mi. NW of Post Falls off Hwy. 53
Pets OK

Hope

Beyond Hope Resort
C $18-27   85   264-5251/877-270-4673   All Year
Hwy. 200, E. to the Hope Peninsula, 1 mi. on Peninsula Rd.
Cable TV Hookups, Hookups, Pets OK, Pull-thru Sites, Reservations, Showers

Island View RV Resort
C $23   60   264-5509   All Year
Hwy. 200 to Peninsula Rd., S. 2 mi.
Cable TV Hookups, Hookups, LP Gas, Mini-Mart, Modem Hookups, Pets OK, Pull-thru Sites, Reservations, Showers, Tenters Welcome, Waterfront, Laundry

Jeb & Margaret's Trailer Haven
C $20   125   264-5406   All Year
Hwy. 200, 12 mi. E. of Sandpoint
Cable TV Hookups, Hookups, Modem Hookups, Pull-thru Sites, Reservations, Showers, Waterfront

Trestle Creek RV Park
C $20   18   35'   264-5894   All Year
Hwy. 200, 12 mi. E. of Sandpoint
Cable TV Hookups, Drinking Water, Dump Station, Hookups, Pets OK, Reservations, Waterfront

---

Campground Name				Phone	
Public/Commercial	Unit Price	#Spaces	Max. Length	Seasons	
Directions					
Amenities/Activities					

Idaho Country Resort
C $25-30   187   264-5505/800-307-3050   All Year
141 Idaho Country Rd.
Cable TV Hookups, Credit Cards OK, Dump Station, Hookups, LP Gas, Mini-Mart, Pets OK, Playground, Pull-thru Sites, Showers, Waterfront, Laundry, Handicap Access

Sam Owen
P   30'   263-5111   Summer, Fall
3 mi. SE on Hwy. 200, 2 mi. W. on Cty. Rd. 1002
Drinking Water, Dump Station, Pets OK, Pull-thru Sites, Reservations, Swimming Pool

Kellogg

Crystal Gold Mine & RV Park
C   783-4653   All Year
I-90, exit 54 to Frontage Rd., N. of freeway then W. 2 mi., 51931 Silver Valley Rd.
Drinking Water, Dump Station, Pets OK, Handicap Access

Big Hank
P   30   22'   752-1221   Summer, Fall
45 mi. N. of Cataldo on Forest Rd. 208
Drinking Water, Vault Toilets

Devils Elbow
P   20   22'   752-1221   Summer, Fall
39 mi. N. of Cataldo on Forest Rd. 208
Drinking Water, Vault Toilets

Kingston

Country Lane Inn & RV Resort
C $22-25   47   682-2698/877-670-5927   All Year

Albert's Place & RV Park
C $12-18   32   682-4179   All Year
I-90, exit 43

Moyie Springs

Twin Rivers Canyon Resort
C $16-25   65   267-5932/888-258-5952   Summer, Fall, Spring
1 mi. E. of Moyie Springs
Credit Cards OK, Drinking Water, Dump Station, Fire Rings, Hookups, Mini-Mart, Modem Hookups, Pets OK, Playground, Pull-thru Sites, Reservations, Showers, Tenters Welcome, Laundry

Hemlocks Resort
C $22   18   267-9822   All Year
Hwy. 2, 9 mi. E. of Hwy. 95, M. P. 73
Credit Cards OK, Dump Station, Hookups, Mini-Mart, Pets OK, Pull-thru Sites, Reservations, Showers, Tenters Welcome

Osborn

Blue Anchor RV Park
C $23   40   100'   752-3443   Summer, Fall, Spring
I-90, exit 57, 45 mi. E. of Coeur d'Alene
Cable TV Hookups, Credit Cards OK, Drinking Water, Dump Station, Hookups, Modem Hookups, Pets OK, Playground, Pull-thru Sites, Reservations, Showers, Tenters Welcome, Laundry

Pinehurst

Kellogg/Silver Valley KOA Kampground
C $22-35   60   70'   682-3612/800-562-0799   Summer, Fall, Spring
I-90, exit 45, 801 N. Division St.
Cable TV Hookups, Credit Cards OK, Dump Station, Hookups, Mini-Mart, Modem Hookups, Pets OK, Playground, Pull-thru Sites, Reservations, Showers, Swimming Pool, Tenters Welcome, Handicap Access

Campground Quick Reference-continued

Plummer

Heyburn State Park
P	$7-18	132	55'	686-1308
				All Year

Hwy. 5 between Plummer & St. Maries

Boating Facilities, Credit Cards OK, Drinking Water, Dump Station, Hookups, Playground, Reservations, Showers, Tenters Welcome, Waterfront

Post Falls

Suntree RV Park
C	$22-24.99	111		773-9982
				All Year

I-90, exit 2, 1 blk. N., 1 blk. E., follow signs

Credit Cards OK, Drinking Water, Dump Station, Hookups, Modem Hookups, Pets OK, Pull-thru Sites, Reservations, Showers, Swimming Pool, Tenters Welcome, Handicap Access

Coeur d'Alene RV Resort
C	$25-29	191		773-3527/888-343-3527
				All Year

I-90, exit 7, N. to Mullan Ave.

Cable TV Hookups, Credit Cards OK, Drinking Water, Dump Station, Hookups, LP Gas, Mini-Mart, Pets OK, Playground, Pull-thru Sites, Reservations, Showers, Swimming Pool, Work-Out Room, Laundry, Handicap Access

Priest Lake

Geisinger
P	None	2		443-2512
				May-September

SE end of Upper Priest Lake, accessible by boat or short trail from nearby Lions Head Campground

Primitive Camping, Restrooms, Biking, Motorized and Non-Motorized Boating, Fishing, Hiking/Backpacking

Priest Lake RV Resort & Marina
C	$10-13	16		443-2405
				All Year

At Kalispell Bay

Handicap Access

Nordman Store RV Park
C	$15	14		443-2538
				All Year

Hwy. 57, M P 37

Hookups, Mini-Mart, Pets OK, Pull-thru Sites, Showers

Inn at Priest Lake
C		12		443-2447
				All Year

Hwy. 57, M P 22, 5 mi. from exit

Dump Station, Hookups, Pets OK, Pull-thru Sites, Reservations, Showers, Swimming Pool, Tenters Welcome, Handicap Access

Kaniksu RV Resort & Marina
C	$18	77		443-2609
				All Year

3.5 mi. N. of Nordman

Credit Cards OK, Drinking Water, Hookups, LP Gas, Waterfront, Laundry, Handicap Access

Beaver Creek - Priest Lake
C		40	35'	443-2512
				Summer, Fall

39 mi. N. of Priest River on Hwy. 57, 12 mi. NE on Forest Rds. 1339 & 2512

Luby Bay
P		52	55'	443-2512
				Summer

2 mi. NE on Forest Rd 1337, 1 mi. N. on Forest Rd. 237

Drinking Water, Dump Station, Reservations, Swimming Pool

Osprey
P		18	20'	443-2512
				Summer

Hwy. 57, 25 mi. N. of Priest River, 2 mi. NE on Forest Rd. 237

Drinking Water, Swimming Pool, Vault Toilets

Outlet - Priest Lake
P		28	22'	443-2512
				Summer, Fall

Hwy. 57, 25 mi. N. of Priest River, 1 mi. NE on Forest Rd. 237

Priest Lake State Park
P	$7-18	151	50'	443-2200
				All Year

Hwy. 57, 22 mi. N. of Priest River

Boating Facilities, Camping Cabins, Credit Cards OK, Drinking Water, Dump Station, Hookups, Mini-Mart, Pull-thru Sites, Reservations, Showers, Tenters Welcome, Vault Toilets, Waterfront, Laundry

Reeder Bay
P		24	50'	443-2512
				Summer

39 mi. N. on Hwy. 57, 3 mi. E. on Forest Rd. 1339

Drinking Water, Reservations, Swimming Pool

Navigation
P	None	5		443-2512
				June-September

Accessible by boat or trail on the NW end of Upper Priest Lake

Group Camping, Restrooms, Biking, Motorized and Non-Motorized Boating, Hiking/Backpacking

Plowboy
P	None	4		443-2512
				June-September

SW end of Upper Priest Lake, accessible by boat or trail

Group Camping, Restrooms, Biking, Motorized and Non-Motorized Boating, Fishing, Hiking/Backpacking

Bartoo Island
P	Yes	17; 2 Group Areas		443-2512
				May-September

Accessible only by boat from Kalispell Bay

Primitive Camping, 2 Vault Toilets, Motorized and Non-Motorized Boating, Fishing, Water Sports

Trapper Creek
P	None	4		443-2512
				May-September

Accessible by boat or trail from Beaver Creek or Lions Head Campground in Priest Lake State Park

Primitive Camping, Restrooms, Biking, Motorized and Non-Motorized Boating, Fishing, Hiking/Backpacking

Priest River

River Country Motel & RV Park
C	$10-500	15	50'	448-1100/866-779-1100
				All Year

Hwy. 2, W. of Priest River

Cable TV Hookups, Credit Cards OK, Drinking Water, Hookups, Pets OK, Playground, Reservations, Showers, Tenters Welcome

Willow Bay Marina & RV Park
C				265-8854
				Summer, Fall, Spring

Albeni Cove Recreation Area
P	$10-14	10		437-3133
				Summer, Fall, Spring

Hwy 41, 1 mi. S. of Hwy. 2, sharp turn onto Cty. Rd. to end

Boating Facilities, Credit Cards OK, Drinking Water, Fire Rings, Pets OK, Pull-thru Sites, Reservations, Showers, Tenters Welcome

Priest River Recreation Area (Mudhole)
P	$3-14	20		437-3133
				Summer, Fall, Spring

1 mi. E. of downtown Priest River, at the confluence of the Priest and Pend Oreille rivers

Boating Facilities, Credit Cards OK, Drinking Water, Dump Station, Fire Rings, Pets OK, Playground, Pull-thru Sites, Reservations, Showers, Swimming Pool, Tenters Welcome, Waterfront, Handicap Access

Riley Creek Recreation Area
P	$14	67		437-3133
				Summer, Fall, Spring

Hwy 2, S. of Laclede onto Riley Creek Rd. 1 mi.

Boating Facilities, Credit Cards OK, Drinking Water, Dump Station, Fire Rings, Hookups, Pets OK, Playground, Pull-thru Sites, Reservations, Showers, Tenters Welcome, Handicap Access

Sagle

Country Inn
C	$35-55	2		263-3333
				All Year

Hwy. 95, 1 mi. S. of Sandpoint

Playground

Campground Quick Reference-continued

Campground Name				Phone
Public/Commercial	Unit Price	#Spaces	Max. Length	Seasons
Directions				
Amenities/Activities				

Travel America Plaza — 263-6522
C $12-17 78 All Year
Hwy. 95, 5 mi. S. of Sandpoint, 468800 Hwy. 95
Credit Cards OK, Drinking Water, Dump Station, Hookups, Mini-Mart, Pets OK, Pull-thru Sites, Reservations, Showers, Handicap Access

Alpine Park — 265-0179
C $15 15 All Year
Hwy. 95 & Sagle Rd., 6 mi. S. of Sandpoint
Hookups, Pets OK

Garfield Bay Resort — 263-1078
C $20-45 24 All Year
16 mi. S. of Sandpoint
Dump Station, Hookups, Pets OK, Reservations, Showers, Handicap Access

Bottle Bay Resort & Marina — 263-5916/866-268-8532
C $75-150 7 25' All Year
1.5 mi. S. of Sandpoint off Hwy. 95, take Bottle Bay Rd. 8.3 miles, left on Resort Rd., follow signs to 115 Resort Rd.
Boating Facilities, Camping Cabins, Credit Cards OK, Drinking Water, Hookups, Limited Access, Pets OK, Reservations, Showers, Waterfront, Laundry, Handicap Access

Wheel People RV Park — 265-4949
C $12 10 40' All Year
Hwy. 95 to Westmond Rd., right
Cable TV Hookups, Drinking Water, Pets OK, Pull-thru Sites, Reservations, Showers, Tenters Welcome, Laundry

Round Lake State Park — 263-3489
P $7-12 53 24' All Year
Hwy. 95, 10 mi. S. of Sandpoint, W. onto Dufort Road for 2 mi.
Credit Cards OK, Drinking Water, Dump Station, Showers, Tenters Welcome, Waterfront

Sandpoint

Best Western Edgewater — 263-3194/800-635-2534
C $15-25 20 All Year
Follow signs to beach
Cable TV Hookups, Dump Station, Hookups, Pets OK, Playground, Reservations, Showers, Swimming Pool, Work-Out Room, Handicap Access

Springy Point Recreation Area — 437-3133
P $14 37 36' Summer, Fall, Winter
1.5 mi. S. of Sandpoint via Hwy. 95, 3 mi. W. on Lakeshore Dr.
Boating Facilities, Credit Cards OK, Drinking Water, Dump Station, Fire Rings, Pets OK, Pull-thru Sites, Reservations, Showers, Tenters Welcome, Waterfront, Handicap Access

Whiskey Rock Bay — 263-5111
P 9 16' Summer, Fall
30 mi. SW on Forest Rd. 278
Pets OK, Vault Toilets

Silverton

Silver Leaf Motel — 752-0222
C $5-10 7 All Year
W. of Wallace

Spirit Lake

Silver Beach Resort — 623-4842
C 40 All Year
Hwy. 41, W. on Maine 2.5 mi.
Dump Station, Hookups, Mini-Mart, Pets OK, Playground, Reservations, Showers

St. Maries

Ed's R&R Shady River RV Park — 245-3549
C $9-10.5 14 All Year
Hwy. 3
Credit Cards OK, Dump Station, Hookups, LP Gas, Mini-Mart, Pets OK, Waterfront

Misty Meadows RV Park — 245-2639
C $8-19 30 All Year
3 mi. E. on St. Joe River Rd. from Hwy. 3 N.
Drinking Water, Fire Rings, Hookups, Pets OK, Reservations, Tenters Welcome, Waterfront

St. Joe Lodge & Resort — 245-3462
C $12-50 20 All Year
35 mi. E. of St. Maries
Credit Cards OK, Dump Station, Hookups, LP Gas, Pets OK, Showers, Waterfront, Handicap Access

Riverside Campground — 245-6737
C $17 15 Summer, Spring
Waterfront

Emerald Creek — 245-2531
P 18 22' Summer, Fall
5 mi. NW on Hwy. 3, 6 mi. S. on Forest Rd. 447
Drinking Water, Vault Toilets

Huckleberry - St. Maries — 769-5030
P $9-12 39 50' Summer, Fall, Spring
5 mi. E. of Calder on St. Joe River Rd.
Drinking Water, Dump Station, Fire Rings, Hookups, Pets OK, Pull-thru Sites, Tenters Welcome, Vault Toilets, Handicap Access

Shadowy St. Joe — 245-2531
P 14 45' Summer, Fall
1 mi. E. on Hwy. 3; 10 mi. E. on Forest Rd. 50
Drinking Water, Swimming Pool, Vault Toilets

Marble Creek — 245-2531
P None 2 June-September
35 miles E of St. Maries on Forest Highway 50, then 6 miles south of Marble Creek Historical Site on FR 321
Primitive Camping, Drinking Water, Restrooms, Cultural/Historic Sites, Fishing, Picnicking

Donkey Creek — 245-2531
P None 2 June-October
35 miles E of St. Maries on Forest Highway 50, then 8 miles south of Marble Creek Historical Site on FR 321
Primitive Camping, Restrooms, Cultural/Historic Sites, Fishing, Picnicking

Camp 3 — 245-2531
P None 4 June-September
35 miles E of St. Maries on Forest Highway 50, then 15 miles south of Marble Creek Historical Site on FR 321
Primitive Camping, Drinking Water, Restrooms, Exhibits, Cultural/Historical Sites, Fishing, Hiking/Backpacking, Horseback Riding, Picnicking

Tensed

RV Park Mile Post — 274-5023
C $10.70 11 All Year
Register at Cross Keys Restaurant, Hwy. 95, 2nd & D St.
Credit Cards OK, Hookups, Mini-Mart, Pets OK, Playground, Showers

Wallace

Down by the Depot RV Park — 753-7121
C $20 45 All Year
1 blk. N. of Wallace Depot, 108 9 Mile
Cable TV Hookups, Dump Station, Hookups, Pets OK, Pull-thru Sites, Reservations, Showers, Tenters Welcome, Laundry, Handicap Access

Lookout Pass Ski Area — 762-5707
C 12 All Year
I-90 at the Idaho/Montana border
Pets OK

Berlin Flats 7 — 69-3000
P 9 22' Summer, Fall
14 mi. N. of Prichard, turn R. 7 mi. up Shoshone Creek on Forest Road 412.
Drinking Water, Vault Toilets

Dining Quick Reference

Price Range refers to the average cost of a meal per person: ($) $1-$6, ($$) $7-$11, ($$$) $12-up. Cocktails: "Yes" indicates full bar; Beer (B)/Wine (W), Service: Breakfast (B), Brunch (BR), Lunch (L), Dinner (D). Businesses in bold print will have additional information under the appropriate map locator number in the body of this section.

MAP No.	RESTAURANT	TYPE CUISINE	PRICE RANGE	CHILD MENU	COCKTAILS BEER WINE	MEALS SERVED	CREDIT CARDS ACCEPTED
2	**Bear Creek Lodge** 5952 Main St, Sandpoint, 267-7268	Steaks/Pasta	$$	Y	B W	BR/D	M V
2	Badger's Den 6551 Main St, Bonners Ferry, 267-1486	American/Coffee	$$	N	N	B/L	M V
2	China Kitchen 6483 Main St, Bonners Ferry, 267-5412	Asian	$$	N	B W	L/D	Major
2	Downtown Pizza 6371 Kootenai St, Bonners Ferry, 267-0891	Pizza	$	N	N	L/D	M V
2	Feist Creek Restaurant 195 Rd 34 #A, Bonners Ferry, 267-8649	Family	$$	Y	N	L/D	M V
2	Jill's Cafe 7211 Main St., Bonners Ferry, 267-1950	Family	$$	Y	N	L/D	M V
2	Kodiaks Steak & Pasta 5952 Main St, Bonners Ferry, 267-1891	Steakhouse	$$	Y	B W	L/D	Major
2	Oriental Garden 6231 Main St, Bonners Ferry, 267-8000	Asian	$$	N	N	L/D	M V
4	J J Cookshack Old Hwy 2, Naples, 267-5757	American/Ethnic	$-$$$	Y	B W	B/L/D	Major
5	Sub Shop 32255 Hwy 200, Kootenai, 263-0244	American	$	N	N	L/D	M V
5	Burger King 476997 Hwy 95, Ponderay, 265-3544	Fast Food	$	Y	N	L/D	M V
5	Hoot Owl Cafe 30784 Hwy 200, Ponderay, 265-9348	Family	$	Y	N	B/L	No
5	Kentucky Fried Chicken 476560 Hwy 95, Ponderay, 263-9503	Fast Food	$-$$	Y	N	L/D	Major
5	McDonald's 205 Bonner Mall Way, Ponderay, 263-5614	Fast Food	$	Y	N	B/L/D	Major
5	Taco Bell 476930 Hwy 95, Ponderay, 255-1570	Fast Food	$	Y	N	L/D	Major
6	**Bangkok Cuisine** 202 2nd Ave, Sandpoint, 265-4149	Thai	$$	N	B W	L/D	M V D
6	**Cafe Trinity** 116 N 1st, Sandpoint, 255-7558	Southern Inspired	$$-$$$	N	B W	L/D	M V
6	**Di Luna's Cafe** 207 Cedar St, Sandpoint, 263-0846	American Bistro	$$	Y	B W	B/L/D	M V D
6	**Ivano's Ristorante Italiano** 102 S First Ave, Sandpoint, 263-0211	Northern Italian	$$-$$$	N	Yes	L/D	Major
6	**The Inn at Sand Creek/Sand Creek Grill** 105 1st St, Sandpoint, 255-5736	Regional/Northwest	$$-$$$	Y	B W	D	M V
6	Arby's 410 N 5th Ave, Sandpoint, 263-3104	Fast Food	$	Y	N	L/D	M V
6	Arlo's Ristorante 330 N 1st Ave, Sandpoint, 255-4186	Fine Dining	$$$	N	B W	L/D	M V
6	Bamboo Chinese Restaurant 417 Church St, Sandpoint, 263-9593	Asian	$	N	N	L/D	Major
6	Beach House Bar & Grill 56 Bridge St, Sandpoint, 255-4947	American/Fine Dining	$$-$$$	Y	Yes	B/L/D	Major
6	Blue Moon Cafe 124 So 2nd Ave, Sandpoint, 265-9953	American	$-$$	Y	B W	B/L	Major
6	Burger King 476997 Hwy 95, Sandpoint, 265-3544	Fast Food	$	Y	N	L/D	M V
6	Cabin On The Green Sandpoint, 263-1642	Family	$	Y	N	L/D	M V
6	Chimney Rock Grill 10000 Schweitzer Mountain Rd, Sandpoint, 255-3071	Fine Dining	$$$	N	B W	D	Major
6	Connie's Restaurant 323 W Cedar St, Sandpoint, 255-2227	American	$$	Y	B W	B/L/D	Major
6	Domino's Pizza 316 N 5th Ave, Sandpoint, 263-6600	Pizza	$-$$	N	N	L/D	M V

Section 1

All Idaho Area Codes are 208

Dining Quick Reference-Continued

Price Range refers to the average cost of a meal per person: ($) $1-$6, ($$) $7-$11, ($$$) $12-up. Cocktails: "Yes" indicates full bar; Beer (B)/Wine (W), Service: Breakfast (B), Brunch (BR), Lunch (L), Dinner (D). Businesses in bold print will have additional information under the appropriate map locator number in the body of this section.

MAP NO.	RESTAURANT	TYPE CUISINE	PRICE RANGE	CHILD MENU	COCKTAILS BEER WINE	MEALS SERVED	CREDIT CARDS ACCEPTED
6	Dub's Drive-in Hwy 2 W, Sandpoint, 263-4300	Family	$	Y	N	B/L	M V
6	Edguapos 209 E Superior St, Sandpoint, 265-4075	Mexican	$-$$	N	N	B/L/D	No
6	Eichardt's Pub Grill & Coffee 212 W Cedar St, Sandpoint, 263-4005	American/Coffee	$-$$	N	B W	L/D	M V
6	Fifth Ave Restaurant 807 N 5th Ave, Sandpoint, 263-0596	American	$$	Y	Yes	B/L/D	Major
6	Golden Dragon 100 Tibbetts Dr, Sandpoint, 265-5425	Asian	$	N	N	L/D	No
6	Panhandler Pies Restaurant & Bakery 120 S 1st Ave, Sandpoint, 263-2912	Family	$-$$	Y	N	B/L/D	M V
6	Pend Oreille Pasta (takeout only) 476534 Hwy 95 Ste B, Sandpoint, 263-1352	Italian	$-$$	N	B W	L/D	No
6	Subway 476534 Hwy 95 Ste A, Sandpoint, 255-7525	Fast Food	$	N	N	L/D	M V
6	Thor's Pizza 166 Village Lane, Sandpoint, 255-5645	Pizza	$	N	N	L/D	No
6	Winter Ridge Cafe & Bakery 701 Lake St, Sandpoint, 255-2079	Café/Bakery	$	N	N	L	Major
7	Klondyke Cafe & Tavern 14873 Hwy 2, Laclede, 255-7223	Café/Tavern	$	Y	B W	B/L/D	No
8	Mr Mun-cheese 311 N Idaho Ave, Oldtown, 437-2160	Family	$	N	N	L/D	Major
8	Riverbank Family Restaurant 402 N Idaho Ave, Oldtown, 437-0892	American	$	Y	B W	B/L/D	M V
8	La Rosa Mexican Restaurant 1305 Hwy 2, Priest River, 448-0333	Mexican	$	N	N	L/D	M V
8	Mangy Moose Cafe & Rv Park 3604 Hwy 2, Priest River, 448-4468	Family	$	Y	N	B/L	Major
8	River Pigs Inn 114 Main St, Priest River, 448-1097	American	$$	N	N	L/D	No
8	Village Kitchen Restaurant 911 Alberni Hwy, Priest River, 448-2293	American	$-$$	Y	B W	B/L/D	M V
9	View Cafe 1947 Hwy 95, Cocolalla, 263-7476	Family	$$	Y	N	B/L/D	No
9	Bottle Bay Resort & Marina 115 Resort Rd, Sagle, 263-5916	American	$$	N	N	L/D	No
9	Captain's Table 1649 Garfield Bay Rd, Sagle, 265-6351	American/Steakhouse	$-$$	N	B W	L/D	M V
9	Travel America Cafe 468810 Hwy 95, Sagle, 265-2862	Family	$$	Y	N	B/L/D	M V
10	Squeeze Inn Hwy 200 & Pine St, Clark Fork, 266-0234	Family	$$	Y	N	D	No
11	Don's Cafe 6th & Main Ave, Bayview, 683-9005	American	$$	N	B W	L/D	No
12	A&W Family Restaurant 6300 E Hwy 54, Athol, 683-8124	Fast Food	$	Y	N	L/D	M V
12	Athol Cafe 6160 E Hwy 54, Athol, 683-2363	Family	$	Y	N	L/D	Major
12	KKJ's Pizza Place 29777 N Hwy 95, Athol, 683-5049	Pizza	$$	N	N	L/D	M V
12	Rib Ranch 30401 N Hwy 95, Athol, 683-2071	Family	$$	Y	N	L/D	Major
12	White Pine Country Cafe 30625 N Hwy 95, Athol, 683-4408	Family	$	Y	N	B/L/D	Major
13	Blanchard Inn Hwy 41, Blanchard, 437-3137	American	$$	N	N	L/D	Major
13	Stoneridge 437-Golf-Restaurant 355 Stoneridge Rd, Blanchard, 437-3565	American	$-$$	N	B W	L/D	Major

Price Range refers to the average cost of a meal per person: ($) $1-$6, ($$) $7-$11, ($$$) $12-up. Cocktails: "Yes" indicates full bar; Beer (B)/Wine (W), Service: Breakfast (B), Brunch (BR), Lunch (L), Dinner (D). Businesses in bold print will have additional nformation under the appropriate map locator number in the body of this section.

MAP NO.	RESTAURANT	TYPE CUISINE	PRICE RANGE	CHILD MENU	COCKTAILS BEER WINE	MEALS SERVED	CREDIT CARDS ACCEPTED
13	Dairy Queen 15570 N Vera St, Rathdrum, 687-2898	Fast Food	$	N	N	L/D	No
13	Domino's Pizza Rathdrum, 687-3480	Pizza	$-$$	N	N	L/D	M V
13	Granny's Pantry 14683 W Hwy 53, Rathdrum, 687-0881	American	$-$$	N	N	B/L/D	Major
13	McDonald's 15973 N Hwy 41, Rathdrum, 687-5560	Fast Food	$	Y	N	B/L/D	Major
13	Taco Bell Express 15963 N Hwy 41, Rathdrum, 687-3987	Fast Food	$	Y	N	L/D	Major
13	Toro Viejo 15837 N Wwood Dr, Rathdrum, 687-3723	Mexican	$$	Y	B W	B/L/D	Major
13	Westwood Saloon 8162 W Main St, Rathdrum, 687-9400	Tavern	$	N	Yes	L	No
13	Zip's Drive In 14480 N Hwy 41, Rathdrum, 687-9144	Family	$	Y	N	L/D	M V
13	Hog-n-Jog Restaurant 32471 N 5th Ave, Spirit Lake, 623-6666	Family	$	Y	N	B/L/D	M V
13	Italian Bay Garden 64 Industrial Park Ave, Spirit Lake, 623-6055	Italian	$	N	N	L/D	M V
14	Arby's 181 W Prairie Ave, Hayden, 762-3653	Fast Food	$	Y	N	L/D	Major
14	Burger King 307 W Prairie Ave, Hayden, 762-8016	Fast Food	$	Y	N	L/D	M V
14	Domino's Pizza Hayden, 772-8210	Fast Food	$-$$	N	N	L/D	M V
14	Everett's On The Lake 3799 E Hayden Lake Rd, Hayden, 762-4876	Fine Dining	$$-$$$	Y	Yes	L/D	Major
14	Kynrede Cafe Inc 8885 N Government Way, Hayden, 772-8643	Family	$	Y	N	L/D	M V
14	Paul's Country Store Classic Deli & Wine Grotto 702 E Prairie Ave, Hayden, 762-8544	Deli/Café	$-$$	N	B W	B/L/D	M V
14	Paupau's Kitchen 9751 N Government Way Hayden, 762-0169	Asian	$$	N	N	L/D	No
14	Pizza Factory 121 W Prairie Ave Ste H, Hayden, 762-9937	Pizza	$	N	N	L/D	M V
14	Rancho Chico Family Mexican Restaurants 8882 N Government Way, Hayden, 762-3310	Mexican	$-$$	Y	N	L/D	M V
14	Rustler's Roost 9627 N Hwy 95, Hayden, 772-6613	Family	$	Y	N	B/L	Major
14	Sargents Restaurant & Lounge 9021 N Government Way, Hayden, 772-4114	Fine Dining	$$$	Y	Yes	L/D	Major
14	Subway 9170 N Hess St, Hayden, 762-1124	Fast Food	$	N	N	L/D	M V
14	The Blue Plate Cafe 10015 N Government Way, Hayden, 772-8399	Family	$-$$	Y	N	B/L/D	Major
14	The Porch Public House 1658 E Miles Ave, Hayden, 772-7711	Fine Dining	$$-$$$	Y	Yes	L/D	Major
14	Noodle Express 305 W Prairie Shpng Ctr, Hayden Lake, 762-8488	Asian	$	Y	B W	L/D	Major
14	Orange Julius 200 W Hanley Ave, Hayden Lake, 762-2212	Fast Food	$	N	N	L	No
14	Owl Cafe 9178 Government Way, Hayden Lake, 772-4912	Family	$	Y	N	B/L	No
14	Starbucks Coffee Company 121 W Prairie Ave Ste E, Hayden Lake, 772-7575	Coffeehouse	$	N	N	B/L	No
14	Susie's Bar & Grill 10325 N Government Way, 762-2533	Fine Dining	$$-$$$	Y	Yes	B/L/D	M V
14	Caruso's Deli 113 W Prairie Shpng Ctr, Hayden Lake, 762-4676	Deli/Café	$	N	N	B/L/D	Major

Dining Quick Reference-Continued

Price Range refers to the average cost of a meal per person: ($) $1-$6, ($$) $7-$11, ($$$) $12-up. Cocktails: "Yes" indicates full bar; Beer (B)/Wine (W), Service: Breakfast (B), Brunch (BR), Lunch (L), Dinner (D). Businesses in bold print will have additional information under the appropriate map locator number in the body of this section.

MAP NO.	RESTAURANT	TYPE CUISINE	PRICE RANGE	CHILD MENU	COCKTAILS BEER WINE	MEALS SERVED	CREDIT CARDS ACCEPTED
14	Daanen's Delicatessen & Gourmet Grocery 702 E Prairie Ave, Hayden Lake, 772-7371	Deli/Café	$	Y	N	B/L/D	Major
14	KFC 279 W Orchard Ave, Hayden Lake, 762-4959	Fast Food	$	Y	N	L/D	M V
14	Lomcevak Restaurant & Lounge Coeur d'Alene Airport, Hayden Lake, 772-4906	American	$$	N	B W	B/L	M V
14	Orlando's Mexican Drive Up 9878 N Government Way, Hayden Lake, 772-3387	Mexican	$-$$	Y	N	B/L/D	Major
14	Papa Murphy's Take 'n' Bake Pizza 301 W Prairie Ave, Hayden Lake, 772-0552	Pizza	$-$$	N	N	L/D	Major
14	Paul Bunyan Too 8625 N Government Way, Hayden Lake, 762-2320	Family	$-$$	Y	N	L/D	Major
14	TCBY 121 W Prairie Ave Ste C, Hayden Lake, 762-3300	Fast Food	$	Y	N	L/D	M V
14	Yellow House 11068 N Government Way, Hayden Lake, 762-1040	American	$	N	N	L	M V
15	Hauser Lake Resort Hauser, 773-3654	Fine Dining	$$-$$$	N	Yes	L/D	Major
15	Burger King 4202 W Expo Pkwy, Post Falls, 777-9397	Fast Food	$	Y	N	L/D	M V
15	Flying J Travel Plaza Thad's Restaurant 3636 W 5th Ave, Post Falls, 773-0597	Family	$	Y	N	B/L/D	Major
15	McDonald's 3820 W 5th Ave, Post Falls, 773-9213	Fast Food	$	Y	N	B/L/D	Major
15	Penny's Family Diner & Pub 2561 W Seltice Way, Post Falls, 773-7250	American	$	Y	B W	B/L/D	Major
16	**Three Sisters Coffee House** 621 N Spokane St, Post Falls, 457-1691	Coffee/Deli	$-$$	N	N	B/L	Major
16	Arby's 1500 E Seltice Way, Post Falls, 777-8200	Fast Food	$	Y	N	L/D	Major
16	Big Cheese Pizza 1790 E Seltice Way, Post Falls, 773-6659	Pizza	$	N	N	L/D	No
16	Denny's Restaurant 1670 E Schneidmiller Ave., Post Falls, 773-6988	Family	$-$$	Y	N	B/L/D	Major
16	Domino's Pizza 112 E Seltice Way, Post Falls, 457-1216	Pizza	$-$$	N	N	L/D	M V
16	Falls Club 611 E Seltice Way, Post Falls, 773-2051	American	$-$$	Y	Yes	B/L/D	Major
16	Godfather's Pizza 1603 E Seltice Way, Post Falls, 773-6700	Pizza	$	Y	N	L/D	M V
16	Golden Dragon 106 W Seltice Way, Post Falls, 457-0137	Asian	$	N	N	L/D	Major
16	Hot Rod Cafe 1610 E Schneidmiller Ave, Post Falls, 777-1712	American	$$-$$$	Y	Yes	L/D	Major
16	La Cabana Mexican Restaurant 604 E Seltice Way, Post Falls, 773-4325	Mexican	$	N	N	L/D	Major
16	Las Canastas Taco Shop 115 W Seltice Way, Post Falls, 777-7278	Mexican	$	N	N	L/D	Major
16	McDonald's 1615 E Seltice Way, Post Falls, 773-5435	Fast Food	$	Y	N	B/L/D	Major
16	Mcduff's Restaurant 115 E Seltice Way, Post Falls, 777-7278	Family	$-$$	Y	N	B/L/D	M V
16	Momiji Japanese Red Maple Restaurant 620 N Spokane St, Post Falls, 457-0123	Asian	$-$$	N	N	L/D	Major
16	Moon's Mongolian Grill 1901 E Seltice Way, Post Falls, 773-0348	Asian	$	N	N	L/D	Major
16	Pizza Hut 920 E Polston, Post Falls, 773-3538	Pizza	$	N	N	L/D	M V
16	Rob's Seafoods & Burgers 104 W Seltice Way, Post Falls, 773-5214	American	$	N	B	L/D	No

Price Range refers to the average cost of a meal per person: ($) $1-$6, ($$) $7-$11, ($$$) $12-up. Cocktails: "Yes" indicates full bar; Beer (B)/Wine (W), Service: Breakfast (B), Brunch (BR), Lunch (L), Dinner (D). Businesses in bold print will have additional information under the appropriate map locator number in the body of this section.

MAP NO.	RESTAURANT	TYPE CUISINE	PRICE RANGE	CHILD MENU	COCKTAILS BEER WINE	MEALS SERVED	CREDIT CARDS ACCEPTED
16	Subway 1603 E Seltice Way, Post Falls, 773-8797	Fast Food	$	N	N	L/D	M V
17	Burger King 780 N Thornton St, Post Falls, 773-8680	Fast Food	$	Y	N	L/D	M V
17	Dairy Queen 3560 E Seltice Way, Post Falls, 773-7097	Fast Food	$	N	N	L/D	No
17	Kentucky Fried Chicken 325 N Ross Point Rd, Post Falls, 773-3534	Fast Food	$-$$	Y	N	L/D	Major
18	Baskin Robbins 31 Ice Cream 101 E Best Ave, Coeur d'Alene, 667-0031	Fast Food	$	N	N	L	M V
18	Burger King 216 W Appleway Ave, Coeur d'Alene, 765-5966	Fast Food	$	Y	N	L/D	M V
18	Dagny's Coffee Company 1820 NW Blvd, Coeur d'Alene, 667-5371	Coffee/Deli	$	N	N	L	No
18	Deli Shop 4055 N Government Way, C d'Alene, 667-8840	Deli/Café	$	N	N	L	No
18	Eat & Run Deli 1735 W Kathleen Ave, Coeur d'Alene, 667-1619	Deli/Café	$	N	N	L	M V
18	Pasty Depot 1801 Lincoln Way #2, Coeur d'Alene, 667-2789	Bakery/Café	$	N	N	L	No
18	Scoops Ice Cream & Chocolate 215 W Canfield Ave, Coeur d'Alene, 762-9312	American	$	N	N	L	M V
19	Hunters Bar And Grill 2108 N 4th Ave, Coeur d'Alene, 765-9388	American	$	N	Yes	L/D	Major
22	Coeur d'Alene Brewing Co 209 E Lakeside Ave, Coeur d'Alene, 664-2739	American	$$	N	B W	L/D	Major
22	Roger's Ice Cream & Burgers 1224 E Sherman Ave, Coeur d'Alene, 765-5419	Family	$	Y	N	L	M V
25	Mission Inn 36179 E Canyon Rd, Cataldo, 682-4435	American	$	N	N	B/L/D	Major
25	Roselake Restaurant 11233 S Hwy 3, Cataldo, 682-4443	American	$-$$	Y	B W	B/L/D	Major
28	Boat Restaurant 47240 Silver Valley Rd, Smelterville, 786-1681	Family	$-$$	Y	N	B/L/D	M V
28	Silver Valley Truck Stop 183 Theater Rd, Smelterville, 783-1134	American	$-$$	N	B	B/L/D	M V
29	C J's Cafe & Coffee Co 234 E Cameron Ave, Kellogg, 783-2600	Coffee/Deli	$	Y	N	B/L	No
29	McDonald's 820 W Cameron Ave, Kellogg, 784-4431	Fast Food	$	Y	N	B/L/D	M V
29	Meister Burger 116 Mckinley Ave, Kellogg, 783-5691	Family	$	Y	N	B/L	No
29	Rancho Chico Family Mexican Restaurants 319 S Main St, Kellogg, 783-4038	Mexican	$	N	N	L/D	M V
29	San Felipe's 120 W Cameron Ave, Kellogg, 784-1360	Mexican	$-$$	N	N	L/D	M V
29	Subway 745 W Cameron Ave, Kellogg, 784-2027	Fast Food	$	N	N	L/D	M V
29	Taco Express 830 W Cameron Ave, Kellogg, 783-1308	Fast Food	$	N	N	L/D	No
29	Terrible Edith's 610 Bunker Ave, Kellogg, 783-2440	American	$	N	N	L/D	No
29	Wah Hing Restaurant 215 Mckinley Ave, Kellogg, 783-3181	Asian	$-$$	N	N	L/D	No
30	Deb's Evergreen Cafe 713 E Mullan Ave, Osburn, 752-2107	Family	$	Y	N	B/L/D	Major
32	Albi's Steak House & Lounge 220 6th St, Wallace, 753-3071	Steakhouse	$$	N	Yes	D	M V
32	Brooks Restaurant 500 Cedar St, Wallace, 752-8171	Fine Dining	$$-$$$	Y	Yes	B/L/D	Major

Dining Quick Reference-Continued

Price Range refers to the average cost of a meal per person: ($) $1-$6, ($$) $7-$11, ($$$) $12-up. Cocktails: "Yes" indicates full bar; Beer (B)/Wine (W), Service: Breakfast (B), Brunch (BR), Lunch (L), Dinner (D). Businesses in bold print will have additional information under the appropriate map locator number in the body of this section.

MAP NO.	RESTAURANT	TYPE CUISINE	PRICE RANGE	CHILD MENU	COCKTAILS BEER WINE	MEALS SERVED	CREDIT CARDS ACCEPTED
32	E J's Ready To Bake Pizza 517 1/2 Bank St, Wallace, 753-5431	Pizza	$$	N	N	L/D	Major
32	Gloria's Steak House & Lodge 21428 Coeur d'Alene River Rd, Wallace, 682-3031	Steakhouse	$$-$$$	N	B W	D	Major
32	Pizza Factory 612 Bank St, Wallace, 753-9003	Pizza	$	N	N	L/D	M V
32	Silver Corner Bar & Grill 601 Cedar St, Wallace, 753-4261	American	$-$$	N	Yes	L	No
32	Silver Lantern Drive-in 5th St & Pine St, Wallace, 753-8471	Family	$	Y	N	L/D	M V
33	Mean Gene's Pizza 206 Earle Ave, Mullan, 744-1290	Pizza	$	N	N	L/D	No
33	Mullan Cafe 312 River Rd, Mullan, 744-1490	American	$	N	N	B/L	No
35	The Landing Restaurant 105 S Coeur d'Alene Ave, Harrison, 689-3895	Fine Dining	$$-$$$	Y	Yes	L/D	M V
36	Gateway Cafe 126 10th St, Plummer, 686-1314	Family	$-$$	Y	N	B/L/D	Major
36	Pemmican Inn 396060 Hwy 95, Plummer, 686-6074	American	$$	Y	B W	B/L/D	Major
36	Steamboat Grill 20 W Jerry Lane, Worley, 686-1151	American	$-$$	N	N	L/D	No
37	Big Eddy Resort 18985 Saint Joe River Rd, St Maries, 245-4075	American/Fine Dining	$$	N	B W	B/L/D	M V
37	Bud's Drive In 101 College Ave, St Maries, 245-3312	American	$	N	N	B/L/D	Major
37	Cabin City Pizza 2242 W Idaho Ave, St Maries, 245-2561	Pizza	$	N	N	L/D	No
37	Gem State Grill 813 Main Ave, St Maries, 245-1649	American	$$	Y	Yes	B/L/D	Major
37	Junction Drive In 213 W College Ave, St Maries, 245-3416	American	$	N	N	L/D	No
37	Pizza Factory 910 Main Ave, St Maries, 245-5515	Pizza	$	N	N	L/D	No
37	Serv-a-burger 127 E College Ave, St Maries, 245-5428	American	$	N	N	L/D	N
37	Western Bar & Cafe Hwy 6, St Maries, 245-1301	American	$	N	Yes	B/L/D	No
38	El Gallo 71 Old River Rd, Avery, 245-3996	Mexican	$	N	N	L/D	M V
38	Calder General Store 1 Railroad Ave, Calder, 245-5278	Family	$-$$	Y	N	L/D	Major
39	Hideout 64019 Hwy 3, Fernwood, 245-0405	American	$$	Y	B W	L/D	No

NOTES:

Motel Quick Reference-Continued

Price Range: ($) Under $40 ; ($$) $40-$60; ($$$) $60-$80, ($$$$) Over $80. Pets [check with the motel for specific policies] (P), Dining (D), Lounge (L), Disabled Access (DA), Full Breakfast (FB), Cont. Breakfast (CB), Indoor Pool (IP), Outdoor Pool (OP), Hot Tub (HT), Sauna (S), Refrigerator (R), Microwave (M) (Microwave and Refrigerator indicated only if in majority of rooms), Kitchenette (K). All Idaho area codes are 208.

MAP No.	HOTEL	NUMBER ROOMS	PRICE RANGE	BREAKFAST	POOL/ HOT TUB SAUNA	NON SMOKE ROOMS	OTHER AMENITIES	CREDIT CARDS
2	**Bear Creek Lodge**							
	5952 Main St, Hwy 95 S, Bonners Ferry, 267-7268	12	$$/$$$		HT	Yes	P/DA/R/M	Major
2	Bonners Ferry Resort/The Lantern							
	6438 Main St, Bonners Ferry, 267-2422	10	$			No	P/K	M/V
2	Carriage House Inn							
	6506 Main St, Hwy 95, Bonners Ferry, 267-7915	12	$$	CB	HT	Yes	P/R/M/K	Major
2	Kootenai Valley Motel							
	6409 S Main St, Bonners Ferry, 267-7567	22	$$		HT	Yes	P/DA/R/M/K	M/V
2	Bonners Ferry Log Inn							
	HCR85, Box 6, Bonners Ferry, 267-3986	22	$$$	CB	HT	Yes		Major
2	Best Western Kootenai River Inn & Casino							
	7169 Plaza St, Bonners Ferry, 267-8511	65	$$$$		IP	Yes	D/L	Major
2	Town & Country Motel & RV Park							
	1540 S Main, Bonners Ferry, 267-7915	12	$$/$$$	CB	S	Yes	P/DA/K	Major
4	Naples AYH Hostel							
	Hwy 2, Naples, 267-2947	18 beds	$			Yes		
5	**Monarch Mountain Lodge**							
	363 Bonner Mall Way, Ponderay, 263-1222	48	$$	CB	HT/S	Yes	P/R/M	Major
5	Motel 6							
	477255 Hwy 95 N, Ponderay, 263-5383	70				Yes	P/DA	Major
6	**Church Street House B&B**							
	401 Church St, Sandpoint, 255-7094	2	$$$$	FB		Yes		Major
6	**Country Inn & RV Park**							
	470700 Hwy 95, Sagle, 263-3333	21	$$	CB	HT	Yes	P/R/M	Major
6	**K2 Inn**							
	501 N 4th Ave, Sandpoint, 263-3441	18	$		HT	Yes	P/R/M/K	Major
6	**The Coit House B&B**							
	502 N 4th Ave, Sandpoint, 265-4035	5	$$$	FB		Yes	P/K	M/V/A
6	Red Lion Hotel - Selkirk Lodge							
	10000 Schweitzer Mtn Rd, Sandpoint, 265-0257	82	$$$$		OP	Yes	D/L/DA/R/M	
6	Red Lion Hotel - White Pine Lodge							
	10000 Schweitzer Mtn Rd, Sandpoint, 265-0257	50	$$$$		IP/HT/S	Yes	P/D/L/DA/K	Major
6	Super 8							
	476841 Hwy 95 N, Sandpoint, 263-2210	60	$$/$$$	CB	HT	Yes	P/DA	Major
6	Sandpoint Quality Inn							
	807 N 5th Ave, Sandpoint, 263-2111	62	$$$		IP/HT	Yes	P/K	Major
6	S & W Motel							
	3480 Hwy 200 E, Sandpoint, 263-5979	12	$$			Yes	P/R/M/K	Major
6	Best Western Edgewater							
	56 Bridge St, Sandpoint, 263-3194	54	$$$$	CB	IP/HT		P/D/L	
6	Lakeside Inn							
	106 Bridge St, Sandpoint, 263-3717							
6	The Inn at Sand Creek							
	105 S 1st Ave, Sandpoint, 255-5736	3	$$$$			Yes	D/L/R/K	M/V/A
6	La Quinta							
	415 Cedar St, Sandpoint, 263-9581	50	$$$$/$$$	CB	IP	Yes	P/DA	Major
6	Meandering Moose Motel							
	310 Hwy 200, Sandpoint, 263-5979	12	$$			Yes	P	M/V
6	Motel 16							
	Hwy 2 W, Sandpoint, 263-5323	16	$$$$/$$$	CB	OP/S	Yes	P/DA/K	Major
6	Chalet Motel							
	3270 Hwy 95 N, Sanpoint, 263-3202	11	$$	CB	OP	Yes	P	Major
6	Country Inn							
	7360 Hwy 95 S, Sandpoint, 263-3333	24	$$/$	CB	HT/S	Yes	P/K	Major
6	La Quinta Inn							
	415 W Cedar, Sandpoint, 263-9581	70	$$$/$$$$	CB	OP	Yes	P/D/L/DA	Major
6	West Shore Lodge							
	Sandpoint, 487-3636							
8	Selkirk Motel							
	1201 Hwy 2, Priest River, 448-1112	6	$$			Yes	P/R/M	Major

Motel Quick Reference-Continued

Price Range: ($) Under $40 ; ($$) $40-$60; ($$$) $60-$80, ($$$$) Over $80. Pets [check with the motel for specific policies] (P), Dining (D), Lounge (L), Disabled Access (DA), Full Breakfast (FB), Cont. Breakfast (CB), Indoor Pool (IP), Outdoor Pool (OP), Hot Tub (HT), Sauna (S), Refrigerator (R), Microwave (M) (Microwave and Refrigerator indicated only if in majority of rooms), Kitchenette (K). All Idaho area codes are 208.

MAP No.	HOTEL	NUMBER ROOMS	PRICE RANGE	BREAKFAST	POOL/ HOT TUB SAUNA	NON SMOKE ROOMS	OTHER AMENITIES	CREDIT CARDS
8	Eagle's Nest Motel 1007 Hwy 2, Priest River, 448-2000	30	$$		S	Yes	P/DA/K	M/V
8	River Country Motel 3566 Hwy 2, Priest River, 448-1100	6	$$/$$$			Yes	P/K	Major
9	Sleep's Cabins 231 Lakeshore Dr, Sagle, 255-2122	6	$$$/$$$$			Yes	L/K	M/V
9	Country Inn & RV Park 470700 Hwy 95, Sagle, 263-3333	21	$$	CB	HT	Yes	P/R/M	Major
10	Clark Fork Lodge 421 E 4th, Clark Fork, 266-1716	15	$$		HT	Yes	P/DA/R/M/K	M/V/D
10	Hotel Hope 126 W Main St, Hope, 264-6004	53	$$$$	FB		Yes	P/D/L/K	Major
11	Bayview Scenic Motel & RV Park 34297 N Main St, Bayview, 683-2215	10	$$/$$$			Yes	P/D/L/K	Major
11	Scenic Bay Marina/JD Marina 17173 E Pier Rd, Bayview, 683-2243							
11	Boileau's Resort & Marina On Lake Pend Oreille, Bayview, 683-2213							
12	Athol Motel 5950 Hwy 54, Athol, 683-3476	9	$			Yes	P/D/R/M/K	Major
14	Affordable Inn 9986 N Government Way, Hayden Lake, 772-4414	21	$$$/$$$$			Yes	K	Major
15	Riverbend Inn 4105 W Riverbend Ave, Post Falls, 773-3583	71	$$$	CB	OP/HT	Yes	DA/K	Major
15	Sleep Inn 157 S Pleasantview Rd, Post Falls, 777-9394	84	$$$/$$$$	CB	IP	Yes	P/DA	Major
15	Howard Johnson Express 3647 W 5th, Post Falls, 773-4541	99	$$/$$$$	CB	IP/HT	Yes	P/DA	Major
16	**Red Lion Templin's Hotel on the River** 414 E 1st, Post Falls, 773-1611	163	$$$$		IP/S/HT	Yes	P/DA/R/M	Major
18	**Best Western Coeur d'Alene Inn & Conference Center** 414 W Appleway, Coeur d'Alene, 765-3200	123	$$$$		IP/HT	Yes	P/D/L/DA/R	Major
18	Boulevard Motel & RV Park 2400 W Seltice Way, Coeur d'Alene, 664-4978	10	$$				P/K	Major
18	Days Inn 2200 Northwest Blvd, Coeur d'Alene, 667-8668	62	$$$/$$$$	CB	HT/S	Yes	P/DA/K	Major
18	Garden Motel 1808 Northwest Blvd, Coeur d'Alene, 664-2743	23	$$		IP/HT	Yes	P/R/M/K	Major
18	GuestHouse Inn 330 W Appleway, Coeur d'Alene, 765-3011	60	$$$	CB		Yes	P/R/M	Major
18	Holiday Inn Express 3175 E Seltice Way, Post Falls, 773-8900	47	$$$$	CB	IP	Yes	P/DA/K	Major
18	Motel 6 416 W Appleway, Coeur d'Alene, 664-6600	109	$/$$$		OP	Yes	P/DA/R/M	Major
18	Rodeway Inn Pine's Resort 1422 Northwest Blvd, Coeur d'Alene, 664-8244	65	$$$/$$$$	CB	IP	Yes	P/D/L/DA	Major
18	Shilo Inns 702 W Appleway, Coeur d'Alene, 664-2300	139	$$$/$$$$	CB	IP	Yes	P/DA/R/M/K	Major
18	Silver Lake Motel Convention & Banquet Center 6160 Sunshine, Coeur d'Alene, 772-8595	48	$$$	CB	HT/OP	Yes	DA/R/M/K	Major
18	Blackwell Island RV Park 800 S Marina Dr, Coeur d'Alene, 665-1300							
18	AmeriTel Inn 333 Ironwood, Coeur d'Alene, 665-9000	118	$$$$	CB	IP/HT	Yes	DA/R/M/K	Major
18	Super 8 505 W Appleway, Coeur d'Alene, 765-8880	94	$$$	CB		Yes	P/DA	Major
18	La Quinta Inn 280 W Appleway, Coeur d'Alene, 765-5500	68	$$$	CB	IP/S	Yes	P/DA	Major
18	Best Value Inn 330 W Appleway, Coeur d'Alene, 765-3011	60	$$$	CB		Yes	P	Major

Motel Quick Reference-Continued

Price Range: ($) Under $40 ; ($$) $40-$60; ($$$) $60-$80, ($$$$) Over $80. Pets [check with the motel for specific policies] (P), Dining (D), Lounge (L), Disabled Access (DA), Full Breakfast (FB), Cont. Breakfast (CB), Indoor Pool (IP), Outdoor Pool (OP), Hot Tub (HT), Sauna (S), Refrigerator (R), Microwave (M) (Microwave and Refrigerator indicated only if in majority of rooms), Kitchenette (K). All Idaho area codes are 208.

MAP #	HOTEL	NUMBER ROOMS	PRICE RANGE	BREAKFAST	POOL/ HOT TUB SAUNA	NON SMOKE ROOMS	OTHER AMENITIES	CREDIT CARDS
19	Fairfield Inn							
	2303 N 4th St, Coeur d'Alene, 664-1649	69	$$$$	CB	IP/HT	Yes	P/DA/R/M	Major
21	Bennett Bay Inn							
	7904 E Coeur d'Alene Lake Dr, Coeur d'Alene, 664-6168	21	$$$		OP	Yes	P/R/K	Major
21	Cedar Motel & RV Park							
	319 Coeur d'Alene Lake Dr, Coeur d'Alene, 664-2278	17	$		OP	Yes	P/R/M/K	Major
21	El Rancho Motel							
	1915 Sherman Ave, Coeur d'Alene, 664-8794	14	$$			Yes	P/R/M/K	M/V/D
21	Holiday Motel							
	219 E Coeur d'Alene Lake Dr, Coeur d'Alene, 765-6760	11	$/$$/$$$			Yes	P/R/M/K	Major
21	The Bates Motel							
	2018 Sherman Ave, Coeur d'Alene, 667-1411	14	$$/$			Yes	P/R/M	Major
21	Japan House Suites							
	2113 Sherman Ave, Coeur d'Alene, 667-0600	22	$$/$$$/$$$$	CB		Yes	DA/R/M	Major
21	La Quinta Inn & Suites							
	2209 Sherman Ave, Coeur d'Alene, 667-6777	62	$$$$	CB	IP	Yes	P/DA	Major
21	Lake Drive Motel							
	316 Coeur d'Alene Lake Dr, Coeur d'Alene, 667-8486	18	$$		OP/HT	Yes	P/R/M/K	Major
21	Monte Vista Motel & RV Park							
	320 Coeur d'Alene Lake Dr, Coeur d'Alene, 765 -2369	9	$/$$/$$$				P	Major
22	**The McFarland Inn**							
	601 E Foster Ave, Coeur d'Alene, 667-1232	5	$$$$	FB	HT	Yes		M/V
22	**The State Motel**							
	1314 Sherman Ave, Coeur d'Alene, 664-8239	13	$$/$$$			Yes	R/M	M/V/A
22	Coeur d'Alene Budget Saver Motel							
	1519 Sherman Ave, Coeur d'Alene, 667-9505	53	$$/$$$	CB	HT	Yes	P/DA/R/M/K	M/V/D
22	Flamingo Motel							
	718 Sherman Ave, Coeur d'Alene, 664-2159	18	$$/$$$		OP	Yes	P/R/M/K	Major
22	La Quinta Inn							
	2209 E Sherman Ave, Coeur d'Alene, 667-6777	62	$$$$	CB	IP/S	Yes	P/R/M	Major
22	Resort City Inns							
	621 Sherman Ave, Coeur d'Alene, 676-1225	17	$$	CB		Yes	P/DA/R/M	M/V
22	Sandman Motel							
	1620 Sherman Ave, Coeur d'Alene, 664-9119	10	$			Yes	R/M	M/V
26	Country Lane Resort							
	Kingston, 682-1698							
29	**Super 8**							
	601 Bunker Ave, Kellogg, 783-1234	61	$$	CB	IP/HT	Yes	P/DA/R/M	Major
29	**The Trail Motel**							
	206 W Cameron, Kellogg, 784-1161	24	$			Yes	P/DA/R	Major
29	Silverhorn Motor Inn & Restaurant							
	699 W Cameron, Kellogg, 783-1151	40	$$/$$$		HT	Yes	P/D/DA	Major
29	Kellogg Rio Hotel							
	201 McKinley Ave, Kellogg, 786-2103	8	$$/$$$			Yes	R/M/K	Major
29	Morning Star Lodge at Silver Mountain							
	602 Bunker Ave, Kellogg, 783-0202	68			HT	Yes	P/D/DA	Major
29	Motel 51							
	206 E Cameron Ave, Kellogg,	11				Yes	P/DA	Major
32	**The Brooks Hotel**							
	500 Cedar St, Wallace, 556-1571	21	$$$			Yes	D/L/K	Major
32	Wallace Inn							
	100 Front St, Wallace, 752-1252	63	$$$		IP/HT/S		P/D/L/DA	Major
32	Stardust Motel							
	410 Pine St, Wallace, 752-1213	43	$$		IP	Yes	P/DA/K	Major
32	Molly B'Damm Motel							
	60330 Silver Valley Rd, Wallace, 753-2031	17	$$			Yes	P/DA/K	
32	Ryan Hotel							
	608 Cedar St, Wallace, 753-6001	14	$$			Yes	P	Major
32	Best Western Wallace Inn							
	100 Front St, Wallace, 752-1252	63	$$$		IP	Yes	P/D/DA	Major

Ultimate Idaho Atlas and Travel Encyclopedia

Motel Quick Reference-Continued

Price Range: ($) Under $40 ; ($$) $40-$60; ($$$) $60-$80, ($$$$) Over $80. Pets [check with the motel for specific policies] (P), Dining (D), Lounge (L), Disabled Access (DA), Full Breakfast (FB), Cont. Breakfast (CB), Indoor Pool (IP), Outdoor Pool (OP), Hot Tub (HT), Sauna (S), Refrigerator (R), Microwave (M) (Microwave and Refrigerator indicated only if in majority of rooms), Kitchenette (K). All Idaho area codes are 208.

MAP #	HOTEL	NUMBER ROOMS	PRICE RANGE	BREAKFAST	POOL/ HOT TUB SAUNA	NON SMOKE ROOMS	OTHER AMENITIES	CREDIT CARDS
32	Silver Leaf Motel							
	Exit 60 Hwy 10, Wallace, 556-8531	8	$$			Yes	K	M/V
33	Lookout Motel							
	201 River, Mullan, 744-1601	16				Yes	DA/R/M	
36	**Coeur d'Alene Casino Resort Hotel**							
	27068 S Hwy 95, Worley, 686-0248	207	$$$/$$$$		IP/HT	Yes	P/D/L/DA	Major
36	Hiway Motel							
	Hwy 95 Jct Hwy 5 & 95, Plummer, 686-1310	16	$			Yes	DA/K	Major
37	The Pines Motel							
	1117 Main St, St. Maries, 245-2545	28	$$/$$$			Yes	P/DA	Major
38	Swiftwater Motel							
	645 Old River Rd, Avery, 245-2845	4	$$$$			Yes	P/M/K	Major
38	Scheffy's Motel							
	95 Milwaukee Rd, Avery, 245-4410	5	$$$			Yes	K	Major

Notes:

GIFT CORRAL

FINE GIFTS AND ACCESSORIES

WWW.GIFTCORRAL.COM

Searching for that perfect western gift or decorative item? Don't miss the huge selection of quality-crafted items at the Gift Corral. A full selection of their signature products are available online, including handmade bath and body products, Moose Drool novelty items, whimsical bear and moose figurines, stuffed animals, wood carvings, Christmas ornaments reflecting the Western spirit, clothing, antler art, handcrafted jewelry, gourmet foods, Montana Silversmiths items, household décor items ranging from lamps to rustic furniture to picture frames, and much, much more!

Montana Silversmiths Elmer Paper Towel Holder Western artist Phyllis Driscoll created this handsome horse piece for Montana Silversmiths. This paper towel holder makes an impressive horse gift. 17" tall, 10" wide. Item # GC36212

J.S. Drake Originals Wolf Toilet Paper Holder Made of heavy gauge metal, triple-coated with copper and sealed with a urethane topcoat, this delightful piece is durable. Complete a fun bathroom look by adding the wolf towel bar and single hook. An American artist known for his wolf, bear and deer switch plates, J.S. Drake created this piece. 10" tall, 6-1/2" long. Item # GC31163

The Huckleberry People Moose Grub Beer Bread Mix
Add one bottle of beer, knead, and bake. Huckleberry People, a Montana company known for its dry mixes, candy bars and cordials, made this delicious bread mix. Add the Moose Grub Huckleberry BBQ Sauce for an amazing food gift. 16 ounces. Item # GC29492

Find these favorites and many more Western items at…

WWW.GIFTCORRAL.COM

SECTION 2

NORTH-CENTRAL AREA

INCLUDING LEWISTON, MOSCOW, OROFINO, AND GRANGEVILLE

From U.S. Hwy 95 travelers can get a glimpse of what is merely the beginning of Hells Canyon, the deepest gorge in North America.

1 Food

Onaway
Pop. 230

Originally known as Bulltown after the pioneering Bull family, this community was renamed after a city in New York State that was home to some of the earliest settlers. The town was founded in the 1880s as a Wells Fargo stage stop from Palouse to Grizzle Camp.

Potlatch
Pop. 791

The word potlatch, for which the town is named, was a Chinook Indian ceremonial feast that involved exchanging gifts in a competitive display of wealth. The community was founded and named in 1905 by the Potlatch Lumber Company, which at one point was recognized as the world's largest steam-powered mill. Until 1952, the company owned the entire town, including all the homes, churches, and stores. Today, buildings and land are privately owned, and the area's lumber industry has dwindled for lack of resources and demand.

Viola
Pop. 100

Initially called "Four Mile," Viola is one of the oldest settlements in Latah County. Established in 1878, the town once served as a stop for the Spokane and Inland Empire Railroad. There are two well-regarded stories as to how this sleepy village received its current name. Some historians claim that the first child born in the area was named Viola and she later became the town's first teacher. The second story suggests that the town's first postmaster donated land for a school to be built with the understanding that the town would then bear his daughter's name.

T Scenic 6 Park
125 Sixth St., Potlatch.

Potlatch's Scenic 6 Park in downtown Potlatch not only offers standard park recreation, but also provides access to important regional history. In 1905, Potlatch Lumber Company was thriving, and with its profits, built up and managed the community. In no time, Potlatch Lumber established itself as the world's largest steam-powered sawmill. Although the mill is now gone, the site of the famous company is visible from Scenic 6 Park. The park also includes a historical steam engine utilized by the Potlatch Railroad and Depot.

T The Palouse River
State Hwy. 6 between Potlatch and Harvard

Paralleling State Hwy. 6 to the south, the Palouse River flows nearly 100 miles and is named after an Indian word describing a rock formation at the head of a stream. Previously, Lewis and Clark dubbed the river "Drewyer" after a Corps of Discovery member, and French Canadian trappers christened it "Pavillon." However, the river's present name reflects the presence of Palouse Indians who historically resided on the river's banks in eastern Washington. The river drains more than 530 square miles in Idaho before dumping into the mighty Snake River west of Lewiston.

Due to damaged riparian habitat resulting from logging, mining, and road construction in the drainage's upper regions, anglers are likely to only find trout near the river's headwaters.

2

Harvard
Pop. 65

Homer W. Canfield, a prosperous landowner along the Washington, Idaho, and Montana rail line, was recognized for his kindness and cooperation during the line's construction. As a measure of thanks, railroad officials hoped to name the town Canfield. Homer, however, refused the title and instead declared that he wanted the new settlement named Harvard. The village was platted and officially dedicated on May 28, 1906, and a post office was ready for service upon the town's establishment.

Princeton
Pop. 100

The Potlatch Lumber Company constructed the Washington, Idaho, and Montana Railroad in this area in a shrewd move to speed up log transfer times from the forests to the Potlatch mill. The town of Princeton lay along these tracks and was founded in 1896 by Orville Clough, a prominent lumberman and donor of the town's school site. Despite popular belief that the town honors the famous American university, Clough actually named the town in honor of his hometown of Princeton, Minnesota. Despite the realtiy behind its title, Princeton became one of eight stops along the line bearing a college name. This tradition began when an engineer named the nearby town of Purdue in recognition of his alma mater. Thereafter, several university students who spent their summers working for the railroad chimed in and started naming new settlements after their own universities.

T Historic Gold Hill Mining Area
4 miles north of State Hwy. 6 between Princeton and Harvard

In 1870, low-grade placer gold and quartz were discovered between Princeton and Harvard, and an ensuing gold rush hit the area. Between 1870 and 1905, hundreds of claims were filed, and the area produced $500,000 worth of ore. However, when more prosperous gold discoveries were found in Alder Gulch, Montana, activity on Idaho's Gold Hill quickly became non-existent.

TV Laird Park
4 miles east of Harvard (turn right at the Laird Park/Camp Grizzly marker). 875-1131.

Nestled next to the Palouse River, Laird Park is surrounded by lush pine and cedar trees and provides access to the undeveloped North Fork of the Palouse River region. Hiking, horseback riding, picnicking, and swimming are all available in the area, and mountain biking is growing in popularity. A ten-mile moderate biking trail leaves Laird Park and travels to nearby Moose Creek Reservoir.

TV White Pine Scenic Area
East of Harvard on the White Pine Scenic Byway (State Hwy. 6). Continue past Laird Park, bearing right at the marked turnoff for Giant White Pine Campground.

The White Pine Scenic Byway is renowned for its giant white pines, but the largest and most scenic white pine is located within the boundaries of north-central Idaho's Giant White Pine Campground. A short trail in the campground leads to Idaho's largest white pine, measuring in at six feet in diameter and soaring 188 feet into the air.

The White Pine Campground and Scenic Area is also home to a network of mountain biking trails. Trail guides are available on-site and describe the moderate to difficult trails ranging in length from one mile to a nineteen-mile loop ride.

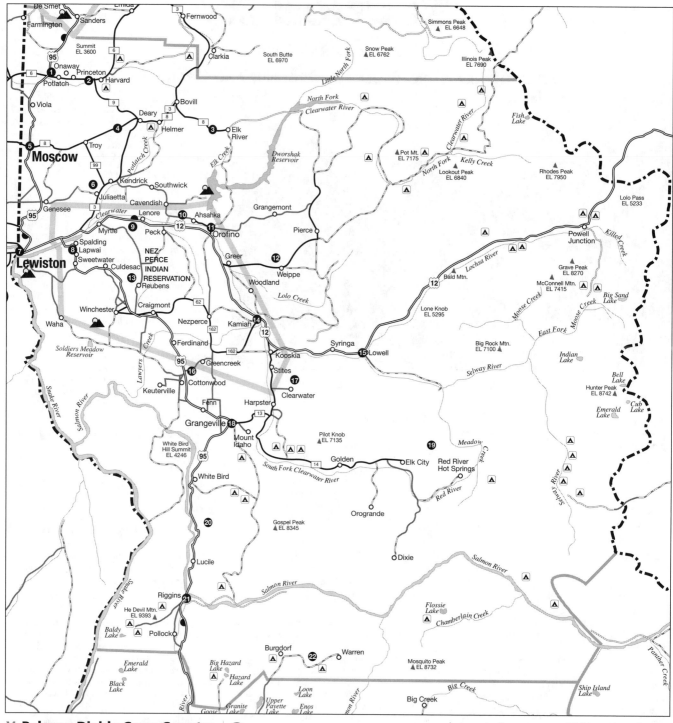

V Palouse Divide Cross-Country Ski Area

23 miles east of Potlatch on State Hwy. 6. Contact the Coeur d'Alene division of Idaho Department of Parks and Recreation at 666-6711.

Eighteen miles of marked trails and panoramic views of the surrounding mountains and valleys await Nordic skiers at the Palouse Divide Cross-Country Ski Area in the St. Joe National Forest. Most of the trails are rated at the beginner level, but a few do require intermediate skills. Approximately 45% of the trails are groomed on a periodic basis. The area is part of Idaho's Park N' Ski system, and permits are required. Permits may be obtained at the Ranger Station and fees are as follows: $25 annual permit (good at all Idaho Park N' Ski areas), $7.50 3-day permit, and $2 day use permit.

3 Food

Bovill
Pop. 305

The town of Bovill was named for Hugh Bovill, who, upon seeing the Idaho territory during a cattle drive from Colorado, vowed he would one day return. And return he did, in 1899, with his wife and two daughters. They purchased a homestead from R. Francis Warren and proceeded to ranch over 550 acres. As more homesteaders, timber crews, and sportsmen arrived in the area, the Bovills decided to take advantage of the economic opportunity at hand and opened a store and lodge instead. Incorporated in 1907, the town received a post office during the same year with Hugh serv-

ing as its first postmaster. Within no time, the quiet landscape that had lured Hugh and his family to the area was overcrowded, so the community founders left in 1911.

Two fires threatened to destroy Bovill in its early years. First, in 1910 a large area north of town burned, but the town was spared. Then, on

Idaho Trivia

State Highway 9 is one of a kind among Idaho's state and U.S. highways. The short route between Deary and Harvard represents Idaho's only unpaved state highway.

Legend

00	Locator number (matches numeric listing in section)
▲	Campsite
⛰	State Park
⛺	Rest stop
▬▬▬	Interstate
═══	U.S. Hwy.
▬▬▬	State Hwy.
▬▬▬	County Road
▬▬▬	Gravel/unpaved road

July 4,1914, a fire destroyed much of the western end of Main Street. The fire's cause was never clearly pinpointed, but law enforcement officials believed that the fire was a case of arson used to conceal a mugging and murder of a man who had recently robbed $1,450 from the town bank.

Elk River
Pop. 156

Elk River was originally called Trumbull after the Trumbull Hunting and Fishing Lodge that stood at the end of the newly laid Milwaukee Railroad tracks. Upon completion of the tracks in 1909, however, an electricity-driven sawmill was constructed under the management of the Potlatch Timber Company. Almost overnight, the area blossomed with activity, attracting workers and their families. Soon, residents decided to rename their growing community after the vast numbers of elk in the area. Although the town flourished and business opportunities increased for over twenty years, the 1927 construction of the Clearwater Timber sawmill in Lewiston spelled hard times ahead for Elk River. As predicted, the town essentially quit growing, and the sawmill was forced to close during the Depression years. Today, it is a recreation hot spot boasting fishing, hunting, horseback riding, mountain biking, swimming, ice fishing, boating, cross-country skiing, and ATV riding.

T Oviatt Creek Fossil Beds
Near Elk River and Bovill. Contact the Clearwater National Forest at 476-4541. From Bovill, drive 11 1/2 miles southeast on State Hwy. 8 to Forest Rd. #1963 located just before mile marker 48. Proceed south on FR 1963 for 3 miles to the intersection of FR 4704 on Oviatt Creek.

The Scene
Imagine a quiet, peaceful lake surrounded by densely forested slopes winding gently down to water's edge. That's what this site looked like 15 million years ago.

However, the forests of that era looked very different from the stands of cold-tolerant conifers found here today. Back then, the climate was warm and humid, more like the present day Southeastern United States. Forests of subtropical species such as bald cypress and redwoods mixed with magnolia, birch, sycamore, avocado, oak, chestnut, and beech covered the mountains and valleys.

Some of these tree species became extinct in North America millions of years ago. For example, the Metasequoia, or dawn redwood, now grows only in a small valley in central China.

What Created the Fossils?
Just like any lakeside forest, gusts of wind blew leaves into the water where they sank, finally resting flat on the lake bottom. At some point, unique geologic events led to heavy, rapid siltation which buried the leaves before they had time to decompose.

Leaves and other botanical parts – and even insects – in the Oviatt Creek fossil beds have not seen the light of day for about 15 million years! By trapping and preserving the fossils in unusually good condition, these sedimentary rocks now offer a rare outdoor treat you must see for yourself.

What You Will Find
Although the lake and subtropical forests are long gone, evidence of that era remains for you to discover at Oviatt Creek.

Fossils here are abundant and extremely well-preserved. Picking through the fine textured gray and tan lake sediments with a knife or rock hammer, you will find a wide variety of conifer and hardwood leaves, stems, seeds, pods, and cones. You might also discover flowers, ferns, moss, and insect remains.

Most of the specimens here are "impression" fossils. Usually brown or tan in color, these are merely imprints left by plants as they decomposed. Most of the world's fossils are of this type.

However, some Oviatt fossils still contain original organic material. Called "compression" fossils, these are usually found deeper in the silt layers where oxidation and weathering haven't penetrated. Not only are the 15 million year old leaves you find in this case still leaves – but the outer and inner layers of specialized cells remain intact, and can be studied under a microscope!

On sites similar to Oviatt Creek, scientists have extracted actual DNA genetic codes from compression fossils of the ancient forests represented here. Only a few other places in the world offer fossils this well-preserved.

Fossils Are a Limited Resource
School children on field trips and professionals researching the natural history of our region are among the many people who enjoy the tremendous educational opportunities these fossils offer the public.

Feel free to take a few fossils, but please don't take more than you need. By conserving these ancient tributes to forest biological history, others may share the treasures and enjoy the site for years to come.

Although some digging may be necessary to get good, complete fossils, please keep disturbance to a minimum. If you do dig, please fill in any holes you create and help keep the area clean.

Enjoy your visit to the Clearwater National Forest. And take home a little memento from the Oviatt Creek fossil beds to help you relive the trip and share it with friends.

Where to Dig
Oviatt Creek, a very small year-round stream, parallels the west side of Forest Rd. 4704 at the intersection with the more heavily traveled and improved Forest Rd. 1963. Park near the 4704 sign, making sure to leave enough room for vehicles to pass safely in any direction.

Just across the stream from where you park is an old road bed backed by a cutbank. This wedge-shaped piece from the creek up to and including part of this old road cut – is the fossil site.

You will see some gray and tan sediments a few feet wide exposed in the cut bank where the fossils are easy to dig out. Since digging undercuts the bank, please be careful. Higher concentrations of fossils can be found in the ground between the cutbank and Oviatt Creek. However, you may need a digging tool such as a shovel or Pulaski to reach the really good fossils. Some can be found close to the surface, but oxidation and disturbance have broken up much of the rock on the top, so the best, most complete specimens are found by going from 6" to 1 1/2' deeper.

Presently, there is no signage at the fossil site, nor is the area extraordinary in any way to the casual traveler passing by. However, by digging around you will locate numerous samples of vegetation millions of years old and some of the most well-preserved fossils found in the world!

Reprinted from a Clearwater National Forest brochure

T Giant Western Red Cedar
10 miles north of Elk River on Forest Rd. 382. Contact the Clearwater National Forest at 883-2301.

Situated in the tranquil Upper Elk Creek Basin, Idaho's largest tree is a 3,000-year-old Western Red Cedar. The tree measures more than 18 feet in diameter and skyrockets over 177 feet. The tree, surrounded by a handicap accessible boardwalk, stands amidst several other old-growth cedars while a stream flows in and around the giant cedar.

T Latah Clay Pits
15 miles west of Bovill

Located on the north side of State Highway 8, the Latah Clay Pits are an important economic industry for Bovill and the surrounding region. Clay extracted from the pits is utilized as filler in quality paper and in manufacturing refractory bricks.

T Ruby Creek
0.5 miles south of Bovill on State Hwy. 8

Running alongside State Highway 8, Ruby Creek was the site of gold-rush mining activity dating back to 1885. Placer claims and lode mines were worked in the area until 1910 with meager profits gained in gold and lead-zinc veins.

T Morris Creek Cedar Grove
10 miles northwest of Elk River via Forest Roads 382 and 1969. Contact Elk River City Information at 826-3299.

Situated beside the Morris Creek tributary in the Elk Creek basin, Morris Creek Cedar Grove contains ninety acres of impressive old-growth cedars. The impressive trees are estimated to be 400 to 500 years old, and a short loop trail winding under the canopy of leaves provides an up-close view.

T Rhodes Peak
Near the Idaho/Montana border

Rising 7,950 feet towards the Idaho atmosphere, Rhodes Peak is named after historic Pierce miner, William "Black Bill" Rhodes. Rhodes was enormously successful in the area, sharing his wealth with all around him and garnering the favor of the entire community. Upon his death, Rhodes' friends buried him fifty miles from Pierce on top of Blackhead Mountain near today's Rhodes Peak.

NEZ PERCE CULTURE IN NORTH-CENTRAL IDAHO

Nez Perce, or Nii Mii Pu, legend states that the Nez Perce people and all of civilization began in north central Idaho. The lifestyle of the Nez Perce has reflected this cultural belief with evidence of regional Native American habitation for thousands of years.

Drawing upon this extensive ancestry and traditional homelands extending into southeastern Washington and northeastern Oregon, the Nez Perce have played an important role in the history of Idaho. Although their ancestors were free to roam the once open lands of the American West, the 1800s brought conflict and change to the Nez Perce. Negotiating with the U.S. government, the Nez Perce were eventually forced onto a reservation where they continue to maintain the reservation as a sovereign nation governed by its own tribal constitution. Of the nearly 3,300 current tribal members, nearly two-thirds still call the reservation home.

While maintaining the long-established reservation, the Nez Perce people also work to pass along the traditions of their ancestors while embracing the future. A Nez Perce language program is thriving, and the tribe has once again started breeding the colorful Appaloosa horses. In addition, the Nez Perce participate in government programs, manage businesses related to forestry and limestone production, and operate popular gaming enterprises.

Today, the Nez Perce are eager to share their culture with the rest of the world. Annual events and community festivities are open to the public and provide an insight into the rich heritage that the Nez Perce people preserve from one generation to the next.

T Potlatch River
Bovill to Lewiston near the route of U.S. Hwy. 12.

Lewis and Clark were the first white men to christen Idaho's present-day Potlatch River. The Corps of Discovery chose to name the waterway "Colter Creek" after their companion and fellow explorer, John Colter. The name was later changed to reflect the presence of the important Potlatch Lumber Company in northern Idaho.

Rising near Bovill, the Potlatch River flows forty miles southwest where it empties in the Clearwater River. The river boasts a few whitewater rafting rapids for the experienced adventurer.

TV Elk Creek Falls Recreation Area
3 miles south of Elk River

Marked by 960 acres of national forest land, Elk Creek Falls Recreation Area is a scenic place to relax or start an active adventure. A deep gorge, several waterfalls with light refracting natural pools, dense timber stands, and impressive views around every corner make the recreation area a popular place year-round. A system of National Recreation Trails winds past three waterfalls with possible sightings of area wildlife. The lush habitat provides a perfect home for bears, moose, elk,

deer, mountain lions, non-game birds, and brook and rainbow trout.

During the winter, the area is transformed into a Nordic paradise. Twenty-four miles of intermittently groomed trails bisect the recreation area. The area is part of Idaho's Park N' Ski system, and permits are required. Permits may be obtained at the nearest Ranger Station, and fees are as follows: $25 annual permit (good at all Idaho Park N' Ski areas), $7.50 3-day permit, and $2 day use permit.

V Moose Creek Reservoir
2 miles north off State Hwy. 8 and 1 mile west of Bovill

Moose Creek Reservoir is a favorite fishing hole encompassing more than 80 acres. Stocked trout, bluegills, pumpkinseeds, and crappies populate the waters, while osprey, Canadian geese, and ducks make the area a popular bird-watching destination. For those seeking a more active adventure, several hiking and mountain biking trails depart from the reservoir and lead to scenic overviews of the area.

V Clearwater River
Contact the Clearwater National Forest in Orofino at 476-4541.

Rising in three branches in northern Idaho's Bitterroot Range, the 190-mile Clearwater River flows through the heart of north-central Idaho before spilling into the Snake River at Lewiston. The river, which drains 9,640 square miles, offers both placid and raging waters, making it ideal for family float trips or experienced whitewater rafters.

The river is also a popular destination for anglers, offering one of the Pacific Northwest's finest steelhead fisheries. Resident fish populations found in the Clearwater include rainbow, cutthroat, and bull trout, mountain whitefish, chinook salmon, and kokanee salmon. The river's tributaries include the Lochsa and Selway Rivers, 450 alpine lakes, and the popular Dworshak Reservoir that houses smallmouth bass.

V Elk Creek Reservoir
Directly south of Elk River. Contact the Elk River City Hall at 826-3209.

Lying in close proximity to Idaho's famous Dworshak Reservoir, Elk Creek Reservoir is much smaller but offers similar recreational possibilities. The reservoir is widely known for its rainbow and brook trout, bullhead catfish, and small and largemouth bass. In addition, the area is ripe with huckleberries making it a favorite destination of both locals and visitors during late summer.

4 Food

Deary
Pop. 552

This small town originally known as Anderson began as a stop on the Washington, Idaho, and Montana rail line. It was renamed for William

Deary, an early settler and manager for the Weyerhaeuser Company. Deary and the company he worked for platted the town in 1907 and constructed the lumber mill as well. The town was officially incorporated in 1912 but was nearly wiped off the map in 1923 when a fire destroyed every building on the west side of Main Street except for the bank.

Helmer
Pop. 45

Helmer prospered in its early years as a shortcut route to homesteads in the upper areas of the Potlatch River and Elk Creek. The small village hosted a post office from 1907 to 1929, and draws its name from timber-cruiser, William Helmer.

Troy
Pop. 798

Like the famous Troy described in both history and literature texts, this small Idaho town has an interesting past filled with legend. In the mid 1880s, the area was known as Huffs Gulch, and according to early homesteaders, Huffs Gulch didn't have much to offer. That all changed in 1890 when millionaire banker John Vollmer arrived. Using his influence as a state agent of the Northern Pacific Railroad, Vollmer persuaded the railroad to build a line running through his town. The same year, the prominent businessman changed the now growing settlement's name to "Vollmer" in honor of his accomplishments.

While Vollmer was popular in the town's early days, he quickly lost favor with residents. During the 1893 area depression, Vollmer foreclosed on several notes, so an election was held to change the town's name. Among the name choices were Vollmer, Romeo, and Troy. Legend has it that a young Greek railroad laborer stood outside the poll site with a large barrel of liquor. For anyone who voted to change the town's name to Troy, the young Greek would allow that person to have as much free liquor as he/she wanted. His bribing technique worked, and at the end of the election, Troy came in with 29 votes, Vollmer with 9, and Romeo with 0.

With a new name, Troy opened its post office doors in 1898. In 1905, the First Bank of Troy began business, and this prosperous bank later became the birthplace of the national Key Bank. As more people moved to the area, Troy became an important regional supply center, and it is even rumored that Cape Canaveral's launch pad is partially constructed of bricks made in Troy.

T Potato Hill
North of Deary

Rising one thousand feet above its valley surroundings, Potato Hill dominates the Deary landscape. At an elevation of 4,017 feet, Potato Hill appears to be a volcanic vent of an undetermined age. Deary's first residents called the unique geological feature "Spud Hill" while the community newspaper continually referred to the landmark as Mount Deary. The present name is a local compromise of these original titles.

T Mica Mountain
5 miles north of Deary

During its long history, Deary was once home to several mica mines. First discovered in 1881 at the head of Swartz Creek, the mica crystals formed in giant pegmatite on the slopes of Mica Mountain. Mining continued in the area as late as World War II, with some pieces that were extracted measuring in at two feet by three feet with weights exceeding 100 pounds. The mica was then shipped for use across the U.S. in stove doors, carriage window panels, and home insulation.

T Tatonka Whitepine Bison Ranch
5 miles east of Troy near the intersection of White Pine Flats Rd. and State Hwy. 8. Contact the Troy Chamber of Commerce at 835-5411.

For curious onlookers interested in seeing where the buffalo roam in the American West, the Tatonka Whitepine Bison Ranch provides a rare opportunity to see the creatures up-close near the highway. These buffalo frequently end up as prized restaurant fare across Idaho.

M Troy Chamber of Commerce
421 Main St., Troy. 835-5411.

5 *Food, Lodging*

Moscow
Pop. 21,291

Originally known to Nez Perce Indians as Tat-Kin-Mah (place of the spotted deer), this community nestled in the heart of Palouse country welcomed the first white settlers in 1869. These first few homesteaders tended to come and go, and the fledgling site became known regionally as "Hog Heaven" because razorback hogs grazed on the area's abundant camas bulb fields. When Almon Ashbury Lieuallen arrived in 1871 as the first permanent settler, however, he decided the area needed a more appealing name if it had any hope of attracting more residents. He changed the name to Paradise Valley, and a post office was established in 1873.

In 1875 the current name of Moscow was adopted. Some claim the idea for the name change came from Lieuallen himself. He supposedly believed the community's problematic solitary landscape was comparable to problems in Russia, as that country was under the rule of Ivan the Terrible. Still others claim the name change came from a postmaster or town business official who decided the area was reminiscent of a

Pennsylvania town known as Moscow. In either case, the name change took hold, and Moscow slowly began to grow.

In the late 1870s and early 1880s, Moscow wasn't much to speak of, but by 1900, the population neared 300. When Congress ceded land from the adjacent Nez Perce reservation in the mid-1800s, Latah County was created, and Moscow was designated as the county seat. The area's reputation was further bolstered when Moscow was selected in 1889 as the site for the land-grant University of Idaho. By 1920, the community had acquired over 4,000 residents, and the town continued its steady growth throughout the twentieth century. Today, Moscow is known for its friendly atmosphere, a culture of superb arts and entertainment, and admirable architecture.

H University of Idaho
Milepost 342.7 on U.S. Hwy. 95

Like this long highway, the University of Idaho links together the northern and southern parts of the state of Idaho.

Established by the territorial legislature, January 30, 1889, the university opened in the fall of 1892. As Idaho's land grant institution, the university was charged to bring the benefits of quality teaching, research, and service to the people of Idaho. Its eight colleges and graduate school now serve thousands of students and is a major center for higher education in Idaho.

T Idaho Forest Fire Museum and Interpretive Center
310 N. Main St., Moscow. 882-4767.

Opened in 1997, the Idaho Forest Fire Museum preserves and interprets the great history surrounding forest fires and heroic firefighters.

Visitors will view one of the U.S.' largest collections of Smoky the Bear memorabilia and learn interesting facts about forest fires, the story of Idaho's famed 1910 forest fire, the tale of Idaho hero, Edward Pulaski, who saved his crew from a raging fire and later developed the tool now bearing his name. The museum is open 9 AM to 4 PM Monday through Friday from January to May. From June through December, the museum is open 9 AM to 5 PM Monday through Friday and 9 AM to 4 PM on Saturdays. Admission is free.

T McConnell Mansion Museum
110 S. Adams St., Moscow. 882-1004.

Moscow has been graced with numerous stately 19th century homes, one of which is the 1886 McConnell Mansion. Built for Idaho's third governor, William "Poker Bill" McConnell, this well-preserved Victorian Gothic house is now home to the Latah County Historical Society. Amid its Victorian furnishings and décor, the museum offers rotating displays of historical information relevant to the region's development plus a treasure hunt for children. Past exhibits have included period dress and photos of early settlers. Here, the historical society also offers a guide to other historical residences and downtown buildings. The mansion is open from 1 PM to 5 PM Tuesday through Saturday from May to September. October through April, the mansion is open from 1 PM to 4 PM Tuesday through Saturday. In addition to the exhibits and hands-on activities at the McConnell Mansion, the Latah County Historical Society offers a research library and photo collection at 327 East 2nd Street from 9 AM to 12 PM and 1 PM to 5 PM Tuesday through Friday.

Moscow
Map not to scale.

Moscow	Jan	Feb	March	April	May	June	July	Aug	Sep	Oct	Nov	Dec	Annual
Average Max. Temperature (F)	34.7	40.1	47.5	56.9	65.3	72.7	82.8	82.5	72.9	60.0	44.4	36.3	58.0
Average Min. Temperature (F)	22.5	26.0	30.6	35.7	41.2	46.3	50.3	49.8	44.1	37.4	30.6	25.0	36.6
Average Total Precipitation (in.)	2.97	2.20	2.26	1.89	2.02	1.64	0.73	0.80	1.23	1.85	3.03	2.93	23.55
Average Total Snowfall (in.)	16.2	9.1	5.0	1.2	0.1	0.0	0.0	0.0	0.0	0.3	5.3	12.4	49.5
Average Snow Depth (in.)	4	2	0	0	0	0	0	0	0	0	0	2	1

T Appaloosa Museum and Heritage Center
5070 Hwy. 8 W, Moscow. 882-5578.

Idaho's state horse, the Appaloosa, is the focus of this museum's exhibits. The spotted, hardy horse draws its name from the Palouse Prairie. When early settlers arrived in the area, these horses dominated the landscape. Thus, many pioneers began referring to the horse as "a Palousey." Eventually, the title was changed to the horse's current proper name, Appaloosa. Celebrated by Nez Perce Indians, the Appaloosa is now fondly remembered in the museum's unique display of historical photos, artifacts, exhibits, and the Appaloosa Hall of Fame. The museum is open Tuesday through Saturday year-round with free admission.

T Camas Prairie Winery
110 S. Main St., Moscow. 882-0214 or (800) 616-0214 Take U.S. Hwy. 95 to Moscow, and locate First St. The winery is situated in a historical brick building on the corner of First and Main Sts.

Under the ownership of Sue and Stuart Schott, Camas Prairie Winery traces its origins back to 1983. However, the Schotts rely heavily upon late 1800s northern Idaho winemaking traditions in producing their fourteen distinctive wine varieties. With humble beginnings in the Schotts' basement and two garages, Camas Prairie Winery eventually grew and moved into a historic building in the heart of Moscow's downtown. Today, patrons can enjoy sips of the Schotts' sparkling wines, honeymeads, Merlot, Lemberger, Riesling, Chardonnay, Cabernet Sauvignon, and other proprietary blends at a wine bar in the winery's new mezzanine. Also displaying local watercolor paintings, the winery is open to visitors Tuesday through Saturday from 12:00 PM to 6:30 PM.

T Life Force Naturals
531 South Main St., Moscow. 882-9158

Life Force Naturals was established in 1989 and showcases the unique wines of beekeeper, Garric Cruz. Utilizing honey almost exclusively from his own bees, Cruz produces award-winning wines, including raspberry, huckleberry, and apricot honey wines, as well as Original and Vandal Gold meads. The winery is open Tuesday through Saturday from 10:00 AM to 5:30 PM and Sundays from 12:00 PM to 5:00 PM.

LAND OF PLENTY

The Palouse Country surrounding Moscow and Troy is a land of plenty when it comes to wheat, peas, lentils, and barley. The area produces more than 90% of America's dry peas, and aids the U.S. in maintaining its position as the world's largest exporter of peas and lentils. The area's wheat is also a valuable commodity with most of it being shipped to Asia and the Middle East for the manufacture of pasta and baked goods.

T Hamilton-Lowe Aquatic Center
830 N. Mountain View Rd., Moscow. 882-7665.

The Hamilton-Lowe Aquatic Center offers a fun way to cool off during Idaho's summer sizzle. Opened in 2000, the center features a 25-yard lap pool, diving boards, an activities pool complete with water slides and interactive water equipment, lounging chairs, and a picnic area.

T Prichard Art Gallery
414 S. Main, Moscow. 885-3586.

Established in 1982 in downtown Moscow, the Prichard Art Gallery is an extension of the University of Idaho's College of Art & Architecture. Year-round exhibitions showcase a variety of regional art as well as the works of college students and faculty. A range of mediums is presented, including fine arts, architecture, ceramics, photography, glass art, fine crafts, computer art, folk art, painting, and sculptures. In addition to the seven to nine different displays hosted annually, the gallery also features lectures, readings, and art workshops. The gallery serves over 13,000 visitors each year, and is open Monday through Saturday free of charge with changing seasonal hours.

T University of Idaho
709 Deakin Ave., Moscow. 885-4636 or 885-6111.

In an attempt to keep northern Idaho from seceding to Washington, the Idaho Territorial Legislature founded the University of Idaho in 1889. Established as a land grant facility, the university is the state's oldest and largest institution of higher learning and is surrounded by the rolling hills of the Palouse. Nearly 12,000 students attend the ten different colleges represented on the main 320-acre campus, and a variety of architectural styles characterize the buildings. The university also boasts the state's largest library with 1.6 million volumes and numerous government documents. Campus tours are available by advance arrangement.

T University of Idaho Hartung Theater
U of I Campus, Moscow. 885-7212.

The university's Hartung Theater is home to the Mainstage Series, a collection of dramas, comedies, musicals, and lectures. Performances are presented throughout the year in this acoustically superior setting seating 417. Call for a complete listing of current events.

T Shattuck Arboretum
West of the U of I Administration Building and north of the President's Residence. U of I Campus, Moscow. 885-5978.

Christened "Shattuck Arboretum" in 1933, this beautiful landscape actually dates back to 1910. Upon his arrival at the University of Idaho, Charles Houston Shattuck noted that the campus was essentially treeless and shrubless. At his own initiation, he began planting a 14-acre parcel with hundreds of trees and shrubs in an effort to beautify the campus. Although Shattuck died in 1931, his efforts live on. Today, the arboretum represents one of the oldest university plantings. The grove of mature trees features a giant sequoia, and provides a peaceful setting for an afternoon stroll or picnic. The arboretum is open to the public free of charge.

T University of Idaho Arboretum and Botanical Garden
U of I campus on Nez Perce Drive, Moscow. 885-5978.

Nestled against the gentle rolling Palouse hills, the 63-acre University of Idaho Arboretum is a crown jewel and represents influences from around the world. The garden features geographical groups of Asian, European, Eastern, and Western North American plants, providing the area with 120 dedicated trees in addition to native Idaho species present.

These trees and shrubs are continually changing, reflecting each season with bright flowers and vibrant fall colors. Visitors can enjoy the range of plants and wildlife habitats through the arboretum's many groves and walking trails while also gaining access to magnificent vistas of Oregon's Blue Mountains. In addition, water features and twenty-seven granite benches add to the area's mystique, and visitors are encouraged to take a stroll or simply relax in the tranquil atmosphere.

Personal guided tours are available from the aboretum's horticultural staff. Those interested should call in advance to schedule a tour and check on availability.

T Kenworthy Performing Arts Center & Moscow Community Theater
508 Main St., Moscow. 882-4127.

In 1926, Milburn Kenworthy opened this historical theater as a vaudeville and silent movie house. As the years passed, remodeling efforts turned the Kenworthy into Moscow's finest theater, and it continued to operate as the stage for Hollywood's latest films until the late 1980s.

After completing its lease with a major cinema provider, the Kenworthy family donated the building to the Moscow Community Theater. By late 2000, the Kenworthy Performing Arts Center was back in business, featuring classic movies, superior foreign films, and live stage productions. Today, the theater is also home to Moscow Community Theater productions as well as various other musical performers. Call for a complete listing of current shows.

T Idaho Repertory Theatre
U of I, Moscow. 1-88-88-UIDAHO.

Affiliated with the University of Idaho Theater Department, the Idaho Repertory Theatre represents one of the Northwest's oldest professional summer theater companies. The troupe was founded in 1935 and offers performances each July and August. Call for a complete listing of events.

T Washington Idaho Symphony

Call (509) 332-3408 for a current events schedule and ticket information.

Established in 1969, the Washington Idaho Symphony specializes in bringing the best classical and contemporary symphonic music to Idaho and Washington residents. The prestigious orchestra includes members from both north central Idaho and eastern Washington, and several concerts are offered annually to the public.

T Idaho Washington Concert Chorale

Call (208) 883-3248 for events schedule and ticket information. www.iwchorale.org.

The Idaho Washington Concert Chorale is an audition-only musical masterpiece consisting of eighty singers from both Idaho and Washington's Palouse Country. The chorale is directed by Washington State University professional, John Weiss, and a range of contemporary and classical pieces are performed at concerts throughout the year.

T Cordelia Lutheran Church

7 miles southeast of Moscow off the paved Lenville Rd.

Cordelia Lutheran Church dates back to 1883 and represents Idaho's oldest Lutheran Church. The church also holds the title for conducting the first Lutheran confirmation ceremony in the American West.

T University of Idaho Geology Displays

Department of Materials Science & Engineering, University of Idaho, Moscow. 885-6376.

The University of Idaho is home to a variety of geology displays showcasing Idaho's geological characteristics and mining history. On the second and third floor hallways of the Materials Science and Engineering Department, visitors will find impressive displays of old mining tools and Idaho gemstones.

T Moscow Mountain Scenic Overlook

From northeast Moscow, follow Mountain View Rd.

Moscow's Mountain View Road provides several opportunities for visitors to overlook the unspoiled countryside and the city of Moscow. Known as Moscow Mountain, the ridge features gravel and dirt roads lined with pines, cedars, ferns, wildflowers, wildlife, and numerous scenic pull-out points.

T University of Idaho Golf Course

1215 Nez Perce Dr., Moscow. 885-6171.

Dating back to 1933, the public University of Idaho Golf Course was first designed by Francis L. James as a 9-hole course. In 1968, Bob Bolduck redesigned the course, adding an additional nine holes to bring the course to its present 18-hole, par 72 status. PGA instruction is available, as well as a driving range, Pro Shop, and club and cart rentals. Advance tee times are recommended.

T East City Park

3rd and Hayes Streets, Moscow. Contact the Moscow Parks and Recreation Dept. at 883-7085.

In addition to standard playground equipment, Moscow's East City Park features a basketball court, horseshoe pits, covered picnic areas, sand volleyball, and a band shelter.

T Ghormley Park

3rd and Home Sts., Moscow. Contact the Moscow Parks and Recreation Dept. at 883-7085.

Ghormley Park is situated near the University of Idaho campus and features two lighted baseball/softball fields, lighted tennis courts, horseshoe pits, a community swimming pool, barbecue pits with group/individual picnic areas, and a child friendly playground.

T Mountain View Park

On Mountain View Rd. on the east edge of Moscow. Contact the Moscow Parks and Recreation Dept. at 883-7085.

Wide open spaces and tranquility characterize Moscow's Mountain View Park. In addition to a peaceful bike path winding next to Paradise Creek, the park features a playground and picnic areas complete with barbecues. Cyclists who travel on the paved bike path will end up at Kiwanis Park/Hordemann Park, which boasts a small fishing pond.

T Virgil Phillips Farm

5 miles north of Moscow off U.S. Hwy. 95. Contact Latah County Parks & Rec. at 883-5709.

Encompassing 160 acres, the Virgil Phillips Farm is not a typical western farm. Visitors to the farm will find two small ponds showcasing ducks, frogs, salamanders, and turtles.

T Moscow Historical Building Tour

Downtown Moscow. Contact the Moscow Chamber of Commerce at 882-1800.

With roots dating back to the late 1860s, Moscow has enjoyed a variety of building periods and architectural styles. The structures listed below represent both the economic and personal character of the ever-growing city.

Skattaboe Block
Southwest Corner of Main and Fourth Streets
Featuring a Romanesque style, the two-story Skattaboe Block has been home to a range of telephone companies since the early 1900s. Taylor and Lauder of Moscow, a prominent masonry company of the day, was responsible for the building's brickwork. The Skattaboe Block is listed on the National Register of Historic Places.

Hotel Moscow
Northwest Corner of Main and Fourth Streets
Constructed between 1891 and 1892, the three-story Hotel Moscow features a Victorian Romanesque style accented with red brick and sandstone trim. Completed at a cost of $30,000, the structure was built as a replacement for the community's first hotel that burned in a devastating 1890 fire. Today, the Hotel Moscow is used for various commercial purposes and is listed on the National Register of Historic Places.

Main and Third Street
Originally home to Dernham and Kaufmann's U.S. Wholesale & Retail General Merchandise store, this building was erected in 1889. In 1900, the business was converted to David & Ely, Inc. and became a renowned Moscow department store. Although the store retains its historic façade from its starting days, the original storefront has been covered with aggregate panels.

Main and First Street
This elaborate cast iron and wood beam structure was built in 1891 as a home for the McConnell-McGuire Department Store. The storefront features a cast iron façade, pressed tin, and gargoyles with wolf faces. The building was remodeled in the 1980s.

Dernham House
221 N. Adams
This two-story house was built for Henry Dernham, co-owner of the Dernham and Kaufmann U.S. Wholesale and Retail General Merchandise Store. The Queen Anne style house was completed in 1885 and features unique hexagonal bay windows with colored glass panes.

Tom Taylor Residence
124 N. Polk at "A" Street
Built around 1885, the former Tom Taylor residence features a Queen Anne cottage style throughout its 1 1/2 stories. The home is accented with Eastlake trim, shaped shingles, and a decorative large round window with stained glass details.

Miller House
325 N. Polk at "C" Street
Known as the "House of Seven Gables," this 2 1/2-story chalet-style mansion was built for local flourmill owner, Mark Miller. A Portland architect designed the home that was built between 1908-1911, and the house features many interesting details. On the exterior, the home includes exposed, curved rafters and stained glass windows, while the interior features oak paneling, built-in bookcases, and numerous bedrooms. At one time, the home also included a ballroom with twelve-foot ceilings, a covered porch for horse drawn carriages, and servants' quarters.

Butterfield Residence
403 N. Polk at "C" Street
Charles Butterfield constructed this home between 1902 and 1903, and the residence reflects Moscow's only example of Georgian Revival architecture. Butterfield modeled the home after his sister's house in Janesville, Wisconsin, but the cost was so exorbitant, Butterfield was forced to rent out the upper story as apartments to pay for the mortgage.

604 N. Polk at "C" Street
This 1 1/2-story home situated across the street from the Butterfield residence was built in the 1800s. The charming home features a Queen Anne architectural style.

528 E. First at N. Polk Street
George Hallum, head carpenter for the University of Idaho, built this two-story, T-shaped home in 1890. Frank David, owner of David's' Department Store in Moscow, was the home's first inhabitant. The home retains its original character, complete with decorative shingles and a screened sleeping porch.

Jerome Day House
430 "A" at Van Buren Street
Jerome Day, brother of Harry Day who discovered the Hercules silver claim in the Coeur d'Alene mining district, was the first owner of this Queen Anne/Colonial style home. After laboring in the mine with his family and receiving an equal share of the profit, Jerome attended Gonzaga College in Spokane and later enlisted in the University of Idaho's cadet corps before returning to the mines. He enrolled in the Western Federation of Miners and soon served as shift boss. In response to the discovery of a second rich vein in the Hercules mine, Jerome enrolled at the University of Idaho at age twenty-six to study mineral chemistry and prepare for a career as an assayer.

After meeting and marrying Lucy Mix in Moscow, Jerome hired a Boston architect to design this home for them in 1902. The two-story home features metal finials on the roof, beveled glass, and a carriage house accented with Mission style gables. Although he studied to become an assayer, Jerome became the Moscow State Bank director in 1904 and later president. He also financed the Idaho National Harvester Company that produced farm equipment in Moscow between 1906 and 1918. Jerome later served in the state senate and moved to Lake Coeur d'Alene in 1923 where he resided until his death in 1941. The mansion he had built for his wife was once rented by the University as the President's home, but currently serves as a private residence.

James Forney Residence
310 "A" Street
Constructed in 1878 for Moscow Judge James Forney, this home is reputed to be the oldest home still standing in the community.

Mason Cornwall House
308 S. Hays at Third Street
Moscow's Taylor and Lauder Masonry Company constructed this unique Victorian Italianate home in 1889 for wealthy businessman, Mason Cornwall. The two-story L-shaped house features sixteen-inch thick walls covered with stucco veneer to simulate cut stone. At one time, the home featured a cupola viewing tower, but the structure was removed in 1940. Mr. Cornwall's name was also once chiseled into the home's siding, but the inscription was later removed. Many locals believe that Cornwall's sons, who did not get along with their father, scratched out the engraving upon their father's death.

Third and Washington Street
Constructed between 1909-1910, this Renaissance-Revival building once served as Moscow's community post office. In 1974, a new post office was built, and plans were made to use this building as a community center.

Moscow-Latah County Library
110 S. Jefferson at Second Street
Crafted in a Mission style, this Carnegie library was designed by a Boise architect in 1905-1906. The library was built at a cost of $10,000 and is one of the few remaining operating Carnegie libraries in the state.

Almon Asbury Lieuallen Residence
101 Almon at First Street
A pioneer stockman and Moscow merchant, Almon Asbury Lieuallen is responsible for providing Moscow with its official name. His twelve-room residence dates back to the 1880s and features the only Mansard roof left in the community. In 1917, the home was remodeled into six apartments, and they were the first in town to feature electric stoves and running water.

Eighth Street and Jackson Street
Encompassing a two-block expanse, a concentrated collection of grain elevators dating from 1885 to 1942 can be found in Moscow. The collection featuring wooden, concrete, and corrugated metal structures is one of the state's finest.

Union Pacific Depot
1/2 block off Jackson Street at Eighth Street
Established in 1885 in Moscow, this Union Pacific Depot stands as one of the three oldest depots in Idaho.

T University of Idaho Life Sciences Building
Southeast corner of University Ave. at the U of I Campus, Moscow. 885-4636.

The University of Idaho's Life Sciences Building is home to the extensive Northwest Mammal Gallery

and the Biological Sciences Bird and Mammal Collection. The building contains full skeletons of elk, moose, bear, deer, mountain lions, and many other native Rocky Mountain animals. The collection also includes skins, skulls, and antler displays along with horns from a Rocky Mountain ram. The collection is open to the public free of charge.

TV Bill Chapman Memorial Trail
Located at the Idaho/Washington border between Moscow and Pullman. Contact the Moscow Chamber of Commerce at 882-1800.

Traversing seven miles from Moscow's University of Idaho campus across the Idaho/Washington border into Pullman, the paved Bill Chapman Memorial Trail is a natural choice for outdoor recreationists. Surrounded by lush scenery, the easy trail is open to cyclists, rollerbladers, walkers, joggers, and those simply interested in taking a leisurely stroll.

TV Robinson Park
3 miles east of Moscow. Contact the Moscow Chamber of Commerce at 882-1800.

Surrounded by the shade of large white pines, Robinson Park offers tranquility and recreation in one setting. A small stream trickles through the park, and several walking trails are available for strolling. The park also features a volleyball court, two softball diamonds, a playground, an ice skating rink, and picnic sites accommodating both small and large gatherings.

V Moscow Mountain Trails
Drive 4.5 miles north of Moscow on U.S. Hwy. 95. Bear right after the overpass, and drive towards the mountain on the main gravel road.

In addition to providing outstanding scenery, Moscow Mountain also offers several winding dirt trails for mountain bike enthusiasts. Most trails require moderate skills, but some are geared towards more advanced riders.

V Spring Valley Reservoir
From Moscow, drive 12 miles east on State Hwy. 8 towards Troy. Approximately 3 miles outside Troy, turn onto the marked Spring Valley Rd. and proceed to the reservoir.

Spring Valley Reservoir was established solely for the purpose of recreation and summer fun. A sandy beach surrounds the 50-acre tranquil lake, and swimmers, sunbathers, and boaters flock to the site. The reservoir is frequently stocked with trout and bass, but only non-motorized boats are allowed on the water. Picnic tables and restrooms are also available on-site.

M Moscow Chamber of Commerce
411 S. Main St., Moscow. 882-1800 or (800) 380-1801. www.moscowchamber.com; staff@moscowchamber.com

6 *Food*

Juliaetta
Pop. 609

Juliaetta was originally called Schupferville by Rupert Schupfer, who founded and platted the town in 1878. The name was changed in 1882 when the post office arrived to honor postmaster, Charles Snyder, and his daughters, Julia and Etta. The initially prosperous town boasted a flourmill in 1882, and by 1911, a local cannery was producing 8,000 cans per day. In 1890, work on the Northern Pacific Railroad halted in Juliaetta while rights-of-way could be obtained to cross the Nez Perce Indian reservation. While the legal battles raged, Lewiston merchants raised nearly $75,000

and purchased most of the right-of-way from the reservation. The railroad had the go-ahead to keep building, but the Panic of 1893 delayed its construction for another six years. Today, activity in Juliaetta has slowed, and the town is most recognized for its "Castle House," a 1906 mansion now home to an area museum.

Kendrick
Pop. 369

Established by John Kirby in 1888 as Latah, this small town's name was changed when the Northern Pacific Railroad came through in 1890. To ensure the line reached the small settlement, its name was changed to honor the railroad's chief engineer. Ties for the line were cut from trees paralleling the intended route, and a railroad bridge was completed in 1898. The town itself was nearly decimated in a 1904 fire, but residents had high hopes for their community and rebuilt the town. Kendrick hosts one of the state's oldest newspapers, the Kendrick Press News, and the small town is known for its beautiful locust trees that bloom each spring.

Genesee
Pop. 946

Jacob Kambitsch first settled Genesee in 1871 and found the soil to be rich and fertile. As word spread of the area's ideal agricultural qualities, settlers arrived in droves. The town's name, however, has nothing to do with the area's soil, but instead is the result of an innocent comment. Legend states that as merchant banker, John Vollmer, and an associate were riding through the area, the associate mentioned that it reminded him of New York State's Genesee Valley. The comment stuck, and when journalist, Alonzo Leland, began calling the valley Genesee, the town adopted the name as well.

When the railroad was erected one mile away from the townsite in 1888, Genesee's residents were forced to relocate near the railroad if they cared about the town's future. Until 1898, Genesee served as the line's terminus, but when the railroad extended its route, the town's population began to decline.

T Castle Museum
202 State St., Juliaetta. 276-3081.

Built in 1906 by New York stonemason, Abram Adams, this three-story mansion is a replica of a Scottish castle and is now home to the community's museum. Inside the impressive nine room museum, visitors will find numerous photos and local mementos, as well as Juliaetta's first movie projector, bank safe, and switchboard. Visitors should call and schedule a private appointment.

T Kendrick Community Park, Swimming Pool, and Murals
Downtown Kendrick. Contact the Kendrick City Hall at 289-5731.

The Kendrick Community Park and Swimming Pool is a favorite recreation spot for both locals and visitors alike. Children and adults can cool off in the community pool during the summer while enjoying a colorful mural surrounding the pool. The painted mural and a mosaic tile mural located near the park restrooms represent the combined talents of local high school students. The park is also home to summer plays, community events, and the Saturday Farmer's Market.

T J. P. Vollmer Building
Walnut and Fir Sts., Genessee. Contact the City of Genesee at 285-1621.

Named after the town's merchant-banker, John Vollmer, the J. P. Vollmer Building features one of the most elegant galvanized iron facades in all of Idaho. The Mesker Brothers of St. Louis, Missouri manufactured the façade in the 1800s. Although the state once boasted ten of these high-quality facades, only three remain intact today.

Constructed in 1898, the building featured Vollmer's wholesale and retail grocery store. Despite extensive remodeling to the interior, the building's exterior retains much of its original character.

V Potlatch River Biking Trail
Kendrick and Juliaetta. 276-7791 or 289-5731.

Created and opened in 2002, the 5.3 mile long Potlatch River Biking Trail provides an excellent means of taking in the scenic Potlatch River running between the small communities of Kendrick and Juliaetta. The trail is paved with asphalt and is open to bicyclists, walkers, joggers, and rollerbladers.

7 *Food, Lodging*

Lewiston
Pop. 30,904

Lewiston is Idaho's lowest lying city at only 739 feet above sea level and just missed earning the distinction as Idaho's first permanent settlement. Ironically, even though the city is 470 miles from the Pacific Ocean, Lewiston serves as an Idaho seaport for Columbia and Snake River barge traffic. It is therefore a very important shipping and packing center.

After Captain E.D. Pierce discovered gold in the area in 1860, the town was established at the confluence of the Snake and Clearwater Rivers. The original settlement was established approximately seventy-five miles east of the present city. Portland advertised the gold strike, and thousands of miners began making their way to Idaho. At the time of the strike, the town site was still located on the Nez Perce reservation. Indian agent, A.J. Cain, threatened to tear down any permanent buildings placed on the land, so miners outwitted him and lived in framed canvas tents. The temporary homes garned the city its "Ragtown" nickname. These canvas dwellings weren't all that comfortable during the winter months, especially during 1861-1862 when Idaho recorded its most severe

---

FOR THE LOVE OF GOLD & HORSES

During the 1800s, gold fever struck Idaho residents with full force, and those who couldn't make an honest living in the mines found creative means of making fortunes. Although counterfeiting is normally thought of as an endeavor of today's craftiest criminal masterminds, some of the most notorious figures in Idaho's Salmon River Country successfully counterfeited thousands of dollars worth of gold coins in the late nineteenth century.

In 1886, the Eddys and their seven children moved to the Shingle Creek area and in no time, had acquired a small herd of cattle without purchasing any of the cows from their neighbors. Settling directly north of the Eddy's settlement, Ike and Stan Splawn along with Stan's brother-in-law, Charley Scroggins, were known as real cowboys addicted to horseracing. Neither the Eddys or the Splawns had any money when they first arrived in north-central Idaho, but a conniving set of circumstances soon changed their meager existence.

When the Nez Perce lands were opened to white settlement, the Native Americans preferred payment in gold coins while white settlers spent inordinate amounts of money wagering bets on racehorses. Seeing a niche that both fulfilled their need for money and their passion for horses, the Splawns and Eddys decided to create their own gold coins and pass them off at regional racing events.

In no time, production was under way with full operations in swing by 1896. The families labored only during the winter, creating wooden molds for $5, $10, and $20 gold pieces that were then filled with plaster and fired. A well-respected gentleman in Wiser, Emmett Taylor, helped the families acquire necessary chemicals and production advice from Chicago, while Ike Splawn (who was then living in Lewiston with his wife) helped pass off the coins in northern

Idaho. The Eddys and Splawns also found it quite easy to pass off the coins at local events, and even though rumors circled about possible cattle theft and counterfeit gold, the families talked their way out of any conviction.

Eventually, the U.S. Treasury Department heard about the suspected counterfeiting operation and sent William Reavis to investigate. Reavis had an interest in racehorses and created a plot to verify that the Eddys and Splawns were indeed responsible for passing out the fake coins. Using his racehorse, Reavis beat one of Jim Eddy's horses in a Lewiston race and subsequently utilized the event to create a friendship with the Eddys.

Reavis hinted that he would give up half-interest of his winning racehorse to the Eddys if he were allowed a cut of the fake gold coins. The Eddys fell for the trick, and Reavis found himself visiting the operation site near Shingle Creek. Although the Eddys and Splawns were initially distrustful of the stranger, Reavis quickly won over the two families when he explained he could pass off the gold coins as far away as Oregon. After three months, Reavis was "in" with the group and garnered enough information to send a message to the Idaho County Sheriff. The sheriff sent out a warrant for Jim Eddy's arrest in a recent cattle theft. Wanting to make sure that all guilty parties arrived in Mount Idaho with Jim, Reavis convinced them all to go and testify on Jim's behalf. Much to the Eddys' and Splawns' surprise, they were all greeted with an arrest in Mount Idaho for their counterfeiting operation.

The Eddys and Splawns, however, still did not realize that Reavis was the detective who turned them in. Under the guise of assisting the Eddy and Splawn women bury the evidence, Reavis returned to the counterfeiting site and helped bury the coins and production equipment. Reavis returned to the site days later, secretly dug up the evidence, and presented all the proof the jury needed to convict the Eddys and Splawns in one of Idaho's most notorious counterfeiting cases.

---

winter ever. If that wasn't bad enough, spring floodwaters drenched the canvas city.

In 1861, in an attempt to name the town and establish some permanency, several men gathered and began suggesting names. Local merchant, Mr. Trevitt, suggested the name Lewiston in recognition of Lewis and Clark's western achievements. It was later discovered that Trevitt really suggested the name in honor of his former home in Lewiston, Maine. Despite the newfound meaning behind the town's moniker, the name was kept, and Lewiston was designated Idaho's territorial capital in 1863. At the time, however, Lewiston was actually still located on Native American reservation land. Conveniently, the U.S. government "renegotiated" the treaty and reduced the size of the reservation so its boundary did not encompass Lewiston.

Such actions, however, seemed fruitless when the area mining activity began to decline, and the capital was moved to the prospering Boise in 1864. In spite of its raucous character, violent crimes, and reputation as a village of loose moral standards, Lewiston continued to attract new residents and was incorporated in 1866. When the government further reduced the Nez Perce Reservation lands in 1895, 540,000 acres were opened up for new homesteads. On November 18, 1895, a cannon was shot from Lewiston, and thousands of settlers rushed forward to make

claims on the coveted land. The railroad didn't reach town until 1898, but when it did, a three-day celebration ensued. Just one year later, a toll bridge was constructed across the Snake River, and thirteen years later, a Clearwater River bridge was finally established. At that time, the states of Idaho and Washington pooled their resources to purchase the Snake River bridge and remove the toll.

Soon, farmers began arriving to work the fertile land, and orchards were established in 1905. Although planted strictly as apple orchards, the orchards later expanded to include cherries, English walnuts, filberts, chestnuts, and grapes. The prosperity of the orchards was short-lived, however, as a plauge of moths nearly destroyed the entire bounty in the 1920s. As a result, the land became more valuable as lots for new homes and businesses, and the town continued its history of expansion.

H Mackenzie's Post
Milepost 316.6 on U.S. Hwy. 95

Early in September 1812, Donald Mackenzie set up a fur trade post near here for John Jacob Astor's Pacific Fur Company.

Disappointed to find that beaver were unavailable in this area, he built only a store and two houses out of driftwood. Then, the War

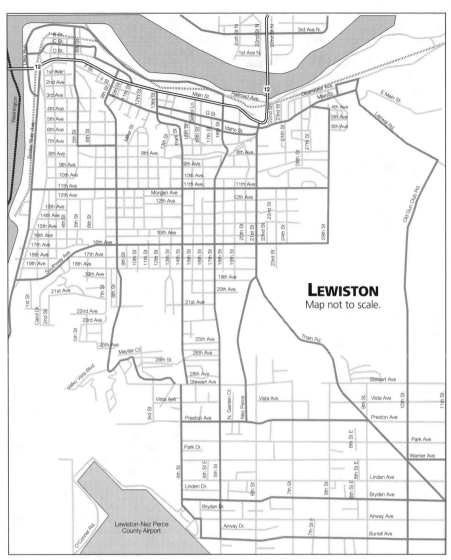

LEWISTON
Map not to scale.

cial center for Idaho miners during their hectic gold rush to Pierce that spring.

Steamboats continued to dock there until 1940, mainly after Columbia and Snake River channel improvements made navigation practical in 1914. Finally, a series of locks and dams made Lewiston a seaport and large-scale river shipping resumed in 1975.

T Craig Mountain Wildlife Management Area
10 miles south of Lewiston. Contact the Idaho Department of Fish and Game at 799-5010.

The Craig Mountain Wildlife Management Area encompasses over 24,000 acres of special habitat, including fourteen miles of land nestled against the Snake River. With elevations ranging from 800 feet to a mile high, a variety of wildlife can be viewed in the area. Bighorn sheep, elk, mule and white-tailed deer, wild turkeys, sharp-tailed grouse, and blue grouse are just a few of the many species calling this area home. The area is accessible via trail or river with access gained off Waha and Redbird Roads outside Lewiston.

T Bryden Canyon Golf Course
445 O'Connor Rd., Lewiston. 746-0863.

Golfers can enjoy spectacular overviews of the Snake and Clearwater Rivers while playing a round on the 18-hole Bryden Canyon Golf Course. The par 71-course features relatively flat fairways and two ponds that create water hazards on some of the holes. Designed for the intermediate and advanced player, the course is open year-round. Green fees start at $18.

T Lewis-Clark Center for Arts and History
415 Main St., Lewiston. 799-2243.
www.artsandhistory.org

This museum and gallery affiliated with the Lewis-Clark State College recollects the strong presence of Chinese immigrants in the region during the late 19th and early 20th centuries. A permanent "Chinese at the Confluence" historical exhibit displays pieces of the 1890 Beuk Aie Temple as well as several artifacts that Chinese miners and their families used for daily living. In addition, the center presents a concert series and numerous rotating displays featuring historical topics and the works of local and regional artists. The museum and gallery are open from 11 AM to 4 PM Tuesday through Saturday year-round.

T Nez Perce County Historical Society Museum
0306 3rd St. at C St., Lewiston. 743-2535.

Formerly known as the Luna House Museum for its placement on the original site of the Luna House Hotel, the Nez Perce County Historical Society Museum is housed within an art deco building constructed by the Works Progress Administration in 1937. Inside the museum, exhibits range from Native American artifacts and history, the fur trade, the gold rush of the 1860s, the Lewis and Clark Expedition, a model pioneer kitchen and bedroom, and several historical photos illustrating the development and progress of the City of Lewiston. A permanent display features artistic works depicting Chief Joseph in his youth, maturity, and old age, and children will delight in the history detective quiz. The museum is open from 10 AM to 4 PM Tuesday through Saturday.

of 1812 and Indian trouble tangled his plans. In May 1813, he abandoned this site, since Astor's venture had failed and was about to be sold to the North West Company of Montreal. "Perpetual Motion" Mackenzie who once had been a "Nor'Wester," rejoined the Canadians in 1816 and finally organized the snake country fur trade.

H Lewis Clark State College
Milepost 316.6 on U.S. Hwy. 95

Lewis Clark State College was created by the Legislature in 1893 as a two-year normal school to train teachers.

After more than half a century of growth, Lewiston State Normal School expanded into a four-year college in 1947. An area vocational school and a nursing education program were added in 1965. Designated a state college in 1971, Lewis Clark continues to specialize in teacher education.

Idaho Trivia

North-central Idaho's Idaho County extends from the Montana state line to the Oregon/Idaho border. As it encompasses so much land, Idaho County is actually larger than the entire state of New Jersey!

H The First Capital
Milepost 317.7 on U.S. Hwy. 95

The organization of Idaho Territory was proclaimed in Lewiston July 10,1863, and the first two legislatures met here.

When Lewiston served as the capital, Idaho Territory included modern Montana and practically all of Wyoming – an area much larger than Texas. Then in 1864, after Montana was established as a separate territory and most of Wyoming was attached to Dakota, the governor and legislature decided to locate the capital of Idaho in Boise, where it has been ever since.

H Lewiston Hill
Milepost 317.7 on U.S. Hwy. 95

When automobile traffic made a steep old wagon road obsolete, a remarkable new highway grade was built down this hill in 1917.

With a series of sharp curves that let cars go 20 or 30 miles an hour – a good speed for that time – a gradual 10-mile, 2,000-foot grade was designed. It still can be used by anyone not in too much of a hurry who wants to see an engineering model of early highway construction.

H Steamboats
Milepost 317.7 on U.S. Hwy. 95

Started May 13, 1861, as a steamboat landing, Lewiston immediately became a primary commer-

T Tsceminicum Sculpture

Located at the Lewis and Clark Interpretive Center in Lewiston at the confluence of the Snake and Clearwater Rivers near the blue Interstate Bridge.

Meaning "Meeting of the Waters" in the Nez Perce language, this was the historic name for the confluence of the Snake and Clearwater Rivers.

The sculpture interprets Native American mythology with a symbolic Earth Mother figure whose body sustains all forms of life and from whose hands the rivers run. The wildlife and legends depicted on the east-facing wall are those of the Clearwater River and its tributaries; on the other side are those of the Snake River. A Coyote, the central "Trickster" character of Native American legend, keeps watch from the north end of the wall.

About the Sculpture

The original scale model for "Tsceminicum" was entered in a 1976 design competition held by the U.S. Army Corps of Engineers as part of the Lewiston Levee Beautification Project and was chosen for the final commission in February 1977. By fall 1978, the full size sculpture, modeled with 850 pounds of non-hardening clay over a wooden framework, had been assembled in a Clarkston warehouse. The clay surface was then covered with many coats of silicone rubber, capturing each detail in a flexible liner that was sprayed with urethane foam to form a 4-inch-thick, rigid, lightweight mold. This was cut away from the clay in sections, transported to the site and carefully reassembled, leaving a cavity into which reinforcing steel and plumbing and electrical connections were placed. Massive formwork, backfilled with a sand-plaster mix, was bolted around the urethane shell to support the 25,000 pounds of concrete that was pumped and vibrated into the mold cavity. Once the concrete was cured sufficiently to remove the bracing and mold, the sculptor completed the necessary patching, coloring, and protective coating. The base of native river rock was then laid.

Idaho artist and sculptor, Nancy M. Dreher, created the sculpture.

Reprinted from U.S. Army Corps of Engineers brochure

T Lewiston Civic Theater

805 6th Ave., Lewiston. 746-3401 or 746-1371.

Performing shows since 1961, the non-profit Lewiston Civic Theater serves up a variety of entertainment to rave reviews every September through June. Housed in the historic Anne Bollinger Performing Art Center, the Lewiston Civic Theater has received several national and international awards for its performances. Individuals should contact the theater for a current listing of events.

Idaho Trivia

Out of the entire U.S., only Alaska possesses more than Idaho's 18 million acres of wild, forested land.

T Lewis-Clark State College

500 8th Ave., Lewiston. (800) 933-5272.

Established in 1893, the four-year Lewis-Clark State College boasts enrollment figures over 3,000 students. The school offers approximately twenty different undergraduate degrees along with two-year vocational programs. In addition to offering quality education, Lewis-Clark State College's campus is a favorite for picnickers and Frisbee golf lovers, while the on-campus sculpture garden memorializes the history of the Nez Perce people.

T Prospect Park

Prospect Ave. west of Lewis-Clark State College, Lewiston. Contact the Lewiston Chamber of Commerce at 743-3531.

Originally a Chinese cemetery for early miners in the Lewiston area whose graves have since been moved, Prospect Park is now a shaded plot of land commanding some of the best views of the entire city. Visitors can enjoy picnic tables, lush grass, and old-growth trees, as well as spectacular sunsets over the Snake River.

T Lewis and Clark Interpretive Center

West end of D St. near the blue Interstate Bridge, Lewiston. Contact the Lewiston Chamber of Commerce at 743-3531.

Situated on top of a levee at the convergence of the Snake and Clearwater Rivers, the Lewis and Clark Interpretive Center offers detailed information regarding the Corps of Discovery's historical expedition and the Nez Perce people. The Army Corp of Engineers built this site featuring outstanding views of the rivers' confluence.

T Lewiston Tree Tour

Downtown Lewiston. Contact the Lewiston Chamber of Commerce at 743-3531.

Throughout the years, Lewiston's earliest settlers and its ensuing generations have made a conscious effort to beautify the landscape with a variety of trees. After years of hard work and care, many of these trees have reached "champion status" (meaning the largest tree of that particular specimen in the state). These trees include box elder, blue ash, flowering dogwood, American chestnut, flowering ash, umbrella black locust, red maple, willows, and several others. For those curious in seeing a natural botanical garden, the Chamber of Commerce offers free brochures providing directions to the city's champion trees.

HORSES AND THE NEZ PERCE PEOPLE

Horse parades are often part of tribal ceremonies and special events. Horses and riders are bedecked in beautiful traditional finery, serving as powerful reminders of the horses' place in Nez Perce history. Horses came to Nez Perce country in the early 1700s from the south. In less than two generations, the horse transformed the Nez Perce way of life, providing unprecedented mobility and becoming a symbol of power, wealth, and prestige.

The Nez Perce bred their horses for agility, strength, and whatever pleased them. Unfortunately, as the reservation shrank with each successive treaty, the great horse herds declined as well. Today, the Nez Perce Tribe has invested time and resources to breed a horse, the *Nimiipuu Sik'em* that has the endurance and strength common in the horses of the past. The horse-breeding program has the added benefit of allowing youth to develop horse skills and reestablish the unique link between the Nez Perce and the horse. What was almost lost has come back, stronger and more meaningful than ever before.

The Nimiipuu have been in this land since time immemorial. Nez Perce National Historical Park tells the story of the Nez Perce, offering all Americans an important perspective about our history as a people. This is not a story told from the Mississippi looking west; it is a view from a homeland looking out, witnessing the march of history and change. It is a park about a people for all people.

Reprinted from National Park Service Newspaper

T Historical Tour of Lewiston

Contact the Lewiston Chamber of Commerce at 743-3531.

Established around 1860, Lewiston has a long-standing history that is still reflected in several of its buildings. The structures not only represent the personal lives of Lewiston's earliest residents, but the town's economic roots as well.

Camas Prairie Railroad Depot
Main & Thirteenth
The Northern Pacific's engineering department designed Lewiston's depot for the Camas Prairie Railroad. The depot was built between 1908-1909 at the site where an old flourmill was demolished. Like many depots of its day, Lewiston's building featured a large waiting room, a men's smoking area, a lady's comfort room, a telegraph office, and a ticket office with perfect views of all approaching trains.

Continued on Page 124

Lewiston	Jan	Feb	March	April	May	June	July	Aug	Sep	Oct	Nov	Dec	Annual
Average Max. Temperature (F)	39.3	46.2	53.7	62.1	70.7	78.8	89.0	88.0	77.8	62.9	48.0	40.7	63.1
Average Min. Temperature (F)	26.7	30.7	34.4	39.6	46.4	53.1	58.9	58.2	50.3	40.8	33.5	28.7	41.8
Average Total Precipitation (in.)	1.25	0.90	1.08	1.21	1.50	1.37	0.62	0.73	0.76	1.00	1.18	1.14	12.73
Average Total Snowfall (in.)	5.8	2.6	1.4	0.1	0.0	0.0	0.0	0.0	0.0	0.1	1.7	4.1	15.8
Average Snow Depth (in.)	1	0	0	0	0	0	0	0	0	0	0	0	0

The Corps of Discovery through Idaho's Native American Homeland, 1805-1806

In 1803, President Thomas Jefferson commissioned Meriwether Lewis and William Clark to find "the most direct and practicable water communication across this continent, for the purposes of commerce." When the Corps of Discovery departed St. Louis in May, 1804, the party destined to cross the continent consisted of Captains Lewis and Clark, 26 volunteers and Army regulars, Clark's black slave York, and Lewis' Newfoundland dog, Seaman. This military unit of experienced outdoorsmen followed the Missouri River through today's Missouri, Iowa, Nebraska, South Dakota, and North Dakota, where they built Fort Mandan, north of present Bismark, and spent the winter of 1804-1805.

While visiting nearby Hidatsa and Mandan villages, the captains hired French trader, Touissaint Charbonneau, as interpreter and guide. Charbonneau's young Lemhi Shoshoni wife, Sacajawea, and their infant son, Jean Baptiste, would prove to be an asset to the expedition when it reached her native homeland in present-day Idaho. Not only were her language skills helpful, but also native peoples were less suspicious of white men traveling with a native woman and child.

By mid-August 1805 their travels brought them to Three Forks, Montana, headwaters of the Missouri River. From there on they needed horses to make what they thought would be an easy portage across the Rocky Mountains to the navigable headwaters of the Columbia. They were beyond the western border of the Louisiana Purchase and for the first time entering land about which they had no knowledge. It was the homeland of the Lemhi Shoshoni, Salish, and Nez Perce people, a land of ancient cultures with networks of travel and trade that spanned thousands of years and stretched from plains to mountains to ocean. A land that nurtured sophisticated societies with resources aplenty, where family was foremost and the elderly were valued. A homeland where oral histories recorded the hospitality of these tribes toward the strangers in their midst.

Expedition members had no idea how they would be received, but realized with each passing mile that their success would depend upon native good will. They knew that rivers flowed westward from the Continental Divide toward the Pacific Ocean, but their hopes of an easy portage over this barrier were thwarted by the realities of the Rocky Mountains, a series of one mountain chain after another. Even with native assistance, for members of the Corps of Discovery, this search for a "Northwest Passage" would prove to be the most difficult part of their entire journey.

Meeting the Lemhi Shoshone (Aqui-Dika)

Captain Lewis led an advance party along an Aqui-dika hunting trail across Lemhi Pass (We-yah-vee) and came upon the Lemhi River (Pah-dye) which he mistook to be the headwaters of "the great Columbia river." There they first beheld the majestic "sea of mountains" – the Bitterroots (Kannah Doyah-Huveed) – an unexpected mountainous barricade. Shoshoni help was critical. But they found no Shoshoni.

Finally they came upon three women digging for wild carrots (Yump). When they sighted the men with "faces pale as ashes" one woman fled while an elderly woman and young girl lowered their heads awaiting certain death. "…They appeared much alarmed but saw that we were too near for them to escape by flight they therefore seated themselves on ground holding down their heads as if reconciled to die which they expected no doubt would be their fate…" Lewis gave the older woman gifts and daubed red paint on her face. The woman later reassured the Lemhi Shoshoni Chief Cameahwait that these men meant no harm. For among the Aqui-dika people, the gift of red paint (Bee-sha) is sacred and symbolizes the giver's prayerful wish for the well-being and safety of the recipient's family and people.

The advance party and the Aqui-dika returned to the forks of the Beaverhead where Clark and the main party were to meet them. They were not there; suspicions mounted. On August 17, in perhaps the most serendipitous moment of the expedition, Clark, Sacajawea, and Charbonneau watched as Lewis and the Aqui-dika rode up to them. Suddenly Sacajawea began to dance for joy. She recognized her people and her brother, Chief Cameahwait. Curious about the strangers, the Shoshoni people welcomed their guests as they gathered at a place Lewis called Camp Fortunate.

Among the Lemhi Shoshone

Clark, Charbonneau, Sacajawea, and eleven others returned across the Divide with Cameahwait to his village on the Lemhi River (Pah-dye). Clark requested geographical information; Cameahwait obliged him with a detailed relief map of the Lemhi, Salmon, and Bitterroot rivers as well as the Bitterroot Mountains. Sacajawea and Charbonneau then remained in the village while Clark led a reconnaissance party to the Salmon River. He hoped they could use that stream to reach the Columbia River but found that it was far too treacherous to gamble their lives on it.

They spent their last few days among the Shoshoni trading for horses. Chief Cameahwait cautiously decided to help them and agreed to provide twenty-nine horses. On August 30 the two groups parted company. The Corps of Discovery headed north to Lost Trail Pass and on to the Bitterroot Valley (Wee-yah Ma-nungwa) of western Montana, into the land of the Salish (Tushepah). They were accompanied by Aqui-dika guides whom they hired, Old Toby (Tee-toby) and his son.

The valley of the North Fork of the Salmon grew more narrow and steep as the small party approached the pass. It snowed, rained, and sleeted; the horses "were in danger of slipping to their certain destruction." Clark and the men broke their last thermometer. To top it off, Old Toby, for unknown reasons, led the party three miles off course. With the weather growing increasingly worse, they crossed Lost Trail Pass on the 4th of September and began their descent to the land of the Salish.

Salish Country: Among the Tushepah (Flathead)

September 4, 1805: As the strangers approached a beautiful valley later known as Ross' Hole, Salish Chief Three Eagles spotted them while out scouting for raiding parties. Observing they had no blankets, he concluded they must have either been robbed or, upon seeing York's black face – no doubt painted for war – had lost their blankets in battle. He returned to his village and advised, "Let us keep quiet and wait for them, they seem to have no intentions of fighting us or harming us."

In the early evening the expedition reached Three Eagles' large village. "Bring the best buffalo skins, one for each man to sit on." They smoked together before setting up camp – a sign of acceptance and protocol for any type of social and business relation. The journals referred to the people as Flatheads, a name erroneously used, possibly because of a sign language gesture, because they had heard of Flatheads at Fort Mandan, or perhaps because someone from the Chinook tribe of the Pacific Coast, where they did flatten their heads, was visiting at the time.

The next morning the Tushepah began trade with the "pale, cold, poorly dressed" and ill-equipped strangers. A Shoshoni boy who lived there was able to translate the final link from English, to French, Hidatsa, Shoshoni, and Salish. Expedition members exchanged flags, medals, and other trade stock for additional mounts to replace their spent horses. On the 6th of September with the Bitterroot Mountains looming ominously to their left, they continued north through the valley to Lolo Creek, where they stayed two days at "Travelers' Rest."

Salish and Ni Mi Pu (Nez Perce) Country

September 11, 1805, they left Travelers' Rest along a trail system so old and used that its depth revealed its antiquity. The Ni Mii Pu (Nez Perce) knew the route as the "Road to Buffalo Country." They traveled annually east to hunt buffalo and trade with people of the Plains. But the road was also important to the Salish. To them it was "The Trail to the Nez Perce," their route to the communal Ni Mii Pu fisheries and to places they could trade with Plateau and Coastal people. Today the trail parallels U.S. Hwy. 12 and Lolo Creek from Travelers' Rest to Lolo Pass.

At Lolo Hot Springs, several roads and animal trails confused their guide Old Toby. He took them a few miles east of the main trail. They continued to climb to the head of Lolo Creek and the mountain pass, then "through open glades, Some of which (were) 1/2 mile wide" (Packer Meadows).

After again accidentally leaving the main route, they followed a Ni Mii Pu fishing trail down to the Lochsa River and camped opposite a small island near an Indian fishing site (Powell Ranger Station). With rations severely depleted, and because "Some of the men did not relish this (portable) soup," they killed a colt. The next morning they proceeded downstream before climbing a ridge to Lolo Trail. It was apparent further travel along the river valley was impossible.

Reaching the main trail from the river was a test of resolve. Travel conditions grew worse. Desperate to find food and help, Clark and six hunters pushed on ahead the morning of the 18th of September. Eleven days from Travelers' Rest, Clark's small party finally emerged from what Sgt. Patrick Gass called "the most terrible mountains I ever beheld."

Among the Ni Mi Pu 1805

On September 22, the advance party of Clark and six hunters came upon three Ni Mii Pu boys in an open plain at the eastern edge of Weippe Prairie (O-yip). The boys feared a raid and immediately hid. Clark found two of them, gave them small pieces of ribbon, and sent them to the nearest village. The boys came into camp wondering what "creatures" they had met. The men had "eyes like fish." Were they human? Were they coming from the past legend times? Chief Red Bear, of a Clearwater River band, cautiously approached them and escorted them into a spacious lodge.

Some men wanted to kill the strangers but the words of an old woman, Wetxuwiis, contributed to their protection. "That is the strange white people I have been telling you about…" She told the people to prepare food for them, recounting her story of being taken captive in the Bitterroots and taken as far east as the Great Lakes. A party of white men helped her return to her people.

Despite their apprehensions, the Ni Mii Pu welcomed the Corps with gifts of food that did not agree with the starving explorers, who became very ill. The natives smoked "peace smoke" with the strangers and received their gifts, which included a Jefferson peace medal. To the Ni Mii Pu, gift giving verified the strangers' humanity. Chief Twisted Hair drew them a detailed map of regional rivers and agreed to guide them west. On the 24th the expedition left Weippe for the Clearwater River, reaching it a few miles east of present day Orofino. There they prepared for the final leg of their long journey to the Pacific Ocean.

Among the Ni Mi Pu on the Clearwater River

On the Clearwater River, across from its confluence with the North Fork, the expedition made camp near Ahsahka, the first of many villages they encountered along the water route. There on September 27, the still suffering men began to build five canoes using a "small, strange looking ax" to shape the pine logs. The Ni Mii Pu watched, then offered to show them a better method: "First burn the log with pitch and dry grass, then chop with an Indian stone ax…made from long black stone (obsidian)." – George Peo Peo Tal likth.

On the 7th of October they resumed their journey. Twisted Hair and Tetoharsky guided them as far as the great falls of the Columbia. Near the mouth of the Potlatch River one of the canoes struck a rock and was nearly cut in two. They towed it ashore, repaired it, and spent the night. Private Joseph Whitehouse noted a number of Indians came to visit them and "behaved with a great deal of friendship…" He said they belonged to the "Flatt-head Nation." That night old Toby and his son left without pay, perhaps because of the canoe accident. Perhaps they worried about being so deep in Ni Mii Pu country, for the two nations were not always on friendly terms.

On October 11, the expedition continued on down the Snake River. Flint Necklace (Looking Glass the Older) traveled by land ahead of the expedition to tell other tribes along the way the strangers were coming. He was "very instrumental in procuring us a hospitable and friendly reception…"

Amont the Ni Mi Pu on the Return Trip

Members of the Corps of Discovery continued down the Snake River to the Columbia and on west to the Pacific Ocean. They spent a wet, miserable winter at Fort Clatsop and began their return trip the end of March, 1806. Along the Columbia River they traded canoes for horses and continued their eastward journey by land.

In May they were again in Ni Mii Pu country. They ascended the Snake and Clearwater Rivers, meeting old friends and making new ones. Near the mouth of the Potlatch River they met Cutnose (Nuus nu Pek'iiwnin). Lewis honored his position by giving him a small Jefferson medal. Their route continued across Big Canyon Creek, up a gentle slope, and across a divide to Twisted Hair's camp on the prairie. They collected their horses and retrieved the cached equipment before proceeding on to Broken Arm's camp on Lawyer's Creek.

Headmen and members of their bands arrived from throughout the Clearwater, Snake, and Salmon River country. They followed Ni Mii Pu protocol of joining in a grand council with Lewis and Clark. Because a young Shoshoni was in camp, they were no longer forced to communicate by sign. The headmen voted unanimously on behalf of their bands to receive future American fur trading houses and to attempt a peace with their enemies. Among the dozens of headmen present, three chiefs agreed to guide them across the mountains.

Camp Chopunnish (Long Camp) on the Clearwater

On May 14, the expedition left Broken Arm's village and established camp on the Clearwater, where they remained until June 10. Besides time spent in Forts Mandan and Clatsop, this was their longest stay among native people. Kamiah was a time to get acquainted – to fiddle, dance, compete in sports, and enjoy one another's company. Many Wounds, grandson of Red Bear, wrote that the Ni Mii Pu liked to watch Cruzatte sing and play the fiddle, they liked to watch York dance "with feet," and watch the others dance to unlike traditional Ni Mii Pu dance. It was also a time to report on the lives and society of the Ni Mii Pu people, from clothing and food preparation to selective horse breeding, as well as the topography, flora, and fauna of the region.

While in Kamiah the men spent most of their time hunting or trading for food. That quest took three men into what we today call Hells Canyon. On the 27th of May, Sgt. John Ordway, Peter Weiser, and Robert Frazer left Camp Chopunnish with some Ni Mii Pu for the lower Salmon River to purchase salmon. They crossed the prairie and descended a "bad hill down a creek" to the Salmon River about 20 miles above its Snake River confluence. The salmon run had not yet reached that far. They then crossed a mountain ridge and down "the worst hills we ever saw a road made down" to a second fishery on the Snake River.

The three men purchased some salmon before returning to Kamiah Valley. What they had expected would be a two-day trip took seven days.

Lolo Trail to Journey's End: 1806

June 10, with an inadequate food reserve but all invalids recovered, the Corps of Discovery resumed its journey east. The Nez Perce had repeatedly warned them snow was too deep beyond Weippe Prairie, but they didn't listen. The Clearwater River had been falling for several days and they took that as "strong evidence that the great body of snow has left the mountains." From Camp Choppunish up "hills which are very high," they traveled to Lolo Creek and on to the eastern edge of Weippe Prairie. There they remained through the 14th, attempting to build up their provisions. The next day, after heavy rain subsided, they began their eastward trek, proceeding "with much difficulty" before camping on Eldorado Creek.

They proceeded on up the creek the next day. Three miles farther up the ridge and "inveloped in snow from 8 to 12 feet deep," they could go no further. They cached unnecessary baggage and returned to Weippe Prairie, their first retreat of the entire expedition.

On June 24, 1806, the group again set out to conquer the mountain trails. Chief Red Bear was one of the three guides. He showed Lewis how to "make snow go fast" so they would not be further delayed. He "made a big fire to the brush and high trees" to melt the snow and clear the trail. They proceeded on across the Lolo Creek, reaching the hot springs on the 29th and Travelers' Rest on the 1st of July. The return mountain trip was much quicker and easier than the 1805 journey.

At Travelers' Rest, Lewis and Clark separated. Lewis took a small party east toward the falls of the Missouri; Clark and his men retraced their route through the Bitterroot Valley and across the Divide to Three Forks. The groups reunited at the Yellowstone and Missouri confluence in mid-August after six weeks apart, and proceeded on down the Missouri River to today's North Dakota.

The expedition reached the Mandan villages on August 13, 1806. Since they no longer needed Toussaint Charbonneau and Sacajawea as interpreters they released them from service and paid them the agreed upon sum of $500.33. Travel downriver was quick, and the party passed through present-day South Dakota, Nebraska, Iowa, Kansas, and into the Missouri by September 15.

On September 23, 1806, Clark wrote these words, "…descended to the Mississippi and down that river to St. Louis at which place we arrived about 12oClock. we Suffered the party to fire off their pieces as a Salute to the Town."

Sacajawea

Sacajawea was a Lemhi Shoshoni (Snake) woman who had been captured and enslaved by the Hidatsa Indians (North Dakota) five years prior to meeting Lewis and Clark at Fort Mandan in 1804. At seventeen, with an infant, she accompanied the expedition all the way to the Pacific and back to Mandan during 1805-1806.

There are three versions concerning the spelling and meaning of her name. "Sacagawea" is the most widely accepted spelling of her name, which follows the use of the hard "g" in the expedition's journals and this entry by Lewis: "a handsome river of about fifty yards in width discharged itself into the (Mussellshell) river...this stream we called Sah-ca-gah-we-ah or bird woman's River...after our interpreter the Snake woman."

Lemhi Shoshoni advocates claim her as "Sacajawea" or "One Who is Carrying a Great Burden." This is a popular local spelling in the Far West. Finally, the North Dakota Hidatsas promote "Sakakawea" from the conjunction of two Hidatsa words for "bird" and "woman."

Sacajawea's son "Pomp," was raised by Captain Clark and was a world traveler and explorer in his own right. Documentary evidence traces Sacajawea's death at Fort Manuel (South Dakota) on December 20, 1812.

Reprinted from Idaho Department of Commerce brochure

Hotel Lewis-Clark
Block of First & Main
Spokane architect, Kirkland Cutter, designed this California Mission style hotel with simplicity in mind. The hotel was erected in 1922 at a cost of $350,000 and featured 144 rooms, three dining halls, and an expansive Italian-style lobby. Although the hotel was nearly demolished in the 1970s, the Ponderosa Inn chain saved the historic hotel from an untimely fate and gave the building a one million dollar renovation. The hotel is still open today for guest reservations.

Luna Building
Third & C Streets
Now home to the county museum, the Luna Building sits on the site of Hill Beachy's 1862 log cabin. The building was quite large for its time, boasting a parlor, kitchen, and dining hall with twenty sleeping quarters on the second floor. When Lewiston held the title of territorial capital from 1863-1864, the log building provided overnight accommodations for several state legislators and territorial officials.

Kettenbach Residence
Southwest corner of Fifth Avenue & Eighth Street
Frank Kettenbach was one of Lewiston's prominent bankers at the turn of the century, and his residence reflected his wealth. The home was built in 1912 for $11,500 and features a sandstone retaining wall.

R. C. Beach Residence
Northwest corner of Fifth Avebye & Eighth Street
Lewiston merchant, R. C. Beach, constructed this home in 1916 for $19,000. At the time, the home's lot represented the community's most expensive residential lot.

St. Stanislaus Catholic Church
Fifth Avenue between Seventh & Sixth Streets
Father Joseph Cataldo founded Lewiston's Catholic Church in 1867-1868, and work began immediately on creating a parish home. Designed by Lewiston architect, James Nave, the present Gothic-style church features stone quarried at nearby Swallow's Nest Rock. Today's stone structure replaced the original frame church in 1905.

Pioneer Park/City Library
North on Fifth Street to Second Avenue
Situated at the confluence of the Snake and Clearwater Rivers, Pioneer Park is home to Lewiston's Carnegie library. The library was built in 1904 with a $10,000 grant and displays a Renaissance Revival style. The park also includes a log home dating back to 1862.

312 Prospect Avenue
Constructed in 1904, this building served as Lewiston's original weather station. Flags and pennants were flown high from a pole at the site, which provided river steamboat pilots below with the day's forecast.

Curtis Thatcher Residence
204 Prospect Avenue
Curtis Thatcher built this impressive home in 1899. The most notable feature is the footing for a staircase that the neighborhood built as a shortcut down to the river. The staircase footing is across the street from the house.

Eben Mounce Residence
113 Prospect Avenue
I. J. Galbraith designed this home for U.S. Marshall, Eben Mounce. Mounce lived in Lewiston, and his home was completed in 1901.

T Potlatch Corporation Tours
Directly east of Lewiston near U.S. Hwy. 12. Contact the Lewiston Chamber of Commerce at 743-3531.

The Potlatch Corporation dates back to 1903 and the acquisition of Minnesota's Northland Pine Company by the Potlatch Lumber Company of Maine. Frederick Weyerhaeuser was among the company's founders, and wealthy investors from across the Midwest leant support to the growing company. In 1906, the Potlatch Company began operating mills north of Moscow, Idaho and in January 1931, the company merged with Clearwater Timber Company and Edward Rutledge Timber Company. At that time, the company adopted the new name, Potlatch Forests, Inc.

Frederick Weyerhaeuser's grandson, John Phillip Weyerhaeuser, served as first president of the new company and helped the corporation triple its net worth in the 1930s and 1940s. As the company's capabilities continued to expand and production increased, so did profits. In 1973, Potlatch Forests, Inc. became the Potlatch Corporation, owning over 614,000 acres of land in Idaho. The company also employs thousands of people across northern Idaho at its sawmills and plywood plants, and the Lewiston plant is home to more than 3,000 industry employees.

Two-hour tours of the massive facility are available year-round on weekdays. The tour, however, is not recommended for children under eight years old.

T Arrow Beach Archaeological Site
10.5 miles east of Lewiston on U.S. Hwy. 12. Contact the Lewiston Chamber of Commerce at 743-3531.

Excavated in 1967, the Arrow Beach Archaeological Site contained artifacts dating back 2,800 years before white man's arrival in Idaho. The site represents the earliest dated home in the entire Columbia Plateau, and Nez Perce occupied the site from approximately 1500 –1850 A.D.

T Palouse Hill Country
Between Lewiston and Moscow on U.S. Hwy. 95

Not only are Idaho's gentle Palouse hills scenic, but they are also important to the state's agricultural economy. Rolling between Lewiston and Moscow, the Palouse Hills produce the world's softest white wheat. Prior to modern day agricultural practices, farmers on the Palouse relied on horses and a multiple hitching system where wheat farmers became hard-working team members.

Although this system worked efficiently for the Idaho farmers, a new agricultural era was ushered in during the 1930s. Skeleton wheel tractors and caterpillar tractors allowed farmers to seed and fertilize more acres per day, and yields dramatically increased. By the 1960s, production had risen from just forty bushels per acre to nearly eighty, and production continues to increase as technology improves.

TV Hells Gate State Park
3620A Snake River Ave., Lewiston. 799-5015. 4 miles south of Lewiston on Snake River Ave

Encompassing 200 acres of land beside the winding Snake River, Hells Gate State Park is situated on the former site of the Nez Perce village, Hasotino. Although signs of this important civilization have long since faded, the site still bustles with activity.

Recreation abounds, and swimming, boating, fishing, camping, hiking, horseback riding, biking, and picnicking are favorite pastimes. Hells Gate Marina provides a perfect launching spot for scenic cruises or water skiing adventures.

The park also boasts interpretive programs, while the informative visitor center provides insight into the history of the Snake and Clearwater Rivers, Lewiston's natural history, and settlement in and around Hells Canyon. Due to year-round mild weather, the park and marina are open daily in all seasons.

V Clearwater and Snake River National Recreation Trail
Begins at Lewiston's Clearwater Park. Contact the Lewiston Chamber of Commerce at 743-3531.

Designated as a National Recreation Trail, the Clearwater and Snake River trail system passes through both Idaho and Washington. Spanning twenty-five miles, the riverside greenbelt provides a paved pathway for walkers, runners, cyclists, and rollerbladers. The trail begins at Lewiston's Clearwater Park, crosses Memorial Bridge, and continues south to the Lewis and Clark Interpretive Center and Hells Gate State Park before winding across the Idaho/Washington border. Benches are available alongside the river, and the sounds of ducks and geese quacking can be heard along the entire trail. The trail is open year-round free of charge.

V Mann Lake
Near Lewiston. Contact the Lewiston Orchards Irrigation District at 798-1806. From the south end of Thain Rd. in Lewiston, bear east on Powers Ave., and proceed to the lake.

The 130-acre Mann Lake features a man-made treasure for anglers of all ages. Under the operation of the Lewiston Orchards Irrigation District, Mann Lake is annually stocked with 25,000 rainbow trout. The lake also holds natural populations of catfish, crappie, and smallmouth bass, and electric motor boats are allowed access to the lake's surface via a nearby boat ramp.

V Snake River Fishing: From Lewiston to Hells Canyon Dam

Bordered by wilderness and making its way through America's deepest gorge, the 108-mile section of the Snake River flowing from Lewiston to Hells Canyon Dam is an angler's dream. The river, which features many portions with "wild and scenic" designation, is a corridor for the migration of Chinook salmon, sockeye salmon, Pacific lamprey, and steelhead. The river also features channel catfish, stocked rainbow trout, smallmouth bass, and white sturgeon. In recent years, some anglers have reeled in sturgeon over nine feet long!

Major tributaries of this Snake River section include Captain John, Granite, and Sheep Creeks. These creeks are known to harbor a large resident population of rainbow, bull, and cutthroat trout.

M Lewiston Chamber of Commerce

111 Main St., Lewiston. 743-3531 or (800) 473-3543. www.lewistonchamber.org; info@lewistonchamber.org

8 Food

Lapwai
Pop. 113

Lapwai ("LAP-way") was established in 1836 as the first mission to the Nez Perce Indians. Reverend Henry Spalding formed the mission under the Nez Perce word meaning "the place of butterflies." The story of Henry is intriguing as he was part of a group of four Presbyterians headed west from St. Louis on a journey to convert the "heathens" to Christianity. Although Henry fell madly in love with Narcissa Prentiss, she did not share his sentiments and instead married Dr. Marcus Whitman. Henry went on to marry Eliza Hart, and despite the awkward feelings of the past, the four set out on their mission together in just one wagon. On July 4, 1836, the quartet reached the Nez Perce territory where their initial fears were put to rest with a warm welcome. Since Narcissa and Eliza safely became the first white women to cross the Rockies, other potential emigrants began to view the West as a place for families, not just men.

After meeting the Nez Perce, the two couples carried out separate plans with Marcus and Narcissa journeying to present day Walla Walla, Washington. Enamored with the possibilities of missioning to the Nez Perce, Henry and Eliza stayed in Idaho. Unfortunately, Marcus and Narcissa did not experience the same long-lasting welcome from their intended missionees, the Cayuse Indians. When a journeying wagon train infected the area with measles, Whitman successfully cured the whites, but his treatment failed to heal the Indians who possessed no natural disease immunity. Subsequently, many Indians died from the measles while in Whitman's care, and the Cayuse thereby assumed that their once trusted friend and missionary was actually killing them. In 1847, the Cayuse retaliated, killing Marcus, Narcissa, and twelve other white mission workers.

Henry and Eliza proceeded to build their mission near Lapwai where Eliza learned to read and write the Nez Perce language. As part of her mission work, she encouraged other area white settlers to do the same and was responsible for teaching several homesteaders the Nez Perce language so that communication barriers were non-existent. In 1838 she gave birth to a daughter,

Eliza, who became the first white child born in Idaho. Henry, meanwhile, built a cabin and taught the Native Americans farming skills. He soon built a sawmill, gristmill, and blacksmith shop and raised corn and potatoes as staples. Word spread of the mission and its agricultural potential, and more Nez Perce began to settle around the mission and cultivate their own plots. In 1839, Henry installed the region's first irrigation system, and the area boomed with activity. After word of the Whitman's massacre reached the Spaldings, however, they decided to leave the area. They moved to the Willamette Valley and resumed farming. Eliza died in 1851, and Henry moved back to Lapwai in 1863 where he later died in 1874. He and Eliza are both buried there. Today, the site of the historic Lapwai mission rests east of Lewiston in the Nez Perce National Historic Park.

In addition to the mission that took the name Lapwai, A U.S. Army Fort was established here in 1862 under the same name. The fort was intended to protect Native Americans and their land from white homesteaders. Ironically, the fort later served to protect the settlers from Native American aggression.

Spalding
Pop. 150

Henry Harmon Spalding, a Presbyterian missionary from New England, and his wife Eliza established the Lapwai Mission in 1836 (see also Lapwai). The Spaldings taught many local Nez Perce Indians the art of irrigated farming, and the town of Spalding is named in his honor. This community became Idaho's first agricultural settlement in 1895, and a post office was built in 1897.

H Ant and Yellowjacket
Milepost 10.9 on U.S. Hwy. 12 near the Idaho/Washington border

According to a Nez Perce Indian legend, the stone arch up the hill was once two fighting insects.

Ant and Yellowjacket had an argument and came to blows over who had the right to eat dried salmon here. Fighting fiercely, they failed to notice Coyote, the all-powerful animal spirit. Even when he ordered them to stop, they kept on struggling. For not heeding his warning, he turned them to stone while their backs were arched and their jaws locked together in combat.

H Spalding's Mission
Milepost 12.2 on U.S. Hwy. 12

Marcus Whitman and Henry Harmon Spalding led Presbyterian missionaries west in 1836 to answer a Nez Perce call for teachers.

Spalding began his mission and school nearby, but moved here in 1838. Believing in secular as well as religious teaching, he taught the Indians farming, brought in the Northwest's first printing press, and built flour and sawmills. But hostility slowly developed, and Spalding left after the Whitman massacre at Walla Walla in 1847. He returned with the gold rush to labor

RECREATION ON THE PALOUSE

Northern Idaho was first explored by white men during the Lewis and Clark Expedition to the Pacific Coast in 1805-1806; then came the fur trappers and the missionaries. In the 1860s, cattlemen were the first settlers to arrive in the area, followed by the homesteading farmers.

Gold was discovered in Idaho in 1860. Early gold strikes were made in the Hoodoo Mountains at the head of the North Fork of the Palouse River. In 1861, gold was discovered along Gold Creek northeast of Potlatch. Mine tailing piles can still be seen along the North Fork of the Palouse as evidence of the early mining activity. Gold mining continues today on active claims throughout the district although at a lower level than in the early years.

At the turn of the century, the timber industry made its debut in the area. Midwestern lumbermen discovered the productive timberlands of northern Idaho, particularly the seemingly endless stands of valuable western white pine. The Potlatch Lumber Company built sawmills in Potlatch (1905) and Elk River. The mill in Potlatch was the largest of its kind in the world, and a company town soon grew up around the mill. Both of these mills are now closed.

Today, the national forest lands of the Palouse Ranger District offer a wide array of recreation attractions including developed campgrounds, group picnic areas, and multiple use trails. Another popular and enjoyable activity on the Palouse is watching wildlife in its natural habitat. Numerous species can be found in the area including various small animals and birds, mountain lion, whitetail deer, black bear, mule deer, moose, and elk. Although wildlife may be seen any time of day, the best time to observe is in the early morning or late evening hours. Good places to see wildlife are in meadows, around ponds, and next to creeks and rivers.

Enjoy your visit to the Palouse, and contact the U.S. Forest Service for more information.

Partially reprinted from a Clearwater National Forest Service brochure

among his converts until his death in 1874. His grave is nearby.

H Saint Joseph's Mission
Milepost 293.1 on U.S. Hwy. 95

When he came to Lewiston in 1867, Father J.M. Cataldo developed a Jesuit Nez Perce mission that continued long after he founded Gonzaga University in Spokane.

A chapel was built a mile up Mission Creek in 1868, but a permanent location was not established until construction of Saint Joseph's Mission was completed at a more secluded site in 1874. It now is open to visitors as part of the Nez Perce National Historical Park.

H William Craig
Milepost 295.4 on U.S. Hwy. 95

"A bluff jolly good fellow," he joined the Rocky Mountain fur trade in 1829, married a Nez Perce in 1838, and settled with the Lapwai band in 1840.

In 1850, the Oregon Donation Land Act gave free farms to pioneers who had come to the Oregon Territory. Craig had the only eligible farm in Idaho (then part of Oregon) and filed a 640-acre claim here. When the Nez Perce reservation was set up, the Indians trusted Craig and let him keep his farm.

H Lapwai Mission
Milepost 300. 5 on U.S. Hwy. 95

Henry Harmon Spaulding established Idaho's earliest mission near here, November 29, 1836, at a campsite chosen by the Nez Perce Indians.

Ever since they met Lewis and Clark in 1805-06, the Nez Perce had wanted to find out more about the white man's ways. In 1831, a Nez Perce delegation went all the way to St. Louis, where they saw Clark again and asked for teachers. Spaulding came west to answer their call. With Indian help, a house and assembly hall were built in 24 days. In two months, Mrs. Spaulding started a mission school. In 1838, the mission was moved north to the Clearwater.

H Coyote's Fishnet
Milepost 306.8 on U.S. Hwy. 95

A Nez Perce Indian legend tells how Coyote and Black Bear had a falling out while fishing here long ago.

Coyote, the all-powerful animal spirit, was having a good time until Black Bear, the busybody, began to tease him. Finally, losing his temper, Coyote tossed his huge fishnet onto the hills across the river. To teach Black Bear a lesson, Coyote threw him to the top of the hill on his side and turned him to stone. The Nez Perce people know just where to look for the net and unfortunate bear.

H Nez Perce Village
Milepost 306.8 on U.S. Hwy. 95

This important archaeological site was occupied for 10,000 years or more and has at least 10 pit houses as much as 5,000 years old.

Two styles of houses were used. Some were fairly square with interior benches dug out for use by a family or two. Others were round – 20 to 30 feet wide and two to three feet deep – but lacked benches. This village reached its height from about 4,100 to 2,600 years ago, but remained important enough that when fur traders arrived in 1812, they made this their main camp.

T Fort Lapwai/Old Fort Lapwai Cemetery
1 mile south of Lapwai on U.S. Hwy. 95. Contact the City of Lapwai at 843-2212.

Established in July 1862, Fort Lapwai was the first Idaho military fort and was erected to protect the Nez Perce from encroaching white settlers. President Lincoln granted the fort official military status in 1864, and the fort operated through the Nez Perce War. It has been abandoned since 1884.

Today, the parade ground is still visible, and a few of the original buildings remain nearby. The Officers' Row, built in 1866, can be seen on the fort's southwest side. The old Fort Lapwai Cemetery is also available for touring on the ridge south of the fort. The cemetery once housed the remains of several U.S. soldiers killed at White Bird during the Nez Perce War.

T Nez Perce Spalding Site
Nez Perce National Historic Park, Route 1, Spalding. 843-2261.

Spalding Site
The Spalding Site, located along U.S. Highway 95, is home to the Headquarters of Nez Perce

National Historical Park. A modern Visitor Center offers a fine museum collection, movie on the history of the Nez Perce people, and a small gift shop. The 99-acre site contains historic cemeteries and buildings, interpretive signs, and a large picnic area.

The present day community and park area of Spalding (officially named in 1897) was originally called Lapwai and served as a traditional homesite for over 11,000 years to the Thlep-thlep-weyma band of Nez Perce. Each summer they moved to higher elevations to hunt, fish, gather roots, berries, and other wild foods, returning each fall in time for the salmon 'run' on the Clearwater River. The location was ideal where Lapwai Creek flowed into the Clearwater River. A large boomground where trees and branches washed downstream by spring floods were deposited provided enough firewood for a village of over 200 people. Winters were usually milder at this 700-foot elevation and the bluffs provided shelter from the winds and storms.

By the late 1800s, Spalding was a thriving community with an Indian Agency, hotels, stores, church, blacksmith, saloon, and a railroad station (called 'Joseph'). Horse racing and stickgames provided entertainment during leisure time. In 1904, the Indian Agency moved and the town gradually grew smaller with the last business (Watson's General Merchandise Store) closing in 1964. In 1935, the Idaho State Legislature established the Spalding Memorial State Park at the site of the old mission. A tree from each State in the Union was planted in the 14-acre arboretum, many of which survive to this day. In 1965, Nez Perce National Historical Park was created by an act of Congress, preserving Nez Perce history for future generations.

Missionaries Come to Nez Perce Country
In 1831, four Nez Perces traveled to St. Louis in search of the 'book of Heaven and the teachers.' In response to that, Henry and Eliza Spalding along with Marcus and Narcissa Whitman were sent as missionaries by the American Board of

Commissioners of Foreign Missions. Eliza and Narcissa were the first white women to cross the Rocky Mountains. The Whitmans settled at Wailatpu near present day Walla Walla, Washington and the Spaldings at Lapwai near Idaho's Clearwater River.

"We rode on and entered the valley. It proved to be larger than we expected. It is on a little stream emptying into Koos Koos from the south. We found it well-timbered with cotton wood, balm of gilead, birch, and a few pine. Soon found good soil. The Indians could scarcely contain themselves for joy when they heard us pronounce the word 'good'". So wrote Rev. Henry Harmon Spalding about his first view of Lapwai Valley in the fall of 1836. Spalding's built their first home at Thunder Hill, 2 miles up Lapwai Creek but heat and mosquitoes forced them to move to the banks of the Clearwater River where morning and evening breezes made for more pleasant living conditions.

Spalding felt the Nez Perces needed a settled existence to learn the Christian religion. He therefore gave out seeds and hoes and taught them farming methods. Orchards were planted and land cultivated. They built a home, meetinghouse, school, mission church, blacksmith shop, sawmill, gristmill, and a series of ditches, dikes, and ponds that provided water to run both mills. Eliza taught school, often with over 200 students at a time.

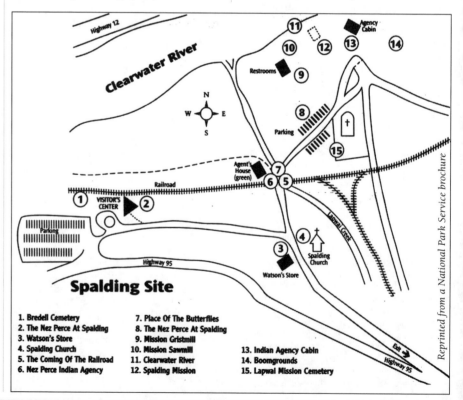

Reprinted from a National Park Service brochure

Spalding Site

1. Bredell Cemetery
2. The Nez Perce At Spalding
3. Watson's Store
4. Spalding Church
5. The Coming Of The Railroad
6. Nez Perce Indian Agency
7. Place Of The Butterflies
8. The Nez Perce At Spalding
9. Mission Gristmill
10. Mission Sawmill
11. Clearwater River
12. Spalding Mission
13. Indian Agency Cabin
14. Boomgrounds
15. Lapwai Mission Cemetery

THE NEZ PERCE NATIONAL HISTORIC TRAIL

Congress passed the National Trails System Act in 1968 establishing a framework for a nationwide system of scenic, recreational, and historic trails. The Nez Perce (Nee-Me-Poo) Trail, extending about 1,170 miles from the vicinity of Wallowa Lake, Oregon, to Bear Paw Battlefield near Chinook, Montana, was added by Congress as a National Historic Trail in 1986.

The Nez Perce Indians, originally composed of independent villages and bands, were long known as friends of the whites. They had welcomed Lewis and Clark, fur trappers, and missionaries to their homeland in the mountains, valleys, and along the rivers of southeastern Washington, northeastern Oregon, and north-central Idaho. In 1855, Washington Territorial Governor Isaac I. Stevens responded to increasing white expansion and negotiated a treaty with Nez Perce chiefs. This treaty recognized Nez Perce peoples' rights to their traditional homeland and established it as a reservation of some 5,000 square miles.

In 1860, prospectors encroached on Nez Perce lands and struck gold. In the ensuing rush, thousands of miners, merchants, and settlers disregarded Steven's treaty, overran large parts of the reservation, took Indian lands and livestock, and heaped mistreatment and injustices on Nez Perces. To cope with the crisis, the U.S. Government engaged angry Nez Perce in new treaty talks in 1863. Nearly all tribal bands were represented.

When the government tried to get some bands to cede all or most of their lands, they refused and left the council. In their absence, other chiefs, without tribal authority to speak for the departed bands, did so anyway, and ceded lands of those who had left the council. Their act resulted in a division of the tribe. The whites praised those who had signed as "treaty" Indians; those who did not sign became known as the "nontreaty" Nez Perce.

For some years, nontreaty bands continued to live on their lands, insisting no one had the right to sell them. But conflicts with growing white populations increased, particularly in the Wallowa country of northeastern Oregon, homeland of Chief Joseph's band. In May 1877, the Army finally ordered nontreaties to turn over their lands to whites and move onto a small reservation at Lapwai, Idaho. Pent-up emotions stemming from years of high-handedness and mistreatment by whites, as well as orders to leave their homelands, moved several embittered young warriors to ride to Salmon River. There, they avenged past murders of tribal members by killing some white settlers. The hope for a peaceful move to the small reservation at Lapwai thus ended, and the flight of the Nez Perce began on June 15, 1877.

Pursued by the Army, nontreaties left Idaho intending to seek safety with their Crow allies on the plains to the east. When this failed, flight to Canada became their only hope. Their long, desperate, and circuitous route as they traveled and fought to escape pursuing white forces is what we now call the Nez Perce National Historic Trail.

This route was used in its entirety only once; however, component trails and roads that make up the route bore generations of use prior to and after the 1877 flight of nontreaty Nez Perce.

Trails and roads created through continued use often became portions of transportation systems, though some were later abandoned for more direct routes or routes better suited for modern vehicles. Most abandoned segments can be located today but are often overgrown by vegetation, altered by floods, powerlines, and other structures, or cross a variety of owernships.

General William Tecumseh Sherman called the saga of the Nez Perce "the most extraordinary of Indian wars." Swept into a fight they did not seek by impulsive actions of a few revengeful young men, nearly 750 non-treaty Nez Perces fought defensively for their lives in some 20 battles and skirmishes. Only 250 were warriors, most were women, children, and old or sick. Together with nearly 2,000 horses, they battled against more than 2,000 soldiers, numerous civilian volunteers, and Indians of other tribes. Their route through four states, dictated by topography and their own skillful strategy, covered over 1,100 square miles before they were trapped and surrendered at Montana's Bears Paw Mountains just short of the Canadian border and safety on October 5, 1877.

The Nez Perce National Historic Trail ends at Bear Paw Battle Site, but the Nez Perce story did not end here. The 431 Nez Perce survivors were taken down the Missouri River by flatboat to an unexpected exile, first at Fort Leavenworth, Kansas, then Indian Territory, Oklahoma. Others captured while trying to return to Idaho from Canada later joined them. Despite efforts of honorable officers and citizens throughout the country, the Nez Perce remained in exile for eight years.

Of nearly 500 Nez Perce exiled to Indian Territory, only 301 survived extreme weather and poor conditions. In 1885, nontreaty Nez Perce returned to the Northwest. Joseph and 149 Nez Perce were re-settled on the Colville, Umatilla, and Nez Perce reservations. Some chose to stay in Canada. Chief Joseph was never again permitted to live in his ancestral home in the Wallowa Valley.

Reprinted from a U.S. Forest Service, Bureau of Land Management, National Park Service, and U.S. Fish & Wildlife Service brochure

THE NEZ PERCE (NEE-MEE-POO) NATIONAL HISTORIC TRAIL

Legend
— NEZ PERCE TRAIL
··· NEZ PERCE HOMELANDS
BLM
NATIONAL PARK
INDIAN RESERVATION
FOREST SERVICE

Chief Timothy and Chief Joseph (father of the now famous Chief Joseph) were the first two to be baptized. As many as 2,000 people attended Sunday services at the height of the Spalding mission efforts. Spalding was often considered stern and unyielding and yet ironically was the most 'successful' of any of the early missionaries, baptizing over 900 Indians before his death in 1874.

Eliza gave birth to four children while at the mission. The oldest, also named Eliza, was the first white child born in Idaho. In 1847, due to the murders of Whitmans and 12 others at Wailatpu, the Spaldings were ordered to close their mission. Eliza died three years later in Brownsville, Oregon. Henry returned to Nez Perce country twice as a teacher and missionary, dying at age 70 in Kamiah, Idaho. Years later, as a fitting memorial to her, the Nez Perces retrieved Eliza's body from Brownsville and placed it beside Henry's grave, just a few yards from their old mission home.

Indian Agency Period
The first Nez Perce Reservation was created by the Treaty of 1855. Due to the large influx of gold miners trespassing on the Reservation, the Bureau of Indian Affairs established the Nez Perce Agency in 1861 at Spalding. The Indian Agent was supposed to keep the peace, mediate between Indians, settlers and the Army, administer treaties, promote the welfare of Indians, represent government interest, and supervise the allotments of supplies and lands on the Reservation. The Agency remained at Spalding until 1904 when it was moved to Fort Lapwai. Today, the Agent's House (painted the original bright green) can still be seen near Lapwai Creek.

Cemeteries

Burial sites are considered sacred by the Nez Perce people, therefore the cemeteries at the Spalding Site are to be respected by all visitors. You may visit these Tribal cemeteries, but please do not stand on marked graves, take rubbings from headstones, or touch memorial items left on the graves. Eating, drinking, or any type of recreational activity within the cemeteries is considered inappropriate behavior.

Reprinted from National Historical Park brochure

T Lewiston Hill
U.S. Hwy. 95 north of Spalding where U.S. 95 and U.S. 12 separate

In the early 1900s, Idaho citizens and elected officials petitioned for better roads, including a safer and more easily traversed route across the Palouse hills. Under the direction of E. M. Booth, a winding highway featuring sixty-four curves and a 2,000-foot climb was completed in 1917 at a cost of $100,000. The road, although certainly more modern than before, was harrowing and prompted officials in the 1970s to create a different route. In 1975, work began on the present highway with the road open to traffic in spring 1979.

T Nez Perce National Historical Park
Visitor Center in Spalding. 843-2261.

A Park About A People, For All People
Long before Meriwether Lewis and William Clark ventured west; before the English established a colony at Jamestown; before Christopher Columbus stumbled upon the 'new world', the Nez Perce, who called themselves Nimiipuu, lived in the prairies and river valleys of north Idaho, Montana, Oregon, and Washington. Despite the challenges of two centuries of threats and assaults on the Nez Perce homeland, their voices are still heard, strong and resilient. The thread of the past meets the future as the language, culture, and traditions of the Nez Perce move forward through the 21st century.

Nez Perce National Historical Park is a park about a people, for all people. It is not one place but many. It is not one story, but a multitude of them. The stories to be discovered are often emotional and sometimes controversial, but they bind us together in a common history and define us as a nation. Today 38 sites in Idaho, Montana, Oregon, and Washington commemorate the legends and the history of the Nez Perce and their interaction with others. This includes other Indian peoples as well as the explorers, fur traders, missionaries, soldiers, settlers, gold miners, loggers, and farmers who moved through and into the Nez Perce homeland. As you travel from site to site you will come to sense the rich and diverse cultural history they represent.

The culture and history of the Nez Perce are intertwined with the land they live in. Two sites, Ant and Yellowjacket near park headquarters in Spalding, Idaho, and Heart of the Monster in

Kamiah, Idaho, preserve features on the landscape that form the basis of stories relating to the origins of the Nez Perce and the beginnings of their relationship with the Land. At Buffalo Eddy along the Snake River outside Asotin, Wash., the ancestors of the Nez Perce left their mark on the landscape in the form of rock drawings or petroglyphs. Weis Rockshelter, close to the Salmon River near the town of Cottonwood, is a site inhabited by the Nez Perce for thousands of years.

Chief Joseph's band lived in the Wallowa Valley in northeast Oregon. The Old Chief Joseph Gravesite is located outside the town of Joseph at the edge of Wallowa Lake. Joseph Canyon Viewpoint, 30 miles north of Enterprise, Ore., on Ore. 3, is an example of the canyon-bottomland environment in which the Nez Perce people lived in the winter.

The arrival of the Lewis and Clark expedition triggered an era of change that would have lasting consequences for the Nez Perce. In 1805, after an arduous journey across the Bitterroot Mountains via the Lolo Trail and Pass, the Corps of Discovery, as the group led by Lewis and Clark was known, arrived in Nez Perce country. Today, U.S. 12 parallels the historic route Lewis and Clark traveled. Those with a high-clearance vehicle can travel U.S. Forest Rd. 500, the Lolo Motorway, a primitive dirt road that roughly follows the overland route taken by the expedition.

Lewis and Clark emerged from the mountains on the Weippe Prairie and came upon the Nimiipuu at a site three miles outside the town of Weippe. Along the Clearwater River, at Canoe Camp, in Orofino, Idaho, Lewis and Clark built the canoes they needed to continue their journey to the Pacific Ocean.

Following in the footsteps of Lewis and Clark came fur trappers and Christian missionaries. Henry H. Spalding built the first Nez Perce mission on the site that is below the visitor center at Spalding, Idaho. The remains of his mission, the Indian Agency it evolved into, and the town of Spalding can be seen. Father Joseph Cataldo established Saint Joseph's Mission, the first Catholic mission in Nez Perce country. The church is still standing, 10 miles southeast of Lapwai.

The establishment of white settlements in the lands of the Nez Perce coincided with the treaties of 1855 and 1863. The treaties divided Nez Perce families and ushered in a period of tumultuous change. Growing resentment over loss of land and unpunished atrocities helped to bring on a war in 1877 between the Nez Perce and the U.S. Government. The first battle of that war was fought in June 1877 in White Bird Canyon and resulted in a Nez Perce victory. White Bird Battlefield, north of the town of White Bird, can be seen from an overlook off U.S. 95 and a self-guiding trail.

The pursuit of the Nez Perce by troops commanded by Gen. Oliver O. Howard led to the battle at Big Hole in western Montana. In August 1877, soldiers surprised the encampment, killing between 60 and 90 Nez Perce men, women, and children. The National Park Service has preserved the site as Big Hole National Battlefield west of Wisdom, Mont. In October 1877, after a 1,100-mile chase, the U.S. Army besieged the Nez Perce at Bear Paw, 40 miles from the U.S.-Canadian border and brought an end to the war. Bear Paw Battlefield, south of the town of Chinook, Mont., appears much as it did more than a century ago during the last battle of the Nez Perce War.

These are only a few of the sites comprising Nez Perce National Historical Park. An auto tour of the entire park is more than 1,000 miles in length. The map shows all 38 sites. Many can be experienced in segments of one or two days travel. Sites associated with the war of 1877 are also part of the Nez Perce National Historic Trail. Check the trail's web site at www.fs.fed.us/npnht for information.

If you intend to stay in Nez Perce country while touring the park's sites, plan ahead. Food, gasoline, and accommodations are not available in the park. Many sites, however, are within easy driving distance of urban centers where services are available. Some park sites have opportunities for recreational activities such as hiking, picnicking, and viewing wildlife. Opportunities for camping and backpacking, while plentiful in the region, are not available in the park. Inquire locally for information.

Remember: All natural and cultural features are protected by federal and state law.

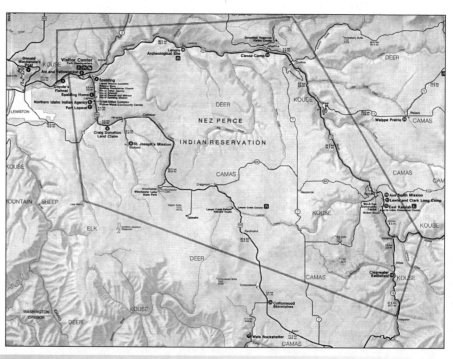

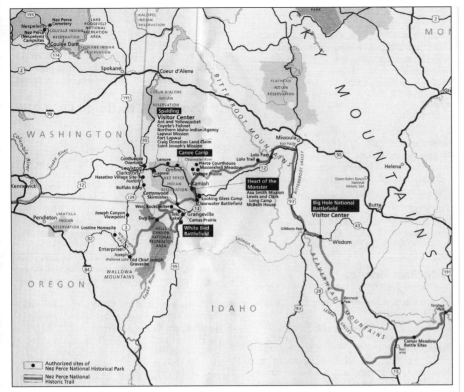

Nimipuu

We Have Always Been Here

The prairies and plateaus of north central Idaho, Oregon, and Washington have always been home to the Nimiipuu, as the Nez Perce call themselves. Here they fished the streams, hunted in the woodlands, and gathered the abundant roots and berries of the high plateaus. The Nez Perce traveled widely on the principal rivers of the region - the Snake, Clearwater, and Columbia - to trade with their neighbors. The acquisition of the horse in the 1700s increased mobility allowing for more frequent travel in company with their Cayuse and Palouse relatives to the Montana bison grounds and Columbia River fishing sites.

During the 1800s the Nez Perce culture underwent profound changes as explorers, fur trappers, traders, missionaries, soldiers, settlers, gold miners, and farmers moved into or through the area. With the arrival of the newcomers looking for land, the Nez Perce, anxious to avoid conflict, met with officials of the U.S. Government and agreed to hold treaty negotiations. In 1855, the Nez Perce signed a treaty that created a large reservation that included most of their traditional homeland as their exclusive domain. In 1863, however, following the discovery of gold on the reservation, settlers and miners forced a new treaty that reduced the reservation to one-tenth of the land originally set aside. Some tribal leaders accepted the treaty, but those who stood to lose their land rejected it, giving rise to the "treaty" and "nontreaty" designations of the respective factions.

U.S. Government efforts to move nontreaty bands onto the new, smaller reservation led, in part, to the Nez Perce War of 1877. When the war ended, many of the nontreaty survivors were relocated to Indian Territory (in present-day Oklahoma). Eventually some Nez Perce were allowed to return to the reservation at Lapwai, Idaho, but others were exiled to the Colville Reservation. Some Nez Perce also made their homes on the Umatilla Reservation.

The last years of the 19th century and the early years of the 20th were difficult ones for the Nez Perce as white values and culture were forced upon them. The Dawes Severalty Act of 1887 gave up to 160 acres of land to individual Nez Perce in the belief that ownership of land would more swiftly assimilate them into the mainstream of American life. The unallotted land was sold to the general public. Soon, more than 90 percent of reservation lands was in white ownership.

Today there are Nez Perce living on the Nez Perce, Colville, and Umatilla reservations as well as in towns and cities across the United States. Regardless of where they live, it is the shared heritage of the Nez Perce that unites them as a people.

1877

The Nez Perce bands who refused to accept the 1863 treaty remained in their homeland for several years. In May 1877, however, with settlers clamoring for access to nontreaty lands, the U.S. Government told the nontreaty Nez Perce that the U.S. Army would forcibly move them onto the new, smaller reservation if they did not do so willingly by June 14.

The leaders of the nontreaty Nez Perce, Cayuse, and Palouse bands, including Young Joseph, Looking Glass, and Toohoolhoolzote, not wishing to lease their homes or to go to war, had hoped for a favorable solution, but to no avail. Before the nontreaty bands could comply with the government order, however, a group of young men, angered by the situation and the lack of justice in murders committed against the Nez Perce, attacked and killed several local settlers.

Fearing reprisal, the nontreaty bands and their allies headed south to a more defensible location near Chief White Bird's village. At White Bird Canyon on June 17, 1877, the Nez Perce inflicted heavy casualties on a superior force of pursuing cavalry. Skirmishes at Cottonwood in early July and a battle on the Clearwater River, July 11-12, proved inconclusive. At Weippe Prairie, the non-treaties decided to cross Lolo Pass into Montana. The bands, totaling about 800 men, women, and children, hoped that their friends, the Crow people, would help them out.

More and more soldiers came after them, eventually totaling more than 2,000 infantry and cavalry by the time the war ended. At Big Hole, August 9-10, the Nez Perce lost between 60 and 90 people in a surprise attack under Col. John Gibbon. The relentless pursuit continued. The expected aid from the Crow people did not materialize. In October 1877, after a 1,100-mile chase, the U.S. Army besieged the Nez Perce and their allies at Bear Paw in northern Montana. Many escaped to Canada or found their way back to the Umatilla and Nez Perce reservations. Others, exhausted from the ordeal, were forced to surrender.

The memory of the 1877 war lingered for many generations. The survivors mourned those who were lost and, as one Nez Perce historian puts it, "We mourn those lost, still. As time passes into the future, we slowly accept our great loss, strengthen our hearts, and continue with the living of today. Such is the teachings of our way. But we will never forget what happened here. To forgive…that is another matter."

Precious Homeland

You may feel that you know us because you have read our story already in the printed words of historians and other chroniclers of "life." You may see around you where the deep canyons of river and creek carvings created living spaces we no longer occupy. You may even taste and smell the air and feel the sun upon your face much as we had once done, so many years ago. Or perhaps you will enter a hall filled with dancers in their fine regalia and hear a prayer or two. Even so, you still may not truly understand us as a people.

The old people talked of these places. They talked of the beauty of "home" and of the abundance of food. They talked of landmarks and special places. They talked longingly of family and relatives of a misty past with whom they enjoyed living each day. And, finally, they talked of having to leave. They remembered starving and being cold. They remembered losing old ones and young ones all along the way. And they remembered the deeper pain of loss-not simply of a precious homeland but of human beings they once knew and loved: "We left many of our people buried out there. We pray they will never more be disturbed."

Today, you may read and hear different forms of their expressions. In English. And you will miss the nuance of expression that comes from the heart of our ancient tongue. Our survivors and historians spoke "nimiputimpki," in the Nez Perce way. It is these stories that were handed down from generation to generation. It is the ancient tongue that truthfully relates our hearts and our truths.

One cannot truly say, in English, what we express in our language. There are many expressions that cannot be directly translated into the language of the "conquering peoples." No, you may not hear our truths as our people had once expressed them. And you may not understand our hearts as a consequence. Today, some are learning to speak that ancient tongue of our heart's expression: our ancestral language. Is it possible that we, too, might convey these histories in the old way, that our past may live in the consciousness of our young people's tomorrow, that they will not forget our origins so easily.

We, the descendents, live far apart from one another in today's world - not only in miles distant, but ideologically and spiritually. We live in a scattered way today. However, we are still the walwama of the Wallowa Valley. We are still the lamtama of the Salmon River country. We are still the kamnaha of the upper Clearwater country. We are still the palucpu and weyiletpu of the Snake River country. We are still the asotans of the lower Clearwater. We are still halalhutsut's people of the treaty bands. And we are all still the cupnitpelu, "the ones who came out of the woods" (nun wisix ikuyn nimipu).

Though you can behold the wonder of this country, you will not fully embrace the great power and strength of a united Nez Perce people before that Treaty of 1855. However that may be, Mother Earth turns upon a newer day and time. Perhaps it will be the young ones who will create a healing place for all our people's future. As you travel through this beautiful country with an eye of wonder, remember us as we once were while greeting us as we are today. In some places we are also visitors, as are you. Remember this when you enter the Salmon and Snake River and the Wallowa Valley countries, that this was also our home... once.

-Albert Andrews Redstar, Chief Joseph band, Colville Confederated Tribes

About Your Visit
Nez Perce National Historical Park has two visitor centers. One is located in Spalding, Idaho, 12 miles east of Lewiston on U.S. 95. Another can be found at Big Hole National Battlefield, 10 miles west of Wisdom, Mont., on Mont. 43. Both facilities have films, exhibits, ranger-led programs, bookstores, and helpful staffs that can answer your questions.

Bear Paw Battlefield is 16 miles south of Chinook, Mont. Information is available at the Blame County Museum in Chinook or by calling 406-689-3155.

For More Information
Nez Perce National Historical Park
39063 U.S. 95
Spalding, ID 83540
208-843-2261
www.nps.gov/nepe

Big Hole National Battlefield
P.O. Box 237
Wisdom, MT 59761
406-689-315
www.nps.gov/biho

Nez Perce National Historical Park is one of more than 380 parks in the National Park System. The National Park Service cares for these special places saved by the American people so that all may experience our heritage. Visit www.nps.gov to learn more about parks and National Park Service programs in America's communities.

Reprinted from a National Park Service/U.S. Department of the Interior brochure

M Nez Perce Tribal Information
PO Box 365, Lapwai. 843-2253. www.nezperce.org

9 *Food*

Lenore
Pop. 25

The Lewis and Clark expedition camped at Lenore's location on October 7, 1805, but before they arrived, the Nez Perce Indian ancestors were here nearly 10,000 years ago. Explored between 1967 and 1971, the archeological site near town revealed numerous artifacts that indicated the Indians used this area for fishing and big game hunting. The site also contained several large oval-shaped pit houses occupied from approximately 900 B.C. to 1300 A.D. This village is one of the oldest and longest-used in the region.

Permanent white settlement began in the late 1800s, and the post office was established here in 1900. Great Northern Railroad officials named the town, but additional history behind the name's selection remains unknown. A series of grain elevators built in the 1930s, 40s, and 50s reflect the area's continued agricultural history.

Peck
Pop. 186

Peck was originally homesteaded in 1896 and welcomed a post office that same year. When the railroad arrived in 1899, the community boomed (slightly). The town memorializes railroad official, George Peck, and relies primarily on the agricultural industry for survival.

Myrtle
The small town of Myrtle is nestled inside the Nez Perce Indian Reservation. Due to its location near the Clearwater River, the area has become a popular recreation site

H Indian Houses
Milepost 27.6 on U.S. Hwy. 12 at Lenore Rest Area

Indians have lived next to this good fishing hole for 10,000 years.

As long as 3,000 years ago, they had large oval houses, 28 feet long by 24 feet wide. To build these houses, they put a bark and mat covering over a frame of 50 or so house posts. Four or more families lived in a house this size. From their village here by the river, they went out to hunt deer or to dig camas. They had to travel widely in their constant search for food.

H Lenore Tram
Milepost 28.3 on U.S. Hwy. 12 outside Lenore

In 1898, after rail service from Lewiston reached Lenore, a tramway was begun to ship grain from Camas Prairie (1,600 feet above) to a new freight stop directly across the river.

Previously, grain wagons descended a long steep hill from the prairie. Gravity moved full tram buckets down, sending empty buckets back up the cable loop. By 1903, the completed system carried up to 100,000 bushels of grain each year. In 1937, a fire destroyed the entire system.

10 *Food*

Ahsahka
Pop. 150

Ahsahka was established in 1898 on the banks of the North Fork of the Clearwater River and was named after an old Native American village located nearby. Although it is agreed that the town's name reflects a Native American term, there are discrepancies as to the word's meaning. While some insist that Ahsahka means "forks of a river," others maintain that the word's translation is "box canyon" or Salish for "brushy country."

Cavendish
Pop. 15

Cavendish was established in the early 1860s along an old trail that led to a small settlement called Snell's Mill. In 1886, E.A. Snell established a post office at the location and officially named it Cavendish after a town in Vermont.

Idaho Trivia

Winding 420 miles through Idaho, the Salmon River is the longest free-flowing river in the continental U.S.

Southwick
Pop. 35

The first settler (name unknown) arrived at this location in 1882. When the post office was established in 1888, this mystery man was appointed as the first postmaster, and the settlement adopted his name.

T Dworshak National Fish Hatchery
4156 Ahsahka Rd., Ahsahka. 476-4591.

Dworshak National Fish Hatchery is the largest combination producer of steelhead trout and spring Chinook salmon in the world. The hatchery, located at the confluence of the North Fork and the main stem Clearwater, three miles west of Orofino in north-central Idaho, is operated by the U.S. Fish & Wildlife Service and was designed and built by the Walla Walla District, U.S. Army Corps of Engineers.

Steelhead and rainbow trout production, begun in 1969, is in conjunction with Dworshak Dam which is the largest and highest straight-axis, concrete-gravity dam ever built in the United States and second largest in the world. Dworshak Dam blocks migrating steelhead from natural spawning grounds on the North Fork of the Clearwater River.

Additional construction, completed in 1982 under the Lower Snake River Compensation Plan, expanded facilities to rear spring Chinook salmon to offset losses caused by dams on the lower Snake River.

Kooskia National Fish Hatchery, 35 miles upriver, became part of the Dworshak National Fish Hatchery Complex in 1978. The two hatcheries are managed closely together for the production of salmon and steelhead.

The hatchery, dedicated in 1969, is the culmination of an intensive cooperative effort by the Army Corps of Engineers, Fish, and Wildlife Service and State of Idaho to perpetuate the return of fish from the Pacific Ocean to the Clearwater River.

The hatchery is unique in that water temperatures for the outside steelhead ponds can be controlled through recirculation similar to an aquarium. There are 84 circulating water-type ponds divided into three reuse or environmentally controlled systems. In these systems, 10 percent of the water used in the ponds is added as fresh water after being filtered, supplemented with minerals, and heated. The water goes through aerators for re-oxygenation before supplying each pond with 600 gallons per minute of flow. When water returns from the ponds, it flows through biological filters where ammonia is oxidized and then reduced to harmless nitrates.

Ability to regulate temperatures and to reuse the water enables the hatchery to use warm water (54 degrees F) in the winter when water temperatures normally run about 39 degrees F. Since growth rates are faster in warmer water, the juvenile steelhead are released the spring following egg hatching at a length of 8 inches. It would take an additional year in colder water to reach the same size.

The hatchery's water system, pumping at a total capacity of 90,000 gallons per minute, is comparable to satisfying the daily drinking needs of all the people residing in the State of Idaho.

Adult steelhead may spawn near the ocean or many miles upstream. The famous Clearwater "B" strain of steelhead, collected at the hatchery from October until May, spawn from January through April. The spring Chinook brood fish return to the river from May until September with egg collection

BIG EDDY

A notorious obstacle for loggers and steamboats, Big Eddy represents the large meandering route around Rattlesnake Point. The Oregon Steam and Navigation Company led the way with Columbia River passenger service in the 1860s and wanted to expand routes to serve north-central Idaho's gold mine rush.

Under the command of Captain Len White, the Colonel Wright became the first steamer to run the rapids of the upper Columbia. Just above Big Eddy in the 1860s, the boat stopped, unloaded its passengers, and the town of Slaterville was born.

But on the boat's next attempt to retrace its route, the Big Eddy wreaked havoc on Colonel Wright. The Oregon Steam and Navigation Company abandoned the route, and without steamboat service, Slaterville withered away.

over a three-week period beginning in late August. The returning adult fish move up the hatchery fishway, or ladder, directly into large holding ponds. These fish are three to five years in age and weigh from 12 to 15 pounds.

Fifteen million eggs are collected annually from the returning adult fish. Some of the eggs can be used to supply the State of Idaho with fish to various planting programs as well as to provide several million smolts (juvenile fish ready to change from fresh water to a salt water environment) for release the following spring.

In a good year, 6,500 eggs from one steelhead spawner would account for 55 adult fish back to the Clearwater River; 3,700 eggs collected from a female spring Chinook returns 10 fish.

At the time of release, yearling salmon and steelhead are discharged directly from the ponds to the river, or pumped onto trucks and transported to off-site locations to begin their downstream migration.

Visitors are welcome to tour the facilities 7:30 AM to 4:00 PM daily. Exhibits describing the hatchery activities and a self-guided tour are available.

Reprinted from a U.S. Fish & Wildlife Service/U.S. Army Corps of Engineers brochure

T Wildlife at Dworshak Dam and Reservoir
Ahsahka. 476-1261 or (800) 321-3198.

Welcome to Dworshak Dam and Reservoir managed by the U.S. Army Corps of Engineers. Bring binoculars and discover the beautiful and amazing creatures that reside here. Whether it's watching bald eagles soar over the dam in winter or hearing elk bugle in the fall, Dworshak offers year-round wildlife opportunities.

Viewing Tips
The ultimate wildlife watching experience is to view animals without interrupting their normal activities. Most animals see, hear, and smell us long before we know they are near. Fighting or fleeing from us robs animals of precious energy. Here are some simple ways you can help blend into the surroundings. Instead of just a glimpse, you can have an encounter, a chance not only to identify the animal, but to identify with it.

Fade into the Woodwork

• Wear natural colors and unscented lotions.

• Walk softly so as not to snap twigs or trample wildflowers.

• Use binoculars or zoom lenses to see close-up.

• Give nests a wide berth. Your visit may lead a predator to the nest, or cause parents to abandon their young.

Let Animals Be Themselves

• Let animals eat their natural foods. Human food can harm wild digestive systems. You'll learn a lot about an animal by watching what food it prefers.

• Resist the temptation to "save" baby animals. The parent is usually watching from a safe distance.

• Let patience reward you. Resist the urge to throw rocks to see birds fly.

Come to Your Senses

• Use your sense of smell, taste, touch, hearing and sight for deeper awareness.

• Look above and below you. Animals occupy niches in all layers of a habitat.

• Peer through a hand lens to enter the world of insects.

Think Like an Animal

• Imagine how the animal you are seeking spends its days. Check field guides to learn the life history and preferred habitats.

• Look in high visitation areas – train intersections, open areas, and drinking sites.

• Dusk and dawn offer best bets for viewing.

Popular Viewing Locations
Magnus Bay & Upper Reservoir

• Western Grebe, Great Blue Heron, Red Breasted Merganzer, American Widgeon, Bald Eagle, Osprey, Spruce Grouse, Bobcat, Moose, Rocky Mountain Elk, Black Bear, Whitetail Deer, Mountain Lion

Dent Acres/Cold Springs

• Canada Goose, Western Grebe, Mallard, Bald Eagle, Osprey, Ruffed Grouse, Turkey, Pileated Woodpecker, Barn Swallow, Columbia Ground Squirrel, Whitetail Deer, Black Bear, Moose

Canyon Creek

• Great Blue Heron, Belted Kingfisher, Osprey, Ruffed Grouse, Turkey, Bobcat, Whitetail Deer, Elk

Big Eddy

• Canada Goose, Western Grebe, Mallard, Osprey, Bald Eagle, Killdeer, Pileated Woodpecker, Whitetail Deer, Black Bear

Visitor Center and Dam

• Great Blue Heron, Bald Eagle, Osprey, Herring Gull, Belted Kingfisher, Violet-Green Swallow, Yellow-Bellied Marmot, River Otter, Whitetail Deer

Common Wildlife Elsewhere at Dworshak
A variety of wildlife is found throughout the Dworshak area. Species include: Osprey, Bald Eagle, Canada Goose, Western Grebe, American Widgeon, Great Blue Heron, Belted Kingfisher, Black-billed Magpie, Ruffed Grouse, Rocky Mountain Elk, Yellow-bellied Marmot, Whitetail Deer, Black Bear, Moose, Bobcat, River Otter, Coyote, Beaver, Porcupine, Mule Deer, Mountain Lion, Western Skink, and Pacific Tree Frog.

Partially reprinted from U.S. Army Corps of Engineers brochure

T Dent Bridge
Eastern side of Dworshak Reservoir. Contact the Idaho Department of Parks and Recreation at 334-4199.

Crossing the eastern side of Dworshak Reservoir, Dent Bridge is an impressive structure modeled

after San Francisco's Golden Gate Bridge. The suspension bridge measures in at 1,050 feet long and is open to traffic year-round.

TV Dworshak Dam and Reservoir
Introduction
The beauty of north central Idaho can be yours year-round at Dworshak Reservoir. The 54-mile-long lake is surrounded by lush, forested mountains, offering recreation for the entire family. Boating, fishing, camping, and picnicking, along with hunting, hiking and wildlife viewing are just some of Dworshak's recreational opportunities. Relax and enjoy the great outdoors the way you want to…casting a line, telling tales around the campfire, or savoring the solitude. Come learn for yourself why Dworshak is a treasure worth discovering.

History of Dworshak
Ancestors of the Nez Perce Indians came to the valley of the North Fork of the Clearwater River more than 8,000 years ago. They called themselves the Nee-mee-poo. The Nez Perce learned to live with the cycle of the river. During the spring flood they hunted on high ground. When the river slowed in the summer, they trapped fish in its eddies and gathered roots and game in the lowlands made fertile by the silt-laden waters.

In the fall of 1805, the Lewis and Clark expedition visited the Nez Perce on their way to the Pacific Ocean. They made a trip up the North Fork in search of suitable timber from which to build canoes. Fur trappers, missionaries, prospectors, settlers and lumberjacks came to the area shortly afterward. As the years passed, settlers moved down to the floodplains. Unable to pick up their homes and move to high ground, settlers tried with little success to hold off the force of the floods.

Lives and property are safer today along the Clearwater River because of flood protection created by Dworshak Dam. It is the highest straight-axis, concrete gravity dam in North America, and the largest of its type ever constructed by the U.S. Army Corps of Engineers. Dworshak Dam is a multipurpose flood control project, completed in 1973, after seven years of construction. Congress authorized the $327 million project for flood control, hydropower production, recreation, natural resource management, and navigation.

Dworshak water levels fluctuate throughout the year to help reduce flood damage, generate power, and to aid juvenile salmon in their migration to the ocean. The reservoir generally reaches its full elevation by mid-June, depending on the snow pack and precipitation of the previous winter and spring.

Dworshak Dam is an integral unit in the comprehensive development of the water resources of the Columbia-Snake River drainage. The dam controls a drainage area of 2,500 square miles in the Clearwater River basin. The powerhouse adds important electrical generation to the Pacific Northwest power system. The hydropower produces market equivalent yields of more than $50 million in revenues annually. Some of that income is used to repay the U.S. Treasury for the construction costs of the dam.

There are three hydroelectric generators in the powerhouse, one with a rated 220,000-kilowatt capacity and two with 90,000-kilowatt capacities. These three generators are capable of producing enough power to light, heat, and cool a city the size of Boise, Idaho. Electricity produced by the generators is transmitted through lines from the powerhouse to the Bonneville Power Administration transmission system for marketing and distribution.

Discover Dworshak Dam & Reservoir
Boating, Swimming, Water Skiing
Whether you are on a ski boat, canoe, sailboat, or personal watercraft, there is plenty of room for everyone on the 19,000-acre reservoir! Launch from your choice of seven boat ramps spread out along the picturesque 184 miles of shoreline. Kayak in a secluded cove. Watch a blue heron fishing in the shallows. Ski behind a powerboat on the open waters. Big Eddy Marina offers fueling facilities, moorage, and a snack shop for your last-minute needs. Convenient floating restrooms are located throughout the reservoir. Floating docks make a great destination for a family picnic and swim.

Hiking Trails
Strap on your pack and head for the hills. A hiker's haven awaits you at Dworshak. Walk softly through the wooded forest on the two-mile-long Canyon Creek Trail. Listen to the music of the songbirds. Enjoy a short walk through the shaded Douglas Fir forest on the Merry's Bay Trail. Retreat from the hot summer sun on the five-mile-long Cold Springs Trail. Explore a wildlife Mecca where you might follow in the fresh tracks of an elk. For the hardiest of hikers, the 10-mile-long Big Eddy Trail offers spectacular cliffside views of the reservoir and quiet seclusion.

Wildlife Watching
Many wildlife species reside at Dworshak. Marvel at the splendor of majestic eagles, hawks, and ospreys soaring. Listen to a bugling bull elk on a crisp fall morning. Black bear, deer, and moose are sometimes seen near the water. Ruffed grouse, known for their springtime drumming rituals, burst from cover in the lowlands. Osprey speed dive into the reservoir to catch the kokanee salmon. With keen senses and a pair of binoculars, wildlife watchers find great rewards at Dworshak.

Picnicking
If you're here for the day, take advantage of beautiful picnic sites. Reserve a group shelter at Dent Acres for your family reunion, company picnic, or friendly gathering. Big Eddy, with its picnic area, marina, and boat ramp, is a great place for kids of any age! The Visitor Center is another great place to relish a nice meal overlooking the dam and reservoir.

Camping
Camping at Dworshak is a memorable experience. Whether it is a primitive camp hugging the shoreline away from the crowds, or your home-away-from-home site with full hookups, Dworshak has it. Over 100 primitive mini-camps dot the shoreline in isolated coves and creeks. Each site has a tent pad, fire ring, picnic table and toilet. If a developed campground is more your style, try Dent Acres or Dworshak State Park, which offer hookups and showers.

Reservations are available for some sites at Dent and Dworshak State Park. Dent Group Camp can accommodate up to 250 people. The Three Meadows Group Camp provides accommodations for up to 100 people with sleeping cabins and a lodge.

Hunting
A variety of game, including whitetail deer, turkey, grouse, mountain lion, black bear, and the prized Rocky Mountain elk are here to challenge any hunter. Hunting is permitted on most Dworshak lands, except developed recreation areas. Play it safe! Boat, hunt, and fish at your own risk. All Idaho state boating, hunting, and fishing laws apply.

Fishing
Catch your limit at Dworshak Reservoir! From the headwaters to the tailwaters, angling opportunities abound. Rainbow trout, smallmouth bass, and kokanee salmon are abundant in the shallow bays, quiet coves, and open water of the reservoir. Below the dam, anglers come from near and far for a chance to hook one of the big ones - the feisty steelhead trout and the massive Chinook salmon. Dworshak has fishing for everyone!

Tour the Dam

Looking for a good family activity? Take a guided tour inside Dworshak Dam, one of the largest dams of its kind in the world! Start out at the Visitor Center located at the top of the dam. Guides are on site to answer questions. Interpretive displays and audiovisual programs are available for your enjoyment. Tours take about an hour and a half. Learn about the complexity of Dworshak and the many competing demands for our natural resources. Call ahead for tour times and schedules. Dworshak welcomes persons with disabilities. Wheelchairs and strollers are available for tours at no charge. All project buildings are accessible.

Dworshak Facts
Reservoir

- 184 miles of shoreline

- 54-mile-long reservoir

- 630 feet deep on the upstream side of the daM-19,000 surface acres at 1,600 mslL- Full reservoir pool is 1,600 feet above mean sea level-Minimum pool elevation is 1,445 msl

- Dworshak lands include approximately 30,000 acres

- Gross water capacity is 3.5 million-acre feet. One acre-foot is about 325,900 gallons of water.

Dam

- Dworshak is the tallest straight axis concrete gravity dam in North America

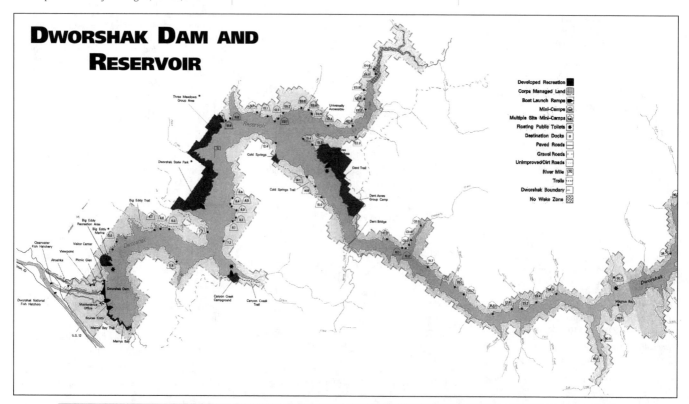

- It is 717 feet high, 3,300 feet long, 535 feet wide at its base, and 35 feet wide at it cresT- The dam contains 6.7 million cubic yards of concrete. (That's approximately enough to pave four lanes of highway from Portland, Oregon, to Salt Lake City, Utah.)

- Construction took seven years at a cost of approximately $327 million

- The power plant, which came on line in March 1973, has three hydropower turbines that can generate 400,000 kilowatts of electricity for homes and industry.

Play it Safe
- Obey posted rules and regulations

- Always wear your personal flotation device

- Avoid boating near the dam itself

- Watch for floating debris and underwater obstructions

- Know how to swim!

- Don't drink alcohol while boating - alcohol and boating don't mix!

- Be aware that water level can change at any time

- Plan for the weather - bring water, sunscreen, and warm clothing

- Build campfires only in designated fire rings

- Use only dead branches or downed trees for your fire

- Carry a shovel, bucket, and axe when camping during fire season.

Contact Information
- Fire and Ambulance: 911

- Clearwater County Sheriff Department: (208) 476-4521

- Dworshak Resource Office: (208) 476-1261

Reprinted from a U.S. Army Corps of Engineers (Walla Walla District) brochure

V Fishing at Dworshak Dam & Reservoir
Ahsahka. 476-1261 or (800) 321-3198.

Welcome to Dworshak Dam and Reservoir! The recreation areas are managed by the U.S. Army Corps of Engineers and Idaho State Department of Parks and Recreation. Among the many recreational opportunities, fishing is always popular.

Dworshak Fishing Fun Facts
Dworhshak is annually stocked with 150,000 rainbow trout at an average size of 10 inches.

Dworshak Reservoir is home to Idaho's largest recorded smallmouth bass, 8 lbs., 15 oz., 22" long, caught by Dan Steigers in 1995. We invite you to try your luck here too, maybe even set a new record.

Fishing Opportunities On and Below Dworshak Reservoir
Kokanee: Good fishing year round. Best times are April to August. The older kokanee reach maximum growth in July/August and then progress upstream to spawn. They generally bite while trolling on maggots and white corn trolled lures.

Bass: The best times are in the spring where creeks enter the reservoir and the bottom is somewhat gravelly. Later in the year when the top layer of water is warm, the bass tend to head to deeper rocky areas with cooler temperatures. They generally bite on nightcrawlers and plastic grubs, but many other baits also work.

Rainbow Trout: Fishing is good year round in all areas of the reservoir. Trout generally bite on nightcrawlers, spinners, and scented baits.

Steelhead Trout: Steelhead are an anadramous type of rainbow trout. They travel all the way from the ocean to try to spawn in the waters of Idaho. Some years large numbers of steelhead are found in the waters below Dworshak Dam and along the mainstem of the Clearwater. The most common fishing methods include slip bobber with jig and shrimp, large flashy spoons or minnow type lures, and drift fishing with bait.

Chinook Salmon: Similar to steelhead, spring Chinook salmon also spawn in this area. During high return years, large numbers of salmon can be found in the waters below Dworshak Dam and concentrated around the hatchery areas. Fishing methods are similar to those for steelhead. Be aware of special regulations for harvest and handling of these fish.

Note: Dworshak and the North Fork of the Clearwater River are home to Bull Trout. No harvest is allowed. Bull trout lack the wormlike markings of Brook Trout and have no spots on their dorsal fin.

Reprinted from U.S. Army Corps of Engineers brochure

V Boating at Dworshak Dam and Reservoir
Ahsahka. 476-1261 or (800) 321-3198.

Welcome to Dworshak Dam and Reservoir managed by the U.S. Army Corps of Engineers. To assure an enjoyable stay while protecting public lands, we've developed these guidelines to make your trip safe and memorable.

Before you head out on the reservoir, be sure to have the following safety equipment on board:

- Personal Flotation Devices (PFD's)

- Throwable PFD

- Fire Extinguisher

- Navigation/Anchor Lights

- Visual Distress Signals

- Sound Producing Devices

- First Aid KiT

Boating Facilities
Big Eddy Marina

- 98 slip marina

- 2 lane launch ramp

- Handling dock, tie-up dock

- Marine dump station

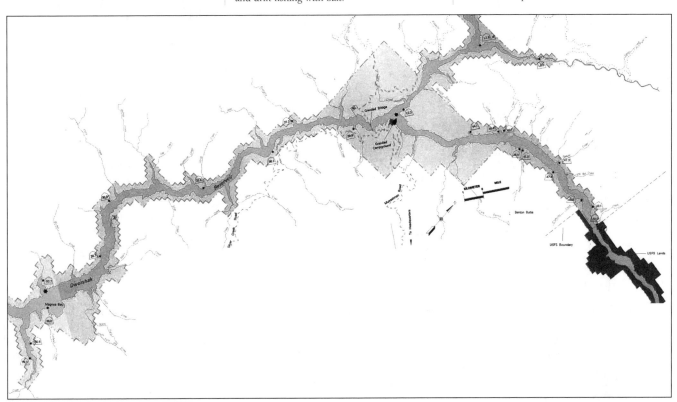

- Floating fuel station
- Fish cleaning station

Bruce's Eddy

- 2 launch ramps (1 single lane)
- Handling dock

Canyon Creek

- 1 lane launch ramp, usable down to water elevation 1560
- Handling dock

Dent Acres

- 2 lane launch ramp, usable down to water elevation 1490
- Handling dock
- Marine dump station
- Fish cleaning station

Freeman Creek

- 2 lane launch ramp, usable down to water elevation 1515
- Handling dock, tie-up dock

Grandad

- 1 lane launch ramp, usable down to water elevation 1540
- Tie-up dock

Destination Docks

Destination docks can be found at both Elk Creek and Indian Creek. They provide a tie-up point for picnics, swimming, and sunbathing.

Life Jackets

All recreation boats must carry one properly fitted personal flotation device for each person aboard. Children fourteen and under must wear a Coast Guard approved life jacket when they are aboard a moving boat 19 feet in length or less.

Float Plan

Fill out a float plan and leave a copy with a friend, relative, or local marina. Float plans include all the important information about a trip, your party, and your boat. This information will help in responding to any emergencies that may occur. You can obtain a float plan at any Corps boat launch on the reservoir. They are collected by the Clearwater County Sheriff's Department.

Reservoir Levels

Reservoir levels change throughout the year for flood control and to help endangered salmon. This can present challenges when tying off a boat and accessing boat ramps. When the reservoir is filling, floating debris can create navigational hazards. Before you go out, be sure to check the lake level.

Reprinted from U.S. Army Corps of Engineers brochure

V Dworshak State Park

4 miles south of Dworshak Dam. 476-5994. From downtown Orofino, proceed to Ahsaka. Next, follow County Rd. P1 to Cavendish before bearing east on Freeman Creek Rd. leading to the park.

Recreation is the name of the game at north-central Idaho's Dworshak State Park. Named afer prominent Idaho senator, Henry Dworshak, the park includes a sandy beach, boating, angling, a fish cleaning station, water-skiing, a boat ramp, camping facilities, volleyball courts, and horseshoes. Trees and open meadows surround the scenic park.

11 *Food, Lodging*

Orofino
Pop. 3,247

In 1860, the gold rush hit Orofino Creek. The name means "pure gold," or "fine gold" in the Spanish language. In 1895, when the Nez Perce reservation was opened to settlement, Clifford Fuller staked a claim and established a trading post. The town itself was founded a year later under the direction of the Clearwater Improvement Company. In 1898, Fuller built a ferry across the Clearwater River, and the Northern Pacific Railroad further enhanced transportation to and from the area when it arrived in 1899.

The post office was established in 1901, and in 1911 the first bridge was built over the river to replace the ferry. Local legend states that the first schoolhouse required too far of a walk for some of the youngest school children. Despite parent pleas to move the school closer to town, school officials declined. So, one morning the locals woke to find the schoolhouse mysteriously and conveniently "relocated" one mile upstream. In 1906, a fire tore through town, destroying the entire Main Street. Brick buildings were constructed to replace the burned wooden structures. Another form of heat, not related to fires, has also been recorded in Orofino. The community holds the record for the state's highest recorded temperature: 118 degrees Fahrenheit on July 8, 1934!

Today the town occupies both banks of the Clearwater River and its economy revolves around the logging industry. Recreation also abounds here, drawing anglers, boaters, hikers, and camping enthusiasts. Heavy winter snowfalls bring in a multitude of snowmobilers and a host of skiers.

Grangemont

This tiny, almost non-existent town was named for the grange that W.W. Deal founded here in approximately 1885.

T Orofino Golf and Country Club

3430 Debertin Dr./Hwy. 12, Orofino. 476-3117.

The Orofino Golf and Country Club is an excellent course to visit while traveling along the historic Lewis and Clark trail. Nestled in the Clearwater Valley, the course is challenging due to its hilly terrain. Golfers can opt to play a 9-hole par 35 game, or select a longer 18-hole game covering 5,414 yards. Green fees are $12 for 9 holes and $17 for 18. The course is open daily April through October.

T Clearwater Historical Museum

315 College Ave., Orofino. 476-5033.
www.clearwatermuseum.org

Clearwater County has a rich heritage that is thoroughly captured in this museum. With exhibits ranging from the Nez Perce Indians to the Lewis and Clark Expedition, this museum is stocked with artifacts. Among the numerous displays are antique guns, Orofino newspapers dating back to 1899, early homesteading and logging industry exhibits, 4,500 historical photos, and artifacts left behind by Chinese miners in Clearwater County's gold mining districts. All exhibits are area donations, and admission is free. The museum is open 1:30 PM to 5:30 PM Tuesday through Saturday from June 1 to September 30. During the remainder of the year, hours are 1:30 PM to 4:30 PM Tuesday through Saturday and private appointments are welcome.

T Orofino Community Pool

H St., Orofino. Contact the Orofino Chamber of Commerce at 476-4335.

Orofino's community pool provides a cool escape from summer's heat. The pool is open to the public during the summer.

T Konkolville Mill Tours

2 miles east of Orofino. 476-4597.

In 1947, Andy and Bernice Konkol purchased a parcel of land near present day Orofino and set to work building a lumber mill. While the first mill produced only one million board feet of lumber, Andy was confident that production would increase. In 1948, he constructed a larger mill and increased his staff.

The new mill included the first automated electric log carriage and has operated continuously for over fifty years. Today, the Konkolville Lumber Company turns out more than 21 million board feet of lumber each year and continues to distribute quality products throughout the entire Northwest region. Visitors interested in viewing the milling process and a relic of history still going strong are invited to schedule a guided tour. Tours are available by reservation Monday through Friday year-round.

Orofino	Jan	Feb	March	April	May	June	July	Aug	Sep	Oct	Nov	Dec	Annual
Average Max. Temperature (F)	37.6	46.9	54.6	64.7	74.1	81.8	91.8	90.5	80.6	64.1	48.0	40.0	64.6
Average Min. Temperature (F)	24.0	28.9	31.4	36.9	43.7	49.9	53.6	52.7	45.4	37.6	32.0	27.7	38.7
Average Total Precipitation (in.)	3.11	2.39	2.32	2.16	2.18	1.96	0.66	0.87	1.19	2.10	2.88	3.48	25.30
Average Total Snowfall (in.)	12.0	3.9	1.3	0.1	0.0	0.0	0.0	0.0	0.0	0.0	1.3	7.9	26.4
Average Snow Depth (in.)	3	2	0	0	0	0	0	0	0	0	0	1	1

T Clearwater National Forest Headquarters

Located on U.S. Hwy. 12 near the Orofino Bridge

The Clearwater National Forest Headquarters provides a clearinghouse of information regarding regional wildlife and history. Displays include a Clearwater National Forest 3D map, large wall paintings of Nez Perce life, and a painting depicting a Clearwater log drive during Idaho's early logging industry. The office also provides visitors access to numerous regional books, and park rangers are available to answer visitor questions.

T Bronze Logger

Downtown Orofino. Contact the Orofino Chamber of Commerce at 476-4335.

Situated in downtown Orofino's Heritage Plaza is an impressive bronze statue of a logger. Logging has been a part of Orofino's culture since its founding days, and the statue is a reminder of the area's economic heritage.

TV Clearwater National Forest

Contact the Forest Supervisor's Office at 476-4541.

Deep, forested gorges and rugged mountain peaks characterize the 1.8 million acre Clearwater National Forest covering much of north-central Idaho. With elevations ranging from 1,600 feet to nearly 9,000 feet, the forest experiences diverse weather patterns. The snow-covered forest is generally inaccessible from December through May, while higher elevations may not be open until early July. During the summer, temperatures may reach 90 degrees Fahrenheit during the day, but evenings find cool temperatures and frequent lightning storms.

Due to its large size and numerous access points, the Clearwater National Forest is a recreationist's dream come true. Horseback riding, whitewater rafting, wildlife watching, hunting, fishing, camping, hiking, and snowmobiling are all popular area pursuits. Those interested in visiting the forest should contact the Clearwater National Forest Supervisor's Office for additional information and forest regulations.

V Bald Mountain Ski Area

28 miles northeast of Orofino. 464-2311 or (800) 794-8742.

Tucked inside Idaho's Clearwater Mountains, Bald Mountain Ski Area offers 140 acres of varied terrain suitable for the beginner to expert skier. Seventeen runs offer uncrowded slopes, and while many of the runs are groomed, a few are left ungroomed for the true powder lover. Serviced by a T-bar and rope tow, the ski area also includes professional lessons, a rental shop, and nearby cross-country skiing and snowmobiling trails.

M Orofino Chamber of Commerce

217 1st St., Orofino. 476-4335. www.orofino.com

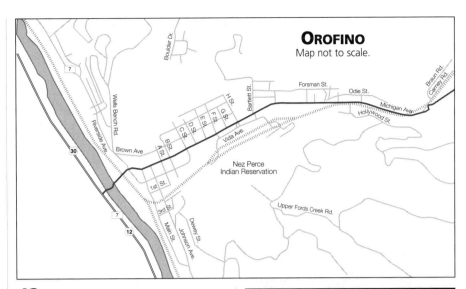

OROFINO
Map not to scale.

12 Food, Lodging

Headquarters
Pop. 300

Headquarters, a company logging town, originated as the end of the railroad line that extended from Orofino. The rails, laid with a $4 million price tag, were placed in the area between 1925 and 1927. One particular ten-mile stretch of line required fifty bridges! Due to the town's isolated nature, the railroad enabled Headquarters to become self-sufficient. Within no time, the town possessed its own power plant, school, dairy, store, community hall, and blacksmith shop. Today, lumber and the Potlatch Lumber Company still drive the economy, but most workers now simply rent company housing during the week, returning to their official residences elsewhere on weekends.

Greer
Pop. 30

Colonel William Craig and Jacob Shultz constructed a ferry over the Clearwater River here in 1861. The ferry served the local miners and packers passing through during the gold rush era, and soon a ferry house was built to further accommodate the travelers. John Greer (for whom the town was named) and John Molly owned the ferry at the time of the Nez Perce War in 1877. During that time, the Indians set the ferry loose in the river and burned the ferry house, thereby making it harder for the Army to chase them. Despite this unfortunate turn of events, Greer persevered and built a new ferry house. He and new business associate, John Dunn, later platted the townsite when the railroad came through town in 1899. A bridge was eventually erected across the river in 1914, making Greer's famous ferry an unnecessary town amenity.

Pierce
Pop. 617

While trespassing onto Nez Perce reservation land on September 30, 1860, Captain Elias D. Pierce discovered Idaho's first gold. Thereafter, thousands of prospectors flocked to the area and turned Pierce into a boomtown. Less than a year later, over 1,600 mining claims had been filed. A courthouse was built in 1862 to handle all the claims. It still stands today and is Idaho's oldest remaining government building. The post office was established in 1863.

Obviously, the town owes its namesake to community founder and prospector, Elias D.

Pierce. Pierce emigrated from Ireland to Virginia when he was fifteen years old, studied law under the guidance of a lawyer, and briefly established his own practice in Indiana. When the Mexican-American war began in 1846, Elias volunteered for service. After nearly ten months of duty and earning a Second Lieutenant rank, Elias returned to Indiana, settled down, and planned to marry Rebecca Jones. However, Elias decided he first should make the couple a fortune. He postponed the wedding and left for California's golden hills. During the journey, Elias supervised the travel progress, and his companions dubbed him "captain," a title that remained with him throughout his life.

Upon Pierce's arrival in California, he abandoned his mining ambitions and turned to the trading business with Native Americans. Next, he worked construction on the doomed Shasta River Canal, became the first person to climb northern California's Mt. Shasta, and became a member of California's Third Legislature. His lust for gold, however, was still on his mind.

Returning to the trading business, Pierce headed to Idaho, found a way to sneak onto the Indian Reservation, and devised his plan to hunt for gold. His plan worked, and Pierce's discovery skyrocketed Idaho Territory into the national spotlight. As for Pierce, he finally returned to Indiana twenty years after his departure, married his fiancee, hunted for more gold prospects in the west, and eventually retired with his wife in Pennville, Indiana. He died in 1897.

Weippe
Pop. 416

Pronounced "wee-ipe," this town draws its name from a Native American term meaning "gathering place." Indeed, Weippe and the surrounding prairie have always been a gathering place for Native Americans as well as white settlers. The site was the end point for travelers on the Lolo Trail, and Indians used the area for annual camas bulb diggings, tribal councils, and as a camping spot on the way to buffalo hunts. On September 20, 1805, the Lewis and Clark Expedition arrived on the prairie and spent a hospitable night in a Nez Perce village located just two miles east of the present day town. Times changed, however, and by 1877, relations between Native Americans and the white American government were strained. During this time, the Weippe Prairie was the scene for the famous Nez Perce retreat to Montana after a bitter battle with General Oliver O. Howard's troops on the Clearwater. Although the town retains its place as an important and sometimes chaotic site in history, Weippe is now a sleepy place on the Idaho prairie.

H Lewis and Clark
Milepost 17.2 on State Hwy. 11

Journeying toward the Clearwater River, six men under William Clark met the Nez Perce Indians not far from here, September 20, 1805.

Clark first saw three frightened Indian boys, who hid in the grass. Finding two, he reassured them with small presents and "sent them forward to the village." The Indian people, though naturally somewhat nervous in greeting the first whites to reach their land, fed Clark's men. The next day, Clark "collected a horse load of roots & 3 Sammon" to send back to the main expedition.

H Chinese Hanging
Milepost 27.5 on State Hwy. 11 outside Pierce

Charged with hacking a prominent local merchant to pieces, five Chinese were hanged here by vigilantes September 18, 1885.

They were just setting out on a long, hard 240-mile trip from Pierce to face trial at the county seat in Murray when the vigilantes struck. A large group of armed, masked men forced the deputy sheriff and his posse to give up the Chinese prisoners and to return to Pierce. A marked trail leads 365 feet from here to the site where this incident occurred.

H Canal Gulch
Milepost 28.6 on State Hwy. 11 north of Pierce

The famous gold rush days of Idaho began on September 30, 1860, when W. F. Bassett struck gold just about here.

E. D. Pierce, who knew the country, had led 12 prospectors, including Bassett, out from Walla Walla in August. After news of the strike spread, about 60 men came in and wintered nearby in spite of snow and Indians. Next spring the stampede was on and by that July this six-month-old county cast the largest vote in Washington Territory.

H Oro Fino City
Milepost 28.6 on State Hwy. 11 north of Pierce

Oro Fino City was the commercial center of Idaho's earliest gold camp in the great days of 1861. It flourished here for more than a year.

Pierce City was only two miles away, but another town sprang up near some rich gold strikes. In its first few weeks, Oro Fino City had "about 60 houses – more going up every day; nine or ten stores, more saloons than are needed, two smith shops, two butcher shops, three families, and about 500 inhabitants." But with the gold rush over, the place was abandoned. The deserted town burned to the ground August 10, 1867.

H Lewis and Clark
Milepost 47.4 on U.S. Hwy. 12

On their way west in 1805, Lewis and Clark descended into Clearwater Canyon on an old Indian Trail across from here.

After more than a month's search, they finally reached a westward river where they could use canoes. From here, they continued another 16 miles with their packhorses before they found a campsite with trees suitable for making canoes. But at this point, they had finished their difficult mountain passage to navigable Columbia water.

H Gold Rush Ferry
Milepost 52.5 on U.S. Hwy. 12

An old ferry near here took thousands of eager fortune hunters to a trail that climbed out of this canyon to rich gold fields discovered at Pierce in 1860.

You still can follow their spectacular route to Weippe Prairie, where in 1805 Lewis and Clark met a Nez Perce band that helped save their expedition. Continuing on, you can reach Idaho's oldest public building – Pierce Courthouse, built in 1862. Take State Hwy. 11.

T Orofino
U.S. Hwy. 11 to Pierce; at the south end of town, merge onto French Mountain Rd. and proceed 0.5 miles up Orofino Creek; Oro Fino was situated 20 miles east of present day Orofino

Named Oro Fino (meaning fine gold) by California miners in the area, this once booming city produced gold so fine that miners had to collect it with quicksilver. Located on Orofino Creek at the mouth of Rhodes Creek, the town quickly became the headquarters for any prospector interested in making a fortune in Idaho. By 1861, the town included more than 1,500 residents, ten stores, several saloons, two butcher shops, two blacksmith shops, and nearly 400 cabins costing anywhere from $500 to $1,000 each. For neighboring towns, the flood of miners to Oro Fino sparked intense jealously, and Oro Fino quickly became known as "Muttonville" in the surrounding area due to its lack of law and order.

While Oro Fino prospered greatly for a few years, it became a memory of the past by 1868. A new Oro Fino was established in 1896 by the Clearwater Improvement Company at Orofino Creek's mouth, but in 1898, the post office changed the spelling to the present day version, Orofino.

T J. Howard Bradbury Logging Memorial Museum
101 S. Main St., Pierce. 464-2531 or 435-4670.

Historically, this region's economy began with and was dependent upon the mining and logging industries. Today, visitors can glimpse into the past at the J. Howard Bradbury Logging Memorial Museum. Situated inside a log cabin built in 1928, the museum displays a photographic timeline of the timber harvest, the machines used, and the hardworking men who made the logging industry thrive. Visitors will also locate equipment used in both mining and logging. The museum is open

from 12 PM to 4 PM Thursday through Sunday from May 15 to October 15.

T Musselshell Meadows
Near Weippe. From Weippe, drive east on Pierce St. At the road's fork, continue on the marked Lolo Creek-Kamiah fork to the meadow. The site is located approximately 13 miles from Weippe.

An important source of food to their ancestors that remains an integral part of Nez Perce culture today, the camas bulb has long been identified with Native American tradition. Today, the Nez Perce honor their tribal legacy with the management of Musselshell Meadows as a camas bulb harvest area. The meadow serves as the last active camas bulb gathering spot in northern Idaho.

T Lewis and Clark Cedar Grove
Near Weippe. From Weippe, drive east on Pierce St. At the road's fork, continue on the marked Lolo Creek-Kamiah fork past Musselshell Meadows to U.S. Forest Service Rd. (FR) 500. Bear left on FR 500, drive 1.2 miles to the Cedar Creek sign, and bear left and continue 1.5 miles to the grove.

The Lewis and Clark Cedar Grove honors the memory of the Corps of Discovery who camped near Cedar Creek on September 19, 1805. The area features an enormous white pine called "Clark's White Pine" and several other impressive cedars. Although logging companies tried to get their hands on the grove in the 1900s, the U.S. Forest Service intervened, preserving the grove for the enjoyment of future generations.

T Bateau Display
West side of Main Street in Pierce. Contact the Pierce Chamber of Commerce at 464-2212.

For those unfamiliar with historical timber operations, a bateau was a boat used to assist "river pigs" (men whose job was to stand in the water and prevent log jams) on log drives. Although hundreds of bateaus once existed in Idaho, only four remain today, one of which is protectively displayed in downtown Pierce.

The Pierce bateau originated with woodcarver, John Cockburn, in Ottawa, Canada. The boat features pine tongue-and-groove planking and the traditional brick coloring received from an oil and jeweler's rouge protective coating. Upon its arrival in Idaho, the bateau became an important part of several Clearwater River log drives. Six to eight men occupied the boat at one time, rowing in unison at the command of the head boatman who stood facing downriver at the boat's bow. With the precision of hardworking bateau crews, log drives became more efficient and boosted Idaho's lumber related economy.

T Historical Discrimination Site
1.5 miles southwest of Pierce on State Hwy. 11. Contact the Pierce Chamber of Commerce at 464-2212.

After Pierce was founded, streams of Chinese miners poured into town to make a living. Although they were prohibited from staking their own claims, these industrious men were allowed to purchase claims abandoned by white men. By 1885, the area proved to be so profitable that nearly 150 Chinese men and just fifteen to twenty Caucasians called Pierce home.

Despite the low white population, Pierce ran rampant with discrimination against the Chinese. The Orientals were often harassed both physically and verbally, and in September 1885, became the unlucky scapegoats for an unsolvable murder.

On that fateful September evening, prosperous town merchant D. M. Fraser was murdered with a hatchet while he slept in the back of his store.

Nothing was stolen, resulting in the sheriff's speculation that the motive was jealousy on the part of storekeeper, Lee Kee Nam. Although no evidence tied Nam to the event, the mere suggestion that a Chinese man was involved was enough to incite rage throughout the white community. White men began using a hangman's noose to coerce confessions out of the local Chinese, but no one could tell which confessions were simply made up out of fright. Finally, the sheriff rounded up five random Chinese men to take them to trial in Murray. But approximately two miles outside of the town, the sheriff was halted by a band of vigilantes who kidnapped the five unlucky souls.

Upon being kidnapped, the Chinese men were doomed. The vigilantes hung all five men just outside town, and a packer later brought the bodies back to Pierce for burial. Learning of the event, the Chinese Consul in San Francisco wrote to the Chinese Minister in Washington, D.C. and requested an investigation. Although the Minister contacted Territorial Governor, Edward Stevenson, for a full report, Stevenson covered up the case's facts. The governor ordered that a full investigation take place, but the report had to clearly state that the five Chinese were hung for their indisputable guilt, not because of their race.

Today, a sign near the road memorializes the tragic event in Idaho's history.

T Rhodes Creek
Near French Mountain Rd. off of State Hwy. 11 in Pierce. Contact the Pierce Chamber of Commerce at 464-2212.

Rhodes Creek is named after a Missouri mulatto man known as William "Black Bill" Rhodes. William was a member of the first party of miners that entered Pierce, and he quickly became successful. Drawing upon his mining experience in California, William struck it rich on this creek, pulling out more than $80,000 worth of gold quartz. William was known for his altruistic ways, and he shared his wealth with anyone in need. The creek was subsequently named after the prosperous, friendly miner liked by all.

T Jaype
4.1 miles north of Pierce on State Hwy. 11

Although no one permanently resides in Jaype, the area is home to an expansive Potlatch Corporation plywood plant. Established in 1967, the plant's mill encompasses seven acres and has reached the capability of producing 150 million square feet of plywood each year. The area was named after early company president, John Phillip Weyerhaeuser.

T Bertha Hill Firetower
From Headquarters on State Hwy. 11, drive 8.6 miles north on the paved road. At the dirt road, turn left and continue 0.5 miles to the Bertha Hill sign. Stay to the right at all times, and travel 4.4 miles to the present lookout tower.

Idaho's Bertha Hill is distinguished as the site of America's first forest fire lookout tower. Interested in protecting its assets, the Clearwater Timber Company built a ladder to a wooden platform in 1902 situated atop 5,520-foot Bertha Hill. A man was employed to spot fires for the timber crew and relay the message back to the company to prevent any major disasters. This tower was located just a few yards off the dirt road 0.6 miles from the present lookout tower site.

Catching on to the idea, the U.S. Forest Service began budgeting for fire towers in 1909, and 5,060 federal, state, and private towers were

built in just 45 years. In 1959, the Clearwater Potlatch Timber Protective Association built a new Bertha Hill fire tower at the present site. The steel tower measures sixty-feet tall, and the protective railing was added in 1962 when a tower employee fell to her death.

The tower is listed on the National Register of Historic Places and is open to the public for viewing.

T Beaver Creek Flume
From Headquarters on State Hwy. 11, drive approximately 24 miles north, ignoring any road forks and staying on the main route. The road parallels Beaver Creek to the west.

Between the trees and grass, traces of the historic Beaver Creek flume can be viewed. The Potlatch Lumber Corporation built the twenty-mile flume to aid in log drives from 1930 to 1942. Although the flume required four million board feet for its construction, it turned out more than 170 million board feet for company profit. When World War II broke out, the flume was abandoned, never to be used again.

THE NEZ PERCE AND BUFFALO

Like other Native American tribes in the Plains and Rocky Mountain West, the Nez Perce people were historically dependent upon the buffalo. Few people truly understand the Native Americans' dependence upon buffalo and the crisis that ensued when white settlers destroyed the large bison herds. The following outlines the many uses of the buffalo to the ancient tribesmen of the west.

Skull
• Religious Rites
• Sun Dance

Brain
• Hide Preparation

Horns
• Cups
• Spoons
• Ladles
• Headdresses

Tongue
• Considered the best part of the buffalo
• Ornaments for clothing and weapons

Muscles
• Sinew was used for sewing thread and bowstrings

Hooves & Feet
• Rattles used in both everday life and religious cermonies
• Glue

Hair
• Headdresses
• Saddles
• Pillows
• Padding Fillers
• Rope Halters

Hide
• Moccasins
• Cradles
• Shoes
• Dolls
• Tipi Coverings

• Lance Covers
• Bags Of All Sizes And Purposes
• Quivers

Bones
• Knives
• War Clubs/Weapons
• Arrow Heads
• Scrapers
• Awls
• Game Dice
• Saddle Trees
• Winter Sleds
• Shovels

Tail
• Ornamental Decorations On Clothing
• Whips
• Fly Swatters

Stomach
• Cups
• Dishes
• Basins
• Buckets

Rawhide
• Headdresses
• Moccasin Soles
• Knife Cases
• Saddles
• Clothing
• Belts
• Armbands
• Stirrups
• Ropes
• Drums
• Buckets
• Shields
• Quirts
• Food
• Storage Containers

From the extensive list above, it is easy to see how disastrously affected the Nez Perce and their fellow Native Americans were when the buffalo population disappeared from the American West. Today, no animal matches the multiple capabilities that the buffalo provided to America's first inhabitants. As a result, the Nez Perce have been forced to diversify as they move towards the future while still maintaining a sense of their heritage.

T Brown's Rock
From Headquarters, drive northeast on Forest Rd. (FR) 246 past the Potlatch facilities. Proceed 5.2 miles to the Brown's Rock sign, turn left, and continue past "A" and "B" Rd.s. Continue 5.5 miles, and park at the abandoned spur on the road's right side. Walk up the spur to a grassy covered knoll.

Lined with trees and brush, the grassy knoll known as Brown's Rock is the site of one of Idaho's most famous battles for timber possession. On August 13, 1900, Charles O. Brown and his

Idaho Trivia
Known to cowboys and homesteaders as the gun that would help them win the American West, the Winchester Rifle is memorialized in Idaho. In the town of Winchester, a replica of the rifle hangs above Main Street to commemorate how the community was named.

21 RANCH: SITE OF THE WAHA FEUD

Situated twenty miles south of Lewiston near Lake Waha is the historic Queen Anne style ranch home of Frank Ward built in 1888. Ward served as ranch foreman for 21 Ranch for several years, but his career ended with a violent twist.

21 Ranch dates back to the 1870s when John Siers and Joseph Schissler became partners and decided to irrigate the pastureland with Lake Waha water. When Schissler died in 1886, Siers took his own portion of the stock and land and leased it to ranch foreman, Frank Ward. While Siers traveled east, Ward married the daughter of Mrs. Goddard, a cantankerous rancher with whom Siers and Schissler had argued many times in the past. When Siers found out the news and returned to the ranch in 1894, he terminated his agreement with Ward. Despite this termination, Siers decided to award Ward, his wife, and Mrs. Goddard with continued residence in the house.

Ward, however, was unhappy with the agreement, sueing Siers for $1,000 which he believed to be owed to him. At the same time, Schissler's heirs sued Siers for not abiding by property lease terms. Pending litigation, Sier's property was placed in the hands of a receiver who then leased the property to Mrs. Goddard.

Deeply distressed by the turn of events, Siers obtained a written note allowing him to return to the ranch to gather some of the personal articles that Mrs. Goddard previously refused to give back. While running an errand with three of his employees in 1895, Siers stopped at the house to gather his belongings. Ward stepped out onto the porch, and as the two men began to quarrel, Mrs. Goddard joined Ward outside. Siers finally decided to leave, but as he turned to go, Ward shot him twice. Siers attempted to fire back, but Mrs. Goddard drew her rifle and shot Siers several times in the back.

As Siers lay motionless, his hired hands moved toward the house. Ignoring Mrs. Goddard's thirteen-year-old son's request to halt, Elmer Shorthill shot Ward dead and landed a bullet in Mrs. Goddard's shoulder.

Although Mrs. Goddard and her son were charged with Siers' death, a jury acquitted them. Shorthill stood trial in Ward's death, but he was found not guilty.

Today, the historic home's upper stories retain their original fancy shingles, and the ranch is the legendary landmark of the Waha Feud.

Idaho Trivia

Although small in size, the community of Culdesac has a large claim to fame in Idaho history. Craig Donation's land claim, situated approximately six miles south of town on U.S. Hwy. 95, represents the first white settler's claim in the state of Idaho.

son, Nat, stood on top of this knoll and surveyed the white pine forest below. Brown was a timber representative for Fred Weyerhaeuser and John Humbird and was seeking more timber for his employers.

After filing a report in Moscow and gathering a crew of six men, Brown headed back to the area and began making survey descriptions so that the company could file on the land. Right on their heels was competitor W. E. McCord who had his own crew surveying the area north from Pierce. Brown and his men used McCord's survey line, and on September 9, Brown went to Lewiston to meet with his boss, John Glover. They filed a railroad script for 30,000 acres of the white pines, just hours before McCord arrived in town with the same objective.

Outraged, McCord went back to the woods intent on surveying new land and filing his rightful claim. But Brown and his associates had other plans. Pleased with Brown's success, Weyerhaeuser, Humbird, and Glover decided they wanted an additional 20,000 acres and sent Brown back into the forest. Both Brown and McCord and their crews worked fiercely to garner the necessary information, each for their own purposes.

While out riding casually one day, Brown learned from one of McCord's crewmembers that McCord had left just three hours earlier, heading to Lewiston to file a claim. Brown refused to let McCord win the forested acres he promised to his employers. He dispatched his son, Nat, who rode feverishly throughout the night and finally overtook his competitor. While McCord rested briefly at a cabin to enjoy a meal, Nat stole his adversary's fresh horse and arrived in Orofino at daybreak. When he arrived, the hired hand at the livery stable mistook Nat for McCord and handed him a note instructing the train engineer to take the young man to Lewiston. Nat cashed in on the ticket, impersonated McCord, and arrived in Lewiston on the train originally chartered for McCord. Glover met him and they filed their claim on the remaining 20,000 acres. Although McCord arrived as the two gentlemen were filing their claims, legality did not hold up, and Brown won the timber race for his employers.

V Musselshell Nordic Ski Trails
Near Pierce and Weippe. Contact the Pierce Chamber of Commerce at 464-2212.

Twenty-four miles of ungroomed cross-country ski trails wind through the forest surrounding Pierce and Weippe. With three access points from Forest Rd. 100, the area is ungroomed and open to beginning and intermediate skiers free of charge.

M Pierce-Weippe Chamber of Commerce
PO Box 416, Pierce. 435-4406.
www.pierceidaho.com; chamber@pierceidaho.com

13 *Food, Lodging*

Craigmont
Pop. 556

Craigmont may seem like a sleepy town, but in the early 1900s there was intense feuding. In 1898 the town started out as "Chicago," but soon the residents learned that having two Chicagos in America wasn't going to cut it. They renamed their town Ilo after a local merchant's daughter and resumed life as usual. In 1906, John Vollmer deceptively bypassed Ilo with the Camas Prairie Railroad by one mile. It was said he did this in order to establish a town under his own name.

The Ilo settlement was bitterly upset, but left with little choice, picked up their town and settled one mile away, just across the tracks from Vollmer. At that point, the feuding escalated. Folks from one town blatantly did not like the folks from the other, and vice versa. Even the post office was located in a neutral spot between the two communities, and it is said the train in Vollmer would oftentimes stop behind a string of boxcars just so the passengers wouldn't have to look at Ilo.

In 1920, after the schools consolidated (despite Ilo fighting the merger to the State Supreme Court), the towns finally agreed on becoming one city. They decided to name themselves after Idaho's first permanent white settler, Colonel William Craig.

Culdesac
Pop. 378

The name Culdesac was given to this community by Charles S. Mellon, the president of the Northern Pacific RR, because the railroad terminated at that location. Roughly translated, the French word "culdesac" means "the bottom of the bag," "blind alley," or "a place with only one outlet." In 1900, when the railroad was being built, there were actually two towns at this juncture. When the Post Office arrived, the townsfolk proposed the name as Cul-de-sac. The Post Office refused and instead named it Magnolia. In July of 1902, the residents petitioned the Post Office, and this time they were successful in changing the name to Culdesac.

Ferdinand
Pop. 145

When the Nez Perce Reservation opened up for settlement in 1895, Frank M. Bieker and ten other settlers homesteaded claims at just $3.75 an acre. Bieker then petitioned for postal services in 1898, naming his new settlement Ferdinand after his mother's hometown of Ferdinand, Indiana.

When the Camas Prairie Railroad built its line, Ferdinand was on the west side of the tracks. Bieker got word that John P. Vollmer, a ruthless millionaire-banker, planned on building another town just one-quarter mile away on the other side of the tracks. Bieker offered to sell Ferdinand's forty town acres to Vollmer if Vollmer would promise to put his proposed community on the west side of the tracks as well. Vollmer never responded to the offer but proceeded to build his town called Steunenberg. He even managed to claim a few of Ferdinand's businessmen. Most of Ferdinand's residents stayed put, however, and Steunenberg's newly established post office soon closed. Realizing his costly mistake, Vollmer eventually sold his land, and the small town was moved across the tracks to join Ferdinand.

Nezperce
Pop. 523

In great anticipation of the subdivision of Nez Perce tribal lands, government officials platted out Nezperce in 1895. More than 5,000 white settlers lined up for a chance to purchase the newly established lots, and the town boomed overnight.

As the town's sensational start began to lose its luster by 1909, Z.A. Johnson and a few local farmers constructed a fourteen-mile rail line that connected Nezperce to Craigmont with the Camas Prairie Railroad. Despite these men's attempts, the town continued to dwindle in size, boasting just 1,800 residents in 1911. Since then, the community has continued to decline in population but retains a peaceful setting.

Reubens
Pop. 72

James Reubens, a Nez Perce Indian who fought alongside United States troops in the War of 1877, is honored by this town's name. James later became a key government interpreter to the Nez Perce. When the Camas Prairie railroad made its way through the small settlement in 1907, the community absorbed the nearby fledgling settlements of Kippen and Chesley. A post office was established in 1906.

Winchester
Pop. 308

Shortly after the Nez Perce Indian Reservation was opened to white homesteaders, Old Winchester sprang up and a post office was established in 1899. In 1900, a town meeting was held to discuss the development of a school district. Agreeing that the district would need an official name, one resident gazed around the room and noted that most individuals present had brought Winchester rifles with them. The suggestion of dubbing the community after the popular gun was offered up, and residents unanimously voted to accept the moniker. When the Craig Mountain Lumber Company came to the area in 1909, residents moved the town to its current site to take advantage of employment opportunities at the newly established sawmill. Today, the area draws large numbers of people visiting Winchester Lake State Park situated just one half mile outside the community.

Waha

Charles Faunce established a new stage station on the shores of Lake Waha in 1882. As the first stage stop on the route from Lewiston to Cottonwood, Waha grew into a tiny settlement primarily serving the needs of stagecoach passengers. Postal services were available from 1890 to 1965, and visitors can still find the post office's historical site located within the saloon/store building Faunce had constructed in 1892. The town is named after a Native American word that translates to "beautiful" or "subterranean water," both of which accurately describe the area.

H Craigmont
Milepost 272.5 on U.S. Hwy. 95 at Craigmont City Park

Not long before Camas Prairie railroad service started here in 1908, rival towns were started on each side of the track.

The town of Vollmer began as a rail and business center on the east, and Ilo (an older town a mile away) moved to an adjacent site on the west. Each had separate schools, churches, stores, newspapers, banks, and other businesses. After 12 years of sharp competition, they finally merged into a united community in 1920.

H Railroad Tunnels
Milepost 285.8 on U.S. Hwy. 95

Seven tunnels – one a horseshoe more than a quarter mile long – had to be blasted in this canyon so that a railroad could be completed to Grangeville in 1908.

Building a railroad up this canyon was exceptionally difficult and expensive. Although they competed in Lewiston, Union Pacific and Northern Pacific officials decided to organize a separate company, in which each of them had an equal interest, to complete a Camas Prairie line. Otherwise, neither would have had enough traffic to operate profitably.

HUNTING IN NORTH CENTRAL IDAHO: A LANDSCAPE MARKED BY SUCCESS

Over 18 million acres of wild forested land and mountains add to Idaho's diverse landscape, and many of those untamed acres can be found in north-central Idaho. Filled with endless rivers, lush forests, and relatively few people, it's no wonder that north-central Idaho is a wildlife paradise to which hunters from around the world flock each year.

The rugged terrain dotting north-central Idaho is home to trophy big game, including moose, mountain goats, bighorn sheep, mountain lions, and nearly half the state's entire population of whitetail deer and elk. Although gray wolves and grizzly bears also roam the region, these threatened species are protected under Idaho and Federal law. But north central Idaho isn't strictly about big game. The area also supports bird hunters interested in finding a coveted Chinese pheasant, forest grouse, California quail, ruffed grouse, or Hungarian partridge.

Licensed guides are available throughout the region to lead visitors on an unforgettable hunting expedition. For those who prefer a trip of their own, licenses, tags, and hunting regulations are available at most retail sporting goods stores throughout Idaho or through the mail. Happy Trails!

T Wolf Education and Research Center
418 Nez Perce, Winchester. 924-6960.

The Wolf Education and Research Center is committed to educating the public and scientific community about the gray wolf and its habitat in the Northern Rocky Mountains. Visitors will find displays about the Sawtooth Pack and will also have an opportunity to view the pack in its natural habitat. The center is open 9 AM to 5 PM daily May through September with guided tours available by reservation. Admission is $5 for adults, $2 for youth ages 6 to 13, and free for those under 6.

T Old Trestles & Tunnels of the Camas Prairie Railroad
U.S. Hwy. 95 from Spalding to Cottonwood. Call 924-6586 for additional information.

In the 1930s, the Civilian Conservation Corp helped construct many of the wooden trestles and tunnels that the Camas Prairie Railroad used on its route. In the fifty-mile stretch between Spalding and Cottonwood, the rail line utilized twenty-eight trestles ranging in length from 50 to 685 feet and seven tunnels to traverse the steep mountainous terrain. Many of these trestles and tunnels can still be seen from U.S. Hwy. 95 as they add character to an already scenic backdrop. Visitors can also opt to take a scenic guided rail car ride across the route.

T Lt. Colonel William Craig's Grave
Four miles west of Culdesac on U.S. Hwy. 95, bear south at Jacques Spur onto the paved road. Proceed approximately 75 yards, and park at the road's left side to locate an overgrown cemetery.

Although Lt. Colonel William Craig may not be as recognized as his more famous counterparts, Craig was a mountain man by definition and played an important role in Idaho history. Born in West Virginia in 1809, Craig wandered out to Oregon Country in 1829 and counted Kit Carson, Jim Clyman, and Jedediah Smith among his closest friends.

Throughout his life, Craig participated in several mountain man activities. He worked for a period of time for the Rocky Mountain Fur Company. He participated in the Battle of Pierre's Hole in present day northeastern Idaho, was present at the Green River Rendezvous, and was alongside Jedediah Smith at a Blackfoot scrimmage near Yellowstone.

When the fur trade petered out, Craig settled in Lapwai with his Nez Perce wife in 1839 and cultivated Idaho's first farm. The Native Americans here held Craig in the highest esteem, and Craig was invaluable in saving the life of missionary, Henry Spalding. Based upon his hospitable relations with the local Indians, Craig was named a Lieutenant Colonel of Washington Territory where he served as an interpreter to the governor.

After retiring his interpreter post, Craig moved his family to Fort Walla Walla where he became the first postmaster and served as a Cayuse Indian Agent in the late 1850s. He later ran a ferry across the Clearwater River, and when he died of a stroke in 1869, he was buried in this cemetery. His wife, Pat-Tis-Sah, is buried next to him.

TV Winchester Lake State Park
Winchester. 924-7563.

Nestled in a forested area at the base of the Craig Mountains, Winchester Lake State Park encompasses 211 acres of pristine land and a 103-acre crystal clear lake. The lake, stocked with rainbow trout, largemouth bass, and bullhead catfish, draws anglers year-round, and a boat ramp provides easy access to this summer playground. Hiking trails double as cross-country ski trails during the winter, and interpretive programs are available.

V Waha Lake
Near Redbird Rd., Lewiston. Contact the Lewiston Orchards Irrigation District at 798-1806.

Managed by the Lewiston Orchards Irrigation District, Waha Lake is a 100-acre fishing hole popular with both Lewiston residents and visitors. The pond is regularly stocked with kokanee and rainbow trout, crappie, and smallmouth bass, and a boat ramp provides easy lake access to both electric and non-electric motors.

V Soldiers Meadow Reservoir
Contact the Lewiston Orchards Irrigation District at 798-1806. From Waha Lake, proceed south to Soldiers Meadow Rd.. Bear east, and continue 3 miles to the reservoir.

The Lewiston Orchards Irrigation District oversees the operation and maintenance of the isolated Soldiers Meadow Reservoir. Anglers will find the

---

Idaho Trivia

Kamiah has long been known for its warm weather. For thousands of years, the Nez Perce flocked to the area for its mild winters, and not much has changed. Kamiah's winters are still warm, so warm in fact that the region is supposedly the hottest spot in the neighboring four state region.

SNOWMOBILING IDAHO

Although relatively overlooked by the masses, Idaho features more snowmobile trails than any other state in the western U.S.! Traveling through scenic forests atop snow-capped mountain ridges, snowmobilers are privy to panoramic views of Idaho's landscape. Miles of both groomed and ungroomed snowmobile trails are available to winter recreationists of all abilities, many of which are found in the northern and north-central areas of the state.

Lolo Pass
Situated near the Idaho/Montana border, Lolo Pass is a snowmobiling mecca available December through April. Groomed trails connect the Lolo and Clearwater National Forests, while ungroomed trails designed for snowmobilers with advance abilities lead to Elk Summit, Beaver Ridge, and the popular Lochsa Lodge. In addition to the trails, Lolo Pass features restrooms, a warming hut, and a visitor center. Three-day and season passes are available, and interested recreationists should contact the Idaho Department of Parks and Recreation at 334-4199.

Buffalo Hump Corridor
The extremely remote Buffalo Hump Corridor is nestled southeast of Grangeville near the scenic Gospel Hump Wilderness. Only backcountry snowmobilers should venture into the area, and proper preparation and safety precautions are recommended at all times. The area is generally open from December through March, and more information is available from the Red River-Elk City Ranger District at 842-2255.

Elk City & Surrounding Area
Ranging in elevation from 3,000 feet to more than 6,000 feet, Elk City, Dixie, and Red River area snowmobile trails provide more than 350 miles of groomed trails in the Nez Perce National Forest. Mountain ridges and fire tower lookouts provide spectacular views of the valley below, and the forest's millions of acres encourage advanced snowmobilers to create their own

trails. Contact the Red River-Elk City Ranger District at 842-2255.

Grangeville Area
Open from November to April, snowmobile trails near Grangeville provide easy access to the Nez Perce National Forest. Featuring both groomed and ungroomed terrain, these trails follow historic Nez Perce Indian routes and gold-rush trails, wind past mining ghost towns, and venture near the Gospel Hump Wilderness with views of the Seven Devils Mountains. Nearby, Winchester State Park boasts an additional 100 miles of groomed trails open to snowmobilers of all abilities. For more information, contact the Grangeville Chamber of Commerce at 983-0460.

Pierce Area
300+ miles of groomed trails and several more miles of ungroomed mountain climbs await riders of all skill levels in the rugged area near Pierce. Trails are open November through April and traverse forests and meadows with spectacular views of mountain peaks and frozen lakes. Wildlife also abounds in the Pierce area with possible sightings of mountain lions, bobcats, moose, and deer. For the historian, the Pierce area allows snowmobilers to travel along some of the trails Lewis and Clark used during their 1804-1806 expedition. Contact the Pierce Chamber of Commerce at 464-2212.

Lewiston Area
The Waha and Craig Mountains south of Lewiston provide snowmobilers with another possible destination from January to March. Offering both open and forested areas, 250 miles of groomed trails are maintained by Nez Perce County with parking available at Waha and Winchester. Contact the Lewiston Chamber of Commerce at 743-3531.

Moscow Area
From January to April, 300 miles of groomed trails are available in Latah County. In the Elk River area, breathtaking views await snowmobilers who climb the hilly landscape, while the smaller Moscow Mountain provides a loop trail leading to the summit. Contact the Moscow Chamber of Commerce at 882-1800.

---

reservoir stocked with kokanee and rainbow trout, crappie, and smallmouth bass, and a boat ramp provides access to fishing on the water's surface.

M Craigmont Chamber of Commerce
PO Box 250, Craigmont. 924-7724.

M Nezperce Chamber of Commerce
PO Box 278, Nezperce. 983-0440.

14 *Food, Lodging*

Kooskia
Pop. 675

In 1895, the U.S. government opened up 104 acres on the Nez Perce Indian reservation for the express purpose of encouraging white settlement and establishing a new town. First named Stuart after Nez Perce surveyor and merchant, James Stuart, the Northern Pacific Railroad changed the name in 1899 as the line already serviced a town by that name. Thus, since 1902, the name of

Kooskia has prevailed. The name is a derivative of the Nez Perce word, "kooskooskia," which Lewis and Clark believed to mean "clear water." Although linguists now believe that the word actually translates to "where the waters join," the name is still appropriate as the town is situated at the convergence of the Clearwater River's Middle and South Forks.

In the 1900s, the town was known by avid equestrians as the home of Decker saddles. Blacksmith and packer, Oliver P. Robinett, moved to Kooskia in 1906 and built the Decker saddle. The model soon established itself as being more efficient and easier to use than other available saddles. The Decker brothers took up making the saddles, named the item after themselves, and sold them all over the west.

Kamiah
Pop. 1,160

Kamiah's name (pronounced KAM-ee-eye) is derived from the Nez Perce word "kamia," meaning "ropes." The Indians collected kame hemp in this area and used it as building material for ropes

and mats. During the early 1800s, the Nez Perce wintered here and fished the Clearwater River for steelhead. Most notably, the Lewis and Clark Expedition camped for four weeks (May 14 to June 9, 1806) just northwest of the present-day Kamiah bridge on the river's east bank. The expedition was headed back to St. Louis, but the party was forced to wait near Kamiah for the last of the winter snows to melt. An official settlement and post office were established here in 1878, and the town developed a reputation for its timber industry. Although the logging industry eventually faded from Kamiah's spotlight, the town still attracts year-round visitors and attention with its numerous community events and beautiful surroundings.

Woodland
Spurred on by news of unclaimed land and rich mineral deposits, several Kansas residents migrated here in the mid 1800s. Upon settling in a flat, wooded area, the new homesteaders christened their small mining camp, Woodland. The town serves as the final stop for a branch of the Northern Pacific Railroad, and a post office operated in the area from 1898 to 1935.

H Asa Smith Mission
Milepost 67.6 on U.S. Hwy. 12

A Massachusetts Congregationalist, Smith spent two years here learning the Nez Perce language and starting a mission.

Coming here May 10, 1839, to study with Lawyer, an important Nez Perce leader, he stayed to work on an Indian dictionary and to hold daily religious classes each spring and winter. After spending six months in a "mere hovel," he finished a comfortable home and started a garden of several acres. But he never got used to pioneer life here. Leaving Kamiah April 19, 1841, he moved to a mission in Hawaii.

H Long Camp
Milepost 67.6 on U.S. Hwy. 12

In 1806, Lewis and Clark waited six weeks for deep snow to melt on the high ridges of the Lolo Trail to the east of here.

Their route home blocked, they spent four of the six weeks (May 14 – June 10) at their long camp across the river. They hunted, fished, and amused themselves showing the Nez Perce Indians "the power of magnetism, the spyglass, the compass, watch, air gun and sundry other articles equally novel and incomprehensible to them." Finally, with three Indian guides, they got away on their long journey back to the United States.

H Looking Glass
Milepost 75.9 on U.S. Hwy. 12

During General O. O. Howard's 1887 Nez Perce campaign, Looking Glass and his band were camped up Clear Creek near here.

Looking Glass told Army authorities: "Leave us alone. We are living here peacefully and want no trouble." But after a July 1 military attack that destroyed his village, ruined his gardens, and captured 750 Nez Perce horses, Looking Glass and his band joined other Nez Perce refugees and soon headed for Montana's buffalo plains. Howard spent three months pursuing Joseph, White Bird, Looking Glass, and their warriors after that fiasco.

T Kooskia Mural
Pankey's Foods Store, Downtown Kooskia. Contact the Kooskia Chamber of Commerce at 926-0855.

The Pankey's Wall Mural Project is a must-see point of interest for regional tourists. Idaho artist, Robert Thomas, and art students from Clearwater

Valley High School collaborated to create the large mural depicting the 1806 Kooskia town site. Based on Thomas' historical oil painting of the region, the mural was then traced onto the wall with projectors. The mural is intended to instill pride in the community's heritage and reflects the valley as the Lewis and Clark Expedition would have found it.

T Old Opera House Theatre
Downtown Kooskia. 926-0094.

Kooskia's Old Opera House Theater dates back to 1912 and was originally called the Mount Stuart Playhouse. Vaudeville acts graced the logging town with their presence until the mid 1920s, after which point the theater simply hosted community events.

In 1994, new owners decided to renovate the theater and bring back the legacy of old-fashioned entertainment. Inside, theater patrons will discover a crystal chandelier, a dessert and Sarsaparilla bar, and waitresses dressed in historic Victorian pieces.

The theater is open year-round and showcases melodramas, musicals, Dixieland jazz, bluegrass, big band music, barbershop quartets, and plays featuring local performers. Call for tickets and a complete schedule of events.

T Idaho's Oldest Protestant Church
3 miles southeast of Kamiah. Contact the Kamiah Chamber of Commerce at 935-2290.

Five early Idaho settlers raised the idea of establishing a Protestant Church near Kamiah in 1871. Three years later, Nez Perce Indians erected the church in 1874 that is now recognized as Idaho's oldest continually running Protestant Church. Although Asa and Sarah Smith served as missionaries to the area as early as 1837, they left in 1839.

In 1871, Reverend H. T. Cowley arrived on the scene and began instructing the Nez Perce. He was a commanding force in erecting the area's Protestant Church. Upon Cowley's departure, Henry Spalding arrived, followed by Sue McBeth. Through the efforts of Sue and her sister, Kate, all young Nez Perce boys and girls received a religious education. The church is used to this day on the Nez Perce Indian Reservation.

T Kooskia National Fish Hatchery
2 miles east of Kooskia on Clear Creek Rd.. 926-4272.

Situated near the confluence of Clear Creek and the Middle Fork of the Clearwater River, the Kooskia National Fish Hatchery was authorized by Congress in August 1961. The fish hatchery was established to rear and preserve populations of spring Chinook salmon, and the facility works closely with the Dworshak National Fish Hatchery.

Every May through August, adult salmon are trapped at the Kooskia Hatchery and transported

for spawning to Dworshak. The eggs are then returned to Kooskia each fall where they incubate, hatch, and are reared for release in eighteen months.

Self-guided tours are available daily, and large groups may make reservations for a guided tour. In addition to visual presentations and instructive displays about Pacific salmon, the hatchery features the new interpretive Mill Pond Trail. The gentle trail winds 300 yards near an old mill pond that is home to a variety of native wildlife. The trail also includes a historic plaque commemorating the 1877 Nez Perce War. The hatchery is open to the public free of charge from 7:30 AM to 4 PM daily excluding major holidays.

M Kamiah Chamber of Commerce
518 Main St., Kamiah. 935-2290. www.kamiahchamber.com

M Kooskia Chamber of Commerce
PO Box 310, Kooskia. 926-4362. www.kooskia.com

15

Lowell
Pop. 30

Established at the confluence of the Lochsa and Selway Rivers, Lowell was founded in 1903 with the arrival of twenty-one settlers. Soon, the settlement was a popular and important stopping place for workers constructing U.S. Hwy. 12. The site continued to grow with its nearness to the Fenn Ranger Station, a prison camp, and the O'Hara CCC Camp along the Selway River.

A New Englander named William Parry is said to have finally provided Lowell with its current name. After finding the lost and half-starved Henry Lowell in the Lochsa River Canyon, Parry proceeded to revive him and nurse him back to health. When the town decided to apply for postal services, Parry requested that the settlement be named after his lucky comrade, who in turn became the first postmaster. Today, the tiny town's economy is based almost completely upon the recreation industry and the tourist dollars of eager backcountry and river enthusiasts who visit the community each summer.

H Whitehouse Pond
Milepost 158.4 on U.S. Hwy. 12

On their westbound journey, Lewis and Clark crossed here, September 15, 1805, after camping four miles upstream at Powell.

Their Shoshoni guide had brought them down an old trail from Lolo Pass to a Lochsa fishery he knew about. To continue west, he had to take them north up this ridge to rejoin their Lolo Trail route. Indian travel through here had to go along high ridges because Lochsa Canyon had too many cliffs and gorges to provide a good horseback route.

H Lolo Trail Crossing
Milepost 171.2 on U.S. Hwy. 12 near the Idaho/Montana border

When Lewis and Clark came up this ridge, June 29, 1806, they ran into "A shower of rain, with hail, thunder, and lightning that lasted about an hour."

But they got out of deep Lolo Trail snow after they reached Rocky Point (directly across from here) and descended to Crooked Fork, below this turnout. They reported that then they "ascended a very steep acclivity of a mountain about two miles" crossing this highway here to reach their old trail to Lolo Pass.

H Lolo Summit
Milepost 174.4 on U.S. Hwy. 12 near the Idaho/Montana border

The Lewis and Clark party crossed this pass September 13, 1805, westbound for the Pacific after a long detour from the south.

From the headwaters of the Missouri, they had crossed the mountains to the Salmon. Finding that river impassable, they traded for packhorses, hired an Indian guide and came north to an Indian trail across the mountains here. Tired and ill-fed, the men had a hard struggle in early snow along the steep ridges which the trail followed for most of its 125-mile course west to the Clearwater River.

T Lochsa Historical Ranger Station
Contact the Lochsa Ranger District at 926-4274

The Lochsa Historical Ranger Station was dedicated in July 1976 as a memorial to the history of the Forest Service efforts to bring management to the National Forests.

The log buildings and simple furnishings represent an era that ended when the station became accessible by road in 1952. During that era, building materials were either harvested from the abundant timber supply or packed in on the backs of horses and mules. The furnishings were simple, but bringing many of them to the station required ingenuity, teamed with backbreaking labor. The desk in the office of the Combination Building was packed on the side of a mule with a large ham and two bales of hay balanced on the other side.

Disastrous forest fires were a part of early day life. In 1934, flames raged around and overhead, but 200-plus men were able to save themselves and the station.

Good examples of early-day craftsmanship have been preserved in the log buildings. The tools and furnishings were either used here or at other backcountry stations during the same era.

To provide information, either a Forest Service guide or volunteer Forest Service retiree is on duty. Feel free to visit with them and ask any questions you might have. We hope you enjoy your visit and come away with a better understanding of the history of management of your National Forests.

Reprinted from Clearwater National Forest brochure

T Lochsa Face
U.S. Hwy. 12 from Lowell to the Idaho/Montana border

On its path to Montana, U.S. Hwy. 12 parallels the Lochsa Face. This 73,000-acre strip of land flows between the Lochsa River and the Selway-Bitterroot Wilderness. In addition to impressive mountain peaks, trout-filled streams, and breathtaking scenery, the Lochsa Face is also home to an array of native wildlife. Passerby may catch a glimpse of elk or moose and maybe even an elusive mountain lion.

Idaho Trivia
The Camas Prairie spans 200,000 acres in north-central Idaho and is covered with delicate blue flowers during late spring and early summer. The prairie was thus named after this blue flower's bulb, the Camas bulb. The prairie is also a hotbed of agriculture, averaging more than 100 bushels of wheat per acre.

THE FATEFUL JOURNEY OF THE CARLIN HUNTING PARTY

In autumn 1893, the Carlin Hunting Party and their ensuing tragic saga became one of Idaho's most notorious outdoor expeditions. Will Carlin, a passionate hunter, organized the fateful trip. Included were his best friend, Abe Himmelwright; his brother-in-law, John Pierce; guide, Martin Spencer; and former hunting companion and camp cook, George Colgate. Although several of Carlin's companions felt Colgate was too old for the excursion, Carlin insisted that Colgate join the group's ranks.

After meeting in Spokane, the group traveled to Kendrick, Idaho where they would begin their trek to the Lochsa River via the Lolo Trail. On September 18, 1893, the men left Kendrick, eager for the hunting to begin. They were equipped with ten horses, four dogs, two cameras, and several guns.

Almost immediately, the group encountered problems. Idaho's fall weather was particularly cold and snowy in 1893, and the men soon noticed that Colgate's limbs were swelling. The men later learned that Colgate had an enlarged prostate, and ignoring his doctor's orders, that he had intentionally left his necessary catheters back in Washington. On top of it all, the men had horrible luck in shooting any game, often missing or only wounding their intended prey.

As the autumn weather turned colder and October cast its shadow on the group, Colgate's condition continued to deteriorate, and Spencer suggested that the party postpone the rest of the expedition and return to Kendrick. But Carlin and Himmelwright refused, stating they had not yet had their fill of hunting in Idaho's wilderness. As the next four days passed, Colgate's legs swelled to twice their normal size, and it was apparent he was suffering from uremic poisoning. Spencer strongly suggested again that the group abandon their hunting pursuits in the name of saving Colgate's life, but Carlin once again refused. Although Spencer and Pierce offered to take Colgate back themselves, Colgate insisted that the group remain together.

Finally, on October 10 with only eight days of provisions remaining, Carlin agreed that the group could return to Kendrick. But due to early winter snows, the Lolo Trail was covered with three feet of snow, and Colgate was in no condition to walk. Although the group thought they may be able to carry Colgate on snowshoes, they soon realized that idea was not feasible.

After discovering that the land route was blocked, the group decided to forge their way back via a water route. Spencer was skeptical of the plan, but the group insisted and set forth to create two log crafts, the Clearwater and the Carlin. On November 2, the boats were ready, and the men loaded the fragile Colgate on board with them. As Spencer predicted, the river's raging rapids and rocky bottom tore the boats to shreds, and Colgate suffered greatly. Back on shore, the group lit a fire to help warm Colgate, whose lungs had by now filled with liquid. But Colgate remained incapacitated, and the group began questioning their next move. Carlin felt that the group had shown more than enough civility to the ailing man whom he doubted would even make it back to civilization alive. Going against their better judgment, the other men agreed they had no choice but to leave Colgate behind in an attempt to save themselves.

Continuing overland through blizzard conditions, the men averaged approximately four miles per day and exhausted all their resources. Finally, out of desperation, the men ate one of their dogs on November 21 and began reconsidering their choice of a land route. While scouting out a possible river route, Carlin and Himmelwright encountered Lieutenant Charles P. Elliott and Sergeant Guy Norton who had been dispatched to rescue the party. When Carlin's father, General Carlin of Fort Sherman, Idaho, received word from a concerned friend of Spencer's that the group had not yet returned from their planned expedition, General Carlin immediately sent out rescue teams in search of his son. The rescue teams left November 7, and much to their surprise, found the group alive two weeks later.

Carlin's party left for Spokane on November 22 and were welcomed with a Thanksgiving feast upon their arrival. As for Colgate, Carlin visited his widow and explained the circumstances of his death. Although Mrs. Colgate appeared to accept the necessity of the hunting party's actions, the general public was appalled. Newspapers across the country slandered the men's actions as a violation of wilderness principle to never leave anyone behind.

As a result of the notorious expedition, General Carlin paid Colgate's wife and their seven children a lump sum of $25 for their loss. Spencer returned to the wilderness with a friend the following June to search for Colgate's body but failed to find the remains. When Lieutenant Elliot and his military party searched the area mid-summer, Colgate's remains were found nearly eight miles from where Carlin's party had left him to die.

T DeVoto Memorial Cedar Grove
2.9 miles east of Powell Junction on U.S. Hwy. 12

Nestled on a flat beside the Lochsa River, the DeVoto Memorial Cedar Grove honors the life of western historian, conservationist, and writer, Bernard DeVoto (1897-1955). DeVoto was born in the west, but through his education at Harvard and subsequent English professorship there, DeVoto found a platform to defend his homeland and the American West's unique culture and beauty.

Throughout his travels, DeVoto frequently visited Idaho and particularly loved this forested area. During his review of Lewis and Clark's journals and subsequent editing, DeVoto camped in this forest grove. When DeVoto died, his friends knew he wished for his ashes to be scattered in a western forest. His friends chose Idaho's Clearwater National Forest, and the grove subsequently memorializes him.

Today, the impressive grove features towering old-growth cedars while dogwood, sword fern, maidenhair and bracken ferns, and foam flowers complement the lush atmosphere. The site features several short trails, interpretive signs, and a picnic area.

T O'Hara Bar
Southeast of Lowell. Contact the Lowell/Syringa Chamber of Commerce at 926-4430. From Lowell, turn southeast off U.S. Hwy. 12 across a bridge, and drive 25 miles to the site.

O'Hara Bar was once home to eleven buildings and served as a base of operations for the Forest Service and the Civilian Conservation Corp. A 1 1/2-story log cabin dating back to 1910 still stands on the valley flat. The Forest Service cabin consists of squared logs and saddle-and-rider joints, and it features a log cellar and vertical-log shelter predating the cabin. At the time it was constructed, the remote cabin was more than thirty miles from the nearest road.

T Selway Falls Guard Station
Southeast of Lowell. Contact the Lowell/Syringa Chamber of Commerce at 926-4430. From Lowell, turn southeast off U.S. Hwy. 12 across a bridge, and drive 38 miles to the site.

Built in 1912, this log structure served as an early ranger station in the area. Rangers who manned the post were given a horse and $75 a month in exchange for fire patrol duty.

T Lochsa Federal Prison Work Camp
7 miles east of Lowell on U.S. Hwy. 12. Contact the Lowell/Syringa Chamber of Commerce at 926-4430.

In 1935, the nation's second federal prison work camp was established on the banks of Idaho's Canyon Creek. 170 prisoners were housed in the area in its first year while they worked eight hours a day constructing the highway. The crew completed eight miles in three years, and by 1943, more than 1,200 prisoners were on-site.

In late 1943, the work camp was turned into a Japanese internment center at the order of President Roosevelt. 135 internees lived at the camp and continued the prisoners' work on the highway until 1945.

T Idaho Batholith
East of Lowell at Split Creek on U.S. Hwy. 12

Encompassing 14,000 square miles, the Idaho Batholith covers a body of granite formed by magma over 80 million years ago. The site represents one of the largest granite masses in the world, most of which is found in the Idaho wilderness. Views of the Batholith, however, are visible from the highway.

T Powell Ranger Station
Just south of Powell Junction on U.S. Hwy. 12, 3.4 miles east of Whitehouse.

Situated on a gravel road and marked with a sign, Powell Ranger Station is more than just an important Forest Service site. The area was first home to the Corps of Discovery. On September 14, 1805, Lewis and Clark and their men camped at the site of the Powell Ranger Station. The men's provisions were running low, and the site marks the legendary killing of one of the Corp's colts for the evening meal.

T Lolo Pass
Idaho/Montana state border on U.S. Hwy. 12

Lolo Pass is reputedly named after the Chinook word meaning "to carry," but some historians suggest the name is actually reflective of an early area trapper. In either case, Lolo Pass marks the border with Montana. Interestingly, no official border existed between the states for nearly forty years as Lolo Pass wasn't surveyed until 1904.

TV Colgate Licks
61.2 miles east of Lowell (8.3 miles east of Saddle Camp Rd.). Contact the Lowell/Syringa Chamber of Commerce at 926-4430.

Colgate Licks is named after early hunter and trapper, George Colgate, who died tragically in the Idaho wilderness. The site features two natural hot springs, a short interpretive trail, and wildlife sightings of deer, elk, and sheep. The site is open year-round free of charge.

V Lochsa Whitewater Rafting
Contact the Clearwater National Forest at 476-4541.

The River and You
As part of the Middle Fork Clearwater Wild and Scenic River system, the Lochsa, with "recreation" river" classification is managed to protect and enhance aesthetic, scenic, historic, fish and wildlife, and other values that will contribute to public use and enjoyment of its clear, free-flowing waters and immediate environment.

The floating season normally extends from May to August. Permits are not required for non-commercial floating.

Throughout the floating season, the Lochsa is fed by melting snow in the surrounding mountains. Water temperatures are in the 30s and 40s. Danger of hypothermia is always high. Wet suits are a must for early season floating. Weather in the Lochsa area is often cool, cloudy, and rainy during the whitewater season.

Professional boatmen consider the Lochsa a hazardous river requiring heavy equipment and much technical maneuvering. They cancel trips or alter runs to avoid certain parts of the river when the water level is above 6.0 feet on the bridge gauges. Below 3.0 feet on the bridge gauges, many rocks begin to appear, and some sections are difficult to float without dragging.

If you have light equipment, little experience, or are unsure of your ability to handle your equipment under extremely difficult water conditions, you should not consider floating the Lochsa without competent accompaniment.

River Management Sections
The Lochsa River is divided into four management sections as determined by floating characteristics.

1) Section One – Confluence of Crooked Fork Creek and White Sands Creek to Indian Grave Creek. In this area, the river valley is wider and flatter. This section contains longer stretches of smooth water with few large rapids. Less technical maneuvering is required for floating this section. This section would be more suitable for open boaters, less experienced kayakers and floaters.

At river levels of 4.5 feet or above (measured at the bridge flow gauges) spray covers for open canoes, use of kayaks or inflatables is recommended. At levels of 6.0 feet recommend only experienced kayakers and rafters with extra safety precautions.

2) Section Two – Indian Grave Creek to Wilderness Gateway Bridge. This section contains large rapids requiring very technical maneuvering. Only skilled kayakers and rafters with good heavy-duty equipment and extra safety precautions should attempt it. Water levels of 6.5 feet and above will find rapids running onto one another, loss of stopping eddies and pooling below major drops and movement of dangerous debris down the river channel.

3) Section Three – Wilderness Gateway Bridge to Split Creek Pack Bridge. This section contains some very large rapids, however requiring less technical maneuvering than in Section Two. Rapids tend to be followed more by pools allowing more time for rest and easier rescue. This area should be attempted only by experienced floaters with heavy-duty equipment and extra safety precautions. At levels below 6.0 feet on the bridge flow gauges, eddies begin to form behind rocks and numerous bank eddies appear. The river is still quite pushy and recommended only for the experts. Above 6.0 feet there are few eddies, rapids run into each other, and tight maneuvering is required on some sharp bends.

4) Section Four – Split Creek Pack Bridge to Lowell. In this section, the river gradient begins to flatten out and the river valley widens. Intensity of the water begins to diminish. This section is used by experienced boatmen when high water levels prohibit floating other areas. Several large rapids must be noted as they come up unexpectedly. Apart from the few large rapids in this section, it is suitable for the less experienced boatmen. At river levels of 8.0 feet on the bridge flow gauges, most stopping points are washed out, noted rapids change considerably and calm areas disappear.

Reprinted from Clearwater National Forest brochure

V Lochsa River
Contact the Clearwater National Forest in Orofino at 476-4541.

Idaho's Lochsa River reflects a Nez Perce term that translates into "rough water." Rising high in the Bitterroot Mountains, the Lochsa parallels the scenic Lolo Hwy. while boasting forty rapids designated as IV or above on the rapid rating scale. As it winds its way to a confluence with the Selway and Clearwater Rivers, the Lochsa provides plenty of whitewater rafting opportunities for adventurous souls. Although permits are not required to run the river, only experienced rafters should attempt to tame the Lochsa's challenging waters.

V Lolo Pass Cross-Country Ski Area
U.S. Hwy. 12 at the Idaho/Montana border. Contact the Idaho Department of Parks and Recreation at 334-4199.

Straddling the Continental Divide at the Idaho/Montana state border, Lolo Pass Cross Country Ski Area features ten miles of groomed trails. The Nordic trails are appropriate for both beginners and those with intermediate skills, and a warming hut is available on-site. The area is part of Idaho's Park N' Ski system, and permits are required. Permits may be obtained at the nearest Ranger Station, and fees are as follows: $25 annual permit (good at all Idaho Park N' Ski areas), $7.50 3-day permit, and $2 day use permit.

V Fenn Pond
Contact the Idaho Department of Game and Fish at 334-3700. At Lowell, merge off U.S. Hwy. 12 and proceed to the pond on the marked Selway Rd..

Located directly across from the Fenn Ranger Station, Fenn Pond is a popular fishing location ideal for both experienced anglers and those who have never before sunk a line. The stocked pond, also commonly referred to as Selway Pond, features boardwalks and fishing piers, and a picnic area provides a great spot to enjoy a picnic lunch or view the area's wildlife.

V Jerry Johnson Hot Springs
77 miles east of Kooskia on U.S. Hwy. 12. Contact the Kooskia Chamber of Commerce at 926-0855.

The undeveloped Jerry Johnson Hot Springs are surrounded by nature's peaceful setting and are open to the public daily from 6 AM to 8 PM free of charge. A signed trail takes visitors on a one-mile hike to the three naturally warm pools that represent one of Idaho's most well-known hot springs.

The springs are named after famous hunter, packer, and trapper, Jerry Johnson, who was born in Prussia. After spending time in New Zealand, Johnson arrived in America eager to work the mines of the great Rocky Mountains. He landed himself in Idaho where he pursued a life of wilderness hunting.

V Weir Creek Hot Springs
67 miles east of Kooskia on U.S. Hwy. 12. Contact the Kooskia Chamber of Commerce at 926-0855.

A marked 0.25-mile hike leads visitors to the popular Weir Creek. The area features two natural hot springs that are open to the public daily year-round free of charge.

V Stanley Hot Springs
48 miles east of Kooskia on U.S. Hwy. 12. Contact the Kooskia Chamber of Commerce at 926-0855.

To enjoy Stanley Hot Springs, visitors must first take a 5.5-mile hike through the scenic wilderness. Many, however, feel the hike is well worth it to enjoy the serenity of the two warm pools situated in the lush forest. The marked trail to the hot springs departs from the Wilderness Gateway Campground.

16 *Food, Lodging*

Cottonwood
Pop. 944

In 1862, a man known as Mr. Allen opened a way station here that he constructed from the black cottonwood trees growing along the nearby creek. Soon, the outpost had grown to include a hotel, saloon, store, and a stage station entitled "The Cottonwood House." Although it was established during the gold rush, the settlement became known as a cattle round-up center and wasn't officially incorporated until 1901. In 1908, the railroad pulled into town, along with a devastating fire that first tore through the saloon before burning the post office and several other buildings to the ground. The fire created $250,000 in damages. However, using the single surviving building (the brick German State Bank) as a foundation, community residents rebuilt their town. Today, the quiet community is a gateway to area recreation and exploration.

Fenn
Pop. 40

Originally called Tharp, Fenn was renamed after Stephen S. Fenn and his son, Frank, in 1907

ANNUAL EVENTS

Lewiston Roundup

Saddle up for one of Idaho's biggest cowboy events! The Lewiston Roundup is held each September and represents the longest continuously running community event in Lewiston. Attracting the nation's top fifteen rodeo professionals, the PRCA event features a full weekend of competitions and is frequently televised nationally on ESPN.

Dogwood Festival

Every spring, the Lewiston landscape blossoms with the pink and white flowers of numerous dogwood trees. Celebrating the arrival of spring, Lewiston's Dogwood Festival includes ten days of garden tours, an arts and crafts fair, concessions, winetastings, concerts, a rodeo, a 10K fun run, and a classic car show.

Hot August Nights

Held in Pioneer Park, Lewiston's Hot August Nights memorializes the 1950's with over 400 vintage cars. River cruises and big time oldies performers highlight the event.

Lewis-Clark State College Artists Series

From June through September, Lewiston becomes a city of culture with the Lewis-Clark State College Artists Series. The series specializes in bringing touring theater, ballet, opera, and classical musical productions to the community.

NAIA World Series

The National Association of Intercollegiate Athletics (NAIA) selected Lewis-Clark State College's Harris Field as the location for the 1984-1991 World Series. Although the college lost its bid to the event for nine years, the World Series has returned to the area for the 2000-2006 season. The field seats a crowd of nearly 5,000, and advance tickets are highly recommended.

Cottonwood Rasberry Festival

Ripe summer raspberries are glorified at the Cottonwood Raspberry Festival. Held each August at St. Gertrude's Historical Museum, the event boasts raspberry concoctions as well as a quilt show, arts and crafts booths, a barbeque, and a vintage car show.

Grangeville Border Days

Also known as "Cut 'Em Loose," Grangeville Border Days is Idaho's oldest rodeo and continues to draw large crowds as it nears its Centennial Celebration. Held over the 4th of July weekend, the event features three days of parades, street vendors, fireworks, and barbeques, as well as street sports, an egg toss, a carnival, a community breakfast, a vintage car show, and the special Art in the Park show.

Lionel Hampton Jazz Festival

Recognized as the world's first jazz festival named after a jazz musician, the Lionel Hampton Jazz Festival has been a hit since its inception in February 1985. Hosted by the University of Idaho's Music School, the festival features Lionel Hampton along with many other big name jazz musicians. The four-day event includes concerts, clinics, and student competitions and has been named by the Los Angeles Times as the world's premier jazz festival. Tickets for the annual February event go on sale in early December, and advance reservations are strongly recommended.

Moscow Farmer's Market

Every Saturday morning from May to October, downtown Moscow bustles with activity. The Farmer's Market offers an array of wares from local farmers, artists, and crafters. In addition, the Market Music and Art Series is held in conjunction with the event. The Farmer's Market is open from 8 AM to 12 PM free of charge, unless of course you buy something!

Salmon River Jet Boat Races

Hosted by the Riggins and Whitebird communities, the annual Salmon River Jet Boat Races arrive in north-central Idaho each April. A world-class event drawing both regional and international competitors, the race provides one of the most technical courses available and represents the first leg of the U.S. Championships. The races conclude with a community BBQ and an awards ceremony.

Riggins Rodeo

The Riggins Rodeo has been bringing western fun to the community and surrounding region for over forty years. Held annually in May, the rodeo draws local cowboys and cowgirls as well as competitors from all across the western U.S.. Rodeo events include roping, bull riding, wild cow milking, barrel racing, and saddle bronc and bareback riding. The event also includes a community breakfast, parade, and dances.

White Bird Days & Rodeo

Held every June for more than 25 years, White Bird Days and Rodeo is packed with action. Rodeos, parades, a cowboy breakfast, a White Bird Battle reenactment, and games and booths downtown round out the weekend events.

White Bird Poker Trail Ride

The White Bird Poker Trail Ride offers individuals the opportunity to relive Idaho history while having some fun. Each May, horseback riders, horse-drawn wagons, and walkers gather together at the White Bird Battlefield Park for a history lesson and a game of poker. Significant historical points are marked on the trail relating pioneer and Native American history, and at each point, participants are given one playing card. Upon the tour's end, prizes are awarded to the individuals with the best poker hands.

Mat'Alyma Root Festival

Mat'Alyma Root Festival in Kamiah honors Nez Perce tradition. The festival includes a Pow Wow complete with full Native American dress, a royalty contest, and dancing contests.

Chief Lookingglass Days

Chief Lookingglass Days in Kamiah is a festive event for the whole family. The celebration includes an outdoor market, a fun run, arts and crafts booths, a parade, a friendship feast, and social and competitive dancing.

Clearwater County Fair & Orofino Lumberjack Days

The Clearwater County Fair and Lumberjack Days Celebration isn't just a standard small town fair. Instead, this event is one of the region's hottest, drawing U.S. and international competitors. In addition to lumberjack competitions, the weeklong event features parades, community breakfasts, an old-fashioned social and auction, truck driving, horse pulling, fun run, skidder contests, carnival rides, and a variety of concessions.

Clearwater Valley Frontier Music Festival

Held in the Kooskia City Park, the Clearwater Valley Frontier Music Festival is one of the regions finest musical events. The festival includes a narrated historical program featuring music, dancing, poetry, and vignettes relating the story of the American West.

Weippe Camas Festival

The two-day Weippe Camas Festival honors the significance of the Weippe Prairie to the Lewis and Clark Expedition and provides families with a weekend of history and traditional celebrations. Festivities include teepee raising, guest speakers, camas gathering, story telling, historical displays, music, food and craft booths, horseshoe tournaments, canoe digging, fun runs, and melodramas and reenactments. The festival is family-oriented and open to the public.

Elk River Fireworks in the Mountains

Although this small town boasts a steady population of less than 200 people, the town booms with excitement every Fourth of July. Nearly 2,500 people flock to Elk River each year for live music, concessions, and regionally renowned fireworks.

Kamiah Labor Day Weekend Celebration

Every Labor Day Weekend, Kamiah bursts with three days of fun and excitement. The event features a spaghetti feed, football game, cowboy breakfast, street sports, fun run, all school reunion, parade, quilt show, historical displays, sidewalk fair, beer garden, a free community barbeque, dancing, a motocross race, and various live entertainment.

Kamiah Christmas Lighting Festival

The Western/Victorian facades of Kamiah's downtown district come to life with holiday cheer at the community lighting festival. The weekend event features caroling, a lighted parade, goodies, and Santa Claus.

Mardi Gras & Beaux Arts Ball

Held annually in March regardless of it being Mardi Gras or not, Moscow's Mardi Gras and Beaux Arts Ball comes to town for the weekend. The event features a parade and several live bands.

Renaissance Fair

Step into history at Moscow's annual Renaissance Fair. Held each May when spring awakens, the fair features Renaissance style events and dress for the whole community.

Rendezvous in the Park

Moscow's Rendezvous in the Park is a favorite of both locals and visitors. Held each summer in East City Park, the event features children's activities along with a variety of musical styles and bands.

Hot Summer Nights

Held annually on the last weekend of July, Riggins' Hot Summer Nights remembers the 1950s and 1960s. The annual event features a classic car show, food, vendors, and more.

Big Water Blowout & River Festival

During the first weekend of June, Riggins celebrates spring at the Big Water Blowout & River Festival. Regional outfitters gather to offer eager crowds whitewater fun. Experienced boaters are encouraged to bring their own equipment, and vendors, live music, and a Dutch Oven cook-off round out the entertainment.

when the first Camas Prairie Railroad Depot was established here. During his life, Stephen was a prosecuting attorney for Idaho County, a delegate to Congress (1874-1876), and a soldier in the Indian War of 1877. Frank Fenn possessed an equally impressive resume. He attended Whitman Academy in Walla Walla, Washington, and entered the U.S. Naval Academy, from which he was expelled in 1872 for hazing a fellow student. Frank later became a Fairfield school teacher and eventually married one of his students. He fought in the Nez Perce War and volunteered for the Spanish-American War, where he attained the rank of Major. In the middle of all that, Frank was postmaster at Mount Idaho, a lawyer in Boise from 1890-1901, and state chairman for the Republican Party. From 1903 to 1920, Frank Fenn served as superintendent for all of the National Forest Reserves in northern Idaho, as well as thirteen reserves in Montana. He later returned to Kooskia and helped his son run a newspaper. Frank died in 1927, but the legend of the two men live on to this day.

Keuterville
Pop. 40

Four Catholic families migrating from Kansas settled this tiny town in 1883. Upon arriving, they immediately started a fund in order to build a church. One of the settlers placed an ad in a St. Louis paper praising the new Catholic settlement. This attracted Henry Kuther, who built the first store and applied for a community post office. Bearing no sons at the time, Henry wanted the town named Kutherville in order to preserve his name; however, the post office misread the postal application and the spelling was forever altered. Luckily for Henry, he later went on to father two sons.

In 1911 a fire destroyed the town church, but it was quickly rebuilt the following year and sustained its role as the community center for numerous years. During the community's first five years of existence, most residents were German, so the town's business and church services were conducted completely in German. This language situation has since changed, but the town retains its distinction as the third oldest settlement on the Camas Prairie.

Greencreek
Pop. 50

Named after Greencreek, Illinois, this small community is rooted in agriculture. Several of the area's first homesteaders had emigrated westward from Illinois; thus, they found it only fitting to honor their past in their new settlement.

H Nez Perce War
Milepost 252.9 on U.S. Hwy. 95

A Gatling gun, firing from the top of a low hill a mile northwest of here, beat off a Nez Perce attack, July 4, 1877.

The next day, Indians just east of here surrounded 17 Mount Idaho volunteers: two were killed and three wounded before cavalrymen from Cottonwood came out to rescue them. Meanwhile, Chief Joseph's people, screened this well-planned diversionary skirmish, crossed the prairie to join their allies on the Clearwater. From there, the Indians retired across the mountains to Montana, where the Nez Perce War ended three months later.

H Lewis and Clark
Milepost 252.9 on U.S. Hwy. 95

On May 31, 1806, Sgt. John Ordway and Pvts. Frazer and Weiser began the return trip from Lewis' River (Snake River) with salmon for Camp Chopunnish (Kamiah).

The men crossed the Camas Prairie near here on their way to rejoin the Corps of Discovery, waiting in Camp Chopunnish for mountain snows to recede before attempting to cross the Bitterroots. At about noon on June 2, the small group arrived with seventeen salmon and some roots they had purchased. Most of the fish were spoiled, but Lewis described those that were sound as "extremely delicious."

H Railroad Trestles
Milepost 268.6 on U.S. Hwy. 95

In order to cross Lawyer's Canyon and other Camas Prairie gorges, a series of high railroad bridges was built in 1908.

This highway goes past two of them here. Most were timber, but a metal structure, 1,500 feet long and 296 feet high, was needed here. A long, high wooden trestle also crossed a nearby side canyon. North Idaho's Camas Prairie Railroad – a joint Northern Pacific and Union Pacific venture – served this region for eight decades.

H Lawyer's Canyon
Milepost 268.6 on U.S. Hwy. 95 between Craigmont and Ferdinand

Named for the Nez Perce Indian leader who served as head chief, 1848-71, and who lived near the lower end of the canyon.

Called "The Lawyer" by early fur traders for his exceptional talents in languages and oratory, he was a friend of the whites. He had learned English before the missionaries came in 1836 and helped them prepare dictionaries and translate the Bible into Nez Perce. He played an important part in all the treaties negotiated with his people before his death in 1876, a year before the Nez Perce war.

H Lewis and Clark
Milepost 268.6 on U.S. Hwy. 95

On May 27, 1806, Sgt. John Ordway and Pvts. Frazer and Weiser were dispatched from Camp Chopunnish (Kamiah) to Lewis' River (Snake River) to obtain salmon.

Guided by Nez Perce Indians, the men crossed the Camas Prairie near here. On May 29, at a Salmon River Indian village, Frazer traded an "old razer" to an Indian woman for two Spanish mill dollars. They reached the Snake River after descending "the worst hills we ever saw a road make down." They were welcomed by Nez Perce and purchased a number of salmon.

H Camas Prairie
Milepost 10.6 on State Hwy. 162

Most of Camas Prairie's wind-blown soil rests upon Columbia River lava flows. Coming from a series of widespread eruptions, they covered older, eroded granite rocks here about six million to 17 million years ago.

Some earlier volcanic extrusions, including the Kamiah Buttes (between which this highway passes), rise above those Camas Prairie lava flows. Perhaps older than 40 million years, they resemble volcanic rocks from Challis, in south-central Idaho, rather than newer lava from farther west. Geologists still are studying how these buttes are related to similar formations elsewhere in Idaho.

T St. Gertrude's Monastery and Museum
Keuterville Road, 2 miles southwest of Cottonwood. 962-3224 or 962-7123.
www.historicalmuseumatstgertrude.com

Striking 97-foot twin towers rise sharply to the sky from the St. Gertrude Monastery. Constructed out of locally quarried stone, the Romanesque convent and priory was built in the 1920s for the Benedictine Sisters and is now home to both male and female monks. The chapel is a popular destination as visitors marvel at the complex, hand-carved alter built without a single nail. Adjoining the monastery is an informative 7,200 square foot museum. Housing more than 70,000 artifacts, the museum displays approximately 12,000 items at any one time including pioneer and mining relics, a mineral collection, handcrafted mountain man utensils, Oriental art, Native American and local history, religious artifacts, and personal collections from early nuns at the monastery. The museum is open 9:30 AM to 4:30 PM Tuesday through Saturday and 1:30 PM to 4:30 PM on Sundays May through September. From October to April, museum hours are 9:30 AM to 4:30 PM Tuesday through Saturday. Admission is $4 for adults, $1 for youth ages 7-17, and free for children age 6 and under. Special group rates are available.

T Tri-State Uplands
Between Grangeville and Lewiston on U.S. Hwy. 95

Geologists dubbed Tri-State Uplands after its gently rolling hills rising from 3,000 to 5,000 feet.

SADDLING INTO HISTORY

Ray Holes' Saddle Shop resides in Grangeville and is one of the most acclaimed in the West. It is the oldest saddle shop in Idaho that has operated under the same name since its conception. Ray Holes was born in Washington State in 1911, and was afflicted by polio as a toddler. He moved to Idaho as a teenager and turned to horsemanship, soon becoming an admirable wrangler despite his disability. After school, Ray worked in a shoe shop and did leather work by hand. He began accepting ranch repair work, fixing everything from boots to bridles – anything leather. Soon he was making his own harnesses, chaps, halters and gun scabbards. In 1933, Ray's real forte was revealed when a cowboy brought him a saddle to repair. With all the repairs made to the saddle, Ray figured it would have been easier to build one, so he did. After some trial and error, Ray succeeded. He had the saddle tested by a cowboy at a round-up and soon obtained his first saddle order.

Ray desired to be the best saddle-maker in the area, but to accomplish that, Ray needed more experience and knowledge about his chosen craft. He traveled the Rockies and Canada in search of those who could teach him what he longed to know. Upon his return to Grangeville in 1936, Ray had his knowledge and standards: durability, beauty and comfort. He made his own laminated tree forks and a modified extra-deep, semi-flat saddletree bar. He also invented a type of free-swinging stirrup leathers that appealed to the Idaho backcountry cowboys. The leather was stamped with a flower pattern that gave the saddles the beauty he was after. Soon, Ray's saddles were a coveted possession by the locals. After retiring in 1972, Ray's son, Jerry Holes, took over the business. Approximately seventy custom riding saddles and one hundred fifty pack saddles are produced yearly for folks across the nation and across the seas. There is, however, about a year's wait for a custom saddle.

Columbia River basalt lava flows measuring 2,000 to 3,000 feet thick produced down-warping in the area responsible for the plateau's current shaping. Today, the area is still lined with faults from ancient lava activity.

T Idaho County Farm and Ranch Museum
Cottonwood Fairgrounds. Contact the Cottonwood Chamber of Commerce at 962-3231.

During fair week each summer, the Idaho County Fairgrounds not only come to life with traditional fair activities, but it also hosts the annual Farm and Ranch Museum. Each Wednesday through

Saturday during the fair, visitors have a chance to view antique farm equipment and machinery used in developing the region's agricultural legacy.

The Cottonwood Lions Club assembled the collection in 1967 which includes an 1887 stationary threshing machine and a 1916 Harvester among other valuable items. The collection has been donated to all people residing in Idaho County.

T Dog Bark Park
U.S. Hwy. 95 near Cottonwood. 983-DOGS.

Dog Bark Park provides an interesting break from driving as it hosts the world's largest beagles. Created by Dennis Sullivan and Frances Conklin, Toby and Sweet Willy Colton are larger than life beagle replicas that measure in at nearly thirty feet tall. The park also boasts picnic tables and chainsaw carvings of bears, wolves, moose, and other animals found in Idaho's wildest places.

T Weis Rock Shelter
Travel south from Cottonwood to a signed county road, bear west, and continue to the rock shelter located on the road's right side. Contact the Cottonwood Chamber of Commerce at 962-3231.

During the summers of 1961 to 1965, archaeologists worked painstakingly in north-central Idaho to investigate possible sites of ancient human activity. The archaeologists found what they were looking for when they discovered several rock shelters along Graves and Rock Creeks. Artifacts, including arrowheads, suggested that ancestors of the Nez Perce cultural tradition thrived in the area from 8,000 to 12,000 years ago. One of these ancient rock shelters/dwellings is visible today tucked around a rock face outside Cottonwood.

T Cottonwood Butte
Keuterville off U.S. Hwy. 95

Cottonwood Butte rises 5,732 against the Keuterville landscape and is a local landmark.

V Cottonwood Butte Ski Area
7 miles west of Cottonwood off U.S. Hwy. 95. 962-3624 or 743-6397.

Cottonwood Butte Ski Area was established in 1967 and offers a full service, family-oriented ski hill. Excellent views of the Camas Prairie can be found on the area's four major runs and several side trails. A 3,000-foot long T-Bar and one rope tow services skiers from beginner to advanced, and the area features an 845-foot vertical drop. Lessons, equipment rentals, snowmobiling, and cross-country skiing are all available, while summer months offer trails for mountain biking and

hiking. Cottonwood's ski season generally runs from mid-December through mid-March depending on trail conditions.

M Cottonwood Chamber of Commerce
506 King Ave., Cottonwood. 962-3231.

17

Clearwater
Pop. 35

The name Clearwater was first attributed to the river, then the town. The name supposedly is the translation of the Nez Perce word, "Kook-Koos-Kai-Kai," which is a traditional Native American adjective used to describe clear water. The community is situated at the headwaters of Clear Creek, and Clearwater's post office was established in 1872.

Mount Idaho
Pop. 75

Established at the foot of the mountain that serves as its namesake, Mount Idaho became the first settlement along the road between Lewiston and the Florence mines. The town's first postmaster, Loyal P. Brown, was responsible for naming the town in 1862, and postal services were active in the area from 1863 to 1922. Although the town was named Idaho County seat in 1865, the designation was later transferred to the larger and more prosperous Grangeville settlement in 1902.

Stites
Pop. 226

White settlers are relatively new to this Idaho area originally limited to Nez Perce Indian tribes until 1895. Even after the reservation was opened up for exploration and purchase, it took two years before a white settler staked a claim. As the first non-native to the area in 1897, New Jersey emigrant Jacob Stites homesteaded a quarter section of land. Under pressure to sell in 1900, Stites sold 60 acres to a land developer with the understanding that he could name the new settlement. By late 1900, the site bearing Stites' name was a growing community that also boasted an area post office. The town later became a stopping point for the Clearwater Branch of the Camas Prairie Railroad and aided in shipping timber from the Meadow Creek area.

H Mount Idaho
Milepost 1.1 on State Hwy. 13 3 miles southeast of Grangeville at Mount Idaho

In 1862, a noted Western scout, Mose Milner, started Mount Idaho on his gold rush trail to Florence. Camas Prairie's major early town soon grew up here.

But when civic leaders resisted a farm effort to organize a grange there in 1874, Grangeville grew up as a better-located town. Although Mount Idaho became county seat from 1875 to 1902 and had an important Chinese community, Grangeville soon surpassed its older rival. Most of its early buildings have disappeared.

Grangeville													
	Jan	Feb	March	April	May	June	July	Aug	Sep	Oct	Nov	Dec	Annual
Average Max. Temperature (F)	36.8	42.3	48.3	56.1	64.0	71.5	81.7	81.8	72.0	59.1	44.7	37.9	58.0
Average Min. Temperature (F)	21.3	24.5	27.7	32.9	39.4	45.7	50.5	49.7	42.3	34.7	27.9	22.6	34.9
Average Total Precipitation (in.)	1.57	1.29	2.18	2.76	3.43	2.86	1.27	1.16	1.69	1.90	1.81	1.57	23.51
Average Total Snowfall (in.)	10.8	7.3	8.5	3.3	0.4	0.0	0.0	0.0	0.0	1.2	5.9	11.2	48.7
Average Snow Depth (in.)	3	2	1	0	0	0	0	0	0	0	1	2	1

H Nez Perce War
Milepost 21.2 on State Hwy. 13

After the Clearwater battle on the heights above here, July 11-12, 1877, the Indians crossed the Lolo Trail to Montana.

Advancing northward along the high ground with 600 troops and artillery, General O. O. Howard found the Indian camp on the flat across the river. But 24 brave Indians blocked his advance and 100 more pinned him in rifle pits for a day. Then the Indians, camp and all, moved slowly northward past Kamiah, while Howard followed without fighting. There the Indians decided to move east away from the troops.

T Harpster

This former town was originally known as both Bridgeport and Brownsville. In the 1860s, William Jackson established a Clearwater River stage station and toll bridge, subsequently naming his tiny settlement Bridgeport. A fire decimated the area during the 1877 Nez Perce War, and Jackson left the area disheartened.

Loyal Brown became the next landowner, eventually selling eighy of his acres to the Clearwater Mining Company in 1893. In Brown's honor, the company mapped out a townsite named Brownsville. When postal services were acquired in 1895, the name changed to Harpster. The name memorializes the life of gold rush era pioneer, Abraham Harpster, who died in the area in 1891.

T Clearwater Battlefield Sites
1 mile south of Stites on State Hwy. 13

Marked by basalt bluffs, the Clearwater Battlefield Site represents one of the fiercest battles of the Nez Perce War. From the top of these bluffs, General Oliver O. Howard attempted to spring a surprise attack on the Nez Perce. Although Howard and his 600 soldiers lobbied cannonball after cannonball against the Nez Perce, twenty-four warriors encamped below the bluffs at the mouth of Cottonwood Creek were able to stay off the attack. As soon as more Nez Perce warriors arrived on the scene, it was clear to Howard that his mission would fail. As the warriors fought bravely against the soldiers, the rest of the encamped Nez Perce were able to withdraw towards present-day Kamiah.

18 *Food, Lodging*

Grangeville
Pop. 3,228

Serving as the seat of Idaho County, Grangeville's first record of habitation dates back to the flood of miners entering the area during the Pierce gold rush. The town's official establishment, however, dates back to the 1863 arrival of cattlemen, Aurora Shumway and John Crooks. Settling on Three Mile Creek, the gentlemen remained in the area even when all the miners left and the area showed little potential for the development of a thriving community. Forming alliances with other

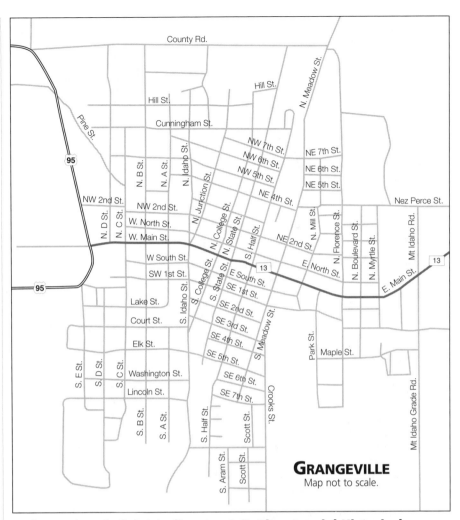

GRANGEVILLE
Map not to scale.

area homesteaders and with the help of Lapwai missionary, Hart Spalding, the men helped organize Charity Grange No. 15 in 1874. Crooks willingly donated land for a building site for the fraternal order, hoping that the construction would spur future growth. Crooks' plan worked, and Grange Hall led to the development of this community. In 1876, a post office was established, as was a flourmill and gristmill. The hall served as a community events center for many years and, enclosed by a stockade, provided a sanctuary and temporary hospital site during the Nez Perce War.

Since then, Crooks' hope for the future has proved itself over and over. Grangeville continues to thrive to this day despite disastrous fires and floods that ripped through town during the early twentieth century.

H Camas Prairie
Milepost 233.6 on U.S. Hwy. 95

Named for the Blue Flowering Camas – an important root food for all interior Northwestern Indians – the Camas prairie is a traditional Nez Perce cultural center.

Tolo Lake – visible below – provided a campground for Chief Joseph's Wallowa band and White Bird's Salmon River band when war broke out on the Salmon River directly south of here, June 14,1877. Both of these bands were under military pressure to settle on the Camas Prairie when three young men from White Bird's band avenged a long series of past wrongs and Army authorities retaliated.

T Bicentennial Historical Museum
305 N. College, Grangeville. 983-2573.

The Bicentennial Historical Museum's mission is to collect and display any artifact related to Idaho County's history. Among the exhibits, visitors will find a permanent mining display as well as several Nez Perce Indian artifacts. The museum is open June 1 through September 30th from 1 PM to 5 PM on Wednesday and Friday afternoons with free admission.

T Smoke Jumpers Base
Grangeville Air Center, Grangeville. 983-1964.

Grangeville is home to a U.S. Forest Service Smoke Jumpers Base. Every June through September, Idaho smokejumpers are available for forest fire assistance across the American West. With only a few bases located in the northern Rockies, the Grangeville base provides visitors with the chance to tour a unique facet of American forest fire fighting. The base also features an air tanker capable of holding 2,000 gallons of fire retardant and a fire management helicopter. Tours are available by advance request.

T Grangeville Mammoth House
Eimers Park on the west side of Grangeville off U.S. Hwy. 95. Contact the Grangeville Chamber of Commerce at 983-0460.

The Grangeville Mammoth House takes visitors back in time to the age of dinosaurs with a displayed 14-foot tall Columbian mammoth. The resin replica reflects the mammoth skeleton unearthed in 1995 at nearby Tolo Lake. The mammoth is believed to

GHOST TOWNS

Moose City
Clearwater County; nine miles from the Idaho-Montana state border

Found in the dense forests of Idaho, few buildings remain standing at Moose City. Gold Rush fever brought thousands of miners to the area in 1862 and the population exploded to 9,000 inhabitants. Word about the community spread and in 1868, a new wave of hopefuls moved into the community. However, the rush was a hoax, and several miners abandoned the community after this event and another false rush in February 1869.

Despite frequent supply shortages due to heavy winter snows that hampered the ability of supply wagons to reach Moose City, several Chinese immigrants remained in the area and reportedly continued to mine until 1880.

Slaterville
35 miles west of Pierce near the mouth of the North Fork Clearwater River

Slaterville's origins began with Seth S. Slater, a gold miner who like others discovered gold in the surrounding area. Although Slaterville is not historically known as a prominent Idaho gold mining town, it is recognized as one of the first communities in Idaho. Settled in 1861, the town eventually grew to include two wood houses, five canvas dwellings, and one saloon. Seth Slater eventually left his namesake town and moved to Lewiston where he opened and operated the first Lewiston store.

Buffalo Hump
32 miles southeast of Grangeville near the Continental Divide

In this area, granite rises to an elevation of 8,926 feet, forming a mountain peak resembling a buffalo's hump. Several historians speculate that miners saw this prominent landmark and dubbed their new community with this name. Others suggest that Native Americans in the area called the natural feature "See-nimp," which can be translated into "buffalo hump." In either case, Buffalo Hump has a vague history. It is known that gold quartz deposits were known to exist in the area as early as 1894. However, the first reported find did not occur until August 8, 1898, which sparked a rush to Buffalo Hump the following winter. By spring 1899, more than 500 people occupied the area, and the dawn of the twentieth century marked prosperity for the community. During the summer of 1900, the town claimed two hotels, five saloons, a livery barn, and several mining tents.

From this point, Buffalo Hump's history becomes more rumor than fact. Some writers suggest that Buffalo Hump incorporated mills that ran until 1915. Others suggest that by 1913, most of the city's businesses and residences had been destroyed in a fire. Still, hope remains in this Idaho area that more riches will be found and Buffalo Hump (known as Humptown to local historians) will again prosper in the future.

Collender
17 miles southwest of Elk City

Collender's (or Calender or Callender) history began in 1900 when the small mining community was officially named after New York prospector Thomas O. Collender. Previously, area miners called the settlement "Hill's Camp." With a new name, the town grew quickly and included a hospital, company store, and a bank. The bank was especially important in Collender's economic success as it was responsible for 400 to 500 men's payrolls from the Big Buffalo and Kerrimack mines. Although the town prospered for a couple years, little is known of the town's history after a 1903 fire destroyed most of Collender.

Midas
Southeast from Grangeville near Dixie

Also known as Midasville, Midas sprang up near the gold rush town of Dixie. Several settlers came to the town when the Ajax mine was built, but as with many other ghost towns, all the residents left when the mine closed.

Freedom
32 miles south of Mount Idaho

Freedom was originally known as "Slate Creek" to settlers in 1861 after the creek running in the area was found containing no placer gravel. Eventually, when Charles H. Wood established the first post office on April 5, 1880, the name was changed to Freedom. Several stories are told concerning the town's namesake. Some historians suggest the community was named after Josh Freedom who was a member of the First Territorial Democratic Convention. Others argue that early miner, Josh Fockler, named the community after the Civil War's freeing of slaves.

Freedom was filled with miners, and other individuals used the community to winter pack trains and cattle. Freedom also claimed rights to the first house built on the Salmon River when Charles Silverman bought land from an area Native American, Captain John. During 1875, the town was so popular that it was considered as a candidate for Idaho County seat. However, Freedom lost this opportunity, and the town soon dwindled in size.

Newsome
24 miles east of Grangeville

Situated near Newsome Creek that empties into the South Fork of the Clearwater River, Newsome was born in 1861 when John Newsome discovered gold along this creek. Along with other early settlers, John Newsome prospered in his digs along Newsome Creek and its tributaries. By 1862, structures were being built in the town, and it appeared that the community would enjoy a long and stable life. But by 1867, many of the settlers' luck had changed, and the town appeared to die.

Newsome saw a rebirth of activity in 1895 when more placer gold was discovered. During World War I to the start of World War II, quartz mining was prevalent in the area, and there was great hope that Newsome would yet prosper. However, these second mining efforts netted only a small $2 million production, and the town eventually disappeared into history.

Pardee
Near upper Clearwater River

Alfred Day Pardee, a Philadelphia capitalist and Pennsylvania coal investor, turned his sights westward in the early 1900's as he began investing in Idaho mining areas near the Clearwater River. The town bearing his name was plotted approximately March 1, 1902, and miners soon arrived to explore a new area of possible wealth. A year later on April 20th, 1902, Pardee was officially established as an Idaho community, and mining continued in the area for several years. Alfred Pardee never visited his namesake town, spending most of his time in France until his 1942 death. Little else is known about the town's history after this date.

Denver
4 miles northeast of Fenn off U.S. Hwy. 95 From the Fenn community store, drive north 1 mile before bearing east at the "L." Continue 1 mile, turn north at "T" and proceed 1.5 miles, and finally bear east 1 mile to the "Y."

Members of the Camas Prairie Land and Town Company plotted the new town of Denver in 1892 on 640 acres. The town quickly emerged as an industry leader in flour production, selling its Prairie Rose flour as far north as Alaska in 1898. This flourmill continued to operate until the 1950s, but when the railroad arrived in Fenn, Denver withered away. The community's buildings and citizens moved to nearby Fenn, and all that remains today is the historic cemetery.

Concord
2 miles south of historic Buffalo Hump; approximately 34 miles southeast of Grangeville

Established in 1899, Concord saw little growth as a prosperous Idaho community, and by 1900, only ten individuals called it home. The town eventually grew to include a hotel, butcher shop, examiner's office, and a few houses, but mining in the area halted at the start of World War II.

Florence
6 miles north of Riggins in Idaho County

John Healy, James Ayers, Lemuel Grigsby, and Hull Rice first discovered placer gold in the area on August 19, 1861 after prospecting for more than two months. Although the men intended to keep their findings a secret, word soon leaked of the new placer gold. More than 350 men were working the area by November, earning as much as $100 a day. Despite harsh winter conditions and a lack of supplies that made the camp undesirable, the miners' held a meeting in late November to map out a new town. Dr. George Furber suggested the town be named Florence in honor of his daughter who lived in California. The name was approved, and by summer 1862, Florence was a booming mine town with more than 10,000 residents. Only one-third of the residents, however, met with any success, and lawlessness plagued the town. Murderers, robbers, and members of the Henry Plummer gang frequented the area, and resident brawls were a common occurrence between Northern and Southern sympathizers of the Civil War. Such injustice has led to one of the most interesting graveyards in Idaho. Residents deemed as moral and just were buried in an east-west direction, while "bad guys" were laid to rest in a north-south direction. Despite a loose legal system, Florence's mine production carried on, and altogether, Florence produced nearly $10 million in gold.

have roamed the area around Grangeville over 11,000 years ago. Today, the Mammoth House provides information about this era in history, along with detailed insight into the mammoth excavation process.

T Grangeville Historical Tour
Contact the Grangeville Chamber of Commerce at 983-0460.

With roots extending back to the 1860s and 1870s, Grangeville has a long history reflected in a few historic buildings still lining the town's main streets.

Grangeville Savings & Trust
Main & State Streets
Lewiston architect, James Nave, designed this unique store that is a commodity within the state of Idaho. The store was erected in 1909 to house the J. C. Penney store. The building retains its original tin ceilings, making it a historic landmark.

First Security Bank
Main & Meadow Streets
The stately First Security bank features an impressive grandfather clock dating back to 1822. Housed in the bank's lobby, the clock measures eleven feet by four feet and reached Grangeville in the mid 1930s.

Alexander & Freidenrich (A & F) Building
Main Street
The Alexander & Freidenrich Clothing Store has operated in Grangeville since the 1870s. The store initially occupied a room in the Charity Grange Hall before moving to a newly framed building in 1879. The clothing store ranks as Idaho's second oldest continuously operating business.

TV Tolo Lake
6 miles west of Grangeville on U.S. Hwy. 95. Contact the Grangeville Chamber of Commerce at 983-0460.

Named after a brave nineteenth-century Nez Perce woman, the forty-acre Tolo Lake is a year-round recreational favorite. In its history, Tolo Lake served as an ice skating rink for Idaho's earliest white settlers. Today, the lake is annually stocked with rainbow trout, bluegill, crappie, and large-mouth bass. The lake also features a boat ramp for non-motorized boats and was the site of a 1995 mammoth dig.

V Snowhaven Ski Area
7 miles south of Grangeville on the Grangeville-Salmon Rd. (Forest Rd. 221). 983-2851.

Nestled on the western edge of the Central Idaho Mountains, Snowhaven Ski Area overlooks Camas Prairie, the Nez Perce National Forest, and the Gospel Hump Wilderness. As a non-profit, city-owned facility, Snowhaven specializes in offering affordable lift tickets for the whole family. The area includes forty acres of ski terrain for beginning and experienced skiers, and features a T-bar, bunny hill, rope tow, night skiing, tubing, and snowboarding. Rentals and lessons are available in the ski shop, and a day lodge offers skiers a place to warm up after spending a day on the slopes. Snowhaven Ski Area is generally open from mid-December to mid-March.

V Fish Creek Meadows
9 miles south of Grangeville on Forest Rd. 221 (Grangeville-Salmon Rd.). Contact the Idaho Department of Parks and Recreation at 334-4199.

Fish Creek Meadows offers Nordic skiers twelve miles of beginner and intermediate trails near the Gospel Hump Wilderness. Although the trails are only groomed once a week, the area's panoramic views are well worth a Nordic trip. The area is part of Idaho's Park N' Ski system, and permits are

required. Permits may be obtained at the nearest Ranger Station, and fees are as follows: $25 annual permit (good at all Idaho Park N' Ski areas), $7.50 3-day permit, and $2 day use permit.

During the summer and fall, the cross-country ski trails double as popular mountain biking, hiking, and horseback riding paths. The scenic area is popular year round, abounding with huckleberries during August.

M Grangeville Chamber of Commerce
Hwy 95 at Pine St., Grangeville. 983-0460. www.grangevilleidaho.com

19 *Food, Lodging*

Dixie
Pop. 10

Although a couple miners discovered gold in Dixie Gulch on August 24, 1862, it wasn't until 1867 that the site caught on with other miners. Even then, no claims were filed until 1884, and it took sixteen more years for Dixie to become a boomtown. The settlement was named for an early prospector, likely someone who emigrated from the South. Eventually, the town produced over $500,000 in gold, but it still didn't catch up with modern society until it received telephone and power lines in 1980. Today, Dixie is home to just a few people year-round but is known for its serene isolation and good snowmobiling in winter months.

Elk City
Pop. 450

Nestled on the edge of a scenic meadow, Elk City holds the distinction as Idaho County's oldest mining town. Upon violating federal law and a previous arrangement with the Nez Perce, fifty-two prospectors explored the South Fork of the Clearwater River. When they discovered gold in August 1861, Elk City became an overnight success. After just three weeks, the town's population swelled to nearly 1,000 with twenty-five buildings already constructed. By 1866, the mines had produced over $3.6 million in gold.

As with many Idaho mining camps, Chinese immigrants swarmed to the area. In 1888 there were 400 Chinese settlers in town, and at one time, there were over 1,400 Chinese and only a dozen white folks in town. The Chinese people were hired to work the claims, but by the late 1880s, discrimination against and mistreatment of the Chinese occured so frequently they had to hire themselves white guards to watch over them while they worked. In 1887, a judge ruled that aliens could not possess mining claims under newly established U.S. mining laws. The alienation laws worked as the discriminating judge had hoped, and several Chinese made a mass exodus.

In 1902, mining began for quartz lode with total production estimated at nearly $5 million. Dredging began in 1935 and raked in nearly $1 million. Today, Elk City supplies hikers, campers, equestrians, and snowmobilers with backcountry necessities.

Idaho Trivia
Lining the Snake River in Idaho and Washington, Hells Canyon is recognized as one of the two deepest gorges in all of North America. Commercial rafting and powerboat tours offer visitors the chance to glimpse the spectacular canyon up close.

Golden
Pop. 50

The settlement of Golden came into existence when mining claims were staked in the area. Originally called Ten Mile Cabin, the town's name was later changed as a reflection of the gold mined there. In addition to its mining activities, the town used to serve as an ideal overnight stop for travelers passing between Grangeville and Elk City. The old mine, which is located approximately one mile below the settlement, remained busy with activity through the 1930s.

Orogrande
Pop. 10

Although Orogrande was placer mined for several years prior to its official founding, it wasn't until 1899 that the small community began to draw permanent settlers. Upon its founding, the town became a hub of trading activity for those working and living in the Buffalo Hump Mining District. The mining boom was short-lived, however, and the remote town's population quickly declined upon the lapse of significant mining claims in 1913. A post office operated in this near ghost town from 1900 to 1934.

H Buffalo Pit
Milepost 47.1 on State Hwy. 14

An exceptionally large hydraulic pit, left by massive placer mining in this area, still can be seen one mile from here.

Buffalo Company miners using hydraulic giants — large metals hoses with nozzles that could direct a stream of water under high pressure — cut away a large hillside deposit of placer gold. Long ditches and flumes were employed to bring water in at an elevation sufficient to gain pressure enough to operate their giants.

H Elk City
Milepost 49.4 on State Hwy. 14

Twenty-two prospectors from Pierce discovered the Elk City mines in May 1861, and a gold rush followed that summer.

Through July, the houses were "nice and airy, being constructed of brush," with bars for doors "to keep out the cayuse horses." Permanent log buildings were begun August 6, and within a month about 40 stores, saloons, and cabins were ready for winter use. Most of the miners rushed off to other new bonanzas that fall, but Elk City still became one of the important Idaho gold camps.

H Nez Perce Trail
Milepost 49.4 on State Hwy. 14

An old Indian trail connected Elk City with mines in Montana when Idaho's gold rush spread there in 1862.

Following a route developed by Nez Perce buffalo hunters, a host of miners and packers ascended a series of ridges overlooking the deep Salmon and Clearwater river canyons on their way to new gold fields. Long after local Indians and miners ceased to travel there, a single-lane forest road was constructed near that traditional Nez Perce thoroughfare in 1934.

T Crooked River Rearing Facility Tours
Near the mining ghost town of Orogrande, 476-3331. Merge off State Hwy. 14 onto the gravel Forest Service Rd. #233 (Orogrande Road), and travel 11 miles to the facility.

Nestled in Idaho's isolated wilderness country, the Crooked River Rearing Facility is a satellite station of the larger Clearwater Fish Hatchery located in

Continud on page 151

LEWIS & CLARK AND THE NATIVE PEOPLE

The Corps Of Discovery Through Idaho's Native American Homeland, 1805-1806

In 1803, President Thomas Jefferson commissioned Meriwether Lewis and William Clark to find "the most direct and practicable water communication across this continent, for the purposes of commerce." When the Corps of Discovery departed St. Louis in May, 1804, they party destined to cross the continent consisted of Captains Lewis and Clark, 26 volunteers and Army regulars, Clark's black slave York, and Lewis' Newfoundland dog, Seaman. This military unit of experienced outdoorsmen followed the Missouri River through today's Missouri, Kansas, Iowa, Nebraska, South Dakota, and North Dakota, where they built Fort Mandan, north of present Bismarck, and spent the winter of 1804-05.

While visiting nearby Hidatsa and Mandan villages, the captains hired French trader Toussaint Charbonneau as interpreter and guide. Charbonneau's young Lemhi Shoshoni wife, Sacajawea, and their infant son, Jean Baptiste, would prove to be an asset to the expedition in present-day Idaho. Not only were her language skills helpful, but also native peoples were less suspicious of white men traveling with a native woman and child.

By mid-August 1805, their travels brought them to Three Forks, Montana, headwaters of the Missouri River. From there on, they needed horses to make what they thought would be an easy portage across the Rocky Mountains to the navigable headwaters of the Columbia.

They were beyond the western border of the Louisiana Purchase and for the first time entering land about which they had no knowledge. It was the homeland of the Lemhi Shoshoni, Salish, and Nez Perce people, a land of ancient cultures with networks of travel and trade that spanned thousands of years and stretched from plains to mountains to ocean. A land that nurtured sophisticated societies with resources aplenty, where family was foremost and the elderly were valued. A homeland where oral histories recorded the hospitality of these tribes toward the strangers in their midst.

Expedition members had no idea how they would be received, but realized with each passing mile that their success would depend upon native good will. They knew that rivers flowed westward from the Continental Divide toward the Pacific Ocean, but their hopes of an easy portage over this barrier were thwarted by the realities of the Rocky Mountains, a series of one mountain chain after another. Even with native assistance, for members of the Corps of Discovery, this search for a "Northwest Passage" would prove to be the most difficult part of their entire journey.

Sites Along Lewis & Clark's Journey

1) Packer Meadows – Interpretive Sign, 1 mile east of Lolo Pass Visitor Center on Forest Road 373

2) Lolo Pass Visitor Center – U.S. Hwy. 12 at the ID/MT border, elevation 5,235 feet. (208) 942-3113.

3) DeVoto Memorial Cedar Grove – 3 miles east of Powell Ranger Station. Bernard DeVoto, Lewis & Clark journal editor, came here to meditate and write in the 1950s. Picnic tables, restrooms, and hiking trail.

4) Powell Ranger Station – 13 miles west of Lolo Pass on U.S. Hwy. 12. A sign nearby identifies the campsite of September 14, 1805, where the party was "compelled to kill a Colt...for the want of meat..." (208) 942-3113.

5) Colgate Licks National Recreation Trail – Rest stop offers toilet facilities and a 1.25-mile interpretive trail.

6) Lochsa Historical Ranger Station – Built in the 1920s, offers the visitor a glimpse of life at a backcountry Forest Service ranger station. Log buildings are outfitted with period furnishings, and volunteers provide a sense of living history. The station is open Memorial Day through Labor Day. (208) 926-2474.

7) Fenn Ranger Station – Built in the late 1930s by the Civilian Conservation Corps, is 5 miles from Lowell, a community at the confluence of the Lochsa and Selway Rivers. (208) 926-4258.

8) Kooskia Kiosks – Interpretive displays located near the intersection of U.S. Hwy. 12 and Idaho Hwy. 13 describe the cultural, historical, and economic heritage of the region.

9) Canoe Camp – Interpretive sign relates how the expedition camped here from September 26 to October 7, 1805, while 5 canoes were built for their journey down the Clearwater, Snake, and Columbia Rivers.

10) Weippe Prairie – Near the town of Weippe on ID Hwy. 11 is the site of the first meeting of the Lewis and Clark Expedition and the Nez Perce people.

11) Musselshell Meadows – From the junction of Forest Service Roads 100 and 500 (24 miles from Kamiah) continue 6 miles on Road 100 to Musselshell Meadows, a Nez Perce cultural site with interpretive sign.

12) Lewis & Clark Campsites – trail 25 begins 0.5 miles east of Pheasant Camp at the junction of Forest Roads 100 and 500. Hike 3 miles to Lewis/Clark Grove, or drive 1 mile east on Road 500 to Road 520, then drive 1.5 miles on Road 520. At Lewis/Clark Grove, Trail 25 continues 5 miles to Small Prairie Camp, or drive 7 miles east on Road 500 from its junction with Road 520. 4WD vehicle recommended to continue east on Road 500.

13) Bradbury Logging Museum – Pierce. Open Fridays and Saturdays mid-June to mid-October. (208) 435-4670.

14) Dworshak Dam – Hatchery and Visitor Center at the north end of the dam, open daily in the summer, Wednesday-Sunday the rest of the year. (208) 476-1255.

15) Clearwater Historical Museum – Orofino, Tuesday through Saturday. (208) 476-5033.

16) Nez Perce National Historical Park Visitor Center – Spalding. Cultural museum of Ni Mii Pu exhibits and artifacts and an auditorium for films and interpretive talks. (208) 843-2261.

17) Lewis & Clark State College – Lewiston. Centennial Mall in the center of campus contains statues of Lewis, Clark, and Nez Perce. Library houses a collection of Lewis and Clark books and journals. (208) 799-2210.

18) Nez Perce County Historical Museum – Lewiston. Open Tuesday through Saturday. (208) 743-2535.

19) Hells Gate State Park – Lewiston. Lewis and Clark botany interpretive display. (208) 799-5015.

20) Lewis & Clark Center for Arts and History – Lewiston. Open Monday through Friday. (208) 799-2243.

21) Chief Timothy State Park – Interpretive Center 8 miles west of Clarkston on U.S. Hwy. 12, on the site of the Alpowai encampment of the Nez Perce people. (509) 758-9580.

22) Heart of the Monster – East Kamiah. Represent the place of creation in Ni Mii Pu mythology. An audio station nearby tells the legend.

23) Long Camp Interpretive Sign – Mile 68 on U.S. 12 near Kamiah. Near the area where the expedition spent 3 weeks among the Nez Perce in late spring 1806. Also called Camp Chopunnish (a word Lewis used for the Ni Mii Pu) or Camp Kamiah.

24) Wolf Education and Research Center – Provides a unique opportunity to view endangered Gray Wolves in their natural habitat. Located on Nez Perce tribal property adjacent to Winchester Lake State Park in Winchester, 2 miles east of U.S. Hwy. 95. (208) 924-6960.

25) Ordway's Signs – Commemorates Sgt. Ordway's May, 1806 trip from Long Camp (Camp Choppunish) to the Salmon and Snake Rivers to procure salmon for the main party of the Corps of Discovery. One sign at mile 253 and another at mile 269 on Hwy. 9.

26) Historical Museum at St. Gertrude – Cottonwood. 3 miles off Hwy. 95. Open Tuesday through Saturday. (208) 962-7123.

Contact the Idaho Division of Tourism Development at (800) 474-3246. Reprinted from Idaho Travel Council brochure.

Riggins	Jan	Feb	March	April	May	June	July	Aug	Sep	Oct	Nov	Dec	Annual
Average Max. Temperature (F)	41.7	49.4	57.3	66.0	74.1	81.6	92.5	92.4	81.6	67.5	50.9	42.6	66.5
Average Min. Temperature (F)	27.7	30.9	34.6	39.5	45.9	52.4	58.3	57.9	50.5	41.9	34.5	29.3	41.9
Average Total Precipitation (in.)	1.22	1.10	1.59	1.74	2.23	1.92	0.81	0.82	1.14	1.31	1.52	1.37	16.76
Average Total Snowfall (in.)	2.9	1.3	0.6	0.0	0.0	0.0	0.0	0.0	0.0	0.0	0.3	1.9	7.0
Average Snow Depth (in.)	1	0	0	0	0	0	0	0	0	0	0	0	0

Ahsahka, Idaho. Fish culturists at the Crooked River station use the latest biological and technological knowledge to help restore dwindling populations of Chinook salmon in the Clearwater River. Tours are available upon request.

TV McAllister Picnic Area
Milepost 11 on State Hwy. 14.

Nestled among an array of wildlife, the McAllister Picnic Area offers a peaceful picnic setting with various birds and elk inhabiting the surrounding landscape. In addition, a one-mile trail leads from the picnic area to the old McAllister mine and homestead. The site is open free of charge to the public when weather permits.

V Selway River
Contact the West Fork Ranger Station of the Bitterroot National Forest at (406) 821-3269.

Whitewater rapids, abundant wildlife, and solitary wilderness are just three of the many attractions luring visitors to the pristine Selway River. Designated a Wild and Scenic River, the Selway is known for its remoteness, and outfitters are only allowed to run one trip per week in an effort to preserve the river's magnificent beauty.

Distinguished as the world's longest free flowing river, the Selway always runs clear as salmon swim their way up the river alongside westslope cutthroat trout. During high water, the Selway possesses some of the most challenging rapids of any other river in the American West, and only experienced rafters or professionals should undertake a whitewater journey. Permits are required to raft the Selway and are available from the U.S. Forest Service.

V Red River Hot Springs
Elk City, 842-2589. Located 25 miles from Elk City on Forest Rd. 234 (Red River Rd.).

Idaho's landscape is dotted with natural hot springs. While ancient inhabitants believed the springs' mineral water possessed mysterious healing effects, early white settlers simply found the springs to be a source of relaxation from the hard pioneer life. Today, the 130-degree springs are protected by the U.S. Forest Service, but they are still open to the public. Red River features a large swimming pool, a hot tub, and private soaking tubs.

M Elk City Area Alliance
PO Box 402, Elk City. 842-2597.
www.camasnet.com/~elkcity/

20 Food, Lodging

H Nez Perce War
Milepost 227 on U.S. Hwy. 95

Near the base of this hill, more than 100 cavalrymen and volunteers met disaster in the opening battle of the Nez Perce War.

Rushing from Grangeville on the evening of June 16, 1877, Captain David Perry planned to stop the Indians from crossing the Salmon River to safety. At daylight the next morning, he headed down the ravine below you. Some 60 to 80 Indians wiped out a third of his force and the survivors retired in disorder. No Indians were killed.

H White Bird Grade
Milepost 227 on U.S. Hwy. 95

For 60 years after construction was completed in 1915, the White Bird Grade (across the valley) served as Idaho's only north-south highway.

Many tortuous curves and switchbacks – which, if placed together made 37 complete circles – let the old road climb 2,900 feet in 14

miles. Gaining an elevation of 4,429 feet at its summit, that route represented a significant engineering and construction achievement. This new grade did not replace it until 1975.

H Salmon River
Milepost 230.9 on U.S. Hwy. 95

A vast mountain wilderness, cut by the mile deep Salmon River Canyon, stretches across Idaho south and east of here.

Travel through the Salmon River Mountains always was hard in the early days. An 1872 railways survey showed the Salmon River Canyon to be too expensive a route to build. Until a highway was finished down White Bird Hill in 1921, only some pack trails and a difficult wagon road crossed the rugged mountain barrier that separated north and south Idaho.

T Lucile
Pop. 30

Judge James Ailshie was influential in helping local miners apply for a settlement post office in 1896. Therefore, when it came time to name the town, he chose to honor his baby daughter, Lucile. The small town was the center of mining activity for the McKinley, Blue Jacket, and Crooks Corral mines until 1939. Lucile was also once home to a few heated feuds between sheep ranchers and area cattlemen.

T White Bird
Pop. 106

Named after a great Nez Perce Indian Chief, White Bird may be a small village, but it is loaded with history. Situated near White Bird Creek and the Salmon River, the first recorded settlers arrived as early as 1863. A. D. Chapman and his Umatilla Indian wife were entrepreneurs. Soon after arriving, the Chapmans began offering ferry services across the Salmon, and more homesteaders began calling the area home. A post office was established in 1866, and a few businesses began appearing in 1874. The town's growth greatly increased when S. S. Fenn built a stage station and hotel in 1891. Within no time, White Bird had grown to include four hotels, a livery stable, a meat market, a general store and saloon, a blacksmith shop, and a school. The area is most recognized, however, for the 1877 Battle of White Bird Hill. This conflict between the Nez Perce and U.S. government was the start of the Nez Perce Indian War.

T Slate Creek Ranger Station
10 miles south of White Bird on U.S. Hwy. 95. 839-2211.

The Slate Creek Ranger Station is the proud owner of a cherished piece of Idaho Forest Service history. A two-story log cabin situated in front of the ranger station was constructed in 1909 and operated with a variety of functions during its day. The cabin served as the Forest Service's first district headquarters, as well as a guard station for fire, trail, and road crews. Today, the cabin serves as an informational Forest Service museum.

T White Bird Battlefield Memorial
North of White Bird on U.S. Hwy. 95.

The 1800s were plagued with Native American and U.S. Government conflict, and in 1877, the conflict flared in north central Idaho. In 1855, a treaty was signed relegating many Nez Perce to reservation lands. Those Nez Perce, however, whose lands were not affected by the treaty, refused to sign the 1855 agreement and continued

to live as "non-treaty" bands for the next two decades. But in 1877, the government decided that all Nez Perce must live on the reservation.

The non-treaty bands of Chiefs Joseph and White Bird gathered together at Tolo Lake, ready to peacefully enter the reservation. But a few young braves were adamantly against this resolution, and they rode out in search of the U.S. Cavalry.

Although different interpretations persist in regards to who fired the first shot, it is known that the Nez Perce fought bravely against the army soldiers. In the end, the army lost thirty-four men while the Nez Perce suffered no losses. The battle, known as White Bird, marked the beginning of the Nez Perce War.

Today, an interpretive shelter above the battlefield and a self-guided auto tour remember and recount the battle.

T Foskett Memorial
8 miles north of Lucile on U.S. Hwy. 95 near the Salmon River's east side

Idaho's Foskett Memorial honors the legacy of one of the finest doctors to grace the American West with his presence. Born in Warsaw, New York in 1870, Doctor Wilson A. Foskett graduated from a Chicago medical school and began practicing medicine in White Bird in 1897.

Doctor Foskett was the icon for early doctors who made a practice of making house calls. Foskett would travel great distances to help anyone in need, and over the span of his career, he delivered babies, performed surgeries, set broken bones, and pulled teeth. On a routine house call on April 13, 1924, Foskett helped deliver a baby in Riggins before being summoned back to Lucile to check on an expectant mother. Although Foskett had been up all night, he refused to sleep and headed on his way to see the young pregnant woman. On his way, however, Foskett fell asleep at the wheel and plunged into the Salmon River. He was found the next morning, and the monument today honors his commitment to help others at any cost.

T White Bird Hill
On U.S. Hwy. 95 near White Bird

Ascending 3,000 feet in 7.2 miles, the White Bird Hill grade was constructed between 1965-1975 at a cost of more than $4 million. Crewmembers often referred to the job as the "white knuckle flight" as they created basalt cuts more than 300 feet deep and frequently drove heavy equipment on slopes angled at forty-five degrees.

T White Bird Bridge
On U.S. Hwy. 95 near White Bird

Using manufactured steel from U.S. Steel of Gary, Indiana, the White Bird Bridge was completed in 1975 at a cost of $1.7 million. The American Institute of Steel Construction awarded the White Bird Bridge design with a first place title in 1976.

TV Hammer Creek Recreation Area/Pittsburg Landing
Hells Canyon National Recreation Area. Contact the Recreation office in Riggins at 682-3916. From White Bird, proceed south on U.S. Hwy. 95, bearing left onto Forest Rd. 493 (Deer Creek Rd.). Proceed 17 miles to the site.

Lined with pictographs and petroglyphs from ancient Native American inhabitants, Hammer Creek Recreation Area and Pittsburg Landing are the only place south of Hells Canyon Dam where visitors can drive down to the Snake River's banks. The area features boat launching and take-out points for rafters, as well as a dock, campground/

picnic ground, and numerous trailheads. Contact the Hells Canyon National Recreation office for further information.

M White Bird Chamber of Commerce
White Bird. 839-2777.

21 Food

Pollock
Pop. 100

Established in 1872 as a mining supply center, Pollock was granted a post office in 1893. Within twenty years of its settlement, the community was prospering as a regional trading post. For unknown reasons, the town site was moved four miles south between 1914 and 1919. It was named for Thomas Pollock, the second postmaster, who donated land for the original townsite's plat. When the location moved south, the name tagged along.

Riggins
Pop. 410

Riggins' roots began with the Nez Perce Indians and Yellow Bull, Little White Bird, and Black Elk, all of whom used the area as a preferred camping ground. In 1863, white men made their presence known when Mike Deasy happened upon the area and discovered gold. Although he didn't immediately delve into the find, he returned a few years later to stake a claim. In 1893, he sold his claim and built the first house in the area where he, his wife, and five boys resided.

Around the same time, Charley, John, and Bud Clay moved to the area and developed an irrigation ditch to help with their intended mining endeavors. In 1894, the area's population was sufficient enough to require a school, and fourteen local children began receiving instruction that year.

Meanwhile, Missouri native, John Riggins, established a ferry on Lightning Creek that traveled to the northern reaches of Riggins. In March 1901, John's son, Richard (Dick), moved to the town site, established a post office, and became one of the fledgling town's most respected businessmen. Serving as a stage driver, farmer, and freighter, Dick made significant contributions to the town's development. Therefore, the town bears his name. Prior to this title, the area was known as Gouge-Eye, Clay, and Irwin Bar.

The town continued to grow when a wagon road was completed to the settlement in 1902. Hotels, houses, churches, and stores soon began to join Dick's previously established businesses, and the town became a livestock and trade center for the surrounding mining towns. Today, the town is ranked as Idaho's whitewater capital, and hundreds of thrill-seekers launch their Salmon River excursions from Riggins every summer. In addition, Riggins boasts convenient access to hunting, fishing, hiking, and other scenic backcountry adventures.

H Fabulous Florence
Milepost 205.6 on U.S. Hwy. 95

Millions in gold, mined mostly in one big year, came from the high mountain basin around Florence, 14 airline miles east of here.

Early prospectors, fanning south from Pierce – Idaho's first gold camp – came unexpectedly upon rich ground in August 1861. Their secret leaked, golden rumors started an eager rush that fall, and winter famine followed. Next spring, thousands stampeded into Florence, even from the California mines. But the rich camp had only 575 men by 1863. Today, scarcely a trace of the town remains among scars of the old diggings. The original town has vanished.

H Hydraulic Mining
Milepost 205.6 on U.S. Hwy. 95

Visible directly across the river is a pit left by large-scale hydraulic mining for gold deposited in ancient gravel beds.

Big nozzles, called "hydraulic giants," shot powerful streams of water against a prehistoric river bed (now the bank of the stream) to expose and wash down gold bearing gravel, which then in the 1860s, remained in use until recent economic changes made gold mining unprofitable. Many pits – some enormously larger than this one – are left as reminders of the mining days gone by.

H Salmon River Canyon
Milepost 211.2 on U.S. Hwy. 95

Some 15 million years ago, the Salmon River ran across great Miocene lava flows above here and started to carve this deep canyon.

Then this part of the earth's surface gradually rose. As the mountains were rising, the river cut down into the older rock below. Many other Northwestern rivers cut similar gorges. The Snake River flows through Hells Canyon – deepest of them all – eight miles west of here.

T Rapid River Fish Hatchery
7 miles southwest of Riggins at the Rapid River Forest Service Trailhead. Contact the Salmon River Chamber of Commerce in Riggins at 628-3778.

Situated in a picturesque canyon, the Rapid River Fish Hatchery was established in 1964 under the management of the Idaho Power Company. The hatchery was constructed to help preserve Chinook salmon by holding them at the hatchery each May through August as their eggs mature. In addition to offering daily year-round tours, the hatchery also features a scenic park for picnicking and hiking.

T Hells Canyon
Near Riggins. Contact the Hells Canyon National Recreation Area in Riggins at 682-3916.

Deeper than Arizona's Grand Canyon, Hells Canyon slices between the Oregon/Idaho border with the Snake River freely flowing through it. Rising from an elevation of 1,480 feet at the

Continued on Page 154

Let Your Senses Be Your Guide!
Welcome to the Hells Canyon National Recreation Area managed by the Wallowa-Whitman National Forest. Hugging the borders of northeastern Oregon and western Idaho, this national showcase holds 652,488 acres of beauty and adventure, where you can let your senses run as wild as the landscape.

The deepest river gorge in North America. Scenic vistas that rival any on the continent. World-class whitewater boating. Spectacular mountain peaks. Vast reaches of remote wilderness. Exciting recreational opportunities. Diverse and abundant wildlife. Artifacts from prehistoric tribes and rustic remains of early miners and settlers...Hells Canyon National Recreation Area truly offers something for everyone, and much to remember.

We know you will enjoy Hells Canyon National Recreation Area, whether you choose to explore by road, trail, or boat.

Look... Over The Edge Of North America's Deepest Canyon
The landscape of Hells Canyon is a study in contrast, from the steep desert like lower slopes and sandbars edging the Snake River, to the rugged peaks and alpine lakes of the majestic Seven Devils Mountains towering almost 8,000 feet above.

Look... across the ever-changing horizon. Enjoy spectacular vistas from the edge of this great abyss at Hat Point, Heavens Gate, or Hells Canyon overlook. Travel deep into the Hells Canyon gorge along the Snake River. Discover the expansive bench country between rim and river where clear streams meander through forest and meadow.

Look... for abundant wildflowers in the canyon during the early spring, or watch miniature high mountain wildflowers show their color in the warm summer months.

Listen... To The Music Of Songbirds And The Cry Of Raptors That Share The Skies
Wildlife enthusiasts will enjoy the opportunity to sport creatures both great and small – from the tiny pika to cougars, bobcats, bears, elk, deer, mountain goats, and bighorn sheep – who claim homes in Hells Canyon's lush forests and craggy ridges. Many species of fish thrive in the waters of the Snake River.

Listen... to the footsteps left by Hells Canyon residents of ages past. Traces of human existence in Hells Canyon date back thousands of years – from prehistoric Native American tribes, Chief Joseph's band of the Nez Perce Indians, to the 1860s gold miners and late 1800s homesteaders. Today, Indian pictographs and petroglyphs, as well as the remains of settlers' homes, dot the landscape. Historical and archaeological sites can be enjoyed, but are fragile, irreplaceable, and protected by federal law. Please leave them for others to discover.

Feel...The Spray Of Water And The Thrill Of Raging Rapids On The Wild And Scenic River

The river holds both world-class whitewater and tranquil stretches of glass-smooth water. Whether you seek the adventure of a whitewater raft trip or the excitement of a powerboat excursion, you'll find both day and overnight trips offered by outfitters to suit your needs. If you prefer the challenge of captaining your own watercraft, contact the National Recreation Area office in Clarkston, WA, for permit requirements and other information.

Feel...the cool, relaxing evening breeze at one of nineteen rustic campsites. You're also welcome to pick a favorite spot most anywhere to camp.

Feel...the quiet solitude of the Hells Canyon Wilderness. Imagine a time without cars, or roads, a time of self-reliance and adventure. You'll find both in the Hells Canyon Wilderness.

Feel...the earth move beneath your feet as you journey over nearly 1,000 miles of trails ranging from easiest to most difficult. Before planning a trip, check at any Forest Service office for trail conditions, acceptable means of travel, and specific regulations for the wilderness area.

Feel...the exhilaration of snowmobiling or cross-country skiing. Try our groomed trails or designated play areas. Stable winter weather ensures powder snow and family fun.

Explore...
Sensational Hells Canyon National Recreation Area

By any measure, Hells Canyon National Recreation Area is immense. First-time visitors may wish to contact a Forest Service office for help in planning a visit.

Here are some pointers to help you get started:

• Local Communities near the Hells Canyon National Recreation Area welcome visitors with lodging, supplies, and services year-round. Discover rural life in America with vibrant turn-of-the-century historic districts. Explore the National Historic Oregon Trail Interpretive Center at Flagstaff Hill, near Baker City. Marvel at bronze sculptures at foundries

in Joseph. Step aboard a jet boat at Lewiston or at Hells Canyon Dam. Begin your trip into the Seven Devils Mountains from Riggins. Area outfitters offer a variety of services. Local and state tourism offices can help you with your travel plans.

• The Wallowa Mountains Visitor Center (one mile West of Enterprise, Oregon on Hwy. 82) offers information and displays on Hells Canyon National Recreation Area and the Wallowa-Whitman National Forest.

• Road Access varies from two-lane paved high-

ways to single lane, steep, gravel or dirt roads. Some roads are open seasonally. Before traveling, check on road conditions and local restrictions at any Forest Service office. The following two routes are part of the National Scenic Byway System.

• The Wallowa Mountain Loop Road (Forest Road 39) is a two-lane paved road that provides the easiest access to the rim of Hells Canyon at the Hells Canyon Overlook, via Forest Road 3965. This loop road is part of the Hells Canyon All American Road – a leisurely five-hour scenic tour from Baker City to Halfway, Joseph, and La Grande, through inviting valley communities and over steep winding roads across the Wallowa Mountains.

• The Hat Point Road (Forest Road 4240) begins at Imnaha and climbs the sheer cliffs of the Imnaha River Canyon along a narrow, steep, single-lane gravel road on its way to the breath-taking vista at Hat Point Overlook. You'll need a full day to complete this drive.

• The Imnaha River Road (Forest Roads 3960 and 3955) follows the Wild and Scenic Imnaha River. Enjoy a picnic or hike the trail up river from the Indian Crossing campground. Allow a half-day to explore this beautiful area along the two-lane gravel Imnaha River Road.

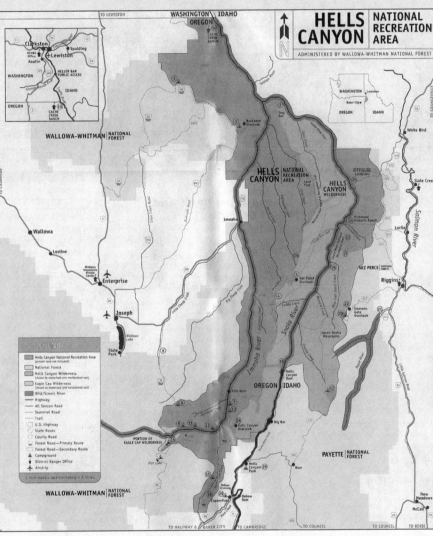

• The Snake River Road between Oxbow Crossing and Hells Canyon Dam takes you deep into the canyon. This two-lane paved road is flanked by steep walls that rise from the dark blue water of Hells Canyon Reservoir and the beginning of the Wild and Scenic Snake River. Stop below Hells Canyon Dam to begin a river trip or enjoy the view. Visit the Hells Canyon Creek Information Station (in summer months). Enjoy camping or boating along Hells Canyon Reservoir. Allow an easy three hours from Baker City, or Enterprise, or Cambridge, to the Hells Canyon Dam.

• Heavens Gate Overlook is thought by many to be the best view into Hells Canyon from Idaho. From the south end of Riggins, allow a half day to reach the Overlook on a very steep and winding gravel road (Forest Road 517).

• The Pittsburg Landing Road (Forest Road 493) is a narrow, steep, gravel road to the Snake River within Hells Canyon. Once an expansive Native American Village site, today Pittsburg Landing is popular for river access and camping. From White Bird, allow a half-day to visit Pittsburg Landing.

• The Dug Bar Road (Forest Road 4260) is as rugged as it is beautiful. Recommended only for high clearance or four-wheel drive vehicles, this steep, narrow, one-lane dirt road is an all-day adventure to the Snake River Inmaha.

Contact the Hells Canyon NRA in Riggins at 628-3916. Reprinted from USDA Forest Service brochure.

The sun sets on pleated terrain north of Riggins that fades into a late evening shower.

canyon floor up to 9,393 feet at He Devil Mountain, Hells Canyon's geography is just as wild as its elevation changes and raging river rapids. Granite peaks soar at its rims, while volcanic rock, limestone, and basalt converge into impressive canyon walls.

Humans and wildlife have inhabited this rugged, federally protected area for years. Evidence of ancient peoples is reflected in petroglyphs and pictographs, while traces of early 1800s and 1900s white settlers have long disappeared. Today, canyon visitors report sighting mountain goats, elk, deer, bighorn sheep, coyotes, bobcats, mountain lions, black bears, peregrine falcons, golden eagles, and bald eagles.

Although wildlife appear to be the only present permanent residents of Hells Canyon, plenty of recreationists find their way to the canyon year-round. Boating, whitewater rafting, fishing, wildlife viewing, and hiking are all popular activities, and interested visitors should contact the Hells Canyon National Recreation Area.

T Upper Pittsburg Landing
Hells Canyon National Recreation Area. Contact the Recreation office in Riggins at 682-3916.

Archaeologists have discovered nearly 1,500 sites suggesting ancient Native American inhabitation in the Hells Canyon National Recreation Area. In addition, petroglyphs and pictographs dating back 7,100 years are visible at Upper Pittsburg Landing.

T Kirkwood Ranch
Hells Canyon National Recreation Area. Contact the Recreation office in Riggins at 682-3916.

When the first settlers arrived in Idaho, a few made their way to Hells Canyon and began ranching. Although many soon left due to the isolated conditions, some cattle and sheep ranchers persevered. Today, the well-preserved Kirkwood Ranch provides an ideal example of early sheep ranching in Idaho. The interpretive site is only available by hiking, biking, or boating in, and interested visitors should contact the Hells Canyon National Recreation office for a map and directions.

T Schoolmarm Peak and Preacher Mountain
Near Riggins

Situated at the confluence of the Little Salmon, the 3,500-foot Schoolmarm Peak draws its name from traditional outings that early Riggins students took to the peak with their teacher every spring. Rising west of town, 4,656-foot Preacher Mountain reflects the legacy of Mr. and Mrs. Hess who settled near the peak.

TV Salmon River
The Salmon River begins its journey four miles north of Alturas, Idaho, high in the Sawtooth Mountains of central Idaho, at an elevation of over eight thousand feet. The river ends 425 miles later when it drains into the Snake River on the border of Oregon and Idaho, about forty-five miles south of Lewiston. At that point, it's at an elevation of 803 feet. No dams are present on the Salmon River because 35% of all steelhead and salmon that make up the Columbia River spawn at its headwaters.

Throughout the course of its journey, the Salmon River flows through mostly rugged, mountainous, timber-covered terrain. Its drainage basin includes over 14,000 acres. The River has an East, Middle, North and South Fork, all of which contribute to its grandeur. For over 180 miles of its trip, the Main Salmon flows through a 6,300-foot deep canyon, which is deeper than the Grand Canyon itself, and second in depth only to Hells Canyon at Lewiston. Unlike the sheer walls of the Grand Canyon, the Salmon flows below wooded ridges rising steeply toward the sky beneath eroded bluffs and ragged crags. Adventurers seek out the waters of the Salmon for its incredible rapids. The North Fork contains Class II and III+ rapids, and the Middle Fork is one of the world's greatest and most popular whitewater locations, attracting adventurers from around the globe. The river boasts over thirty rapids, most of them Class IV in nature. Hot springs also line the banks of the river, tempting weary water travelers. Some of the attraction of the Middle Fork is that it's more hidden from civilization than is the Main Fork. The Main

Fork, however, contains the biggest waves and deepest holes in its rapids and has many sandy beaches along its banks. Both rivers offer many historical sites along their shores, including pioneer and hermit cabins, Indian camps and pictographs, sites associated with the Sheepeater Campaign of 1879, and old mining camps.

The Lewis and Clark Expedition traveled through this area and camped in the Lemhi Valley. On August 21, 1805, Captain Lewis was the first white man to visit the waters, and therefore they named it "Lewis River." The local Shoshone Indians told Captain Clark the Salmon River Canyon was impassable. Clark decided to find out for himself what the canyon was like and traveled to the high side of the canyon for a better view. From there he could see the Class IV Pine Creek Rapids far below in the deep gorge. With the high, rocky walls on either side, Clark determined that the canyon was indeed impassable. He returned to the camp and instructed the expedition to detour to the north around the canyon. In later years, some pioneers did float some sections of the upper Salmon, but paddling upstream against the strong current was impossible, thus earning its nickname of "The River of No Return." The name of the river was later changed to Salmon, because of the salmon found below its surface.

TV Gospel Hump Wilderness
East of Riggins. Contact the Salmon River Ranger District at 839-2211.

Named after Gospel Peak to the west and Buffalo Hump on the east, Idaho's 206,053-acre Gospel Hump Wilderness Area was created in 1978. Closed to motor vehicles, mining, and other modern marvels, the wilderness area ranges in elevation from 1,970 feet to 8,940 feet. 200 streams, 35 lakes, and densely forested areas support a variety of wildlife, including sockeye and Chinook salmon, steelhead, trout, elk, deer, black bears, moose, mountain goats, and mountain lions. A popular area for primitive recreation, such as backpacking and horseback riding, the Gospel Hump Wilderness area is usually open and free of snow from mid-July through mid-October.

TV Seven Devils Mountains
Located between the Snake and Salmon Rivers in the Hells Canyon National Recreation Area. Contact the Hells Canyon National Recreation Area in Riggins at 628-3916.

Nicknamed "Idaho's Northern Rockies," the Seven Devils Mountains rise sharply up from north central Idaho's landscape. Soaring up to 9,393 feet high, the rugged peaks of the Seven Devils are aptly named He Devil, She Devil, Tower of Babel, Devil's Tooth, Devil's Throne, Goblin, and Belial.

Despite their sinister names, these mountains are nothing short of majestic. Horseback riders and hikers have access to some of the most awe-inspiring landscapes in all of Idaho, and wildlife abounds around every corner. Shaggy mountain goats, abundant fish species, and bighorn sheep straddle the cliffs, lakes, and streams. Contact the Hells Canyon National Recreation Area for detailed trail maps.

TV Papoose Cave
Contact the Nez Perce National Forest Headquarters in Grangeville at 983-1950. 7 miles north of Pollock, merge west off U.S. Hwy. 95 onto Squaw Creek Rd. Proceed 1.5 miles northwest up Squaw Creek, and at the road's left fork, bear southwest. Continue driving 5 miles, park, and walk 1.5 miles further up Papoose Creek.

Featuring miles of winding passages, Papoose Cave was formed more than 200 million years ago and represents Idaho's largest limestone cave. With depths of more than 600 feet, the cave is also one of America's ten deepest caverns.

For the experienced explorer, the cave contains a plethora of underground treasures that can be accessed with ropes and ladders. Waterfalls, vertical obstacles, and formations highlight the cave's interior. The cavern's entrance is locked to protect the general public, but the Forest Service will provide a key to experienced cave climbers and explorers.

V Fishing the Salmon River Drainages

Mouth to Horse Creek
Recognized as a crucial migration passage for steelhead and Chinook and sockeye salmon, the Salmon River from its mouth to Horse Creek features a variety of fish species. Although the Gospel Hump and Frank Church-River of No Return Wilderness Areas protect some of the river, anglers still have luck in finding smallmouth bass, sturgeon, and rainbow, cutthroat, and bull trout. This portion of the Salmon River includes the Chamberlain Creek tributary.

Horse Creek to North Fork
Running fifty miles through the heart of Lemhi County, the Horse Creek to North Fork portion of the Salmon River is known for a myriad of fish species. Wild and natural steelhead, Chinook salmon, westslope cutthroat trout, and small populations of white sturgeon populate the Salmon River and its Panther, Indian, Colson, Pine, and Corn Creek tributaries.

Little Salmon
The Little Salmon River drains 516 square miles and begins in Adams County at Meadows Valley. On its course to the confluence with the Salmon River in Riggins, the river flows through forests, meadows, and agricultural pastures. The river and its tributaries, including Goose Creek, Hazard Creek, Boulder Creek, Rapid River, Fish Lake, Goose Lake, Hazard Lake, and Brundage Reservoir, feature numerous fish species. Anglers will find mountain whitefish, non-game species, steelhead, Chinook salmon, and rainbow, bull, brook, and cutthroat trout.

South Fork
Contained within the state's Valley and Idaho Counties, the South Fork of the Salmon River flows north through the Idaho batholith and features widely divergent terrain. Flowing from steep canyons through lush meadows, the river contains wild steelhead, mountain whitefish, kokanee, and rainbow, cutthroat, brook, bull, and lake trout. This portion of the Salmon River Drainage system includes thirty-seven lakes and flows for 515 miles.

Middle Fork
The Middle Fork of the Salmon River Drainage System is isolated and extremely rugged, draining 2,830 square miles of some of Idaho's most pristine landscapes. Held inside the Frank Church-River of No Return Wilderness Area, the river drainage is accessible by boat, aircraft, or hiking trails. For anglers who take the time and make the preparations to enter this remote landscape, the Middle Fork rewards their efforts with populations of Chinook salmon, steelhead, mountain whitefish, bull trout, and cutthroat trout. Interestingly, the cutthroat population has recently been identified as possessing a unique westslope strain not yet discovered in any other Idaho drainage.

Although most of the tributary streams remain in pristine condition due to wilderness protection, the quality of some were affected by historical mining activity and cattle grazing.

North Fork to Headwaters
The North Fork to Headwaters portion of the Salmon River runs 173 miles through mountainous terrain and glacially carved valleys. A portion of the river is situated inside the Sawtooth National Recreation Area, and tributaries include the Lemhi, Pahsimeroi, East Fork of the Salmon, and Yankee Fork Rivers. Due to the area's granitic watershed, the river's large lakes are frequently sterile and cannot naturally produce fish. The river and area lakes, then, are annually stocked with over 100,000 hatchery rainbow trout. Included in this drainage area are Redfish and Alturas Lakes, which support populations of sockeye and kokanee salmon.

East Fork
The East Fork of the Salmon River drains 540 square miles on its thirty-three mile journey to the confluence of the Salmon River's South and West Forks. Encompassing the White Cloud Peaks and the Boulder Mountains, the drainage is one of Idaho's most important salmon spawning regions. The river also features hatchery steelhead.

Yankee Fork
Although the Yankee Fork of the Salmon River was once home to extensive mining operations, this twenty-six mile river stretch continues to support a variety of fish species. Anglers will locate hatchery steelhead along with rainbow, bull, and cutthroat trout.

V Wapiti River Guides
128 N. Main St., Riggins. 628-3523 or (800) 488-9872. www.doryfun.com

Not a herd animal? Rather run with a small pack? Want personalized attention from informative guides? Then journey on Idaho's Lower Salmon River with Wapiti River Guides. Unlike most outfits, Wapiti's micro-sized trips fit you individually. Favoring a genuine natural experience not possible with huge groups, Wapiti offers whitewater by dory/raft/kayak, driftboat fishing, and chukar hunts. Inspirational fun with nature lore is aimed at all skill levels. As natural interpreters, guides help you read the landscape to better appreciate the tour area. Engaging nature the "Wapiti Way," guides blend in science, history, and culture to broaden your awareness. Camp where large groups can't. Sneak up on wildlife, and enjoy the leisurely solitude of small group travel. Think small for big adventure. See, do, and have more fun with the Wapiti clan.

M Heath Realty
318 S. Main St., Riggins. 628-3322 or (877) 628-3300 or 628-3829, residence. www.heathrealty.com

Opened in 1975 and under the brokerage/ownership of Vickie Heath since 1987, Heath Realty is recognized as Riggins' longest established real estate firm. The brokerage, which specializes in Salmon River properties in and around Riggins, offers everything from residential homes to sprawling ranches, land, and commercial listings. As an added bonus, Vickie's husband operates Heath Construction, providing clients with building and remodeling services. Vickie strives to be fair and ethical to every buyer and seller so that informed real estate decisions can easily be made. In addition, Vickie's area residency dates to 1974, ensuring that she has the knowledge to acquaint residents with their cozy new community. When your search for the perfect home or investment property leads you to Riggins, rely on the proven experience of Heath Realty!

M Jaclyn Truppi, Main Salmon River Real Estate
101 N. Main St., Riggins. 628-3441 or (866) 578-1681. www.mainsalmonriverrealestate.com

Surfing the market for a real estate professional? Catch the wave with REALTOR® Jaclyn Truppi at Main Salmon River Real Estate in association with Blevins Agency. Whether you're a first-time homebuyer or an experienced investor or seller, Jaclyn can provide information about choosing property, making an offer, negotiating, financing, mortgage rates, moving, and everything involved in making informed real estate decisions in today's market. Property listings are available in or near Riggins, New Meadows, Whitebird, Hells Canyon, the Snake River, and the Salmon River. Born and raised in the heart of Salmon River country and a recreational enthusiast, Jaclyn has the knowledge to answer your questions about this year-round center for outdoor fun. When you're ready to take the plunge and discover life in Idaho, trust Jaclyn Truppi's dedication to honesty, hard work, friendly professionalism, and 100 percent client commitment! Equal Housing Opportunity and member of the Multiple Listing Service.

M Riggins - Salmon River Chamber of Commerce
126 N. Main, Riggins. 628-3778. www.rigginsidaho.com

WATERFALLS

Selway Falls

U.S. Highway 12 to Lowell; turn southeast, proceeding 18 miles on Selway River Road #1614

Tumbling 50 feet in multiple threads as the Selway River divides, Selway Falls is situated at an elevation of 1,700 feet in the Moose Creek Ranger District of the Nez Perce National Forest and is easily viewed roadside.

Horsetail Falls

Drive along U.S. Highway 12 paralleling the Lochsa River; proceed to a turnout between mile markers 114 and 115 to view the falls at an elevation of 2,000 feet across the Lochsa River

Located within the Middle Fork Clearwater Wild and Scenic River area of the Lochsa Ranger District, Horsetail Falls drops 60 to 100 feet. Falling from an unnamed stream, this cataract is accessible by vehicle.

Shoestring Falls

U.S. Highway 12 northeast of Lowell; peer across the river between mile markers 115 and 116

An unnamed creek descends 150 to 200 feet in five tiered sections to form Shoestring Falls. Dropping into the Lochsa River, Shoestring Falls are found at an elevation of 1,920 feet within the Middle Fork Clearwater Wild and Scenic River area.

Wild Horse Creek Falls

U.S. Highway 12 northeast of Lowell; locate between mile markers 115 and 116

Wild Horse Creek Falls tumble 40 to 60 feet in two tiers and are located within the Clearwater National Forest's Lochsa Ranger District. After locating the falls via the road, visitors can use caution and gain a close-up view of the falls by walking along U.S. Highway 12 for 0.1 mile.

Tumble Creek Falls

U.S. Highway 12; gaze east between mile markers 113 and 114

Before falling into the Lochsa River below U.S. Highway 12, Tumble Creek Falls descends 20 to 30 feet. Contained within the Clearwater National Forest's Lochsa Ranger District, this waterfall is not marked but visitors can view the cataract from the road.

Carey Falls

Exit U.S. Highway 95 1 mile south of Riggins; follow Big Salmon Road #1614 for 23 miles to the Wind River Pack Bridge; advance 0.4 mile to view the falls

Acting as the boundary separating the Gospel Hump and Frank Church River of No Return Wildernesses, Carey Falls is found on the Salmon River. Unlike many other waterfalls, Carey Falls cascades in rapids from several small streams and is easily viewed from the road.

Elk Falls

Follow Scenic Route 8 south for 16 miles from Bovilli toward Elk River; bear south (right) at the marked entrance road, continuing 1.6 miles to a turnout at Elk Creek Canyon Trailhead

Also known as Elk Creek Falls, this waterfall at a 2,550 foot elevation descends vertically for 125 to 150 feet and affords visitors an outstanding scenic feature. Visitors must take a moderate day hike to reach the highest of Elk Creek's six

waterfalls, but most will find the trip worth the effort.

From the trailhead, locate the left fork of the road next to this trail and hike the moderately steep fork for 2 miles to an open area. Rapidly descend to the canyon's grassy north rim and head right on a trail amid the green slopes to access several viewing areas over 0.2 mile.

Upper Elk Falls

Drive on Scenic Route 8 south of Bovilli toward Elk River for 16 miles; at the marked access road, turn south (right) and continue 1.6 miles to Elk Creek Canyon Trailhead's parking area

As one of several waterfalls located in the Clearwater National Forest's Palouse Ranger District, Upper Elk Falls tumbles 30 to 50 feet from a narrow stream into a small pool below. At an elevation of 2,660 feet, Upper Elk Falls does require visitors to take a moderate day hike.

At the trailhead, locate the fork in the road. Taking the left fork, hike along the moderately steep road for 2 miles until reaching a small clearing. At this point, climb down to the canyon's grassy north rim and then turn left. To reach the falls' viewing area in approximately 0.3 mile, follow the grassy trail into the woods toward Elk Creek.

Twin Falls and Small Falls

Access the falls in the Clearwater National Forest's Palouse Ranger District by taking Scenic Route 8; drive south from Bovilli toward Elk River for 16 miles, turning right at a marked access road; continue to the Elk Creek Canyon Trailhead's parking area in 1.6 miles located beside a fork in the road

Dropping as a series of falls with a large watershed, visitors should expect a moderate day hike to reach the viewing area. From the trailhead, hike on the road's left fork and proceed 2 miles on the steep trail until reaching a clearing. Here, walk down to the hills of the canyon's north rim, turning right onto a grassy trail. Continue downstream past Elk Falls for 0.3 miles. At this point, both falls can be viewed at the same time. While Twin Falls drops in 10 to 20 foot segments, Small Falls tumbles vertically for another 10 to 20 feet.

Bull Run Creek Falls

Take Scenic Route 8 south of Bovilli to Elk River for 16 miles; bearing south (right) at a marked access road, continue 1.6 miles to the Elk Creek Canyon Trailhead's parking area; do not park here, but instead proceed forward along the unnamed road's right fork to reach another parking area in 1.5 miles

Bull Run Creek Falls cascades 75 to 100 feet and is situated in an undeveloped area of the Elk Creek Falls Recreation Area in Clearwater National Forest. To reach the cataract's 2,480 feet elevation, visitors should take a moderate day hike along a narrow, faint trail heading to the falls.

Lower Bull Run Creek Falls

To reach the waterfall's 2,420-foot elevation, drive 16 miles south of Bovilli to Elk River along Scenic Route 8; turn right at the marked access road and proceed 1.6 miles to the parking area near Elk Creek Canyon Trailhead; instead of parking here, locate the unnamed road's right fork and continue driving 1.5 miles to a second parking area

Rushing down 30 to 50 feet beside Bull Run Creek, these falls are recommended only for experienced, determined hikers ready for a difficult excursion. From the parking area, take the faint, small trail and hike past Bull Run Creek Falls. Proceed downstream 0.1 mile along the ridge and beyond a marshy area. To reach the creek at the base of Lower Bull Run Creek Falls, cautiously climb down the steep tree-lined grade.

Lower Elk Falls

Drive 16 miles south of Bovilli toward Elk River on Scenic Route 8 until reaching a signed entrance road; turn south (right) and continue 1.6 miles to the Elk Creek Canyon Trailhead's parking area located near a fork in the road

Losing contact with its bedrock surface, Lower Elk Falls drops 75 to 100 feet in the Clearwater National Forest's Palouse Ranger District. With a large magnitude, Lower Elk Falls is the most powerful waterfall near Elk Creek. However, viewing of this waterfall is recommended only to visitors with strong hiking boots who are ready for modest rock climbing along an undeveloped trail.

Taking the left fork at the trailhead, hike for 2 miles until reaching an open area. Next, descend to the canyon's north rim of green hills and turn right onto a grassy trail. Proceed 0.6 miles past Elk Falls, Twin Falls, and Small Falls to the trail's end. For excellent views, walk along a faint trail to the top of a basaltic ledge. However, visitors should use caution at all times as the viewing area is unfenced.

Middle Elk Falls

Follow Scenic Route 8 to Elk River 16 miles south of Bovilli and turn south (right) at the marked access road; drive 1.6 miles to the Elk Creek Canyon Trailhead's parking area located beside a fork in the road

Situated in the Palouse Ranger District of the Clearwater National Forest, Middle Elk Falls is a favorite location of avid fishermen and determined backpackers fond of creating their own trail. Descending 20 to 30 feet, these falls are most readily viewed from a distance.

At the parking area, travel along the road's left fork and hike 2 miles along the moderately inclined trail to a small clearing. Here, descend to the green slopes of the canyon's north rim, turning right onto a trail amid the grassy hills. Locate Elk Falls and then proceed 0.2 mile downstream. To view the falls trailside, gaze down into the chasm.

Jerry Johnson Falls

To access, proceed on U.S. Highway 12 until locating Warm Springs Creek Trail #49, approximately 1 mile east of the Jerry Johnson Campground; park here and use the footbridge to cross the Lochsa River and reach Warm Springs Creek

At an elevation of 3,900 feet, Jerry Johnson Falls requires sightseers to take a fairly difficult day hike, and visitors are recommended to wear appropriate footwear. Found within the Powell Ranger District of the Clearwater National Forest, the falls are formed as Warm Springs Creek tumbles 40 to 70 feet into a large pool below.

After reaching Warm Springs Creek, continue hiking upstream 1.5 miles to the Jerry Johnson Hot Springs. Many visitors choose to rest in these thermal waters, but you will quickly become secluded as you advance past the springs. In approximately 1 mile, the trail crosses a tributary creek. Follow the trail as it rises above Warm Springs Creek for viewing of the falls in 1 more mile.

The following Idaho waterfalls are also located in this section with limited directions/ access available:

Hoodoo Creek Falls

Found within the Selway-Bitterroot Wilderness area, Hoodoo Creek Falls lies in Idaho County in central Idaho. Although the falls are located on Hoodoo Creek, access to the falls is uncertain.

Bimerick Falls

Bimerick Falls cascades within Lowell County of Idaho's Clearwater National Forest. Although topographic maps suggest a rough trail leads to the cataract, little access information is known about this waterfall.

Dead Elk Creek Falls and Patsy Ann Falls

Located in Idaho County in the general vicinity of Warm Springs Creek, both Dead Elk Creek Falls and Patsy Ann Falls are found on detailed topographic maps of this northern Idaho region. While Dead Elk Creek Falls does not appear accessible, Patsy Ann Falls may be viewable from a distance for hikers who carve their own trail.

Slippy Creek Falls

Slippy Creek Falls is located in Idaho County in the general area of the Salmon Wild and Scenic River Area. Topographic maps, however, indicate that the cataract is not likely reachable.

Hazard Falls

Found within Idaho County, Hazard Falls is appropriately named. Topographic maps suggest that the cataract may be accessible, but only after taking a difficult hike. Determined viewers ready for a challenge should be prepared to make their own trail as no developed road leads to this waterfall.

22

Warren
Pop. 35

This near ghost town's beginning, like many other isolated Idaho settlements, originated with the search for mining riches. In 1862, James Warren led Matthew Bledsoe and several other prospectors from Florence through the Salmon River Canyon to the meadows surrounding this area. Upon discovering gold, a rush of miners moved in, and the mining camp was informally dubbed "Warren's Diggings" after its founder. During its heyday, Warren supported a population of nearly 2,000 inhabitants, and the settlement was a popular destination for Chinese miners who arrived in the area during the 1870s and 1880s. When early white miners to the area realized that their claims were fading, they decided to make a profit off the unsuspecting Chinese laborers. It is reported that some Chinese workers paid up to $8,000 for a single claim.

Since the town was so remote and supply lines were often limited, the cost of living in the area was extremely high. One boarding house owner in the 1860s charged $3 per meal, a steep price during that time. Due to rising costs and dwindling luck with claims, many Warren settlers left in search of better prospects. Despite some spotty mining successes over the last century, Warren has never again attained its initial popularity. Today, the town at the end of Forest Road 21 boasts a few historic buildings, including an old hotel, an examiner's office, and a saloon.

T Burgdorf
U.S. Hwy. 55 35 miles north of McCall on Lake Creek

Burgdorf is best known for its hot springs and was first called "Warm Springs." Officially named after German immigrant, Frederick C. Burgdorf, who moved to the area from San Francisco in 1864 as part of the gold rush, Burgdorf changed the name of the location to "Resort" after purchasing rights to the hot springs in 1865. Burgdorf established himself as the town's postmaster and built a twenty-room hotel capitalizing on his hot springs. Since "Resort" was located along the main trail leading to popular mining communities in the area, Burgdorf built a successful business and was listed in 1913-1914 as the town's only taxpayer. When Burgdorf married a singer from Denver, Colorado in 1902, she renamed the town after her husband, and this name finally stuck. Although the town's prosperity has waned, Burgdorf's famous hotel and its furnishings still remain.

SCENIC DRIVES

Heavens Gate

Experience the nation's deepest river gorge atop the 8,429 foot Heavens Gate scenic overlook. Heavens Gate is the highest elevation viewpoint in the area and offers spectacular views of Hells Canyon and the Seven Devils Mountains.

The route begins south of Riggins on Forest Road #517 at the turnoff for Seven Devils Campground. The 18.5-mile single lane, gravel/dirt road has a steady uphill grade and some switchbacks throughout its entirety, so is not suitable for RV's or trailers. The scenic drive is generally accessible from mid-July to mid-October, but travelers should check at the local ranger station for current road conditions.

Iron Phone Junction

Situated at an elevation of 5,300 feet, Iron Phone Junction offers travelers a scenic vista of the impressive Hells Canyon. The route begins north of Riggins on Race Creek Road #241 and traverses a steeply graded, single lane gravel road. The scenic drive does have turnouts but is not suitable for RV's or trailers. Iron Phone Junction is normally accessible from mid-June to mid-October, but travelers should check at the local ranger station for current road conditions. Travelers should plan at least two hours for this 30-mile roundtrip drive.

Sawpit/Low Saddle Loop

Distant views of the Seven Devils Mountains and a gorgeous view of Hells Canyon down to the Snake River can be found along the Sawpit/Low Saddle loop drive. The elevation climbs from 4,800 feet to nearly 7,000 feet while driving on the narrow, gravel/dirt roads. To access the route, drive north of Riggins to Race Creek Road #241. From here, proceed along Forest Roads #2060 and #1819 to locate the viewpoints and make a loop drive. The route is recommended only for high clearance vehicles, and travelers should be comfortable in

their ability to drive on remote, backcountry roads. The area is generally accessible mid-June to mid-October, but travelers should check at the local ranger station for current road conditions.

The Palouse Country Discovery Tour

Discover the farmlands, canyons, forests, and rural towns of Latah County on a scenic drive through the fertile rolling hills of Northern Idaho. Beginning in Lewiston, cross the Clearwater River on Highway 12 and reach the junction for Highway 3. At this junction, proceed northeast on Highway 3.

1. Juliaetta and Kendrick are the first stops along this tour. This area inside the Potlatch Canyon is known for its mild climate and long growing season. It's no surprise, then, that both communities are major fruit and vegetable producers. While driving down Juliaetta's Main Street, notice the brick building with a corner entrance. This structure was built in 1889 and served as the community's first bank. Driving just four miles to Kendrick, note the many historic buildings lining the business district. Most were constructed after the town experienced a devastating fire in 1904.

2. From Kendrick, merge off Highway 3 onto Highway 99 and drive up Brady Gulch to the Scandinavian town of Troy. Proceed east on Highway 8 to Dreary, taking in the beautiful sights at Spring Valley Reservoir as well as numerous opportunities for nature walks and fishing.

3. At Dreary, drive 10 miles along Highway 8 to the once thriving community of Bovill. Named after Lord Hugh and Lady Charlotte Bovill, the town was once a busy recreational spot for fishermen and hunters. The downtown area boasts the Hotel Bovill and a two-story opera house as reminders of the town's glory days. Continue through the forests on Highway 8 to Elk River. This community once boasted a prosperous logging business. Today, it is most known for its trail access to the beautiful Elk River Falls. After visiting the waterfall, drive back to Dreary on Highway 8.

4. Upon reaching Dreary again, drive northwest on Highway 9 to the town of Harvard and the junction with Highway 6 and 95A. Follow Highway 6 and 95A 3.5 miles before bearing right on Palouse River Road. Follow the road to 120-acre Laird Park. Maintained by the U.S. Forest Service, the park offers a scenic picnic area and a swimming hole the whole family is sure to love.

5. Back in Harvard, proceed along Highway 6 to Princeton and Potlatch. In 1905, the Potlatch Lumber Company constructed America's largest steam-driven mill here and the community of Potlatch quickly sprang up. Although the mill was torn down in 1983, the site still boasts the Scenic Six Historic Park. Be sure to stop at the City Hall and pick up a brochure for the self-guided tour of the town's historic district.

6. From Potlatch, bear north onto Highway 95 and proceed to the turnoff for McCroskey State Park. Dedicated to the memory of pioneer women, the park boasts mountain crests, spectacular vistas of the Palouse country, and several picnic tables scattered along the windy, dirt road. After taking in the scenery, return to Highway 95 and proceed south to Moscow.

7. The lively cultural and educational center of Moscow serves as Latah County seat. The area is characterized by a rich history, and the Chamber of Commerce provides walking tour brochures of historic downtown and residential districts.

8. After taking time to explore Moscow, drive south on Highway 95 through rich farmlands to the summit of Lewiston grade. At 2,400 feet, this point provides panoramic views of the Clearwater and Snake Rivers and the city of Lewiston. Proceed down the highway's steep grade to end the tour back in Lewiston.

French Creek Loop

Explore mountain lakes, forests, hot springs, historic areas, and waterfalls along the 115-mile scenic French Creek Loop into Idaho's backcountry. The route begins near Shore Lodge in McCall where travelers should merge off Highway 55 onto Warren Wagon Road. This road served as an important pack trail in the 1800s mining days and later became a well-traveled wagon road. Many old wagon ruts are still visible near the highway.

Continue on past Big Payette Lake to North Beach State Park. Depending on how much time you have available, stop for a swim, picnic, or a stroll along the beach. From the park, the road winds through granite cliffs lined with pine, fir, and aspen trees to the popular fishing spot at Upper Payette Lake. Proceed past Secesh Summit (where many visitors have reported moose-sightings) and continue to the trip's 27.3-mile mark. Here, travelers should cross the Lake Creek Bridge and bear left on windy Forest Road 246, a road that was unbelievably considered a state highway in the late 1800s.

Now on Road 246, continue to the historic Burgdorf Hot Springs. Established by German immigrant, Fred Burgdorf, the hot springs are listed on the National Register of Historic Places. Continue winding through the forest as the road climbs to its high point at mile 37.7 before descending down several hairpin turns into Salmon River country. At mile 42.1, note a pioneer cabin on the road's left side. Built in 1900, a man named Edmundson lived there with his family until 1930 and it was a popular freight stop along the French Creek Road.

At mile 53.6, travelers will reach the junction of French Creek and Salmon River Roads. Proceeding left, the road winds through scenic canyons along the Salmon River. Many visitors stop for a stroll on the river's banks or for a dip in the river. Swimmers, however, are highly urged to wear lifejackets as the river's rapids can be dangerous.

The one-lane, steel Manning Bridge appears at the trip's 58.3-mile mark. The Civilian Conservation Corps constructed the bridge in the 1930s, and although it appears rickety, it is safe for automobile crossings. Upon crossing the bridge, drive past the Spring Bar Campground and Allison Creek picnic area to the junction with Highway 95. Turn left here and proceed back to McCall. Along the way, check out the Rapid River Hatchery where salmon are raised, the waterfall on the Little Salmon River, Zim's Hot Springs, and Packer John's Cabin State Park. Travelers should allow at least 6 hours for this drive that primarily follows gravel roads.

Magruder Road Corridor

The 101-mile primitive Margruder Corridor Road winds through a vast undeveloped area, offering solitude and pristine beauty as well as expansive mountain views.

The landscape is much the same as when the Nez Perce Indians and other early travelers crossed the area.

The road has changed little since its construction by the Civilian Conservation Corps (CCC) in the 1930s. It has also been known as the Southern Nez Perce Trail, Elk City to Darby Road, Montana Road and the Parker Trail.

Area History & Lloyd Magruder

Gold was discovered near Pierce, Idaho, in 1861 and near Bannack, Montana in 1862. Many miners and traders used the Southern Nez Perce Trail as the most direct route from Elk City, Idaho, to Bannack or Virginia City, Montana.

In 1863, Lloyd Magruder and companions were returning along this route from Virginia City after making a handsome profit of gold dust from selling supplies to miners. Four other travelers joined the Magruder group. A few days later, the travelers attacked, murdered, and robbed Magruder and his companions in the dark of the night. The murderers burned and buried the evidence of their crime and fled to San Francisco with their stolen booty. Hill Beachy, Magruder's friend, pursued the murderers and brought them back to stand trial in Lewiston, Idaho. The trial resulted in the first legal hanging in the Idaho Territory.

Lloyd Magruder had been a successful California merchant. He was a well-respected man and had many friends. Prior to his ill-fated trip, he had agreed to represent the Idaho Territory in Congress.

As a result of this event, many places bear the name "Magruder," among them the road on which you are traveling.

Wilderness

The corridor was created in 1980 when the Central Idaho Wilderness Act was passed, leaving a unique road that enables a traveler to drive between two wildernesses: the 1.2-million-acre Selway-Bitterroot Wilderness to the north, and the 2.3-million-acre Frank Church-River of No Return Wilderness to the south. Together, they represent the largest unroaded block of land in the lower 48 states and are nearly twice as large as the combined states of Delaware and Rhode Island.

To help safeguard the naturalness of wilderness, practice "leave no trace" techniques to ensure the country you came to enjoy will remain intact for future generations. Another safeguard is the use of certified weed-free products. As of January 1, 1996, all forage or mulch used on national forest lands in Idaho must be noxious weed free.

Remember the use of motorized or mechanized equipment or vehicles is not permitted in a designated wilderness.

Area Access

The Magruder Road, Forest Road #468, is mostly unimproved. The west end intersects Forest Road #222, 0.3 mile south of the old Red River Ranger Station (65 miles east of Grangeville, Idaho). The east end is 0.8 miles south of West Fork Ranger Station (18 miles southwest of Darby, Montana).

Road Conditions

This primitive one-lane road is rough, steep, and winding with few turnouts for passing oncoming vehicles. It is suitable for high clearance vehicles, pickup trucks, motorcycles, and mountain bikes. The Forest Service does not recommend towing trailers because there are several hairpin turns along the route. Motor homes with low clearance should not travel the road.

Snow begins to fall in early October and persists into July; however, snowstorms are possible at any time. Four-wheel-drive is recommended when the road is snow covered or muddy.

Remember you are traveling through an extensive undeveloped area with no services for 117 miles. Be sure you start with a vehicle in good operating condition, a full tank of gas, and a spare tire. At all times, be alert for other traffic, washouts, fallen trees, and other debris on the road.

The road is busiest during the Idaho hunting season: mid-September through mid-November.

Travel Time

Travel time varies, but it takes eight to ten hours to travel from Red River to Darby without rest stops. The average speed will be 12-15 miles per hour. A two-day trip is ideal with an overnight stay at one of the dispersed or primitive campsite locations.

Take your time, absorb the solitude, and enjoy the remoteness far from the hassles of crowded highways.

Area Highlights

The Magruder Corridor is lined with campgrounds and scenic wonders, all of which add to the mystique of this scenic drive. Below are some of the most popular stopping points along the corridor.

Poet Creek Campground: Poet Creek Campground lies directly north of the Magruder Road. Here in the Magruder Corridor and adjacent wildernesses, diverse plant communities fill habitat needs for a variety of mammals, birds, reptiles, and amphibians.

Large mammals include black bear, sheep, goats, and four deer family members – whitetail and mule deer, elk, and moose. Deer are the most commonly seen animals. There are many smaller mammals, such as badger, wolverine, pine marten, mink, and weasels, but count yourself lucky if you see one. However, you will see ground squirrels, golden-mantle squirrels, red squirrels, and two kinds of chipmunks. You can differentiate between chipmunks and golden-mantle squirrels, as the chipmunk's white stripes extend onto its head. Be alert while traveling to increase your chances of seeing wildlife.

Sabe Vista: Passing Sabe Saddle, the road climbs up to Sabe Vista, which offers many scenic views. Elevation is 7,490 feet at the vista. This portion of the road is very narrow and sometimes very steep. There are few places to pass another vehicle.

A large burn, which was part of the Ladder Creek Fire complex, is visible at Sabe Vista. In 1988, three lightning strikes started three different fires, which eventually merged into one fire. Nearly 70,000 acres were burned in three National Forests (Nez Perce, Bitterroot, and Payette). Fire is a natural source which rejuvenates the environment.

Salmon Mountain Area: The Old Salmon Mountain Ranger Station site was established in 1911. Nearby is the Salmon Mountain base camp, a very popular trailhead during hunting season. It has stock facilities. A one-mile trail leads to the Salmon Mountain lookout tower which is staffed by volunteers during fire season. The elevation is 8,944 feet. Mountain goats are often seen on the rocky crags and talus slopes of Salmon Mountain.

This area is one of the few places in America where you can see the subalpine larch. The larch is the only deciduous coniferous tree, meaning that its needles turn yellow and drop off in the fall. "Ribbon forest" are visible on the slopes in this area. These are elongated narrow forest strips growing perpendicular to prevailing wind directions and alternating with narrow bands of moist-wet snow glades. Also, you can find good examples of "ghost" trees on the mountain. These whitebark pines were killed by a combination of mountain pine beetles and blister rust attacks. They became bleached from the summer sun, giving them a ghost-white appearance. Near the peak of the mountain are "banner" or "flag" trees and stunted trees called "krummholz," which are often hundreds of years old and only two feet high.

Magruder Crossing Bridge: The only place in the upper Selway drainage you can drive across the Selway River is at Magruder Crossing. This steel pony-truss bridge was built by CCC's in 1935.

Indian Creek Hatchery: The Indian Creek hatching channel was constructed in 1964 so that spring Chinook salmon eggs could be planted in the Selway River drainage. Fish had been unable to reach the Selway since the construction of the Lewiston Dam in 1929.

A total of approximately two million eggs were planted each year from 1965 to 1981 and again in 1985. In the spring, the emerging fry were trapped and distributed in the upper Selway by vehicle, stock, and aircraft. This supplemented the naturally spawning Chinook salmon in the Selway River. Chinook salmon are found throughout the Selway River, however, they are usually seen during peak spawning activity in late August and early September.

Magruder Guard Station: The Magruder Guard Station is located 1/2 mile from Road #468. The elevation is 4,100 feet. After the widespread forest fires of 1910 and 1919, the Forest Service built many low-standard roads into the area. The road along Deep Creek was first surveyed in 1919-1920 and the road was constructed to the newly established tent camp known as Deep Creek Ranger Station. The name was later changed to Magruder. The office/residence and ranger's house were built by Ole Tangen, a Forest Service employee. The CCC constructed the bar, corral, and woodshed.

The station is eligible for nomination to the National Register of Historic Places. The structures are excellent examples of rustic log construction and interior craftsmanship.

Deep Creek Bridge: The Deep Creek Bridge is a beautiful example of arched native cut-stone construction. It was built by Lithuanian stonemasons who were assisted by CCC enrollees in the 1930s.

Nez Perce Pass: The elevation at Nez Perce Pass is 6,598 feet. An information board at the pass interprets the history of the area and provides visitors with general information about this spectacular area.

Partially reprinted from Nez Perce and Bitterroot Forests brochure

Lewiston to Moscow Scenic Drive
Known locally as "Spiral Highway," this road winds to the top of Lewiston Hill over the course of sixty-four switchbacks. On its journey to Moscow, the road travels up a canyon rim, offering panoramic views of the Snake and Clearwater Rivers, and the cities of Lewiston, Idaho and Clarkston, Washington.

North Fork-Superior Scenic Drive
Winding beside the North Fork of the Clearwater River 160 miles to Superior, Montana, the North Fork-Superior backcountry road was constructed by the Civilian Conservation Corp in 1935.

Although no services are available on the route, the drive promises scenery around every corner with loads of potential for wildlife enthusiasts.

The route begins in Orofino, traveling along the Grangemont Road to State Highway 11. Bear left at this intersection, proceeding down the highway as it carves a path through dense forest and becomes Forest Road (FR) 247. The road continues past Beaver Creek to Bungalow Ranger Station where the road splits.

Here, proceed east on FR 250 to Kelly Forks Ranger Station. For 4-wheel drive vehicles, continue on FR 250 through Black Canyon to Deception Gulch. RV's should take FR 255 through the Moose City ghost town, meeting back up with FR 250 at Deception Gulch. From the gulch, continue your drive eastward towards the Continental Divide and Montana.

Palouse Divide Scenic Drive
Following the well-maintained, dirt Forest Road (FR) 377, the Palouse Divide Scenic Drive provides a backcountry view of some of the area's finest landscapes. The route wanders down the Palouse Divide, providing travelers with magnificent views of Palouse Country and distant mountain peaks.

After driving on FR 377 for 17 miles, travelers should bear onto FR 447 at a well-marked T-intersection. FR 447 continues 14 miles back to State Highway 6. The route is open to vehicles from late spring to late autumn, while cross-country skiers and snowmobilers rule the road during winter.

Salmon River Scenic Drive
Constructed by the Civilian Conservation Corp between 1933-1939, the Salmon River Road winds upstream twenty-seven miles beside the famous River of No Return. The road requires extreme caution at all times, and drivers should be prepared to proceed slowly. For those willing to take the time, however, the drive offers several points of interest.

Located two miles from Riggins, Shorts Bar is named for early settler, William H. Short. After traveling across America, Short finally settled on the Snake River in 1879 to undertake a hydraulic mining operation. Today, scars from his mining operations are still evident, although the area's large, white sandbar provides plenty of opportunities for summer fun.

Six miles from Shorts Bar, travelers will encounter Lake Creek Bridge. In 1964, a mountainside up Lake Creek slid into the drainage, slamming down a wall of water and debris that that washed out the bridge's northern portion. Just one mile further down the road, drivers will spot Ruby Rapid named after the industrial-grade garnets lining the area.

Fifteen miles from Riggins, the Civilian Conservation Corp constructed the Manning Bridge. The bridge is named after a crewmember who died when he fell off the bluff near the bridge's right end. The road then winds another mile to Elkhorn Creek, which was a ferry site operated by Frederick and Susan Shearer during the area's mining boom.

French Creek, situated twenty miles from Riggins, was named for eight French miners. At one time, a state bridge crossed the creek, and in 1901, the road was an official state highway. When the bridge blew down later that year, the highway ceased to exist. Seven miles down the road from French Creek, Chittam Rapid marks the end of the scenic drive as well as a popular takeout point for Salmon River boat trips.

Doumecq and Joseph Plains/Optional Rice Creek and Rocky Canyon Side Trip
Approximately 17 miles north of Lucile on U.S. Highway 95. Merge northwest off U.S. Highway 95, and in 1 mile, cross over the Salmon River Bridge. Turn right (north) on the Canfield Road.

The Doumecq-Joseph Plains is a high plateau bounded by the Salmon River Canyon and Hells Canyon that covers over 250 square miles. The region has always been the land of cattle with the first homesteaders arriving in the mid 1800s. The drive features plains dotted with old corrals, abandoned buildings, and fields of waving grass.

The route also provides drivers with other sightseeing options. Instead of proceeding to the top of the Doumecq-Joseph Plains, bear right down Rice Creek for four miles to cross the Salmon River at the head of Rocky Canyon. The route continues eleven miles up Graves Creek before reentering U.S. Highway 95 at Cottonwood. This route is inundated with western history. During the 1800s, the old Boise Trail traversed the canyon walls and rivers on its path to the Camas Prairie. In 1908, an official road was constructed through Rocky Canyon, which was then replaced in 1950 by an Army Corps of Engineers route.

Pittsburg Landing & Saddle
Approximately 17 miles north of Lucile on U.S. Highway 95. Merge northwest off U.S. Highway 95, and in 1 mile, reach the Salmon River Bridge. At the bridge's west end, bear left (south).

Winding near the Snake River, this backcountry drive promises travelers an array of spectacular scenery. From its start, the route travels thirteen miles over the picturesque Pittsburg Saddle, offering views of the Snake and Salmon River gorges below. The route then drops to Pittsburg Landing, often noted as one of the prettiest places in Idaho during spring.

The Pittsburg Landing and Saddle regions have been inhabited since the dawn of man. Evidence of Native American habitation has been discovered in the area, and sheepherders and ranchers settled the region in the early 1900s. Today, traces of these early dwellers are still visible, and a picnicking and camping area are found at the historic landing.

Lewis & Clark on the Lolo Trail
Layers of History
The edges of time blur when you follow the Lolo Trail, a route traveled by the Lewis and Clark expedition in 1805 and 1806; the Nez Perce, Salish, and other Indian tribes for centuries before the explorers arrived; miners, trappers and settlers for a century after their arrival. Most of the route is primitive, the landscape much the same as it was when Lewis and Clark traveled it.

Lewis and Clark reached the Bitterroot Valley in Montana mid-September 1805. The weather was beginning to change, with frost at night and snow on the surrounding mountains. To the west lay the mountains they knew they had to cross. They left Traveller's Rest near present-day Lolo Montana, September 11.

From Traveller's Rest they traveled westerly, crossing the Bitterroot Divide and climbing to follow ridge tops, descending to traverse saddles. Clark and six hunters broke out of the mountains September 20 and found themselves at the edge of a prairie near what is now the small town of Weippe, Idaho.

Buffalo Road
For the Nimiipuu (the Nez Perce) the Lolo Trail was the "Road to Buffalo Country," a route they

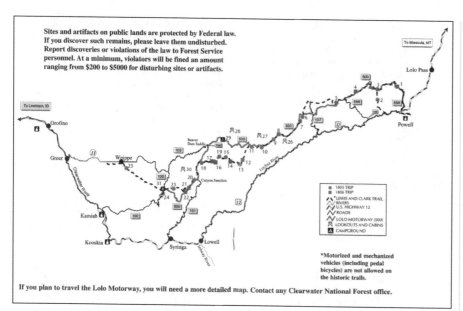

Sites and artifacts on public lands are protected by Federal law. If you discover such remains, please leave them undisturbed. Report discoveries or violations of the law to Forest Service personnel. At a minimum, violators will be fined an amount ranging from $200 to $5000 for disturbing sites or artifacts.

*Motorized and mechanized vehicles (including pedal bicycles) are not allowed on the historic trails.

If you plan to travel the Lolo Motorway, you will need a more detailed map. Contact any Clearwater National Forest office.

traveled annually to hunt buffalo and trade with Plains Indians. For the Salish, it was the "Trail to the Nimiipuu," a route to salmon fishing and trading with Plateau and Coastal Indians.

The Nimiipuus hunted and gathered food across their homeland, from the Bitterroots to the Blue Mountains in present-day Oregon. Each summer Nimiipuu families traveled the Lolo Trail to the buffalo grounds on the Great Plains.

In the early 1700s, horses spread north from Spanish colonies in New Mexico, eventually reaching the Nimiipuu homeland, becoming part of the Nimiipuu way of life and providing a means to travel the Lolo Trail and beyond faster and farther than ever before.

Nearly two centuries later, in 1877, five bands of Nimiipuu followed the Lolo Trail in their attempt to elude General O. O. Howard and the U.S. Army charged with moving them onto a reservation.

The journey across the 1,170-mile route lasted nearly four months. It began near Wallowa Lake, Oregon (the homeland of Chief Joseph's band), and ended at the Bear Paw Mountains near Chinook, Montana.

The route was designated the Nez Perce (Nee-Me-Poo) National Historic Trail in 1986.

Wagon Road

In May 1866, sixty years after Lewis and Clark journeyed east across the Lolo Trail, an engineer by the name of Wellington Bird left Lewiston, Idaho, with construction workers, cooks, teamsters, blacksmiths, the surveyor Sewell Truax and others. The Secretary of the Interior had hired Bird to build a wagon road from Missoula, Montana, to Lewiston.

The road was to be a commerce route for mining traffic from Bannack and Virginia City, Montana, to Lewiston and beyond.

After scouting the area, Bird realized he could not build the road on the budget allowed him. Instead, he and his crew relocated and improved the most difficult sections of the Lolo Trail. They widened the trail into a road on the west end, from Weippe to an area called Musselshell. By the end of September 1866 they had finished their work.

For decades, the trail remained basically the way they left it, used by the Nimiipuu, prospectors, trappers and settlers. In 1893 the infamous Carlin hunting party ventured onto the trail. Deep snow nearly trapped the men. They got out alive but left their ill cook George Colgate behind to die.

Forest Service Road

In 1897, President Cleveland proclaimed the establishment of the Bitter Root Reserve, and the Lolo Trail fell within its boundaries.

The Bitter Root Reserve became the Clearwater and Lolo National Forests, and in 1907, crews cleared decades of brush and fallen trees from the Lolo Trail.

In 1909, Forest Service rangers set up stations at Powell and Elk Summit and began the business of overseeing the vast country for the United States government.

The Forest Service managing the Lolo Trail on the Idaho side of the Bitterroot divide was headquartered at Kooskia.

Over the years crews built trails, constructed fire lookouts, strung phone lines across the forest to join headquarters with lookouts and remote ranger stations. And, of course, they fought fires started from summer lightning storms.

Model Ts to SUVs

In 1925 road construction began near the Lolo Trail on the east end, starting at Lolo Hot Springs in Montana and ending west of the divide at Powell in 1928.

In 1930, the Forest Service appealed to Congress for money to build roads for fire fighting. They needed low standard "motor ways" or "truck trails." They got both money and permission to proceed.

The Civilian Conservation Corps worked in conjunction with the Forest Service. Construction was finished in 1934. The Lolo Motorway became a reality, following the general route of the Lolo Trail.

No one anticipated that the public would use the road much, but that's exactly what happened.

In the '30s it was Model Ts. Today it's SUVs.

The Motorway Today

The Lolo Motorway, Forest Road 500, winds along ridges above the Lochsa River. Don't let the term "motorway" fool you. It's an old-fashioned term from the early days of automobile travel when people didn't take drives; they "motored."

You will find no gas stations, stores, developed water sources, or other services along this high elevation, precipitous dirt road. You will find 100 miles of breathtaking scenery set in a sea of mountains.

Mountain lakes and ridge-top vistas beckon travelers. Trails meander alongside and away from the motorway, offering paths for hiker explorers.

Near Weitas Meadows, you can cross a rustic boardwalk made by volunteers dedicating their labor and time to protect the fragile meadow.

In the summer, wildflowers blaze in glorious colors across hillsides and meadows. In the autumn, foliage and underbrush put on their color, and berries hang on bushes ripe for picking.

A few lookout towers loom above treetops on remote ridges. Once used for fire detection, these days they're used for getting away from it all, rented by people seeking a quiet experience with inspiring views.

The history of the motorway is rich. Many sites along the route are revered by American Indians. Others are valued for their primitive state. All sites deserve our respect and protection. Enjoy them, but take only photographs and memories with you. Only take photographs of the American Indians with their permission.

Historic Crossing

The Lewis and Clark Expedition traveled across the Lolo Trail in 1805 and 1806.

The following sites are listed and numbered east to west as you will find them on your travels across the Lolo Trail and the Lewis and Clark route along the Lolo Motorway.

On their westward journey in 1805 members of the expedition struggled to survive, often starving, cold and ill. They made the trip in nine days.

On their eastward journey in 1806, they made the trip in five days with the help of Nimiipuu guides. They started their journey once without guides but turned back because of deep snow.

1) 13 Mile Camp - June 28, 1806
Lewis wrote, "we continued our rout along the dividing ridge passing one very deep hollow and at the distance of six miles passed our encampment of the [15th] of September [1805]...about eleven O'clock we arrived at an untimbered side of a mountain with a Southern aspect just above the fishery here we found an abundance of grass for our horses as the Indians had informed us. as our horses were very hungary and much fatiegued and from information no other place where we could obtain grass for them within the reach of this evening's travel we determined to remain at this place all night having come 13 miles only."

"I observed a range of high mountains Covered with Snow... Their top bald or void of timber…From this mountain I could observe high ruged mountains in every direction as far as I could See." -Captain William Clark

2) Wendover Ridge Rest Site - September 15, 1805
Stopping to wait two hours for those at the rear to catch up, Clark wrote in his journal: "about 2 hours the rear of the party came up much fatigued & horses more So, Several horses Sliped and roled down Steep hills which hurt them verry much The one which Carried my desk & Small trunk Turned over & roled down a mountain for 40 yards & lodged against a tree, broke the Desk the horse escaped and appeared but little hurt."

3) Snowbank Camp - September 15, 1805
Expedition members completed the difficult climb up Wendover Ridge and finally arrived back on the Lolo Trail. Clark described their situation: "[W]hen we arrived at the top As we Conceved, we could find no water and Concluded to Camp and make use of the Snow we found on the top to cook the remn. of our Colt & make our Supe, evening verry cold and cloudy." They awoke to four inches of new snow the next morning.

4) Bears Oil and Roots -June 27, 1806
Lewis wrote, "[We] arrived at our encampment of September [16, 1805]... and again ascended to the

dividing ridge on which we continued nine miles when the ridge became lower and we arrived at a situation very similar to our encampment of the last evening tho' the ridge was somewhat higher and the snow had not been so long desolved of course there was but little grass. here we encamped for the night having traveled 28 miles over these mountains without releiving the horses from their packs or their having any food .... our meat being exhausted we issued a pint of bears oil to a mess which with their boiled roots made an agreeable dish."

5) Lonesome Cove Camp - September 16, 1805
Private Whitehouse described this campsite: "towards evening we descended the mountain down in a lonesome cove on a creek where we Camped in a thicket of Spruce pine & bolsom fir timber. all being tired & hungry, obledged us to kill another colt and eat the half of it this evening, it has quit Snowing this evening, but continues chilley and cold." Clark wrote, "I have been wet and as cold in every part as I ever was in my life, indeed I was at one time fearfull my feet would freeze in the thin mockersons which I wore…"

6) The Sinque Hole - September 17, 1805
Private Whitehouse noted: "Camped at a Small branch on the mountain near a round deep Sinque hole full of water. we being hungry obledged us to kill the other Sucking colt to eat."

7) The Smoking Place -June 27, 1806 (Please respect The Smoking Place, a site special to the Nimiipuu)
Lewis wrote, "the road still continued on the heights of the same dividing ridge... to our encampment of the 17th of September last. about one mile short of this encampment on an elivated point we halted by the request of the Indians a few minutes and smoked the pipe."

8) Greensward Camp -June 26, 1806
Lewis wrote, "we ascended and decended severall lofty and steep hights...late in the evening much to the satisfaction of ourselves and the comfort of our horses we arrived at the desired spot and encamped on the steep side of a mountain convenient to a good spring. here we found an abundance of fine grass for our horses. this situation was the side of an untimbered mountain with a fair southern aspect where the snows from appearance had been desolved about 10 days. the grass was young and tender of course and had much the appearance of the greenswoard."

9) Dry Camp - September 18,1805
The expedition split this morning, Clark moving ahead with six hunters to look for game, Lewis following with the main party, equipment and supplies. Lewis wrote in his journal that evening, "We marched 18 miles this day and encamped on the side of a steep mountain; we suffered for water this day passing one rivulet only; we wer fortunate in finding water in a steep raviene about ° maile from our camp. this morning we finished the remainder of our last coult. we dined & suped on a skant proportion of portable soupe, a few canesters of which, a little bears oil and about 20 lbs. of candles form our stock of provision."

10) Spirit Revival Ridge - September 19, 1805
Clark and his party saw the Camas Prairie (north of present-day Grangeville, Idaho) for the first time from Sherman Peak. Lewis described their reactions: "[T]he ridge terminated and we to our inexpressible joy discovered a large tract of Prairie country lying to the S. W. and widening as it appeared to extend to the W. through that plain the Indian informed us that the Columbia river, in

which we were in surch run. this plain appeared to be about 60 Miles distant, but our guide assured us that we should reach it's borders tomorrow the appearance of this country, our only hope for subsistence greately revived the sperits of the party already reduced and much weakened for the want of food."

11) Sherman Saddle - September 19, 1805
They left Sherman Peak and traveled through a pass now known as Sherman Saddle. Private Whitehouse described it: "[We] descended down the mountn, which was verry Steep descent, for about three miles. then assended another as bad as any we have ever been up before. it made the Sweat run off the horses & ourselves."

12) Cache Mountain -June 17, 1806
When the expedition reached Cache Mountain, they had to turn back. The snow was deep, and they feared they would not find enough food for themselves or their horses. They cached their equipment and returned to the Weippe Prairie. Clark wrote, "having come to this resolution, we ordered the party to make a deposit of all the baggage which we had not immediate use for, and also all the roots and bread of Cows which they had except an allowance for a fiew days to enable them to return to Some place at which we could Subsist by hunting untill we precured a guide."

Note: The following seven sites lie along a section of trail hazardous to travel, thick with brush, with no visible trail tread and no signs posted.

13) Hungery Creek - September 18, 1805
Clark wrote, "I proceded on in advance with Six hunters to try and find deer or Something to kill…and Encamped on a bold running Creek passing to the left which I call Hungery Creek as at that place we had nothing to eate."

14) Retreat Camp -June 17, 1806
After they cached their supplies and turned back to the Weippe Prairie, Lewis wrote, "the party were a good deel dejected....this is the first time since we have been on this long tour that we have ever been compelled to retreat or make a retrograde march."

15) Portable Soup Camp - September 19, 1805
Even though revived by the sight of the Camas Prairie, Lewis and his party were weak from hunger. He wrote, "having traveled 18 miles over a very bad road. we took a small quantity of portable soup, and retired to rest much fatiegued. Several of the men are unwell of the disentary. brakings out, or irruptions of the Skin, have also been common with us for some time."

16) Jerusalem Artichoke Camp -June 25, 1806
After several hours of travel, the expedition stopped for the day. At their campsite Lewis came upon "a parcel of roots of which the Shoshones Eat. it is a Small knob root a good deel in flavour and Consistency like the Jerusolem artichoke.... after dinner we continued our rout to hungary creek and encamped about one and a half miles below our Encampment of the 16" [of September 1805]."

17) Horse Steak Meadow -June 16, 1806
The expedition set out early this morning, retracing their route of September 1805. Clark wrote, "We found much dificulty in finding the road, as it was So frequently covered with Snow. we arived early in the evening at the place I had killed and left the flesh of a horse for the party in my rear last Septr. here is a Small glade in which there is Some grass, not a Sufficency of our horses, but we thought it adviseable to remain here all night as

we apprehended if we proceeded further we should find less grass."

18) Hearty Meal Stop - September 20, 1805
Lewis and his party stopped here to eat their midday meal. Clark and his hunting party had gone ahead of the others and had left them meat for their sustenance. Lewis wrote, "at one oclock we halted and made a hearty meal on our horse beef much to the comfort of our hungry stomachs."

19) Gass Creek - September 1805 & June 1806
Gass Creek (named decades later for Sergeant Patrick Gass) is a tributary of Hungery Creek. Twelve miles of the expedition's route passed through the drainage in 1805. They returned to the area in June 1806. From the Gass Creek interpretive sign along the Lolo Motorway, you can look down into the Hungery Creek drainage.

20) Full Stomach Camp - September 20, 1805
Lewis and his men bedded down this night with full stomachs following days of difficult travel with little food. Lewis wrote, "we encamped on a ridge where ther was but little grass for our horses, and at a distance from water. however we obtained as much as served our culinary purposes and suped on our beef."

21) Salmon Trout Camp -June 18, 1806
The expedition camped and rested here for three days. Lewis wrote, "we proceeded on to Collin's Creek [today called Eldorado Creek] and encamped in a pleasant situation at the upper part of the meadows about 2 ms. above our encampment of the 15th [of September 1805]. we sent out several hunters but they returned without having killed anything. they saw a number of salmon in the creek and shot at them several times without success. we directed Colter and Gibson to fix each of them a gigg in the morning and indevour to take some of the salmon."

22) Small Prairie Camp -June 15, 1806
The expedition set out from Weippe in a hard rain. Lewis wrote, the road which was very Sliprey, and it was with great dificulty that the loaded horses Could assend the hills and Mountains...incamped near a small prarie in the bottom land. the fallen timber in addition to the slippry roads made our march slow and extreemly laborious on our horses. the country is exceedingly thickly timbered with long leafed pine, some pitch pine, larch, white pine, white cedar or arborvita of large size, and a variety of firs."

23) Lewis and Clark Grove - September 19, 1805
Clark and six men camped after 22 miles of travel. He wrote, "passed over a mountain, and the heads of branch of hungary creek, two high mountains, ridges and through much falling timber (which caused our road of to day to be double the derect distance on the Course) Struck a large Creek passing to our left which I Kept down for 4 miles and left it to our left & passed [down the] mountain bad falling timber to a Small Crek passing to our left and Encamped."

24) Pheasant Camp -September 21, 1805
Lewis and his men made their way west to Lolo Creek. Lewis wrote, "encamped in a small open bottom where there was tolerable food for our horses. I directed the horses to be hubbled to prevent delay in the morning being determined to make a forced march tomorrow in order to reach if possible the open country. we killed a few Pheasants, and I killd a prarie woolf which together with the balance of our horse beef and some crawfish which we obtained in the creek enabled us to make one more hearty meal, not knowing where the next was to be found."

25) Weippe Prairie - September 20, 1805
Clark wrote, "Set out early and proceeded on through a Countrey as ruged as usial...and at 12 miles decended the mountain to a leavel pine proceeded on through a butifull Countrey for three miles to a Small Plain in which I found maney Indian lodges... a man Came out to meed me with great Caution...proceeded on with a Chief to his Village 2 miles in the Same Plain, where we were treated kindly in their way and continued with them all night" Lewis and his men joined them two days later.

Roads to Reach the Lolo Trail System
Several roads lead to the Lolo Motorway. You're a long way from anywhere, so check with local Forest Service offices for current road conditions. Pack provisions, including a Clearwater National Forest map, spare tire, food, water and gas.

Your sight distance and opportunities to pass or pull over are often limited, and you need to travel slowly.

East to west, from U.S. Highway 12:
- Parachute Hill Road 569 - 110 miles west of Lolo Pass, 0 mile east of turnoff to Powell. Gravel surface.
- Doe Creek Road 566 - 8 miles west of Powell to Fishing Creek Road 108 turnoff; mile to Road 566. Narrow one-lane dirt road.
- Saddle Camp Road 107 - 34 miles west of Powell at milepost 140. Gravel surface.
- Smith Creek Road 101 - 1 mile west of Syringa. Gravel surface.

West to east:
- Beaver Dam Saddle - Follow Road 100 east out of Kamiah, turn north onto Road 103, turn east at the junction with Road 104 at Beaver Dam Saddle. Or follow Road 100 east out of Weippe to Road 103, then turn east at the junction with Road 104.
- Canyon Junction - Follow Road 100 east out of Kamiah to Road 500, or follow Road 100 east out of Weippe then south to connect with Road 500.

Getting There
From the east, take Parachute Hill Road 569. It leaves U.S. Highway 12 just east of the turnoff to Powell Ranger Station. Or take Saddle Camp Road 107, which leaves Highway 12 twenty-seven miles west of Powell Ranger Station. (Caution! You may encounter logging traffic on these roads.)

From the west, follow the national forest access sign posted alongside Highway 12 by the bridge that crosses the Clearwater River at Kamiah. Turn onto Kamiah-Pierce Road 100. Follow Road 100 to Lolo Forks Campground.

You'll cross a bridge and turn right onto Forest Road 500. Fourteen miles and 45 minutes later, you'll come to Canyon junction, a five-point intersection. Road 500 turns into a narrow, unsurfaced travel way at this junction and remains that way as you continue eastward along the route. It's 73 miles from Canyon Junction to Powell Junction where Road 569 meets Road 500. This segment is the historic Lolo Motorway. From Kamiah to Powell, you'll travel 119 miles.

Or, from the west, get to Road 100 by driving east from Weippe, off Idaho State Highway 11, which leaves Highway 12 at Greer.

Drive with Care!
The Lolo Motorway is narrow, a one-lane road with nothing more than what nature supplies as a surface. Some stretches hold big rocks that can scrape the underside of a low-clearance vehicle. It's best to drive a tough vehicle with high clear-ance and good tires. Towing trailers or driving RVs or motor homes on many stretches of the Motorway is not advised.

The high elevation route is open and free of snow generally from July through September, sometimes longer. Lightning storms are common in July and August, and snow can come early.

Selecting a Campsite
- Look for established sites where others have already camped rather than start new sites.
- Please use a stove, or limit campfires to occasional small fires on pans that you can clean up completely.
- If you have a campfire, avoid building new rock rings, and collect only small deadwood from the ground. (Large logs and standing dead trees provide homes for wildlife like the pileated woodpecker.) Make sure to put out your fire completely, scatter charcoal, restore the site, and pack out unburned items.
- High mountain lakes and surrounding areas are especially susceptible to damage, so avoid soft, wet soil, and camp a good distance from water sources.
- Keep all soap and food particles out of creeks, lakes, and springs.
- Summer storms can bring lightning to high ridges. If you see storm clouds coming in, move to a lower elevation until the storm passes.
- Pack out all garbage. You'll find no garbage receptacles along the Lolo Motorway.
- Toilets are few and far between. Where bathroom facilities aren't provided, use a trowel or shovel and bury human waste at least 200 feet away from water, in a common latrine (for groups) or in individual "cat holes" 6-8 inches deep.
- Make sure pets are under your control at all times.

Leave No Trace!
The high elevation ground of the Lolo Trail Corridor is easily damaged by people, stock animals, and vehicles. Respect road and trail restrictions. Travel and camp only where permitted. Make no new trails or campsites. Leave no trace of your visit, and take no mementos. Instead, take photographs, and recall your memories of time spent along the route.

Places to Camp or Stop
You'll find scattered campsites along the route and places to stop to stretch your legs or have a picnic.

29) Rocky Ridge Lake - 12 miles east of Canyon Junction along Road 500. Clearwater National Forest. 5 campsites, restroom, no drinking water.

23) Lewis and Clark Grove - 20 miles east of Kamiah via Roads 100 and 500. Clearwater National Forest. No camping. Restroom, no drinking water. Short 1/2-mile hike.

31) Lolo Campground - 23 miles east of Kamiah along Road 100. Clearwater National Forest. 5 campsites, restrooms, no drinking water.

There are a few retired fire lookouts and one historic cabin you can rent along the route across the Clearwater National Forest. You need to contact the Kooskia Ranger Station to book your stay.

26) Castle Butte Lookout - 85 miles east of Kooskia via U.S. Highway 12, Roads 107 and 500.

27) Liz Butte Cabin - 26 miles east of Canyon junction via Road 500.

28) Weitas Butte Lookout - 52 miles east of Kamiah via U.S. Highway 12, Roads 100, 103, 104, 500 and 557.

30) Austin Ridge Lookout - 32 miles east of Kamiah via Roads 100, 500, 520 and 523.

Reprinted from a U.S. Forest Service-Clearwater National Forest brochure

Elk City Wagon Road
Picture yourself on a wagon 100 years ago. The rough road makes your ride bumpy, and you hang on as the wagon moves forward. In the winter you're atop a sleigh drawn by horses wearing snowshoes. They plod their way through drifts as high as ten feet. The air is cold. It's rough going.

Travel along the Elk City Wagon Road, and follow the same road miners and freighters took to the gold fields of Elk City.

Traveling the Road Today
How to get there: The Elk City Wagon Road begins at Harpster, a small town on the South Fork of the Clearwater River. Harpster is between Grangeville and Kooskia at milepost 13 (about 13 miles from each town). It's located along State Highway 13, part of the Northwest Passage Scenic Byway.

If you're traveling from Grangeville, go past the Harpster store into the small community. Turn right at the sign describing the wagon road. If you're traveling from Kooskia, turn left at the wagon road description sign once you're in Harpster.

Tour length: Starting at Harpster, you'll wind your way 53 miles to Elk City. The tour will take you 4-6 hours with travel of 10-15 mph. The route is marked at each mile and road junction with brown and white "Elk City WR" markers. Reset the mileage counter in your vehicle at zero when you begin your tour.

Road conditions: Most of this single-lane road is unpaved. Drive slowly when conditions are dry and dusty. There are few turnouts. Some stretches of road are narrow, and there are some tight switchbacks. Vehicles with high clearance travel the route well, although passenger cars can make the trip if driven with caution. Large recreational vehicles and vehicles towing trailers are not recommended for travel along the Elk City Wagon Road. Overhanging branches and rocks protruding from the roadway can cause serious damage. Snow at higher elevations restricts travel to summer (late June through September). Check with the Clearwater or Red River Ranger Districts for current road conditions.

Facilities: There are no gas stations along the Elk City Wagon Road. Gas is available at Kooskia, Harpster, Grangeville or Elk City. There are no campgrounds along the route, but there are places to pull off and set up a tent. There are picnic and toilet facilities near the Newsome Creek Cabin.

When you reach Elk City, you'll find a small, full-service community with hotels, restaurants and gas stations. Your return trip to Harpster via State Highway 14, a 50-mile drive, takes 1 1/2 hours.

Traveling the Road 100 Years Ago
On a spring day in 1900, a wagon made its way along the Elk City Wagon Road. Loaded with mining supplies and mail, a team of several horses pulled the wagon. The driver knew he'd have to switch from wagon to sleigh when he encountered snow, but the road was well used and snow packed. If he could make it to Mountain House Way Station before nightfall, he could get a good meal and a place to sleep. With a little luck and no breakdowns, the freight would reach Elk City in another three days.

So it was along the Elk City Wagon Road from 1895 to 1932. The freight and stage route was prominent in the mining and homesteading history of central Idaho.

Starting at Harpster on the South Fork of the Clearwater River 80 miles upstream from Lewiston, the road stretched about 50 miles to the mining town of Elk City. A branch of the road ran from Stites and joined the main route at the town of Clearwater. Beginning in the South Fork River valley at an elevation of about 1600 feet, the road climbed as high as 6200 feet in the Baldy Mountain vicinity and then dropped into the Elk City basin at around 4000 feet.

The first route in this area was the Southern Nez Perce Trail. Indian tribes used the trail to travel from the Camas Prairie in Idaho to the Bitterroot Valley in Montana. The Southern Nez Perce Trail remains significant to the Nimiipuu, the Nez Perce people.

The first gold miners from Pierce used the trail on their way to explore the Elk City area in 1861. The trail became a thoroughfare and was modified for pack strings and wagons in the mining boom that followed. By 1890, several way stations had been built along the trail: Harpster, Newsome House, and a rest station for mail carriers called Ten Mile.

In 1894 construction started on the Elk City Wagon Road. The road was finished in 1895. It closely followed the original trail, overlaying it in a few places. By 1896, there were way stations at Switchback, Mountain House, Corral Hill, and Mud Springs, providing room and food for travelers. These stations were some of the first homesteads in the area.

A stage trip from Stites to Elk City took two days in the summer. Leaving Stites at 6 a.m., the stage arrived at Mountain House by noon and at Newsome by nightfall. There, travelers spent the night. In the winter, the trip to Elk City took five days, with overnight stops at Switchback, Mountain House, Newsome, and Mud Springs. The stage fare from Stites to Elk City was $6 in 1910.

The Journey Begins
(Mile locator in parentheses)

1) Harpster (0.0)
Prospectors came through here from the Camas Prairie on their way to the gold fields of central Idaho in the 1860s. It's reported that Abraham Harpster camped here in 1861. Pioneers began settling in the valley by 1864. The settlement was called Jackson Bridge, Clearwater Station, Brownsville, Riverside and Bridgeport. Finally, in 1893, it was named Harpster.

Harpster's claim to "dill pickle fame" was the sale of homemade pickles to places as far away as Spokane, Washington. Pickles were delivered to the Davenport Hotel there in the 1920s.

From mile 1.0-1.6, remnants of the original Wagon Road are visible on the left side of the road.

2) Wall Creek Bridge (3.2)
The original Wagon Road continued up Wall Creek, but today the road is impassable beyond two miles. Follow the Elk City WR markers to the left.

Jacob and Fronia Riebold operated Riebold Station, a 14-room overnight and livery station one mile up Wall Creek. The house was constructed of boards milled on the property. Jacob died in 1911.

In 1916, Fronia married Reverend Knox, who preached the gospel to miners on a peak near Florence above the Salmon River, known today as Gospel Peak.

Follow the Elk City Wagon Road markers to the left.

3) Clearwater (6.6)
This town is located on the original Nez Perce Trail and a branch of the Wagon Road.

The railroad reached Stites in 1902, and Clearwater became a town with a sawmill, livery stable, blacksmith shop, and general store. Caulder's sawmill was at the foot of the hill 1/2 mile north.

At mile 7.5 the road forks. Follow the Elk City WR markers to the left. Take the other fork only in good weather.

At mile 8.7 on a flat covered with small trees, you'll come to the site of the Folden Sawmill, which operated in the 1940s.

4) Four Ways Went Junction (9.5)
The original Wagon Road crosses here. The unmaintained fork to the left is the original route not passable by highway vehicles. Downhill to the west is Nolen Way Station, the only remaining original building along the Wagon Road.

To see the site, turn right. Proceed 0.3 miles. The old wooden house sits below the road to the left. Nolen Station provided comfort and shelter to travelers and teams.

5) Limestone Rock Outcrop (10.5)
The Ulmer family operated a kiln and sold lime to freighters. They quarried this vein of limestone, and their kiln was on the original road 600 feet uphill. You can walk to the site, but it's a steep climb.

Lime was available self-service. Customers left payment in an unlocked box. Lime was used to bond rock for concrete foundations.

Junction with Sears Creek Road #1106 (mile 12.4). Turn left.

6) The Initial Tree (12.8)
The road joins the route of the original Wagon Road. One-half mile west is a living monument of the Elk City Wagon Road. Follow the trail to the left to reach a ponderosa pine several hundred years old.

Travelers carved their initials, dates, and brands in the tree. Some marks, barely visible,

may have been made by Indian tribes en route to Montana. The tree is 5 1/2 feet in diameter and has survived many lightning strikes. Remnants of the original road are also visible to the right one-tenth of a mile above.

Junction with Road #284 (mile 13.2). Turn right.

7) Switchback Station (13.4)
Built in 1895, Switchback provided a full-service overnight facility and the first major stopover en route to Elk City. The large barns could accommodate 100 head of stock. Patches of nettles grow over the manure-rich soil where the barns were located.

The original switchback of the Elk City Wagon Road is a few yards beyond these nettle patches to the north. Stay clear of these patches. Nettles sting!

8) Haysheds (13.7)
Freighters switched loads from wagons to sleighs in winter. A pole structure was used to store hay and supplies at a commonly used transfer site near here.

9) Water Spout (14.8) - Wall Creek
Freighters filled water containers from a spout eight feet above the road. (Play it safe. Don't drink the water!) Many of these sites were reference points rather than significant landmarks.

Storm Creek Saddle (mile 15.2). Junction with Road #1851; follow Elk City WR markers to the left.

10) Corral Hill (17.0)
Built in 1896, Corral Hill Station provided lodging and a livery stable. The house was north above the road; the barn and stock facilities were on the ridge to the south. A spring and a house platform remain.

The mountains to the south are (left to right) Pilot Rock, Buffalo Hump, the Gospels, and the Seven Devils.

11) Southern Nez Perce Trail (17.5)
Here the Elk City Wagon Road intersects the original Southern Nez Perce Trail. Used for centuries by Nez Perce Indians to journey between the

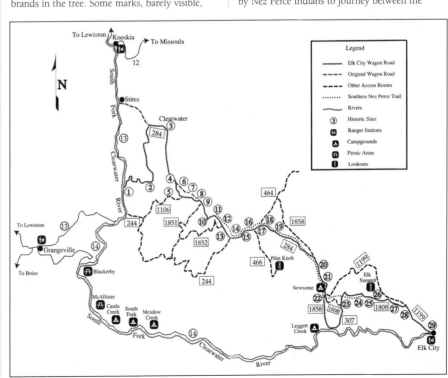

Camas Prairie and Montana, the trail was the main route east before the wagon road was built. The road intersects the trail in several places ahead.

Lloyd Magruder, Elk City merchant well-known and respected in the Idaho Territory, followed the Indian Trail to transport goods from Lewiston to his store in Elk City. In 1863 robbers murdered him and his traveling companions, taking the gold dust miners had paid them for goods purchased in Magruder's Elk City store. (Ask for your copy of the Magruder Road Corridor brochure at local Forest Service offices.)

12) Ten Mile Cabin (18.9)
You are at the junction with Road #1852. Here, ten miles from Riebold Station, a small log cabin was used by mail carriers in winter. It provided a bunk, fireplace, and bare essentials for preparing meals.

The road for the next half-mile was reconstructed in 1987 to harvest timber in Clear Creek to the north. Follow the signs as you continue on your journey.

Junction with Clear Creek Road #1855 (mile 19.6). Stay right.

13) Grangeville Tree (19.8)
A large fir tree once marked the spot where stage drivers stopped to give passengers their first view of Grangeville and the Camas Prairie.

14) China Point (20.2)
This landmark was named for three Chinese who lived nearby. Legend claims the men were evicted from the Newsome area and later murdered. The site bears no trace of historic debris.

Near this site, the Forest Service built the Jackpot Ranger Station early in the 1900s.

15) Log Corduroy (21.0)
The next two miles traverse the highest elevations on the route (6,000-6,280 feet). Snowdrifts are common until late June. The road may be muddy.

Freighters placed logs in the worst mud holes all along the Wagon Road. Remnants of this original 'log corduroy" are still visible in a couple of spots.

16) Mountain House (23.0)
The three-story log structure that sat here was especially important in winter. Freighters were often stopped here by heavy snows. Passengers on snowshoes sometimes broke trail for the horses. The building sites and a few timbers are all that remain.

Junction with Pilot Knob Road #466 (23.4). Stay left.

17) Pilot Rock (23.5)
Pilot Rock, seen one-half mile to the south (elevation 6,952 feet), is important to Nez Perce Indian tradition and culture.

18) Big Switchback (24.3)
This was a tight turn for wagons pulled by many teams. From here the Wagon Road descends six miles to Newsome Creek. This road is steep. Drive with caution on this stretch. Gear down!

19) Toothacher Springs (25.2)
Named for a nearby spring with cold water, this area was a rest stop for freighters coming out of Elk City hauling heavy loads.

20) Newsome Townsite (30.4)
The main stop at Newsome was a hotel with excellent food operated by the Shissler family. There were several buildings here, including a post office. There was a morgue for temporary storage of bodies to be transported to Grangeville. Gold dredging in the 1940s eliminated all remnants of the buildings. A cemetery still exists between the Wagon Road and private roads. The dwellings here are privately owned. Please respect private property.

Junction with Newsome Creek Road #1858 (30.5). Turn right.

21) Newsome Cabin (32.0)
The Forest Service now maintains toilet and picnic facilities at the site.

Across Newsome Creek is the site where Sing Lee, a Chinese miner, fed and sheltered travelers in the late 1890s. The site is now a campground with toilets and picnic facilities.

22) Elk City Wagon Road (33.9)
The original Wagon Road to the left follows Smith Gulch up Vicory Creek. This 2.2-mile segment is on the National Register of Historic Places. It is closed to vehicle traffic by slides. Continue going straight.

Allison Creek Road #307 (36.6). Turn left.

23) Elk City Wagon Road (40.0)
The route rejoins the original Wagon Road. Stay right.

24) Mud Springs (41.0)
This site included a roadhouse built in 1896. The old roadbed is still evident. Several buildings and a pond were built below the spring area in recent years.

25) The Big Mailbox (43.5)
A log structure about five feet square was anchored between two trees here. It served as a mailbox and supply drop for the South Fork Mines located down the ridge on the breaks of the South Fork of the Clearwater River. The box was placed high so people could reach their mail even when the snow was 6-7 feet deep.

26) Whiskey Creek Flat (44.7)
Some freighters, so heavily laden they could not reach established way stations within a day, camped here.

27) Montgomery Cabin (45.0)
This is the site of one of the earliest mines in the Elk City Mining District. An old prospector stayed on for years without much success. An ore crusher can still be seen at the site.

28) Buffalo Gulch (46.9)
Here was another campsite used by heavily loaded freighters. The original road is to the left, not passable by vehicles. Continue going straight.

Junction with Elk Summit Road #1199 (48.5). Continue straight on the original Wagon Road route.

29) Elk City (51.5)
You have reached the junction with State Highway 14 and are almost to Elk City. The town was established in 1861. It burned almost completely in 1930. Several old cabins in the basin and a store on Main Street remain from the early mining days.

Be Prepared for Your Trip!
Take with you: Food, water, insect repellent, Nez Perce National Forest map, and a camera and binoculars.

Wear: Serviceable shoes

Be sure to have: A full tank of gas!

Reprinted from a U.S. Forest Service-Nez Perce National Forest brochure

HIKES

For information on additional area trails, please contact the Forest Service Ranger Districts listed at the back of this section.

Dworshak Reservoir Area Trails
Distance: varies
Climb: gentle
Difficulty: easy
Usage: heavy
Location: Various access points are found near or within Dworshak State Park.

For those camping at Dworshak State Park, the 10 mile Big Eddy Trail leads to the Big Eddy Recreation Area north of Dworshak Dam. After crossing a small peninsula, this trail predominantly follows the reservoir's shoreline. Another hike can be accessed south of Dworshak Dam. Merry's Bay Trail winds along the south shoreline of Dworshak Reservoir for 0.8 miles. The Canyon Creek Trail is a suitable option for families. At just 1 mile roundtrip, this trail begins near Canyon Creek Campground and wanders near the south shoreline. The final trail begins near the Wells Bench Road. At 2.5 miles one-way, the Cold Springs Trail leads to the Cold Springs Group Camp while following the reservoir's shoreline. All four trails offer outstanding vistas of the reservoir, and fishing opportunities abound along the shore. Best months for hiking are June through September.

Frank Church – River of No Return Wilderness Area

Bear Point, Sheep Hill, and Rattlesnake Lake
Distance: 21 miles roundtrip (Bear Point)
Climb: moderate
Difficulty: moderately difficult
Usage: moderate (light usage last half of trek)
Location: From Grangeville, drive 9 miles west on State Highway 13 and merge onto State Highway 14. Continue on Highway 14, and just before reaching Elk City, bear right onto Forest Road (FR) 222. Proceed 13.5 miles, passing the Red River Ranger Station, and turn left onto FR 468 (Montana Road). Continue 27.5 miles, passing Mountain Meadows, Bargamin Creek, Granite Springs, and Poet Creek Campground to reach Trail 575 at the Dry Saddle Trailhead.

A continuous up and down hike along a wildflower painted ridge offers hikers continual views of the Frank Church-River of No Return and Selway-Bitterroot Wilderness areas as well as access to fourteen alpine lakes providing great fishing opportunities. As Trail 575 begins, hikers will climb past Trilby Lakes, Spread Point Lake, and Lake Creek Lakes. Lake Creek Lakes is very popular for its renowned fishing, so if you plan to hike down a side trail to the lakes, expect company. After passing by Lake Creek Lakes, climb to a low saddle that separates Lake Creek and Rattlesnake Creek and locate a three-way junction. Taking the left trail, proceed to Bear Point. This area provides an outstanding vista of the Salmon River flowing 5,300 feet below and it is common to see bears here as well. To access Sheep Hill, proceed on the right fork at the junction. This trail climbs to the 8,000-foot Deadman's Saddle, then climbs another 400 feet in less than a mile to Sheep Hill Lookout. Bighorn sheep often frequent the area, and Sheep Hill provides access to the four lakes enclosing Sheep Hill. Proceeding on the middle fork, hikers will drop into Rattlesnake Lake along a very faint, unmaintained trail. Best months for hiking are late July to mid-September.

Goose Hump Wilderness Area

Hanover Ridge

Distance: 8 miles roundtrip
Climb: moderate
Difficulty: moderate
Usage: heavy
Location: At Grangeville, drive 32 miles south on County Road 221 (which turns into Forest Road 221). At the junction for FR 444 (Gospels Road), turn left and proceed on FR 444 13.3 miles to the Hanover Mountain Trailhead. FR 444 is a steep, washboard, loose gravel road and four-wheel drive is strongly recommended.

Climbing through meadows lined with wildflowers and forests that are prime elk and mountain lion territory, hikers will find outstanding views of the Gospel Hump Wilderness, Umbrella Butte, Seven Devils Mountains, and Buffalo Hump. A moderate day hike along Hanover Ridge, this trail is well-maintained until the switchback ascent leading to the 7,966-foot peak of Hanover Mountain. Best months for hiking are July and August.

Oregon Butte and Vicinity

Distance: 7 miles roundtrip
Climb: gradual
Difficulty: moderate
Usage: very light
Location: From Grangeville, drive 42 miles east on State Highway 14 to Crooked River Road. Turning onto this gravel road, continue 14 miles, passing the old mining town of Orogrande. At Forest Road (FR) 233 (Orogrande Summit Road), turn right and proceed to a road junction on top of Orogrande Summit. Bear left, driving past Lake Creek Campground, Hump Lake, and a private airstrip, arriving at the Jumbo Camp trailhead near the road's end at Jumbo Mine. Accessing this trailhead requires four-wheel drive as the road is badly worn and steep bedrock areas on the road are often difficult to climb even with four-wheel drive.

Beginning in a marshy meadow, hikers will soon reach an intersection for FR 201 and Trail 202. Staying to the left, continue 2.25 miles on Trail 202 through Jumbo Canyon to a junction at Teepee Flats saddle. Take the right, switchback trail to reach an outstanding vista of the Salmon River Canyon and Oregon's Wallowa Mountains from the top of Oregon Butte. Hikers will likely also see mountain goats and bighorn sheep in the area and shouldn't be surprised to find the lookout tower on Oregon Butte still staffed. Best months for hiking are mid-July through August.

Optional Hikes: 0.25 miles past the junction of FR 201 and Trail 202 is a trail on the right leading to Brandon Lakes. Passing over the rugged Quartzite Ridge populated with mountain goats, hikers will reach the lakes situated in two different cirques.

After hiking 1 mile through Jumbo Canyon, a short, clearly marked trail leads down to Deer Lake.

Approximately 200 yards before reaching Tepee Flats Saddle, hikers can take a faint trail that leads to great fishing at Round Lake. Following a stream, the trail descends into a cirque and passes through a thick spruce forest before ending at the lake.

At the junction on Tepee Flats Saddle, take the left West Fork Trail leading down to the West Fork of Crooked Creek. Continuing 0.5 miles further on the West Fork Trail, find a well-defined side trail leading to Oregon Butte Lake. Although few fish are found in this lake, the hike is very scenic.

For hikers interested in Idaho's mining history, Trail 230 at the Jumbo Camp Trailhead steeply descends into a valley with old mining buildings visible on your left. After crossing Jumbo Creek, mine tailings appear next to the trail which lead to the old mine and mill in 0.25-miles.

While driving along FR 233 (Orogrande Summit Road), reach Orogrande Summit and proceed 1.75 miles on the left fork to the Fish Lake Trailhead. The 2-mile moderate trail ends at Fish Lake, and numerous moose are rumored to inhabit the surrounding area.

After reaching Orogrande Summit on FR 233, proceed 2 miles along the right fork in the road leading to Wild Horse Lake. Park at Wild Horse Lake and climb 1,500 feet on a difficult 2-mile trail ending at the North Pole Mountain's pinnacle.

Hells Canyon Area

Rapid River

Distance: variable – from 1 mile to 40 miles
Climb: begins gradually, but becomes steeper after the first 11 miles
Difficulty: easy to difficult in areas
Usage: heavy
Location: Drive 4 miles south from Riggins on U.S. Highway 95, exiting onto the road leading to the Rapid River fish hatchery. Park at the top of the fish hatchery's loop road.

Following the main fork of the Rapid River, this trail winds through a scenic canyon designated as a unit of the National Wild and Scenic Rivers System. Although most hikers opt for a short 1-2 mile day hike, several options abound for those interested in a longer, more strenuous trip. After 1.5 miles, hikers will reach the first river crossing. Trail engineers have placed bridges at all river crossings during the first 11 miles to make the trail accessible for hikers of all experience levels. In another 1.5 miles, hikers have a unique opportunity to view a Pacific Yew, a special evergreen tree commonly found near the ocean. At the 4-mile mark, hikers can opt to take the trail fork leading to the West Fork of Rapid River and eventually to the base of the Seven Devils Peaks. For those who stay on the main trail, the route passes Castle Creek, Copper Creek, Paradise Cabin, and ends at Frypan Creek. Here, hikers must either ford the river or bushwhack 2 miles beyond the ford point. After doing so, hikers can choose to take a loop along the North Star Trail or follow the Black Lake Fork of the Rapid River that climbs to the Seven Devils. Both of these trails are strenuous and require a multi-day backpacking trip. Best months for hiking are May and September when temperatures are moderate and foliage and wildlife are at their best. However, the canyon is often accessible from mid-March until mid-November. Summer months require caution as temperatures soar in the canyon, and later months can also be dangerous due to icy patches on the trail.

Seven Devils Loop

Distance: 29 mile loop
Climb: steep
Difficulty: difficult
Usage: moderate
Location: From Riggins, head south on U.S. Highway 95, bearing west (right) onto Forest Road (FR) 517. Continue on FR 517 17 miles to the Windy Saddle Trailhead at Windy Saddle Campground.

Wandering through the peaks of the rugged Seven Devils Mountains, hikers will experience breathtaking views of the 8,000-foot deep Hells Canyon, likely encounter wildlife, and have an opportunity to camp at some of the 30 lakes found in the area.

The area is known for violent summer thunderstorms, so hikers should use caution at all times and be aware of their surroundings. After climbing the first 5 miles to Iron Phone Junction, proceed straight ahead to Bernard Lakes, keeping right at all further trail junctions until reaching the Dry Diggins Lookout. This point provides views of the Snake River and Hells Canyon, and mountain goats are commonly found in the area. From the lookout, continue on the main trail to the right and hike to the sign for Potato Hill and Little Granite Creek Trails. Take the left Potato Hill Trail, and in 0.3 miles, reach a side trail leading to Echo Lake. Many hikers opt to take this 1-mile roundtrip detour to view the forested Echo Lake with the 9,393-foot He Devil Peak rising at the lake's base. Back on the main trail, proceed to another possible side hike in 1.5 miles. This 2 mile roundtrip side trail leads to the heavily used Baldy Lake where views of He Devil, Mount Belial, Devils Throne, and Twin Imps Peaks are offered. Following the main trail, reach Horse Heaven Junction and continue on Boise Trail past Hanson Creek to the heavily used Cannon Lakes. A short side trail leading to the lakes will provide hikers with views of Goblin, She Devil, and the Tower of Babel peaks. From the lakes, it is another 2.5 miles to the trailhead. Best months for hiking are mid-July to mid-September.

Lochsa River Historical Trail

Distance: varies
Climb: moderate
Difficulty: moderate
Usage: heavy
Location: Find various access points along U.S. Highway 12.

Hikers will wind along a historical pack trail built in the 1920s that served as the precursor to U.S. Highway 12 and was named part of Idaho's Centennial Trail in 1990. To access the Split Creek Trail, travel to milepost 111.4 on Highway 12 and hike 16 miles to the Sherman Creek Trailhead at milepost 122.6. Hikers can also opt to access the Beaver Flat Trailhead. At Highway 12 milepost 118, turn onto Beaver Flat Road to locate a trail on the road's north side. Best months for hiking are June through September.

Lowell Area

Fish Creek

Distance: 6 miles roundtrip
Climb: gentle
Difficulty: easy
Usage: heavy
Location: Drive 23 miles east of Lowell on U.S. Highway 12. After crossing Fish Creek Bridge, locate the Fish Creek Trailhead.

Fish Creek Trail offers visitors an easy but scenic hike. The trail is suitable for day hikes, and most visitors choose to hike only as far as Willow Creek.

Boulder Creek Trail

Distance: 8 miles roundtrip
Climb: moderate
Difficulty: moderate
Usage: heavy
Location: On U.S. Highway 12, drive 26 miles east of Lowell to the Boulder Creek Trailhead.

Hikers who have some experience backpacking find the Boulder Creek Trail a natural option for a moderate day hike to Lochsa Saddle. For those more adventurous, the Boulder Creek Trail also offers a difficult entry point leading to the Selway Crags area.

Warm Springs Creek

Distance: 4 miles roundtrip
Climb: moderate
Difficulty: moderate
Usage: heavy during first half of trip; light at destination point
Location: From Lowell, drive 55 miles east on U.S. Highway 12 to the trailhead for Warm Springs Creek.

The first portion of Warm Springs Trail is heavily used due to the popularity of the hot springs found next to the trail. However, for those hikers interested in a more peaceful atmosphere, the trail continues to an old-growth cedar grove that is rarely frequented.

Mallard-Larkins Proposed Wilderness Area

Larkins Lake

Distance: 14 miles roundtrip
Climb: moderate
Difficulty: moderate
Usage: heavy
Location: Drive east on U.S. Highway 12 48 miles from Lewiston to Greer. Merge onto State Highway 11 and proceed through the towns of Weippe and Pierce to Headquarters. Directly north of Headquarters, bear right onto Forest Road (FR) 246 and drive 4 miles to the fork with FR 251. Taking FR 251, drive 10 miles to the junction with FR 247. Proceed 7 miles along FR 247 and cross the Clearwater River. Bear left after the river crossing to reach Isabella Creek in 1 mile. Turn right at this creek onto FR 700 (Smith Ridge Road) and continue 9 miles to Trail 240 at the Smith Ridge Trailhead.

Cutthroat trout thrive in the 12-acre Larkins Lake and moose, elk, deer, black bears, and mountain goats reside in this forested area. Due to the trail's popularity, much of the wildlife has become "tame," so hikers need to make sure all food and cooking supplies are hung each evening out of reach of elk standing on their hind feet. After hiking 4.5 miles through lush trees, wildflowers, and huckleberries, hikers can opt to take a side trail on the left of Trail 240 leading north to Larkins Peak. To reach Larkins Lake, bear left from Trail 240 onto Trail 108 after 5.5 miles. In another 0.75 miles, hikers should take the far left (southerly) trail at the four-way junction leading to the lake and several camping spots in 0.5 miles. Best months for hiking are mid-July through mid-October.

Ice Lake, Pete Ott Lake, and Vicinity

Distance: 5 miles roundtrip to Pete Ott Lake
Climb: gentle
Difficulty: moderately easy
Usage: moderate
Location: Drive 48 miles east of Lewiston on U.S. Highway 12 to Greer. Merge left onto State Highway 11 and travel to Pierce. Just south of Pierce, turn onto Forest Road (FR) 250 (French Mountain Road). After crossing the North Fork Bridge, turn right and continue on FR 250 approximately 15 miles to FR 711 (Cold Springs Road). After driving 1.7 miles on FR 711, bear right on FR 5295 and proceed to FR 5297. Drive along FR 5297, then turn onto FR 5297A that leads to the Trail 176 trailhead. Visitors must have a four-wheel drive vehicle to access the trailhead.

Situated in a forested area offering vistas of the Clearwater Mountains and access to icy lakes, hikers only stay on Trail 176 for a short distance. After traveling past Ring Lake, hikers will veer to the right on Trail 445 and reach Ice Lake in 0.3 miles. Continuing another 0.3 miles leads to the unmarked trail on the right that descends to Pete Ott Lake. Best months for hiking are late-July to mid-September, with fall foliage particularly beautiful in the area during September.

Optional Hikes: Continue on Trail 445 past the unmarked trail to Pete Ott Lake, which rises high above Pete Ott Creek. From here, hikers have extensive views of the Elizabeth Lakes. Proceed past this vantage point to descend to the North Fork of the Clearwater River.

Meadow Creek Area

Meadow Creek

Distance: 28 miles roundtrip
Climb: moderate
Difficulty: moderate
Usage: heavy
Location: Drive 114 miles east on U.S. Highway 12 from Lewiston to Lowell. After crossing over a bridge, proceed 19 miles east on Forest Road (FR) 223 (Selway River Road) to the Meadow Creek Trailhead located at the south end of Slims Campground.

Winding beside Meadow Creek through a fern-lined canyon, this trail's first 3 miles sparkles with mica and is canopied with old-growth cedars. Arriving at Little Creek, hikers face a 1.5-mile difficult switchback climb to a hillside overlooking Meadow Creek before the trail eventually descends back to the creek shore. After dropping down to the junction of Meadow Creek and Indian Hill Creek, continue on the same trail 7 miles to your destination at Meadow Creek Guard Station. Meadow Creek is known for its rainbow and cutthroat trout, but use caution while fishing as the creek is also home to the protected Chinook salmon. Best months for hiking are early April to November, although autumn months will find the trail active with hunters.

Optional Hikes: Just prior to the junction of Meadow Creek and Indian Hill Creek is Trail 603 leading to the left. Hikers may opt to take this 13-mile roundtrip to Indian Hill Lookout but should be prepared for a 3,000-foot climb to the lookout's 6,810-foot elevation.

Another optional hike is found near the Lark Creek Bridge approximately 1 mile after reaching Indian Hill Creek. Hikers who climb west on Trail 608 will eventually reach Anderson Butte.

Proposed Great Burn Wilderness Area

Goat Lake

Distance: 11 miles roundtrip
Climb: gradual to moderate in places
Difficulty: moderate
Usage: light
Location: Drive 164 miles east on U.S. Highway 12 from Lewiston to Forest Road (FR) 569 (Parachute Hill Road). Proceed north 2.7 miles on FR 569 to a three-way fork, and continue on the middle road 1.7 miles until reaching another fork. Keeping left at this fork, drive 1.6 miles to Powell Junction and merge onto FR 500. After passing Papoose Saddle, proceed an additional 11.5 miles to Cayuse Junction and bear right onto FR 581. Follow FR 581 8.2 miles to the unmarked right turn leading to Blacklead Mountain. Turn off here and proceed 0.5 mile, parking at the first trailhead in the area. From here, walk on this jeep road the final 0.75 miles to the desired trailhead for Trail 508. Do not take Deer Creek Trail 513 which leads to the north, but instead proceed on the unmarked Trail 315 leading east (right). Trail users should note that the 28-mile dirt/gravel road leading to the trailhead often requires four-wheel drive as well as a 4 to 5 hour drive.

While traveling to the trailhead, backpackers will drive along a portion of the Lolo Indian Trail that Lewis and Clark used in 1805 and 1806 to traverse these Idaho mountains. At the trailhead, the Goat Lake Trail quickly descends over several switchbacks into a meadow lined with lodgepoles, and in 1.5 miles, the trail splits. Staying to the left, hikers face two stream crossings before reaching Goat Lake. Surrounded by a 1,000-foot cirque wall, Goat Lake offers visitors fishing opportunities as well as views of nearby Williams Peak and Rhodes Peak. From Goat Lake, hikers can opt to head back to the trailhead or proceed on to numerous other lakes, Cayuse Creek, and eventually the Bitterroot Divide. Best months for hiking are mid-July through mid-September.

Steep Lakes Loop

Distance: 22 miles
Climb: moderate
Difficulty: moderately difficult
Usage: light
Location: Located 150 miles east of Lewiston, access is easiest from Superior, Montana. From this town, drive west on Forest Road (FR) 250 over Hoodoo Pass to the junction of Long Creek and Lake Creek. At the junction, proceed 7 miles on FR 295 to a barrier near Siam Creek and locate the Lake Creek Trailhead for Trail 419. ATV's and motorcycles are allowed on the first five miles of this trail, so hikers should use caution.

After hiking 3 miles along Trail 419 through a narrow canyon, hikers reach a junction where Trail 419 becomes Trail 478. Continuing 2 miles to Fish Lake, locate Stateline Trail 738 directly beyond Fish Lake. Now crossing from Montana into Idaho, this ridgeline trail follows the Bitterroot Divide and provides excellent views of more than twenty alpine lakes, as well as possible encounters with elk, moose, deer, and wolves. To reach these lakes, hikers will have to do some off-trail exploring, and camping in the area also requires climbing down off the ridge each night. Proceeding along the trail, hikers will pass Goose Lake, Siamese Lakes, Straight Lake, and eventually reach the steep ascent over rugged cliffs surrounding Steep Lakes. Lower Steep Lake is known for the rare California golden trout, and the fish limit here is two. After enjoying Steep Lakes, continue on Trail 738 past Goose Lake and locate the junction for Goose Creek Trail 414. Continue on Trail 414 to the Goose Creek Trailhead, and then walk 4 miles along FR to reach your car at the Lake Creek Trailhead. Hikers should use precaution while traveling along the ridgeline as dangerous summer thunderstorms occur and there is no water on top of the divide. Best month for hiking is August as hikers will encounter snowdrifts in early July and September weather is generally cold.

Selway-Bitterroot Wilderness Area

Coolwater to Selway Crags

Distance: 7 miles to Louse Lake and 10 miles to Selway Crags, one way
Climb: moderate
Difficulty: moderate
Location: Drive east on U.S. Highway 12 114 miles from Lewiston to Lowell. At Lowell, proceed 0.3 miles east on Forest Road (FR) 223 (also called Selway River Road). After passing Three Rivers Resort, turn left onto FR 317 (Coolwater Mountain Road) and continue 8 miles. At the top of Coolwater Ridge, drive past the road leading to Idaho Point and proceed 4.7 miles to the undeveloped trailhead at Remount. Four-wheel drive on FR 317 is highly recommended, as the road is slippery when wet and extremely rocky.

LOSING VALUABLE GROUND

The Palouse Country surrounding Moscow and lining U.S. Hwy. 95 on its journey towards Lake Coeur d'Alene is slowly losing valuable ground. According to the U.S. Soil Conservation Service, the area is pulverized from agricultural use and loses nearly 17 million tons of soil each year. As a result, Palouse Country is distinguished as the U.S. site experiencing the greatest annual soil erosion. Despite the Conservation Service's attempt to sway farmers to use no-till or minimum-till agricultural practices, little else has been done to remedy the problem.

Following a trail that is vulnerable to severe summer afternoon thunderstorms, hikers will experience incredible views of mountain peaks, forests, and meadows throughout this ridgeline trek. During the second mile, the trail steers left of Point 6,761 and this is often a point of confusion as the old, unmaintained trail appears to the right. After bearing left around this point, hikers will cross the old trail and should keep to the right. If you head into a heavy forest, backtrack as you are now on the wrong trail. Despite this potentially confusing area, this trail is well-worth its effort as it leads hikers to Ghost Mountain, Louse Lake, and the Gateway to the Selway Crags. Best months for hiking are mid-July through mid-September.

Lower Selway River

Distance: 12 miles roundtrip
Climb: gentle
Difficulty: easy
Usage: moderate
Location: Drive 114 miles east on U.S. Highway 12 from Lewiston to Lowell. At Lowell, continue east across the Clearwater River onto Forest Road (FR) 223 (Selway River Road). Proceed 18 miles past Selway Falls to the trailhead at Race Creek Campground.

Sparkling with mica, this trail winds through a granite canyon along the north side of the Selway River. The trail offers several resting opportunities along the numerous sand beaches and under the large pine and cedar trees, so it is an appropriate trail for families. However, children should be watched as the trail does follow cliff ledges in some areas. Proceeding six miles, hikers will reach their destination at the beach and rapids of Cupboard Creek. Cupboard Creek abounds with a variety of fish, and area wildlife includes moose, elk, deer, otters, beavers, black bears, and wolves. Best month for hiking is September due to colorful foliage; however, the trail can easily be accessed from the beginning of June.

Optional Hikes: At Cupboard Creek, the unmarked Big Fog Saddle Trail (Trail 710) exits the river trail. Involving a difficult climb, hikers will pass the Big Fog Saddle and end at Fog Mountain Road. Several backpackers choose to enter the Selway Crags from Fog Mountain. Best months for hiking are mid-July to mid-September.

Another difficult, multi-day hike takes backpackers further into the Selway Wilderness. From Cupboard Creek, continue upstream along the river trail. Hikers will eventually reach the Selway River crossing at Magruder's Road and locate the river's headwaters in the Frank Church-River of No Return Wilderness.

Selway Crags via Big Fog and Legend Lakes

Distance: 8.5 mile loop
Climb: steep
Difficulty: difficult
Usage: light
Location: Drive east from Lewiston 114 miles to Lowell on U.S. Highway 12. At Lowell, proceed 17 miles east on Forest Road (FR) 223 (Selway River Road). After crossing Gedney Creek, turn onto FR 319 (Fog Mountain Road). FR 319 is extremely steep, rocky, and narrow, so four-wheel drive is highly recommended. Continue 14 miles on FR 319 to the multiple trail trailhead at Big Fog Saddle. Follow Fog Mountain Trail 343.

Panoramic views, glacier-carved valleys, alpine lakes, and wildlife await hikers on this ridgeline trail winding deep into the rugged Selway Crags. After hiking 1.5 miles to Big Fog Mountain, bear left onto Trail 363 that leads north through both marshes and rocky areas to the cirques where Big Fog Lake and Legend Lake lie. Trail 363 is faint at times, but getting lost is hard as the ridgeline is steep on both the east and west sides. Bushwhacking is required to reach Big Fog Lake from the east side of Legend Lake. Topographic maps are highly suggested, and best months for hiking are July through mid-October.

Optional Hikes: After reaching Big Fog Mountain, continue east and follow Trail 693 to join the South Three Links Lakes Trail. Upon reaching these lakes at an elevation of 6,780 feet, climb over Jesse Pass and descend towards Cove Lakes. Cove Lakes is one of the most popular destinations in the area, and Cove Lakes Trail will return hikers to the Big Fog Saddle trailhead. This is an extremely difficult hike, and best months for hiking are July through mid-October.

White Cap Creek

Distance: 43 miles roundtrip
Climb: moderate
Difficulty: difficult
Usage: light
Location: From Grangeville, follow State Highway 13 9 miles west to State Highway 14. Bearing right, proceed towards Elk City on Highway 14. Nearing Elk City, exit onto Forest Road (FR) 222 and drive to the Red River Ranger Station. 0.5 miles past this station is FR 468 (also known as Montana Road and Magruder Corridor). Bear left onto this road and follow the road signs leading to Paradise Ranger Station and White Cap Creek. The trailhead for Trail 24 begins at the ranger station near an outfitter's camp.

Winding through a narrow canyon near White Cap Creek, hikers will soon find themselves deep within the wilderness where rattlesnakes and black bears are a common occurrence. Requiring a multi-day trip, the following are suggested camping stops on the first leg of the trip: Day 1 – 7 mile hike from the trailhead to Cooper Flat; Day 2 – 7 mile hike from Cooper Flat to Cliff Creek; Day 3 – 7.5 miles from Cliff Creek to Triple Lakes. After passing Cliff Creek, hikers will view Patzy Ann Falls and reach a trail junction for Trail 701. Continue on Trail 24, ascending 2,000 feet to the fabulous fishing afforded at Triple Lakes. Trail 701 leads hikers another strenuous 5 miles to White Cap Creek Lakes over a rough, and sometimes faint, path. All backpackers should be prepared for several difficult creek crossings. Best month for hiking is August due to significant runoff in early summer months.

INFORMATION PLEASE

All Idaho area codes are 208

Road Information

ID Road & Weather Conditions
888-432-7623 or local 884-7000
Idaho State Police 736-3090

Tourism Information

Idaho Travel Council 800-VISIT-ID outside Idaho
334-2470 in Idaho
www.visitid.org
North CentralID Travel Association
800-473-3543
983-2175
www.northcentralidaho.info

Airports

Cottonwood	962-3231
Grangeville	983-1565
Lewiston	746-7962
Pullman	397-9910

Government Offices

Idaho Bureau of Reclamation	334-1466
	www.usbr.gov
Idaho Department of Commerce	
(800) 847-4843 or 334-2470	
www.visitid.org or http://cl.idaho.gov/	
Idaho Department of Fish and Game	
(800) ASK-FISH or 334-3700	
http://fishandgame.idaho.gov	
Idaho Department of Parks and Recreation	
	334-4199
www.idahoparks.org	
State BLM Office	373-3889 or 373-4000
	www.id.blm.gov
Bitterroot National Forest	(406) 363-7161
Bureau of Land Management	
Cottonwood Field Office	962-3245
Clearwater National Forest	476-4541
Frank Church-River of No Return Wilderness	
	634-0700
Gospel Hump Wilderness Area	983-1950
Hells Canyon National Recreation Area	
	628-3916
Nez Perce National Forest	983-1950
Nez Perce National Historical Park	843-2261
Selway-Bitterroot Wilderness Area	983-1950

Hospitals

St. Mary's Hospital • Cottonwood	962-3251
Syringa General Hospital • Grangeville	983-1700
St Joseph Regional Medical Center	
Lewiston	743-2511
Gritman Medical Center • Moscow	883-6393
Clearwater Valley Hospital • Orofino	476-4555

Golf Courses

Grangeville Country Club	
Grangeville	983-1299
Bryden Canyon • Lewiston	746-0863
Eagles Pointe Golf Course • Lewiston	746-7401
University of Idaho • Moscow	885-6171
Orifino Golf and Country Club	
Orofino	476-3117
Kayler's Bend Golf • Peck	486-6841

Bed & Breakfasts

Dog Bark Park • Cottonwood	962-3647
Texas Rodge B &B • Deary	877-1888
Silver Spur Outfitters • Dixie	842-2417
Gospel View • Grangeville	983-7067
Quilt House B&B • Kamiah	935-7668

Dreamis B&B • Kooskia	926-7540
Reflections Inn • Kooskia	926-0855
Carriage House Inn B&B • Lewiston	746-4506
Kirby Creek Lodge • Lewiston	746-6276
Anna Italianna Inn • Lewiston	743-4552
Garden Court B&B • Lewiston	743-0679
Acres For Kids B&B • Lucile	628-3569
Ivy B&B • Moscow	883-0748
Journey's End • Moscow	882-5035
Peacock Hill B&B • Moscow	882-1423
Old Willow Inn • Potlatch	875-0861
Lodge B&B • Riggins	628-3863
Canyon House • White Bird	839-2777

Guest Ranches & Resorts

Sable Trail Ranch • Elk City	842-2672
Flying B Ranch • Kamiah	935-0755
Outback Adventures • Pierce	464-2171
Deer Cliff Inn • Preson	852-0643
Bar H Bar Ranch • Soda Springs	547-3082
River Mountain Ranch • White Bird	839-2243

Vacation Homes & Cabins

Prospector Cabins • Elk City	842-2557
Elk River Lodge & General Store Elk River	826-3299

Car Rental

C&B Towing and Auto • Grangeville	983-2378
Budget Car and Truck Rental Lewiston	746-0488
Enterprise • Lewiston	746-2878
Hertz • Lewiston	746-0411

Idaho Car Sales • Lewiston	746-6455
Nice Cars Auto Rental • Lewiston	746-3638
Sears • Lewiston	746-7700
Valley Car Rentals • Lewiston	743-9371
Ambassador • Moscow	882-2722
KDM Towing & Recovery • Moscow	882-8697
Hanson Garage Inc • Orofino	476-5536

Outfitters & Guides

F=Fishing H=Hunting R=River Guides
E=Horseback Rides G=General Guide Services

Id Outfitters & Guides Association	800-49-IDAHO
Outfitters & Guides Licensing Board	327-7380
Wapiti River Guides	FHR 628-3523
62 Ridge Outfitters & Guides	FHERG 476-7148
Dixie Outfitters, Inc	HEG 842-2417
Shattuck Creek Ranch Outfitters	FHERG 826-3284
Holiday River Expeditions	RG 983-1518
Cayuse Outfitting	HE 935-0859
Flying B Ranch	FHERG 935-0755
Ralph Oswold	935-0068
Ridge Runner Outfitters	FHE 935-0757
Ridgerunner Outfitters	FHE 935-0757
Selway Ridgerunner Outfitters	FHEG 935-1042
Weitas Creek Outfitters	FHE 983-0900
Weitas Creek Outfitters	FHE 983-9267
Lochsa River Outfitters	FHERG 926-4149
Lost Lakes Outfitters	FHERG 926-4988
Rivers West Outfitters, Inc	FHERG 926-4988
Barker River Trips, Inc	FHR 743-7459
Beamer's Landing Inc	FHR 758-4800

Corral Creek Ranch	H 743-6529
High Roller Excursions	FR 746-6276
Intermountain Excursions LLC	FH 746-7035
Snake River Adventures	FHR 746-6276
Vogel Outdoor Adventures LLC	FH 798-7701
Gospel Mountain Outfitters	FHEG 628-3553
Salmon River Experience	HFR 882-2385
B-Bar-C Outfitters	FHER 476-7074
Bungalow Outfitters, LLC	476-3982
Clearwater Outfitters	FHEG 476-5971
Barker Trophy Hunts	H 924-7809
Boulder Creek Outfitters	FHERG 486-6232
Triple "O" Outfitters, Inc	FHERG 464-2349
Northwest Voyagers	FHERG 628-3021
Red Woods Outfitter	FH 628-3673
Bigfoot Outfitters, Inc	FHE 628-3539
Exodus Wilderness Adventures	FHR 628-3484
Heaven's Gate Outfitters	H 628-3062
Natsoh Koos River Outfitters	HFR 628-3131
Hells Canyon Jet Boat Trips	FH 839-2255
Lockey U Outfitters	FGE 983-1802
Yellow Wolf Ranch	H 983-1288

Downhill Ski Areas

Bald Mountain • Grangemont	464-2311

Snowmobile Rentals

Elk River Recreation • Elk River	826-3663
Triple "O" Outfitters • Pierce	464-2349

Bike Rentals

Trailhead Rentals • Moscow	883-3005

Notes:

Campground Quick Reference

Ahsahka

Grandad Creek
P
476-1255/800-321-3198
Summer, Fall
20 mi. N. of Orofino at Dworshak Reservoir

Burgdorf

Burgdorf
P   None   6
634-0400
June-September
30 miles N of McCall on FR 21 and FR 246
Primitive Camping, Restrooms, Biking, Hiking/Backpacking, Off Highway Vehicles, Water Sports, Winter Sports

Chinook Campground & Horse Camp
P   Yes   5; 5 Group Sites
634-0400
June-October
36 miles N of McCall on FR 21, then 1 mile S on FR 378
Primitive Camping, Group Camping, Restrooms, Cultural/Historical Sites, Biking, Non-Motorized Boating, Fishing, Hiking/Backpacking, Horseback Riding, Hunting, Off Highway Vehicles, Scenic Driving, Water Sports, Wildlife Viewing

Cottonwood

Pine Bar
P   26'
962-3245
All Year
15 mi. S. on Graves Creek Rd.
Boating Facilities, Drinking Water, Fire Rings, Pets OK, Tenters Welcome, Vault Toilets, Waterfront

Craigmont

The Station & RV Park
C $12-17.5   7
924-7724
All Year
401 E. Main St.
Hookups, Reservations, Handicap Access

Deary

Little Boulder Creek
P $8   17   35'
875-1131
Summer, Fall
4 mi. E. of Deary on Hwy. 8, 3 mi. SE on Cty. Rd. 1963
Drinking Water, Pets OK, Tenters Welcome, Vault Toilets

Dixie

Dixie Motel & Mercantile
C $15   2   35'
842-2358
All Year
30 mi. S. of Elk City
Camping Cabins, Credit Cards OK, Drinking Water, Dump Station, Fire Rings, Hookups, Hot Springs, LP Gas, Mini-Mart, Modem Hookups, Pets OK, Playground, Reservations, Showers, Tenters Welcome, Laundry

Elk City Junction Lodge
C $16-45   14
842-2459
All Year
Hwy. 14, 6 mi. W. of Elk City

Mud Springs
C $10-35   2
983-3528
All Year
near Elk City

Red River
P   40   16'
842-2255
Summer, Fall
3 mi. SW on Hwy. 14, 14 mi. SE on Cty. Rd. 222, 6 mi. NE on Cty. Rd. 234
Drinking Water, Reservations, Vault Toilets

Poet Creek
P   None   4
842-2245
July-October
17 miles SE of Elk City on Hwy. 14 and FR 222, then 21 miles E on FR 468
Developed Campground, Restrooms, Fishing, Hiking/Backpacking, Horseback Riding, Hunting, Picnicking, Wildlife Viewing

Elk River

Huckleberry Heaven RV Park
C   20
826-3405
All Year
Cable TV Hookups, Credit Cards OK, Dump Station, Fire Rings, Hookups, Pets OK, Pull-thru Sites, Reservations

Elk River Recreation Campgrounds
C $5-7   25
826-3569
All Year
Dent Rd., Elk Creek Reservoir
Dump Station, Pets OK, Playground, Reservations

Grangeville

Mountain View M/H RV Park
C $10-16.5   24
983-2328/800-452-8227
All Year
Hwy. 95/13 junction (Main St.), E. on Main St. .5 mi. to Hall St., N. .5 mi.
Cable TV Hookups, Hookups, Pets OK, Pull-thru Sites, Reservations, Showers, Tenters Welcome

Sundown RV Park
C $16   28
983-9113
Summer, Spring
Hwy. 13/95 junction, 102 N. C St
Credit Cards OK, Hookups, Pets OK, Pull-thru Sites, Reservations, Showers, Laundry

Harpster Riverside RV Park
C $20-22   24
983-2312/800-983-1918
All Year
Hwy. 13, 13 mi. from Grangeville or Kooskia
Cable TV Hookups, Credit Cards OK, Drinking Water, Dump Station, Hookups, LP Gas, Mini-Mart, Modem Hookups, Pets OK, Pull-thru Sites, Reservations, Showers, Tenters Welcome

Country Court RV Park
C $10   5
983-2587/888-832-5251
All Year
1 mi. N. of Grangeville, Hwy 95
Hookups, Playground, Pull-thru Sites, Showers, Laundry, Handicap Access

Christmas Ranch RV Resort
C $25   21   100'
983-2383
Summer, Fall, Spring
3/4 mi. S. of Grangeville on Hwy 95 & Fish Hatchery Rd.
Cable TV Hookups, Credit Cards OK, Drinking Water, Dump Station, Game Room, Hookups, Modem Hookups, Pets OK, Pull-thru Sites, Reservations, Showers, Laundry

Castle Creek
P   8   22'
983-1950
Summer, Fall
1 mi. E. on Hwy. 13, 10 mi. SE on Cty. Rd. 17; 6 mi. SE on Hwy. 14
Drinking Water, Dump Station, Swimming Pool, Vault Toilets

Fish Creek
P   16'
983-1950
Summer, Fall
1 mi. E. on Hwy. 13; 1 mi. S. on Cty. Rd. 17, 7 mi. SE on Forest Rd. 221
Vault Toilets

South Fork
P   8   22'
983-1950
Summer, Fall
9 mi. S. on Hwy. 13, 6.5 mi. E. on Hwy. 14
Drinking Water, Swimming Pool, Vault Toilets

Christmas Ranch of Idaho
P
983-2383
All Year

Meadow Creek
P   None   3
983-1963
June-October
9 miles S of Grangeville on Hwy. 13, then 9 miles E on Hwy. 14
Developed Campground, Restrooms, RV Sites, Fishing, Hiking/Backpacking, Picnicking, Scenic Driving

Harvard

Pines RV Campground
C $14   17
875-0831
All Year
M P 12.5 on Hwy. 6
Hookups, LP Gas, Mini-Mart, Pets OK, Playground, Pull-thru Sites, Showers, Tenters Welcome

Campground Quick Reference - continued

Giant White Pine

P	$8	14	30'	875-1131 Summer, Fall, Spring

7 mi. N. of Harvard on Hwy. 6

Drinking Water, Pets OK, Tenters Welcome, Vault Toilets

Kamiah

Lewis Clark Resort

C	$17-65	180		935-2556/800-264-9943 All Year

Hwy. 12, 1 mi. E. of Kamiah

Cable TV Hookups, Dump Station, Hookups, Mini-Mart, Pets OK, Playground, Pull-thru Sites, Reservations, Showers, Swimming Pool, Handicap Access

Long Camp RV Park

C	$20	21		935-7922 All Year

Hwy. 12, E., M P 68

Drinking Water, Hookups, Pets OK, Reservations, Showers, Tenters Welcome, Waterfront, Handicap Access

Kooskia

River Junction RV Park

C	$10-25	35		926-7865 All Year

Hwy. 12, M P 74.1

Drinking Water, Dump Station, Hookups, Pets OK, Pull-thru Sites, Reservations, Showers, Tenters Welcome, Laundry

Lewiston

Aht'Wy Plaza RV Park

C	$12-20	33		750-0231 All Year

4 mi. E. on Hwy. 95/12

Drinking Water, Dump Station, Hookups, LP Gas, Mini-Mart, Modem Hookups, Pets OK, Pull-thru Sites, Showers, Swimming Pool, Tenters Welcome, Laundry, Handicap Access

Hells Gate State Park

P	$12-16	93	60'	799-5015

Please Call

4 mi. S. of Lewiston on Snake River Ave.

Boating Facilities, Camping Cabins, Credit Cards OK, Drinking Water, Dump Station, Hookups, Mini-Mart, Playground, Pull-thru Sites, Showers, Tenters Welcome, Handicap Access

Myrtle Recreation Site

P	$8	15		All Year

15 miles east of Lewiston at Myrtle on Highway 12

Drinking Water, Hookups, Tenters Welcome, Vault Toilets, Waterfront

Lowell

Three Rivers Resort & Rafting

C	$15-97	50		926-4430/888-926-4430 All Year

Hwy. 12

Camping Cabins, Credit Cards OK, Hookups, Mini-Mart, Pets OK, Playground, Pull-thru Sites, Showers, Swimming Pool, Waterfront

Apgar Creek

P	$6	7	22'	926-4274 Summer, Fall

29 mi. E. of Kooskia on Hwy. 12

Drinking Water

O'Hara Bar

P		32	20'	926-4274 Summer, Fall

24 mi. E. of Kooskia on Hwy. 12, 7 mi. SE on Rd. 223, 1 mi. S. on Forest Rd. 651; Selway River Area

Drinking Water, Reservations, Swimming Pool, Vault Toilets, Handicap Access

Wild Goose

P	$6	6	22'	926-4274 Summer, Fall

20 mi. E. of Kooskia on Hwy. 12

Drinking Water, Pets OK, Vault Toilets

Wilderness Gateway

P	$8	91	40'	926-4274 Summer, Fall

49 mi. E. of Kooskia on Hwy. 12

Drinking Water, Dump Station, Pets OK, Playground, Pull-thru Sites, Reservations, Swimming Pool, Vault Toilets

Elk Summit

P	None	15; 1 Group Site		942-3311 July-October

67 miles E of Lowell on Hwy. 12, then 5.5 miles S on FR 111, then 14 miles S on FR 360

Developed Campground, Handicap Accessible Restrooms, RV Sites, Non-Motorized Boating, Fishing, Hiking/Backpacking, Horseback Riding, Picnicking, Scenic Driving, Wildlife Viewing

Hoodoo Lake

P	None	2		942-3113 June-September

67 miles E of Lowell on Hwy. 12, then 17 miles S on FR 111 and FR 360

Primitive Camping, Restrooms, Hiking/Backpacking, Horseback Riding, Wildlife Viewing

Lucile

Riverfront Gardens RV Park

C	$20-22	32		628-3777 All Year

Hwy. 95, M P 210.5, 15 mi. N. of Riggins

Prospector's Gold RV & Campground

C	$4-17	50		628-3773 All Year

9 mi. N. of Riggins

Drinking Water, Dump Station, Hookups, Mini-Mart, Modem Hookups, Pets OK, Pull-thru Sites, Showers, Tenters Welcome, Waterfront

Nezperce

Nezperce RV Park

C	$10	6		937-2454 All Year

4th @ Maple St.

Cable TV Hookups, Dump Station, Hookups, Pets OK, Playground, Pull-thru Sites, Reservations, Showers, Handicap Access

Orofino

Hidden Village

C	$15-20	20		476-3416 All Year

Cable TV Hookups, Dump Station, Pets OK, Showers, Tenters Welcome, Laundry

Canoe Camp RV Park

C	$15-18	28		476-7530 All Year

Near historic canoe camp on the Lewis & Clark trail

Cable TV Hookups, Hookups, Pets OK, Reservations

Canyon Creek

P		12	22'	476-1255/800-321-3198 Summer, Fall

11 mi. N. on Orofino-Elk River Rd.

Vault Toilets

Dent Acres

P	$16	50	35'	476-1255/800-321-3198 Summer, Fall, Spring

20 mi. N. of Orofino

Drinking Water, Dump Station, Hookups, Playground, Showers

Dworshak State Park

P	$7-10	105	50'	476-3132

Please Call

N. of Ahsahka, near Orofino

Drinking Water, Dump Station, Playground, Showers, Swimming Pool

Pink House Recreation Site

P	$18	15	40'	962-3245 All Year

3 mi. W. on Hwy. 12

Boating Facilities, Drinking Water, Fire Rings, Hookups, Pets OK, Pull-thru Sites, Tenters Welcome, Vault Toilets, Waterfront, Handicap Access

Campground Quick Reference - continued

Campground Name				Phone
Public/Commercial	Unit Price	#Spaces	Max. Length	Seasons
Directions				
Amenities/Activities				

Pierce

Aquarius
476-4541
P $5 7 22' Summer
11 mi. N. on Hwy. 11; 25 mi. NE of Headquarters on Forest Rd. 247

Hidden Creek
476-4541
P $7 13 22' Summer, Fall
1 mi. S. on Hwy. 11, 55 mi. NE on Forest Rd. 250
Drinking Water, Pets OK, Tenters Welcome, Vault Toilets

Kelly Forks
476-4541
P $5 14 32' Summer, Fall
1 mi. S. on Hwy. 11; 47 mi. NE on Forest Rd. 250
Drinking Water, Pets OK, Vault Toilets

Noe Creek
476-4541
P $7 6 22' Summer, Fall
1 mi. S. on Hwy. 11, 40 mi. NE on Forest Road 250
Drinking Water, Pets OK, Tenters Welcome, Vault Toilets

Washington Creek
476-4541
P $7 23 32' Summer, Fall
1 mi. S. on Hwy. 11, 39 mi. NE on Forest Rd. 250, 6 mi. W on Forest Rd. 247
Drinking Water, Pets OK, Tenters Welcome, Vault Toilets

Weitas
476-4541
P None 6 June-September
30 miles E of Pierce on FR 250
Developed Campground, Restrooms, RV Sites, Biking, Fishing, Hiking/Backpacking, Horseback Riding, Scenic Driving

Cedars
476-4541
P None 5 June-September
66 miles NE of Pierce on FR 250
Developed Campground, Restrooms, RV Sites, Biking, Fishing, Hiking/Backpacking, Horseback Riding, Hunting, Off Highway Vehicles, Picnicking, Scenic Driving

Potlatch

Scenic 6 Park
875-0708
C $12 24 All Year
Hwy. 95, 16 mi. N. of Moscow, 1 mi. E. on Hwy. 6
Drinking Water, Dump Station, Hookups, Pets OK, Playground, Pull-thru Sites, Vault Toilets, Handicap Access

Laird Park
875-1131
P $8 31 35' Summer, Fall
3 mi. NE on Hwy. 6; 1 mi. SE on Forest Rd. 447
Drinking Water, Pets OK, Playground, Swimming Pool, Tenters Welcome, Vault Toilets

McCroskey State Park
666-6711
P 20' Summer, Fall, Spring
Hwy. 95, 9 mi. N. of Potlatch
Tenters Welcome, Vault Toilets

Powell

Jerry Johnson
926-4274
P $6 15 22' Summer, Fall
56 mi. SW of Lolo, Mt. on Hwy. 12
Drinking Water, Pets OK, Vault Toilets

Powell
926-4274
P $8-15 35 40' Summer, Fall
44 mi. SW of Lolo, Mt. on Hwy. 12
Drinking Water, Hookups, Pets OK, Pull-thru Sites, Vault Toilets

Wendover
942-3113
P $8 25 35' Summer, Fall
48 mi. SW of Lolo, Mt. on Hwy. 12
Drinking Water, Pets OK, Vault Toilets

White Sand
942-3113
P $6 7 32' Summer, Fall
48 mi. W. of Lolo, Mt. on Hwy 12, 1 mi. S. on Elks Summit Rd.
Drinking Water, Pets OK, Swimming Pool, Vault Toilets

Whitehouse
942-3113
P 32' Summer, Fall
48 mi. SW of Lolo, Mt. on Hwy. 12
Drinking Water, Pets OK, Vault Toilets

Red River Hot Srpings

Deep Creek
(406) 821-3269
P None 3 June-October
55 miles E of Red River on FR 468
Primitive Camping, Restrooms, Fishing, Hiking, Hunting

Riggins

Pinehurst Resort Cottages & RV Park
628-3323
C $8-13 8 All Year
21 mi. N. of New Meadows, 13 mi. S. of Riggins
Credit Cards OK, Drinking Water, Hookups, LP Gas, Mini-Mart, Pets OK, Reservations, Waterfront

River Village RV Park
628-3443
C $20 33 All Year
Hwy. 95, N. end of town
Cable TV Hookups, Dump Station, Hookups, Pets OK, Pull-thru Sites, Reservations, Showers, Tenters Welcome, Laundry

Canyon Pines RV Resort
628-4006
C $20-24 54 50' All Year
Hwy. 95, M P 185
Cable TV Hookups, Credit Cards OK, Drinking Water, Dump Station, Fire Rings, Game Room, Hookups, LP Gas, Modem Hookups, Pets OK, Pull-thru Sites, Reservations, Showers, Tenters Welcome, Waterfront, WiFi, Laundry, Handicap Access

Seven Devils
628-3916
P 10 Summer, Fall
17 mi. SW of Hwy. 95 on Forest Rd. 517 (Trailers not advised)
Fire Rings, Pets OK, Tenters Welcome, Vault Toilets

Spring Bar
839-2211
P 18 20' Summer, Fall
1 mi. S. on Hwy. 95, 10 mi. E. on Forest Rd. 1614
Drinking Water, Swimming Pool, Vault Toilets

Windy Saddle
628-3916
P 5 Summer, Fall
17 mi. SW on Hwy. 95, Forest Rd. 517 (Trailers not advised)
Fire Rings, Pets OK, Tenters Welcome, Vault Toilets

Shorts Bar Recreation Site
962-3245
P 20 40' All Year
1 mi. E. on Salmon River Road
Boating Facilities, Fire Rings, Pull-thru Sites, Tenters Welcome, Vault Toilets, Waterfront

Black Lake
628-3916
P 5 Summer, Fall
FS Rd. 112, 15 mi. N. of Bear Work Center (High clearance vehicle recommended)
Fire Rings, Pets OK, Tenters Welcome, Vault Toilets

Papoose
839-2211
P None 2 June-September
4 miles W of Riggins on FR 517. The road is not suitable for trailers and RVs.
Primitive Camping, Restrooms, Hiking/Backpacking, Horseback Riding, Hunting, Off Highway Vehicles, Picnicking, Scenic Driving

Weippe

Timberline Cafe & RV Park
435-4763/866-284-6237
C $16-18 9 All Year
1022 N. Main St.
Cable TV Hookups, Credit Cards OK, Drinking Water, Dump Station, Hookups, Pets OK, Reservations, Showers

Watts RV Park
435-4140
C All Year
Hwy. 11, 705 Pierce St. W.
Cable TV Hookups, Drinking Water, Dump Station, Hookups, Pull-thru Sites, Tenters Welcome

Campground Quick Reference - continued

Campground Name Public/Commercial	Unit Price	#Spaces	Max. Length	Phone Seasons
Directions				
Amenities/Activities				

Campground Name Public/Commercial	Unit Price	#Spaces	Max. Length	Phone Seasons
Directions				
Amenities/Activities				

Irby's Blue Spruce Lodge
C $7-18   12   435-4890 / All Year
1090 Lackey Rd.

White Bird

Hoots Motel & Cafe
C $38-50   6   839-2265/888-801-9790 / All Year
Mini-Mart, Showers

Swiftwater RV Park
C $20-22   25   65'   839-2700 / All Year
After Hoots Cafe, or 1/16 mile north M P 222, exit towards Hammer Creek; go 1/2 mile; RV Park on left before crossing Silver Bridge
Cable TV Hookups, Credit Cards OK, Drinking Water, Dump Station, Hookups, LP Gas, Mini-Mart, Pets OK, Pull-thru Sites, Reservations, Showers, Tenters Welcome, Waterfront, Laundry

River Ranch Inn
C   839-2340 / All Year
6 mi. S. of White Bird

Hells Canyon Jet Boat Trips & Lodging
C $20-25   18   839-2255/800-469-8757 / All Year
1 mi. S. of White Bird, on Old Hwy. 95

Angel's Nook RV Park
C $14-20   12   55'   839-2880 / All Year
1.5 mi. E. of Hwy. 95
Cable TV Hookups, Dump Station, Hookups, Pets OK, Pull-thru Sites

Hammer Creek
P $10   8   26'   962-3245 / All Year
1.5 mi. S. on Hwy. 95, 1.5 mi. N. on Cty. Rd.
Boating Facilities, Drinking Water, Dump Station, Fire Rings, Pets OK, Tenters Welcome, Vault Toilets, Waterfront, Handicap Access

Slate Creek
P $10   6   26'   962-3245 / Summer, Fall, Spring
10 mi. S. on Hwy. 95
Boating Facilities, Drinking Water, Dump Station, Fire Rings, Pets OK, Pull-thru Sites, Tenters Welcome, Waterfront, Handicap Access

Pittsburg Landing
P $8   28   628-3916 / Summer, Fall
22 mi. SW of White Bird on County Rd. 493
Boating Facilities, Drinking Water, Fire Rings, Pets OK, Tenters Welcome, Vault Toilets, Handicap Access

Upper Pittsburg Landing
P   628-3916 / All Year
Hwy. 95, 22 mi. on County Rd. 493. Steep, one-lane gravel road. Hike-in campsites.
Fire Rings, Pets OK, Vault Toilets

Rocky Bluff
P   None   4   839-2211 / June-September
From Whitebird, drive to Slate Creek, and then travel 16 miles E on FR 354
Developed Campground, Handicap Accessible Restrooms, RV Sites, Biking, Fishing, Hiking/Backpacking, Horseback Riding, Hunting, Off Highway Vehicles, Picnicking, Scenic Driving

Wilderness

Indian Creek
P   None   7   (406) 821-3269 / June-October
From Darby, MT: 4 miles S on Hwy 93, then 14 miles SW on County Rd 473, then 37 miles W on FR 468, and 5 miles N on FR 6223
Primitive Camping, Restrooms, RV Sites, Biking, Fishing, Hiking/Backpacking, Horseback Riding, Hunting

Raven Creek
P   None   2   (406) 821-3269 / July-October
From Darby, MT: 4 miles S on Hwy 93, then 14 miles SW on County Rd 473, then 37 miles W on FR 468, and 2 miles N on FR 6223
Primitive Camping, Restrooms, Cultural/Historic Sites, Biking, Fishing, Hiking/Backpacking, Horseback Riding

Magruder Crossing
P   None   4   (406) 821-3269 / June-October
From Darby, MT: 4 miles S on Hwy 93, then 14 miles SW on County Rd 473, and 37 miles W on FR 468
Primitive Camping, Restrooms, Cultural/Historic Site, Biking, Fishing, Hiking/Backpacking, Horseback Riding, Off Highway Vehiclese, Scenic Driving

Big Creek Airfield
P   Yes   4   634-0600 / July-October
18 miles NE of Yellow Pine on FR 412, FR 340, and FR 371
Developed Campground, Handicap Accessible Drinking Water, Handicap Accessible Restrooms, Visitor Center, Biking, Fishing, Hiking/Backpacking, Horseback Riding, Hunting, Picnicking, Scenic Driving

Winchester

Miss Lily's Saloon & Buggy Stop
C $14   12   924-5048 / All Year
Hwy. 95 business loop
Hookups, Reservations

Winchester Lake State Park
P $12-16   70   40'   924-7563 / All Year
1 mi. W. on Hwy. 95
Credit Cards OK, Drinking Water, Dump Station, Hookups, Pull-thru Sites, Reservations, Showers, Yurts/Teepees, Tenters Welcome, Vault Toilets

NOTES:

Dining Quick Reference - continued

Price Range refers to the average cost of a meal per person: ($) $1-$6, ($$) $7-$11, ($$$) $12-up. Cocktails: "Yes" indicates full bar; Beer (B)/Wine (W), Service: Breakfast (B), Brunch (BR), Lunch (L), Dinner (D). Businesses in bold print will have additional information under the appropriate map locator number in the body of this section.

MAP NO.	RESTAURANT	TYPE CUISINE	PRICE RANGE	CHILD MENU	COCKTAILS BEER WINE	MEALS SERVED	CREDIT CARDS ACCEPTED
1	Camas Cafe 123 W Main St, Grangeville, 983-1019	American	$$	Y	B W	B /L/D	Major
1	Ireland's Inn 5497 Hwy 95, Potlatch, 875-1362	Family	$$-$$$	Y	N	B/L/D	No
3	Pizza To Go 112 S Front St, Elk River, 826-1600	Pizza	$	N	N	L/D	Major
4	Fuzzy's 408 2nd Ave, Deary, 877-9991	American	$$	N	Yes	B/L/D	No
4	White Horse Cafe 401 2nd Ave, Deary, 877-7750	American	$	Y	Yes	B/L	No
5	Basilios Steak & Seafood Ristorante 313 S Main St, Moscow, 892-3848	Steaks & Seafood	$$-$$$	Y	B W	L/D	Major
5	Blimpie Subs & Salads 1330 W Pullman Rd, Moscow, 882-7827	Fast Food	$	Y	N	L	Major
5	Breakfast Club 501 S Main St, Moscow, 882-6481	Family	$	Y	N	B	M V
5	Casa De Oro 415 S Main St, Moscow, 883-0536	Mexican	$	N	N	L/D	M V
5	Domino's Pizza 1104 S Main St, Moscow, 883-1555	Pizza	$-$$	N	N	L/D	M V
5	El Mercado Family Mexican Restaurant & Cantina 1420 S Blaine St, Moscow, 883-1169	Mexican	$-$$	Y	N	L/D	Major
5	Gambino's Italian Restaurant 308 W 6th St, Moscow, 882-4545	Italian	$$	Y	N	L/D	Major
5	Jack in the Box 710 W Pullman Rd, Moscow, 883-8212	Fast Food	$	Y	N	L/D	No
5	Kentucky Fried Chicken 1420 S Blaine St, Moscow, 882-8363	Fast Food	$-$$	Y	N	L/D	Major
5	La Casa Lopez 415 S Main St, Moscow, 883-0536	Mexican	$	N	N	L/D	M V
5	LocoGrinz Hawaiian Plate Lunch 113 N Main St, Moscow, 883-4463	Ethnic	$	N	N	L/D	M V
5	McDonald's 862 Troy Rd, Moscow, 882-1953	Fast Food	$	Y	N	B/L/D	Major
5	McDonald's 1404 W Pullman Rd, Moscow, 882-2900	Fast Food	$	Y	N	B/L/D	No
5	Mikey's Greek Gyros 527 S Main St, Moscow, 882-0780	Greek	$	N	N	L/D	No
5	Mingles Bar & Grill 102 S Main St, Moscow, 882-2050	American	$	N	Yes	L/D	No
5	Mongolian BBQ Express 1420 S Blaine St, Moscow, 882-7723	Asian	$-$$	N	N	L/D	Major
5	New Hong Kong Cafe 214 S Main St, Moscow, 882-4598	Asian	$	N	N	L/D	Major
5	Old Peking Restaurant 505 S Main St, Moscow, 883-0716	Asian	$	N	N	L/D	M V
5	One World Cafe 533 S Main St, Moscow, 883-3537	Bakery/Coffeehouse	$	N	N	B/L	M V
5	Papa John's Pizza 602 S Main St, Moscow, 892-2345	Pizza	$	N	N	L/D	M V
5	Papa Murphy's Take 'N' Bake Pizza W 3rd St, Moscow, 883-9508	Pizza	$$	N	N	L/D	M V
5	Patty's Mexican Kitchen & Catering 450 W 6th St, Moscow, 883-3984	Mexican	$	N	N	L/D	No
5	Pizza Hut 1429 S Blaine St, Moscow, 882-0444	Pizza	$	N	N	L/D	M V
5	Pretzel Maker 1904 W Pullman Rd, Moscow, 883-1817	American	$	N	N	L	M V
5	Quiznos Sub 317 W 6th St, Moscow, 882-8800	Fast Food	F	N	N	L/D	M V

Price Range refers to the average cost of a meal per person: ($) $1-$6, ($$) $7-$11, ($$$) $12-up. Cocktails: "Yes" indicates full bar; Beer (B)/Wine (W), Service: Breakfast (B), Brunch (BR), Lunch (L), Dinner (D). Businesses in bold print will have additional information under the appropriate map locator number in the body of this section.

MAP NO.	RESTAURANT	TYPE CUISINE	PRICE RANGE	CHILD MENU	COCKTAILS BEER WINE	MEALS SERVED	CREDIT CARDS ACCEPTED
5	Rathaus Pizza Shoppe 215 N Main St, Moscow, 882-4633	Pizza	$	N	N	L/D	No
5	Red Door 215 S Main St, Moscow, 882-7830	America/Fine Dining	$$-$$$	Y	Yes	D	Major
5	Rudy's Delicious Burgers 1420 S Blaine St, Moscow, 882-7839	Family	$-$$	N	N	L/D	M V
5	Subway 307 W 3rd St, Moscow, 883-3841	Fast Food	$	N	N	L/D	Major
5	Super China Buffet 1896 W Pullman Rd, Moscow, 883-4886	Asian	$	N	N	L/D	M V
5	Taco Time Restaurants 401 W 6th St, Moscow, 882-8226	Fast Food	$	N	N	L/D	M V
5	Ted's Burgers 321 N Main St, Moscow, 882-4809	Family	$	Y	N	L/D	No
5	The Ale House 226 W 6th St, Moscow, 882-2739	American	$-$$	N	Yes	L/D	Major
5	The Pita Pit 212 S Main St, Moscow, 882-7482	Fast Food	$	N	N	L/D	M V
5	Wendy's Restaurant 1030 W Pullman Rd, Moscow, 883-8112	Fast Food	$	Y	N	L/D	M V
5	Wingers American Diner 1484 S Blaine St, Moscow, 882-9797	American	$-$$	Y	B W	L/D	Major
5	Zip's Restaurant 1222 W Pullman Rd, Moscow, 883-0678	Family	$	Y	N	L/D	Major
5	Zume Bakery & Cafe 403 S Main St, Moscow, 882-4279	Bakery/Café	$	Y	N	B/L/D	Major
5	Arby's/Pasta Connection 150 Peterson Dr, Moscow , 882-4223	Fast Food	$	Y	N	L/D	Major
5	Pizza Perfection 428 W 3rd St, Moscow , 882-1111	Pizza	$	N	N	L/D	M V
6	First Bank Of Pizza 3rd & Main St, Juliaetta, 276-7061	Pizza	$	N	N	L/D	M V
6	Antelope Inn 707 E Main St, Kendrick, 289-5771	American	$	N	Yes	L	No
7	Antonio's Pizza & Pasta 1407 Main St, Lewiston, 746-6262	Pizza/Family	$	Y	N	L/D	Major
7	Anytime Tavern & Grill 1350 Main St, Lewiston, 746-6230	American	$	N	B W	L/D	M V
7	Arby's 721 21st St, Lewiston, 746-7227	Fast Food	$	Y	N	L/D	Major
7	Arby's/T.J. Cinnamons 248 Thain Rd, Lewiston, 798-8000	Fast Food	$	Y	N	L/D	Major
7	Baskin-Robbins 1430 21st St, Lewiston, 746-1482	Fast Food	$	Y	N	L	M V
7	Burger King Restaurant 920 21st St, Lewiston, 743-3961	Fast Food	$	Y	N	L/D	M V
7	Curley's North 315 20th St N, Lewiston, 746-0858	American	$$	N	N	B/L/D	No
7	Dairy Queen 1302 Main St, Lewiston, 746-2831	Fast Food	$	N	N	L/D	No
7	Domino's 3206 5th St, Lewiston, 743-9595	Pizza	$-$$	N	N	L/D	M V
7	Domino's Pizza 316 18th St, Lewiston, 746-9595	Pizza	$-$$	N	N	L/D	M V
7	Domino's Pizza 3206 1/2 5th St, Lewiston, 743-9595	Pizza	$-$$	N	N	L/D	M V
7	EL Sombrero Mexican Restaurant 629 Bryden Ave, Lewiston, 746-0658	Mexican	$	N	B W	L/D	Major
7	Finnagen's 301 Main St, Lewiston, 746-8333	American	$$	N	N	L/D	M V

Section 2

All Idaho Area Codes are 208

Dining Quick Reference - continued

Price Range refers to the average cost of a meal per person: ($) $1-$6, ($$) $7-$11, ($$$) $12-up. Cocktails: "Yes" indicates full bar; Beer (B)/Wine (W), Service: Breakfast (B), Brunch (BR), Lunch (L), Dinner (D). Businesses in bold print will have additional information under the appropriate map locator number in the body of this section.

MAP NO.	RESTAURANT	TYPE CUISINE	PRICE RANGE	CHILD MENU	COCKTAILS BEER WINE	MEALS SERVED	CREDIT CARDS ACCEPTED
7	Fun & Tasty Express 138 Thain Rd, Lewiston, 798-7600	American	$	N	N	L/D	No
7	Godfather's Pizza 2004 19th Ave, Lewiston, 746-1301	Pizza	$	N	N	L/D	M V
7	Golden Dragon 2404 N-S Hwy, Lewiston, 743-1952	Asian	$	N	N	L/D	Major
7	Helm Restaurant 1826 Main St, Lewiston, 746-9661	American	$-$$	Y	B W	B/L/D	Major
7	Henry J's Cafe 908 16th Ave, Lewiston, 743-1777	Fine Dining	$$$	Y	N	L/D	Major
7	Jack in the Box 203 19th St, Lewiston, 798-7410	Fast Food	$	Y	N	L/D	No
7	Jeffrey's Restaurant 244 Thain Rd, Lewiston, 746-9482	Family	$	Y	N	B/L/D	Major
7	Kentucky Fried Chicken 600 21st St, Lewiston, 746-2171	Fast Food	$-$$	Y	N	L/D	Major
7	Main St Grill 625 Main St, Lewiston, 746-2440	American	$$	Y	N	L/D	Major
7	Mandarin Pine Restaurant 833 21st St, Lewiston, 746-4919	Asian	$$	Y	N	L/D	Major
7	McCaullen's 1516 Main St, Lewiston, 746-3438	Steaks/Seafood/American	$-$$$	Y	Yes	L/D	Major
7	Meriwether's Bar & Grill 621 21st St, Lewiston, 746-9390	American	$$$	Y	B W	L/D	Major
7	Old Country Buffet 2305 Nez Perce Grade, Lewiston, 746-5124	Family	$$	N	N	L/D	Major
7	Papa Murphy's Take 'N' Bake Pizza 148 Thain Rd, Lewiston, 746-7272	Pizza	$	N	N	L/D	M V
7	Pizza Hut 1307 21st St, Lewiston, 746-5920	Pizza	$	N	N	L/D	Major
7	Pizza Perfection 247 Thain Rd, Lewiston, 743-5000	Pizza	$	N	N	L/D	No
7	Quizno's Classic Subs 2331 Thain Grade, Lewiston, 746-8899	Fast Food	$	N	N	L/D	M V
7	Rascal's Cafe 301 Main St, Lewiston, 743-8383	Family	$	N	N	L	M V
7	Red Lobster Restaurant 2115 Thain Grade, Lewiston, 746-9096	Seafood	$$	Y	N	L/D	Major
7	Rowdy's Texas Steakhouse And Saloon 1905 19th Ave, Lewiston, 798-8712	Steakhouse	$$-$$$	Y	Yes	L/D	Major
7	Rusty's Ranch 2418 N-S Hwy, Lewiston, 746-5054	Family	$	Y	N	B/L/D	M V
7	Shari's 2122 Nez Perce Grade, Lewiston, 798-0309	Family	$$	Y	N	L/D	M V
7	Skipper's Seafood 'N Chowder House 719 21st St, Lewiston, 746-0242	Seafood	$	Y	B W	L/D	Major
7	Strike & Spare Bar & Grill 244 Thain Rd, Lewiston, 743-4742	American	$$	N	Yes	L/D	Major
7	Subway 2112 8th Ave, Lewiston, 743-4000	Fast Food	$	N	N	L/D	M V
7	Subway 247 Thain Rd, Lewiston, 746-6000	Fast Food	$	N	N	L/D	M V
7	Super China Buffet 1928 19th Ave, Lewiston, 798-4931	Asian	$	N	N	L/D	M V
7	Taco Bell 1717 21st St, Lewiston, 746-1799	Fast Food	$	N	N	L/D	M V
7	Taco Johns 99 Sway Ave, Lewiston, 746-3498	Fast Food	$	N	N	L/D	M V
7	Thai Taste Restaurant 1410 21st St, Lewiston, 746-6192	Asian	$-$$	N	N	L/D	M V

Dining Quick Reference - continued

Price Range refers to the average cost of a meal per person: ($) $1-$6, ($$) $7-$11, ($$$) $12-up. Cocktails: "Yes" indicates full bar; Beer (B)/Wine (W), Service: Breakfast (B), Brunch (BR), Lunch (L), Dinner (D). Businesses in bold print will have additional information under the appropriate map locator number in the body of this section.

Section 2

All Idaho Area Codes are 208

MAP NO.	RESTAURANT	TYPE CUISINE	PRICE RANGE	CHILD MENU	COCKTAILS BEER WINE	MEALS SERVED	CREDIT CARDS ACCEPTED
7	The Bait Shop Grill 3206 5th St, Lewiston, 746-1562	American	$$	Y	N	L/D	Major
7	The China Inn 2007 16th Ave, Lewiston, 746-7876	Asian	$-$$	N	N	L/D	M V
7	The Clearwater River Casino Clearwater River, Lewiston, 746-0723	American	$	N	N	B/L/D	M V
7	Waffles Cafe 1421 Main St, Lewiston, 743-5189	Family	$-$$	Y	N	B/L	M V
7	Wendy's Old-Fashioned Hamburgers 1819 21st St, Lewiston, 743-1212	Fast Food	$	N	N	L/D	M V
7	Who's On First 631 Main St, Lewiston, 746-2440	American	$$	Y	B W	L/D	Major
7	Zany's 2004 19th Ave, Lewiston, 746-8131	American	$$	Y	B W	L/D	Major
8	Donald's Family Dining 304 N Us Hwy 95, Lapwai, 843-7273	American	$-$$	N	N	B/L/D	M V
8	Pi-nee-waus Cafe Main St & Beaver Grade, Lapwai, 843-2121	American	$	N	N	L/D	No
9	Canyon Inn Restaurant & Tavern 20289 Big Canyon Rd, Peck, 486-9991	American/Tavern	$-$$	Y	Yes	B/L/D	Major
10	The Woodlot Tavern 4166 Northfork Dr, Ahsahka, 476-4320	Tavern	$	N	B W	L/D	Major
11	Becky's Burgers 105 Michigan Ave, Orofino, 476-7361	American	$	N	N	L	No
11	China Palace 115 College Ave, Orofino, 476-7721	Asian	$	N	N	L/D	M V
11	Fiesta En Jalisco 203 Johnson Ave, Orofino, 476-7506	Mexican	$	N	N	L/D	Major
11	Flamingo Cafe 235 Johnson Ave, Orofino, 476-0200	Deli/Coffee	$	N	N	B/L	M V
11	Krystal Cafe 130 Johnson Ave, Orofino, 476-4982	Deli/Coffee	$	N	N	B/L	Major
11	M& M Pizza & Pub 12740 Hwy 12, Orofino, 476-7605	Pizza	$	N	B W	L/D	No
11	Pizza Factory 307 Michigan Ave, Orofino, 476-5519	Pizza	$	N	N	L/D	M V
11	Ponderosa Restaurant & Brass Rail 220 Michigan Ave, Orofino, 476-4818	American	$-$$	Y	B W	B/L/D	Major
11	Subway 11330 Hwy 12, Orofino, 476-9968	Fast Food	$	N	N	L/D	M V
12	Wink & Smile Family Restaurant 703 S Main St, Pierce, 464-2681	Family	$$-$$$	Y	N	B/L/D	M V
12	Timberline Cafe & Rv Park 1022 N Main St, Weippe, 435-4763	American	$-$$	Y	B	B/L/D	Major
13	Camas Club 101 W Main, Craigmont, 924-5801	American	$	Y	Yes	L/D	No
13	Jacques Spur Junction Cafe 29212 Mission Creek Rd, Culdesac, 843-2410	American	$$	Y	B W	B/L/D	Major
13	The Halfway Club Ferdinand, 962-5168	American	$-$$	N	Yes	L/D	No
13	Hi-Land Inn 518 Joseph, Winchester, 924-7351	American	$-$$	N	Yes	B/L/D	No
14	Lolo Trail 308 3rd St, Kamiah, 935-2821	American	$-$$	Y	B W	B/L/D	M V
14	Palenque Mexican Restaurant 714 3rd St, Kamiah, 935-7700	Mexican	$-$$	N	N	L/D	M V
14	Pizza Factory 814 Hwy 12, Kamiah, 935-2134	Pizza	$	N	N	L/D	M V
14	Sacajawea Cafe Rt 1 Box 17-X, Kamiah, 935-2233	American	$-$$	N	B W	B/L/D	Major

Ultimate Idaho Atlas and Travel Encyclopedia

Dining Quick Reference - continued

Price Range refers to the average cost of a meal per person: ($) $1-$6, ($$) $7-$11, ($$$) $12-up. Cocktails: "Yes" indicates full bar; Beer (B)/Wine (W), Service: Breakfast (B), Brunch (BR), Lunch (L), Dinner (D). Businesses in bold print will have additional information under the appropriate map locator number in the body of this section.

MAP NO.	RESTAURANT	TYPE CUISINE	PRICE RANGE	CHILD MENU	COCKTAILS BEER WINE	MEALS SERVED	CREDIT CARDS ACCEPTED
14	The Hub Bar & Grill 406 Main St, Kamiah, 935-2211	American	$$-$$$	N	Yes	L/D	M V
14	China Cafe 118 S Main St, Kooskia, 926-4800	Asian	$-$$	N	N	L/D	M V
14	Rivers Cafe 18 N Main St, Kooskia, 926-0986	American	$$	N	B W	B/L/D	M V
16	Country Haus Restaurant & Village Motel 407 Foster, Cottonwood, 962-3391	American	$$	Y	B W	B/L/D	M V
16	Keuterville Pub & Grub Hc3 Box 413, Keuterville, 962-3090	American	$-$$	Y	B W	L/D	No
18	Copper Hood Pizza Parlor 521 W Main St, Grangeville, 983-2642	Pizza	$	N	N	L/D	M V
18	Little Italy Restaurant 500 E Main St, Grangeville, 983-5400	Italian	$$	Y	N	L/D	M V
18	Oscar's Restaurant 101 E Main St, Grangeville, 983-2106	American	$$	Y	Yes	B/L/D	M V
18	Pizza Factory 126 W Main St, Grangeville, 983-5555	Pizza	$	N	B	L/D	Major
18	Subway Sandwiches 179 Greenacres Ln, Grangeville, 983-3054	Fast Food	$	N	N	L/D	Major
18	The Shanghai Restaurant 124 W Main St, Grangeville, 983-0485	Asian	$$	N	N	L/D	Major
19	Reno Club 308 Main St, Elk City, 842-2292	American	$	N	B W	L/D	Major
20	Hoots Cafe US Hwy 95, White Bird, 839-2265	American	$-$$	N	B W	B/L/D	Major
21	J C's River Grill 232 Hwy 95, Riggins, 628-2374	American	$-$$	Y	N	B/L/D	M V
21	Salmon River Inn 129 S Main St, Riggins, 628-3813	Deli/American	$-$$	N	B W	L/D	Major
21	This Old House Restaurant 1149 S Main St, Riggins, 628-3338	American	$-$$	N	N	B/L/D	Major

NOTES:

Motel Quick Reference

Price Range: ($) Under $40 ; ($$) $40-$60; ($$$) $60-$80, ($$$$) Over $80. Pets [check with the motel for specific policies] (P), Dining (D), Lounge (L), Disabled Access (DA), Full Breakfast (FB), Cont. Breakfast (CB), Indoor Pool (IP), Outdoor Pool (OP), Hot Tub (HT), Sauna (S), Refrigerator (R), Microwave (M) (Microwave and Refrigerator indicated only if in majority of rooms), Kitchenette (K). All Idaho area codes are 208.

MAP No.	HOTEL	NUMBER ROOMS	PRICE RANGE	BREAKFAST	POOL/ HOT TUB SAUNA	NON SMOKE ROOMS	OTHER AMENITIES	CREDIT CARDS
5	Best Western University Inn 1516 Pullman Rd, Moscow, 882-0550	173	$$$$		IP/OP/HT	Yes	P/D/DA	Major
5	Super 8 175 Peterson Dr, Moscow, 883-1503	60	$$/$$$ $	CB		Yes	P/DA	Major
5	Amerihost 185 Warbonnet Dr, Moscow, 882-5365	76		CB	IP/HT	Yes	DA/R/M	Major
5	Feather River Motel HC 87, Moscow, 653-2310	10	$$$			Yes	P/R	Major
7	Red Lion Hotel Lewiston 621 21st St, Lewiston, 799-1000	183	$$$$	FB	IP/OP/HT	Yes	P/D/DA/R/M	Major
7	Holiday Inn Express 2425 Nez Perce Dr, Lewiston, 343-4900	80	$$$$	CB	IP	Yes	R	Major
7	Super 8 3120 N S Hwy, Lewiston, 678-7000	59	$$/$$$	CB		Yes	P/DA	Major
7	Comfort Inn 2128 8th Ave, Lewiston, 798-8090	52	$$$/$$$$	CB	IP	Yes	P/DA	Major
7	Inn America 702 21st St, Lewiston, 746-4600	61	$$	CB	OP	Yes	R/M	Major
7	Howard Johnson 1716 Main St, Lewiston, 743-9526	66	$$$	CB	HT	Yes	P/DA/R	Major
7	GuestHouse 1325 Main St, Lewiston, 746-3311	58	$$$		OP		D/DA	Major
7	Econolodge 1021 Main St, Lewiston, 743-0899	42			OP	Yes	P	Major
7	Bel Air Motel 2018 N & S Hwy, Lewiston, 798-4444	10	$			Yes	P/R/M/K	
7	El Rancho Motel 2250 3rd Ave, Lewiston, 743-8517	24	$			Yes	P/DA/K	Major
11	Best Western at River's Edge 615 Main St, Orofino, 476-9999	49	$$$/$$$$	CB	IP	Yes	P/D/DA	Major
11	Helgeson Hoel Suites 125 Johnson Ave, Orofino, 476-5729	20	$$	CB	HT	Yes	R/M/K	Major
11	Konkolville Motel 2000 Konkolville Rd, Orofino, 476-5584	40		CB	OP	Yes	P/R/M	Major
11	White Pine Motel 222 Brown Ave, Orofino, 476-7093	18	$$			Yes	R/M	Major
12	Pierce Motel 509 S Main St, Pierce, 464-2324	16	$$			Yes	R/M	Major
12	Timber Inn 2 S Main St, Pierce, 464-2736	5	$			Yes	D	Major
13	Minnie Motel 420 Algoma, Winchester, 924-7784	4	$$			No	P/R/M	
14	Kamiah Inn Motel 216 3D, Kamiah, 935-0040	19	$$/$	FB		Yes	P	
14	Sundown Motel 1004 3rd St, Kamiah, 935-2568	14	$			Yes	P/R/M	Major
16	Village Motel 407 Foster St, Cottonwood, 962-3391	6	$$	CB		Yes	D/DA	Major
18	Super 8 801 W S 1st St, Grangeville, 983-1002	39	$$$	CB	IP	Yes	DA	Major
18	Elkhorn Lodge 822 S W First St , Grangeville, 983-1500	17	$$/$$$			Yes	P/R/M	Major
18	Downtowner Inn 113 E N St, Grangeville, 983-1110	20	$$/$$$			Yes	P/R/M/K	Major
19	Boar Hoager Inn 309 Main St, Elk City, 842-2735		$$$/$$$$			Yes	P/R/M/K	Major
19	Elk City Motel 289 Main St, Elk City, 842-2452	12	$$$			Yes	P/R/M/K	Major
19	Prospector Lodge & Cabins Main St, Elk City, 842-2597	5	$$/$$$			Yes	P/DA/K	Major

Section 2

All Idaho Area Codes are 208

Motel Quick Reference - continued

Price Range: ($) Under $40 ; ($$) $40-$60; ($$$) $60-$80, ($$$$) Over $80. Pets [check with the motel for specific policies] (P), Dining (D), Lounge (L), Disabled Access (DA), Full Breakfast (FB), Cont. Breakfast (CB), Indoor Pool (IP), Outdoor Pool (OP), Hot Tub (HT), Sauna (S), Refrigerator (R), Microwave (M) (Microwave and Refrigerator indicated only if in majority of rooms), Kitchenette (K). All Idaho area codes are 208.

MAP No.	HOTEL	NUMBER ROOMS	PRICE RANGE	BREAKFAST	POOL/ HOT TUB SAUNA	NON SMOKE ROOMS	OTHER AMENITIES	CREDIT CARDS
19	Dixie Motel 101 Main St, Dixie, 842-2358	6	$$$			Yes	P/L/R/M/K	Major
20	Hoots Motel US 95, White Bird, 839-2265	16	$$			Yes		Major
20	White Bird Motel White Bird, 839-2308	10	$$			No	P/R	M/V

Notes:

SECTION 3

SOUTHWEST AREA

INCLUDING BOISE, MCCALL, CASCADE, NAMPA, AND CALDWELL

The Idaho State Capitol Building in Boise

1 *Food, Lodging*

New Meadows
Pop. 533

Located amid a scenic meadow landscape, New Meadows received its first white inhabitants in 1864 when a pioneer homesteaded on Goose Creek in 1864. In 1877, Tom Cooper and Bill Jolly joined the scene with sixty head of horses, and the area became known as Whites Mail Station. Three years later, the Tom Clay family moved into the area, and the region was well on its way to establishing a community foothold in Idaho Territory.

In 1911, the Pacific and Idaho Northern Railroad arrived in this partially settled area and built a brick depot. Their original intentions were to terminate the line at the already established town of Meadows, but that never evolved due to disagreements between Meadows officials and Col. E.M. Heighho. Therefore, they laid the tracks one and one-half miles east of Meadows in the tiny homesteaded area, and many of nearby Meadows' residents and businesses relocated. The railroad, however, never prospered greatly from hauling meager loads of cattle and lumber, and in 1979 the line from Tamarack to New Meadows was abandoned. Today, New Meadows is developing into one of Idaho's newest recreational hot-spots and resort areas.

Meadows
Pop. 170

This small town lies in the middle of rich grazing, livestock, and farmland, and draws its name from its fertile landscape. A post office was established in 1883, but when the railroad came to the area and situated its tracks one and one-half miles west of town, most of the residents and businesses up and moved to that location. That site still prospers and is called New Meadows.

H Packer John's Cabin
Milepost 153 on State Hwy. 55 at Packer John's Park

John Welch, always known as Packer John, hauled supplies from Lewiston to Idaho City during a major Boise Basin gold rush of 1863-64.He built a cabin (one-quarter mile north of here) that immediately became an Idaho landmark. Territorial political conventions (Republican in 1863 and Democratic in 1864) used his cabin as a point where north Idaho leaders could meet with southern representatives to choose congressional candidates. This site was a state park and is now an Adams County park.

T Meadow Creek Golf Course
1 Meadow Creek Ct., New Meadows. 347-2555. www.meadowcreekresort.com On U.S. Hwy. 95, travel 2 miles north of New Meadows along the 45th Parallel.

A kaleidoscope of scenery awaits golfers at every turn on the Meadow Creek Golf Course. The towering Granite and Brundage Mountain peaks cap the skyline as the 6,696-yard course meanders in and out of meadow valleys and evergreen forests. The well-maintained championship course was established in 1982 and provides players with 18 holes of challenging par 72 play. Along the way, many golfers also report seeing a variety of wildlife. Green fees are $29 Monday through Thursday and $35 on weekends.

T Zims Hot Springs
4 miles north of New Meadows on U.S. Hwy. 95. 347-2686.

Surfacing at 145 degrees Fahrenheit, the natural Zims Hot Springs are cooled to ideal soaking temperatures with aeration in two large pools. The commercial site features a 93-degree Olympic size pool and a 104-degree soaking pool. The springs, which are closed on Mondays, are open year-round with a small admission charge. Picnicking is also available in the area.

T 45th Parallel
2.5 miles north of New Meadows on U.S. Hwy. 95

Immediately north of the U.S. Hwy. 95 and State Hwy. 55 junction, travelers will find the imaginary line of the 45th Parallel. A sign and small rest stop marks the parallel line designating the halfway point between the Equator and the North Pole

T Packer John's Cabin and Adams County Park
3 miles southeast of New Meadows on State Hwy. 55. Contact the Meadows Valley Chamber of Commerce at 347-2647.

From 1862 to 1864, John Welch earned a living transporting supplies to gold miners from the city of Lewiston over Boise Trail to Idaho City. During late winter 1862, Packer John (as he was affectionately nicknamed) reached Little Salmon Meadows only to find the trail completely blocked with snow. Unable to continue the trek, Packer John and his fellow packers constructed an eighteen by twenty-four foot cabin in the Goose Creek Valley just south of present day New Meadows where they spent the winter.

As winter thawed and the men were able to resume their journey, Packer John's Cabin became a local landmark symbolizing the connection of northern Idaho with the rest of Idaho Territory. Originally known as the Cottonwood House, the small cabin was selected as the site for the first Idaho Republican Convention in 1863 and as the Democratic Convention site in 1864. During these conventions, the territorial boundaries of Idaho were voted upon and mapped.

Although once a hotbed of political activity, Packer John's Cabin fell to the ghosts when the Boise Basin gold rush ended in 1864 and Boise Trail traffic decreased significantly. As the cabin began to fall apart, pictures recorded its decay with the site becoming a popular picnic ground at the turn of the 20th century.

Realizing the historic value of the cabin, the Idaho Legislature appropriated $500 to the State Historical Society in 1909 to preserve the structure. John Hailey was responsible for much of the restoration, paying others to move the cabin, replace decaying boards with fresh logs, and install a new roof and floor. During its reconstruction, the cabin emerged with a new design much different than Packer John's original structure, but the site nevertheless became a popular state attraction.

Upon its restoration, the park was originally maintained privately in Salmon Meadows as a summer resort. However, this system soon failed, and Idaho legislators set aside the cabin as a state park on March 6, 1951. Since then, the cabin has lost its state title but remains a county park under the management of Idaho's Adams County. The scenic and historic sixteen-acre park and campground surrounding the cabin is open during the summer, and a state historic marker identifies the area.

T Pacific and Idaho Northern Railroad Depot
South end of New Meadows on State Hwy. 55. Contact the Meadows Valley Chamber of Commerce at 347-2647.

In 1911, the Pacific and Idaho Northern Railroad arrived in New Meadows and purchased a large plot of land outside the original city site. Railroad

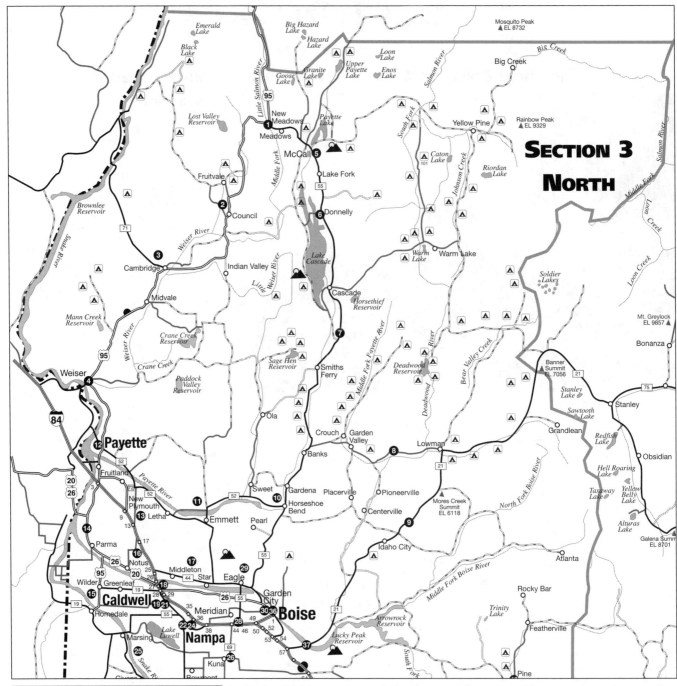

Legend

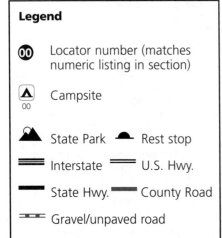

00 Locator number (matches numeric listing in section)

A Campsite
00

▲ State Park **⬣** Rest stop

═══ Interstate **───** U.S. Hwy.

━━━ State Hwy. **━━━** County Road

▬▬▬ Gravel/unpaved road

---

officials ordered the construction of a $30,000 brick depot, one of the most elaborate in the state. The line was primarily important in transporting mining, lumber, and agricultural supplies and operated until 1979. Today, the historic depot has been renovated into a combination museum and library.

T Meadows Valley
Directly north of New Meadows on U.S. Hwy. 95

For approximately ten miles, the Meadows Valley extends northward from New Meadows along the path of U.S. Hwy. 95. Geologists have concluded that the valley once contained a glacial lake before the hands of time transformed the area into a lush valley. Native Americans utilized the valley as a rich hunting and fishing ground, and a few Oregon Trail pioneers developed the land as a cattle ranching mecca. Charles Campbell was one such pioneer, and his 1884 Circle C Ranch

became one of the American West's largest cattle operations. Today, the valley is home to summer residences.

M The Crawford Company Real Estate Services, Inc.
410 Virginia St., New Meadows. 347-2323. www.thecrawfordcompany.com

M Meadows Valley Chamber of Commerce
PO Box 170, New Meadows. 347-2647. http://newmeadowsidaho.org; meadowsvalleychamber@hotmail.com

2 *Food, Lodging*

Council
Pop. 816

Council was named because the valley where it lies used to be the gathering grounds for Native American trading, peace talks, and tribal games.

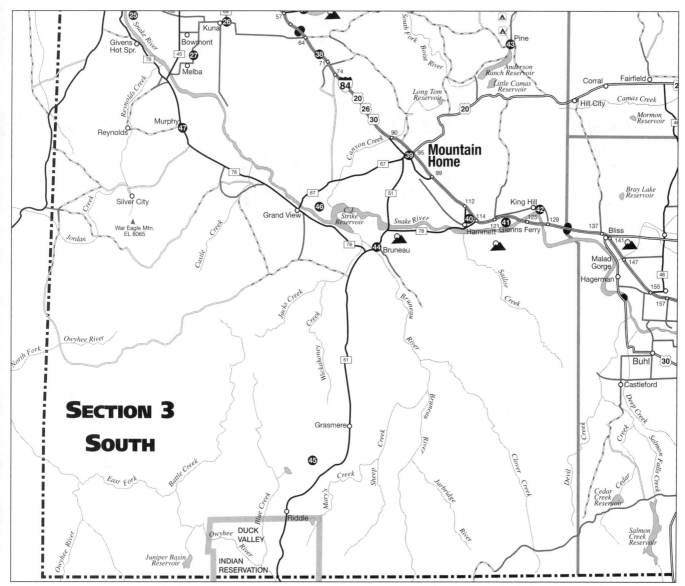

SECTION 3
SOUTH

Many of the councils were held on the butte, and the first white pioneers didn't arrive until 1876. George Moser and his family were the first to build a cabin in town. The couple eventually built a second, two-story frame structured home in which they housed travelers. The hogs and cattle they raised produced meat and butter, which the Mosers sold to the local miners. One spring day when George Moser set out to find the grizzly bear that had been preying on his dogs, the bear unfortunately found him first and tore his legs up. The damage was irreparable, and ill health plagued Moser for the rest of his life. In 1894, his condition finally led him back to Arkansas where he died shortly thereafter. More settlers arrived throughout the years in response to the Seven Devils mining boom, and in 1901, the railroad arrived. The town was eventually incorporated in 1903, and today serves as an access point to recreation in the Seven Devils Mountains.

Indian Valley
Pop. 30

Located along the Weiser River, Indian Valley attracted early Native American Indians who wintered in the area due to its relatively mild climate. A post office was established here in 1873. Today, the valley takes advantage of its favorable climate, basing its economy upon farming and ranching.

Fruitvale
Pop. 50

Fruitvale lies on the northern edge of an agricultural valley near Council and reflects its positioning near the region's numerous orchards. The post office has operated here since 1904.

H Mesa Orchards
Milepost 128 on U.S. Hwy. 95

For more than half a century after 1910, an exceptionally large apple orchard covered these hills around Mesa. An eight-mile wooden flume brought water to these slopes. Chicago and other distant investors bought ten-acre shares in an orchard company to pay for this expensive, 1,500 acre project. A town for fifty orchard workers was built here, and a 3 1/2-mile gravity tram hauled apples to a railroad siding below Mesa. This ambitious operation lasted until 1967.

H Old Railroads
Milepost 135.8 on U.S. Hwy. 95 at Council City Park

An ambitious railroad project to a high Seven Devils copper mine (elevation 6,800 feet) created a lot of excitement here in 1898-99. This would have been Idaho's highest mountain railroad if funding had been available to complete it. Construction began near a canyon rim more than a vertical mile above the Snake River. Although it never got anywhere, that grade still can be seen near Kinney Point. Remains of an old mining smelter at Landore also survive from that time.

McCall	Jan	Feb	March	April	May	June	July	Aug	Sep	Oct	Nov	Dec	Annual
Average Max. Temperature (F)	30.5	35.7	41.6	50.7	61.2	69.6	80.7	80.0	70.0	57.5	40.3	31.5	54.1
Average Min. Temperature (F)	11.0	13.2	18.1	26.0	33.8	39.8	44.2	41.9	35.0	28.2	21.9	14.4	27.3
Average Total Precipitation (in.)	3.54	2.84	2.54	2.01	2.31	2.05	0.71	0.83	1.38	2.02	2.99	3.54	26.76
Average Total Snowfall (in.)	37.1	25.3	18.7	5.3	0.8	0.0	0.0	0.0	0.1	1.8	16.2	31.9	137.3
Average Snow Depth (in.)	26	33	27	6	0	0	0	0	0	0	3	14	9

T Cuprum
28 miles northwest of Council off U.S. Hwy. 95

Meaning "copper" in Latin, Cuprum was located in the Seven Devils Mining District on Indian Creek. Established in 1897, Cuprum was characterized by its immense copper deposits and grew to include three saloons, two general stores, the Imperial Hotel, an examiner's office, and a newspaper. With its rapid prosperity, Cuprum drew the attention of New York City's Metropolitan Trust Company. This company leased the Blue Jacket mine and funded the construction of a smelter in Cuprum. Unfortunately, the smelter was inefficient, and after two operations, it was sold to another Idaho mining district. Today, Cuprum reportedly still holds vast copper deposits, but the area is now a sleepy village of summer cabin vacationers.

T Helena
10 miles north of Cuprum (approximately 38 miles northwest of Council)

Now characterized by a few decaying structures, Helena was a thriving mining camp on Indian Creek during the first few years of the twentieth century. While the town's discovery is credited to the Peacock copper mine, the story of the town's name is more vague. Some historians suggest that the town was named after the first girl born in the settlement. Many more speculate that the Peacock mine operators I.I. Lewis and Levi Allen named the mining community after their hometown of Helena, Montana. In 1910, miners' hopes were high as the P & IN Railroad made plans to construct a passage from Weiser to Helena to haul Peacock ore. The railroad never arrived, and the town died in disillusionment.

T Council Mountain Golf Course
1922 U.S. Hwy. 95 South, Council. 253-6908.

The Council Mountain Golf Course utilizes the natural terrain to create moderately sloped greens. Offering 9-holes at a par 37, this 3,236 yard course was built in 1967. Players will find that many of the tee boxes and greens are elevated. For golfers interested in an extended game, an extra set of tees is available for 18-hole play. The course is open daily March 15 to November 15, with green fees at $11.50 during the week and $13.50 on weekends.

T Charles Winkler Memorial Museum/Council Valley Museum
100 S. Galena St., Council. 253-4201.

The history of Council and the surrounding area begins primarily after the 1889 arrival of George and Elizabeth Winkler. The Winklers had six children, all of whom made significant contributions to Idaho politics, law, and the economy, as well as serving in World War I. This museum honors these contributions as well as other area families who have helped turn Council into what it is today. Visitors will find an extensive photo collection, Civil War diaries, Native American relics, memorabilia from the Prohibition era, area newspapers dating back to 1877, cemetery records, and much more. The museum is open from 10 AM to 4 PM Tuesday through Saturday and 1 PM to 4 PM on Sundays from Memorial Day to Labor Day.

T Kinney Point, Horse Mountain, and Sheep Rock Overlooks on Hells Canyon
Northwest of Council via the Kleinschmidt Grade. Contact the Hells Canyon National Recreation Area at 628-3916. From Council, drive northwest up Hornet Creek Rd. and continue as it turns into Forest Road (FR) 002. At the junction of FR 002 and FR 105, proceed north on FR 105 and drive past Bear and the junctions with FR 110 and 112. Turn off on FR 108 and continue to the lookout sites.

Hells Canyon, America's deepest river gorge, divides the Idaho/Oregon state border with relatively few lookout points found on the Idaho side. Kinney Point, Horse Mountain, and Sheep Rock, however, reward dedicated travelers with phenomenal vistas of the scenic canyon and surrounding Wallowa Mountains. The forest roads leading to the vantage points wind through the heart of historic mining districts and beautiful forest scenery. The seasonal road is closed in conjunction with wintry weather conditions, so interested visitors should call for road information prior to departure.

T Hixon-Sharptail Preserve
On U.S. Hwy. 95 near Council. Contact The Nature Conservancy at 788-2203.

Spanning 379 acres, The Nature Conservancy's Hixon-Sharptail Preserve is part of a 30,000 acre protected Bureau of Land Management area. The preserve combines rolling grassland hills with steep canyon slopes in an area set aside to protect the Colombian sharptail grouse. This rare species lives primarily in southwestern Idaho's lush grasslands, and the preserve contains four of Idaho's six remaining sharptail mating grounds. The area is open year-round for birdwatching, photography, and hiking. The preserve also boasts an excellent range of native wildflowers. The free site is open daily during daylight hours.

T White Licks Hot Springs
Halfway between Council and Donnelly on Forest Service Rd. 186. Contact the Council Chamber of Commerce at 253-6830.

Nestled against the Payette National Forest border, White Licks Hot Springs is tucked inside a remote, free camping area. The site features two bathhouses, each containing one small concrete soaking pool that can tightly accommodate up to three people. Each concrete pool includes a wooden plug that soakers can use to control the water temperature by stopping either the 90-degree or 110 degree Fahrenheit hot water pipes. The clear springs are rarely crowded and are open seasonally when road conditions allow.

T Cottonwood Creek: Home of Idaho's Most Notorious Outlaw
2.5 miles south of Council on U.S. Hwy. 95 at the Cottonwood Creek culvert

In 1908, the Whitney family and their seven children migrated from the Hells Canyon area to Idaho's Cottonwood Creek. After spending their teenage years helping the family develop a cattle and sheep ranch, Hugh and Charlie Whitney moved to Cokeville, Wyoming in 1910 where they pursued work as herders on the Pete Olsen ranch.

Despite the boys' hardworking and honest upbringing, trouble was brewing. When the foreman found out Hugh frequently used his pistol to herd sheep, the brothers were immediately fired. Hugh refused to accept the order and dealt the foreman a mortal beating. Hugh was quickly apprehended, but he escaped while waiting transfer to his manslaughter trial. Hugh's life as an outlaw had begun.

Hugh's trail took him to Montana where the outlaw developed a reputation as a sore gambler. In one particular game in Monida, Hugh, Charlie, and a friend lost hundreds of dollars. Refusing to be losers, Hugh held up the saloon the next day and demanded the return of the trio's money at gunpoint.

Discovering that intimidation and robbery seemed to work for him, Hugh decided to delve into train robbery. In June 1911, he attempted to rob the Oregon Short Line Railroad. When the conductor recognized him as a wanted man, though, Hugh panicked and shot the conductor dead. In his flight from authorities, Hugh also wounded a sheriff. In just a little over a year, Hugh established himself as one of the West's most wanted outlaws. His flight lead him south through Idaho back to Cokeville, Wyoming where he and Charlie successfully stole $700 from the town's First National Bank. The robbers were never caught and virtually seemed to disappear from society.

Although their outlaw past disappeared, the Whitney brothers were alive and well. They fled to Wisconsin, and worked in Minnesota and Texas before using their savings to purchase a Glasgow, Montana ranch. Taking a break from ranch life to enlist under assumed names, the brothers served in World War I in France. Upon their return to the ranch, Hugh and Charlie's partnership lasted three years before Hugh married and moved to a Canadian ranch. Charlie stayed on at the Montana ranch and became one of the community's most well-respected citizens. He served on the school board and led an honorable life. The brothers' secrets may have remained hidden had Hugh's conscience not faltered. On his deathbed in 1951, Hugh revealed his true identity and cleared his brother's name in all criminal activity except the Cokeville bank robbery. Upon hearing the news of his brother's dying admission, Charlie divulged his identity to Montana's governor. In an act of generosity and in light of Charlie's reformed ways, the Montana governor pleaded with Wyoming's governor to dismiss any charges against the rancher. Wyoming's governor wholeheartedly agreed, and Charlie Whitney remained on his Montana ranch until his 1955 death.

COPPERFIELD: THE SNAKE RIVER'S SIN CITY

During the boom and bust cycle of Idaho and Oregon's early twentieth century, Copperfield earmarked itself as one of the most lawless and notorious communities in the entire Pacific Northwest. Although the town was founded upon hard work and bright hopes for the future, martial law snuffed out the town's abhorrent ways.

After the discovery of copper at the nearby Iron Dyke mine, plans were laid for the extension of a railroad to the mine. At the same time, the Idaho-Oregon Light and Power Company acquired water and property rights for the establishment of a large hydro power plant. Upon hearing the news of the impending building boom, a group of Baker, Oregon businessmen pooled their resources to purchase the 160-acre Copperfield Ranch. The men then platted a townsite and began selling lots. Within just two years, every lot was sold, and droves of new settlers moved to Copperfield.

Due to the town's location, most of Copperfield's residents were hardworking construction workers of all nationalities. Few families settled within Copperfield's city limits, and governing law was lax. As a result, the tough laborers capped off their long workday with boisterous and sometimes violent revelry. At the height of Copperfield's boom, approximately 700 men were employed for the railroad or power company. Main Street was lined with wooden buildings, including gambling halls, two boarding houses, eleven saloons (each complete with its own house of ill-repute), a post office, butcher shop, general stores, a livery barn, jail, and a few hotels.

As the men gambled, drank, brawled, and frequented the brothels into the wee hours of the morning, nearly 400 family men who had settled nearby grew weary of Copperfield's increasingly raucous nightlife. The town's atmosphere worsened further around 1913 when the power company went bankrupt. Storeowners literally fought in the streets for customers, and arson became a regular occurrence. Finally, the town's schoolteacher and fifty other residents contacted Oregon Governor, Oswald West, for help.

West was appalled at the report and immediately sent a decree to Copperfield's Sheriff Rand. West ordered the sheriff to clean up his community by Christmas or face state interference. Rand scoffed at the order, but West was serious. When Rand failed to meet the governor's demands, West created a plan of action that would eventually lead to the demise of the lawless town.

West immediately sent his intelligent twenty-five year old secretary, Fern Hobbs, to Copperfield as an intermediary. Seven veteran soldiers and military men dressed in civilian clothes accompanied the young lady as she read the resignation request for all city officials. When the officials refused to follow the order and sign her papers, Hobbs declared immediate placement of martial law. The disguised soldiers who accompanied her arrested the mayor and city councilmen, stating that all liquor, bar tools, and gambling equipment had to be removed from Copperfield establishments by the next afternoon. If residents failed to meet this deadline, the soldiers led by Lieutenant Colonel B. K. Lawson would drag these items to the streets and set fire to them. Forced to hand over their weapons, Copperfield residents were speechless as Hobbs boarded the train and returned to Governor West's office.

Copperfield city officials promptly hired attorneys to protect their rights, but Lieutenant Colonel Lawson ignored all interference from lawyers. Instead, he and other soldiers gathered every ounce of liquor and all gambling materials and shipped them to a Baker, Oregon warehouse for safekeeping. Copperfield's fate was sealed, and by 1914, only thirty-two residents were counted. By 1935, a string of fires had destroyed most of the community's buildings, and the town once called "Gomorrah on the Snake" was left in ashes.

Copperfield can be found near Oxbow Reservoir on State Hwy. 71 north of Cambridge.

TV Ben Ross Reservoir

South of Council off U.S. Hwy. 95. Contact the Idaho Department of Parks and Recreation at 334-4199. Merge off U.S. Hwy. 95 at Alpine and proceed through Indian Valley to the reservoir.

Ben Ross Reservoir is situated amidst the scenic Indian Valley and provides recreationists with a remote setting for summer fun. The 350-acre reservoir offers boating, boat docks, fishing, water skiing, and a few primitive campsites.

TV Lost Valley Reservoir

North of Council. Contact the Idaho Department of Parks and Recreation at 334-4199. From Council, drive 16 miles north on U.S. Hwy. 95 to the Pine Ridge community. Bear west here on Lost Valley Reservoir Rd., and proceed 4 miles to the reservoir.

Encompassing 800 acres in southwest Idaho, Lost Valley Reservoir is an ideal setting for angling and camping outings. The reservoir features excellent fishing, and two developed campgrounds are available.

M Council Chamber of Commerce

108 Illinois, Council. 253-6830. www.councilidaho.net

3 Food, Lodging

Cambridge
Pop. 360

Cambridge obtained its name from the location of Harvard University, the alma mater of the president of the Pacific & Idaho Northern RR. When the railroad originally came to the area in 1899-1900, the plan was to run the track through a settlement called Salubria. However, one landowner was asking too much money for the right-of-way. A rancher across the Weiser River offered to donate every other lot of his property if the railroad would come by that route. Unable to pass up a deal like that, the PINRR changed its plans and relocated to the other side of the river, foregoing Salubria. While Cambridge evolved, Salubria perished. Many of Salubria's businesses moved to the new townsite.

The original town of Salubria was located about two miles east of present day Cambridge and across the river. Settlers began homesteading there and ranching the land in the early 1880s. Silver and copper were also mined in the Seven Devils mine between 1880 and 1905. John Cuddy, an Irish emigrant, came to the area in 1870 to erect a grist mill on Rush Creek. It had the capacity to produce three tons of flour a day. The mill was a couple miles from Salubria, and as the town grew, Cuddy relocated the mill within the city limits. Today, Cambridge is still a farming and ranching community, economically reliant upon cattle, dairy, and hay production.

Midvale
Pop. 176

Based upon its name, it comes as no surprise that Midvale lies in the middle of two other valleys: the Weiser and Salubria valleys. Previously called Middle Valley, this settlement arose in 1868 with the arrival of John Reed and his family. Upon their arrival, the Reeds constructed a log cabin along the Weiser River and created a sawmill. Despite the sawmill's promising potential, growth was slow through the 1870s. In 1881, the population boomed with the arrival of forty Oregon Trail emigrants weary of further traveling. Two years later, a wooden bridge was erected over the river, but high flood waters every spring frequently washed out the dirt embankments holding the span in place. In 1896, this annual occurence created a fiasco for a young couple residing on the river's east side. As the young lovebirds were unable to cross over to attend their own wedding, the officiant stood on the river's west side and shouted out the vows. Finally, in 1911, a steel bridge was built at approximately the same location. With the 1899 arrival of the P & IN Railroad, Midvale grew as a prominent sheep ranching location. The large quantities of lambs and wool production sustained the community's economy from 1905 to 1930.

H Brownlee Ferry
Milepost 2 on State Hwy. 71 at Idaho Power Park

Guiding Oregon Trail emigrants and a party of prospectors who had discovered gold in Boise Basin, Tim Goodale opened a new miners' trail through here in August 1862. A gold rush followed that fall, and John Brownlee operated a ferry here from 1862 to 1864, before leaving to work his own Boise Basin mine. A new ferry commenced here a year after James Ruth and T.J. Heath discovered silver mines on Brownlee Creek in 1874, with service continuing until after 1920.

H Seven Devils Mines
Milepost 2 on State Hwy. 71 at Idaho Power Park

More than a century ago, miners faced a hopeless problem of hauling copper ore to this canyon for shipment to smelters. They started with Albert Kleinschmidt's road grade down from their mine, more than a vertical mile above the Snake River about 30 miles downstream from here. After a steamboat failed in 1891, a railroad (now under water) was built past here to their river landing. That did not work either. Large ore trucks finally solved the problem in 1968.

H An Early Industry
Milepost 101 on U.S. Hwy. 95 at the Midvale Hill Rest Area

At the top of this hill 3,000 to 5,000 years ago, prehistoric men had a rock quarry where they made a variety of stone tools. Projectiles, knives, and scrapers were among the tools made by these early people who camped at the foot of the hill. These nomads hunted deer and other game, collected plant foods and fished in the river here. They had spears and spear throwers

Continued on page 189

Southwest Area

Including Boise, Cascade, McCall, Nampa, and Caldwell

Emmett Cherry Festival

Join in some old-fashioned fun while celebrating Idaho's agricultural heritage at the annual Emmett Cherry Festival. Known for its bountiful orchards, Gem County has observed this early June festival for over 70 years. With a different theme each year, the festival features a parade, hot-air balloon races, cherry-pit spitting contests, pie-eating contests, square dancing, a carnival, food, craft, and expo booths, pancake feeds, fun runs, sporting events, live entertainment, and the Miss Gem County Contest. For additional information, contact the Gem County Chamber of Commerce at (208) 365-3485.

Parade America

The Northwest's largest patriotic parade is hosted in Nampa the weekend before Memorial Day. Held for nearly 40 years, the parade features numerous patriotic floats, horses, antique cars, and several marching bands.

Snake River Stampede & Snake River Dayz

The Professional Rodeo Cowboys Association recently rated the Snake River Stampede Rodeo as one of the top twelve rodeos in the U.S.. Originating in 1913 as part of Nampa's Harvest Festival, the rodeo finally separated and became its own event in 1937. Today, the weeklong event features a Buckaroo Breakfast, large horse parade, and world-renowned rodeo pros competing in bull riding, steer wrestling, barrel racing, bareback and saddle bronc riding, and individual and team roping. In addition, the rodeo includes the annual Miss Rodeo Idaho Pageant, plus a special Mutton Busting event for children ages 5-7. The rodeo is held each July in the 120,00 square foot Idaho Center Arena.

In conjunction with the Stampede, Snake River Days provides families with a week full of fun. The festival features games, clowns, magicians, face painting, fiddlin' contests, arts and crafts booths, and pancake stacking contests.

Canyon County Fair

The Canyon County Fair offers locals and visitors old-fashioned fun at a reasonable price for a week in July. Annual events include expo shows, livestock shows, cook-off contests, a carnival, a tractor pull, pie-baking and milk-drinking contests, and a range of daily entertainment. Contact the Caldwell Chamber of Commerce at (208) 459-7493 for additional information.

Caldwell Night Rodeo

Held annually for more than 70 years, the Caldwell Night Rodeo attracts more than 40,000 fans during the event's six nights of rodeo thrills each August. The rodeo has been christened as one of America's top 20 PRCA-sanctioned events and includes team roping, barrel racing, steer wrestling, and Mini Mite Barrel Racing for 5-7 year olds as just some of the many events. For additional information, contact the Caldwell Chamber of Commerce at (208) 459-7493.

Three Island Crossing Reenactment

During the summer, the Glenns Ferry community sponsors an annual reenactment of the Oregon Trail crossing at Three Island Crossing State Park. This popular event, which is held every August, often includes living history presentations and a historic skills fair, although variations from year to year are possible.

Council 4th of July Celebration/ Porcupine Race

Council celebrates the 4th of July with a full day of entertainment. The day includes a free community breakfast in the park, parade, carnival, quilt show, live music, food booths, sawing contests, fireworks, and the event's signature porcupine races.

Alive After Five

Boise residents and visitors can sample good food and the sounds of live music from May through August in the city's downtown plaza. Alive After Five is held every Wednesday evening beginning at 5 PM.

Capital Rotunda Art Show

Idaho's State Capitol Building in Boise reflects the inspiring colors and paintings of Idaho Watercolor Society artists each spring. The annual two-week display is open to the public free of charge.

Council Quilt Show

Although Council may be small, it draws the attention of quilt enthusiasts from all across America each summer at its annual quilt show. The event features over 150 old and new quilts, along with antiques, crafts, and a quilt block contest.

Hyde Park Street Fair

Boise's annual Hyde Park Street Fair is a late summer extravaganza featuring more than 100 different booths beckoning visitors to browse. The fair includes both local and regional arts and crafts booths, live music, a beer and wine garden, and food booths.

Idaho Aviation Festival

The annual Idaho Aviation Festival is held in the Boise Centre on the Grove and includes a myriad of educational presentations and displays. The three-day festival features safety and general interest seminars, teacher's and children's aviation workshops, and a large tradeshow.

Idaho Gem Club Show

Held towards the beginning of the year, the annual Idaho Gem Club Show showcases rare gems, minerals, and fossils. The two-day event also includes children's activities, raffles, dealer showcases, demonstrations, a garnet dig, and lectures about Idaho's precious rocks.

Pine Festival

The community of Pine may be tiny, but it still hosts a regional festival that draws crowds from miles around. The Pine Festival features arts and crafts booths, a Wild West shootout, food, games for the whole family, a street dance, and performances by the Treasure Valley Cloggers.

Soul Food Extravaganza

Boise's Julia Davis Park is turned into an aromatic and taste bud delight each summer with the annual Soul Food Extravaganza. The one-day event features ethnic foods like jambalaya, fried catfish, barbeque beef, pork, and chicken, collard greens, and sweet potato pie. In addition, a range of music, children's activities, and African storytelling awaits crowds. All proceeds are donated to Boise charity organizations.

Art & Roses

Every summer, the Rose Garden in Boise's Julia Davis Park is transformed into a wonderland of art. The event strictly features the fine art of Idaho residents with a portion of the proceeds donated to the upkeep of Julia Davis Rose Garden.

Art in the Park

The three-day Art in the Park festival draws original works from Pacific Northwest artists to Julia Davis Park each autumn. The outdoor event also includes a variety of food booths and live performances, and all event proceeds are donated to the Boise Art Museum.

Art for Kids

The Boise City Arts Commission is dedicated to educating children about art and its objective is partially achieved through the annual Arts for Kids event. Held weekly from June through July, the event includes 45-minute hands-on art workshops. The free event is open to children ages 3 to 12 and is held on the Grove Plaza in downtown Boise.

Basque Picnic

Celebrate Basque culture each summer at the annual Basque Picnic held in Mountain Home's Basque Park. The one-day event features games for both children and adults, cultural dancing, arts and craft booths, and an array of native food. The event concludes with a community street dance.

Beaux Arts Societe Holiday Sale

The Beaux Arts Societe Holiday Sale is a Boise holiday tradition held each November. The event features handcrafted items from over 340 nationally and regionally acclaimed artisans. Proceeds from the sale are given to the Boise Art Museum.

Boise Tours Annual Holiday Lights Tours

The Boise Tours Annual Holiday Lights Tours offer heated trolleys and mini-buses that carry tour participants to Boise's finest decorated homes and businesses. The tour takes place on one of the first weekends in December, and participants are encouraged to bring along hot chocolate.

Family Holiday Concert

Boise State University's Music Department treats Boise residents and visitors to affordable family entertainment at its annual holiday concert. The Christmas concert includes musical performances from university groups and soloists.

Washington County Fair & Cambridge Rodeo

Every August, the Washington County Fair draws crowds from far and wide to witness arts, crafts, baking, needlework, and flowers and horticulture exhibits along with a livestock show, parade, and live entertainment. From Thursday through Saturday, the fair boasts the annual Cambridge Rodeo offering the finest in western tradition.

A Taste of the Harvest

One of Idaho's newest annual festivals, A Taste of the Harvest features an array of the state's finest homegrown and homemade products. The event includes samples of specialty foods and wine, live music, and educational displays about Idaho's agriculture scene.

Canyon County Fair & Festival

Held mid-summer, the Canyon County Fair and Festival transports spectators back to the good old days with an old-fashioned fair. The festival also includes contests, livestock shows, and affordable live entertainment suitable for the whole family.

Court Street Cruise

The annual Court Street Cruise is held in Weiser's City Park each August. Spectators will find hula-hoop contests and dancing, a classic car show, sidewalk art sales, radio control car races, airplane drops, and an ugly art contest.

Eagle Fun Days
Eagle Fun Days is exactly that – fun. The summer weekend event begins with a community golf tournament on Friday, and a Fun Run and community breakfast kicks off Saturday's events. The festival also includes Idaho's wettest parade, a huge waterfight where spectators are guaranteed to get wet, over eighty food vendors, a professional bicycle race, arts and crafts booths, and a community worship service.

Elmore County Fair & Rodeo
In addition to hosting standard fair and 4-H events, the Elmore County Fair and Rodeo provides live entertainment, a carnival, charros, and Hispanic music along with traditional dancers.

Emmett Spring Horse Race Meet
The Emmett Spring Horse Race Meet dates back to 1964 and annually offers the first horse race of the season in Idaho. The event offers three days of racing at the end of April each year. Featured horses include quarter horses, thoroughbreds, Appaloosas, and paints.

Fall Festival in the Park
Horseshoe Bend's Fall Festival is held each October in the community park. The event includes a community breakfast, children's activities, and arts and crafts booths.

Fiesta Idaho
Nampa residents and visitors kick off autumn's arrival with the annual Fiesta Idaho. The festival celebrates southwestern Idaho's Hispanic heritage. Features include Mexican music, Menudo cook-off, traditional food, Mexican folk arts, a mariachi concert, children's bullfighting, and a classic low-rider car show.

Fruitland Family Fun Day
As its name suggests, Fruitland Family Fun Day is geared towards families and is held each September. The event is held in the community park and features live entertainment, arts and crafts, quilt show, street dance, and a Beer Garden for the adults.

Garden Tour
Garden Tour is one of southwestern Idaho's most unique annual events. Spectators can watch as regional artists paint in a garden setting in Mountain Home. The artwork that is created is auctioned off later in the day. The event, held in early summer, also includes music, food, and wine.

Gene Harris Jazz Festival
Boise State University's Gene Harris Jazz Festival is annually held in April in honor of one of Idaho's greatest jazz musicians. The late Gene Harris enjoyed a distinguished career in which he inspired several young musicians. The renowned festival features national and local jazz artists on piano, trumpet, guitar, and sax, along with vocal performances. The three-day event also includes student competitions and clinics.

Music in the Garden
The Idaho Botanical Garden in Boise is transformed into a music wonderland every Thursday evening during summer. The beautiful garden features live music along with food and beverage vendors. Spectators can purchase fine food at the garden or pack along their own picnic.

Griddles & Fiddles Festival
Nampa's Griddles and Fiddles Festival is a traditional western celebration held in the park every summer. The two-day event features a pancake breakfast, Kidz Korral, Kidz Kreative Korner, live entertainment, clowns, magicians, pony rides, a petting zoo, a three-on-three basketball tourney, a skateboard park, fun run, and a free fiddling concert.

Harvest Fest
During autumn's annual Harvest Fest, Emmett's Main Street is lined with arts and crafts booths and plenty of tempting food vendors. Merchants join in the fun with special sidewalk sales.

Hells Canyon Days, Bull-A-Rama & Farm Toy Show
Nestled on the Idaho/Washington border, Cambridge comes alive with activity at the annual Hells Canyon Days, Bull-A-Rama, and Farm Toy Show. The one-day summer event includes a community breakfast, car show, sidewalk sales, antique power equipment show, square dancing, a barbeque, museum open houses, Weiser River Trail activities, barrel racing, team roping, and a farm toy show featuring new and antique farm toys and collectibles.

Horseshoe Bend Banjo Contest & Festival
Break out the banjos and prepare yourself for a bluegrass extravaganza at the annual Horseshoe Bend Banjo Contest & Festival. The two-day event features a banjo contest with cash prizes, and although pre-registration is not necessary, it is recommended.

Horsehoe Days
In addition to its main Tuttle Blacksmith Horseshoe Tournament, New Plymouth's Horseshoe Days features a plethora of events. The one-day festival includes a community yard sale, the Park in the Park Show n' Shine Car Show, a library book sale, food and craft vendors, live entertainment, and the Noble Duck Race.

Huckleberry Festival
Donnelly's Huckleberry Festival draws hundreds of berry lovers each August. The two-day community event includes a pancake breakfast, live music and entertainment, a parade, and a competitive huckleberry dessert contest.

Mad Hatter's Tea Party
Idaho Botanical Gardens in Boise makes children's dreams come true and provides fun for the whole family during autumn's Mad Hatters Tea Party. The day includes all the characters of Alice in Wonderland along with games, shopping, live entertainment, and children's activities.

Idaho City Arts & Crafts Festival
Every June, Idaho City's John Brogan Park hosts an annual one-day arts and crafts fair. The event features children's craft activities, live entertainment, over eighty art booths, and numerous food vendors.

Idaho Shakespeare Festival
Showcased in a stunning outdoor amphitheater, Shakespeare has been coming to life in southwestern Idaho every June through September since 1976. Performed by the Idaho Shakespeare Festival in Boise, the summer showcases the bard's favorites, and spectators are encouraged to pack along a picnic. Food and beverages are also available for purchase.

Jaialdi
Boise and many other communities in southwest Idaho contain large populations of Basque people. This heritage is celebrated every five years at Boise's international Jaialdi Festival. The festival celebrates every aspect of Basque culture, featuring sports, music, dancing, food, and much more. The most recent Jaialdi Festival is scheduled for July 2005 with the next festival to follow in 2010.

Juneteenth
Boise and the surrounding area celebrate slavery's abolition at the annual Juneteenth Festival. The event, held at Boise's Julia Davis Park and Nampa's Ridgecrest Golf Course, features ethnic specialties, children's games, the Silly Olympics, live music, and plenty of food vendors.

Kuna Days
Kuna's past and future are celebrated at the annual Kuna Days. The two-day summer event draws hundreds of area residents and visitors for a community barbeque, parade, live entertainment, an arts and crafts fair, a quilt show, and a fireworks extravaganza.

McCall Winter Carnival
The weeklong McCall Winter Carnival is Idaho's hottest spot every January/February. Although the town normally boasts a tiny population, it's not unusual for more than 20,000 people to pour into town to partake in the renowned winter festivities. Snow-sculpture lined streets welcome visitors to the festivities, which include a world-class ice sculpting contest, parades, fireworks displays, sled dog and snowmobile races, snowshoe golf tournaments, a variety show, sledding, ice skating, and a Snowflake Ball.

Meadow Valley Days
New Meadows' annual three-day Meadow Valley Days extravaganza features activities sure to please the whole family. The event includes parades, arts and crafts booths, and a community barbeque, antique car show, and an amateur logging competition.

Meridian Dairy Days
Meridian has a long history as a major Idaho dairy location, and this heritage is celebrated annually at Meridian Dairy Days. The three-day event features a massive pancake feed, a dairy-themed parade, a cattle show, and a carnival. Merchants also participate with special sales and community events.

Murphy Outpost Days
Every summer, the Owyhee County Historical Museum draws hundreds of visitors to its Murphy Outpost Days. The two-day event takes visitors back in time with its pioneer skills and lost art demonstrations, soap making booths, pinecone basket weaving, and horsehair braiding events. The festival also includes Native American dancers, horny toad races, country music, cowboy poetry readings, parades, pie and food vendors, and a community dance.

Nampa Festival of the Arts
Held annually in August, the Nampa Festival of the Arts draws hundreds of artisans and those who appreciate handmade crafts. The event includes booths featuring a plethora of hand-crafted arts and crafts.

National Old Time Fiddlers' Contest & Festival
Situated along U.S. Hwy. 95, Weiser turns into a

fiddlin' mecca each summer when the National Old Time Fiddlers' Contest and Festival arrives in town. More than 350 of America's top fiddlers compete for national titles at this five-day event. In addition to the contest, the festival includes three live entertainment stages, free instructional workshops, a huge parade, and arts and crafts booths.

Oktoberfest
Autumn's beauty comes to life in Boise at the annual Oktoberfest held in the Idaho Botanical Garden. Event participants have the opportunity to learn original folk dances, eat and drink traditional German food and beverages, and enjoy the sounds of lively polka music.

Payette Apple Blossom Festival
Western Idaho blooms with the beauty and fragrance of apple blossoms each spring, and this annual sighting is celebrated every April or May (depending on the year) at the Payette Apple Blossom Festival. The two-week event features a parade, arts and crafts booths, ice cream socials, a chamber breakfast, pie-eating contests, lawn mower races, the Apple Core Open Golf Tournament, a classic car show, talent shows, pig wrestling, a mud volleyball tournament, fireman's challenge and games, and a carnival, rodeo, mountain man encampment, and live entertainment.

Payette Neighborhood Renaissance Fair
The family-oriented Payette Neighborhood Renaissance Fair is held annually each fall with the intent of uniting regional residents as neighbors. The one-day event includes a period costume contest, live music, arts and crafts booths, games, pie vendors, food booths, and face painting. Visitors will find all event vendors and booths decked out in Renaissance fare.

Scarecrow Festival
Meridian residents imbibe the autumn air while taking part in the annual Scarecrow Festival. The two-day citywide contest and festival features a historical scavenger hunt, pumpkin bowling contests, arts and crafts booths, and, of course, titles for the winning scarecrows.

Thunder Mountain Days
Thunder Mountain Days annually arrives in Cascade just in time for the Fourth of July. The two-day event includes children's activities, a parade, a community barbeque, concerts, a poker run, a dance, a burnout demonstration at the regional airport, and a show & shine car display.

Weiser Valley Round-Up
The Weiser Valley Round-Up is known throughout Idaho as one of the state's finest summer shows. The three-day professional rodeo event originated in 1916 with the first rodeo staged on a high school athletic field. Since then, the rodeo has developed its facilities, and the round-up continues to grow in popularity each year.

Western Idaho Fair
As one of Idaho's largest fairs, the Western Idaho Fair arrives for ten days of fun and excitement each August. The fair features 4-H exhibits, live stock shows, nationally recognized live entertainment, a carnival, game booths, and plenty of food.

Winter Games of Idaho
Held each winter in a variety of venues, the Winter Games of Idaho is a month-long event created for state and regional athletes of all ages. The sports festival competitions include figure skating, snowboarding, ice hockey, and alpine and Nordic races held in Salmon, Kellogg, Sun Valley, Idaho Falls, McCall, and Boise.

Winter Garden Aglow
Boise's Idaho Botanical Garden features the warm glow of the holiday season each December at the Winter Garden Aglow. The garden events features more than 150,000 twinkling lights, carolers, bonfires, hot cocoa, and cookies. The family-oriented event is open nightly from 6 PM – 9 PM.

Yellow Pine Harmonica Contest
Hosted in a town that reflects Idaho's historical gold-mining roots, the Yellow Pine Harmonica Contest is an amateur contest paying tribute to the harmonica's role in the Old West. The three-day festival features plenty of foot-stompin' music as well as food and craft vendors.

Payette Lakes Craft & Antique Fair
As the summer sun casts its glow and melts away McCall's prized snow, artisans gear up for the Payette Lakes Craft and Antique Fair. The weekend event is held annually in July and features hundreds of local craft and antique vendors selling an array of wares.

McCall Folk Music Festival
Under the direction of the McCall Folklore Society, the McCall Folk Music Festival draws hundreds of spectators for three days every July. The evening concerts feature both national and local musicians specializing in the sounds of jazz, blues, swing, and country.

Kaleidoscope Children's Festival
McCall's Kaleidoscope Children's Festival is held annually on the second Saturday of July and specializes in presenting interactive art booths. The free event encourages children to experiment with various art mediums while adults are entertained with a variety of live musical acts. The McCall Arts and Humanities Council sponsors the event that is open to both area residents and visitors.

Spring Boat Races
Marsing's Jet Sprint Boat Park on the Snake River is home to the hottest action in town each summer. The park, which was the first of its kind in America, hosts sprint boat races on the first Saturday of each month from June through September.

Air Force Appreciation Day
In appreciation and honor of the airmen stationed at Mountain Home Air Force Base, Mountain home celebrates the annual Air Force Appreciation Day the first weekend after Labor Day. The one-day event includes live entertainment, a community barbeque, a patriotic parade, and a fly-by by some of the base's most experienced pilots.

Festival of San Inazio of Loyola
Ever since his death on July 31, 1556, the Basque St. Ignatius has been honored with annual festivals around the world. Boise celebrates the saint's life with athletic contests, dancing, Basque food, a picnic, and plenty of drink. The festival is held every July.

Boise River Festival
Established in 1990 as a ploy to draw tourists to the area, the Boise River Festival is a must-see among Boise's annual summer events. The free festival held every June was revamped in 2003 and provides live performances from music headliners, hot air balloons, parades, and activities for the whole family. The weekend event regularly draws more than 100,000 people and is one of the state's most popular summer attractions.

Boise Baroque
A regionally acclaimed chamber orchestra, the recently established Boise Baroque features weekly concerts of classical Baroque music in intimate production settings. Concerts are held every Friday at 8 PM at the Albertson College of Idaho in Caldwell as well as at 3 PM in Boise's Cathedral of the Rockies. Interested patrons are encouraged to call for further information.

First Thursday
Downtown Boise turns into a weekly street fair the first Thursday of every month. Known as "First Thursday," the monthly event features an art gallery stroll, dining specials, shopping, live music, dancing, and a free downtown trolley service. The event is free, unless of course strollers decide to purchase one of the event's many bargains.

Boise Kite Festival
Drawing thousands of spectators and hundreds of novice and professional kite flyers, the annual Boise Kite Festival breezes into town at the end of March. Usually held in the scenic Ann Morrison Park, the festival features stunt kites, noisemaker kites, tiny kites, box kites, and every other imaginable kite ever designed. The event is free to spectators.

Race to Robie Creek
Race to Robie Creek, considered one of the Pacific Northwest's toughest races, has been a southwestern Idaho tradition since the mid 1970s. In 1975, Jon Robertson invited twenty-five of his closest friends to join him on a summer night's fun run to Robie Creek. Winding through sagebrush covered hills along the 1860s stagecoach road that led to Idaho City, Robertson and friends finally made it to Robie Creek in good spirits.

Reflecting on the experience, Robertson decided to expand his "fun-run" into a regional tradition. Featuring unique starting calls, from weddings to motorcycles to exploding balloons, the Race to Robie Creek is a 13.1-mile test of stamina. Every year, more than 3,000 walkers and runners gear up for the eight-mile climb to 4,797 foot Aldape Summit and subsequent five-mile descent down to the creek. Upon reaching the creek and finishing the race, participants and their family and friends are treated to a catered picnic, entertainment, and awards and prizes. All race entry fees are pooled and donated to selected charities.

Boise Greek Festival
Held annually in June under the direction of Saints Constantine and Helen Greek Orthodox Church, the Boise Greek Festival is a two-day event celebrating the finest in Greek culture. Festival visitors are treated to Greek dancing and music, historic church tours, ethnic booths, and traditional Greek cuisine and pastries. Although the event is free, donations are suggested.

International Women's Challenge

Many of the world's finest female bicyclists grace Boise with their presence each summer at the annual International Women's Challenge. The women's bicycling event features a variety of terrain and requires competitors to perform on both flat surfaces and in the toughest mountain and desert biking conditions. Selection committees closely watch the race for possible Olympic hopefuls, and thousands of fans cheer on their favorite competitor from the sidelines.

Women's Fitness Celebration

Founded in September 1993, the Women's Fitness Celebration is a three-day event featuring a Women's Expo as well as a 5K Run, Walk, or Stroll. The event, which has never been about speed or endurance, encourages health and wellness among women and draws over 25,000 attendees each year. The run/walk, which starts at the Idaho State Capitol Building and finishes at Boise's Ann Morrison Park, represents Idaho's largest road race as well as America's second-largest women-only run/walk event. The free event concludes with an awards ceremony.

Atlanta Days

For all those looking for some good old-fashioned summer fun, Atlanta is the place to be in late July. The near ghost town comes to life under the shadow of the majestic Sawtooth Mountains with a community breakfast, street dance, and a horseshoe tournament.

for hunting and fishing, and mortars and pestles for grinding roots and berries. Archaeologists have not yet determined when this industry shut down.

T Salubria
Drive 1 mile east of Cambridge on U.S. Hwy. 95; bear south (right) on the first paved road and proceed 1 mile to the Salubria Rd. intersection

In the early 1880's, settlers began staking homesteads in the Salubria Valley, also known as the Weiser Valley, near the Weiser River. At the same time, Irish emigrant John Cuddy erected a flour mill on the nearby Rush Creek. As he saw the community of Salubria grow, Cuddy moved his mill to the new town and was soon producing three tons of flour per day. By 1890, the town included Cuddy's mill, a bank, a saloon, several blacksmith shops and livery stables, a mercantile, feed and hardware stores, the seventeen-room Salubria Hotel, a two-story schoolhouse, the newspaper office for the "Salubria Citizen," and an Odd Fellows Hall. By all accounts, the town was filled with hope of prospering for years to come, and the construction of the Pacific and Idaho Northern Railroad through town was to ensure this positive fate. However, a land dispute in Salubria and a better land offer near the present town of Cambridge caused the railroad to change its course. As the railroad bypassed Salubria, the community faded and many residents relocated to Cambridge.

T Cambridge Historical Museum
15 N. Superior St., Cambridge. 257-3485 or 257-3571.

The Cambridge Historical Museum, located in a false front wood store building, is home to an extensive collection preserving the region's history.

The North Fork of the Payette River meanders through trees near Smiths Ferry.

Beginning with the first settlers' arrival in 1869, the museum carries visitors through the 1930s. Exhibits cover topics such as geology, Native Americans, local farming and logging history, pioneer life, the Seven Devils Mining boom, and the importance of the railroad. The museum also houses a research library and genealogy collection. With free admission, the museum is open 10 AM to 4 PM Wednesday through Saturday and 1 PM to 4 PM Sunday from June 1 to August 31. Private appointments can be made at other times during the year.

T Big Bar and Black Point
On Hells Canyon Rd. near the Oregon/Idaho border. Contact the Hells Canyon National Recreation Area at 628-3916.

As Idaho Highway 71 winds into Oregon, becomes Oregon Highway 86, and then veers northerly back into Idaho, the road climbs up the Kleinschmidt Grade towards Big Bar. In the 1890s, John Eckels developed Big Bar along the Snake River as a premier fruit and vegetable orchard. His agricultural business boomed as he carried his produce to miners at the top of Kleinschmidt Grade in the Seven Devils Mining District. Today, none of his award-winning strawberry fields can be found, but the area is home to a few primitive camping spots. Big Bar has also received considerable attention from archaeologists who unearthed hundreds of classifiable artifacts in the region. Historians believe that prior to John Eckels' settlement, the region was home to Native American populations since the early 1600s. Directly north of Big Bar, a pullout at Black Point provides stunning vistas of the Snake River and rugged Hells Canyon. The seasonal road is closed in conjunction with wintry weather conditions. Although open to all passenger vehicles, the one-lane road leading to the sites is steep and marked with relatively few guardrails.

T Salmon River Stock Driveway
State Hwy. 71 along Pine Creek

As State Highway 71 winds northwest beside Pine Creek through the Pine Creek Valley, drivers follow the historical Salmon River Stock Driveway. During Idaho's prosperous era of sheep ranching, more than 80,000 sheep were moved from their

wintering range in Idaho's southern canyons to their Long Valley summer habitat. Thousands of sheep ranchers passed by State Hwy. 71 through Cambridge on their trek, with most activity occurring between 1918 and 1958.

T Eagle Bar and Red Ledge Mine
Approximately 7 miles north of Big Bar on Hells Canyon Rd. near the Oregon/Idaho border. Contact the Hells Canyon National Recreation Area at 628-3916.

Eagle Bar, an old mining settlement, is visible on the west side of Hells Canyon Road as drivers proceed towards Hells Canyon Reservoir. Tom Heady staked the first copper claim in 1894, and subsequent area mining activity resulted in the development of the Red Ledge Mine. The mine drew its name from the oxidized pyrite coloring the area. After Heady convinced Idaho's state mining inspector, Robert Bell, of the claim's validity, mining activity increased and continued until World War I. After the war, the Idaho Copper Corporation controlled the deposit from 1925 to 1928. When the corporation was found guilty of mail fraud, Cooley Butler acquired property rights. Today, Red Ledge includes over twenty patented mining claims and several unpatented acres. Although no substantial amount of ore has been recovered, approximately 2,400 feet of underground work has been accomplished.

T Midvale Hill
2.5 miles southwest of Midvale on U.S. Hwy. 95. Contact the Southwest Idaho Travel Association at 344-7777.

Midvale Hill is the source of an extensive archaeological recovery of ancient artifacts. In 1963, the north slope of Midvale Hill was excavated, unearthing a treasure trove of items indicating that Native peoples seasonally occupied this area thousands of years ago. Projectile points found in the area suggest that members of the Plateau culture occupied the hill from 3,000 to 5,000 years ago.

T Mesa Hill and Mesa Orchards Company
13 miles north of Cambridge on U.S. Hwy. 95

As U.S. Highway 95 travelers wind north from Cambridge through Indian Valley, the former site of the 3,000+-acre Mesa Orchards Company rises on the horizon. Between 1908 and 1910, the

WEISER'S BASEBALL CLAIM TO FAME

For a fleeting year in the early twentieth century, the fertile heartland of Weiser, Idaho was home to a baseball legend. Although Walter Perry "Big Train" Johnson was born on a Humboldt, Kansas farm on November 6, 1887 and didn't move to Weiser with his family until 1906, Weiser still honors the famous baseball pitcher as one of their own.

From a young age, Johnson showed an uncanny aptitude for baseball, and his right-handed pitching skills continued to improve as he grew into his 6'1", 200-pound frame. After moving to Weiser, it was only one year until the Washington Senators recruited the natural athlete in 1907. At just 19 years old, Johnson left Weiser behind on a $9 train ticket ride.

It wasn't long until Johnson established his trademark nickname. Recognized for delivering a fastball with the speed of a loco-motive and sharp breaking curveballs, Johnson soon became "Big Train" to his teammates, fans, and baseball rivals. The quiet, stoic man was both feared and respected, known for his good sportsmanship and gentlemanly manners both on and off the field. Unlike some of his counterparts, Johnson adamantly declined to knock out opposing batters with inside pitches, and he was looked up to as a role model of generous spirit and clean living.

Many baseball experts agree that Big Train was probably the greatest pitcher in the sport's entire history. During his baseball tenure, Johnson claimed 416 victories, second only to the all-time record of Cy Young. He also compiled a 2.17 career earned run average, played in the World Series in 1924 and 1925, maintains the shutout record with 110, and was one of five elected to the first class of the National Baseball Hall of Fame inductees in 1936.

After leaving the playing field, Johnson continued his fascination with baseball from the management angle. From 1929 to 1932, Big Train managed the Washington Senators and moved to the Cleveland Indians from 1933 to 1935. Widowed in 1930, Big Train remained an important force in the baseball arena until his 1946 death in Washington, D.C.

Weiser Valley Land and Water Company acquired the property from area homesteaders and turned the land into one of the world's largest privately owned fruit farms at the time. Within no time, the orchard was home to several working families dedicated to the project's success. Picking season lasted six weeks every fall, and the orchard served as an area economic resource during the Great Depression.

Despite it's initial success, however, the orchard ended up in the hands of a credit association who in turn sold it to A. H. Burroughs in 1943. Throughout the ensuing years, the orchard changed ownership several times with each new owner adding something new to the orchard's operation and history. After severe freezes in the 1950s ruined thousands of apple bushels, the owners lost enthusiasm, and the property disintegrated. Today, the once active fruit orchard is nothing but a memory.

TV Brownlee, Oxbow, and Hells Canyon Reservoirs
Northwest of Cambridge on State Hwy. 71. Contact the Idaho Department of Fish and Game at 334-3700.

Twisting through the forests and deserts on its way to Hells Canyon, the Snake River passes through three reservoirs before finally diving into North America's deepest canyon. Scattered ponderosa and Douglas fir trees combine with sagebrush and bitterbrush steppes to surround each reservoir's shore, and boating, camping, and picnicking are available at each reservoir free of charge. Created by one of the world's highest rock-fill dams, Brownlee Reservoir is situated approximately twenty miles northwest of Cambridge. The reservoir is known as one of the best cat-fishing sites in the state. Nine miles past Brownlee, drivers will encounter Oxbow Reservoir. When State Hwy. 71 ends, travelers should continue on Forest Road 454 to locate Hells Canyon Reservoir.

TV Woodhead Park
State Hwy. 71 at Brownlee Reservoir. Contact Idaho Power Parks Information at (503) 785-3323.

The Idaho Power Company established Woodhead Park in 1959 in honor of Ed Woodhead, the Chief Construction Engineer for Hells Canyon's Brownlee Power Plant. As the largest Idaho Power Park in the Hells Canyon Area, Woodhead Park was reconstructed in 1995 for a total of sixty-five acres. The park includes several gazebos, shaded picnic areas with tables and fire rings, numerous boat launching ramps and docks, a fish-cleaning station, and hundreds of tent and RV campsites with electricity and water hookups.

TV McCormick Park
State Hwy. 71 at the south end of Oxbow Reservoir. Contact Idaho Power Parks Information at (503) 785-3323.

McCormick Park, established in 1958 under Idaho Power Company management, honors the life and company contributions of Fred McCormick. Beginning his Idaho Power Company career in 1935, McCormick served as Chief Engineer during the Brownlee Power Plant construction and worked up until his death in 1958.

Today, the twelve-acre park rests underneath a canopy of mature trees on the Snake River banks. Park features include a few tent and RV overnight sites as well as picnic areas and a grassy day-use area. Nearby, the McCormick Overflow area and Carter's Landing provide unimproved, free campsites on the reservoir.

TV Hells Canyon Park
East shore of Hells Canyon Reservoir near State Hwy. 71. Contact Idaho Power Parks Information at (503) 785-3323.

Featuring mature trees and a large grassy area alongside the Snake River, Hells Canyon Park was constructed in 1967. The small, beautifully land-scaped Idaho Power park features a few RV campsites with limited tent spaces, a picnic area with tables and grills, a boat ramp, and four boat docks.

TV Crane Creek Reservoir
Southeast of Midvale and U.S. Hwy. 95 on Crane Creek Rd. Contact the Idaho Department of Parks and Recreation at 334-4199.

Highly regarded for its isolation and lack of crowds, Crane Creek Reservoir is named after its year-round white crane residents. The large 3,700-acre lake boasts boat ramps, primitive camping areas, and excellent opportunities for anglers to catch crappie, largemouth bass, cutthroat trout, and bullhead catfish.

4 Food, Lodging

Weiser
Pop. 5,343

Situated at the convergence of the Snake and Weiser Rivers, this town's history dates back to the mid 1800s, but the origin of the town's name still remains controversial. Several historians suggest that the town and nearby river were named after Revolutionary War veteran, Peter Weiser, who served as cook for the Lewis and Clark Corps of Discovery from 1804 to 1806. Others tend to believe that the town was named after trapper turned miner, Jacob Weiser. After striking it rich in Idaho's Florence Basin, Weiser along with William Logan and Thomas Galloway settled in this area in 1863. In 1864, Reuben Olds acquired a franchise from the Territorial Legislature and began operating a ferry on the Snake River near town. This business greatly increased Weiser's population, and a post office was established in 1866. In 1881, the population surged again as the Oregon Shortline Railroad built a line through town. Today, this town that was once known for frequent shoot-outs serves as the seat for Washington County and supports an agricultural and ranching lifestyle. The town is also recognized as the site of the National Old-Time Fiddler's Contest and Festival held each June.

H 11,000 Years of Indian Occupation
Milepost 82.4 on U.S. Hwy. 95

The Weiser Valley provided an abundant environment for early hunters and food gatherers. Archaeological excavation along Monroe Creek in conjunction with U.S. 95 realignment yielded one of the most significant prehistoric sites in the region. Spear and arrow points and radio-carbon dates suggest the site was occupied for 11,000 years. Inhabitants hunted deer, mountain goat, and rabbit and gathered salmon, roots, berries, and seeds. Artifacts were found 10 feet below the ground surface.

T Intermountain Cultural Center and Washington County Museum
2295 Paddock Ave., Weiser. 549-0205.

Inside the Intermountain Cultural Center and Washington County Museum, visitors will find artifacts and memorabilia of the region's Native Americans, as well as special collections of clothing, costumes, and music. The museum, previously known as the Snake River Heritage Center, is open 12 PM to 4:30 PM Sunday, Monday, Thursday, Friday, and Saturday from April 15 to October 15. During the winter season, the museum operates from 12 PM to 4:30 PM on Sunday, Monday, Friday, and Saturday.

T Fiddler's Hall of Fame
Weiser Community Center, 10 E. Idaho St., Weiser. 414-0452.

Weiser is known for its fiddle festival, but for those visitors who miss out on the fun, the Fiddler's Hall of Fame captures a glimpse of the event. The museum is home to fiddle memorabilia from past to present and pictures of past champions (including Mark O'Connor). The museum is open 9 AM to 5 PM Monday through Friday year-round with free admission.

T Weiser Historical Tour

Contact the Weiser Chamber of Commerce at 414-0452.

Among all Idaho cities, Weiser is reputed above most others for its architectural variety and extravagance. No building style was too fancy or modern for Weiser's earliest residents and business owners, and several structures remain as a testament to this affluent attitude.

Oregon Short Line Depot
State St.

The Oregon Short Line Railroad arrived in Weiser in 1883, but it was not until 1907 that a depot was built to serve the line. Operated under the direction of the Union Pacific, the Oregon Short Line Railroad Depot required two years of construction to complete its ornate Queen Anne architectural style. The brick building, which was schedule for demolition in 1987, was saved and has since been restored to its status as an impressive city gateway.

Sommercamp House
W. Idaho and 411 W. Third

After her husband fell to his death in a Silver City mineshaft, Mary Sommercamp and her four children left the mining life behind. Upon the family's arrival in Weiser, a Boise architectural firm designed this house for Mary in 1899. Mary's children grew into prominent Weiser citizens and were responsible for establishing several stores in the area.

Herman Haas House
253 W. Idaho and W. Third

At the young age of fourteen, Herman Haas emigrated from Germany to Oregon in 1853. After establishing himself as a successful businessman in America, Haas moved to Weiser and founded the community's first store in 1882 while serving as vice-president of the town's first bank. With his wealth, Haas had a Boise architectural firm draw up plans for an elaborate Queen Anne style home in 1900. The home features a distinctive octagonal east bay, stained glass windows, ornamental trim, a corner tower, and decorative interior woodwork that have been preserved.

Pythian Castle
30 E. Idaho St.

Weiser's major architectural landmark, the Pythian Castle, was constructed in 1904 as an Idaho lodge of the fraternal Order Knights of Pythias. The lodge had established a Weiser membership in 1897, and by 1904, had grown to include 170 member Knights. Needing a new meeting hall, the Order enlisted the help of Tourtellotte and Company of Boise who designed the castle façade structure. Featuring a medieval castle design, the structure was constructed from rock locally quarried near the Weiser River with a completed price tag of $9,000. The building, the only one of its kind in all Western fraternal orders, has retained most of its original features. Visitors will find arched, pressed tin ceilings, stained glass, and grand staircases.

Gerwick House
206 W. Main and W. Second

James Gerwick, a prosperous sheep rancher, prune farmer, and saddle maker, constructed this impressive Queen Anne style home in 1898. After completing all the work himself, Gerwick only resided in the house seven years before retiring from city life and moving to a nearby ranch.

Colonel E. M. Heigho House
541 W. Third and W. Court St.

When Lewis Hall moved to Weiser from New York in 1900 to serve as the Pacific and Idaho Northern Railroad President, this Queen Anne style home

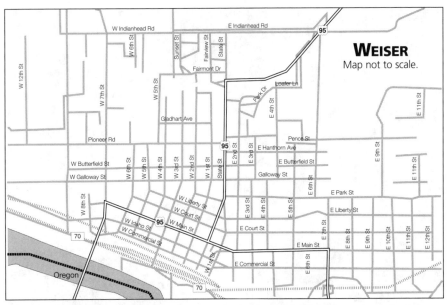

was built for the fine businessman. Seven years later, when Hall abandoned his post, Colonel Edgar Heigho stepped in to fill Hall's position and acquired this property at the same time. Heigho was a well-respected gentleman who served as the company president until an illness forced an early 1919 retirement.

Walter "Big Train" Johnson Residence
49 W. Park and W. First

A Kansas native, Walter "Big Train" Johnson moved with his family to this humble Weiser abode in 1906 at age 18. In July 1907, 19-year-old Johnson was recruited into the major league baseball world with the Washington Senators. He became one of baseball's greatest pitchers of all time and was one of the first five players inducted into the Baseball Hall of Fame.

Commercial and E. First Sts

This unassuming building, now home to a grain storage facility, was originally known as the Clinton Rooms. In Weiser's early days, the Clinton Rooms was Weiser's most notorious house of ill repute. Local legend suggests that the ladies frequently attempted to barter their services for other goods. The most reported version involves a woman who attempted to seduce a mailman to avoid the cash on delivery charge she owed him.

St. Agnes Catholic Church
E. Liberty and E. Second

St. Agnes Catholic Church was erected in 1911 and features an Italianate architectural style. The brick church's most stunning feature is the stained glass windows lining the sanctuary.

Galloway Residence
1120 E. Second and Hanthorne Ave.

After living in Oregon and working in the Cariboo and Boise Basin mines, Thomas Galloway settled in Weiser as the first permanent resident. In 1868, Thomas met and married Mary Flournoy, and the couple moved to a two-room log cabin where they raised nine children. While Mary was busy tending the children, Thomas worked as a rancher, grazing his horses on ten square miles of range. When woolgrowers moved into the area, however, Thomas knew his horse herding days were over, and he sold all 800 head. With his profits, Thomas decided to build a new home for his wife and family. In 1900, this historic Queen Anne style was completed for $5,000 and became the most expensive residence in all of Weiser.

Featuring triple brick construction and a design from a Boise architectural firm, the mansion features twelve rooms highlighted with leaded glass windows and fine woodwork. The Galloway's heirs sold the home in 1966, and today, the residence is listed as a Nationally Registered Historic Place.

Buildings lining the grassy oval area on Paddock Ave.

In 1899, Reverend Edward Paddock decided it was time to open up the doors to high school education for young people from rural areas who wanted to learn but whose families could not afford to pay for school. His dream became a reality, and with the philanthropy and support of scholars from across America and local residents, the Intermountain Institute was born.

During the institute's early years, the school's acreage far outnumbered its pupils. But word of the unique school quickly spread and hundreds of applications began pouring in, resulting in waiting lists year after year. As the student demand rose, the school expanded into five concrete buildings. Age and religious discrimination was forbidden, and both girls and boys received a college preparatory curriculum in math, science, history, English, art, and music. While girls supplemented their curriculum with domestic science and kitchen skills, boys received training for farm chores and manual tasks.

Although the highly regarded education was free in the sense that students were not required to pay cash for tuition, students were required to work for their keep. While not in class or taking their one hour mandatory recreation period, students performed farm chores, baked goods in the Institute's kitchen to sell in Weiser stores in exchange for other necessities, made brooms in the school's own broom factory, and helped with other necessary school operations.

The school eventually became nearly self-sufficient, but when the Depression hit and demand for agricultural goods sank, the school floundered. After educating over 2,000 students, Paddock was forced to close his institute in 1933. Upon the institute's closure, the campus buildings were used for a variety of causes. The National Youth Administration first used the campus as a vocational training center before Weiser High School garnered ownership. The public school district occupied the buildings until 1967. Today, the buildings house the Intermountain Cultural Center and Museum, classrooms are used for art,

T Weiser Brick Company
Intersection of Indianhead Rd. with U.S. Hwy. 95

In 1901, the Weiser Brick Company built its headquarters in the brick barn on the north side of this intersection. Alexander Gordon and his son were the company's first owners, molding bricks for many of Weiser's first commercial buildings and private dwellings. In 1922, the father/son team leased the company to Reader and Lowe. The barn's location near ochre sand and clay pits was ideal for unlimited brick production. After being mixed with water, the clay was poured into wooden molds, air dried, and then fired for a week at 1,700 degrees Fahrenheit.

T Indianhead Mountain
West of Weiser. Contact the Weiser Chamber of Commerce at 414-0452.

Rising grandly along Weiser's western horizon, Indianhead Mountain is a famous local landmark known for its striking image of a Native American overlooking the valley. Visitors can glean stunning views of the valley below from the top of the picture-worthy mountain.

T Walter Johnson Memorial Park
Hanthorn and 3rd Sts, Weiser. Contact the Weiser Recreation Department at 549-0301.

Memorializing past Weiser resident and one of baseball's greatest pitchers, Walter "Big Train" Johnson, this park provides playing fields for a variety of sports. Visitors will find baseball fields, a football field, tennis courts, picnic tables, barbeque grills, a playground, and a municipal swimming pool.

T Rolling Hills Golf Course
50 W. Indianhead Rd., Weiser. 549-0456. www.weiserrollinghillsgc.com

Appropriately named after its location on the rolling Snake River Valley hills, Weiser's Rolling Hills Golf Course provides a unique, tree-lined course encompassing over 6,000 yards. The challenging 9-hole course offers three sets of tees, two practice greens, and a driving range for a reasonably priced green fee.

T Star Theater and the Illustrious Onion Skin Players
342 State St., Weiser. Contact the Weiser Chamber of Commerce at 414-0452.

A Weiser landmark, the Star Theater has provided eighty-eight years of movies and live theater to community residents and visitors. A. C. Gordon constructed the facility in 1917 as a forum for vaudeville troupes and dubbed his new playhouse, the "Wheaton Theater." When he later added a movie screen to showcase silent movies and increase profits, he renamed his pet project, "Star Theater."

Gordon's Star Theater was wildly successful, drawing crowds in for live piano entertainment, silent movies, and poker nights. This success continued when Bruce Gordon acquired the theater in 1939. He spent $40,000 on an art deco remodeling project, adding tapestry wall coverings and a marquee that are still used today. Since 1997, the theater has provided a home for the community's Illustrious Onion Skin Players. The acting troupe was organized in 1985 and draws upon talented actors from across the state. The players produce traditional melodramas appropriate for people of all ages and perform to sold-out crowds during their annual presentation each March. For its illustrious history and contributions to the Weiser community, the Star Theater was added to the National Register of Historic Places in 1999. Those interested in seeing an annual March performance should call for tickets and a complete schedule of dates and times.

music, and photography workshops, and the auditorium provides a venue for local drama, dance, and film productions.

All of Paddock's original buildings remain on-site in their original placement. Situated in the grassy oval, the buildings from north to south are:

1) Billings Memorial Gymnasium: Elizabeth Billings, a Northern Pacific heiress, donated $40,000 to build this gymnasium in 1929. The facility was once the finest high school gym in the state and featured a sixty-foot long swimming pool in the basement.

2) Slocum Hall: Mrs. Russell Sage donated $30,000 towards the construction of Slocum Hall in 1909. The building served as a boy's dormitory.

3) Hooker Hall: In 1924, Hooker Hall was completed at a cost of $100,000. The building, which once held the school offices and twenty-two class-

rooms, is named after Fannie Hooker Forbes and Mary Hooker Dole who made significant monetary contributions to defray construction costs. Today, the hall is home to the Intermountain Cultural Center and Museum.

4) Beardsley Hall: This building, completed in 1907 with sixteen-inch thick walls, is the oldest facility on the campus. The building contained a dining hall in the basement, a school chapel on the first floor, and female dormitories on the second and third floors. The attic served as an informal gym. In 1913, the hall caught fire, but the walls were luckily undamaged and allowed for the interior's reconstruction.

5) Carnegie Library: Recognized as the only high school library funded by the Carnegie Foundation, this educational center was completed with a grant in 1919 and once contained over 5,000 books.

T City Park

Court St., Weiser. Contact the Weiser Recreation Department at 549-0301.

Weiser's City Park is located adjacent to the Washington County Courthouse and provides a relaxing atmosphere in the midst of town. Playground equipment entertains children, newly constructed picnic facilities provide an ideal luncheon outing, and a covered gazebo hosts several community events throughout the year.

T Idaho Almaden Quicksilver Mine

East of Weiser on S. Crane Creek Rd. at Nutmeg Mountain. Contact the Weiser Chamber of Commerce at 414-0452.

Discovered by a sheepherder and developed as a commercial site in 1937, the Idaho Almaden Quicksilver Mine was a profitable component of the Weiser economy through the 1970s. During it's initial years, the open-pit Cinnabar (a relative of mercury) mine was under the management of President Herbert Hoover's sons. The mine was instantly successful and eventually possessed America's largest rotary mercury kiln. Throughout its commercialized life, this mine produced over $3.7 million in mercury and pozzolana, a mineral used to harden cement.

TV Mann Creek Reservoir Recreation Area

15 miles north of Weiser on U.S. Hwy. 95. Contact the Bureau of Reclamation at 382-4258.

Established in 1967, Mann Creek Reservoir Recreation Area is situated in the rolling foothills of the Hitt Mountains. The Bureau of Reclamation manages this year-round recreation destination that provides camping, picnicking, five miles of shoreline, boat launching sites, and over 280 acres of ideal fishing waters. The reservoir is stocked annually, and anglers will find abundant numbers of largemouth bass, crappie, and rainbow trout. In addition, the entire 936-acre recreation area is open to bird watching and photography.

TV Weiser River

Flowing 112 miles in a southwesterly direction, the Weiser River drains 1,660 square miles before dumping into the Snake River near the city of Weiser. Although the drainage does not feature any mainstream reservoirs, private irrigation reservoirs include Lost Valley, Crane Creek, Manns Creek, and C. Ben Robs. Anglers on the Weiser drainage will find largemouth and smallmouth bass, crappie, mountain whitefish, and rainbow trout. Bull trout, which are listed as an endangered species candidate, are also occasionally found.

V Clay Peak Trails

Near Weiser. Contact the BLM – Idaho State Office at 373-4000.

Situated on the bluffs lining the scenic Payette River, Clay Peak Trails offer a variety of short rides accommodating mountain bikers of all expertise. While some trails are level, many others are steep and require expert handling. The entire trail system is free and can be completed with just an hour's ride. The trails are closed seasonally, so interested users should first contact the BLM State Office for additional information.

M Weiser Chamber of Commerce

309 State St., Weiser. 414-0452.
www.ruralnetwork.net/~weisercc/;
weisercc@ruralnetwork.net

McCALL
Map not to scale.

5 *Food, Lodging*

McCall
Pop. 2,084

McCall lies at the head of Long Valley and is one of Idaho's premier resort and recreation areas. The town was founded in 1899 when Thomas McCall and his family became enamored with the area upon camping on Lake Payette's shore. Instead of continuing west with the rest of their wagon train companions, the family stayed behind and purchased the east side of town from homesteader, Sam Devers. McCall then platted the town in 1901, and a post office was established that same year. When the Union Pacific Railroad came through, the settlement was renamed Lakeport. However, residents objected and changed it to McCall in honor of the town's founding father.

For nearly eighty years, lumber was manufactured along Payette Lake. However, the lumber industry went belly-up here after a series of sawmill fires, and the last mill closed in 1977. Since then, McCall has relied on its ideal recreational location to draw tourists year-round. During winter, residents and visitors are treated to an average of 151 inches of snow (the most in the state) perfect for skiing and snowboarding, while summer brings lake recreation, hiking, and mountain biking.

T Lake Fork
Pop. 10

Located near Donnelly and McCall, Finnish immigrants originally settled in this lake area from 1896 to 1910. Initially, there were only two Finnish settlements in the entire state, but by 1915, eighty-five Finnish families lived here as hardworking farm owners. Dave Collender established a trading post and post office here in 1931.

Today, most area inhabitants consider themselves McCall residents, and Lake Fork is primarily just the lake itself. The Finnish Evangelical Lutheran Church built in 1916-1917 still stands on a hilltop and is maintained by the Ladies Aid Society. The Nationally Registered Historic Site is only used for Bible studies, weddings, and funerals due to the absence of a presiding minister.

T Yellow Pine
Pop. 35

Located east of McCall, fourteen miles from the famous Stibnite mines, Yellow Pine Basin was discovered in 1902 with Al Behne arriving as the first settler. More homesteaders soon arrived in response to the Thunder Mountain Boom of 1902-1907. The community of Yellow Pine was appropriately named after the abundant ponderosa pines characterizing the area. Serving as an early supply center to both miners and ranchers, Yellow Pine acquired a post office in 1906.

T Jug Mountain Ranch
E. Lake Fork Rd., McCall. 634-5072.
www.jugmountainranch.com From McCall, proceed 5 miles south on State Hwy. 55. At E. Lake Fork Rd., bear east and head to the course.

Internationally renowned course designer, Don Knott, laid out the 18-hole Jug Mountain Ranch course in 2004, and it is quickly gaining regional acclaim. Offering awe-inspiring views, the course provides a combination of challenging play, varied terrain, and unbeatable scenery. Meandering through forests and meadows, the course offers several water hazards and is appropriate for both beginners and experienced players. The course, which is open from 8 AM to 8:30 PM daily, offers $35 adult and $25 junior green fees Monday through Friday. On Saturdays, Sundays, and holidays, green fees are $45 for adults and $35 for juniors.

T McCall City Golf Course
1000 Reedy Ln., McCall. 634-7200.
www.mccallcitygolfcourse.com From State Hwy. 55 in McCall, bear right on E. Lake St. Continue to Spruce Ave. and turn right. At Davis Ave., bear left and continue to the right-hand turn for Reedy Ln. and the course.

Ponderosa State Park provides the incredible scenic backdrop to this course established in 1968 under designer, Robert Muir Graves. Tree-lined fairways, flat greens, natural playing hazards, and a variety of wildlife characterize this course providing golfers with three separate 9-hole tracks. Players can opt to play just one round or all 27 holes while enjoying mountain vistas. Green fees on this easy to walk course are $29 Monday through Thursday and $35 on weekends. For a single round, weekday green fees are $18 with weekends at $25. Due to weather, the course is closed November through April.

T Central Idaho Cultural Center and Museum
1001 State St., McCall. 634-4497.

From 1936 to 1937, the Civilian Conservation Corp constructed eight buildings in the McCall area. These historic buildings that were once a summer home for the governor and served as the Southern Idaho Timber Protective Association headquarters from 1938 to 1992 are now home to a regional museum. The center features several exhibits relating to mining, logging, recreation, fire suppression, forest management, and local history. Hours of operation are Monday through Friday from 10 AM to 4 PM.

T The B-23 "Dragon Bomber" Crash Site and Wreck
Contact the Payette National Forest Headquarters in McCall at 634-0700.

The Event
On January 29, 1943, the B-23 "Dragon Bomber" went down at Loon Lake (elevation 5,280') with eight men aboard. The plane was returning to McChord Field in Tacoma, Washington from a training mission in Nevada when it flew into a heavy snow storm near Pendleton, Oregon. Unable to maintain altitude, the pilot decided to attempt a landing in Boise. The approach was hampered by heavy icing and a failed radio. An order to prepare to parachute was given at 13,000'. Just then a hole developed in the cloud cover. A frozen lake was spotted and a landing was attempted.

Frozen flaps caused the first approach to be abandoned. In a successful second approach, the plane touched down on the frozen lake, sliding across the ice and through the trees. With both wings sheared off, the plane came to rest 150 feet from the shore of Loon Lake in the timber. All eight men survived. A broken kneecap was the only injury.

After waiting five days for rescue, the crew selected three men to go for help. On February 3rd, the three left Loon Lake with a shotgun and chocolate rations. They followed the Secesh River downstream. Then, hiking over Lick Creek Summit, elevation 6,700', they reached the Lake Fork Guard Station. Once inside, an exhausted crewmember picked up the telephone and spoke to the operator in McCall. The three men had hiked for fourteen days and approximately 42 miles through waist deep snow.

On February 18th, the wreckage was spotted by bush pilot, Penn Stohr, of Cascade, Idaho. He returned and notified authorities. Stohr made two more flights, landing on the frozen lake to fly the crew out. After some 21 days in the harsh winter climate of Idaho's primitive area, all eight men were rescued.

The Plane
The B-23 "Dragon Bomber," a 1939 twin engine aircraft, was developed from the Douglas B-18 and the DC-3. It was the first United States airplane equipped with tail gunners. Only 38 B-23's were manufactured. Most were assigned to the 34th Bomb Squadron at McChord Field in Washington State. By the time of the bombing on Pearl Harbor on December 7, 1941, more advanced aircraft such as the B-17 and B-24 made the B-23 obsolete. It never saw combat use. B-23's were used instead for training purposes.

Locating the Site
From Chinook Campground in the Payette National Forest, take Trail 080. Trail 080 follows the Secesh River south towards Loon Creek. Just above Loon Creek, take Trail 084 west. Trail 084 becomes rocky and steep with many switchbacks, rising 800 feet in elevation in 1.3 miles. Trail 084 intersects with Trail 081. Here there are two choices:

1) Continue south along 081, leaving the trail to bushwhack your way south along the east side of the lake.

2) Continue south along 081 to the junction of Trail 084. Head west again on 084. This trail runs 1.75 miles south along the west side of Loon Lake. Where the trail meets Loon Creek, leave the trail to follow the creek north to Loon Lake. The wreckage is on the south side of Loon Lake,

approximately 150 feet into the trees. You may return the way you came, or you may follow Trail 081 back north to Chinook Campground. Be aware that on 081, you must cross the Secesh River to reach the campground and there is no bridge. This is not advised during late spring and early summer or any time there is high water. The hike is approximately ten miles roundtrip.

While hiking, apply Leave No Trace principles. Practicing a Leave No Trace ethic is very simple – make it hard for others to see or hear you and Leave No Trace of your visit:

1) Leave your campsite cleaner than you found it.

2) Build your campfire away from tree roots, overhanging branches, and reflector rocks.

3) Pack out what you pack in.

4) Bury human waste six to eight inches deep and at least 200 feet from water.

5) Don't contaminate lakes and streams with soap or detergents. They are harmful to aquatic life.

Reprinted from a Payette National Forest brochure

T Payette National Forest Smokejumper Base
605 S. Mission, McCall. 634-0390.

Established as an experiment in 1939, the McCall Smokejumper Base quickly displayed its merit as an integral part of fighting western forest fires. Today, the base is one of four smokejumper training centers in the U.S.. On average, McCall hosts seventy smokejumpers each summer, all of whom receive hours of training and physical conditioning before being shipped across the U.S. to wage war against wildfires. The smokejumper base includes a training unit, forest dispatch office, paraloft, and the McCall air tanker base. Free tours are available year-round during the morning and afternoon, and interested visitors should call for further details.

T Burgdorf Hot Springs
800 W. Lakeside Ave., McCall. 634-0700. Travel 30 miles north from McCall on Warren Wagon Rd. to Burgdorf Junction. Bear left, and continue the remaining short distance to the springs.

Established around 1865, Burgdorf Hot Springs is the area's oldest developed hot springs area. The springs first catered to regional miners and loggers, and today, some of the springs' rustic character has been preserved. The large natural hot springs pool features 104-degree spring water extending five feet deep complete with log siding and a sand bottom. Moose and elk roam the hillsides surrounding the pool, and rustic cabins are available for overnight stays. Although open year-round with a small admission fee, the springs are only accessible by snowmobile during winter.

T McCall Fish Hatchery
300 Mather Rd., McCall. 634-2690.

The U.S. Fish and Wildlife Service happily welcomes visitors to the McCall State Fish Hatchery that was established in 1980. On a mission to restore the Salmon River's disastrously low Chinook salmon populations, the McCall Fish Hatchery can accommodate over a million Chinook salmon at one time. Hatchery personnel also work with cutthroat and rainbow trout, releasing many of them each summer into alpine lakes and area rivers. The hatchery is open year-round with no admission fee. Self-guided tours are available daily from 8 AM to 5 PM, while guided group tours can be scheduled in advance.

T Art Roberts Park
E. Lake St., McCall. Contact the McCall Chamber of Commerce at 634-7631.

Locally known as Shaver's Beach Park, the small Art Roberts Park offers outstanding views of McCall's scenic landscape. A grassy slope in the park features both lake and mountain vistas while the municipal dock and a sandy wading/swimming beach provide convenient water access.

T Community Park
Corner of State Hwy. 55 and Lenora St., McCall. Contact the McCall Chamber of Commerce at 634-7631.

Serving primarily as a convenient travelers' rest area, Community Park beckons visitors to relax awhile amid its grassy expanses.

T Davis Beach
West end of Diamond St., McCall. Contact the McCall Chamber of Commerce at 634-7631.

Davis Beach Park is a local favorite with its sandy beach and swimming area. Although privately owned, two boat docks at the park are open to courteous public users.

T Legacy Park
Corner of 3rd and E. Lake Sts., McCall. Contact the McCall Chamber of Commerce at 634-7631.

Established with the proceeds of a bond sale, Legacy Park is destined to be a McCall centerpiece with extensive landscaping planned. In addition to volleyball courts and picnic areas, the park features a public swimming beach.

T Brown Park
North of the corner of E. Lake St. and Hemlock St., McCall. Contact the McCall Chamber of Commerce at 634-7631.

Overlooking scenic Payette Lake, Brown Park was formerly known as Mill Park. The developed and well-maintained park includes a playground, game tables, boardwalks, walking trails, and benches.

T Rotary Park
N. Fork of the Payette River, McCall. Contact the McCall Chamber of Commerce at 634-7631.

Rotary Park rests in the shade of mighty old-growth ponderosa stands adjacent to Payette Lake. Park features include playground equipment, a lake swimming beach, and numerous picnic tables.

T Riverfront Park
N. Fork of the Payette River across from the airport on Mission St., McCall. Contact the McCall Chamber of Commerce at 634-7631.

Riverfront Park, also commonly referred to as Riverside Park, is nestled against the banks of the Payette River. Once home to a gravel pit, the wetland area park is now being developed to include baseball fields, river access, and walking trails.

T University of Idaho Field Campus
Near downtown McCall. 634-3918 or 634-8444.

Operating under an extension from the University of Idaho in Moscow, the McCall UI Field Campus spans eleven acres of heavily forested terrain. The campus provides Idaho forestry students with an ideal setting for studying and researching an array of native vegetation. Occasionally, the campus offers non-students environmental education workshops and natural resource management extension courses. In addition, the naturally landscaped campus also hosts several community events.

T Profile Summit
Near Yellow Pine on Profile Gap Rd. (off S. Fork Poverty Flat Rd.)

During the late 1800s and early 1900s, legendary local, Profile Sam Wilson, lived the life of a griz-

zled prospector desperately searching for Idaho's elusive treasure. Despite his hard work, Profile Sam never achieved success and committed suicide in his tiny cabin in 1935. The old fortune seeker is buried in Yellow Pine, and his friends erected a memorial at this 7,605-foot summit.

T Big Creek
North of Yellow Pine and Edwardsburg on Profile Gap Rd.

The outpost of Big Creek was established alongside its namesake to serve the needs of regional miners. In 1937, Jim Carpenter, Joe Powell, and Dick Cowman constructed the prominent log lodge marking the only real sign of civilization in this scenic backcountry place. Today, the lodge continues to rent rooms during summer and autumn, catering primarily to recreation and hunting enthusiasts.

TV Ponderosa State Park & Payette Lake
2 miles northeast of McCall's City Center. 634-2164.

Ponderosa State Park encompasses a 1,000-acre peninsula on scenic Payette Lake, and many residents consider the park one of Idaho's finest. During Idaho's timber era, the peninsula was never subjected to logging and today boasts old-growth ponderosa pines that are more than 400 years old. In addition to these gigantic 150-foot tall ponderosa pines, several other pine, evergreen, and fir trees rise impressively on the lake's shores.

At the park's entrance, visitors will find an informative visitor center complete with park maps and rangers. Rangers happily provide answers to visitor questions as well as information about the park's interpretive campfire programs that are held nightly during summer months at the park's amphitheater. In addition to such historical information and scenic wonders, Ponderosa State Park is prized throughout the region for its wide array of year-round recreation.

Summer recreation opportunities include boating, canoeing, kayaking, floating, swimming, camping, fishing, hiking, mountain biking, and picnicking. Self-guided, easy nature trails abound, and the park service also offers guided walks with park naturalists, small boat rentals, and carriage rides. Winter recreationists will find nearly eleven miles of groomed Nordic trails, some of which are lit for night-skiing from 6 PM to 11 PM.

Amid the park's topography of dense forests, lakefront beaches, and sagebrush flats, visitors will find two camping units. The North Beach Unit, located on Payette Lake's northern end, includes the lake's largest public beach, a boat ramp, canoe rentals, Payette River access, and a primitive camping area. The larger Lakeview Village offers eighty-four park administered camping sites, along with a swimming beach, grassy group area, and a boat launch. Wildlife abounds at both sites and throughout the entire park. Visitors may glimpse bears, muskrats, deer, beaver, wood ducks, Canada geese, red-tailed hawks, bald eagles, and mallards.

Ponderosa State Park is open year-round with a $4 per car entrance fee. Those interested in camping at the park should plan to make early reservations as sites book quickly for the summer season.

TV Payette River
Contact the Cascade Ranger District at 382-7400.

The Payette River is a clean mountain river featuring a variety of terrain sure to please whitewater enthusiasts and anglers of all experience and skill levels. The river honors the legacy of Canadian fur trapper and explorer, Francois Payette, who came

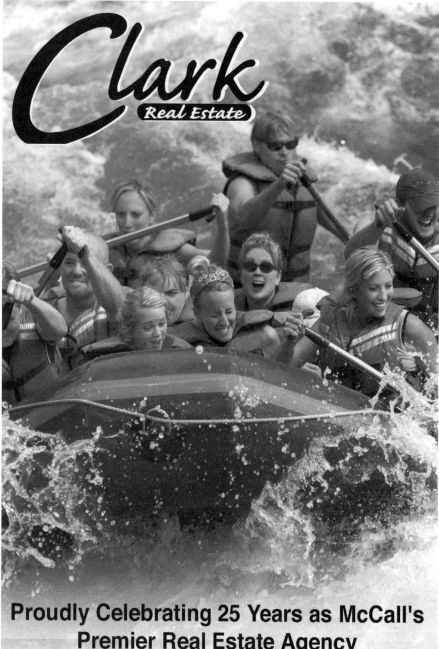
TV Payette National Forest
McCall. Contact the Payette National Forest Headquarters at 634-0700.

Nestled between the Salmon River Canyon and Hells Canyon, the 2.3 million acre Payette National Forest covers much of west-central Idaho. The spectacular forest features hundreds of pristine alpine lakes as forest elevations range from 1,500 feet to as high as 9,500 feet.

The outdoor paradise provides recreationists with year-round adventures. With over 2,100 miles of trails and 15,000 miles of streams, there's a trail or river suitable to anglers, rafters, hikers, and mountain bikers of all skill levels and preferences. Other popular activities include rock climbing, hunting, bird watching, and wildlife viewing.

For those who prefer winter to summer, the Payette National Forest delivers with over 600 miles of groomed snowmobile trails easily accessible from downtown McCall. Backcountry skiing, Nordic skiing, snowshoeing, and snowboarding are also local favorites.

The forest requires no access fees and is easily reached year-round. Visitors are encouraged to contact the Payette National Forest Headquarters for maps and additional information

V Brundage Mountain Resort
Goose Lake Rd., McCall. 634-4151 or (800) 888-7544. www.brundage.com
8 miles north of McCall off State Hwy. 55.

Boasting a thirty-year history of providing skiers and snowboarders with some of Idaho's finest powder, Brundage Mountain Resort provides 1,300 acres of lift-served terrain. With a maximum vertical drop of 1,800 feet, the mountain showcases exceptional views of the Seven Devils Mountains, the Salmon River Mountains, Payette Lake, and Oregon's Eagle Cap Wilderness Area. A high-speed quad chair, two triple chairs, and two surface lifts service the mountain that offers groomed runs for all skill levels. Snowboarding, Nordic skiing, snowmobiling, and snowcat adventures are also available along with rentals and lessons.

During summer, the winter wonderland is transformed into a mountain biker's dream with single-track trails winding fifteen miles around the mountain. In addition, the resort area's amphitheater hosts summer concerts in the full glory of its mountain splendor.

The resort is open year-round with the typical ski season running from mid-November to mid-April.

V McCall Power Sport Rentals
302 N. 3rd St., McCall. 634-8200.
www.mccallpowersportrentals.com

McCall Power Sport Rentals combines the latest top of the line sports equipment with unbeatable customer service. Guaranteeing that entry level or outdated equipment is never rented here, the professional staff works diligently with suppliers to provide market-leading selections at low prices. During winter, explore McCall's mountainous landscape on a snowmobile meeting your need for luxury, performance, or a combination of both. Summer beckons with the latest jet skis, pontoon boats, ski boats, wakeboards, skis, and tubes. In

to the region in 1818 on a North West Fur Trading Company expedition.

The river, which is lined with forested banks, is comprised of three forks all showcasing their own unique features. Draining 3,240 square miles on its 175 mile journey to the Snake River, the Payette ranges significantly in elevation, providing an array of recreational diversity. The South Fork of the Payette is a wild river requiring advanced whitewater skills. On the intermediate level, many portions of the North Fork of the Payette combine stretches of scenic, peaceful water with areas boasting rapids up to a Class III rating. The Main Fork of the Payette is the calmest of all, offering a suitable floating trip for families as well as beginning kayakers and canoeists. On all stretches, rafters should expect company overhead from hawks and osprey riding the air currents in search of their day's fresh catch.

For anglers, the varying elevations results in several different types of resident fish. Mountain whitefish, smallmouth and largmouth bass, channel catfish, black crappie, rainbow trout, and brown trout all line the river's banks. In the tributaries of Black Canyon, Sagehen, Paddock, Cascade, and Deadwood Reservoir, yellowperch, coho salmon, kokanee, and rainbow and cutthroat trout try to evade their predators. Numerous alpine lakes in the drainage feature stocked arctic grayling and rainbow, cutthroat, golden, brook, and hybrid trout.

All users are encouraged to contact the Cascade Ranger District for current information about river conditions. For those unsure of their whitewater or angling skills, several area outfitters provide guided Payette River excursions.

addition to offering the area's latest fleet of equipment and delivery service, McCall Power Sport Rentals provides high-quality safety and comfort gear, including sanitized life jackets, wetsuits, snowmobile suits, boots, helmets, and gloves. Whether you need to accommodate a single rental or large group order, call today to reserve a memorable adventure!

V Cheap Thrills Rentals
303 N. 3rd St., McCall. 634-7472 or (800) 831-1025. www.cheapthrillsrentals.com

Family-owned Cheap Thrills Rentals has been serving the sport rental needs of area residents and visitors since 1994. Featuring new equipment arrivals each season and the guaranteed lowest prices in McCall, Cheap Thrills Rentals specializes in providing year-round fun. During summer, check out Payette Lake on a Waverunner, boat, wakeboard, or a pair of water-skis. Winter brings its own fun with hundreds of miles of groomed snowmobile trails. Cheap Thrills Rentals offers a variety of SkiDoo snowmobiles, allowing customers to discover the hot springs, ghost towns, mountains, and incredible forested backcountry surrounding McCall. Dedicated to making fun easy, Cheap Thrills Rentals includes all gear, delivery, and pickup with every rental. Come explore this beautiful paradise!

VS Gravity Sports
503 Pine St., McCall. 634-8530.

Visit McCall's outdoor specialists. Gravity sells and rents bikes, canoes, and lake kayaks during summer, and Cross Country ski equipment and snowshoes during winter. Boasting a large selection of Alpine and backcountry equipment, Gravity Sports also stocks a variety of backpacking, camping, hiking, biking, and boating gear. Patrons will find the finest brand names on the market and the latest in technical apparel, footwear, and accessories as well as gift items. In addition, experienced technicians are on-hand to provide bicycle repairs and tune-ups, quality ski and race tunes, the fastest waxes, and information on local snow and trail conditions. Whether you are skiing at the

hill, biking local trails, or exploring rivers and backcountry, Gravity Sports can help you enjoy the best of McCall with a friendly, service-oriented approach.

V Manchester Ice and Event Centre
200 E. Lake St. in downtown McCall. 634-3570.

After McCall residents spent years twirling on an outdoor ice skating rink, individuals are now able to hone their skills indoors at the Manchester Ice and Event Centre. Patrons are treated to beautiful views of nearby Payette Lake and snowcapped peaks as they slide across the large, well-maintained indoor ice skating rink. The centre is open daily year-round with both private and public skate times available. Skate rentals are also furnished on-site.

V Activity Barn Tubing Park
Approximately 2 miles south of McCall off Moonridge Rd. 634-2222. From downtown McCall, drive 0.5 miles west on Deinhard Ln. to Mission St.. Bear left on Mission St. and continue 1.6 miles before turning right on Moonridge Rd. Drive 0.6 miles to the park, watching for pedestrians and skiers at all times.

The Activity Barn Tubing Park is one of McCall's newest attractions, claiming rights as Idaho's only lift-served snow tubing park. The 700 foot long tubing hill treats users to four levels of difficulty and a maximum drop of eighty-five feet that allows tubers to reach speeds up to forty-five miles per hour! Lighted night tubing is available, and tubers can warm themselves by the bonfire on weekends. The tubing park is open Wednesday through Sunday during ski season, and a small admission fee is charged.

V Activity Barn Nordic Trail
Approximately 2 miles south of McCall off Moonridge Rd. 634-2222. From downtown McCall, drive 0.5 miles west on Deinhard Ln. to Mission St. Bear left on Mission St., and continue 1.6 miles before turning right on Moonridge Rd. Drive 0.6 miles to the park, watching for pedestrians and skiers at all times.

One of McCall's newest attractions, the Activity Barn has expanded its services to include a groomed four-mile Nordic skiing trail. The scenic trail meanders through a working cattle ranch near the Payette River and is appropriate for beginning and intermediate skiers. The trail is open to the public free of charge, but donations are appreciated to help with trail maintenance.

V Little Ski Hill
3 miles northwest of McCall on State Hwy. 55. 634-5691.

Under the management of the Payette Lakes Ski Club, McCall's Little Ski Hill has been serving community residents and visitors since 1937.

Established merely as a diversion for bored forest workers, the hill has grown into a community gathering spot and breeding ground for local Olympic champions. Operating with the intent of fostering lifelong affinity for winter sports in people of all ages, Little Hill offers something for everyone. 405 vertical feet of alpine terrain awaits skiers and snowboarders, while an extensive thirty-mile Nordic system provides hours of groomed touring experiences during daylight hours. The Nordic system features both skating and traditional tracks, and lighted night skiing is offered every Friday and Saturday night. In addition to its outdoor recreation, Little Ski Hill offers a certified ski school with lessons available to both downhill and cross-country skiers, a small lodge, and live music every Friday night. Downhill day passes are a mere $6, while the Nordic trail fee is just $3 a day.

V Slick Rock Mountain
East of McCall. Contact the McCall Ranger District at 634-0400. From McCall, drive east on Lick Creek Rd. past the Lake Fork Campground. At the Slick Rock sign, park in the pullout, cross the creek, and hike 15 minutes to the base of the rock wall.

Slick Rock Mountain, surrounded by the dense Payette National Forest, is situated in Lick Creek Canyon. The large rock face boasts one of Idaho's longest continual technical climbs and is a popular destination for climbers seeking routes with a 5.3 to 5.6-difficulty rating. The site is free and open seasonally when road conditions allow access.

V McCall Area Snowmobile Trails
McCall. Contact the McCall Chamber of Commerce at 634-7631.

In a December 1998 issue of *Sno-West Magazine*, McCall and the surrounding region were listed as a top reader pick for picture-perfect snowmobiling. Today, the McCall Area Snowmobile Trails remain one of the most popular systems of snowmobile trails in all of Idaho. Connecting the communities of Cascade, Donnelly, and McCall, the well-groomed trail system also leads through

Idaho Trivia

Minnesota may technically hold the distinction as the "Land of Lakes," but Idaho offers some stiff competition. More than 200 of Idaho's many lakes can be found within a 100-mile radius of McCall.

Idaho Trivia

As the second oldest winter recreation area in the state, McCall is home to a wide variety of winter sports and recreational venues. With its ideal location, unrivaled powder, and numerous winter amenities, McCall frequently hosts the U.S. Junior Olympics. The weeklong winter event draws contestants and crowds from across the U.S. and

THE LIFE BEHIND TIM GOODALE: LEGENDARY MOUNTAIN MAN & TRAIL EXPLORER

Famous for opening up a new mining route near Cambridge, Idaho, mountain man, Tim Goodale, was a legend in his own era. The wilderness expert migrated to Colorado in 1839 where he hunted sheep and antelope and honed his trapping skills. In 1850, Goodale joined forces with Kit Carson, driving horses to Fort Laramie and later trailing sheep from New Mexico to California. Always leading the life of a wanderer and explorer, Goodale's next adventures took him to Green River, Wyoming where he operated a ferry from 1854 to 1856. During his stint in Wyoming, Goodale assisted railroad and military survey crews, and worked closely with Jim Bridger in discovering Colorado's Berthoud Pass.

By the 1860s, Goodale had made his way north to Idaho Territory. Goodale helped Oregon Trail pioneers cross the Snake River and then escorted them on alternate routes that decreased both mileage and travel time. Goodale's cutoffs (as they were regionally known) were scattered throughout Idaho, including routes in southeastern Idaho and one that traveled near Cambridge through the Pine Creek Valley. Although Goodale eventually left Idaho, historians estimate that seven out of every ten wagons that passed through Idaho after 1862 followed at least one of Goodale's routes.

mountain meadows and provides backcountry access to Goose Lake, Granite Lake, and Brundage Reservoir. The trail system is free and open to the public during daylight hours.

F Lardos Grill & Saloon
600 W. Lake St., McCall. 634-8191.
www.frontiernet.net/~lardoS

The family-style Lardos Grill & Saloon has been serving up good food, good times, and friendly, prompt service since 1973. Priding itself on stocking fresh, high quality products that are prepared in-house, Lardos provides a full service bar and an extensive menu with an array of cuisine. Weekly lunch specials, summer dinner specials, a cozy atmosphere highlighted with history, covered patio dining, and a staff that is knowledgeable about the McCall area further enhance Lardos' charming

customer appeal. Always open at 11:30 AM with the bar operating until 2 AM on busy nights, Lardos Grill closes during the summer at 11:00 PM Sunday through Thursday and 12:00 AM Friday and Saturday. During winter, the restaurant closes at 10:00 PM Sunday through Thursday and 11:00 PM on weekends.

F McCall Brewing Company
807 N. 3rd St., McCall. 634-3309.

FS The Pancake and Christmas House
209 N. 3rd St., McCall. 634-5849.

Opened in 1952 and under the same ownership since 1983, The Pancake House is McCall's oldest restaurant and a local favorite for huge portions of scrumptious homemade food. Housed in a new lodge facility since 2002, the restaurant offers an extensive breakfast menu, including "Those Potatoes" – a famous recipe of hashbrowns, bacon bits, and cheese once featured in *Country Living Magazine*! Hungry for lunch? Select from homemade soups and breads, sandwiches, burgers, and salads. While waiting for your order, stroll through the on-site Christmas House. The Christmas House was added in 1986 and displays Santa's, nativity scenes, themed trees, and an endless ornament and gift selection. The Pancake and Christmas House is open daily from 6 AM-2 PM (excluding Christmas and Thanksgiving) and invites you to discover its five decade tradition of excellence!

L Accommodation Services
302 N. 3rd St., McCall. 634-7766 or
(800) 551-8234.
www.accommodationservices.com

Accommodation Services is proud to offer McCall's largest selection of premier vacation property rentals. They offer cabins, condos, and homes in a wide variety of sizes, locations, and amenities that are sure to accommodate your individual taste and budget. Located on the shore of the 5,330-acre glacial Payette Lake, McCall offers year-round activities including swimming, boating, water skiing, Nordic and alpine skiing, snowshoeing, and over 500 miles of groomed snowmobile trails. Accommodation Services features approximately 150 properties ranging in price from $85-$1,500

per night. There is always something for the entire family to enjoy. They look forward to serving you.

L McCall RV Resort & Northfork Lodge
200 Scott St., McCall. 634-1418 or
(800) 709-9739. www.mccallrvresort.com

Indulge yourself in the warmth of a fine resort in a beautiful wilderness setting at the McCall RV Resort & Northfork Lodge. Located on the North Fork of the Payette River, McCall RV Resort is open year-round as one of the Pacific Northwest's most amenity-rich RV resorts. Spacious sites include 30, 50, and 100 amp service, paved drives, phone and cable hook-ups, and big rig and pull throughs. The resort's centerpiece is the stunning Northfork Lodge. The lodge's cozy atmosphere welcomes patrons with a pool, spa, exercise room, billiards lounge, and library. For guests' convenience, free wireless Internet access is offered, an events coordinator is on-site, and ample room is available for indoor and outdoor gatherings. On your next destination getaway or journey across scenic Idaho, discover a new kind of RV experience!

L The Hunt Lodge Holiday Inn Express
210 N. 3rd St., McCall. 634-4700.
www.thehuntlodge.com

The Hunt Lodge is an award-winning Holiday Inn Express Hotel & Suites nestled in Idaho's Payette National Forest. Located near Brundage Mountain and Tamarack Ski Resorts and just 0.75 miles from Payette Lake, the lodge welcomes visitors with rich ambience and convenient access to restaurants, shopping, the arts, and numerous outdoor activities. Guests also enjoy complimentary deluxe continental breakfast with their stay. The completely smoke-free hotel features 85 beautifully decorated rooms and suites complete with air conditioning, voice mail, free local calls, coffeemakers, hair dyers, remote TV, free high speed internet access, iron and board, with suites including refrigerators and microwaves and nine Jacuzzi suites. The hotel also offers an indoor heated pool and spa, fitness center, business center, guest laundry, free parking, movie rentals, and meeting/banquet facilities accommodating up to 300 people.

CHUKAR HUNTING: FLOCKING TO THE HIGH DESERT

For those unfamiliar with the high desert terrain encompassing several western U.S. regions, most individuals will be just as unfamiliar with the unique upland bird known as the chukar. At first mention of the word, some may think the bird is nothing more than another jackalope tale of folklore creation used to trick non-natives into asking stupid questions or doing unbelievably strange things just to catch a glimpse of the elusive creature. But alas, the chukar is real, and chukar hunters agree that few creatures rival this intelligent, isolating bird.

So if chukars are real and chukar hunting is a huge phenomenon, why have so few people heard about it? The reason is simple. The non-native birds, which were introduced into the U.S. during the 1800s, crave wide-open spaces. Naturally, the birds flocked to some of the most remote terrain in the entire country – the western U.S. – and carved out a niche in the most arid regions where human habitation has remained nearly non-existent. For years, the birds lived undetected in the wilds of Nevada, Oregon, and Idaho's Snake River Plain and the Owyhee Canyonlands. But when modern transportation combined with western man's innate desire to explore the foothills, mountains, and deserts around him, the handsome bird was discovered along with the advent of chukar hunting.

Preferring rugged terrain to flat ground, chukars are found amid deep canyons, rocky hillsides, and sparse vegetation in some of the west's most unforgiving landscapes. Although the birds are capable of eating a diverse array of food sources, the chukar diet does require routine cheatgrass feedings and watering at least twice per day. These simple facts regarding the chukar's nutritional needs certainly narrow the possible hunting areas, but the bird still frequently manages to evade both novice and experienced hunters. With wingspans of seventeen inches and low body weights, chukars can fly with ease up and over rugged hillsides while their predators pant dejectedly behind them in a fruitless chase.

In cases such as these, many hunters new to the sport chalk the day up to experience and pursue upland birds less bent on making their predators work for a trophy catch. For chukar hunters, however, the difficult pursuit through remote canyons and across high desert plateaus is what brings them back for more each hunting season. Successful chukar hunters enjoy the views of raging canyon rivers, distant mountains, and the silence of non-civilization just as much as the hunt itself, and they're known for their attention to detail. Noticing things on a nearly microscopic level, these outdoor enthusiasts learn to detect every small sign of a chukar's presence, including rocky lookout perches, distinctive droppings, and natural rainwater bowls where the bird may have drank during the day. These and other indicators lead smart and patient hunters to their pride and joy.

Chukars are distinguished from other upland birds by their rapid movements, fifteen-inch bodies, and red beaks, legs, and feet that stand in stark contrast to their gray chests and nude colored bellies. With white necks, throats, and chins and bold vertical barring on their sides, chukars are unlike any other regional bird and are easily identified when spotted. Taunting those who seek them with rhythmic clucking, chukars are most easily bagged from late summer through late fall. For those who successfully snag the hardy bird, chukars provide a tasty campfire or Dutch oven meal. The light meat bird can be seasoned, cooked, and served in a variety of ways, but preparation should include plenty of liquid as chukars tend towards dryness when cooked.

While visitors to western states can't believe everything they're told, they should believe chukar tales and respect the regional value of chukar hunting. It's a call of the wild only the western U.S. boasts and a hunting experience that will keep true bird lovers flocking in hot pursuit to the high desert.

north of Boise. McCall Real Estate Company has the largest and most knowledgeable team of real estate professionals in central Idaho. Agents provide exceptional customer service. Because they love living here, they're always happy to share their extensive knowledge of the Valley and surrounding areas with clients. They'll help you find the home, building site, or investment property that's right for you – and be there for you through every step of the transaction. So whether you're looking for rustic simplicity, luxurious amenities, or something in between, McCall Real Estate Company can help you experience some of Idaho's finest living.

M Clark Real Estate
1010 N. 3rd St., McCall. 634-7924 or (888) 551-8901. www.clark-realestate.com

Located on the road to your dreams, Clark Real Estate was founded in 1980 and has since set the area's industry standard for unsurpassed service. The brokerage boasts twenty-five years of continuous service to McCall, Donnelly, Cascade, and New Meadows and has established a reputation for consistency, honesty, integrity, and unparalleled service. Offering the area's largest inventory of waterfront and mountain-view home sites, ranches, acreages, and commercial property, Clark Real Estate also provides professional and experienced agents who know how to help clients find just the right property, even if it isn't listed! Whether you're looking for a vacation retreat or a year-round home or business amid one of Idaho's finest recreational playgrounds, contact Clark Real Estate in McCall to make your real estate dreams come true!

M Fields & Hopkins Realtors
309 E. Lake St., McCall. 634-7755. www.fandhrealtors.com

Make your dream of owning real estate in McCall, ID a reality. Whether you're searching for a vacation home, permanent residence, recreation property, rustic mountain cabin, or weekend getaway, the dedicated professionals of Fields & Hopkins Realtors will help you locate your ideal Valley County property. Under the management of Julie Fields, Owner, and John Hopkins, Broker, the brokerage offers unsurpassed excellence and a commitment to warmth and integrity. In promoting and serving both buyers and sellers, the office adheres to the following principles: service, responsibility, reliability, integrity, interaction, reachability/communication, professionalism, marketing, technology/internet, and honesty in pric-

S Heart to Heart Gifts
317 Lake St., McCall. 634-4512. www.hearttoheartgifts.com

Established in 1988, Heart to Heart Gifts offers friendly service and high quality gifts and home décor. Patrons will find collectibles along with wildlife, country western, and lodge and cabin décor. Select from custom hand-painted furniture and garden items, hand-painted themed checkerboards, linens, antique furniture, woodcarvings, art, and Idaho antler products, chandeliers, and carvings. A large selection of dog and cat items caters to pet lovers, while country rooster items, Christmas ornaments, and a variety of jewelry ensures that Heart to Heart Gifts provides something for everyone. In addition, the store proudly sells sports-related gifts, gourmet foods, and huckleberry jam, syrups, and candy. When you need a unique gift or are simply looking to redecorate, visit the friendly staff of Heart to Heart Gifts in downtown McCall or online!

M The McCall Real Estate Company
301 E. Lake St., McCall. 634-2100. www.McCallRealEstate.com

Tired of the rat race? Discover life in the friendly mountain town of McCall – just two scenic hours

THE SNAKE WAR 1864-1868

As eastern pioneers poured westward through Idaho along the Oregon Trail, tensions between area Native Americans and white settlers ran high. Disgusted at the closing of Fort Boise and continual destruction of their hunting and trading grounds, the Shoshone Indians in Boise Basin and the Owyhees grew even more displeased as a wave of miners arrived in southern Idaho. Unsettled by the influx of gold seekers and the establishment of mines on sacred ground, the Shoshone Indians began sporadically attacking bands of miners headed to the Boise Basin in the early 1860s.

In response to the attacks, a group of Boise Basin miners was organized in 1863 under the direction of Jeff Standifer to ward off any hostile Native Americans in the area. Despite leading a few successful fights against the raiding Shoshones, the Indian raids continued and a seven-foot Indian named Ouluck continually harassed miners.

Learning of the tensions, the War Department finally intervened and sent Major Pinckney Lugenbeel and two troops of volunteers to reestablish Fort Boise. With the military's presence, surely the raids would end. But the Shoshone attacks continued and were too much for the small volunteer corp to handle. Stepping up military support, the First Oregon Cavalry under Colonel R.F. Maury's command was sent to Fort Boise on August 28, 1864. By that time, the continuous conflicts had become known as the Snake War (as area white men called the Shoshone "Snakes"). In 1865, Lieutenant Charles Hobart and his line of Oregon Cavalry arrived and established Camp Lyon twenty miles from the major Owyhee mines. Still, the attacks persisted. The Shoshones did not seem to care about the military's presence, and the miners' lives were still in jeopardy.

After the volunteer troops were replaced by regular U.S. Army troops returning from Civil War duty, the War Department dispensed Major L.H. Marshall in May 1866 to oversee the Boise District's continually expanding military camps. Just a few days after his arrival, Marshall led a successful four-hour campaign against the Indians at the Owyhee River on May 11. However, while Marshall was recovering from wounds, the Shoshones retaliated and scalped 150 Chinese men headed to the Boise Basin mines. Outraged that the military had not been able to protect these men, white settlers began loudly protesting and calling for increased intervention and support. Two new military camps were constructed, and General H.W. Halleck replaced Major Marshall with the famous Indian fighter, Lieutenant Colonel George Crook, in December 1866.

Crook began operations immediately, setting out on a winter campaign in 1867. Crook staged several surprise attacks against the Shoshone with heavy Native American losses. When he discovered that the Indians were receiving supplies from comrades in northern California, Crook sought vengeance and waged the two-day Infernal Caverns Battle on September 27-28, 1867. Slowly but surely, Indian raids on stagecoaches and miners became less frequent, and after being chased by Crook for over a year, the Shoshones' resistance was growing weak. Following the Castle Rock Battle, the Shoshone Indians called for a peace agreement in May 1868. By September 1868, Crook settled on peace terms with head chief Wewawewa that offered federal protection from white harassment. Unlike most treaties of the day, Crook was bold and did not offer a reservation or federal funding to the warring bands. Satisfied with the terms, the Shoshones' relations with white miners and pioneers improved and the Snake War was officially ended.

hydromassage for a small admission fee. The springs open daily at 10 AM, but are closed every Tuesday.

T Long Valley
Between Cascade and McCall on State Hwy. 55

Cradled within the alpine fingertips of mountain grandeur and remote scenic lakes, Long Valley holds Cascade and McCall within its grasp. The North Fork of the Payette River connects this scenic valley with Payette Lake and twenty-mile long Lake Cascade. Although fur trappers discovered Long Valley as early as the mid 1800s, permanent white settlement did not occur in the area until the 1880s. The valley's small population once dominated by livestock ranchers has now been replaced with outdoor enthusiasts.

V Tamarack Resort
2099 W. Mountain Rd., Donnelly. 325-1000.

Nestled on the scenic shores of Lake Cascade, Tamarack Resort is Idaho's newest year-round recreational destination. Winter 2004 marked the resort's inaugural ski season with more than 1,100 skiable acres, 600 of which are groomed. Recognized for feather-light powder snow, the ski area features a maximum vertical drop of 2,800 feet and a wide variety of terrain. From steep mogul runs to long cruisers and terrain parks to powder bowls, Tamarack has an appropriate run for every skiing and snowboarding ability. In addition, the resort features a 30K Nordic ski trail, snowshoeing trails, snowcat skiing, and snowmobiling.

During summer, Tamarack keeps going strong with 360-degree views of the surrounding mountains, forests, meadows, and Lake Cascade. Summer visitors have access to kayaking, floating, hiking, biking, and golf. Tamarack is open from 8 AM to 4 PM daily with prices varying according to season and activity.

L Boulder Creek Inn & Suites
629 Hwy. 55, Donnelly. 325-8638 or (866) 325-8638. www.bouldercreekinn.com

Experience comfort and convenience at the Boulder Creek Inn & Suites. Newly opened in July 2004, the four-season inn provides access to year-round recreation. After spending a summer day on the trail, lake, or golf course, revive yourself with scenic Jug Handle Mountain views and clean rooms. Guests may reserve single or double standard rooms, kitchenette units, family suites, or a special King Jacuzzi suite. All rooms feature free wireless DSL, Internet, cable TV, and HBO, and guests enjoy on-site laundry facilities and a continental breakfast featuring fresh waffles. If your travel plans involve visiting Donnelly during winter, the inn provides easy access to Tamarack and Brundage ski resorts and an array of other winter activities. Pets are welcome, and daily, weekly, and monthly rates are available.

---

ing. Clients are always treated with respect, and customer satisfaction is of utmost importance. Discover for yourself the appeal of this mile high resort town, and contact the experienced professionals at Fields & Hopkins Realtors today!

M Jan Kangas, Clark Real Estate
1010 N. 3rd St., McCall. 634-7924 or (888) 551-8901. www.mccall4sale.com

M McCall Area Chamber of Commerce
102 N. 3rd St., McCall. 634-7631. www.mccallchamber.org

6 Food, Lodging

Donnelly
Pop. 138

Founded by Finnish immigrants and named for the founding Donnelly family in the 1890s, this tiny establishment blossomed with economic activity upon the railroad's 1912 arrival. It's thriving economy, however, wasn't destined for a prosperous future. When the Richmond & Samuel Pea Company and the CCC shut down during World War II and the logging camp moved to New Meadows in 1940, Donnelly became a sleepy little town. The area, however, is known for its wintry

sleigh rides that take visitors through the woods to gain a close-up view of a massive elk herd. These magnificent animals have attained a safe haven from winter hardships and hunters here in Donnelly, and the sleigh rides are a longstanding annual tradition.

T Valley County Museum & Roseberry Townsite
1.5 miles east of town, Donnelly. 325-8871.

The history of Valley County is thoroughly presented in this small-town museum commonly referred to as Long Valley Museum. Exhibits include the old Roseberry townsite, a turn of the century church, school, and city hall, logging and woodworking tools, plus a spinning wheel and loom used by Finnish pioneers who settled in the area. The museum is open 1 PM to 5 PM Friday through Sunday from June through August, and 1 PM to 5 PM on Sundays in May and September.

T Gold Fork Hot Springs
South of Donnelly. 890-8730. 1.5 miles south of Donnelly on the highway's east side, bear south on Gold Fork Rd. and proceed to the springs.

Situated outside Donnelly beside the Gold Fork River, Gold Fork Hot Springs offers year-round relaxation in its naturally warm water. The commercialized site features six mineral pools and

L Long Valley Motel
161 S. Main St., Donnelly. 325-8271

Maintaining a quaint, cozy atmosphere, Long Valley Motel is located within minutes of Tamarack Resort, Gold Fork Hot Springs, and the must-see Roseberry General Store and Museum. The motel features eight clean and affordable rooms, each room possessing its own unique theme. Interconnected, fully-equipped kitchenettes along with additional bedrooms offer convenience and the ability to accommodate any size group. Guests also enjoy free DSL and HBO, and pets are always welcome. Nonsmoking rooms are also available. The motel is committed to offering affordable stays, and special rates are available. For those staying six nights, the seventh day is free, while guests who make ten individual stays will enjoy the first night of their eleventh stay for free! Explore Donnelly without breaking your budget, and make reservations today at Long Valley Motel!

S Roseberry General Store
1 mile east of Donnelly at the intersection of E. Roseberry and Farm to Market Rd., Donnelly. 325-5000.

Step back in time at the Roseberry General Store. Constructed in 1905, the building was restored in 1995 to a 1920s general store atmosphere and opened in 2003 as a general store and museum. Shelves stocked with history complement the store's merchandise, which includes groceries, antiques, collectibles, clocks, porcelain and Raggedy Ann dolls, cast iron banks and figurines, fine beers and wines, and vintage toys, hats, and candy. For those with worldly tastes, the store boasts Russian woodcarvings, Finnish handmade knives, and Scandinavian food and gifts. In addition, Roseberry General Store serves as an authorized dealer for Old World Christmas, Byer's Carolers, Breyer Horses, Radio Flyer Wagons, and Steger Mukluks. The coffee is always on, and the store welcomes visitors 10 AM to 6 PM Wednesday through Sunday.

7 *Food, Lodging*

Cascade
Pop. 997

Cascade Falls, located on the North Fork of the Payette River, used to be a spectacular site to behold. In 1948, when the dam was built, the falls became all but hidden by Cascade Reservoir.

Nonetheless, the town of Cascade derived its name in 1912 from those original falls. Although a lumber mill was initially responsible for a large sector of the community's economy, Cascade today relies on agriculture, ranching, and a significant tourism industry for sustenance.

Warm Lake
24 miles east of Cascade. Contact the Cascade Chamber of Commerce at 382-3833.

Situated near the crystal clear waters of Warm Lake in Boise National Forest, the town of Warm Lake is primarily a resort and summer home community. A variety of wildlife dominates the scenic landscape, and an array of recreational activities abound throughout the year, including boating and fishing.

Smiths Ferry
Pop. 15

A post office operated here from 1910 through the 1960s. The town's name recognizes Caldwell resident, E.J. Smith, as he operated a popular ferry on the North Fork of the Payette River in the early 1890s.

H Long Valley Ambush
Milepost 115.4 on State Hwy. 55

While hunting for stolen horses on August 20, 1878, William Monday, Jake Groseclose, Tom Healy, and "Three Finger" Smith were ambushed by Indians in a rocky basin about a mile from here.Monday and Groseclose were killed immediately and Healy wounded; Smith, "being a man of experience in such matters," fled. He made it 40 miles to Salmon Meadows. Infantrymen buried the three, marked the spot, and took up the Indian trail. Smith estimated there were 75 Indians; Army trackers finally concluded there were only five – but they never caught them.

T Stibnite
Valley County; from Cascade, Idaho, drive east on the paved road for 24 miles until reaching Warm Lake; here, proceed east 4.5 miles on the E. Fork of the South Fork of the Salmon River to the Profile Gap/Stibnite Junction; Stibnite is located 9.5 miles southeast of this junction.

In 1913, Albert Hennessey found gold and antimony ore on Meadow Creek near Stibnite during the Thunder Mountain Mining District rush. Stibnite grew slowly as it was isolated, but the area eventually became the fourth richest Idaho mining district. With abundant antimony, gold, and cinnabar deposits, Hennessey prospered with his claims before selling them in 1921 to the United Mercury Mines Company. In 1928, F.W. Bradley leased the claims from United Mercury Mines before eventually forming his own open-pit mine in the area in 1937. In 1940, U.S. Bureau of Mines drilling crews discovered high-grade tungsten, and Stibnite quickly became the leading U.S. tungsten producer during World War II. Although the mines saw tremendous success, they eventually closed in 1952 but not without a wealthy history. Between 1932 and 1952, the Stibnite mines produced $24 million in antimony, $21 million in tungsten, $4 million in gold, $3 million in mercury, and $1 million in silver.

Most of Stibnite's residents left by 1959, and many of the houses and buildings were moved to new locations. However, the U.S. Bureau of Mercury Mines suggests that nearly $50 million in antimony deposits still remain in the Stibnite area.

T Cascade Golf Course
117 Lakeshore Dr., Cascade. 382-4835.

The Cascade Golf Course overlooks scenic Cascade Reservoir, and the hilly terrain and open

fairways make this public course popular. Designed with 9 holes, the course features multiples sets of tees allowing golfers to play a round as long as 5, 246 yards. While the lake does present itself as a hazard in four of the holes, the course is suitable for golfers of all experience levels. Green fees are $12 for 9 holes and $17 for 18 holes Monday through Thursday. On weekends, fees are $15 for 9 holes and $20 for 18 holes. The course is closed November through March due to the weather.

T Molly's Hot Springs
Near Cascade. Contact the Cascade Chamber of Commerce at 382-3833. From Cascade, travel on Forest Road (FR) 22 to the S. Fork of the Salmon River. Here, bear south on FR 474, following the route 2 miles to the springs.

Molly's Hot Springs is a local favorite among the area's numerous non-developed hot springs. Volunteers and hot springs users constructed a primitive rock pool to contain the area's naturally hot water drawn from several hot springs. The free area is open seasonally depending upon weather and road conditions.

T Vulcan Hot Springs
Near Cascade. Contact the Cascade Chamber of Commerce at 382-3833. From Cascade, travel on Forest Rd. (FR) 22 to the S. Fork of the Salmon River. Here, bear south on FR 474, pass by Molly's Hot Springs, and continue 5 miles to a primitive campground and parking area.

After taking an easy one-half mile hike from the parking area through a scenic forested area, visitors are welcomed with remote relaxation at Vulcan Hot Springs. Boiling area springs are cooled to a nearly constant temperature of 105 degrees Fahrenheit in a rocky dammed pool. The isolated area offers no facilities, so visitors should plan accordingly. The non-developed site is open seasonally depending upon weather and road conditions.

T Trail Creek Hot Springs
Near Cascade. Contact the Cascade Chamber of Commerce at 382-3833. From Cascade, travel on Forest Road (FR) 22 alongside Trail Creek to a small parking area, and then hike to the pool below.

Situated beside its namesake, Trail Creek Hot Springs features a small pool built into the creek bed. Filled with 122 degree Fahrenheit spring water, the pool's location allows users to mix in cold creek water to adjust the water temperature and create the perfect soaking conditions. The isolated area offers no facilities, so visitors should plan accordingly. The non-developed site is open seasonally depending upon weather and road conditions.

T Alpine Playhouse
Hemlock Ave., McCall. Contact the McCall Chamber of Commerce at 634-7631.

Since 1969, McCall's Alpine Playhouse has provided a venue for Idaho performing arts. Due to the efforts of dedicated actors, playwrights, and community businesses, the community's old Catholic Church was recreated into a 110-seat community theater. The playhouse not only provides local artists with a place to gather and inspire one another but also plays host to several various productions each year. Past performances have included *Steel Magnolias*, *Bye Bye Birdie*, high school drama productions, Shakespeare in the Parks presentations, children's plays, and original plays by local writers. For those interested in catching an Alpine Playhouse production, call for tickets and a complete schedule of events and workshops.

WATERFALLS

Big Fiddler Creek Falls and Long Gulch Falls

Exit I-84 at Mountain Home; continue 20 miles north on U.S. Hwy. 20; merge onto Rd. #134 and drive for 5 miles; turn left onto Rd. #113 and continue 2 miles to Prairie; at the junction, turn left (west) and drive 2.4 miles to the Rd. #189 junction; turn west onto Rd. #189 and proceed into S. Fork Canyon for approximately 5.7 miles.

At an elevation of 4,000 feet within the Mountain Home Ranger District of Boise National Forest, Big Fiddler Creek Falls claims the title of Idaho's highest officially measured waterfall. Descending 252 feet, this waterfall can be impressive if viewed during early and late spring before Big Fiddler Creek dries up in the summer's heat.

The 100 to 125 foot plunge of Long Gulch Falls is also viewable from the same area. At an elevation of 3,600 feet, this waterfall has a medium watershed and descends into the South Fork Boise River. After driving 2 miles into South Fork Canyon and locating the viewing area for Big Fiddler Creek Falls, gaze toward the near side of the canyon to find this cataract.

Little Salmon Falls

U.S. Hwy. 95; 11 miles north of New Meadows; park at the unmarked turnout directly next to the falls.

Located at an elevation of 3,640 feet near the Payette National Forest's New Meadows Ranger District, this waterfall offers visitors scenery and easy accessibility. Following the Salmon River, these falls cascade 10 to 15 feet with a large watershed.

Lower Little Salmon Falls

U.S. Hwy. 95; 10.3 miles north of New Meadows.

The Little Salmon River descends rapidly for 5 to 10 feet to form Lower Little Salmon Falls near the Payette National Forest. Immediately north of the Smoky Boulder Rd. junction, park at the turnout and walk to the falls.

Fall Creek Falls

U.S. Hwy. 95; 18 miles north of New Meadows near an unmarked highway turnout.

Before slipping into the Little Salmon River under U.S. Hwy. 95, Fall Creek plunges 15 to 25 feet at an elevation of 2,920 feet.

Lost Creek Falls

U.S. Hwy. 95 south; turn west onto Lost Valley Valley Reservoir Rd. #089 and follow 5.3 miles; continue south for 2.7 miles on Rd. #154.

Found within the Payette National Forest's Council Ranger District, Lost Creek Falls is situated at an elevation of 4,380 feet and is easily accessible. Dropping 5 to 10 feet from Lost Creek into a pool below, these falls provide visitors with a peaceful picnic backdrop in the wooded surroundings. While Lost Creek Falls is visible from the roadside, visitors will find up-close views by taking one of the various fishermen's trails leading to the cataract.

Little Falls and Big Falls

Exit Scenic Route 55 at Banks, ID onto S. Fork Rd.; continue 21.7 miles to Little Falls and 23.9 miles to Big Falls.

Little Falls drops along the South Fork Payette River within Boise National Forest's Lowman Ranger District. At an elevation of 3,350 feet, Little Falls descends 5 to 10 feet as a wide band from the broad river. For more waterfall scenery, continue past Little Falls 2.2 miles until reaching Big Falls' 25 to 40 foot drop into a pool below. This cataract is best viewed from a slight distance, so park where the gravel road broadens and gaze upstream. Big Falls may then be found 100 to 150 feet below on the canyon floor.

Indian Bathtub Falls

Take Scenic Route 51 to Bruneau; merge onto Hot Springs Rd.; after 7.2 miles, turn right onto Indian Bathtub Rd. and follow 0.7 mile to Sugar Creek Rd.; turn left and proceed 2.9 miles to a nameless dirt road; continue 0.9 mile to a parking area.

Found on land that the Bureau of Land Management administers, Indian Bathtub Falls drips 7 to 12 feet into a small hot springs pool. Many find the waterfall uninspiring, but the thermal springs surrounding the cataract draws several visitors eager to soak in the warm water. Visitors are cautioned to bring appropriate footwear as the hot springs basin may contain broken glass from previous users.

Deadman Falls

I-84 to Glenns Ferry; merge onto Frontage Rd. and follow 1.7 miles west to Sailor Creek Rd.; turn left (south) and proceed 5.8 miles to Deadman Canyon.

The seasonal eroding force of Deadman Creek and Deadman Falls formed the gorge now known as Deadman Canyon on land overseen by the Bureau of Land Management. Visitors expecting to see a powerful cataract, however, will likely be disappointed. Although a 125 to 175 foot rocky ridge characterizes the canyon, a small dam prohibits Deadman Creek from dropping down this ledge most of the year. However, visitors lucky enough to visit after a severe thunderstorm may catch a glimpse of the falls.

Jump Creek Falls

Drive south along U.S. Hwy. 95 2.5 miles past the junction for Scenic Route 55; merge onto Poison Creek Rd. and follow for 3.5 miles; as the paved road sharply turns right, bear south (left) onto a nameless gravel road; proceed 0.5 mile before heading west (right) onto a dirt road marked "No Trespassing;" disregard this warning as the road is the designated public access to Jump Creek Canyon; after driving 0.4 mile, visitors will reach a fork in the road; stay on the upper road at the right of the fork as this will lead to the mouth of the canyon in approximately 1 mile (the lower road leads to a private home); at the upper road's end, park your vehicle and follow the trail into the canyon.

Descending vertically for 40 to 60 feet along Jump Creek, Jump Creek Falls is found at an elevation of 2,640 feet on land governed by the Bureau of Land Management. Visitors who take a fairly easy hike will discover this cataract falling amidst unusual rock formations. Upon locating the trailhead, follow the 0.2-mile path leading to the canyon floor. Viewers will climb over and under massive boulders and jump across a small creek before reaching the cataract.

Smith Creek Falls

Exit I-84 at Mountain Home and drive north on U.S. Hwy. 20 for 20 miles; at Rd. #134 (marked Anderson Ranch Dam/Prairie), proceed 5 miles to the dam and then turn west (left) onto Rd. #113; continue 2 miles to Prairie, and at the junction, bear westward for 2.4 miles; upon reaching the junction with Rd. #189, turn left onto Rd. #189 and drive toward South Fork Canyon for approximately 3.7 miles; locate the cattle guard in the road about 0.1 mile before entering the canyon and continue forward approximately 200 feet; at the wide spot in the road, park your vehicle.

Since no developed trail leads to Smith Creek Falls, access is limited and recommended only to adults with no physical limitations. For those willing to take a difficult day hike, however, Smith Creek Falls provides outstanding scenery with its 80 to 120 foot plunge into a cavern formed by Smith Creek. At an elevation of 3,700 feet, this cataract is located within the Boise National Forest's Mountain Home Ranger District and is rarely visited.

After parking your vehicle, begin your trek by crossing the 5 to 10 foot wide irrigation canal that may be knee or waist deep. Next, cross through the sagebrush toward Smith Creek. After walking approximately 100 feet, you will reach views of the cataract from South Fork Canyon's rim. Visitors are urged to use caution while hiking near these unfenced cliffs.

The following Idaho waterfalls are also located in this section with limited directions/access available:

Wildhorse Falls and Bear Creek Falls

Both Wildhorse and Bear Creek Falls lie within Adams County in the Payette National Forest. Wildhorse Falls is shown cascading near an unnamed 4-wheel drive road on topographic maps while Bear Creek Falls appears to have no roads or trails providing visitors with access.

Benton Creek Falls, Rush Falls, and Lower Rush Falls

These three waterfalls are located at different points all within the Payette National Forest and Washington County. Benton Creek Falls cascades down Benton Creek and topographic maps pinpoint the cataract alongside an unnamed trail. Both Rush Falls and Lower Rush Falls are mapped away from any developed trail, and access to both falls is uncertain.

Gold Fork Falls, Sixmile Creek Falls, and Upper Sixmile Creek Falls

Found in the Boise National Forest under the Garden Valley Ranger Station's jurisdiction, all three of these cataracts lie within Idaho's Valley County. Topographic maps illustrate Gold Fork Falls tumbling next to a gravel road. However, little information exists about the exact location of this road. Both Sixmile Creek Falls and Upper Sixmile Creek Falls can likely be seen from a distance. Maps illustrate a gravel road winding near the Middle Fork Payette River with views of the falls gained by gazing across the river from this road.

Falls Creek Falls

Falls Creek Falls plunges in Boise National Forest's Mountain Home Ranger District near the South Fork Canyon. Located north of the

Anderson Ranch Reservoir and Dam, the cataract is shown falling near Forest Rd. #123.

Swan Falls

Located on Bureau of Land Management land within Jump Creek Canyon, Swan Falls is found near U.S. Hwy. 95. On the Snake River, a small dam creates Swan Falls and the cataract is shown on maps as a point of interest.

Austin Butte Falls, Camel Falls, The Falls (Sugarloaf), Sheepshead Draw Falls (Section 3)

Austin Butte Falls is found near Scenic Route 51 as it flows into Bruneau Canyon. Visitors can create their own trail to the falls using back roads. Camel Falls, The Falls (Sugarloaf), and Sheepshead Draw Falls are also located in the same vicinity. However, topographic maps suggest that these Idaho cataracts are inaccessible.

Clover Creek Falls

Found near Deadman Canyon southwest of Glenns Ferry, ID, Clover Creek Falls is a small, segmented cataract. For adventurers willing to take time to locate the waterfall, Clover Creek Falls can be viewed after following an old four-wheel drive trail to this destination.

T Cascade Dam and Idaho Power Plant

0.5 miles from Cascade on State Hwy. 55. Contact the Cascade Chamber of Commerce at 382-3833.

Situated atop igneous granite rock, Cascade Dam was constructed in 1942 under the direction of the Bureau of Reclamation. The dam, which was established in conjunction with the Black Canyon Irrigation Project, is notched 107 feet high into a bedrock ridge. Although construction began in 1942, work crews were forced to halt for World War II. Building continued in 1946 with the dam and newly formed Cascade Reservoir completed in 1948.

In 1983, a $24 million Idaho Power Plant was erected at Cascade Dam's base. The plant features twin turbines capable of producing up to 12.8 megawatts of electricity at any given moment. The power plant is open daily for spectators interested in gaining an up-close perspective of how water is transformed into electricity.

TV Lake Cascade State Park

Near Cascade off State Hwy. 55. 382-6544.

Lake Cascade State Park, spanning 4,450 acres, is a sportsman's paradise. Extending itself through more than twenty miles of rolling hills, the park is situated amid majestic mountain views and offers year-round recreation. The lake itself is the main attraction, and the prevailing winds make it especially popular for sailing, windsurfing, and boating. Anglers have access to perch, rainbow trout, smallmouth bass, bullhead and channel catfish, and coho salmon in both summer and winter. Since the lake is known for its consistent catches, the park is one of the most frequented areas in the entire state.

The park also supports 300 well-maintained campsites, several hiking, biking, and cross-country skiing trails, and a playground and horseshoe pits. Boat ramps and docks offer convenient water access, and group yurts are available for rent. Park admission does require a $4 vehicle fee.

V Crawford Nordic Ski Trail

4 miles east of Cascade on Warm Lake Rd. Contact the Idaho Department of Parks and Recreation at 334-4199.

Crawford Nordic Ski Trail is an ideal option for intermediate skiers seeking a day in Idaho's pristine forests. Seven miles of marked trails are periodically groomed, and skiers should expect abrupt turns on a few of the downhill sections. The trail is open to the public free of charge during daylight hours.

V Cascade-Smith's Ferry Area Snowmobile Trails

Off State Hwy. 55 in Cascade and Smith's Ferry. Contact the Cascade Chamber of Commerce at 382-3833.

The region surrounding Cascade and Smith's Ferry is just one of wintry Idaho's many snowmobiling destinations. Near Smith's Ferry, recreationists will find 400 miles of trails at the Wellington Snow Park. 250 of those miles are groomed terrain offering access to Cascade, McCall, Ola, Stanley, Warm Lake, and Garden Valley. Another popular route, Winter Wonderland Trail, departs from downtown Smith's Ferry and winds through the scenic backcountry surrounding Cascade and Donnelly. The area trail systems are free and open to the public during daylight hours.

V Railroad Trail Pass Snowmobile Trails

20 miles north of Cascade on Warm Lake Rd. Contact the Cascade Ranger District at 382-7400.

The Railroad Trail Pass Snowmobile Trails are some of the most remote trails in all of Idaho. The trails wind through the backcountry of southwestern Idaho, connecting the old mining areas of Yellow Pine, Warm Lake, and Deadwood on their journey. Services are unavailable in the area, so trail users should pack along plenty of water, food, fuel, and winter provisions. The trails are free and open to the public daily during daylight hours.

V West Mountain Snowmobile Trails

Cascade. Contact the Cascade Ranger District at 382-7400.

The crowning feature of the West Mountain Snowmobile Trails outside Cascade is the panoramic vista of Long Valley stretching between Cascade and McCall. The groomed trail is open daily to the public free of charge during daylight hours.

V Clear Creek Mountain Biking

8 miles south of Cascade on Forest Rd. 409. Contact the Cascade Chamber of Commerce at 382-3833.

For those interested in catching some rays along with beautiful scenery, Forest Road 409 offers a gentle ride ideal for beginning and intermediate mountain bikers. Known locally as Clear Creek Rd., the route meanders beside trickling Clear Creek through a canopy of pine trees. The narrow road promises scenic landscape vistas and possible wildlife sightings. The route is open to bicyclists and picnickers free of charge before winter settles in for the season.

M Cascade Area Chamber of Commerce

126 N. Main, Cascade. 382-3833. www.cascade-chamber.com

Banks
Pop. 50

Banks is located on the Payette River where the North Fork and the South Fork merge and was named after early settlers W. B. Banks and Emma Banks. Today, the quiet village awakens with activity each summer when the river's renowned whitewater draws many rafters and kayakers.

Crouch
Pop. 154

Located on the Middle Fork of the Payette River, Crouch was named after the Garden Valley's first owner of platted land, William Crouch. A hub of gardening activity during its early years, Crouch served as headquarters for a large group of men serving in the 1930s with the Civilian Conservation Corp. Today, the once productive post office now operates as the local mercantile and is one of the state's oldest buildings. With all necessities and businesses within walking distance of each other, this friendly mountain town takes travelers back in time to a slower pace of life.

Lowman
Pop. 15

Although first settled by homesteader, Nathaniel Lowman, in the late 1800s or early 1900s, this city didn't actually receive telephone service until 1982. Prior to that, long distance phone calls were transmitted via microwave to Mesa, Idaho's Cambridge Telephone Company. Today, the town is a hotbed of activity for Boise National Forest recreationists.

Garden Valley
Pop. 150

Established in approximately 1870 with a post office following in 1871, Garden Valley draws its name from the area's scenic, fertile, and geothermal characteristics. During the gold rush era, Garden Valley supported year-round greenhouses full of fresh vegetables that were then sold to area miners. Today, the community is still home to the state's largest wholesale greenhouse. The valley, which is located on the Wildlife Canyon Scenic Byway, is flanked by two mountain ranges, and the South Fork and Middle Fork of the Payette River bisect the heart of the picturesque landscape.

H Lowman
Milepost 72.8 on State Hwy. 21

In 1907, Nathaniel W. Lowman settled here, and four years later, when he started a post office in his large log house, this community was named for him. Only a few scattered settlers lived here then. Lowman got all its supplies once a year from a large freight wagon over a state road built in 1894 to provide access to north Idaho. This highway followed in 1939. Eventually a one-room schoolhouse was moved here from Garden Valley. It still serves Lowman.

H Emma Edwards
Milepost 77.7 on State Hwy. 21

A talented artist, Emma Edwards went to work in 1890 to design Idaho's state seal when she was only 18 years old. Although her father had moved to California after serving as governor of Missouri (1844-1848), Emma preferred to spend much of her time in Idaho. After her marriage to John G. Green, a Boise Basin miner, they took up a land claim along Emma Creek and Green Creek in 1906 and lived here for many summers. Her seal design designated syringa, which blooms on these hills, as Idaho's state flower.

H Emile Grandjean
Milepost 95.4 on State Hwy. 21

An emigrant from Denmark, where he had studied forestry, Grandjean came to this part of Idaho in 1883 to mine, hunt, and trap.Before Idaho became a state in 1890, he built a winter cabin below Grandjean Peak at a site later occupied by the Grandjean ranger station. Because of his European studies, he became a professional forester here. He served as supervisor of the Boise National Forest from 1906-22.

T Terrace Lakes Golf Course
101 Holiday Dr., Garden Valley. 462-3314. www.terracelakes.com From Boise, drive north approximately 40 miles on State Hwy. 55 to Banks. At Banks, bear right onto Lowman Hwy., and continue 8 miles. At Middle Fork Rd., turn left and continue another 4 miles, staying left at all times. Finally, turn left on Warm Springs Creek Rd. and follow the signs leading to the course and Terrace Lakes Lodge.

The Terrace Lakes Golf Course is situated just fifty miles north of Boise at an elevation of 3,300 feet. Established in 1965, the 18-hole championship course provides panoramic views of Scott Mountain and the Middle Fork Range. Surrounded by tall forests and streams, the course plays like two different 9-hole courses, but all holes are challenging on the tight fairways. While the front 9 is a bit more expansive, the back 9 is squeezed between lush trees and a mountain stream, so there is little room for error. Players shouldn't be surprised to see deer, elk, fox, and wild turkeys gazing on as curious spectators. The course is open to the public Monday through Friday with green fees starting at $28. Advance tee times are required.

T Starlight Mountain Theater
850 S. Middlefork Rd., Garden Valley. 462-5523.

Amidst the surrounding mountain and river splendor, Starlight Mountain Theater treats Garden Valley residents and visitors to professional Broadway musicals. Featuring actors from all across America, the theater showcases family-oriented productions at affordable rates. Past performances have included *Grease*, *Oklahoma*, and *Joseph and the Amazing Technicolor Dreamcoat*. Call for advance tickets and a complete event schedule.

T Bonneville Hot Springs
18 miles east of the Lowman Ranger Station on State Hwy. 21. Contact Boise National Forest Headquarters at 373-4100.

Situated within the Boise National Forest, Bonneville Hot Springs is an undeveloped site featuring a user-built rock pool with sand and silt bottoms. The small pool's temperature varies considerably with steaming water occasionally reaching 101 degrees Fahrenheit. The site is open year-round and receives considerable use.

T Kirkham Hot Springs
4.2 miles east of Lowman on State Hwy. 21. Contact the Boise National Forest Headquarters at 373-4100.

Nestled on the Payette River's south fork at an elevation of 3,900 feet, Kirkham Hot Springs features rock pools with sand and rock bottoms. The odor free pools range in temperature from 102 to 118 degrees Fahrenheit with a steaming hot waterfall as the site's main attraction. The non-commercialized springs are open year-round, but autumn and winter are generally best for soaking due to less congestion. The popular pools are closed daily from 10 PM to 6 AM.

T Sacajawea Hot Springs
East of Lowman. Contact the Boise National Forest Headquarters at 373-4100. From the Lowman Ranger Station, drive 22 miles east on Hwy. 21. Bear right on Forest Rd. 524 (Grandjean Rd.), and proceed 5.2 miles to the springs.

Sacajawea Hot Springs is a natural spring area located within the Boise National Forest at an elevation of 5,600 feet. The beautiful surroundings house several river rock, gravel lined pools with water temperatures varying extensively within each pool. Visitors should plan to visit during low water periods, as the pools can submerge during spring run-off. Deer and elk are frequently sighted in the area, and bull trout are known to inhabit the water surrounding the springs.

T Banks Beach
Off State Hwy. 55 near Banks. Contact the Emmett Ranger District at 365-7000.

Although the Payette River is primarily known as a whitewater extravaganza, Banks Beach provides residents and tourists with easy access to a calmer stretch of the river. The seasonal site does require a small entrance fee and accepts the Visit Idaho Playgrounds Pass.

T Chief Parrish Picnic Area
Near Garden Valley. Contact the Emmett Ranger District at 365-7000.From Banks, bear east on Garden Valley Rd. (Wildlife Canyon Scenic Byway).

Nestled amid spacious mountain wilderness, the Chief Parrish Picnic Area provides a peaceful picnic setting with easy access to the Payette River. The area is a premier wildlife habitat, home to elk, deer, eagles, migratory birds, and hundreds of other mammals. The picnic area is open during summer, fall, and winter and requires a small entrance fee or a Visit Idaho Playgrounds Pass.

T Silver Creek Plunge
2345 Silver Creek Rd., Garden Valley. 585-3134.

Nestled in the Boise National Forest on the Middle Fork of the Payette River, Silver Creek Plunge combines hot springs relaxation with mountain splendor. The hot springs also includes horseshoes, volleyball, basketball, a snack bar/grocery area, and campsites. The springs are open year-round for a small admission fee but are only accessible in winter by snowmobile.

T Rocky Canyon, Fire Crew, and Boiling Springs Natural Hot Springs
Near Crouch. Contact the Boise National Forest Visitor Center at 373-4007. From Crouch, drive on Forest Rd. (FR) 698 (Middle Fork Rd.) past several campgrounds. Approximately 1.5 miles upstream from Hardscrabble Campground, locate Rocky Canyon Hot Springs. At Trail Creek Junction, bear left to continue on FR 698 to Fire Crew Hot Springs and Boiling Springs.

The forested stretches of the Middle Fork of the Payette River north of Crouch are lined with numerous natural hot springs popular with both locals and visitors. Nestled within the Boise National Forest, all three hot springs feature their own unique character and scenic wonders. The first of the springs on Forest Road 698, Rocky Canyon Hot Springs is located across the river from the road and requires users to cautiously wade through the Payette. Upon reaching the highly visible hot pools at the base of Rocky Canyon, visitors will find a large soaking pool set upon the river's bank with a few smaller pools amid the rocky ledges. The pools are filled with runoff from a 120-degree spring flowing down the canyon's steep walls.

After continuing on Forest Road 698 at the Trail Creek Junction, a fork veers off to the left in approximately 0.5 miles. Visitors who take the short road spur will wind down to the Payette River and Fire Crew Hot Springs. Named after the local fire crew who frequently takes dips in the hot pools, Fire Crew Hot Springs is naturally protected from view with the dense woods lining this stretch of the river. Since the pools' water temperatures maintain a consistent 128 degrees Fahrenheit, soaking in the rock-lined pools is generally most comfortable during early spring.

Last but not least, Forest Road 698 winds its way to the Boiling Springs Guard Station and natural hot springs. Located next to the cabin are the popular Boiling Springs. Rushing out of fissures in a rocky cliff, steaming 185 degree Fahrenheit water cascades down the hillside in a large waterfall, passes through a meadow, and eventually dumps into rock-lined pools at the Payette River edge. Although the water cools slightly on its course through the mountain meadow, the water temperatures remain piping hot. Users are encouraged to use caution at all times to avoid possible scalding.

All three natural pools are open to the public free of charge when road and weather conditions permit. Nude bathing is highly discouraged as the pools receive considerable use.

T Payette Forest Fire Interpretive Signs
Along the Ponderosa Pine Scenic Byway (State Hwy. 21) near Lowman.

While providing scenic treasures to passerby, the grand old ponderosa pines lining State Hwy. 21 have been subjected to nature's fury. In 1989, the Lowman Complex fires raged out of control through the area, singing over 72 square miles and devastating everything in its path. Although few Idaho residents thought things could get much worse, a horrible fire season swept over the area just five years later. During the course of the 1994 fire season, more than 100,000 acres were charred near Idaho City, Star Gulch, and Rabbit Creek. To this date, both natural evidence and man-made markers recollect nature's wrath. Interpretive signs along the highway highlight forest regeneration areas.

T Bonneville Hot Springs
18 miles east of the Lowman Ranger Station on State Hwy. 21. Contact Boise National Forest Headquarters at 373-4100.

Situated within the Boise National Forest, Bonneville Hot Springs is an undeveloped site featuring a user-built rock pool with sand and silt bottoms. The small pool's temperature varies considerably with steaming water occasionally reaching 101 degrees Fahrenheit. The site is open year-round and receives considerable use.

TV Deadwood Reservoir
Northeast of Garden Valley off State Hwy. 21. Contact the Boise National Forest Headquarters at 373-4100. Drive east from Garden Valley on S. Fork River Rd. At Forest Rd. 555 (Scott Mountain Rd.), bear north and proceed 26 miles to the reservoir.

The scenic, 3,000-acre Deadwood Reservoir is a year-round alpine delight for hikers, campers, anglers, and boaters. Cutthroat and rainbow trout are frequently caught here along with Atlantic Chinook and kokanee salmon. In fact, Idaho's state record for an Atlantic salmon was set at Deadwood Reservoir in 1995 when a thirteen pound, four ounce whopper was snagged. The reservoir is free but does require navigating back-country forest roads that are steep and occasionally washed out. Interested visitors should call the Forest Service Headquarters for the latest road conditions prior to departure.

V Garden Valley Snowmobile Trails
Garden Valley. Contact the Garden Valley Chamber of Commerce at 462-5003.

Beginning at Terrace Lake Resort, the Garden Valley Snowmobile Trail System provides 137 groomed miles of fun through Idaho's frosty landscape. The free trail system connects with several other area trails, including trails that depart from Smith's Ferry. Groomed Garden Valley trails lead to Silver Creek, Six Mile, Boiling Springs, and more, while miles of ungroomed trails wind to the top of Garden Mountain. The trails are open to the public during daylight hours.

M Garden Valley Chamber of Commerce
PO Box 10, Garden Valley. 462-5003.
www.gvchamber.org; gvchamber@micron.net

9 Food, Lodging

Idaho City
Pop. 458

When Idaho City was founded in 1862, it was the most important mining town in the Boise Basin, producing more gold than all of the Alaskan mines! Naturally, prospectors swarmed to the area in search of their fortune, bringing with them gamblers, "ladies," and lawmen by the hundreds. The town had its share of saloons and law offices, as well as two bowling alleys, a bookstore, painter's shop, mattress factory, two jewelry stores, a photographer's gallery, and a hospital. The town also possessed two main streets, each said to be one-half mile long. At one time larger than Portland and recognized as the largest city in the northwest, Idaho City boasted a population of nearly 20,000 by 1864. It wasn't all fun and games, however, as fires ripped through the city in 1865, 1867, 1868 and 1871, causing extensive damage each time. By 1870, when several Chinese emigrants began to arrive, most of the gold had been taken from the streams. These foreigners, who frequently suffered intense discrimination, soon accounted for one-half of the city's population. Throughout the next decade, the fading town clung to life with a few quartz-lode claims and sparse gold mining activity.

Today, Idaho City is a sleepy historic town, with dredges and evidence of hydraulic mining covering the land as a reminder of the community's heritage and past economic vitality.

Atlanta
Pop. 50

Founded in approximately 1863 in the shadow of the Sawtooth Mountains, this remote mountain village was once home to as many as 500 miners and their families. The "Atlanta Lode," a quartz-gold deposit about one and a half miles long and twenty feet wide, promised large rewards, but its inaccessibility challenged the miners. The ore from Atlanta was high in silver, but as it was processed, much of the silver was lost, thereby reducing its value by nearly three-quarters. Because of this and the lack of effective transportation and technology, work in the Atlanta mines was slow through the early and mid 1870s. At its peak, from 1878-1884, high-grade ore was taken from the hills, but once that was exhausted, work again diminished as mining the low-grade, large ore deposits became economically inefficient.

In 1932, St. Joseph Lead Company purchased the claims and began operating an amalgamation-flotation concentrator method of extraction. This resolved many of the accessibility issues, and once a road was built between Atlanta and Boise in 1936, the transportation issues were resolved as well. During that time, from 1932-1936, the Atlanta Mining District was Idaho's leading gold producer. A nearby mine, the Talache (one mile from Atlanta) also produced outstanding amounts of gold after World War II, and when that closed in 1953, the total mining efforts of the Atlanta area had reached $16 million!

Today, the town of Atlanta is home to just a handful of people and numerous ghosts of its past. Despite losing it's mining economic staple, the near ghost town has managed to preserve its history, pioneer-era buildings, and serene setting near the Sawtooth Wilderness boundary. Even the old jail still stands in the town's Community Historic Park.

Centerville
Approximately 7 miles northwest of Idaho City

Founded during the spring of 1863, Centerville drew its name from its prime location between the settlements of Placerville and Idaho City. Once considered by many as the prettiest town in the Boise Basin, Centerville reached a peak population of 3,000 residents before becoming a ghost town. Today, Protestant and Catholic cemeteries are all that mark this former town site. A new Centerville still exists and is situated approximately three miles south of the original community site.

Pioneerville
7.1 miles north of Centerville in Boise County

J. Marion Moore and other members of the Splawn-Grimes discovery party set out in the fall of 1862 in search of gold. After just one month of searching, the party staked claims on October 7, and Moore established Pioneerville, the first town in the Boise Basin. Moore's party quickly ran out of supplies, so several men left for Walla Walla and Lewiston to gather needed materials for the site. Fearing an Indian attack, the remaining miners constructed a twelve-foot high wall around their town and remained inside until supplies arrived six weeks later. At the same time, Jefferson Standifer and other prospectors arrived in Pioneerville. Noting that all the claims had been staked, Standifer nicknamed the town "Fort Hog'em" before leaving Pioneerville. Once the community was adequately supplied again, the first post office in Boise Basin was established in 1864 with the population swelling to 2,000. Although Pioneerville is now just another ghost town, it is remembered as producing some of the richest gold ore in Idaho with values reaching up to $20,000 per ton.

H The Old Toll Road
Milepost 20.3 on State Hwy. 21

The Old Toll Road to Idaho City crossed the ridge from Boise through the lowest point you can see in the skyline across the valley. Climbing the More's Creek canyon wall, it crossed this highway about here and swung north. The road was built, and stage services began in 1864 when Idaho City was the largest town in the Pacific Northwest. Even though the road was shorter than today's highway, it was a long, hard day's trip from Boise to Idaho City. A stage from this run is in the Idaho Historical Museum.

H Grimes' Creek
Milepost 28.9 on State Hwy. 21

Named for George Grimes, who with Moses Splawn led the party that on August 2, 1862, made the strike that started the Boise Basin gold rush. The party was searching for a rich basin described to Splawn a year earlier by an Indian. Further up this creek, they found the gold they were looking for. A few days later, Grimes was killed at Grimes' Pass (it was blamed on Indians), and his partners had to bury him in a prospect hole nearby.

H Idaho City
Milepost 38.8 on State Hwy. 21

This roaring metropolis was founded early in October 1862, about 10 weeks after gold was discovered in Boise Basin. By the next summer, this was the largest city in the Northwest, with 6,275 people – 5,691 of them men! Families followed, and respectable businesses, schools, libraries, good theaters, churches and fraternal orders soon came. The town survived several disastrous fires and remained an important mining center until the war shut down gold production in 1942.

T Atlanta Historical Society
Drive north of Idaho City on State Hwy. 21. Proceed to downtown Atlanta via the well-maintained Crooked River Rd. 384, Swanholm Creek Rd. 327, and Middle Fork Rd. 268. www.atlantaidaho.org

In the isolated old mining town of Atlanta, the Historical Society is on a mission to preserve the town's heritage. The town's 1910 jail now houses historic photos and artifacts of Rocky Bar and Atlanta from its mining heyday. Next door, a restored 1870s cabin provides visitors with a glimpse into early pioneer life on the Idaho frontier. The museum is open in the summer from 10 AM to 9 PM and year-round by appointment.

T Boise Basin Historical Museum
402 Montgomery St. (at the corner of Montgomery and Wall Sts.), Idaho City. 392-4550.

Idaho City's gold mining heritage is captured in this informative museum emphasizing the region's history from 1863 to 1890. Housed in a building utilized as a post office in 1867 and later as a Wells Fargo station, the museum is home to several old mining tools, regional artifacts, memorabilia, and historic photos. Costumed hosts lead visitors through several interpretive displays and present a video about Boise Basin's history. The museum also explores historic buildings in the village as well as the 1864 territorial penitentiary. With free admission, the museum is open daily 11 AM to 4 PM Memorial Day to Labor Day, and 11 AM to 4 PM on Saturdays and Sundays the rest of the year.

T Idaho City Historical Building Tour
Contact the Idaho City Chamber of Commerce at 392-6000.

Once a bustling city boasting a population larger than Portland, Oregon, Idaho City's golden days are indisputably long gone. However, many buildings that witnessed the hustle and bustle of this rich gold mining camp remain.

Masonic Temple
Wall St.
In 1864, Idaho City received its long-requested charter for a Masonic Temple, and construction on the two-story, white building began in 1865. Although lodge meetings were moved to Boise in 1920, temple members still gather at the Idaho City Temple each June to honor their forefathers. The temple is reputedly the oldest Masonic Temple west of the Mississippi that is still used.

Idaho Territorial Penitentiary
Wall St.
Built entirely out of hand-hewn logs, the Idaho Territorial Penitentiary was constructed in 1864 at a cost of $10,000. Before a larger penitentiary was built in Boise, this prison served not only Boise County, but also all of Idaho Territory. During its history, the prison housed 106 convicts, twenty-six of whom were paroled and seventeen that escaped and were never caught. The building was once located west of the city but was moved to its present locale in 1953.

Boise Basin Museum
Corner of Montgomery St.
Distinguished by its iron window shutters, this brick building was constructed in 1867 as the Central News Depot Post Office and James Pinney Bookstore. Today, the historic building appropriately houses the Boise Basin Historical Museum's extensive collection of area photographs, artifacts, and tools.

511 Montgomery St.
This small board structure was built in 1870 to house the Idaho City fire station. From 1920 to 1930, the building doubled as the Boise County Jail.

Idaho City Schoolhouse
West side of Main St.
Built in 1891, this three-story white clapboard building served as Idaho City's school until a new structure was built in 1962. Today, the historic building serves dually as the City Hall and a community church.

Miner's Exchange Saloon
Main and Wall Sts.
The brick Miner's Exchange and Saloon building was once one of the most active sites in all of Idaho City. Miners brought their precious gold dust here in hopes of exchanging it for a hefty amount of cash they could then spend on the saloon's booze. Today, the structure is home to the County Recorder and Auditor's Offices.

Boise County Courthouse
Main and Wall Sts.
Built in 1873 to house a community general store, this structure next hosted a hotel before being revamped into the Boise County Courthouse in 1909.

Idaho World Building
On the east corner of Main and Commercial Sts.
Constructed in 1867, the Idaho World Building serves as headquarters for the state's oldest functioning newspaper.

Boise Basin Mercantile
On the west corner of Main and Commercial Sts.
Complete with four arched doorways, this brick building was erected in 1865 as the Boise Basin Mercantile. To date, it is one of Idaho's oldest continuously operating general stores.

St. Joseph Catholic Church
Wallula St.
The white, wooden St. Joseph Catholic Church was constructed in 1863 in just thirty days. The religious center represents the first Idaho Catholic Church built specifically for white settlers.

Kestlers
Corner of Wallula and Main Sts.
Kestlers was originally constructed as a blacksmith shop and once housed a community newspaper.

Idaho City Hotel
Corner of Wallula and Montgomery Sts.
Operating during Idaho City's mining hey-day, the Idaho City Hotel is still going strong and welcomes guests year-round. The country inn is complemented with several antiques.

I.O.O.F. Hall
North of St. Joseph Catholic Church on Wallula St.
Constructed in 1875, Idaho City's I.O.O.F. Hall is recognized as the oldest Odd Fellows Lodge west of the Mississippi River. The two-story building still serves a faithful group of members.

Pon Yam House
Corner of Commercial and Montgomery Sts
The Pon Yam House was once home to Idaho City's most prosperous Chinese miner and businessman. During its golden mining years, Idaho City hosted more Chinese miners than any other mining settlement of similar size in Idaho. It is estimated that at one time, more than one-third of Idaho City's population was Chinese.

Pioneer Cemetery
West of North Main St. on Centerville Rd.
On the outskirts of town lies Pioneer Cemetery. Of the first 200 people buried there, rumor suggests that only twenty-eight died of natural causes. Many of the historic graves are enclosed with ornate wooden and iron fences.

T Idaho City Visitor Center
Corner of Main St. and State Hwy. 21, Idaho City. 392-6040.

The Idaho City Visitor Center greets guest with open arms to this historic mining camp. The center, staffed with knowledgeable employees, provides a plethora of community and regional information and happily answers questions. The center is open daily during summer.

T Atlanta Hot Springs
Directly east of Atlanta on Forest Rd. 227. Write info@atlantaidaho.org for additional information.

Tucked against the base of the Sawtooth Mountains, Atlanta is known for its easily accessible natural hot springs. One such spring bearing the town's name is a particular favorite. Situated underneath a large stand of gigantic old-growth ponderosa pines, Atlanta Hot Springs is a roadside spring consisting of a six by twelve foot rock and masonry pool. The pool's temperature maintains a fairly consistent 105 degrees, and a hand-hewn bench inside the pool provides the utmost in soaking comfort. The free pool is generally usable by late spring.

T Chattanooga Hot Springs
Directly east of Atlanta on Forest Rd. 227. Write info@atlantaidaho.org for additional information. After passing Atlanta Hot Springs, take a spur road leading north to a grassy bluff area. Park here, and then climb down the steep path leading to the springs.

Chattanooga Hot Springs near Atlanta is ranked among Idaho's finest natural, undeveloped hot springs. Situated on the Middle Fork of the Boise River beneath scenic cliffs, Chattanooga not only delivers breathtaking scenery, but also a 122 degree Fahrenheit waterfall that cascades over a bluff into a rock-lined pool. The sandy-bottomed pool naturally maintains ideal soaking temperatures year-round with adjacent river access providing the opportunity for a cool-down. Hidden just fifty feet west of the main pool is a little known about hot pool complete with its own steaming waterfall shower. Chattanooga Hot Springs is frequently visited, so users are encouraged to use discretion as far as swimsuits are concerned.

T Grimes Pass
North of Pioneerville At Idaho City, merge off State Hwy. 21. Continue through Centerville and Pioneerville on the improved dirt road.

Named after the Splawn-Grimes discovery party that staked numerous area claims, Grimes Pass rests at an elevation of 5,099 feet. The steep pass features a memorial to miner, George Grimes, near the roadside. From the pass, drivers wind down a steep grade across the South Fork of the Payette River, eventually arriving in Garden Valley.

T More's Creek Summit
North of Idaho City on State Hwy. 21

As drivers wind north from Idaho City through the forested landscape shrouding State Hwy. 21, More's Creek Summit awaits at an elevation of 6,117 feet. Between Idaho City and the summit, extensive evidence of the area's mining history is recorded in the presence of roadside ditches.

TV Boise National Forest
North and east of Boise. Contact the Boise National Forest Headquarters at 373-4100.

Surrounding the city of Boise and encompassing 2,612,000 forested acres, the Boise National Forest has weathered years of gold mining, logging, and homesteading as it has transformed itself into a recreational hot spot. The forest ranges in elevation from 2,600 to 9,800 feet with mixed stands of ponderosa pines, Douglas fir, Engelmann spruce, subalpine fir, and lodgepole pine. With the Boise, Payette, and the South and Middle Fork of the Salmon Rivers running through the forest along with miles of hiking and biking trails, forest visitors have endless recreation opportunities. Visitors are greeted with more than eighty campgrounds and picnic areas, all providing their own unique glimpse into this scenic ecosystem. The forest is open year-round for ATV riding, backcountry skiing, snowmobiling, camping, hiking, horseback riding, hunting, mountain biking, rafting, and wildlife viewing with no access fee assessed.

V Banner Ridge Nordic Ski Trails
22 miles north of Idaho City on State Hwy. 21. Contact the Idaho Department of Parks and Recreation at 334-4199.

Banner Ridge offers intermediate and expert skiers sixteen miles of periodically groomed trails. The area's groomed trails include Elkhorn Loop, Alpine Loop, Banner Loop, Cougar Trail, and Snowshoe Loop. Area highlights also include breathtaking views from the ridgetop along with access to off-trail skiing and fresh powder in several open bowls. The area is part of Idaho's Park N' Ski system, and permits are required. Permits may be obtained at the nearest Ranger Station, and fees are as follows: $25 annual permit (good at all Idaho Park N' Ski areas), $7.50 3-day permit, and $2 day use permit.

V Gold Fork Nordic Ski Trails
20 miles northeast of Idaho City on State Hwy. 21. Contact the Idaho Department of Parks and Recreation at 334-4199.

Comprised of long groomed loops and shorter side loops, the Gold Fork Nordic Ski Trail System offers twenty-one miles of winter fun. The trails, which accommodate practiced beginners to experts, are groomed weekly and include the Gold Fork Loop, Lodgepole Loop, Double Dip Loop, Moose Loop, Summit Trail, Skyline Loop, Beaver Trail, Ralph's Trail, and Ridge Trail. Those skiers with advanced skills also enjoy access to powder bowls and steep downhill runs. The area is part of Idaho's Park N' Ski system, and permits are required. Permits may be obtained at the nearest Ranger Station, and fees are as follows: $25 annual permit (good at all Idaho Park N' Ski areas), $7.50 3-day permit, and $2 day use permit.

V Whoop-Um-Up Nordic Ski Trails
18 miles northeast of Idaho City on State Hwy. 21. Contact the Idaho Department of Parks and Recreation at 334-4199.

Covering nearly seven miles of terrain, the Whoop-Um-Up Nordic Ski Trails are most appropriate for intermediate to expert level skiers. Many of the loops feature short, steep sections, and several of the downhill areas require technical maneuvering. Area trails include the Whoop-Um-Up Loop, Upper Lamar Loop, Pilgrim Loop, Lower Lamar Loop, Valley Trail, and Wagon Trail. Although the trails are marked, they are not groomed. The area is part of Idaho's Park N' Ski system, and permits are required. Permits may be obtained at the nearest Ranger Station, and fees are as follows: $25 annual permit (good at all Idaho Park N' Ski areas), $7.50 3-day permit, and $2 day use permit.

M Idaho City Chamber of Commerce
180 Main St., Idaho City. 392-6000. www.idahocitychamber.com

10 Food

Ola
Pop. 25

A small store, old church, cemetery, and plenty of character make up this quiet ranching community platted alongside the banks of Squaw Creek.

Horseshoe Bend
Pop. 770

Established on a horseshoe-shaped bend in the Payette River, Horseshoe Bend began as a gold mining settlement in 1890. Mahlon B. Moore, who arrived in 1862 or 1863, is reportedly credited as the town's first settler. The post office was established in 1867, and the railroad completed a line to the town in 1910.

Gardena
Pop. 60

Located on the North Fork of the Payette River, Gardena received its name from Oregon Short Line Railroad officials in 1914. Some say the name was chosen to make the area sound appealing to potential settlers. However, the name did little to attract homesteaders, and the town retains its historic small population.

Placerville
Pop. 60

In December of 1862, a group of California men founded this small mining town. It became the first mining camp miners and freighters encountered when they entered the Boise Basin along Harris Creek and the Payette River. Due to its ideal location and abundant mining opportunities, the tiny village quickly grew to encompass more than 3,200 residents within a year from its founding. Placer mining was visible everywhere from Main St., and the town's name reflects this activity. By 1869, manmade ditches and flumes aided in the operation of twenty hydraulic mining machines. Eventually, the ore ran thin through Placerville's creeks, and today the area is a virtual ghost town. The Henrietta Penrod Museum stands in what was once the Magnolia Saloon, and a community cemetery rests just outside of town. One particular gravestone states, "Fiddlers murdered in Ophir Creek," and serves as the source of an interesting tale about early justice in the Wild West.

According to legend, in 1863, two fiddlers had played at a Placerville dance and were walking to nearby Centerville the following morning when they came upon the mugging and subsequent murder of a wealthy miner. The perpetrator, desiring no witnesses to the crime, then killed the two innocent fiddlers. When the victims were discovered, John Williams and two of his partners were arrested on hearsay alone. The evidence was meager, and the district court found them not guilty. A special grand jury then charged Williams with assault and robbery. Since there was no criminal law in place in 1863, Williams' attorney argued that Williams had not committed any crimes. You see, in the Organic Act of Idaho Territory, Congress neglected to transfer the use of the old Washington Territorial code and failed to declare its own territorial laws. Therefore, Idaho had no criminal law until one year later when the Territorial Legislature passed the Criminal Practices Act. Based upon that, Williams was released. He fled from the area, and no one was ever convicted of the fiddlers' murders.

Sweet
Pop. 65

This tiny town is situated at the bottom of Squaw Creek Valley at the mouth of Squaw Creek, and traces its origins back to the 1870s. Setting out from Ohio, Ezekiel Sweet arrived in the valley in 1877. Here, he met his wife, Isabel, and the couple settled in the valley. During this time, the area was a popular freight stop on the journey to the Buffalo Hump mining district. In 1884, Ezekiel

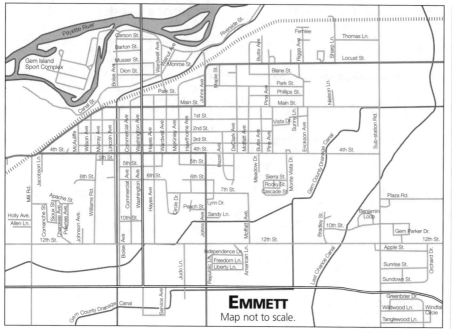

EMMETT
Map not to scale.

decided to open a post office to better serve residents' needs. Although he hoped to name the town "Squaw Creek," the postal service balked at the length of the name, and the town was then christened "Sweet" after its first postmaster. The town's most prosperous year came in 1905 with the gold rush to Thunder Mountain in the Chamberlain Basin. The economy rapidly grew, and the town was soon home to a bank, hotel, flourmill, saloons, lodge halls, a newspaper, and a church. Unfortunately, as the mining boom ended, so did most business activity in Sweet. Today, Sweet is a sleepy village where visitors can still find the town's namesake buried in Sweet-Montour Cemetery, as well as a local park marking a natural spring where freight horses drank during the late 1800s.

H Horse Shoe Bend
Milepost 64.4 on State Hwy. 55 at Horseshoe Bend City Park

Gold was struck in Boise Basin (over the ridge to the east) in 1862, and the rush to these new mines came through here. Traffic came by steamer up the Columbia to Umatilla and then overland. At first there were only pack and saddle trains, but in 1864, John Hailey, a famous Idaho pioneer, ran stages this way. A toll road up Harris Creek was opened shortly. Though other routes to the Basin also developed, freighters continued to come through Horse Shoe Bend for many years.

T Thunder Mountain Line
120 Mill Rd., Horseshoe Bend. 793-4425

Traveling through scenic Payette country, the Thunder Mountain Line carries travelers back to Idaho's golden days. Under the operation of the Idaho Northern and Pacific Railroad, the Thunder Mountain Line offers three different rides. For a two and one-half hour mountain experience, the Horseshoe Bend Express carries passengers from Horseshoe Bend to Banks while the Cabarton Flyer travels through the nation's shortest solid rock tunnel on its journey from Cascade to Smith's Ferry. Those passengers with more time may opt for the five-hour Cascade Limited train that winds through the Boise National Forest and up steep grades into the mountains. All scenic train rides offer beautiful mountain vistas and the opportunity to view regional wildlife. Adventurous passen-

gers may wish to ride the train one-way and then take a rafting trip back down the Payette River. Ticket prices vary according to age, and excursions are offered year-round on weekends with an extended summer schedule.

T Bread Loaf Rock
5 miles south of Horseshoe Bend on State Hwy. 55

Aptly named after its striking resemblance to a freshly cut loaf of bread, Bread Loaf Rock is nestled approximately 300 yards below State Hwy. 55's eastern shoulder. The giant loaf has been shaped entirely through the natural process of time and erosion.

TV Sage Hen Reservoir
Immediately north of Ola off State Hwy. 52. Contact the Idaho Department of Parks and Recreation at 334-4199.

Tucked in the shadows of mountains and densely wooded forests, Sage Hen Reservoir encompasses 270 scenic acres. The reservoir features a few developed campsites, a boat ramp for motorboats, and a 0.5-mile nature trail. Waterskiing is prohibited to protect the lake's ecosystem, and anglers will find healthy populations of rainbow trout. For picnickers, the Sagehen Dam Picnic Area offers a day-use fee site on the reservoir's west side. The reservoir is situated in known bear country, so visitors are encouraged to follow all bear safety precautions.

M Horseshoe Bend Chamber of Commerce
112 Ada, Horseshoe Bend. 793-2363.
www.horseshoebendchamber.com

11 *Food, Lodging*

Emmett
Pop. 5,490

The year 1862 saw the arrival of the first emigrants to this area. They traveled over Freezeout Hill and across the Payette River where Emmett now lies. Some members of the group were headed to Oregon; others wanted to find their way to the Florence Basin mines. In 1864, two men, Nathaniel Martin and Jonathan Smith, settled at the Emmett townsite and built a roadhouse and ferry. They charged $1.00 for a team and $.25 for an individual to cross over. The two men named their growing settlement Martinsville.

In 1870 a post office was established seven miles from Martindale. Thomas Cahalan was named the first postmaster and thereby received authority to dub the town Emmettsville after his son, Emmett. In 1900, the name was shortened to Emmett. Six years later, the post office was moved to Martinsville, and the name Emmett followed.

James Wardell is recognized for organizing and platting the townsite in 1883. He laid out the streets, and in 1884, a bridge was built across the Payette River. When the Rossi irrigation ditch was established, orchards were planted with apples, cherries, peaches, and apricots. The orchards' profit potential increased greatly when the Oregon Short Line Railroad linked the town to large markets in 1902. By 1928, Emmett had established itself as the largest export stop along the Union Pacific line, shipping out not only fruit, but also lumber, livestock, and ice. Wool was also distributed through Emmett, sheared from the 100,000 sheep that were raised in the area. Before the construction of the Black Canyon Dam which interfered with spawning, salmon fishing used to be a significant industry in the area. Today, most of the industries that helped establish Emmett remain as economic mainstays.

Letha
Pop. 100

Founded along the Union Pacific Railroad and the Enterprise Canal, Letha was named after Letha Wilton, the only daughter of railroad official, W.W. Wilton. Mr. Wilton helped sponsor the New Plymouth railroad extension to Emmett, and postal services were established here in 1912.

H Pearl
Milepost 11 on State Hwy. 16 at the Scenic Overlook

Long after its discovery in 1867, a mining camp flourished next to a gold lode below Crown Point on this ridge 4 miles west of here. Pearl boasted 3 stores, 4 saloons, a butcher shop, a fire station, a church, a school, 2 hotels, and an Odd Fellows' Lodge before it declined. A revival was considered as late as 1982, when high gold prices had increased Pearl's early production value to $12,000,000.

H Freezeout Hill
Milepost 11 on State Hwy. 16 at the Scenic Overlook

In 1862, Tim Goodale opened an Oregon Trail cutoff that descended a steep ridge just west of here into the valley below. Later that year a gold rush to Boise Basin came up Payette Valley, and the next summer farmers along the river started raising crops to supply the mines. For a year or more they were troubled by a notorious band of horse thieves based at Pickett's Corral located at the head of the valley before you. Late in 1864, the farmers organized the Payette Vigilance Committee and drove out the Pickett Corral gang.

H Black Canyon Dam
Milepost 39.1 on State Hwy. 52 at Black Canyon Dam Park

Constructed in 1924, this $1.5 million concrete gravity dam has a 1,039-foot crest and a 183-foot structural height. A 29-mile-long canal, along with lesser ditches, serves 58,250 acres of Boise and Payette valley farms. A power plant at Black Canyon Dam generates electricity for commercial use as well as for irrigation pumping. Farms far from early riverside canals benefit from this project.

T Freezeout Hill
7 miles southeast of Emmett on State Hwy. 16

Overlooking the lush Valley of Plenty and city of Emmett, Freezeout Hill marks a historic point on the Oregon Trail. In 1862, mountain man Tim Goodale led a train of Oregon Trail travelers down the long, steep hill, across the Payette River, and to the present site of Emmett. In order to safely traverse the trail, pioneers were forced to lock or "freeze" up their wagon wheels so they could slide down the hill, thus giving the area its name. This frightening route became known as Goodale's Cutoff, and a portion of the trail can still be found just west of the highway on Freezout Hill. Every April, this historic site is home to Emmett's Blossom Sunday. Lined with orchards and flowers, the valley below is a beautiful kaleidoscope of color.

T Squaw Butte
From downtown Emmett, drive north on State Hwy. 52 to Emmett Bench. Drive straight on Van Deusen Rd. and then bear right onto Butte Rd. At Lookout Rd. turn left and continue 7 miles to the butte.

Throughout much of southwestern Idaho, the shadow of Squaw Butte's 5,906-foot towering peak is visible. The butte draws its name from the valley's early Native Americans who saw the profile of an Indian maid watching over them from the butte. Squaw Butte became an officially developed site in 1933 when the Bureau of Land Management developed a lookout on the summit. Although the original cabin burned, the present two-story log cabin constructed in 1981 is still staffed each summer. Today, Squaw Butte affords visitors panoramic views of southwestern Idaho and has also become a popular launching point for hang gliders.

T Picket's Corral
4 miles north of Emmett on the east side of State Hwy. 52

Formed from lava cliffs cradling a tight canyon, Picket's Corral is the infamous site of horse thieves, bandits, murderers, and bogus gold mine operators who wreaked havoc on Emmett during its early days. In the 1860s, numerous outlaws hid stolen horses and merchandise in the corral before selling it in Oregon, and pioneers lived in fear of the rowdy gang. Eventually, the Payette Vigilantes formed under the direction of future Idaho governor, William J. McConnell, and the outlaws were brought to justice. Today, these cliffs are visible from the highway, and the remains of the first structure built in the Emmett Valley can be found here bordered with a ten-foot stockade.

T Roystone Hot Springs
10 miles north of Emmett

Upon its founding in the early 1900s, these hot springs were developed into a rich fruit and vegetable farm with the produce given to area miners. In 1923, Roy Stone and his wife purchased the springs, and Mrs. Stone was responsible for turning the area into a lucrative summer resort and health spa. With temperatures reaching up to 151 degrees, most of the hot springs are now part of a private residence. However, a large open-air swimming pool is still open to the public and is a popular area attraction among locals and tourists.

T Emmett City Golf Course
2102 Salesyard Rd., Emmett. 365-2675.

This 2,910 yard, par-36 course stretches amid narrow fairways and numerous water traps. Most interesting, however, is that the airport runway runs right through the course! Green fees for this challenging 18-hole course are $12 Monday through Thursday and $15 on weekends. Golfers are urged to schedule tee times at least two days in advance for weekends and holidays.

T Firebird Raceway
7 miles south of Emmett on State Hwy. 16. 938-8986. www.firebirdonline.com

Racing enthusiasts across southwestern Idaho and the western U.S. flock to Firebird Raceway for more than 45 different races held each year from late March through October. As a National Hot Rod Association member track since 1968, the raceway hosts a variety of events including roadster shows and junior drag racing. The track's largest weekend of racing occurs in August at the annual Pepsi Nightfire Nationals, and a schedule of events can be found online.

T Gem County Historical Museum
501 E. 1st St., Emmett. 365-9530 or 365-4340.

The Gem County Historical Museum opened in 1973 and is committed to preserving the history of life from past to present in Emmett and the surrounding area. Exhibits focus upon such areas as the Native Americans who once inhabited the area, fur trappers, miners, early settlers, a full-sized display of a general store, parlor, and early 20th century laundry room, and an old doctor's and dentist's office. In addition, several period pieces of clothing, pianos, office equipment, and photos are displayed. The museum is free of charge and is open from 10:30 AM to 5:30 PM Wednesday through Friday and 12 PM to 5 PM on Saturdays in the summer and 10:30 AM to 4 PM Wednesday through Friday during the winter.

TV Black Canyon Dam and Reservoir
4.5 miles northeast of Emmett on State Hwy. 52. 365-2682 or 365-2600.

Originating in 1905 with an idea to divert water from the Payette River into the Emmett Valley, the 183-foot Black Canyon Dam was completed in 1924 at a cost of $1.5 million. Built for the Bureau of Reclamation as part of the Boise reclamation project, the dam is situated on natural basalt formations and still provides water to Emmett's agricultural community.

The resulting large Black Canyon Reservoir accommodates a variety of water sports, including swimming, boating, waterskiing, and fishing. Locals and tourists alike can enjoy the many day use areas located along the reservoir's shores for a small fee. Wild Rose Park is a popular picnic area surrounded by a rose garden and gazebo. On the eastern shore, visitors will find Triangle Park with its boat ramp and dock. To the west is Black Canyon Park. Perhaps the most used day area, this park offers a designated swimming area, sandy beaches, shaded picnic sites, and a boat-launching ramp.

TV Montour Wildlife & Recreation Area
East of Emmett off State Hwy. 52. Contact the Gem County Chamber of Commerce at 365-3485.

East of Emmett lies the former town of Montour. During the late 1800s, Montour flourished as a stage stop for those heading to the Boise Basin's prosperous mines. When the railroad arrived in 1900, a line was built through town and the community's population and economic vitality surged. But when the Great Depression hit and the Black Canyon Dam was formed, Montour's bright hopes for the future disintegrated. Water from the newly constructed dam began seeping into town, and residents were forced to move. When the Bureau of Reclamation bought out all the landowners in 1976, Montour was developed into a recreation area and wildlife sanctuary. Today, the 1,100-acre preserve is a popular wildlife viewing destination home to raptors, mammals, upland game birds, and numerous waterfowl. In addition, outdoor enthusiasts will find plenty of opportunities for angling, hunting, camping, and picnicking.

M Emmett - Gem County Chamber of Commerce
127 E. Main St., Emmett. www.emmettidaho.com; chamber@emmettidaho.com

12 *Food, Lodging*

Payette
Pop. 7,054

Located where the Payette and Snake Rivers merge, this community was first called Payettenville. A store operated here in 1867, and in 1871 the town boasted the only post office between Baker, Oregon and Boise. The name was later changed to honor Francois Payette, Hudson Bay Company's operator at Fort Boise (see also Parma). Francois was regarded as one of the West's most hospitable gentleman before he moved to Canada upon retiring. The town truly owes its existence and subsequent boom to two factors. The first factor which drove up the population was the 1882 arrival of the Oregon Short Line Railroad. During that time, the nearby railroad camp was called Boomerang, and some of the workers stayed in the region upon the railroad's completion. The brothers A.B. and Frank Moss were the second influence on the community. They were originally railroad employees who later opened the popular Merchant Mercantile in Boomerang. When the railroad construction crews picked up camp, the brothers picked up their business and moved it to Payette. The business in turn brought area settlers to the fledgling settlement for supplies, and the rest is history!

Fruitland
Pop. 3,805

Once known as Zeller's Crossing (for A. Zeller, who plotted the town in 1908), Fruitland is renowned for its apple and prune orchards. During peak production from 1916-1930, six packing sheds and an evaporator were needed to keep up with the abundant supply of fruit. Dirt-covered cellars were built to store the apples until they could be packed in winter months. Today, temperature-controlled storage warehouses contain thousands of bins of fruit as well as frozen

Payette	Jan	Feb	March	April	May	June	July	Aug	Sep	Oct	Nov	Dec	Annual
Average Max. Temperature (F)	36.7	45.6	57.3	66.6	75.2	83.2	92.5	90.9	81.1	67.6	50.7	39.3	65.6
Average Min. Temperature (F)	20.2	24.7	30.8	36.4	44.3	51.3	56.8	54.9	45.8	35.7	28.0	22.5	37.6
Average Total Precipitation (in.)	1.53	1.07	0.98	0.83	1.02	0.77	0.23	0.35	0.41	0.68	1.24	1.51	10.61
Average Total Snowfall (in.)	6.7	2.6	0.3	0.0	0.0	0.0	0.0	0.0	0.0	0.0	1.4	5.6	16.6
Average Snow Depth (in.)	2	1	0	0	0	0	0	0	0	0	0	1	0

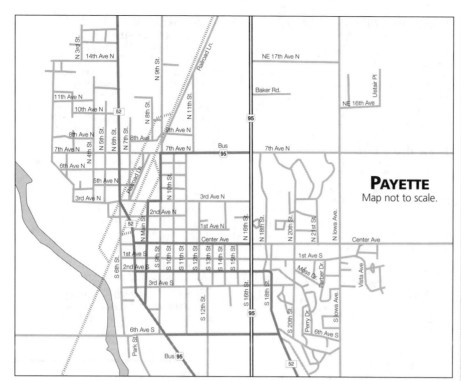

PAYETTE
Map not to scale.

FRUITLAND
Map not to scale.

products from the area's orchards. The agricultural community is often jokingly referred to as "The Big Apple of Idaho."

H Snake River
Milepost 1, Eastbound on I-84, at the Snake River View Rest Area

The valley of the snake, historic passage from the Midwest to the Northwest, has been a primary route for travel since the days of Indians and fur traders. The Oregon Trail forded the river at Old Fort Boise, the Hudson's Bay Co. post 23 miles upstream. Many a famous early westerner saw the valley you now see – though the look of the land has changed since white settlement brought irrigated farms. Today, the river provides both irrigation and power along its 1,000-mile course from the Yellowstone country to the Columbia River. Hwy.s, railroads, and airlines follow its open valley east of here; but to the north, Hells Canyon of the Snake River is still almost impassable to man.

H Salmon Festival
Milepost 1, Eastbound on I-84, at the Snake River View Rest Area

Long before fur hunters explored here in 1811, an annual Indian festival was held each July in this area. Indian people came great distances to trade and celebrate and arrange intertribal marriages. Cheyenne and Arapaho bands brought elegant tipi poles from Colorado. Crow and Shoshoni buffalo hunters supplied meat and hides from Montana and Wyoming. Nez Perce and Walla Walla horsemen marketed superior stock they had developed, and Paiute weapon and toolmakers provided obsidian from central Oregon. All were attracted to this river area for its excellent salmon fishing.

T Payette County Historical Museum
90 S. 9th St., Payette. 642-4883.

Payette's rich heritage is captured in this well-maintained museum. The town's intriguing architectural history lends itself to a self-guided walking tour, and the museum features vintage

clothing, furniture, and photos depicting Payette's development. One of the most popular exhibits is baseball memorabilia from Payette native, Harmon Killebrew. Killebrew played twenty-two years in the major league and earned the reputation as one of the league's greatest home-run hitters during his time. The museum is open 12 PM to 4 PM Wednesday through Saturday with free admission.

T Centennial Park
Northwest end of Payette near the Idaho/Oregon border on State Hwy. 52. Contact the Payette Chamber of Commerce at 642-2362.

Payette's Centennial Park was established in 1988 in celebration of the community's centennial. The ten-acre park has grown to include picnic tables and grills, sports fields, and a boat ramp providing convenient access to the adjacent Snake River. The park is a popular summer launching spot for water skiers and jet-skiers.

T Central Park
Center Ave, Payette. Contact the Payette Chamber of Commerce at 642-2362.

Central Park in Payette mixes history and recreation for a one-of-a-kind park atmosphere. Situated on the founding site of Payette's 1885 schoolhouse, the park includes war memorials, a canon used in World War I, picnic tables, rose gardens, a playground area, and basketball courts. The park is also home to the Payette Public Library.

T Scotch Pines Golf Course
10610 Scotch Pines Rd., Payette. 642-1829. From Payette, proceed north on U.S. Hwy. 95 and bear right on 7th Ave. N. At Iowa Ave, turn left and continue to Airport Rd. Here, turn right, and drive to Scotch Pines Rd. Bear left here, and proceed to the course.

The rolling hills above Payette are home to the municipal, 18-hole Scotch Pines Golf Course. Dubbed after the Scotch Pines lining a majority of the fairways, this mature course was established in 1961 under the direction of designer, William Graham. The course offers a challenging round of golf along with crowned greens. Green fees are $21 daily with a special $15 rate available Monday

and Tuesday mornings before 12 PM. The course is occasionally closed during the winter due to bad weather.

T Payette Historical Tour
Contact the Payette Chamber of Commerce at 642-2362.

The quiet town of Payette is alive with history around every corner. The community's downtown area and surrounding residential neighborhoods are littered with nationally registered historic buildings representing a range of architectural styles, from Queen Anne to French Regency, Arts and Crafts to Art Deco.

Payette High School Gymnasium
6th Ave S. near Sixteenth St.
Defined by its white igloo shape, the Payette High School gymnasium features a ninety-foot tall fiberglass dome. North American Rockwell designed the dome in 1958 for $5 million for the U.S. Air Force as a radar installation base. Although the dome was fitted atop Dooley Mountain in Baker, Oregon for a few years, it was designated "surplus property" in 1972.

At no cost, the Payette School District acquired the dome, disassembled it, and then reassembled the geodesic dome on a new cement block foundation on the school premises. The dome created a 37,000 square foot gymnasium lit with a six-ton chandelier and mercury vapor lights.

Coughanour Buildings
1st Ave N. and 7th St.; 1st Ave N. and 8th St.
After successfully managing a Boise Basin gold mine for fifteen years, Bill Coughanour arrived in Payette in 1885. Coughanour, commonly referred to as "Knot Hole Billy," was a jack-of-all-trades. Not only did Coughanour build these two connected buildings bearing his name, but he also operated a local sawmill, invested in agriculture, served as Payette mayor for seven terms, and served in the state senate in 1896.

2nd Ave. N. and 8th St.
Originally constructed to house the A. B. Moss Merchant Mercantile, this brick building turned into the Golden Rule Store in 1926 before finally receiving its final purpose as the local Senior Citizens Center. The building's distinguishing feature is the decorative chevrons located in the façade.

1st Ave. and S. 9th St.

Featuring an adaptation on the Gothic Revival architectural style, Payette's former Methodist Episcopal Church is constructed from both bricks and clapboards. The building, now home to the Payette County Historical Society Museum, features several ornate gothic stained glass windows.

St. James Episcopal Church
1st Ave. and N. 10th St.
The brick St. James Episcopal Church was established in 1892 and is regarded for its tall wooden steeple. The church is used to this day.

First Church of Christ, Scientist
215 N. 9th St.
This small church dates back to 1907 and was designed to inspire balance. The structure achieves this goal with a perfectly balanced architectural style featuring two entrances joined with a centrally located Gothic window.

Historic Chase Residence
N. 9th St. and 3rd Ave.
Constructed for Payette's first railroad depot agent, the Chase residence retains much of its original splendor. Campbell and Hodgson designed the two-story, fifteen room brick house in 1890 with all the finest amenities. The interior featured cut glass and golden oak, which the Chase family accented with Chippendale furniture from the 1700s. The Chase family, who occupied the house for over fifty years, also decorated their home with collections of statues, fine lamps, antiques, Havilland dinnerware, and pioneer photographs.

T Kiwanis Park Complex
Located on the Payette River in Payette. Contact the Payette Chamber of Commerce at 642-2362.

Payette's Kiwanis Park spans over twenty-seven prized acres beside the Payette River. In addition to providing scenic views and river access, the park boasts picnic tables and shelters, a skateboard park, a historic band shelter, tennis and basketball courts, indoor and outdoor swimming pools, and a Jacuzzi. The park is open to the public during daylight hours.

T Snake River View Visitor Center
Idaho/Oregon State Border on I-84

Located just inside the Idaho border, the Snake River View Visitor Center welcomes travelers to the great state of Idaho year-round. The center is open daily from 9 AM to 5 PM and offers state tourist information.

TV Paddock Valley Reservoir
Near Payette. Contact the Idaho Department of Fish and Game at 334-3700. Southeast of Payette, merge off State Hwy. 52 onto Little Willow Rd. Follow this road to the reservoir.

Nestled in the agricultural bounty surrounding the communities of Fruitland, New Plymouth, and Payette, Paddock Valley Reservoir is under the management of the Idaho Department of Fish and Game. The reservoir is recognized as a prime crappie fishing area, and a boat ramp on the reservoir's southern edge provides quick and easy water access.

V Clay Peak Motorcycle Park
Located on the outskirts of Payette on State Hwy. 52. Contact the Payette Chamber of Commerce at 642-2362.

Clay Peak Motorcycle Park is a delight for off-road enthusiasts. The county park was designed specifically for motorcycles, ATV's, off-road vehicles, and trail bikes. The park and trails are open during daylight hours.

M Fruitland Chamber of Commerce
200 Whitley Dr., Fruitland. 452-4350. www.fruitlandcofc.com; frtlndcc@fmtc.coM

M Payette Chamber of Commerce
2nd N. Main, Payette. 642-2362.

13 Food

New Plymouth
Pop. 1,400

New Plymouth was established to promote irrigation projects and prove to the world that small farm communities were capable of thriving in arid regions. This plan for a model village originated in Chicago in 1894 with the National Irrigation Congress. Folks from Boston and the lush midwest region lined up 250 families who made their way to Idaho in 1895 to begin this planned community. The town was platted in a horseshoe shape, and prior to migrating to the destination of their new lives, settlers were told they would be provided with one acre of farmland on the horseshoe's "sole." Farmers were also restricted to living no more than two miles away from their crops, and the sale of alcohol was banned for over forty years to keep the farmers sober and well-mannered at all times. After all, New Plymouth was a model village, and it needed to possess model citizens!

Although the plan sounded ideal at its start, the National Irrigation Congress' plan was exactly that - just an ideal. Mud plagued the town's first residents every time it rained, and irrigation canal pipes frequently broke with a mess of floods to follow. Despite such hardships, the settlers persevered, and 1,000 acres had been successfully cleared and planted by 1896. Eventually, the National Irrigation Congress' plan was abandoned, and local farmers bought the rights to the local irrigation company. Now in control of their own fate, the farmers developed better canals and established prosperous gardens and orchards. Up until the Great Depression, New Plymouth provided over 40% of Idaho's available fruit. Today, fruit is still a main crop, but agriculture in the valley has diversified signficantly.

H New Plymouth
Milepost 26.5 on U.S. Hwy. 30 at Triangle Park

In 1894, the National Irrigation Congress designed a model town and canal system. New Plymouth was founded to demonstrate it, and farming began here in 1896. Organizers and settlers came from Cleveland, Boston, and Chicago to try out their plan for locating all their farmhouses in a central town. New Plymouth streets and parks still reflect that plan, but small, adjacent farms here have grown into a much larger irrigated tract.

T Tuttle Blacksmith Shop
116 W. Maple, New Plymouth. 278-5846.

The Tuttle Blacksmith Shop was established in 1896 and remains in business in the same building. The historic blacksmith shop is open for tours Monday through Friday or by appointment where visitors are treated to blacksmithing and tool demonstrations. The free tour is available year-round.

M New Plymouth Chamber of Commerce
PO Box 26, New Plymouth. 278-3696.

Parma
Pop. 1,771

Until 1883, this town situated alongside the Oregon Trail was known as Lower Boise. The area, however, was first home to Fort Boise. The fort was located just outside town where the Snake and Boise Rivers meet. The Hudson Bay Company used to run fur trades through the fort under the direction of Frenchman Francois Payette. Operating from 1834 to 1855, the fort was renowned for its hospitality, and Native Americans, trappers, pioneers, and traders all frequented the site. Today the fort no longer stands, but a monument marks the site.

When the fort closed, the area remained unpopulated for just a few short years. Between 1862 and 1864, a few farmers noted the site's river location and began homesteading in the region. When the Oregon Short Line Railroad laid its tracks here in 1883, the railroad officials decided to rename the area. Albert Fouch, who arrived in Parma at the same time and opened the first store, complied with the railroad's wishes and named the settlement after Parma, Italy.

In 1888, the Sebree Canal was constructed, and farming conditions in the area greatly improved. Word spread of the irrigation system, and farmers and ranchers from the midwest arrived in droves during the late 1800s. By its 1904 incorporation date, Parma was home to an opera house, schoolhouse, bank, and creamery. The area also experienced an apple production boom in the early 1900s, but the Depression, increasing costs, and toxic soil destroyed the orchards by 1930. Luckily, the soil problems were later resolved. Today, sugar beets, onions, and potatoes produce bumper crops each year.

H Marie Dorian
Milepost 46.7 on U.S. Hwy. 95 at Old Fort Boise Park in Parma

An Iowa Indian who came through here with Wilson Price Hunt's fur trappers in 1811, Marie Dorian spent an incredible winter in this region in 1814. She and her two infant children were the sole survivors of a mid-January Bannock Indian clash at John Reid's fur trade post four miles west of here. So they had to set out with two horses on a 200-mile retreat through deep mountain snow. Finally, a Columbia River band of Walla Walla Indians rescued them in April.

H Old Fort Boise
Milepost 46.7 on U.S. Hwy. 95 at Old Fort Boise Park in Parma

An important Hudson's Bay Company Fur trade post was established in 1834, two miles west of here on the bank of the Snake River. Fur trading declined, but this British post became famous for its hospitality to American travelers on the Oregon Trail. An 1845 report spoke of "two acres of land under cultivation…1,991 sheep, 73 pigs, 17 horses, and 27 meat cattle" – a welcome oasis at the ford of the Snake River after 300 thirsty miles from Fort Hall. A flood in 1853 washed away the adobe buildings and Indian trouble forced the company to abandon the post two years later.

T Motor-Vu Drive In
Parma. Take exit 26 off I-84, and bear right at the Motor-Vu sign.

Thought the days of drive-in movie theaters were over? Think again. In Parma, movie lovers can travel back to the past at the Motor-Vu Drive In while listening to a movie over FM radio. The

Motor-Vu Drive In plays newly released films and is open on weekends during the summer months. Ticket prices are $6 per person on Friday and Saturday evenings, $5 on Sundays, and free admission to children under 11 who are accompanied by an adult.

T Old Fort Boise Replica and Museum
20847 Old Fort Boise Rd. (at the east entrance to Parma on U.S. Hwy. 95), Parma. 722-5138.

The Old West comes alive at Parma's Old Fort Boise Replica and Museum. Constructed by the Hudson's Bay Company in 1834 as competition for nearby Fort Hall, Old Fort Boise became an important supply post along the Oregon Trail. The fort was abandoned, however, in 1854 after severe flooding and increased skirmishes with area Native Americans. In 1863, a new Fort Boise was constructed in present day Boise, but a replica of the first fort can still be found near the original site. Although the replica is not completely accurate, it still offers visitors a taste of what life would have been like in the mid 1800s. The replica offers a historical museum and pioneer cabin amid the fort's reconstructed concrete walls. The facility is open from 1 PM to 3 PM Friday through Sunday from June through August or by appointment. In June, watch out for the arrival of Old Fort Boise Days complete with period costumes, craft fairs, a community parade, and a chili cookoff.

T Parma Ridge Vineyards
24509 Rudd Rd., Parma. 722-6885.

Planted on an old apple orchard overlooking the Boise River, Parma Ridge Vineyards originated in 1998 under the ownership of Dick and Shirley Dickstein. At an elevation of 2,400 feet, the vineyard includes Merlot, Chardonnay, Syrah, Gewurtraminer, Viongier, and Zinfandel grapes. These grapes are processed quickly after harvest as the winery is on site with Dick acting as chief winemaker, Carlos Navarrete as assistant winemaker, and Shirley as design and marketing director. To sample Parma Ridge Vineyards' fine wine, please call for a private appointment.

T Snake River Winery and Arena Valley VineyardS
24013 Arena Valley Rd., Parma. 722-5858.

In 1998, Scott and Susan DeSeelhorst purchased the mature Arena Valley Vineyards dating back to 1981. After making several improvements to balance the vineyard, reduce excessive grape shading, and improve grape flavor, the DeSeelhorsts built a winery in 2000. Drawing upon Scott's background in culinary arts and constructing wine lists, the DeSeelhorsts' mission has always been to produce a variety of affordable, food-friendly wines that can be enjoyed year round. Production includes thousands of cases of Chardonnay, Cabernet Sauvignon, Merlot, White Riesling, Syrah, and Zweigelt. For wine tasting, please call and schedule a private appointment.

TV Fort Boise Wildlife Management Area
30845 Old Fort Boise Rd., Parma. 722-5888. From Parma, travel north on U.S. Hwy. 95. Bearing west off the highway at Old Fort Boise Rd., proceed to the management area.

Under the management of the Idaho Department of Fish and Game, the Fort Boise Wildlife Management Area offers history and recreation in one setting. Spanning 1,500 acres alongside the confluence of the Boise and Snake Rivers, the preserve encompasses the former site of the Hudson's Bay Company's 1834-1855 Fort Boise. A concrete marker decorated with British accents pinpoints the fort's approximate location and is available year-round for viewing. In addition, area visitors will find plenty of fishing, boating, and waterfowl hunting opportunities. A boat ramp provides easy access to the nearby river, and the site is open free of charge. Recreational users are reminded to follow preserve regulations and all seasonal hunting restrictions.

15 _Food, Lodging_

Greenleaf
Pop. 862

Greenleaf bears the name of poet, John Greenleaf Whittier. Founded in the early 1900s by a group of Quakers and incorporated in 1972, the town and all of its activity originally centered upon the Friends Church and Greenleaf Academy (1908). The Academy is still located there despite declining populations of residents with Quaker roots and beliefs.

Wilder
Pop. 1,462

Established in 1911, Wilder attained its current name as a favor to a reputable magazine editor. Learning about the town, Marshall P. Wilder agreed to write a favorable article describing the town in his popular women's magazine, The Delineator. In return, the editor requested that his last name be adopted as the settlement's official title. Prior to this event, the town was nearly called "Golden Gate" by wealthy western investors. These investors planned to develop a line of the San Francisco, Idaho, and Montana Railroad running from Butte, Montana to San Francisco. In the process, the financiers had great plans to turn the small Idaho settlement into a miniature San Francisco. The plan was dropped, however, upon learning of the community's agreement with Marshall P. Wilder.

Wilder has supported a prosperous agricultural lifestyle since its inception. The area is home to several potato, sugar beet, corn, wheat, barley, and onion farming operations. The town is also nationally recognized for its hops production. Grown in only four states, hops requires extensive labor and production costs. The Wilder area, which is responsible for most of Idaho's hops production, has mastered production of this crop. Area farmers are frequently recognized as having America's highest average yield.

Homedale
Pop. 2,528

Jacob and Ada Mussell created a ferry across the Snake River at this location in 1898. In need of a name for the new townsite, townsfolk placed suggestions in a hat. Jacob Mussel's entry was randomly selected, and the name stuck. To increase access to the fledgling community, Jake plowed a road to the neighboring Roswell settlement and began negotiating for a connecting road leading to Parma. With these innovations and the arrival of a railroad line in 1906, traffic to the area gradually increased, and an official townsite was platted in

1912. As a result of increased traffic flow, the ferry was replaced with a steel bridge in 1920, and the town was finally incorpated that same year. In 1970, the steel bridge was updated to concrete and has remained ever since. Today, much of the town's population traces its roots back to the community's founders and first residents.

T River Bend Golf Course
18981 Fish Rd., Wilder. 482-7169.
www.golfriverbend.com

The 18-hole, par 72 River Bend Golf Course in Wilder offers golfers outstanding views of the Snake River Valley and ample opportunity to view wildlife. Wide, tree-lined fairways await golfers, and sand bunkers and water hazards come into play on several holes. A driving range and large practice green are also available for those wishing to polish their skills. Weather permitting, the course is open year-round, and green fees range from $11 to $16.

T Cana Vineyards
28372 Peckham Rd., Wilder. 482-7372.

Situated on the slopes of Arena Valley overlooking the Snake River, Cana Vineyards is recognized as one of Idaho's oldest vineyards. After reviving Idaho pioneer Lou Facelli's vineyards and winery, the Lawrence Dawson family has seen great success. Specializing in red wines, the Dawsons often have difficulty keeping up with the increasing demand for the vineyard's renowned Merlot and Cabernet vintage wines; thus, winetasting at the vineyard has been restricted. However, patrons can sample the wines every Saturday from May through October at Boise's Capitol City Market.

M Homedale Chamber of Commerce
PO Box 845, Homedale. 337-4693

16 _Food_

Notus
Pop. 458

Originally called Lower Boise and situated on the Boise River, Notus boasts four theories as to the origin of its present name. The first theory links the name to the area arrival of the Oregon Short Line Railroad in 1883. Officials supposedly thought the word meant "it's all right" in some Native American tongue. Locals contend that the name is drawn from an Oregon Trail incident where some weary travelers refused to continue their westward journey, declaring, "Not Us." Another story relates that the town is actually named after an ancient North African city. How the term migrated to Idaho is beyond explanation. The last explanation is derived from the mythological Notus figure, who was the Greek god of the south wind and the son of Eos and Astraeus. Regardless of the meaning behind its name, Notus has been an Idaho presence since the late 1800s.

From 1886 to 1887, an irrigation canal was constructed in the area that granted farmers and ranchers more prosperity than they had ever known. When the Black Canyon Dam was built nearby in 1921, the town's popularity grew still greater, and the town gained an adequate population base to finally be incorporated into the state.

H Lower Boise
Milepost 16.1 on U.S. Hwy. 20 at Notus City Park

Confederate refugees from Missouri started farming in this area in 1863 and 1864, when gold and silver mining camps created a great demand for flour and cattle. Driven out from their Missouri River homes below Kansas City by extremely bitter Civil War border warfare, they got a new start by digging riverside canals and planting crops.

They helped make Idaho an overwhelmingly southern Democratic territory from 1864 to 1880. Settlements from Caldwell to Notus were known as Dixie, and those farther west were called Lower Boise.

17 *Food*

Middleton
Pop. 2,978

Established just two miles north of the Oregon Trail in the early 1860s, Middleton is located at the midway point of Boise City and Keeney's ferry at the mouth of the Boise River. As a result of its location, it incorporated in 1865 and became an important stopping point for weary travelers. Today, the town is recognized as one of the state's oldest settlements, and a post office has operated here since 1866.

Star
Pop. 1,795

Nestled in the hubbub of Boise Valley, Star was founded in 1863. The community was one of the region's first settled villages. Despite its proximity to larger, more metropolitan cities, Star maintains its heritage as a small town.

T River Birch Golf Course
3740 Pollard Ln., Star. 286-0801. From Boise, drive west on State St., and then proceed north on State Hwy. 16. At Beacon Light Rd., bear left and continue to Pollard. Turn right on Pollard to locate the course.

River Birch, designed by John Boehm, is the newest golf course in Idaho's Treasure Valley. Opened during summer 2004, the course, and its wide fairways border the Eagle Knoll vineyards. Its most interesting feature appears to be the sandy delta that wanders in and out of play on several holes, creating numerous water hazards. With flat terrain, the course is easy to walk and suited to players of all levels. A large practice facility can also be found onsite. Adult green fees are $20 daily for 18 holes, and junior green fees are just $15. After 3 PM, adult golfers will receive the discounted $15 twilight rate, and juniors accompanied by an adult are free after 3 PM. Tee times are requested one week in advance.

18 *Food*

Caldwell
Pop. 25,967

This beautiful city lies on the north banks of the Boise River. Known as "Bugtown" and "Hamburg" during the early years when it served as a campsite for the railroad workers, Caldwell was later named for former Kansas U.S. Senator C.A. Caldwell, who was the president of the Idaho and Oregon

Land Improvement Company. Mr. Caldwell owned and platted the townsite in 1883, and in 1890, the town was officially incorporated as part of Canyon County. The city obtained the title of county seat in 1894. At one time, an electric street-car provided service between Caldwell and Boise; the trip required one hour and twenty minutes of travel time.

The completion of the Deer Flat dams and Lake Lowell in 1908 further increased the area's amenities, providing irrigation for alfalfa, hybrid sweet-corn seed, beans, onions, hops, and sugar beets. In 1941, the J.R. Simplot Company opened its doors and began dehydrating onions. During World War II, potatoes were added to the company's lineup, and today, the plant is one of the world's largest potato processing factories. As its history has illustrated, Caldwell and Canyon County in general is one of the nation's most prosperous agricultural regions.

H Emigrant Crossing
Exit 26 on I-84; follow signs east 0.25 miles on old U.S. Hwy. 30 before bridge

After reaching the Boise River, emigrant wagons had to travel 30 miles to find a good crossing about 1/4 mile north of here.They had to avoid a wide zone of shifting channels, so they descended Canyon Hill, where the route is still visible. In 1853, Maria Belshaw "crossed Boise River at ford, 15 rods wide 3 feet deep, beautiful river, gravel bottom, very clear, large salmon in it." After crossing, the road headed westward along a route that became U.S. 20.

H The Ward Massacre
Milepost 27.2 on U.S. Hwy. 20

Only two young boys survived the Indian attack on Alexander Ward's 20-member party, which was Oregon-bound on August 20, 1854.Military retaliation for the slaughter so enraged the Indians that Hudson's Bay Company posts Fort Boise and Fort Hall had to be abandoned, and the Oregon Trail became unsafe without army escort. Eight years of conflict followed. Finally, the 1862 gold rush brought powerful forces, civilian and military, that gradually subdued the tribes.

T Ward Massacre Site
5 miles northeast of Caldwell on U.S. Hwy. 20/26

Pioneers faced numerous risks while traveling west along the Oregon Trail, and encounters with hostile Native Americans were just one of the many worries plaguing early travelers. A particularly brutal meeting occurred 25 miles east of Boise on August 20, 1854.

After a long day of traveling, the Missourian Alexander Ward wagon train settled down to dinner. Unfortunately, their peaceful meal was interrupted by a surprise Indian horse thief. After catching and shooting the thief in the act, the party met with the revenge of the Shoshone Indian's tribe. Eighteen of the twenty wagon train members were captured and killed, and the Indians stole all the pioneers' livestock and personal belongings. After leaving the Ward party, the Indians carried out further attacks, and six more people in the general area were murdered.

Unbeknownst to the warring Native Americans, two of the Ward children survived the attack.

While the nine-year-old boy hid amid the sagebrush, his fourteen-year-old brother walked with an arrow piercing his lung to Fort Boise where he reported the incident. Troops were immediately dispatched under the direction of Captain Haller and Captain Olney to investigate the massacre and punish the perpetrators. Upon finding the small band of Indians, the troops shot three, hung three others at the massacre site, and imprisoned several more.

The bodies of the eighteen victims are buried in a common grave at the site, and a granite marker lists the names of those who tragically lost their lives here in search of the American West.

T Purple Sage Golf Course
15192 Purple Sage Rd., Caldwell. 459-2223. Merge off I-84 at Exit 25, and proceed east on Hwy. 44. Bear north on Hwy. 30, and at Purple Sage Rd., drive east to the course.

Open year-round, the Purple Sage Golf Course is one of the Treasure Valley's finest courses. Spreading over 6,754 yards, the well-maintained par-71 track is lined with pine trees and purple sage bushes. Its flat layout provides an easy walk, and the mature course has hosted several amateur tournaments since its 1962 origination. Green fees for the 18-hole course are $18 Monday through Thursday and $20 on the weekends, with a 9-hole rate of $12 daily. Cart rentals are also available.

19 *Food*

T Caldwell Memorial Park
The corner of Kimball and Grant Sts., Caldwell.

A leisurely day awaits visitors at Caldwell Memorial Park. The park's amenities include several old shade trees, a community swimming pool, four tennis courts, and sand volleyball. In addition, the park offers playground equipment, three baseball fields, a basketball court, a popular skateboarding area, and is host to the Caldwell Blues Festival held during late summer/early autumn.Another popular event, Fiesta Cultural, is held on Cinco de Mayo in the park and celebrates Caldwell's growing Hispanic population. Thousands of people attend the event to dance, listen to mariachi bands, and eat authentic Mexican cuisine.

TV Oregon Trail Centennial Greenway
Centennial Way and Chicago St., Caldwell.

Enjoy the scenery alongside the Boise River while catching up on the history of the area. Numerous historical markers and an Oregon Trail monument are highlights along this greenway enjoyed by joggers, bicyclists, walkers, and fishing enthusiasts.

20 *Food, Lodging*

T Luby Park Rose Garden
Near Illinois Ave. off the north side of Exit 28, Caldwell. 455-3060.

The sweet scent of nearly 2,000 roses perfumes the air in Caldwell's Luby Rose Park. Planted in the late 1930s during the Depression era, the roses are in full bloom from May to September. Wander through the beautifully manicured gardens, rest

Caldwell	Jan	Feb	March	April	May	June	July	Aug	Sep	Oct	Nov	Dec	Annual
Average Max. Temperature (F)	37.1	45.4	56.3	65.9	74.4	82.6	92.4	90.3	79.7	66.6	50.1	39.2	65.0
Average Min. Temperature (F)	20.5	25.7	30.7	36.6	43.7	50.4	55.9	53.0	44.2	35.7	28.0	22.5	37.2
Average Total Precipitation (in.)	1.36	1.06	1.09	0.97	1.00	0.79	0.27	0.28	0.52	0.77	1.21	1.27	10.60
Average Total Snowfall (in.)	6.8	2.9	0.8	0.2	0.0	0.0	0.0	0.0	0.0	0.1	1.5	4.3	16.5
Average Snow Depth (in.)	1	0	0	0	0	0	0	0	0	0	0	0	0

under the shade of the flower-adorned gazebo, or enjoy the park's more active attractions, including baseball fields, and basketball and tennis courts.

T Fairview Golf Course
816 Grant St., Caldwell. 455-3090. Take Exit 28 off I-84, and proceed south on 10th Ave. Bear right on Grant St. to locate the course.

The Fairview Golf Course is a gem among Idaho's municipal golf courses. Built in the 1930s, a park-like setting surrounds golfers on this 2,572-yard, par-35 course. The course featured the first annual Idaho Seniors Golf Tournament in 1967 and is home today to a mature putting green and a 150-yard practice area. Green fees for the 9-hole course are $10 Monday through Thursday and $14 on weekends and holidays.

T Our Memories Museum
1122 Main St., Caldwell. 459-1413.

Life in the late 1800s and early 1900s is captured in this turn-of-the-century residence now housing an interesting museum. Inside the 19-room home are a vintage kitchen, pantry, parlor, and several bedrooms furnished with period furniture. Also on display are household appliances, vintage clothing, toys, office equipment, photographs, and local history exhibits. Organized by Earl Archie and Opal Gulley with a private foundation, the museum is open from 10:30 AM to 4:30 PM on Fridays, 1:00 PM to 4:30 PM on Sundays, and also by appointment. Admission is free.

T Van Slyke Agricultural Museum
S. Kimball and Irving Sts., Caldwell. 459-1597.

This open-air museum is situated inside Caldwell Memorial Park and provides visitors with insight into agricultural history. The museum features a variety of antique farm machinery, two 1864 pioneer log cabins complete with period furnishings, and a pair of 1950s railroad cars as the railroad was integral in shipping goods produced on Western farms. The facility is open by appointment only, and interested visitors should call for additional information.

T Caldwell Historical Tour
Contact the Caldwell Chamber of Commerce at 459-7493.

Caldwell's agricultural landscape is dotted with architectural beauties representing the community's past and hopes for the future. Visitors will find a sampling of some of Caldwell's most historic sites described below.

Memorial Park
S. Kimball and Grant Sts.
Memorial Park commemorates Caldwell's agricultural past with a presentation of antique farm equipment upon which the earliest settlers relied. In addition, the park boasts two historic log structures. Dating back to 1864, the first cabin was home to Dave, Dennis, and Tom Johnston for over fifty years. The hospitable, clean-living gentlemen were all bachelor ranchers. The second cabin was also constructed in 1864. The cabin features cottonwood logs pinned together with wood pegs.

Union Pacific Depot
S. Seventh Ave.
Caldwell became home to a Union Pacific Depot in 1907. The Queen Anne style building stands elegant to this day, even though many of its ornamental fixtures no longer remain.

Saratoga Hotel
624 Main St.
The four-story Saratoga Hotel is a Caldwell landmark constructed between 1903 and 1904. After founding several farm equipment/hardware stores

throughout the region, Howard Sebree had an architect design the elaborate hotel. The hotel featured octagon turrets, and its canopied entrance made a grand statement to all hotel patrons and passerby.

William Isaacs Residence
823 Albany St.
Once dubbed the finest residence in town, this home was built for sheep rancher, William Isaacs, and his bride-to-be just prior to their forthcoming 1890 marriage. Local contractors completed every step of the home-building process.

William Boone House8
16 Belmont St.
This two-story frame house built in 1890 for Presbyterian minister, William Boone, sits atop a lava-rock foundation. Boone founded the College of Idaho (Albertson College) in 1891 and served as College President until 1936.

John Johnson Home
904 Belmont St.
This two-story home was erected in 1890 for local resident, John Johnson. Recognized as Caldwell's finest example of Queen Anne architecture, the historic residence features toothed shingles, a large wraparound porch, and corner turrets.

M Caldwell Chamber of Commerce
704 Blaine St., Caldwell. 459-7493.
http://chamber.cityofcaldwell.com/index;
chamber@ci.caldwell.id.us

21 *Food, Lodging*

H Albertson College of Idaho
Exit 29 on I-84, Caldwell Business Loop

Planned by the Presbyterians of southern Idaho in 1884 and opened with 19 students in 1891, this is Idaho's oldest college. William Judson Boone, the founder, remained president for 45 years. From a modest beginning with a faculty of eight (including two later governors and a chief justice), it grew to full college status and moved in 1910 to this site, then an alkali desert. A Boise Valley electric railroad served the college, and an interurban station, always known as the "Hat," still stands on the campus as a reminder of the college's pioneer days.

T Albertson College of Idaho
2112 E. Cleveland Blvd., Caldwell.
(800) 224-3246 or 459-5011.

Cultural events abound at Albertson College, one of the West's most renowned liberal arts colleges. The 43-acre campus boasts the Jewett Auditorium, a fine place to catch a concert or thought-provoking lecture. Every year between October and April, the Caldwell Fine Arts Council sponsors a renowned concert series here. Past performances have included jazz pianists, Native American theater, and wind quartets. If drama, dance, or visual arts sounds more appealing, check out the performance listings for the Langroise Center for the Performing and Fine Arts. For the art connoisseur, numerous rotating exhibitions are offered at the Rosenthal Gallery of Art.

T Orma J. Smith Museum of Natural History
2101 Fillmore St., Caldwell. 459-5507.

Housed on the campus of Idaho's Albertson College, the Orma J. Smith Museum of Natural History is the only collection of natural history in southwestern Idaho, southeastern Oregon, and

northern Nevada. The notable museum features anthropology, entomology, and archaeology collections from Idaho, the western U.S., and Baja California. Both national and international experts frequent the museum and utilize the elaborate research library. The museum is open Monday through Friday during the college's academic year and also by appointment. Self-guided tours are free, but guided tours can be taken for a small admission fee.

T Glenn and Ruth Evans Gem and Historical Collection
Albertson College, 2112 E. Cleveland Blvd., Caldwell. 224-3246

Located in the Boone Science Hall, the Glenn and Ruth Evans Gem and Historical Collection is literally an Idaho treasure. Amid the collection's common and rare gems is Bruneau jasper and Owyhee jasper found in southwestern Idaho. Call for additional information regarding hours of operation.

T Ste. Chapelle Winery
19348 Lowell Rd., Caldwell. 459-7222 or (877) 783-2427. From I-84, take Exit 35 to State Hwy. 55 S. Proceed 13 miles, and turn left on Lowell Rd. where signs direct visitors to the winery on the road's left side.

Ste. Chapelle is recognized as Idaho's largest and oldest winery, as well as one of the Pacific Northwest's most revered wine producers. Named after King Louis IX's La Sainte Chapelle (Saint's Chapel) in Paris, Ste. Chappelle started out small in 1976 but has successfully grown to produce more than 150,000 award-winning cases of wine each year. Distributing its wine throughout the world, Ste. Chapelle produces bulk sparkling wines, Chardonnay, Fume Blanc, Riesling, Chenin Blanc, Cabernet Sauvignon, Merlot, and Syrah at the hands of winemaker Chuck Devlin. Complimentary wine tastings are offered each day in a winery that recreates the feel of La Sainte Chapelle while overlooking the vineyards, orchards, and Snake River winding in the valley below. The winery also offers guided tours through the fermentation, aging, and bottling cellars, and monthly wine education classes are becoming increasingly popular. Patrons may also enjoy the winery's picnic grounds and its renowned Jazz at the Winery summer concert series featuring jazz and blues music Sunday afternoons at the winery's two-acre park. Ste. Chapelle is open Monday through Saturday from 10 AM to 5 PM and Sundays from 12 PM to 5 PM with tours starting on the hour. Call them for additional information regarding the Jazz at the Winery Series.

T Hells Canyon Winery
18835 Symms Rd., Caldwell. 454-3300 or (800) 318-7873. Merge off I-84 at Exit 35, and follow the signs for State Hwy. 55 S. Proceed 13 miles before bearing east (left) on Lowell Rd. At Chicken Dinner Rd., turn right and drive to Symms Rd. Turn left here and follow the signs to the winery.

Drawing its name from the famous canyon created by Idaho's Snake River, Hells Canyon Winery was founded in 1980. Owners/winemakers, Steve and Leslie Robertson, blend their passion for fine wine with an enthusiastic spirit as they annually create 3,000 cases of Chardonnay, Cabernet Sauvignon, Cabernet Franc, Syrah, and Merlot wines reflecting the character of the Mountain West. Each wine is barrel fermented and the limited production wine is bottled with unique wildlife labels reflecting the Robertsons' love of the Northwestern wilderness. In addition, the Robertsons faithfully

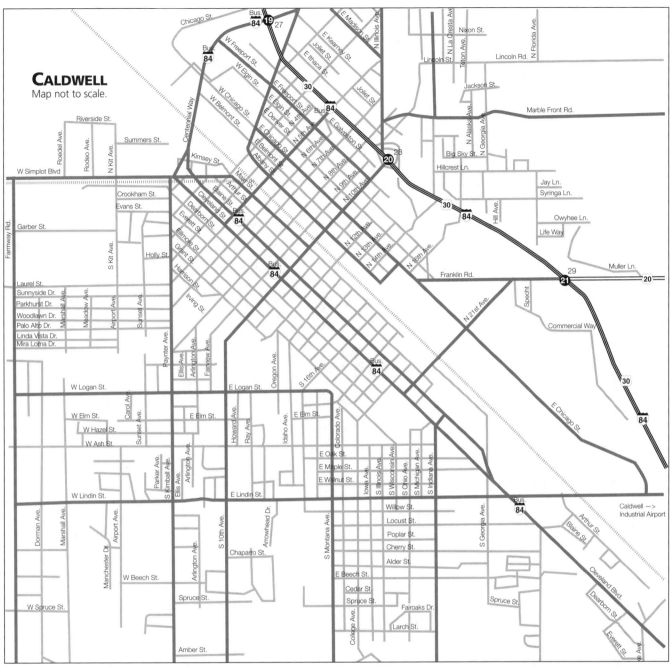

CALDWELL
Map not to scale.

---

donate a portion of the winery's proceeds to wildlife conservation organizations. To sample some of the award winning wines, wine tasting is available on weekends from 12:00 PM to 5:00 PM. The winery also hosts an open house each Thanksgiving Weekend, and a bed and breakfast with private wine tasting is available.

T Weston Winery

16316 Orchard St., Caldwell. 459-2631. Merge off I-84 at Exit 35 and follow State Hwy. 55 South. Proceed 12 miles to locate the winery on the highway's west side.

When Cheyne and Murray Weston moved to the Sunny Slope area in 1981, they created what would become a family winemaking tradition. As the second oldest Idaho winery, Weston Winery boasts one of the highest vineyards in the Northwest at an elevation of 2,750 feet. With 20 acres of grapes, the Weston's produce affordable, high quality Riesling, Chardonnay, Pinot Noir, Cabernet Sauvignon, Merlot, Cabernet Franc, and

Zinfandel wines. The River Runner label on each bottle reflects Idaho's vast rivers and mountainous regions as well as Cheyne Weston's enthusiasm as a river guide on Idaho's Salmon and Selway Rivers. The Weston Winery is open Friday and Saturday from 1 PM to 5 PM and also by appointment.

T Vickers Vineyards

15646 Sunny Slope Rd., Caldwell.

Specializing in handcrafted Chardonnays distinguished by rich fruit and oak flavors, Kirby and Cheryl Vickers began growing Vickers Vineyards in 1981. Over a decade later, the Vickers released their first barrel-fermented vintage and have become well known across the region. Although the vineyard does not have a visitor tasting facility, the Chardonnays are featured at Boise's best restaurants and can also be purchased at the Boise Consumer Co-op.

T Koenig Distillery and Winery

20928 Grape Ln., Caldwell. 455-8386. Merge off I-84 at Exit 35. At the stoplight, turn north, then bear left on Karcher Rd. Proceed for 13 miles, turning right on Lowell Rd. Bear right on Plum Rd., then turn right again on Grape Ln.

Reflecting their family heritage and an entrepreneurial spirit, Andy and Greg Koenig are the proud owners of the Koenig Distillery and Winery. While spending three years in their father's hometown of Lustenau, Austria, the brothers learned from family the European tradition of making brandy from pears and apples. Upon returning to Idaho, the brothers utilized their European education as well as the family's history of winemaking during the Great Depression to begin developing 70 acres of Merlot and Cabernet Sauvignon grapes, pears, Italian prunes, apricots, and peaches above the Snake River. After much hard work and dedication, the brothers have succeeded in producing renowned handcrafted wines, and a new winery and distillery showcases a wine tasting

www.ultimateidaho.com

215

Section 3

SOUTHWEST AREA

INCLUDING BOISE, CASCADE, MCCALL, NAMPA, AND CALDWELL

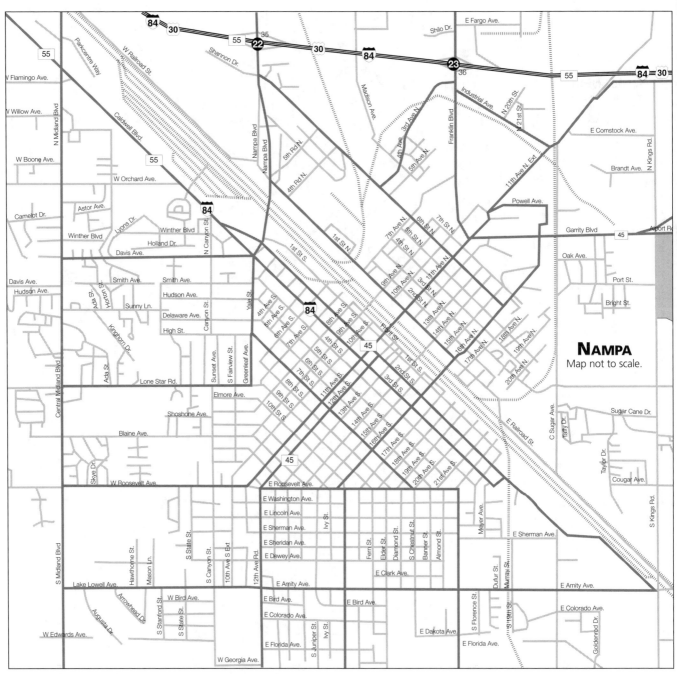

NAMPA
Map not to scale.

room. With Andy serving as distiller and Greg as winemaker, the Koenig Distillery and Winery has a goal of turning Idaho fruit into world-revered wines and fruit brandies. The winery is open for visitation on Saturdays and Sundays from 12 PM to 5 PM April through December. The wines and brandies are also available at fine wine shops and Idaho State Liquor Stores.

T Bitner Vineyards
16645 Plum Rd., Caldwell. 454-0086.

Ron Bitner, an Idaho native, entomologist, and expert grape grower, began planting Bitner Vineyards in 1982. With the first production in 1985, Bitner has successfully maintained twelve acres of Chardonnay, Cabernet Sauvignon, and Johannisburg Riesling grapes each following year. Today, many of the grapes from Bitner Vineyards are used at the nearby Koenig Distillery and Winery.

22 *Food, Lodging*

Nampa
Pop. 51,867

Located on Indian Creek and initially called New Jerusalem, the community of Nampa draws its name from the Shoshone word "nambe," or "nam-buh," meaning "foot" or "moccasin print." However, some historians speculate that the word is based upon a Shoshone renegade named Namp ("foot") Puh ("big"). Regardless of its origin, the Oregon Short Line Railroad gave the community its name in 1883 when they established a station house and water tank. Alexander Duffes, a railroad promoter and land developer, homesteaded 160 acres that were bisected by the tracks. He platted the townsite and Nampa began to grow.

In 1887, the community welcomed its first post office, and three years later, the town was incorporated. Col. William Dewey, a wealthy mining gentleman, built a luxurious hotel in 1901, for $243,000. The eighty-one room, four-story hotel known as the Dewey Palace Hotel occupied an entire city block! Extensively elaborate for its time, the hotel boasted oak paneling, elevators, electric lights, a banquet hall, ballroom, bowling alley, billiard room, barber shop, saloon, and laundry services. In addition, the hotel possessed its own well and water tank, an electric generator, hot water, and radiant heat. Three months after the hotel's grand opening in February 1903, Dewey passed away at the age of seventy-nine. The hotel closed in 1956 and was torn down in 1963 because of deterioration.

By 1903, the railroad business in Nampa had grown so popular that a new depot on Twelfth Ave. was constructed. The depot, now home to a museum, quickly established itself as one of the nicest railway stations in the entire state. It was an important railroad center for the region. Today, the town is an agricultural hub home to America's largest sugar beet plant.

T Nampa Civic Center
311 3rd St. S., Nampa. 465-2252.

The Nampa Civic Center is an outstanding facility for business conferences, arts and crafts exhibitions, cultural events, and performing arts. The center hosts over 750 different events throughout the year, and the 648-seat auditorium is the perfect venue for concerts and plays. To learn about upcoming events, call for more information or drive by as all events are listed outside the center.

T Amalgamated Sugar Company
138 E. Karcher Rd., Nampa. 466-3541. Merge off I-84 at Exit 35, and proceed north on Northside Blvd. Turn east onto Karcher Rd.

Established in Nampa in 1942, the Amalgamated Sugar Company is a huge economic force in Nampa as well as in the world's agricultural climate. The company purchases over six million tons of sugar beets each year, producing nearly two billion pounds of sugar annually. Such production capabilities have landed Nampa's famous company recognition as the largest sugar beet factory in the U.S. and the second largest in the world. More than ten percent of all sugar available to Americans is manufactured in the Nampa plant. Although tours are not available, the plant's exterior and the unique odor of sugar beets are worth the sight and smell.

23 Food, Lodging

T Lakeview Park
Garrity Blvd and 16th Ave. N., Nampa.

This small park offers something for everyone amid its shade trees and brightly colored rose garden. Locals and visitors alike appreciate the picnic tables, swimming pool, horseshoe pits, volleyball, basketball, and tennis courts, softball fields, duck pond, and fun waterpark. The park is also home to many of Nampa's annual community events.

T Farm to Market Agricultural Tours
Nampa Area. Contact the Chamber at (208) 466-4641.

One hundred years ago, the area surrounding Nampa was desert country. But with the innovative efforts of early settlers and modern irrigation, Canyon County is now Idaho's most productive agricultural area. Vegetable and fruit stands line country roads, and passerby are encouraged to stop at one of the many orchards to pick their own fruit. Visitors can explore this fertile land and enjoy some of the best produce available for miles on the self-guided Farm to Market Agricultural Tour. Tour pamphlets are available at the Nampa Chamber of Commerce at 1305 3rd Street South.

T Brandt Center/Friesen Art Galleries
Northwest Nazarene University, 623 Holly St., Nampa. 467-8795.

The John and Orah Brandt Fine Arts Center opened in 1997 on the campus of Northwest Nazarene University. Today, the facility's 1,500 seat Swayne Auditorium is a popular venue for a variety of musical and cultural events. Among the numerous performers is the Boise Philharmonic, which offers monthly performances in the center during the September through April symphony season. Call for the most recent schedule of events.

Also included in the Brandt Center is the Friesen Art Galleries. This gallery celebrates the visual arts and the creative spirit inherent in all

human life. Open to the public for viewing, the gallery also provides educational opportunities for elementary, junior high, high school, and college students.

T Native American Pictographs
From Lake Lowell Ave. in Nampa, drive 14.7 miles south on State Hwy. 45 (12th Ave. Rd.) before bearing right on a road following the Snake River's north bank. Proceed 6 miles to the pictograph site on the road's right side.

The ancient history of Idaho's original settlers is recorded near the banks of the Snake River. Interested passerby will locate a sizeable rock near the road comprising one of the largest single Indian pictographs ever discovered. The pictographs explore topics such as the Snake River, western Wyoming's Jackson Lake, and a few other geographical areas in Idaho and Wyoming.

T Canyon County Historical Museum
1200 Front St., Nampa. 467-7611.

The Canyon County Historical Museum is packed with a variety of historic memorabilia. Situated in the 1902 Oregon Short Line Depot listed on the National Register of Historic Places, the museum preserves the region's heritage while educating both locals and visitors. In addition to old farm equipment, medical equipment, printing presses, newspapers dating to 1881, and historic photographs, the museum is also home to a 1940s era railroad caboose and a 1917 Steam Derrick. The museum is open from 1 PM to 5 PM Tuesday through Friday and 10 AM to 3 PM on Saturdays during the summer. In the winter, operating hours are 1 PM to 5 PM Tuesday through Friday and 11 AM to 3 PM on Saturdays. Admission is free, but donations are highly suggested.

T Sawtooth Winery
13750 Surrey Ln., Nampa. 467-1200. On I-84, take Exit 36 onto Franklin Ave.. Proceed to 11th Ave. and turn right. Continue north, turning left on Third St . S. which jogs over to 12th Ave. S. Follow 12th Ave. south, and then bear right onto Missouri Rd. At Sky Ranch Rd., turn left and follow the signs leading to the winery.

Previously known as Pintler Cellars, the winery was founded in 1987 on fifteen acres of land owned by Charles Pintler. Set amidst vast vineyards and blue skies, the winery sits on the rim of Hidden Valley and offers views of the Boise Valley and Owyhee Mountains. In 1998, Pintler Cellars joined the Corus Brands family of Woodinville, Washington and changed its name to Sawtooth Winery. The label reflects Idaho's jagged Sawtooth Mountains and scenic wilderness areas, and the winery is known for its distinctive, high-quality wines. With Brad Pintler serving as winemaker, the winery features Riesling, Chenin Blanc, Chardonnay, Cabernet Sauvignon, Semillon, Merlot, and Pinot Noir. Now encompassing more than 600 acres and producing 10,000 cases of wine annually, the winery's goal is to produce white wines that are not too earthy and red wines that possess a distinctive taste and structure. The

winery is open for wine tasting Friday through Sunday from 12:00 PM to 5:00 PM and a special Mother's Day Wine and Food Festival as well as a Thanksgiving Weekend Open House are offered. Call in advance for winery tours.

T Music Theater of Idaho
203 9th Ave. S., Nampa. 468-2385.

Producing family-oriented musicals, Music Theater of Idaho draws audiences from across Idaho's Treasure Valley as well as from neighboring states. Five musicals are regularly performed each year, with different productions showcased annually. Past performances have included *Beauty and the Beast*, *The Wizard of Oz*, *The Secret Garden*, *West Side Story*, *Seussical*, and several others. The theater encourages young children to discover drama, and performance opportunities are available for children. Those interested in seeing a performance should call for a complete schedule of events and tickets.

T Northwest Nazarene College
623 Holly St., Nampa. 1-877-668-4968. Located near E. Dewey and E. Amity Ave.

Founded in 1913 under the affiliation of the Church of the Nazarene, Northwest Nazarene College is situated on an eighty-five acre park-like campus. The school offers accredited four-year undergraduate programs as well as graduate studies in spiritual formation, social work, ministry, business, and education.

TV Deer Flat National Wildlife Refuge at Lake Lowell
13751 Upper Enbankment (near the intersection of Lake and Lake Lowell Avess), Nampa. 467-9278.

With over 11,585 acres, the Deer Flat National Wildlife Refuge provides outstanding opportunities to view both resident and migratory wildlife. Designated by President Theodore Roosevelt as a national wildlife refuge in 1909, the area is managed by the U.S. Fish and Wildlife Service and is a popular stop for migratory birds. During December's peak migration season, nearly 12,000 geese and 100,000 ducks have been observed at the refuge. Although ducks and geese are by far the largest residents here, several other species have been noted: pelicans, loons, herons, bald eagles, hawks, peregrine falcons, and sandpipers. A visitor center provides information about the refuge's natural history, and a nature trail explores some of the area vegetation while winding down to the lakeshore. This center is open 8 AM to 4 PM Monday through Friday.

While not being enjoyed by birdwatchers, the refuge and Lake Lowell offer numerous opportunities for horseback riding, mountain biking, swimming, boating, waterskiing, hunting, fishing, ice-skating, and cross-country skiing. To protect the refuge, recreational users should note the boating, hunting, and fishing regulations enforced at various times throughout the year.

Idaho Trivia

Idaho may be most famous for its potatoes and wild outdoors, but the legacy of Nampa's cheerleaders shouldn't be missed. The high school squad is famous in the cheerleading world and has secured top awards in international competitions.

V Nampa Recreation Center
131 Constitution Way, Nampa. 465-2288.

For an active day indoors, the massive 140,000 square foot Nampa Recreation Center offers a host of recreational options blending fitness and fun. The facility includes three collegiate sized basketball courts, an indoor track, racquetball, three dance studios, a large gymnastics floor, an aerobics area, weight machines, a children's play center, five indoor swimming pools, a Jacuzzi, sauna, and steam room, and one of the largest indoor climbing walls in the state. Rental equipment is available. The center is open 5 AM to 10 PM Monday through Friday, 8 AM to 7 PM on Saturdays, and 11 AM to 6 PM on Sundays. Admission is $6.25 for adults, $5 for seniors over 55, $4.25 for youth ages 12-17, $3.25 for children ages 6-11, and $1 for toddlers age 0-5.

M Nampa Chamber of Commerce
1305 3rd St. South, Nampa. 466-4641.
www.nampa.com; info@nampa.com

24 Food, Lodging

H Northwest Nazarene University
Exit 38 on I-84, Nampa Business Loop

In 1913, Eugene Emerson started a Christian school that his church developed into an accredited college on a campus he donated. The college, located on a campus 2 miles southwest of here, moved to university status in 1999. Northwest Nazarene University continues to maintain its church relationship as reflected in its mission statement. "The basic mission of Northwest Nazarene University is the development of Christian character within the philosophy and framework of genuine scholarship."

T Centennial Golf Course
2600 Centennial Dr., Nampa. 467-3011. Take Exit 38 off I-84 in Nampa, and proceed south on Franklin Blvd. Bear left onto Industrial Rd. to 11th Ave. Turn left, and at Centennial Dr., proceed left again.

Established in 1987, the Centennial Golf Course is one of Idaho's most popular courses and is perfect for golfers of all abilities. This 18-hole, par-72 municipal course is situated near I-84 and offers hills, open fairways, and large putting greens at an exceptional value. Green fees are $16.25 Monday through Thursday and $19.25 on the weekends.

T Ridgecrest Golf Club
3730 Ridgecrest Dr., Nampa. 468-9073.

Designed by John Harbottle III in 1996, this 18-hole Scottish-links style course was recently rated by Golf Digest as a 4-star course. The creatively designed course incorporates a ridge, water, and large waste bunkers in addition to its wide fairways. Ridgecrest also offers a Wee-Nine par 3-4 course perfect for beginner golfers. Green fees are $23 Monday through Thursday and $27 on weekends.

T Swiss Village Cheese Factory
Merge off I-84 at Garrity Blvd. Exit 38, and proceed right on Franklin 1.5 miles, Nampa. 467-4424.

Visitors can learn everything there is to know about cheese while touring the Swiss Village Cheese Factory. On this free tour, 35 different varieties of cheese are produced, pressed, and packaged right in front of onlookers. Upstairs, a gallery displays old cheese-making tools, historical photographs, and outlines the origins of several popular cheese varieties. As a bonus, free cheese samples are provided. From the famed "squeaky cheese curds" to standard cheddar, the Swiss Village Cheese Factory offers an informative tour geared to both young and old. Operating hours are 7 AM to 7 PM Monday through Saturday and 10 AM to 5 PM on Sundays.

T Nampa's Idaho Center
16200 Can-Ada Rd. (off I-84 at Exit 38), Nampa. 468-1000.

Cultural events, athletic games, and entertainment abound at Nampa's Idaho Center. The indoor arena and outdoor amphitheater host the Idaho Stampede basketball team, numerous equestrian events, the annual Snake River Stampede pro rodeo, concerts by popular musicians, and trade shows. Call for additional information regarding upcoming events.

T The Berry Ranch
Nampa. 1-800-801 3860 or 466-3860. From Garrity Blvd., drive north 6 miles on Franklin Rd. At the junction with U.S. Hwy. 20/26, bear right and locate the ranch to the northeast.

Located just north of Nampa along the historic Oregon Trail, the family operated Berry Ranch blossoms with old-fashioned fun. The working western ranch raises an assortment of small fruits, vegetables, and livestock, and provides visitors with an opportunity to learn and play. Antique farm machinery displays, livestock corral tours, picnic lunches, and a historic dairy farm are just the beginning of what's available. During growing season, guests can pick their own vegetables and fruit. Guests can pick strawberries in June, raspberries in July, blackberries in August, and pumpkins in October. Summer picking hours are 8 AM to 12 PM Monday through Saturday and 6 PM to 8:30 PM on Tuesday and Thursday evenings. Pumpkins can be picked in October from 4 PM to 6:30 PM Monday through Friday and 10 AM to 6:30 PM on Saturdays.

In addition to these standard activities, the ranch also offers hayrides, a giant straw maze in the fall, spring blossom tours, and four annual festivals, including the Strawberry Festival, Raspberry Festival, Sheep Shearing Day, and a Harvest Festival. The Berry Ranch is open 10 AM to 6:30 PM Monday through Saturday from April to October and by appointment November through March.

T Wilson Ponds Fish Hatchery
3608 S. Powerline Rd., Nampa. 465-8479.

Wilson Ponds Fish Hatchery provides five ponds open to trophy catch and release trout fishing, bird watching, and nature walks. Adjacent to the ponds is a fish hatchery offering children an opportunity to feed fish and view outdoor raceways between thousands of large and small trout. For detailed information about the area, step inside the Fish and Game office where displays about nature and bird watching are found.

T Warhawk Air Museum
201 Municipal Dr., Nampa. 465-6446. www.warhawkairmuseum.org

This 20,000 square foot museum located at the Nampa Municipal Airport opens up a world of aviation and war history. The museum's mission is to teach and preserve World War II history from the home front to the war front and aviation history from the first flight to modern space exploration. Encouraging visitors to have an educational experience about the technology and cultural changes in North America since World War II, the museum offers an array of interesting exhibits. Sweetheart pillows, ration books, V-Mail, Mother's Flags, survival gear, a Norden Bombsight, and Victory Puzzles are just a few of the many smaller artifacts housed at the museum. Also on display is an impressive line of historic aircraft. Two of the world's few remaining Curtiss P-40 World War II fighter airplanes and a rare World War II P-51C razorback Mustang fighter airplane have found their home at Warhawk. Besides historic aircraft, the museum recently added the NASA Space Place Club explaining the most advanced flight technology known to man today. The museum and gift shop are open April 2 to October 14 from 10 AM to 5 PM Tuesday through Saturday and 11 AM to 5 PM on Sundays. From October 15 to April 1, museum hours are 10 AM to 4 PM Tuesday through Friday and 10 AM to 5 PM on Saturdays. Admission is $5 general, $4 for seniors, $3 for kids ages 3-10, and free for those under 3.

T Wood River Cellars
2606 San Marco Way, Nampa. (888) 817-7294.

Established in 1994 with a small vineyard of Merlot, Cabernet Franc, and Point Gris grapes, Wood River Cellars has continued to expand under the ownership of Wendy Thompson. Dennis McArthur serves as winemaker, and with the expertise of local award-winning winemaker, Bill Stowe, Wood River Cellars has added Chardonnay and Cabernet Sauvignon wines to the production list. To visit, call for more information.

T For the Birds
1510 N. Happy Valley Rd. (Near Exit 38 off I-84), Nampa. 466-0364.

For the Birds is a privately owned rehabilitation and educational center for birds and mammals. The nine-acre facility features over 800 birds representing ninety different species. In addition, visitors will find lizards, leopards, cougars, tigers, and lemurs at this unique family-owned operation. Free tours are available Monday through Saturday from 10 AM to 1 PM and by appointment.

25 Food, Lodging

Marsing
Pop. 890

Earl Q. Marsing and Mark Marsing settled in this area in 1913. After purchasing forty-four acres, the two men and C. A. Johnson platted out a new town and began selling lots. The gentlemen originally named the settlement "Butte" after the nearby geologic wonder of Lizard Butte, and Walter Volkmer became the community's first settler. When Volkmer applied for postal services in 1922, however, the post office rejected the town's name in because there were too many other regional towns operating under the same title. Therefore, the town was named after its founders, the Marsings. The small settlement originally served as the area's trade center. Before a bridge was built across the river in 1921, one upstream and one downstream ferry carried travelers and supplies back and forth from their intended destinations. Today, Marsing is one of Owyhee County's largest communities and retains its economic heritage as an agricultural center.

Idaho Trivia

For all those who love the mall scene, Nampa's Karcher Mall is a historical must in the state of Idaho. The mall represents the state's first large-scale indoor shopping center and today boasts over seventy stores.

H Froman's Ferry
Milepost 2.6 on State Hwy. 55 at Island Park in Marsing

In 1888, George Froman built a ferry about a mile downstream from here. It operated until a bridge was built here in 1921. The ferry barge was connected by ropes to a pulley that slid along a cable spanning the river. By angling the barge into the swift current, the ferryman could make it across the stream in either direction with no other power. Ferries of this type were a common solution to the transportation problem imposed on the pioneers by Western rivers. There were several others not far upstream.

H Givens Springs
Milepost 11.5 on State Hwy. 78

Natural hot water available here has been a popular attraction for thousands of years. A winter village site for about 5,000 years, these hot springs had large pit houses typical of plateau communities northwest of here from 4,300 to about 1,200 years ago. After that, small huts used by Great Basin tribes became fashionable. Deer, rabbits, and river mussels sustained this winter camp. After 1842, emigrants using an Oregon Trail alternate also patronized Givens Springs.

T Givens Hot Springs
11 miles south of Marsing on State Hwy. 78. 495-2000.

For thousands of years, Native Americans used this popular Idaho site as a winter village and medicinal mecca. When Oregon Trail pioneers began migrating west, Givens Hot Springs took on new patronage with enthusiastic travelers reveling in the springs' naturally restorative hot water.

As the springs' attraction continued to grow, Oregon Trail pioneers, Milford and Mattie Givens, decided to abandon the rest of their westward migration in favor of staking a claim at the springs. In 1881, the couple built a home on the site, and a pool, bathhouse, and hotel were added in the late 1880s. Within no time, Givens Hot Springs was one of the Oregon Trail's premier destinations, providing weary travelers with comfortable accommodations and relaxation in the constant 95 to 100 degree water.

When Milford and Mattie divorced in 1898, Mattie stayed on the property and remarried Gus Yanke. With Gus' help, a restaurant, ice-cream parlor, barbershop, post office, shady picnic grounds, and a school were added, further boosting the area's business. Although the hotel burned to the ground in 1939 and was never rebuilt, a new poolhouse was added in 1952.

Today, the 1952 poolhouse houses an Olympic-size pool, private soaking tubs, and a snack bar. Outside, visitors have access to baseball, volleyball, horseshoe pits, picnicking, and fishing on the nearby Snake River. The springs are open year-round from 12 PM to 10 PM daily, and a small admission fee is charged.

T Lizard Butte
Directly north of Marsing on State Hwy. 55. Contact the Marsing Chamber of Commerce at 896-4123.

Overlooking the Snake River, the dramatic Lizard Butte keeps watch over Marsing. The butte, which is comprised of an extinct volcano, resembles a large one-legged lizard basking in southwestern Idaho's glorious sunny days. At one time, the lizard formation purportedly possessed two legs, but an eager claims seeker drilled into one of the legs to test for coal deposits and permanently dis-

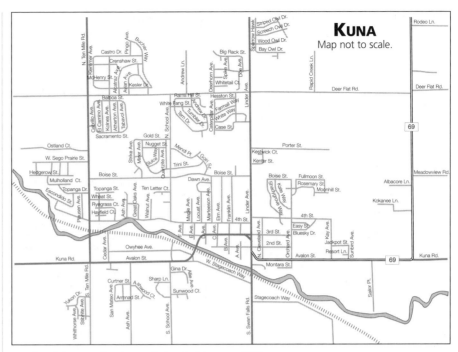

KUNA
Map not to scale.

membered the natural sculpture. Archaeologists have also suggested that ancient Native Americans once performed sacrificial ceremonies on top of the bluff. While the butte is impressive from below, visitors can gain outstanding vistas of the surrounding area by taking a short walk to the butte's summit.

T Island Park
Near Marsing on the bridge's upriver side. Contact the Marsing Chamber of Commerce at 896-4123.

As the shadow of Lizard Butte stands guard, Island Park offers travelers and Marsing residents with a well-maintained setting for outdoor fun. The park features a large grassy area complete with picnic tables, grills, and an occasional wandering duck that may decide to join you for lunch. The park's location near the Snake River also provides anglers with convenient access to smallmouth bass.

T Sunny Slope and Symms Fruit Ranch
Northeast of Marsing on State Hwy. 55.

Marsing and Caldwell encompass one of Idaho's most productive agricultural regions and are especially renowned for the longstanding Sunny Slope orchards covering more than 25,000 acres. Although several productive growers have made their living off the Sunny Slope, Symms Fruit Ranch's history dates back to 1913. Relocating from Kansas, R. A. Symms planted Sunny Slope roots in 1913 when he purchased an eighty-acre homestead. Within just a few years, Symms had row after row of apples, peaches, and plums, and his sons partnered with their father during the 1930s. Although the original Symms Fruit Ranch owner died in 1934, the ranch is still going strong. With the addition of packing houses and cold storage, the ranch's operations expanded. Today, the ranch is known for its superior asparagus, cherries, raspberries, apricots, peaches, nectarines, prunes, plums, and apples. Reportedly, the ranch packs and sells more than 500,000 boxes of apples annually!

M Marsing Chamber of Commerce
PO Box 247, Marsing. 896-4123.

26 Food

Kuna
Pop. 5,382

A man named E. P. Vining, with the aid of an Indian language dictionary, gave Kuna ("Q-na") its name. At the time, he believed the term meant "snow," but others say it means "end," "green leaf," or "good to smoke." The area first served as an Oregon Short Line Railroad stop in 1884, and in autumn 1905, Mr. F.H. Teed and his wife filed a 200-acre Desert Land Act claim to become the town's first permanent settlers. At first, the only other area home was thirteen miles away, and water had to be hauled ten miles to Kuna from the Snake River.

In 1907, the Teeds decided to open a post office for their tiny village, but business was expectedly low. In the first three months of operation, receipts totaled just 16 cents. Gradually, pioneers from Iowa and Missouri settled in this area. Today, farms, ranches, and a winery surround the town along with a wide open, beautiful landscape. The Birds of Prey National Conservation Area lies just south of town.

H Initial Point
Exit 44 on I-84 at Storey Park in Meridian

All Idaho land surveys refer to a beginning point – "Initial Point" – 16 miles directly south of here. When he began surveying Idaho in 1867, Lafayette Cartee, first surveyor general of Idaho Territory, established the initial point on a volcanic hill visible for many miles. Everywhere in Idaho, surveyors depend upon this essential point in establishing land boundaries. The city of Meridian is name for the Boise Meridian – the surveyors' north-south line that runs through Initial Point.

T Falcon Crest Golf Course
11102 S. Cloverdale Rd., Kuna. 362-8897. www.falconcrestgolf.com Merge off I-84 at Exit 46 and proceed south on Eagle Rd. At Overland Rd., bear left, and drive to Cloverdale Rd. Turn right, and proceed 7 miles to the course.

Designer Hons Borbonus created this premier golf facility in 2000 to provide a challenge to golfers of varying skill levels. A grassy ocean offers golfers unhurried play, and the well-maintained 18-hole course intertwines its natural beauty with water, sand, and stone playing hazards. On its way to becoming a recognized facility throughout the entire Pacific Northwest, Falcon Crest Golf Course provides magnificent vistas of the Boise Valley and distant mountains. In addition to its traditional course, Falcon Crest also offers beginner golfers and junior players a chance to practice up at a reduced rate on the 9-hole Robin Hood Course. A thirty-acre driving range can also be found with more than 18,000 square feet of putting space. Tee times can be scheduled up to seven days in advance. Green fees are $39 on weekdays and $49 on weekends and include carts. Youth under 18 are admitted at a $20 daily rate. For those desiring to walk, standard green fees are reduced by $10.

T Indian Creek (Stowe) Winery
1000 N. McDermott Rd., Kuna. 922-4791. On I-84, take Exit 44, 2 miles west of Kuna, turn right on N. McDermott Rd., and continue 0.5 mile to locate the winery on the road's right side.

Utilizing vineyards planted from 1982-1984, Indian Creek Winery is a family affair with production by Bill, Mui, Will, Greg, and Tammy Stowe, and John and Mary Ann Ocker. While winemaker Bill Stowe's white Pinot Noirs are most popular, the winery also produces red Pinot Noirs, Chardonnay, Riesling, Cabernet Sauvignon, Merlot, and occasional Gewurztraminers and ice wines. Consistently winning both regional and national wine competitions, the Stowes' transfer their love of winemaking into their high-quality wines. Visitors to the winery usually have an opportunity to speak to Bill at length while sampling one of the winery's latest vintages. Indian Creek Winery is open Friday through Sunday from 12:00 PM to 5:00 PM or by appointment.

T Sandstone Vineyards and Silver Trail Winery
188 8 E. Rodeo Ln., Kuna. 922-2111. Merge off I-84 at Exit 44, and proceed 6 miles south. On Rodeo Ln., bear east to locate the winery between Hubbard Road and Deer Flat Rd.

Located in a natural farming area, Sandstone Vineyards and Silver Trail Winery are family owned and operated. Under the direction of Larry and Kathy Hansen, eight acres of Merlot, Lemberger, Pinot Noir, Chardonnay, Chenin Blanc, and Riesling grapes have been planted. The Hansens pride themselves on their all-natural products and no pesticides are used on the vineyards. To visit the winery, call for an appointment.

T Snake River Birds of Prey Conservation Area
3 miles south of Kuna on Swan Falls Rd. Contact the BLM – Four Rivers Field Office at 384-3300.

The Snake River Birds of Prey Conservation Area was established in 1993 and includes eighty-one miles of terrain on the rugged Snake River Canyon. The canyon's natural crevices, ledges, cracks, and pinnacles provide an ideal habitat for birds of prey, and the area is now home to the continental U.S.' largest concentration of these birds. As the raptors soar on the vertical air currents rising above the canyon, visitors have plenty of opportunity for wildlife viewing and photography. The area is home to golden eagles, prairie falcons, short-eared owls, burrowing owls, red-tailed hawks, sharp-shinned hawks, Swainson's hawks, kestrels, and northern harriers. This unique conservation region is open year-round during daylight hours free of charge.

T Kuna Butte
6.2 miles south of Kuna along Swan Falls Rd. Contact the Kuna Chamber of Commerce at 922-9254.

Kuna Butte dominates Kuna's southern skyline as an ancient shield volcano. Erupting more than a million years ago, the butte hurled molten lava across the region and helped shaped the Snake River Plain's landscape. Covered with moss, lichen, and perennial grasses, the butte provides views into western Oregon and is home to burrowing owls and other birds of prey.

T Kuna Cave
South of Kuna on Kuna Cave Rd. Contact the Kuna Chamber of Commerce at 922-9254. From Kuna, proceed south across Indian Creek. At Kuna Way, bear west for 3.7 miles before turning south on Robinson Blvd. After following Robinson Blvd. for 4.5 miles, head 1.8 miles due east to a dirt road with a southeastern fork. Follow the fork 1.1 miles to the cave.

During ancient times, Kuna and the surrounding region was a hotbed of volcanic activity, and Kuna Cave is a reminder of the area's geological history. A 1,000-foot long lava tube, Kuna Cave rests amidst a popular recreational site. Near the area's rock ring, cave explorers will find a thirty-five foot iron ladder descending into the tube. Although the tube appears small from its opening, explorers are greeted with large open areas at the bottom of the ladder.

Legend states that prehistoric Native American tribes used Kuna Cave to access the Snake River on an underground journey, but no proof has ever been found to solidly verify this folklore tale. The cave, however, does hold an intriguing story dating back to its founding in 1890. Boise lawyer, Claude Gibson, happened upon the cave one afternoon, and using a rope attached to his wagon, lowered himself into the dark abyss. Upon entering the cave, Gibson discovered a human skeleton near a pile of rocks. Historians speculate that the skeleton is the remains of an unfortunate Native American who may have accidentally fallen in with no way of exiting, but the bones remain a mystery.

The cave is open free of charge when weather permits, and users are cautioned to practice safety at all times. Visitors are also encouraged to bring along plenty of flashlights.

T Initial Point and Dedication Point
South of Kuna. Contact the Kuna Chamber of Commerce at 922-9254. From Kuna, proceed south across Indian Creek to Kuna Way. Drive 3.7 miles west on Kuna Way before turning onto Robinson Blvd. Drive north 3.5 miles to Bennett Rd., turning due east and continuing 4 miles to Swan Falls Rd. After turning onto Swan Falls Rd., proceed 7 miles to a spur road leading east. Follow this spur road 1 mile to Initial Point.

Rising to an elevation of 3,240 feet, Initial Point's raised lava butte not only provides breathtaking scenery, but also is historically significant. In 1867, Initial Point was selected as the Boise Meridian Point, marking the starting point for all of the fledgling territory's official land surveys. After taking a short, easy hike to the historic point's summit, visitors have access to views of the Owyhee Mountains and the Snake River Plain.

Just a few miles further down the spur road, Dedication Point greets travelers with a pullout parking area near a canyon rim. A short nature trail winds through the area with interpretive signs providing insight into the area's distinctive landscape and wildlife.

TV Swan Falls Dam, Museum, and Park
28 miles south of I-84 near Kuna. Contact the Kuna Chamber of Commerce at 922-9254.

In the late 1800s and early 1900s, Colonel William Dewey was no ordinary Idaho pioneer. Possessing a vivacious entrepreneurial spirit, Dewey was also a dreamer with the ability to influence all those around him. Desiring to make the most profit out of his Silver City mine, Dewey convinced the powers that be to construct a dam that would generate enough electric power to supply an electric railway to his mine.

Although Dewey's intended vision never fully materialized, his suggested Swan Falls Dam was constructed as he requested. A. J. Wiley, a young Boise engineer, designed the dam for the Trade Dollar Consolidated Company, and construction began in 1900. Just one year later, the 288-foot long concrete dam was complete, and electricity was extended to the citizens of Murphy and Silver City up until World War II. As for Dewey's expected electric railway, the plans never came to fruition.

Today, the dam is recognized as the state's oldest operating hydroelectric site on the Snake River. After several repairs were made to improve the efficiency of the original power plant, a new facility was constructed at the dam in the mid 1990s. The old power building was renovated into a historical power display full of regional memorabilia and interesting informational tidbits.

Also on-site, Swan Falls Park is situated within the Snake River Birds of Prey National Conservation Area. The park provides a grassy picnic area as well as access to fishing, upland game bird and waterfowl hunting, rafting, boating, mountain biking, and hiking.

M Kuna Chamber of Commerce
123 Swan Falls Rd., Kuna. 922-9254. www.kunachamber.com

27 *Food*

Bowmont
Pop. 50

Bowmont, originally known as Newell, was founded in 1911. The community honors the contributions of village founder, J.F. Bow, and is regarded for its production of potatoes, lettuce, onions, and clover seed.

Melba
Pop. 439

Melba bloomed along the Union Pacific Railroad in the heart of grain country. The town was officially settled in 1912 after the Boise Project made water available to potential inhabitants. The post office arrived that same year, and town founder C.C. Todd, named the community after his daughter.

H Steamer Shoshone
Milepost 10.3 on State Hwy. 45

The boat was built in 1866 to provide easy river travel for a part of the route from the Columbia River to Boise and Silver City. It was intended to ply 105 miles between here and Old's Ferry. Once it even explored the river for 60 miles above here, astonishing the jackrabbits with its ambitious whistle. But business was poor, and firewood for boilers was scarce. Service stopped after a few trips. Finally, in a hair-raising tide, the 136-foot, 300-ton boat was run through Hells Canyon to the Columbia.

T Walter's Ferry
South of Nampa on State Hwy. 45

In 1863, John Fruit and a partner developed a lucrative ferry crossing at this site. After just five years, the two sold the business to Lewellyn and Augusta Walter, and the new Walter's Ferry became a crossroads of pioneer activity. Numerous Oregon Trail travelers crossed the Snake River on the roughly constructed log ferry, and stage lines at the site connected Boise, Silver City, and San Francisco. Ferry services ended in 1923 when a bridge was built connecting the river's shorelines. Today, the site is a popular boat launching area for Snake River enthusiasts.

T Swayne's Ferry Museum
South of Nampa on State Hwy. 45 to Walter's Ferry.

Local resident Pappy Swayne (1887-1976) created what has become a conglomeration of historical museum, botanical gardens, animal farm, and religious arena. After Pappy's death, his widow, Cleo, took over operations and has since added an extensive collection of both life-size and smaller works from artist Gary Lee Price. Upon entering the "museum," visitors will encounter numerous birds strutting around, lizards, squirrels, and a swan-filled lake. Moving ahead, a nature trail loops through a forest dotted with gnome statues, past Pappy's grave, and to a prayer garden. This unique experience sometimes referred to as "Cleo's Ferry Museum" is free, but donations are always welcome.

T Celebration Park
Southwest of Melba at 5000 Victory Ln.
495-2745.

Established in 1989 beside the Snake River, Celebration Park represents Idaho's only archaeological park. The area was fashioned nearly 15,000 years ago during the aftermath of the massive Bonneville Flood. A few thousand years later, Paiute Indians began using the area as a wintering ground. Archaeologists estimate that the area's earliest habitation dates back nearly 12,500 years.

While wintering here, the Paiute Indians left behind walls of unique petroglyphs. Although many have hypothesized about the art's significance, the true meaning remains a mystery. Later "artwork" was added by Oregon Trail pioneers on their westward migration, all of which can still be found throughout the park.

Individuals visiting the high desert park will also find an informational center staffed with knowledgeable naturalists, scenic land features and flora, and the historic Guffey Bridge. The bridge was constructed in 1897 to carry railroads across the Snake River to the prosperous mining community of Silver City. The railroad tracks never made it to their proposed destination, but the bridge remains. Closed to vehicle traffic, the historic structure is open to walkers, bicyclists, and equestrians.

The park requires a $2 day use fee per person and is open year-round from 9 AM to 4 PM daily.

T Guffey Railroad Bridge
7 miles north of Walter's Ferry. Contact the Southwest Idaho Travel Association at 344-7777. From Walter's Ferry, bear right on the paved Ferry Rd., and continue 2 miles to a "T" in the road. Turning right on Hill Rd., proceed 4.2 miles to the next right turn on Sinker Rd. Follow the gravel road 2.8 miles to its dead end.

Erected in 1897, the doubled-arched iron Guffey Railroad Bridge was constructed for Colonel William Dewey's Boise, Nampa, and Owyhee Railroad. Dewey planned to extend his railroad

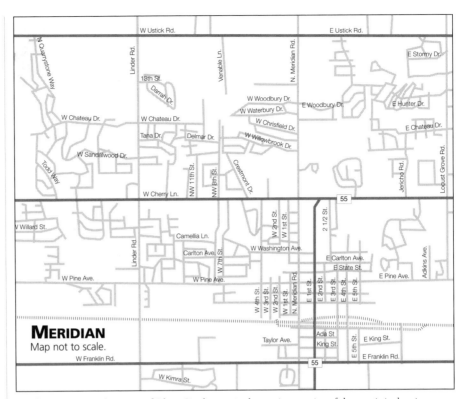

line from Nampa to the mines of Silver City, but his well-laid plans never materialized. The line only made it to Murphy, and the Guffey Railroad Bridge was an instrumental link in the railroad's brief success of transporting livestock. Dominating the horizon around the Guffey Railroad Bridge are benches of Melon gravel. Resembling boulders, these rock deposits date back more than 30,000 years to the Bonneville Flood. Geologists speculate that the river measured at least three hundred feet deep here during the height of the flood's devastation.

T Bernard's Ferry
North of Walter's Ferry. Contact the Southwest Idaho Travel Association at 344-7777. Drive 0.6 miles north of Walter's Ferry on State Hwy. 45 to Map Rock Rd. Bear west, and drive 5.3 miles to a large boarded building.

British Columbia native, James Bernard, came to Idaho Territory in 1864. He and his wife, Ada, immediately set to work building a fourteen-room home where they raised their large family and frequently hosted celebrated social gatherings. As soon as the residence was completed, Bernard began operating an expedited freight service between the Owyhee mines and Caldwell. Bernard's drivers were recognized for boasting the region's fastest delivery times, and the company's freight teams received the highest quality care. Bernard later developed a ferry system that catered to Owyhee Road traffic. The rustic barn on the river's west side is all that remains of Bernard's famous freight and ferry company.

T Map Rock
North of Walter's Ferry. Contact the Southwest Idaho Travel Association at 344-7777. Drive 0.6 miles north of Walter's Ferry on State Hwy. 45 to Map Rock Rd. Bear west, and drive 9.3 miles to the site.

The large basalt boulder dubbed Map Rock rests beside the road and presents passerby with an array of petroglyphs. Although archaeologists surmise that a winding serpent shape represents the course of a regional river, no one knows for sure

the precise meaning of these artistic drawings crafted thousands of years ago.

28 *Food, Lodging*

Meridian
Pop. 34,919

First named Hunter in 1898, the name changed after the Meridian Lodge was built. The name change was the result of the townsite being laid out on the Boise Meridian, the prime north-south line from which all lands in Idaho are surveyed. Despite a disastrous fire that devoured the lodge in 1923, the incorporated city held its own and established a reputation as Idaho's dairy capital. At one time, the city claimed to have more cows per acre than any other region in America! Today, suburban sprawl from Boise has eaten up much of the farmland, and Meridian has joined its capital city neighbor as part of Idaho's fastest growing region.

T Foxtail Golf Course
990 W. Chinden Blvd., Meridian. 887-4653. In Meridian, proceed on Chinden Blvd./U.S. Hwy. 20 to the course located 3 miles west of Eagle Rd.

The par-61 Foxtail Golf Course was created in 1993, and its expansive fairways provide a perfect course for players of all abilities. Featuring a fun layout complete with water and other natural hazards, the course is flat and can easily be walked. Foxtail also provides a covered driving range, putting green, and chipping green. Green fees are $16 on weekdays and $17 on weekends, and tee times are requested at least one week in advance.

T Roaring Springs Water Park
Adjacent to I-84 in Meridian. 884-8842.

Spanning fifteen acres, the family-oriented Roaring Springs Water Park features a 16,000 square foot wave pool, waterfalls, a kiddie park and pool, float tubing, and numerous water slides, one of which plunges more than 350 feet. The park is open mid-May through mid-September with various ticket prices and day passes available.

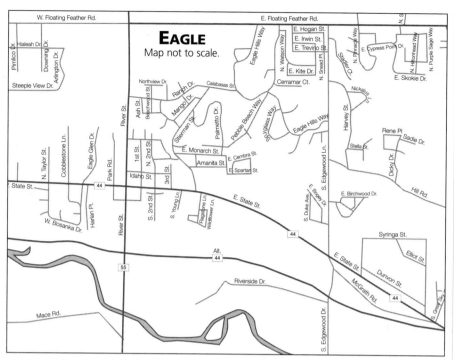

EAGLE
Map not to scale.

T Historic Pine Street School
Downtown Meridian. Contact the Meridian Chamber of Commerce at 888-2817.

The Pine Street School celebrates Meridian's pioneer days and the era of one-room schoolhouses. The historic structure was restored for the city's Centennial Celebration in 1993 and now displays a museum of rural memorabilia. The school recently received the Idaho Governor's Award for Historic Preservation.

T Idaho Peace Officers Memorial
South of Meridian on Stratford Dr. Contact the Meridian Chamber of Commerce at 888-2817.

Located on the grounds of the Idaho State Law Enforcement Headquarters, the Idaho Peace Officers Memorial was dedicated on May 15, 1998 in honor of all Idaho officers who have lost their lives in the line of duty. The memorial was built with funds contributed by police officers, family and friends of law enforcement officials, and community fundraisers from all across Idaho.

Designed as a five-point star badge, the memorial is laid in a red-bricked walkway accented with five flowering pear trees. In the star's center is the memorial centerpiece composed of three sandstone boulders inlaid with granite. Each granite slab is engraved with the names of fallen Idaho officers, and the inscription "Blessed are the Peacemakers" towers above. Names of the fallen date back as far as the 1880s.

The memorial is open daily during daylight hours, and a small interpretive center is being built on-site to provide visitors with additional information about Idaho's peacekeepers.

T Cherry Lane Golf Club
4200 W. Talamore, Meridian. 888-4080.

Meridian's Cherry Lane Golf Club was built in 1978 with nine new holes added during a 1997 course redesign. The city-owned 18-hole course spans 6,500 yards and features small challenging greens intermingled with water hazards. The par-72 course is open year-round with affordable green fees.

T Storey Park
Main St. and Franklin, Meridian. Contact the Meridian Chamber of Commerce at 888-2817.

Meridian's Storey Park is the center for community activity and annual festivals. As one of the community's newest recreational sites, Storey Park features picnic tables and shelters, softball fields, a playground, and substantial grassy areas. In addition, the park's large visitor center provides detailed information about the community, and a historical marker explains the origination of the town's name.

M Meridian Chamber of Commerce
215 E. Franklin Rd., Meridian. 888-2817. www.meridianchamber.org

29 *Food, Lodging*

Eagle
Pop. 11,085

This town is the second in Idaho to be named such. The first "Eagle" settlement lay just west of Murray, in Idaho's panhandle. This particular Eagle no longer exists. It had been Coeur d'Alene's first gold rush camp and the home of Wyatt Earp's infamous 1884 tent saloon.

The current town of Eagle is located just outside Boise and boasts the remarkable Oliver Short house. Utilizing building materials gathered from the Boise River, this home dates to 1906 and is the largest remaining river rock house in Idaho. The house originally contained fifteen rooms and was two-stories high. Since then the interior has been altered. Oliver himself originated from Kansas. After Indians killed his father, Oliver was sent to live with his uncle on Eagle Island near this present day community. After managing the ranch for years, Oliver eventually purchased most of it.

The Eagle Flour Mill, which still stands on Main St., was built in the 1920s and operated for over forty years before closing. It was the last flour mill in the state to close.

T Banbury Golf Club
2626 N. Marypost Place, Eagle. 939-3600.

Architect John Harbottle III designed the championship, 18-hole Banbury Golf Club. Rated by *Golf*

Digest as Idaho's second best course, Banbury encompasses 6,812 yards with a Scottish golf-links style. The course, which is nestled beside the winding Boise River, is rated a par 71 and features manicured greens, natural hazards, wetlands, and spectacular river views. The course is open year-round, and tee-times may be reserved up to seven days in advance.

T Eagle Hills Golf Course
605 N. Edgewood Ln., Eagle. 939-0402. www.eaglehillsgolfcourse.com Proceed on State Hwy. 55 past Floating Feather Dr. and bear left on Edgewood Lane

Eagle Hills Golf Course is renowned for its immaculate care and mature character. Originating in 1967, the par 72 course was remodeled in 1977, and further improvements have helped this course rank as one of southern Idaho's best. Situated in an older neighborhood, the flat 4,922-yard course presents golfers with plenty of challenges on its notorious water traps. Be sure to book a tee-time for this 18-hole course as it is a popular venue for wedding ceremonies and other special celebrations. Green fees are $24 on weekdays and $31 on weekends.

T The Winery at Eagle Knoll
3701 State Hwy. 16, Eagle. 286-9463. Turn north on State Hwy. 16, and head toward Firebird Raceway. Drive past Floating Feather Rd. to Beacon Light Rd., and turn left into the driveway.

After growing up in Oregon and paying several visits to California wine country, it came as no surprise when Mike and Joy Kaufman decided to develop their love of fine wine into their own vineyard and winery. With the help of their family and thirty-two acres to their name, the Kaufmans planted the vineyards' first five acres in Spring 2000 and an additional eight in 2001. Since that time, more grapes have been planted and a 3,400 square foot winery has been built, including grape crushing equipment, barrels, bottling facilities, and a lab. Right next to the winery is a new 3,100 square foot tasting room where patrons can sample nine different wines crafted by winemaker, Keith Green, as well as foods from the Kaufmans' new smokehouse. The winery is open from 11 AM to 6 PM daily.

TV Eagle Island State Park
2691 Mace Rd., Eagle. 939-0696. From Boise, drive 8 miles west on U.S. Hwy. 20/26 to Linder Rd. and follow signs leading to the park.

Although Eagle Island State Park only includes 545 acres of day-use facilities, the park is far from short on fun. Originally home to a livestock ranch, the popular site now offers a swimming beach adjacent to a fifteen-acre lake, a water slide, and a grassy area dotted with countless picnic tables. In addition, five miles of equestrian trails criss-cross throughout the park, and horseshoe pits and a volleyball area are available. The park is open daily during the summer, with the waterslide operating from 12 PM to 8 PM on weekends. A $4 vehicle entrance fee is required, and those wishing to make their way down the waterslide should expect to pay an additional $4 for 10 rides or $8 for unlimited turns.

M Eagle Chamber of Commerce
67 E. State St., Eagle. 939-4222.
www.eaglechamber.com; info@eaglechamber.com

30

Boise
Pop. 185,787

Boise, meaning "wooded" in French, serves as the State Capital and is frequently referred to as the "City of Trees." The forested area brought much relief to the French-Canadian trappers who were weary of walking over the territory's treeless, sage-filled plains. Although there were visitors to this area as early as 1811, the region wasn't officially named until approximately 1824.

Between 1854 and 1860, several members of Oregon Trail wagon trains were massacred on their journey west. After the occurence of the Ward and Otter party massacres, General George Wright recommended that the U.S. Army build a fort in the region as protection. In 1863, his request was put in motion by the pinpointing of the fort's exact location. Shortly thereafter, a handful of men from the area gathered together and decided upon the location for the city of Boise. They mapped out the townsite and set to work donating choice lots to prospective businessmen, thereby attracting many new settlers to the city. After starting as a supply center for the farmers and miners, Boise continued as the hub for commercial and cultural activities in southwestern Idaho.

In 1863, one year after the gold rush reached the territory, Boise was officially founded and swiped the State's capital title from Lewiston. The capital building was erected in 1879 with local sandstone. Additionally, some of the 400 buildings built during the first five years of the city's life can still be seen today in Old Boise and Warm Springs. In the early years, engineers also devised irrigation canals and an extensive geothermal heating system using the water from the local hot springs on the east end of town. It was the world's first heating system of its kind.

In 1887, the Oregon Short Line Railroad branched in from Nampa and provided a much needed outlet for the increasing amount of produce emerging from the Boise area. By 1910 the

Diversion Dam and the New York Canal were completed, and the county was populated by nearly 11,500 farmers and included roughly 1,500 acres of irrigated land. After World War II, Boise's population grew with the addition of two Air Force training bases.

Today, Boise is a well-rounded, down-to-earth city providing an array of cultural events and recreational activities. Hikers, mountain bikers, and skiers flock to the hills; rafters, fishermen and inner-tubers float down the river through town; and the local townspeople stroll the streets on summer evenings. Recognized as early as 1963 as a metropolitan community, Boise proclaims itself as a very safe city with a low crime rate and friendly folks all around. The state capital city serves as Idaho's professional, business, financial, and transportation center and now includes nearly 15% of the entire state's population.

T Boise Master Chorale
344-7901. www.boisemasterchorale.org.

Featuring 110-talented members, the Boise Master Chorale is recognized as Idaho's premier symphonic chorus. The renowned choral group is dedicated to providing audiences with the highest caliber musical performances during their September through May concert season. Several concerts are offered throughout the season with ticket prices varying by performance.

T Opera Idaho
345-3531. www.operaidaho.org.

For those who savor fine opera performances, Opera Idaho delivers grand opera meeting the highest professional standards. The organization offers a performance for every season, and an array of storylines is presented. Past productions have included Carmen, Met to Broadway, La Traviata, Nosferatu (Dracula), and special Christmas opera extravaganzas. Ticket prices range from $15 to $55 depending upon the performance, and advanced tickets are recommended. Call for a complete schedule of the current season's events.

T Treasure Valley
Boise

Containing the cities of Boise, Nampa, Meridian, and outlying areas, Idaho's Treasure Valley is recognized for its year-round mild climate and rich volcanic soil that results in bumper fruit and vegetable crops. Historically, the valley attracted six different regional Native American tribes on an annual basis for a two-month salmon bake and trade fair. Today, high tech industries combine with more than seventy different agricultural cash crops (including grapes!) to make Treasure Valley one of Idaho's most economically diverse regions.

S The Headboard Antiques, Vintage Furniture, & Collectables
11133 Ustick Rd., 1/4 mile west of Five Mile in Boise. 322-7778. Fax 323-2750.
Email: ustickbeeboard@msn.com

31 Food, Lodging

TV Boise Foothills and Mountains
Contact the Boise Visitors Bureau at 344-7777.

Rising directly north of Boise, the Boise Foothills extend into the rugged Boise Mountain Range. With elevations starting in the Boise River Valley at just barely over 2,000 feet, the peaks of the Boise Mountains skyrocket to elevations above 6,000 feet. Historically, the area was populated with abundant wildlife, and Native Americans used the area as a primary hunting ground. Although the wildlife populations have since declined, the area's unique vegetation remains quite the same. Dry land bunch grasses and sage-brush combine with rare flowering plants and riparian corridors to create a unique landscape. Encompassing 80,467 acres, the foothills and mountains provide opportunities for hiking, biking, and scenic photography.

32 Food, Lodging

Garden City
Pop. 10,624

Idaho's "second" Garden City has merged with Boise and is considered part of Boise's western downtown metro area.

T Old Idaho Penitentiary
2445 Old Penitentiary Rd., Boise. 334-2844.

Named to the National Register of Historic Places in 1974, Boise's Old Idaho Penitentiary is just one

Boise	Jan	Feb	March	April	May	June	July	Aug	Sep	Oct	Nov	Dec	Annual
Average Max. Temperature (F)	35.9	41.9	50.6	58.6	67.6	78.0	87.8	86.5	75.9	62.1	45.7	37.0	60.6
Average Min. Temperature (F)	22.4	26.0	31.8	36.3	42.1	49.0	56.6	56.7	49.2	39.9	29.8	22.9	38.6
Average Total Precipitation (in.)	2.15	1.90	2.21	2.01	1.98	1.03	0.48	0.45	0.99	1.23	2.16	2.29	18.89
Average Total Snowfall (in.)	13.2	10.0	7.0	3.2	0.4	0.0	0.0	0.0	0.0	0.3	8.3	13.6	56.0
Average Snow Depth (in.)	4	3	1	0	0	0	0	0	0	0	1	2	1

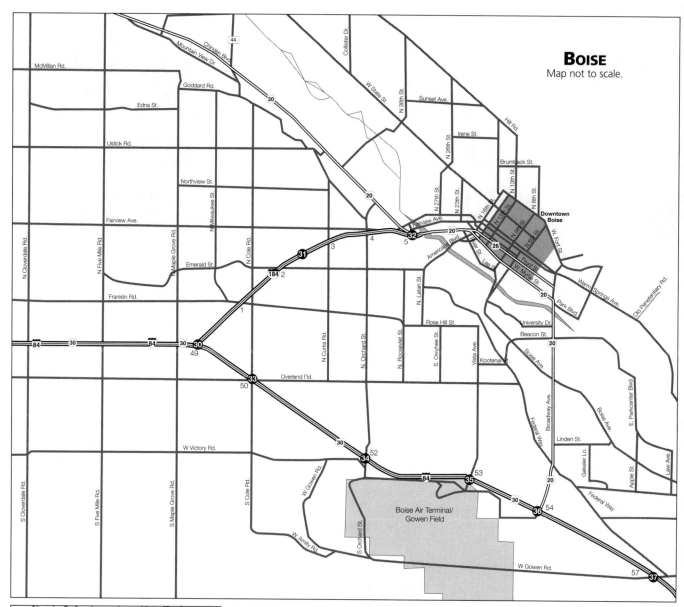

BOISE
Map not to scale.

Boise Downtown- Map not to scale.

of four territorial prisons still standing as a reminder of America's heritage. The penitentiary opened as a single cellhouse in 1870, but prisoners were soon put to work hand cutting and constructing the sandstone buildings and towering walls now comprising the historical institution. Despite

no internal plumbing, the complex was used until December 3, 1973 and housed more than 13,000 prisoners during its operation. After numerous inmate uprisings against the archaic conditions, government officials finally approved construction of a new facility with the old penitentiary remaining as a historical site.

Today, the ominous facility is a captivating museum. Visitors will learn about some of Idaho's most notorious inmates, including Harry Orchard, convicted of killing the governor in 1905, as well as Lady Bluebeard, who was found guilty of poisoning her fourth husband for insurance money and suspected of involvement with her previous husbands' mysterious deaths. Lady Bluebeard actually escaped the prison and had married her fifth husband by the time officials arrested her and brought her back to the prison. Along with such notable stories, the self-guided walking tour also explores daily prison life, the women's ward that housed 215 women during its lifespan, solitary confinement, Death Row, and a rose garden that served as the site for the prison's gallows and the state's only hanging (in 1957). The tour takes approximately 90 minutes and features a museum displaying prisoners' contraband weapons and photos of several inmates' self-designed tattoos.

On-site and included with admission to the Old Penitentiary is an electricity museum featuring hands-on exhibits and a few old electrical appliances. The Idaho Transportation Museum displays the vast array of transportation modes people have used throughout the growth and development of the state. Numerous early model vehicles are displayed, as well as some horse-drawn carriages. The site is open 10 AM to 5 PM daily from Memorial Day to Labor Day and 12 PM to 5 PM daily during fall, winter, and spring. Admission is $5 for adults, $4 for seniors, $3 for children ages 6-12, and free to those under 6. Discounted admission is available to groups of ten or more.

T Pierce Park Greens
5812 N. Pierce Park Ln., Boise. 853-3302.

Views of the surrounding mountains and tree-lined fairways await players at Pierce Park Greens. This 9-hole, par 36 course features hilly greens and was designed for golfers of all abilities. Weather permitting, the course is open daily from 8 AM to dusk. Green fees are $9 for adults, $8 for seniors, $7 for juniors, and $5 for peewee players.

T Basque Museum and Cultural Center
611 Grove St., Boise. 343-2671.
www.basquemuseum.com

In 1864, early Boise resident and wealthy merchant, Cyrus Jacobs, built what is now the city's oldest surviving brick building. This building, which Jose Uberuaga later used for a Basque sheepherders' boardinghouse, is now included as part of the extensive Basque Museum and Cultural Center. The museum explores the Basque culture in the U.S. and abroad and includes several artifacts unique to the Basques. The center is open Tuesday through Saturday year-round with free admission.

T Boise Art Museum
670 S. Julia Davis Dr., Boise.
345-8330. http://boiseartmuseum.org

Originating in 1931 as the Boise Art Association, today's Boise Art Museum is the only AAM (American Association of Museums) accredited Idaho art museum. After years of volunteer management, the museum received its first professional staff in the mid 1960s, and in 1988, it received its initial accreditation. Throughout its history, the Boise Art Museum has strived to collect and display regional and national artwork, as well as nationally acclaimed exhibitions. The museum houses an extensive permanent collection of works, including the nationally recognized American Realist works of Glenn C. Janss.

The Boise Art Museum is also on a mission to educate the public. With community support, the museum created a schedule of education programs, including such events as the studio art program, school tours, lectures, family days, after hours promotional events that include regular jazz concerts, and September's Art in the Park festival. It is estimated that the museum reaches out to more than 13,000 students every year. With more than a dozen different exhibitions each year, the museum offers instant access to culture often only found in more metropolitan areas. The museum is open 10 AM to 5 PM Tuesdays, Wednesdays, and Friday through Sunday. On Thursdays, the museum is open from 10 AM to 8 PM with extended hours to 9 PM on the first Thursday of each month. Admission is $5 general, $3 for seniors and college students, $1 for youth in grades 1-12, and half price admission on the first Thursday of each month.

T Discovery Center of Idaho
131 Myrtle St., Boise.
343-9895. www.scidaho.org

Boise's Discovery Center of Idaho situated within the Julia Davis Park teaches physics to both kids and adults in a fun atmosphere. The center boasts more than 160 unique hands-on exhibits that teach visitors of all ages about electricity, light, sound, liquids, and much, much more. Striving to make science fun, the center and its staff host science discovery day camps and operate the site's Science Educational Resource Center. The center is open May 31 to August 31 from 10 AM to 5 PM Monday through Saturday and 12 PM to 5 PM on Sundays. During the rest of the year, operating hours are 9 AM to 5 PM Tuesday through Friday, 10 AM to 5 PM on Saturdays, and 12 PM to 5 PM on Sundays. There is an admission charge, and visitors should plan more than an hour to adequately partake in all the center's exhibits.

T Idaho Black History Museum
508 Julia Davis Dr., Boise. 433-0017. www.ibhm.org

Founded in 1995, the Idaho Black History Museum's mission is to educate all races about African American history and culture, particularly emphasizing the experience of Idaho's African Americans. Displaying several historical photos, crafts, and artifacts reflecting the heritage of Idaho's African American culture, the museum's building is also part of Idaho's African American legacy. The museum is housed in the former St. Paul Baptist Church. Erected in 1921, the building is one of the oldest structures constructed by Idaho African Americans. The non-profit museum is open 10 AM to 4 PM Tuesday through Saturday and 1 PM to 4 PM on Sundays during the summer. Winter hours are 11 AM to 3 PM Wednesday through Saturday.

T Idaho Botanical Garden
2355 Old Penitentiary Rd., Boise.
343-8649. www.idahobotanicalgarden.org

The Idaho Botanical Garden is a living museum committed to appreciation of gardening, horticulture, and conservation and educating the public on these topics. Situated on 50 acres of land that served as the farm and nursery at the old Idaho State Penitentiary, the once defunct land was turned into beautiful gardens beginning in 1984. Today, visitors will find thirteen different theme gardens: Herb, Rose, Alpine, Contemporary English, Outlaw Field, Butterfly and Hummingbird, Iris, Meditation, Water, Cactus, Peony, Children, and Idaho Native Plants and Outdoor Classroom. The garden is open 9 AM to 5 PM Monday through Friday and 10 AM to 6 PM Saturday and Sunday from May through October. November to April, the garden is open 9 AM to 5 PM Monday through Friday and 12 PM to 4 PM on weekends.

T Idaho State Historical Museum
610 N. Julia Davis Dr., Boise. 334-2120.
www.idahohistory.net/museum.html

Founded in 1907, the Idaho State Historical Museum is Idaho's largest and most frequently visited museum. Recounting the state's rich heritage of progress from prehistoric times to early white settlement, the museum is filled with a variety of interesting exhibits. Visitors will find displays about Native American, Chinese, and Basque cultures, the fur-trading and mining eras, and pioneer settlers. Just outside the museum, a Pioneer Village preserves several of the earliest buildings constructed in Boise with some dating back as far as the 1860s. The museum attracts an especially large crowd annually on the last Saturday of September when the "Museum Comes to Life" is held. Costumed interpreters bring to life such exhibits as an Old West saloon, a Chinese apothecary's shop, and other historical crafts and activities relevant to Idaho's legacy. The museum is open 9 AM to 5 PM Tuesday through Saturday and 1 PM to 5 PM on Sunday from May through September. October through April, the museum is open from 9 AM to 5 PM Tuesday through Friday and 11 AM to 5 PM on Saturdays. Admission is $2 for adults, $1 for youth ages 6-18, and free for those under 6.

T Idaho State Capitol Building
700 W. Jefferson, Boise. 332-1007.

Nestled in the heart of downtown Boise, the Idaho State Capitol rises impressively as a smaller version of the nation's capital building. Boise architect, J.E. Tourtelloutte, drew the plans for the building at the dawn of the 20th century with construction beginning in 1905. Featuring a neoclassical design, the capital was finally completed in 1920 with a $2.3 million price tag.

The majestic building's exterior is composed of multi-ton Boise sandstone quarried by convicts behind the old Idaho State Penitentiary. Inside, marble from Alaska (gray), Georgia (red), Vermont (green), and Italy (black), distinguishes the rotunda topped with a 5'7" bronze eagle. Sixty-foot tall faux marble pillars support a dome showcasing Idaho's title as the forty-third state with forty-three stars painted against a blue background. The four-story interior also features the handiwork of state agencies and special-interest groups with several changing exhibits. Idaho history and information about the state's major industries is displayed along with sculptures, tapestry murals, and photo-

A SPORT FOR ALL ENTHUSIASTS

Sports enthusiasts will be delighted upon visiting Boise to discover that the city offers a wide range of spectator sports sure to please all athletic enthusiasts. From baseball to drag racing to football and more, Boise's professional teams and venues provide thrills and spills in every season!

Boise Hawks

For sports lovers, Boise's professional baseball team serves up a professional take on an All-American favorite. The Boise Hawks serve as the short-season affiliate of the Chicago Cubs and play a full schedule from mid-June through early September every year. The team functions as a breeding ground for tomorrow's major league stars, and interested spectators are encouraged to reserve tickets for the games played at Memorial Stadium. 322-5000.

Firebird Raceway

Those who crave the need for speed should head north of Boise to the Firebird Raceway. The raceway hosts all types of racing April through October, including the Nightfire Nationals. Interested racing fans should contact the raceway at 938-8986 for a complete schedule of events.

Idaho Stampede Basketball

Competing as a member of the Continental Basketball Association, Idaho Stampede Basketball provides fans with heart-pounding action at affordable prices. The team plays other association members, providing top-quality games suitable for a wide range of audiences. For an annual schedule and ticket information, call 388-4667.

Idaho Stallions Arena Football

The Boise-based Idaho Stallions are members of the Indoor Professional Football League. Playing home games at the Bank of America Center from April through August, the Idaho Stallions drive home wall-to-wall action in every quarter. Call 331-TIXS for tickets and further information.

Idaho Steelheads

As members of the West Coast Hockey League, the Idaho Steelheads serve up reasonably priced hockey games every October through March. Games are held in the Bank of America Centre with ticket prices ranging from $15 to $25. For additional information, call 424-2200.

Idaho Sneakers

Offering a change of pace from traditionally silent tennis tournaments, the Idaho Sneakers encourage fans to yell and have some fun. The team is a franchise of World Team Tennis and play summer home matches in the Bank of America Centre.

Les Bois Park

For equestrian lovers, Les Bois Park provides an outlet for thoroughbred and quarter horse racing every April through August. Numerous famous jockeys have started their careers at this very park, and races occur three times each week. On non-race days, horse enthusiasts can hone their betting skills and wager on horse races via satellite television. For further schedule and racing information, call 376-7223.

---

graphs of Idaho's territorial governors. On the fourth floor, visitors may slip into the House and Senate galleries for a glimpse of Idaho lawmakers in action.

Complete with a replica of the Liberty Bell and a Civil War era cannon, the capitol building offers a discovery tour of Idaho. Free self-guided tour brochures are available from the first floor visitor information counter, and guided tours are available by advance arrangement. The capitol building is open Monday through Friday from 7 AM to 6 PM and on Saturdays and Sundays from 9 AM to 5 PM.

T Idaho Museum of Mining and Geology

2455 Old Penitentiary Rd., Boise. 368-9876.

Located in an outbuilding just outside the Old Idaho State Penitentiary, the Idaho Museum of Mining and Geology is the place for geology lovers and history buffs interested in the state's mining tradition. Mining was one of Idaho's first industries and has remained an important component of the state's economy. Inside this museum, visitors will find old mining artifacts and photos relating the story of Idaho's mining history. The museum is open from 12 PM to 5 PM on weekends April through October and also by appointment.

T Shadow Valley Golf Course

15711 State Hwy. 55, Boise. 939-6699. www.shadowvalley.com From downtown, proceed northwest on State St. At Hwy. 55, bear right, and proceed 5 miles to the course

Established in 1973, the mature Shadow Valley Golf Course offers tremendous views of the Boise Valley in a natural environment. The par-72 course features expansive sloping greens, waterfalls, ponds, flower gardens, and elevation changes amid its 5,514 yards. It is consistently rated one of Boise's best courses. Green fees are $25 for 18 holes and $15 for 9 holes Monday through Thursday with $20 twilight games offered after 3 PM. On weekends, green fees are $33 for 18 holes with a $25 twilight game after 3 PM. The course is also proud of its loyalty program, whereby visitors earn a free round of golf after spending $250 (on games, buckets of balls, or cart rentals).

T Quail Hollow Golf Course

4520 N. 36th St., Boise. 344-7807. On 36th St., drive 1 mile north of Hill Rd.

Although short in length, this par 70 course offers an extended day of play amid its numerous natural challenges. Large sloping greens, sand, water, and elevation changes greet golfers around every bend, and the course provides skilled practice for target golf. Designed by Bruce Devlin and Robert Von Hage, Quail Hollow was established in 1978 amid the Boise foothills and offers outstanding views of the Treasure Valley and city skyline. Weekday green fees are $34 with a cart, and weekend fees are $39 with a cart.

T Idaho Anne Frank Human Rights Memorial

Off Capitol Blvd. between the Log Cabin Literary Center and the Boise Public Library, Boise. 345-0304.

Nestled in the heart of Boise's cultural district, the Anne Frank Human Rights Memorial reminds visitors of the terrible price paid for failing to intervene in human rights issues. The memorial, which includes over sixty quotes from renowned human rights leaders, two reflection pools, three waterfalls, an amphitheater, a reading circle, and a bronze statue of Anne Frank, is designed to trigger people's spiritual instincts and desire for good will toward others.

T Kathryn Albertson Park

1000 Americana Blvd., Boise. Contact the Boise Parks Department at 384-4240.

The forty-acre Kathryn Albertson Park is a tranquil wildlife preserve nestled in the heart of Boise. Joe Albertson, founder of the national grocery chain, dreamed of creating a wildlife sanctuary left behind as a legacy to his wife. Albertson's plans quickly came to fruition, and over the course of fourteen months, the once abandoned horse pasture was transformed into this landscaped oasis. Due to its Boise River bank location and abundant riparian vegetation, the park attracts a myriad of wildlife. A paved path meanders around several ponds and two gazebos, and the park is a popular destination for a quiet picnic. Also housing the world's largest known ponderosa pine tree, the Kathryn Albertson Park is dedicated to preserving wildlife habitat, so swimming and fishing are prohibited in the area.

T Veterans Memorial Park

State St. and Veterans Parkway (at the corner of N. 36th St.), Boise. Contact the Boise Parks Department at 384-4240.

Veterans Memorial Park provides a peaceful escape from the surrounding hubbub of downtown Boise. The large park connects with the Boise River Greenbelt and features a small lake ideal for skipping rocks, floating, swimming, and fishing for rainbow trout, bluegill, bullhead, crappie, and largemouth bass. While the park's front corridor features neatly landscaped greens, pruned evergreen trees, an amphitheater, and several memorials to Idaho veterans and those who fell in the line of duty, the park's back side is a web of dense overgrowth providing a canopy of shade for greenbelt users. The park is accessible year-round.

T Ann Morrison Park

Between Americana Blvd. and Capitol Blvd., Boise. Contact the Boise Parks Department at 384-4240.

Stretching itself over 155 acres along the Boise River, the level, grassy Ann Morrison Park offers something for everyone. The 0.75-miles of shoreline provides floaters and anglers with easy river access, while numerous picnic groves, grills, an illuminated fountain display, reflecting pool, and a wood-themed playground provide a tranquil family outing. For those seeking a more active day in the park, the area also boasts soccer fields, tennis courts, lighted softball fields, an archery range, and horseshoe pits. The park is accessible year-round during daylight hours.

T Camel's Back Park and Reserve

North of Hyde Park off 13th St., Boise. Contact the Boise Parks Department at 384-4240.

Camel's Back Park is aptly named after the two large grassy humps rising 100 feet above the rest of the park's flat surface. The expansive grassy area features a large playground, shade trees, tennis courts, and a soccer field. The park is accessible year-round.

T Julia Davis Park

Capitol Ave. and Front St., Boise. Contact the Boise Parks Department at 384-4240.

Encompassing ninety-acres near the Boise River, Julia Davis Park is home to some of Boise's most popular attractions, including the Idaho Historical Museum, Boise Art Museum, and Zoo Boise. In addition, the park features picnic shelters, tennis courts, playgrounds, horseshoe pits, boat rentals, and a bandshell that provides free summer concerts.

The park's namesake honors the legacy of early Boise residents, Thomas and Julia Davis. In 1863, Thomas Jefferson Davis came to the region with his brother and homesteaded 360 acres. Selling the vegetables they raised to Boise Basin miners, the brothers saw the potential for a new Idaho Territory city. On July 7, 1863, Thomas and his brother gathered with a group of other area homesteaders to plot out a new city. Their resulting city of Boise ignited like wildfire, and homesteaders from near and far moved to the new community.

Julia McCrum of Ontario, Canada was one of the new settlers who came to Boise, and in 1871, she married Thomas. Together, the couple built an agricultural empire encompassing hundreds of prime city acres. Just prior to the dawn of 1900, Thomas and Julia decided to donate forty acres along the Boise River for a community park. The park was completed in 1907 and bears the name of Thomas' beloved wife.

T Zoo Boise
355 N. Julia Davis Dr., Boise. 384-4260.

Representing eighty-three different species with more than 200 animals, Zoo Boise is situated inside Boise's beautiful Julia Davis Park. The zoo is a member of the American Zoo and Aquarium Association and is dedicated to providing animals with the highest quality care. Featuring everything from tiny walking sticks to rare tigers, the zoo strives to educate visitors and provide a fun learning experience for all. Except for major holidays, the zoo is open daily with a small admission charge. In mid-May, visitors should watch for "Zoo Daze," which offers discounted admission and several special events targeted at children.

T Downtown Boise, The Grove, and Warehouse District
Contact the Boise Visitors Bureau at 344-7777.

Downtown Boise is one of the most culturally vibrant and eclectic areas in all of Idaho. Intriguing architecture from the city's late 19th and early 20th century roots combine with modern sidewalk cafes, pubs, and an array of shops to create a one-of-a-kind friendly hometown atmosphere. Although one-way streets line the district, this eco-conscious downtown area is pedestrian friendly with diverse offerings sure to keep people of all ages entertained.

Situated between 8th and 9th Sts. south of Main St., The Grove is Boise's premier gathering place. Surrounding a central water fountain where children and adults alike can't resist getting wet, the large brick plaza is home to numerous community events. Benches line the plaza, late night musicians often strum free tunes, and the Bank of America Centre provides a 5,000-seat arena accommodating events ranging from sports to renowned music concerts. The Grove's most well-known feature, however, is the weekly "Alive After Five" summer concert series where children and adults gather for live music and dancing.

Across from The Grove is the 8th Street Marketplace, originally known as the "Warehouse District" in the early 1900s. Today, the marketplace is exactly that – a market of shops, boutiques, restaurants, and a historic candy company dating back to 1909.

T Boise Tour Train and Trolley
Julia Davis Dr. in Julia Davis Park, Boise. Contact the Boise Visitors Bureau at 344-7777.

Pulled by a miniature replica of an 1890s steam locomotive, the Boise Tour Train departs daily from a small depot in Julia Davis Park and provides visitors with a one-hour narrated tour. The train carries passengers through Julia Davis Park, Old Fort Boise, the capitol area, historic Warm Springs residential neighborhood, and the historic downtown area. Visitors will learn interesting tidbits and fun facts about Boise's history and development as a major Idaho city. Four to five tours are offered daily during summer, with limited daily tours offered the remainder of the year. Winter passengers miss out on the replica steam engine and instead are treated to an enclosed, heated trolley.

T Julia Davis Rose Garden
Julia Davis Park, Boise. Contact the Boise Visitors Bureau at 344-7777.

The Julia Davis Rose Garden is a summer attraction whose fragrant aroma drenches Julia Davis Park and the surrounding area with the sweet perfume of roses. Garden visitors are treated to more than 300 vibrantly colored rose varieties amid the 1,600 lovingly maintained rose bushes. The garden is open free of charge during park hours.

T Downtown Boise's Public Art
Contact the Boise Visitors Bureau at 344-7777.

Boise is known as one of Idaho's cultural meccas, littered with art, theater, and music around every corner. Downtown Boise reflects this commitment to the arts with a phenomenal public art collection lining the streets. From painted murals to stained glass windows, the art is as varied as each creator.

A Legend of Dreams, The Idaho Historic Statehouse Murals (1994)
Jefferson St. at the Idaho State Capitol, 4th Floor
Idaho's southeastern, southwestern, and northern regional history comes to life in this large fabric mural. Artist: Dana Boussard.

Steunenberg (1927)
Capitol Blvd. & Jefferson St.
Frank Steunenberg served as Idaho's governor from 1897-1901, and this memorial honors the fallen political figure who was assassinated in 1905. Artist: Gilbert Riswold.

Alley History (1992)
Ninth St. Alley, between Bannock & Idaho Sts.
Combining history and popular imagery in a whimsical pattern, this ceramic wall mural features graffiti, painted advertisements, nightclub mementos, and product logos. Artist: Kerry Moosman.

Stained Glass Window (1999)
9th St. & Idaho St.
Featuring unique pieces from the Boise Peace Quilt Project, this stained glass site marks the entryway to 9th Street. Artist: Michael Pilla.

River of Trees (1999)
9th St. & Idaho St.
Inspired by the Boise River, this sidewalk art piece

features bronze leaves scattered amid iron cast tree grates. Artists: Judith and Daniel

Caldwell Spring Run (1994)
Spring Run Plaza, between Main St. & Idaho St.
Located on the building's south wall, viewers will find a school of sixty ceramic fish and six metal bear heads curiously looking on as the annual spring run that takes place in several of Idaho's wild rivers is depicted. Artist: Marilyn Lysohir.

Boise Totems (1993)
Corner of 8th St. & Idaho St.
Capturing the imagery of the Pacific Northwest's Native American tribes, these three bronze columns are situated in the heart of downtown. Artist: Rod Kagan.

Stearns Motor Car (2000)
Idaho St. between 6th St. & Capitol Blvd.
This mural was gifted to the City of Boise at the dawn of the 21st century. The unique painting is the work of The Letterheads, an international group of sign painters. Artists: The Letterheads.

Les Bois (1992)
Capitol Terrace Parking Garage, Idaho St. Exit
Les Bois provides striking visual imagery with its scattered pattern of leaf images etched into twenty-four white steel plates. As passerby walk past, the leaves appear to dissolve, become whole, and then disappear again. Artists: Bruce Poe and Dennis Proksa.

Sidney's Niche (1992)
8th St. Escalator, between Main St. & Idaho St.
Constructed from bulletin enamel, this site-specific painting is highlighted with a fun and fanciful quality. Artist: Rick Thomson

Egyptian Windows (2001)
Corner of Capitol Blvd. & Main St.
The historic qualities of the Egyptian Theater building are preserved in this creative work of art. Silkscreened theater photos from 1927 and 1946 were placed on glass, back painted, detailed in gold leaf, and finally lit up with tiny fiber optic lights. Artist: Classic Design Studio.

CYC Wall of Fame (1997)
City Hall Entryway on Capitol Blvd.
Boise, also known as the City of Trees, is memorialized in this ceramic tile wall mural. Artist: Michael Corney with the help of Community Youth Connection's Youth Hall of Fame inductees.

Through the Cottonwoods, One Could See the Games Being Played (1978)
City Hall's 3rd floor Les Bois Room on Capitol Blvd.
The Shoshone tribe has historically met under the canopy of cottonwoods, and this tapestry reflects that cultural heritage. The artwork features rich colors, textures, and symbolism. Artist: Dana Boussard.

Laiak (2000)
Capitol Blvd. & Grove St.
Marking the entrance to the Basque Block, these two steel and stone monuments honor the culture and history of the Basque people. The sculptures were erected in memory of Pat and Eloise Bieter. Artist: Ward Hooper.

River Sculpture (1999)
Corner of Front St. & Capitol Blvd. at the Grove Hotel
Nature's creation and gifts of water and light are celebrated in this fifty-foot tall sculpture. The work is comprised of painted aluminum, neon, granite, fused glass, and fog misers to create a one-of-a-kind piece. Artist: Alison Sky.

Historical Sight: Boise Chinatown (2001)
Three locations: The Grove; Capitol Blvd. near Front St.; Capitol Blvd. across from Grove St.
Chinese came to Idaho in droves during the gold rush era and consequently helped shape the history of southwestern Idaho. The presence of Chinese nationals in Boise and the surrounding region is explored in historical photos viewed through unique stereoscopic devices. Artist: Dwaine Carver

1867/The Miner (1984)
The Grove, behind U.S. Bank on Main St.
Two miles of barbed wire weighing in at 700 pounds forms this unique art piece. The piece's name reflects the historical protection of miner's gold at the First National Bank of Idaho. Artist: Bernie Jestrabek-Hart.

Keepsies (1985)
In the middle of The Grove off Main St.
Three children playing an old-fashioned game of marbles are memorialized in this nostalgic bronze sculpture. Artist: Ann LaRose.

Great Blues (1990)
In the middle of The Grove off Main St.
Nature arrives in the middle of the city setting with this sculpture of blue herons resting in a stream. The sculpture is crafted out of stainless steel. Artist: David Berry.

Untitled (1988)
Wells Fargo Plaza near The Grove on 9th & Main Sts.
Nestled amid winding concrete sidewalks, this black painted steel sculpture presents an abstract form. The sculpture fulfills its intended goal of reflecting the contemporary building structure of the nearby Wells Fargo. Artist: Guy Dill.

Basque History Mural (2000)
Capitol Blvd. between Grove & Front St.
The Letterheads, an international sign painting organization, gifted the City of Boise with this mural in 2000. The painting recognizes the long history of Basque culture in Idaho. Artist: The Letterheads.

Homage to the Pedestrian (2002)
The Grove
This innovative sculpture's distinguishing characteristic is its involvement of and dependence upon passerby. The sculpture interacts with pedestrians, translating motion into unique sounds. Artist: Patrick Zentz.

Boise Visual Chronicle (1996-Present)
Interior lobby areas of Boise City Hall and Boise Centre on the Grove
An array of perspectives capturing the life and times of Boise provides a visual history display. The ongoing masterpiece features over forty art and literary works to this date. Artist: Various Idaho Artists.

Flow (1998)
Interior Lobby of Boise Centre on the Grove
The changing of seasons, water bodies, tree groves, and the environment in general serves as the subject for this inspirational piece. Created from glass, wood, steel, and silver leaf, the artwork spans sixty feet and serves as a lobby centerpiece. Artists: Dwaine Carver & Christ Binion.

Natural Bridge (1994)
In front of the Boise Public Library on Capitol Blvd.
The culture of Idaho's Native American tribes comes to life in this steel sculpture near the Boise River. Artist: David Berry.

A Ribbon of Hope (1998)
The lobby of Boise Public Library on Capitol Blvd.
What do you get when you combine the talents of an artist, writer, and a creative group of young people? "A Ribbon of Hope" answers that question in its unique mixed media presentation. Artists: Shannon Fausey, Geno Sky, and Community Youth Connection Hall of Fame inductees.

Point of Origin (1978)
On the grounds of the Boise Art Museum on Julia Davis Dr.
Originally positioned in front of the Boise City Hall, this geometric sculpture was formerly entitled, "Northwest Passage." Now under a new name, the sculpture remains the first public art piece to grace Boise's downtown area. Artist: John Mason.

Boise Art Museum Sculpture Garden
Behind the Boise Art Museum on Julia Davis Dr.
The Boise Art Museum Sculpture Garden is a revolving display of impressive sculptures. Artwork gathered from both Pacific Northwest and national artists is showcased in the outdoor sculpture garden. Artist: Various Artists.

Capitol Bridge Tiles
On the Capitol Bridge pillars on Capital Blvd.
An unremembered 1930s artist created ornately painted ceramic tiles on the pillars of Capital Blvd. The tiles honor the thousands of pioneers who made the long journey across Idaho on the Oregon Trail.

T Hyde Park
13th St. between Alturas and Brumback, Boise. Contact the Boise Visitors Bureau at 344-7777.

Recognized as one of the hippest neighborhoods in town, Boise's Hyde Park is a designated historic district oozing old world charm mixed with modern comforts. Hyde Park features a charming atmosphere adorned with unique specialty stores, antique shops, and a variety of cafes, restaurants, and independently owned coffeehouses.

T Golf & Recreation Club
5803 O'Hara Ct., Boise. 344-2008. From W. State St., merge onto Ellens Ferry Dr., then N. Bluegrass Ave. to O'Hara Ct.

The Golf & Recreation Club in Boise provides public golfing opportunities every spring through autumn. The 1,235 yard, 9-hole course is rated a par 27.

T Boise Philharmonic
516 S. 9th St. (off Myrtle St.), Boise. 344-7849. www.boisephilharmonic.org.

Performing for over 58,000 people annually, the Boise Philharmonic is the foremost symphony orchestra in the Pacific Northwest. The orchestra has long provided a legacy of musical excellence in the Treasure Valley and traces its origins back to the 1887 founding of the Boise City Orchestra. The organization later changed its name to the Boise Civic Symphony Orchestra, and since 1960,

the group has performed under its Philharmonic title. The orchestra continues to grow with every passing season, offering audiences more performances during the regular September through April concert season. Ticket prices range from $15 to $40 depending upon the performance, and advanced tickets are recommended as concerts generally play to sold-out crowds.

T City Hall Plaza
Capitol Blvd., Boise. Contact the Boise Visitors Bureau at 344-7777.

Located in front of Boise's City Hall, the City Hall Plaza is a downtown landmark offering a retreat from urban exploration. The park includes historical artifacts, flag displays, a fountain, and an arboretum providing visitors with plenty of shade.

T C.W. Moore Park
5th and Grove Sts., Boise. Contact the Boise Visitors Bureau at 344-7777.

In 1863, Canadian native, Christopher W. Moore, arrived in Boise and founded the First National Bank of Idaho. He quickly established a reputation for philanthropy, and upon his death, donated two city lots that he owned for park development. Moore's wishes were fulfilled, and one of Boise's most interesting parks was developed. Today, the park features historic treasures and architecture from Boise's pioneer days, a working waterwheel that once irrigated Boise's lawns and trees, and an idyllic setting in the midst of town.

T Ballet Idaho
501 S. 8th St., Ste. A, Boise. 343-0556. www.balletidaho.org

Ballet Idaho, a professional ballet company featuring a permanent corps de ballet, produces a diverse mix of contemporary and classical performances. The nationally recognized and acclaimed company offers several productions throughout its regular September through March season, including the holiday favorite, *The Nutcracker*. Performances generally sell out, so advanced tickets are recommended. Call for a complete schedule of major season productions and ticket prices.

T Boise Contemporary Theater
854 Fulton St. in the Fulton St. Theater, Boise. 331-9224. www.bctheater.org

Established in 1998 as a poor theater company performing plays wherever it could find a venue or empty storefront, the Boise Contemporary Theater Company has expanded its horizons and reputation. The theater company is now at home in the Fulton Street Theater and is dedicated to producing and presenting theatrical works of the highest quality. Presentations are aimed at reflecting and exploring contemporary life, and patrons become just as much a part of the play as the playwright, director, and actors. Contemporary favorites as well as works by up and coming playwrights are presented throughout the year. Actor Matt Damon even graced the company with a theater benefit when he premiered his 2002 film, "The Bourne Identity" in Boise. Ticket prices vary with each performance, and patrons are encouraged to call for advanced tickets and a complete schedule of events.

T Idaho Supreme Court Building
451 W. State St., Boise. Contact the Boise Visitors Bureau at 344-7777.

Recognized for extravagance, the Idaho Supreme Court Building in Boise is often referred to as the "Palace of Justice." Located in the same vicinity as the State Capital, the court building displays granite-chip floors and travertine-limestone walls. The building was constructed for a hefty $2 million, a price tag that remains controversial among today's critics.

T Idaho Department of Commerce
700 W. State St., Boise. Contact the Boise Visitors Bureau at 344-7777.

The Idaho Department of Commerce is contained within the stately Joe R. Williams Office Building near the Idaho State Capitol. With windows that function like mirrors, the building showcases spectacular views of Idaho's Capitol while serving as a headquarters for tourist information about the entire state.

T GAR Hall
714 W. State St., Boise.

The tiny GAR Hall located in Boise's Capitol neighborhood was built in 1892 as the meeting site for the Grand Army of the Republic. The organization, comprised of Union soldiers who fought in the Civil War, held regular meetings at this building to commemorate the soldier's bond and their service to America.

T Boise Historical Tour
Contact the Boise Visitors Bureau at 344-7777.

Historically recognized as a farming and mining supply center, Boise has developed into the site of premier cultural and commercial activity. Home to the state's capital, Boise and its promising future is based upon the groundwork of the city's earliest settlers. Many contributions from these pioneering dreamers remain, and Boise's streets are filled with historical businesses and private residences from days gone by.

Idanha Hotel
928 West Main St.
Characterized by tall corner turrets and a French Chateau architectural style, the Idanha Hotel is a regional landmark. After W.S. Campbell completed the hotel's innovative design, construction began immediately with an opening date of New

IDAHO'S BASQUE CULTURE AND THE OINKARI BASQUE DANCERS

While the eastern seaboard is known for its dense populations of Irish and Italian descendants, the western U.S. is graced with the presence of one of the world's most courageous and unique cultures. California, Nevada, Wyoming, Oregon, Utah, and Idaho are all recognized for their dense Basque populations. Idaho alone harbors over 12,000 Basque-Americans, many of whom reside in Boise.

The Basque's scenic homeland of Euskadi is located between the Spanish-French border near scenic ocean shores and is covered with lush forests and verdant pastures. Accustomed to this beautiful and fertile terrain, the Basque people honed their skills as premier shipbuilders, whalers, farmers, and mariners. These skills, however, did little to help improve the economic situation of young siblings in large Basque families. Traditional Basque culture dictated that only the oldest child would inherit the family fortune while younger siblings were forced to create their own destiny. Hearing tales of easy gold fortunes made in America's Wild West, many of these young Basque packed their bags, left their homeland behind, and bravely made their way to the New World.

Upon arriving in the American West, the Basque people faced a culture shock. The Basque's distinct language, which linguists have failed to relate to any other world language, posed a communication barrier with other settlers. In addition, the high desert landscape featured no job opportunities to which the Basque were accustomed. In response, a few Basque pursued employment in the gold mines while others sought the solitary life of sheepherding. Although the Basque had no experience with sheepherding, the job was available to anyone,

regardless of one's ability to speak English. Within no time, the Basque proved themselves as reliable hard workers.

Over time, the Basque's reputation and their increased knowledge of the English language allowed them to assimilate into life in Idaho territory. Their integration, however, did not translate into denial of their heritage. The Basque culture is honored to this day and evident throughout Boise. In addition to annual festivals and Basque cultural museums, Boise is home to the celebrated Oinkari Basque Dancers.

In 1949, Basque descendant, Juanita Uberuaga Hormaechea, was known as a prized "jota" dancer (the traditional Basque dance). Deciding that all children of Basque heritage should be exposed to their unique cultural traditions, Hormaechea began providing Boise and regional children with Basque dancing lessons. The well-respected teacher quickly earned a reputation for her prized students' skills, and in 1960, she took a group of her students to the Basque homeland. While there, the young Boise dancers watched and practiced with the native Oinkari professional dancing group. Hormaechea's students learned new skills from the native group, and lifelong friendships formed. When it was time for the Boise dancers to return to America, the Oinkari troupe requested that Hormaechea and her young dancers name themselves "Oinkari" after the native Basque troupe that had inspired them all. Hormaechea kindly accepted the honor, and Boise's Oinkari dancing troupe began its journey to international recognition.

Today, the dance troupe maintains respect for their cultural heritage with lively dances of flying feet, snapping fingers, and shouts of joy. Boise's Oinkari has performed at numerous World's Fairs, Washington D.C. folk festivals, international Basque festivals, and at regional Basque gatherings in Nevada, California, and Idaho. Proud of their heritage, the Oinkari dancers and Basque people in general invite visitors to discover their unique culture while visiting Boise.

Year's Day, 1901. At a total cost of $125,000, the hotel was the most elite in the entire state. The Idanha was Idaho's first six-story building and featured the state's first electric elevator. An instant success, the 103-room hotel was accessorized with the finest amenities, including claw foot tubs, luxurious tapestries and furnishings, and bay windows. As the hotel's reputation spread far and wide, the Idanha became known as the finest hotel west of the Mississippi and welcomed such famous guests as Theodore Roosevelt, Wild Buffalo Bill, William Borah, and John and Ethel Barrymore. Today, the historic building has been refurbished into private apartments.

The Book Shop
908 Main St.
Located in mid-block, The Book Shop is housed in one of Boise's oldest buildings and is frequently referred to as the best independent bookstore in all of Idaho.

Idaho First National Bank
Capitol Blvd.
Rising 267 feet against the Boise business backdrop, Idaho First National Bank was constructed in 1978 and holds the title as the state's tallest building. The bank charter dates back to 1864

with the original building located just one block away. Despite its massive size, the building supposedly uses at least one-third less energy than comparably sized facilities due to its positioning and computer controlled heating and cooling system.

Egyptian (Ada) Theater
Northwest Corner of Main and Capitol Sts.
The 1922 discovery of Egyptian King Tut's tomb and the Los Angeles Egyptian Theater inspired the development of this unique building in 1926 and 1927. Designed by Frederick Hummel and erected at a cost of $160,000, the theater has long been considered the finest representation of Egyptian Revival architecture in all of the Pacific Northwest. Although the theater was once doomed to demolition, the historic building was saved and features its original, working pipe organ used to provide all the music and sound effects for early twentieth century silent films.

U.S. Assay Office
Main St. between 3rd and 2nd Sts.
This National Historic Landmark was federally authorized in 1869 and opened in 1872, quickly becoming one of the most important buildings during the state's gold rush era. The site, donated by Alexander Rossi, was selected to ease the ship-

ping burden and costs for miners in Silver City and the Boise Basin.

At the time of its construction, the sandstone building cost $73,000 and included assayer's offices, vaults, melting rooms, safes, a guard's room, and living quarters for the head assayer and his family. The office quickly established itself as the region's premier place for gold and silver evaluation and business boomed. From 1895 to 1906, the office shipped out more than $1.5 million in gold mint bars collected from miner's gold deposits. But when World War I hit, business went bust, and the office was finally closed in June 1933. In 1972, the building was donated to the Idaho Historical Society. Today, the building is open from 9 AM to 5 PM on weekdays.

Eoff Mansion
140 Main St.
J.F. Tourtellotte designed this home in 1897 for prominent town banker, Alfred Eoff. Alfred and his wife, Victoria, shelled out $10,000 for the home that would later serve as James Brady's governor's mansion from 1908 to 1909.

Regan House
110 Main St.
Built for Timothy Regan between 1903 and 1904, this Colonial Revival House features an elaborate oak, birch, maple, and sycamore interior. Regan drew his wealth from investments in the Golden Chariot and Oro Fino mines near Silver City.

Warm Springs Ave.
In general, Boise's Warm Springs Avenue is known for its gracious historic homes and was once recognized as the city's most prestigious residential area. In 1890, a geothermal well was developed in the area, and the 170 degree Fahrenheit water was used to heat the street's historic residences. Eventually, nine miles of pipe linked the geothermal heating system with several residences for a mere $3.00 a month. The system is still used in some of the Warm Springs Ave. homes today.

Warm Springs Center
Corner of Warm Springs Ave. and Bruce St.
In 1920, Cynthia Mann donated this block of land for Boise's Children's Homes. Supported by the Idaho Legislature and several women's groups, the home was designed by Tourtellotte & Company as an institution for orphaned and abused children. The building contained classrooms, dining rooms, a kitchen, hospital, and male and female dormitories. The building now houses a center that assists mentally and emotionally disturbed youth.

Joseph Kinney House
Corner of 904 Warm Springs Ave. and Elm St.
Joseph Kinney, longtime owner of a Boise saloon, occupied this Queen Anne style house in 1904.

C.C. Anderson Home
929 Warm Springs Ave.
C.C. Anderson was the owner of Boise's first Golden Rule store on Main Street. He was so successful, he expanded his local store into a chain store encompassing five western states and twenty-one stores. Using some of his profits, Anderson had this English Country style home built in 1925. Famous Spokane architect, Kirtland Cutter, designed the home especially for Anderson.

William Regan Residence
1009 Warm Springs Ave.
This Mission-style home was built in 1911 for William Regan and his wife. Regan was the son of wealthy mine investor, Timothy Regan, and he served as Boise Artesian Water Company's Director. Together with his wife, Regan raised seven children in this home before relocating in 1939.

Moore-Cunningham Mansion
Southeast corner of Warm Springs and Walnut Aves.
The Moore-Cunningham Mansion is one of the most admired homes in all of Boise and dates back to 1891. Boise architect, James King, designed the French Chateau residence, which was built for $17,000. The fourteen-room residence housed C.W. Moore, the founder of the Idaho First National Bank and president of a local water company, along with his family. The home was the first in America to be heated with geothermal water, and the interior is accented with cherry, oak, and redwood. The mansion's hyphenated name reflects the title of Moore's daughter, Laura Cunningham.

R. M. Davidson Mansion
1205 Warm Springs Ave.
Butte, Montana mining millionaire, R.M. Davidson, had this massive Georgian Revival home built in 1901. Constructed at a cost of $15,000, the fifteen-room mansion features locally quarried granite.

Selden Kingsbury Residence
1225 Warm Springs Ave.
Boise architect, James King, designed this sandstone home in 1896 for Boise attorney, Selden Kingsbury. An English sculptor and his two young sons cut and sculpted the ornate sandstone walls by hand.

Lindley Cox Home
1308 Warm Springs Ave.
This Georgian Revival home was constructed in 1906 for Lindley Cox and his family. Cox served as a partner in a major Boise land development firm important to Boise's early commercial climate.

Jacob Wagner Home
1420 Warm Springs Ave.
This Queen Anne style home was built for early Boise resident, Jacob Wagner, in 1894 at a cost of $1,500. Although the home was originally located about twelve blocks west of its present location, the home was moved in 1977 when expansion of the local hospital threatened the home's future.

Bishop's House
Across the street from the Old Idaho Penitentiary entrance on Penitentiary Rd.
Boise architect, James King, was renowned during his time for resplendent Boise homes, and the Bishop's House bolsters his reputation. Originally built in 1889, the home was enlarged in the 1890s with a third story. The residence was first home to Reverend Daniel Tuttle, the first Episcopal Bishop in Idaho. In 1899, Bishop Funsten expanded the home to accommodate his wife and five children. Funsten was a great entertainer, and the home reportedly hosted William Borah, Marian Anderson, and Wild Buffalo Bill Cody during Funsten's residence. After seeing a slew of owners, the home was scheduled for a 1974 demolishment. However, when a group of community volunteers pooled their efforts, the home was saved and moved to this location in 1976 from its original placement on Idaho and Second Sts.. Today, the residence is leased out for both public and private functions.

Morrison-Knudsen Company Headquarters
East side of Broadway Ave. at Myrtle St.
In 1905, fifty-year-old Danish immigrant and former Nebraska farmer, Morris Knudsen, arrived in Idaho to help construct the New York Canal. While working on the project, Knudsen met twenty-seven-year-old Harry Morrison, a concrete superintendent for the Reclamation Service. Merging their money and equipment, the two decided to start their own construction firm. In 1912, Morrison-Knudsen opened its doors with

$600 in capital and a few scrapers and wheelbarrows.

Although the company lost money on its first project, the owners gained experience and soon saw their profits rise out of the red. While the company's first contracts included building logging roads, railways, and irrigation canals, the company incorporated in 1923 when it hit the million-dollar mark.

Leaving its meager beginnings behind, the company began building storage depots, ships, and airfields during World War II, and eventually expanded into construction in over sixty countries. Famous past company projects include the Manned Spacecraft Center, Minuteman missile silos, locks and channels on the St. Lawrence Seaway, and over 100 major dams across the world. Although both of the original owners are now deceased, the company maintains its position as one of America's largest engineering-construction firms.

St. Michael's Episcopal Cathedral
Eighth and State Sts.
Constructed between 1899-1902, St. Michael's Episcopal Cathedral was designed by the national Episcopal Church. The sandstone structure features stained-glass windows from New York's famous Tiffany Studios. A Memorial Peace Tower was added in 1949.

St. John's Cathedral
Northwest corner of Eighth and Hays Sts.
Representing the Boise Diocese, this Catholic cathedral features a Romanesque style. The church was built between 1906 and 1920 at a total cost of $246,000.

United Methodist Church
N. Eleventh St.
Constructed from Arizona flagstone, this Gothic style church was erected between 1958-1960. Often referred to as the "Cathedral of the Rockies," the church features thirty-foot tall stained glass windows. The large church was built with a $2 million price tag.

Bush Mansion
1020 Franklin St.
After making his mark as president of Capital State Bank and owner of the Central Hotel, John Bush had this mansion built in 1892. The elaborate home originally cost $6,000.

Congregation Beth Israel Synagogue
Northwest Corner of W. State and Eleventh St.
This Moorish revival temple is distinguished as the oldest active synagogue west of the Mississippi River. The church, founded by the Falk brothers and Moses Alexander (who would become America's first Jewish Governor in 1915), was erected in 1895. The synagogue was entirely refurbished in 1981.

Boise Cascade Corporation
Thirteenth St.
Occupying an entire city block, this five-story building was constructed between 1969 and 1972 under the architectural design of Skidmore, Owings, and Merrill. The building serves as headquarters for the Boise Cascade Corporation, a large lumber company established in 1947. The unique building features an interior landscaped plaza and bridges that connect each floor.

Harrison Blvd.
During the 1890s, Harrison Blvd. was created as a northern city alternative to Warm Springs Ave. located on Boise's southeast side. The wide street, modeled after Europe's landscaped drives, was named after President Benjamin Harrison. In 1891, Harrison graced Boise with his presence on a short visit.

Looney House
4 blocks from Harrison on Eastman Street
Eugene Looney was a prominent sheep rancher who invested his profits in personal property. After purchasing this entire city block on Eastman, Looney had a three-story Queen Anne style home constructed in 1906 and developed the rest of the block into a prune orchard. The home was sold in 1957 to Robert Hansbergers.

Lewis Heaston
1301 West Sixteenth
Featuring a Queen Anne style, this home was built for Lewis Heaston in 1906. The home features a corner tower and corner porch entry. Despite its inherent charm, the home has a history of frequently changing owners.

Arthur and Mary Golden
1403 Harrison
After moving to Boise from the mining fields of Rocky Bar and Atlanta, Arthur Golden found employment in the Falk Wholesale Company. Arthur's employment was lucrative, and in 1906, this home was built for him and his wife, Mary.

T Steunenberg Park
Capitol Blvd. and Jefferson St., Boise. Contact the Boise Visitors Bureau at 344-7777.

Situated across from the Idaho State Capitol's main entrance, Steunenberg Park honors the life of former governor, Frank Steunenberg. In 1896, Steunenberg became the youngest Idaho Governor and served for two terms. While Steunenberg held office, he was forced into the battle of warring mine union workers who demanded better wages. Although Steunenberg was a union supporter, he was forced to suppress the union uprising at the Bunker Hill Mine near Coeur d'Alene with martial law in 1899. His involvement in squelching the Bunker Hill strike created several Steunenberg enemies bent on retaliation.

When Steunenberg's terms were completed in 1900, several friends and influential political figures encouraged the gentlemanly figure to run for Congress. Steunenberg, however, declined any future activity with politics, retreating to his position at a Caldwell Bank and as founder of a local lumber company. Despite his best-laid plans to live out a peaceful future, Steunenberg was assassinated on December 30, 1905 with a dynamite bomb outside his home's front gate.

Police immediately suspected Harry Orchard who had holed himself up in Caldwell's Saratoga Hotel. Orchard confessed to the murder and also implicated other members of the Western Federation of Miners. He was eventually sentenced to death but later had his sentence changed to life imprisonment. Though Orchard became a model prisoner in the State Penitentiary and petitioned for a pardon, his application was denied. Orchard died at age eighty-eight in 1954 behind prison walls.

While Orchard repented for his crimes in prison, a park and memorial were created to honor the assassinated former governor. In May 1927, a commission granted sculptor, Gilbert Riswold, $12,500 to cast a figure of Steunenberg. Griswold completed the statue in December 1927 and suffered a stroke shortly thereafter.

TV Boise River Greenbelt
Downtown Boise. Contact the Boise Parks Department at 384-4240. From downtown, proceed 4 miles west on State St.. At Willow Ln., bear left and drive to the tennis courts and park. The trail begins immediately in front of the tennis courts.

Winding under a canopy of towering trees amid lush greenery, the twenty-five-mile paved Boise River Greenbelt connects the city's most popular parks. Up until the 1960s, the Boise River banks

were nothing more than a trash-dumping site. But with community action, the banks were groomed into their present state over the course of several years in the 1960s and 1970s. Today, the greenbelt offers bicyclists, walkers, joggers, skaters, wildlife observers, and anglers free paved trails on both sides of the river. Abundant wildlife, including deer, fox, beaver, muskrat, bald eagles, blue herons, and great horned owls dot the pathway that is open year-round to recreational use. Major access points include Julia Davis Park, Ann Morrison Park, and Veterans Memorial Park.

V Bogus Basin Mountain Resort
2405 Bogus Basin Rd., Boise. (800) 367-4397 or 332-5100.

Bogus Basin Mountain Resort is an enviable alpine and Nordic ski center just 16 miles north of Boise. With a base elevation of 6,100 feet and a peak of 7,590 feet, the 2,600-acre ski area welcomes both skiers and snowboarders on all trails. 58 runs and 7 chairlifts with short lift lines await those eager to explore the alpine setting and reputable deep powder. In addition, 32 kilometers of groomed trails await Nordic skiers, and snowboarders will find a separate mogul field, rail slides, quarter pipes, and half pipes. Bogus Basin is most famed, though, for its lighted runs allowing skiers to extend their winter play. In fact, Bogus Basin offers more night skiing than any other ski area in the northwestern U.S..

During the summer, Bogus Basin's breathtaking scenery can still be enjoyed. The resort offers a system of interpretive trails in the Boise National Forest for beginning to intermediate mountain bikers and also plays host to numerous private events, including weddings and receptions.

In addition to its ski area, Bogus Basin provides its users with lodging, food, ski lessons, rentals, daycare, a racing program, adaptive skiing programs for physically disabled skiers, and bus service to Boise. The season generally begins around Thanksgiving and continues through March. The area is open daily during ski season until 10 PM and snow reports are available by calling (208) 342-2100.

V Boise Front Mountain Bike Trails
Directly north of Boise. Contact the Ridge to Rivers Trail System at 384-3360. From downtown Boise, head straight north out of town on 8th St..

The Boise Front, comprised of a vast tract of wild land known unofficially as the Boise Foothills, is one of the most widely used recreation areas in all of Idaho. The area is comprised of both Forest Service and Bureau of Land Management terrain and offers a network of beginner to advanced mountain bike trails with spectacular Boise vistas. Since the area is exceedingly popular, bikers should use caution at all times to avoid collisions on blind corners. The area is open year-round free of charge during daylight hours.

V Riverside Pond
Corner of Riverside Drive and Glenwood near the Glenwood Bridge, Boise. Contact the Boise Visitors Bureau at 344-7777. Take Exit 5 off I-184 onto Chinden Blvd. Proceed west to a right turn on N. Glenwood, and continue 1 mile.

Boise's Riverside Pond provides a family-friendly setting for a day of peaceful fishing. The pond is home to rainbow trout and bluegill and is open to the public free of charge when weather conditions permit.

V Rhodes Park
Between 15th and 16th Sts. on Front St., Boise. Contact the Boise Visitors Bureau at 344-7777.

Rhodes Park in Boise is named after retired contractor, Glenn Rhodes, and is the newest skateboarding park to hit the Boise scene. Believing that Boise's youth needed a safe place away from the downtown streets, Rhodes created this free park under the concrete bridges connecting 15th and 16th Sts. in Boise. The park features basketball hoops, rail slides, a half pipe, and quarter pipes.

C Fiesta RV Park
11101 Fairview, Boise. 375-8207 or toll free 888-784-3246. Fax 322-2499. www.fiestarv.com

S Mayfair Antiques & Collectables
5777 Glenwood, across from fairgrounds in Boise. 378-9507 or toll free 866-378-9507. Fax 375-7411. www.mayfairantiques.com or email:mayfairantiques@earthlink.net

Mayfair Antiques & Collectables offers 7,500 square feet of merchandise representing more than 60 dealers under one roof. The family owned and operated business is overseen by Terry and Margaret Van Der Mark, with over 15 years of experience. Browse furniture from the 18th, 19th, and 20th centuries, art, carpets, glassware, clocks, porcelain, toys, jewelry, and more. Find a large selection of antiques to suit every budget and taste. They specialize in European antiques and collectables with containers arriving from Europe every three to four months. They also carry wonderful American antiques and collectables, including shabby chic. Open daily, Monday through Saturday 10 AM to 6 PM and Sundays 12 PM to 6 PM Ample parking for all sizes of vehicles.

M Boise Convention and Visitors Bureau
312 S. 9th St., Ste. 100, Boise. 344-7777. www.boise.org

33 *Food, Lodging*

T Peregrine Fund World Center for Birds of Prey
6 miles south of I-84 at 5668 West Flying Hawk Ln., Boise. 362-8687. www.peregrinefund.org

Recently voted "Boise's Best Place to Take Out of Town Guests," the Peregrine Fund World Center for Birds of Prey is the world's largest privately endowed setting for raptor breeding, research, and education. In 1970, Tom Cade founded the Peregrine Fund to preserve and increase the dwindling peregrine falcon population. Since then, the fund has bred and released more than 4,000 peregrines into 28 states.

Under the operation of this conservationist fund, Boise's World Center for Birds of Prey offers visitors an incredible look at the lives of eagles, falcons, hawks, owls, and other raptors. The

Velma Morrison Interpretive Center offers interactive displays for people of all ages, multimedia shows exploring the status of endangered birds of prey throughout the world, and close-up views of several birds. Outside, visitors can see several caged eagles unable to survive on their own in the wild. The center is open 9 AM to 5 PM daily March through October and 10 AM to 4 PM daily November through February. Admission is $4 for adults, $3 for seniors ages 62 and over, $2 for youth ages 4-16, and discounted rates for pre-arranged group tours.

34 Food

T Indian Lakes Golf Club
4700 S. Umatilla Dr., Boise. 362-5771.
www.indianlakesgolf.com

This tree-lined, manicured public course offers a naturally contoured landscape and gentle rolling hills that are easy to walk. The 18-hole, par 70 course will challenge players of all experience levels, and scenic views of the Owyhee Valley abound. Green fees are $21 on weekdays and $26 Friday through Sunday. The course is open year-round depending on the weather.

T Idaho Military History Museum
4748 Lindbergh St., Building 924, Boise.
422-4841. http://inghro.state.id.us/museum

The Idaho Military History Museum was established in 1995 and is committed to preserving and interpreting Idaho's connection to the U.S. military's lasting legacy. The museum covers a wide array of military history utilizing historical photos and artifacts. Visitors can view Gowen Field as it appeared during World War II, a small arms collection dating back to the early 20th century, numerous armored vehicles, and much more. The museum is open from 12 PM to 4 PM Tuesday through Sunday with free admission.

T Boise Ranch Golf Course
6501 S. Cloverdale Rd., Boise. 362-6501. Merge off I-84 at Exit 52 onto Orchard St. Bear right onto W. Victory Rd,. and proceed to a left turn onto S. Cloverdale Rd.

Boise Ranch Golf Course was established in 1994 under the design of Russ Isbell. The 18-hole, par-72 championship course features multi-tiered greens and numerous water hazards scattered amid 6,691 yards. Green fees are less than $20, and the course is open year-round.

35 Food, Lodging

T Boise Depot and Platt Gardens
2603 Eastover Terrace (off Vista Ave.), Boise.
384-9591.

The Union Pacific Railroad built this impressive depot in 1925 as a premier stop on its passenger railway. When the Union Pacific rolled up its line, Amtrak stepped in with passenger service until 1997. Today, the city of Boise owns the historic building and has turned it into a must-see stop on a downtown tour. Railroad cars are exhibited outside the depot, while inside, visitors will find railroad memorabilia, an accessible bell tower, and magnificent views of Boise's scenic city and foothills landscape.

Surrounding the depot are the renowned Platt Gardens. The exquisitely landscaped grassy knoll features trees, small ponds, and water fountains. The gardens and depot are open limited hours

Monday through Friday. A small admission fee is charged for children and adults over twelve years of age.

T National Interagency Fire Center
3833 S. Development Ave. (next to the Boise Airport), Boise. 387-5512.

Under the joint management of the Forest Service, Bureau of Land Management, Fish and Wildlife Service, National Park Service, National Weather Service, and Bureau of Indian Affairs, the National Interagency Fire Center serves as America's national logistics support center for emergency operations and wildfire fighting. In addition, the center also features the largest warehouse of firefighting equipment. More than 5,000 hand held radios are found amid aisles of Pulaskis, hoses, fire shelters, and other essential firefighting equipment, and droves of dispatchers, pilots, smokejumpers, and communications specialists arrive at the center every summer.

In advance, interested visitors can arrange free center tours. Tour highlights include an infrared mapping system, remote solar weather stations, radio communication shops, automatic lightning detection systems, and a warehouse featuring more than 3,000 fire related items. Visitors should note that tours are only available in the off-season when wildfires are infrequent.

36 Food, Lodging

H Airmail Service
Milepost 50 on U.S. Hwy. 20 at the BSU Campus

U.S. commercial airline service began with a Varney Air Lines flight from Pasco to Boise, which landed here April 6, 1926. Army planes had delivered airmail before that time. After Varney Air Lines was merged with newer companies to become United Airlines, this flight was recognized as United's initial flight. A year later, Charles A. Lindbergh landed here on national tour after his solo flight to Paris. Boise's municipal airport continued to serve planes here until 1940, when 8,800-foot runways were built at its present site.

H Boise State University
Milepost 50 on U.S. Hwy. 20 at the BSU Campus

Expanding from a two-year community college (1932-1965) to a campus with a graduate program, Boise State was designated as a university in 1974. Originating as an Episcopalian academy founded in 1892, this institution was located a mile north until 1940, when Boise's municipal airport, located here, became available for a large new campus. Christ's Chapel, Boise's original Episcopalian church building which was built downtown in 1886, was moved to this site for permanent preservation in 1963.

T Hemingway Western Studies Center
Boise State University, Boise. 426-1999.

Located on the campus of Boise State University, the Hemingway Western Studies Center focuses on studying and preserving the Western way of life, and a small art gallery strives towards this mission. The center is also dedicated to the memory of writer and Idaho enthusiast, Ernest Hemingway. Inside, visitors will find pictures of Hemingway's home in Ketchum, letters he wrote to his editor, and other miscellaneous Hemingway memorabilia. Admission is free, and operating hours are 8 AM to 5 PM Monday through Friday.

T Morrison Center for Performing Arts
1910 University Dr., Boise. 426-1609.

Situated on the Boise State University campus alongside the Boise River banks, the Morrison Center for Performing Arts proudly hosts an array of musical, artistic, and cultural events throughout the year. Harry K. Morrison, founder of Morrison-Knudsen Company, dreamed of a fine performing arts center. Upon Morrison's death, his widow Velma continued providing financial endowment, and the center became a reality in 1984. Today, the performance hall is considered one of the U.S.' most acoustically perfect sites and seats up to 2,000 people. Past performances have included ballet, Broadway musicals, opera ensembles, and symphonies. Ticket prices vary with each production, and advance tickets are recommended. For a complete listing of events or to schedule a private tour, contact the center's box office.

T Fort Boise Park and Military Reserve Park
Fort St., Boise. Contact the Boise Parks Department at 384-4240. Merge off I-84 at Exit 54. Proceed north to Fort St.

Remains of the original 1863 Fort Boise are the highlight of the sixty-seven acre Fort Boise Park. Spotting the large athletic fields are old parade and polo grounds, as well as the newer additions of the Fort Boise Community Center, Boise Art Center, and the Boise Little Theater. Behind Fort Boise Park is the 466-acre Military Reserve Park. Sagebrush covered foothills provide miles of hiking and biking trails, from which users are guaranteed stunning city views. The park also includes the historic O'Farrell Cabin, Boise's first permanent residence.

T MK Nature Center
600 S. Walnut (off W. Beacon St. and Park Blvd.), Boise. 368-6060.

The Idaho Department of Fish and Game's MK Nature Center is a serene wildlife haven amidst Boise's fast-paced city atmosphere. Offering a small sample of wild Idaho, the 4.5-acre preserve and botanical garden features several of the state's widely divergent ecosystems. The indoor/outdoor facility takes visitors along the life of a mountain stream with viewing windows providing close-up views of many Idaho native fish species in their favorite stream habitat. Ponds with bridges, nature trails, interpretive signs, and interactive exhibits provide hours of fun for people of all ages as fish, waterfowl, mammals, and songbirds move about the Nature Center.

The MK Nature Center also features an informative Visitor Center staffed with Idaho wildlife experts. The visitor center provides hands-on displays and continually rotating exhibits about Idaho fish and wildlife. While the outdoor trails are open year-round, the Visitor Center features seasonal hours. The Nature Center is free but donations are appreciated.

T World Sports Humanitarian Hall of Fame
Boise State University Campus at the southwest end of Bronco Stadium, Boise. 343-7224.
www.sportshumanitarian.com

Located on the campus of Boise State University, the World Sports Humanitarian Hall of Fame was founded with the mission of celebrating and showcasing athletes who act nobly and participate in humanitarian causes. The museum inducts several world-class athletes every year who have not only excelled on the playing field but also in making contributions to the betterment of others. Among the many past inductees are Kirby Puckett, Mary Lou Retton, Roberto Clemente, Jacki Joyner-Kersee, David Robinson, and Bonnie Blair. The museum features informational exhibits about each inductee, an authentic Heisman trophy, and articles about great humanitarians. Open Monday through Friday from 8 AM to 5 PM, the museum encourages all sports enthusiasts and those with a humanitarian spirit to visit.

T Boise State University
Near the Boise River in Boise. 426-1011. www.boisestate.edu. Merge off I-84 at Exit 54, and proceed to University Dr.

Originating in 1932 as a private school, Boise State University opened under the charter of the Protestant Episcopal Church as Boise Junior College. Although the school was accredited, church funding was withdrawn in 1934 due to the Depression, and the college was forced to rely on community donations until 1939. At that time, the State Legislature signed a bill to help fund junior colleges, saving the small university from imminent closure. In 1940, the school expanded and relocated to its present 110-acre site, further expanding services in 1965 when the Legislature granted the school four-year status as Boise College. In 1974, the school finally received its current title of Boise State University. Today, the college serves over 15,000 graduate and undergraduate students in a diverse array of programs. Presently, the school possesses the largest enrollment of all Idaho universities and colleges, and tours are available Monday through Friday.

T Boise Little Theater
100 E. Fort St., Boise. 342-5104. Merge off I-84 at Exit 54, and proceed north to East Fort St.

Boise Little Theater is recognized as Idaho's oldest community theater and consistently performs to sold-out crowds. Producing everything from comedies to drama for more than fifty years, the reportedly haunted theater and acting troupe cater to a wide range of audiences. Past performances have included *Grapes of Wrath*, *A Christmas Carol*, *One Flew Over the Cuckoo's Nest*, *A Man for All Seasons*, and many other acclaimed features. Season passes or individual tickets may be purchased, and interested patrons should call for further information and a complete schedule of events.

T Spontaneous Productions
1011 Williams St., Boise. 363-7053. Merge off I-84 at Exit 54 and proceed north to Boise Ave. Williams St. is immediately located off Boise Ave.

Spontaneous Productions has developed a reputation as Boise's alternative theater. The unique acting troupe specializes in producing dramas, musicals, and comedies all featuring some sort of plot twist. Past productions have included *The Rocky Horror Show*, *Hollywood Nights*, *Drag Queens on Trial*, and several other performances sure to keep audiences engaged. Ticket prices range from $8 to $22, and interested attendees should call for a complete schedule of events and ticket reservation.

T ParkCenter
385 W. ParkCenter Blvd., Boise. Contact the Boise Visitors Bureau at 344-7777. Merge off I-84 at Exit 54, and proceed north to Beacon St. Turn east, and continue to the junction of Beacon and ParkCenter Blvd.

Encompassing nearly fourteen acres in the heart of Boise, ParkCenter offers an array of entertainment for the entire family. The park features a picnic area, playground, volleyball course, a par golf course, and an eight-acre pond popular for float tubing, windsurfing, and fishing.

T Pioneer Cemetery
Intersection of Warm Springs and Broadway Aves., Boise. Contact the Boise Visitors Bureau at 344-7777.

Boise's forefathers and earliest residents are buried in the town's idyllic Pioneer Cemetery. Simple graves mark the resting spots for Julia Davis and her husband, Thomas Davis, early Idaho governors, and some of Boise's first entrepreneurs and business owners. The gravestones remain unencumbered by fences, allowing visitors a close-up look at the history of Boise's founders.

T Greenbelt Wildlife Preserve
Off ParkCenter Blvd. at River Run Dr., Boise. Contact the Boise Parks Department at 384-4240. Merge off I-84 at Exit 54, and proceed north on S. Broadway. Next, drive east on Linden, turn north on S. Gekeler Ln., bear east on Pennsylvania St., and turn north on ParkCenter Blvd. Proceed to River Run Dr..

Located along the Boise River Greenbelt and open only to pedestrian traffic, the Greenbelt Wildlife Preserve is a sanctuary for regional wildlife. Visitors will catch glimpses of deer, fox, beaver, birds of prey, and several waterfowl species. The preserve is open daily during daylight hours free of charge.

T Boise State University Gallery of Art
1910 University Dr., Boise. 426-3994 or 426-1230.

Home to both regional and national artists, the Boise State University Gallery of Art features an array of art mediums with its rotating exhibits. In addition, student and faculty artwork is displayed. The gallery is open free of charge Monday through Saturday from September through May.

TV Table Rock
East of Boise. Contact the Ridge to Rivers Trail System at 384-3360. Take Exit 54 off I-84, and proceed north to Fort Boise and Reserve St. Follow Reserve St. from Fort Boise to Shaw Mountain Rd. Bearing right at Table Rock Rd., continue driving to the dirt road. Mountain bikers can begin their journey here.

Table Rock rises to the east of Boise and is a prominent mesa on the city's horizon. The rock is comprised of a hot spring deposit of silica and chalcedony and is the site of popular summer and fall recreation. Mountain bike trails wind to the top of the rock, providing stunning views of Boise sprawled below. Rock climbers also frequent the area as it's recognized for intermediate bouldering routes. The site is open during daylight hours free of charge, and additional information is available from the Ridge to Rivers Trail System Association.

37 Food

H The Oregon Trail
Milepost 7.4 on State Hwy. 21 (Warm Springs Ave.)

The Oregon Trail is still clearly visible coming off the rimrock across the river. Here the westbound emigrants after 1840 came gratefully down into this green valley. The first cart passed here with Henry H. Spalding and Marcs Whitman, pioneer missionaries, in 1836. After 1842, thousands of emigrant wagons cut a broad track, later called the Overland Road. The tide of travel declined when the railroad was completed in 1883, but emigrant wagons continued to use this road until after 1900. The tracks of the wagons and stages can still be followed for miles east in the desert.

H Beaver Dick's Ferry
Milepost 7.4 on State Hwy. 21 (Warm Springs Ave.)

In 1863 and 1864, overland packers hauling supplies from Salt Lake City to Idaho City crossed here and took a direct route northward to More's Creek. They cut a steep grade from the Oregon Trail down to Beaver Dick's Ferry, which served as a crossing only a short distance below here. After gold rush excitement ended, Idaho City traffic came through Boise and used a toll road further north to Boise Basin.

H Diversion Dam
Milepost 8.4 on State Hwy. 21

Diversion Dam was completed in 1909 to lift water into an already constructed New York Canal system, greatly expanding its irrigated farmlands. After a quarter-century of failing to dig a large canal above Diversion Dam, United States Reclamation Service funding enabled a group of Boise Valley irrigation districts to complete this project. Then in 1912, a generating plant was installed to provide power to construct Arrowrock Dam. It has been preserved as a historical display by the Bureau of Reclamation.

H More's Creek
Milepost 17.1 on State Hwy. 21

More's Creek is named for J. Marion More, leader of the party of miners who founded Idaho City, October 7, 1862. Like most of Idaho's early miners, he came originally from the South. Unlike most of them, he struck it rich. During the Idaho gold rush, he had profitable investments in many important mining camps. Hardly anyone else did as much to build Idaho during the early days.

H Arrowrock Dam
Milepost 17.1 on State Hwy. 21

Higher than any other dam from 1915 until 1934, Arrowrock still is an essential part of the Boise Valley's irrigation system. Located six miles upstream from here, Arrowrock is 350 feet high and 1,150 feet wide. Built at a cost of $4,725,000 to provide additional water storage to get 2,635 valley farms through dry summer seasons, it had enough capacity to take care of more than 1,000 new farms as well. Its 18-mile canyon reservoir holds 280,000 acre-feet of water.

T Warm Springs Golf Course
2495 Warm Springs Ave., Boise. 343-5661. www.cityofboise.org

Ranging from 5,660 to 6,719 yards, the Warm Springs Golf Course originated in 1972 and is a popular municipal course nestled just minutes away from downtown Boise. The relatively flat course is lined with trees and includes large putting greens, well-maintained sand bunkers, and beautiful views of the Boise River. The 18-hole, par 72 course prides itself on its mature layout and ease of use for all ages. Green fees are $21 on weekdays, $25 on weekends, and a $16 twilight fee is charged after 5:30 PM.

T Boise Municipal Park
East of downtown Boise off Warm Springs Ave.. Contact the Boise Parks Department at 384-4240.

Boise Municipal Park stretches twenty-eight acres along the Boise River and is the quintessential picnic destination for small gatherings or large reunions. The shady park offers picnic shelters, fire pits and grills, and a playground. Summer reservations for the picnic shelters book completely full as early as April, so visitors should plan accordingly.

T Barber Park
Eastern edge of Boise. Contact the Boise Parks Department at 384-4240.

The Boise River is undoubtedly Barber Park's greatest attraction. More than 250,000 river rafters and floaters launch from the park every summer, and wildlife observation is increasingly popular in the area. The park is also a prime picnicking area from late spring through early fall. Barber Park is accessible year-round with considerably less crowds once the summer heat has been squelched.

T Boise Natatorium
1811 Warm Springs Ave., Boise. 345-9270.

Fueled by a geothermal discovery in 1890, the Boise Natatorium was designed by John C. Paulsen and constructed in 1892. Featuring over 15,000 square feet of luxurious space, the Natatorium's distinctive Moorish towers and arches beckoned visitors to come and play in the 65 by 125 foot geothermal heated pool. The four-story decadent facility also included rooms for all occasions, and the pool was capable of holding a wooden dance floor above it. At the turn of the century, the Natatorium was known as Boise's best place to host a dance, party, or political inauguration, and its reputation for fun was further enhanced when the White City Amusement Park was constructed behind the building.

In 1934, the Natatorium's successful history began to crumble. A horrific windstorm damaged the building beyond repair, and the facility was torn down. Today, the historic building site is home to an elementary school and a new Boise City Parks and Recreation Department swimming pool. Open daily during summer, the outdoor pool features a wildly popular hydrotube slide open to both children and adults. Nothing remains of the historic Natatorium, but visitors can visit the new facility for a small admission fee.

T Oregon Trail Ruts
2 miles southeast of Barber Dam Rd. on State Hwy. 21 near Boise

As travelers leave the Boise River Valley and head north on State Hwy. 21, traces of the past have been engraved in the landscape. Oregon Trail pioneers traveled through this same valley on their journey west, and their heavily loaded wagons left deep impressions. These ruts, which run directly beside the highway, are still visible today.

T Boise Diversion Dam & New York Canal
Approximately five miles northeast of Boise on State Hwy. 21

Recognized as possessing one of the oldest operating federal power plants, the Boise Diversion Dam is listed as a Nationally Registered Historic Place. Despite the dam's relatively smooth operating history over the course of the twentieth century, the construction process was wrought with conflict, lawsuits, and financial catastrophes.

During the 1860s, a flood of Idaho mining activity brought with it a flurry of agricultural opportunists. As increasing numbers of farmers saw the potential to make a huge profit off the food needs of hungry miners, eager farm owners made the trek to Idaho Territory in droves. Although more than 80,000 acres of Idaho Territory was farmland by 1880, limited irrigation hampered further agricultural expansion. Seeking an opportunity to help out the farmers while also making a profit, a group of New York investors joined forces in June 1882 to create the Idaho Mining and Irrigation Company. Full of high hopes, the company planned to construct a seventeen foot deep and forty-seven foot wide canal that would irrigate over 500,000 acres. The project, named New York Canal, would flow for seventy-five miles and be completed by 1887.

Company engineer, Arthur DeWint Foote set to work immediately surveying the main ditch in hopes of promoting the project to additional investors. Despite his well-laid plans, the construction process was immediately filled with controversy. Competitors, lawsuits, and bankruptcy forced Foote into a panic. As the five-year completion deadline came and went, the canal was nowhere near finished.

Hearing of the company's plight, Denver, Colorado construction contractor, W. C. Bradbury, arranged to extend the Phyllis Canal from Nampa to the western end of the New York Canal. After completing the thirty-five mile extension, Bradbury contracted with the Idaho Mining and Irrigation Company to continue work on the New York Canal. Bradbury sunk his heart and soul into the project, employing hundreds of men and over 250 teams of horses. But his well-laid plans were partially shot down in March 1891 when the Idaho Mining and Irrigation Company was forced out of business over a bondholder dispute.

Bradbury persevered a few more months, using $386,000 of his own money to continue the New York Canal. After a financial panic hit in 1893, the project came to a screeching halt. What was supposed to have been finished in 1887 was still miles away from operation. Over the course of the next few years, litigations and the organization of the private Farmers' Canal Company kept the canal project in limbo. Finally, the U.S. Reclamation Service stepped in to take care of the messy project. The project was finally completed more than twenty years after its start, and the New York Canal headgates opened for the first time in February 1909. In 1912, the present day power plant was completed on the Boise Diversion Dam's south side.

Today, the infamous dam and canal irrigates over 300,000 acres of southwestern Idaho farmland. Larger than originally planned, the Boise Diversion dam rises sixty-eight feet high above the extensive New York Canal. The dam is available for viewing, and the power plant is open daily during summer for curious passerby.

TV Arrowrock Reservoir
20 miles east of Boise off State Hwy. 21. Contact the Boise National Forest Headquarters at 373-4100. From Boise, drive 8 miles east on State Hwy. 21 to Lucky Peak Reservoir. Take the turnoff leading to Lucky Peak, and proceed an additional 12 miles to Arrowrock.

Arrowrock Reservoir is situated inside an eighteen-mile canyon on the Boise River and encompasses more than 280,000 acre-feet of water. A sixty-mile shoreline and boat ramps provides access for boating and windsurfing, and anglers can test their skills while trying to catch rainbow trout, whitefish, yellow perch, and kokanee salmon. A few primitive campsites are available in the area, and the reservoir is accessible year-round.

TV Boise River
Southwestern Idaho. Contact the Boise Parks Department at 384-4240.

The 190-mile Boise River, a tributary of the Snake River, winds approximately seventy-five miles through southwestern Idaho. The river was first explored during the 1811 Astoria Expedition where it drew its original name, "Reed's River." Rising in three separate forks, the river is responsible for draining a portion of the Sawtooth Mountains and the western Snake River Plain.

Today, the Boise River is an outdoor adventure destination. Float tubing and whitewater rafting is increasingly popular, while the river is an angler's dream. The river boasts excellent populations of wild and hatchery rainbow trout, bull trout, mountain whitefish, largemouth and smallmouth bass, channel catfish, brown trout, brook trout, redband trout, and cutthroats. In addition to the river, 224 alpine lakes and Anderson Ranch, Arrowrock, and Lucky Peak Reservoirs provide further angling opportunities. The most frequented river stretches run through the middle of Boise with access points at several of the community's major parks.

TV Lucky Peak State Park
10 miles east of Boise on State Hwy. 21. 336-9505.

Lucky Peak State Park, designated in *Travel Magazine* as one of the Pacific Northwest's top twenty-five parks, is a haven for Boise residents and visitors. The day-use-only park revolves around its namesake, Lucky Peak Reservoir and Dam, which the Army Corps of Engineers completed in 1955 at a cost of $19 million. Within just a few years of its completion, the 2,340-foot-long dam and reservoir gave way to Discovery State Park. Renamed Lucky Peak State Park, the area consists of three different units, each providing their own recreational diversions.

Discovery Unit features a grassy park nestled next to the riverbank. The unit is ideal for picnickers and anglers, offering easy river access as well as several picnic tables and grills. Situated at the base of Lucky Peak Dam, Sandy Point is one of the most popular units with its beaches, picnic tables, raft and tube rentals, concession stands, and frequent summer concerts. The third unit, Spring Shores, is the only unit actually situated on Lucky Peak Reservoir itself. Spring Shores is most appropriately suited to anglers and boaters with its boat docks, ramp, boat trailer parking, and marina. Water-skiers, jet skiers, sailboarders, and sailboats all frequent the high-desert lake, while anglers will find whitefish, perch, kokanee, trout, and smallmouth bass. The park is open seasonally from May 1 through Labor Day, and a $4 vehicle entrance fee is required.

V Idaho Ice World
7072 S. Eisenman Rd., Boise. 331-0044. Take Exit 57 off I-84 and proceed to E. Gowen Rd. Bear left on E. Gowen, and turn left again on S. Eisenman Rd.

Idaho Ice World is an indoor ice skating facility. Maintained for year-round fun, the facility features ice-skating, ice hockey, and lessons. The rink is open daily, and group rates and rentals are available.

V Lucky Peak Rock Climbing Wall
East of Boise. Contact the BLM – Idaho State Office at 373-4000. Drive east of Boise on Warm Springs Ave. to State Hwy. 21. Follow the highway to the Diversion Dam where the rock wall is located adjacent to the highway.

An unsuspecting rock wall that juts out near the highway as the Boise River tumbles from a diversion dam is one of the most popular regional rock climbing destinations. Situated just before Lucky Peak Reservoir, the wall face features several easy to intermediate routes on the river's north side with more advanced routes on the south side of the riverbanks. The wall is a common practice site for avid regional climbers wishing to hone their climbing and rappelling skills before tackling more technical terrain. The rock wall is closed annually from January to May to protect the area's nesting birds of prey.

V Black Cliffs
7 miles east of downtown Boise on the north side of Warm Springs Ave./State Hwy. 21. Contact the Boise Visitors Bureau at 344-7777.

Featuring a variety of pitches, Black Cliffs is a basalt outcropping located on the outskirts of Boise's historic district. The cliffs are recognized as one of the most popular rock-climbing destinations in the region.

38

Mayfield
The Corder family ran a stage station near here from 1865 to 1887, and thus the settlement was originally named after them. The post office was established in 1883, and the second postmaster, Authur Mayfield, changed the name of the town in 1887 to honor himself. Today, Mayfield is surrounded by a dry-farming region, and lacks a stable population.

H Oregon Trail
Milepost 62.2, Eastbound on I-84, at Blacks Creek Rest Area

Indians, trappers, and emigrants who came this way before 1900 used a more direct route to get between Boise and Glenns Ferry. Their road still can be seen at Bonneville Point, five miles from here. Following close to a line of hills bordering a broad, rolling plain, their route had water and grass essential for horses and oxen. It also gave them a spectacular view of the Boise valley. To see that site, follow directional signs when you reach Interchange 64 at Blacks Creek, one mile beyond here.

H Basque Country
Milepost 62.4, Westbound on I-84, at Blacks Creek Rest Area

Idaho has a large Basque community that preserves its ancient European traditions in a new land of opportunity. Coming here originally to herd sheep on mountain and desert ranges, they shifted into other occupations as quickly as possible, making way for more of their countrymen to follow. Their sheep wagons often can be seen on grazing lands, and a Basque museum (611 Grove St. in Boise) interprets their life here.

T Bonneville Point
10 miles east of Boise. Contact the BLM – Idaho State Office at 373-4000. Merge off I-84 at the Black Creek Exit (Exit 64), and proceed 4 miles north on Black Creek Rd. Follow the signs to Bonneville Point.

When Captain Bonneville and his men arrived in the American West, they surveyed the Boise River Valley in 1833 and named the region, "Les Bois." Today, visitors can stand in the same spot as Bonneville and his men for the same vantage point of the surrounding valley. The free day-use area includes a historical marker, interpretive displays, and well-preserved Oregon Trail ruts. Visitors to the point also have access to picnicking and wildlife viewing.

V Danskin Trails
Northeast of Boise. Contact the Mountain Home Ranger District at 587-7961. Merge off I-84 at the Black Creek Rd. Exit (Exit 64), and proceed east approximately 10 miles.

Situated in the high desert territory of Mountain Home, the Danskin Trails are a large system of interconnected ATV, motorcycle, and mountain biking trails. Users should keep in mind that the trails, which range in difficulty from beginner to intermediate, can become slick when wet. The free trails are closed seasonally, so users should contact the ranger district for current trail conditions.

V Indian Creek Reservoir
19 miles east of Boise on the south side of I-84 near Exit 71. Contact the Idaho Department of Fish and Game at 334-3700.

Indian Creek Reservoir provides easy access to an array of fish. The reservoir is stocked annually with rainbow trout and also is home to cutthroat trout, largemouth bass, bluegill, bullhead, and catfish. The free site is open when reservoir levels are high and weather conditions permit.

39 *Food, Lodging*

Mountain Home
Pop. 11,143

Originating as the Rattlesnake Stage Station, Mountain Home actually owes its upbringing to the Oregon Short Line Railroad. While working to install a line in the area, OSL Railroad officials created the tent town of Tutville in 1882 to house railroad construction workers and traveling pioneers. Eventually, residential and commercial lots were sold for $25, and the new town began to prosper. At the turn of the century, the city boasted several general stores, two weekly newspapers, a school, three churches, two hotels, and an array of merchants and saloons. The city's ideal shipping location helped secure the town's presence on the Idaho frontier, and wool was frequently shipped from the site.

The name Tutville was eventually dropped, and the wife of first postmaster, John Lemmon, selected "Mountain Home" after the distant mountains forming the surrounding county's northern boundary. Ironically, at an elevation of only 3,180 feet, the town isn't even in the mountains, and the town is frequently the warmest civilized spot in the state. Although once boasting an economy based upon the shipping industry, Mountain Home's current economy rests prominently upon Mountain Home Air Force Base.

Mountain Home	Jan	Feb	March	April	May	June	July	Aug	Sep	Oct	Nov	Dec	Annual
Average Max. Temperature (F)	38.1	45.0	53.8	63.1	72.8	83.0	93.1	91.5	80.9	67.4	49.8	39.5	64.8
Average Min. Temperature (F)	20.4	24.2	28.9	34.5	42.2	49.9	56.5	54.4	45.2	35.3	27.3	21.5	36.7
Average Total Precipitation (in.)	1.34	0.87	1.05	0.83	0.88	0.72	0.27	0.28	0.50	0.63	1.17	1.32	9.87
Average Total Snowfall (in.)	4.5	1.9	0.3	0.1	0.0	0.0	0.0	0.0	0.0	0.0	1.0	3.0	10.8
Average Snow Depth (in.)	1	0	0	0	0	0	0	0	0	0	0	1	0

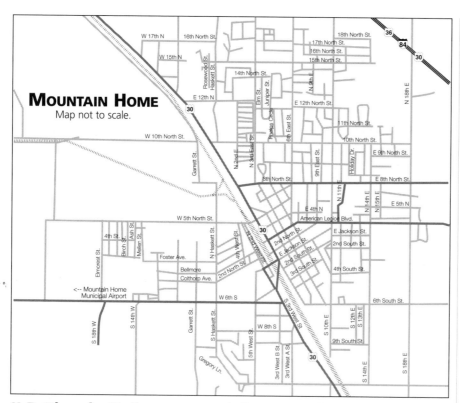

MOUNTAIN HOME
Map not to scale.

<-- Mountain Home
Municipal Airport

H Rattlesnake Station
Milepost 102.7 on U.S. Hwy. 20 near Mountain Home

At the junction of the Rocky Bar road with the Oregon Trail, this was a major stage line stop for 20 years.Stage service commenced in 1864, and a connection to the Rocky Bar mines was moved here in 1870. In 1878, the station owners thought it would sound a lot better to call their place Mountain Home instead of Rattlesnake. Then the Union Pacific – built out in the valley in 1883 – replaced the freight wagons and stage lines that came through here. So Mountain Home was moved on down Rattlesnake Creek to its present location on the railroad.

T Desert Canyon Golf Course
1880 E. 8th N., Mountain Home. 587-3293. www.ci.mountain-home.id.us Merge off I-84 at Exit 95 and bear right, proceeding to the course.

Desert Canyon Golf Course strives to give players a pleasurable golfing experience at a competitive price. Established in 1962, the course provides two unique 9-hole courses. While the front nine is situated on a broad, tree-lined fairway, the treeless back nine meanders through a narrow canyon. With these options, nearly every golfer can find a round suitable to him or her. Green fees for nine holes are $12 on weekdays and $16 on weekends with special pricing plans available to traveling golfers and youth. Unadvertised specials are also usually available upon request and can be used on the course, driving range, putting green, or chipping green.

T Elmore County Historical Museum
180 S. 3rd St. E., Mountain Home. 587-6847.

With a mission to preserve and promote the appreciation of Elmore County, the Elmore County Historical Museum displays artifacts significant to the region's history. Among the exhibits are old farming tools, memorabilia from early settlers, and artifacts from Native Americans and

Chinese miners. Call for more information and hours of operation.

T Mountain Home Air Force Base
10 miles southwest of Mountain Home on State Hwy. 67. Contact Public Affairs at 828-6800 or the Visitor's Center at 828-6797.

With a mission to develop and nurture airmen that are prepared to deploy and ready to fight, Mountain Home Air Force Base is the only major military installation in all of Idaho. Construction on the base began in November 1942, and the base was opened for operation on August 7, 1943.

Although the base was slated as a B-24 crew training school, it was deactivated in 1945. After several more years of activation and deactivation, the base was finally permanently reactivated and became home to the 366th Fighter Wing in 1972. With the arrival of these "gunfighters," Mountain Home Air Force Base became the only Air Expeditionary Wing in the entire Air Force. To this date, the base retains this distinction, and in 1991, the 366th was designated as the Air Force's premier air intervention composite wing. Crews trained at Mountain Home have carried out countless missions across the world and have received numerous "outstanding unit" awards.

Public base tours are offered through advance arrangement, and a Visitor's Center is available on-site. A one-day annual open house is also held every summer.

T Desert Mountain Visitor Center
2900 American Legion Blvd., Mountain Home. 587-4464.

Conveniently located near Exit 95 on I-84, the Desert Mountain Visitor Center provides travelers with a wealth of regional information. For visitors' convenience, the center is staffed with knowledgeable individuals pleased to address visitors' questions or concerns. The center is open daily year-round with limited hours during winter.

T Teapot Dome
Near Mountain Home off U.S. Hwy. 20. Contact the Mountain Home Chamber of Commerce at 587-4334. Bear off I-84 onto U.S. Hwy. 20 at Exit 95. Proceed to milepost 102.7, distinguished with a Rattlesnake Station Historical Marker. Across from the marker on the west side of the highway, turn southeast, and proceed 3 miles down a gravel road.

Teapot Dome may sound like a forgettable destination at first mention, but the natural site retains historical significance as a popular and important point on the Oregon Trail. While some early pioneers elected to cross the Snake River near Hagerman, others opted for a northerly alternative route leading to Teapot Dome. Those who chose to travel to Teapot Dome were by no means disappointed with their choice as they were greeted with excellent camping grounds and natural hot springs that soothed their road-weary bodies. Historic journal entries document the springs' popularity with Oregon Trail travelers who reconnected with the main Oregon Trail just a short distance from Teapot Dome. Today, Oregon Trail ruts can still be found near the rhyolite cliffs frequented by eagles, and the region is popular for day hikes.

T Volcanic Crater Rings
West of Mountain Home. Contact the Mountain Home Chamber of Commerce at 587-4334. From N. Main St. in Mountain Home, proceed to Third W. St. Driving north, bear west onto Frontage Rd., continuing 5.4 miles to Cinder Butte Rd. Bear south here to locate a dirt track road in approximately sixty feet. After turning left on the dirt track, drive southwesterly for 2.7 miles.

Located in the basalt of the Bruneau Formation, the 200-foot deep twin Crater Rings were formed over 1.4 million years ago. Geologists speculate that the lava flow encompassed over 100-square miles, and the craters were formed with a sudden drop in area gas pressure.

M RE/MAX CastleRock Realty
1355 Airbase Rd., W. 6th St. S., Mountain Home. 587-2800 or (800) 916-2800. www.castlerockre.com

An Idaho native with an Idaho family history dating back seven generations, Gini Johnson possesses the area knowledge clients need when making informed real estate decisions. Passionately committed to and enthusiastically embracing her profession, Gini established her own real estate office in Mountain Home in 1991 before joining the RE/MAX franchise as a Broker/Owner in 2001. At RE/MAX CastleRock Realty, Gini offers clients thirty successful years of industry experience and is dedicated to acquainting newcomers with Idaho's treasures. Service to customer needs is of utmost importance, and the brokerage's talented agents have the knowledge to help clients buy or sell a diverse range of property. For the resources of a national corporation combined with unbeatable hometown quality service, call Gini Johnson and her agents today at RE/MAX CastleRock Realty!

40

Hammett
Pop. 200

The Oregon Short Line Railroad mapped out Medbury, as it was originally called, as an agricultural town in 1883. The small town didn't develop quickly, but when the post office arrived in 1908, the town grew slightly. Hammett owes its present name to Charles Hammett, a King Hill irrigation project promoter.

T Cold Springs Winery
Cold Springs Rd., Hammett.

As one of the newest Idaho wineries, Cold Springs Winery opened during fall 2003 and is under the ownership of William F. Ringert. For additional information, call the Hammett Area Chamber of Commerce.

41 *Food, Lodging*

Glenns Ferry
Pop. 1,611

Glenns Ferry is named for Gustavus P. Glenn who operated a ferry across the Snake River from 1865 to 1889. The ferry was established to shorten the route from Kelton to Boise by twenty miles and afforded Oregon Trail emigrants an extra ounce of safety as they no longer had to make a dangerous ford of the river. The route also helped Glenn's brothers as they owned freight teams and traveled that route regularly. In 1879, enough settlers had remained in the area surrounding the ferry to acquire postal services. Just four years later, the town was formally platted when the arrival of the Oregon Short Line Railroad ensured the community's hopes for the future. In 1908, the first Snake River Bridge was constructed here.

H Oregon Trail
Exits 120 and 121 on I-84, Glenns Ferry Business Loop on Bannock Rd.

A perilous ford at Three Island Crossing State Park was a formidable Oregon Trail barrier. Those who could not cross here faced a longer, more difficult southern route. No other ford between Missouri and Oregon troubled them so much. This was their largest river. Using two of three islands, they crossed three channels, but sometimes lost stock and wagons. Many emigrants depended upon Shoshoni Indian guides to get them across safely.

H Glenn's Ferry
Exits 120 and 121 on I-84, Glenns Ferry Business Loop on Bannock Rd.

Heavy Boise freight traffic from Pacific rail terminals in Utah and Nevada led Gus Glenn to start a ferry here in 1870. This crossing (just below I-84's bridges) connected to a shorter and better freight road. James S. Reynolds noted its advantages: "By it King Hill, Clear Creek Hill, and that horrid road between Canyon Creek and Rattlesnake are avoided." Indians captured and sank Glenn's ferry during a Bannock War skirmish here in 1878. But overland stage service started here in 1879, and lasted until Glenns Ferry became an important railroad center in 1883.

T Vineyard Greens Golf Course
795 W. Madison, Glenns Ferry. 366-7531.

Players can enjoy magnificent views of Carmela Vineyards while playing a round of golf at one of Idaho's many wineries. Encompassing 2,369 yards, the par-34 course provides a new angle to southwestern Idaho's wine country as it winds its way through fifty acres of grapes. The course is short enough to accommodate beginners, but challenging enough to test the skills of the best players. Green fees are $10 for 9 holes and $16 for 18 holes on weekdays, with weekend rates at $13 for 9 holes and $21 for 18 holes. Cart rentals are available.

T Glenns Ferry Historical Museum
200 W. Cleveland, Glenns Ferry. 366-7706.

The Glenns Ferry Historical Museum is committed to preserving the rich heritage of the Glenns Ferry, Hammett, and King Hill areas. The museum building itself is a significant piece of history. Opened in 1909, the sandstone structure served as the area school until 1965. In 1987, the schoolhouse was named to the National Register of Historic Places and became the local museum shortly thereafter. Inside, visitors will find exhibits on topics such as early Native Americans, pioneer life on the Oregon Trail, memorabilia from the Oregon Shortline Railroad and King Hill Irrigation Project, as well as numerous school and household artifacts. As part of its mission, the museum also serves as a source for historic printings, including old newspapers, letters, journals, and other documents important in tracing one's genealogy. The museum is open from 12 PM to 5 PM on Fridays and Saturdays from June 1 to September 30 with no admission fee.

T Carmela Vineyards
795 W. Madison, Glenns Ferry. 366-2313. Take I-84 to the Glenns Ferry exit, and proceed to Three Island State Park; the winery is adjacent to the park.

Under the ownership of Roger and Nancy Jones since July 1997, Carmela Vineyards was established in 1988. Situated next to Three Island State Park, an impressive stone winery overlooks the Snake River. With more than 48 acres of grapes, Carmela Vineyards grows and bottles its own wines, including Chardonnay, Cabernet Sauvignon, Merlot, Johannesburg Riesling, Semillon, Lemberger, Muscat, Cannelli, and the most popular Cabernet Franc. Recognizing that many wine connoisseurs enjoy a good meal along with their wine, Carmela Vineyards also offers a family-style restaurant serving lunch and dinner daily with a full Sunday brunch. In addition to the winery and restaurant, Carmela Vineyards offers a 9-hole golf course winding through the vineyard acres, a golf pro shop, a gift shop, wine tasting room, full bar, banquet-conference rooms, and an outside veranda. Patrons are asked to call first to arrange tours of the vineyards and winery. Carmela Vineyards is open from 9:00 AM to 9:00 PM during the summer for wine tasting.

T Three Island Crossing State Park
1083 S. Three Island Park Dr., Glenns Ferry. 366-2394.

Three Island Crossing State Park is situated on one of the most famous crossing points on the Snake River, where pioneers and emigrants following the Oregon Trail were forced to ford the river. The crossing was often dangerous with many pioneer diaries telling of lost wagons and lost lives. Today, the 613-acre park commemorates this historic crossing point with access to picnic areas, hiking, fishing, and a full-service campground as well as access to the admission free Three Island History and Education Center. The education center, however, is closed during the fall and winter from October 10 through April 30. There is a $4.00 per vehicle park entry fee.

M Glenns Ferry Chamber of Commerce
108 E. 1st Ave., Glenns Ferry. 366-7345. http://glennsferryidaho.org

42

King Hill
Pop. 100

Now located near the Snake River, the original town site was one mile east of its present location. With the inception of the King Hill irrigation project, the town was moved to a more central irrigation location. Stage drivers found the large, crown-shaped hill rising north of town particularly difficult to navigate on their route from Kelton, UT to Boise. Some claim the town did indeed derive its name from this hill, while others claim the name came from Mr. King of the Big Wood Irrigation Company. In either case, the post office accepted the community's application for service in 1908.

43 *Lodging*

Pine
Pop. 30

Formerly known as Pine Grove, this small town came into existence with the building of the Anderson Ranch Dam. Mining was also prevalent as is evidenced by the remaining mine dumps. After the completion of the dam, some of the buildings at the location were moved upstream to the present location of Pine. The name of the town is derived from the area's abundant yellow pine groves. A post office operated here from 1888 to 1929.

H Toll Gate
Milepost 107 on U.S. Hwy. 20

An 1868 toll road to Rocky Bar provided better access to early gold mines 40 miles north of here. Julius Newberg's south Boise wagon road had reached Rocky Bar in 1864, but a route through this canyon was needed to avoid steep Syrup Creek grades on Goodale's Cutoff eight miles

Continued on page 241

GHOST TOWNS

Landore
49 miles northwest of CounciL
The history of Landore is spotty at best. It is rumored that the town was named after Landore, Glamorgan in Wales for its meaning, "land of ore." The first hopeful miners moved into the area in 1898, but the town wasn't officially established until 1919 when a post office began operations. The town's settlers may have numbered as many as 1,500 at one time, but like many other settlements in the area, the wealth soon disappeared and so did Landore's residents.

Iron Springs and Paradise
40 miles northwest of Council
During the Seven Devils Mining District rush, Iron Springs was born. Eastern Capital established a town mill, and soon the community also included a hotel, livery stable, numerous saloons, and nearly thirty houses. Although the boom lasted a few years, it eventually died out and only a few decrepit buildings remain in Iron Springs.Situated near Iron Springs beside Paradise Creek was the community of Paradise. During its heyday, Paradise was still nothing more than a tiny suburb of Iron Springs. Today, one dilapidated building marks the townsite.

Rankins Mill
46 miles northwest of CounciL
A once booming neighboring town to Iron Springs, Rankins Mill is now little more than a shadow of its past. Visitors will find remains of a few buildings at the site, including an old mining mill.

Banner City
35 miles northeast of Placerville
Established in 1864, Banner City was originally named Silver City after its inclusion in the Silver Hill Mining District. From the moment of Banner City's origination, problems plagued the town. From late 1864 through early 1865, the community received no supplies due to severe winter conditions and snowfalls regularly exceeding eight feet. The community also lacked a developed road to the site for several years, so hopeful miners often had difficulty reaching the town. In 1872, Banner City believed its bad luck had ended when a mill was built. However, the mill remained non-operational for 10 years. When the mill finally was used, it aided Banner City in the extraction of more than $3 million of silver. Bad luck struck the town again, though, as the mill closed and mining ended in 1921.

Beaver City
North fork of the Boise River
Beaver City is best known as a mystery camp. Records only indicate that the town was settled on the north fork of the Boise River in February 1864.

Boston
Between Placerville and Idaho City
Henry C. Clark, a businessman who moved to Boise County, Idaho from Boston, Massachusetts is credited with naming this community. Located on Grimes Creek approximately two miles south of another ghost town (Centerville), Boston's history is vague other than Clark's attempt to operate a store in the community.

Eureka
Approximately 35 miles northeast of Placerville
Situated near the Banner City mine, Eureka arrived in Idaho during August 1864. Little else is known about the community's history.

Forest City
Approximately 35 miles northeast of Placerville
Forest City's presence in Idaho is extremely vague. Historians suggest the town was established a few miles northeast of Banner City.

Granite City
Boise County
Once known as Granite Creek, Granite City was established in 1862 as the first community for the workers of Gold Hill mine. Named after the immense number of granite rocks in the area, Granite City prospered until 1882 before becoming part of the Quartzburg community.

Jerusalem
North of Horseshoe Bend
Prospectors weary of panning for gold near present-day Centerville struck out and founded Jerusalem in 1862 on the Payette River. After scouring the area, prospectors soon left for better opportunities and more supplies in Walla Walla.

Comeback
North of Centerville
Logging was the initial industry of men near the town of Comeback. However, when a logger discovered gold in 1924, Comeback was formally established. Comeback never achieved much popularity in Boise County as the town's population peaked at two-dozen people.

Golden Age Camp
North of Pioneerville
Golden Age Camp was once distinguished in the area for its numerous town structures. Settled by a man named Wells, the community was once home to a school, recreation hall, two mills, several houses, two bunkhouses, and a hotel. The hotel was most frequently used as it housed company offices and a popular dance hall.

Pomona
Between Centerville and Idaho City
Located directly below the historic Gold Channel and Quartz Gulch junction, Pomona entered the Idaho mining scene as a small camp in 1864. By 1881, the town founded by John Wallace and Company was prospering, but little else is known about the town's doomed fate.

Quartzburg
3 miles northwest of Placerville
One of the most extensive areas containing quartz deposits in Boise County once existed at the settlement of Quartzburg. After the Gold Hill mine was discovered, W.W. Raymond established a twenty-stamp mill on Granite Creek, and Quartzburg was subsequently founded. The first operation of the mill proved unsuccessful, but a new owner attempted to run the facility until 1895. After the property was sold at a sheriff's auction, the next owner ran the mill until 1923. After closing for a short period of time, ownership changed yet again in 1926 and remained in operation until the 1930's Depression. Although it appeared that the mill would have weathered the Depression, a severe forest fire in 1931 closed the business' doors as well as destroyed most of the community. The

only remaining business was the 1884 post office, and it was soon forced to close due to lack of residents.

Summit City
North Boise River
Summit City in Boise County was a short-lived community founded in February 1864 on the North Boise River.

Alturus City
Elmore County
Alturus City drew its name from Spanish and Native American origins. For Spaniards, "alturus" means "heights," while Native Americans believe "alturus" translates into "heavenly heights." Both meanings are relevant in the case of Alturus City, and it is suspected that California prospectors named the settlement found at the mouth of the Yuba River. While the community was established in 1864, nothing remains at the site today.

Clifden
Elmore County
Settled in 1864, Clifden was a small mining community found near the mouth of Quartz Gulch in present day Elmore County. The town, located approximately one-half mile from the now non-existent community of Rocky Bar, was short-lived. By 1880, all of Clifden's residents had moved on to explore new prospects.

Eastman
Elmore County
Eastman is yet another Idaho mystery. The only fact known about this mining settlement is that it was located approximately seven miles south of the Twin Springs community.

Esmeralda
Elmore County
The Spanish tent city of Esmeralda is difficult to locate in Idaho's landscape due to conflicting stories about its location. Some suggest that the settlement was located three-fourths of a mile north of Rocky Bar. Another historian places it twelve miles north of Pine. Still others suggest it was on the south fork of the Boise River or perhaps three miles from Featherville. At any rate, the first Esmeralda settlement was named Alturas County's county seat in 1864, but the town withered away before the county became official. When Elmore County was formed later in 1864, Esmeralda's tent community sprang up again and the population reached nearly 3,000 inhabitants. The rest of Esmeralda's life is vague and left to speculation.

Fredericksburg
Near State Hwy. 21 in Elmore County
Fredericksburg was a small mining community established three-fourths of a mile north of Rocky Bar. The town sprang up with the establishment of the Ada Elmore mine, but the rest of the community's history is lost.

Graham
Elmore County
Graham is perhaps best known as the United State's biggest lie in mining history. Funded in part with the British capital of Matt Graham and American capital totaling $1 million, the community grew to a population numbering 300 men and 41 women. The settlement included boarding houses, a restaurant, jail, butcher shop, blacksmiths, livery stables, and a community hall. Oddly enough, the immense silver ore

in the area was never mined. Instead, Matt Graham used his capital and American investments to create a bogus mine. Next, a mile-long tram was developed to connect his "mine" with a $350,000 mill. Finished in August 1888, this mill operated for a scarce eight hours before being shut down and sold at auction. However, many of the settlers were ingenious and knew how to make a profit on the fake mine. Brothers Mose and Charlie McKee transported freight and passengers to the Graham "mine," charging twelve cents per pound for freight and three dollars for every passenger. Today, the foundations of Graham's mill remain as a testimony to the town's exaggerated mining legacy.

Happy Camp
Elmore County near Elk Creek
Happy Camp, located above the mouth of Bear Creek on Elk Creek, was established four miles from Rocky Bar in 1863. The community boomed, and by fall of 1863, more than thirty-five crews of prospectors were mining in the area. It is estimated that the town's population may have reached 175 inhabitants with the average miner earning $12 to $25 each day before the wealth disappeared.

Marysville
Elmore County
This community was the first Marysville to arrive in Idaho. Settled in 1863 by hopeful miners, the town was dead within a year. Today, a new Marysville is still in existence in Fremont County.

Pine Grove
Elmore County
Now flooded with water from the Anderson Ranch Dam, Pine Grove first served as a stagecoach stop. In 1864, the town included two general stores, a blacksmith, saloon, and a hotel. The town's early history as a stage station was quickly forgotten when miners entered the area around 1886 or 1887. The post office later shortened the town's name to Pine in 1890 before its fated water burial. In anticipation of the flooded townsite, a few residents created a new townsite named Pine nearby. This settlement is still in existence.

Ridgeville
Elmore County
Ridgeville, founded in 1864, was part of Idaho's mining heyday for only a short period of time. The settlement was located between the Feather River and another fated ghost town, Red Warrior.

Red Warrior
Elmore County
Red Warrior's history is vague. Few details exist about the community other than its location one mile from the settlement of Rocky Bar.

Volcano
Elmore County on the Malad River
Found between Camas Prairie and the Snake River Plain near the eastern Bennett Mountains, Volcano sprang to life with the Pioneer Company's March 12, 1864 mine discovery. Hopeful miners rushed to the area, and in 1865, a ten-stamp mill began operating. However, test runs found the mill produced only ten dollars of ore per ton, and the mill was abandoned. Still, mining continued in the area until the mid 1930's.

Yuba City
Elmore County
Yuba City's fate was sealed when the Alturus Mining Company's president ordered a halt to the delivery of a mill and lumber to the Atlanta mining lode near Yuba City. Instead of developing as a community, the lumber meant to erect structures in Yuba rotted away. Yuba City eventually died and was replaced by Atlanta.

DeLamar
State Hwy. 78 near Jordan Creek
Captain Joseph R. DeLamar (the community's namesake) came to Idaho in 1886 after studying chemistry and metallurgy in Chicago and a recent failure at mine operation in Colorado. Deciding to test his luck in Idaho, DeLamar settled in the Owyhee mining district and bought a few claims on what is now DeLamar Mountain. From his purchase and with capital from Chicago investors, DeLamar formed the Wilson mine, and in 1889, he successfully opened a twenty-stamp mill. In less than three years, DeLamar had made $1.5 million. So, in 1891, DeLamar decided to sell his mining operation for $500,000 to the DeLamar Mining Corporation in London. This sale was the only profitable British investment in Idaho's mining boom, and the mine continued to produce a wealth of silver and gold. Although DeLamar sold his properties and left his life as a politician, leading town citizen, and prosperous businessman in 1892 to move to New York, the community continued to prosper. At the height of its success in 1896, the town boasted a population of 950 residents, a thirty-room hotel, a hundred houses, a miner's bunkhouse, and amenities such as electric lights, running water, telephone lines, and a telegraph system. The edge of DeLamar also had a reputation. Known as "Tough Town," this portion of DeLamar was characterized by saloons and houses of ill-repute. According to legend, Long-toe Liz was one of the most popular ladies in the district.

Dewey
Owyhee County near Jordan Creek
J.C. Boone and twenty-eight other prospectors came to this southern Idaho area in 1863 and founded "Booneville." The town, like the area's mining endeavors, was short-lived. But as a new rush of prospectors began searching for gold in the 1890's, Colonel William Henry Dewey saw promise in the settlement. In 1896, Colonel Dewey bought most of Booneville and rebuilt the town. With his own funds, Dewey started a twenty-stamp mill, laid out a city water system, and had a grand, three-story hotel built. The hotel was by far the town's finest attraction as it included steam heat, electricity, and modern plumbing. For his contribution to the town, Colonel Dewey dubbed his new community "Dewey." Unfortunately, Dewey's mill produced hardly enough ore to outweigh the operation costs, and the potential of Dewey being a stop for the Boise, Nampa, and Owyhee Railroad vanished. Colonel Dewey died in 1903, and in 1905, his grand hotel burned to the ground. Today, a large power plant building and a mine dump are all that remain of this town once filled with dreams for success.

Fairview
Owyhee County
Once located two miles east of another mining town (Silver City), Fairview was founded in 1863 after some minor mining activity began in the area. When Charles William Lee came to town, he decided Fairview needed a post office. Thus, on August 27, 1872, Lee established the first post office and served as the only postmaster. Disaster hit Fairview in 1875 when a fire created more than $100,000 worth of damage to the town's structures. Fortunately, a quartz mine was soon located in the area, and the town was brought back to life. However, these mining efforts were short-lived, and Fairview soon became another Idaho boom-town run dry.

Flint
Owyhee County
Discovery of ore in the area during the 1860s led to Flint's development. The town reached a peak population of nearly 1,500 residents and for a short period of time, a mill and smelter operated in the mining settlement. Today, pieces of this mill remain standing as well as remnants of other town structures. The graves of William Black (who was killed by Indians) and his daughter-in-law, Emma Myers, can also be found on a hill near town.

Ruby City
Owyhee County
Miners flocked to this Idaho area after the first discovery of gold on Reynolds Creek near Happy Camp. As more and more settlers moved to the area, existing settlements became cramped so Ruby City was established in 1863 to allow for an increasing population. In 1864, the community was named county seat for Owyhee County, and it held this recognition until the seat was moved to the nearby boomtown of Silver City. This transfer of power marked the beginning of Ruby City's demise. Lured by Silver City's promising mining and business opportunities, all of Ruby City's residents gradually moved away and most of the town's buildings were moved to Silver City. Today, Ruby City's cemetery is the only marker paying tribute to the town's site.

Deadwood City
Valley County near Deadwood River
Numerous prospectors migrated to an area west of the Deadwood River during the 1863 summer in search of riches. By October 17, 1864, another Idaho mining district was full of activity. Unfortunately, the land provided little wealth. Miner Nathan Smith, however, had faith in his Idaho mining plan. In August 1867, Smith relocated the Deadwood District to land he speculated had more potential. By 1868, word had spread of the new community, and nearly 100 men were employed in the district's mines. The rush was only temporary. In 1869, the Loon Creek rush attracted Deadwood City miners. This small community was completely abandoned by 1876 except for a few minor lead and zinc mining operations between 1924 and 1932.

Lake City
Valley County near the Payette Lakes
Founded in 1863, Lake City was appropriately named after its positioning near Idaho's Payette Lakes. Little else is known about this now defunct community.

Logan
Valley County on Logan Creek
Mining had its ups and downs in the small min-

ing camp of Logan near Logan Creek. The settlement was a small placer camp that disappeared along with the absence of riches in the area.

Thunder Mountain City
Valley County near Monumental Creek
Thunder Mountain City was a typical boom camp established in the Thunder Mountain Mining District near Monumental Creek. The camp suffered harsh winters and as new miners arrived, many more settlers left in search of more prosperous camps. Although a few miners were lucky and left with wealthy pockets, the riches were soon gone and the mining camp disappeared.

Roosevelt
Valley County near Monumental Creek
Three miles upstream from Thunder Mountain City on Monumental Creek was the settlement of Roosevelt. In a rush to arrive in Idaho's Thunder Mountain Mining District, many hopeful miners actually believed Thunder Mountain was made of pure gold. Two of these prospectors were Ben and Lew Caswell who laid claims in the area on July 10,1894. After their claims were staked and other workers arrived in the area, the town of Roosevelt was formed and a full-fledge boom was in action by 1902. With the mining advice of expert Colonel William Henry Dewey and financial support from Pittsburgh, Roosevelt continued on successfully until 1909. Unfortunately, a natural disaster in 1909 spelled the end for Roosevelt. After a mudslide blocked Monumental Creek, a lake was formed that buried most of Roosevelt. Today, some of Roosevelt's buildings can be seen partially sticking out of the water. The rest of the town's structures are buried in murky water.

Marble City
Valley County near Monumental Creek
Located near Roosevelt, Marble City sprang up as a community that supported the mining industry in nearby communities. Mining was never a major industry in the settlement. Instead, Marble City's residents participated in trade and transportation sectors. As mining activities dwindled in the surrounding areas, so did Marble City's economic stability and the town disappeared.

Heath
Washington County
T.J. Heath and James Ruth made the first discovery of gold here in October 1864 and word spread quickly of new mining activity. By June 28, 1875, Heath and Ruth's find had launched another prosperous Idaho mining district and the new community of Heath. This community was home to a smelter and a railroad mine. New discoveries near Heath occurred frequently, sustaining the area until the 1920's. After this date, the Bunker Hill-Sullivan Mining Company leased T.J. Heath's mines. However, World War II brought the sale of Heath's smelter, and most of the town's cabins were destroyed. Today, the smelter's bunker is all that remains of this community.

Mineral
22 miles northwest of Weiser in Washington County/
During the summer of 1880, John A. James and his cousin, Jim Peck, established the settlement of Hancock (named after their favorite presidential candidate that year). The camp quickly grew into a town that included two butcher shops,

two livery stables, a blacksmith shop, two general stores, an assay office, two hotels, a barber, nine saloons, several houses of ill repute, a small crusher mill, and a smelter. During this period of rapid growth, the community also decided to change its name to Mineral. Supplies, especially lumber, were scarce in Mineral, so residents were forced to use ingenuity in constructing town buildings. House roofs were frequently made from canvas or from flattened cyanide cans. Other residents opted to use molten slag from the smelters that had been molded into blocks, while still others preferred to create dugouts in the hills rising above Mineral. With these frequent supply shortages, it is not surprising that the town wavered between prosperity and disaster. Times were hard during the 1890's, but by 1900, residents' outlooks had changed and a new, sixty-ton smelter was built. 1905 marked another bust for the community and much of the population left Mineral. Except for a short period of mining in World Wars I and II, the town has slowly withered away. Today, only one building and a graveyard remain.

Ruthburg
38 miles north of Weiser in Washington County
Originally dubbed Brownlee by the U.S. Postal Service, Ruthburg began as a mining settlement in 1875. The first post office was established in 1878 and operated until 1909. On April 21, 1881, the community's residents voted against the name "Brownlee" and adopted the new town name of Ruthburg. Although Ruthburg no longer boasts any residents, its memory lives on in the Idaho state seal where Ruthburg's mill is pictured.

Empire City
Owyhee County
Established as a small mining camp, Empire City was founded near Silver City on War Eagle Mountain. Little else is known about the town's mining history and eventual abandonment.

Wagontown
Owyhee County
Established along Jordan Creek, Wagontown was an important stage stop on the road from Silver City to Winnemucca, Nevada. With the aid of the stagecoach, prospectors eventually arrived in the area and Wagontown soon became a center for mining activity. J.W. Stoddard discovered the first mine in the area, and soon the Webfoot, Last Chance, and the Garfield mines were in operation. Wagontown also included a mill important in handling the tailings that arrived from the De Lamar mill. Today, visitors will find evidence of mine dredging in the area as well as the old Wagontown cemetery.

Decorah
31 miles northwest of Council in Adams County
Located three miles northeast of the ghost town of Cuprum (now a popular summer vacation destination), Decorah was a small mining settlement established in the early 1900s. Miners working along Garnet Creek resided in Decorah for short period of time, and the town competed with nearby Landore for supplies.

Garnet Town
Adams County
Just a few miles north of Decorah along Garnet Creek was the small settlement of Garnet Town. Founded in the early 1900s, Garnet Town was comprised of only three small cabins, all of which can still be found.

Placer Basin
Adams County
Rich ore was discovered in Placer Basin as early as 1890, but production of the ore did not begin until the early 1930s. After Tom Williams struck gold in the area in 1930, he sold out his claim. The new owners constructed a mill that operated in 1935 and 1936 and produced more than $3 million in free milling gold. The mill stands to this day, but the rest of Placer Basin's buildings are falling apart.

Black Lake Town
Adams County
Rugged mountains, Black Lake, and rushing streams provide the backdrop for the old mining camp called Black Lake Town. With the mine located above Black Lake and the mill located below, miners used cable tramways to transport the ore to the mill. Due to the distance between the mine and the town, miners generally stayed at the large boarding house built next to the mine, and Black Lake Town was known for its heavy alcohol consumption. Mining in the area died out within a few years of its start, and during World War II, the mill was dismantled for scrap metal.

Millers Camp
Valley County
Serving as the residence for miners working the Ruby Meadows, Millers Camp was built on a ridge overlooking Ruby Creek. Forest fires eventually destroyed the camp that was once nicknamed Ruby City. Although no original cabins can be found in the area, a dredge from more recent activity in Ruby Meadows remains.

Marshall Lake Mining District
Idaho County
Several small settlements arose in the Marshall Lake Mining District, but no large towns ever prospered in the area. The Golden Anchor mine was discovered in 1915, and it soon became the area's mining headquarters with its few surrounding buildings and a school. For several years, state mine inspector, J.A. Czizek, owned the mine. When the mine reopened in 1940, a post office with the name Czizek was established. World War II, however, forced the closure of the mine and settlers at Czizek moved away. Nearby, on a ridge above Bear Creek, was the tent town of Bungville. Established in 1902, the community was short-lived as it was primarily composed of miners from Florence waiting for snows to melt to begin prospecting again. As soon as the roads opened up, Bungville's residents packed up camp, and the tent town disappeared as quickly as it arose.

Spanish Town
Elmore County
Located near the mouth of Elk Creek's East Fork, Spanish Town was established when early settlers arrived in the area in the late 1800s. As these early miners began prospecting, they discovered artifacts suggesting that Spaniards had reached the area long before them, and they dubbed their new settlement Spanish Town. Once host to a large mining operation, Spanish Town is now falling apart. Visitors will find caved in mine tunnels, dilapidated buildings, and remnants of an old mill.

Brownstown and China Basin
Elmore County
As settlers arrived in the Yuba City area, several miners branched out to form their own

camps/settlements nearby. As a result, the mining camp of Brownstown was established near the Little Queens River, but the camp never achieved popularity. In the same vicinity, Chinese immigrants formed their own camp on the north side of Boise River. This camp was appropriately named China Basin, and many Chinese remained in the area for years to work the placer mines.

Neal
Near Boise
Arthur Neal discovered ore along the summit of Upper Blacks Creek Road in 1889, and a small rush to the area ensued. Several mines and mine dumps were established near Neal, but the town was ill-fated. A few run-down cabins and remains of a stamp mill can be found in the area.

Edwardsburg
8.5 miles north of Profile Summit on Profile Gap Road near Big Creek
William Edwards, a prestigious gentleman who graduated from both Emory College and Georgetown University Law School, established the village of Edwardsburg between Yellow Pine and Big Creek in 1904. Despite spending ten lucrative years employed at the Assistant Attorney General's Office in Washington, D.C., William's health failed him and he decided to move west. Bringing his wife, Annie, and son, Napier, with him to Spokane, William longed to be part of Idaho's treasure seeking madness. When William heard news of the Thunder Mountain boom, he packed up his family and belongings and headed for some of Idaho's most remote backcountry. Although Edwards loved his new surroundings and believed that

nearby Logan Creek contained valuable ore deposits, the intelligent Annie detested her new home. Accustomed to her aristocratic Georgia upbringing and life as an honor graduate of Wesleyan University, the tiny cabin her family now called home was too much for her to handle. As William put his mining law training to work in an attempt to convince wealthy friends to invest in his Copper Camp Mining Company, Annie slowly began to go crazy. In the end, William's theory about Logan Creek proved itself false, and the family was destitute. Annie eventually ended up dying in the state mental asylum in Blackfoot while William retreated to Nampa. Today, this tiny community founded upon great plans and dreams is little more than a scenic area filled with summer-use cabins.

South Mountain City
20 miles southeast of Jordan Valley, Oregon in Idaho's Owyhee County
In 1872, the settlement of Bullian City was established twenty-two miles south of the booming Silver City. As more miners flooded to the area, Bullian City was granted a post office and the town's name was changed to South Mountain City. One of the earliest mining camps in Owyhee County, South Mountain City acquired the first smelter in Idaho to aid in production of the following lead and silver mines: Crown Point, Golconda, Bay State, and Black Giant. South Mountain City's mining activities eventually died out, but a new boom occurred for a few years in the 1950s. Today, visitors will find a black slag pile from the early smelter furnace, as well as some buildings from the 1950s boom.

T Trinity Mountains
West of Featherville. Contact the Idaho Department of Parks and Recreation at 334-4199.

Rising in the remote landscape of southwestern Idaho, the Trinity Mountains are comprised from the massive granite Idaho Batholith. With craggy peaks featuring crystal-lined granite faults, the mountains possess diverse terrain suitable to a variety of recreational pursuits. Open, high elevation forests filled with subalpine fir, whitebark pine, and aspens combine with sagebrush flats and wildflower meadows for a truly unique mountain experience. Due to the remote setting's popularity, a 204-acre Trinity Mountain National Recreation Area was established in 1995 to provide wilderness users with further access to backcountry recreation.

T Johnson's Bridge Hot Springs
Northeast of Mountain Home off U.S. Hwy. 20. Contact the Idaho Department of Fish and Game at 334-3700. From Mountain Home, drive northeast on U.S. Hwy. 20. Approximately 3 miles past the Little Camas Reservoir, bear left on Forest Rd. (FR) 152. At FR 61, turn left again and continue to Johnson's Bridge at the South Fork of the Boise River.

Johnson's Bridge Hot Springs is a popular year-round destination for outdoor enthusiasts and those who crave the natural relaxation of non-commercial mineral pools. Situated on the South Fork of the Boise River, Johnson's Bridge Hot Springs provides several pools on both the north and south ends of the bridge. Each pool is brimming with piping hot water from the natural spring located on the river's eastern bank.

T Trinity Springs
Northeast of Mountain Home between Pine and Featherville. 653-2363.

Located in a quartz-granite aquifer, Idaho's Trinity Springs borders the Sawtooth and Boise National Forests. Bubbling out of the ground from a natural spring where no manmade drilling or pumping equipment is required, Trinity Springs is a 2.2-mile deep source of crystal pure water dated at more than 16,000 years old.

The springs have also given way to the environmentally friendly water bottling company, Trinity Springs Incorporated (formerly known as Underground Water People). Situated near a natural wetland, the company headquarters and springhouse were designed to complement the pristine natural surroundings. Both the springhouse and company headquarters utilized the ancient art of Geomancy during all construction phases, and only the most natural building materials were selected. Visitors will find a hand-hewn stone springhouse next to the straw, bamboo, wood, and stone operations facility. Staffed with environmentally friendly, health-conscious employees, Trinity Springs Incorporated sells its pure Idaho water all across America. Tours of the unique facility are available upon advance notice.

T Baumgartner Hot Springs
East of Featherville on Forest Rd. 227 at Baumgartner Campground. Contact the Idaho Department of Parks and Recreation at 334-4199.

Baumgartner Hot Springs dates back to the early twentieth century and the mining claim of John Baumgartner. While slaving away in the mines, Baumgartner realized he had an opportunity to provide area residents with much-needed relaxation. Upon discovery of hot springs on his land, Baumgartner maintained the primitive site for public use until his death in 1941. At Baumgartner's passing, the hot springs and his surrounding land claim were donated to the

northwest of here. Tolls were collected here for 20 years to maintain it, and James Porter's splendid hotel and dairy attracted travelers for many miles.

H Goodale's Cutoff
Milepost 124.4 on U.S. Hwy. 20

An old emigrant road headed west across Camas Prairie and then descended to the valley below on its way to rejoin the Oregon Trail 20 miles southwest of here. This route, discovered by Donald Mackenzie's fur trade party in 1820, came into use for emigrant wagons in 1852. Indian hostility along the regular Oregon Trail to the south led Timothy Goodale to bring a large emigrant party of Idaho pioneers this way in 1862. After that, the road was known as Goodale's Cutoff.

H Castle Rock
Milepost 124.4 on U.S. Hwy. 20

Up toward Camas Prairie, this road goes by Castle Rock and other eroded granite outcrops that were landmarks on Goodale's Cutoff, an Oregon Trail route that came this way. Emigrants generally had not seen large granite rock formations of this kind, and Idaho offered a number of good opportunities, both for Oregon and California travelers. Castle Rock and its neighbors were outstanding examples along Goodale's Cutoff. The trail was used primarily from 1862 until automobiles replaced wagon traffic more than 40 years later.

H Gold Mines
Milepost 126.3 on U.S. Hwy. 20

More than a century ago, Rocky Bar, Happy Camp, and a number of other south Boise min-

ing towns flourished in a remote wilderness 30 miles northwest of here. Discovered early in 1863, they were so hard to get to that they could not be worked successfully for more than 20 years. But wealthy investors from New York and London finally put up enough capital that large mills and underground tunnels produced more than $6 million. That gold now is worth more than $120 million.

T Featherville
Off U.S. Hwy. 20 north of Mountain Home

Also known as Junction Bar, Featherville was located at the mouth of the Feather River. The community served as a stagecoach stop on the route to Rocky Bar, and gold was mined in the area from 1922 to 1927. During its short life, 33,000 ounces of gold were found in the area, and today, a few vintage structures remain at the settlement.

T Rocky Bar
South of Atlanta on Forest Rd. 156

H.T.P. Comstock, the originator of Nevada's Comstock Lode, founded Rocky Bar in December 1863. Located at the convergence of Bear and Steel Creeks north of the Featherville settlement, Rocky Bar served as Alturas and Elmore County's first county seat. On September 1, 1892, disaster struck the prospering mining community. A forest fire swept through the area destroying several buildings and all of Chinatown. The settlers were determined to keep their community alive, however, and the town was rebuilt. Today, some of the community's antiquated structures still remain as a glimpse into Idaho's mining history.

Forest Service in accordance with the miner's wishes. The area was subsequently developed into a popular campground, and the primitive sand-lined pool was refashioned into a large concrete hot springs wonder. Today, the fifteen by twenty foot pool is complete with steps, railings, and filters, and the pool is drained, cleaned, and refilled daily during the summer season. Surrounded by nature's beauty and occasional deer and elk passerby, the pool is open daily from mid-May through September until 10 PM. Swimsuits are required at all times, and the road leading to the pool is seasonally closed from October through mid-May.

TV Anderson Ranch Reservoir Recreation Area
20 miles east of Mountain Home off U.S. Hwy. 20 on Forest Rd. 134. Contact the Desert Mountain Visitor Center at 587-4464.

Anderson Ranch Reservoir was created in 1950 when the Bureau of Reclamation constructed the 1,350 foot long earthen Anderson Ranch Dam. Stopping the South Fork of the Boise River, the dam created a perfect segue for the formation of a reservoir recreation area. Today, the seventeen-mile long reservoir is home to an array of year-round outdoor adventures. With fifty miles of shoreline, Anderson Ranch Reservoir provides anglers with easy access to world-class fishing. The recreation area is known to harbor smallmouth bass, rainbow trout, Chinook salmon, and kokanee, while several boat ramps afford boaters and water-skiers the opportunity to cool off in the summer heat. The recreation opportunities don't end with the arrival of winter, however. The area maintains nearly 250 miles of groomed snowmobile trails that wander around the reservoir and through historic mining areas. The recreation area is open year-round free of charge. Nearby area services include a marina, RV and tent camping sites, restaurants, fuel stations, and convenience stores.

TV Little Camas Reservoir
Northeast of Mountain Home. Contact the Idaho Department of Fish and Game at 334-3700. From Mountain Home, drive northeast on U.S. Hwy. 20. At Forest Road 160, bear north and continue to the reservoir.

Lost in the limelight of its more popular Anderson Ranch Reservoir neighbor, Little Camas Reservoir provides outdoor enthusiasts with a serene Magic Valley setting. The scenic reservoir situated in the Boise National Forest is stocked with rainbow trout, and a Forest Service boat dock on the reservoir's north end provides easy water access.

V Pine-Featherville-Trinity Lakes Area Snowmobile Trails
North of Mountain Home near Pine. Contact the Mountain Home Ranger District at 587-7961.

Starting at a base elevation of 4,200 feet, the Pine-Featherville-Trinity Lakes Area Snowmobile Trails climb to nearly 10,000 feet in the scenic Trinity Mountains. More than 380 miles of well-marked groomed trails provide an array of options for snowmobilers of all ages and experience levels. The most frequently used trails in the area include Trinity Lakes, Pfifer Creek, James Creek, Wagon Town Loop, Idaho City, Burnt Creek, Nesters, Pine, Fall Creek, Rocky Bar, Atlanta, Featherville, Deer Creek, and Smith's Prairie.

44 Lodging

Bruneau
Pop. 100

This small town founded in the 1870s takes its name from the Bruneau River; however, some folks claim the name came from Bruneau John, an old Indian who warned several white people of an Indian uprising and saved their lives. The opposite is true, in fact. The old Indian was named after the town.

During the town's early years, the area's desert-like terrain was ideal for spring animal grazing, but accessing water was an ongoing problem for local ranchers. For those who wished to make a profit at ranch living, water had to be hauled in over twenty miles to the sheep herds dwelling in the desert. The Air Force ended sheep grazing when they began using the area for aerial gunnery and bombing practice missions. Today, interestingly enough, a tiny snail unique to the area has been classified "endangered" by the government, and residents have been placed under fairly strict orders to protect it. Think snails are cute? Not if you ask the locals. Most are not impressed by the restrictions placed on their hometown.

T Bruneau Dunes State Park
South of Mountain Home on State Hwy. 51. 366-7919.

Established in 1970 and encompassing 4,800 acres of arid terrain directly south of the Snake River, Bruneau Dunes State Park is one of the state's largest and most unique destinations. While all other dunes on the North American continent form at the edge of a basin, the Bruneau Dunes formed at the center of a natural basin 15,000 years ago during the catastrophic Bonneville Flood. Today, the dunes retain their shape due to southeast and northwest winds that blow roughly equal amounts of time. In addition to their unique formation, the Bruneau Dunes are also recognized as the tallest, single-structured sand dunes on this continent. One of the dunes rises nearly 470 feet from the basin floor!

While the pristine dunes are closed to all motorized activity, visitors may hike up to the crest to catch incredible views of the Snake River Plain. A few established hiking trails meander around the dunes' base, and several small lakes dot the landscape. Fishing and paddleboats are allowed on the water, and visitors will likely glimpse sight of the area's diverse wildlife population. Thousands of ducks frequent the lakes' shorelines, while coyotes, jackrabbits, and squirrels play in the dunes. Swimming in the lakes is not recommended as they are known to harbor larval parasites resulting in "swimmers' itch."

In addition to its natural attractions, the park includes a grassy, forty-eight site campground with one of the longest open seasons in all of southern Idaho. A visitor center includes information regarding the dunes' historical and geological background, fossils, and mounted specimens of area species. The park's observatory is also open, offering visitors a twenty-five inch telescope and several other smaller scopes ideal for stargazing.

The park is open year-round and special stargazing programs are offered on Friday and Saturday nights March through October. A motorized park entrance fee of $4 per vehicle is required at the park's entrance.

T Bruneau Canyon Overlook
19 miles southeast of Bruneau on Hot Springs Rd. Contact the BLM – Four Rivers Field Office.

The raging Bruneau River glimmers below in the desert heat from the spectacular Bruneau Canyon Overlook. The area offers the only accessible overlook of the scenic gorge where visitors can peer down 800 feet for views of the 1,300-foot wide dramatic desert canyon. Bighorn sheep and antelope populate the area, and the free overlook is usually accessible during spring, summer, and fall. Visitors should call for the latest road conditions prior to departure.

TV Bruneau and Jarbidge Rivers
South of Mountain Home on State Hwy. 51. Contact the BLM – Four Rivers Field Office at 384-3300.

The Bruneau River, one of the west's most remote canyonland rivers, is frequently dubbed Idaho's best-kept secret and honors historic Northwest Fur Trading Company employee, Jean-Baptiste Bruneau. Fifty miles of turquoise waters rage through the tall, narrow red rock canyon carved into ancient lava flows, and many visitors refer to the area as the Sistine Chapel of all American river canyons. The Class III and IV rapids feature natural hot springs shaded in the canopy of steep canyon walls, and sixty different bird species habiting the area add to the mystique of this popular whitewater destination.

Nearby, the twenty-five mile long Jarbidge River serves as the Bruneau's largest feeder stream. The challenging river flows through an impressively steep, narrow canyon whose shores are lined with rocks and juniper trees. The scenic river is clogged with log jams and boulders, and only highly experienced rafters should attempt the Jarbidge.

Both the Bruneau and Jarbidge Rivers have been nominated for National Wild River status, and the rivers are generally run together in white-water outings. Due to the region's desert conditions, the best months for river running are April, May, and June. The rivers and their tributaries also include redband trout and limited populations of bull trout for interested anglers.

45 Lodging

Riddle
Pop. 25

Established near the northern border of the Duck Valley Indian Reservation, Riddle draws its name from historic area ranch owners, Frank W. and Grant Riddle. The town's post office operated from 1898 until 1963.

Grasmere
State Hwy. 51 south of Bruneau

In the remote desert land of Idaho's Owyhee County, Grasmere stands as a solitary outpost amid miles of badland canyons and sagebrush flats. The area serves as the final stop of civilization for kayakers and rafters headed east on wild Bruneau Canyon excursions.

TV Duck Valley Indian Reservation & Mountain View Reservoir
South of Riddle on State Hwy. 51. 757-3161.

Established in 1877 under a federal government order, the Duck Valley Indian Reservation stretches from southern Idaho into northern Nevada in the isolated desert region surrounding Idaho State Hwy. 51. Although the 293,000-acre reservation was initially founded as a home for the Western

Shoshone, an Idaho gubernatorial decree forced a tribe of Northern Paiute Indians onto the reservation in 1886. In 1938, these two tribes were merged under the Indian Reorganization Act and formed a tribal governing body composed of eight elected members.

Today, the reservation's unemployment rate is chronically high, and most of the 1,600 plus members rely on the tribal income garnered from fishing permit sales on Mountain View Reservoir. The lake was built in 1969 and is stocked annually with rainbow trout. Those interested in testing their angling skills must first purchase a tribal permit at the reservation headquarters on the Idaho/Nevada state line.

46 Food, Lodging

Grand View
Pop. 330

Grand View was founded around 1880 as a placer mining town, and a post office was established there at that time. It wasn't until 1908, however, that the settlement really grew. Named after the view of the surrounding Owyhee valley, Grand View also boasts arid ranchlands.

T The Otter-Van Orman Massacre
3 miles north of State Hwy. 78 on Castle Creek between Murphy and Grand View

Although most emigrants along the Oregon Trail wished for nothing more than a peaceful journey and a fortuitous end on the Western coast, some white men were not as scrupulous. After robbing, murdering, and raping many of the Native American peoples, white men and pioneers heading west earned an unfavorable reputation and became the target of revenge. Numerous massacres occurred along the way, and pioneers quickly learned to live in fear of encounters with the native peoples. One of the most horrific tragedies along the Oregon Trail occurred in Owyhee County.

Led by Elijah Otter, forty-four emigrants in a train of eight wagons were traveling west on September 9, 1860 when a band of Shoshone Indians waged a surprise attack. Over the two day siege, nine of the pioneers were killed and the covered wagons were set on fire, leaving the emigrants destitute. As the initial battle ended and the emigrants attempted to leave the scene, the group was ambushed again, bringing the death count to twenty-three with four children kidnapped. The eighteen remaining pioneers were left stranded in the desert, forced to walk towards safety. Facing extreme weather conditions and a lack of food, water, and supplies, six of the pioneers died and became a source of food for the desperate survivors. A military rescue party eventually met the survivors near the Owyhee River, and Army personnel were sent in search of the missing children.

T Lawson's Emu-z-um
22142 River Rd., Grand View. 834-2397.

Formerly an emu ranch, Lawson's Emu-z-um provides a glimpse into the past on the banks of the Snake River. This museum is filled with memorabilia of southwestern Idaho's colorful past, and its primary attraction is the authentic replica of a 1860s Idaho pioneer settlement. Among the many other displays is a hand built automobile, historic clothing, antique farm equipment, Native American artifacts, and local artwork. The museum is open mid-March through mid-September on weekends from 9 AM to 5 PM. Throughout the rest of the year, museum tours are available by appointment.

TV C. J. Strike Reservoir and Wildlife Management Area
21 miles south of Mountain Home. Contact the Desert Mountain Visitor Center at 587-4464.

Spanning 8,000 acres, the high desert C. J. Strike Reservoir was established in 1952 under the name of Idaho Power Company employee, Clifford J. Strike. Strike served as the company president from 1938 to 1948, and the reservoir and wildlife management area honor his company contributions.

Surrounded by steep, rocky cliff faces, the reservoir is popular with boaters and anglers for its year-round boat launching sites. Anglers will find plenty of bass, bluegill, crappie, catfish, perch, and even an occasional sturgeon, while area hikers are likely to locate Oregon Trail wagon ruts.

The 12,500-acre C. J. Strike Wildlife Management Area was established in the same location and is composed of the reservoir and surrounding land. The area serves as a protected sanctuary each winter for migratory geese and ducks.

The C. J. Strike area is open year-round free of charge and includes twenty-six campground sites for overnight visitors.

47 Lodging

Murphy
Pop. 75

Before becoming an official townsite, the region surrounding Murphy was home to the Oregon Trail's south alternate route. By 1891, however, settlers began to stay, and cattle ranchers and sheepherders prospered. Quickly establishing itself as a regional livestock center, Murphy eagerly welcomed the 1892 arrival of the Boise, Nampa, and Owyhee Railroad. At that same time, area residents decided to christen their town after Pat Murphy. Pat was a Silver City mining engineer and close friend of Colonel William Dewey, and Dewey had played an instrumental role in bringing the line to Murphy. Although Dewey fully intended to connect Murphy to nearby Silver City by rail, the plan never materialized, and Murphy remained the end of the line. Nevertheless, the railroad was key in establishing Murphy as the Pacific Northwest's largest livestock and agricultural shipping point in the early 1900s. Based upon this economic factor and the town's location near the Snake River, Murphy obtained rights from Silver City as county seat in 1934.

Today, a lone parking meter stands in front of the courthouse, reminding locals to watch where they park. Local lore also states that the meter is supposed to remind visitors that this town may in fact be America's smallest county seat.

Idaho Trivia

Owyhee County in southwestern Idaho represents the state's second-largest county, encompassing nearly five million acres. Despite its massive land size, Owyhee County's population remains fairly stagnant due to the remote high desert terrain. In 1866, the county population hovered at 5,000. Now, nearly 150 years later, the county's population has only risen to a meager 10,227 residents.

Reynolds
9 miles west of Murphy on Reynolds Creek in Owyhee County

As one of many prospectors from Walla Walla, Washington who came to Owyhee County in the 1870s, John Reynolds serves as this community's namesake. John Reynolds was known as the laziest prospector in the party, preferring to sit in camp all day while the other members prospected, gathered supplies, and located food. Noticing Reynolds' apathy, his comrades named the nearby creek Reynolds Creek as both failed to move quickly, and the post office established in 1877 adopted his name as well. In 1884, residents renamed their community Brunzel, but in 1915, the town's name returned to Reynolds. The town post office operated until 1915 when it was forced to close its doors due to a dwindling population.

H War Eagle Mines
Milepost 34.1 on State Hwy. 78 at the Silver City junction

For a decade after 1864, most of Silver City's fabulous mineral wealth came from upper War Eagle Mountain, which rises a vertical mile above here. With lodes far richer than those found elsewhere, War Eagle miners fought a series of violent wars for control of valuable claims. Troops from Fort Boise finally had to intervene in one armed clash in 1868. San Francisco bank failures ended production there in 1875, and thriving camps became ghost towns.

H Diamond Gulch
Milepost 34.1 on State Hwy. 78

In December 1865, Idaho's governor – Caleb Lyon of Lyonsdale – set off a wild rush to Diamond Gulch, visible a few miles west of here, with a story that was too good to be true. He told miners in Silver City that a prospector had given him some priceless diamonds from that area. Enough gems of interest to rock hounds were found there to maintain a diamond frenzy that winter. A similar excitement followed in 1892, but no actual diamonds ever were recovered in Diamond Gulch.

H Owyhee Country
Milepost 14.1 on U.S. Hwy. 95

The name applied to these mountains and the whole surrounding region is an outdated spelling of the word "Hawaii." Fur-trading ships brought Hawaiian natives – then called "Owyhees" – to the Northwest. In 1818, Donald Mackenzie brought the first big brigade of fur hunters to the Snake River Valley. He sent several Owyhees to trap in this region – and they never came back. Ever since then, this has been called the Owyhee country and Owyhee County carries the name. (Pronounce "Owyhee" and "Hawaii" aloud – they sound similar.)

T Silver City
Drive 5 miles south of Murphy on State Hwy. 78; exit west off this highway onto a 23-mile road leading through Striker Creek Basin Gulch (Note: The road is generally open by June 1, but avoid traveling during rainy conditions as the steep mountain passes become very dangerous when wet.)

Silver City is a treasure among American ghost towns. Complete with forty remaining buildings, Silver City is a popular attraction where visitors can glimpse into Idaho's mining history. Initially, mining in the area focused on placer gold, but most of the findings were insignificant. In 1864, though, riches were struck as vast deposits of silver and gold were found on War Eagle Mountain east of present day Silver City. Silas Skinner, Colonel W.H. Dewey, and Michael Jordan knew the mines would prosper with adequate supplies. Together, these men requested a fifteen-year franchise to build a toll road from Jordan Valley to Silver City and then seventy miles down Reynolds Creek to Boise City. Silas Skinner completed this road May 19, 1866, and supplies from Chico, California began reaching the settlement in just four days.

As supplies poured in and the Oro Fino and Morning Star mines on War Eagle Mountain prospered, New York investors sent capital to the area to develop more mills along Jordan Creek. By 1866, eighty-two mills were fully operating, producing $70,000 each week. In the first ten years, the mines boasted a total of $30 million in profits.

Silver City's population surged as more mines were developed on War Eagle. In 1866, the community was named Owyhee county seat, and an 1867 population of 3,000 enabled construction and business growth. The town boasted two schools, the elegant fifty room Idaho Hotel, six general stores, a brewery, eight saloons, a miner's hospital, several houses of ill-repute, a Masonic Temple, and Catholic and Protestant Churches. During the same time period, the *Idaho Avalanche* began reporting area news and acquired the first telegraph service in the area. Silver City also had a large population of Chinese miners. These men were forced into Chinatown, an area separated from the rest of the city by the narrow Deadman's Alley.

With great riches also came great conflict. In 1865, the Poorman mine opened on the already existing claim of Hays and Ray (an illegal action as determined by the apex mining doctrine). Determined to maintain their claim, Poorman employees armed themselves and built Fort Baker at the entrance to their mine. While some high-grade ore was sent to Portland, Oregon before the standoff ended, a judge soon ruled that the Poorman was on the same vein as the Hays and Ray and fined the Poorman owners. Afterwards, the two mines decided to work together and by January 1867, the Hays-Poorman mine had made nearly $1 million.

As the Hays-Poorman miners learned to work together, another conflict was brewing. D.H. Fogus staked the Ida Elmore mine while Hill Beachy claimed the Golden Chariot mine in September 1867 on War Eagle. With tensions running high between the two competing mines, Golden Chariot workers shot their way into the Ida Elmore shaft on March 25, 1868. For three days, workers from both mines were involved in an underground gun battle that killed three people. Although the underground war eventually ended, the conflict continued on the evening of April 1, 1868. On that fateful night, J. Marion Moore (co-owner of the Ida Elmore mine) encountered Golden Chariot mine representative, Sam Lockhart, on the porch of the Idaho Hotel. After heated words were exchanged, shots broke out between the two, and both were mortally wounded. Reinforcements were called in, and Governor D.W. Ballard sent deputy marshal, Orlando Rube Robbins, to read a cease-fire proclamation to the workers. Apparently, the remaining company leaders hammered out an agreement ending the conflict, but Governor Ballard ensured the community's safety by sending ninety-six Fort Boise soldiers to the area for four days.

After the conflict was settled, mining on War Eagle Mountain continued steadily and peacefully, and production by the end of 1868 yielded more

than $3 million in profits. Mining continued in the area steadily until the Great Depression, but activity declined so much that the county seat was eventually awarded to Murphy. At the start of World War II, mining restrictions forced the last of Silver City's operating mines to shut their doors, and the community soon became a ghost town.

Known today as one of the most well-preserved ghost towns in the American West, the popular Silver City still maintains its two main streets, Jordan and Washington. Stop in at the 1860's Idaho Hotel on Jordan Street which still occasionally offers rooms during the summer. Next door, visitors will find the remains of the Wells Fargo office. A few yards from the hotel is the still standing newspaper office. Among other structures in the town, sightseers will locate some elaborate houses, the Silver City Cemetery, and Our Lady of Tears Catholic Church. And last, but not least, stop in at the old schoolhouse that has now been turned into an interesting museum. The schoolhouse features several historic newspaper articles, stories of Silver City's heyday, and the history of the surrounding area. Operating hours are 10 AM to 6 PM daily June to October, and admission is $.50 for adults and $.25 for youth.

T Owyhee County Museum
190 Basey St., Murphy. 495-2319.

The Owyhee County Museum offers an excellent collection of well-preserved historical buildings as well as a small research library. Visitors will find a one-room schoolhouse, a pioneer log cabin with the kitchen still intact, the old Marsing railroad depot complete with a Union Pacific caboose, antique farm machinery, Oregon Trail information, and a reconstructed mining stamp mill complete with equipment used in old Owyhee mines. In the library, nearly 4,000 photos illustrate the region's growth and development, and microfiche newspapers preserve local history back to 1865. The museum is open from 10 AM to 4 PM Tuesday through Saturday year-round.

T 45 Ranch Conservation Area
In the Owyhee Canyonlands near Murphy. Contact The Nature Conservancy at 788-2203.

The Nature Conservancy and several Idaho government agencies work jointly to preserve the unique desert canyon environment and its wildlife at the 45 Ranch Conservation Area. Including nearly 70,000 acres of terrain stretching from the Oregon border to the Nevada stateline, the conservation area is one of the only inhabited developments in the entire Owyhee Canyonlands region. In addition to hosting mountain lions, sage grouse, chukkar, antelope, mule deer, bobcats, river otter, and several fish species, the conservation area is home to the world's largest population of threatened California Big Horn Sheep. The ranch is open for wildlife viewing year-round free of charge during daylight hours.

TV Owyhee River
South of Boise in the state's southwestern corner. Contact the Southwest Idaho Travel Association at (800) 635-5240.

Winding through dramatic, multi-colored canyons, the uninhabited Owyhee River may be Idaho's most remote and scenic water passage. The river's name, which is a phonetic spelling of Hawaii, dates back to Donald McKenzie's 1818 scouting expedition. During the trip, two native Hawaiians accompanying the group vanished forever into the river's remote canyon setting. As tales of the account spread, misspellings and pronunciations garnered the river its current name and spelling.

On its journey from Nevada headwaters, the river flows northerly through Idaho and Oregon before eventually dumping into the Snake River. In 1979, 192 miles of the secluded river were signed into the National Wild and Scenic Rivers System, and today, the river is known as a premier whitewater rafting destination. Ranging from intermediate to advanced runs, the Owyhee River offers the best rafting from April to early June. Even though the best running season technically occurs in spring, temperature changes in the Owyhee River Canyon can be extreme with searing afternoon heat plunging rapidly to below freezing temperatures at night. Anglers will find excellent populations of redband trout, and Lahontan cutthroat trout has recently been introduced. All river users should plan accordingly for the isolated, desert setting.

TV Owyhee Canyonlands
South of the Snake River in Owyhee County. Contact the BLM – Idaho State Office at 373-4000.

Owyhee Canyonlands includes some of Idaho's most wild and remote territory and has been recommended for both Wilderness and Wild and Scenic River designations. The high mountain desert terrain is home to whitewater adventures on the Snake, Owyhee, and Bruneau Rivers and boating on the ever-popular C. J. Strike Reservoir. For hikers and mountain bikers, the breathtaking canyonlands provide miles of adventurous trails steeped in solitude and ghost town history. Due to the desert conditions, trails are accessible year-round. Visitors to this free natural area are encouraged to follow all safety and backcountry precautions. The land is remote and users should be adequately prepared at all times for a range of weather conditions and temperatures. Maps and more specific Owyhee Canyonlands information is available from the Bureau of Land Management State Office in Boise.

V Hemingway Butte
23 miles south of Nampa near Murphy. Contact the BLM – Idaho State Office at 373-4000. Traveling west of Boise on I-84, take Nampa Exit 38 and proceed south to 12th Ave. S. and Hwy. 45. After crossing the Snake River at Walter's Ferry, drive approximately one mile to the butte's access point on Reynolds Creek Road.

Hemingway Butte is the site of an extensive ATV trail system that continues to grow in popularity. Situated on the front range of the Owyhee Mountains, the landscape offers riders of all abilities a variety of terrain ranging from flat land to desert foothills to high ridges and buttes. The area is open year-round free of charge.

SCENIC DRIVES

French Creek Loop
Explore mountain lakes, forests, hot springs, historic areas, and waterfalls along the 115-mile scenic French Creek Loop into Idaho's backcountry. The route begins near Shore Lodge in McCall where travelers should merge off Highway 55 onto Warren Wagon Road. This road served as an important pack trail in the 1800s mining days and later became a well-traveled wagon road. Many old wagon ruts are still visible near the highway.

Continue on past Big Payette Lake to North Beach State Park. Depending on how much time you have available, stop for a swim, picnic, or a stroll along the beach. From the park, the road winds through granite cliffs lined with pine, fir, and aspen trees to the popular fishing spot at Upper Payette Lake. Proceed past Secesh Summit (where many visitors have reported moose-sightings) and continue to the trip's 27.3-mile mark. Here, travelers should cross the Lake Creek Bridge and bear left on windy Forest Road 246, a road that was unbelievably considered a state highway in the late 1800s.

Now on Road 246, continue to the historic Burgdorf Hot Springs. Established by German immigrant, Fred Burgdorf, the hot springs are listed on the National Register of Historic Places. Continue winding through the forest as the road climbs to its high point at mile 37.7 before descending down several hairpin turns into Salmon River country. At mile 42.1, note a pioneer cabin on the road's left side. Built in 1900, a man named Edmundson lived there with his family until 1930 and it was a popular freight stop along the French Creek Road.

At mile 53.6, travelers will reach the junction of French Creek and Salmon River Roads. Proceeding left, the road winds through scenic canyons along the Salmon River. Many visitors stop for a stroll on the river's banks or for a dip in the river. Swimmers, however, are highly urged to wear lifejackets as the river's rapids can be dangerous.

The one-lane, steel Manning Bridge appears at the trip's 58.3-mile mark. The Civilian Conservation Corps constructed the bridge in the 1930s, and although it appears rickety, it is safe for automobile crossings. Upon crossing the bridge, drive past the Spring Bar Campground and Allison Creek picnic area to the junction with Highway 95. Turn left here and proceed back to McCall. Along the way, check out the Rapid River Hatchery where salmon are raised, the waterfall on the Little Salmon River, Zim's Hot Springs, and Packer John's Cabin State Park. Travelers should allow at least 6 hours for this drive that primarily follows gravel roads.

Owyhee Uplands Backcountry Byway

Starting through hay meadows, rolling hills and the winding course of Jordan Creek, you'll soon climb into the mountains and gnarled stands of juniper woodlands. Numerous mountain ranges frame the picturesque desert, with Idaho's Owyhees rising to the north. From expanses of sagebrush and wildflowers, to rough, rock-walled rivers and streams, the Owyhee Uplands represent what many people believe the real West is all about.

The loop begins 80 miles southwest of Boise. It can be reached from the west through Jordan Valley, Oregon, and from the east, on Idaho 78 near Grand View, Idaho. The route is mostly one and one-half lanes of graveled road. The byway is usually impassable from late November through March because of snow. Also, precipitation can make the road treacherously slick. The best times of year to drive the byway are early summer and fall. The byway is 101 miles, and from Boise, it is an all-day trip.

Reprinted from Idaho Department of Transportation brochure

Western Heritage Historic Byway

When President Lincoln turned his attention from the Civil War to proclaim Idaho a U.S. Territory, migration south from Fort Boise had already begun. Huge silver and gold discoveries had been made in the Owyhees. Emigrants trudged trails south and twenty-horse teams moved mine machinery over rattlesnake-infested volcanic rifts and down the steep sides of the Snake River Canyon.

Today, where trails once existed, a broad new highway passes through farmlands to Indian Creek and the town of Kuna. This historic place was first an Indian crossing – then a traveler's

way-station – then the Shortline railhead, and finally, the growing farm community it is today.

Here, the byway turns south down Swan Falls Road. Just a few miles past Kuna, the scene moves abruptly from gold and green fields stitched together by silver irrigation canals, to rugged terrain unchanged since wild horse herds roamed and the great hoards of jack rabbits made settlers' lives miserable.

Now, thousands of folks visit the Birds of Prey National Conservation Area, Initial Point, Snake River Canyon, Dedication Point, and Swan Falls Dam each year.

From Meridian, Idaho Highway 69 begins on the southbound road from exit 44 off I-84 and runs for 8 miles to East Avalon Avenue in Kuna. Turn south on Swan Falls Road and continue for 21 miles through the National Conservation Area Birds of Prey to Swan Falls Dam. Idaho 69 is a new 5-lane roadway to Kuna. Swan Falls Road is a two-lane highway to the Swan Falls Dam. The final mile is a steep grade from the Snake River Canyon rim to the dam site. Ice patches occur infrequently during winter weather. The byway can be seen year-round, but birds of prey migrate in and are active March to late June. Travelers should allow at least 1 hour for this 30-mile trip.

Reprinted from Idaho Department of Transportation brochure

Ponderosa Pine Scenic Byway

The Ponderosa Pine Scenic Byway starts in Boise. It follows Idaho 21 north to the historic mining town of Idaho City, where you can still pan for gold in a nearby streambed. Campgrounds and fishing opportunities dot the route from Idaho City to Lowman along the South Fork of the Payette River, as you slowly climb along the byway's northeasterly route.

At the cutoff road to Grandjean, the roadway leaves the Payette River and squeezes between two of Idaho's wilderness areas. On the right, the Sawtooth Wilderness and its 217,000 pristine acres of coniferous forest lands and wilderness lakes. To the left, the Salmon-Challis National Forest, entryway to the 2.3-million-acre Frank Church River of No Return Wilderness, with more contiguous acres of roadless wilderness than anywhere else in the lower 48 states.

From Banner Summit, one of Idaho's highest at 7,056 feet, you begin a descent into the town of Stanley. As the roadway grooves through the steep foothills and thick forest, you can catch glimpses of the Sawtooth Mountains ahead; finally, as you drop into Stanley, they come into full, magnificent view.

The byway follows a narrow, winding road with some steep grades. There are two lanes with some passing lanes. There usually is a snow floor north of Lowman during winter. Severe avalanche conditions exist in the Banner Summit area and road closures can be frequent. Check conditions before traveling in winter. Travelers should allow at least 3 hours for this 130.9-mile trip.

Reprinted from Idaho Department of Transportation brochure

Wildlife Canyon Scenic Byway

Herds of elk numbering near one hundred are not an unusual sight along the Wildlife Canyon Scenic Byway, especially near the Danskin river access. Along with elk are mule deer, whitetail deer, chukars, wild turkeys, eagles, ospreys, cougars, bears, and wolves. Several campgrounds along the byway have natural hot springs for visitors to enjoy, as well as several trails for hiking and biking. Fishing and rafting are also enjoyable activities afforded along the route. In winter months,

summer hiking trails provide miles of snowmobile and skiing adventure. You will also find motels, bed and breakfasts, a musical theater, and even a golf course.

Wildlife Canyon Scenic Byway joins two other scenic byways, forming a one-day drive from Boise. It can be accessed either by the Ponderosa Pine Scenic Byway on Idaho 21 or by the Payette River Scenic Byway on Idaho 55. Either route connects with this 33-mile trip through some of the most powerful canyon scenery offered in the state. A one-day trip from Boise affords visitors a glimpse of the pioneering spirit of early Idaho and the awesome beauty of Idaho's wildlife and whitewater.

The route travels along the Banks-Lowman road. It can be accessed either at Banks along Idaho 55 or at Lowman along Idaho 21. Either point of access brings the traveler back to a route leading to Boise. The byway is a two-lane roadway with no passing lands, but there are several turnouts for scenic viewing. The paved roadway is maintained year-round but often has a snow floor during winter months. There is exceptional elk viewing in winter and spring. Travelers should allow one hour for the byway, and three hours for the loop from Boise and back.

Reprinted from Idaho Department of Transportation brochure

Payette River National Scenic Byway

From the junction of Idaho 44 and Idaho 55 west of Idaho's capital city of Boise, this byway heads north on Idaho 55 to Horseshoe Bend where it meets the Payette River. From there, it passes through the Boise and Payette National Forests and the popular resort towns of Cascade and McCall before reaching the northern end of the byway at New Meadows.

For motorists, it can be a distracting drive as the river crashes and tumbles its way over the rocks through this narrow river valley. Depending on where you are on the river, it can be a mild ripple or a wild torrent. There are occasional pull-offs where you can view the wilder parts and treat your senses to the sight, sound, smell, and rhythm of Idaho's famous whitewater.

Along this byway are some great locations for camping, hiking, boating, fishing, and guided float trips. Outfitters offer river excursions that range from half-day to three-day outings in rafts or kayaks.

The mountain resort town of McCall sits next to Payette Lake and is a great year-round getaway. It is particularly famous for the annual Winter Carnival, when the streets are lined with ice sculptures.

The byway follows a narrow, winding, two-lane road with occasional passing lanes and slow vehicle turnouts. The byway can be viewed year-round, and travelers should allow at least 2 hours and 15 minutes for this 111.7-mile trip.

Reprinted from Idaho Department of Transportation brochure

Hells Canyon Scenic Byway

The Hells Canyon Scenic Byway winds its way along the east side of this massive rift that separates Idaho from neighboring Oregon. While the view from the road is breathtaking, a guided float trip or jet boat tour of the Hells Canyon National Recreation Area is a must. Towering cliffs of black and green basalt hang so high above the Snake River and its sandy beaches that boaters strain their necks to see these places. Outfitters offer one to six day trips.

During the summer months, visit the Hells Canyon Creek Visitors Center just below Hells

Canyon Dam, the entrance to the wild and scenic part of the Snake River. The surrounding area was the home of Chief Joseph's band of Nez Perce Indians. Other tribes, including the Shoshone, bannock, North Paiute and Cayuse Indians, were frequent visitors to the area. These tribes were drawn to the region by relatively mild winters, lush foliage, and plentiful wildlife.

Today, walls of the canyon are like a museum, where pictographs and petroglyphs display evidence of the Indians' early settlements.

Follow Hells Canyon Road from Oxbow Bridge near Copperfield, Oregon, north along the Idaho side of the Snake River to Hells Canyon Dam. Hells Canyon road is a narrow, 22-mile winding road with several steep grades. It is maintained all year, and travelers should allow 3 hours roundtrip from Cambridge.

Reprinted from Idaho Department of Transportation brochure

Emigrant Foothills Backcountry Road

As it turns into Foothills Road, Mayfield Road, and Blacks Creek Road, the Emigrant Road takes drivers into the backcountry surrounding the Mountain Home and Boise landscape. The twenty-five mile route follows the historic Oregon Trail and features numerous pullouts along the way. Several short nature hikes appropriate for individuals of all ages are available from these pullouts. The road is open year-round, but drivers should contact the Bureau of Land Management for the latest road conditions prior to departure.

Salmon River Stock Driveway

As State Highway 71 winds northwest beside Pine Creek through the Pine Creek Valley, drivers follow the historical Salmon River Stock Driveway. During Idaho's prosperous era of sheep ranching, more than 80,000 sheep were moved from their wintering range in Idaho's southern canyons to their Long Valley summer habitat. Thousands of sheep ranchers passed by State Highway 71 through Cambridge on their trek, with most activity occurring between 1918 and 1958.

HIKES

For information on additional area trails, please contact the Forest Service Ranger districts listed at the back of this section.

Anderson Ranch Reservoir Recreation Area

Camp Creek Trail

Distance: 11.4 miles roundtrip
Climb: steep
Difficulty: moderate
Usage: moderate
Location: From the Anderson Ranch Reservoir Recreation Area, locate the Camp Creek trailhead off Forest Road (FR) 128 (Lester Creek Road).

Open to ATV's and motorcycles, this trail climbs to a steep ridge where hikers will access views of the South Fork of the Boise River, Pine, and Featherville. Best months for hiking are June through August.

Boise Area

Hulls Gulch National Recreation Trail

Distance: 7 miles roundtrip
Climb: gentle
Difficulty: easy
Usage: heavy

Location: Outside Boise's northern city limits, drive along North 8th Street to the pavement's end. Continue 6.5 miles, passing the lower trailhead, to a parking area the upper trailhead.

A Bureau of Land Management interpretive hike, this trail takes visitors just outside of Boise for a detailed description of the area's natural features, including wildlife, ecology, and soil. Most hikers report glimpses of lizards, porcupines, rabbits, and the occasional coyote and badger. Best months for hiking are May through September.

Mores Mountain Trail

Distance: 4 miles roundtrip
Climb: gentle
Difficulty: easy
Usage: heavy
Location: Locate the Bogus Basin Road and drive 20 miles from Boise to the trailhead at Shafer Butte picnic area.

This easy nature trail offers families the opportunity to view the Treasure Valley and the Sawtooth Range at a distance. Best months for hiking are June through September.

Crouch Area

Stolle Meadows and Warm Lake

Distance: variable
Climb: moderate
Difficulty: moderate
Usage: moderate
Location: From Crouch, head north on Forest Road (FR) 698 (Middle Fork Road) to Trail Creek Junction. At the junction, proceed left on FR 698 7 miles to the Boiling Springs Campground Trailhead.

Passing through meadows and forest, this trail leads to the serene Stolle Meadows and Warm Lake. Along the way, many hikers opt to take a side trip leading to Moondipper and Pine Burl Hot Springs on Middle Fork Trail 033, while others choose to veer onto Trail 102 leading past Bull Creek to Bull Creek Hot Springs. Best months for visiting are July through September.

Frank Church-River of No Return Wilderness Area

Big Baldy-Indian Creek Loop

Distance: 52 mile loop
Climb: steep
Difficulty: very difficult
Usage: very light
Location: Drive 1 mile north of Cascade on State Highway 55, bearing east (right) onto Warm Lake Road. Proceed 37 miles, pass Landmark Ranger Station, and locate a four-way junction. Turn right onto Forest Road (FR) 447 (Burntlog Road) and drive 14.3 miles to the Buck Creek Trailhead, staying to the left at all times.

For experienced, conditioned backpackers, this trek leads to some of the most beautiful views of Idaho's mountains, rivers, canyons, old-growth forests, and wilderness areas. Beginning on Trail 090 (Buck Creek Trail) climb 0.7 miles and turn left onto Trail 088 (Summit Trail). After passing Chilcoot Pass, locate a jeep road at the 3.5-mile mark and turn right. At the 4.2-mile mark, hike left along the signed "hiking trail" and reach the junction for Trail 227 (Baldy Ridge Trail). Bearing right onto Trail 227, wind through pine trees, passing Buck Lake and reaching a side trail leading to the Big Baldy Mountain lookout at the 16 mile mark. Continue on the main trail to a left fork with Trail 226. Proceed on Trail 226 until reaching the Grays Peak Trail at the 22.5-mile

mark. Bear left onto Grays Peak Trail and cross Indian Creek. After this crossing, proceed left onto Trail 225 (Indian Creek Trail). This trail leads to Kwiskwis Creek, Kwiskwis Hot Springs, through forested gorges, and eventually to Kiwah Meadows. At the 39-mile mark, hikers will reach a junction with Trail 224 (Big Chief Trail). However, hikers should stay to the left on Trail 225 (Indian Creek Trail) and wind along the faint trail through some deadfall. At the 46.5-mile mark, hikers will reach Pistol Spring and should merge back onto Trail 088 (Summit Trail). Continue to the Trail 227 (Baldy Ridge Trail) junction, where hikers should take Trail 227 and retrace their steps the last 5 miles to the trailhead. Best months for hiking are July through September.

Rainbow Lake and Shell Rock Lake

Distance: 5 miles roundtrip to Rainbow Lake; 9 miles roundtrip to both Rainbow Lake and Shell Rock Lake
Climb: moderate
Difficulty: moderate
Usage: light
Location: Drive 1 mile north of Cascade on State Highway 55, bearing east (right) onto Warm Lake Road. Proceed 35.5 miles and turn left onto Forest Road (FR) 413, continuing another 15 miles. Directly south of Halfway Ranger Station, bear left onto FR 410 and follow this road 11 miles to the trailhead. This route does require a four-wheel drive vehicle.

Located in the Salmon River Mountains, this trail is an excellent choice for beginning backpackers interested in wildlife viewing opportunities and scenic subalpine lakes surrounded by wildflowers and old-growth fir, spruce, and pine. Following Trail 094, hike 0.4 mile through logged forest and locate the marked Rainbow Lake Trail leading uphill. Continue straight ahead another 2.1 miles to arrive at Rainbow Lake. To reach Shell Rock Lake, backtrack 0.6 miles from Rainbow Lake to an unmarked trail leading to the west. Proceeding on this trail, ascend towards the bench on Shell Rock Peak's north side. On top of the bench, continue on this faint trail through trees and huckleberry bushes and descend steeply south into Shell Rock Lake, located 4.5 miles from the trailhead. Shell Rock Lake is situated in a granite cirque, and despite its beauty, is rarely visited. Best months for visiting are late June to late September.

Snowshoe Summit to Pistol Lake

Distance: 11 miles roundtrip
Climb: moderate
Difficulty: moderate
Usage: moderate
Location: South of Landmark, turn onto Forest Road (FR) 447. This road is also known as Mud Lake Road and Artillery Dome Road. After crossing Johnson Creek, stay to the right at the road junction. Keeping to the left at Sand Creek Road, proceed past Mud Lake and turn right onto FR 447E (Artillery Dome Road). Continue 3 miles along this steep road to Summit Trail 008 located at Summit Trail Trailhead.

Following the ridgeline above Pistol Creek, this trail takes hikers across scenic mountain saddles and subalpine meadows before dropping into a cirque containing Pistol Lake, marshes, and waterfalls. Follow Summit Trail 008 through the dense forest and climb up to the saddle of Little Baldy. Continue on this trail, and at the 4.8-mile mark, locate a trail to the right leading over the top of another ridge. This trail, which is faint at times, descends steeply into Pistol Lake. Best months for hiking are mid-July to mid-August.

Kuna Area

Swan Falls Dam Trail
Distance: 5 miles roundtrip
Climb: moderate
Difficulty: moderate
Usage: moderate
Location: Locate the Birds of Prey Area south of Kuna. From here, drive 1 mile upriver from the Swan Falls Dam and park near an old corral.

Winding upstream, this trail offers river views and climbs to a Nature Conservancy wetland. Best months for hiking are May through September.

Optional Hikes: After parking below the Swan Falls Dam, locate several trails along the north shore leading to Swan Falls.

Wees Bar Trail
Distance: 6 miles roundtrip
Climb: moderate
Difficulty: moderate
Usage: moderate
Location: Locate the Birds of Prey Area south of Kuna and drive to the Swan Falls Dam. Cross the dam's spillway to locate the trailhead.

Visitors will glimpse into ancient history while hiking downstream to Wees Bar. Petroglyphs characterize the area, and visitors are reminded not to touch the drawings so they can be preserved for future generations. Best months for hiking are May through September.

Lick Creek Mountains

Lava Lakes
Distance: 8.5 miles roundtrip
Climb: moderate
Difficulty: moderate
Usage: light
Location: Drive 6 miles west of McCall on State Highway 55, bearing right onto Forest Road (FR) 257. Continue 3 miles, then bear left and continue north on FR 257 leading to Brundage Mountain Ski Resort. After traveling 3 more miles, stay to the left at the Y-junction and continue on FR 257. Pass Hard Creek Guard Station and Hazard Lake Campground, reaching the Clayburn Trailhead after traveling a total of 26 miles from McCall.

Hike into solitude along this trail that climbs deep into the mountains and offers an occasional glimpse of wildlife. Beginning at the Clayburn Trailhead, ignore Trail 347 and hike 100 yards down to the Trail 505 junction heading east. While Trail 505 is faint in places, hikers can head east to Clayburn Creek and locate the trail again at the creek crossing. From the creek, climb up to the basaltic and granite Lava Ridge and view Seven Devils' peaks distantly rising above the Rapid River, Little Salmon River, and Salmon River, as well as Patrick Butte and portions of the Gospel Hump area. At Lava Ridge, proceed left on Trail 149 and descend 4.2 miles to Lava Lakes. Hikers should note that topographic/trail maps of the area are outdated. Best months for hiking are mid-July through mid-September.

Loon Lake Loop
Distance: 10 mile loop
Climb: gentle
Difficulty: moderate
Usage: moderate
Location: Drive north from McCall on Forest Road (FR) 22 (Warren Wagon Road) toward Burgdorf. At the Burgdorf junction, keep right and proceed 7 miles before merging onto Chinook Campground Road. Continue 1.5 miles to the Chinook Campground Trailhead and locate Trail 080.

Winding along the Secesh River through trees and huckleberry patches, this trail ultimately brings hikers to the famous Loon Lake set amidst rugged mountain peaks. Loon Lake is best known for saving the lives of a bomber crew in February 1943. Flying from Nevada to Idaho's Mountain Home Air Force base in a snowstorm, the pilot became disoriented and soon realized the plane was running out of gas. As the pilot pointed the nose downwards, Idaho's Salmon River Mountains appeared in front of him and it seemed that the flight was doomed. At the last possible moment, though, a large field surrounded by mountain peaks and trees emerged, and the crew landed with no serious injuries. This field was actually the frozen Loon Lake, and the aviators found their own trail back to civilization. Today, hikers will walk in several of the same areas as these brave men. To begin the hike, follow Trail 080 3.5 miles to a junction near the Secesh River bridge crossing. After crossing the bridge and merging onto Trail 084, continue to the right and avoid an abandoned trail leaving to the left. Upon reaching a junction for Trails 084 and 080, proceed left 0.25 miles to another junction. Going left on Trail 081 takes hikers to Loon Lake's outlet while proceeding right on Trail 084 takes hikers around the lakes north side. To make the return loop and head up Loon Creek Canyon, hikers should proceed 0.3 miles to the head of Loon Lake and then turn right onto Trail 081. Continuing through both burned and unburned forest areas, the trail descends to the Victor Creek bridge crossing. Just past the bridge is a three-way trail junction. Proceed 3 miles along the right trail back to Chinook Campground. Best months for hiking are late June through September, but September offers cooler temperatures, fewer insects, and more colorful foliage.

Boulder-Louie Lakes Loop
Distance: 6 mile loop
Climb: moderate
Difficulty: moderate
Usage: heavy
Location: Follow State Highway 55 0.5 miles south of McCall and bear east (left) onto ELO Road. Drive 2.1 miles, then turn east on the road leading to Boulder Lake. Watching for heavy traffic and blind curves, proceed past the Louie Lake Trailhead to reach the Boulder Meadows Reservoir Trailhead. This trailhead is 7.8 miles from the turnoff from State Highway 55.

Surrounded by wildlife, forests, and wildflower-covered meadows, this trail climbs up numerous switchbacks, leading hikers to popular fishing lakes as well as offering views of Jughandle Mountain. From the trailhead, hike 2 miles along Trail 105 to the natural Boulder Lake. Travel along the lake's south shore for approximately 0.2 miles and reach a stone-marked fork in the road. Take the right fork and climb along a ridge just east of the Twin Peaks, reaching the glacial Louie Lake in 2.8 miles. From here, proceed 0.8 mile on a jeep road, then bear right onto the main trail. Continue 0.4 miles back to the trailhead. Best months for hiking are July through late September.

Optional Hikes: Continue 0.3 miles beyond Boulder Lake to reach the trail junction of Paddy Flat and Kennally Creek (0.1 mile past the stone-marked trail leading to Louie Lake). To discover several alpine lakes set amidst rugged granite peaks, continue on the 20-mile long Kennally Creek Trail. This trail is moderately difficult, and best months for hiking are July through early September.

Box Lake
Distance: 8 miles roundtrip
Climb: moderate
Difficulty: moderate

Usage: moderate
Location: In McCall, take Park Street to Davis Street to Forest Road (FR) 48 (Lick Creek Road). Travel 13 miles through the scenic, but busy, Lake Fork Canyon to reach Trail 110 at the Black Lee Trailhead.

This trail takes hikers through rugged, glacier carved granite peaks before ending at one of Lick Creek Mountains' largest lakes. From the trailhead, proceed northwest on Trail 110 next to Black Lee Creek under fir and spruce tree branches. At 1.6 miles, ford Black Lee Creek, then continue 1.1 miles to an overlook area of Box Lake. Hike another 0.5 miles and Box Lake's shores will appear. To reach the lake's outlet area and Box Lake Creek's beginning, continue 0.8 miles where visitors will find an old dam and a rocky beach area. Best months for hiking are August through mid-September. The trail can be reached as early as late June, but hikers will wade through snow and fording Black Lake Creek will be extremely difficult.

Snowslide Lake
Distance: 4 miles roundtrip
Climb: steep
Difficulty: difficult
Usage: moderate
Location: In McCall, take Park Street to Davis Street to Forest Road (FR) 48 (Lick Creek Road). On Lick Creek Road, locate the trailhead for Snowslide Lake Trail (which requires fording Lake Fork Creek).

This rocky trail winds up the rugged mountains to the remote Snowslide Lake. Best months for hiking are July through mid-September as Lake Fork Creek's water levels make fording the creek dangerous during late spring and early summer months.

Duck Lake and Surrounding Area
Distance: 2 miles roundtrip
Climb: gentle
Difficulty: easy
Usage: moderate
Location: From McCall, drive along Forest Road (FR) 48 past Little Payette Lake and Lick Creek Summit to the trailhead located on the road's left side.

This trail provides families with perfect wildlife viewing opportunities of deer, elk, and ducks. Leading to Duck Lake, the trail crosses vast meadows, and Duck Lake offers mediocre fishing potential. Best months for hiking are June through August.

Optional Hikes: Directly below Duck Lake, locate Trail 083 leading to Hum Lake. This trail is much more difficult than the path to Duck Lake as the trail quickly climbs 1,000 feet to a mountain ridge, then steeply descends 1,000 feet to Hum Lake. Along the path, hikers have outstanding vistas of the surrounding mountains and of both Duck Lake and Hum Lake.

Lowman Area

Crooked River Trail
Distance: 19 miles roundtrip
Climb: moderate
Difficulty: moderate
Usage: moderate
Location: Take State Highway 21 between Lowman and Idaho City and locate Forest Road (FR) 384 (Crooked River Road). Take FR 384 to the Crooked River trailhead.

Hikers will wind up and down a narrow canyon with outstanding views of Crooked River running near the trail. Best months for hiking are June through August.

Clear Creek Trail
Distance: 4 miles roundtrip
Climb: gradual
Difficulty: easy
Usage: moderate
Location: From Lowman, travel northeast and locate the Clear Creek trailhead off Forest Roads (FR) 582 and 515.

This trail is suitable for families with small children as it winds next to small mountain streams through pine trees and wildflower covered meadows. Best months for hiking are June through August.

McCall/New Meadows Area
Twenty Mile Trail
Distance: 40 miles roundtrip
Climb: moderate
Difficulty: moderate
Usage: moderate
Location: From McCall, drive north on Forest Road (FR) 22 (Warren Wagon Road) to locate the Twenty Mile Trailhead.

While motorized vehicles are not allowed on this trail, it is not uncommon to see horses along the trek. For those simply interested in wildlife viewing, the first 3 miles provides easy access to wildlife. Continuing along the trail requires more perseverance as the trail gradually becomes steeper to its end at area alpine lakes. Best months for hiking are July through mid-September.

Victor Creek Trail
Distance: 25 miles roundtrip
Climb: moderate
Difficulty: moderate
Location: From McCall, drive north on Forest Road (FR) 22 (Warren Wagon Road) to locate the Victor Creek Trailhead.

This trail winds through an area burned in Idaho's 1994 Blackwell fire, but the hike still offers outstanding scenery. Visitors may opt to take the whole trek, or simply hike a little over 1 mile to reach a wildflower-covered meadow. From this meadow, hikers will have distant views of the mountain range surrounding the Payette River. Best months for hiking are July through mid-September.

Josephine Lake
Distance: 1 mile roundtrip
Climb: steep
Difficulty: difficult
Usage: heavy
Location: From McCall, drive north on Forest Road (FR) 22 (Warren Wagon Road) toward Burgdorf Hot Springs. Merge onto FR 316 (Josephine Creek Road) to locate the lake's trailhead.

A must see for avid fly-fisherman, the 13-acre Josephine Lake is set in a granite cirque. While the short trail does lead to the famed lake, its steepness requires hikers to have a moderate physical fitness level. Best months for visiting are mid-June through September.

Powerline Trail
Distance: 2 miles roundtrip
Climb: gentle
Difficulty: easy
Usage: heavy
Location: From State Highway 55, exit onto Forest Road (FR) 257 (Brundage Mountain Road) and locate the trailhead for Powerline Trail.

Families with young children will enjoy this easy hike ending at the scenic Goose Creek Falls. The

trail begins with a slight descent, and then climbs gently uphill to the cascade. Best months for hiking are mid-June through September.

Twin Lakes
Distance: 2 miles roundtrip
Climb: moderate
Difficulty: moderate
Usage: heavy
Location: From State Highway 55, exit onto Forest Road (FR) 257 (Brundage Mountain Road) and locate the Twin Lakes Trailhead.

Twin Lakes is a popular fishing destination for Idaho residents and hikers should expect to have company on the trail. The trail is appropriate for families with young children. Best months for hiking are mid-June through September.

Big Hazard Lake
Distance: 1 mile roundtrip
Climb: gentle
Difficulty: easy
Usage: heavy
Location: From State Highway 55, exit onto Forest Road (FR) 257 (Brundage Mountain Road) and locate the trailhead leading to Big Hazard Lake.

Appropriate for most age and fitness levels, this trail wanders through the Corral fire region. Best months for hiking are mid-June through September.

Upper Hazard Lake
Distance: 4 miles roundtrip
Climb: gentle
Difficulty: moderate
Usage: heavy
Location: From State Highway 55, exit onto Forest Road (FR) 257 (Brundage Mountain Road) and locate the trailhead leading to Upper Hazard Lake at Hazard Lake Campground.

Winding through wildflowers and green meadows, this trail reaches its destination at Upper Hazard Lake. Best months for hiking are July through September.

Last Chance Springs
Distance: 1 mile roundtrip
Climb: gentle
Difficulty: easy
Usage: heavy
Location: Exit off State Highway 55 2 miles after passing the Brundage Mountain Road exit and park near Goose Creek.

A rock pool filled with 102-degree mineral water is this hike's main attraction and destination. The trail, which winds next to scenic Goose Creek, is appropriate for a leisurely family walk. Best months for hiking are mid-June through September.

Mesa/Council Area
Laurel Hot Springs
Distance: 4 miles roundtrip
Climb: gentle
Difficulty: easy
Usage: light
Location: Driving north on U.S. Highway 95, locate the small town of Mesa. Directly north of Mesa, exit U.S. Highway 95 and merge onto Forest Road (FR) 186 (Middle Fork Road). Proceed 9 miles on FR 186 until locating the Trail 203 trail marker on the road's left side.

Situated in Indian Valley and the West Mountains, Laurel Hot Springs is a remote destination where

most visitors encounter more cows than other hikers. Hiking along a wooded slope, visitors will find shallow, hot pools waiting for them at the end of the trek. Best months for visiting are June through September.

Sheep Rock Nature Trail
Distance: 1 mile roundtrip
Climb: gentle
Difficulty: easy
Usage: moderate
Location: From Council, locate Hornet Creek Road and proceed northwest. Hornet Creek Road eventually turns into Forest Road (FR) 002. Continue on FR 002 until reaching a junction with FR 105. Bear north on FR 105 and continue to the junction with FR 108. Turn onto FR 108 and drive 9 miles to Sheep Rock.

Owyhee-Bruneau Canyonlands Proposed National Monument Area
Big Jacks Creek
Distance: 3 miles roundtrip
Climb: gentle
Difficulty: easy
Usage: very light
Location: Exit State Highway 78 2 miles west of Bruneau and merge south onto State Highway 51. Proceed 25 miles to the junction for Wickahoney Road and bear west (right). Continue 5 miles to a junction with a bumpy dirt road and turn north (right). Drive 3 miles along this road to a Y intersection, then proceed left and follow the road to its end at the trailhead.

Hikers will travel into isolation on this trail that winds through a remote rhyolite canyon. Surrounded by rugged canyon walls, needles, and pinnacles, hikers are likely to encounter numerous bighorn sheep, antelope, bats, and raptors. From the trailhead, descend 1.5 miles to the scenic Big Jacks Creek. Here, hikers can opt to return to the trailhead, or proceed upstream or downstream. Traveling downstream brings hikers to the canyon's end, while traveling upstream carries visitors deeper into Big Jacks Canyon. For those continuing onward in search of exits from Big Jacks Creek into other area canyons, caution and expert map-reading skills are urged. No water is available, and falls in these canyons often prove fatal. Best months for hiking are May, June, and October.

Bald Mountain Ridge and Surrounding Area
Distance: 1.5 miles roundtrip to Bald Mountain Ridge Saddle; 3.5 miles roundtrip to Bald Mountain Summit; 5.5 miles roundtrip to West Fork Shoofly Canyon overlook
Climb: moderate
Difficulty: moderate
Usage: very light
Location: Locate State Highway 78 south of Grandview. Proceed east for 1.5 miles before bearing south onto the well-marked Owyhee Uplands National Backcountry Byway (Mud Flat Road). Pass the Oreana intersection and Poison Creek picnic area, locating the trailhead parking area across from Fall Creek at the 22.2-mile mark.

This trail offers hikers a remote look at spectacular canyon scenery as well as panoramic overviews of distant mountains and sagebrush covered deserts. Begin by hiking south and climbing a northern slope leading to a ridge between Poison and Shoofly Creeks. From the ridge, continue uphill toward the Bald Mountain ridgeline. Two saddles will appear, but follow the faint trail leading to the eastern saddle. This trail leads to Bald Mountain

Ridge and breathtaking views of Rough Mountain, Poison and Birch Creeks, and the Snake River Plain. Best months for hiking are April through late May and October.

Optional Hikes: From the ridge, continue hiking southwest 1.5 miles to the summit of Bald Mountain. While hiking to the summit, the Jarbidge, Independence, and Santa Rosa Mountains rise on the horizon.

An additional canyon hike begins at the Bald Mountain saddle. Hike southeast to the West Fork of Shoofly Creek. Visitors will discover red cliffs as well as an overlook into Shoofly Canyon.

Bruneau Dunes State Park
Distance: 5 mile loop; 2 mile loop; 1 mile loop
Climb: moderate
Difficulty: moderate for long loop; easy for shorter loops
Usage: heavy
Location: From Mountain Home, drive 15.6 miles south on State Highway 51 before merging east onto State Highway 78. On Highway 78, proceed 1.8 miles to the marked road leading to Bruneau Dunes State Park. The 5 mile loop trailhead is found at the Visitor Center's northwest corner. The trailhead for the 2 mile loop is at the Big Dune Picnic Area, and the observatory at Observatory Picnic Area provides access to the 1 mile loop.

Contained within a 4,640-acre state park, these trails wind through hot, desert hiking conditions, but lead visitors to the tallest sand dunes in North America. To take a 5 mile trek, head south from the visitor center, following the white and red trailposts to a marshy area. After circling around the marsh and reaching Big Dune (the area's tallest dune), hike between the dunes and two lakes to reach the lakes' isthmus. From here, drop down off the dunes and head to the Observatory Picnic Area. For the 2-mile loop, follow the obvious trail from Big Dune Picnic Area. After climbing Big Dune, hike to the lakes' isthmus and drop back down to the picnic area. The 1-mile loop, appropriate for small children and families, heads northeast from the observatory. After walking across a grassy area, locate a well-marked trail leading around the small lake and back to the Observatory Picnic Area. Best months for hiking are March through May and September through November. Visitors should be prepared to pay a $2.00 entrance fee and should not bring dogs along the hikes as the sand can burn animals' feet. Water, sunscreen, and insect repellant should be carried at all times, and caution should be used while swimming in the lakes as flatworm larva is present.

Smith's Ferry Area
Joe's Creek to West Peak
Distance: 10 miles roundtrip
Climb: moderate
Difficulty: moderate
Usage: moderate
Location: From Smith's Ferry, travel along U.S. Highway 55, exiting onto FR 644. Following the road signs, proceed along FR 644, 626, and 614 leading to Sagehan Creek and Antelope Campgrounds. Between these two campgrounds, locate the trailhead for Joe's Creek Road (which becomes Joe's Creek Trail #137).

Hikers will wind north along the forested Joe's Creek before reaching the summit of West Peak's 8,086-foot elevation. Panoramic views of the surrounding area are offered atop the peak, and the area is prized for its profuse morel mushrooms. Best months for hiking are June through September.

Trinity Mountains Area
Rainbow Lakes
Distance: 9 miles roundtrip
Climb: moderate
Difficulty: moderate
Usage: moderate
Location: At Mountain Home, exit off Interstate 84 and merge northeast onto U.S. Highway 20. Drive 20 miles, then turn onto the Anderson Ranch Reservoir Dam Road. Proceed across the dam to a fork in the road. Bear right at this fork onto Forest Road (FR) 113 and proceed 8.5 miles to Fall Creek. At Fall Creek, bear left onto the gravel FR 123 and continue 5 miles to the junction with FR 129. Turning onto FR 129, proceed 2 miles before reaching another junction. At this junction, bear right and continue on this steep, narrow road to Rainbow Lakes Trail located at the Big Trinity Lake Campground and Trailhead.

With nearly continuous views of the Trinity Mountain rising in the distance, this trail leads hikers through exceptional wildflower covered meadows past nine alpine lakes filled with rainbow and brook trout. Climbing steeply during the first mile, the trail levels out and hikers soon reach Rainbow Basin Divide and a side trail leading to Green Island Lake. The side trails to all of the area's lakes are well marked with approximate distances. Hikers may opt to take all or none of these side trails; however, each lake is scenic and fishing opportunities are outstanding in each. Continuing on the main trail, reach Little Rainbow Lake after another 2.5 miles. After passing this lake, proceed 0.7 miles to the Rainbow Lakes Basin and Parks Creek Divide. Here, follow the steep, obvious trail leading to the right to reach the area's most remote lake, Hideaway Lake, in 0.2 miles. Best months for hiking are late July through August.

Weiser Area
Weiser River Trail
Distance: 84 miles one-way
Climb: moderate
Difficulty: moderate
Usage: moderate
Location: From U.S. Highway 95, exit into Weiser and locate the trailhead for the Weiser River Trail.

Hikers will step into history while following one of Idaho's first rail lines that the Pacific and Idaho Northern Railway utilized for years. Ending at New Meadows, the route weaves in and out of civilization amid alpine meadows and high desert canyons. The trail is open to hikers, mountain bikers, and equestrians. Best months for hiking are May through September.

After viewing the surrounding Hells Canyon and Wallowa Mountains, locate the interpretive nature trail. The hike passes twenty-one descriptive points and leads to Sheep Rock Overlook. Best months for hiking are June through September.

INFORMATION PLEASE

All Idaho area codes are 208

Road Information

ID Road & Weather Conditions
888-432-7623 or local 884-7000
Idaho State Police   736-3090

Tourism Information

Idaho Travel Council 800-VISIT-ID outside Idaho
334-2470 in Idaho
www.visitid.org
Southwest ID Travel Association   800-635-5240
www.swita.info

Airports

Boise	383-3110
Mountain Home	587-3585
Nampa	442-2786

Government Offices

Idaho Bureau of Reclamation	334-1466
	www.usbr.gov
Idaho Department of Commerce	
	(800) 847-4843 or 334-2470
www.visitid.org or http://cl.idaho.gov/	
Idaho Department of Fish and Game	
	(800) ASK-FISH or 334-3700
http://fishandgame.idaho.gov	
Idaho Department of Parks and Recreation	
	334-4199
www.idahoparks.org	
State BLM Office	373-3889 or 373-4000
www.id.blm.gov	
Boise National Forest	373-4039
Bureau of Land Management Boise -	
Four Rivers Office	384-3300
Payette National Forest	634-0700

Hospitals

Intermountain Hospital • Boise	377-8400
Saint Alphonsus Regional Medical Center	
Boise	357-2135
West Valley Medical Center	
Caldwell	459-4641
Cascade Medical Center • Cascade	382-4242
Walter Knox Memorial • Emmett	365-3561
St Lukes Meridian Medical Center	
Meridian	706-5000
West Valley Medical Center	
Middleton	459-4641
Elmore Medical Center	
Mountain Home	587-8401
Mercy Medical Center • Nampa	463-5000
Weiser Memorial Hospital • Weiser	549-0370

Golf Courses

Boise Ranch Golf • Boise	362-6501
Golf and Recreation Club • Boise	344-2008
Indian Lakes Public Golf Course	
Boise	362-5771
Pierce Park Green • Boise	853-3302
Quail Hollow • Boise	344-7807
Shadow Valley• Boise	939-6699
Warm Springs Golf Club • Boise	342-6397
Falcon Crest Golf Club • Boise	362-8897
Warm Springs Golf Course • Boise	726-3715
Caldwell City - Golf Courses	
Caldwell	455-3090
Purple Sage Municipal Golf	
Caldwell	459-2223
Cascade Golf Course • Cascade	382-4835
Council Mountain • Council	253-6908
Banbury Golf Club • Eagle	939-3600
Eagle Hills Golf Course • Eagle	939-1301
Gem County Golf Association	
Emmett	365-2675
Carmela Vineyards • Glenns Ferry	366-2313
Falcon Crest • Kuna	362-8897
Waterhole Lodge • Lake Fork	634-7758
Jug Mountain Ranch - Golf Course	
McCall	634-5072
McCall Golf Course • McCall	634-7160
Foxtail Golf Course • Meridian	887-4653
Desert Canyon Municipal Golf Course	
Mountain Home	587-3293
Desert Wind Golf Range	
Mountain Home	587-6099
Centennial Golf Course • Nampa	467-3011
Ridgecrest • Nampa	468-9073

Meadowcreek Forty-Fifth Parallel

New Meadows	347-2555
Rolling Hills Golf • Payette	549-0456
Scotch Pines • Payette	642-4866
Rolling Hills Golf Course • Weiser	549-0456
River Bend Golf Course • Wilder	482-7169

Bed & Breakfasts

Robie Creek B&B • Boise	345-5096
Quail Hollow • Council	253-0013
Revel Inn • Garden Valley	888-6510
Walk on the Wild Side B&B Garden Valley	462-8047
Great Basin B&B • Glenns Ferry	366-7124
Guest House Of Idaho City Idaho City	392-2273
Northwest Passage B&B • McCall	634-5349
Red Fox Ridge Retreat • McCall	634-3055
Pink Tudor B&B • Nampa	465-3615
Hartland Inn And Motel New Meadows	347-2114
Last Resort New Meadows	628-3029

Guest Ranches & Resorts

Brundage Mountain Resort • McCall	634-4151
McCall RV Resort & Northfork Lodge McCall	634-1418
Beaver Lodge • Atlanta	864-2132
Allison Ranch • Boise	376-5270
Gillihan's Lodge • Boise	327-0907
Shepp Ranch • Boise	343-7729
Mackay Ranch • Boise	800 854-9904
4D Longhorn Guest Ranch Cascade	466-9527
Sawtooth Lodge • Lowman	259-3331
Sourdough Lodge • Lowman	259-3326
Brundage Inn • McCall	634-8573
Brundage Inn, Bungalows, Cabins McCall	634-2344
Hotel McCall & Jug Mountain Ranch and Golf Course • McCall	634-8105
Tamarack Resort • McCall	325-1000
Whitetail Club: A Club for All Seasons McCall	630-0225
Deer Creek Lodge • Mountain Home	653-2454
Meadow Creek Golf Resort New Meadows	347-2584
Pinehurst Resort • New Meadows	628-3323
Fall Creek Resort • Pine	653-2242
Fall Creek Resort & Marina Pine (Fall Creek)	653-2242
Cougar Mountain Lodge Smiths Ferry	382-4464
Wapiti Meadow Ranch • Warm Lake	633-3217
Warm Lake Lodge and Resort Warm Lake	632-3553
Zena Creek Ranch • Yellow Pine	382-4336

Vacation Homes & Cabins

John L Scott Real Estate Garden Valley	462-8070
Jan Kangas • McCall	634-7766
Golden Rule KOA Mobile Home Park Mountain Home	587-5111

Forest Service Cabins

Boise National Forest
Beaver Creek
21 mi. NE of Idaho City 392-6681
Cap: 6 Nightly Fee: $45 Available: Year Round
Living room, 2 bedrooms, kitchen, propane cook stove and refrigerator, indoor privy and sink (available only in summer), and wood heat stove. No elec.

Atlanta Cabin
67 mi. E of Idaho City 392-6681
Cap: 6 Nightly Fee: $45 Available: 5/31-9/30
Has electricity, living room, propane cook stove and wood heat stove, indoor privy and shower, and drinking water.

Barber Flat Cabin
26 mi. E of Idaho City 392-6681
Cap: 6 Nightly Fee: $40 Available: 5/31-9/30
Living room, 1 bedroom, propane cook stove and refrigerator, indoor privy and bathtub, wood heat stove. No elec.

Deer Park
39 mi. E of Idaho City 392-6681
Cap: 4 Nightly Fee: $35 Available: 5/31-9/30
Living room, propane cook stove, wood heat stove, outdoor privy. No elec. Outside water pump.

Dutch Creek
46 mi. E of Idaho City 392-6681
Cap: 6 Nightly Fee: $40 Available: 5/31-9/30
Propane stove and refrigerator, indoor privy, shower, drinking water. No elec.

Graham
40 mi. E of Idaho City 392-6681
Cap: 6 Nightly Fee: $35 Available: 7/17-9/30
Wood cooking/heating stove, sink for washing. No electricity, propane or drinking water. Stock allowed.

Cottonwood Bunkhouse
25 mi. E of Boise, 1 mi. from Arrowrock Reservoir 587-7961
Cap: 8 Nightly Fee: $35 Available: 5/15-10/15
Located at Cottonwood Guard Station. Propane heat, refrigerator, cooking stove, indoor water, bathroom fac. No bathtub or shower. Outdoor fire ring/grill, picnic table. Firewood provided w/splitting maul and axe. No livestock fac. Generator provided, lighting limited to few hours daily, but not guaranteed. Alternative lighting required. Candles not permitted at bunkhouse. Four bunk bed set w/mattress.

Big Trinity
80 mi. NE of Mountain Home 587-7961
Cap: 6 Nightly Fee: $30 Available: 7/15-9/30
Wood heat, cooking stove, hand pump drinking water, outdoor privy. Fire ring/outdoor grill, picnic table. No fac. For livesock or tents. Firewood provided with splitting maul and axe. Near 3 mountain lakes and campgrounds. Motorized and hiking trails within ° mi. No elec. Nearest phone 19 mi. in Featherville.

Boiling Springs
25 mi. N of Crouch 365-7000
Cap: 6 Nightly Fee: $40 Available: Year Round
Propane/wood stove, propane refrigerator, outdoor privy. No fac. For livestock. Bring potable water. Managed by concessionaire.

Third Fork
18 mi. N of Ola 365-7000
Cap: 4 Nightly Fee: $40 ($50 fr. 4/15-5/23)
Available: 4/15 to last weekend in Oct.
Propane/wood stove, propane refrigerator, indoor restroom fac. No fac. For livestock. Outdoor fire ring. Bring potable water. Managed by concessionaire.

Deadwood Lookout
15 mi. E of Garden Valley 365-7000
Cap: 2-6 Nightly Fee: $30 Available: 7/1-10/15
Wood cook/eat stove. Two beds (plus four may sleep on floor) Outdoor privy. Bring firewood. Outside fire ring for campfires.

Elk Creek Cabin #1
35 mi. NE of Lowman 259-3361
Cap: 10+ Nightly Fee: $40 Available: 11/15-5/15
Fireplace insert, wood cook and heat stove. Outdoor privy. Cross-country ski or snowmobile access only on popular snowmobile trail. Firewood provided, must be split.

Elk Creek Cabin #2
35 mi. NE of Lowman 259-3361
Cap: 6-10 Nightly Fee: $35 Available: 11/15-5/15
Wood cook/heat stoves. Outdoor privy. Cross-country or snowmobile access only on popular snowmobile trail. Firewood provided, must be split.

Warm Springs Guard Station
18 mi. E of Lowman 259-3361
Cap: 2-6 Nightly Fee $30 Available 11/15-5/1
Cross-country or snowshoe in only. Wood heat stove. Camp stove rec. for cooking. Outdoor privy. Emergency telephone available. Firewood provided, must be split.

Stolle Meadow Guard Station
25 mi. E of Cascade, then 6 mi. off Warm Lake Hwy. On Rd. 474 382-4271
Cap: 5 Nightly Fee: $40
Available: Year Round except 4/1-5/15
Wood heat and propane cook stove. Beds and mattresses provided. Outdoor privy. Drinking water available. Room for livestock nearby. Access by cross-country ski or snowmobile in winter.

Payette National Forest
Buck Park
12 mi. NE of Council 549-4200
Cap: 3 Nightly Fee: $15 Available: 7/1-11/7
Wood stove, 3 single bunks w/mattresses. Outdoor privy. Bring firewood and potable water. Room for stock nearby.

Summeris Grove
12 mi. NW of Council 549-4200
Cap: 6 Nightly Fee: $15 Available: 7/1-11/7
Wood stove, 6 single bunks w/mattresses. Outdoor privy. Bring firewood and potable water. Room for livestock nearby.

Car Rental

All American • Boise	342-7795
Avis Boise Municipal Airport • Boise	383-3350
Budget • Boise	322-7874
Budget • Boise	343-0561
Budget Car and Truck • Boise	383-3090
Budget Car and Truck • Boise	343-2600
Budget Car and Truck • Boise	331-2131
Budget Car and Truck • Boise	853-4832
Dollar • Boise	658-9097
Dollar • Boise	345-1658
Dollar Boise Airport • Boise	345-9727
Enterprise • Boise	336-8777
Enterprise • Boise	345-0004
Enterprise • Boise	344-4054
Enterprise • Boise	672-0585
Enterprise • Boise	381-0650
Enterprise • Boise	321-7936
Executive Leasing • Boise	322-8585
Hertz • Boise	383-3100
Lithia Chrysler • Boise	342-6811
Nationals • Boise	383-3210
Practical • Boise	344-3732
Thrifty • Boise	336-1904
Thrifty • Boise	342-7795
Hertz • Caldwell	455-9500
Tom Scott Honda • Caldwell	466-3248
Enterprise • Garden City	672-1650
Collins Auto Rental • McCall	634-8440

Section 3

All Idaho Area Codes are 208

McCall Aviation Inc • McCall	634-7137	Middle Fork Lodge	FHEG 333-0783	Bogus Basin • Boise	332-5100
Enterprise • Meridian	321-7936	Middle Fork Rapid Transit	FHR 338-9162	Jug Mountain Ranch • McCall	634-5074
Enterprise • Meridian	888-3559	Northwest River Company	FG 344-7119		
Budget • Mountain Home	587-8466	Shepp Ranch	FHEG 343-7729	**Downhill Ski Areas**	
Dennis Dillon Truck & Auto		Sulphur Creek Ranch	FHE 377-1188	**Brundage Mountain • McCall**	634-7462
Mountain Home	580-1000	Hughes River Expeditions, Inc	FRE 257-3477	Kelly Canyon • McCall	538-6261
Mountain Home Auto Ranch		Middle Fork Lodge	333-0783	Bogus Basin • Boise	332-5100
Mountain Home	580-1000	Snowbank Outfitters	EG 382-4872	Tamarack • Boise	388-3800
Affordable Auto Rental • Nampa	467-3078	Wapiti Meadow Ranch	FHEG 633-3217	Hitt Mountain • Cambridge	355-2256
Budget • Nampa	442-1540	Seven Devils Ranch	G 258-4431	Big Basin Butte • McCall	345-3223
Dan Wiebold Ford • Nampa	475-1100	Tamarack Resort	RG 325-1000		
Enterprise • Nampa	468-2330	Elk Creek Outfitters	FH 365-3895	**Snowmobile Rentals**	
Enterprise • Nampa	463-1221	Korell Outfitters	FHE 365-5393	**Cheap Thrils Rentals • McCall**	634-4787
Thrifty Car Rental • Nampa	468-3732	R & R Outdoors	HFRG 462-3999	**McCall Power Sports Rentals**	
		Sawtooth Wilderness Outfitters		McCall	634-8200

Outfitters & Guides

F=Fishing H=Hunting R=River Guides
E=Horseback Rides G=General Guide Services

Id Outfitters & Guides Association			FHERG 462-3416	Outdoor Adventures • Boise	386-9846
	800-49-IDAHO	Three Forks' Safaris	HE 462-6600	Power Trip Rentals • Cascade	382-5232
Outfitters & Guides Licensing Board	327-7380	Juniper Mountain Outfitters	HFE 454-1322	Bear Creek Lodge • McCall	634-3551
Brundage Mountain Adventures		Cascade Raft & Kayak	RG 793-2221	Xtreme Adventure Rentals • Meridian	884-4614
	FREG 634-4151	Lazy J Outfitters, Inc	FH 922-5648		
Bar Nunn Outfitters	HF 362-2976	Crystal Creek Camp	HG 836-5644	**Bike Rentals**	
Custom River Tours	FHRG 939-4324	Cascade Adventures	FRG 634-4909	**Gravity Sports • McCall**	**634-8530**
Diamond D Ranch, Inc	FHGE 336-9772	Whiskey Mountain Outfitters	FHE 466-4121	Bikes 2 Boards Outfitters• Boise	343-0208
Flying Resort Ranches, Inc	FHEG 756-6378	Flying V Outfitters	H 347-2760	Idaho Mountain Touring • Boise	336-3854
Greylock Mountain Company	G 376-4106	Wind River Outfitters	FHE 278-3706	Screamin' Toad Cycles Inc • Boise	367-1899
Mackay Wilderness Trips	FHERG 344-9904			Skiers Edge • Boise	336-3854

Cross-Country Ski Centers

Gravity Sports • McCall	634-8530
Brundage • McCall	634-4151

NOTES:

_____

_____

_____

_____

_____

_____

_____

_____

_____

_____

_____

_____

_____

_____

_____

_____

_____

_____

_____

_____

_____

_____

_____

_____

_____

_____

_____

_____

Campground Quick Reference

Atlanta

Neinmeyer
P | 8 | 22' — 392-6681 — Summer, Fall
27 mi. W. on Forest Rd. 268
Vault Toilets

Power Plant
P | 24 | 22' — 392-6681 — Summer, Fall
1.5 mi. NE on Forest Rd. 268
Drinking Water, Fire Rings, Pets OK, Vault Toilets

Riverside - Atlanta
P | 8 | 22' — 392-6681 — Summer, Fall
Left on FS Rd. 268, 1 mi.
Drinking Water, Fire Rings, Hot Springs, Pets OK, Vault Toilets

Banks

Big Eddy
P | $10 | 4 | 30' — 365-7000 — Summer, Fall
15 mi. N. on Hwy. 55
Pets OK, Tenters Welcome, Vault Toilets, Waterfront

Canyon
P | $10 | 6 | 30' — 365-7000 — Summer, Fall
19 mi. S. on Hwy. 55
Drinking Water, Pets OK, Tenters Welcome, Vault Toilets, Waterfront

Cold Springs - Banks
P | $10 | 5 | 22' — 365-7000 — Summer, Fall
9.5 mi. N. on Hwy. 55
Handicap Access

Swinging Bridge
P | $10 | 11 | 28' — 365-7000 — Summer, Fall
8 mi. N. on Hwy. 55
Drinking Water, Pets OK, Tenters Welcome, Vault Toilets

Boise

Fiesta RV Park
C | $20-32 | 145 — 375-8207/888-784-3246 — All Year
I-84, exit 46, W. on Eagle Rd., right on Fairview
Dump Station, Hookups, LP Gas, Modem Hookups, Pets OK, Reservations, Showers, Swimming Pool, Laundry, Handicap Access

Mountain View RV Park - Boise
C | $21-24 | 63 — 345-4141/877-610-4141 — All Year
I-84, exit 54, S. right to Commerce, right on Development, right on Airport Way
Credit Cards OK, Drinking Water, Dump Station, Hookups, Modem Hookups, Pets OK, Pull-thru Sites, Reservations, Showers, Laundry, Handicap Access

Americana RV Park
C | $20-24 | 90 — 344-5733
I-84, exit 49 to River St., right onto Americana Blvd. cross the river, right on Americana Terrace
Credit Cards OK, Dump Station, Hookups, LP Gas, Modem Hookups, Pets OK, Pull-thru Sites, Waterfront

On The River RV Park
C | $20-25 | 215 — 375-7432/800-375-7432 — All Year
I-84, exit 50, N. on Cole Rd., left on Mountain View Blvd., right on Glenwood for .8 mi. to Marigold St.
Cable TV Hookups, Dump Station, Hookups, Modem Hookups, Pets OK, Playground, Pull-thru Sites, Reservations, Showers, Handicap Access

Hi-Valley RV Park
C | $27-300 | 194 — 939-8080/888-457-5959 — All Year
Camping Cabins, Credit Cards OK, Drinking Water, Dump Station, Hookups, Modem Hookups, Pets OK, Playground, Pull-thru Sites, Reservations, Showers, Work-Out Room, Laundry

Shafer Butte

Shafer Butte
P | 7 | 22' — 587-7961 — Summer, Fall
16 mi. NE on Bogus Basin Rd, 3 mi. N. on Forest Rd. 374, 1.5 mi. E. on Shafer Butte Rd.
Drinking Water, Pets OK, Reservations, Vault Toilets

Bruneau

Bruneau Dunes State Park
P | $12-16 | 73 | 80' — 366-7919 — All Year
18 mi. S. of Mountain Home on Hwy. 51, E. on Hwy. 78 2 mi.
Camping Cabins, Credit Cards OK, Drinking Water, Dump Station, Hookups, Pets OK, Reservations, Showers, Tenters Welcome, Handicap Access

Caldwell

Caldwell Campground & RV Park
C | $13-21 | 85 | 40' — 454-0279/888-675-0279 — All Year
I-84, exit 26
Cable TV Hookups, Credit Cards OK, Drinking Water, Dump Station, Fire Rings, Hookups, LP Gas, Mini-Mart, Pets OK, Pull-thru Sites, Reservations, Showers, Tenters Welcome, Laundry

Towns Village RV Park
C | 40 — 455-1940 — All Year
I-84, exit 26
Cable TV Hookups

Country Corners Campground & RV Park
C | $15-22 | 75 — 453-8791 — All Year
I-84, exit 17
Cable TV Hookups, Credit Cards OK, Dump Station, Hookups, Mini-Mart, Modem Hookups, Pets OK, Playground, Pull-thru Sites, Reservations, Showers, Tenters Welcome, Handicap Access

Cambridge

Frontier Motel & RV Park
C | $5-15 | 9 — 257-3851 — All Year
Hwy. 95 in Cambridge
Dump Station

Brownlee
P | 11 | 16' — 253-0100 — Summer, Fall, Spring
16.6 mi. NW on Hwy. 71, 1 mi. E. on Forest Rd. 044
Drinking Water, Pets OK, Tenters Welcome, Vault Toilets

Copperfield Park
P | $12 | 62 | 45' — 388-2231/800-422-3143 — All Year
Hwy 71 to Oxbow, Or, Hwy 86, 900 ft. to entrance
Drinking Water, Dump Station, Fire Rings, Hookups, Pets OK, Pull-thru Sites, Showers, Tenters Welcome, Waterfront

Hells Canyon Park
P | $12 | 24 | 45' — 388-2231/800-422-3143 — All Year
Hwy. 71 to Oxbow, Or, Hwy 86, toward Hells Canyon Dam. 7 mi. N. of Oxbow
Boating Facilities, Drinking Water, Dump Station, Fire Rings, Hookups, Pets OK, Pull-thru Sites, Showers, Tenters Welcome, Waterfront

McCormick Park
P | $12 | 34 | 45' — 388-2231/800-422-3143 — All Year
Hwy. 71, right just before the Snake River Bridge
Boating Facilities, Drinking Water, Dump Station, Fire Rings, Hookups, Pets OK, Pull-thru Sites, Showers, Tenters Welcome, Waterfront

Woodhead Park
P | $12 | 124 | 45' — 388-2231/800-422-3143 — All Year
Hwy. 71 toward Brownlee Dam
Boating Facilities, Drinking Water, Dump Station, Fire Rings, Hookups, Pets OK, Pull-thru Sites, Showers, Tenters Welcome, Waterfront

Big Bar
P | None — 253-0100 — Undeveloped April-November
29 miles N of Cambridge on Hwy 71, then 9 miles N on FR 454
Primitive Camping, Restrooms, Cultural/Historic Sites, Boat Ramp, Motorized and Non-Motorized Boating, Caving, Climbing, Fishing, Hiking/Backpacking, Hunting, Picnicking, Scenic Driving, Water Sports, Wildlife Viewing

Campground Quick Reference - continued

Cascade

Arrowhead RV Park
382-4534
C $23-32   110   40'   All Year
Hwy. 55, 1.5 mi. S. of Cascade
Cable TV Hookups, Camping Cabins, Credit Cards OK, Dump Station, Hookups, LP Gas, Mini-Mart, Pets OK, Showers, Yurts/Teepees, Waterfront, Work-Out Room, WiFi, Laundry, Handicap Access

Water's Edge RV Resort
382-3120/800-574-2038
C $25-32   120   75'   Summer, Fall, Spring
Just off of Scenic Highway 55, East side of Hwy 55, N end of Cascade.
Cable TV Hookups, Camping Cabins, Credit Cards OK, Drinking Water, Hookups, Hot Springs, LP Gas, Modem Hookups, Pets OK, Pull-thru Sites, Reservations, Showers, Tenters Welcome, Waterfront, Laundry, Handicap Access

The Pines RV Park
382-5060
C $25   30   Summer, Fall, Spring

Cable TV Hookups, Drinking Water, Dump Station, Hookups, Mini-Mart, Pets OK, Pull-thru Sites, Reservations, Showers

Big Sage
382-6544
P   Summer, Fall, Spring
2.9 mi. S of Cascade
Credit Cards OK, Drinking Water, Pets OK, Swimming Pool, Tenters Welcome, Vault Toilets, Waterfront

Cabarton 1
382-6544
P $4-8   70   32'   Summer, Fall, Spring
3.2 mi. S. of Cascade
Drinking Water, Pets OK, Vault Toilets, Waterfront

Crown Point
382-6544
P $7-22   31   32'   Summer, Fall, Spring
On Cascade Reservoir
Drinking Water, Pets OK, Pull-thru Sites, Tenters Welcome, Vault Toilets, Waterfront

Curlew Tent Area
382-6544
P   Summer, Fall, Spring
21.5 mi. N. of Cascade
Credit Cards OK, Drinking Water, Pets OK, Tenters Welcome, Vault Toilets, Waterfront

French Creek
382-7400
P $10   21   30'   Summer, Fall
SW shore of Cascade Reservoir on West Mountain Rd.
Drinking Water, Reservations, Vault Toilets

Huckleberry - Cascade
382-6544
P $7-22   28   32'   Summer, Fall, Spring
21 mi. N. of Cascade, W. side of Cascade Reservoir
Credit Cards OK, Drinking Water, Pets OK, Pull-thru Sites, Tenters Welcome, Vault Toilets, Waterfront

Poison Creek
382-6544
P $7-22   18   32'   Summer, Fall, Spring
23.5 mi. N. of Cascade, W. side of Cascade Reservoir
Credit Cards OK, Drinking Water, Pets OK, Pull-thru Sites, Tenters Welcome, Vault Toilets, Waterfront

Shoreline
382-7400
P $10   25   40'   Summer, Fall
1 mi. N. on Hwy. 55, 24 mi. NE on Forest Rd. 22, 1 mi. SW on Forest Rd. 489
Drinking Water, Reservations, Swimming Pool, Vault Toilets

Sugarloaf
382-6544
P $7-22   45   32'   Summer, Fall, Spring
8.8 mi. N. of Cascade
Credit Cards OK, Drinking Water, Pets OK, Tenters Welcome, Vault Toilets, Waterfront

Van Wyck Main
382-6544
P $7-22   22   32'   Summer, Fall, Spring
Lake Cascade State Park
Boating Facilities, Credit Cards OK, Drinking Water, Dump Station, Pets OK, Pull-thru Sites, Tenters Welcome, Vault Toilets, Waterfront

Van Wyck Central
382-6544
P $7-22   40   32'   Summer, Fall, Spring
Lake Cascade State Park
Credit Cards OK, Drinking Water, Pets OK, Pull-thru Sites, Tenters Welcome, Vault Toilets, Waterfront

West Mountain
382-6544
P $7-22   26   32'   Summer, Fall, Spring
23 mi. N. of Cascade, W. side of Cascade Reservoir
Credit Cards OK, Drinking Water, Dump Station, Pets OK, Pull-thru Sites, Tenters Welcome, Vault Toilets, Waterfront

Blue Heron
382-6544
P $7-22   10   32'   Summer, Fall, Spring
Lake Cascade State Park
Boating Facilities, Credit Cards OK, Drinking Water, Pets OK, Tenters Welcome, Vault Toilets, Waterfront

South Fork Salmon River
382-7400
P   11   30'   Summer, Fall
23 mi. NE on Forest Rd. 22
Drinking Water, Vault Toilets

Council

Hodges RV Park
253-6042
C $20   14   55'   Summer, Fall, Spring
Hwy. 95, W. at Bleeker to end, left to 415 S. Hornet St.
Drinking Water, Dump Station, Hookups, Pets OK, Pull-thru Sites, Reservations, Showers, Tenters Welcome, Laundry, Handicap Access

Big Flat
P $8   13   45'   Summer, Fall
12 mi. S. on Hwy. 95; 14 mi. SE and E on Forest Rd. 50206
Drinking Water, Pets OK, Tenters Welcome, Vault Toilets

Cabin Creek
253-0100
P $8   12   22'   Summer, Fall
4 mi. S. on Hwy. 95, 10 mi. E. on Forest Service Rd. 186
Drinking Water, Pets OK, Vault Toilets

Huckleberry - Council
253-0100
P $8   8   16'   Summer, Fall
30 mi. NW on Forest Rd. 002, 5 mi. NE on Forest Rd. 105, 1 mi. E. on Forest Rd. 110
Drinking Water, Fire Rings, Pets OK, Tenters Welcome, Vault Toilets

Lafferty
253-0100
P   Yes   8   June-October
24 miles NW of Council on FR 002
Developed Campground, Drinking Water, Restrooms, RV Sites, Fishing, Hunting, Picnicking

Evergreen
347-0300
P   Yes   12   June-September
14 miles N of Council on Hwy. 95
Developed Campground, Drinking Water, Restrooms, RV Sites, Biking, Fishing, Picnicking

Donnelly

Chalet RV Park
325-8223
C $22-120   76   40'   Summer, Fall, Spring
Hwy. 55, S. end of Donnelly
Credit Cards OK, Drinking Water, Dump Station, Fire Rings, Hookups, Modem Hookups, Pets OK, Pull-thru Sites, Reservations, Showers, Tenters Welcome, Laundry

Mountain View RV Park - Donnelly
325-8055/208-325-8573
C $15-190   40   All Year
.75 mi. W. of Hwy. 55

SISCRA RV Campground
325-8130
C $6-10   175   All Year
SW of Donnelly on Siscra Rd.
Dump Station, Hookups, Pets OK, Pull-thru Sites, Reservations, Showers

Campground Quick Reference - continued

Campground Name Public/Commercial	Unit Price	#Spaces	Max. Length	Phone Seasons
Directions				
Amenities/Activities				

Westside RV Park   325-4100
C $15   35   Summer, Fall, Spring
.5 mi. W. of Hwy. 55 on Roseberry Rd.
Dump Station, Hookups, Pets OK, Reservations, Showers, Tenters Welcome

Emmett

Holiday Motel & RV Park   365-4479
C $42-48   15   All Year
12th & Washington Ave.
Cable TV Hookups, Credit Cards OK, Hookups, Limited Access, Pets OK, Laundry

Capitol Mobile Park   365-3889
C   15   All Year

Cable TV Hookups, Mini-Mart, Pets OK, Reservations, Showers, Laundry

Antelope   365-7000
P   28   32'   Summer, Fall
10 mi. NE on Forest Rd. 618, 6.7 mi. on Forest Rd. 626, 2.3 mi. NE on Forest Rd. 614

Eastside   365-7000
P $10   6   32'   Summer
10 mi. NE on Forest Rd. 618, 6.7 mi. NE on Forest Rd. 626, 4 mi. NE on Forest Rd. 614
Drinking Water, Pets OK, Vault Toilets, Waterfront

Hollywood Point   365-7000
P $10   6   22'   Summer
10 mi. NE on Forest Rd. 618, 6.7 mi. NE on Forest Rd. 626, 4.5 mi. E. on Forest Rd. 614
Drinking Water, Pets OK, Vault Toilets, Waterfront

Sagehen Creek   365-7000
P $10   15   32'   Summer
10 mi. NE on Forest Rd. 618, 6.7 mi. NE on Forest Rd. 626, 3.5 mi. NE on Forest Rd. 614
Drinking Water, Pets OK, Pull-thru Sites, Reservations, Vault Toilets, Waterfront

Montour Wildlife Area   383-2211
P $5   17   32'   Summer, Fall, Spring
10 mi. NE on Hwy. 52
Drinking Water, Dump Station, Tenters Welcome, Vault Toilets

Featherville

Abbott   764-3202
P $3   7   16'   Summer, Fall
2 mi. E. on Forest Rd. 70000
Tenters Welcome, Vault Toilets

Baumgartner   764-3202
P $10-20   29   28'   Summer, Fall
11 mi. E. on Forest Rd. 227
Drinking Water, Hot Springs, Pets OK, Reservations, Tenters Welcome, Vault Toilets

Bowns   764-3202
P   30'   Summer, Fall
23.2 mi. E. of Featherville on Forest Rd. 227
Drinking Water, Pets OK, Tenters Welcome, Vault Toilets

Chaparral   764-3202
P $2   7   22'   Summer
3.1 mi. E. of Featherville on Forest Rd. 227
Pets OK, Pull-thru Sites, Tenters Welcome, Vault Toilets

Fruitland

Neat Retreat   452-4324
C $23   41   150'   All Year
Hwy. 95, between Ontario & Payette, .75 mi. N. of junction of Hwys. 30/95
Cable TV Hookups, Credit Cards OK, Drinking Water, Dump Station, Hookups, LP Gas, Modem Hookups, Pets OK, Pull-thru Sites, Reservations, Showers, Tenters Welcome

Exit 3 RV Park   452-4232
C $15   25   All Year
I-84, exit 3 and junction of Hwy. 95, behind Shell Station
Dump Station, Hookups, Mini-Mart, Pets OK, Pull-thru Sites

Garden Valley

Silver Creek Plunge   585-3134
C   All Year
22 mi. N. of Crouch
Camping Cabins, Credit Cards OK, Drinking Water, Fire Rings, Mini-Mart, Playground, Handicap Access

Riverpond Campground   853-2326
C $8-12   15   Summer, Fall, Spring
Banks-Lowman Rd. to Middle Fork Rd., left towards Crouch
Hookups, Tenters Welcome, Waterfront

Boiling Springs   365-7000
P $8   7   30'   Summer, Fall
2.5 mi. W. on Hwy 17, 23 mi. N. on Forest Rd. 698
Drinking Water, Pets OK, Tenters Welcome, Vault Toilets, Waterfront

Hardscrabble   365-7000
P $8   6   30'   Summer, Fall
2.5 mi. W. on Hwy. 17, 14 mi. N. on Forest Rd. 698
Pets OK, Tenters Welcome, Vault Toilets, Waterfront

Hot Springs   365-7000
P   35'   Summer, Fall
2 mi. E. on Hwy. 17
Drinking Water, Hot Springs, Pets OK, Pull-thru Sites, Reservations, Tenters Welcome, Vault Toilets, Waterfront

Rattlesnake   365-7000
P $10   11   35'   Summer, Fall
2.5 mi. W. on Hwy. 17, 18 mi. N. on Forest Rd. 698
Drinking Water, Pets OK, Pull-thru Sites, Reservations, Tenters Welcome, Vault Toilets, Waterfront, Handicap Access

Silver Creek   365-7000
P   5   30'   Summer
2.5 mi. W. on Hwy. 17, 19 mi. N. on Forest Rd. 698, 7 mi. NE on Forest Rd. 671
Drinking Water, Pets OK, Pull-thru Sites, Tenters Welcome, Vault Toilets

Tie Creek   365-7000
P $10   8   30'   Summer, Fall
2.5 mi. W. on Hwy. 17, 11 mi. N. on Forest Rd. 698
Drinking Water, Pets OK, Tenters Welcome, Vault Toilets, Waterfront

Trail Creek - Garden Valley   365-7000
P   35'   Summer, Fall
2.5 mi. W. on Hwy. 17, 19 mi. N. on Forest Rd. 698

Silver Creek Plunge   739-3400
C   Yes   May-September
2.5 miles W of Garden Valley on Hwy. 17, then 19 miles N on FR 698, then 7 miles NE on FR 671
Developed Campground, Group Camping, Drinking Water, Restrooms, RV Sites, Biking, Fishing, Hiking/Backpacking, Hunting, Off Highway Vehicles Picnicking, Winter Sports

Glenns Ferry

Trail Break RV Park   336-7745
C $15-20   35   40'   All Year
E-bound - Exit 120 W-bound - Exit 121 & Frontage Rd., West 1/2 mi.
Cable TV Hookups, Hookups, Pets OK, Pull-thru Sites, Showers, Tenters Welcome, Laundry

Three Island Crossing State Park   366-2394
P $12-22   101   60'   All Year
2 mi. W. on Madison St.
Camping Cabins, Credit Cards OK, Drinking Water, Dump Station, Hookups, Reservations, Showers, Tenters Welcome

Campground Quick Reference - continued

Campground Name				Phone
Public/Commercial	Unit Price	#Spaces	Max. Length	Seasons
Directions				
Amenities/Activities				

Grand View

C.J. Strike Parks   388-2231/800-422-3143
P   50   40'   All Year
Hwy. 67 to Grandview, SE on Hwy. 78, left at High School, N. to three parks at C.J. Strike Dam
Boating Facilities, Drinking Water, Fire Rings, Pull-thru Sites, Tenters Welcome

North Fork - Owyhee Uplands   384-3300
P   7   16'   Summer, Fall, Spring
30 mi. E. of Jordan Valley, OR. on Owyhee Uplands Byway
Vault Toilets

Cove   384-3300
P   27   36'   Summer, Fall, Spring
2 mi W. on Hwy 51, E. on Hwy 78, C.J. Strike Reservoir
Drinking Water, Dump Station, Pets OK, Pull-thru Sites, Vault Toilets, Waterfront

Homedale

Snake River RV Resort LLC   337-3744
C $20-25   50   All Year
Hwy. 95, 1 mi. S. of Homedale, E. on Pioneer Rd.
Boating Facilities, Credit Cards OK, Drinking Water, Fire Rings, Game Room, Hookups, Modem Hookups, Pets OK, Pull-thru Sites, Showers, Tenters Welcome, Laundry

Idaho City

Trudy's Kitchen, RV & Cabin   392-4151
C $19-60   9   All Year
Next to Trudy's Kitchen Restaurant
Cable TV Hookups, Credit Cards OK, Drinking Water, Hookups, LP Gas, Mini-Mart, Pets OK, Pull-thru Sites

Bad Bear
P $10   6   22'   Summer, Fall, Spring
Hwy. 21, 10.5 mi. N. of Idaho City
Drinking Water, Fire Rings, Pets OK, Handicap Access

Black Rock
P   11   22'   Summer, Fall, Spring
2 mi. NE on Hwy. 21, 18 mi. E. on Forest Rd. 327
Drinking Water, Fire Rings, Pets OK, Reservations, Vault Toilets

Edna Creek
P   9   16'   Summer, Fall
Hwy. 21, 19 mi. N. of Idaho City
Drinking Water, Fire Rings, Pets OK, Vault Toilets, Handicap Access

Grayback Gulch   392-6681
P $10   20   22'   Summer, Fall
2.4 mi. S. on Hwy. 21
Drinking Water, Fire Rings, Pets OK, Reservations, Vault Toilets, Handicap Access

Hayfork   392-6681
P   12   22'   Summer, Fall, Spring
10 mi. NE on Hwy. 21
Drinking Water, Fire Rings, Pets OK, Reservations, Vault Toilets, Handicap Access

Ten Mile   392-6681
P $10   15   22'   Summer, Fall, Spring
9.3 mi. NE on Hwy. 21
Drinking Water, Fire Rings, Pets OK, Vault Toilets, Handicap Access

Willow Creek
P   9   Summer, Fall, Spring
Hwy. 21, 19 mi. E. of Boise, 23 mi. E. on Forest Rd. 268
Drinking Water, Pets OK, Vault Toilets, Handicap Access

Whoop-Um-Up   392-6681
P $10   8   30'   Summer, Fall, Spring
Equestrian campground, 18 mi. N. on Hwy. 21
Drinking Water, Fire Rings, Pets OK, Pull-thru Sites, Vault Toilets, Handicap Access

Lowman

Sawtooth Lodge   259-3331
C   23   Summer, Fall
27 mi. E. of Lowman, in Grandjean
Dump Station, Hot Springs, Showers, Handicap Access

New Haven Lodge   259-3344
C $7-110   9   All Year
Hwy. 21, M P 76, S. Fork Payette River
Cable TV Hookups, Credit Cards OK, Drinking Water, Dump Station, Hookups, Limited Access, LP Gas, Swimming Pool, Waterfront

Sourdough Lodge & RV Resort   259-3326
C $45-89   4   All Year
Hwy. 21, M P 84, E. of Lowman

Barney's   269-3361
P $8   9   30'   Summer, Fall
36 mi. NE on Hwy. 21, 28 mi. W. on Forest Rd. 579, 7.5 mi. S. on Forest Rd. 555
Drinking Water, Limited Access, Pets OK, Reservations, Vault Toilets

Bear Valley   269-3361
P   10   22'   Summer, Fall
36 mi. NE on Hwy. 21, 12 mi. N. on Cape Horn Turnoff
Limited Access, Pets OK, Vault Toilets

Bonneville   269-3361
P $10   12   30'   Summer, Fall
19 mi. NE on Hwy. 21, .6 mi. N. on Forest Rd. 025
Drinking Water, Pets OK, Reservations, Vault Toilets

Bull Trout Lake   269-3361
P $10   38   60'   Summer, Fall
34 mi. NE on Hwy 21, 2 mi. SW on Forest Rd. 520
Drinking Water, Limited Access, Pets OK, Reservations, Vault Toilets

Cozy Cove   269-3361
P $8   11   16'   Summer, Fall
36 mi. NE on Hwy. 21, 28 mi. W. on Forest Rd. 579, 11 mi. S. on Forest Rd. 555
Drinking Water, Limited Access, Pets OK, Reservations, Vault Toilets

Grandjean   727-5000/800-260-5970
P   31   22'   Summer, Fall
7 mi. off Hwy 21 on S. Fk. Payette River
Drinking Water, Fire Rings, Pets OK, Tenters Welcome, Vault Toilets

Helende   269-3361
P $8   10   Summer, Fall
9 mi. E. on Hwy. 21
Drinking Water, Limited Access, Pets OK, Reservations, Vault Toilets

Hower's   269-3361
P $8   8   22'   Summer, Fall
36 mi. NE on Hwy. 21, 28 mi. W. on Forest Rd. 579, 7.5 mi. S. on Forest Rd. 555
Drinking Water, Limited Access, Pets OK, Reservations, Vault Toilets

Kirkham Hot Springs   269-3361
P $10   16   32'   Summer, Fall
4.2 mi. E. on Hwy. 21
Drinking Water, Limited Access, Pets OK, Pull-thru Sites, Reservations, Vault Toilets

Mountain View   269-3361
P $10   14   32'   Summer, Fall
.6 mi. E. on Hwy. 21
Drinking Water, Pets OK, Pull-thru Sites, Reservations, Vault Toilets, Waterfront

Park Creek - Lowman   269-3361
P $8   26   32'   Summer, Fall
.3 mi. E. on Hwy. 21, 3 mi. NE on Forest Rd. 582
Drinking Water, Limited Access, Pets OK, Pull-thru Sites, Reservations, Vault Toilets

Pine Flats   269-3361
P $10   25   32'   Summer, Fall
5 mi. W. on Banks-Lowman Rd.
Drinking Water, Limited Access, Pets OK, Pull-thru Sites, Reservations, Vault Toilets

Section 3

INCLUDING BOISE, CASCADE, MCCALL, NAMPA, AND CALDWELL

SOUTHWEST AREA

Campground Quick Reference - continued

Campground Name Public/Commercial	Unit Price	#Spaces	Max. Length	Phone Seasons
Directions				
Amenities/Activities				

Deer Flat 269-3361
P   None   5   July-September
36 miles NE of Lowman on Hwy. 21, then 22 miles E on Landmark-Stanley Rd/FR 579
Primitive Camping, Restrooms, Horseback Riding, Wildlife Viewing, Winter Sports

Bench Creek 838-2201
P   None   5   July-September
Near Banner Summit, east of Lowman on Hwy. 21
Developed Campground, Drinking Water, Restrooms, RV Sites, Biking, Fishing, Hiking/Backpacking, Off Highway Vehicles, Picnicking, Scenic Driving

Marsing

Givens Hot Springs 495-2000
C $20-25   25   All Year
Hwy. 78, 11 mi. S. of Marsing
Hookups, Hot Springs, Pets OK, Playground, Reservations, Showers, Swimming Pool, Handicap Access

River Haven RV Park 8   96-4268/800-852-9263
C $8-15   45   All Year
Old Bruneau Hwy., 2.5 mi. S. of Marsing
Dump Station, Hookups, LP Gas, Mini-Mart, Pets OK, Showers, Waterfront, Handicap Access

McCall

Lakeview Village RV Park 634-5280
C $12-16   84   All Year

Credit Cards OK, Drinking Water, Hookups, Limited Access, LP Gas, Pets OK, Showers, Waterfront, Handicap Access

McCall Campground 634-5165
C $8-20   29   All Year
Hwy. 55, 1.5 mi. S. of Payette Lake
Credit Cards OK, Drinking Water, Dump Station, Hookups, Pets OK, Playground, Pull-thru Sites, Reservations, Showers, Tenters Welcome

McCall RV Resort - Northfork Lodge 634-1418/800-709-9739
C $36-119   45'   All Year
Hwy. 55 to Deinhard, W. to Mission St., Left on Mission 2/10 of a mile to Scott St. Go right to resort.
Business Center, Cable TV Hookups, Camping Cabins, Credit Cards OK, Drinking Water, Dump Station, Fire Rings, Game Room, LP Gas, Mini-Mart, Modem Hookups, Pets OK, Pull-thru Sites, Reservations, Showers, Swimming Pool, Waterfront, Work-Out Room, WiFi, Laundry, Handicap Access

Amanita 382-7400
P   22' Summer, Fall, Spring
4.8 mi. SW on Cty. Rd. 422

Buckhorn Bar 634-0400
P   10   22'   Summer, Fall
30 mi. NE on Forest Rd. 48, 7.5 mi. S on Forest Rd. 674
Drinking Water, Fire Rings, Pets OK, Tenters Welcome, Vault Toilets

Lake Fork 634-0400
P $8   9   22'   Summer, Fall
9.5 mi. E. on Forest Rd. 48
Drinking Water, Fire Rings, Pets OK, Tenters Welcome, Vault Toilets

Ponderosa 634-0400
P $8   14   20'   Summer, Fall
31 mi. NE on Forest Rd. 48
Credit Cards OK, Drinking Water, Fire Rings, Pets OK, Tenters Welcome, Vault Toilets

Ponderosa State Park 634-2164
P $12-16   170   35'   Summer, Fall
2 mi. NE of McCall City Center
Boating Facilities, Camping Cabins, Credit Cards OK, Drinking Water, Dump Station, Hookups, Pull-thru Sites, Reservations, Showers, Yurts/Teepees, Tenters Welcome, Vault Toilets, Waterfront

Rainbow Point 382-7400
P $10   12   22'   Summer, Fall
4.7 mi. SW on Cty. Rd. 422
Drinking Water, Pull-thru Sites, Reservations, Swimming Pool, Vault Toilets

Upper Payette Lake 634-0400
P $8-10   19   22'   Summer, Fall
18.5 mi. N. on Forest Rd. 21
Drinking Water, Pets OK, Reservations, Tenters Welcome, Vault Toilets, Handicap Access

Kennally Creek 634-0400
P $8-10   14   26'   Summer, Fall
3 mi. N. on Hwy. 55, 10 mi. E. on Forest Rd. 388
Drinking Water, Fire Rings, Pets OK, Tenters Welcome, Vault Toilets, Handicap Access

Secesh River Horse Camp 634-0600
P   Yes   5   June-October
31 miles NE of McCall on FR 48
Primitive Camping, Restrooms, Non-Motorized Boating, Whitewater Rafting, Fishing, Hiking/Backpacking, Horseback Riding, Hunting, Picnicking, Scenic Driving

Camp Creek 634-0600
P   Yes   4   May-November
30 miles NE of McCall on FR 48, then 9.5 miles S on FR 674
Developed Campground, Handicap Accessible Restrooms, RV Sites, Biking, Fishing, Hiking/Backpacking, Horseback Riding, Hunting, Picnicking, Scenic Driving

Fourmile 634-0600
P   Yes   4   May-November
30 miles NE of McCall on FR 48, then 11 miles S on FR 674
Developed Campground, Handicap Accessible Restrooms, RV Sites, Biking, Fishing, Hiking/Backpacking, Horseback Riding, Hunting, Picnicking, Scenic Driving

Kennally Creek 634-0400
P   Yes   10   June-September
7 miles S of McCall on Hwy. 55, then 15 miles E on FR 388 and FR 387
Developed Campground, Drinking Water, Restrooms, RV Sites, Biking, Fishing, Hiking/Backpacking, Horseback Riding, Hunting, Off Highway Vehicles, Picnicking, Scenic Driving, Wildlife Viewing

Upper Payette Lake 634-0400
P   Yes   19; 5 Group Sites   June-October
15 miles N of McCall on FR 21 to the group site; 16 miles N to the single site campground
Developed Campground, Handicap Accessible Group Camping, Drinking Water, Handicap Accessible Restrooms, Handicap Accessible RV Sites, Boat Ramp, Biking, Fishing, Hiking/Backpacking, Hunting, Off Highway Vehicles, Picnicking

Meridian

The Playground RV Park 887-1022/800-668-7529
C $22   72   60'   All Year
I-84, between exits 44 & 46
Credit Cards OK, Drinking Water, Dump Station, Hookups, LP Gas, Mini-Mart, Modem Hookups, Pets OK, Playground, Pull-thru Sites, Reservations, Showers, Swimming Pool, Tenters Welcome

Mountain Home

Mountain Home KOA 587-5111
C   43   Summer, Fall, Spring
I-84, exit 90 westbound to Stinker Station, right; exit 95 eastbound to 3rd signal light, then right
Cable TV Hookups, Camping Cabins, Credit Cards OK, Dump Station, Hookups, LP Gas, Pets OK, Playground, Pull-thru Sites, Reservations, Showers, Tenters Welcome, Laundry

The Wagon Wheel 587-5994
C $15-20   10   All Year
I-84, exit 95, American Legion Blvd. to 18th E.
Cable TV Hookups, Drinking Water, Hookups, Pets OK, Reservations, Showers, Tenters Welcome

Campground Quick Reference - continued

Fort Running Bear RV Park
653-2494
C $20-45   72   All Year
Hwy. 20, 26 mi. NE of Mountain Home
Camping Cabins, Drinking Water, Dump Station, Hookups, LP Gas, Modem Hookups, Pets OK, Playground, Pull-thru Sites, Reservations, Showers, Swimming Pool, Yurts/Teepees, Laundry

Cottonwood RV Park
587-4426
C $16.50   19   All Year
Exit 95 to Main, left on Hwy. 51 to Air Base Rd., right at light to Bradford
Cable TV Hookups, Dump Station, Modem Hookups, Pets OK, Pull-thru Sites, Reservations, Showers, Tenters Welcome, Laundry

Nampa

Mason Creek RV Park
465-7199/800-768-7199
C $16-27   78   42'   All Year
I-84, exit 36, Franklin Blvd. .5 mi. S.
Cable TV Hookups, Credit Cards OK, Drinking Water, Dump Station, Hookups, LP Gas, Modem Hookups, Pets OK, Pull-thru Sites, Reservations, Showers, Laundry

Garrity Blvd. RV Park
442-9000/877-442-9090
C $10-22   88   All Year
Exit I-84 at Garrity, 1 mi. S.
Credit Cards OK, Dump Station, Hookups, Mini-Mart, Modem Hookups, Pets OK, Playground, Pull-thru Sites, Showers, Work-Out Room, Laundry

New Meadows

Meadows RV Park
347-2325/800-603-2325
C $12-20   37   50'   Summer, Fall, Spring
Hwy. 55, 2.5 mi. E. of New Meadows
Credit Cards OK, Dump Station, Hookups, Modem Hookups, Pets OK, Pull-thru Sites, Reservations, Showers, Laundry

Zim's Hot Springs
347-2686
C $9-18   12   Summer, Fall, Spring
Hwy. 95, 4 mi. N. of town, 13 mi. W. of McCall
Credit Cards OK, Drinking Water, Dump Station, Game Room, Hookups, Hot Springs, Pets OK, Showers, Swimming Pool, Tenters Welcome, Waterfront

Cold Springs - New Meadows
634-0400
P $8-10   30   22'   Summer, Fall
8 mi. SW on Hwy. 95, 2.5 mi. W. on Forest Rd. 089, 1 mi. W. on Forest Rd. 50091
Drinking Water, Fire Rings, Pets OK, Reservations, Tenters Welcome, Vault Toilets

Hazard Lake
347-0300
P $8   12   22'   Summer, Fall
6 mi. E on Hwy. 55, 19 mi. N. on Forest Rd. 50257, 1 mi. E. on Forest Rd. 50259
Drinking Water, Fire Rings, Pets OK, Tenters Welcome, Vault Toilets, Waterfront

Last Chance
347-0300
P $8-10   23   45'   Summer, Fall
4 mi. E. on Hwy. 55, 2 mi. N. on Forest Rd. 453
Drinking Water, Fire Rings, Pets OK, Tenters Welcome, Vault Toilets

Grouse Campground
347-0300
P $4/night   6   June 15-September 15
6 miles E of New Meadows on Hwy. 55, then 9 miles N on FR 257
Developed Campground, Drinking Water, Restrooms, Boat Ramp, Biking, Motorized and Non-Motorized Boating, Fishing, Hiking/Backpacking, Horseback Riding, Hunting, Picnicking, Scenic Driving, Water Sports, Wildlife Viewing

Parma

Old Fort Boise RV Park
722-5138
C $7-13   9   Summer, Fall, Spring
Hwy. 95, E. side of Parma
Dump Station, Hookups, Pets OK, Showers, Tenters Welcome, Handicap Access

Payette

Lazy River RV Park
642-9667
C $10   12   All Year
Hwy. 95, 4 mi. N. of town
Dump Station, Hookups, Pets OK, Showers, Laundry

Pine

Nester's Riverside Campground
653-2443
C $7.50   10   All Year
Anderson Ranch Recreation Area
Mini-Mart, Pets OK, Reservations

Pine Resort
653-2323
C $10-150   16   All Year
Anderson Ranch Recreation Area
Credit Cards OK, Dump Station, Hookups, Limited Access, LP Gas, Pets OK, Waterfront, Handicap Access

Deer Creek Lodge
653-2454
C $15   24   All Year
Hwy. 20, N. of Mountain Home, W. at M. P. 127 for 15 mi.
Credit Cards OK, Drinking Water, Hookups, LP Gas, Modem Hookups, Reservations, Tenters Welcome, Waterfront

Fall Creek Resort & Marina
653-2242
C $10   30   All Year
Hwy. 20, N. of Mountain Home, W. at M. P. 116, 11 mi.
Boating Facilities, Credit Cards OK, Drinking Water, Dump Station, Fire Rings, Game Room, Hookups, LP Gas, Mini-Mart, Reservations, Showers, Tenters Welcome, Vault Toilets, Waterfront, Work-Out Room, Handicap Access

Anderson Ranch Reservoir Campgrounds
587-7961
P   200   32'   Summer
30 mi. NE on Hwy. 20, 15 mi. NE on Forest Rd. 61
Boating Facilities, Vault Toilets

Big Roaring River Lake & Big Trinity Lake
587-7961
P   29   22'   Summer, Fall
30 mi. NE on Hwy. 20, 29 mi. NE on Forest Rd. 61, 15 mi. NW on Forest Rd. 172, 3 mi. S. on Forest Rd. 129
Drinking Water, Vault Toilets

Dog Creek
587-7961
P $8-12   12   22'   Summer, Fall
34 mi. NE on Hwy 20, 24 mi. N. on Forest Rd. 61
Drinking Water, Reservations, Vault Toilets

Elks Flat
587-7961
P   35   55'   Summer, Fall
29 mi. NE on Hwy. 20, 22 mi. NE on Forest Rd. 61
Drinking Water, Pets OK, Reservations, Vault Toilets

Warm Lake

Warm Lake Lodge & Resort
632-3553
C $15   7   All Year
26 mi. E. of Cascade at Warm Lake
Camping Cabins, Credit Cards OK, Drinking Water, Fire Rings, LP Gas, Mini-Mart, Reservations, Showers, Tenters Welcome

Poverty Flat
382-7400
P   25'   Summer, Fall, Spring
25 mi. E. on Warm Lake Rd. (Forest Rd. 22), 15 mi. N. on S. F. Salmon River Rd. (Forest Rd. 474)
Drinking Water, Fire Rings, Tenters Welcome, Vault Toilets

Warm Lake
382-7400
P $10   12   30'   Summer, Fall
1 mi. N. on Hwy. 55; 26 mi. NE on Forest Rd. 22, 1/8 miles SE on Forest Rd. 579RA
Drinking Water, Pull-thru Sites, Reservations, Swimming Pool, Vault Toilets

Buck Mountain
382-4271
P   None   4   June-October
35 miles E of Cascade on Warm Lake Rd, then 2 miles N on Johnson Creek Rd
Primitive Camping, Restrooms, Fishing, Hiking/Backpacking, Horseback Riding, Off Highway Vehicles, Picnicking

Summit Lake
382-4271
P   None   3   June-October
32 miles E of Cascade on Warm Lake Rd
Primitive Camping, Restrooms, Fishing, Hiking/Backpacking, Picnicking, Scenic Driving, Winter Sports

Section 3

INCLUDING BOISE, CASCADE, MCCALL, NAMPA, AND CALDWELL

SOUTHWEST AREA

Campground Quick Reference - continued

Campground Name				Phone	
Public/Commercial	Unit Price	#Spaces	Max. Length	Seasons	
Directions					
Amenities/Activities					

Shoreline Campground
P $10   25; 1 Group Site   382-4271   May-November
25 miles E of Cascade on Warm Lake Rd
Developed Campground, Group Camping, Drinking Water, Restrooms, RV Sites, Boat Ramp, Biking, Motorized and Non-Motorized Boating, Fishing, Picnicking, Water Sports

Picnic Point
P $5/night   8   382-4271   May-November
25 miles E of Cascade on Warm Lake Rd
Developed Campground, Drinking Water, Restrooms, Biking, Non-Motorized Boating, Fishing, Water Sports

Boundary Creek
P   Yes   14   879-4101   June-September
70 miles E of Cascade on Warm Lake Rd, then S and E on Landmark-Stanley Rd, then 13 miles N on FR 668
Developed Campground, Drinking Water, Restrooms, RV Sites, Boat Ramp, Non-Motorized Boating, Whitewater Rafting, Fishing, Hiking/Backpacking, Horseback Riding, Picnicking, Scenic Driving

Fir Creek
P   None   5   269-3361   July-Septebmer
70 miles E of Cascade on Warm Lake Rd, then S and E on Landmark-Stanley Rd
Primitive Camping, Restrooms, Hiking/Backpacking, Horseback Riding, Wildlife Viewing

Weiser

Gateway RV Park
C $16-20   20   40'   549-2539   All Year

Cable TV Hookups, Hookups, Pets OK, Reservations, Showers

Indian Hot Springs
C $8-15   11   549-0070   All Year
6 mi. NW of Weiser
Dump Station, Hookups, Pets OK, Showers, Swimming Pool

Indianhead Motel & RV Park
C $22   9   549-0331   All Year
Hwy. 95 at Indianhead Rd.
Credit Cards OK, Hookups, Pets OK, Pull-thru Sites, Reservations, Showers

Monroe Creek Campground & RV Park
C $13-20   46   549-2026   All Year
1.5 mi. N. of Weiser
Dump Station, Hookups, Mini-Mart, Modem Hookups, Pets OK, Playground, Pull-thru Sites, Reservations, Showers

Steck Park
P $8   46   36'   384-3300   Summer, Fall, Spring
8 mi. W. Cty. Rd 70, 1 mi. N. Eaton Rd, 11 mi W. Olds Ferry Rd.
Drinking Water, Dump Station, Pets OK, Pull-thru Sites, Tenters Welcome, Vault Toilets, Waterfront

Mann Creek
P $8   12   45'   383-2211   Summer, Fall, Spring
Hwy. 95, 18 mi. N. of Weiser
Drinking Water, Pets OK, Pull-thru Sites, Tenters Welcome, Vault Toilets, Waterfront

Paradise/Justrite
P   7   20'   549-4200   Summer, Fall
12.5 mi. N. on Hwy. 95; 13 mi. NW on Forest Rd. 009
Pets OK, Vault Toilets

Spring Creek - Weiser
P $8   14   45'   549-4200   Summer, Fall, Spring
12.5 mi. N. on Hwy. 95, 11.5 mi. N. on Cty. Rd. & Forest Rd. 009
Drinking Water, Pets OK, Tenters Welcome, Vault Toilets, Handicap Access

Yellow Pine

Murph's RV Park
C $20   22   633-2233   Summer, Fall, Spring
.25 mi. NE of Yellow Pine on Big Creek-Stibnite Rd.
Drinking Water, Hookups, Playground, Reservations, Showers, Tenters Welcome, Laundr

Zena Creek Ranch
C   6   382-4336   All Year
On Secesh River, 30 mi. E. of McCall, 20 mi. W. of Yellow Pine

Alpine Village Lodge
C   8   385-0271   All Year
Yellow Pine
Hookups, Showers

Golden Gate
P   9   22'   382-7400   Summer, Fall
2 mi. S. on Forest Rd. 413
Vault Toilets

Pen Basin
P   6   22'   382-7400   Summer, Fall
30 mi. S. on Forest Rd. 413, 3 mi. S. on Forest Rd. 579
Vault Toilets

Yellow Pine
P   14   22'   382-7400   Summer, Fall
1 mi. S. on Forest Rd. 413
Drinking Water, Vault Toilets

Ice Hole
P   None   8   382-4271   June-October
35 miles E of Cascade on Warm Lake Rd, then 19 miles N on Johnson Creek Rd
Developed Campground, Drinking Water, Restrooms, Fishing, Hiking/Backpacking, Horseback Riding, Off Highway Vehicles, Picnicking, Wildlife Viewing

NOTES:

Dining Quick Reference

Price Range refers to the average cost of a meal per person: ($) $1-$6, ($$) $7-$11, ($$$) $12-up. Cocktails: "Yes" indicates full bar; Beer (B)/Wine (W), Service: Breakfast (B), Brunch (BR), Lunch (L), Dinner (D). Businesses in bold print will have additional information under the appropriate map locator number in the body of this section.

MAP NO.	RESTAURANT	TYPE CUISINE	PRICE RANGE	CHILD MENU	COCKTAILS BEER WINE	MEALS SERVED	CREDIT CARDS ACCEPTED
1	Granite Mountain Cafe 213 Virginia Ave, New Meadows, 347-2513	American	$-$$	N	N	B/L/D	M V
1	Subway Hwy 55 & 95, New Meadows, 347-4000	Fast Food	$	N	N	L/D	M V
2	Burgers & More 106 Michigan Ave, Council, 253-0089	Family	$	Y	N	L/D	No
2	Rivers Edge Café 102 Mosher St, Council, 253-4855	Family	$	Y	N	B/L	No
2	Seven Devils Cafe 116 Illinois Ave, Council, 253-1177	Family	$$	Y	N	B/L/D	M V
2	The Branding Iron Steak House 103 Illinois Ave, Council, 253-4499	Steakhouse	$$	Y	Yes	B/L/D	Major
3	Bucky's Cafe & Motel Hwy 95 & 71, Cambridge, 257-3330	Family	$	Y	N	L/D	Major
3	Gateway Cafe Hwy 71, Cambridge, 257-3531	American	$	Y	B W	B/L/D	M V
3	Gobbler Cafe 20 E Central Blvd, Cambridge, 257-3561	Family/Fine Dining	$$-$$$	Y	N	B/L/D	Major
3	The Round Up Coffee House Cambridge, Cambridge, 257-3406	Coffee/Deli	$	N	N	B/L	No
4	Beehive Family Restaurant 611 Hwy 95, Weiser, 549-3544	Family	$$	N	N	B/L/D	Major
4	Judy's Weiser In 1800 E 6th St, Weiser, 414-4962	American	$$$	Y	B W	B/L/D	Major
4	La Tejanita Mexican Food 622 E Commercial St, Weiser, 549-2768	Mexican	$	N	N	L/D	M V
4	Ruszoni's Pizzeria 540 State St, Weiser, 549-1093	Pizza	$	N	N	L/D	No
5	**Lardos Grill & Saloon** 600 W Lake St, McCall, 634-8191	American	$$-$$$	Y	Yes	L/D	Major
5	**McCall Brewing Company** 807 N 3rd St, McCall, 634-3309	American	$$	Y	B W	L/D	M V
5	**The Pancake and Christmas House** 209 N 3rd St, McCall, 634-5849	Family	$$	Y	N	B/L	M V
5	Bryan's Burger Den Fast Food 600 N 3rd St, McCall, 634-7964	Fast Food	$	Y	N	B/L/D	M V
5	Club House Restaurant 1001 Reedy Ln, McCall, 634-4867	American	$	N	N	B/L	Major
5	Home Town Pizza 617 1/2 N 3rd, McCall, 634-2596	Pizza	$	N	N	L/D	M V
5	Panda Chinese Restaurant 317 E Lake St, McCall, 634-2266	Asian	$-$$	N	N	L/D	Major
5	Subway 320 N 3rd, McCall, 634-2855	Fast Food	$	N	N	L/D	M V
5	The Taco Maker / Taco & More 147 N 3rd, McCall, 634-3671	Mexican	$	N	N	L/D	No
5	Silver Dollar Grill Yellow Pine, 633-6207	American	$-$$	N	B W	B/L/D	No
6	Donnelly Club 256 W Main, Donnelly, 325-8770	American	$	N	F B	B/L/D	Major
6	Fearless Farris Service Station - grocer 119 W Roseberry Rd, Donnelly, 325-8501	American	$	N	N	L	Major
7	Buzz City 301 S Main St, Cascade, 382-5498	Coffee/Deli	$	N	N	B/L	Major
7	Cascade Chef's Hut 806 S Hwy 55, Cascade, 382-4496	Family	$	Y	N	B/L/D	M V
7	Cougar Mountain Lodge 9738 Hwy 55, Cascade, 382-4464	American	$$	N	B W	B/L/D	M V
7	Howdy's Gas & Grub 503 N Main, Cascade, 382-6712	American	$	N	N	B/L/D	Major

Dining Quick Reference - continued

Price Range refers to the average cost of a meal per person: ($) $1-$6, ($$) $7-$11, ($$$) $12-up. Cocktails: "Yes" indicates full bar; Beer (B)/Wine (W), Service: Breakfast (B), Brunch (BR), Lunch (L), Dinner (D). Businesses in bold print will have additional information under the appropriate map locator number in the body of this section.

MAP NO.	RESTAURANT	TYPE CUISINE	PRICE RANGE	CHILD MENU	COCKTAILS BEER WINE	MEALS SERVED	CREDIT CARDS ACCEPTED
8	Banks Store and Cafe 54 Hwy 55, Banks, 793-2617	American	$$	Y	B W	L/D	Major
8	Carla's Kitchen 837 S Middlefork Rd, Garden Valley, 462-3200	Family	$$	Y	N	B/L/D	M V
8	Country Inn Banks Lowman Rd, Garden Valley, 462-3152	Family	$	Y	N	B/L	Major
8	Longhorn Restaurant & Saloon 1049 Old Crouch Rd, Garden Valley, 462-3108	American	$$	N	Yes	B/L/D	M V
8	Terrace Lakes Ranch Restaurant 101 Holiday Dr, Garden Valley, 462-3933	Family	$$	Y	N	B/L/D	M V
8	Longhorn Restaurant & Saloon 1 Hida Way # 17, Lowman, 462-3108	Steak/American	$$-$$$	Y	Yes	B/L/D	M V
9	Calamity Jayne's 201 Main, Idaho City, 392-4453	Family	$-$$	Y	N	B/L	M V
9	Diamond Lil's Steakhouse & Saloon 405 Main, Idaho City, 392-4400	Steakhouse	$-$$$	Y	Yes	L/D	Major
9	Gold Mine Eatery & Spirits 312 Hwy 21, Idaho City, 392-2233	American	$$-$$$	Y	Yes	B/L/D	Major
10	Cowboy Kettle Restaurant & Espresso 531 Hwy 52, Horseshoe Bend, 793-3374	Coffee/American	$$	Y	B W	B/L/D	Major
10	El-tennampa 400 Hwy 55 # C, Horseshoe Bend, 793-3258	Mexican	$-$$	N	B W	L/D	Major
10	Ola Inn 22001 Sweet Ola Hwy, Horseshoe Bend, 584-3737	Casual Fine Dining	$-$$	N	B W	B/L/D	No
10	Riverside Inn 101 Riverside Dr, Horseshoe Bend, 793-2651	Steak/American	$$-$$$	Y	B W	B/L/D	Major
10	Subway 459 Hwy 55, Horseshoe Bend, 793-3277	Fast Food	$$$	N	N	L/D	M V
10	Ola Inn 22001 Main, Ola, 584-3737	American	$	N	B	L	No
10	Calamity Jaynes 201 S Main St, Placerville, 392-4453	Family	$	Y	N	B/L	Major
11	Ann Roe Drive-in 929 S Washington Ave, Emmett, 365-9926	American	$	N	N	L/D	No
11	Arctic Circle 1205 S Washington Ave, Emmett, 365-1172	Fast Food	$	Y	N	L/D	M V
11	Beijing 913 S Washington Ave, Emmett, 365-3400	Asian	$$	N	N	L/D	Major
11	Blue Ribbon Cafe & Bakery 515 S Washington Ave, Emmett, 365-3290	Bakery/Café	$	Y	N	L/D	No
11	Bon Chente Mexican Store 142 E Main St, Emmett, 365-2139	Mexican	$$	N	N	L/D	Major
11	Emmett Chinese Cafe 414 S Washington Ave, Emmett, 365-5374	Asian	$	N	N	L/D	Major
11	GeriKen's Pancake & Steakhouse 2001 S Washington Ave, Emmett, 365-4703	Family/Steakhouse	$	Y	N	B/L	Major
11	Hometown Pizza 1109 S Washington Ave, Emmett, 365-7760	Pizza	$	N	N	L/D	No
11	La Costa 517 N Washington Ave, Emmett, 365-1567	Mexican	$-$$	N	N	L/D	Major
11	McDonald's 1335 S Washington Ave, Emmett, 365-1281	Fast Food	$	Y	N	B/L/D	Major
11	Pizza Factory 102 W 5th St B, Emmett, 398-7777	Pizza	$	N	B	L/D	M V
11	Pizza Hut 1580 S Washington Ave, Emmett, 365-5550	Pizza	$	N	N	B/L/D	No
11	Subway 620 Hwy 16, Emmett, 365-1100	Fast Food	$	N	N	L/D	Major
11	Swing Scene 1825 Hwy 16, Emmett, 365-4999	Casual Fine Dining	$$	Y	B W	B/L/D	Major

Dining Quick Reference - continued

Price Range refers to the average cost of a meal per person: ($) $1-$6, ($$) $7-$11, ($$$) $12-up. Cocktails: "Yes" indicates full bar; Beer (B)/Wine (W), Service: Breakfast (B), Brunch (BR), Lunch (L), Dinner (D). Businesses in bold print will have additional information under the appropriate map locator number in the body of this section.

MAP NO.	RESTAURANT	TYPE CUISINE	PRICE RANGE	CHILD MENU	COCKTAILS BEER WINE	MEALS SERVED	CREDIT CARDS ACCEPTED
11	Tacos Don Chente 114 N Commercial Ave, Emmett, 365-3948	Mexican	$	N	N	L/D	M V
11	Tik's Tavern 101 E Main St, Emmett, 365-3108	Tavern	$	N	Yes	L	Major
11	Timbers Restaurant 300 Hwy 16, Emmett, 365-6915	Steak/Seafood	$$	Y	B W	L/D	Major
11	Triangle Restaurant 8770 N Hwy 52, Emmett, 584-3246	Casual Fine Dining	$	Y	B W	B/L/D	M V
12	A&W Restaurant 2001 Hwy 30 W, Fruitland, 452-4236	Fast Food	$	Y	N	L/D	M V
12	Apple Bin 314 S W 3rd, Fruitland, 452-4173	Family	$	Y	N	B/L	Major
12	Country Choice Pizza 301 N Whitley Dr, Fruitland, 452-2300	Pizza	$	N	N	L/D	Major
12	Dolphie's Pizza 1619 N Whitley Dr, Fruitland, 452-7999	Pizza	$	N	N	L/D	Major
12	El Tenampa 1619 N Whitley Dr, Fruitland, 452-7533	Mexican	$	N	N	L/D	M V
12	Palisades Bar & Grill 4998 Sand Hollow Rd, Fruitland, 452-9303	American	$	N	Yes	L/D	Major
12	Subway 1611 N Whitley Dr, Fruitland, 452-6040	Fast Food	$	N	N	L/D	Major
12	A&W Restaurant 340 S Main, Payette, 642-2539	Fast Food	$	Y	N	L/D	M V
12	Burger King 305 S 16th St, Payette, 642-9519	Fast Food	$	Y	N	L/D	M V
12	Field Of Dreemz 120 N Main, Payette, 642-1877	Pizza	$	N	N	L/D	Major
12	Grandma's Kitchen 501 N 16, Payette, 642-8261	Family	$	Y	N	B/L/D	M V
12	Homestyle Pizza 844 6th Ave S F, Payette, 642-0177	Pizza	$	N	N	L/D	M V
12	Keystone Pizza 17 S Main, Payette, 642-9333	Pizza	$	N	N	L/D	M V
12	Mandarin Restaurant 107 N Main, Payette, 642-3567	Asian	$	N	N	L/D	M V
12	Arctic Circle 500 S 16th, Payette, 642-1038	Fast Food	$	Y	N	L/D	M V
12	Subway 18 S Main, Payette, 642-1080	Fast Food	$	N	N	L/D	M V
12	Tips Restaurant 136 S Main, Payette, 642-4109	American	$	N	N	L/D	M V
13	Stinker Stations Restaurant 5240 Black Canyon Exit 13, Caldwell, 454-8448	Family	$	Y	N	B/L/D	Major
13	Double Diamond Steakhouse & Bar 127 N Plymouth Ave, New Plymouth, 278-9282	Steakhouse	$	N	Yes	L	No
13	Palisades Bar & Grill 4998 Sand Hollow Rd, New Plymouth, 452-9303	American	$	N	Yes	L/D	No
13	Red Carpet Pizza & Cafe 116 S Plymouth Ave, New Plymouth, 278-5700	Pizza	$	N	N	L/D	M V
13	Todd's Burger Den 112 W Idaho, New Plymouth, 278-3580	Family	$	Y	N	B/L/D	Major
14	Frosty Palace Drive-inn Restaurants 203 N 9th St, Parma, 722-7007	Family	$	Y	N	L/D	M V
14	The Pizza Place 206 N 1st St, Parma, 722-6048	Pizza	$	N	N	L/D	M V
15	Greenleaf Cafe 21513 W Main St, Greenleaf, 459-8334	Family	$	Y	N	B/L	Major
15	Cindy's Coffee Shop 10 N Main St, Homedale, 337-5070	Coffee/American	$-$$	Y	N	B/L/D	Major

Dining Quick Reference - continued

Price Range refers to the average cost of a meal per person: ($) $1-$6, ($$) $7-$11, ($$$) $12-up. Cocktails: "Yes" indicates full bar; Beer (B)/Wine (W); Service: Breakfast (B), Brunch (BR), Lunch (L), Dinner (D). Businesses in bold print will have additional information under the appropriate map locator number in the body of this section.

MAP NO.	RESTAURANT	TYPE CUISINE	PRICE RANGE	CHILD MENU	COCKTAILS BEER WINE	MEALS SERVED	CREDIT CARDS ACCEPTED
15	Homedale Drive In 305 E Idaho Ave, Homedale, 337-4243	Family	$	Y	N	B/L/D	M V
15	Taco Bell 101 E Idaho Ave, Homedale, 337-5639	Fast Food	$	N	N	L/D	M V
15	Tc's 24-7 3 S Main St, Homedale, 337-4814	Pizza	$-$$	N	N	L/D	Major
16	Sandhollow Country Market Exit 17, Sand Hollow/Caldwell, 454-8686	American	$	N	N	L/D	Major
17	Farm Boy Drive In 103 W Main, Middleton, 585-9962	Family	$	Y	N	L/D	No
17	Garbonzo's Pizza 206 E Main, Middleton, 585-3083	Pizza	$	Y	N	L/D	M V
17	Jim's Burger Den 308 W Main, Middleton, 585-3097	Family	$	Y	N	L/D	No
17	Mr Moms Take N Bake 525 S Middleton Rd, Middleton, 585-9122	Pizza	$	N	N	L/D	M V
17	North St Cafe And Donut Shop 307 E 1st St , Middleton, 585-9160	Family	$	Y	N	L/D	No
17	Taco Bell 7 E Main, Middleton, 585-2896	Fast Food	$	Y	N	L/D	M V
17	The Sunrise Cafe 200 E Main, Middleton, 585-9700	Family	$-$$	Y	N	B/L/D	Major
17	Cup of Soul 10706 W State , Star, 286-7252	Coffee/Deli	$	Y	N	L	M V
17	Star Country Cafe 10883 W State, Star, 286-7799	Family	$$	Y	N	B/L/D	M V
18	Lakey's Cafe 5016 Hwy 20-26, Caldwell, 455-8654	Family	$	Y	N	L/D	M V
19	Covey Cafe 510 Simplot Blvd, Caldwell, 402-0011	American	$	Y	B W	B/L	Major
19	Frosty Palace Drive Inn 1302 Paynter Ave, Caldwell, 455-9699	Family	$	Y	N	L/D	No
19	Gem In & Out 322 E Cleveland Blvd, Caldwell, 459-0922	American	$	Y	N	L/D	No
19	Lundy Ranch Cafe 313 S Kimball Ave, Caldwell, 453-4895	Family	$	Y	N	B/L	M V
19	Sportsman Bar & Cafe 117 Everett St, Caldwell, 459-9881	American	$	N	Yes	L/D	Major
20	Acapulco Mexican Restaurant 702 Main St, Caldwell, 454-0425	Mexican	$$	N	N	L/D	Major
20	Brewed Awakenings Espresso 1102 E Cleveland Blvd, Caldwell, 454-9387	Coffee/Deli	$$	N	N	B/L/D	Major
20	Campos Market 517 Main St, Caldwell, 453-9311	Grocery/Deli	$$	N	N	L/D	No
20	Canton Cafe 902 E Cleveland Blvd, Caldwell, 454-1582	Asian	$-$$	N	N	L/D	Major
20	Carl's Junior 611 S 10th Ave, Caldwell, 455-2435	Fast Food	$-$$	Y	N	B/L/D	Major
20	Domino's Pizza 1123 E Cleveland Blvd, Caldwell, 454-8888	Pizza	$-$$	N	N	L/D	M V
20	Fiesta Guadalajara 420 N 10th Ave, Caldwell, 455-8605	Mexican	$$	N	N	L/D	Major
20	Golden Palace Restaurant 703 Main St, Caldwell, 459-4303	Asian	$-$$	Y	N	L/D	Major
20	Hamburger Connection 423 S 10th Ave, Caldwell, 454-8477	Family	$	Y	N	L/D	No
20	Jack In The Box 703 N 10th Ave, Caldwell, 454-6441	Fast Food	$	Y	N	L/D	No
20	Jack's Drive-In 1124 Cleveland Blvd, Caldwell, 459-9771	Family	$	Y	N	L/D	No

Dining Quick Reference - continued

Price Range refers to the average cost of a meal per person: ($) $1-$6, ($$) $7-$11, ($$$) $12-up. Cocktails: "Yes" indicates full bar; Beer (B)/Wine (W), Service: Breakfast (B), Brunch (BR), Lunch (L), Dinner (D). Businesses in bold print will have additional information under the appropriate map locator number in the body of this section.

MAP NO.	RESTAURANT	TYPE CUISINE	PRICE RANGE	CHILD MENU	COCKTAILS BEER WINE	MEALS SERVED	CREDIT CARDS ACCEPTED
20	Kentucky Fried Chicken 1003 E Cleveland Blvd, Caldwell, 454-1211	Fast Food	$	Y	N	L/D	Major
20	Las Enchiladas 420 N 5th Ave, Caldwell, 459-3003	Mexican	$	N	N	L/D	Major
20	Mariscos La Costena 320 N Kimball Ave, Caldwell, 453-1301	Mexican	$	N	N	L/D	M V
20	Mr V's Coffee Shop 407 N 10th Ave, Caldwell, 454-9778	Coffee/Deli	$	N	N	B/L	M V
20	Orphan Anne's Bar & Grill 801 Everett St, Caldwell, 455-2660	American	$	N	Yes	L/D	Major
20	Papa Murphy's Take 'N' Bake Pizza 922 Blaine St, Caldwell, 454-0444	Pizza	$	N	N	L/D	Major
20	Pizza Hut 710 N 10th Ave, Caldwell, 454-1341	Pizza	$	N	N	L/D	M V
20	Ritas Mexican Food & Grocery 707 Main St, Caldwell, 454-2200	Mexican	$	N	N	L/D	Major
20	Subway 319 N 10th Ave, Caldwell, 455-1225	Fast Food	$	Y	N	L/D	Major
20	The Dutch Goose 2502 E Cleveland Blvd, Caldwell, 459-9363	American	$	Y	Yes	L/D	M V
21	Airport Cafe 4601 Aviation Way, Caldwell, 453-2121	American	$$	N	N	L/D	Major
21	Beuk's Bagel and Deli 2609 Blaine St, Caldwell, 455-7842	Café/Deli	$	N	N	B/L	M V
21	Cattlemen's Cafe 1900 E Chicago St, Caldwell, 454-1785	Steakhouse	$$	Y	N	L/D	Major
21	Cooky's Famous Potato House 14949 Hwy 55, Caldwell, 459-8200	Family	$-$$	Y	N	B/L/D	Major
21	Creeks Grill 2805 Blaine St, Caldwell, 455-0100	American	$-$$	Y	Yes	L/D	Major
21	Daily Perks 101 N 21st Ave, Caldwell, 455-0300	Coffee/Deli	$-$$	N	N	B/L	Major
21	Dairy Queen 2324 Blaine St, Caldwell, 454-9927	Fast Food	$	N	N	L/D	No
21	Flying J 3512 Franklin Rd, Caldwell, 453-9225	Family	$	Y	N	B/L/D	Major
21	Golden Dragon Chinese & American Buffet 211 S 21st Ave, Caldwell, 455-7410	Asian/American	$$	N	N	L/D	Major
21	Great Western Pizza 2610 Blaine St, Caldwell, 459-1676	Pizza	$-$$	N	N	L/D	Major
21	Hometown Pizza 5210 E Cleveland Blvd, Caldwell, 459-2402	Pizza	$	N	N	L/D	Major
21	Idaho Pizza Company 4816 E Cleveland Blvd, Caldwell, 454-3000	Pizza	$	N	B W	L/D	Major
21	Imelda's Restaurant 2414 E Cleveland Blvd, Caldwell, 454-8757	Mexican	$	N	N	L/D	Major
21	Kentucky Fried Chicken/A&W 5102 E Cleveland Blvd, Caldwell, 454-8118	Fast Food	$	Y	N	L/D	Major
21	Mancino's Subs & Pizza 2412 E Cleveland Blvd, Caldwell, 459-7556	Pizza/American	$	N	N	L/D	M V
21	McDonald's 5108 Cleveland Blvd, Caldwell, 402-0024	Fast Food	$	Y	N	B/L/D	Major
21	McDonald's 2923 E Cleveland Blvd, Caldwell, 454-2993	Fast Food	$	Y	N	B/L/D	Major
21	Midway Lunch 6124 E Cleveland Blvd, Caldwell, 459-9944	Family	$	Y	N	L	No
21	Pepperoni's 3512 Franklin Rd, Caldwell, 454-7222	Pizza	$	N	N	L/D	Major
21	Perkins Restaurant & Bakery 909 Specht, Caldwell, 459-2904	Family	$-$$	Y	N	B/L/D	Major

Dining Quick Reference - continued

Price Range refers to the average cost of a meal per person: ($) $1-$6, ($$) $7-$11, ($$$) $12-up. Cocktails: "Yes" indicates full bar; Beer (B)/Wine (W), Service: Breakfast (B), Brunch (BR), Lunch (L), Dinner (D). Businesses in bold print will have additional information under the appropriate map locator number in the body of this section.

Section 3

MAP NO.	RESTAURANT	TYPE CUISINE	PRICE RANGE	CHILD MENU	COCKTAILS BEER WINE	MEALS SERVED	CREDIT CARDS ACCEPTED
21	Que Huong Vietnamese Restaurant 3110 E Cleveland Blvd, Caldwell, 454-0757	Asian	$	N	N	L/D	Major
21	Sage Travel Plaza 2929 Franklin Rd, Caldwell, 454-2084	Family	$	Y	N	B/L/D	Major
21	Subway 2803 Blaine St, Caldwell, 454-7827	Fast Food	$	Y	N	L/D	Major
21	Subway 5216 E Cleveland Blvd, Caldwell, 459-8887	Fast Food	$	Y	N	L/D	Major
21	Sunrise Family Restaurant 2601 E Cleveland Blvd, Caldwell, 459-8557	Family	$	Y	N	B/L/D	Major
21	T C B Y Treats 2609 Blaine St, Caldwell, 455-7842	Fast Food	$	Y	N	L/D	M V
21	Taco Bell 2807 E Cleveland Blvd, Caldwell, 454-9869	Fast Food	$	Y	N	L/D	M V
21	Taco Time 2605 Blaine St, Caldwell, 459-0211	Fast Food	$	Y	N	L/D	M V
21	Tacos Michoacan 605 N 5th Ave, Caldwell, 454-1583	Mexican	$	N	N	L/D	M V
21	Wendy's Old Fashioned Hamburgers 600 N 10th Ave, Caldwell, 459-7535	Fast Food	$	Y	N	L/D	M V
22	Applebee's Neighborhood Grill & Bar 1527 Caldwell Blvd, Nampa, 461-5330	American	$$	Y	Yes	L/D	Major
22	Arbys 1360 Caldwell Blvd, Nampa, 442-2969	Fast Food	$	Y	N	L/D	Major
22	Bamboo Garden 623 Caldwell Blvd, Nampa, 465-3552	Asian	$	N	N	L/D	Major
22	Blimpie Subs & Salads 2207 N Cassia St, Nampa, 467-5332	Fast Food	$	Y	N	L	Major
22	Carl's Junior 2034 Caldwell Blvd, Nampa, 461-1991	Fast Food	$	Y	N	L/D	No
22	Champions Sports Pub & Grill 1125 Caldwell Blvd, Nampa, 467-9722	American	$	N	B W	L/D	Major
22	Chicago Connection Pizza 1515 N Midland Blvd, Nampa, 467-1177	Pizza	$-$$	N	N	L/D	Major
22	Dairy Queen 809 Caldwell Blvd, Nampa, 466-2595	Fast Food	$	N	N	L/D	No
22	Denny's Restaurant 607 Nampa Blvd, Nampa, 467-6579	Family	$-$$	Y	N	B/L/D	Major
22	El Mineral Restaurant 2501 Caldwell Blvd, Nampa, 465-4616	Mexican	$	N	N	L/D	M V
22	Elliott's Sports Pub & Grill 1125 Caldwell Blvd, Nampa, 467-6811	American	$$	N	B W	L/D	Major
22	Garibaldi's 525 Caldwell Blvd, Nampa, 461-1420	Mexican	$$-$$$	Y	N	D	Major
22	Great Western Pizza 732 Caldwell Blvd, Nampa, 467-3336	Pizza	$	N	N	L/D	M V
22	J B's Family Restaurants 117 N Chaparral St, Nampa, 318-0044	Family	$-$$	Y	N	B/L/D	Major
22	Jade Garden Restaurant 1514 Caldwell Blvd, Nampa, 467-6611	Asian	$$	N	N	L/D	Major
22	Kentucky Fried Chicken 177 Caldwell Blvd, Nampa, 467-5529	Fast Food	$-$$	Y	N	L/D	Major
22	l Tenampa 248 Caldwell Blvd, Nampa, 466-4460	Mexican	$$	N	N	L/D	Major
22	Leonardi's Pizza 2020 Caldwell Blvd, Nampa, 466-3485	Pizza	$	N	N	L/D	M V
22	McDonald's 148 Caldwell Blvd, Nampa, 467-2012	Fast Food	$	Y	N	B/L/D	Major
22	Mongolian B B Q 1123 Caldwell Blvd, Nampa, 465-7860	Asian	$-$$	N	N	L/D	Major

Dining Quick Reference - continued

Price Range refers to the average cost of a meal per person: ($) $1-$6, ($$) $7-$11, ($$$) $12-up. Cocktails: "Yes" indicates full bar; Beer (B)/Wine (W), Service: Breakfast (B), Brunch (BR), Lunch (L), Dinner (D). Businesses in bold print will have additional information under the appropriate map locator number in the body of this section.

MAP NO.	RESTAURANT	TYPE CUISINE	PRICE RANGE	CHILD MENU	COCKTAILS BEER WINE	MEALS SERVED	CREDIT CARDS ACCEPTED
22	New York Burrito 2107 N Cassia St, Nampa, 466-2991	Mexican	$	N	N	L/D	M V
22	Outback Steakhouse 2011 W Karcher Rd, Nampa, 461-4585	Steakhouse	$-$$	Y	B W	L/D	Major
22	Papa Murphy's Take 'N' Bake Pizza Nampa 920 Caldwell Blvd, Nampa, 465-3555	Pizza	$$	Y	N	L/D	M V
22	Pizza Hut 140 Caldwell Blvd, Nampa, 467-4252	Pizza	$	N	N	L/D	M V
22	Quizno's 1240 Caldwell Blvd, Nampa, 461-4555	Fast Food	$	N	N	L/D	M V
22	Red Robin America's Gourmet Burgers & Spirits 2222 Cassia, Nampa, 463-8300	American	$	N	N	L/D	M V
22	Shanghai Restaurant 332 Caldwell Blvd, Nampa, 466-2921	Asian	$$	N	N	L/D	Major
22	Shari's Restaurant 1807 Caldwell Blvd, Nampa, 442-9631	Family	$$	Y	N	L/D	Major
22	Sizzler Restaurant 501 Caldwell Blvd, Nampa, 466-8570	Family	$$	Y	N	L/D	Major
22	Skipper's Seafood 'N Chowder 1124 Caldwell Blvd, Nampa, 467-3781	Seafood	$$	Y	N	L/D	Major
22	Subway 1104 Caldwell Blvd, Nampa, 466-7189	Fast Food	$	Y	N	L/D	M V
22	Taco Bell 1415 Caldwell Blvd, Nampa, 465-8030	Fast Food	$	Y	N	L/D	M V
22	Vip's Restaurant 607 Nampa Blvd, Nampa, 467-6579	Family	$$	Y	N	L/D	M V
22	Wendy's Old Fashioned Hamburgers 1028 Caldwell Blvd, Nampa, 466-9599	Fast Food	$	Y	N	L/D	M V
22	Yen Ching Express Nampa 2101 N Cassia St, Nampa, 467-9100	Asian	$	N	N	L/D	M V
23	Arctic Circle 1008 3rd St S, Nampa, 466-5256	Fast Food	$	Y	N	L/D	M V
23	Beefy's 1104 Garrity Blvd, Nampa, 466-6225	American	$	Y	N	L/D	M V
23	Blazen Burgers 216 1st Ave S, Nampa, 463-1985	American	$	N	N	L/D	No
23	Blimpie Subs and Salads 1507 12th Ave Rd, Nampa, 442-0022	Fast Food	$	Y	N	L	Major
23	Burger King 90 2nd St S, Nampa, 466-5517	Fast Food	$	Y	N	L/D	M V
23	Chicago Connection Pizza 523 12th Ave Rd, Nampa, 467-6444	Pizza	$-$$	N	N	L/D	Major
23	Cobby's Sandwich Shops 608 12th Ave S, Nampa, 461-3740	American/Deli	$	N	N	L/D	No
23	ConTreras Restaurant 1512 1st St S, Nampa, 442-0557	Mexican	$	Y	N	L/D	Major
23	Copper Canyon Restaurant 113 13th Ave S, Nampa, 461-0887	Fine Dining	$$-$$$	N	B W	L/D	Major
23	Dairy Queen 1211 12th Ave Rd, Nampa, 463-7739	Fast Food	$	N	N	L/D	No
23	Domino's Pizza 1011 12th Ave S, Nampa, 465-5555	Pizza	$-$$	N	N	L/D	M V
23	Dutch Inn-Quik Wok Restaurant 1120 12th Ave Rd, Nampa,	Asian	$	Y	N	L/D	Major
23	El Charro Cafe 1701 1st St N, Nampa, 467-5804	Mexican	$	N	N	L/D	M V
23	El Rinconcito 824 1st St S, Nampa, 466-6963	Mexican	$$	Y	N	L/D	Major
23	El Rodeo 908 3rd St S, Nampa, 463-1700	Mexican	$	N	N	L/D	M V

Dining Quick Reference - continued

Price Range refers to the average cost of a meal per person: ($) $1-$6, ($$) $7-$11, ($$$) $12-up. Cocktails: "Yes" indicates full bar; Beer (B)/Wine (W), Service: Breakfast (B), Brunch (BR), Lunch (L), Dinner (D). Businesses in bold print will have additional information under the appropriate map locator number in the body of this section.

MAP NO.	RESTAURANT	TYPE CUISINE	PRICE RANGE	CHILD MENU	COCKTAILS BEER WINE	MEALS SERVED	CREDIT CARDS ACCEPTED
23	Elmer's Breakfast Lunch & Dinner 1411 Shilo Dr, Nampa, 466-7945	Family	$	Y	N	B/L/D	Major
23	Goyito's Restaurant 1512 1st St S, Nampa, 442-0557	Mexican	$$	Y	N	D	Major
23	Idaho Pizza Company 104 W Iowa Ave, Nampa, 467-1900	Pizza	$	N	N	L/D	Major
23	Jack In The Box 804 12th Ave Rd, Nampa, 467-2023	Fast Food	$	Y	N	L/D	No
23	Jack In The Box 1700 Franklin Blvd, Nampa, 463-0301	Fast Food	$	Y	N	L/D	No
23	La Parrila Juarez 16 12th Ave S, Nampa, 465-0073	Mexican	$$	N	N	L/D	Major
23	Le Baron's Honker Cafe 1210 2nd St S, Nampa, 466-1551	Family	$	Y	N	B/L	Major
23	Mancino's Baked Subs & Pizza 220 1/2 Holly St, Nampa, 466-2129	Pizza	$	N	N	L/D	M V
23	McDonald's 2100 12th Ave Rd, Nampa, 466-7228	Fast Food	$	Y	N	B/L/D	Major
23	McDonald's 1108 12th Ave Rd, Nampa, 463-4077	Fast Food	$	Y	N	B/L/D	Major
23	Noodle's Pizza-Pasta-Pizzazz 1802 Franklin Blvd, Nampa, 466-4400	Pizza/Italian	$	N	N	L/D	M V
23	Papa John's Pizza 604 12th Ave S, Nampa, 461-4600	Pizza	$	N	N	L/D	M V
23	Papa Murphy's Take 'N' Bake Pizza Nampa 2420 12th Ave Rd, Nampa, 466-8777	Pizza	$$	Y	N	L/D	M V
23	Pizza Hut 611 12th Ave Rd, Nampa, 466-6005	Pizza	$	N	N	L/D	M V
23	Round Table Pizza 2310 12th Ave S, Nampa, 468-7800	Pizza	$	N	N	L/D	Major
23	Sawtooth Pizza Company 16466 Franklin Rd, Nampa, 468-1500	Pizza	$	N	N	L/D	M V
23	Shilo Inn Restaurant 1401 Shilo Dr, Nampa, 465-5908	Family	$	Y	N	L/D	Major
23	Southern Barbeque Grill 218 12th Ave S, Nampa, 465-4510	American	$$	N	N	L/D	Major
23	Squeezers Giant Burgers 2121 12th Ave Rd, Nampa, 466-5455	Family	$$	Y	N	L/D	Major
23	Subway 16476 Franklin Blvd, Nampa, 466-3310	Fast Food	$	Y	N	L/D	M V
23	Subway 604 12th Ave Rd, Nampa, 466-2332	Fast Food	$	Y	N	L/D	M V
23	Subway 2410 12th Ave Rd, Nampa, 442-0335	Fast Food	$	Y	N	L/D	M V
23	Super Pollo Mexican Grill 1204 12th Ave S, Nampa, 466-6112	Mexican	$	N	N	L/D	M V
23	Taco Jalisco 219 11th Ave N, Nampa, 465-5788	Mexican	$	N	N	L/D	M V
23	Taco John's 624 12th Ave Rd, Nampa, 466-0946	Fast Food	$	N	N	L/D	M V
24	El Chalateco 2707 Garrity Blvd, Nampa, 442-8813	Mexican	$$	Y	N	L/D	Major
24	Kentucky Fried Chicken 145 E Maine Ave, Nampa, 466-4584	Fast Food	$-$$	Y	N	L/D	Major
24	McDonald's 4412 Garrity Blvd, Nampa, 466-9096	Fast Food	$	Y	N	B/L/D	Major
24	Mega Bites Restaurant 3008 Garrity Blvd, Nampa, 467-3990	Family	$	Y	N	B/L/D	Major
24	Runway Cafe 101 Municipal Dr, Nampa, 468-3033	American	$	N	N	B/L	Major

Ultimate Idaho Atlas and Travel Encyclopedia

Dining Quick Reference - continued

Price Range refers to the average cost of a meal per person: ($) $1-$6, ($$) $7-$11, ($$$) $12-up. Cocktails: "Yes" indicates full bar; Beer (B)/Wine (W), Service: Breakfast (B), Brunch (BR), Lunch (L), Dinner (D). Businesses in bold print will have additional information under the appropriate map locator number in the body of this section.

MAP NO.	RESTAURANT	TYPE CUISINE	PRICE RANGE	CHILD MENU	COCKTAILS BEER WINE	MEALS SERVED	CREDIT CARDS ACCEPTED
24	Saigon Restaurant 3107 Garrity Blvd, Nampa, 463-9001	Asian	$$	N	N	L/D	Major
24	Tj Milanos Pizzerias 2817 Garrity Blvd, Nampa, 463-1888	Pizza	$	N	N	L/D	M V
25	Caba's Restaurant & Lounge Marsing, 896-4182	American/Tavern	$-$$	N	Yes	L/D	Major
25	Pepe's Pizza 429 Main St, Marsing, 896-4555	Pizza	$-$$	N	N	L/D	M V
25	Sandbar River House Restaurant 18 Sandbar Ave, Marsing, 896-4124	American	$-$$	Y	B W	L/D	Major
25	Whitehouse Drive Inn & Motel 909 W Main St, Marsing, 896-4130	American	$	N	N	B/L/D	No
26	Arctic Circle Restaurant 710 E Avalon, Kuna, 922-4200	Fast Food	$	Y	N	L/D	M V
26	El Gallo Giro 482 W Main St, Kuna, 922-5169	Mexican	$	N	N	L/D	M V
26	Fiesta Guadalajara 780 W Avalon, Kuna, 922-4311	Mexican	$	N	N	L/D	M V
26	Fresh Express Take N Bake 290 W Main St, Kuna, 922-4100	Pizza	$	N	N	L/D	Major
26	Hong Kong Express 726 E Avalon, Kuna, 922-4951	Asian	$	N	N	L/D	M V
26	Idaho Pizza Co 331 Ave E, Kuna, 922-5032	Pizza	$	N	N	L/D	M V
26	Quik Wok Restaurant 361 W Main St, Kuna, 922-4088	Asian	$	N	N	L/D	M V
26	Red Eye 414 W Main St, Kuna, 922-5086	Tavern	$	N	Yes	B/L/D	Major
26	Taco Bell 330 W Main St, Kuna, 922-5492	Fast Food	$	N	N	L/D	M V
27	Blue Canoe 16479 State Hwy 78, Melba, 495-2269	Fine Dining	$$$	Y	B W	D	Major
27	Cook's Two Hole Bar & Grill 313 Broadway Ave, Melba, 495-9784	American	$-$$	N	B W	L/D	No
28	Beacon Light Subway 12795 Hwy 55, Meridian, 938-6237	Fast Food	$	N	N	L/D	Major
28	Burger King 6350 N Discovery Wy, Meridian, 321-1935	Fast Food	$	Y	N	L/D	M V
28	Jack in the Box 6030 N Eagle Rd, Meridiane, 938-5606	Fast Food	$	Y	N	L/D	No
28	Lindy's Steak House 6290 N Meeker Ave, Meridian, 375-1310	Steakhouse	$$-$$$	N	Yes	L/D	Major
28	Papa Murphy's 13613 W McMillan Rd, Meridian, 938-0005	Pizza	$	N	N	L/D	M V
28	Taco Del Mar 13613 W McMillan Rd, Meridian, 939-4750	Fast Food	$	N	N	L/D	M V
28	Andrade's Mexican Restaurant 2031 E Fairview, Meridian, 401-0138	Mexican	$-$$	N	B W	L/D	Major
28	Applebee's Neighborhood Grill & Bar 1460 N Eagle Rd, Meridian, 855-0343	American	$$	Y	Yes	L/D	Major
28	Arbys 1270 N Eagle Rd, Meridian, 855-9599	Fast Food	$	Y	N	L/D	Major
28	Arctic Circle 1625 W Franklin Rd, Meridian, 898-9200	Fast Food	$	Y	N	L/D	M V
28	Baja Taco 1735 W Franklin Rd, Meridian, 888-4142	Mexican	$	N	N	L/D	M V
28	Bangkok House Thai Restaurant 1890 E Fairview Ave, Meridian, 884-0302	Asian	$-$$	N	N	L/D	Major
28	Blimpie Subs & Salads 521 N Main St, Meridian, 887-1234	Fast Food	$	Y	N	L	Major

Price Range refers to the average cost of a meal per person: ($) $1-$6, ($$) $7-$11, ($$$) $12-up. Cocktails: "Yes" indicates full bar; Beer (B)/Wine (W), Service: Breakfast (B), Brunch (BR), Lunch (L), Dinner (D). Businesses in bold print will have additional information under the appropriate map locator number in the body of this section.

MAP NO.	RESTAURANT	TYPE CUISINE	PRICE RANGE	CHILD MENU	COCKTAILS BEER WINE	MEALS SERVED	CREDIT CARDS ACCEPTED
28	Bolo's Pub & Eatery 601 S Main St, Meridian, 884-3737	American/Tavern	$-$$	N	B W	L/D	Major
28	Burger King 300 E Fairview Ave, Meridian, 887-2198	Fast Food	$	Y	N	L/D	M V
28	Cabin Fever Pizza & Treats 965 E Ustick Rd, Meridian, 887-6672	Pizza	$	N	N	L/D	M V
28	Carl's Junior 1320 N Eagle Rd, Meridian, 855-2370	Fast Food	$	Y	N	B/L	Major
28	China Wok 993 S Progress Ave, Meridian, 884-1555	Asian	$-$$	N	N	L/D	Major
28	Corona Village 21 E Fairview Ave, Meridian, 887-9348	Mexican	$$-$$$	Y	Yes	L/D	Major
28	Dairy Queen 107 E Watertower Ln, Meridian, 888-9029	Fast Food	$	N	N	L/D	No
28	Dancing Dog Coffee House 10 W Franklin Rd, Meridian, 887-3684	Coffee/American	$	N	B W	L	Major
28	Domino's Pizza 1701 W Cherry Ln, Meridian, 887-6400	Pizza	$-$$	N	N	L/D	M V
28	El Tenampa 906 N Main St, Meridian, 888-4089	Mexican	$$	N	B W	L/D	Major
28	Epi's Basque Restaurant 1115 N Main St, Meridian, 884-0142	Ethnic	$$	N	B W	D	Major
28	Express Cafe 400 E Fairview Ave, Meridian, 888-3745	Family	$-$$	Y	N	B/L/D	Major
28	Fiesta Guadalajara 704 E Fairview Ave, Meridian, 884-0161	Mexican	$$	N	B W	L/D	Major
28	Goodwood Barbeque Company 1140 N Eagle Rd, Meridian, 884-1021	American	$$-$$$	Y	Yes	L/D	Major
28	Harry's Bar & Grill 704 N Main St, Meridian, 888-9868	American	$$	N	Yes	L/D	Major
28	Hometown Pizza 1800 N Locust Grove Rd, Meridian, 884-4725	Pizza	$	N	N	L/D	M V
28	Idaho Pizza Company 405 E Fairview Ave, Meridian, 888-4441	Pizza	$	N	N	L/D	M V
28	International House Of Pancakes 3525 E Fairview Ave, Meridian, 888-1216	Family	$-$$	Y	N	B/L/D	Major
28	J B's Restaurant 1565 S Meridian Rd, Meridian, 887-6722	Family	$-$$	Y	N	B/L/D	Major
28	Jack in the Box 207 E Fairview Ave, Meridian, 884-8992	Fast Food	$	Y	N	L/D	No
28	Johnny Carino's Italian Restaurant 3551 E Fairview Ave, Meridian, 888-7801	Italian	$$-$$$	Y	Yes	L/D	Major
28	Kentucky Fried Chicken/A&W 677 E 1st St, Meridian, 888-7446	Fast Food	$-$$	Y	N	L/D	Major
28	Kahootz Pub & Eatery 1603 E 1st St, Meridian, 895-9861	American	$-$$	Y	B W	L/D	Major
28	Lotus Garden Chinese Restaurant 2120 E Fairview Ave, Meridian, 288-2772	Asian	$$	N	N	L/D	Major
28	Louie's Pizza & Italian Restaurant 2500 E Fairview Ave, Meridian, 884-5200	Pizza/Italian	$$	Y	B W	L/D	M V
28	McDonald's 603 S Eagle Rd, Meridian, 288-1687	Fast Food	$	Y	N	B/L/D	Major
28	McDonald's 1710 E Fairview Ave, Meridian, 887-1565	Fast Food	$	Y	N	B/L/D	M V
28	McDonald's 195 E Central Dr, Meridian, 888-4348	Fast Food	$	Y	N	B/L/D	Major
28	Miss Tami's Cottage And Tea Room 1031 N Main St, Meridian, 888-6829	Teahouse/Fine Dining	$$	N	N	B/L	M V
28	Mongolian Grill 519 E Fairview Ave, Meridian, 288-2288	Asian	$	N	N	L/D	Major

Dining Quick Reference - continued

Price Range refers to the average cost of a meal per person: ($) $1-$6, ($$) $7-$11, ($$$) $12-up. Cocktails: "Yes" indicates full bar; Beer (B)/Wine (W), Service: Breakfast (B), Brunch (BR), Lunch (L), Dinner (D). Businesses in bold print will have additional information under the appropriate map locator number in the body of this section.

MAP NO.	RESTAURANT	TYPE CUISINE	PRICE RANGE	CHILD MENU	COCKTAILS BEER WINE	MEALS SERVED	CREDIT CARDS ACCEPTED
28	Panda Express 1500 N Eagle Rd, Meridian, 288-2203	Asian	$-$$	N	N	L/D	Major
28	Papa John's Pizza 1526 N Main St, Meridian, 888-7272	Pizza	$	N	N	L/D	M V
28	Papa Murphy's Take 'N' Bake Pizza 3317 W Cherry Ln, Meridian, 884-8333	Pizza	$-$$	N	N	L/D	Major
28	Pier 49 Pizza 1551 W Cherry Ln, Meridian, 888-4921	Pizza	$-$$	N	N	L/D	M V
28	Pizza Hut 675 S Progress Ave, Meridian, 888-1771	Pizza	$	N	N	L/D	Major
28	Port of Subs 3355 E Fairview Ave, Meridian, 888-7827	American/Deli	$	N	N	L/D	M V
28	Primo's 3909 E Fairview Ave, Meridian, 855-0288	Pizza/Italian	$	Y	N	L/D	M V
28	Quarter Circle Diamond Bbq 7080 W Mcmillan Rd, Meridian, 286-7115	American	$$-$$$	Y	B W	L/D	Major
28	Quik Wok Restaurant 3055 E Fairview Ave, Meridian, 888-3373	Asian	$	N	N	L/D	M V
28	Quizno's 3909 E Fairview Ave, Meridian, 888-6060	Fast Food	$	N	N	L/D	M V
28	Ram Restaurant & Brewery 3272 E Pine Ave, Meridian, 888-0314	American	$-$$	Y	Yes	L/D	Major
28	Round Table Pizza 499 S Main St, Meridian, 887-1100	Pizza	$	N	N	L/D	M V
28	Royal Dynasty Chinese Rstrnt 72 E Fairview Ave, Meridian, 888-6262	Asian	$	N	N	L/D	Major
28	Sa-Wad-Dee Thai Restuarant 1890 E Fairview Ave, Meridian, 884-0701	Asian	$$	N	N	L/D	Major
28	Shari's Restaurant 895 S Progress Ave, Meridian, 884-1100	Family	$-$$	Y	N	L/D	Major
28	Smoky Mountain Pizza & Pasta 114 E Idaho, Meridian, 884-1067	Pizza/Italian	$	N	N	L/D	M V
28	Sonic Drive In 2160 E Fairview Ave, Meridian, 888-7110	Fast Food	$	N	N	L/D	M V
28	Subway 1890 E Fairview Ave Ste A, Meridian, 888-4204	Fast Food	$	N	N	L/D	M V
28	Subway 1518 N Main St, Meridian, 887-7756	Fast Food	$	N	N	L/D	M V
28	Subway 3030 E Magic View Dr, Meridian, 288-2454	Fast Food	$	N	N	L/D	M V
28	Sunrise Bakery & Cafe 805 N Main St, Meridian, 888-4517	Bakery/Café	$	Y	N	L/D	No
28	Taco Bell 645 N Main St, Meridian, 884-0091	Fast Food	$	Y	N	L/D	M V
28	Taco Bell 3101 E Magic View Dr, Meridian, 884-1729	Fast Food	$	Y	N	L/D	M V
28	Taco Del Mar 1535 W Franklin Rd, Meridian, 884-0829	Fast Food	$	N	N	L/D	M V
28	Taco Time 785 S Progress Ave, Meridian, 887-1973	Fast Food	$	N	N	L/D	M V
28	Teriyaki Stix 1835 W Cherry Ln, Meridian, 288-1896	Asian	$	Y	N	L/D	Major
28	Texas Roadhouse 3801 E Fairview Ave, Meridian, 887-9401	Steak/American	$$-$$$	Y	Yes	D	Major
28	Tony Romas - Famous For Ribs 790 Progress Ave, Meridian, 895-8466	Steakhouse	$$-$$$	Y	Yes	D	Major
28	Vina Vietnamese Restaurant 1534 N Main St, Meridian, 888-1378	Asian	$$	N	N	L/D	Major
28	West Of Philly Cheese Steaks 3355 E Fairview Ave, Meridian, 895-0144	American	$-$$	Y	N	L/D	Major

Dining Quick Reference - continued

Price Range refers to the average cost of a meal per person: ($) $1-$6, ($$) $7-$11, ($$$) $12-up. Cocktails: "Yes" indicates full bar; Beer (B)/Wine (W), Service: Breakfast (B), Brunch (BR), Lunch (L), Dinner (D). Businesses in bold print will have additional information under the appropriate map locator number in the body of this section.

MAP NO.	RESTAURANT	TYPE CUISINE	PRICE RANGE	CHILD MENU	COCKTAILS BEER WINE	MEALS SERVED	CREDIT CARDS ACCEPTED
28	Whitewater Pizza & Pasta 1510 N Eagle Rd, Meridian, 888-6611	Pizza/Italian	$	Y	N	L/D	Major
28	Winger's Diner 1701 E Fairview Ave, Meridian, 888-1030	American	$$	Y	B W	L/D	Major
29	Casa Mexico 393 W State St, Eagle, 939-7795	Mexican	$	N	N	L/D	Major
29	Chicago Connection Pizza 344 W State St, Eagle, 939-9100	Pizza	$-$$	N	N	L/D	Major
29	China Palace Restaurant 625 E State St, Eagle, 939-8938	Asian	$$	N	N	L/D	Major
29	DaVinci's 190 E State St, Eagle, 939-2500	Italian	$$	Y	Yes	L/D	Major
29	Domino's Pizza 498 E State St, Eagle, 939-4440	Pizza	$	N	N	L/D	M V
29	McDonald's 178 S Eagle Rd, Eagle, 938-0031	Fast Food	$	Y	N	B/L/D	Major
29	Mongolian Of Eagle 362 S Eagle Rd, Eagle, 938-0585	Asian	$$	N	N	L/D	M V
29	Pizza Hut 398 S Eagle Rd, Eagle, 938-9090	Pizza	$	N	N	L/D	Major
29	Quiznos 664 Rivershore Ln, Eagle, 319-0358	Fast Food	$	Y	N	L/D	Major
29	River Rock Alehouse 228 E Plaza, Eagle, 938-4788	American	$$	N	Yes	L/D	Major
29	Road House BBQ 1059 E Iron Eagle Dr , Eagle, 939-8108	American	$$	Y	B W	L/D	Major
29	Roque's 3210 E Chinden Blvd, Eagle, 938-6111	Mexican	$-$$	Y	B W	B/L/D	M V
29	Round Table Pizza 395 W State St, Eagle, 939-2900	Pizza	$	N	N	L/D	No
29	Sakura Sushi 3210 E Chinden Blvd 138, Eagle, 938-1599	Asian	$$	Y	N	L/D	Major
29	Smoky Mountain Pizza & Pasta 34 E State St, Eagle, 939-0212	Pizza/Italian	$$	Y	B W	L/D	Major
29	Subway Sandwiches & Salads 182 E State St, Eagle, 939-4567	Fast Food	$	N	N	L/D	Major
29	The Banbury Restaurant 2626 N Marypost Place, Eagle, 939-4600	Family	$	Y	N	L/D	M V
29	The Blue Moose Cafe 79 E Aikens Rd, Eagle, 939-3079	Family	$	Y	N	L/D	M V
29	Villano's Specialty Market & Deli 3220 E Chinden Blvd, Eagle, 939-7001	Deli	$	N	N	L	Major
29	Wendy's Old Fashioned Hamburgers 65 E Eagle River Dr, Eagle, 939-8717	Fast Food	$	Y	N	L/D	Major
31	A&W Family Restaurant 350 N Milwaukee, Boise, 375-3074	Fast Food	$	Y	N	L/D	Major
31	American Catering 7700 Goddard Rd, Boise, 375-5333	American	$		N	L	Major
31	Applebee's Neighborhood Grill & Bar 7845 W Emerald, Boise, 378-1890	American	$$	Y	Yes	L/D	Major
31	Arby's 5941 Fairview Ave, Boise, 376-4448	Fast Food	$	Y	N	L/D	Major
31	Arby's 989 N Milwaukee, Boise, 672-8807	Fast Food	$	Y	N	L/D	Major
31	Bad Boy Burgers 2 7000 Fairview Ave, Boise, 373-0020	Family	$	Y	N	B/L/D	Major
31	Baja Fresh Mexican Grill 992 N Milwaukee, Boise, 327-0099	Mexican	$	Y	N	L/D	Major
31	Bangkok Thai Restaurant 477 N Milwaukee, Boise, 375-0946	Asian	$	N	N	D	Major

Ultimate Idaho Atlas and Travel Encyclopedia

Dining Quick Reference - continued

Price Range refers to the average cost of a meal per person: ($) $1-$6, ($$) $7-$11, ($$$) $12-up. Cocktails: "Yes" indicates full bar; Beer (B)/Wine (W), Service: Breakfast (B), Brunch (BR), Lunch (L), Dinner (D). Businesses in bold print will have additional information under the appropriate map locator number in the body of this section.

MAP NO.	RESTAURANT	TYPE CUISINE	PRICE RANGE	CHILD MENU	COCKTAILS BEER WINE	MEALS SERVED	CREDIT CARDS ACCEPTED
31	Blimpie Subs & Salad 9140 W Emerald , Boise, 321-9222	Fast Food	$	Y	N	L	Major
31	Blue Jeans Cafe 9140 W Emerald 300, Boise, 658-5053	American	$	N	N	L/D	Major
31	Boise Towne Square - Dairy Queen 350 N Milwaukee St Ste 2053, Boise, 378-0303	Fast Food	$	N	N	L/D	No
31	Borders Books, Music, Movies, & Cafe 1123 N Milwaukee, Boise, 322-6669	Coffee/Café	$	N	N	L	M V
31	Burger King 280 N Milwaukee St, Boise, 323-0171	Fast Food	$	Y	N	L/D	M V
31	By the Sea 350 N Milwaukee St, Boise, 375-3665	Seafood	$-$$	Y	N	L/D	M V
31	Cafe' Ole' Restaurants 210 N Milwaukee, Boise, 322-0222	Mexican	$$	Y	Yes	L/D	Major
31	California Market 8069 W Fairview Ave, Boise, 378-0566	American	$-$$	N	N	L/D	M V
31	Carl's Junior 493 N Milwaukee, Boise, 658-7746	Fast Food	$	Y	N	B/L/D	M V A
31	Casa Mexico 10332 Fairview Ave, Boise, 375-0342	Mexican	$-$$	Y	Yes	L/D	M V A
31	Chef Express Chinese Food 1098 N Orchard St (near Exit 4), Boise, 331-2885	Asian	$	N	N	L/D	M V
31	Chiang Ma Thai Restaurant 4898 Emerald St, Boise, 342-4051	Asian	$$	N	N	L/D	Major
31	Chicago Connection Pizza 7070 Fairview Ave, Boise, 377-5551	Pizza	$$	Y	N	L/D	Major
31	Chili's Grill & Bar 7997 W Franklin Rd, Boise, 327-0088	American	$$	Y	Yes	L/D	Major
31	Chuck E Cheese's 6255 W Fairview Ave, Boise, 322-1833	Pizza/Family	$	N	N	L/D	M V
31	Crescent "No Lawyers" Bar & Grill 5500 W Franklin Rd, Boise, 322-9856	American	$$	N	Yes	L/D	Major
31	Dairy Queen 5711 W Franklin Rd, Boise, 343-0239	Fast Food	$	N	N	L/D	No
31	Domino's Pizza 10384 Fairview Ave, Boise, 377-5201	Pizza	$-$$	N	N	L/D	M V
31	Edo Japan 350 N Milwaukee, Boise, 377-4652	Asian	$-$$	N	N	L/D	Major
31	Elmer's Breakfast-Lunch-Dinner 6767 Fairview Ave, Boise, 376-6767	American	$-$$	Y	B W	B/L/D	Major
31	Fresh Off The Hook Seafood 507 N Milwaukee, Boise, 322-9224	Seafood	$$-$$$	Y	B W	L/D	Major
31	Golden Corral 8460 W Emerald, Boise, 373-7118	American	$$-$$$	N	N	B/L/D	M V
31	Golden Wheel Drive-In 11100 W Fairview Ave, Boise, 375-4262	Family	$	Y	N	L/D	No
31	Idaho Pizza Company 7100 Fairview Ave, Boise, 375-4100	Pizza	$-$$	N	B W	L/D	Major
31	International House Of Pancakes 7959 W Emerald St, Boise, 322-4467	Family	$-$$	Y	N	B/L/D	Major
31	Jack In The Box 205 N Milwaukee, Boise, 327-0100	Fast Food	$	Y	N	L/D	No
31	Jack In The Box 3220 N Cole Rd, Boise, 322-5005	Fast Food	$	Y	N	L/D	No
31	JJ North's Country Buffet 6681 Fairview Ave, Boise, 375-7161	American	$-$$	N	N	L/D	M V
31	Kim's Oriental Restaurant 8061 Fairview Ave, Boise, 321-7800	Asian	$-$$	N	N	L/D	Major
31	Kyoto Japanese Steak House & Sushi Bar 6002 Fairview Ave, Boise, 378-8808	Asian	$-$$	N	N	L/D	Major

Dining Quick Reference - continued

Price Range refers to the average cost of a meal per person: ($) $1-$6, ($$) $7-$11, ($$$) $12-up. Cocktails: "Yes" indicates full bar; Beer (B)/Wine (W), Service: Breakfast (B), Brunch (BR), Lunch (L), Dinner (D). Businesses in bold print will have additional information under the appropriate map locator number in the body of this section.

MAP NO.	RESTAURANT	TYPE CUISINE	PRICE RANGE	CHILD MENU	COCKTAILS BEER WINE	MEALS SERVED	CREDIT CARDS ACCEPTED
31	Little Caesars Pizza 1471 N Milwaukee, Boise, 672-9334	Pizza	$	N	N	L/D	Major
31	Lone Star Steakhouse & Saloon 8799 W Franklin Rd, Boise, 377-5565	Steakhouse	$$-$$$	Y	Yes	L/D	Major
31	Los Mariachis Mexican Restaurant 6565 Fairview Ave, Boise, 323-5917	Mexican	$-$$	Y	N	L/D	Major
31	Marie Callender's Restaurant & Bakeries 8574 Fairview Ave, Boise, 375-7744	American/Bakery	$-$$$	Y	Yes	B/L/D	Major
31	Mario's Pizza 350 N Milwaukee, Boise, 322-1722	Pizza	$-$$	N	N	L/D	M V
31	McDonald's 9804 Fairview Ave, Boise, 321-0922	Fast Food	$	Y	N	B/L/D	Major
31	McDonald's 350 N Milwaukee, Boise, 375-7707	Fast Food	$	Y	N	B/L/D	Major
31	McDonald's 2510 Fairview Ave, Boise, 344-9040	Fast Food	$	Y	N	B/L/D	Major
31	McDonald's 8571 W Franklin Rd, Boise, 375-0444	Fast Food	$	Y	N	B/L/D	Major
31	Mongolian Stir Fry 8037 Fairview Ave, Boise, 376-3662	Asian	$-$$	Y	N	L/D	Major
31	Olive Garden Italian Restaurant 320 N Milwaukee, Boise, 322-3327	Italian	$$-$$$	Y	Yes	L/D	Major
31	Panda Express 350 N Milwaukee, Boise, 323-8697	Asian	$-$$	N	N	L/D	Major
31	Panda Express #810 1124 N Milwaukee, Boise, 321-0350	Asian	$-$$	N	N	L/D	Major
31	Papa John's Pizza 3379 N Five Mile Rd, Boise, 377-5050	Pizza	$	N	N	L/D	M V
31	Papa Murphy's Take 'N' Bake Pizza 7320 Fairview Ave, Boise, 658-1155	Pizza	$	N	N	L/D	M V
31	Pizza Hut 10659 W Fairview Ave, Boise, 375-2919	Pizza	$	N	N	L/D	M V
31	Pizza Hut 5859 Fairview Ave, Boise, 376-3291	Pizza	$	N	N	L/D	M V
31	Pojos 7736 Fairview Ave, Boise, 376-6981	Family	$-$$	Y	N	L/D	Major
31	Popeye's Famous Fried Chicken 8840 Fairview Ave, Boise, 376-1266	Fast Food	$$	Y	N	L/D	Major
31	Quizno's 8665 W Franklin Rd, Boise, 323-4516	Fast Food	$-$$	Y	N	L/D	Major
31	Red Lobster 550 N Milwaukee St, Boise, 672-1188	Seafood	$$	Y	N	L/D	Major
31	Red Robin America's Gourmet Burgers & Spirits 267 N Milwaukee, Boise, 323-0023	Family	$	Y	N	L/D	M V
31	Rio Grande 1950 Fairmeadow Dr, Boise, 377-8810	Mexican	$	Y	N	L/D	Major
31	Rockies Car Hop 4822 Fairview Ave, Boise, 323-0787	Family	$	Y	N	L/D	Major
31	Romano's Macaroni Grill 980 N Milwaukee, Boise, 323-4445	Italian	$$-$$$	Y	Yes	L/D	Major
31	Saigon Grill 8053 W Emerald, Boise, 375-7655	Asian	$$	N	N	L/D	Major
31	Sam's Place 3395 N Five Mile Rd, Boise, 376-0074	American	$$	N	Yes	L/D	M V
31	Shari's Restaurant 8521 W Franklin Rd, Boise, 322-3696	Family	$$	Y	N	L/D	Major
31	Sizzler Restaurants 459 N Cole Rd, Boise, 322-2930	Family	$$	Y	N	L/D	Major
31	Skipper's Seafood 'n Chowder House 5588 Fairview Ave, Boise, 377-4370	Seafood	$$	Y	N	L/D	Major

Ultimate Idaho Atlas and Travel Encyclopedia

Dining Quick Reference - continued

Price Range refers to the average cost of a meal per person: ($) $1-$6, ($$) $7-$11, ($$$) $12-up. Cocktails: "Yes" indicates full bar; Beer (B)/Wine (W), Service: Breakfast (B), Brunch (BR), Lunch (L), Dinner (D). Businesses in bold print will have additional information under the appropriate map locator number in the body of this section.

MAP NO.	RESTAURANT	TYPE CUISINE	PRICE RANGE	CHILD MENU	COCKTAILS BEER WINE	MEALS SERVED	CREDIT CARDS ACCEPTED
31	Sockeye Grill & Brewery 3019 N Cole Rd, Boise, 658-1533	American	$$	N	B W	L/D	Major
31	Sonic Drive In 10480 W Ustick Rd, Boise, 323-1172	Fast Food	$-$$	Y	N	L/D	M V
31	Subway 1120 N Milwaukee, Boise, 672-8146	Fast Food	$$	N	B W	L/D	Major
31	Subway 7180 Fairview Ave, Boise, 322-3434	Fast Food	$-$$	Y	N	L/D	M V
31	Subway 10715 W Fairview Ave, Boise, 375-8525	Fast Food	$-$$	Y	N	L/D	M V
31	T G I Friday's 600 N Milwaukee, Boise, 373-0889	American	$$	Y	Yes	L/D	Major
31	Taco Bell 6521 Fairview Ave, Boise, 378-4548	Fast Food	$	N	N	L/D	M V
31	Taco Time 350 N Milwaukee, Boise, 322-1707	Fast Food	$	N	N	L/D	M V
31	Taco Time 7965 Fairview Ave, Boise, 376-3281	Fast Food	$	N	N	L/D	M V
31	Taj Mahal 10548 Fairview Ave, Boise, 327-4500	Ethnic	$$-$$$	Y	B W	L/D	Major
31	The Capri Restaurant 2520 Fairview Ave, Boise, 342-1442	Family	$$	Y	N	B/L	Major
31	The Great Steak & Fry Company 350 N Milwaukee, Boise, 376-5011	Steakhouse	$-$$	N	B W	L/D	Major
31	Vien Dong Vietnamese Restaurant 8716 Fairview Ave, Boise, 376-9881	Asian	$$	N	N	L/D	No
31	Wendy's Old Fashioned Hamburgers 8100 W Franklin Rd, Boise, 377-5900	Fast Food	$	N	N	L/D	M V
31	Wendy's Old Fashioned Hamburgers 6615 Fairview Ave, Boise, 375-4441	Fast Food	$-$$	Y	N	L/D	M V
31	Wok-Inn Noodle 4912 W Emerald, Boise, 343-7262	Asian	$	N	N	L/D	M V
31	Yen Ching Express 132 N Milwaukee, Boise, 375-7557	Asian	$$	N	N	L/D	Major
32	A&W Restaurant 13375 W Chinden Blvd, Boise, 938-3437	Fast Food	$	Y	N	L/D	Major
32	Addie's 501 W Main, Boise, 388-1198	Family	$$	Y	N	B/L	Major
32	Angell's Bar & Grill 999 W Main St, Boise, 342-4900	American	$$$	Y	Yes	L/D	Major
32	Applebee's Bar & Grill 7253 W State St, Boise, 853-2330	American	$$	Y	Yes	L/D	Major
32	Applebee's Bar & Grill 7025 Glenwood St, Boise, 853-2330	American	$$	Y	Yes	L/D	Major
32	Aquacuisine 12554 W Bridger St Ste 120, Boise, 323-2782	Seafood	$$	N	N	L/D	Major
32	Asiago's Downtown 1002 W Main St, Boise, 336-5552	Italian/Fine Dining	$	N	N	L/D	Major
32	Aubergine 250 S 5th St, Boise, 381-0034	American	$$	N	N	B/L	M V
32	Balcony 150 N 8th St Ste 224, Boise, 336-1313	Tavern	$$	N	N	L/D	M V
32	Bar Time Lounge 10th & Main, Boise, 336-9100	Tavern	$	N	Yes	L/D	Major
32	Bardenay Restaurant & Distillery 610 Grove, Boise, 426-0538	International	$$-$$$	N	Yes	L/D	Major
32	Basque Pub & Eatery-Bar Gernika 202 S Capitol Blvd, Boise, 344-2175	Ethnic/Basque	$$	N	BW	L/D	Major
32	Big City Coffee & Cafe 5517 W State, Boise, 853-9161	Coffee/Café	$	N	N	L	M V

Dining Quick Reference - continued

Price Range refers to the average cost of a meal per person: ($) $1-$6, ($$) $7-$11, ($$$) $12-up. Cocktails: "Yes" indicates full bar; Beer (B)/Wine (W), Service: Breakfast (B), Brunch (BR), Lunch (L), Dinner (D). Businesses in bold print will have additional information under the appropriate map locator number in the body of this section.

MAP NO.	RESTAURANT	TYPE CUISINE	PRICE RANGE	CHILD MENU	COCKTAILS BEER WINE	MEALS SERVED	CREDIT CARDS ACCEPTED
32	Bittercreek Ale House 246 N 8th St, Boise, 343-3119	American	$$-$$$	N	BW	L/D	Major
32	Blimpie Subs & Salads 1781 W State, Boise, 333-8888	Fast Food	$	Y	N	L	Major
32	Blimpie Subs & Salads 233 S Capitol Blvd, Boise, 472-3698	Fast Food	$	Y	N	L	Major
32	Boise Cafe 219 N 10th, Boise, 343-3397	Bakery/Deli	$	N	N	L	M V
32	Boogie Woogie 800 W Idaho, Boise, 367-0040	American	$$	N	Yes	L/D	Major
32	Burger King 1700 W State St, Boise, 343-6565	Fast Food	$	Y	N	L/D	M V
32	Burger King 6770 Glenwood St, Boise, 853-8389	Fast Food	$	Y	N	L/D	M V
32	Burger n Brew 4295 W State, Boise, 345-7700	American	$$	Y	Yes	L/D	Major
32	Cafe Ole Restaurant & Cantina 404 S 8th Ste 216, Boise, 322-0222	Mexican	$$	Y	Yes	L/D	Major
32	Casa Mexico 1605 N 13th, Boise, 333-8330	Mexican	$-$$	Y	Yes	L/D	M V A
32	Cazba-Downtown Mediterranean & Greek Food 211 N 8th, Boise, 381-0222	Greek/Mediterranean	$$	Y	Yes	L/D	Major
32	Chicago Connection Pizza 310 N 4th St, Boise, 345-3278	Pizza	$$	Y	N	L/D	Major
32	Corona Village 4334 W State St, Boise, 338-9707	Mexican	$$	N	B W	L/D	Major
32	Cottonwood Grille 913 W River, Boise, 333-9800	American	$$-$$$	Y	Yes	L/D	Major
32	Domino's Pizza 5000 W State, Boise, 853-6060	Pizza	$-$$	N	N	L/D	M V
32	Eddie's Diner 3095 N Lakeharbor Ln, Boise, 853-9800	Family	$$	Y	N	B/L/D	Major
32	Elmer's Breakfast-Lunch-Dinner 1385 S Capitol Blvd, Boise, 343-5714	American	$-$$	Y	B W	B/L/D	Major
32	Emilio's 245 S Capitol Blvd, Boise, 333-8002	Italian	$-$$	Y	Yes	L/D	Major
32	Falcon Tavern 780 W Idaho, Boise, 947-3111	Tavern	$-$$	N	Yes	L/D	Major
32	Fanci Freez 1402 W State, Boise, 344-8661	Fast Food	$	Y	N	L/D	M V
32	Flying Pie Pizzaria 4320 W State St, Boise, 384-0000	Pizza	$-$$	N	N	L/D	M V
32	Gino's Italian Ristorante 150 N 8th, Boise, 331-3771	Italian	$-$$$	Y	B W	L/D	Major
32	Grape Escape Wine Bar 800 W Idaho, Boise, 368-0200	Latin	$$-$$$	N	B W	L/D	Major
32	Guido's Original New York Style Pizza 235 N 5th, Boise, 345-9011	Pizza	$-$$	N	B W	L/D	No
32	Harrys Of Hyde Park 1501 N 13th, Boise, 336-9260	American	$-$$	Y	B W	L/D	Major
32	Highlands Hollow Brewhouse 2455 Harrison Hollow, Boise, 343-6820	American	$$-$$$	Y	B W	L/D	Major
32	Idaho Pizza Company 6840 Glenwood, Boise, 853-1224	Pizza	$-$$	N	B W	L/D	Major
32	Jades Chopstick 6970 W State, Boise, 853-1302	Asian	$-$$	N	N	L/D	M V
32	Jan's Cafeteria 650 W State, Boise, 336-3663	American	$-$$	N	N	B/L/D	M V
32	Jim's Coffee Shop 812 W Fort, Boise, 343-0154	Coffee/Café	$-$$	N	N	L/D	M V

Dining Quick Reference - continued

Price Range refers to the average cost of a meal per person: ($) $1-$6, ($$) $7-$11, ($$$) $12-up. Cocktails: "Yes" indicates full bar; Beer (B)/Wine (W), Service: Breakfast (B), Brunch (BR), Lunch (L), Dinner (D). Businesses in bold print will have additional information under the appropriate map locator number in the body of this section.

MAP NO.	RESTAURANT	TYPE CUISINE	PRICE RANGE	CHILD MENU	COCKTAILS BEER WINE	MEALS SERVED	CREDIT CARDS ACCEPTED
32	Joe's Crab Shack 2288 N Garden, Boise, 336-9370	Seafood	$$	Y	N	L/D	Major
32	Kentucky Fried Chicken 13373 W Chinden Blvd, Boise, 938-3437	Fast Food	$-$$	Y	N	L/D	Major
32	Kentucky Fried Chicken 3220 W State St, Boise, 342-8162	Fast Food	$-$$	Y	N	L/D	Major
32	Korea House 160 N 8th, Boise, 345-6262	Asian	$-$$	N	N	L/D	Major
32	Las Fuentes 6882 W State, Boise, 853-6770	Mexican	$-$$	Y	N	L/D	Major
32	Le Cafe De Paris 204 N Capitol Blvd, Boise, 336-0889	French	$-$$	Y	N	L/D	Major
32	Los Mariachi's Mexican Restaurant 8305 W State St, Boise, 853-0290	Mexican	$-$$	Y	N	L/D	Major
32	Louie's Pizza & Italian Restaurant 620 W Idaho, Boise, 344-5200	Pizza/Italian	$-$$	Y	N	L/D	Major
32	Lucky 13 Pizza 1602 N 13th, Boise, 344-6967	Pizza	$-$$	N	N	L/D	Major
32	Madhuban Indian Cuisine 6930 W State, Boise, 853-8215	Ethnic	$-$$$	Y	N	L/D	Major
32	Mai Thai Restaurant & Bar 750 W Idaho, Boise, 344-8424	Asian	$-$$	N	N	L/D	M V
32	Manhattan Grill 622 W Idaho St, Boise, 331-1131	Family	$-$$	Y	N	L/D	Major
32	McDonald's 4825 Glenwood St, Boise, 323-1094	Fast Food	$	Y	N	B/L/D	M V
32	Merritt's Country Cafe 6630 W State, Boise, 853-9982	Family	$-$$	Y	N	L/D	M V
32	Milkyway 816 W Bannock St Ste C, Boise, 343-4334	American	$$	Y	N	L/D	Major
32	Mona Lisa Fondue Restaurant Downtown, Boise, 336-8699	Eclectic	$$	N	N	L/D	M V
32	Mongolian BBQ 6920 W State, Boise, 853-7964	Asian	$-$$	Y	N	L/D	Major
32	Montego Bay 3000 N Lakeharbor Ln, Boise, 853-5070	Fine Dining	$$-$$$	Y	B W	L/D	Major
32	Mortimer's Idaho Cuisine 110 S 5th, Boise, 338-6550	Regional	$-$$	Y	N	L/D	Major
32	Mosaic Gallery Bar 500 W Main, Boise, 338-5006	Fine Dining	$$-$$$	N	Yes	L/D	Major
32	M's Wine Bar 10th & Main, Boise, 336-9100	Tavern	$$	N	B W	L/D	Major
32	Mulligans' Golf Pub & Eatery 1009 W Main, Boise, 336-6998	American	$-$$	N	B W	L/D	Major
32	New York Burrito 1754 W State, Boise, 424-1950	Mexican	$	N	N	L/D	M V
32	North End Chinese Rest 1806 W State, Boise, 343-1080	Asian	$$	N	N	L/D	M V
32	Old Chicago 730 W Idaho, Boise, 363-0037	Pizza/Italian	$$	Y	B W	L/D	Major
32	O'Michael's Pub & Grill 2433 Bogus Basin Rd, Boise, 342-8948	American	$$	N	Yes	L/D	Major
32	Pac-Out 2315 Harrison Blvd, Boise, 338-9627	American	$	N	N	L/D	M V
32	Pair Restaurant 601 Main St, Boise, 343-7034	Casual Fine Dining	$-$$	Y	N	L/D	M V
32	Pantry Restaurant 1545 Shoreline Dr, Boise, 344-5486	American	$-$$	Y	N	B/L	Major
32	Papa Joes Pizza 1301 S Capitol Blvd, Boise, 344-7272	Pizza	$	N	N	L/D	M V

Dining Quick Reference - continued

Price Range refers to the average cost of a meal per person: ($) $1-$6, ($$) $7-$11, ($$$) $12-up. Cocktails: "Yes" indicates full bar; Beer (B)/Wine (W). Service: Breakfast (B), Brunch (BR), Lunch (L), Dinner (D). Businesses in bold print will have additional information under the appropriate map locator number in the body of this section.

MAP NO.	RESTAURANT	TYPE CUISINE	PRICE RANGE	CHILD MENU	COCKTAILS BEER WINE	MEALS SERVED	CREDIT CARDS ACCEPTED
32	Papa Murphy's Take 'N' Bake Pizza 1736 W State, Boise, 336-0011	Pizza	$	N	N	L/D	M V
32	Papa Murphy's Take 'N' Bake Pizza 7084 W State, Boise, 853-8882	Pizza	$	N	N	L/D	M V
32	Pizza Hut 818 Ann Morrison Park Dr, Boise, 344-7041	Pizza	$	N	N	L/D	M V
32	Pizzalchik 7300 W State, Boise, 853-7757	Pizza/Salad/Chicken	$$	N	N	L/D	Major
32	Poblanos 199 N 8th St, Boise, 395-7000	Mexican	$$	N	N	L/D	Major
32	Pollo Rey Mexican Rotisserie 222 N 8th St, Boise, 345-0323	Mexican	$$	Y	N	L/D	M V
32	Quizno's 6944 W State, Boise, 854-1914	Fast Food	$-$$	Y	N	L/D	Major
32	Quizno's 9351 W State St, Boise, 853-6100	Fast Food	$-$$	Y	N	L/D	Major
32	Reef 125 S 6th, Boise, 287-9200	Casual Fine Dining	$$-$$$	Y	N	L/D	Major
32	Richard's Bakery & Cafe 1513 N 13th St, Boise, 368-9629	Bakery/Café	$	Y	N	L/D	Major
32	Roque's 2870 W State, Boise, 343-7211	Mexican	$$	Y	B W	L/D	M V
32	Santa Maria Barbeque Co 5459 Glenwood St, Boise, 938-6128	American	$$	N	N	L/D	M V
32	Satchel's Grill 705 W Bannock, Boise, 344-3752	American	$$	N	N	L/D	Major
32	Save On Café 106 S 16th, Boise, 342-9022	Family	$	Y	N	L/D	M V
32	Senor Fresh Mexican Eatery 12375 Chinden Blvd, Boise, 378-1888	Mexican	$$	N	N	L/D	M V
32	Shige Japanese Cuisine 100 N 8th, Boise, 338-8423	Asian	$$	N	N	L/D	Major
32	Smoke Inn 3912 W State, Boise, 344-7334	American	$$	N	N	L/D	Major
32	Smoky Mountain Pizza & Pasta 1805 W State, Boise, 387-2727	Pizza/Italian	$-$$	N	N	L/D	Major
32	Square 750 W Main, Boise, 345-7782	French	$$	N	B W	L/D	M V A
32	State Court Cafe 2907 W State, Boise, 367-0751	Deli	$$	N	B W	L/D	Major
32	Stubs Sports Pub 12505 Chinden Blvd, Boise, 378-8273	American	$$	N	B W	L/D	Major
32	Subway 3220 W State, Boise, 336-2224	Fast Food	$-$$	Y	N	L/D	M V
32	Sunrise Family Restaurant 7135 W State, Boise, 853-2037	Family	$-$$	Y	N	L/D	M V
32	TableRock Brewpub & Grill 705 Fulton, Boise, 342-0944	American	$$	N	B W	L/D	Major
32	Tepanyaki Japanese Steak House 2197 N Garden, Boise, 343-3515	Asian	$$	Y	B W	L/D	Major
32	The Edge Pastry Shop 1105 W Idaho, Boise, 344-5383	Bakery/Café	$	N	N	B/L	Major
32	The Pita Pit 746 W Main, Boise, 388-1900	Fast Food	$-$$	N	N	L/D	M V
32	The Sports Zone 245 S Capitol Blvd, Boise, 472-3333	American	$$	N	B W	L/D	Major
32	Top Wok 12375 Chinden Blvd, Boise, 327-8889	Asian	$$	Y	B W	L/D	Major
32	Viking Drive In 3790 W State, Boise, 342-7289	Family	$	Y	N	L/D	M V

Dining Quick Reference - continued

Price Range refers to the average cost of a meal per person: ($) $1-$6, ($$) $7-$11, ($$$) $12-up. Cocktails: "Yes" indicates full bar; Beer (B)/Wine (W), Service: Breakfast (B), Brunch (BR), Lunch (L), Dinner (D). Businesses in bold print will have additional information under the appropriate map locator number in the body of this section.

MAP NO.	RESTAURANT	TYPE CUISINE	PRICE RANGE	CHILD MENU	COCKTAILS BEER WINE	MEALS SERVED	CREDIT CARDS ACCEPTED
32	Wendy's Old Fashioned Hamburgers 3680 W State, Boise, 344-8284	Fast Food	$-$$	Y	N	L/D	M V
32	Yen Ching Chinese Restaurant 305 N 9th, Boise, 384-0384	Asian	$$	N	N	L/D	Major
32	Zen Bento 103 N 10th, Boise, 388-8808	Asian/Sushi	$$	Y	N	L/D	Major
32	Zutto Japanese Restaurant 615 W Main, Boise, 388-8873	Asian	$$	Y	N	L/D	Major
32	Arbys 8117 W Chinden Blvd, Garden City, 672-8806	Fast Food	$	Y	N	L/D	Major
32	Boise's Ultimate Sports Bar 5504 Alworth St, Garden City, 376-6563	American	$	N	Yes	L	Major
32	Burger King 6770 Glenwood St, Garden City, 853-8389	Fast Food	$	Y	N	L/D	M V
32	Chapala Mexican Restaurant 5697 Glenwood St, Garden City, 321-8262	Mexican	$-$$	N	N	L/D	Major
32	China One International Buffet 5181 Glenwood St, Garden City, 373-5806	Asian	$	N	N	L/D	Major
32	Cobby's Sandwich Shops 4348 W Chinden Blvd, Garden City, 322-7401	American/Deli	$	N	N	L	Major
32	El Gallo 5165 Glenwood St, Garden City, 321-0355	Mexican	$	Y	N	L/D	Major
32	Fortune Wok 5161 Glenwood St, Garden City, 378-4645	Asian	$	N	N	L/D	Major
32	Golden Wok 3948 W Chinden Blvd, Garden City, 336-3399	Asian	$	N	N	L/D	Major
32	Howard's Cafe 6932 W State St, Garden City, 853-4641	American	$	N	N	L	M V
32	Madhuban Indian Cuisine 6930 W State St, Garden City, 853-8215	Ethnic	$$	N	N	D	Major
32	McDonald's 4825 Glenwood St, Garden City, 323-1094	Fast Food	$	Y	N	B/L/D	Major
32	Michael's Kitchens 410 E 41st St, Garden City, 424-7743	American	$$	N	N	L/D	No
32	Mongolian Barbeque 6920 W State St, Garden City, 853-7964	Asian	$$	N	N	L/D	Major
32	Moxie Java 9275 W Chinden Blvd, Garden City, 375-7562	Coffee/Deli	$	N	N	L	Major
32	Pizza Hut 5285 Glenwood St, Garden City, 322-5562	Pizza	$	N	N	L/D	Major
32	Players Pub and Grill 5504 Alworth St, Garden City, 376-6563	American	$	N	N	L	M V
32	Round Table Pizza 5865 Glenwood St, Garden City, 658-7800	Pizza	$	N	N	L/D	Major
32	Shari's Restaurant 8121 W Chinden Blvd, Garden City, 378-4700	Family	$$	Y	N	L/D	Major
32	Taco Bell 8109 W Chinden Blvd, Garden City, 377-2888	Fast Food	$	N	N	L/D	M V
32	Granny's Restaurant 6736 Glenwood St, Garden City, 853-4327	Family	$	Y	N	B/L	Major
33	A Taste of Heaven Bakery 10703 W Smoke Ranch Dr, Boise, 888-2727	Bakery	$	N	N	B/L	M V
33	Big Bun Drive In 5816 Overland Rd, Boise, 375-5361	Family	$	Y	N	L/D	M V
33	Blimpie Subs & Salads 5120 Overland Rd, Boise, 333-0444	Fast Food	$	Y	N	L	Major
33	Burger King 4800 Overland Rd, Boise, 343-8991	Fast Food	$	Y	N	L/D	M V
33	Casa Mexico 1459 S Vinnell Wy, Boise, 321-8302	Mexican	$-$$	Y	Yes	L/D	M V A

Dining Quick Reference - continued

Price Range refers to the average cost of a meal per person: ($) $1-$6, ($$) $7-$11, ($$$) $12-up. Cocktails: "Yes" indicates full bar; Beer (B)/Wine (W), Service: Breakfast (B), Brunch (BR), Lunch (L), Dinner (D). Businesses in bold print will have additional information under the appropriate map locator number in the body of this section.

MAP NO.	RESTAURANT	TYPE CUISINE	PRICE RANGE	CHILD MENU	COCKTAILS BEER WINE	MEALS SERVED	CREDIT CARDS ACCEPTED
33	Catalinas Taco Loco 4518 W Overland Rd, Boise, 368-9654	Mexican	$	N	N	L/D	M V
33	Chicago Connection Pizza 3931 W Overland Rd, Boise, 344-6838	Pizza	$-$$	N	N	L/D	Major
33	Chicago Connection Pizza 5 Mile & Overland, Boise, 323-0126	Pizza	$-$$	N	N	L/D	Major
33	Chuck A Rama Buffet 7901 W Overland Rd, Boise, 327-4800	American	$$	N	N	L/D	Major
33	Cracker Barrel Old Country Store 1733 S Cole Rd, Boise, 321-8280	Family	$-$$$	Y	N	B/L/D	Major
33	Dairy Queen 10264 W Overland Rd, Boise, 323-2658	Fast Food	$	N	N	L/D	No
33	Domino's Pizza 8966 W Ardene, Boise, 658-5555	Pizza	$-$$	N	N	L/D	M V
33	Eat-A-Burger 601 N Cole Rd, Boise, 323-9412	Family	$	Y	N	L/D	M V
33	Eddie's Restaurant 7067 Overland Rd, Boise, 377-3340	Family	$-$$	Y	N	B/L/D	Major
33	El Gringo 5506 Overland Rd, Boise, 377-2387	Mexican	$	N	N	L/D	Major
33	Guido's Original New York Pizza 3415 N Cole Rd, Boise, 322-9045	Pizza	$-$$	N	B W	L/D	No
33	Idaho Pizza Company 4218 Overland Rd, Boise, 343-5455	Pizza	$-$$	N	B W	L/D	Major
33	Jack in the Box 10496 W Overland Rd, Boise, 658-0508	Fast Food	$	Y	N	L/D	No
33	Johnny Carino's Italian Restaurant 1700 S Entertainment Ave, Boise, 373-4968	Italian	$$-$$$	N	B W	L/D	Major
33	Kentucky Fried Chicken 8440 W Overland Rd, Boise, 322-6372	Fast Food	$-$$	Y	N	L/D	Major
33	Kentucky Fried Chicken 3575 Overland Rd, Boise, 344-1573	Fast Food	$-$$	Y	N	L/D	Major
33	McDonald's 7222 W Overland Rd, Boise, 377-1808	Fast Food	$	Y	N	B/L/D	M V
33	McDonald's 7222 Overland Rd, Boise, 375-7381	Fast Food	$	Y	N	B/L/D	Major
33	McDonald's 8300 W Overland Rd, Boise, 376-7340	Fast Food	$	Y	N	B/L/D	Major
33	McGrath's Fish House 1749 S Cole Rd, Boise, 375-6300	Seafood	$$-$$$	Y	Yes	L/D	Major
33	Mike's Hillcrest Restaurant & Lounge 5264 Overland Rd, Boise, 345-5572	Steakhouse	$-$$	N	Yes	L/D	Major
33	On The Border Mexican Grill & Cantina 7802 Spectrum, Boise, 322-8145	Mexican	$$	Y	N	L/D	Major
33	Outback Steakhouse 7189 Overland Rd, Boise, 323-4230	Steakhouse	$$-$$$	Y	B W	L/D	Major
33	Panda Garden 2801 W Overland Rd, Boise, 433-4235	Asian	$-$$	N	N	L/D	Major
33	Papa Murphy's Take 'N' Bake Pizza 10545 Overland Rd, Boise, 375-8700	Pizza	$	N	N	L/D	M V
33	Pollo Rey Mexican Rotisserie 7709 Overland Rd, Boise, 375-4642	Mexican	$$	Y	N	L/D	M V
33	Port Of Subs 8162 W Overland Rd, Boise, 378-4900	American/Deli	$	N	N	L/D	Major
33	Pronto Pups & State Fair Lemonades 7709 W Overland Rd, Boise, 377-1425	Family	$	Y	N	L/D	No
33	Raedeans Restaurant 4969 Overland Rd, Boise, 336-2201	American	$$	Y	N	L/D	Major
33	River Rock Alehouse 8915 W Overland Rd, Boise, 322-8288	American	$$	N	B W	L/D	Major

Dining Quick Reference - continued

Price Range refers to the average cost of a meal per person: ($) $1-$6, ($$) $7-$11, ($$$) $12-up. Cocktails: "Yes" indicates full bar; Beer (B)/Wine (W), Service: Breakfast (B), Brunch (BR), Lunch (L), Dinner (D). Businesses in bold print will have additional information under the appropriate map locator number in the body of this section.

MAP NO.	RESTAURANT	TYPE CUISINE	PRICE RANGE	CHILD MENU	COCKTAILS BEER WINE	MEALS SERVED	CREDIT CARDS ACCEPTED
33	Rockies Diner 3900 Overland Rd, Boise, 336-2878	Family	$	Y	N	L/D	Major
33	Round Table Pizza 10412 Overland Rd, Boise, 672-7878	Pizza	$$	N	N	L/D	M V
33	Round Table Pizza 5120 Overland Rd, Boise, 331-7979	Pizza	$	N	N	L/D	M V
33	Shakey's Pizza Parlor 4903 Overland Rd, Boise, 344-1234	Pizza	$	N	N	L/D	M V
33	Sonic Drive-In 8777 W Overland Rd, Boise, 322-2605	Fast Food	$-$$	Y	N	L/D	M V
33	Sports Pub & Grill 7609 W Overland Rd, Boise, 377-1819	American	$$	Y	Yes	L/D	M V
33	Taco Bell 7070 Overland Rd, Boise, 323-2857	Fast Food	$	N	N	L/D	M V
33	Taco Time 6940 Overland Rd, Boise, 376-3621	Fast Food	$	N	N	L/D	M V
33	The Chef's Hut 164 S Cole Rd, Boise, 376-3125	Family	$	Y	N	L/D	M V
33	The Pizza Pipeline 10489 W Overland Rd, Boise, 321-9800	Pizza	$$	N	N	L/D	Major
33	West Of Philly Cheese Steaks 7609 W Overland Rd, Boise, 658-1781	American	$-$$	N	N	L/D	M V
33	Yen Ching Overland Restaurant 7609 W Overland Rd, Boise, 378-5888	Asian	$$	N	N	L/D	Major
33	Zone Idaho 3085 N. Cole Rd, Boise, 321-1118	American	$$	N	N	L/D	Major
34	Burger Time 1273 S Orchard, Boise, 385-9951	Family	$	Y	N	L/D	M V
34	Golden Star Restaurant 1142 N Orchard, Boise, 336-0191	Family	$-$$	Y	N	L/D	M V
34	Jack In The Box 1302 S Orchard, Boise, 342-2666	Fast Food	$	Y	N	L/D	No
34	McDonald's 510 N Orchard, Boise, 336-0711	Fast Food	$	Y	N	B/L/D	Major
34	Quiznos 1216 N Orchard, Boise, 336-8102	Fast Food	$-$$	Y	N	L/D	Major
34	Sonic Drive-In 851 N Orchard, Boise, 327-9999	Fast Food	$-$$	Y	N	L/D	M V
34	Tsuru 303 N Orchard, Boise, 323-8822	Asian	$$	N	N	L/D	Major
34	Wendy's Old Fashioned Hamburgers 1450 S Orchard, Boise, 344-4411	Fast Food	$-$$	Y	N	L/D	M V
35	Anton Airfood Of Boise Inc 3201 Airport Way , Boise, 424-1042	American	$$	N	Yes	L/D	Major
35	Bad Boy Burgers 815 S Vista Ave, Boise, 331-1580	Family	$	Y	N	B/L/D	Major
35	Big Juds 1289 Protest Ave, Boise, 343-4439	Family	$-$$	Y	N	L/D	Major
35	Cheyenne's Vista Bistro 650 N Vista, Boise, 713-4495	American	$$	N	B W	L/D	Major
35	Denny's Restaurant 2580 Airport Way, Boise, 344-9092	Family	$-$$	Y	N	L/D	Major
35	Din Fung Buffet 925 S Vista Ave, Boise, 367-1688	Asian	$-$$	Y	N	L/D	Major
35	Domino's Pizza 1013 S Vista Ave, Boise, 343-5995	Pizza	$-$$	N	N	L/D	M V
35	Europe Delicious 1204 Vista Ave, Boise, 367-9109	Ethnic	$-$$	N	N	L/D	Major
35	Johnny's 1201 S Vista Ave, Boise, 331-1173	American/Caribbean	$-$$	N	N	L/D	Major

Dining Quick Reference - continued

Price Range refers to the average cost of a meal per person: ($) $1-$6, ($$) $7-$11, ($$$) $12-up. Cocktails: "Yes" indicates full bar; Beer (B)/Wine (W), Service: Breakfast (B), Brunch (BR), Lunch (L), Dinner (D). Businesses in bold print will have additional information under the appropriate map locator number in the body of this section.

MAP NO.	RESTAURANT	TYPE CUISINE	PRICE RANGE	CHILD MENU	COCKTAILS BEER WINE	MEALS SERVED	CREDIT CARDS ACCEPTED
35	McDonald's 1185 S Vista Ave, Boise, 336-4110	Fast Food	$	Y	N	B/L/D	Major
35	McDonald's 2323 S Vista Ave, Boise, 345-9545	Fast Food	$	Y	N	B/L/D	Major
35	McDonald's 2828 Airport Way, Boise, 367-9221	Fast Food	$	Y	N	B/L/D	Major
35	Papa Murphy's Take 'N' Bake Pizza 1340 S Vista Ave, Boise, 345-2220	Pizza	$	N	N	L/D	M V
35	Pizza Hut 2450 S Vista Ave, Boise, 343-0199	Pizza	$	N	N	L/D	M V
35	Quinn's Restaurant & Lounge 1005 S Vista Ave, Boise, 342-9568	Steakhouse	$$	Y	Yes	L/D	Major
35	Rooster's Eatery & Deli 930 S Vista Ave, Boise, 336-9300	Family/Deli	$$	Y	N	L/D	Major
35	Subway 3201 Airport Way, Boise, 343-3010	Fast Food	$-$$	Y	N	L/D	M V
35	Taco Time 405 S Vista Ave, Boise, 343-0932	Fast Food	$	N	N	L/D	M V
35	Varsity Sports Bar And Grill 3201 Airport Way, Boise, 344-2874	American	$$	N	Yes	L/D	Major
36	Aladdin Egyptian Restaurant 111 Broadway Ave, Boise, 368-0880	Ethnic	$$	N	BW	B/L/D	M V
36	Arby's 3500 S Findley Ave, Boise, 344-0735	Fast Food	$	Y	N	L/D	Major
36	Aubergine 415 E Parkcenter Blvd, Boise, 429-8775	American	$$	N	N	B/L	M V A
36	Bandara Grill Park Center Blvd, Boise, 343-3430	Steakhouse	$$	Y	Yes	L/D	Major
36	Berryhill & Co Cafe And Wine Bar 2170 Broadway Ave, Boise, 387-3553	Fine Dining	$$-$$$	Y	BW	L/D	M V
36	Blimpie's 2475 S Apple, Boise, 345-4250	Fast Food	$	Y	N	L	Major
36	Burger King 1121 Broadway Ave, Boise, 336-9544	Fast Food	$	Y	N	L/D	M V
36	Buster's Restaurant 1326 Broadway Ave, Boise, 345-5688	American	$$	Y	Yes	L/D	Major
36	Carl's Junior 226 Broadway Ave, Boise, 344-7664	Fast Food	$	Y	N	B/L/D	M V A
36	Chili's Grill & Bar 916 Broadway Ave, Boise, 389-2200	American	$$	Y	Yes	L/D	Major
36	Cobby's Sandwich Shops 1030 Broadway Ave, Boise, 345-0990	American	$-$$	Y	BW	L/D	M V A
36	College Drive-In 1295 University Dr, Boise, 344-5774	Family	$	Y	N	L/D	M V
36	Cricket's Bar & Grill 1228 Oakland Ave, Boise, 344-6235	American	$	N	Yes	L/D	No
36	Domino's Pizza 2164 Broadway Ave, Boise, 345-5551	Pizza	$-$$	N	N	L/D	M V
36	Fiesta Guadalajara 3552 S Findley Ave, Boise, 424-8580	Mexican	$-$$	N	B W	L/D	No
36	Ha' Penny Bridge Irish Pub & Grill 855 Broadway Ave, Boise, 343-5568	Irish	$-$$	N	B W	L/D	Major
36	Idaho Pizza Company 1677 Broadway Ave, Boise, 343-1011	Pizza	$-$$	N	B W	L/D	Major
36	Jack In The Box 2611 Broadway Ave, Boise, 336-8088	Fast Food	$	Y	N	L/D	No
36	Jaker's Park Center Blvd, Boise, 343-3430	Steakhouse	$$$	Y	Yes	L/D	Major
36	La Tapatia Restaurant 401 E Parkcenter Blvd, Boise, 343-6403	Mexican	$-$$	Y	B W	L/D	Major

Dining Quick Reference - continued

Price Range refers to the average cost of a meal per person: ($) $1-$6, ($$) $7-$11, ($$$) $12-up. Cocktails: "Yes" indicates full bar; Beer (B)/Wine (W), Service: Breakfast (B), Brunch (BR), Lunch (L), Dinner (D). Businesses in bold print will have additional information under the appropriate map locator number in the body of this section.

MAP NO.	RESTAURANT	TYPE CUISINE	PRICE RANGE	CHILD MENU	COCKTAILS BEER WINE	MEALS SERVED	CREDIT CARDS ACCEPTED
36	Mancino's 1016 Broadway Ave, Boise, 319-0485	Pizza/Italian	$-$$	Y	N	L/D	M V
36	McDonald's 2516 S Apple, Boise, 342-6608	Fast Food	$	Y	N	B/L/D	Major
36	McDonald's 1375 Broadway Ave, Boise, 338-9110	Fast Food	$	Y	N	B/L/D	Major
36	Murphy's Seafood Bar & Grill 1555 Broadway Ave, Boise, 344-3691	Seafood/American	$-$$	N	B W	L/D	Major
36	Northern Lights Cafe 650 E Boise Ave, Boise, 424-9111	Coffee/Café	$$-$$$	Y	B W	L/D	M V
36	Papa John's Pizza 1323 Broadway Ave, Boise, 367-9200	Pizza	$	N	N	L/D	M V
36	Papa Murphy's Take 'N' Bake Pizza 2412 S Apple, Boise, 344-0070	Pizza	$	N	N	L/D	M V
36	Perkins Restaurant & Bakery 300 Broadway Ave, Boise, 395-1531	Family	$$	Y	N	B/L/D	Major
36	Quik Wok Restaurant 2775 Broadway Ave, Boise, 342-1515	Asian	$-$$	N	N	L/D	M V
36	Quizno's 2241 University Dr, Boise, 389-1177	Fast Food	$-$$	Y	N	L/D	Major
36	Ram Restaurant and Brewery 709 E Park Blvd, Boise, 345-2929	American	$$-$$$	Y	Yes	L/D	Major
36	Royal Delight Chinese Restaurant 408 W Arizona Ln, Boise, 342-3562	Asian	$-$$	N	N	L/D	M V
36	Royal Dynasty Chinese Restaurant 415 E Parkcenter Blvd, Boise, 336-3113	Asian	$-$$	N	N	L/D	M V
36	Senor Fresh Mexican Eatery 590 Broadway Ave, Boise, 344-1888	Mexican	$$	N	N	L/D	M V
36	Skippers Seafood N Chowder House 220 Broadway Ave, Boise, 336-8652	Seafood	$$	Y	N	L/D	Major
36	Sonic Drive-In 2145 Broadway Ave, Boise, 333-8100	Fast Food	$-$$	Y	N	L/D	M V
36	Stubs Sports Pub 3662 S Findley Ave, Boise, 336-7882	American	$$	N	B W	L/D	Major
36	Taco Bell 1420 Broadway Ave, Boise, 384-0744	Fast Food	$	N	N	L/D	M V
36	Vicious Fish Tacos 404 E Parkcenter Blvd, Boise, 424-3888	Seafood	$	N	N	L/D	M V
36	Wendy's Old Fashioned Hamburgers 1180 Broadway Ave, Boise, 336-1700	Fast Food	$-$$	Y	N	L/D	M V
36	Wok-King On Broadway 2146 Broadway Ave, Boise, 345-1779	Asian	$$	N	N	L/D	Major
37	Blimpie Subs & Salads 7072 S Eisenman Rd, Boise, 338-5556	Fast Food	$	Y	N	L	Major
37	Burger King 6490 S Eisenman Rd, Boise, 367-0679	Fast Food	$	Y	N	L/D	M V
37	Chalet Drive-In 249 Hwy 21, Boise, 392-4542	Family	$	Y	N	L/D	M V
37	Crow Inn 6781 Warm Springs Ave, Boise, 342-9669	Seafood	$	N	B W	L/D	Major
37	International House Of Pancakes 3599 Federal Wy, Boise, 426-9125	Family	$-$$	Y	N	B/L/D	Major
37	Jack In The Box 6875 Federal Way, Boise, 388-8452	Fast Food	$	Y	N	L/D	No
37	Kentucky Fried Chicken/A&W 3545 S Federal Way, Boise, 331-0921	Fast Food	$-$$	Y	N	L/D	Major
37	McDonald's 6574 Federal Way, Boise, 368-9703	Fast Food	$	Y	N	B/L/D	Major
37	Perkins Restaurant & Bakery 6801 Federal Way, Boise, 331-8538	Family	$$	Y	N	B/L/D	Major

Dining Quick Reference - continued

Price Range refers to the average cost of a meal per person: ($) $1-$6, ($$) $7-$11, ($$$) $12-up. Cocktails: "Yes" indicates full bar; Beer (B)/Wine (W), Service: Breakfast (B), Brunch (BR), Lunch (L), Dinner (D). Businesses in bold print will have additional information under the appropriate map locator number in the body of this section.

MAP NO.	RESTAURANT	TYPE CUISINE	PRICE RANGE	CHILD MENU	COCKTAILS BEER WINE	MEALS SERVED	CREDIT CARDS ACCEPTED
37	Shy Simon's Pizza 6564 Federal Way, Boise, 433-1112	Pizza	$$	N	N	L/D	Major
37	Trolley House 1821 Warm Springs Ave, Boise, 345-9255	American	$$	N	N	B/L/D	Major
37	Warm Springs Golf Club Warm Springs Cafe 2495 Warm Springs Ave, Boise, 342-6397	American	$$	N	Yes	L/D	Major
39	Aj's Restaurant & Lounge 1130 Hwy 20, Mountain Home, 587-2264	American	$-$$	Y	B W	L/D	No
39	Burger King 3870 Ditto Creek Rd, Mountain Home, 587-1189	Fast Food	$	Y	N	L/D	M V
39	Carlos' Mexican Style Family Dining 210 E 5th N, Mountain Home, 587-2966	Mexican	$	Y	N	B/L/D	M V
39	Domino's Pizza 950 Airbase Rd, Mountain Home, 587-5000	Pizza	$-$$	N	N	L/D	M V
39	Eggrolls Asian Food To Go 224 N Main St, Mountain Home, 580-0073	Asian	$	N	N	L/D	M V
39	Golden Crown Restaurant 2005 American Legion Blvd, Mt Home, 587-7192	Asian	$$	N	N	L/D	Major
39	Grinde's Diner 550 Airbase Rd, Mountain Home, 587-5611	American	$	Y	B W	B/L/D	Major
39	Jack in the Box 3100 Foothills Ave, Mountain Home, 587-2007	Fast Food	$	Y	N	L/D	No
39	Jade Palace Restaurant 1525 American Legion Blvd, Mt Home, 587-2856	Asian	$$	N	N	L/D	Major
39	Kentucky Fried Chicken 1060 Hwy 20, Mountain Home, 587-9775	Fast Food	$-$$	Y	N	L/D	Major
39	Kurley's Sports Bar & Grill 124 E Jackson St, Mountain Home, 587-3836	American	$-$$	N	Yes	L/D	Major
39	l Herradero 2644 Sunset Strip St, Mountain Home, 587-0694	Mexican	$-$$	Y	N	L/D	Major
39	Little Caesars 1035 Airbase Rd, Mountain Home, 587-3213	Pizza	$	N	N	L/D	Major
39	Los Pinos Restaurant 815 S 3rd W, Mountain Home, 587-7441	Mexican	$-$$	Y	N	L/D	M V
39	Maple Cove 135 Bitterbrush Ct, Mountain Home, 580-2537	American	$-$$	N	B W	B/L/D	Major
39	McDonald's 755 W 6th S, Mountain Home, 587-8942	Fast Food	$	Y	N	B/L/D	Major
39	McDonald's 2840 American Legion Blvd, Mt Home, 587-8650	Fast Food	$	Y	N	B/L/D	Major
39	Papa Murphy's Pizza 425 American Legion Blvd, Mt Home, 580-0222	Pizza	$$	N	N	L/D	M V
39	Pizza Hut 605 Airbase Rd, Mountain Home, 587-4404	Pizza	$	N	N	L/D	Major
39	Steaks & Suds 4175 S 130th W, Mountain Home, 832-1085	Steakhouse	$-$$	Y	B W	L/D	Major
39	Stoney's Desert Inn 1500 Sunset Strip St, Mountain Home, 587-9931	American	$-$$	N	B	B/L/D	Major
39	Subway 515 Airbase Rd, Mountain Home, 587-8387	Fast Food	$	N	N	L/D	M V
39	Taco John's 495 N Main St, Mountain Home, 587-5832	Fast Food	$	N	N	L/D	M V
39	Thaihut 2195 W 6th S, Mountain Home, 587-5425	Asian	$$	N	N	L/D	Major
39	Top Hat Barbeque 145 N 2nd E, Mountain Home, 587-9223	American	$-$$	Y	N	L/D	Major
39	Wendy's Old Fashioned Hamburgers 2910 American Legion Blvd, Mt Home, 587-3190	Fast Food	$	Y	N	L/D	M V
41	Carmela Vineyards Restaurant 795 W Madison Ave, Glenns Ferry, 366-2539	Casual Fine Dining	$$	N	Yes	L/D	Major

Ultimate Idaho Atlas and Travel Encyclopedia

Motel Quick Reference

Price Range: ($) Under $40 ; ($$) $40-$60; ($$$) $60-$80, ($$$$) Over $80. Pets [check with the motel for specific policies] (P), Dining (D), Lounge (L), Disabled Access (DA), Full Breakfast (FB), Cont. Breakfast (CB), Indoor Pool (IP), Outdoor Pool (OP), Hot Tub (HT), Sauna (S), Refrigerator (R), Microwave (M) (Microwave and Refrigerator indicated only if in majority of rooms), Kitchenette (K). All Idaho area codes are 208.

MAP No.	HOTEL	NUMBER ROOMS	PRICE RANGE	BREAKFAST	POOL/ HOT TUB SAUNA	NON SMOKE ROOMS	OTHER AMENITIES	CREDIT CARDS
1	Hartland Inn Hwy 95, New Meadows, 347-2114	22	$$/$$$/$$$$			Yes	DA/K	Major
1	Meadows Motel Hwy 95 N, New Meadows, 347-2175	16	$$	CB			P/DA/K	Major
2	Starlite Motel 102 N Dartmouth, Council, 253-4868	12	$				P	M/V
3	Frontier Motel 240 S Superior St, Cambridge, 257-3851	16	$$			Yes	P	Major
3	Bucky's Motel Hwy 95 & 71, Cambridge, 257-3330	3	$			Yes	P	Major
4	Colonial Motel 251 E Main, Weiser, 549-0150	24	$$/$$$			Yes	P/R/M	Major
4	Indianhead Motel 747 Hillcrest Ave, Weiser, 549-0331	8	$$/$$$			Yes		Major
4	State Street Motel 1279 State St, Weiser, 414-1390	13	$$			Yes	P/D	Major
5	**McCall RV Resort & Northfork Lodge** 200 Scott St, McCall, 634-1418	12	$$$$		IP/HT/S	Yes	P/R/M/K	M/V/D
5	**The Hunt Lodge Holiday Inn Express** 210 N 3rd St, McCall, 634-4700	85	$$$$	CB	IP/HT	Yes	DA	Major
5	McCall Super 8 Lodge 303 S 3rd St, McCall, 634-4637	61	$$$	CB	HT	Yes	P/DA/K	Major
5	Bear Creek Lodge Hwy 55, McCall, 634-3551	13	$$$$		HT	Yes	D/DA/M	Major
5	Best Western 415 3rd St, McCall, 634-6300	79	$$$/$$$$	CB	IP/HT	Yes	P/DA/R/M	Major
5	Brundage Inn 1005 W Lake St, McCall, 634-8573	22	$$$/$$$$			Yes	P/K	Major
5	Scandia Inn Motel 401 N 3rd St, McCall, 634-7394	16	$$		S	Yes	K	Major
5	Brundage Inn, Bungalows, Cabins 1005 W Lake St, McCall, 634-2344	22	$$$/$$$$				P/K	Major
5	Woodsman Motel & Cafe 402 N 3rd St, McCall, 634-7671	53	$/$$			Yes	P/K/D	Major
5	Yellow Pine Lodge Main St, Yellow Pine, 633-3300	12	$$			Yes	P/D/DA	Major
6	**Boulder Creek Inn & Suites** 629 Hwy 55, Donnelly, 325-8638	43	$$$	CB		Yes	P/DA/R/M/K	Major
6	**Long Valley Motel** 161 S Main St, Donnelly, 325-8271	8	$$$			Yes	P/K	Major
7	The Ashley Inn 500 N Main St, Cascade, 382-5621	67	$$$$	FB	IP/HT	Yes	R/M	Major
7	Bears Knight Inn 403 N Main, Cascade, 382-4370	7	$$			Yes	K	M/V
7	Mountain View Motel 762 S Main, Cascade, 382-4238	26	$$			Yes	P/R/M	Major
7	Pinewood Lodge Motel 900 S Main St, Cascade, 382-4948	10	$$$			Yes	P/DA/R/M	M/V
7	The Chief Hotel & High Country Inn Main St, Cascade, 382-3315	12	$$				P/D/K	M/V
7	Alpine Cottage Motel 519 N Main St, Cascade, 382-4800	3	$$$/$$$$			Yes	K	Major
8	Garden Valley Motel 1111 Banks-Lowman Rd, Garden Valley, 462-2911	12	$$$			Yes	P/DA/K	Major
9	Idaho City Motel Idaho City, 392-4290	5	$			Yes	P	Major
9	Prospector Motel 507 Main, Idaho City, 392-4290	7	$$			Yes	P/DA/K	Major
11	Holiday Hotel 1111 S Washington Ave, Emmett, 365-4479	20	$$			Yes	P/D/DA	Major

Motel Quick Reference - continued

Price Range: ($) Under $40 ; ($$) $40-$60; ($$$) $60-$80, ($$$$) Over $80. Pets [check with the motel for specific policies] (P), Dining (D), Lounge (L), Disabled Access (DA), Full Breakfast (FB), Cont. Breakfast (CB), Indoor Pool (IP), Outdoor Pool (OP), Hot Tub (HT), Sauna (S), Refrigerator (R), Microwave (M) (Microwave and Refrigerator indicated only if in majority of rooms), Kitchenette (K). All Idaho area codes are 208.

MAP No.	HOTEL	NUMBER ROOMS	PRICE RANGE	BREAKFAST	POOL/ HOT TUB SAUNA	NON SMOKE ROOMS	OTHER AMENITIES	CREDIT CARDS
12	Payette Motel 625 S Main St, Payette, 642-4548	10	$					
14	The Court Motel & Grocery 712 Grove St, Parma, 722-5579	11	$$			Yes	P	Major
15	Sunnydale Motel 2 E Columbus, Homedale, 337-3302	8				Yes	DA/K	Major
20	Holiday Motel 512 Frontage Rd, Caldwell, 455-3550	21	$					Major
20	Sundowner Motel 1002 Arthur St, Caldwell, 459-1585	65	$$	CB		Yes	P/DA/M/R	Major
20	I-84 Motor Inn 505 Hannibal St, Caldwell, 459-1536	28	$$				P	Major
21	Best Western Inn & Suites 908 Specht Ave, Caldwell, 454-7225	69	$$$$	CB	IP/S	Yes	D/DA	Major
21	La Quinta 601 Specht Ave, Caldwell, 454-2222	65	$$$/$$$$		IP/HT	Yes	K/DA/P	Major
22	Super 8 624 Nampa Blvd, Nampa, 467-2888	62	$$/$$$	CB		Yes	DA	Major
22	Days Inn 130 Shannon Dr, Nampa, 442-0800	61	$$$/$$$$	CB	HT/S	Yes	P/DA/K	Major
22	Shilo Inn Suites 617 Nampa Blvd, Nampa, 465-3250	83	$$$$	FB	IP/OP/HT/S	Yes	P/D/L/DA/R/M	Major
22	Inn America 130 Shannon Dr, Nampa, 442-0800	61	$$/$$$	CB	OP	Yes	DA/R	Major
23	Sleep Inn 1315 Industrial Rd, Nampa, 463-6300	81	$$$/$$$$	CB	IP	Yes	DA	Major
23	Shilo Inn Suites 1401 Shilo Dr, Nampa, 465-3250	83	$$$$	FB	IP/S	Yes	P/DA	Major
23	Budget Inn 908 3rd St S, Nampa, 466-3594	45	$$			Yes		Major
23	Desert Inn 115 9th Ave S, Nampa, 467-1161	40	$$	CB	OP	Yes	P/DA	Major
23	Hampton Inn and Suites 5750 E Franklin Rd, Nampa, 442-0036	101	$$$$	CB	IP	Yes	P/DA	Major
23	Starlite Motel 320 11th Ave N, Nampa, 466-9244	16	$$/$			Yes	P	Major
24	Hostel Boise - A Country Place 17322 Can Ada Rd, Nampa, 467-5868	4	$				K	Major
25	Whitehouse Motel 909 Main St, Marsing, 896-4130	5	$				P/DA	
28	Best Western 1019 S Progress Ave, Meridian, 887-7888	61	$$$/$$$$	CB	IP/S	Yes	D/DA	Major
28	Comfort Suites 2610 East Freeway Dr, Meridian, 288-2060	77	$$$$	CB	IP	Yes	DA	Major
28	Motel 6 1047 S Progress Ave, Meridian, 888-1212		$$			Yes	P/DA/R/M	Major
28	Microtel Inn and Suites 1047 S Progress, Meridian, 888-1212	68	$$$/$$$$	CB	IP	Yes	DA	Major
28	Mr. Sandman Motel 1575 S Meridian, Meridian, 888-3822	106	$$/$$$/$$$$		OP/HT	Yes	DA/R	Major
28	Holiday Inn Express 800 S Allen, Meridian, 288-2100	67	$$$$	CB	IP/HT	Yes		Major
29	Hilton Garden Inn 145 E Riverside Dr, Eagle, 938-9600	98	$$$$	CB	IP	Yes	D/R/M/P	Major
31	AmeriTel Inn 7965 W Emerald, Boise, 378-7000	124	$$$$	FB	IP/S	Yes	DA/K	Major
31	Red Lion Hotel Boise Downtowner 1800 Fairview Ave, Boise, 344-7691	182	$$$$		OP/HT	Yes	P/D/L/DA	Major
31	Plaza Suite Hotel 409 N Cole Rd, Boise, 375-7666	38	$$$$	CB	IP/S	Yes	DA	Major

Section 3

Motel Quick Reference - continued

Price Range: ($) Under $40 ; ($$) $40-$60; ($$$) $60-$80, ($$$$) Over $80. Pets [check with the motel for specific policies] (P), Dining (D), Lounge (L), Disabled Access (DA), Full Breakfast (FB), Cont. Breakfast (CB), Indoor Pool (IP), Outdoor Pool (OP), Hot Tub (HT), Sauna (S), Refrigerator (R), Microwave (M) (Microwave and Refrigerator indicated only if in majority of rooms), Kitchenette (K). All Idaho area codes are 208.

MAP No.	HOTEL	NUMBER ROOMS	PRICE RANGE	BREAKFAST	POOL/ HOT TUB SAUNA	NON SMOKE ROOMS	OTHER AMENITIES	CREDIT CARDS
31	Bond Street Motel Apartments 1680 N Phillippi, Boise, 322-4407	57	$$/$$$			Yes	P/R/M/K	Major
31	Budget Inn 2600 Fairview Ave, Boise, 344-8617	44	$$			Yes	P/DA	Major
31	Econolodge 4060 Fairview Ave, Boise, 344-4030	52	$$	CB		Yes	P/DA	Major
31	Holiday Motel 5416 Fairview Ave, Boise, 376-4631	19	$			No	P/DA	Major
31	Rodeway Inn 1115 N Curtis Rd, Boise, 376-2700	100	$$$/$$$$	CB	IP/S	Yes	P/D/DA	Major
31	AmeriSuites Hotel 925 N Milwaukee, Boise, 375-1200	128		FB	IP	Yes	P/DA/R/M	Major
31	Travelers Motel 5620 Fairview Ave, Boise, 376-3691	17	$				K	
32	Shilo Inn Suites Riverside 3031 Main St, Boise, 343-7662	112	$$$$	CB	OP/HT/S	Yes	P/DA/K	Major
32	Best Western Safari Motor Inn 1070 Grove St, Boise, 344-6556	103	$$$$/$$$	CB	OP	Yes	D/DA	Major
32	Boise Centre Guest Lodge 1314 Grove St, Boise, 342-9351	48	$$			Yes	DA	Major
32	Cabana Inn 1600 Main St, Boise, 343-6000	50	$		HT	Yes	P	Major
32	Doubletree Club Hotel 2900 Chinden Blvd, Boise, 343-1871	304	$$$/$$$$		OP	Yes	P/D/DA	Major
32	Owyhee Plaza Hotel 1109 Main St, Boise, 343-4611	100	$$$/$$$$		OP	Yes	P/D/L/DA	Major
32	Seven K Motel 3633 Chinden Blvd, Boise, 343-7723	23	$$		OP/HT	Yes	P/DA/K	Major
32	State Motel 1115 N 28th St, Boise, 344-7254	12	$$				P/K	Major
32	Statehouse Inn 981 Grove St, Boise, 342-4622	112	$$$/$$$$			Yes	D/DA	Major
32	Sun Liner Motel 3433 Chinden Blvd, Boise, 344-7647	27	$$					Major
32	West River Inn 3525 Chinden Blvd, Boise, 338-1155	21	$				P/K	M/V
32	Chinden Motor Inn 4678 W Chinden Blvd, Garden City, 322-8668							
33	AmeriTel Inn 7499 W Overland, Boise, 323-2500	133	$$$$	FB	IP/S	Yes	DA/K	Major
33	Budget Host Inn 8002 Overland Rd, Boise, 322-4404	87	$$$	CB	OP	Yes	P/DA	Major
33	Hilton Garden Inn 7699 Spectrum St, Boise, 376-1000	98	$$$$		IP	Yes	D	Major
35	Super 8 2773 Elder St, Boise, 344-8871	108	$$/$$$	CB	IP	Yes	P/DA	Major
35	Comfort Inn Airport 2526 Airport Way, Boise, 336-0077	60	$$$	CB	IP/HT	Yes	DA/R/M	Major
35	Best Western Airport Motor Inn 2660 Airport Way, Boise, 384-5000	50	$$$$	CB	OP	Yes	DA/R	Major
35	Best Western Vista Inn 2645 Airport Way, Boise, 336-8100	87	$$$$	CB	OP	Yes	D/L/DA/R	Major
35	Motel 6 2323 Airport Way, Boise, 344-3506	86	$$		OP	Yes	P/DA/R/M	Major
35	Inn America 2275 Airport Way, Boise, 389-9800	73	$$$	CB	OP	Yes	DA/R	Major
35	Extended StayAmerica 2500 S Vista Ave, Boise, 363-9040	107	$$$/$$$$			Yes	P/R/M/K	Major
35	Holiday Inn Express 2613 S Vista Ave, Boise, 388-0800	63	$$$$	FB	IP/HT	Yes	DA	Major

Motel Quick Reference - continued

Price Range: ($) Under $40 ; ($$) $40-$60; ($$$) $60-$80, ($$$$) Over $80. Pets [check with the motel for specific policies] (P), Dining (D), Lounge (L), Disabled Access (DA), Full Breakfast (FB), Cont. Breakfast (CB), Indoor Pool (IP), Outdoor Pool (OP), Hot Tub (HT), Sauna (S), Refrigerator (R), Microwave (M) (Microwave and Refrigerator indicated only if in majority of rooms), Kitchenette (K). All Idaho area codes are 208.

MAP No.	HOTEL	NUMBER ROOMS	PRICE RANGE	BREAKFAST	POOL/ HOT TUB SAUNA	NON SMOKE ROOMS	OTHER AMENITIES	CREDIT CARDS
35	Holiday Inn 3300 Vista Ave, Boise, 343-4900	265	$$$$	CB	IP/HT	Yes	P	Major
35	Comfort Suites Airport 2906 Vista Ave, Boise, 472-1222	83	$$$/$$$$	CB	IP/S	Yes	DA/R/M	Major
35	Fairfield Inn 3300 S Shoshone Dr, Boise, 331-5656	63	$$$$	CB	IP/HT	Yes	DA/R/M	Major
35	Hampton Inn 3270 Shoshone, Boise, 331-5600	64	$$$$	CB	IP	Yes	P/DA	Major
36	Best Value University Inn and Best Value Safari 2360 University Dr, Boise, 345-7170	82	$$$/$$$$		OP/HT	Yes	P/DA/R	Major
36	Red Lion Park Center Suites 424 E ParkCenter Blvd, Boise, 342-1044	238	$$$/$$$$	CB	OP/HT	Yes	P/L/DA/K	Major
36	Best Western Northwest Lodge 6989 Federal Way, Boise, 287-2300	69	$$$$	CB	IP/HT	Yes	DA/R/D	Major
36	Shilo Inn Suites Airport 4111 Broadway, Boise, 343-7662	125	$$$$	CB	OP/HT/S	Yes	P/D/DA/R/M/K	Major
36	Anniversary Inn 1575 S Lusk, Boise, 387/4900	41	$$$$	CB	HT	Yes	DA	Major
36	Courtyard by Marriott 222 S Broadway, Boise, 331-2700	162	$$$/$$$$		IP/HT	Yes	P/L/DA	Major
36	Doubletree Club Hotel 475 W ParkCenter Blvd, Boise, 345-2002	158	$$$/$$$$		OP	Yes	P/D/DA	Major
36	Ralfroy Motel 2223 Federal Way, Boise, 343-6077	13	$					
36	Residence Inn by Marriott 1401 Lusk Ave, Boise, 344-1200	104	$$$/$$$$	CB	OP/HT	Yes	P/DA/K	Major
36	West Coast ParkCenter Suites 424 E ParkCenter Blvd, Boise, 342-1044	238	$$$$		IP/HT	Yes	DA/K	Major
39	Towne Center Motel 410 N 2nd St E, Mountain Home, 587-3373	31			OP	Yes	P/DA	Major
39	Hilander Motel 615 S 3rd St W, Mountain Home, 587-3311	32	$$		OP	Yes	P/K	Major
39	Sleep Inn 1180 Hwy 20, Mountain Home, 587-9743	60	$$$	CB		Yes	P/DA	Major
39	Best Western Foothills Inn 1080 Hwy 20, Mountain Home, 587-8477	173	$$$$		OP/HT	Yes	P/DA	Major
39	Motel Thunderbird 910 Sunset Strip, Mountain Home, 587-7927	27	$$			Yes	R	Major
40	Oasis Ranch Motel Hammett, 366-2025	6	$					M/V
41	Redford Motel 525 W 1st Ave, Glenns Ferry, 366-2421	11	$/$$			Yes	P/K	M/V
41	Hanson's Motel 102 E 1st St, Glenns Ferry, 366-9983	9	$$			Yes	D/R	Major
43	Nester's Mountain Motel 54 E Nester Dr, Pine, 633-2210	14	$$$			Yes		Major
43	Featherville Saloon & Motel 411 N Pine, Featherville, 653-2310	10	$$				D	M/V
47	Idaho Hotel (Summer Only) Silver City Ghost Town, 583-4104	18	$$/$$$			Yes	DA	

NOTES:

Ultimate Idaho Atlas and Travel Encyclopedia

SECTION 4

CENTRAL AREA

INCLUDING KETCHUM, SUN VALLEY, SALMON, ARCO, AND CHALLIS

This section of Idaho boasts the most awe-inspiring land in the contiguous U.S. The Sawtooth mountains are just one of the ranges that make up this beautiful area.

1 *Food, Lodging*

North Fork
Pop. 170

The North Fork of the Salmon River joins the main river branch at this location, thus providing this small community with its name. Historically, the Lewis and Clark Expedition traveled near here in the fall of 1805. Today, the town serves as the headway leading to a popular whitewater launching area.

Gibbonsville
Pop. 125

Gold was discovered here in 1872, and this tiny community was unofficially established in 1877. A post office was erected just one year later, but the townsite itself wasn't chartered until 1899. Formerly known as Dahlongs or Gibtown, Gibbonsville was eventually named for Colonel John Gibbon who attacked Chief Joseph's Nez Perce encampment in this area just prior to the 1877 Battle of the Big Hole. Most notably, the Lewis and Clark expedition graced the area with their presence during the fall of 1805.

H Lewis and Clark
Milepost 345 on U.S. Hwy. 93

On their way north searching for a route over Idaho's mountain barrier, Lewis and Clark left this canyon and ascended a high ridge to reach the Bitterroot Valley in early September, 1805.No Indian trail came this way, but Tobe, their experienced Shoshoni guide, got them past the ridge anyway. They had to follow a difficult ridge top divide over peaks more than 1,000 feet higher than this highway. They met some Flathead Indians who surprised them by speaking a language stranger than anything they had ever heard.

H Lewis and Clark
Milepost 326.1 on U.S. Hwy. 93

Hoping for an easy river trip up to the Pacific, William Clark explored the first few miles of the rugged canyon of the Salmon River below here

late in August 1805. His small advance party camped near here with poor but friendly Indians. Clark reported that the Salmon "is almost one continued rapid," and that passage "with canoes is entirely impossible." So the expedition had to buy packhorses and go 110 miles north to an Indian trail across the mountains.

H Nez Perce Trail
Milepost 332 on U.S. Hwy. 93

Following high ridges, buffalo hunters cut an old Indian trail along a direct route from Lewiston past here to Lemhi Valley. This trail was not available to Lewis and Clark in 1805, but an early missionary – Samuel Parker – crossed it with a Nez Perce trading party 30 years later. During an 1862 Montana gold rush, eager miners joined Lewiston merchants who sent pack trains over it with supplies for new gold camps. But bandits and robbers made wilderness travel unsafe along it.

H Gibbonsville
Milepost 337 on U.S. Hwy. 93

British investment in a large Gibbonsville mine after 1880 made this an important gold camp until 1899. Discovery of a major lode here in 1877 and construction of a good wagon road to a Utah and Northern Railway terminal in Montana brought prosperity when mining was not suspended because of litigation. With close to 100 buildings, two sawmills, a roller mill, five stamp mills, a newspaper and six to eight saloons, Gibbonsville produced about $2 million in gold.

T Shoup
East of North Fork on Forest Rd. 030

Mining was the predominant industrial activity in Shoup with the first claims staked in 1882. Remaining a small mining camp until the early 1900s, Shoup eventually grew to a population of 600 and served as the community center and post office for the Mineral Hill Mining District. Today, the town is still active with fishermen and tourists.

T Wagonhammer Springs
Approximately 2 miles south of North Fork on U.S. Hwy. 93 at Milepost 234.4. 865-2477.

Located in the heart of the central Idaho Rocky Mountains, Wagonhammer Springs is situated on the banks of the Salmon River. The favorite picnic site earned its name from the 1880s wagons that were constructed here. Years later, an old wagon hammer was found when a sawmill was established here, and the site has been known as "Wagonhammer" ever since.

In addition to picnicking, the area offers convenient access to canoeing, fishing, hiking and mountain biking in the nearby Wagonhammer Springs Canyon. Wildlife viewers are encouraged to bring their cameras as the area boasts frequent visits from bighorn sheep, mountain goats, elk, deer, moose, and various upland birds and waterfowl.

T Lost Trail Pass
46 miles north of Salmon at the junction of U.S. Hwy. 93 and State Hwy. 43 at the Idaho/Montana border

Situated at an elevation of 7,014 feet, Lost Trail Pass separates Idaho and Montana. The steep, rocky pass draws its name from the historical crossing of Lewis and Clark. In 1805, after parting ways with the Shoshone, the Corps of Discovery headed north with a Shoshoni guide in an attempt to find a route to the Bitterroot River. Although the Corp hoped this route would provide a safer and easier passageway than the Salmon River, the group still encountered treacherous conditions. Struggling in the cold and snow, the explorers lost many of their horses and at times, lost sight of their intended route. Today, the exact route of the expedition has been lost, but historians do know that it is in the vicinity of Lost Trail Pass.

At the top of the pass, a visitor's center provides relevant area information. The center is open daily during the summer. The pass also provides access to Lost Trail Powder Mountain Ski Area, situated just across the border in Sula, Montana.

V The Continental Divide National Scenic Trail in Idaho and Montana
Contact the Idaho Department of Parks and Recreation at 334-4199.

General Information

The Continental Divide National Scenic Trail (CDNST) was established by Congress under the National Trails System Act of 1968. The trail will extend 3,200 miles, in its entirety, from Canada to Mexico. This northern-most portion follows the backbone of the Rocky Mountains for approximately 980 miles through Montana and Idaho. It passes through some of our nation's most spectacular scenery – Glacier National Park, ten national forests with wildernesses such as the Bob Marshall and Anaconda Pintler, several Bureau of Land Management Resource Areas, State lands, and short segments of private lands.

This segment begins at the U.S./Canada border between Glacier and Waterton Lakes National Parks, following a route near the divide and through the Blackfeet Indian Reservation to Marias

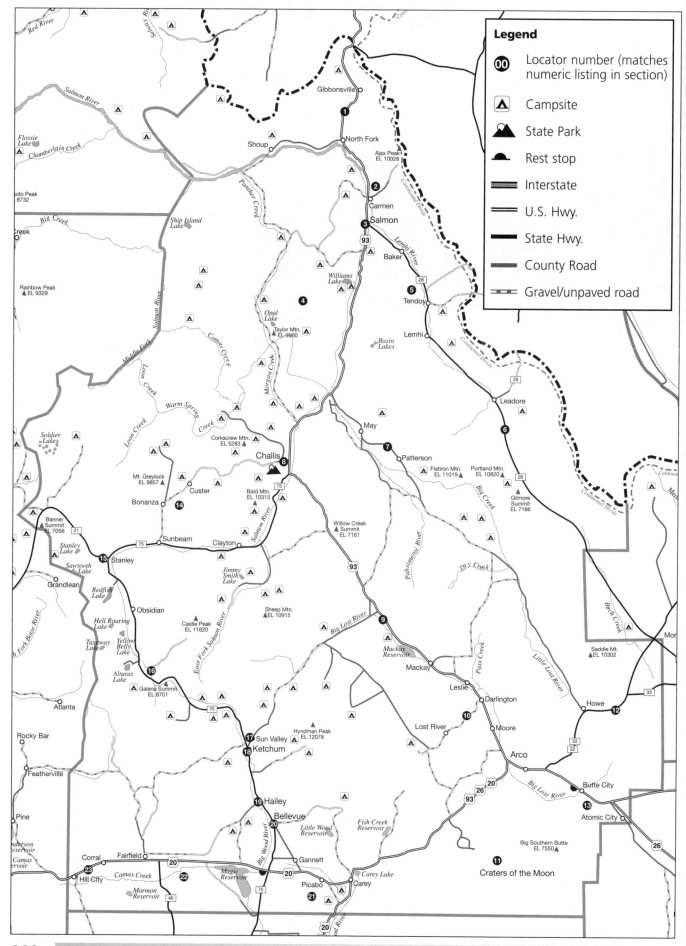

All Idaho Area Codes are 208

Legend

- **00** Locator number (matches numeric listing in section)
- **⛺** Campsite
- **⛰** State Park
- **⬤** Rest stop
- ═══ Interstate
- ━━━ U.S. Hwy.
- ▰▰▰ State Hwy.
- ━━━ County Road
- ▭▭▭ Gravel/unpaved road

Pass. Southward the trail passes through the Bob Marshall and Scapegoat Wildernesses, skirting the Chinese Wall. After crossing Rogers and MacDonald Passes, it continues through historic mining districts and ghost towns. West of Anaconda the trail traverses the length of the Anaconda Pintler Wilderness, reaching the Montana-Idaho border near Lost Trail Pass on the 1805 route of Lewis and Clark.

Winding through the Beaverhead Mountains of the Bitterroot Range, the trail passes high above Big Hole National Battlefield, scene of conflict between the Nez Perce Tribe and the U.S. Army in 1877, and on to Lemhi Pass, headwaters of the Missouri River and marked by the Sacajawea Memorial. Continuing on through the Bitterroots, it crosses Monida Pass and winds along the crest of the Centennial Mountains above Red Rock Lakes National Wildlife Refuge. Staying near the divide, the trail crosses Raynolds and Targhee Passes with views of Henry's Lake to the south and Hebgen Lake to the north, before continuing on to the end of this segment of the CDNST, at the western boundary of Yellowstone National Park.

Elevations along the trail through Montana and Idaho vary from 4,200 feet at Waterton Lake to approximately 10,200 feet at Horse Prairie Peak on Elk Mountain in the Beaverhead Mountains of the Bitterroot Range. Over 90 percent of the trail is within 5 miles of the Continental Divide, and much is on the divide itself; the furthest that it deviates from the divide is 8 miles. Annual precipitation varies from 120 inches in Glacier National Park to only 20 inches near Rogers Pass. Because much comes as snow, portions of the trail are passable only in July, August, and September. Temperatures often drop below freezing, and snowstorms can occur, even during the summer. All travelers are urged to contact local Forest Service Ranger Stations and other agencies' offices for more specific information.

Interim Routes
Only 57 of the 795 miles of this northern portion of the trail do not currently exist as constructed trail or primitive road. Temporary "interim routes" serve as detours, pending construction of the preferred route. Another special interim route exists in Glacier National Park. Because there are no Canadian Customs officials at Waterton Lake, an interim route for the trail begins at Chief Mountain Customs Station on Montana State Hwy. 17.

Modes of Travel
While the National Trails System Act intended the trail be established primarily for hiking and horseback use, motorized uses are permitted where previously established. Of the total 795 miles of road and trail, several hundred miles permit some type of motorized use, including snowmobiles in winter; primitive roads serve as the trail route for 160 miles. Most of the route is lightly used and visitors can expect considerable solitude.

Special Restrictions
- Glacier National Park: Special regulations apply to travel, camping, and stock use. Motorized vehicles are prohibited.
- Wilderness: Travel and camping permits are not required, but some restrictions may apply, including party size limits; motorized transport and bicycles are prohibited. Some wilderness areas may require a permit – contact the local Forest Service, Park Service, or BLM office prior to traveling.

- Stock Use: Contact agencies managing the trail for restrictions on grazing, feeding, and tying stock.

Resupply
There are 34 points on or near roads along this segment of the trail where travelers could prearrange for resupplies of food and equipment. Though land management agencies cannot provide this service, they can help you identify those points.

Precautions
Travelers are responsible for recognizing risks inherent in backcountry travel and taking appropriate precautions. Here are some things to consider:

Bears: All of the CDNST in Montana and Idaho is in occupied black bear habitat, and much is also frequented by grizzly bears. To prevent bear-human conflicts, special practices need to be followed in cooking and disposal of wastes; overnight camping may be prohibited in places.
Terrain & Weather: The trail passes through remote and rugged terrain. Travelers may encounter a variety of dangerous conditions and face the inherent risks of inclement weather, lightning, isolation, physical hazards, and minimal communications.
Water: Water in springs, streams, and lakes should not be considered safe to drink without proper treatment.
Mixed Uses: Use caution where the trail crosses roads or highways, or where motorized use is allowed on the trail.

Be Considerate
Five miles of the trail lie within the Blackfeet Indian Reservation, and other short sections cross private lands. Please respect these lands and observe special restrictions to ensure they will remain open to travelers in the future. Visitors can expect to observe various management activities, such as logging, mining, and grazing on both public and private land along the trail. Agency land management plans and the comprehensive plan for the trail provide for these activities.

All CDNST users should practice Leave No Trace principles. Respect those who will follow your footsteps, and leave no trace of your visit.

Reprinted from U.S. Forest Service brochure

FL 100 Acre Wood Resort and B&B
2356 Hwy. 93 N., North Fork.
www.100acrewoodresort.com

Welcoming vacationers year round, the 100 Acre Wood Resort has provided outdoor adventures and indoor pampering in Idaho's Beaverhead Mountains since 1996. Situated 25 miles north of Salmon near the Frank Church-River of No Return Wilderness, the three-story log lodge features a variety of room choices, crackling fires, outdoor hot tubs, and hearty breakfasts. During the day, experience the area's sheer beauty on an adventure tour. Horseback riding, cattle drives, bear viewing, trout fishing, 4X4 backcountry

drives, hiking, rafting, hunting, mountain biking, snowmobiling, and several other tours provide hours of outdoor exploration. For guests who pre-order dinner, exquisite evening meals are available, including seafood, steaks, pasta, and much more. Discover a vacation of a lifetime and see why previous guests have distinguished this resort as a little slice of heaven on earth!

2 *Food*

Carmen
Pop. 10

Established in the 1890s, Carmen was named for either Benjamin Carmen or Martha Carmen (his wife). Benjamin constructed a sawmill on Carmen Creek in the 1870s, and the post office operated here from 1902 to 1965.

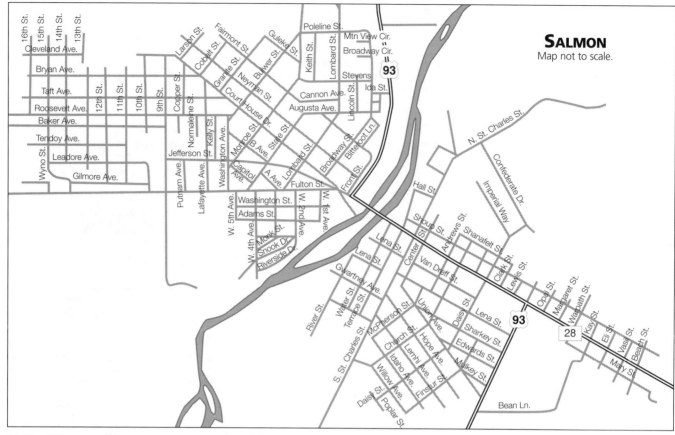
H **Fort Bonneville**
Milepost 310 on U.S. Hwy. 93 at Carmen

In a grove of cottonwoods across the river, Captain B.L.E. Bonneville established a winter fur trade post, September 26, 1832. His fort – described by a rival trapper as "a miserable establishment" – "consisted of several log cabins, low, badly constructed and admirably situated for besiegers only, who would be sheltered on every side by timber, brush, etc." But several bands of friendly Flathead and Nez Perce Indians camped nearby, and Bonneville fully enjoyed his hunter's life here in the midst of "a wild and bustling scene."

H **Historic Lemhi County**
Milepost 310 on U.S. Hwy. 93 at Carmen

In 1866, gold was discovered at Leesburg by Elijah Mulkey, William Smith, F.B. Sharkey, Joseph Rapp, and Ward Girton. Mining has continued in Lemhi County, with production of $30 million in gold and nearly $35 million in copper, lead, tungsten, silver, etc. Sixty-three mineral species have been found. In August 1805, Meriwether Lewis and William Clark entered the Lemhi Valley 20 miles south of here and later crossed Idaho 75 miles north of here on their way to the Pacific Ocean. In 1832, Captain Bonneville occupied the valley four miles north, representing the U.S. in Oregon Territory. In 1855, a Mormon settlement was established at Fort Lemhi near the place where Lewis and

Clark first encamped. It was abandoned in 1858. Agriculture and stock were established in 1870.

V **Richie Outfitters**
742 Hwy. 93 N., Carmen. 756-3231.
www.richieoutfitting.com

Experience trophy big game hunting, fly fishing, and camping in Idaho's primitive Selway-Bitterroot Wilderness area with Richie Outfitters. Due to the region's remoteness, trophy animals are the rule rather than the exception. Hunt elk, deer, bear, moose, and mountain lions in exclusive territory covering 300 square miles of forests, rivers, mountain lakes, and streams. Fair chase hunts are available year-round, so don't let winter deter you. Wildlife is often best seen during winter, and Richie Outfitters offers days of telemarking, cross-country skiing, and snowshoeing. During summer, take a backcountry trail ride and fish amidst majestic mountain scenery. Offering the expertise of a second generation, family owned business,

Richie Outfitters provides comfortable camps, first-rate gear, excellent food, great service, and tons of fun in the heart of Idaho's best game country!

3 *Food, Lodging*

Salmon
Pop. 3,122

In 1832, Salmon was a popular winter nesting place for famous mountainmen, including Jim Bridger, Joe Meek, Henry Fraeb, Captain Bonneville, and Kit Carson. That year, it also became home to the Hudson Bay Trading Company, the Rocky Mountain Fur Company, and the American Fur Company. Despite these early visits from white men, the town waited over three more decades for its official establishment.

Situated at the convergence of the Lemhi and Salmon Rivers, this scenic community boomed in 1866 as a supply center for Leesburg Basin miners. In 1867, Idaho's first governor, George L. Shoup, gathered help from his influential associates and platted out the Salmon City townsite. Named after the abundant salmon that once populated the region's rivers, the town shortened its name in 1869 when a post office was established and it became seat of Lemhi County.

Today, the town serves as a recreational launching site for whitewater enthusiasts, anglers, hikers, campers, equestrians, and hot springs lovers.

Salmon													
	Jan	Feb	March	April	May	June	July	Aug	Sep	Oct	Nov	Dec	Annual
Average Max. Temperature (F)	30.0	38.2	51.0	61.1	70.1	78.6	87.9	86.5	75.6	60.8	42.4	30.7	59.4
Average Min. Temperature (F)	12.2	17.4	26.3	32.4	39.6	46.3	51.1	49.1	40.7	31.4	23.1	13.7	31.9
Average Total Precipitation (in.)	0.69	0.47	0.53	0.78	1.39	1.40	1.05	0.80	0.77	0.60	0.75	0.73	9.95
Average Total Snowfall (in.)	8.0	4.0	1.9	1.1	0.1	0.0	0.0	0.0	0.0	0.1	3.8	7.6	26.6
Average Snow Depth (in.)	5	3	0	0	0	0	0	0	0	0	0	2	1

T Leesburg

12 miles northwest of Salmon in Lemhi County on Leesburg Stage Rd.

In hopes of finding wealth in Idaho, Montana residents E.B. Sharkey, Elijah Mulkey, Joseph Rapp, William Smith, and Ward Girton set out in spring 1866. Prospecting near Napias Creek, the men struck gold on July 16, 1866, and a new mining district was formed on August 10. As miners rushed to the area, the settlement of Leesburg was formed, honoring Civil War General Robert E. Lee. The town quickly grew to a population of 3,000 residents and included nearly one hundred businesses, hotels, general stores, restaurants, saloons, and liveries. Although Leesburg area mines easily produced $6,250,000 in placer gold, living in the community was not as easy. With frequent winter snows averaging five feet, supply wagons had difficulty reaching the town over an 18-mile toll road. Also, tensions ran high between Northern and Southern sympathizers living in the area, and brawls were an everyday occurrence. Today, this once frantic site of mining activity is quiet with many of the town buildings falling apart.

T Sacajawea Interpretive Cultural and Education Center

200 Main St., Salmon. 756-1188.
www.sacajaweacenter.org

The city of Salmon salutes its leading lady and most famous descendant at the Sacajawea Interpretive Cultural and Education Center. With its grand opening on August 15, 2003, the center boasts a seventy-one acre park commemorating the life and contributions of Sacajawea. The center interprets Sacajawea's history and her role in the Lewis and Clark Expedition, presents the unique aspects of the Corp of Discovery while it traveled in Lemhi County, brings a greater understanding and appreciation for the Lemhi Shoshone (Sacajawea's native people), and provides a lasting legacy of Native American history in the Salmon area.

Walking through the Sacajawea Gateway Grove, visitors first enter the visitor's center. Numerous exhibits are continually updated, and the center strives to promote local community arts, educational, and recreational programs. Outside the interpretive center are a monument of Sacajawea and an easy 0.7-mile self-guided interpretive trail that includes wildlife art and tepee encampments. The School of Discovery offers educational programs for individuals of all ages. Visit this cultural wonderment from May 1 through October 30. The facility is open 9 AM to 6 PM Tuesday through Saturday in May, September, and October. June through August, operating hours are 9 AM to 6 PM daily. Admission is $4 per person over age 6, $12 per family, or $2 for those visiting as part of a group tour.

T Lemhi County Historical Society

210 Main St., Salmon. 756-3342.
www.sacajaweahome.com/boardnmuseum.htm

Lemhi County is home to one of the most recognized Native Americans in the country. As the birthplace of Sacajawea, Lewis and Clark's famed interpreter and aide, the Lemhi County Historical Society is devoted to portraying historically accurate information about her and the valley in which she was born. Exhibits include Native American artifacts such as peace pipes and headdresses,

interpretations of the Lewis and Clark journey, an extensive Ray Edward oriental collection from early Chinese settlers, and information regarding famed sharp shooter, Elmer Keith. The museum is open from 9 AM to 5 PM Monday through Saturday from April 15 through October. Admission is $2 for adults with free admission for youth under 16.

T Salmon Valley Golf Course

Southeast of Salmon on State Hwy. 28. 756-4734.

Established in 1986, the public Salmon Valley Golf Course provides 6,434 yards of prime golf on bent grass greens. The tree-lined fairways and rolling greens feature several water hazards, and a tributary of the Salmon River trickles through the course. Rated a par-72, the course offers both 9 and 18-hole games, and players must wear a collared shirt. Green fees are reasonably priced under $20,

and the course is open from March 1 through October 31.

T Salmon Hot Springs

4 miles south of Salmon at 506 Main St. 756-4449.

Known among locals as a classic Idaho soaking spot, Salmon Hot Springs is nestled in the hills surrounding Salmon. Although developed, the springs still retain a sense of privacy, and the warm mineral pool is well-maintained. A small daily use fee is charged.

V Salmon Area Snowmobile Trails

Near Salmon. Contact the Salmon-Challis National Forest at 756-5100.

Receiving an average 150 to 200 inches of snowfall per year, the snowcapped mountains of Lemhi

County near Salmon are a snowmobiling mecca. Nestled in the shadow of the Continental Divide, the area boasts several groomed trails appropriate for riders of all ages and experience levels. Nearly 300 miles of trails intersect the area's backcountry, and several access points are available.

The most popular route in the Salmon area follows an old stagecoach road. The trail winds to the mining ghost town of Leesburg, where many of the buildings are now decaying. Other popular excursions include riding the Continental Divide trail and the miles of paths departing from trailheads at Williams Creek and in Warm Springs near the Agency Creek Road. For maps and detailed route directions, contact the Salmon-Challis National Forest.

V Idaho Adventures
30 Courthouse Dr., Salmon. 756-2986 or (800) 789-9283. www.idahoadventures.com

Unleash your adventurous spirit and discover western hospitality with Idaho Adventures. Operating since 1973, Idaho Adventures prides itself on offering safe whitewater rafting, scenic floats, guided fishing, and mountain bike tours. From half-day options to multi-day adventures, the company offers something for everyone. Wind your way through the Frank Church-River of No Return Wilderness on a Salmon River rafting trip, navigate the Owyhee Canyonlands, or try your hand at steelhead fishing. As exclusive offerings, Idaho Adventures maintains 7,000 private acres for fishing on the Lemhi River, and wooden scow trips provide a glimpse of history on a 2 1/2 hour interpretive float. Every professional guide is certified, maintaining safety as the number one priority. With Idaho Adventures, discover firsthand why living the journey is just as important as the destination!

VL Geertson Creek Trail Rides
151 Geertson Creek Rd., Salmon. 756-2463. www.geertson.com

Discover ranch life or take a scenic trail ride in the beautiful Lemhi Valley with Geertson Creek Trail Rides. Offering trips tailored to customers' unique requests, the ranch boasts professional guides and gentle mountain horses custom-fit to riders of all ages and experience. Travel through breathtaking scenery and catch a glimpse of native wildlife on rides ranging from two hours to all day to overnight. Ranch guests and those on overnight excursions will enjoy scrumptious cuisine and a cozy homestead cabin. For children, the ranch provides supervised pony rides and a farm animal petting zoo where children can bottle-feed baby calves. Family-owned and operated, Geertson Creek Trail Rides is licensed through the Outfitters Guide Association and promises a safe and memorable experience. Reservations are recommended.

F Bertram's Brewery & Restaurant
101 S. Andrews St., Salmon. 756-3391. www.salmonidaho.com/bertrams

Established in a 100-year-old brick building in 1998, Bertram's Brewery & Restaurant features a unique, smoke-free ambience with original pressed metal ceilings, hardwood floors, and

Africana and Rockies décor. As Salmon's only brew pub, Bertram's handcrafts six distinctive microbrews and serves lunch and dinner. From family dining to fine dining, selections include steaks, seafood, pastas, homemade soups, an extensive salad bar, and much more. Bertram's also specializes in a variety of "Pub Grub." For award-winning beers, fine wines, homemade sodas, and tasty food, visit this downtown legend. Reservations aren't required, wireless Internet is available, and tours of the brewery are occasionally provided. Winter hours are 11 AM – 9 PM Monday through Thursday and 11 AM – 10 PM Friday and Saturday. Summer hours are 11 AM – 10 PM Monday through Saturday.

F The Shady Nook Restaurant
501 Hwy. 93 N., Salmon. 756-4182. www.salmonidaho.com/shady/

Situated inside a historic building once home to a hospital, The Shady Nook Restaurant has offered fine dining since the late 1940s. Serving dinner daily from 4 PM to 10 PM, the restaurant features scrumptious meals. House specialties include prime rib, fresh seafood and salmon, Idaho rainbow trout, chicken, pasta, and more, while homemade desserts add the finishing touch. Compliment any meal with a drink from the full cocktail lounge, or enjoy Happy Hour Monday through Friday from 5:30 PM to 6:30 PM. The lounge offers a fun atmosphere with theme nights, and beer, specialty cocktails, and an extensive wine list ensure a perfect choice for everyone. Outside dining and seasonal lunches are available during the summer, and children under 12 are treated to their own menu.

L Twin Peaks Ranch
18 miles south of Salmon on Hwy. 93, Salmon. 894-2290 or (800) 659-4899. www.twiwpeaksranch.com

Adjoining the Salmon River amid towering mountains, Twin Peaks Ranch invites guests to experience western ranch life and breathtaking adventurous activities. After resting in the ranch's original cabins, spacious deluxe cabins, or a suite, wake up to buffet breakfasts and prepare for a day of horseback riding, fly-fishing, lake fishing, whitewater rafting, cattle drives, and/or hiking. Guests may also go trapshooting, relax in the hot tub and swimming pool, play volleyball and horseshoes, take a wilderness overnight excursion,

SACAJAWEA – THE MOST RECOGNIZED NATIVE AMERICAN WOMAN IN THE U.S.

America's history is intertwined with the Native American people, and while famous battles and heroic chiefs are frequently highlights in this history, so is the life of an intriguing Shoshone Native American woman. Known as Sacagawea (meaning Bird Woman) and also as Sacajawea (Boat Launcher), this woman and her life have captured American interest for over 200 years.

Sacajawea's Early Years

During the 1700s and 1800s, Shoshone Indian tribes inhabited parts of Idaho, Utah, and northern Nevada, and one particularly important tribe called the area near Salmon, Idaho home. In 1787, Sacajawea was born into this tribe and lived in the Lemhi Valley until age 12. Tragically, on a family hunting expedition to Montana in 1800, Sacajawea was captured by a raiding party of Hidatsa Indians, a sworn enemy of the Shoshone people. Carried from her native homeland in the Rocky Mountains to the Hidatsa-Mandan villages near present-day Bismarck, North Dakota, Sacajawea was traded as a squaw (prostitute) among the area natives. Eventually, Sacajawea ended up as the property and wife of French-Canadian fur trapper and interpreter, Toussaint Charbonneau. Charbonneau, a polygamist possessing other Native American wives, fiercely mistreated Sacajawea, beating her and using her as a prostitute and slave. Before long, Sacajawea was pregnant, and she and Charbonneau wintered at Fort Mandan in North Dakota. While waiting for the February 11,1805 arrival of their son, Jean-Baptiste Charbonneau, seventeen-year-old Sacajawea and her husband met with the Corp of Discovery who were also wintering at the fort. This encounter would influence the rest of Sacajawea's life.

Sacajawea Joins Lewis and Clark

Upon meeting Charbonneau and learning of his expertise with the Hidatsa and French languages as well as his knowledge of the surrounding area, Lewis and Clark hired him as an interpreter and guide. The expedition's captains insisted, however, that Charbonneau bring along Sacajawea and Jean-Baptiste. Not only would Sacajawea and her son help the party establish a peaceful nature, but she would also be an invaluable asset in helping the Corp understand Native American culture and trade for necessary stock and supplies. In May 1805, the expedition left North Dakota and headed on its journey to discover the Pacific Northwest. Sacajawea would be the only woman to accompany the expedition's thirty-three permanent members to the Pacific Ocean and back.

Sacajawea's Contributions to the Corp of Discovery

While Captain Meriwether Lewis made little mention of Sacajawea in his journals, Captain William Clark grew quite fond of the young woman and her son, whom he affectionately nicknamed "Pompy" or "Pomp" for short. Clark detailed Sacajawea's contributions on several occasions. On May 14, 1805, the boat Sacajawea was riding in nearly capsized. Clark credited her with saving many important papers and supplies crucial to the expedition's success, and she was continually thanked for her calmness and quick-thinking. Sacajawea also provided information about the mountainous terrain and helped secure supplies and trail guides through her ability to negotiate with other Native American tribes. When the food supply ran short, Clark noted in his journal that Sacajawea gathered roots, nuts, berries, and any other edible plant that could be used to nourish the expedition's members. Sensing that Sacajawea seemed respected by most of the party, Charbonneau grew jealous and beatings against Sacajawea began to occur more frequently. Despite mistreatment at her husband's hands, Sacajawea continued to provide key information to Lewis and Clark, and the Corp finally reached the outlet of the Columbia River on November 24, 1805. On January 7, 1806, Sacajawea's dream of seeing the great Pacific Ocean came true. Captain Clark personally led her there as payment for her services along the trek.

Life After the Expedition

When the Corp of Discovery returned to the Hidatsa-Mandan villages on August 14, 1806, Charbonneau was given $500 and 320 acres of land as payment for his interpretive skills while Sacajawea received no material award. Instead, Lewis and Clark named a river in her honor.

Sacajawea remained with Charbonneau but did travel to St. Louis, Missouri for a short time. In 1812, Sacajawea gave birth to a daughter, Lisette, and the family settled in present day South Dakota at the Missouri Fur Company trading post known as Fort Manuel. Lisette's birth, however, appears to have aggravated an infection Sacajawea had battled for months. On December 12, 1812, Sacajawea died at the age of 25. While her contemporaries suspected smallpox, tuberculosis, or scarlet fever as the cause of her death, medical researchers now speculate that Sacajawea suffered from a serious illness most of her adult life that ultimately resulted in her death. Concerned about the welfare of Sacajawea's children at the hands of the abusive Charbonneau, Clark legally adopted Jean-Baptiste and Lisette and returned to Missouri. Nothing else is known about Lisette's fate, but Clark educated "Pomp" until age 18 and then sent him to study in Europe with a German prince.

Intrigue Surrounds Sacajawea's Death

While most historians agree that Sacajawea died in 1812 due to an illness, Shoshone oral history, 20th century scholars, and movies have perpetuated the myth that Sacajawea lived a healthy life until 1884. These tales report the woman's name as Porivo, and she supposedly rejoined Jean-Baptiste in Wyoming's Wind River Mountains. The oral accounts also state that Sacajawea remarried several times, had numerous other children, and died in Wyoming. Based on these tales, a monument to Sacajawea was erected at Porivo's gravesite at Fort Washakie, Wyoming.

While no one is absolutely positive about Sacajawea's ultimate fate after the Lewis and Clark Expedition and different historians and scholars provide varying tales, it is known that Sacajawea played a tremendous role in the Corp of Discovery. With her aid, Lewis and Clark discovered the northwestern corridor and opened up America for future exploration.

or talk business with the aid of group planning services and meeting rooms. Each evening, saddle up to hearty western cuisine, go on a hayride, and gather 'round the campfire for singing and dancing. Whether you're visiting for work or play, let Twin Peaks Ranch show you the Northern Rockies!

L Syringa Lodge
13 Gott Ln., Salmon. 756-4424 or (877) 580-6482. www.syringalodge.com

Situated on a bluff overlooking the Salmon community and the surrounding valley, the Syringa Lodge boasts panoramic vistas. Constructed from large spruce logs, the lodge features uniquely decorated bedrooms furnished with a queen or king sized bed and private bath. When you're not enjoying the views from your room or delighting in the home-cooked breakfasts, escape to one of the lodge's six porches, walk the lodge's Salmon River trail, sip coffee in the library as the sunset lights up the snowcapped Bitterroot Mountains, or cozy up to the great room fireplace with its beautifully carved pine mantel. Guests also enjoy high speed and wireless Internet service, quick access to downtown Salmon and outdoor recreation, and frequent wildlife sightings. For comfort and convenience in a pristine setting, make reservations at the Syringa Lodge.

L Greyhouse Inn Bed & Breakfast
1115 Hwy. 93 S., Salmon. 756-3968 or (800) 348-8097. www.greyhouseinn.com

S McPherson's
301 Main St., Salmon. 756-3232 or (888) 725-3890. www.mcphersonsonline.com

Established in 1902, McPherson's department store still occupies the same building on Salmon's Main Street and offers antiques, gifts, and name brand men's and women's clothing. Along with an extensive clothing line, the Men's Department features the building's original wood floors and a collection of old cowboy hats worn by local ranchers. In the Women's Department, shoppers will find a unique blend of casual and dressy sportswear along with an excellent section of souvenir t-shirts featuring Salmon, Idaho and the Lewis and Clark Expedition. Blending the old with the new, McPherson's Antique and Gift Department emphasizes rural Idaho's lifestyle. Gifts include dinnerware, candles, wine accessories, blankets, and decorative accessories, while antiques are primarily furniture. For quality service and an unbeatable selection of clothing and home items, stop at McPherson's.

M Esther England, Mountain West Real Estate
521 Main St., Salmon. 756-1800, (866) 466-3778, or 756-7019 (Cell). www.mtnwestrealestate.com

M Mountain West Real Estate
521 Main St., Salmon. 756-1800, (866) 466-3778, or 756-7231 (Cell). www.mtnwestrealestate.com

M Hometown Realty
529 Main St., Salmon. 756-6900 or (888) 701-2946. www.salmonidahorealty.com

M Town & Country Realty
534 Main St., Salmon. 756-4910 or (888) 460-7029. www.t-crealestate.com

Broker Leila Jarvis opened Town & Country Realty in 2004, formerly Benedict Realty since 1982. The office continues as a successful independent real estate brokerage in Salmon. Possessing years of experience, the friendly and professional full-time realtors offer expertise in residential, commercial, and land purchases with a history of sales and marketing productivity. The brokerage is a member of the Salmon Exchange Listing and Multiple Listing Service and boasts a user-friendly website with continually updated real estate listings. The office is also home to a fine collection of Leila Jarvis' watercolor paintings with prints available for purchase. When you're in the market to buy or sell property in the pristine Salmon community, contact the personable agents at Town & Country Realty to make your real estate dreams come true!

M Lee Bilger, Realtor at Cook Real Estate
525 Main St., Salmon. Home: 756-2206; Cell: 940-0251. www.salmonidaho.com/web.html?go=8

Lee Bilger, realtor at Cook Real Estate, is an Idaho native and has been a licensed agent since 1991 in the Salmon/Mackay area and also in Winnemucca,

Nevada. She prides herself on professionalism, and her dedication to providing quality service is evident. As a result of her commitment to customers, Lee has received numerous real estate awards, including Top Listing Sales Associate, Master's Club, and Million Dollar Club. In addition, Lee was one of five Idaho agents in 1994 to receive the coveted Centurion Award for customer satisfaction and service. Whether you're interested in selling your business or home or purchasing a dream house in the beautiful Salmon and Mackay region, Lee has the knowledge and experience to provide outstanding results for all your real estate needs!

M Robie Real Estate
531 Main St., Salmon. 756-4159. www.salmonidaho.com/robie

Drawing upon their familiarity with Salmon and the Lemhi Valley, Robie Real Estate has provided professional real estate services for over 30 years. Under the management of Erin and Linda Robie who were born and raised in Idaho, Robie Real Estate is dedicated to providing high quality results to sellers and buyers. The brokerage possesses the experience and market knowledge to help potential homeowners find the property that matches their needs. Sellers enjoy the office's commitment to utilize the latest technology to market the property and find the right buyer at a fair price. Maintaining several licenses, Robie Real Estate's friendly agents are experienced in all aspects of buying and selling ranching, commercial, and residential property. Contact them today and let them illustrate what they can do for you!

M Salmon Real Estate
818 Main St., Salmon. 756-3201 or (877) 756-2201. www.salmonidaho.com/salmonrealestate

Founded on experience and integrity, Salmon Real Estate welcomes you to Salmon, Idaho. We are a full-service company: residential, ranches, acreages, and commercial. Come let us provide you with a packet containing all the available properties with the Salmon Multiple Listing Service. On the Internet, you can view any one of the listings in the region simply by clicking on the MLS number we give you. From our website, you

can conveniently link to every realtor's current listings in Salmon. As a Salmon area native, Broker/Owner, Steve Sayer, offers you first-hand knowledge about the area's vast year-round recreational opportunities. From Salmon Real Estate, you can expect confidentiality, professional advice, and a new friendship with us. Come live by the River of No Return, "Where Dreams Become 'Realty'."

M Salmon Valley Chamber of Commerce
200 Main St., Ste. 1, Salmon. 756-2100. www.salmonbyway.com; info@salmonbyway.com

4

H Michel Bourdon
Milepost 245.3 on U.S. Hwy. 93

This valley was discovered in 1822 by a party of Hudson's Bay Company trappers led by Michel Bourdon. Bourdon had come to the Northwest with David Thompson, who had started the Idaho fur trade in 1808-09. Trappers searched everywhere for beaver and were active south of here for years before Bourdon took them farther into this mountain wilderness. Fur hunting went on for another decade in these parts before the country was trapped out and abandoned by the fur traders.

T Cronks Canyon
Approximately 20 miles north of Challis on U.S. Hwy. 93. Contact the Challis Chamber of Commerce at 879-2771.

Often called the Royal Gorge of Idaho, Cronks Canyon extends for two scenic miles on U.S. Hwy. 93. Winding through an exposed Swauger Quartzite hill next to the Salmon River, the road passes by steep canyon walls and twisted rock layers. Ancient volcanic flows shaped the narrow gorge, and at one time, the area was recognized for its natural hot springs pools. Both historically and recently, the area has afforded numerous sightings of resident bighorn sheep.

T Elk Bend Hot Springs
Located 22 miles south of Salmon on U.S. Hwy. 93 near mile marker 282. Contact the Salmon Valley Chamber of Commerce at 756-2100 for more information. Near mile marker 282, merge off U.S. Hwy. 93 onto the unsigned Warm Springs Creek Rd. Follow the gravel road 0.2 miles to a parking area.

Marked with shade trees, cascading waterfalls, and incredible mountain vistas, the undeveloped Elk Bend Hot Springs (a.k.a. Goldbug Hot Springs) is a natural hideaway often referred to as Idaho's most magnificent soaking spot. From huge pools to smaller soaking spots ideal for couples, Elk Bend boasts eleven separate pools at last count in an unabashedly romantic setting. Water temperature hovers around 102 degrees Farenheit, and most natives soak au natural.

To access the pools, follow the trail up the hillside from the parking area that leads across the valley floor and several footbridges. Passing by the old sheepherder's cabin, camping area, and outhouse, continue hiking into a narrow draw. Here, the hike becomes more difficult, climbing 200 yards up an extremely steep slope. The first pool can be found on the left as the trail flattens. To locate the remaining pools, continue walking upstream past the huge boulders to another footbridge. The hottest pool lies to the right near this bridge, and five other pools are located in this same vicinity. The remaining pools are located just twenty feet down the trail.

The area is particularly noted for its beautiful sunsets, and a general code of ethics for the springs does exist. The area is not recommended for children, and the hike does require a moderate level of physical fitness. Glass containers are prohibited, but visitors can bring food and other beverages to the site. Cameras are also highly recommended to capture the true beauty of this remote mountain wonderland. As a final note, all visitors are asked to treat this natural site with respect so that future generations may enjoy the springs for many years to come.

T Birch Creek Conservation Area

Contact the Nature Conservancy District Headquarters at 788-2203. Located south of Salmon between the Lemhi and Beaverhead Mountains

Operated under a joint partnership of the Nature Conservancy and the Bureau of Land Management, the Birch Creek Conservation Area was established between the Beaverhead and Lemhi Mountains. The 1,160-acre preserve is nestled in a valley where fifty springs join together to create the headwaters of Birch Creek. In addition to boasting the world's largest known alkali primrose population, Birch Creek offers fishing, hiking, hunting, and wildlife viewing. The area is open year round free of charge.

T Pahsimeroi River Hatchery

Contact the Idaho Department of Fish and Game at 334-3700. Located on Pahsimeroi Valley Road 19 miles northeast of Challis near the community of Ellis.

The Idaho Power Company constructed Pahsimeroi River Hatchery in 1967 near the convergence of the Pahsimeroi and Salmon Rivers. Operating with a supplemental-conservation focus, the facility rears Chinook salmon and steelhead trout. The hatchery is surrounded by mountain views and is open for guided tours.

TV Salmon River

The Salmon River begins its journey four miles north of Alturas, Idaho, high in the Sawtooth Mountains of central Idaho at an elevation of over 8,000 feet. The River ends 425 miles later when it drains into the Snake River on the border of Oregon and Idaho, about forty-five miles south of Lewiston. At that point, it's at an elevation of 803 feet. No dams are present on the Salmon River because 35% of all steelhead and salmon that make up the Columbia River spawn at its headwaters.

Throughout the course of its journey, the Salmon River flows through mostly rugged, mountainous, timber-covered terrain. Its drainage basin includes over 14,000 acres. The River has an East, Middle, North and South Fork, all of which contribute to its grandeur. For over 180 miles of its trip, the Main Salmon flows through a 6,300-foot deep canyon, which is deeper than the Grand Canyon itself, and second in depth only to Hells Canyon at Lewiston. Unlike the sheer walls of the Grand Canyon, the Salmon flows below wooded ridges rising steeply toward the sky beneath eroded bluffs and ragged crags. Adventurers seek out the waters of the Salmon for its incredible rapids. The North Fork contains Class II and III+ rapids, and the Middle Fork is one of the world's greatest and most popular whitewater locations, attracting adventurers from around the globe. The river boasts over thirty rapids, most of them Class IV in nature. Hot springs also line the banks of the river, tempting weary water travelers. Some of the

attraction of the Middle Fork is that it's more hidden from civilization than is the Main Fork. The Main Fork, however, contains the biggest waves and deepest holes in its rapids and has many sandy beaches along its banks. Both rivers offer many historical sites along their shores, including pioneer and hermit cabins, Indian camps and pictographs, sites associated with the Sheepeater Campaign of 1879, and old mining camps.

The Lewis and Clark Expedition traveled through this area and camped in the Lemhi Valley. On August 21, 1805, Captain Lewis was the first white man to visit the waters, and therefore they named it "Lewis River." The local Shoshone Indians told Captain Clark the Salmon River Canyon was impassable. Clark decided to find out for himself what the canyon was like and traveled to the high side of the canyon for a better view. From there he could see the Class IV Pine Creek Rapids far below in the deep gorge. With the high, rocky walls on either side, Clark determined that the canyon was indeed impassable. He returned to the camp and instructed the expedition to detour to the north, around the canyon. In later years, some pioneers did float some sections of the upper Salmon, but paddling upstream against the strong current was impossible, thus earning it the nickname of "The River of No Return." The name of the river was later changed to Salmon because of the salmon found below its surface.

TV Pahsimeroi River and Valley

17.3 miles north of Challis. Contact the Challis Chamber of Commerce at 879-2771.

Marking the boundary between Custer and Lemhi Counties in north-central Idaho, the Pahsimeroi River joins forces with the mighty Salmon River north of Challis. Hundreds of explorers, mountain men, and trappers traversed the scenic valley surrounding the Pahsimeroi River during the 1800s. Most notably, Warren Ferris from the American Fur Company and his company of men camped in the Pahsimeroi Valley during the winter of 1831-1832. They succeeded in killing a record 100 bison during their short stay. Although the bison have long been killed off in the area, the valley is now home to an ever-expanding antelope population.

On its journey to join the Salmon River, the Pahsimeroi River drains 845 square miles. Although the drainage's trout populations have steadily been declining for the last decade, anglers still have access to whitefish and limited amounts of rainbow, bull, cutthroat, and brook trout.

V Williams Lake

Contact the Salmon Ranger District at 756-3724. On U.S. Hwy. 93, travel 9 miles south of Salmon, and bear west on Forest Service Rd. 028. Proceed 3 miles to the lake.

Named after early pioneer rancher, Henry Williams, Williams Lake is nestled in north-central Lemhi County at an elevation of 5,252 feet. Researchers speculate that the 180-acre lake formed over 6,000 years ago when an earthquake triggered a landslide that blocked Lake Creek, the lake's primary source of inflow. The Idaho Department of Fish and Game stocked the lake annually with rainbow trout from 1941 to 1983. However, when they discovered that the trout population was self-sustaining, they discontinued the practice. Today, the 185 foot deep lake features wild rainbow trout weighing up to two pounds. The site is open year round for fishing and ice fishing, while summer months also provide boating

FRANK CHURCH – RIVER OF NO RETURN WILDERNESS

The Frank Church-River of No Return

Wilderness, encompassing 2,366,757 acres all within Idaho's borders, is the largest single wilderness area in the lower 48 states. Frank Church was a U.S. Senator from Idaho who was essential to the passage of the Wilderness Act of 1964. His name was added to the Wilderness shortly before his death in 1984. The Salmon River Mountains rise to over 10,000 feet in the middle of the wilderness, and include the Twin, General, Bald, Jordon and Tango Peaks. The Bighorn Crags are an incredible series of summits surrounded by fourteen clear water lakes. For as far as the eye can see, the great forest of Douglas fir and lodge pole pine trees stretches out. Spruce and ponderosa pines also cover the terrain, as do grassy meadows and open prairies. Wildlife is abundant in the forest, despite the arid climate.

The wilderness is very accessible as all the interior mining and logging roads are maintained. Instead of being allowed to become overgrown once the wilderness was established, the roads were grandfathered into the landscape with the government allowing them to remain as is. Because of the numerous roads, access to many trailheads is available throughout the area. In fact, 2,616 miles of maintained trails are available within the wilderness; therefore, hiking and horseback riding are popular activities in the vast forest. Despite the many trails, 1.5 million acres remain trail free.

and swimming opportunities. Three and a half miles of shoreline await visitors, along with two campgrounds and two boat ramps.

V Williams Creek Snowmobile Trails

Contact the Salmon-Cobalt Ranger District at 756-5200. Drive 4 miles south of Salmon on U.S. Hwy. 93. At Forest Rd. 021, bear west.

Snowmobilers in the scenic mountains near Salmon not only have access to winter recreation, but also to a piece of Idaho mining history. In 1866, the mining camp of Leesburg was established after a monumental discovery of placer gold. Although the area produced millions in gold, winters in the region wreaked havoc on the community's living conditions. Within no time, Leesburg residents fled in search of warmer weather and easier living. Today, the quiet ghost town remains tucked in the mountains, and a free snowmobile trail follows Williams Creek to the historic site. The remote area is generally accessible from December to April.

V Fishing the Salmon River Drainages

Mouth to Horse Creek

Recognized as a crucial migration passage for steelhead and Chinook and sockeye salmon, the Salmon River from its mouth to Horse Creek fea-

Continued on page 297

SALMON-CHALLIS NATIONAL FOREST

With the mighty Salmon River at its heart, the 4.3-million-acre Salmon-Challis National Forest is a study in contrasts. A distance of almost two vertical miles separates the climber atop Mt. Borah (12,662 feet), located on the southern end of the Forest, from the river rafter floating the lowest portion of the main Salmon River Canyon (2,800 feet), on the northern end of the Forest. And everywhere, the forest offers unsurpassed scenery and outdoor adventures. The rich history of Native Americans, explorers, pioneers, and miners all took place on this landscape shaped by millions of years of volcanic events, earthquakes, glaciers, wind, water, and fire. Here, much of the land remains only lightly touched by civilization, and native plants and wildlife thrive. Each spring, snowmelt from the high mountain slopes feeds the rivers, bringing renewed life to this incredible landscape.

River Recreation
Humans are drawn to the Salmon River for many reasons. They enjoy the challenge of negotiating surging rapids in a rubber raft. They celebrate when the hook an elusive trout. They relax while floating quiet water in the depths of a river canyon. They capture the river's unique beauty with the camera lens, or simply find solace in the music of the river. On its long journey to join the Snake River, the Salmon River flows for 400 miles. The river passes through portions of the Salmon-Challis National Forest, slowly eroding and sculpturing the face of the land as it gives life to an arid country. Visitors to the river are witness to what eons of time and flowing water have accomplished.

Two National Wild and Scenic Rivers flow through the Salmon-Challis National Forest. The Middle Fork of the Salmon River carries boaters into pristine, primitive landscapes where every bend of the river brings amazing scenery. The alert traveler will be rewarded by sightings of birds and other wildlife along these rivers. The world-class whitewater of the Middle Fork provides a truly wild float trip.

The recreation section of the Salmon Wild and Scenic River runs from North Fork, past the mouth of the Middle Fork, to Corn Creek, where the river enters the Frank Church – River of No Return Wilderness. The 79-mile section of the river from Corn Creek to Vinegar Bar boasts one of the deepest canyons in North America, where crashing rapids alternate with long quiet stretches. Jetboats also navigate the waters of this section of the river.

History-Human & Natural: A Steady Beat of Change
Evidence of the raw, rugged history of the West is clearly visible in and around the Salmon-Challis National Forest. Here, remnants of the lives and societies of Native Americans, gold and silver miners, missionaries, boatmen, explorers, pioneers, trappers, and mountain men are scattered across the land. You can follow the Lewis and Clark Trail to the place where the American flag was first unfurled west of the Rocky Mountains. A rich geological history is also found here, from natural arches along remote trails, to large areas affected by volcanic upheavals, to mountain ranges built by the action of plate tectonics. On October 28, 1983, a magnitude 7.3 earthquake centered near Challis formed a six-foot high scarp that still stretches for several miles along the western slope of the Lost River Range. This earthquake disrupted groundwater flows as far away as Yellowstone National Park, where it affected the eruptions of Old Faithful Geyser. Geologists estimate than an earthquake of similar magnitude has occurred in this area every 3,300 years for many millennia.

The Neighborhood: Arteries to a Wondrous Neighborhood
Located along the network of Scenic Byways, Backcountry Byways, and scenic routes in and around the Salmon-Challis National Forest is a vast spectrum of scenery and points of interest. Scores of opportunities exist to explore, hike, or camp near these roads and highways. You can drive along the high ridge dividing the Salmon-Challis from the Bitterroot National Forest. A trip to Stanley, Idaho, will take you to the only place in the United States where three National Forest Scenic Byways converge: the Sawtooth, Ponderosa Pine, and Salmon River. Nearby are impressive natural and historic wonders, including Mount Borah, the highest point in Idaho, and an earthquake interpretive site at the foot of the mountain. Or visit the Yankee Fork's historic mining district on the Custer Motorway, with its interpretive center near Challis. Silver and molybdenum mines, a unique floating gold dredge, ghost towns, and other historic structures are all within the mining district.

Seasonal Recreation: Circulating Through the Seasons
Spring approaches hesitantly on the Salmon-Challis National Forest. In the valleys and on the lower slopes of the mountains, new plant life begins to stir by April. But cold rains and snowstorms are still frequent, the winter snowpack remains unmelted, and camping and hiking are limited by cold nights and poor access to roads and trails. In late May and early June, however, visitors will begin to notice wildflowers and will often see deer and elk fawns trailing their mothers through budding aspen groves and conifer forests. On the rangelands near Challis, new foals join a wild horse herd.

Early summer brings warm days that begin to melt the mountain snows. As the snowpack melts, creeks and rivers rise swiftly, in some years bringing flooding. Be aware that although days may be warm, streams are still very cold. Hot weather usually begins by the end of June, but snow may linger in the high elevations well into July. Nights are cool at most elevations, and thunderstorms are frequent. Snow in the high elevations is not unknown at this time of year, so be prepared for any type of weather during your outdoor experience. As trails dry out and open, hikes into the Lemhi and Salmon River Mountains followed by a soothing soak in hot springs such as the one at Warm springs Creek, are a wonderful way to spend a weekend. Warm temperatures also bring thermal wind currents, which attract high gliders to King Mountain on the Lost River Ranger District.

Autumn usually arrives in the mountains by the first week of September, even before the leaves of aspen and gooseberry have turned to gold and crimson. The deep canyons of the Salmon River are busy with the rush of late season boaters and fishermen. They days are still warm, native trout and salmon are migrating upstream to spawn, and black bears fatten on wild berries for their winter hibernation. The eerie whistling calls of elk echo through the forest. Birds are on the move; ravens descend to lower elevations while sandhill cranes and ospreys migrate out of the area.

The first heavy winter snows usually arrive by mid-November. A few late elk hunters brave the cold, while skiers, snowmobilers, and ice fishermen enjoy the forest on clear days between storms.

Higher elevation roads and trails are inaccessible in winter. Ice builds up along the riverbanks. At Deadwater, on the main Salmon River below North Fork, a rock shelf stretching across the river begins to capture floating ice. In some years, this ice jam may stretch upriver for over 25 miles to the town of Salmon. While bear and some small mammals hibernate, others are active, and mountain sheep, elk, and deer move to south facing slopes and lower elevations to forage for food. Many bald eagles and other raptors winter in the valleys, feeding on carrion, rabbits, and smaller birds.

Wilderness: A Wild Pristine Treasure Surrounding the Heart
Much of the Salmon-Challis National Forest is untrammeled by man, with 80% of its land either roadless or in the Frank Church – River of No Return Wilderness. Both the Middle Fork and the Main Salmon River flow through portions of this 2.4-million-acre Wilderness. Navigating the wild, treacherous river below the confluence of the Middle Fork was a challenge for boatmen of the past, who delivered goods and passengers in wooden scows to miners and homesteaders. Since traveling back upstream was impossible, the scows were then dismantled for use as building material, leading to the nickname "River of No Return." Today's Wilderness is a wonderland of abundant wildlife, pristine lakes, and breathtaking scenery. The Salmon-Challis administers 1.2 million acres of "The Frank," sharing its vast boundaries with the Boise, Payette, Nez Perce, and Bitterroot National Forests.

Leave No Trace
- Camp and travel on durable surfaces.
- Plan ahead and prepare properly.
- Pack out what you bring into the forests.
- Properly dispose of what you can't pack out.
- Leave natural things where and how you found them.
- Minimize the use and impact of campfires.

Fire: Key to the Cycle of Life in the Forest
Lightning is nature's fire-starter. In the summer of 2000, lightning triggered an unprecedented number of large wildfires on the Salmon-Challis National Forest. The result of those fires will be visible for years, and where the fire burned intensely, revegetation will take many years. In areas where the fire burned more moderately, signs of new life stimulated by the fires are visible. The natural introduction of wildland fire can benefit a landscape.

Visitors will discover:
- Fire is a natural occurrence that can trigger rejuvenation of a forest ecosystem.
- Some cones and seeds need fire in order to germinate.

- Fire thins forest undergrowth and removes excess plants and trees.
- Large trees can survive cooler, low intensity fires.
- Most forest fires burn in a mosaic pattern, leaving islands of unburned vegetation.
- Fire can improve rangeland and stimulate the growth of grasses and forbs.
- Some wildlife actually need fire-adapted areas to thrive.
- Too much fire prevention eventually damages forest health.
- When all fires are suppressed, fuels build up and fires become larger and more destructive.
- Intense fires can destroy habitat needed by wildlife to survive and raise their young.

Remember:
- Fire can cause loss of life and damage to property and natural and historic resources.
- Under the right conditions, fire can benefit the forest.
- Only fire management experts should prescribe and monitor fires needed for forest health.

Be careful and use fire wisely to avoid starting a destructive wildland fire. Make sure your campfire is dead-out before leaving your campsite. Extinguish cigarettes, break matches, use spark arresters on equipment, and park your vehicle over bare ground. And always remember, fireworks are prohibited on National Forests.

Contact the Salmon-Challis National Forest at 756-5100. Reprinted from a U.S. Forest Service brochure

tures a variety of fish species. Although the Gospel Hump and Frank Church-River of No Return Wilderness Areas protect some of the river, anglers still have luck in finding smallmouth bass, sturgeon, and rainbow, cutthroat, and bull trout. This portion of the Salmon River includes the Chamberlain Creek tributary.

Horse Creek to North Fork
Running fifty miles through the heart of Lemhi County, the Horse Creek to North Fork portion of the Salmon River is known for a myriad of fish species. Wild and natural steelhead, Chinook salmon, westslope cutthroat trout, and small populations of white sturgeon populate the Salmon River and its Panther, Indian, Colson, Pine, and Corn Creek tributaries.

Little Salmon
The Little Salmon River drains 516 square miles and begins in Adams County at Meadows Valley. On its course to the confluence with the Salmon River in Riggins, the river flows through forests, meadows, and agricultural pastures. The river and its tributaries, including Goose Creek, Hazard Creek, Boulder Creek, Rapid River, Fish Lake, Goose Lake, Hazard Lake, and Brundage Reservoir, feature numerous fish species. Anglers will find mountain whitefish, non-game species, steelhead, Chinook salmon, and rainbow, bull, brook, and cutthroat trout.

South Fork
Contained within the state's Valley and Idaho Counties, the South Fork of the Salmon River flows north through the Idaho batholith and features widely divergent terrain. Flowing from steep canyons through lush meadows, the river contains

wild steelhead, mountain whitefish, kokanee, and rainbow, cutthroat, brook, bull, and lake trout. This portion of the Salmon River Drainage system includes thirty-seven lakes and flows for 515 miles.

Middle Fork
The Middle Fork of the Salmon River Drainage System is isolated and extremely rugged, draining 2,830 square miles of some of Idaho's most pristine landscapes. Held inside the Frank Church-River of No Return Wilderness Area, the river drainage is accessible by boat, aircraft, or hiking trails. For anglers who take the time and make the preparations to enter this remote landscape, the Middle Fork rewards their efforts with populations of Chinook salmon, steelhead, mountain whitefish, bull trout, and cutthroat trout. Interestingly, the cutthroat population has recently been identified as possessing a unique westslope strain not yet discovered in any other Idaho drainage. Although most of the tributary streams remain in pristine condition due to wilderness protection, the quality of some were affected by historical mining activity and cattle grazing.

North Fork to Headwaters
The North Fork to Headwaters portion of the Salmon River runs 173 miles through mountainous terrain and glacially carved valleys. A portion of the river is situated inside the Sawtooth National Recreation Area, and tributaries include the Lemhi, Pahsimeroi, East Fork of the Salmon, and Yankee Fork Rivers. Due to the area's granitic watershed, the river's large lakes are frequently sterile and cannot naturally produce fish. The river and area lakes, then, are annually stocked with over 100,000 hatchery rainbow trout. Included in this drainage area are Redfish and Alturas Lakes, which support populations of sockeye and kokanee salmon.

East Fork
The East Fork of the Salmon River drains 540 square miles on its thirty-three mile journey to the confluence of the Salmon River's South and West Forks. Encompassing the White Cloud Peaks and the Boulder Mountains, the drainage is one of Idaho's most important salmon spawning regions. The river also features hatchery steelhead.

Yankee Fork
Although the Yankee Fork of the Salmon River was once home to extensive mining operations, this twenty-six mile river stretch continues to support a variety of fish species. Anglers will locate hatchery steelhead along with rainbow, bull, and cutthroat trout.

5

Baker
Pop. 100

Located along the Lemhi River in the heart of cattle and sheep country, Baker honors the life of pioneer rancher William R. Baker. The businessman, who was previously employed as a railroad buffalo hunter, patented his claim on March 24, 1884. In 1889, a post office was established under William's name.

Tendoy
Pop. 50

This small town located on the Lemhi River near the mouth of Agency Creek is named after Native American, Chief Tendoy. A peaceable man, Chief Tendoy oversaw a band of 500 Lemhi and lived in the Lemhi Valley from 1857 to 1907. The area was

known for its mining activities at the nearby Copper Queen mine, as well as for sheep, cattle, and horse ranching.

Lemhi
This settlement on the banks of the Lemhi River draws its name from the historic and religious Fort Lemhi established near here in 1855. Although Fort Lemhi lost its right to postal services in 1907, this tiny outpost bearing the same name was awarded postal services in 1911.

H Lewis and Clark
Milepost 115.7 on State Hwy. 28

After crossing Lemhi Pass, 12 miles east of here, Meriwether Lewis unfurled the American flag for the first time west of the Rockies. Lewis met with three Shoshoni Indians near here on August 13, 1805. "…Leaving my pack and rifle I took the flag which I unfurled and advanced toward them," Lewis reported. The Warm Springs Road leads to a marker at the site, about eight miles from here.

H Fort Lemhi
Milepost 117.3 on State Hwy. 28

In 1855, a group of Mormon missionaries came north from Utah to found a remote colony just below the bench east of here. A religious settlement rather than a military fort, Salmon River Mission grew to more than 100 settlers before Indian trouble forced them to abandon the valley in 1858. By that time, the missionaries had baptized 100 Indians and had begun irrigated farming in spite of ruinous summer frosts and plagues of grasshoppers. Some of the old mission ditches are still used, and part of an old adobe mission wall still stands at Fort Lemhi.

H MacDonald's Battle
Milepost 119.9 on State Hwy. 28

Whooping and yelling, Blackfeet Indians and white trappers "fought like demons" in the defile before you in 1823. After the Hudson's Bay Company trappers burned the Indians out of a strong position by starting a large brush fire, the Blackfeet lost 10 warriors in a hot battle. Though he came out the victor, Finnan MacDonald decided that before he would return to trap anywhere around here again, "The beaver will have a gould skin."

H Lewis and Clark
Milepost 122.4 on State Hwy. 28

After crossing the Continental Divide southeast of here, August 12, 1805, Meriwether Lewis camped with a Shoshoni band near here August 13-14. Lewis had to obtain Indian horses so his men could get from the upper Missouri to a navigable stream flowing to the Pacific. So he persuaded the Shoshoni to accompany him to the expedition's main camp east of the mountains. There he found the

Idaho Trivia

Known to Lewis and Clark as "The River of No Return," Idaho's Salmon River continues to hold legendary status. The river originates in the community of Salmon, providing the town with its nickname, "The Whitewater Capital of the World." The Salmon also remains one of America's few undammed rivers, making it that much more wild for whitewater adventure seekers.

Shoshoni chief to be Sacajawea's brother. With horses and help from Sacajawea's people, Lewis and William Clark came to this valley August 26 on their way north to the Lolo Trail and the Clearwater.

H **Sacajawea**
Milepost 122.4 on State Hwy. 28

Sacajawea returned to her homeland in this valley in 1805 as an interpreter for Meriwether Lewis and William Clark when they explored these mountains.When she was about 14 years old, she had been captured by Indians in Montana, where her people were out hunting buffalo in 1800. Reunited with her family, she helped Lewis and Clark obtain Indian horses and a Shoshoni guide to show them how to reach their Columbia River destination.

T **Fort Limhi**
U.S. Hwy. 28 in Lemhi County

Named after King Limhi in the Book of Mormon, this fort was established in 1855 by Salt Lake City missionaries belonging to the Church of Jesus Christ of Latter Day Saints. Migrating to the area in hopes of converting area Native Americans, these missionaries developed a fort with mud walls measuring seven feet high and 265 feet long. Inside the walls, the 39 residents built several small cabins, a blacksmith shop, and a sawmill. Once an irrigation ditch was built, the missionaries successfully planted crops and raised cattle. The U.S. government, however, was not happy with the arrival of Mormons in the area, and President Buchanan sent 2,500 troops to stop a possible Mormon uprising. Realizing the politics between the Mormons and the U.S. government and surmising that the U.S. would not punish them for harassing the missionaries, area Shoshone and Bannock Indians attacked Fort Limhi in February 1858. Two of the missionaries were killed, and all of the cattle were stolen. In response, Brigham Young sent 150 armed Mormon men to escort the remaining missionaries back to Salt Lake City, and Fort Limhi was abandoned.

Today, visitors will find a portion of the fort's wall still intact as well as part of the first irrigation ditch. The fort is also remembered in Idaho history as the namesake for Lemhi County and the current town of Lemhi.

T **Lemhi Pass**
Contact the Salmon-Challis National Forest at 768-2500 for current road conditions and weather. Turn off State Hwy. 28 at the Tendoy Community Store, and proceed to the intersection for Agency Creek Rd. and Warm Springs Rd. Agency Creek Rd. winds 12 steep miles to Lemhi Pass and is not appropriate for RV's or towing of any kind. To follow Warm Springs Rd., bear left at the intersection, and continue 3 miles to the right hand turn for Warm Springs Road. This gentler route leads to Lemhi Pass in 22 miles.

Situated at an elevation of 7,323 feet along the Continental Divide between Montana and Idaho, Lemhi Pass is a rounded saddle in the Beaverhead Mountains linked to westward expansion. On August 12, 1805, Lewis and Clark and the Corps of Discovery first laid eyes on the Columbia River's headwaters that would eventually become the state of Idaho. Unfurling the first U.S. flag to hit western territory, the expedition then crossed over America's historic western boundary into uncharted, unclaimed territory.

In 1960, Lemhi Pass was designated a National Historic Landmark for its significance to the Lewis and Clark Expedition and U.S. history. For the Corp, the pass was a point of hope as they eagerly anticipated meeting the Shoshone people.

At the same time, the pass was a bitter disappointment as it proved there was no safely navigable waterway leading to the Pacific Ocean through the myriad of mountains.

Although there were fewer pine and fir trees on the hillsides and more beaver dams along the streams, the Lemhi Pass region is much the same as it was 200 years ago. Native sagebrush and bunch grasses remain along with Douglas fir and lodgepole pine trees. The spectacular vista of distant mountains also stands the same.

Dedicated to maintaining the natural, historic landscape of Lemhi Pass, the Forest Service has not overly developed the site. Interpretive signs relating the area's history are available to visitors during the summer.

The road is open to the public generally from June through October. However, the route may be deeply rutted and very rocky, so high clearance vehicles are highly recommended. The weather on the road is frequently cool and unpredictable, and snow is possible throughout the entire year. Summer months bring severe thunderstorms, and road travel is not suggested during wet conditions. Before exploring Lemhi Pass, all visitors are urged to contact the Salmon-Challis National Forest for current road condition and weather information.

T **McFarland Recreation Site**
Located at Milepost 103.6 approximately 5 miles south of Lemhi on State Hwy. 28. 765-5400.

Operated by the Bureau of Land Management, the McFarland Recreation Site provides roadside access to picnicking and fishing. The site offers a few picnic tables, fishing on both the upstream and downstream sections of the Lemhi River, and opportunities to view sandhill cranes, heron, and geese.

T **Chief Tendoy's Grave**
At the Tendoy Post Office, bear east and continue 0.1 miles to a T. Turn right, proceed 0.2 miles, and then turn left up Agency Creek Rd. Continue 1.5 miles on Agency Creek and turn right. Crossing over two cattle guards, follow the road as it curves west to a knoll overlooking the valley.

Chief Tendoy, nephew of the famous Sacajawea, became chief of the Lemhi Band (a mixture of Shoshone and Bannock Native Americans) in 1863. He was a firm disbeliever in warfare and established a reputation as being a friend to both whites and Indians. He strived for peace with the white settlers, and upon his death, hundreds of Native Americans and nearly 400 white men paid respects to Tendoy at his funeral. Today's visitors can pay their own respects to the famous chief outside the town now bearing his name. Nestled on top of a knoll overlooking the scenic Lemhi Valley, Tendoy's grave bears a sandstone marker that his white friends erected in 1924.

T **Corps of Discovery: Cameahwait's Village**
5 miles north of Tendoy at the mouth of Kenney Creek on the highway's east side

After crossing Lemhi Pass in August 1805, Lewis and Clark separated briefly. Lewis, along with eleven other expedition members and guide, Cameahwait, moved camp to this site on August 14. The site served as the expedition's base through August 29 while Clark scouted out a potential route down the Salmon River. Although the site was peaceful at that time, its heritage cannot say the same.

In 1823, Finian MacDonald and his party of Hudson Bay trappers started a fire in the area in an attempt to smoke out a party of Blackfoot warriors. The Blackfeet lost ten warriors in the skirmish and MacDonald vowed never to return to the area.

TV **Lemhi River Drainage**

Flowing through the lush agricultural plain situated between the Bitterroot and Lemhi Mountain Ranges, the Lemhi River drains 1,290 square miles. The river, which is appropriated for irrigational use, merges with the Salmon River near the community of Salmon. Although stream alterations and irrigation has negatively affected populations of migrating salmon and steelhead, the river still possesses a few spawning offspring. In addition, the Lemhi drainage features rainbow, cutthroat, and bull trout along with limited populations of brook trout.

V **Lemhi Pass Scenic Mountain Bike Trail**
21 miles south of Salmon. Contact the Salmon-Challis National Forest at 756-5100.

In 1805, Lewis and Clark's Corp of Discovery climbed the Continental Divide to Lemhi Pass that now straddles the Idaho/Montana border. Although the rough Lewis and Clark Backcountry Byway allows vehicles to retrace the journey, recreationists are encouraged to imbibe the open air and explore the route on a mountain bike.

Winding 39.1 strenuous miles, the gravel Lemhi Pass Scenic Trail is not for the faint at heart as the route climbs to a summit elevation exceeding 7,000 feet. Mountain bikers, however, are rewarded with stunningly scenic views of both Idaho and Montana atop the high pass in the Beaverhead Mountains.

Users should practice caution at all times as cars may also be on the road. Primitive campsites are available, and the route is generally open from June through August.

6 *Food, Lodging*

Leadore
Pop. 90

This small town, once the site of celebrated mining activity, was named for the lead-silver ore found in its surrounding hills. The post office was established in 1911.

H **Charcoal Kilns**
Milepost 61 on State Hwy. 28

Charcoal for a smelter, active from 1885-89 across the valley at Nicholia, was produced in 16 kilns six miles west of here. Discovered in 1881, the Viola mine became an important source for lead and silver from 1886-88. Ore also was hauled from Gilmore to the Viola smelter. British capital kept the Viola mine going until 1889, when the hoisting works burned. Low prices for lead and silver kept the smelter shut down after 1889, and charcoal production ceased here. You are invited to take a self-guided tour of the kilns, provided by the Targhee National Forest.

H **Cote's Defile**
Milepost 61 on State Hwy. 28

A French Canadian who came to southern Idaho in 1818, Joseph Cote found this valley while trapping beaver. Though he was miles from his Canadian base in Montreal, he had years of experience in Pacific Northwest exploration. With Michael Bourdon, who also discovered valleys near here, he had joined David Thompson's 1811 Columbia River explorers. Early trappers knew this valley as Cote's Defile because of his contribution to the regional fur trade.

H **Gilmore**
Milepost 73.2 on State Hwy. 28

Lack of a good transportation system delayed serious lead and silver mining at Gilmore from

1880 to 1910. Construction of a branch railroad from Montana to serve this mining area resulted in the production of $11.5 million worth of ore before a power plant explosion halted operations here in 1929. Old Gilmore and Pittsburgh Railway grades visible north of here and remnants of Gilmore – a ghost town abandoned many years ago a mile west of here – preserve visible evidence of that bygone mining era.

H Bannock Pass
Milepost 13.6 on State Hwy. 29 at the Montana State Line

This traditional Indian route provided access from Montana's buffalo country to Snake and Salmon River fishing streams. Hudson's Bay Co. trapping expeditions came this way after 1822, and prospectors followed, searching for mines. Then in 1877, Nez Perce war combatants returned from Montana to Idaho through Bannock Pass on their way from Big Hole battleground to Yellowstone Park and Canada. From 1910 to 1939, railroad trains from Dillon to Salmon steamed through here. Old Gilmore and Pittsburgh railroad tunnels and grades still can be seen from this highway.

T Gilmore
Proceed south from Leadore on State Hwy. 28. Near milepost 73, merge onto Forest Rd. 002. Continue approximately 1 mile to the ghost town.

Gilmore was once a big money mining town. The mining district that was established here in 1880 reportedly produced more than $40 million in silver and lead. To handle production demands, a line of the Gilmore and Pittsburgh Railroad was added in 1910, and ore was shipped out just as fast as it was produced. Although work had been steady, the mines were forced to close in 1929 in advent of the Depression and a devastating power plant explosion.

Today, the ghost town retains its recognition of John T (Jack) Gilmer of the Gilmer and Salisbury Stage Company. Jack was an intelligent and entrepreneuring pioneer in the American West's stagecoach business. When the post office was established here in 1903, a postal clerk miscopied the name, thereby establishing the name's current spelling.

T Birch Creek Charcoal Kilns
774-3531. From Leadore, drive south on Hwy. 28 over Gilmore Summit. Take the marked turnoff on the road's west side that leads to the kilns in 6 miles.

In the 1880s, the Birch Creek Valley was active with mining activity at the Viola smelter. To fuel the essential smelter, Warren King of Butte, Montana built several beehive shaped rock ovens in 1883. Immediately upon the kilns' completion, charcoal production began. Charcoal is produced from burning wood in the absence of air. Employing over 300 Irish, Italian, and Chinese immigrants, the kilns measured over twenty feet tall and twenty feet in diameter and could hold up to thirty-five cords of wood. With a production capability of 500 pounds of charcoal per one cord of wood, the kilns were highly successful in maintaining the operations of the Viola smelter nearby.

On average, each charcoal kiln produced 45,000 to 50,000 bushels of charcoal per month. The coal was then transferred to the smelter via covered wagons, and the process of cutting down Douglas fir trees and placing them in the kiln began anew. At its peak, the Birch Creek site was home to sixteen kilns, and historians suggest that over 150,000 cords of wood were burned during the kilns' lifespan from 1885-1889. Due to brick salvaging by early settlers, only three kilns remain standing today. The site was added to the National Register of Historic Places in 1972, and a short interpretive trail surrounds the kilns.

CHIEF TENDOY – THE LAST LEMHI SHOSHONE CHIEF

Known as a friend to the white man and one of the greatest Indian chiefs of his time, Chief Tendoy was born in the Boise River area in 1834. As the proud son of a Bannock father and Shoshone mother and nephew of the legendary Sacajawea, Tendoy's character and abilities were recognized at an early age. He defended his tribe against warring Crows, Flathead, and Sioux, and he moved to the Lemhi Valley with distinction.

When the Plummer gang murdered the former chief, his uncle, in 1863, Tendoy became the tribe's new chief. Overseeing a band of more than 500 members, Tendoy decided early on that it was easier to establish peaceful relationships with incoming white settlers instead of making war. In 1868, Tendoy traveled to Virginia City, Montana to sign an agreement that would establish a reservation for the Lemhi Shoshones in north-central Idaho. Congress failed to approve the treaty and as a result, Tendoy and his band were forced to fend for themselves. As the influx of miners had disturbed their sacred hunting grounds, the tribe had no means of gathering food and was not equipped with the knowledge or skills to grow their own food. Tendoy's tribe became destitute until the government finally appropriated some funds for food.

Shortly after these funds were approved, the Indian Commissioner urged the government to move the tribe onto the Fort Hall Indian Reservation. Chief Tendoy refused to move, and his white friends in the area plead with the government for the tribe to be left alone in the Lemhi Valley. In 1875, President Grant agreed to the wishes of Tendoy and his friends, and the 160 square mile Lemhi Reservation was created. For now, Tendoy was free to focus on the problems of other Native Americans.

While it was difficult for him to watch the troubles plaguing many other Native American tribes in the area, Chief Tendoy was adamantly opposed to war. He successfully persuaded his tribe to remain peaceful during the 1877 Nez Perce War. In 1878, he again squelched any plan the tribe may have had to engage in the Bannock War, and he maintained the reputation as a peaceful leader throughout his entire life. Despite conflicts with the Indian Commissioner, Tendoy kept his peaceful resolve. In one instance where Tendoy's grandson was being forced to attend the reservation school, Tendoy boldly stated his opposition and finally succeeded in pulling his grandchild from the school.

Unfortunately, the U.S. Government was not at peace with Chief Tendoy. In 1880, Tendoy and a select number of respected tribal members were sent to Washington, D.C. The Interior Department persuaded Tendoy to sign an agreement where he would move his tribe to the Fort Hall Reservation in return for a $4,000 stipend over the following twenty years. When Tendoy returned to Idaho and presented the plan to his tribe, he soon rethought his decision. Since the agreement was not ratified by a two-thirds approval vote of the Lemhi males, Tendoy backed out on his agreement and refused to move.

Growing weary of Tendoy's resistance, the government sent an order in 1905 that the tribe had no choice but to move. When Tendoy met the federal agent carrying the order, Tendoy finally submitted against his heart's true desire. Speaking earnestly to his tribe about the situation, Tendoy convinced the members that the move was for the best. While the tribe abided by his wishes and moved to the Fort Hall Reservation in June 1907, Tendoy never had to give up his pride. Dying just one month earlier, Tendoy's funeral was attended by his tribe, Native Americans from afar, and nearly 400 white men who called Tendoy "friend."

T Bell Mountain
15 miles south of Gilmore Summit on State Hwy. 28

Rising on the crest of the Lemhi Mountains, Bell Mountain soars 11,600 feet into the Idaho sky. The mountain honors Englishman, Robert Bell, who lived in Lemhi County for twelve years and served as the state mining inspector in the early 1900s.

T Gilmore Summit
Approximately 17 miles south of Leadore on State Hwy. 28

Traveling on State Hwy. 28, visitors will crest the highway's tallest point at Gilmore Summit. The summit is situated at an elevation of 7,186 feet. The summit is named after the ghost town, Gilmore, nestled just one and a half miles from the highway.

T Gilmore and Pittsburgh Historic Railroad Bed
Extending seven miles north from Gilmore Summit on State Hwy. 28

Driving northwest on State Hwy. 28 through the Birch Creek Valley, the old Gilmore and Pittsburg Railroad bed can be seen on the highway's east side. Financed by Northern Pacific Railroad for $4.8 million, the line was completed in 1910 and connected the productive Gilmore mines with smelters in Butte, Montana. However, the railroad was doomed to failure from its start. The railroad was saddled with heavy debt, and improved roads in the area outpaced the line's effectiveness. Once the Gilmore mines were closed, the railroad's fate was sealed. In April 1939, the last train ran, and in 1940, the rails were removed for scrap iron.

T Bannock Pass
State Hwy. 29 northwest of Leadore at the Idaho/Montana border

Situated at an elevation of 7,672 feet, the treeless slopes of Bannock Pass provide an overlook of the surrounding area. Native Americans and miners used the route extensively, although the most famous use probably came in 1877. After the Battle of Big Hole in the Nez Perce War, the Nez Perce Indians crossed here on the morning of August 13 during their flight to Yellowstone National Park.

7 Food

Patterson
Pop. 4

Silver was discovered in a nearby drainage in 1879 by John Patterson, the town's namesake. A post office operated here from 1900 to 1924.

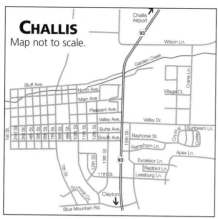

CHALLIS
Map not to scale.

May
Pop. 60

The small community of May lies in the heart of the Pahsimeroi Valley farming district. The post office was established in the spring of 1897. The wife of postmaster, Rudolph Wright, chose the name at the request that the name be short. Since the application was made in May, the name seemed appropriate to her, and the postal department wholeheartedly agreed.

8 *Food, Lodging*

Challis
Pop. 909

This mile-high city was founded in 1878 and honors the contributions of Alvah P. Challis, an early settler who assisted in surveying and platting the town's lots. The settlement became a trading center for the nearby mines and was connected to Custer by a toll road. The town also thrived as a cattle ranching town. In 1967, Challis' economy diversified further when the Cyprus Mine Corporation unearthed a nearby molybdenum deposit, which is used as a hardening agent in steel. Molybdenum is mined here to this day and is responsible for nearly 20% of the world's production.

H Bison Jump
Milepost 243.9 on State Hwy. 75

Before settlers came to Idaho in 1860, buffalo used to roam through this valley. Most of them had left here by 1840. After they acquired Spanish horses, 18th-century Shoshoni buffalo hunters could drive a small herd over a cliff to make their work easier. Directly north of here, an old buffalo jump, used before mining commenced in this region, can be clearly seen. Archaeologists also have found stone weapon factories near it.

T Bayhorse
Drive 8 miles south of Challis on State Hwy. 75. Bear east on Forest Rd. 051 (Bayhorse Creek Road) to locate the ghost town in just a few miles.

Idaho's Bayhorse Creek was a popular spot for prospectors, but it was not until 1872 that a claim was laid in the area. However, the claim was found too minimal to insight any significant mining

activity. Tim Cooper changed the area's dim prospects when he discovered a rich lead-silver deposit in March 1877. Soon, the Ramshorn, Skylark, and Excelsior mines were in full operation and Bayhorse arose as a prominent mining community complete with its own smelter.

Although the U.S. Postal Service initially refused to list the town by the local name, Bayhorse, the post office finally backed down from its stance. The town once listed as Aetna officially became recognized as Bayhorse in 1888, and the community produced nearly $10 million in ore prior to the 1898 mining district's closure.

Mining has continued in the Bayhorse area sporadically since its official 1898 closing. Workers attempted to operate area mines during 1910, 1920-1925, 1935, and 1967-1968. Today, visitors will find six charcoal kilns that are now managed on U.S. Forest Service land. The ghost town itself is located nearby on private property and visitors will be able to see remnants of some of the community's early structures.

T Challis Golf Course
Upper Garden Creek Rd., Challis. 879-5440. www.challisgolfcourse.homestead.com Located on U.S. Hwy. 93 near Challis

The Challis Golf Course is nestled in central Idaho and offers outstanding views of the Lost River Mountain Range. This relatively new course measures 3,311 yards and is a par 36. Guests have rated this links type course as one of the best 9-holes in the state. Green fees start at $10 for 9 holes with optional extension to 18 holes.

T North Custer Museum for Regional History
1205 S. Main St., Challis. 879-2846.

After significant planning and fundraising, the North Custer Museum opened its doors in 1998. The North Custer Historical Society operates the museum and relies on volunteer help in displaying both permanent and traveling exhibits. The museum is open Memorial Day through the last weekend in October. Call for additional information about museum hours.

T Idaho Land of Yankee Fork Historical Museum & Interpretive Center
Junction of U.S. Hwy. 93 and State Hwy. 75 south of Challis. 879-5244.

As early as 1870, eager prospectors arrived in droves in the Yankee Fork area, hungry for gold. As more miners arrived, the area boomed with economic activity. Although the mining boom eventually died out, visitors can still explore one of the primary activities of early Idaho settlers at the Idaho Land of Yankee Fork Historical Museum. Housed inside a building modeled after an old mining mill, the interpretive center provides visitors with historical exhibits, general information about frontier mining, and audiovisual presentations. Just outside the museum is a sixty-foot cliff used by Shoshone Indians from the 13th to 19th centuries as a buffalo jump to slaughter large herds of bison. Call for additional information regarding operating hours.

T Land of the Yankee Fork Historic Area
Contact the Challis Ranger District at 879-4321 or the Idaho Department of Parks and Recreation Challis Office at 879-5244.

Coming to Idaho
Known as the last state discovered by white explorers, Idaho remained largely unexplored long after the settlement of surrounding states. Its rugged terrain and harsh winters, particularly in central Idaho, discouraged most settlers and prompted local Indians to call the region the "land of deep snows." Not until the 1860s did the discovery of gold bring Idaho both national attention and Gold Fever. The resulting surge of activity and renewed interest in this land once passed by, led to the establishment of the state of Idaho on July 3, 1890.

As the new century arrived, new strikes grew fewer and existing ones less dependable. The glory days of gold mining in Idaho ceased, leaving behind the relics of this great adventure. Abandoned communities and unforgotten stories are scattered throughout the state, yet none are more intriguing than those of the Yankee Fork.

To commemorate the contribution of frontier mining to Idaho culture and preserve its history, the Yankee Fork Historic Area was established. Within the Historic Area you will discover the dreams and hear the stories of these resourceful people who grew to love this beautiful country, the Land of the Yankee Fork.

Yankee Fork Gold
Prospectors first entered the region in the 1860s when a group of northerners sought their fortune along a large tributary of the Salmon River. Finding little success, the group departed leaving behind the stream they called the "Yankee Fork" and an undetected wealth of gold.

A more earnest search for gold began in 1870 and soon the Yankee Fork regularly received hopeful prospectors. Most miners arrived with only the possessions on their backs. Too busy mining and packing in supplies to build cabins,

Challis													
	Jan	Feb	March	April	May	June	July	Aug	Sep	Oct	Nov	Dec	Annual
Average Max. Temperature (F)	30.3	37.8	47.4	58.0	67.6	75.7	85.5	83.8	74.0	61.5	43.5	32.1	58.1
Average Min. Temperature (F)	9.4	15.3	22.9	30.6	38.6	45.4	51.0	48.9	40.8	31.9	21.1	12.0	30.7
Average Total Precipitation (in.)	0.47	0.34	0.44	0.56	1.10	1.18	0.65	0.60	0.66	0.44	0.43	0.52	7.40
Average Total Snowfall (in.)	4.3	2.5	2.0	0.5	0.1	0.0	0.0	0.0	0.0	0.2	2.3	3.7	15.7
Average Snow Depth (in.)	1	1	0	0	0	0	0	0	0	0	0	1	0

these men lived in tents and cooked over open fires. Their optimism was reflected in the names of their mines such as the Lucky Boy and the Golden Sunbeam, and in the name of the Yankee Fork's first settlement, Bonanza, (Spanish for prosperity).

Mining camps evolved into mining towns. Completion of a toll road from Challis through the mountains to these remote mining communities allowed freighting of much needed equipment and the eventual use of stages. In 1880, the construction of a large mill in Custer to process the rich ore of the General Custer Mine prompted a period of growth and abundance on the Yankee Fork.

Life on the Yankee Fork became more family oriented as the number of women and children increased. Preferred social activities turned from gambling and drinking in local saloons to dances at the Miner's Union hall and events such as talent plays and melodramas. The town of Bonanza possessed playing fields for both croquet and baseball.

Prosperity was fleeting, however, and the cyclic nature of frontier gold mining held true. Lower grade ore and rising production costs forced mines to close and workers to relocate. By 1910, the feverish activity along the Yankee Fork fell silent and its colorful residents disappeared, leaving behind the dreams they cherished and the country they loved.

Enjoying the Historic Area

Imagine the excitement of early prospectors as they knelt over cold mountain streams, swirling gravel in their pans hoping to see that brilliant splash of gold color. The same thrill of discovery can be experienced by you as you explore the Yankee Fork Historic Area in the beautiful northern Rocky Mountains.

Begin at the Interpretive Center near Challis where exhibits, audiovisual programs, mining artifacts, and publications describe the frontier mining history of the region. Personnel are available year round to answer your questions and help you get the most out of your visit to the Historic Area.

At the Sunbeam Dam Overlook, you will find information on the Historic Area, the Sawtooth National Recreation Area, and the historic Sunbeam Dam. Constructed in 1910 to generate electricity, the dam's use was limited and it also blocked migrating fish. In 1934, the south abutment was dynamited. The Sunbeam Dam remains the only dam ever constructed on the Salmon River.

Those seeking to explore the backcountry may drive the Custer Motorway Adventure Road. Following much of the original Toll Road, the motorway takes its travelers past numerous historic sites and scenic vistas between Custer and Challis. The Motorway is not recommended for low-clearance autos, large motorhomes, and travel trailers.

Opportunities to enjoy the rugged beauty of the Yankee Fork Historic Area abound. The world famous Salmon River offers whitewater rafting and excellent fishing. The nearby Frank Church-River of No Return Wilderness offers backcountry solitude for both hiker and horseman in the largest wilderness in the lower 48 states.

Numerous camping and picnic sites may be found and the region is renowned for its abundance of wildlife including elk, mule deer, bighorn sheep, mountain goats, and more. Through countless possible adventures in every season, the Yankee Fork Historic Area provides you that unique thrill of discovery.

Up the Yankee Fork Road, the remains of the once booming towns of Custer and Bonanza are found. Visit the Custer Museum. Learn to pan for gold and walk the self-guided trail. Your imagination allows you to hear the creaking of passing wagons and the thundering noise of the General Custer Mill. Above Bonanza is the Bonanza Cemetery where you can get a unique glimpse into the lives of those who lived and worked on the Yankee Fork.

Operating from 1940 to 1952, the Yankee Fork Gold Dredge began a new era of gold mining on the Yankee Fork and today is the only remaining floating dredge in Idaho. Tours of this carefully restored 988-ton machine are available.

Keep in Mind

- Historic sites are protected by law. We ask that you leave them undisturbed for others to enjoy.
- Within the Historic Area are numerous private lands and mining claims. Please respect private property rights.
- Portions of the Historic Area are located in remote areas and are open on a seasonal basis only.
- Old buildings and mine shafts are unstable and dangerous. Please do not enter these structures.
- Most lands within the Historic Area open to mining have been claimed. Claimants' permission is required before recreational panning or dredging. Please respect private property rights.

Reprinted from U.S. Forest Service, BLM, and Idaho Parks and Recreation brochure

T Historic Shoshone Buffalo Jump Site
100 feet west of Mile Marker 244 on State Hwy. 75 near Challis. Contact the Challis Chamber of Commerce at 879-2771.

Surrounded by stream cut canyons, this site is known as a favorite buffalo jump site utilized by generations of Native Americans. Archaeologists believe that the buffalo were lured off the edge by Native Americans who then camped downstream to butcher their prey. Researchers believe the site was used as early as 800 A.D. and as late as the mid 1800s. Artifacts found at the site include tip points, drills, glass beads, hand-held skinning knives, and hundreds of bison bones. Today, the bison are gone, but they have been replaced with bighorn sheep that frequent the area during winter and spring.

T Challis Cliffs
Approximately 2 miles north of Challis on U.S. Hwy. 93. Contact the Challis Chamber of Commerce at 879-2771.

Lining the skyline above the Salmon River, the Challis Cliffs represent one of U.S. Hwy. 93's most unique geological formations. Volcanic eruptions spanning more than five million years spewed massive amounts of ash across the Idaho landscape. Geologists speculate that nearly 10,000 feet of ash was layered over the Idaho batholith, and over time, the ash was compressed into solid cliffs. Due to erosion and the everchanging landscape, these cliffs are currently only a fraction of their original size.

T McNabs Point
Approximately 6 miles north of Challis on U.S. Hwy. 93. Contact the Challis Chamber of Commerce at 879-2771.

McNabs Point marks the spot where dark basaltic lava bluffs formed during ancient volcanic eruptions near the present route of U.S. Hwy. 93. During the early 1900s, the old highway featured a sharp curve here and was appropriately nicknamed Deadman's curve after a series of severe accidents. Today, the area is remembered as the historical nesting site for several peregrine falcons.

T Challis Historic Tours
Contact the Challis Forest Service Office on U.S. Hwy. 93 at 879-4321.

Platted in 1876, Challis boomed with buildings, many of which remain today. The Challis Ranger District Office provides a self-guided tour brochure detailing the community's historic structures. The sites, all built between 1877 and 1914, include the original jail, an old schoolhouse, and several pioneer-era homes. Supposedly, Challis' collection of pre-1900 log structures is the largest in Idaho.

T Challis Hot Springs
5 miles south of Challis on State Hwy. 75. 634-0700.

Used since the 1800s mining era, the historic Challis Hot Springs is now a developed area situated on the scenic Salmon River banks. The springs range in temperature from 90 to 127 degrees Fahrenheit, and the outdoor hot mineral pool is open year-round. The area also features a boat launching site, horseshoes, volleyball courts, a picnic area, wildlife viewing, and convenient fishing access. A small admission fee is charged.

TV Mosquito Flat Reservoir
15 miles west of Challis on Forest Rd. 080. Contact the Challis Ranger District at 879-4321.

Established in 1950 after the construction of the earthen Mosquito Flat Dam, Mosquito Flat Reservoir was originally intended for irrigation purposes. Although the reservoir does contribute to area agriculture, the site is best known for angling and boating. Surrounded by towering trees, Mosquito Flat Reservoir is a popular rainbow trout fishing destination, and a boat ramp provides easy water access. For overnight visitors, a free campground lies nearby.

V Salmon River Scenic Run
Junction of Hwy.s 75 and 93, Challis. 879-2249 or (800) 479-1295. www.scenicriver.com

Owning 140 miles of licensed river, Salmon River Scenic Run (SRSR) specializes in fly-fishing for magnificent steelhead in both spring and fall. Professional guides follow the steelhead as they migrate upriver through scenic Salmon River country, and they are pleased to share their beloved region with guests. In addition to steelhead fishing, SRSR offers trout fishing from July through mid-October, and fly-fishing lessons are available in the SRSR outdoor classroom. Each fishing trip utilizes drift boats and includes hot Dutch Oven lunches. For a family rafting trip appropriate for all ages, SRSR boasts years of experience and features limited whitewater. So fish on or take a scenic float while touring some of Idaho's most beautiful country with the licensed and bonded Salmon River Scenic Run!

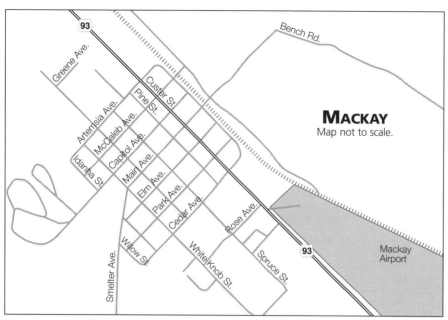

MACKAY
Map not to scale.

Mackay
Airport

and phones. Rooms also feature full baths with a shower and nice touch amenities including lotion, shower gel, and shampoo dispensers to complement extra nice linens and towels. Roomy horse corrals with water are available. The motel is situated adjacent to the city park and horseshoe pits. Shoes are provided for this entertaining game, and the motel welcomes pets. Beginning in April 2005, DSL access is available. All rooms feature drive-up access, and rooms are ninety percent non-smoking. For a personal touch on your next vacation or business trip, stay at the friendly Holiday Lodge Motel that is owner-managed with care.

M Salmon River Realty
1 Hwy. 93, Challis. 879-2225 or 876-4100.
www.challisidahorealestate.com

Experience the beauty of north-central Idaho and make your real estate dreams come true with the professional service guaranteed at Salmon River Realty! A full service real estate organization in central Idaho since 1965, Salmon River Realty has the expertise to help buyers and sellers with a range of real estate transactions. Preston Dixon, Broker, has resided in Custer County since 1976. He is qualified to assist customers with residential, farm, ranch, and business transactions as well as backcountry listings and acreage. He also has extensive knowledge about community amenities, regional recreation, and anything else you may need to know in relocating to the Challis area. For fast, friendly service where customer relations are always a priority, call on Salmon River Realty.

M Challis Area Chamber of Commerce
7th & Main, Challis. 879-2771.

9 *Food, Lodging*

Mackay
Pop. 566

Mackay ("MACK-ee") was founded unofficially thanks to a copper boom in 1884 and 1885. In 1901, George Mackay, an Irish immigrant, built a smelter in the town's present location. Soon after, he platted the town and named it after himself. Although the mine failed after just two years, town residents remained and later consolidated their population with that of Carbonate and Houston. A post office was established here in 1901. Today, this town that is tucked in the shadow of the Lost River Mountains, serves as the final supply point for those tackling the challenging Borah Peak. The area is also known for holding abundant trout populations in the nearby Mackay Reservoir and Big Lost River.

H Mount Borah
Milepost 131.2 on U.S. Hwy. 93 near Mackay

Idaho's highest peak, 12,662 feet, is named for William E. Borah, who served in the United States Senate from 1907 until his death in 1940. Ten or a dozen large but shallow inland seas have covered this area in the past billion years. They became a graveyard for countless generations of sea creatures: bones, shells, coral, and microscopic remains piled up through the

IDAHO'S WILD TURKEYS

The area surrounding Challis and the Sawtooth National Recreation Area is known for its abundant wildlife. Mammals include badgers, martens, minks, weasels, bobcats, lynx, fisher, raccoons, muskrats, red foxes, and marmots. These animals have inhabited the area for as long as written history has been recorded, and Native Americans and early mountain men relied on the animals for food and pelts. In 1990, however, a new species was added to the area's long list of wildlife. In an agreement with the state of South Dakota, the state of Idaho traded forty martens for 120 wild turkeys. These wild turkeys and their offspring inhabit the pastures located near Watts Bridge directly downstream from Challis and can be seen from the highway.

V Mile High Outfitters, Inc.
PO Box 1189, Challis. 879-4500.
www.milehighoutfitters.com

Since the 1990s, Mile High Outfitters, Inc. has been providing quality hunting, fishing, and wildlife viewing experiences in Idaho's Frank Church Wilderness. With a professional guide,

discover the wilderness firsthand on a big game hunting trip. Expeditions include elk, mountain lion, moose, mountain goat, bighorn sheep, deer, black bear, and upland bird hunting. Specialty Alaska hunts are also available. Guides pride themselves on offering well-maintained equipment with gentle horses and mules, and high success rates are guaranteed. Not interested in hunting? Mile High Outfitters also offers stream and lake fishing, as well as wolf viewing trips. All guests are hosted in large wall tents featuring cots, foam pads, wood stoves, floors, and a shower. Bag your own wildlife experience with the knowledgeable and friendly guides of Mile High Outfitters!

L Holiday Lodge Motel
Hwy. 93 N., Challis. 879-2259 or (866) 879-2259.

Holiday Lodge Motel is a small, quiet, personal motel of surprising hospitality. Rooms include refrigerators, microwaves, coffee service, cable TV,

Idaho Trivia

Although at first glance, Mackay may not seem to be at the "top of Idaho," it didn't stop the small town from giving itself this nickname. With an elevation of 5,897 feet and a close proximity to Idaho's tallest peak, Mount Borah, Mackay residents figured they might as well be at the "top of Idaho." For the past several years, the small town has used this nickname widely in promoting area tourism and recreation.

eons into a clay and imestone deposit thousands of feet thick. During the past 10 or 20 million years, part of this deposit has been thrust upward into the towering ridge you see before you.

H Earthquakes
Milepost 131.2 on U.S. Hwy. 93

On October 28, 1983, a major earthquake fracture, 26 miles long and seven miles deep, surfaced as the Lost River Valley slid away from Mount Borah.During that rock shift, Mount Borah's ridge front rose about six inches, while this valley subsided nine feet. This kind of movement has been going on here for 10 to 20 million years as subsurface rock has been pulled apart during gradual but persistent range and valley building. You can drive to a spectacular fracture that shattered this side road 2.5 miles from here.

T River Park Golf Course
717 Capital Ave., Mackay. 588-2296.

Designed by Mike Marinac, the River Park Golf Course opened in 1986. The course is nestled beside the Big Lost River, which creates several challenging water hazards throughout play. With 9 demanding holes, the course is rated a par 31 and is open daily from April 1 to October 31. Green fees for 9 holes are $7 on weekdays and $8 on weekends while 18 holes are $10 on weekdays and $11 on weekends.

T Lost River Museum
One block off U.S. Hwy. 93 at 312 Capital Ave., Mackay. 588-3148.

Operated by the South Custer Historical Society, Mackay's Lost River Museum showcases a variety of artifacts from pioneer days in the valley. Housed within a 100-year-old church, the museum displays mining tools, ranching equipment, vintage clothing, household utensils, railroad memorabilia, and historical photographs. Lost River Museum is open 1 PM to 5 PM Saturday and Sunday from Memorial Day Weekend through September or by appointment.

T Mackay Reservoir
4 miles north of Mackay on U.S. Hwy. 93. Contact the Mackay Business Association at 588-2400.

Situated on the Big Lost River, the Mackay Reservoir was formed after the construction of the Mackay Dam. The original dam was established in 1906, but due to construction problems, the dam was rebuilt by the Utah Construction Company at a cost of $3.5 million. Today, the reservoir is a popular destination for water sports, boating, and excellent fishing.

T Earthquake Visitor Center
North of Mackay at a well-marked turnoff from U.S. Hwy. 93. Contact the Mackay Business Association at 588-2400.

On the morning of Friday, October 28, 1983, Mother Nature wreaked havoc and created millions in damages in central Idaho. At 8:06 AM, the Lost River Fault centered at Idaho's highest peak, Mount Borah, suddenly ruptured open. During forty seconds of devastation, the earthquake raised Mt. Borah two feet and lowered the valley below with tremors rocking Salt Lake City, Portland, Seattle, and Canada. The earthquake measured 7.3 on the Richter scale, caused $15 million in property damages, and killed two children on their way to school in nearby Challis. The twenty-one mile tear in the earth's surface measure's fourteen feet deep in places and split apart at nearly 5,000 miles per hour.

The U.S. Forest Service has created an enclosure surrounding the fault, and an interpretive site at the fault line describes the earthquake's natural

causes. To this date, the quake remains the worst in Idaho history and one of the most damaging quakes in the Pacific Northwest.

T Mackay State Fish Hatchery
Contact the Hatchery Headquarters at 588-2219. From Mackay, travel 12 miles north on U.S. Hwy. 93. At the marked turnoff, proceed 6 miles up the paved road to the facility.

The Mackay State Fish Hatchery was established in 1925 and is one of the state's oldest fish hatcheries. A specialty fish production station, the hatchery uses artesian spring water to produce rainbow trout, cutthroat trout, arctic grayling, and Kokanee salmon ranging in length from one to sixteen inches. The hatchery also affords wildlife viewing opportunities, and facility tours are available upon advance arrangement. The hatchery is free to the public and open daily year round from 8 AM to 4:30 PM.

T Chilly Slough Conservation Area
Contact the Nature Conservancy District Headquarters at 788-2203. Located at the base of Mt. Borah near Mackay.

Developed in the 1980s through a partnership of the Nature Conservancy, private landowners, and several state and federal agencies, the Chilly Slough Conservation Area is nestled against the Lost River Mountains' western slope. Humans have used the unique high-desert, spring-fed wetland for thousands of years. Shoshone-Bannock Indians once gathered plants here and hunted game, and white settlers homesteaded the area from the late 1880s until the 1920s.

Created by a flat valley topography combined with numerous natural underground springs, the wetland has historically experienced earthquakes and is still geologically unstable. However, the area remains a popular wildlife habitat and recreational destination. More than 134 different species of birds call the area home, while twenty-seven mammal, six reptile, three amphibian, and three fish species also reside here. The area is open year-round for birdwatching, canoeing, hiking, fishing, and hunting. Visitors should note that no developed restroom or recreation facilities are available.

T Grandview Canyon and Willow Creek Summit
14 miles southeast of Challis on U.S. Hwy. 93. Contact the Challis Chamber of Commerce at 879-2771.

As U.S. Hwy. 93 winds down into the Big Lost River Valley, the road passes by Warm Springs Creek and through Grandview Canyon. Once a solid knob of Devonian dolomite, the narrow, short canyon formed here when a creek eroded a pathway through the rocks. After climbing out of the canyon, travelers will reach Willow Creek Summit at an elevation of 7,160 feet. The summit offers travelers plenty of wildlife viewing opportunities, especially during colder months when elk arrive to winter here.

T Lost River Mountain Range
Between Challis and Arco on U.S. Hwy. 93. Contact the Lost River Ranger District at 588-2224.

Stretching seventy miles between Challis and Arco in the Big Lost River Valley, this semi-arid mountain range is one of the most isolated regions in Idaho. To the west, the Big Lost River Valley and Salmon River flank the range, while the Little Lost and Pahsimeroi Rivers flow to the east. In addition to boasting Idaho's two highest peaks, Mount Borah and Leatherman Peak, the Lost River

Mountain Range claims rights to seven of the state's nine 12,000+ foot peaks. These peaks include: Peak 11,367, Borah, Idaho, Peak 11,967, White Cap, Leatherman, Bad Rock, Church, Donaldson, and Breitenbach.

10

Darlington
Pop. 10

This near abandoned town was originally established in the 1890s as a mining town and boasted stores, stations, and a post office from 1902 to 1927. The town was named after early miner, Wayne Darlington, and later became the community's first postmaster.

Moore
Pop. 196

Moore is located along U.S. Hwy. 93 and the Union Pacific Railroad. Founded as a livestock center in the early 1880s, Moore finally began receiving postal services in 1901. The town was named after the first postmaster who also happened to own the entire townsite acreage.

Lost River
Pop. 28

Appropriately named after its location on the Lost River, the settlement of Lost River was established on November 12, 1885 when William Matthews opened the first area post office. Just as the nearby Big and Little Lost Rivers disappear into the Snake River Plain's horizon, this small mining camp disappeared into history as well. By 1911, the camp was nearly deserted, and the post office was forced to shut its doors. Today, only a handful of residents remain.

H Goddin's River
Milepost 118.5 on U.S. Hwy. 93

Known as Goddin's River in the days of the fur trade, this stream originally was named for the fur

ARCO
Map not to scale.

they could not avoid lava stretches. But they slowly crept along, leaving their road strewn with parts of broken wagons. J.C. Merrill noted in 1864 that "at one place, we were obliged to drive over a huge rock just a little wider than the wagon. Had we gone a foot to the right or to the left, the wagon would have rolled over."

H Atoms for Peace
Milepost 248.1 on U.S. Hwy. 93 at Bottolfsen Memorial Park in Arco

An important page in atomic history was written here on July 17, 1955, when the lights of Arco were successfully powered from atomic energy. Chosen by the Atomic Energy Commission as an experiment in the peaceful use of atomic power, Arco, Idaho, became the first town in the free world to be served by electrical energy developed from the atom. The energy for this experiment was produced at the National Reactor Testing Station in the Arco desert southwest of here.

T Arco Number Hill
Outside Arco. Contact the Arco Chamber of Commerce/Lost River Visitor Center at 527-8977.

Known as "Number Hill" the graffiti tattooed hill near town has served as a monument for every graduating class since 1920. Each year, the seniors march up the hill and paint the class year on the hillside, forever preserving the event and maintaining a unique tradition. Although visitors are occasionally told that the numbers represent "high water levels" from the Big Lost River, this explanation has no merit.

T Arco Natural Bridge
Near King Mountain at Arco Pass in the Lost River Mountain Range. Contact the Lost River Visitor Center at 527-8977, or visit them in downtown Arco at 132 W. Grand Ave.

Framing the southern flanks of the weathered, spruce-covered terrain of King Mountain, the Arco Natural Bridge is one of eastern Idaho's most unusual scenic features. The natural limestone arch spans nearly eighty feet and is accessible to hikers. Following a county road several miles east of Arco off U.S. Hwy. 20/26, proceed up Arco Pass to a trail leading up Bridge Canyon. The climb is steep and traverses talus slopes at times, so hikers should use caution. Trail maps are available from the community visitor center.

T Bottolfsen Park
Downtown Arco. Contact the Arco Chamber of Commerce/Lost River Visitor Center at 527-8977.

Maintained by the City of Arco, Bottolfsen Park is a popular gathering spot for both locals and community visitors. The park features a playground, lighted baseball field, barbeque pits, and picnic facilities.

T Idaho Science Center
Adjacent to U.S. Hwy. 20/26 in Arco. Contact the Arco Chamber of Commerce/Lost River Visitor Center at 527-8977.

The proposed 3.5-acre site of the Idaho Science Center welcomes visitors to Arco. Plans are being made to construct a large museum that will house artifacts and related scientific highlights of historical projects undertaken at the Idaho National Engineering and Environmental Laboratory (INEEL). Although the museum is not yet complete, visitors today can view the decommissioned sail of the U.S.S Hawkbill, a nuclear submarine. The sail was presented to the city in honor of the submarine designs that INEEL has created throughout its history and also in remembrance of over 40,000 sailors who trained near Arco during the Cold

trapper who discovered it. Thyery Goddin, a prominent Iroquois who explored this river in 1819 or 1820, had come here with Donald Mackenzie's fur hunters who worked for the North West Company of Montreal. Well-stocked with beaver until it was trapped out in 1824, Goddin's River offered a wealth of furs to early trappers. Then, after the fur trade was over, the river's original name was forgotten. Later, settlers called it the Lost River because it sinks into the desert lava.

T Blue Jay Canyon
Near Leslie off of U.S. Hwy. 93 Fifty feet from the highway in Leslie, bear northeast across the railroad tracks, curve left, and continue 1.8 miles to an intersection marked with a BLM sign. Continuing in the same direction, drive up the road adjacent to Pass Creek.

Tucked inside the Lost River Range, Blue Jay Canyon is recognized as one of Idaho's most spectacular gorges. The surprising crevice was created when a small creek eroded the soft, sedimentary limestone. Sheltered in the shadow of precipitous cliffs, the canyon's creek bottom is inundated with Douglas fir, Engelmann spruce, juniper, and limber pine. According to local legend, Blue Jay Canyon at one time harbored Idaho's greatest population of bootleggers.

11 *Food, Lodging*

Arco
Pop. 1,026

This small city arose as the Root Hog Stage Station five miles south of its present location during the late 1870s. As more and more people began settling around the stage station, the name was changed to

"Junction," and the townspeople decided to apply for a post office. However, since Junction was such a popular community name during the era, the U.S. Postal Department denied the request and instead suggested the name "Arco" in honor of a European Count visiting the nation's capitol at the time. The settlers unanimously accepted the name, and Arco received its post office in 1880. When the Oregon Short Line Railroad arrived in 1901 and stage services became antiquated, the community moved to its present location.

Today, this community nestled at the base of the Lost River Mountains is recognized as the first city in the world to receive atomically powered electric services. Two million watts of electricity flowed through town for nearly two hours on July 17, 1955 when scientists at the National Reactor Testing Station (about 18 miles east of town) threw the switch to start the chain reaction. Parades, a rodeo, craft shows, dancing, and nuclear exhibits entertain the community every summer during "Atomic Days," a celebration of the historical event.

Arco also boasts the Idaho state distance records for hang gliding. Directly north of town, King Mountain is a popular launching site for the sport and annually hosts the King Mountain Hang-Gliding Championships.

H Goodale's Cutoff
Milepost 218.2 on U.S. Hwy. 93

When emigrants began to take their westbound wagons along an old Indian and trappers' trail past this lava, they had to develop a wild and winding road.At this spot, like many others, they had barely enough space to get by. At times

War. Also on-site is a decommissioned flight simulator. The simulator was used to train astronauts who participated on Mercury, Gemini, and Apollo space missions.

⊤ Craters of the Moon National Monument
Contact the Craters of the Moon National Monument Headquarters in Arco at 527-3257 or the BLM - Shoshone Field Office at 886-2206.

Introduction
"The strangest 75 square miles on the North American continent," one early traveler dubbed the Craters of the Moon landscape. Others deemed it "a weird lunar landscape," "an outdoor museum of volcanism," and "a desolate and awful waste." Virtually unknown until 1921, the area became a national monument in 1924 and, in 2000, expanded to encompass the entire Great Rift Zone, an area more than 50 miles long. The monument protects an entire ecosystem and is managed cooperatively by the National Park Service and the Bureau of Land Management. This expanded area protects and preserves this outstanding landscape for you and for future generations. Help us safeguard this special place by treating it with care.

In the past, the extensive lava flows affected all visitors to southern Idaho. The combination of jagged rock and the extreme hot and cold climate of the high desert influenced travel and use of the area. Shoshone Indians never inhabited the area in large numbers, but they hunted here. Emigrants in covered wagons skirted the lava flows. Later, ranchers grazed their cattle and sheep on vegetated areas, as they still do today. Visitors to this odd landscape see an example of our Earth's awesome forces.

Surface patterns and formations found here are typical of basaltic lava associated with volcanism throughout the world. "Where is the volcano?" you might ask. There is not just one, for here the Earth opened a great fissure and lava spewed out. These fissure vents, volcanic cones, and lava flows of the Great Rift Zone began erupting about 15,000 years ago and ceased only 2,000 years ago. Geologists predict that the landscape will erupt once again, but don't worry - it will give us ample warning.

A Moon-Like Landscape Comes to Life
Garnering livelihoods from this alien, moon-like landscape are some 2,000 insect, 169 bird, 48 mammal, eight reptile species, and a lone amphibian, the western toad. Mule deer are sometimes seen near Paisley, Inferno, and Broken Top cones.

Secretive predators, bobcats and great horned owls, hunt here. Prairie falcons prey on other birds and small mammals with lightning-fast dives. In campgrounds, look for chipmunks and golden-mantled ground squirrels.

More than 375 species of plants are found in this apparently desolate landscape. Big sagebrush, antelope bitterbush, and rubber rabbitrbrush are established on the older lava flows. On younger flows, mockorange, and tansybush may fill deeper crevices where soil and organic matter have accumulated.

Wildflowers carpet Craters of the Moon from early May until late August. The more delicate annuals bloom during late May and early June when snowmelt and occasional rains provide fair amounts of moisture. With summer's dryness, the more drought resistant plants continue to grow and bloom.

Silent Evidence of a Powerful Past
Basalt lava flows are grouped by appearance. Most common here are 'a'a and pahoehoe, pronounced AH-ah and paHOY-hoy. These Hawaiian terms, one explorer noted, mean "unfriendly" and "friendly" respectively! 'A'a can cut hands and boots. Pahoehoe is relatively smooth. 'A'a actually means "hard on the feet." Pahoehoe means "ropy."

'A'a lava was more viscous on emerging. 'A's highly irregular surface consists of rubble encrusted with stubbly spines, making it impassable to foot travelers.

Pahoehoe lava was more fluid upon emerging, and it hardened in pleats like hot fudge poured from a pan. Pahoehoe contains more dissolved gas than 'a'a and is more frequently associated with impressive lava fountains.

A third lava flow form, block lava, is less common at Craters of the Moon National Monument. This type forms angular blocks that may be almost three feet wide. There are three classes of lava bombs: spindle, ribbon, and breadcrust. Lava bombs - ranging in length from 1/2 inch to three feet - form as airborne blobs of molten lava, cool, and harden as they fall to Earth.

How Did Lava Tubes Form?
When the fluid, molten lava flowed out of the ground it behaved like a stream of water working its way downhill. But soon the "stream" surface cooled and hardened. This crust insulated the molten lava inside, enabling it to keep flowing. The lava inside the crust eventually flowed out leaving the crust as the walls of a lava tube or cave.

You can explore some of these fascinating caves. Some contain stalactites that were created by the dripping of molten lava before cooling. Others contain ice year-round. Some are inhabited by blind insects. In summer, swallows, ravens, and great horned owls nest near cave openings.

This cinder crag is part of a cinder cone that broke off and floated away on a lava flow.

Visitor Center
Stop at the visitor center for information and to see the film and exhibits. The film explains how lava flowed from fissures to create the cinder cones, lava flows, and other volcanic features in the monument. Exhibits tell about the wildflowers

and animals you may see here. You will also gain insight into the human history of this area, hardly a hospitable environment.

Accessibility
The visitor center and a trail at Devils Orchard are accessible to visitors with disabilities. Please ask for details. The staff is here to help you.

Safety and Regulations
Watch those rocks! Lava surfaces are sharp. Stay on trails and wear sturdy footgear. Never climb on spatter cones or monoliths. Be careful in caves. Carry a strong flashlight and extra batteries. Do not enter caves that are marked as closed. The climate is dry, so carry water and drink extra liquids to avoid dehydration. Leashed pets are welcome in the campground and on roads in the developed area; pets are not permitted on trails or in the wilderness. Wood fires are not permitted. Rocks, plants, and natural features are protected by federal law; collecting is prohibited. A day-use permit is required for hiking or biking in the area north of U.S. 20/26/93. Regulations may differ between NIPS and BLM portions of the monument. Ask for details.

Seasons
The best season to visit here depends on your interests. The visitor center is open year-round except for holidays in winter. The loop road is open from late April to mid-November. Snow closes the road in winter. The campground is open from May to October. In winter, the loop road makes an excellent trail for skiers and snow-shoers. Call ahead for a skiing report and information.

Camping, Water, and Restrooms
Camping in the 52-site campground is available on a first-come, first-served basis; no reservations are accepted. Water, restrooms, charcoal grills, and picnic tables are provided. There are no hookups. From October through May, water and other services are limited or unavailable. Water and restrooms are provided at the visitor center. Water is not available elsewhere in the monument. Waterless restrooms are at parking lots at Devils Orchard, Tree Molds Area, and Caves Area.

For More Information
Craters of the Moon National Monument Box 29 Arco, ID 83213 208-527-3257 (for TDD help call ATT Intercept) www.nps.gov/crmo

Shoshone Field Office Bureau of Land Management PO Box 2B Shoshone, ID 83352 208-886-2206 www.id.blm.gov/craters

Exploring Craters of the Moon by the Loop Road
Craters of the Moon National Monument encompasses more than 750,000 acres. What at first appears monotonous is really a landscape full of detail and surprises. This guide to selected features helps you see the monument at your own pace. The larger story unfolds as you tour the loop road.

1) Visitor Center
Begin at the visitor center. Here you will find publications, maps, and a bookstore. Check activity

Arco	Jan	Feb	March	April	May	June	July	Aug	Sep	Oct	Nov	Dec	Annual
Average Max. Temperature (F)	28.8	34.6	44.0	57.2	67.6	76.8	85.7	84.0	74.1	61.5	42.9	31.2	57.4
Average Min. Temperature (F)	3.8	8.7	19.0	28.3	36.9	43.6	48.8	46.4	38.1	29.0	18.1	7.6	27.4
Average Total Precipitation (in.)	0.90	0.88	0.66	0.79	1.20	1.14	0.59	0.68	0.65	0.49	0.67	0.92	9.58
Average Total Snowfall (in.)	10.5	6.3	2.7	0.8	0.4	0.0	0.0	0.0	0.0	0.2	2.3	8.0	31.1
Average Snow Depth (in.)	4	2	1	0	0	0	0	0	0	0	0	1	1

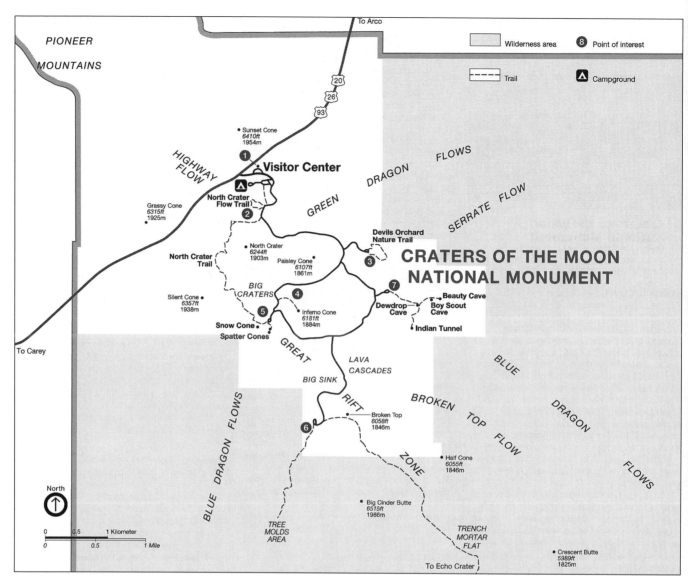

PIONEER
MOUNTAINS

To Arco

☐ Wilderness area   ⑧ Point of interest

--- Trail   ▲ Campground

HIGHWAY FLOW

• Sunset Cone
6410ft
1954m

① **Visitor Center**

North Crater
Flow Trail ②

GREEN

DRAGON   FLOWS

SERRATE FLOW

Grassy Cone
6315ft
1925m

**North Crater
Trail**

• North Crater
6244ft
1903m

Paisley Cone
6107ft
1861m

Devils Orchard
Nature Trail

③

**CRATERS OF THE MOON
NATIONAL MONUMENT**

*BIG
CRATERS*

④

⑦

Silent Cone •
6357ft
1938m

⑤

• Inferno Cone
6181ft
1884m

Dewdrop
Cave

• **Beauty Cave**
**Boy Scout
Cave**

Snow Cone •
Spatter Cones

• **Indian Tunnel**

To Carey

GREAT

*LAVA
CASCADES*

BIG SINK

RIFT

BLUE

DRAGON

TOP   FLOW

BROKEN

*BROKEN TOP
6058ft
1846m*

FLOWS

BLUE DRAGON FLOWS

⑥

ZONE

• Half Cone
6055ft
1846m

North
⬆

0   0.5   1 Kilometer
0   0.5   1 Mile

*TREE
MOLDS
AREA*

• Big Cinder Butte
6515ft
1986m

*TRENCH
MORTAR
FLAT*

• Crescent Butte
5989ft
1825m

To Echo Crater

schedules for ranger-led walks and evening programs. Rangers can answer questions and help you plan your visit.

The seven-mile loop road takes you deeper into Craters of the Moon's scenic attractions. Side trips lead to points two through seven. Most of the drive is one way. Spur roads and trailheads help you explore the monument even further. The trails invite foot travel. You can make the drive, including several short walks, in about two hours.

2) North Crater Flow
At this stop a short trail crosses the flow to a group of monoliths or crater wall fragments transported by lava flows. This flow is one of the youngest, and here the Triple Twist Tree suggests, because of its 1,350 growth rings, that these eruptions ceased only 2,000 years ago. You will see fine examples of ropy pahoehoe lava and block lava on North Crater Flow. Up the road is North Crater Trail. Take this longer, steep trail to peer into the vent of a volcano.

3) Devils Orchard
On the east side, after the road skirts Paisley Cone, is Devils Orchard. This group of lava fragments stands like islands in a sea of cinders. A short spur road leads to a self-guiding trail through these weird features. As you walk this 1/2-mile trail, you will see how people have had

an impact on this lava landscape and how it is being protected today. This barrier-free trail is designed to be accessible to all people.

4) Inferno Cone Viewpoint
A volcanic landscape of cinder cones spreads before you to the distant mountain ranges. Cool moist north slopes of the cones have noticeably more vegetation than the drier south slopes. From the summit of Inferno Cone - a short, steep walk - you can recognize the chain of cinder cones along the Great Rift Zone.

Big Cinder Butte to the south towers above the lava plain in the distance. This is one of the largest purely basaltic cinder cones in the world.

5) Big Craters and Spatter Cones Area
Spatter cones formed along the Great Rift fissure where clots of pasty lava stuck together when they fell. The material and forces of these eruptions originated at depths of nearly 37 miles within the Earth. To protect these fragile volcanic features, you are required to stay on trails in this area.

6) Trails to Tree Molds and Wilderness
A spur road just beyond Inferno Cone takes you to trails that lead to the Tree Molds Area, Trench Mortar Flat, and the Craters of the Moon Wilderness area. Tree molds formed where molten lava flows encased trees and then hardened. The cylindrical molds that remained after the wood

rotted away range from a few inches to just under three feet in diameter.

7) Cave Area
At this last stop on the loop road, take a 1/2-mile walk to the lava tubes and see Dewdrop, Boy Scout, Beauty, and Indian Tunnel. These are natural, wild caves, and exploring them can be hazardous. There are no developed pathways or handrails. Except in Indian Tunnel, you must carry flashlights and extra batteries. The caves have low ceilings, sharp projectiles, and loose rocks. Ask a ranger about safety precautions. Warning - especially hazardous sections of the caves are marked with signs or barriers. For your safety, stay out of these areas.

Rift Volcanism on the Snake River Plain

Light playing on cobalt blue lavas of the Blue Dragon Flows caught the inner eye of explorer Robert Limbert: "It is the play of light at sunset across this lava that charms the spectator. It becomes a twisted, wavy sea. In the moonlight its glazed surface has a silvery sheen. With changing conditions of light and air, it varies also, even while one stands and watches. It is a place of color and silence…"

Limbert explored the Craters of the Moon lava field in Idaho in the 1920s and wrote those words for a 1924 issue of *National Geographic Magazine.* "For several years I had listened to stories told by fur trappers of the strange things they had seen while ranging in this region," wrote Limbert, a sometime taxidermist, tanner, and furrier from Boise, Idaho. "Some of these accounts seemed beyond belief." To Limbert, it seemed extraordinary "That a region of such size and scenic peculiarity, in the heart of the great Northwest, could have remained practically unknown and unexplored…"

On his third and most ambitious trek, in 1920, Limbert and W. C. Cole were at times left speechless by the lava landscape they explored. Limbert recounted his impressions in magazine and newspaper articles whose publication was influential in the area's being protected under federal ownership. In 1924, part of the lava field was proclaimed as Craters of the Moon National Monument, protected under the Antiquities Act. It was created "to preserve the unusual and weird volcanic formations." The boundary has been adjusted and the park enlarged since then. In 1970, a large part of the national monument was designated by Congress as the Craters of the Moon Wilderness. It is further protected under the National Wilderness Preservation System.

Until 1986, little was known about Limbert except for those facts recounted above. That year, however, a researcher compiling a history of the national monument located Limbert's daughter in Boise. The daughter still possessed hundreds of items, including early glass plate negatives, photographs, and manuscripts of her father, and that shed more light on his life, the early days of Idaho, and Craters of the Moon. Some of these photographs served as blueprints for the National Park Service in the rehabilitation of fragile spatter cone formations that have deteriorated over the years of heavy human traffic. The Limbert collection has been fully cataloged by Boise State University curators and has already proven to be a valuable resource to historians interested in Limbert and this fascinating part of Idaho. Preservation of the area owes much to Limbert's imaginative advocacy in the true spirit of the West in its earlier days.

Local legends, beginning in the late 1800s, held that this area resembled the surface of the moon, on which - it must now be remembered - no one had then walked! Geologist Harold T. Stearns first used the name Craters of the Moon when he suggested to the National Park Service, in 1923, that a national monument be established here. Stearns found "the dark craters and the cold lava, nearly destitute of vegetation" similar to "the surface of the moon as seen through a telescope." The name Craters of the Moon would stick after Limbert adopted it in *National Geographic Magazine* in 1924. Later that year the name became official when the area was set aside by President Calvin Coolidge as a national monument under the Antiquities Act.

Like some other areas in the National Park System, Craters of the Moon has lived to see the name that its early explorers affixed to it proved somewhat erroneous by subsequent events or findings. When Stearns and Limbert called this lava field Craters of the Moon, probably few persons other than science fiction buffs actually thought that human beings might one day walk on the moon and see firsthand what its surface is like. People have now walked on the moon, however, and we know that its surface does not, in fact, closely resemble this part of Idaho. Although there are some volcanic features on the surface of the moon, most of its craters were formed by the impact of meteorites colliding with the moon.

Moonscape or not, early fur trappers avoided the lava flows along the base of the Pioneer Mountains at the north of today's park. In doing so, they followed Indian trails such as one found by Limbert that "resembled a light streak winding through the lava. When the sun was directly overhead it could be seen to advantage, but at times was difficult to follow. Think of the years of travel," Limbert marveled, "necessary to make that mark on rock!" At least one Indian trail was destined to become part of Goodale's Cutoff, an alternative route on the Oregon Trail that pioneers in wagon trains used in the 1850s and 1860s. Many adjectives early used for this scene - weird, barren, exciting, awe-inspiring, monotonous, astonishing, curious, bleak, mysterious - still apply. It is not difficult today to see why pioneering folk intent on wresting a living from the land did not tackle this volcanic terrain.

Geologists possessed the proper motivation to tackle it, however. Curiosity aroused by this lava field has led several generations of geologists, beginning with Israel C. Russell in 1901 and Harold T. Stearns in the 1920s, into a deeper understanding of its volcanic origins. With ever increasing penetration of its geological history, the apparent otherworldliness of Craters of the Moon has retreated, but not entirely. The National Aeronautics and Space Administration (NASA) brought the second set of astronauts who would walk on the moon to this alien corner of the galaxy before their moonshot. Here they studied the volcanic rock and explored an unusual, harsh, and unforgiving environment before embarking on their own otherworldly adventure.

Most types of volcanic features in the park can be seen quite readily by first stopping at the visitor center and then driving the Loop Road. Far more features can be seen if you also walk the interpretive trails at the stops along the Loop Road. Still more await those who invest the time required to come to feel the mysterious timelessness and raw natural force implicit in this expansive lava field. Many travelers are en route to Yellowstone National Park and spend only a couple of hours visiting Craters of the Moon. This is ironic because here you are on the geological track of Yellowstone. In fact, Craters of the Moon represents what Yellowstone's landscape will resemble in the future, and both areas can supplement your insight into what happens when the Earth's unimaginable inner forces erupt to its surface.

Although Idaho is famous for forests, rivers, and scenic mountain wilderness, its Snake River Plain region boasts little of these attributes. This plain arcs across southern Idaho from the Oregon border to the Yellowstone area at the Montana-Wyoming border. It marks the trail of the passage of the Earth's crust over an unusual geologic heat source that now brings the Earth's incendiary inner workings so close to its surface near Yellowstone. This heat source fuels Yellowstone's bubbling, spewing, and spouting geothermal wonders. Craters of the Moon therefore stands as a geologic prelude to Yellowstone, as its precursor and the ancestral stuff of its fiery secrets.

When did all this volcanism at Craters of the Moon happen? Will it happen again? According to Mel Kuntz and other U.S. Geological Survey geologists who have conducted extensive field research at Craters of the Moon, the volcanic activity forming the Craters of the Moon lava field probably started only 15,000 years ago. The last eruption in the volcanic cycle ended 2,000 years ago, about the time that Julius Ceasar ruled the Roman Empire.

Craters of the Moon is a dormant, but not extinct, volcanic area. Its sleeping volcanoes could become active again in the near future. The largest earthquake of the last quarter century in the contiguous United States shook Idaho's tallest mountain, Borah Peak, just north of here in 1983. When it did, some geologists wondered if it might initiate volcanic activity at Craters of the Moon. It did not. According to Kuntz, however, this is no reason not to expect another volcanic eruption here soon, probably "within the next 1,000 years."

Today's Craters of the Moon National Monument encompasses 83 square miles of the much larger Craters of the Moon lava field. Reaching southeastward from the Pioneer Mountains, the park boundary encloses a series of fissure vents, volcanic cones, and lava flows known as the Great Rift volcanic zone. This volcanic rift zone is a line of weakness in the Earth's crust that can be traced for some 60 miles across the Snake River Plain. Recent volcanism marks much of its length. You can explore the Great Rift and some of its volcanic features via the park's 7-mile Loop Drive. In the park's northern part you will find spatter cones, cinder cones, lava flows, lava caves, and an unexpected variety of wildflowers, shrubs, trees, and wild animals. The much larger southern part of the park, designated by Congress in 1970 as the Craters of the Moon Wilderness Area, is a vast and largely untraveled region of stark volcanic features flanking the Great Rift. It offers a challenge to serious hikers and explorers - latter day Robert Limberts - who are prepared for rugged wilderness travel.

Despite its seeming barrenness, Craters of the Moon is indeed home to a surprising diversity of plant and animal life. As Limbert noted in 1924: "In the West the term 'Lava Beds of Idaho' has always signified a region to be shunned by even the most venturesome travelers - a land supposedly barren of vegetation, destitute of water, devoid of animal life, and lacking in scenic interest.

"In reality the region has slight resemblance to its imagined aspect. Its vegetation is mostly hidden in pockets, but when found consists of pines, cedars, junipers, and sagebrush: its water is hidden deep in tanks or holes at the bottom of large 'blow-outs' and is found only by following old Indian or mountain sheep trails or by watching the flight of birds as they drop into these places to quench their thirst. The animal life consists principally of migrant birds, rock rabbits, woodchucks, black and grizzly bears: its scenery is impressive in its grandeur."

Years of patient record-keeping by scientists have fit numbers to Limbert's perceptive observations. The number of species identified includes more than 300 plants, 2,000 insects, 8 reptiles, 140 birds, 30 mammals - and one amphibian, the western toad. We now call Limbert's "rock rabbit" the pika. The grizzly is long gone here. With few exceptions, the park's denizens live mostly under conditions of great environmental stress.

Near constant winds, breeze-to-gale in strength, sweep across the park to rob moisture from all living things. Scant soils, low levels of precipitation, the inability of cinder cones to hold rainwater near the surface, and the heat of the summer sun - intensified by heat-absorbing black lavas - only aggravate such moisture theft. Cinder surfaces register summer soil temperatures of over 150°F and show a lack of plant cover. Plants cover generally less than 5 percent of the total surface of the cinder cones. A recent study found that when the area is looked at on a parkwide basis, most of the land is very sparsely vegetated (less than 15 percent vegetative cover). On a scale of sand trap to putting green, this would approach the sand trap end of the scale.

Into this difficult environment wildlife researcher, Brad Griffith, ventured to count, mark, and scrutinize the mule deer of Craters of the Moon in May 1980. Griffith, of the University of Idaho, conducted a three-year study of the park's mule deer population because the National Park Service was concerned that this protected and productive herd might multiply so much that it would eventually damage its habitat. Among other things, he would find that the herd has developed a drought evasion strategy that makes it behave unlike any mule deer population known anywhere else.

"By late summer," Griffith explains, "plants have matured and dried so that they no longer provide adequate moisture to sustain the deer in this landscape that offers them no free water. Following about 12 days of warm nights and hot days in late July, the deer migrate from 5 to 10 miles north to the Pioneer Mountains. There they find free-flowing creeks and the cool, moist shade of aspen and Douglas-fir groves and wait out summer's worst heat and dryness. Early fall rains trigger the deer's return to the park's wilderness from this oasis in late September to feed on the nutritious bitterbrush until November snowfalls usher them back to their winter range."

The pristine and high-quality forage of the Craters of the Moon Wilderness Area, historically nearly untouched by domestic livestock grazing, has inspired this migratory strategy for evading drought. In effect, the mule deer make use of a dual summer range, a behavioral modification unknown elsewhere for their species.

"Their late summer and fall adaptations simply complete the mule deer's yearlong strategy for coping with the limits that this volcanic landscape imposes on them," Griffith explains.

Taking a walk in the park on a mid-summer afternoon gives you a good opportunity to experience the influence of wind, heat, and lack of moisture. The park's winds are particularly striking. The lava that has flowed out of the Great Rift has built up and raised the land surface in the park to a higher elevation than its surroundings so that it intercepts the prevailing southwesterly winds. Afternoon winds usually die down in the evening. As part of the dynamics of temperature and mois-

ture that determine mule deer behavior, this daily wind cycle helps explain why they are more active at night than are mule deer elsewhere. These deer do not move around as much as mule deer in less ecologically trying areas. They have adapted behaviors to conserve energy and moisture in this environmentally stressful landscape.

Early mornings may find park rangers climbing up a cinder cone to count the deer, continuing the collection of data that Brad Griffith set in motion with his three-year study. The rangers still conduct spring and late summer censuses: over a recent three-year period, the deer populations averaged about 420 animals. Another several years of collecting will give the National Park Service a body of data on the mule deer that is available nowhere else.

The uniqueness of this data about the park's mule deer population would surely please the booster aspect of Robert Limbert's personality. Likewise, the research challenges involved in obtaining it would appeal to his explorer self. History has justified Limbert on both counts. Publicity arising from his explorations led to creation of the national monument. Furthermore, that publicity put forth a rather heady claim that history has also unequivocally borne out: "Although almost totally unknown at present," Limbert prophesied in 1924, "this section is destined some day to attract tourists from all America…

"Every year tens of thousands of travelers fulfill Robert Limbert's prophecy of more than a half-century ago.

Geology of the Craters of the Moon

A 400-mile-long arc known as the Snake River Plain cuts a swath from 30 to 125 miles wide across southern Idaho. Idaho's official state highway map, which depicts mountains with shades of green, shows this arc as white because there is comparatively little variation here compared to most of the state. Upon this plain, immense amounts of lava from within the Earth have been deposited by volcanic activity dating back more than 14 million years. However, some of these lavas, notably those at Craters of the Moon National Monument, emerged from the Earth as recently as 2,000 years ago. Craters of the Moon contains some of the best examples of basaltic volcanism in the world. To understand what happened here, you must understand the Snake River Plain.

Basaltic & Rhyolitic Lavas

The lavas deposited on the Snake River Plain were mainly of two types classified as basaltic and rhyolitic. Magma, the molten rock material beneath the surface of the Earth, issues from a volcano as lava. The composition of this fluid rock material varies. Basaltic lavas are composed of magma originating at the boundary of the Earth's mantle and its crustal layer. Rhyolitic lavas originate from

crustal material. To explain its past, geologists now divide the Snake River Plain into eastern and western units. The following geologic story relates to the eastern Snake River Plain, on which Craters of the Moon lies.

On the eastern Snake River Plain, basaltic and rhyolitic lavas formed in two different stages of volcanic activity. Younger basaltic lavas mostly lie atop older rhyolitic lavas. This portion of the plain runs from north of Twin Falls eastward to the Yellowstone area on the Wyoming/Montana border. Drilling to depths of almost 2 miles near the plain's midline, geologists found 1/2 mile of basaltic lava flows lying atop more than 1-1/2 miles of rhyolitic lava flows. How much deeper the rhyolitic lavas may extend is not known. No one has drilled deeper here.

This combination - a thinner layer of younger basaltic lavas lying atop an older and thicker layer of rhyolitic lavas - is typical of volcanic activity associated with an unusual heat phenomenon inside the Earth that some geologists have described as a mantle plume. The mantle plume theory was developed in the early 1970s as an explanation for the creation of the Hawaiian Islands. According to the theory, uneven heating within the Earth's core allows some material in the overlying mantle to become slightly hotter than surrounding material. As its temperature increases, its density decreases. Thus it becomes relatively buoyant and rises through the cooler materials, like a tennis ball released underwater toward the Earth's crust. When this molten material reaches the crust, it eventually melts and pushes itself through the crust and it erupts onto the Earth's surface as molten lava.

The Earth's crust is made up of numerous plates that float upon an underlying mantle layer. Therefore, over time, the presence of an unusual heat source created by a mantle plume will be expressed at the Earth's surface - floating in a constant direction above it - as a line of volcanic eruptions. The Snake River Plain records the progress of the North American crustal plate - 350 miles in 15 million years - over a heat source now located below Yellowstone. The Hawaiian chain of islands marks a similar line. Because the mechanisms that cause this geologic action are not well understood, many geologists refer to this simply as a heat source rather than a mantle plume.

Two Stages of Volcanism

As described above, volcanic eruptions associated with this heat source occur in two stages, rhyolitic and basaltic. As the upwelling magma from the mantle collects in a chamber as it enters the Earth's lower crust, its heat begins to melt the surrounding crustal rock. Since this rock contains a large amount of silica, it forms a thick and pasty rhyolitic magma. Rhyolitic magma is lighter than the overlying crustal rocks, therefore, it begins to rise and form a second magma chamber very close to the Earth's surface. As more and more of this gas-charged rhyolitic magma collects in this upper crustal chamber, the gas pressure builds to a point at which the magma explodes through the Earth's crust.

Explosive Rhyolitic Volcanism

Rhyolitic explosions tend to be devastating. When the gas-charged molten material reaches the surface of the Earth, the gas expands rapidly, perhaps as much as 25 to 75 times by volume. The reaction is similar to the bubbles that form in a bottle of soda pop that has been shaken. You can shake the container and the pressure-bottled liquid will retain its volume as long as the cap is tightly sealed. Release the pressure by removing the bottle cap, however, and the soft drink will spray all over the room and occupy a volume of space far larger than the bottle from which it issued. This initial vast spray is then followed by a foaming action as the less gas-charged liquid now bubbles out of the bottle.

Collectively, the numerous rhyolitic explosions that occurred on the Snake River Plain ejected hundreds of cubic miles of material into the atmosphere and onto the Earth's surface. In contrast, the eruption of Mount Saint Helens in 1980, which killed 65 people and devastated 150 square miles of forest, produced less than 1 cubic mile of ejected material. So much material was ejected in the massive rhyolitic explosions in the Snake River Plain that the Earth's surface collapsed to form huge depressions known as calderas. (Like caldron, whose root meaning it shares, this name implies both bowl-shaped and warmed.) Most evidence of these gigantic explosive volcanoes in the Snake River Plain has been covered by subsequent flows of basaltic lava. However, traces of rhyolitic eruptions are found along the margins of the plain and in the Yellowstone area.

Quiet Outpourings of Basaltic Lava
As this area of the Earth's crust passed over and then beyond the sub-surface heat source, the explosive volcanism of the rhyolitic stage ceased. The heat contained in the Earth's upper mantle and crust, however, remained and continued to produce upwelling magma. This was basaltic magma that, because it contained less silica than rhyolite, was very fluid.

The basalt, like the rhyolite, collected in isolated magma chambers within the crust until pressures built up to force it to the surface through various cracks and fissures. These weak spots in the Earth's crust were the results of earlier geologic activity, expansion of the magma chamber, or the formation of a rift zone.

Upon reaching the surface, the gases contained within the lava easily escaped and produced rather mild eruptions. Instead of exploding into the air like earlier rhyolitic activity, the more fluid basaltic lava flooded out onto the surrounding landscape. These flows were fairly extensive and often covered many square miles. After millions of years, most of the older rhyolitic deposits have been covered by these basaltic lava flows.

The Great Rift and Craters of the Moon
Craters of the Moon National Monument lies along a volcanic rift zone. Rift zones occur where the Earth's crust is being pulled in opposite directions. Geologists believe that the interactions of the Earth's crustal plates in the vicinity of the Snake River Plain have stretched, thinned, and weakened the Earth's crust so that cracks have formed both on and below the surface here. Magma under pressure can follow these cracks and fissures to the surface. While there are many volcanic rift zones throughout the Snake River Plain, the most extensive is the Great Rift that runs through Craters of the Moon. The Great Rift is approximately 60 miles long and it ranges in width from 1/2 to 5 miles. It is marked by short cracks - less than 1 mile in length - and the alignment of more than 25 volcanic cinder cones. It is the site of origin for more than 60 different lava flows that make up the Craters of the Moon Lava Field.

Eight Major Eruptive Periods
Most of the lavas exposed at Craters of the Moon formed between 2,000 and 15,000 years ago in basaltic eruptions that comprise the second stage of volcanism associated with the mantle plume theory. These eight eruptive periods each lasted about 1,000 years or less and were separated by

Craters of the Moon is a rugged landscape characterized by volcanic rifts & numerous lava formations.

periods of relative calm that lasted for a few hundred to more than 2,000 years. These sequences of eruptions and calm periods are caused by the alternating build up and release of magmatic pressure inside the Earth. Once an eruption releases this pressure, time is required for it to build up again.

Eruptions have been dated by two methods: paleomagnetic and radiocarbon dating. Paleomagnetic dating compares the alignment of magnetic minerals within the rock of flows with past orientations of the Earth's magnetic fields. Radiocarbon dating makes use of radioactive carbon-14 in charcoal created from vegetation that is overrun by lava flows. Dates obtained by both methods are considered to be accurate to within about 100 years.

A Typical Eruption at Craters of the Moon
Research at the monument and observations of similar eruptions in Hawaii and Iceland suggest the following scenario for a typical eruption at Craters of the Moon. Various forces combine to cause a section of the Great Rift to pull apart. When the forces that tend to pull the Earth's crust apart are combined with the forces created as magma accumulates, the crust becomes weakened and cracks form. As the magma rises buoyantly within these cracks, the pressure exerted on it is reduced and the gases within the magma begin to expand. As gas continues to expand, the magma becomes frothy.

At first the lava is very fluid and charged with gas. Eruptions begin as a long line of fountains that reach heights of 1,000 feet or less and are up to a mile in length. This "curtain of fire eruption" mainly produces cinders and frothy, fluid lava. After hours or days, the expansion of gases decreases and eruptions become less violent. Segments of the fissure seal off and eruptions become smaller and more localized. Cinders thrown up in the air now build piles around individual vents and form cinder cones.

With further reductions in the gas content of the magma, the volcanic activity again changes. Huge outpourings of lava are pumped out of the various fissures or the vents of cinder cones and form lava flows. Lava flows may form over periods of months or possibly a few years. Long-term eruptions of lava flows from a single vent become the source of most of the material produced during

a sustained eruption. As gas pressure falls and magma is depleted, flows subside. Finally, all activity stops.

When Will the Next Eruption Occur?
Craters of the Moon is not an extinct volcanic area. It is merely in a dormant stage of its eruptive sequence. By dating the lava flow, geologists have shown that the volcanic activity along the Great Rift has been persistent over the last 15,000 years, occurring approximately every 2,000 years. Because the last eruptions took place about 2,000 years ago, geologists believe that eruptions are due here again - probably within the next 1,000 years.

Geological Highlights
Indian Tunnel
Indian Tunnel looks like a cave, but it is a lava tube. When a pahoehoe lava flow is exposed to the air, its surface begins to cool and harden. A crust or skin develops. As the flow moves away from its source, the crust thickens and forms an insulating barrier between cool air and molten material in the flow's interior. A rigid roof now exists over the stream of lava whose molten core moves forward at a steady pace. As the flow of lava from the source vent is depleted, the level of lava within the molten core gradually begins to drop. The flowing interior then pulls away from the hardening roof above and slowly drains away and out. The roof and last remnants of the lava river inside it cool and harden, leaving a tube.

Many lava tubes make up the Indian Tunnel Lava Tube System. These tubes formed during the same eruption within a single lava flow whose source was a fissure or crack in the Big Craters/Spatter Cones area. A tremendous amount of lava was pumped out here, forming the Blue Dragon Flows. (Hundreds of tiny crystals on its surface produce the color blue when light strikes them.) Lava forced through the roof of the tube system formed huge ponds whose surfaces cooled and began to harden. Later these ponds collapsed as lava drained back into the lava tubes. Big Sink is the largest of these collapses. Blue Dragon Flows cover an area of more than 100 square miles. Hidden beneath are miles of lava tubes, but collapsed roof sections called skylights provide entry to only a small part of the system. Only time, with the collapse of more roofs, will reveal the total extent of the system.

Stalactites
Dripped from hot ceilings, lava forms stalactites that hang from above.

Mineral deposits
Sulfate compounds formed on many lava tube ceilings from volcanic gases or by evaporation of matter leached from rocks above.

Ice
In spring, ice stalactites form on cave ceilings and walls. Ice stalagmites form on the cave floor. Summer heat destroys these features.

Wildlife
Lava tube beetles, bushy-tailed woodrats (packrats), and bats live in some dark caves. Violet-green swallows, great horned owls, and ravens may use wall cracks and shelves of well-lit caves for nesting sites.

Cinder Cones
When volcanic eruptions of fairly moderate strength throw cinders into the air, cinder cones may be built up. These cone-shaped hills are usually truncated, looking as though their tops were sliced off. Usually, a bowl or funnel-shaped crater will form inside the cone. Cinders, which cooled rapidly while falling through the air, are highly porous with gas vesicles, like bubbles. Cinder cones hundreds of feet high may be built in a few days. Big Cinder Butte is a cinder cone. At 700 feet high, it is the tallest cone in the park. The shape develops because the largest fragments, and in fact most of the fragments, fall closest to the vent. The angle of slope is usually about 30 degrees. Some cinder cones, such as North Crater, the Watchman, and Sheep Trail Butte, were built by more than one eruptive episode.

Younger lava was added to them as a vent was rejuvenated. If strong winds prevailed during a cinder cone's formation, the cone may be elongated - in the direction the wind was blowing - rather than circular. Grassy, Paisley, Sunset, and Inferno Cones are elongated to the east because the dominant winds in this area come from the west. The northernmost section of the Great Rift contains the most cinder cones for three reasons: 1) There were more eruptions at that end of the rift. 2) The lavas erupted there were thicker, resulting in more explosive eruptions. (They are more viscous because they contain more silica.) 3) Large amounts of groundwater may have been present at the northern boundary of the lavas, and when it came in contact with magma, it generated huge amounts of steam. All of these conditions lead to more extensive and more explosive eruptions that tend to create cinder cones rather than lava flows.

Spatter Cones
When most of its gas content has dissipated, lava becomes less frothy and more tacky. Then it is tossed out of the vent as globs or clots of lava paste called spatter. The clots partially weld together to build up spatter cones. Spatter cones are typically much smaller than cinder cones, but they may have steeper sides. The Spatter Cones area of the park (Stop 5 on the map of the Loop Drive) contains one of the most perfect spatter cone chains in the world. These cones are all less than 50 feet high and less than 100 feet in diameter.

Idaho Trivia

Although home to several historic sites and the most mountain ranges in the lower 48 states, Idaho boasts only one national monument, distinguished as Craters of the Moon.

Plants Adapt to a Volcanic Landscape
Water is the limiting factor in plant growth and reproduction both on the lava fields of Craters of the Moon and on the surrounding sagebrush steppe. Plants have developed a combination of adaptations to cope with drought conditions. There are three major strategies:

1) Drought tolerance
Physiological adaptations leading to drought tolerance are typical of desert plant species. The tissues of some plants can withstand extreme dehydration without suffering permanent cell damage. Some plants can extract water from very dry soils. Sagebrush and antelope bitterbrush exemplify drought tolerance.

2) Drought avoidance
Certain structural modifications can enable plants to retain or conserve water. Common adaptations of this type include small leaves, hairiness, and succulence. The small leaves of the antelope bitterbrush expose less area to evaporative influences such as heat and wind.

Hairs on the scorpionweed reduce surface evaporation by inhibiting airflow and reflecting sunlight. Succulent plants such as prickly-pear cactus have tissues that can store water for use during drought periods. Other plants, such as wire lettuce, avoid drought by having very little leaf surface compared to their overall volume.

3) Drought escape
Some plants, such as mosses and ferns, escape drought by growing near persistent water supplies such as natural potholes and seeps from ice caves. Many other drought escapers, such as dwarf monkeyflower, simply carry out their full life cycle during the moist time of the year. The rest of the year they survive in seed form.

Plant Microhabitats
Lava flows
Most plants cannot grow on lava flows until enough soil has accumulated to support them. The park's older volcanic landscapes, where soils are best developed, are clothed with sagebrush/grassland vegetation. On younger lava flows, bits of soil first accumulate in cracks, joints, and crevices. It is in these microhabitats that vascular plants may gain footholds. Narrow cracks and joints may contain desert parsley and lava phlox. Shallow crevices will hold scabland penstemon, fernleaf fleabane and gland cinquefoil. Deep crevices can support the syringa, various ferns, bush rockspirea, tansybush, and even limber pine. Not until full soil cover is achieved can the antelope bitterbrush, rubber rabbitbrush, and sagebrush find suitable niches.

On lava flows, soils first form from eroded lava and the slow decomposition of lichens and other plants able to colonize bare rock. These soils can be supplemented by windblown soil particles until vascular plants gain footholds. As plants begin to grow and then die, their gradual decomposition adds further soil matter. These soil beginnings accumulate in cracks and crevices, which also provide critical shade and wind protection. Deep crevices provide lower temperatures favoring plant survival.

Cinder gardens
Compared to the lava flows, cinder cones are much more quickly invaded by plants. Here, too, however, volcanic origins influence plant growth. Compared to the relatively level lava flows, steeply sloping cinder cones introduce a new factor that

controls the development of plant communities: topography. Here you can find marked differences in the plant communities between the north and south facing slopes. South-facing slopes are exposed to prolonged, intense sunlight, resulting in high evaporation of water. Because of the prevailing winds, snow accumulates on northeast sides of cones, giving them far more annual water than southwest-facing sides receive. The pioneering herbs that first colonize cinder cones will persist on southwest-facing slopes long after succeeding plant communities have come to dominate north-facing slopes. It is on these north-facing slopes that limber pine first develops in the cinder garden. South-facing slopes may never support the limber pine but may be dominated by shrubs. Unweathered cinder particles range in size from 3 to 4 inches in diameter down to very small particles. They average about 1/4 inch in diameter.

Wildflowers
Wildflowers carpet Craters of the Moon's seemingly barren lava fields from early May to late September. The most spectacular shows of wildflowers come with periods of precipitation. In late spring, moisture from snowmelt, supplemented now and then by rainfall, sees the blossoming of most of the delicate annual plants.

Many of the park's flowering plants, having no mechanisms for conserving moisture, simply complete their life cycles before the middle of summer. This is particularly true of those that grow on the porous cinder gardens into which moisture quickly descends beyond reach of most plants' root systems.

As summer continues and supplies of moisture slowly dwindle, only the most drought-resistant of flowering plants continue to grow and to bloom. With the onset of autumn rains, only the tiny yellow blossoms of the sagebrush and rabbitbrush remain.

Indians, Early Explorers, and Practicing Astronauts
Not surprisingly, archeologists have concluded that Indians did not make their homes on this immense lava field. Astronauts would one day trek about Craters of the Moon in hopes that experiencing its harshly alien environment would make walking on the moon less disorienting for them. No wonder people have not chosen to live on these hot, black, sometimes sharp lava flows on which you must line the flight of doves to locate drinking water.

Indians did traverse this area on annual summer migrations, however, as shown by the developed trails and many sites where artifacts of Northern Shoshone culture have been found. Most of these archeological sites are not easily discerned by the untrained eye, but the stone windbreaks at Indian Tunnel are easily examined. Rings of rocks that may have been used for temporary shelter, hunting blinds, or religious purposes, numerous stone tools, and the hammerstones and chippings of arrowhead making are found scattered throughout the lava flows. Some of the harder, dense volcanic materials found here were made into crude cutting and scraping tools and projectile points. Such evidence suggests only short forays into the lavas for hunting or collecting by small groups.

The Northern Shoshone were a hunting and gathering culture directly dependent on what the land offered. They turned what they could of this volcanic environment to their benefit. Before settlement by Europeans, the vicinity of the park boasted several game species that are rare or absent from Craters of the Moon today. These

Ultimate Idaho Atlas and Travel Encyclopedia

included elk, wolf, bison, grizzly and black bear, and the cougar. Bighorn sheep, whose males sport characteristic headgear of large, curled horns, have been absent from the park since about 1920.

Military explorer, U.S. Army Capt. B.L.E. Bonneville, left impressions of the Craters of the Moon lava field in his travel diaries in the early 1800s. In *The Adventures of Captain Bonneville*, which were based on the diaries, 19th-century author Washington Irving pictures a place "where nothing meets the eye but a desolate and awful waste, where no grass grows nor water runs, and where nothing is to be seen but lava." Irving is perhaps most famous for *The Legend of Sleepy Hollow*, but his *Adventures* is considered a significant period work about the West and provided this early, if brief, glimpse of a then unnamed Craters of the Moon.

Pioneers working westward in the 19th century sought either gold or affordable farm or ranch lands so they, like the Northern Shoshone, bypassed these lava wastes. Later, nearby settlers would venture into this area in search of additional grazing lands. Finding none, they left Craters of the Moon substantially alone.

Early pioneers who left traces in the vicinity of the park did so by following what eventually came to be known as Goodale's Cutoff. The route was based on Indian trails that skirted the lava fields in the northern section of the park. It came into use in the early 1850s as an alternate to the regular route of the Oregon Trail. Shoshone Indian hostilities along the Snake River part of the trail - one such incident is memorialized in Idaho's Massacre Rocks State Park - led the emigrants to search for a safer route. They were headed for Oregon, particularly the Walla Walla area around Whitman Mission, and were family groups in search of agricultural lands for settlement. Emigrants traveling it in 1854 noticed names carved in rocks and trees along its route. It was named in 1862 by travelers apparently grateful to their guide, Tim Goodale, whose presence, they felt, had prevented Indian attacks. Illinois-born Goodale was cut in the mold of the typical early trapper and trader of the Far West. He was known to the famous fur trade brothers, Solomon and William Sublette. His name turned up at such fur trade locales as Pueblo, Taos, Fort Bridger, and Fort Laramie over a period of at least 20 years.

After the discovery of gold in Idaho's Salmon River country, a party of emigrants persuaded Goodale to guide them over the route they would name for him. Goodale was an experienced guide: in 1861, he had served in that capacity for a military survey west of Denver. The large band of emigrants set out in July and was joined by more wagons at Craters of the Moon. Eventually their numbers included 795 men and 300 women and children. Indian attacks occurred frequently along the Oregon Trail at that time, but the size of this group evidently discouraged such incursions. The trip was not without incident, but Goodale's reputation remained sufficiently intact for his clients to affix his name to the route. Subsequent modifications and the addition of a ferry crossing on the Snake River made Goodale's Cutoff into a popular route for western emigration. Traces of it are still visible in the vicinity of the park today.

Curiosity about this uninhabitable area eventually led to more detailed knowledge of Craters of the Moon and knowledge led to its preservation. Geologists Israel C. Russell and Harold T. Stearns of the U.S. Geological Survey explored here in 1901 and 1923, respectively. Taxidermist-turned-lecturer, Robert Limbert, explored the area in the early 1920s. Limbert made three trips. On the first two, he more or less retraced the steps of these geologists. On his third and most ambitious trek,

Limbert and W. L. Cole traversed what is now the park and the Craters of the Moon Wilderness Area south to north, starting from the nearby community of Minidoka. Their route took them by Two Point Butte, Echo Crater, Big Craters, North Crater Flow, and out to the Old Arco-Carey Road, then known as the Yellowstone Park and Lincoln Hwy. These explorations and their attendent publicity in *National Geographic Magazine* were instrumental in the proclamation of Craters of the Moon as a national monument by President Calvin Coolidge in 1924.

Since Limbert's day, astronauts have walked both here and on the moon. Despite our now detailed knowledge of the differences between these two places, the name and much of the park's awe-inspiring appeal remains the same. It is as though by learning more about both these niches in our universe we somehow have learned more about ourselves as well.

Reprinted from a National Park Service brochure and National Park Service handbook

V Blizzard Mountain
West of Arco. Contact the Arco Chamber of Commerce/Lost River Visitor Center at 527-8977.

Maintained by the Arco Lions Club, Blizzard Mountain is situated west of Arco on a knoll just north of Craters of the Moon's boundaries. The ski area was developed during the mid 1900s to help promote tourism in the area while serving as another attraction to Craters of the Moon visitors. The ski area offers one lift that transports skiers to the top of the few groomed downhill runs. The ski area is open during years with sufficient snowfall.

M Arco Chamber of Commerce/ Lost River Tourism
213 W. Grand Ave., Arco. 527-8295 or 527-8977.

12 *Food*

Howe
Pop. 20

Pioneer E.R. Hawley arrived in central Idaho in the early 1880s, and before long, area settlers decided to apply for a post office. Using founder Hawley as the preferred site's name, community residents were disappointed to learn the request had been denied. As it turns out, the post office decided that Hawley looked and sounded too similar to the already established town of Hailey, Idaho. Subsequently, the postal department concocted the town's present name in 1884.

H John Day's River
Milepost 16.5 on State Hwy. 33

Fur traders named this stream for John Day, a pioneer trapper who died 12 miles north of here, February 16, 1820. John Day had started west with John Jacob Astor's Pacific Fur Company party that discovered the Snake River Valley to the south of here in 1811. After 1816, he joined Donald Mackenzie's band of fur hunters, who finally spent the winter of 1819-20 in what now is known as Little Lost River Valley. For many years, trappers and mapmakers

referred to Mackenzie's Fallert Springs campground as John Day's Defile, a major fur trade landmark.

T Volcanic Lands
State Hwy. 22 between Howe and the junction with State Hwy. 28

Under the operation of the Idaho National Engineering Laboratory, this reserve of lowland borders the northwestern edge of the Lost River Sinks. The land is comprised of extensively deep lava that soaks up the flow of the Big and Little Lost Rivers and Birch Creek. Scientists have drilled 1,400 feet into the lava bed, and although the exact depth is unknown, electrical resistance in the area suggests the lava may extend 5,900 feet deep.

13

Atomic City
Pop. 25

Originally dubbed "Midway," Atomic City lies between Arco and Blackfoot and derived its present name in 1950 when the town incorporated and nearby Hwy. 26 received a $2 million facelift. The townsfolk were hoping the population would boom after the improvements to the highway were completed. That wasn't the case. This small town is, however, the gateway to the U.S. Department of Energy's Idaho National Engineering Laboratory (a huge mass of off-limits land). The Lab is a reactor testing station and was established in 1949.

Butte City
Pop. 76

Located just a few miles southeast of Arco, this small community was named after the county in which it lies.

H Nuclear Reactors
Milepost 265 on U.S. Hwy. 20 at the Big Lost River Rest Area

Since 1949, more nuclear reactors – more than 50 of them – have been built on this plain than anywhere else in the world. This 900-square mile Idaho National Engineering and Environmental Laboratory is the birthplace of the nuclear Navy. Commercial power reactor prototypes, including reactors that breed more fuel than they consume, were developed here. Also, internationally renowned for its materials testing reactors and reactor programs, this laboratory has become a major research center for developing peaceful uses of atomic energy.

H Lost River
Milepost 265 on U.S. Hwy. 20 at the Big Lost River Rest Area

When its water is not diverted for upstream irrigation, the Lost River flows past here into a sink 14 miles to the northeast. Lava flows in the Snake River plains buried old channels of the Lost River, Little Lost River, and Birch Creek. No longer able to reach the Snake River on the surface, they went underground. After a 120-mile journey under the lava plains, water from the Lost River eventually emerges through numerous large springs below Twin Falls, making up a small part of the flow of Thousand Springs near Hagerman.

H Big Butte
Milepost 272.8 on U.S. Hwy. 20

Towering 2,500 feet high, two overlapping rock domes form a 300,000-year-old butte that dominates this lava plain.

After a hot flow of molten rhyolite (acidic rock) boiled up through older lava, a second rhyolite dome pushed up a block of earlier basalt on its northwest side. They took many thousands of years to reach their present shape, but geologically, they are very recent structures.

H Three Buttes
Milepost 272.8 on U.S. Hwy. 20

Rising above this level plain of lava flows and windblown soils, these high landmarks are recent additions to Idaho's landscape.

East Butte (farthest east) flowed up and cooled quickly about 600,000 years ago, while Big Southern Butte (south of here) emerged about 300,000 years ago. Although East Butte and Middle Butte have a similar general appearance, they were formed in different ways. A dome of melted rock called rhyolite that rose up through a volcanic fissure became East Butte. Middle Butte, however, is a block of hard lava (basalt) pushed up by volcanic activity from below.

T Idaho National Engineering and Environmental Laboratory
50 miles west of Idaho Falls on U.S. Hwy. 20 encompassing Butte City and Atomic City. 526-0050 or (800) 708-2860. www.atomictourist.com

The Idaho Engineering and Environmental Laboratory (INEEL), although situated near Arco, maintains a home base in Idaho Falls and is Idaho's single largest employer. The site houses nuclear, engineering, and environmental work stations and provides a historical look at nuclear power in the U.S. On December 20, 1951, INEEL made history with its Experimental Breeder Reactor-I (EBR-1). On this date, EBR-1 became the first nuclear reactor to produce usable amounts of electricity. For this feat in atomic power, EBR-1 was added to the Register of National Historic Landmarks. After this accomplishment, engineers attempted to build nuclear powered bomber aircraft in the following years. The models, however, were so large they would require a ten-mile runway to take off and land. In addition, crewmen would be exposed to large quantities of radiation as protective shielding would prohibit the aircraft's ability to fly.

Despite the obvious problems with atomic aircraft, INEEL became the site of major nuclear experimentation in 1955. The X-39 engine was developed and tested on-site in conjunction with a nuclear aircraft power plant. In January 1956, two atomic X-39 engines operated successfully. However, the radiation shields were so heavy, the engines were not flyable. Over the next two years, engineers attempted to remodel the X-39 engines. While the final attempt did produce an engine that could power an aircraft at 460 mph for 30,000 miles non-stop, radiation levels were still a serious problem that eventually led scientists to abandon the idea of atomic aircraft.

Today, the historic EBR-1 and the two X-39 engines are on display at INEEL along with videos and other public exhibits. The free site is open daily from 9 AM to 5 PM Memorial Day through Labor Day. Private tour appointments can be made during the remainder of the year.

T East Butte
Northwest of Atomic City on U.S. Hwy. 26.

Located three miles from Middle Butte, East Butte is a rhyolite dome situated at 6,572 feet above sea level. The butte is estimated to be about 600,000 years old and was formed from small magma chambers during the region's ancient volcanic activity.

T Middle Butte
3.7 miles northwest of Atomic City on U.S. Hwy. 26.

In this land of ancient lava flows, unusual geographical formations line the landscape. Middle Butte is situated at an elevation of 6,392 feet and is estimated to be approximately 300,000 years old. The butte, visible on the highway's north side, was formed when a magma flow thrust the basalt rock off the flat landscape.

TV Big Southern Butte
Near Atomic City. From Atomic City, drive west on Cox's Well-Atomic City Rd. After crossing the railroad tracks, turn right on Cedar Butte Rd. and then left on Cedar Big Butte Rd. Proceed clockwise around the butte's south and west sides until reaching the major intersection at Frenchman's Cabin. Turn southeast, and proceed 1.5 miles to a gate near the butte's base.

Big Southern Butte is a visible landmark from most of southeastern Idaho. Rising 2,500 feet above the rest of the landscape, the butte was formed with a volcanic eruption of rhyolite. Unlike the area's more common black basalt eruptions that had time to spread out across the surface before cooling, rhyolite is much thicker. As a result, the substance solidified so quickly that it formed the light colored butte now towering above the plains

Ambitious visitors can actually climb to the top of the butte's summit on a 3.5-mile hike. Atop the summit, outstanding views of Wyoming's Grand Teton Mountains and the surrounding landscape can be found.

14

Clayton
Pop. 27

This town came to life in the 1870s when several area mines were developed, and the Salmon River Mining and Smelting Company established a smelter. However, the smelter was short-lived, existing only from 1902 to 1904. The town was named after Clayton Smith, who was quite popular with the miners for opening a house of ill-repute. Today, the area still maintains several active mines. The most notable, the Clayton Silver Mine, dates back to 1929 and employs approximately thirty-five people.

Sunbeam
Pop. 5

This nearly extinct town was established at the mouth of the Yankee Fork during the 1880s. As prospectors arrived in herds at the Loon Creek area in 1869, some of these miners eventually decided to branch out on their own. One such miner was Ebenezer E. Cunningham who migrated to the area in hopes of striking it rich. In an attempt to locate placer gold, Cunningham planned to divert water from a nearby stream and form a ditch. With this grand scheme in mind, Cunningham built the area's first cabin (which later became the area's first store) and named his town "Junction Bar" after the point where the ditch was to be completed. Cunningham soon ran out of funds, so he sold his dream and claim to the Sunbeam Mining Company. Bearing the mine's name, this tiny community operated a post office from 1907 to 1912.

H Clayton Smelter
Milepost 222.9 on State Hwy. 75

Lead-silver mineral discoveries 12 miles north of here on Bayhorse Creek in 1864 and 1872 led Joel E. Clayton to locate a large smelter here in 1880. Doubled in size in 1888,

Clayton's smelter had enough variety of ores from local mines to continue production until 1902. A modern flotation plant followed for six years after 1919. When silver prices rose in 1935, Clayton became southern Idaho's primary silver producer, operating steadily for more than 50 years.

T The First Permanent Salmon River Crossing
On State Hwy. 75 directly north of the East Fork of the Salmon River's junction with the main fork.

The mighty Salmon River saw its first permanent crossing erected in 1880. On October 1, Chas Carson of Blackfoot, Idaho completed the fourteen-foot wide, 172-foot long bridge. The bridge stood six feet above the Salmon's highest watermark, and the old cement foundation is still visible from this historic bridge.

T Bonanza and Boothill Cemetery
At Sunbeam, bear north off State Hwy. 75 onto FR 013. Follow FR 013 to the site.

Located on the Yankee Fork River, William A. Morton discovered gold in the area as early as 1875. In 1879, Morton decided to operate a post office, and the Bonanza postal service opened its doors on June 16, 1879. As word of the new camp spread, people flocked to the area, including Charles Franklin who began laying out a new town in 1878. Although no roads officially led to Bonanza at the time, Franklin believed if he created a town, a road would be built. True to Franklin's beliefs, a road was soon built connecting Bonanza with other Idaho mining camps. With Franklin's solid expertise in community planning, Bonanza grew to include 100 private dwellings, a butcher shop, two general stores, furniture and hardware stores, three saloons, a café, dance hall, a town newspaper titled "The Yankee Fork Herald," and the Dodge Hotel (also called the Franklin House Hotel) run by Franklin himself. By 1881, the town reached a population of 600 residents. When fires in 1889 and 1897 destroyed much of the town, most of Bonanza's residents moved to the neighboring town (now also a ghost town) of Custer. However, Bonanza has not been lost to history as it holds one of the greatest mysteries from Idaho's early mining era.

During Bonanza's early boom in the summer of 1878, London natives Richard and Agnes Elizabeth King decided to move to the new community. Richard was an avid real estate market player as well as a prospector, while Agnes "Lizzie" opened and successfully managed the Arcade Saloon and Yankee Fork Dance Hall. It was no surprise that the industrious couple quickly became friends with Charles Franklin. Unfortunately, Richard King was killed in a local tavern during a heated argument with a business partner. His young wife was distraught, so Franklin rushed to her side and aided the widow in selecting three burial plots on Boot Hill: one for Richard, one for Lizzie, and one for himself. After Richard's burial, townspeople noticed that Lizzie and Franklin were fast becoming more than friends. By all accounts, the new couple was expected to wed during the 1880 summer. But Franklin's romantic plans were ended with the arrival of poker dealer Robert Hawthorne. Instead of marrying Franklin, Lizzie gave her vows to Hawthorne that summer.

The newlyweds enjoyed their new life together for just one week. On August 11, 1880, Lizzie and Hawthorne were found murdered in their log home. Although Franklin was the prime suspect in the case, no weapon was ever found and he was never charged. Instead, Franklin assumed responsibility for burying Lizzie next to her first husband. The plot that he had intended for himself was filled with Hawthorne's body. Visitors to Boot Hill Cemetery will notice that Franklin ignored Lizzie's new surname, leaving it "King" on her tombstone and listing her date of death as the day she actually married Hawthorne. Heartbroken, Franklin became increasingly agitated and ten years later, he moved to a placer claim near Stanley Creek. Living as a recluse, Franklin's badly decomposed body was discovered two years later in his bed by a pair of prospectors new to the area. In his hand, Franklin clutched a locket to his heart that contained Lizzie's picture. Franklin was buried in an unmarked grave behind his cabin.

More recently, Bonanza was home to one of Idaho's largest dredges. Brought in by Chinese laborers, the Bonanza dredge operated on the Yankee Fork River from October 1939 to November 1942 and then again from 1944 through 1952. It is reported that this dredge produced more than $11 million in gold, and visitors can still see the well-preserved dredge slowly sinking into the river.

T Custer: A Historical Building Tour

Contact the Challis Chamber of Commerce at 879-2771 At Sunbeam, bear north off State Hwy. 75 onto Yankee Fork Rd. (Forest Rd. 013).

Custer History

Although gold had been discovered as early as 1870 in Jordan Creek, it wasn't until 1875-77 that lode ores were found on the mountains surrounding Jordan Creek and Yankee Fork. The richest claim, the General Custer, was named after General George Armstrong Custer who was killed during the battle of the Little Big Horn on June 26, 1876.

Instead of working his mining claims along the Yankee Fork, Sammy Holman sold them as lots for a new town. Established in 1879, Custer City became the support center for the General Custer, the Lucky Boy, the Black, and other mines on Custer Mountain. Businesses catering to the needs of miners, mostly single, were soon springing up in the new town. Saloons, boarding houses, and cabins lined the "one street" town of Custer. Like many western mining towns, Custer had a Chinese population that lived in "Chinatown" at the southern end of main street.

Bonanza, Custer's older sister city, continued to be the social and business center for the Yankee Fork. However, disastrous fires in 1889 and 1897 destroyed much of Bonanza and many merchants re-established their businesses in Custer. As Bonanza's population declined, Custer's increased. By 1896, Custer had a population of 600 and gradually became the new business and social center for Yankee Fork. A new schoolhouse, jail, Miner's Union Hall, post office, and even a baseball team, completed this transition.

By 1903, the glory days of mining on the Yankee Fork were slipping away. Although the General Custer had closed in 1888, many of the smaller mines continued to be worked. The General Custer was purchased in 1895 by the Lucky Boy group and hopes ran high that it would be reopened - it never was. One by one, the various mines played out. In 1905, even the Lucky Boy failed. Business slumped and a general depression settled down on Custer and Bonanza. Each season found fewer and fewer people in Custer. In 1910, the post office was moved back to Bonanza and, by the time winter closed in on Yankee Fork, Custer had become a ghost town.

In 1966, the Challis National Forest took ownership of the few remaining buildings and, in 1981, Custer was placed on the National Register of Historic Places. Although the Forest had an overall planning strategy for interpreting and preserving the site, funding was generally lacking and Custer slipped further into decay. Only through the efforts of the Friends of Custer Museum was the site kept open for the public's enjoyment. In 1990, the Idaho Department of Parks and Recreation joined the Forest Service in managing Custer. This led to the establishment of the "Land of the Yankee Fork" State Park and National Forest Historic Area.

Historic Tour

1) Custer Schoolhouse: J.F. Davis of Custer, Idaho was awarded a contract to build a 24' x 36' schoolhouse in Custer on September 4, 1900. Abandoned for many years, Tuff and Edna McGown established a museum here in 1960. Purchased by the Challis National Forest in 1966, the old school was restored in 1990 and still houses the Custer Museum.

2) Johnson Graves: On the night of February 2, 1890, an avalanche came down Bald Mountain and carried the frame home of Nels and Maria Johnson across the Yankee Fork. Although Mr. and Mrs. Johnson escaped the destruction, their three daughters, Ulga, Anna, and Josephine, were killed. The family buried the children here so they could be close to their friends - the people of Custer.

3) Stone Cabin Ruins: Ed Treolor commissioned a stonemason to build this one-room cabin for his sister Louise Treolor Short after her husband left her destitute. "Miss Lou," as her many friends called her, moved from Custer to Challis in 1904. The cabin, the only known stone structure in Custer, was constructed of native stone from the hillside around it. It finally collapsed from neglect and the heavy snows of many winters.

4) Storehouse: This small, frame building is probably a recent addition to Custer and is believed to have been built during the depression of the 1930s. During those times, many unemployed men and their families reoccupied the old town and prospected for gold. The few ounces they found reworking some of the old claims got them through the lean years.

5) Pfeiffer House: Known as the Pfeiffer House, this handsome frame structure was purchased by Charles Pfeiffer after his marriage to Ellen Olson in 1890. Mr. Pfeiffer was the manager of the Pfeiffer Store in Custer, and as his family increased, he added the bedroom and kitchen on the north side and the rambling shed on the back of the house. After the mines failed, the Pfeiffer family moved to Challis.

6) Garage and Shop: This garage and shop is also believed to have been built during the depression of the 1930s.

7) Blacksmith Shop (Site): This is the site of one of the many blacksmith shops located in Custer. Blacksmiths made and repaired mining equipment, shod horses and mules, and repaired wagons and carriages. The original structure was destroyed in 1964 by a grass fire started by a cigarette thrown from a passing car.

8) Jail (Site): This is the site of the Custer jail. This small jail was constructed of 2" by 6" lumber with boards laid flat, similar to building with logs. The jail was also destroyed by the 1964 grass fire, but will be rebuilt as funds become available.

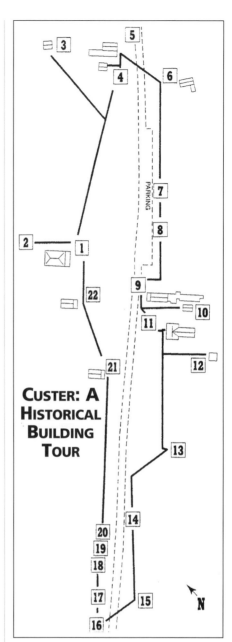

9) Empire Saloon: At first a saloon, this large building was later converted into the office and home of Custer's last doctor, Dr. Charles Kirtley. Dr. Kirtley moved to Custer in 1903 and married Josie Malm in 1907. The Kirtleys lived in the old saloon until 1910 when they moved to Salmon. This building will be restored to its original use as a saloon.

10) Ice House: Ice houses were constructed as storage for ice harvested from the Yankee Fork during the winter months. Covered with sawdust, large blocks of ice could be stored for use during the warmer months. The cool interior of the building was also used to store meats, vegetables, and other perishables before the development of modern refrigeration.

11) McKenzie's House: This large log house was constructed by Kenneth McKenzie in 1880. Billed as one of the finest homes in Custer, the original one-room cabin was added to until it became a rambling, ranch-style home. Mr. McKenzie was one of the more astute businessmen of Custer and owned McKenzie's Saloon, McKenzie's Feed and Livery Stable, and McKenzie's Buggy Shed.

Occupied until about 1914, this building was later converted into a garage, but will be restored to its original use as a home.

12) Frank Tully's Cabin: This one-room frame cabin was originally an addition to a much larger log cabin that has since rotted away. Frank Tully, a bachelor miner, lived in the cabin for many years. Like the McKenzie House, this cabin was also converted into a garage/shop during the 1930s.

13) "Flagpole Grave": Although his name has been lost in history, a young man competing in a flagpole climbing contest was killed here when he fell from the pole during a 4th of July celebration. In commemoration, his friends buried him near the flagpole.

14) McKenzie's Livery Stable (Site): McKenzie's Livery Stable was a large, two-story frame structure with horse stalls on the lower floor and a hay loft upstairs. The livery stable was a necessary business in all towns during the days of the horse. Animals belonging to individuals were boarded here for $1.50 per day. A person could also rent, sell, or buy horses, mules, wagons, and buggies.

15) "Bawdy House" (Site): Like all western mining camps, Custer had houses of ill repute. Shunned by most respected women, prostitutes provided companionship to the many single men who had left families and friends back east. These "ladies of the evening" were well known for the care they provided in times of sickness and for their generous donations to the poor.

16) Deardon & McGown Store (Site): George Deardon and Arthur McGown, Sr., constructed a large, two-story frame mercantile store here about 1897. Typical of general stores throughout the West, the list of items in stock included almost everything from foodstuffs to hardware. Fresh meats and produce could be stored in an ice house set into the hillside at the rear of the store. The two men also established a butcher shop 150 feet to the south of the store.

17) Burton's Rooming House (Site): After the death of her husband in 1895, Estella Burton operated a rooming house at this site. It was a small, one-story building with a false front. Mrs. Burton also operated a restaurant adjacent to the rooming house.

18) Thompson's Furniture Store (Site): George and Belle Thompson constructed a large, two-story frame furniture store here in 1879. It was one of the first business establishments in Custer. The furniture store was on the first floor, while single men lodged in the upstairs. An elevated walkway led from the second story to the Thompson's family home on the hillside behind the hall. Later, the furniture store was converted into a social center, and the building became known as "Thompson's Dance Hall."

19) Judge Davis' Carpenter Shop (Site): J.F. Davis, who served as Justice of the Peace and was popularly known as "Judge" Davis, operated a carpenter shop here. In a small, log structure with a false front, Mr. Davis, a carpenter and cabinet maker by trade, made most of the coffins used in Custer and Bonanza.

20) Casto & McGee Saloon (Site): Bill Casto and "Red" McGee established a saloon at this site. The saloon was a single-story building with the front and porch painted white. This saloon boasted a pool table and specialized in stud poker. Prize fights between the champion boxer of the Yankee Fork and champions from other mining camps were often staged here.

21) Charlie Raine's Cabin: This small log cabin was Charlie Raine's home. He owned a mine up on Custer Mountain and worked it himself or with the help of a few other men. He was a typical example of small mine owners on the Yankee Fork who never struck it rich, but were respected members of the community.

22) Brockman Cabin: This small log cabin was just being constructed when Custer became a ghost town in 1910. The owners abandoned it before it was fully completed. In 1958, the unfinished cabin was moved to a mining claim near Boot Hill cemetery. The remains of the structure were donated to the Friends of Custer Museum, and in 1987, the cabin was moved back to its original location and restored.

Reprinted from an Idaho Department of Parks & Recreation brochure

T Sunbeam Hot Springs

On the Salmon River's north bank at the community of Sunbeam on State Hwy. 75

Possessing more hot springs than any other state, Idaho is an outdoor lover's paradise, and north central Idaho is renowned for its fair share of soaking spots. One of these natural hot spots is located near the tiny community of Sunbeam.

Sunbeam Hot Springs first attracted tourists in 1824 when Alexander Ross and his fellow fur trappers arrived on a chilly October day. The men revived their spirits while luxuriating in the hot pools, and the rest is history. After hundreds more tourists followed in Ross' footsteps, the Civilian Conservation Corps built a bathhouse and tubs on the site in 1937. This original building has since fallen into disrepair and the tubs are long gone, but the natural pools are still open for the public's use free of charge.

A trail and stairways lead down to the pools bubbling with 90-degree water. Only four to six people fit in the most popular and largest pool, so it is not uncommon for lines to form during the peak season in July and August. Skinny-dipping is strictly prohibited, as are glass containers.

T Indian Riffles Overlook

16 miles north of Stanley on State Hwy. 75 between mileposts 205 and 206. Contact the Stanley-Sawtooth Chamber of Commerce at 774-3411.

Perched just four miles downriver from Sunbeam, the Indian Riffles Overlook provides visitors with a tremendous vista of the surrounding mountains and forests. In addition, the site provides an extraordinary look at traditional Salmon spawning beds below.

T Yankee Fork Gold Dredge

13 miles east of Stanley on State Hwy. 75 near Sunbeam. Contact the Stanley-Sawtooth Chamber of Commerce at 774-3411.

When gold was first discovered in the heart of Idaho's wilderness near the Yankee Fork of the Salmon River, a rush of eager miners swept into the area. Many of these miners enjoyed limited success from mining and panning, and the once booming mine towns turned into ghosts of their past seemingly overnight.

Although much of the initial mining excitement had dissipated by the dawn of the twentieth century, the Snake River Mining Company decided to test the Yankee Fork waters one more time. In 1939, they tested the river for gold dredging, and the results were astonishingly good. They immediately contracted with Bucyrus-Erie Company for a dredge, which was assembled on-

site in 1940.

The 988-ton dredge operated from 1940 until August 1952 and recovered gold from the riverbed in a process of separating out rock, dirt, and gold. Today, the 112 foot long, 54 foot wide, and 64 foot high dredge has been preserved as a historic look at Yankee Fork mining operations. From the last weekend in June through Labor Day, the dredge is open daily from 10 AM to 5 PM. Dredge tours are free, but donations are highly encouraged.

T Historic Sunbeam Dam

11 miles east of Stanley on State Hwy. 75. Contact the Stanley-Sawtooth Chamber of Commerce at 774-3411.

Visible in the river below the highway's north shoulder, the remnants of the Sunbeam Dam mark a significant point in Salmon River history. After surveying the area in 1909, the manager of the Sunbeam Consolidated Gold Mines Company decided to build a dam on the river in an effort to supply hydroelectric power to mining operations near the booming town of Bonanza.

Poured from more than 300 tons of cement, the Sunbeam Dam was completed in 1910 and provided power to the Sunbeam mining mill for nearly a year. But the area's poor quality gold ore couldn't justify the expense of operating the dam any longer, and the Sunbeam Consolidated Gold Mines Company went bankrupt in 1911. In an auction that year, the dam was sold for a pittance.

Although the dam was no longer in use as a power source, it wreaked havoc on the Salmon River for over twenty years. The only dam ever built on the Salmon River, the Sunbeam Dam blocked salmon migration and created irreparable harm to the sockeye salmon population. Finally, in 1934, the dam was dynamited to restore the salmon's river run. Today, the restored Salmon River remains one of the American West's last free-flowing rivers, and the salmon species is slowly reclaiming its territory.

T State Hwy. 75's Natural Hot Springs

Contact the Stanley-Sawtooth Chamber of Commerce at 774-3411.

Heading east, the section of State Hwy. 75 between Stanley and Sunbeam is littered with natural hot spring soaking spots. At mile marker 193, Mormon Bend Hot Spring is situated on the far side of the Salmon River. As with the other area hot springs, scenery abounds and the hot water is always relaxing. Seven miles east of Stanley, Basin Creek Campground Hot Spring awaits and is a popular soaking spot with area campers. The springs receive considerable use since they are located next to the highways, so nude soakers should not be encountered.

T West Pass Hot Springs

Near Clayton. Contact the Sawtooth National Recreation Area at 727-5013. 5 miles east of Clayton, merge northeast off State Hwy. 75 onto Forest Rd. 120 (East Fork Salmon River Rd.). After traveling 29 miles and crossing West Pass Creek, immediately turn left on a road that ascends the hillside. A parking area rests on a flat, and a short trail leads to the tubs.

Nestled on a hillside, West Pass Hot Springs offers a world of secluded soaking. As the white bedrock of West Pass Creek shimmers in the sunlight, soakers can choose from three different tubs. Rubber hoses from an old mine shaft feed each tub, and users can simply divert the hoses to change the water temperature. Although the area does possess a moderate sulfur smell, most visitors find that the privacy, lack of bugs, and plentiful wildlife far outweigh any negative aspects. The free area is only accessible from May to December due to seasonal road closures.

T Bowery Hot Springs
Near Clayton. Contact the Sawtooth National Recreation Area at 727-5013. 5 miles east of Clayton, merge northeast off State Hwy. 75 onto Forest Rd. 120 (East Fork Salmon River Rd.). At the West Pass Creek Junction, continue straight ahead on FR 120 to a parking area. Hike approximately 100 yards towards the Bowery Forest Service Guard Station, cross the bridge, and proceed a short distance further to the spring.

Characterized by fabulous mountain scenery and plenty of privacy, Bowery Hot Springs is nestled beside the East Fork of the Salmon River. The site features an old fiberglass spa built into a deck, upon which sits a bucket and two plugs. In order to soak here, visitors must insert the plugs into the spa and then fill the tub using the rubber hose that transports hot water from the spring to the spa. It takes approximately one hour for the spa to fill, at which time, users can either wait for the water temperature to cool down or manually adjust the temperature by using the bucket to pour in cold river water. The bug-free site emits a moderate sulfur smell and is only open from May to December due to seasonal road closures.

T Elkhorn Hot Springs
Slightly east of mile marker 192 on State Hwy. 75 between Stanley and Sunbeam. Contact the Stanley-Sawtooth Chamber of Commerce at 774-3411.

Despite its close proximity to the highway, Elkhorn Hot Springs receives relatively little use and retains a feeling of seclusion. Several rock-lined seasonal pools are available as well as one medium-sized tub accommodating about eight people. The crystal clear water is ideal for long soaks, and the tub is available for soaking year-round. The well-maintained rock-lined pools are accessible when river levels are low.

T Kem Hot Springs
Directly east of mile marker 197 on State Hwy. 75 between Stanley and Sunbeam. Contact the Stanley-Sawtooth Chamber of Commerce at 774-3411.

Situated at an elevation of 6,100 feet beside the Salmon River, Kem Hot Springs is home to an abundant deer and elk population and features a cluster of several semi-secluded pools. Formed from rocky walls with a gravel and rock bottom, each pool provides a leisurely soak during low water. During high water, the pools are submerged in the river. The area is accessible year-round, but the pools are restricted to day-use only.

15 *Food, Lodging*

Stanley
Pop. 100

Nestled in Stanley Basin at the foot of the Sawtooth Mountains, the small community of Stanley serves as the southern access point into the Sawtooth Wilderness Area. As with many other Idaho towns, Stanley's roots lie in the mining era. In the summer of 1863, Captain John Stanley led a group of twenty-three prospectors from Warrens to this area. The men found insignificant traces of placer gold in the basin and quickly moved on in search of better prospects. However, Stanley's name remained, and in 1890, the first settlers and business owners moved in. Although a post office began operating in 1892, Stanley

wasn't officially recognized as a town until 1919. The town's picture perfect setting has been recognized in *The New York Times* and *National Geographic*, and a variety of recreational users help support Stanley's economy.

H Bears Ploughed Field
Milepost 190 on State Hwy. 75

Long before miners and ranchers settled the Stanley Basin, bears dominated this area. When Alexander Ross and his Hudson's Bay Company trappers stopped here, September 20, 1824, they "observed at some distance the appearance of a ploughed field and riding up towards it, found a large piece of ground more than four acres in extent, dug up and turned over. On getting to the spot, we observed no less than nine black and grizzly bears at work, rooting away" eating camas, onions, and wild celery.

H Stanley Ranger Station
Milepost 190 on State Hwy. 75

When the Challis National Forest was established here in 1908, this site became an administrative center. An early log ranger station stood here from 1909 to 1934. Expanding Forest Service responsibilities led to construction of a larger ranger station, as well as other buildings still preserved here. When a new ranger station four miles south of here replaced this one in 1971, this site became a Sawtooth Interpretive and Historical Association Museum.

T Seafoam
At Banner Summit, bear north onto Forest Rd. (FR) 008 (Seafoam Rd.) Continue past the Seafoam Ranger Station, eventually bearing southwest on FR 009.

Seafoam was established in 1886 in response to known silver and lead deposits in the area. Due to its remote location, Seafoam's mining history was short. Visitors with four-wheel drive will still be able to locate the Seafoam mill building as well as several other large town buildings.

T Sawtooth Fish Hatchery
Stanley. 774-3684.

The Sawtooth Hatchery is an essential stop on your visit through the Sawtooth Valley. Constructed in 1985, it is part of the Lower Snake River Compensation Program, which is a federal mitigation program for the lower Snake River dams. It is operated by the Idaho Department of Fish and Game. The facility was built to rear spring Chinook salmon and collect eggs from steelhead trout.

Visitors can see adult steelhead at the Sawtooth Hatchery from late March through early May. Adult Chinook salmon can be seen at the hatchery or from overlooks along Hwy. 75 from late July through early September. Catchable rainbow trout are also held at the hatchery for stocking in lakes and streams in the valley. Our visitor center is open year round from 8:00 AM to 5:00 PM daily. Tours are available from Memorial Day through Labor Day at 1:30 PM. In season, the adult fishing trap is emptied at 9 AM daily.

Reprinted from an Idaho Fish and Game brochure

T Redfish Rock Shelter
5 miles south of Stanley on Redfish Lake Rd. near State Hwy. 75. Contact the U.S. Forest Service Redfish Lake Visitor Center at 774-3376.

Tucked on the north side of Redfish Lake Road near the popular Redfish Lake is a historic point tracing the area's habitation back nearly 9,500 years. Archeologists discovered a rock overhang used as a shelter for indigenous people thousands

of years ago. Researchers also believe that in more recent years, the Sheep Eater (Tukudeka) Band of Northern Shoshone used the shelter as an overnight camping spot on regular sheep hunting expeditions. A short trail leading to the site begins between the highway and Little Redfish Lake's northern shore.

T Stanley Museum
0.5 miles north of the junction of State Hwy.s 21 and 75, Stanley. 774-3517.

The Stanley Museum is situated in the 1933 Valley Creek Ranger Station and provides visitors with a glimpse into Stanley's history. Exhibits include historical photographs of the area, logging and mining artifacts, pioneer life, and the growth and development of the Sawtooth Valley. The museum is open 11 AM to 5 PM daily from Memorial Day through Labor Day with free admission.

T Redfish Lake Osprey Viewing
5 miles south of Stanley on State Hwy. 75. Contact the Redfish Lake Visitor Center at 774-3376.

In addition to hosting numerous year-round recreationists, Redfish Lake is also home to a large osprey nesting population. Osprey inhabit the lake's eastern shore and are frequently seen swarming over the lake in search of their evening meal. Osprey also occasionally can be viewed at the junctions of State Hwy.s 75 and 21.

T McGowan Peak
Near Stanley on State Hwy. 75.

Looming over Stanley from the Sawtooth National Recreation Area, rugged McGowan Peak pokes the sky at 9,191 feet. The foothills surrounding the peak and lying to the east are known as the Stanley Gold and Uranium Belt. Although the hills are recognized for their generous mineral deposits, all of the minerals belong to the U.S. Government and are not available for prospecting, mining, or removal.

T Basin Creek Hot Springs
8.3 miles north of Stanley on State Hwy. 75 between mileposts 197 and 198. Contact the Stanley-Sawtooth Chamber of Commerce at 774-3411.

Basin Creek Hot Springs is a popular and free natural soaking spot nestled amid the scenery of Idaho's Sawtooth Mountains. Due to the labor of previous users, small pools surrounded with rocks have been created for soaking and relaxing. Users should be cautious, however, as the water flowing into the pools is a toasty 170 degrees Fahrenheit before it is cooled with the nearby river water.

T Elk Mountain Overlook
Contact the Stanley-Sawtooth Chamber of Commerce at 774-3411. From Stanley, travel 5 miles west on State Hwy. 21, turning onto Stanley Lake Rd. between mileposts 126 and 127. Proceed 4 miles, and at the road junction, stay to the right. Drive 2.5 miles to the overlook.

Visitors to Elk Mountain Overlook outside Stanley may feel like they're at the top of the world. The overlook provides spectacular views of the tranquil Stanley Lake resting in the shadow of the rugged Sawtooth Mountains. The dirt road leading to the overlook is generally passable during dry weather conditions.

T Sawtooth Valley Pioneer Park
Wall St., Stanley. Contact the Stanley-Sawtooth Chamber of Commerce at 774-3411.

Surrounded by nature, Stanley's Sawtooth Valley Pioneer Park offers scenery combined with traditional outdoor fun. The park includes swings, slides, a picnic area, a baseball diamond, and the historic Shaw Homestead Cabin in addition to captivating views of the Sawtooth Mountains.

Idaho Trivia
Renowned for its breathtaking setting adjacent to the Sawtooth National Recreation Area, Stanley is also recognized for its striking weather patterns. Occasionally reaching minus fifty degrees Fahrenheit during winter, Stanley holds the state record for the lowest recorded temperature. In addition, the small community boasts the state's lowest mean annual temperature, measuring in at just seventeen degrees Fahrenheit!

T Stanley Ranger Station
2.5 miles south of Stanley on State Hwy. 75 between mileposts 187 and 188. 774-3000.

Operated by the U.S. Forest Service, the Stanley Ranger Station provides general national forest information and specific area maps. In addition, the facility provides narrative automobile tour tapes describing highlights of the surrounding landscape. The office is open daily during the summer and Monday through Friday the rest of the year.

T Old Stanley Basin
Contact the Stanley-Sawtooth Chamber of Commerce at 774-3411. On State Hwy. 21, drive 5 miles west of Stanley and turn on Stanley Creek Rd. Follow the road approximately 1.5 miles to the historic basin.

The oldest recorded discovery of Stanley Basin dates back to 1824 when Alexander Ross and his fellow Hudson Bay Company fur trappers arrived in the area. Although Ross hoped to find a land rich with beaver pelts, Stanley Basin disappointed him. Word quickly spread that the area was bereft of beaver, and until 1831, the land remained dormant.

Traveling up the Salmon River, William Ferris arrived in Stanley Basin in 1831 and camped out for ten days in his search of beaver. But again, the area was a disappointment, and Ferris considered the trip a failure. One year later, John Work and his trapping comrades passed through, and Captain Benjamin Bonneville spent Christmas Day in the area. With so many reported accounts of a non-existent beaver population, Stanley Basin simply retained its rugged beauty in isolation for the next thirty years.

Civil War veteran, Captain John Stanley, and a large prospecting party passed through Stanley Basin on a hunt for gold in 1863. When just an insignificant amount of placer gold was found in the area streams, the party moved on but left behind their name.

Today, Stanley Basin retains much of the same mystique and landscape that the first area arrivals would have witnessed. The rugged landscape still features incredible mountain views, and the area's ranching operations capture a flavor of the old west.

TV Redfish Lake & Visitor Center
5 miles south of Stanley on State Hwy. 75. Contact the U.S. Forest Service Redfish Lake Visitor Center at 774-3376.

Nestled in the heart of the Sawtooth Mountains, Redfish Lake is named after the sockeye salmon that once spawned in its waters. When the fish would spawn, their scales turned a vibrant shade of orange-red, thus providing the lake with its name. Although sockeye salmon no longer inhabit the area, the lake still draws a variety of recreationists. Boasting a breathtaking backdrop formed from Mount Heyburn's 4,000-foot granite

---

walls, Redfish Lake is the largest body of water in the Sawtooth National Recreation Area and also one of the most popular.

Located near the lakeshore, the Redfish Lake Visitor Center offers interpretive displays and slide shows about the lake and the Sawtooth Wilderness plus several unique children's activities. During fair weather, guided hikes and campfire programs are available. A self-guided, half-mile interpretive trail also departs from the visitor center and is appropriate for individuals of all ages and physical abilities.

The lake itself provides a hotbed of activity year round. During the summer, the northeast shore's Sandy Beach Day Use Area is populated with swimmers and sunbathers, while boaters make use of the area's boat ramp. Located near the visitor center, the North Shore Picnic Area provides another convenient beach access area. Day use areas are open from 6 AM to 10 PM daily. Visitors wishing to take to the water may bring their own canoes, fishing boats, sailboats, and ski boats or simply rent one from the nearby Redfish Lake Lodge.

In addition to watersports, horseback riding, day hiking, mountain biking, and camping are also available. All recreationists, however, are urged to familiarize themselves with the boundaries of the Sawtooth Wilderness as it borders the lake to the south and west.

V Sawtooth Fishing Guides
Stanley. 774-TROUT (8768). www.sawtoothfishingguides.com

Discover the thrill of Idaho fishing with Sawtooth Fishing Guides. As local residents and passionate anglers, guides ensure that clients experience the best fishing destinations, learn new techniques, and hopefully catch one of the Salmon River's or other area river's or lake's famous trout and Steelhead. For a full fishing day, reserve a drift boat or a walk and wade fishing trip. Trout on these trips measure up to 20 inches, while Steelhead range from 20 to 42 inches! For a combination fishing and wilderness experience, take a guided hike to an alpine lake. Those with less time can opt for a half-day walk and wade or a customized casting and equipment clinic. With diverse trip offerings, Sawtooth Fishing Guides is your destination for a one-of-a-kind Idaho fishing experience!

V Mountain Bike Rides in the Sawtooth National Recreation Area
Near Stanley. Contact the Sawtooth National Recreation Area at 774-3000 for more information.

The following mountain bike routes are popular excursions in the Sawtooth National Recreation Area north of Galena Summit. Bordering the White Cloud and Boulder Mountains, the trails provide miles of outstanding scenery.

1) Valley Creek
North of Stanley off State Hwy. 21
This 7-mile ride follows the old valley road through cattle pasture and rustic ranches. You can loop back on Hwy. 21 at Stanley Creek turn-off. Elevation gain is minimal.

2) Stanley Basin/Anderson Creek/Basin Butte
West of Stanley with access at the Stanley Creek turn-off
The 10-mile route will take you to Basin Butte Lookout. Elevation is 6,400 to 8,950 feet. The road is narrow and used by all types of vehicles but offers panoramic views.

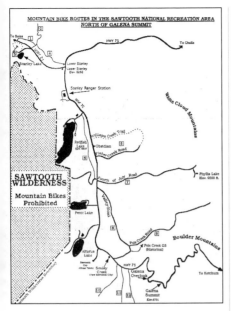

MOUNTAIN BIKE ROUTES IN THE SAWTOOTH NATIONAL RECREATION AREA
NORTH OF GALENA SUMMIT

3) Elk Mountain Loop Trail

Access is from the Stanley Lake Rd.

This trail was designed with mountain bikes in mind. The trail is 12 miles and circles Elk Mountain past Elk Meadows and back to Stanley Lake. Follow the Stanley Lake Road for 3 miles, park at Forest Service Road #649 or Elk Mountain Road to start the loop. Elevation on the trail varies from 7,174 to 7,674 feet.

4) Nip and Tuck Loop

Nip and Tuck Road runs through the southern portion of the Stanley Basin. Interestingly, the town of Stanley is not located in the Stanley Basin. This rolling hill ride provides spectacular views of the northern end of the Sawtooth Range and Sawtooth Valley. Exit State Hwy. 21 at the Stanley Creek turn-off and follow Forest Service Road #652 for 2 miles. Turn right onto Forest Service Road #633. Nip and Tuck enters Hwy. 75 in Lower Stanley after a 10-mile ride. An additional 7 miles (1 on State Hwy. 75 and 6 on State Hwy. 21) will complete the loop ride. Elevation ranges from 6,480 feet to 6,200 feet from Stanley Creek to Lower Stanley.

5) Fisher/Williams Creek Loop

This 18-mile loop is a regional favorite. Park vehicles at the Williams Creek trailhead and ride south on State Hwy. 75 to the Fisher Creek Road or access at Fisher Creek Road. Trail elevations range between 6,640 feet to 6,800 feet.

6) Decker Flat Loop

Forest Service Road #210 parallels Hwy. 75 on the Salmon River's west side. Forest Service Road #210 access if off the Redfish Lake Road (0.25 miles from Hwy. 75); turn left on road #210. This road extends to Decker Flat and the Hell Roaring Creek/Mays Creek area. After the 12-mile ride, a loop may be made by using Hwy. 75. Elevations rise from 6,480 feet to 8,800 feet.

7) Fourth of July Creek Road

This road takes you into the White Clouds from Hwy. 75. The 10-mile road is narrow; watch for vehicle traffic. Elevations range from 6,800 feet to 8,800 feet.

8) Valley Road

This 12-mile road takes you through the southern Sawtooth Valley paralleling State Hwy. 75 past ranches and pastureland. Look for sage grouse and sandhill cranes. Pole Creek Road & Hwy. 75 provide the connection for the rest of the loop ride.

9) Pole Creek

From Hwy. 75 near Smiley Creek, follow the Pole Creek Road 2 miles. Use a side road to the historic Pole Creek Guard Station (2 mile roundtrip to guard station). Continue on Pole Creek Road #197 for 5 miles to Pole-Germania Divide. Elevations rise from 7,200 feet to 8,400 feet.

10) Smiley Creek

Forest Service Road #007 extends 9 miles. Private property blocks the access to the old mining area.

11) Frenchman Creek

Follow Forest Service Road #195 for 6 miles. Elevations rise from 7,340 feet to 8,600 feet.

12) Salmon River/Chemeketan

Follow Forest Service Road #195 and Trail #215 for 9 miles to the summit. Elevations rise from 7,350 feet to 8,600 feet.

Partially Reprinted from a U.S. Forest Service brochure

V Stanley Lake

Contact the Stanley Ranger Station at 774-3000. Drive 5 miles west of Stanley on State Hwy. 21. Turn on Stanley Lake Rd., and continue 2.5 miles to the lake.

Stanley Lake is the largest lake in the northern portion of the Sawtooth National Recreation Area, and its easy accessibility makes it a favorite year-round recreational destination. Recognized as one of the most scenic lakes in the Sawtooth Mountains, Stanley Lake rests in the shadow of Mount McGowan, which seems to rise right out of the water. In addition to stunning views, the lake offers fishing, motorized boating, and waterskiing. The lake is open year-round, and waterskiing is permitted from 10 AM to 6 PM daily.

The lake is also home to the mountain biking trailhead leading to Elk Mountain. The challenging trail loops 12.5 miles north through Elk Meadows and around Elk Mountain. The trail is a local favorite for wildlife viewing.

V Stanley Lake-Elk Mountain Bicycle Trail Loop

Contact the Stanley-Sawtooth Chamber of Commerce at 774-3411. Travel 5 miles west of Stanley on State Hwy. 21. Between mileposts 126 and 127, turn on Stanley Lake Rd. and proceed 1.5 miles to the marked trailhead on the road's right side.

Winding 12.5 miles over gravel roads and single and double track trails, the Stanley Lake-Elk Mountain Bicycle Trail Loop promises spectacular vistas of the Sawtooth Mountains. The trail is moderately difficult, and users should have previous mountain biking experience.

V Stanley Area Snowmobile Trails

Contact the Stanley Ranger Station at 774-3000 or the Stanley-Sawtooth Chamber of Commerce at 774-3411.

With the White Cloud Mountains rising to the east, the Salmon River Range towering across the northern skies, and the Sawtooth Mountains dominating the western and southern horizon, the Stanley Basin Snowmobile Trail System surrounding the small community of Stanley offers spectacular views at every turn. In fact, the region is so magnificent that *Snow West Magazine* recently rated the area America's #2 destination for outstanding scenery! On top of its amazing vistas, the Stanley Basin Snowmobile Trail System is consistently ranked as one of the top ten snowmobiling trail systems in the west, and it's no surprise.

Experiencing average annual snowfalls in excess of 220 inches, the City of Stanley takes advantage of its location and grooms 185 miles of trails for beginners to experts. Basin Butte and Bear Valley offer open meadows with untouched powder, Kelly Creek Loop provides a technical ride leading to summit views of the Sawtooth Mountains, while many other destinations lead to giant bowls and scenic lookouts perched at over 10,000 feet. Some trails even lead right into the heart of town. For those snowmobilers who prefer to carve their own path, the Stanley area also offers unlimited off-trail riding leading to lakes and wide-open meadows.

The area's snowmobiling season generally begins the first of December and runs through March or April. Users are encouraged to contact the Stanley Ranger Station for snow conditions prior to hitting the trail.

V Knapp Creek – Valley Creek Cruiser Trail

15 miles west of Stanley near Banner Summit. Contact the Sawtooth National Recreation Area at 727-5000.

The Knapp Creek – Valley Creek Cruiser Trail is an easy to moderate twenty-mile loop through the beautiful high-elevation meadows of Knapp Creek and Valley Creek. Boasting just 500 feet of climbing, the trail features nearly twelve miles of single track with the remaining mileage covering a gravel double track. Users should expect company from fellow mountain bikers and a variety of regional wildlife.

V Park Creek Nordic Ski Trails

7 miles west of Stanley. Contact the Stanley Ranger Station at 774-3000.

Rolling over open meadows, the Park Creek cross-country ski trails are appropriate for beginning and intermediate Nordic skiers. Under the operation of the Sawtooth Ski Club, the trails are groomed periodically and offer four possible loop routes of varying lengths. The Lupine Loop is the shortest at 0.5 miles, the Shooting Star and Camas Trail loops measure in at 0.75 miles and 2.5 miles respectively, and the Skyrocket Trail is the longest route at 2.6 miles. Although no set fee governs the area, donations are appreciated to offset grooming expenses.

V Stanley City Park Nordic Ski Trail

Off State Hwy. 21 in Stanley near the community elementary school. Contact the Stanley-Sawtooth Chamber of Commerce at 774-3411.

The Stanley City Park is turned into a winter wonderland for alpine enthusiasts each year. The Sawtooth Ski Club periodically grooms a 1.24-mile trail that is open to the public free of charge. Donations to cover grooming expenses are not required but are much appreciated.

V Cape Horn Area Snowmobile Trails

20 miles west of Stanley at Cape Horn Creek. Contact the Sawtooth National Recreation Area at 727-5000.

Situated in the Salmon River Mountains, the Cape Horn Area Snowmobile Trails offer gentle, tree-covered mountain slopes with a range of riding conditions for people of all ages and experience levels. The trail system connects with the communities of Lowman, Warm Lake, and Yellow Pine and is part of the 150-mile groomed Hwy. to Heaven Trail. The trail is generally accessible from December to April, and no fees currently govern the area.

FL Mountain Village Resort
Hwy.s 21 & 75, Stanley. 774-3661 or
(800) 843-5475. www.mountainvillage.com

Nestled in Stanley Basin with spectacular views of the rugged Sawtooth peaks and Salmon River, Mountain Village Resort is located within scenic driving distance of Sun Valley, Twin Falls, and Boise. Remodeled and redecorated, Mountain Village's quality rooms and suites feature coffeemakers, telephones, and satellite TV. Whether you're snowmobiling the area's renowned trails, floating or fishing the famous Salmon, hiking or biking the mountains, or searching for trophy game, start and end your day with a delicious meal at the on-site restaurant. A lounge, gift shop, service station, and convenience store are also available, and the on-site meeting room accommodates up to 40 with all standard meeting amenities included. For majestic views and western hospitality that will leave you longing for more, experience Mountain Village Resort!

FLC Sunbeam Village Resort
100 Yankee Fork Rd., Stanley. 838-2211.

Situated on the Yankee Fork and Salmon Rivers at the historical Sunbeam Dam, the year-round Sunbeam Village Resort provides family-oriented lodging, food, and recreation. Sleeping fifty-five people, the lodge and cabins offer comfort, scenery, and meeting rooms. An on-site restaurant boasts outdoor seating while serving scrumptious breakfasts, lunches, and dinners daily. Catering is available. For campers, tent sites and RV hookups await, while the historic general store serves as the area's only grocery store. The store also sells souvenirs, outdoor sporting goods, camping supplies,

Idaho Trivia

Although far removed from the creature comforts of nearby towns, Idaho's Sawtooth Wilderness is still linked to the world. In fact, the wilderness is so connected that anyone who packs along a radio on their next outdoor adventure will discover a world of wavelength options. Music stations from thousands of miles away broadcast loud and clear in the pristine mountain setting. The Sawtooth's high elevation is to blame for the unbelievable reception.

and fishing and hunting licenses. A natural Salmon River hot springs is just minutes away, and whitewater rafting is available onsite and in the historical Yankee Fork. For your next vacation, business trip, or special event, experience the completely non-smoking Sunbeam Village Resort. Sorry, no pets allowed.

L Valley Creek Motel & RV Park
62 Eva Falls Ave. on Hwy. 21, Stanley. 774-3606.
www.stanleyidaho.com

Nestled in the heart of the Sawtooth Mountains, Valley Creek Motel & RV Park is conveniently located near Stanley dining and entertainment venues. Room features include queen beds, remote control color TVs with HBO, private phones and bathrooms, kitchenettes, picture windows that showcase beautiful mountain views, and a back balcony overlooking Valley Creek. For a fortunate few RV travelers, Valley Creek offers five beautiful sites with hookups for water, sewer, and 30/50 amp electric service. Both motel and RV guests can try their hand at fishing and a lucky few may even catch sight of a migrating Chinook salmon in nearby Valley Creek. For the comforts of home nestled in Idaho's wilderness beauty, stay with the friendly staff of Valley Creek Motel & RV Park.

L Riverside Motel & Sawtooth Rentals
13 River Rd. (Hwy. 75), Stanley. 774-3409 or
(800) 284-3185. www.riversidemotel.biz

Enjoy the sights and sounds of the Sawtooth Valley at Riverside Motel & Sawtooth Rentals. Centrally located, the motel provides area recreation access along with numerous lodging choices. The Salmon River tumbles outside your door in the Riverside Units, each featuring a log cabin ambience, outdoor decks, grills, and kitchenettes. For a cozier stay, reserve the four-person Cabin.

Idaho Trivia

Known for its magnificent mountain splendor, Stanley also boasts a one of a kind American trait. In the entire U.S., Stanley is the only location where three National Scenic Byways intersect. These highways are the Sawtooth, the Ponderosa Pine, and the Salmon River Scenic Byways.

The Sawtooth 4-Plex provides four homes away from home with Sawtooth Mountain views, while the River Annex offers two quaint hideaways. Both facilities include kitchenettes and satellite TV. In addition to clean, comfortable lodging, the motel's friendly staff offers canoe and raft rentals for both whitewater adventures and scenic floats. On your next visit to Stanley, stop and stay awhile while enjoying some of Sawtooth Valley's finest amenities!

L Idaho Rocky Mountain Ranch
9 miles S. of Stanley on Hwy. 75, HC 64, Box 9934, Stanley. 774-3544. www.idahorocky.com

Nestled on 1,000 acres amid scenic Sawtooth Mountain vistas, Idaho Rocky Mountain Ranch is one of Idaho's finest guest ranches and is a Nationally Registered Historic Place Although handcrafted in 1930 as a private facility, the ranch now welcomes everyone with cozy cabin and lodge rooms featuring handcrafted furnishings. Guests start each day with buffet breakfasts and then create their own outdoor adventure, selecting from horseback riding, hiking, fishing, biking, whitewater rafting, kayaking, rock climbing, and ghost town tours. After a day in the wild, congenial staff serve five course dinners, barbeques, and Dutch oven feasts, while the ranch's natural hot springs swimming pool invites relaxation. Discover for yourself why the *New York Times* and travel magazines rave about this magical ranch and its abundant western hospitality!

LS Salmon River Cabins & Motel and Jerry's Country Store
Hwy. 75, 1 mile NE of Stanley. 774-3566 or
(800) 972-4627. www.lowerstanley.com

Enjoy unobstructed Sawtooth Mountain views on the scenic Salmon River banks at Salmon River Cabins and Motel in Lower Stanley. Watch wildlife from the balcony or deck of a private log cabin featuring Direct TV and private baths. For a more standard lodging experience, motel units are available and feature two queen beds, color TV, table and chairs, and a private bath. Kitchenette units are supplied with major appliances, dishes, and utensils. On-site, Jerry's Country Store has been nicknamed America's "Biggest Little Grocery Store" and carries a full line of groceries and non-food items to supply your stay or outdoor adventure. Whether you're looking for rest and relaxation with a magnificent view or easy access to world-class recreation, visit Salmon River Cabins & Motel and Jerry's Country Store year-round.

ANNUAL EVENTS

Boulder Mountain Tour
Held in the pristine mountain conditions of Sun Valley, the annual Boulder Mountain Tour is distinguished as one of America's largest cross-country ski races. The 30 kilometer Nordic race regularly draws over 700 skiers from both the U.S. and Canada each year.

Hailey Springfest
The Hailey Springfest honors spring's arrival with a community celebration drawing both locals and tourists alike. The two-day event features music, plays, historical exhibits, sporting events, arts and crafts booths, and a variety of food vendors.

Sun Valley Ice Show
Sun Valley Resort is more than a winter destination. In addition to an array of summer recreational activities, the resort also hosts a star-studded line of Olympic skaters. Every June through September, previous gold medalists and world-class ice skaters perform by the light of the moon in front of sold-out crowds. Advance tickets for the performances are necessary.

Salmon River Days
The Fourth of July Weekend fires up with excitement in downtown Salmon for the community's annual River Days. The three-day event features a parade, fishing derby, family reunions, arts and crafts booths, a demolition derby, boat and mountain bike races, and an impressive fireworks display lighting up the town's mountainous backdrop.

Sawtooth Mountain Mama Arts & Crafts Fair
Featuring the handiworks of more than 150 talented artisans, the Sawtooth Mountain Mama Arts and Crafts Fair is a juried two-day event. The fair is held each summer and draws talent and spectators from all across the Pacific Northwest.

Sun Valley Summer Symphony
Held throughout the first two weeks in August, the Sun Valley Summer Symphony brings the sounds of classical music to Sun Valley/Ketchum residents and visitors. The free music series features twelve classical concerts hosted in an outdoor tent at the Sun Valley Lodge.

Northern Rockies Folk Festival
The Northern Rockies Folk Festival is held in Hailey each summer and provides two-days of fun for the whole family. The event features arts and crafts booths and renowned folk musicians. Past performers have included the Nitty Gritty Dirt Band in 1998, and in 1999, Elvin Bishop and the Amazing Rhythm Aces graced the crowd with its presence.

Sun Valley Arts & Crafts Festival
The outdoor Sun Valley Arts and Crafts Festival draws talented artisans from all medians. Professional artists, avid art collectors, and local gallery owners judge the two-day event that has been ranked in the top 80 of more than 2,000 art festivals nationwide. In addition to the competition, the event showcases handknit sweaters and hats, personalized wood puzzles, handcrafted canoes, baskets, pottery, blown glass, paintings featuring a variety of mediums, unique jewelry, and much more.

Sacajawea Heritage Days
As the birthplace of Sacajawea and home to the Lewis and Clark Trail, Salmon celebrates its famous past with two days of fun at the Sacajawea Heritage Days. Held each August, the event is also known as "The Great Salmon Valley Balloon Fest" and features arts and crafts booths along with an impressive hot air balloon festival.

Custer Days
Custer comes to life and honors the town's founding legacy with Custer Days. The two-day event is held each summer and features Dutch oven cooking demonstrations and historic mining exhibitions, along with rug weaving, soap making, and broom making lessons.

Ketchum Wagon Days
Held each autumn, Ketchum Wagon Days features three-days of community fun. The event includes a rodeo, car collector's auction, antique show, community barbeque, a western shootout, live music, and the Pacific Northwest's longest non-motorized parade.

Sun Valley Jazz Jamboree
The sounds of jazz fill the air in Sun Valley each October as the five-day Jazz Jamboree comes to town. The event features bands from the U.S., Australia, Canada, and Sweden performing ragtime, jazz, and swing favorites from the early 1900s through the 1940s.

Trailing of the Sheep Festival
Historically, Ketchum was home to hundreds of sheep ranchers. This history is honored with the annual Trailing of the Sheep Festival held each October. The three-day festival features events related to sheep ranching, a parade, and a "trailing" where hundreds of sheep are herded down Main St.

Wood River Farmer's Market
Every June through October, downtown Ketchum bustles with activity at the Tuesday Farmer's Market. The market features growers from as far away as south-central Idaho who specialize in providing Wood River Valley residents with fresh, organic produce. In addition, market visitors will also find various environmental information and booths.

Days of the Old West
Held annually over the Fourth of July weekend, Hailey's Days of the Old West light up the town with action. The multi-day event features a full rodeo, parade, community barbeque, and traditional fireworks extravaganza.

Jazz on the Green
Every June, the sound of jazz fills the air at the Wood River Valley's Elkhorn Resort. On Thursday nights, individuals are encouraged to pack a picnic dinner and listen to three hours of live jazz music. The concerts are free and held in the resort's courtyard.

Paw & Pole
In a region where dogs are frequently welcome in public establishments, it's no surprise that the Wood River Valley hosts an event dedicated to man's best friend. Held annually each March at the Warm Springs Golf Course, the Paw and Pole is an unusual cross-country event featuring all breeds of dogs and their owners. Among the many awards given are "best team spirit," "best costume," and "fastest team." All event proceeds are donated to the local animal shelter.

White Knob Challenge
Rising 10,000 feet and forming a scenic backdrop in Mackay, the White Knob Mountains play host to the annual White Knob Challenge. Held each August, this mountain bike race begins on Main Street and makes a 19-mile loop toward White Knob Peak across old mining roads. The racecourse climbs nearly 2,600 feet in the first nine miles and draws hundreds of enthusiastic participants.

Mackay Community Barbeque
Think this is just an ordinary town gathering? Think again. The Mackay Community Barbeque has reached massive proportions and is a legendary September event drawing visitors from all over the region. The free barbeque is welcomed in with the greeting, "Tons of meat – it's Mackay's treat!"

M Stanley-Sawtooth Chamber of Commerce
Community Bldg on Hwy. 21, Stanley. 774-3411 or (800) 878-7950. www.stanleycc.org

16

H Galena
Milepost 151.8 on State Hwy. 75

After Warren P. Callahan located a rich lead-silver mine here, April 26,1879, thousands of eager treasure-hunters joined in a rush to Wood River in 1880. Successful prospectors discovered valuable lodes from here to Bellevue. Galena had a hotel, four general stores, a livery stable, several saloons and dining halls, a shoe store, and daily stage service to Hailey. After a ruinous decline in silver prices in 1888, its mines were shut down. But Galena continued as a recreation center.

H Alexander Ross
Milepost 156.1 on State Hwy. 75

Searching the mountain wilderness for beaver, Alexander Ross came up the Wood River and discovered this summit September 18, 1824. Leading a large brigade of Hudson's Bay Company trappers, he wondered whether he could get through unknown mountains and rocky defiles that obstructed his passage back to his base of operations at present Challis. Unwilling to turn back, he pressed on to explore Stanley Basin and the difficult canyon beyond. When he reached Challis on October 6, he had traveled this highway route from Bellevue to Salmon, mostly through unexplored land.

H Salmon River
Milepost 160.9 on State Hwy. 75

Rising as a small stream in the valley to the south, the Salmon River winds 420 miles across Idaho before flowing into the Snake River. Discovered in 1805 by Meriwether Lewis and William Clark, and explored with great difficulty by fur traders and prospectors, the Salmon River drains a vast tangle of rugged mountains and deep canyons. Until 1950, boats could not ascend the main canyon, so the Salmon got the name "River of No Return." Large tracts of

untamed wilderness still are found in the Salmon River Mountains.

H Vienna Ghost Town
Milepost 164.1 on State Hwy. 75

Levi Smiley found gold on Smiley Creek in 1878, and E.M. Wilson discovered a still richer lode 8 miles above here near Vienna, on June 4, 1879. Before shutting down in 1886, Vienna was a thriving mining camp with a $200,000 twenty-stamp mill to crush gold ore nearby. Miners here supported 14 saloons, 3 stores, 2 meat markets, a bank, a hotel, a sawmill, 2 livery stables, 6 restaurants, and, in 1882, a newspaper. More than 200 buildings disappeared when Vienna became a ghost town shortly after 1900.

H Sawtooth City
Milepost 166.8 on State Hwy. 75

Gold discoveries on Beaver Creek in 1879 led to mining activity near here that summer. But major production was delayed until 1886. By 1882, Sawtooth City had three saloons, two restaurants, a meat market, a store, a Chinese laundry, an assay office, a blacksmith shop, two quartz mills, a sawmill and 80 or 90 construction workers building their town. Four more years went by, though, before miners worked out a system to process their gold ore. Although 200 miners were employed in 1886, very little could be done after that. One disaster after another led to suspension of work there in 1892.

T William's Peak
South of Stanley near Obsidian on State Hwy. 75

Located on the eastern horizon of the White Cloud Mountain, William's Peak rises 10,700 feet against central Idaho's clear blue skies. The peak honors the legacy of local outfitter and guide, David M. Williams, who was reportedly the first to reach the mountain's summit. Williams accomplished the feat in 1934, accompanied by local residents Mr. and Mrs. Underhill.

T Obsidian
South of Stanley on State Hwy. 75

Although quiet now, Obsidian was a prosperous Idaho community in the early 1900s. The town was originally named Pierson for a local resident, but when a post office arrived in 1916, the name Obsidian was chosen. The town drew its name from the low-grade obsidian rocks located near town. Although the town now fails to exist, its namesake is still going strong. The volcanic gray and black glass used by Native Americans for arrowheads is now used by some plastic surgeons in scalpel blades The glass blades are preferred for their known ability to produce fine incisions with minimum scarring. Although plenty of obsidian can be found in the area, collecting this unique glass is strictly prohibited.

T Russian John Hot Springs
Near mile marker 146 on State Hwy. 75 near Galena Summit. Contact the Sawtooth National Recreation Area at 727-5013.

Situated just 100 yards west of the highway at an elevation of 6,900 feet, Russian John Hot Springs is nestled in the midst of the beautiful Sawtooth National Forest. The area features a small pool shaped with mortar reinforced rock walls, and a firepit rests nearby. Visitors with children should note that many individuals soak in the non-commercial pools au natural. The springs are open year-round and are heavily trafficked in the summer.

T Easley Hot Springs
8 miles north of the Sawtooth National Recreation Area (SNRA) Headquarters on State Hwy. 75. 726-7522.

For those who enjoy relaxing in hot springs but who shy away from undeveloped springs in the wild, Easley Hot Springs offers a solution. Situated in the Sawtooth National Recreation Area, Easley Hot Springs has been developed to include a pool and showering/changing facilities. A small day use fee is charged.

T Pole Creek Ranger Station
Contact the Sawtooth National Recreation Area Headquarters at 727-5013. Bear east onto Forest Rd. 194 near the bottom of the Galena Summit grade on State Hwy. 75.

Constructed in 1909, the Pole Creek Ranger Station was the first Forest Service structure estab-

lished in the Sawtooth National Forest. Built by District Ranger, Bill Horton, the ranger station is listed on the National Register of Historic Places. At one time, the now quiet forest road leading past the ranger station was the major route used to traverse the Sawtooth Valley.

T White Cloud Mountains
State Hwy. 75. Contact the Sawtooth National Recreation Area at 727-5013.

Although not contained in any designated wilderness area, Idaho's White Cloud Mountains still offer the same pristine atmosphere. Rising over 11,000 feet, the White Cloud Peaks are nearly 1,000 feet taller than their famous counterparts, the Sawtooths. The highest point, Castle Peak, boasts an 11,815-foot summit after which mountain climbers salivate.

In the 1960s, mining companies surveyed the mountains for profitable molybdenum deposits and proposed an open-pit mine. However, all mining operations were called off when Congress established the Sawtooth National Recreation Area. As a result, the area retains its breathtaking scenery. Amid the mountains' numerous hiking and biking trails, visitors will find over 125 scenic alpine lakes, waterfalls, abundant granite, and an array of wildlife. Visitors may encounter mountain lions, elk, deer, bighorn sheep, mountain goats, coyotes, foxes, beavers, badgers, and black bears.

TV Galena Summit & Scenic Overlook
30 miles north of Sun Valley on State Hwy. 75.

Rising to an elevation of 8,701 feet, Galena Summit marks the divide between the Salmon River and Wood River drainages. The Columbia and Beaver Mining Company constructed the first route over the summit in 1881 at a total cost of $13,000. The route was known as the Sawtooth Grade, serving miners scattered throughout the Sawtooth Valley in the late 1800s. Between 1918 and 1919, an improved route was completed, and finally in 1953, the present route was established. Just one mile shy of the summit at a marked turnout on the highway's southwest side, drivers have access to an incredible overlook of the Sawtooth National Recreation Area and its jagged mountain peaks rising sharply against Idaho's clear blue skies. The peaks are part of the thirty-mile long Sawtooth Range that began uplifting over 100 million years ago.

For avid outdoor recreationists, the original Sawtooth Grade that wreaked havoc on 1880s travelers is still accessible. The mountain bike trail begins approximately one-quarter mile north of the summit across the highway from the overlook.

V North Valley Nordic Trails
Blaine County Recreation District, 1050 Fox Acres Rd., Hailey. 788-2117. Located between Lake Creek and Galena Lodge on State Hwy. 75 north of Ketchum.

Affording seventy miles of groomed trails for both skate and classic cross-country skiing, the North Valley Nordic Trail system is the premier Idaho destination for cross-country skiing. Professional grooming cats maintain the trail system, and the area is closed to motorized travel to provide high-quality pathways for Nordic skiers. One of the most popular loops is the ten mile Lake Creek Trail which runs near the Big Wood River's west side. The trails operate on a user-pay system with fees used to groom and maintain trails as well as provide maps and interpretive trail signs. User fees are $9 for adults, $2 for dogs and children over 7, and free for those under 6. A $30 seven-day pass is also available.

V Galena Lodge Mountain Bike Trails

24 miles north of Ketchum on State Hwy. 75 at Galena Lodge. 726-4010.

Offering twenty-five miles of trails for both beginning and seasoned riders, the Galena Lodge Mountain Bike Trail System provides spectacular views of the Boulder and Smokey Mountains around every bend. Following dirt forest service roads, ski trails, and single-track pathways, the trail system winds past old mining sites, historic cabins, wildflower meadows, towering pines, and abundant wildlife. The trails are open daily during the summer, and bike rentals and maps are available at the Galena Lodge.

V Alturas Lake

Contact the Stanley Ranger Station at 774-3000. Traveling south of Stanley on State Hwy. 75, bear west onto paved Forest Rd. 205 (Alturas Lake Rd.).

Alturas Lake is the second largest lake in the Sawtooth National Recreation Area and is dammed with a glacial moraine formed over 20,000 years ago. Alturas Lake, meaning "mountain heights" in Spanish, encompasses 1,200 acres and measures up to 300 feet deep. In 1881, fisherman caught nearly 2,600 pounds of Blueback Salmon here, which they then hauled to miners in Atlanta and Rocky Bar. Although the lake does not currently boast such record numbers, anglers will still find plenty of Rainbow Trout and Kokanee Salmon. In addition to fishing, the lake is a popular destination for picnicking, camping, sailing, motorboating, and waterskiing. Visitors will also find an old mining road in the area offering an ideal route for hiking, horseback riding, and mountain biking. The lake is free to all users, and waterskiing is prohibited from 6 PM to 10 AM.

V Perkins Lake

Contact the Stanley Ranger Station at 774-3000. Travel south of Stanley on State Hwy. 75, bearing west onto paved Forest Rd. 205 (Alturas Lake Rd.). The lake is situated approximately 0.5 miles before Alturas Lake.

Nestled in the heart of the Sawtooth National Recreation Area, the undeveloped Perkins Lake provides visitors with a tranquil water experience. Spanning just over 100 acres, Perkins Lake was formed more than 20,000 years ago during glacial movement and subsequent boulder deposits. The lake is closed to motorized boats, but canoeing, float tubing, kayaking, and fishing are allowed.

V Petit Lake

Contact the Stanley Ranger Station at 774-3000. Travel south of Stanley on State Hwy. 75, bearing west on Forest Rd. 208. The 2.5-mile road is traversable once the valley snow melts.

Encompassing 395 acres, Petit Lake provides a scenic destination for kayakers, canoeists, and motorboats along with a sand ramp for easy watercraft launches. Boasting a few primitive campsites, the lake is also a popular starting point for backcountry hikes into the neighboring Sawtooth Wilderness.

V Yellow Belly Lake

Contact the Stanley Ranger Station at 774-3000. Travel south of Stanley on State Hwy. 75, bearing west on Forest Rd. 208. Continue 2.5 miles, and park at Petit Lake.

Midway up the eastern shore of Petit Lake, a short trail leads north to Yellow Belly Lake. The undeveloped, small lake is open to non-motorized boating only and is a popular fishing destination. During winter, cross-country skiers make tracks across the frozen, snow covered lake.

V Alturas Lake Nordic Ski Trail

Contact the Stanley Ranger Station at 774-3000. Travel south of Stanley on State Hwy. 75. A plowed parking area is located directly north of Forest Rd. 205 (Alturas Lake Rd.).

Winding near Alturas Lake Creek, the Alturas Lake Nordic Ski Trail provides a 7.2 mile groomed trail ideal for winter fun. Heading west from the parking area, the trail meanders past Perkins Lake before ending at Alturas Lake's eastern shore. The trail is renowned for its scenery and wildlife viewing opportunities.

V Boulder Mountain Nordic Ski Trails

Galena Summit on State Hwy. 75. Contact the Sawtooth National Recreation Area Headquarters at 727-5013.

Winding down from Galena Summit to the Sawtooth National Recreation Area Visitor's Center, the Boulder Mountain Nordic Ski Trails provide miles of unbeatable forest and mountain scenery. Although users can opt to stay on the main trail, several side trails add potential for an additional loop outing. Day use trail fees are $9.

V Billy's Bridge Nordic Ski Trail

11 miles north of Ketchum on the east side of State Hwy. 75. Contact the Sawtooth National Recreation Area Headquarters at 727-5013.

Nestled in the Prairie Creek area of the Sawtooth National Recreation Area, Billy's Bridge Nordic Ski Trail provides winter enthusiasts with a five-mile loop route and incredible views. The trail is an offshoot of the renowned Boulder Mountain Nordic Ski Trail, and a day use fee of $9 is charged. Cross-country skiers may bring their dogs along on this trail.

V Prairie Creek Nordic Ski Trail

11 miles north of Ketchum on the west side of State Hwy. 75. Contact the Sawtooth National Recreation Area Headquarters at 727-5013.

The four-mile Prairie Creek Nordic Ski Trail is tucked inside the Sawtooth National Recreation Area in Idaho's high country. The loop trail winds up and down its namesake and is an offshoot of the popular Boulder Mountain Nordic Ski Trail. Dogs are not allowed on the trail, and all users are assessed a $9 day use fee.

V North Fork Trail System

Sawtooth National Recreation Area Headquarters near Galena Summit on State Hwy. 75. 727-5013.

Departing from the Sawtooth National Recreation Area Headquarters, the North Fork Trail System meanders beside the North Fork of the Big Wood River. The easy 2.5-mile trail is appropriate for novices, and dogs are allowed. As an offshoot of the Boulder Mountain Nordic Ski Trail, the North Fork Trail does require a $9 day use fee.

17 *Food*

Sun Valley
Pop. 1,427

Situated just outside Ketchum, Sun Valley is a small town whose economy centers upon the Sun Valley Company's business activities. Home to the famous Sun Valley Lodge and Sun Valley Inn, this community's name is most widely associated with the renowned Sun Valley Resort.

After watching the 1932 Winter Olympics at Lake Placid, New York, W. Averell Harriman came up with a business plan that would eventually make him famous. An avid skier as well as chairman of the board of directors of the Union Pacific Railroad, Harriman dreamed of a world-renowned resort that guests could only reach via the railroad. To find the perfect site for his plan, Harriman sent Austrian Count Felix Schaffgotsch across the American West. Finally, the Count stumbled upon Ernest F. Brass' 3,888-acre ranch in Ketchum, which Harriman promptly purchased for $39,000. Development of the resort began immediately with the help of several important figures: the Count picked the site for the 220-room lodge; U.S. Olympic Ski Team member, Charlie Proctor, developed the ski runs on Dollar Mountain and Proctor Mountain; railroad engineer, James Curran, designed and installed the first chair lifts; and popular resort marketer, Steve Hannagan, named the ski resort and advertised it to the world. In December 1936, the resort was finally ready for business, and Harriman's idea became an instant success. Although the resort has been sold twice since its opening and new runs have been developed on the technical Bald Mountain, some things remain the same. It has always been a world-class resort rivaling some of the most luxurious skiing destinations in Europe, and Sun Valley has continued to attract the rich and famous from near and far for decades.

T Sun Valley Golf Course

1 Sun Valley Rd., Sun Valley. 622-2251. www.sunvalley.com From State Hwy. 75 in Ketchum, bear east on Sun Valley Rd., and locate the course past the lodge

The Sun Valley Resort Golf Course is world-famous for its magnificent mountain vistas and challenging track. First established in 1936, the course was later redesigned under the direction of Robert Trent Jones, Jr. The well-maintained 18-hole course is characterized with elevated tees, broad fairways, and numerous natural and artificial hazards challenging even the most skilled players. Green fees are $110, and advance tee times are required on this 6,650-yard course.

T Bigwood Golf Course

125 Clubhouse Dr., Sun Valley. 726-4024. On Hwy. 75, locate the course midway between Ketchum and Sun Valley.

Stunning views of three adjacent mountain ranges await players at the Bigwood Golf Course.

Ketchum/Sun Valley	Jan	Feb	March	April	May	June	July	Aug	Sep	Oct	Nov	Dec	Annual
Average Max. Temperature (F)	30.0	35.9	40.2	52.1	63.9	71.3	82.5	81.6	72.3	60.5	44.0	32.4	55.6
Average Min. Temperature (F)	0.3	3.6	9.5	21.5	29.2	34.5	38.3	37.0	29.9	22.8	14.4	3.6	20.4
Average Total Precipitation (in.)	2.59	1.61	1.17	0.96	1.61	1.67	0.73	0.84	0.89	0.93	1.64	2.61	17.26
Average Total Snowfall (in.)	36.0	19.0	13.8	4.0	1.4	0.0	0.0	0.0	0.5	2.3	12.1	32.0	121.0
Average Snow Depth (in.)	23	29	24	4	0	0	0	0	0	0	2	12	8

Designed by Robert Muir Graves, the 9-hole, 3,270-yard course is rated a par-36 and features four sets of tees catering to a wide range of abilities. Players can opt for an 18-hole, 6,535 yard round if they so desire. Green fees are $25 for 9 holes and $38 for 18 holes. The course is open from 7 AM to 6 PM, and tee times can be scheduled up to two weeks in advance.

T Sawtooth National Recreation Area Visitor's Center
7 miles north of Ketchum/Sun Valley on the east side of State Hwy. 75. 727-5013.

The Sawtooth National Recreation Area (SNRA) Visitor's Center is located in the Wood River Valley near the SNRA's western boundary. The site offers a large selection of natural-history books, and outdoor lovers will find a wealth of informational exhibits and recreational flyers. Visitors will also find a free audiotape tour of Hwy. 75, offering an interpretation of scenic sights along the highway's path.

T Ernest Hemingway Memorial: A Tribute to Famous Sun Valley Writer
Known to his friends and family as "Papa," Ernest Hemingway not only left his mark on the literary world, but also on the community of Sun Valley, Idaho. Although Hemingway visited Sun Valley often and resided there during his final years, his life began in the Midwest and took a varied course.

Hemingway was born in 1899 in Oak Park, Illinois where he excelled in school. Upon his high school graduation, Hemingway worked as a reporter for the *Kansas City Star* before serving in World War I as a Red Cross ambulance driver. During a stint in Italy, Hemingway suffered wounds from machine gun bullets and shell fragments and was awarded a medal for courage.

After the war, Hemingway moved to Paris with other American expatriates where he began fervent work on his first book, *In Our Time*, published in 1925. Hemingway returned to his military roots in the 1930s, serving as a correspondent in Spain during the Spanish Civil War. In World War II, the young writer escorted American troops to the Battle of the Bulge, D-Day, and the liberation of Paris. For his efforts, he garnered a bronze star.

At the invitation of Sun Valley Resort owner, Averell Harriman, Hemingway first visited Idaho's Wood River Valley in the fall of 1939. He stayed in Suite #206, hob-knobbed with other invited celebrities, recreated in the area's beautiful outdoors, and began working on *For Whom the Bell Tolls*. During the autumn of 1940 and 1941, Hemingway returned to his newfound haven and made several visits throughout the next two decades.

Upon his marriage to fourth wife, Mary Welsh Hemingway, the now famous writer and his wife resided in Cuba. While there, Hemingway was granted the Pulitzer Prize in 1953 for *The Old Man and the Sea* while 1954 awarded him with the Nobel Prize for Literature. When Fidel Castro overthrew the Cuban president in 1958, Hemingway and his wife decided to return to America and establish a permanent residence in the Wood River Valley.

During his travels to and residence in Sun Valley, Hemingway worked on several novels, including *The Dangerous Summer, A Moveable Feast, Islands in the Stream*, and *The Garden of Eden*. The Wood River Valley became his refuge as he wrote in the morning, and hunted, fished, and skied in the afternoons. Despite the idyllic setting and evenings spent socializing with friends in local restaurants and taverns, Hemingway was not at peace with himself. Throughout the course of his Idaho residency, Hemingway made several trips to the Mayo Clinic in Minnesota where he was diagnosed with hypertension, possible diabetes, and pigmentary cirrhosis due to his alcoholism. Hemingway, deeply depressed, made his last visit to the clinic on June 30, 1961 and returned to his wife in Sun Valley.

On July 1, 1961, Hemingway and his wife dined at the author's favorite local French restaurant, The Christiania, where as usual he requested a small table on the dining room's southwest side. Early the next morning, Hemingway took his own life with a shotgun, just as his own father had done. His grave lies in the Ketchum/Sun Valley community cemetery where he rests beneath a flat granite slab located in the fore-center of the cemetery. Upon his death, Hemingway's legacy included eight novels, three non-fiction works, and over fifty short stories. He has had more non-literary copy written about him than any other twentieth-century American writer. Upon his wife's death in 1981, the family home in Ketchum was donated to the Nature Conservancy. The residence is not open to the public. In addition, Hemingway's son, Jack, fought to preserve the natural wildlife refuge at Silver Creek where the writer spent many afternoons. Today, the Nature Conservancy's Silver Creek Preserve encompasses 8,700 acres.

Hemingway's legacy is honored with a memorial situated near Trail Creek Cabin a short distance from the Sun Valley Lodge up Trail Creek Road. Dedicated on July 21, 1966, the memorial includes a simple bronze bust of the author designed by Robert Berks. A plaque affixed to the memorial reads: *Best of all he loved the fall, the leaves yellow on cottonwoods, leaves floating on trout streams and above the hills, the high blue windless skies…now he will be a part of them forever.*

Hemingway wrote the dedication himself as a eulogy for his friend, Gene Van Guilder, who was killed in 1939 in a hunting accident. The inscription, however, is truly appropriate for honoring the life and passions of one of the twentieth century's greatest American writers.

T Sun Valley Ballet School
Sun Valley. 726-2985. www.sunvalleyballet.com

Under the management of volunteers, the Sun Valley Ballet School has a longstanding tradition of providing fun and inspiring ballet performances throughout the Wood River Valley. Each season, the school showcases its hardworking students' abilities in two to three ballet performances. Those interested in seeing a performance should contact the school for the latest schedule of events.

T New Theater Company
Sun Valley. (208) 726-2271.

Founded in 1994, Sun Valley's New Theater Company is the largest employer of actors in the Wood River Valley. The company works hard to provide a range of spectacular performances throughout the year. Productions run the gamut, from emotional dramas to humorous sketches of human life to the works of Shakespeare. In addition, the company offers free public workshops throughout the year featuring resident professionals and highly respected directors from across the U.S. For a complete listing of productions and show times, contact the theater.

T Trail Creek Cabin
1.5 miles east of Sun Valley. 622-2135.

Nestled in the woods of Sun Valley, Trail Creek Cabin is a Wood River Valley icon. The log and stone cabin was constructed in 1937 and has since seen visitors ranging from locals to Hollywood's most famous. Ernest Hemingway, Clark Gable, Gary Cooper, and Ava Gardner favored the retreat during their prime, and the cabin remains a favorite among Sun Valley guests. The cabin now boasts dinner sleigh rides each winter and is host to summer concerts and numerous Wood River Valley events.

V Sawtooth National Recreation Area & the Sawtooth Wilderness
The Sawtooth National Recreation Headquarters is located 7 miles north of Ketchum/Sun Valley on the east side of State Hwy. 75. 727-5013.

Established in 1972 to preserve scenic, historic, and wildlife values, the Sawtooth National Recreation Area (SNRA) encompasses 765,000 acres of mountain grandeur and tranquility. With the Smoky Mountains and the Sawtooth Mountains standing to the west and the Boulder Mountains and White Cloud range skyrocketing against the eastern horizon, the SNRA features a breathtaking skyline with more than fifty mountain summits measuring 10,000 feet tall. The SNRA also includes more than 300 alpine lakes and the pristine 217,000-acre Sawtooth Wilderness.

The SNRA offers a variety of recreational activities for outdoor lovers interested in exploring America's Alps. Fishing, boating, and sailing are all popular pastimes, and numerous horseback riding and hiking trails await equestrians and backpackers in the wilderness areas. SNRA users are reminded that the wilderness is closed to all motorized vehicles and mountain bikes in an effort to protect the serene alpine setting. Although government officials have pushed for the SNRA to be granted national park status, no official ruling has yet been decided. For now, the area's steep granite mountains simply remain a recreational and photographic treasure trove.

V Sun Valley Ski Resort
Sun Valley. 635-8261 or (800) 786-8259.

Featuring the Olympic sized Bald Mountain (frequently referred to as "Baldy") and the smaller Dollar Mountain, Sun Valley Ski Resort offers a variety of terrain suitable for skiers and snowboarders of all abilities. Throughout its long history, Sun Valley has repeatedly been voted America's finest ski resort, and the first U.S. Olympic skiing medalist, Gretchen Fraser, declared Sun Valley "the greatest mountain in the world."

Baldy offers the most terrain for intermediate and advanced skiers and is Sun Valley's main attraction. The mountain features a 3,400-foot vertical drop, and the 2,054 skiable acres offer seventy-eight perfectly groomed runs. Boasting seven quads, five double chairs, and seven triple

KETCHUM
Map not to scale.

chairs, Baldy's lift capacities hover at more than 23,000 skiers per hour, which makes for nearly non-existent lift lines. The ski area prides itself on providing consistently pitched runs, along with some runs stretching up to three miles long. After a full day of skiing, numerous day lodges welcome winter enthusiasts with luxury, cozy fires, and great food.

Dollar Mountain, although operating on a much smaller and less grander scale, provides relatively uncrowded slopes ideal for beginners. The mountain boasts four lifts and a handle tow with a maximum vertical of 628 feet. In addition, Dollar Mountain lift tickets are about half the price as those for the larger, more famous Baldy.

V Bald Mountain Biking Trails
Located at the top of Bald Mountain Ski Area in Sun Valley. Contact the Sun Valley/Ketchum Chamber & Visitors Bureau at 726-3423.

Recognized worldwide for skiing, Sun Valley's Bald Mountain becomes a mountain biker's dream during warmer months. For the price of a $15 lift ticket, outdoor enthusiasts have access to two intermediate trails situated atop Baldy. The Cold Springs Trail traverses 11.5 miles, while the Warm Springs Trail covers 14.6 miles. Both trails offer stunning views of the surrounding rugged mountains and scenic valleys.

V Penny Hill
Across the Street from the Sun Valley Barn on Sun Valley Rd., Sun Valley. Contact the Sun Valley/Ketchum Chamber of Commerce at 726-3423.

Sun Valley's Penny Hill may not be Bald Mountain, but it captures the same infamous name recognition among area residents. A favorite among local children, Penny Hill takes advantage of the area's abundant winter weather and is dubbed one of the state's best sledding hills. From plastic trash bags to the latest in sled technology, all sled types and people of all ages are welcome.

V Sun Valley Nordic Center
Near the Sun Valley Resort Lodge. 622-2251.

During the winter, the Sun Valley Resort professionally grooms its golf course to create a well-maintained Nordic Center. Twenty-five miles of trails wind through the beautiful landscape, and the easily accessible area is extremely popular with the local crowd. An area of narrowly spaced tracks is set aside just for children, and skate skiing is the norm. Users should expect company, as many valley residents head to the center for their daily workout. Trail fees are $12 for adults, $9 for senior citizens, and $6.50 for children ages 6-12. Lessons are available for beginners, and the center also provides rental skis and poles.

V Fox Creek & Oregon Gulch Mountain Biking Trails
Contact the Sun Valley/Ketchum Chamber of Commerce at 726-3423.

Located on the west side of State Hwy. 75, the Fox Creek and Oregon Gulch trails provide experienced mountain bikers with a more secluded getaway. Loop rides range in length from three to ten miles, and all trails require excellent maneuvering abilities as the trails are physically demanding. To access Fox Creek, travel four miles north of Ketchum on Hwy. 75 and turn off at the Lake Creek Trailhead. To reach Oregon Gulch, drive seven miles north of Ketchum on Hwy. 75 and locate the trailhead on Forest Road 143.

Idaho Trivia
Situated in Idaho's Sawtooth National Recreation Area, the White Cloud Peaks earned their name after a common natural phenomenon in the area. Soaring high into the atmosphere, the white limestone peaks are often hard to distinguish from the white clouds that streak the summer sky.

Sun Valley Associates
Real Estate Brokers

A TRADITION IN THE WOOD RIVER VALLEY

www.svassociates.com • 700 Sun Valley Rd. • 208-622-4100 • email: judy@svassociates.com

Tom Monge

Bill Casey

Terry Palmer

Alex Higgins

Jed Gray

Jim Figge

Ketchum
Pop. 3,003

David Ketchum staked the first Wood River mining claim here in 1879, but the town's name did not reflect his significance until later. Leadville was the first name applied to the growing settlement, but when the post office arrived in 1880, it rejected the name and honored the first settler instead. The town's population boomed when the area became the smelting center for the Warm Springs mining district. Once mining activity in the area declined, the area turned to agriculture and sheep ranching for its economic livelihood. From 1895 to 1930, Ketchum served as the American West's largest sheep-shipping center.

Ketchum's rural agricultural atmosphere changed drastically in the mid 1930s when W. Averell Harriman bought the 4,300 acre Ketchum Brass Ranch and built a 220-room luxury lodge and the world-famous Sun Valley Ski Resort. His intentions were to build a first-class ski resort community, and he quickly succeeded. Clark Gable and Errol Flynn visited the resort shortly after its opening in December of 1936. Soon after, the world's first chairlift was constructed on Dollar Mountain, and Ketchum's legacy as a first-class recreational destination began.

H Ski Lifts
Milepost 130.8 on State Hwy. 75 at Ketchum near the Sun Peak Picnic Area

When Sun Valley Lodge was built in 1936, Union Pacific engineers developed chair lifts to transport skiers uphill. Starting with two modest ski slopes on Dollar Mountain and Proctor Mountain, chair lifts were used for all Sun Valley ski runs. Far superior to tow ropes and similar devices employed before 1936, they quickly became popular at ski resorts everywhere. New designs were adopted for additional Sun Valley ski runs, but one 1936-style chair lift still is preserved four miles up Trail Creek Road from here.

T Ore Wagon Museum
E. Ave. and 5th St., Ketchum.

Ketchum's heritage is rooted in the mining industry, and visitors can catch a glimpse of early Lewis Ore Wagons on display at the unstaffed Ore Wagon Museum. These high, narrow wagons loaded with millions of dollars of silver and lead were towed in strings from the area's mines to the Wood River Valley smelters. Displayed behind glass most of the year, the wagons are the prominent feature in the area's annual Wagon Days and Parade.

T Sun Valley Center for the Arts and Humanities
620 Sun Valley Rd. E., Ketchum. 726-9491. www.sunvalleycenter.org

Ketchum/Sun Valley is becoming increasingly important in the art scene, and visitors will find

S Venus Fine Furs
631 Sun Valley Rd., Sun Valley. 726-7625.

Experience timeless elegance with Venus Fine Furs. German owner, Brigitte Luise Esswein, caters to a wide audience with casual, elegant, fun, and exceptional furs rarely even found in a large city. Vests, jackets, and full-length coats are available in full and sheared beaver, mink, fox, chinchilla, Russian sable, and more. Accessorize your wardrobe with a hat, purse, scarf, or gloves accented in fur, silk, or cashmere. For those with artistic sense or a cowgirl spirit, Venus Fine Firs also carries wearable art in silk and contemporary Western leather. Silk items include hand-painted, hand-pleated scarves, blouses, and ponchos, while all leather items are hand-stitched from Montana. From international and designer furs to unique accessories, Venus Fine Furs has the selection to make your wardrobe dreams a reality!

Idaho Trivia

Due to its geographical location and high elevation, the Sun Valley/Ketchum area is known for its amazingly long summer days. Most summer days average a minimum of fifteen hours of sunshine!

M George Ruiz, RE/MAX of Sun Valley
360 Sun Valley Rd., Sun Valley. 450-9358 or (877) 823-6113. www.georgeruizrealtor.com

George Ruiz of RE/MAX of Sun Valley markets homes for all their worth and helps buyers locate the best buys. With client satisfaction as his number one priority, George is dedicated to every client's unique needs and prides himself on forming solid relationships resulting in success. For buyers' and sellers' convenience, George also offers free real estate reports twenty-four hours a day at the website above and a toll free hotline listed above. Simply dial the following extensions: for Luxury Sun Valley homes, ext. 2049; for Zero Down/First-time Buyers, ext. 2051. Sellers can enjoy useful over-the-net marketing tips and may receive a Free-Over-the-Net Home Evaluation. Gain the knowledge you need to be a wise homebuyer or seller by visiting George's Success Website.

M Sun Valley-Ketchum Chamber & Visitors Bureau
PO Box 2420, Sun Valley. 726-3423 or (866) 305-0408. www.visitsunvalley.com; chamberinfo@visitsunvalley.com

numerous galleries while browsing downtown. The Sun Valley Center for the Arts and Humanities offers a variety of contemporary works for perusing. During the summer, the center works closely with the Sun Valley Gallery Association to lead guided gallery tours to anyone who is interested. The tour begins on 4th and Main Streets in Ketchum and is offered every Thursday from 10 AM to 12 PM in July and August.

T Ketchum-Sun Valley Heritage and Ski Museum

180 1st Street E., Ketchum. 726-8118.

The Ketchum-Sun Valley Historical Society is dedicated to preserving, interpreting, and displaying the Upper Wood River Valley's history. Accordingly, the society operates the Ketchum-Sun Valley Heritage and Ski Museum where visitors will find exhibits about the town's rich history. Topics include fur trappers, Native Americans, the construction of the Sun Valley Lodge, and the arrival of Hollywood stars in the resort communities populating the region. Admission is free, and the museum is open 11 AM to 3:30 PM Monday through Friday and 1 to 4 PM on Saturdays.

T Atkinson Park

3rd Ave. and 8th St., Ketchum. 726-7820.

Atkinson Park is a popular year-round destination for both Sun Valley visitors and residents. In addition to standard park features, Atkinson Park includes public use tennis courts, a soccer field, and a large recreation facility boasting ping-pong and air hockey tables. During the winter, the soccer field is turned into a free ice skating rink where free skates and helmets are available for the entire family. Throughout the year, Atkinson Park is also the venue for numerous community events.

T Sun Valley Opera

540 Second Ave. N., Ketchum. (800) 294-2748.

Sun Valley has long been known for its wide acceptance of the arts, featuring talented musicians, artists, and actors for decades. Opera, however, was not among the list of available fine art venues until 2001. Believing that the Sun Valley/Ketchum area could easily support full-scale opera productions, Floyd McCracken, Frank Meyer, and Marsha Ingham ushered in the twenty-first century with the formation of Sun Valley Opera. After a brief organizational period, the company showcased its first performance in February 2002 to a sold-out crowd.

Today, Sun Valley Opera is dedicated to providing three to five top-quality opera concerts annually in the Wood River Valley. Each concert features singers from across the U.S. and foreign countries, and performances are aimed at appealing to audiences of all ages. Presented at affordable prices, each opera performance is generally sold out, so advance tickets are necessary.

T Wood River Valley Historical Tours

Contact the Sun Valley/Ketchum Chamber of Commerce at 726-3423.

In addition to the arts, fine dining, and year-round recreation, the Wood River Valley is also home to a plethora of interesting history. The Sun Valley/Ketchum Chamber of Commerce provides free information and a map for self-guided tours of approximately thirty historical points of interest.

SUBURBAN SPRAWL OF IDAHO'S WOOD RIVER VALLEY

With resorts bearing the same name as the communities in which they're nestled, understanding what is incorporated as an actual town in the state of Idaho may be confusing. In the Wood River Valley, this is especially true. Known locally as a mini-opolis, the Ketchum/ Sun Valley region is composed of resort areas and towns. Ketchum is an incorporated city and the largest service provider in the area. Nestled at the base of Bald Mountain's north side just a short distance from Ketchum is the area commonly referred to as Warm Springs. Although not an official town, Warm Springs carries the same amenities as a well-established community, including hotels, vacation rentals, and numerous dining and nightlife options. To the northeast of Ketchum is the infamous Sun Valley. Also granting its name to the world-class ski resort, Sun Valley is essentially the ski resort's company town and is incorporated as a small Idaho community. The area features glitzy homes and condos, as well as company restaurants and stores catering to Sun Valley Lodge and Sun Valley Inn guests. Directly south of Sun Valley is an area known as Elkhorn. Like Warm Springs, Elkhorn is not an official town, but serves as the activity center for the Dollar Mountain activity center. The town is also a hub of more affordable residential abodes for those workers who commute to nearby Ketchum and Sun Valley.

T Sawtooth Botanical Garden

5 miles south of Ketchum on State Hwy. 75 at 11 Gimlet Road. 726-9358. www.sbgarden.org.

The non-profit Sawtooth Botanical Garden has been celebrating plants and inspiring people since its 1994 establishment. Supported in part by the Global Environmental Project Institute, the five-acre public garden encourages individuals to appreciate and live in balance with the natural world around them.

In addition to providing gardening education and year-round workshops for adults, the garden also focuses on children and the natural world. On-site, the Sunflower Children's Center provides educational classes and activities for children ages 2-11. In addition, the garden features an array of annual events, including a plant sale in June, the Bug and Butterflies Children's Festival, a Garden Tour and Party, Harvest Festival, and a bulb sale each autumn.

Self-guided tours of the Sawtooth Botanical Garden are available daily from 10 AM to 4 PM.

T Environmental Resource Center

680 N. Main, Ste. D, Ketchum. 726-4333. www.ercsv.com

A non-profit community environmental education organization, the Environmental Resource Center was established in 1993 with the motto of "making a difference today for tomorrow." The center works not only to increase environmental and conservation awareness, but also to enhance outdoor experiences. In doing so, the facility maintains a museum, store, classroom, and a stockpile of environmental information. Regular video presentations and lectures are offered in hopes of promoting a more sustainable community for Wood River Valley residents and visitors. The center is open free of charge Monday through Friday.

T Warfield Hot Springs

11 miles west of Ketchum on Warm Springs Rd. Contact the Sun Valley/Ketchum Chamber of Commerce at 726-3423.

Among the many natural hot springs dotting the Wood River Valley landscape, Warfield Hot Springs is a favorite. The easily accessible spring is open year-round.

T Sun Valley Repertory Company

Ketchum. 725-0814.

The Sun Valley Repertory Company has established its productions as a must see each Christmas season and during the summer. Featuring professional actors, the company showcases plays in Ketchum at the nexStage Theatre. Past productions have included *A Midsummer Night's Dream*, *A Christmas Carol*, and *The Fantasticks*. Actors usually perform to sold-out crowds, so advance tickets are required. Call for tickets and a complete listing of upcoming events.

T Laughing Stock Theater Company

Ketchum. 726-3576.

Presenting family-oriented musicals and comedies for over twenty years, the Laughing Stock Theater Company was founded by Kathy Wygle and is composed of both professional and semiprofessional actors and actresses. The company showcases two annual performances in a variety of venues in both Ketchum and Sun Valley and also sponsors the Camp Little Laugh summer program for children. Past performances have included *The Sound of Music* and *Rumors*, and shows are generally sold-out. Call for tickets and a complete listing of upcoming events.

T Art Gallery Tours

Downtown Ketchum. Contact the Sun Valley Gallery Association at 726-5079.

Ketchum and Sun Valley have long been noted as possessing many of America's finest galleries. Art lovers and those who are simply curious about art will find that Ketchum harbors numerous galleries within walking distance of one another. Each gallery features its own artistic emphasis and showcased artists, and a tour of all of the town's galleries could realistically take an entire day. For a complete listing of galleries and more information about the Wood River Valley art scene, contact the Sun Valley Gallery Association.

T Historical Ketchum Buildings

Contact the Sun Valley/Ketchum Chamber of Commerce at 726-3423.

Like its Wood River Valley neighbors, Ketchum is home to a few downtown historical buildings worth noting.

Golden Rule Market

Corner of Main Street & Second Ave.

Established in 1887, Ketchum's Golden Rule Market represents Idaho's oldest continuously operating grocery store. It prides itself on a reputable history of serving all of Wood River Valley's mercantile needs.

Historic Lane Mercantile

Corner of Main Street & Sun Valley Road

Thomas Teague and Walt Clark erected this red

brick building in 1887 as a general store. In 1916, the Lane Mercantile opened here and operated until 1946. Today, the historic structure houses a community bank.

T Sun Valley Historical Lift
Contact the Sun Valley/Ketchum Chamber of Commerce at 726-3423. From Ketchum's Main St., follow Sun Valley Rd. 1 mile east, and then bear south onto Dollar Rd. Proceed 0.7 miles to the 4-way stop, continuing straight on Fairways Rd. Follow the route 1.1 miles to the lift site.

Sun Valley Resort has come a long way since its inception and original use of wooden towers and chairlifts. Although most traces of Sun Valley's historic past have faded into glitz and high technology, one of the original chairlifts was saved and reassembled. The historic lift once serviced one of the resort's ski jumps. The lift is visible on Fairways Road's right side.

T Original Sun Valley Lodge
Contact the Sun Valley/Ketchum Chamber of Commerce at 726-3423. From Ketchum's Main St., drive 1.2 miles east on Sun Valley Rd. At the short loop road, bear right and proceed to the lodge.

When Averell Harriman selected the Sun Valley/Ketchum area as his destination of choice for a new, world-class ski resort, he also knew he would need to develop lodging appealing to guests from far and wide. With no expense too grand and no amenity too lavish, construction began on the $1.5 million dollar lodge in May 1936.

Pressured to complete the European-style hotel by ski season, over 400 workers raced to piece together the concrete "imitation wood" hotel. On December 23, 1936, the lodge welcomed guests for Sun Valley's first winter season. It is often noted that as guests were arriving in the

front, the builders and tradesmen were putting on the finishing touches and sneaking out the back door. The lodge's first guests, including several prominent figures from Hollywood and the entire world, were treated to service from imported French chefs and Australian ski instructors.

Today, the lodge reflects its history of multiple renovations but still retains a sense of the original grandeur that Harriman intended. The paneled and Idaho-stone décor features a plethora of skiing memorabilia, and the lodge retains its purposefully chosen location as the first place in Sun Valley where the rising sun shines.

T Copper Basin
Contact the Sun Valley/Ketchum Chamber of Commerce at 726-3423. From Ketchum's Main St., drive 6.2 miles east on Sun Valley Rd. to the pavement's end. Continue straight ahead on the gravel/dirt road, ascend Trail Creek Summit, pass by Big Fall Creek and Kane Creek, and arrive at the Mackay-Copper Basin Junction. Taking the right fork, proceed 18 miles.

Situated at an elevation of 7,800 feet, Copper Basin spans thirty-six miles of high altitude, barren desert. Although not as scenic as some areas surrounding the Wood River Valley, Copper Basin was carved by glaciers thousands of years ago and serves as the finest example of glacial activity in all of central Idaho.

TV Penny Lake
4 miles west of Ketchum on Warm Springs Rd. Contact the Sun Valley/Ketchum Chamber of Commerce at 726-3423.

Among the many ideal fishing holes found in the Wood River Valley, Penny Lake provides an opportunity for novice anglers and children to join in the fun. The two-acre lake is annually stocked

with nearly 3,000 fish, and anglers are allowed to take home a limited number of their day's catch. In addition to fishing, the area is also a popular family picnicking destination.

V Adams Gulch Loop Mountain Bike Trail
Contact the Sun Valley/Ketchum Chamber & Visitors Bureau at 726-3423. Drive 1.5 miles north of Ketchum to Adams Gulch Rd. Turn left, and proceed 0.75 miles to a gravel parking area.

Featuring a seven-mile loop requiring moderate to advanced mountain biking skills, the Adams Gulch Loop Mountain Bike Trail features opportunities to view magnificent scenery as well as area wildlife. The double and single track trail is the most popular in the Ketchum area, so users should expect a crowd during the summer.

V Trail Creek Mountain Bike and Nordic Ski Trail
Contact the Sun Valley/Ketchum Chamber & Visitors Bureau at 726-3423.

Winding alongside its namesake, the paved Trail Creek Mountain Bike Trail offers outstanding views of Bald Mountain, Sun Valley, and Ketchum. The trail takes riders past the Ernest Hemingway Memorial and Trail Creek Cabin on its short journey. The trail is open free of charge year-round, and in the winter, is utilized for cross-country skiing. The trail is accessible from both Ketchum and Sun Valley.

V Sun Valley-Ketchum Area Snowmobile Trails
Sun Valley and Ketchum. Contact the Ketchum Ranger District at 622-5371.

Although Sun Valley and Ketchum are instantly associated with world-famous skiing, the region's abundant snow also affords plenty of snowmobiling opportunities. Every year, Blaine County grooms 120 miles of beginner to expert trails. Offering fantastic scenery, the trails are located north of Ketchum near Baker Creek and west of Hailey in the Wood River Recreation Area. In addition to miles of groomed adventures, the area offers numerous off-trail options appropriate for experienced riders. The free trails are generally accessible from the beginning of December to April.

V Wood River Valley Backcountry Skiing
Contact the Ketchum Ranger District at 622-5371.

Wood River Valley may be known for its meticulously groomed runs at the Sun Valley Resort, but the surrounding mountains also boast a thrill for the more adventurous types. Backcountry skiing is wildly popular in the pristine landscape, and acres of untouched powder abound. For novices, guide services are available in Sun Valley and Ketchum. Experienced backcountry skiers are urged to take all necessary precautions and should access the Ketchum Ranger District's 24-hour Avalanche and Snow Condition Report at 622-8027 prior to departure.

V Sun Valley Trail System
Contact the Sun Valley/Ketchum Chamber of Commerce at 726-3423.

The paved Sun Valley Trail System was designed as a walking and biking path leading through the scenic Wood River Valley. The ten-mile trail travels from Ketchum, looping around Dollar Mountain on its path to Sun Valley and Elkhorn. The trail eventually connects with the more extensive Wood River Trail System and is open to the public free of charge.

F Ketchum Grill
520 E. Ave., Ketchum. 726-4660.
www.ketchumgrill.com

The smoke-free Ketchum Grill opened in 1991 and offers an exquisite, flavorful menu. Utilizing twenty-nine years of perfected culinary experience, Owner/Chef, Scott Mason, creates fresh meals featuring local produce. In addition to appetizers, soups, and salads, homemade selections include gourmet pizzas, pasta, chicken, steak, Idaho elk, hamburgers, lamb, daily fresh fish specials, and much more. Complement your meal with an award-winning wine, and conclude with a decadent dessert or homemade ice cream. Named one of the "eight best ski town restaurants" by *Snow Country Magazine*, the Ketchum Grill also hosts private functions with capacities ranging from 30 to 100 people. With an elegant, yet rustic, ambience and food garnering national attention, Ketchum Grill is Sun Valley's fine dining destination! The restaurant opens nightly for dinner at 5:30 PM, and reservations are accepted.

F Cristina's Restaurant
540 E. 2nd St., Ketchum. 726-4499

Since its 1993 establishment, Cristina's Restaurant has garnered a reputation for extraordinary food, style, and presentation. Owner, Cristina Cook, draws upon her rural Tuscany upbringing to develop simple European-style bistro foods. Menu and bakery selections include breads, soups, pasta, summer salads, grilled vegetables, cakes, pastries, tarts, cookies, and much more. Customers ranging from locals to celebrities line up to sample Cristina's freshly prepared items where summer and winter menus change weekly. A deli displays European meats and cheeses while a summer patio offers quiet dining. For unpretentious, elegant meals, visit Cristina's Restaurant for breakfast, lunch, Sunday brunch, private dinners, and occasional public dinners. Hours are Monday through Saturday from 7 AM to 5:30 PM and Sundays from 9 AM to 3 PM. Take-out, catering, and wedding cakes are available.

F Chandler's Restaurant & Baci Italian Cafe
200 S. Main St., Ketchum. Chandler's: 726-1776. Baci: 726-8384. www.svrestaurantventures.com

Offering superb fine dining experiences since 1994, Chandler's Restaurant features a warm, inviting atmosphere. Experienced restaurateur, Rex Chandler, manager, Sam Fugate, and chef, Keith Otter, have joined forces to serve valley residents and visitors unique, freshly prepared creations reflecting the traditions of American Northwest cuisine. Award winning wines complement each meal's layers of flavor, ensuring that Chandler's will satisfy every palate. For a casual fine dining experience, sample Keith Otter's creations at the nearby Baci Italian Café & Wine Bar. Combining the freshest ingredients, cutting edge cuisine, an extensive wine list, and a comfortable, fun atmosphere, Baci Italian Café offers wonderful meals every night of the week. For their exquisite creations and attention to detail, it's no wonder that both Chandler's and Baci are among the most highly regarded Sun Valley eateries!

F Perry's Restaurant
131 W. 4th St., Ketchum. 726-7703.

A community staple since 1985, Perry's serves daily breakfasts and deli style lunches alongside free wireless Internet. A full breakfast menu abounds with delectable options, while espresso and the on-site bakery turn out tantalizing aromas of freshly ground coffee and baked goods prepared from scratch. For lunch, a full grill menu showcases hamburgers, fries, reubens, and more, while deli sandwiches, salads, baked potatoes, and four to eight daily soup varieties accommodate all taste preferences. Planning an adventurous outing? Call Perry's for fast take-out service ideal for lunches on the slopes, lakes, or trails. Perry's proudly caters most fishing guide lunches with take-outs ready as early as 7 AM. Welcoming large groups and bus tours, Perry's operates 7 AM – 5 PM Monday through Friday and 7 AM – 4 PM Saturday and Sunday.

L Best Western Kentwood Lodge
180 S. Main St., Ketchum. 726-4114 or (800) 805-1001.
www.bestwestern.com/kentwoodlodge

Located in the heart of Ketchum, the Best Western Kentwood Lodge has received the Best Western International Best of the Best Award. Guests are within walking distance of nightlife, restaurants, and live theater, and the lodge's fine ambience is enhanced with numerous amenities. The non-smoking facility features deluxe rooms, high speed wireless Internet, balconies, fireplaces, honeymoon and kitchen suites, air conditioning, a fitness center, indoor heated pool and spa, elevators, covered parking, on-site Esta Restaurant, wood and rock appointments, a conference room, and microwaves, refrigerators, hair dryers, and coffeemakers in each unit. Many rooms showcase ski slope views, and a free shuttle carrying visitors to the slopes and around town departs just across the street. For world class service, superior cleanliness, and a memorable experience, stay at Best Western Kentwood Lodge.

L Clarion Inn of Sun Valley
600 N. Main St., Ketchum. 726-5900 or (800) 262-4833. www.resortswest.net

Relax in downtown Ketchum at the Clarion Inn of Sun Valley and conveniently access restaurants, shopping, galleries, and the free bus route leading to the slopes and outdoor adventure. Standard and deluxe king and double rooms are provided with some featuring gas fireplaces, and a Jacuzzi suite is available. All smoking and non-smoking rooms include microwaves, refrigerators, coffeemakers, and individually controlled heat and air-conditioning. Guests are also privileged to a fitness center, year-round outdoor heated pool and spa, an office center, fax and copy services, high speed wireless Internet, and a conference room. An on-site salon, tanning beds, barbershop, Continental Beer Garden, the Rustic Moose Restaurant, and fully furnished condominium units round out the amenities and make the Clarion Inn of Sun Valley a true home away from home!

LM Sun Valley Ultimate Services LLC

201 Washington Ave., Ketchum. 725-2226.
www.sunvalleyultimateservices.com

Sun Valley Ultimate Services LLC is dedicated to helping visitors secure beautiful vacation rentals in Sun Valley, Ketchum, Warm Springs, and Elkhorn. They offer the valley's finest non-smoking condos, townhouses, and private homes with a range of nightly, weekly, and monthly rates. Sun Valley Ultimate Services specializes in customer satisfaction while matching individuals with the perfect property. In addition to exquisite rentals, many of which are listed on the company website, Sun Valley Ultimate Services provides concierge services including everything from airport shuttles to baby-sitters. A complete itemized service list is available on the website with all services designed to accommodate travelers' every need. On your next visit, feel like Sun Valley has always been your home with Sun Valley Ultimate Services' finely appointed properties and personalized services!

S Dream Catcher Gallery

200 S. Main St., Ketchum. 726-1305 or
(888) 588-6457. www.dreamcatchergallery.com

Carrying an array of museum-quality pieces and gifts, Dream Catcher Gallery is a proud Indian Arts and Crafts Association member and represents a wide range of artists. Gallery inventory

Idaho Trivia

Boasting eighty distinct mountain ranges, Idaho is recognized as America's most mountainous state. While the entire state boasts mountains ranging from miniscule to magnificent, central Idaho is often regarded as possessing the most spectacular. Peaks from the Bitterroot, Boulder, White Cloud, and Sawtooth Mountains rise against the skyline in all directions, and the Sawtooth Mountains are frequently dubbed "America's Alps."

includes fetiches, dream catchers, Southwestern pottery, beadwork, jewelry, the Northwest's largest storyteller collection, and original and limited edition paintings from award-winning artists whose works are displayed in the Smithsonian and other renowned museums. Almost all works are artist signed, and handmade furniture features Northwest and Southwest inspired carvings. For those interested in studying Native American culture, the gallery sells both children's books and texts about Native American art. For hand-crafted pieces and friendly staff dedicated to helping you answer your questions about particular Native American tribes, artists, or pieces, visit the Dream Catcher Gallery in downtown Ketchum.

S Friesen Gallery & Gallery DeNovo

320 N. 1st Ave., Ketchum.
Friesen Gallery: 726-4174, www.friesengallery.com
Gallery DeNovo: 726-8180, www.gallerydenovo.com

Just off the corner of Sun Valley Road and First Ave. North, in the same building, you'll find both the Friesen Gallery and Gallery DeNovo. Both galleries exhibit contemporary works including paintings, glass, and sculpture by nationally and internationally represented artists. The knowledgeable staff members in both galleries are committed to artistic vision and enjoy working with both beginning and expert art collectors. Friesen Gallery, with over eighteen years experience, follows a mission to represent artists who continually push themselves with intelligent and intriguing results. Gallery DeNovo, a newer gallery, was started by collectors with a passion for helping exceptional artists gain exposure to the U.S. art market. The exhibitions change frequently, and artists' works are viewable on the respective websites listed above.

S Zantman Art Gallery of Sun Valley

360 E. Ave. N., Ketchum. 727-9099.
www.zantmangallery.com

Zantman Art Gallery of Sun Valley is an international destination known for excellence in fine art since 1959. As Idaho's premier art gallery, Zantman displays a variety of paintings, sculpture, and artifacts by acclaimed local and international artists, and the elegant showrooms showcase an atmosphere of tradition and quality. The gallery is

dedicated to the fine arts and artistic expression, and the friendly, knowledgeable staff prides itself on representing unique artists in all classic mediums. Whether patrons possess an extensive collection or are just delving into the art world, Zantman Art Gallery is happy to assist with all fine art needs. Discover for yourself why Zantman Art Gallery of Sun Valley has been a favorite destination for art lovers for several years! Open daily.

S Kneeland Gallery

271 1st Ave. N, Ketchum. 726-5512 or
(800) 338-0480. www.kneelandgallery.com

Kneeland Gallery, a presence in Ketchum since 1982, has established itself as an authority on traditional landscapes and still life subjects. The gallery's annual Plein Air Exhibition is a highly regarded three-day event drawing collectors from all over the west to watch as the gallery's top landscape painters create new masterpieces throughout the Wood River Valley. In addition to its high quality landscapes and still lifes, the gallery is also becoming recognized for its secondary focus on contemporary western art, including the works of Thom Ross, Dave McGary, and Jennifer Lowe. Other established artists featured at the gallery include Steven Lee Adams, Linda St. Clair, Andrzej Skorut, and Mary Roberson, among others. Plan to visit frequently as exhibitions are changed on a monthly basis according to Ketchum's popular gallery walks.

S Ozzie's Shoes

407 N. Leadville Ave., Ketchum. 726-3604.

From boots to shoes to sandals, Ozzie's Shoes offers signature products featuring Masai Barefoot Technology (MBT). Swiss engineer, Karl Mueller, developed the world's smallest gym when he created this ultimate walking and circuit product appropriate for both young and old, fit and weak. Featuring a sole that makes the sneaker rock with every step, MBT shoes tighten and tone muscles in the feet, ankles, calves, hamstrings, upper and inner thighs, buttocks, stomach, and back. By taking the pressure off the body's main joints and spine, the shoe promises to improve wearer's overall posture and create a younger, healthier, and better sense of self. To get the most out of your next pair of shoes, let Ozzie's Shoes in downtown Ketchum find the perfect pair for you!

M Classic Realty
201 Washington Ave., Ketchum. 726-9161.
www.classicrealtyllc.com

M Sun Valley Brokers LLC
680 Sun Valley Rd., Ketchum. 622-7722.
www.svbrokers.com

M RE/MAX of Sun Valley
360 Sun Valley Rd., Ketchum. 726-4901 or
(877) 822-6507. www.remax-sunvalleyid.com

M Pam Goetz, RE/MAX of Sun Valley
360 Sun Valley Rd., Ketchum. 726-4901 or
(877) 822-6507. www.pamgoetz.com

Pam Goetz, of Sun Valley's RE/MAX shares tirelessly of herself and is committed to meeting every client's unique needs. Pam first became a licensed Realtor in Seattle, Washington in 1972. Since then, she has received the Certified Residential Specialist, the Accredited Buyer Representative, and the RE/MAX Top 10 Sales Award for Idaho. Her experience and enthusiasm has also garnered her a RE/MAX Hall of Fame distinction. When Pam moved to the Sun Valley area, she further developed her dedication to the real estate profession and surrounding community. Her commitment to education has benefited her clients in successful closings on all types of real estate transactions, including residential, farm/ranch, vacant land, and commercial properties. Receive a guaranteed commitment to customer service and success with Pam Goetz at RE/MAX of Sun Valley!

M Joanne Wetherell, RE/MAX of Sun Valley
360 Sun Valley Rd., Ketchum. 726-4901 or
(800) 576-1823.
www.SunValleyResortProperties.com

From the first-time homebuyer, to an owner looking to sell, to the seasoned investor, in-depth knowledge of the local market is essential. RE/MAX of Sun Valley Broker/Owner, Joanne Wetherell, possesses that knowledge plus professional certifications and proven experience. A Wood River Valley resident since 1980 and a licensed Realtor® since

1992, Joanne is committed to providing her clients with outstanding results. Her integrity, education, and superior service set a gold standard, and she is recognized as one of America's top 100 RE/MAX agents. Buyers can count on Joanne to actively listen to their property needs and desires, while sellers can feel confident that their property will be well-marketed to a target audience. For local expertise and full-time commitment to your real estate needs, view the valley with Joanne Wetherell.

M Marty Bacher, RE/MAX of Sun Valley
360 Sun Valley Rd., Ketchum. 726-4901.
www.SunValleyHomesAndCondos.com

A real estate agent's role is to guide clients through the buying and selling process. Marty Bacher of RE/MAX of Sun Valley promises to fulfill that responsibility. Acting as a community youth advocate and a full-time real estate agent, Marty boasts extensive Wood River Valley knowledge. His property management and resort rental background strengthen his expertise in the Sun Valley area vacation home and condo rental market. Honesty, integrity, and exceptional customer service form the foundation of his customer relationships. He is dedicated to fulfilling clients' unique needs with the highest level of professionalism. Whether you're in the market to locate a primary residence, a second home, or an investment property, Marty Bacher possesses the market knowledge and experience to guarantee success.

M Daren Pennell, Classic Realty
201 Washington Ave., Ketchum. 726-9161 or
720-2619.

Being raised in a family real estate business, it was natural for Daren Pennell of Classic Realty to pursue real estate full-time when he and his daughters moved to Sun Valley in 2000. Daren uses his focused, sincere, and fun personality to create long lasting client relationships based on integrity

and professionalism. Drawing upon local market knowledge and years of experience ensures that your time will be effectively used to show you properties that are appropriate for your family. He utilizes the Internet to share listings and latest market dynamics, educating clients about the local market and helping them recognize opportunity when they see it and make timely decisions with confidence. Discover the joy of Wood River Valley living and let Daren help you find that special place called Home.

M Yvette Lane, Sun Valley Brokers LLC
680 Sun Valley Rd., Ketchum. 622-7722 or
578-0450. www.svbrokers.com

Yvette Lane brings to the Sun Valley Brokers team ten successful years of client satisfaction and a record for matching clients with their ideal property. Her past property management career paved a smooth transition into real estate sales and provides for rental income analysis services. Listing resort, residential, vacant land, and investment properties, Yvette has an outgoing personality that has earned her numerous customer service awards. Past customer, Dr. Robert Applebaum, states, "After the close of escrow, Yvette went beyond the call of the realtor role to help with the process of getting the home put together with the various trades and local services that have made the entire process much easier." Offering a variety of real estate and relocation services, Yvette Lane puts the 'real' in realtor!

M Sun Valley Associates, Real Estate Brokers
700 Sun Valley Rd., Ketchum. 622-4100 or
(866) 526-4100. www.svassociates.com

M Rachel Cooper, McCann Daech Fenton Realtors
271 Leadville Ave., Ketchum. 726-3317 or
727-6638. www.mdfrealtors.com

In its 28th year, McCann Daech Fenton Realtors LLC is the leading real estate brokerage firm in the Wood River Valley. Realtor® Rachel Cooper adds

Continued on page 333

GHOST TOWNS

Section 4

Alturas

Northwestern Blaine County near U.S. Hwy. 93
Once a mining town located near Alturas Lake, the community of Alturas is a ghost from the past with no visible structures remaining to testify of its existence.

Bradford

1 mile west of Bellevue in Blaine County
This mining community surfaced in 1879 and was originally called Jacobs City after early settler, Frank W. Jacobs. This name only held for a year, and by the end of 1880, Bradford was recognized as the community's official name. Bradford is best known as a community of conflict between miners and mine supervisors. When the Hills mine told workers in January 1885 that wages had to be decreased from $4 to $3.50 per day due to low silver and lead market prices, the miners were outraged. After rebelling against the pay cut, the miners lost their jobs as the mine was forced to close. Soon after the Hills mine closure, the Minnie Moore mine faced the same predicament. On February 4, 1885, workers went on strike. Attempting to reconcile the conflict, mine officials, union and non-union miners, the U.S. attorney, the county sheriff, a probate judge, an Army Brigadier General, and Idaho Governor Curtis met together and finally resolved the problem. By late March 1885, both the Minnie Moore and Hills mines were operating again with wages of $3.50 per day.

Doniphan

15 miles southwest of Hailey
Doniphan, named after Judge James Doniphan, prospered for a few short years during the early 1880s. James Doniphan oversaw the Camus Number 2 mines in the area, but the community never attracted large crowds. At the peak of its popularity, the settlement included a saloon, a few houses, and a post office. Little remains of this mining community.

Galena

29 miles northwest of Ketchum near U.S. Hwy. 93
Dating back to 1879, Galena held the distinction as the first town established on the Wood River. Once a small mining camp, the community was named when shoe shop owner, Martin Barry, fathered the first white child in the town and named the baby, William Galena Barry. With a stage connection to the neighboring community of Hailey, Galena prospered and reached a population of nearly 800. The town included a hotel, four general stores, a post office, numerous restaurants and saloons, and a livery stable. However, residents eventually left the area in search of more prosperous opportunities, and Galena was nothing more than a memory in 1890.

Gimlet

Between Ketchum and Hailey in Blaine County
Located near Greenhorn Gulch, Gimlet was primarily recognized as an ore loading station for other mining camps in the area. Settled in 1882, Gimlet was once home to a saloon, a post office, and four houses.

Muldoon

18 miles east of Hailey
In 1881, a mine was discovered in the surrounding area, and workers quickly dubbed this new claim "Muldoon" after a champion wrestler famous in the early 1880s. The town that sprang up near the new mine adopted the name and soon grew to a population of 1,500. Optimistically hopeful about the quality of the mine's ore, two forty-ton smelters were brought to the town in 1882. However, only $200,000 of ore was produced and by 1887, the town sheriff auctioned off the smelters. Realizing the town's fate, all of Muldoon's residents retreated in defeat. Today, only a few pieces of charcoal kilns remain at the town site.

Sawtooth City

Blaine County
Situated 2.5 miles west of Beaver Creek at the base of the Sawtooth Mountains, Sawtooth City was formalized on November 29, 1879 and quickly became a bustling mining settlement. With the establishment of a post office on September 30, 1880, the town grew to include twenty-five houses, meat markets, an examiner's office, a blacksmith shop, several saloons and restaurants, numerous general stores, and separate laundry quarters for Chinese miners. To aide in transferring supplies to the community, $60,000 was spent on creating a stage line to Ketchum. With its booming industry, miners were hopeful in the area and a $40,000 ten-stamp quartz mill was erected and in full operation in 1886. However, the mill failed to produce large yields of ore and it was closed just one year later. In 1887, the area's Silver King mine was the only active mine which operated with varying degrees of success until 1892. At this time, a large fire destroyed the mine's shaft, hoist, and air and water pumps. Although Sawtooth City's population had been dwindling since 1888 with the post office closing in 1890, the 1892 fire sealed the end of Sawtooth City as an active community. Mining continued in the area until 1938 when most of the mines were determined to be dormant.

Stanton

13 miles south of Bellevue
Stanton drew its name from postmaster, Clark Stanton, who opened and operated the area post office beginning on February 26, 1884. When the small mining camp went bust, the post office subsequently closed and the town was officially dead in 1915.

Vienna

Blaine County near Smiley Creek in Smiley Canyon
Vienna was a large mining community founded upon silver and lead claims. On January 16, 1882, a post office was established, and the settlement was formally recognized as a growing Idaho community. Once characterized by nearly 200 buildings, Vienna included three stores, a sawmill, meat markets, six restaurants, fourteen saloons, two livery stables, two hotels, and a newspaper, "The Vienna Reporter." These growing businesses were primarily supported with the mining successes of The Vienna Consolidated, which operated a twenty-stamp mill from 1879 to 1885. In 1888, miners attempted to create a tunnel into the mountain near the Vienna mine, but they staked no claims. By 1904, the once prosperous Vienna Consolidated was sold for tax purposes and the town died out. In 1917, several miners attempted to revive Vienna in a new area. A new settlement and mill were constructed, but little production caused Vienna's second fall. No buildings remain at either of Vienna's town sites.

Antelope

20 miles north of Arco in Butte County
Settled in April 18, 1882 on the Big Lost River, Antelope was a hub for mining and ranching activities. The community's post office, run by Mathew Boyle, operated until 1904 when Antelope's population could no longer support any postal service.

Cedarville

10 miles north of Howe in Butte County
Situated on Spring Creek's east side, Cedarville's founding and ending dates are uncertain. However, historians do know that Cedarville's residents were primarily active as workers in the Daisy Black mines. Today, visitors will still find signs of the small community with a few remaining building foundations, cellars, and rubble present in the area.

Era

16 miles southwest of Arco in Butte County
After Frank Martin laid claim to the Horn silver mine on Champagne Creek in 1885, the mining camp of Era arose. Although starting out slowly, Era saw its population grow to 1,000 residents in 1887 as the area was rich in silver ore. Historians estimate that nearly $1 million in silver was mined near Era and subsequently crushed in the town's dry crusher. With significant support from its profitable mines, Era soon became a desirable business center. At its height, the town included several private houses, a Pacific Express office, a drug store, three general stores, hardware and mining equipment stores, two livery stables, an opera house, six saloons, and numerous prostitution houses. Today, this once prospering community is now a nearly forgotten moment in Idaho history with just a single building foundation remaining at the town site.

Martin

Butte County
Soon after Jack Hood and Fred Winterhoff founded the Park and Elkhorn mines in 1881, the community of Martin attracted miners hoping to get rich quick. To ensure that these miners had contact with distant family members and friends, Samuel Martin began operating the Martin post office on August 12, 1882. During its peak period, Martin boasted nearly 800 residents with three general stores, a drug store, a hardware store, and five saloons. Mining, however, was the primary occupation with most men working in the nearby Horn silver mine and mill.

Carrietown

20 miles northwest of Hailey in Camas County
Located in the Little Smokey Mining District, Carrietown's founding date is unknown. A community of relatively small mining importance, Carrietown peaked at a population of 300 to 400 individuals before its mining and business activity faded away. Today, the town site is simply a popular summer destination for nearby county residents.

Humphreys

25 miles southwest of Hailey in Camas County
Samuel N. Humphrey declared himself postmaster of the new Humphrey post office on December 7, 1887. Located on Solider Creek, the town never attracted large crowds, and the site was completely vacated by the mid 1890s. Another Humphreys was later formed in present day Clark County (Section 6). Named after a Union Pacific Railroad employee, this community faced a similar fate as the previous Humphrey's in Camas County. After the post office closed in 1951, the community disappeared.

Alder City

6 miles southeast of Mackay in Custer County
Established in 1884 at the mouth of Alder Creek, the settlement of Alder was a copper camp that relied on the Big Copper mine for its prosperity. The community was primarily a tent town with most businesses also operating out of tents until the copper boom ended in the area.

Cliff

Custer County
Established in 1884, Cliff was a renowned mining town operating the only two-stack smelter in the state. As more miners moved to the area, Cliff grew to include twenty houses, a general store, and two saloons. While early mining successes allowed a new fifty-ton smelter to be built, the mines eventually ran dry and Cliff's residents disappeared.

Crystal

Custer County
Early 1880s residents first named this community Wagon or Wagontown, but as more settlers began arriving, the town's name was changed to Crystal. Located at the mouth of the Salmon River's East Fork, Crystal was the largest town in Custer County in 1884 and was considered a candidate for county seat. When Crystal lost the vote to Challis, Crystal's doomed fate was sealed.

Frost

18 miles south of Challis in Custer County
Located on the Salmon River, Frost was a small mining camp named after the town's first postmaster, Charles P. Frost. While Frost began as a boom camp in 1885, fortunes quickly ran out. By 1887, most of the miners had left in search of better prospects, and on November 30, Mr. Frost was forced to close the town's post office.

Garden City

Located on Garden Creek (and named after such), Garden City used to serve as a distributing point for the Bayhorse Mining district. The town of Challis eventually absorbed the small community.

Loon Creek

Custer County
California prospector, Nathan Smith, discovered a loon and gold on an area creek and named his new mining camp Loon Creek in 1869. Mining activity in the area was short-lived with all placer mining ending by 1873. During its short life, Loon Creek produced more than $500,000 in gold.

Oro Grande

Custer County
Meaning "big gold" in Spanish, Oro Grande was established on a high bar west of another mining settlement (Loon Creek) in the early 1870's. Due to scarcity of supplies and high lumber costs, Oro Grande grew slowly and peaked at a population of 200 in 1871. By the spring of 1872, mining activities in the area were dwindling, but a few hopeful Chinese immigrants remained in the area. On February 12, 1879, the Sheepeater Indians massacred all but one of the Chinese left in Oro Grande. In response, the U.S. Army waged the Sheepeater Campaign in the summer of 1879, but by then, Oro Grande was a ghost town.

White Knob

Custer County
Mining activities began in the area in 1881 as the Mackay Meadows mine was established. As word of the mine's rich copper deposits spread, a rush to the area occurred in 1883-1884, and White Knob was officially formed in 1885. In addition to several private dwellings, White Knob's residents also had access to a post office, boarding house, a school, two general stores, a theater, and three pool halls. Employing most of White Knob's residents, the Mackay Meadows mine once boasted the largest copper production in Idaho.

Cobalt

Lemhi County
Idaho miners and settlers knew as early as 1901 that large deposits of cobalt were present in this area of Lemhi County, but significant mining activity did not begin until 1939. As miners began full-scale cobalt mining operations in the Blackbird Mining District (earlier used as a mine for copper and gold deposits), the new settlement of Cobalt was formed. However, the community was originally called Forney after early settler, Hank Forney, and the town retained this name until 1950. During its 21-year run, the Blackbird District produced 14 million pounds of cobalt worth an estimated $50 million. With this prosperity, the town's population once numbered 2,500 and was home to a recreation hall, school, post office, grocery store, and service station. Today, most of the businesses are deserted and only a few residents remain with the hope that the mines and town will prosper again.

Grantsville

Lemhi County
Originally known as the Tenderfoot mining camp, Grantsville became the favored name as the Civil War dominated miners' thoughts in the early 1860s. Established in 1866, the town was filled with Northern sympathizers who stubbornly refused to belong to the neighboring settlement of Leesburg. As the Civil War ended, Grantsville and Leesburg grew together and the new, larger community retained the Leesburg name.

Hahn

Lemhi County
Hahn was established in 1884 as a community center for miners of the Spring Mountain Mining District. The mining company was quite prosperous, operating a thirty-ton smelter, ore houses, and a boarding house. As more miners arrived in the area, including a Missouri man named Hahn who constructed a new smelter in 1907, Hahn's population grew to 100 residents. In 1907, the mining camp was officially proclaimed an Idaho town and was granted a post office. This post office closed just two years later, and today, only a few cement foundations remain at the town site.

Kingville

Lemhi County
Established near the Nicholia mines in the late 1800s, Kingville was a short-lived settlement. The town was predominantly populated with men who worked in the kilns supplying charcoal to the Nicholia smelter.

Lava

Lemhi County
In 1881, miners in the Nicholia area discovered the Viola mine, and a rush to the area resulted in the establishment of Lava. The town and surrounding mine were largely developed with the aid of British capital, and lead, silver, and copper were mined in the area. Today, nothing remains of Lava.

Leadville

East of Leadore in Lemhi County
Leadville was appropriately named after lead mining activities in the area that supported the town's growth for a short period of time. Today, a few abandoned mine entrances and cabins remain.

Smithville

Lemhi County
Located three miles from Leesburg farther north on Napias Creek, Smithville was established in 1866 under the direction of William Smith. Smithville was composed of several cabins and a general store and once reached a population of 500. Today, nothing remains of this town that withered away in 1870, the same year William Smith was killed in a Salmon City gunfight.

Summit City

Lemhi County
James Glendenning established Summit City in 1867 and named the town after its lofty elevation. A small town located six miles east of Leesburg, Summit City was a stopping point on the wagon road leading from Salmon City to Leesburg. Summit City's history is sketchy, but historians believe that the town's population never exceeded more than 400 residents. When gold findings were exhausted, employees of the Pioneer Mining Company were forced to move in hopes of finding better prospects.

Reno
Lemhi County
Located southwest of Gilmore, Reno was established in 1885. Although it is known that the Reno family served as the community's namesake, there is some discrepancy as to which individual it honors. Some historians argue that early rancher, Frank Reno, is the town's namesake. More likely, however, is that the settlement was named after Agnes B. Reno who served as the community's first postmaster.

Yellowjacket
Lemhi County
When Nathan Smith and Doc Wilson discovered placer gold on Yellowjacket Creek on September 23, 1869, miners at Loon Creek rushed to the area to develop the placer beds. Soon, the thirty-stamp, water powered Yellowjacket mill was in full operation. With a peak population of 400 miners, Yellowjacket reached the height of its production between 1890 and 1900. As with other area mines, though, Yellowjacket's gold claims were overrated, and labor costs eventually outweighed production values. In all of its operation, the Yellowjacket mill only produced $1 million in revenue. A boom and bust town throughout the course of its history, Yellowjacket is now a quiet testimony to Idaho's miners with several town buildings remaining abandoned but intact.

Boulder Basin
Blaine County
Characterized by rock ridges and alpine lakes, Boulder Basin is one of the most scenic ghost towns in Idaho. Due to the rugged landscape, mining was difficult, and freight wagons found the trip to Boulder Basin problematic. Despite the terrain, Boulder Basin was home to the Golden Glow, Ophir, Trapper, Tip Top, Bazouk, and Sullivan mines. At the Golden Glow mine, the old mill and several small cabins can still be found, as well as several tunnels used by early miners.

Gillman City, North Star, & East Fork City
Blaine County
As the mining town of Galena prospered, several prospectors set out on their own in the 1880s to explore new territory along the Big Wood River. As a result of these prospecting efforts, the small mining camps of Gillman City, North Star, and East Fork City were born. The North Star camp was likely the most profitable, opening the Independence Lead-Silver Mine in 1883 and the Triumph Mine in 1884. As quickly as these sites arose, Gillman City and East Fork City were soon abandoned. In 1917, an avalanche roared into North star, destroying much of the camp and killing several residents. Today, all that remains in the area are a few sludge ponds.

Washington Basin
Custer County
In 1879, African-American miner, George Washington Blackman, accompanied a group of prospectors to Idaho. Settling amid the rugged mountains and timberline landscape, Blackman and his party worked the area later dubbed Washington Basin throughout the summer of 1879. Although some members of his party never came back to the area after 1879, Blackman always returned to Fourth of July Creek to work new claims, and other miners soon joined him. At the height of its production, Washington Basin included a mill and several log dwellings. When the snows forced Blackman to leave the area, he headed south. But every year, residents of neighboring communities knew Blackman would return. Throughout his life, Blackman was one of the most well-respected miners in Washington Basin and he serves as this location's namesake.

Mammoth
Custer County
Located at the bottom of Mammoth Canyon, the small mining town of Mammoth never saw much prosperity. Only a few small claims were made, and the area's mill was eventually dismantled for scrap metal. All that remains of Mammoth are a few old cabins surrounded by rocky ridges and evergreen trees.

Ivers
Custer County
When young Clarence Eddy struck gold in the area in 1902, a rush to the newly established Lost Packer Mine resulted. Assuming that the area would be quite prosperous, the town of Ivers was born and a supply road was constructed to Custer. By 1905, a 100-ton smelter was complete, and the town boasted a population of 200 residents. At its peak, Ivers included a large mill, a general store, a saloon, and several private cabins. Ivers was occupied until the early 1930s, but a devastating forest fire rolled through the area in 1931. Most of the town was destroyed, and today, only a few rotting cabins and part of the rusting mill remain.

Ulysees
Lemhi County
Early prospectors staked gold claims along Indian Creek as early as 1895, but major production in the area didn't occur until 1901. With knowledge of these early claims, the Kittie Burton Gold Mining Company bought most of the important claims and a rush of mining activity followed. As more settlers poured into the area, Ulysees was established and was composed of several houses, a miners' boardinghouse, and the Kittie Burton Mill. Two prominent mines were established surrounding Ulysees: the Kittie Burton Mine and the Ulysees Mine. Ore from both mines was sent via cable tramways to a fifteen stamp mill. Eventually, production ran dry and the mill was closed. Although the mill has since collapsed, visitors will still find several original houses from the mining boom.

Nicholia
Proceeding south from Leadore, merge northeast off State Hwy. 28 onto Nicholia Rd.
In 1881, while searching for his lost horses in the Birch Creek Valley, William McKay stopped to pick up a rock and noted that the rock felt extremely dense. After noticing the same type of rock being loaded into railroad cars at the town of Hailey, McKay returned to the spot and staked the Viola claim. Later, McKay sold this claim to Charles Rustin. Within a matter of months, the LaPlata Mining and Smelting Company of Leadville, Colorado sent New York mining engineer, Ralph Nichols, to inspect Rustin's claim. Upon receipt of Nichols report, they bought the Viola claim for $117,000 and Nichols became the manager of the newly established Viola Mining Company. As word of the mine spread, the settlement of Nicholia was established at the mouth of Smelter Gulch. By 1882, the town boasted more than 400 residents, and by 1886, voting records indicate that 1,500 men voted at Nicholia. During its prosperous run from 1882 to 1894, the Viola mine produced one fourth of all lead mined in the U.S. However, this designation also came with a heavy price. The smelter frequently produced lead poisoning that killed several miners as well as most animals in the area. Today, only a few collapsing buildings remain at the town site.

Carbonate, Houston, and Mackay
Custer County
While Carbonate was a relatively small mining community, Houston prospered from June 1885 until 1901. At its peak, Houston was home to nearly 200 residents as well as 70 homes and businesses. Although Houston's residents hoped the new railroad would run through town, line engineers bypassed Houston. To capitalize on the new railroad, Carbonate and Houston residents joined forces to form the town of Mackay. Named after successful miner, John W. Mackay, the new settlement prospered for years mostly due to the town's rail station.

Custer
At Sunbeam, merge north off State Hwy. 75 onto FR 013. Upon reaching Bonanza, proceed east on FR 074, which becomes 070 and leads to the townsite.
Bonanza Justice of the Peace Samuel Halman established a new community near the prominent General Custer mine in 1878. Based on the settlement's location, early residents christened their town Custer, and by 1888, the town was booming. At its height, Custer's population neared 3,500, and the town boasted three general stores, two restaurants, a shoe and harness store, three boarding houses, a butcher shop, two liveries, a furniture store, two barber shops, carpentry services, a dance hall, five saloons, several houses of ill-repute, a Wells Fargo office, a hotel, and a Chinatown containing Custer's only church. Most of Custer's residents were involved in mining production at the General Custer mine. In its first ten years of operation, the town's mine produced more than $8 million in ore. When the mine began operating under another company, the Lucky Boy vein was discovered and another $1 million was produced before the mines closed in 1911. With the halt of all mining activities, Custer's prosperity withered away.

to that reputation with her enthusiasm, a great attitude, and the ability to handle your residential real estate needs. Whether you're a first-time homebuyer, relocating, investing, or looking for a vacation getaway, she can help you find the perfect property. Rachel relies on her firm's almost three decades of experience, commitment to technology, and interoffice networking to provide you with current market information. In the fast-pace, ever-changing real estate market, you want a reputable brokerage firm and a hardworking Realtor® on your side. From single family homes to condos to vacant land or whatever your real estate need, e-mail Rachel at rachel@mdfrealtors.com or call her today.

M InterMountain Media
411 6th St., Ketchum. 726-6455.
www.intermtnmedia.com

InterMountain Media is a full-service copy center dedicated to professional, friendly service and attention to detail with fast project turnaround. Providing local businesses with affordable black and white, color, and architectural copies, InterMountain Media's services include large format printing, custom paper stock, folding, binding, collating, lamination, FTP drop, and engineering scanning. Color posters may be sized up to 42 inches wide. Realtors receive special pricing on real estate spec sheets and flyers, while orders over $100 receive free delivery. For those with simpler projects, self-service copying and a facsimile are available. The next time your individual or business needs call for the help of a professional copying service, rely on the experience of InterMountain Media.

19 *Food, Lodging*

Hailey
Pop. 6,200

In 1880, John Hailey purchased 440 acres along the Wood River and laid out several blocks for a townsite. The site was originally named Marshall, but the title soon changed to honor its founder. By the time John Hailey moved to Boise in 1881, the town already had eighteen saloons and twelve gambling parlors and was thriving as a mining boom town. The railroad arrived in 1883, and along with it, additional prosperity and technology. Because of the railroad, Hailey received telegraph services shortly after its founding as well as the region's first telephone system. In addition, Hailey also claimed rights to Idaho's first electrical light system in 1889.

In the 1880s, Hailey was so populated and busy that it boasted three daily newspapers and two weekly papers. This was during the town's most prosperous years (1881-1889). At one point, Hailey's Chinese population was the largest in the state. In the end, the local mines produced nearly $60 million in lead, gold, and silver. Even the business-district fires that occurred in 1883 and 1889 can't destroy those figures!

Today, the quiet town at the edge of Idaho's wealthiest and most developed resort area is home to several turn-of-the-century buildings, a thriving art scene, and year-round recreation. The town also retains the distinction as the birthplace of Ezra Pound, famous twentieth-century poet and political activist.

H Wood River Mines
Milepost 112.8 on State Hwy. 75

Rich strikes in 1879 led to a rush to the lead-silver mines of this valley. Eventually, the famous Minnie Moore Mine alone produced a total of $8.4 million worth of ore. Mining quickly brought a railroad and prosperity, and for a time this was the leading region of Idaho. Hailey had Idaho's earliest phone service (1883) and three daily newspapers. A Ketchum smelter pioneered electric lighting in Idaho. But times changed: lodes ran out, mining declined, and now these hills attract more skiers than miners.

T Bullion
7 miles west of Hailey in Blaine County. In Hailey, cross Main St., and follow Bullion Rd./Croy Creek Rd. 4.3 miles to the pavement's end. Proceed another 3 miles on the gravel road to Bullion Gulch.

Commodore Perry Croy and George W. Edgington filed mining claims on June 4, 1880, and a flood of settlers rushed to the new Bullion mine. As the settlement spread, the name Bullion was applied to the community. With a boom period lasting from 1880 through 1893, Bullion once reached a population of over 700 residents with more than 500 men working in the area mines. The settlement grew to include a drug store, two general stores, shoe shops and butcher shops, a post office, an examiner's office, a school, boarding houses, a miners' union hall, livery stables, seven saloons, and a stage line providing visitors, residents, and supplies with a direct route to the community. The town was also proud of its water pipeline featuring hydrants, fireplugs, hoses, and reels. Unfortunately, as with the neighboring communities of Warm Springs, Jacobs, Deer Creek, and Greenhorn, Bullion's boom ended abruptly in 1890 and the post office closed its doors on October 15.

T Blaine County Historical Museum
218 N. Main St., Hailey. 788-1801.

A wide variety of exhibits await visitors at the Blaine County Historical Museum. Idaho's first telephone switchboard can be found, as well as several old mining and farming tools, relics from Chinese miners, and a model mine tunnel. Open Memorial Day through Labor Day, the museum is free. During the remainder of the year, the museum is open by appointment only.

T Liberty Theater & Company of Fools
110 N. Main St., Hailey. 788-3300.
www.companyoffools.org.

Established in 1938, the Liberty Theater is now under the management of Hollywood legend,

Bruce Willis. The historic theater has been completely refurbished with a modern sound system, and in 1996, the theater joined forces with the Virginia based Company of Fools. Artistic Director, Rusty Wilson, started the professional, non-profit Company of Fools in 1992. When Bruce Willis invited him to continue his work in Idaho's Wood River Valley, Wilson accepted the offer and moved operations to Hailey. The acting troupe and theater are committed to providing educational programs to students of all ages, encouraging individuals to rejoice in creative expression. In addition to telling stories of the human heart and discovering the joys and trials of daily life, Liberty Theater hosts several special events throughout the year. Contact the theater for a complete list of upcoming events and educational programs.

T Hailey Skateboard Park
Located across from the airport in Hailey. Contact the Hailey Chamber of Commerce at 788-2700.

For skateboard enthusiasts, the Hailey Skateboard Park is a must-see. Dreamland Skateparks built the 12,500 square foot facility with features that are the first of their kind west of the Mississippi. In addition to numerous other highlights, the park features a sixteen-foot full radius concrete pipe as well as a sixteen-foot roll-in with handrails. The park is open from late spring through early fall.

T Ezra Pound's Birthplace
Corner of 2nd Ave. and Pine St., Hailey.

Tucked in the Wood River Valley, Hailey claims rights as Ezra Pound's birthplace. In the 1880s, Homer Pound and his wife, Isabel Weston, moved to Hailey where Homer would serve as the first recorder for a new government land office there. After building this 1 1/2-story frame house, the couple gave birth on October 30, 1885 to their one and only child, Ezra Loomis Pound. Although Pound only lived in Hailey for the first two years of his life, he remained fascinated with his Idaho roots into his final years.

After leaving Idaho to preserve Isabel's fragile health, the Pound family moved to Pennsylvania where Homer obtained a high-ranking position at the Philadelphia Mint. As a boy genius, Pound learned nine languages and developed a sense of defying conventional wisdom, teachings, and authority. After earning a master's degree in Spanish at the University of Pennsylvania, Pound sought employment as a professor at Wabash College. However, after a misunderstanding of events, Pound was fired.

In 1907, Pound moved to Europe in hopes of pursuing doctoral research. Upon arriving in London, however, Pound discovered an interest in poetry. Just one year later, he published his first book of poetry while working as a translator, editor, and critic. Word of Pound's genius quickly spread throughout the literary world. He befriended and inspired William Butler Yeats, T.S. Eliot, William Carlos Williams, and E.E. Cummings. He also edited many of Ernest Hemingway's first manuscripts and forced Robert Frost to pursue publication.

In 1920, Pound moved to Paris, and in 1925, relocated to Rapallo, Italy. Although once eloquent, Pound's work began to take on a note of paranoia and Fascist ideals. In the early 1940s, Pound made nearly one hundred broadcasts from Italy espousing his anti-American and anti-Semitic beliefs. Although his broadcasts were intellectually lofty and hard to interpret, Pound's beliefs backfired on him. When the Allies overtook Italy in 1945, Pound surrendered to an American soldier and was promptly arrested for treason.

Upon his arrest, Pound was taken to an Army Detention Training Center in Pisa where he was forced to stay outside in a 6 x 6 1/2 foot cage. Now sixty years old, Pound was allowed a Bible, a book of Confucius, and a few pencils and paper, but all visitors and any conversation with fellow prisoners or guards was forbidden. At his onset of amnesia, hysteria, and claustrophobia, Pound was transferred to a medical tent where he spent three months in recovery. Three months later, Pound and his wife flew to the U.S. where Pound stood trial for treason in February 1946 at the Lunacy Inquisition. A panel of psychiatrists dubbed Pound as having an unsound mind, and he was committed for the next thirteen years to St. Elizabeth's Hospital in Washington D.C.

In 1958, lawyers serving Pound argued that in the interest of justice, Pound should be released. The judge agreed, and in 1958, Pound and his wife returned to Italy where they maintained a ten-year public silence. Pound continued to write, and some of his writings make reference to the jagged Sawtooth Mountains and beautiful scenery of his birthplace.

In 1969, Pound returned briefly to America with the full intention of visiting Idaho's Wood River Valley one more time. However, finding that the trip may compromise his health, Pound decided against the journey and returned to Italy, leaving the U.S. behind for good. In 1971, two days after his eighty-seventh birthday, Pound died in Italy in his sleep. He is buried next to legendary composer, Igor Stravinsky, in a cemetery in Venice. His famous birthplace still stands in Hailey, and the

University of Idaho in Moscow has honored this native Idahoan with a special collection of more than 300 books written by or about Pound.

T Blaine County Aquatic Center

1020 Fox Acres Rd., Hailey. 788-2144.

The Blaine County Aquatic Center in Hailey is the source for spring and summer fun for the entire family. The center's 25-yard heated pool features six lanes, and a wading pool for children is also available. The pool is open May through August with a small admission fee.

T Hop Porter Park

209 W. Bullion St., Hailey. Contact the Hailey Chamber of Commerce at 788-2700.

Although downtown Hailey offers locals and visitors several options when it comes to parks, Hop Porter Park is one of the most popular. The tree-lined park features a children's playground, grills, and picnic tables and covered shelters. In addition, the park hosts several community events and area festivals throughout the year.

T Roberta McKercher Gateway Park

State Hwy. 75 in Hailey. Contact the Hailey Chamber of Commerce at 788-2700.

Roberta McKercher Gateway Park is nestled in downtown Hailey and offers an ideal setting for picnics and outdoor fun. In addition to standard playground equipment and a sports field, the park features picnic facilities and a walking/bicycle path.

T Hailey Historical Building Tour

Contact the Hailey Chamber of Commerce at 788-2700.

Founded in the 1880s at the edge of what would become one of America's most legendary ski destinations, Hailey retains much of its historical character in several well-preserved business structures and homes.

Blaine County Historical Museum
Corner of N. Main & Galena St.

Home to regional relics and Idaho's first telephone switchboard, the Blaine County Historical Museum is appropriately housed in one of the town's oldest buildings. The structure was erected in 1882.

Alturas Hotel
First Ave. S.

Built between 1883-1886 at a cost of $35,000, Hailey's Alturas Hotel was once considered the finest hotel between Denver and the Pacific Ocean. With funds contributed by Thomas Mellon of Pittsburgh, the original eighty-two room brick hotel offered guests wood stoves in every room. In 1913, the Hiawatha Land and Water Company purchased the hotel, remodeled it, and tapped a nearby hot springs to provide the hotel with a swimming pool and radiant heat. Unfortunately, in the 1970s, an arsonist destroyed much of this historic landmark.

Blaine County Courthouse
First Ave. S.

The Blaine County Courthouse was established in 1883 as the community's initial boom continued

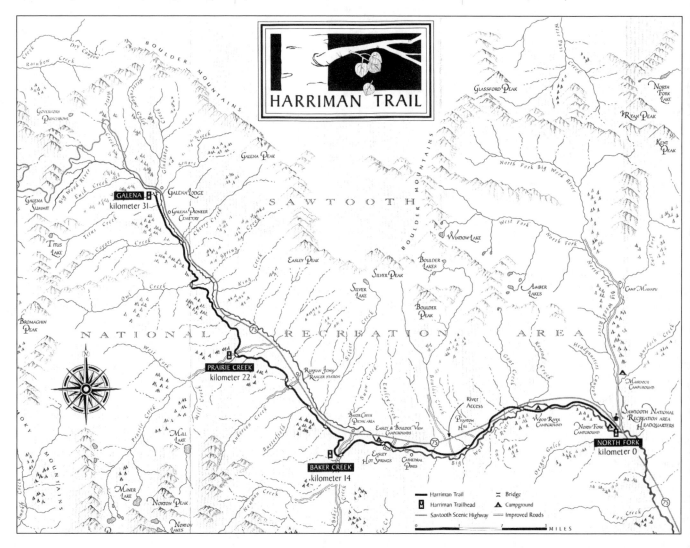

to attract new residents from far and wide. The three-story courthouse features both brick and stonework.

Historic Hailey Church
Northwest corner of Pine St.
In 1913, a large Catholic congregation erected this Gothic-Revival Church at a cost of $7,200. The parish was originally home to the St. Charles of the Valley Church but now operates under a new name with a different congregation of believers.

Ezra Pound Home
Northeast corner of Second Ave. S.
Famous poet and outspoken war critic, Ezra Loomis Pound, was born in Hailey on October 30, 1885. This 1 1/2-story frame house served as the Pound family home until the author was just two years old. Although Pound and his family moved to Philadelphia, the Pound home has been well-maintained and is a local landmark.

Emmanuel Episcopal Church
Southwest corner of Bullion St.
Dating back to 1885, the Emmanuel Episcopal Church epitomizes a Gothic Revival style. The church's distinguishing characteristic is its narrow, arched belfry.

V Harriman Trail
Contact the Blaine County Recreation District in Hailey at 788-2117.

Welcome to the Harriman Trail. Along its eighteen mile course, the Harriman rolls next to the Big Wood River, alternating through spacious meadows, aspen stands, and lodgepole forest, always with the majestic Boulder Mountain Range as a scenic backdrop.

Named in honor of W. Averell Harriman, the founder of Sun Valley, the trail began with a pledge from the Mary W. Harriman Foundation in 1991. This initial gift was magnified by partners in both the public and private sectors to begin construction in 1996. Working partners of the Harriman project include the Sawtooth National Forest, the Harriman Foundation, the Idaho Transportation Department, and Federal Hwy. Administration, and the Blaine County Recreation District, which has been designated as the managing agency.

The Harriman is Many Things
A Corridor
The trail provides a key transportation connection through the scenic corridor, linking the Sawtooth NRA Headquarters on its south end to U.S. Forest Service campgrounds, Easley Hot Springs, and finally Galena Lodge at its northern terminus. The trail has been designed to accommodate wheelchair access and invites a larger spectrum of recreationists to the upper Big Wood River Valley who might not venture into this landscape in the absence of a strong directional trail system.

A Bike Path
Along its length, the Harriman rolls over gentle swells, over small streams, and through impressive rock formations, offering a very backcountry setting, yet the trail grade rivals any urban paved bike path.

A Hiking Network
Not only is hiking along the Harriman a great option, but the trail also provides the adventurous hiker access to any number of canyons and forest stands radiating from the trail to the west.

An Equestrian Trail
The trail is open to horses from Murphy Bridge north.

A Cross-Country Ski Trail
In winter, the trail is groomed for cross-country skiing, serving as a vital link in the North Valley Trails system.

A Place to Experience Nature
Fishing along the route, scanning the trailside for birds and wildlife, identifying wildflowers in bloom – the Harriman is a place to learn about our relationship to the natural world. Along the trail, interpretive sites engage the visitor in self-guided outdoor education about the living systems through which the Harriman winds its way.

The Trail Has Three Segments
North Fork to Baker Creek (7 Miles)
This trail reach connects the Sawtooth National Recreation Headquarters with several campgrounds, Easley Hot Springs and camp, and several private summer home areas. Equestrians – please note that horse use is restricted to north of Murphy's Bridge. No camping with horses is permitted in the campgrounds adjacent to the trail.

Baker Creek to Prairie Creek (6.3 Miles)
This trail section passes through beautiful lodgepole forest with stunning glimpses of the Boulder Mountains and upper Big Wood River. Parking and easy access to the trail is available at Baker Creek.

Prairie Creek to Galena (5.5 Miles)
This section of the Harriman provides the most intimate views at the high peaks of the Boulder Range. Hawk Hill, the steepest grade on the trail, occurs at mile 1.6 and provides stellar views of the mountains. The Community Bridge occurs at mile 4.2.

Trail Etiquette
- Be courteous to all users, regardless of their speed or skill.
- Don't block the trail.
- Slower traffic has the right-of-way.
- Keep right except to pass.
- Bikers – yield to traffic when crossing trails and roads.
- Yield to pedestrians and equestrians.
- Keep the trail clean. Don't litter – pack your trash.
- Horses are permitted ONLY from Murphy Bridge to Galena.
- Always speak to horses so they don't spook.∑
- Use caution when approaching or overtaking another. Make your presence known in advance.
- Control your speed and approach turns in anticipation of someone around the bend or at intersections.
- Control your dog. Leash dogs that cannot be voice controlled. ALWAYS leash dogs through campgrounds.
- Stay on designated trails – avoid tramping native vegetation and minimize potential erosion by not using muddy trails or shortcutting switchbacks.∑
- Bikers – always wear a helmet.
- Use lights at night.
- Know your limit – ride within it!

Reprinted from U.S. Forest Service brochure

V Wood River Trail System
Extending between Hailey and Sun Valley. Contact the Hailey Chamber of Commerce at 788-2700.

Once used as the Union Pacific Railroad right of way linking the communities of the Wood River Valley, the Wood River Trail System today is open to non-motorized traffic. Twenty-two miles of paved paths link Hailey, Ketchum, and Sun Valley

while providing access to public lands and the Big Wood River. The pathway is open to biking, rollerblading, walking, running, horseback riding, and cross-country skiing year-round free of charge.

F CK's Real Food
320 S. Main St., Hailey. 788-1223.

CK's Real Food, managed by husband/wife team Chris and Rebecca Kastner, specializes in fresh cuisine and casual, yet elegant dining. Serving as owners and chefs, the Kastners are long-time Sun Valley residents, and Chris has been a chef since 1978. Both culinary artisans emphasize local organic vegetables and regional products in their taste creations, and every meal is prepared from scratch in-house. As a result, guests are greeted with scrumptious menu offerings, including Idaho lamb, crab cakes, local trout, homemade breads, ravioli, potato chips, and desserts, and much more. In addition to excellent food, the restaurant features an energetic atmosphere showcasing music from around the world. Complete with outdoor summer dining and offsite special events catering, CK's Real Food is your one-stop source for a uniquely fresh dining experience!

F The Red Elephant Restaurant & Saloon
107 S. Main St., Hailey. 788-6047.

Offering a rustic, family-friendly atmosphere with appetite-whetting aromas, The Red Elephant Restaurant & Saloon is situated in a 100-year-old historic Hailey building. Salvatore Caredda, Italian owner and chef, draws upon extensive experience as both a renowned chef and business owner and has established The Red Elephant as a regarded Hailey restaurant. Featuring a bar/saloon and a separate full-scale dining area, The Red Elephant treats customers to steakhouse items along with delectable seafood and Italian specials. Sample aged and marinated prime rib or try the juicy hamburgers, tender filet mignon, or pasta dishes highlighted with Caredda's Italian touch. An extensive variety of wines complement the cozy restaurant's meals, and private dinner parties can accommodate up to eighty-five people. The restaurant opens daily at 4 PM with happy hour from 4 to 6 PM.

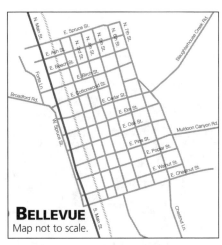

BELLEVUE
Map not to scale.

M Cornerstone Realty Group
Hailey. 788-2646. www.findmycorner.com

Leading the way to helping clients find their corner of the Wood River Valley, Cornerstone Realty Group provides service with insight, integrity, commitment, expertise, energy, technical savvy, and vast local knowledge. Most of the brokerage's highly educated agents have been helping individuals buy and sell Central Idaho property since the late 1980s, providing clients with the professional representation they deserve. Cooperating with all other Sun Valley brokerages, Cornerstone Realty Group offers residential, commercial, vacant land, and subdivision development listings. The dedicated agents use proven "systems" to help clients with every detail of the buying and selling process, and agents are happy to provide extensive relocation information. When it's time to find your corner of the Idaho real estate market, depend on Cornerstone's commitment to personal attention, follow-through, and knowledgeable service!

M Hailey Chamber of Commerce
513 N. Main St., Hailey. 788-2700 or 788-3484. www.haileyidaho.com

20 *Food, Lodging*

Bellevue
Pop. 1,876

Offering easy access to the scenic Wood River Valley, Bellevue was established in 1880 under the nickname, "Gate City." The town was settled in response to the Minnie Moore and Queen of the Hills mine discoveries and grew quickly under its original name of Biddyville. In 1890, when the town was chosen as the Logan County seat, the Idaho Territorial Legislature decided that the community needed a more proper sounding name. Thus, Bellevue acquired its present name and received a city charter. To this day, Bellevue remains the only Idaho city possessing charter status.

T Wood River Valley
Encompassing the communities of Bellevue, Hailey, Ketchum, and Sun Valley

In 1824, Alexander Ross and a band of 140 Hudson Bay Company trappers arrived in Wood River Valley. Historians speculate that this trapping expedition represented the first white exploration of Wood River Valley. Although the area is known for its beauty, Ross and his party quickly left the valley due to nearly non-existent beaver populations.

T Henry Miller Mansion
0.7 miles south of Bellevue on State Hwy. 75. Contact the Bellevue Chamber of Commerce at 788-7788.

Built in the 1880s, this two-story home canopied with trees was once home to mining giant, Henry Miller. Miller owned the highly successful Minnie Moore Mine, which he eventually sold for $500,000 in 1884 to a British company.

At the same time that he was making his fortune, Miller fell madly in love and married Annie Gallagher, the daughter of a Bellevue boarding house owner. After sending her to Europe to receive a worldly education, Miller began work on the fabulous mansion that would become the new couple's home. When Annie returned to Idaho, she was greeted with a stunning home complete with a library, ballroom, parquet floors, and five bedrooms.

The couple lived happily in the home for several years until Miller died in 1907 at age sixty-five in a Salt Lake City Hospital. Seven years later and over the process of several weeks, the home was moved two miles from downtown Bellevue to this new site. Interestingly, while the home was in transit, the cook remained inside to prepare meals as usual. As for the young widow, she eventually remarried, dying at a ripe old age in 1941.

TV Big Wood River
Wood River Valley. Contact the Sun Valley/Ketchum Chamber of Commerce at 726-3423.

Extending through most of central Idaho and draining nearly 3,000 square miles, the Big Wood River is often referred to as the quintessential mountain fly-fishing stream. Although the lower stretches of the river begin near Shoshone and are frequently called the "Malad River", the upper river is notably more popular and receives significantly heavier usage.

Often referred to as one of the American West's finest fishing rivers, the Big Wood offers an outstanding fishery due to strategically planned management policies. The river boasts both catch and release fishing as well as areas where anglers are allowed to take home a limited amount of their day's trophies. Big Wood River fish species include rainbow trout, brook trout, brown trout, yellow perch, largemouth and smallmouth bass, and bluegill. Sixteen alpine lakes in addition to the drainage's Magic, Little Wood, Fish Creek, and Mormon Reservoirs bolster the river's distinction as possessing the most productive trout habitat in all of south-central Idaho. The best fishing generally begins in July, but fall fishing also frequently provides anglers with stunning results. The river is accessible from several points alongside State Hwy. 75.

V Silver Creek
Southeast of Bellevue. Contact the Bellevue Chamber of Commerce at 788-7788.

Rising from alkaline springs located in the high desert west of Picabo, Silver Creek winds its way through open meadows on its journey to the Little Wood River. Ernest Hemingway idolized the fishing in Silver Creek, and the tributary remains a legend among anglers worldwide. The creek is populated with prized rainbow and brown trout and is often referred to as a fishing oasis.

L Bell Mountain Inn
1241 S. Main St., Bellevue. 788-0700.

Bell Mountain Inn is a newly remodeled, refurnished, friendly motel offering affordability and handicapped access. Although situated just fifteen miles from Sun Valley, the inn is hundreds of miles from resort town prices. All rooms include microwaves, refrigerators, coffeemakers, cable TV, and wireless high-speed Internet, while some cater to extended-stay travelers with full kitchens, living rooms, and DVD players. Guests may also use the on-site barbeque, and a nearby bike/Nordic trail is easily accessible. Dining options are conveniently close, and world-famous Silver Creek fly-fishing is just fifteen short minutes away. Whether you're staying a night, a week, or a month, Bell Mountain Inn guarantees affordable excellence!

M Cathy Erwin, Realtor®, Sun Land Investments
114 Equus Loop, Bellevue. 720-1685 or fax, 788-4636.

Cathy Erwin is a licensed realtor dedicated to helping her clients find the perfect property or dream home in the beautiful Sun Valley area. As an area resident for the past eleven years, Cathy possesses extensive knowledge about the Wood River Valley as well as the surrounding region, including the communities of Ketchum, Hailey, Bellevue, Fairfield, Carey, and Shoshone. Cathy's commitment to customer service ensures that clients' real estate dreams become a reality, and she is happy to provide customers with a range of area information, from the economy to education to the endless year-round recreational opportunities. She looks forward to having you as a Wood River Valley neighbor and guarantees that you will settle right in and love the area as much as she does!

21

Carey
Pop. 513

This small agricultural town on the banks of the Little Wood River was established in 1884 and named after James Carey, the community's first postmaster.

Gannett
Pop. 20

Gannett, founded in 1916, maintains its long history of agricultural activity. The town honors early settler, Lewis E. Gannett, who originally owned the townsite's acreage but donated it to the community. The post office was established here in 1911.

Picabo
Pop. 50

The word "picabo" is a Native American term translated in English as "come in" or "silver water." The town stands as a trading post and shipping center for livestock. The area is also known for its quality fisheries and draws hundreds of enthusiastic anglers each year.

H Magic Dam
Milepost 91 on State Hwy. 75

Completed in 1910 at a cost of $3 million, Magic Dam stores water for 89,000 acres of irrigated farms near Shoshone and Richfield.Rising 129 feet high, it is 700 feet wide. An adjacent 1,600-foot embankment with a concrete spillway helps retain more than 190,000 acre-feet of spring floodwater for summer use downstream. A four-mile desert road reaches Magic Dam, which provides fishing and recreational opportunities in a broad valley northwest of here.

T Silver Creek Preserve
3 miles west of Picabo on U.S. Hwy. 20. 788-2203 or 726-3007.

During his residence in the Wood River Valley, Ernest Hemingway's favorite fishing hole was at Silver Creek. Decades later, Hemingway's son arranged to have the natural wildlife refuge sold to the land-conservation organization, The Nature Conservancy. The organization works year-round to keep the preserve and surrounding valley in pristine condition. Today, the preserve encompasses 8,700 acres along with 25 miles of streambeds. The preserve also includes a small visitor information center offering interpretive displays and selling conservation related items.

From the informational center, visitors also have the opportunity to take a short nature walk. The trail loops down to Silver Creek and features a boardwalk that takes visitors right over the crystal clear water. The trail is appropriate for people of all ages and physical abilities.

The preserve is open to the public free of charge, but donations are highly suggested.

T Maybelle Hill
3.5 miles north of the U.S. Hwy. 20/State Hwy. 75 Intersection

Maybelle Hill, an important point on the Oregon Trail, rises to the west on State Hwy. 75. The popular Goodale's Cutoff ran just north of this hill, crossing Poverty Flat and then heading southwest on the trail towards Rock Creek.

22 *Food, Lodging*

Fairfield
Pop. 395

Situated in the shadow of the Soldier, Smoky, and Pioneer Mountains, Fairfield was formerly known as "Soldier" and exists because the railroad bypassed Soldier. Its residents relocated nearer the tracks, naming their new settlement New Soldier and later Fairfield. Its current name reflects its location in a beautiful valley lined with expansive fields of camas lilies. Early Native Americans harvested the abundant and succulent camas bulbs until the 1940s. Once a staple in the early Indian diet, the camas bulb and its violet-blue flowers have now turned Fairfield into a photography masterpiece.

H Magic Reservoir
Milepost 170.1 on U.S. Hwy. 20

Water from deep snow that falls on high mountain ridges north of here is stored each spring in this reservoir to irrigate farmland near Shoshone and Richfield.The Big Wood River flows past some hills that separate this valley from a broad plain of lava and windblown soil. This border area provides an excellent storage site for more than 190,000 acre-feet of irrigation water. Magic Reservoir, created in 1910, provides recreation opportunities and a home for fish and wildlife in a desert setting.

T Worswick Natural Hot Springs
Contact the Fairfield Ranger District at 764-3202. From Fairfield, proceed north up Soldier Creek Rd. towards Soldier Mountain Ski Area. Bear right at the fork in the road leading towards Ketchum, and proceed on Forest Rd. 095. Cross over Couch Summit, and turn right at the next intersection. Continue approximately 4 miles to the hot springs outhouse.

A local favorite, Worswick Natural Hot Springs is situated near the confluence of Worswick and Little Smoky Creeks in the Sawtooth National Forest. The idyllic setting has been featured in *National Geographic Traveler*, and the site boasts several crystal clear, sulfur-free pools dammed with logs and rocks. One pool even includes a rope swing! Visitors are urged to use caution at all times, however, as the pools vary widely in temperature with some boasting extremely hot water. The hot springs are inaccessible from November through mid-May, and prime soaking season is in late July and late October. An outhouse is available on-site for changing.

T Stapp-Soldier Creek Preserve
Contact the Nature Conservancy District Headquarters at 788-2203. Located at the base of Soldier Mountain near Fairfield.

The 120-acre Stapp-Soldier Creek Preserve is located near the base of Soldier Mountain and is open to the public free of charge year-round. Characterized by beaver ponds, cottonwood trees, and native grasslands, Soldier Creek houses the Wood River Sculpin, a rare fish species distinctive to this Idaho region. The preserve is open to bird-watching, hiking, and fishing.

T Camas Prairie Centennial Marsh Wildlife Management Area
Contact the Camas Chamber of Commerce in Fairfield at 764-2222. On U.S. Hwy. 20, drive 10 miles west of Fairfield to Wolf Ln. Bear south on Wolf Ln. to locate the marsh.

In 1987, Ducks Unlimited, the Idaho Department of Fish and Game, and The Nature Conservancy joined forces to create the Camas Prairie Centennial Marsh Wildlife Management Area. Nestled against the Bennett Hills and surrounded by mountains, the once 360-acre preserve now encompasses over 3,100 acres.

Comprised of sedges, juncos, camas, silver sagebrush, basin big sagebrush, rabbit brush, bitterbrush, and Great Basin wild rye, the preserve is a sanctuary for numerous species of birds. Sandhill cranes, blue herons, golden eagles, peregrine falcons, prairie falcons, and owls either permanently reside in the area or temporarily rest here during annual migration. In addition, pronghorn antelope and mule deer frequent the area. The preserve is open for wildlife watching year-round, and visitors are encouraged to bring spotting scopes or binoculars. The preserve is especially beautiful in mid to late spring when the camas bulbs bloom and turn the marsh into a vibrant sea of purple.

T Preis Hot Springs
Contact the Camas Chamber of Commerce in Fairfield at 764-2222.Directly south of Soldier Mountain Ski Area on Soldier Creek Rd., bear east on Forest Rd. (FR) 094. Proceed to the junction with FR 227 and continue on FR 227, ignoring all other road junctions, to locate the springs on the road's right side.

The almost hidden Preis Hot Springs is located northeast of Fairfield near the babbling Little Smoky Creek at an elevation of 5,500 feet. Although the springs are easy to miss, the area boasts outdoor relaxation ideal for one to two people. Preis Hot Springs features a sunken wooden box pool with built-in seating. Footwear is recommended, and the springs are closed October through mid-May due to seasonal road closures.

T Clovis Archaeological Site
6 miles east of Fairfield on U.S. Hwy. 20. Contact the Camas Chamber of Commerce at 764-2222.

North America's finest stockpile of Clovis projectile points was discovered here in 1967. After studying the pieces, archaeologists now believe that Bannock-Shoshone bands and their Native American ancestors have used the land for over 11,000 years.

T Minard School and Monument
Contact the Camas Chamber of Commerce at 764-2222. From Fairfield, drive 3 miles east on U.S. Hwy. 20 before bearing east on a marked gravel road. Proceed 1.9 miles to the monument on the road's west shoulder.

In the tradition of many areas across the newly expanded West, north-central Idaho was home to its fair share of country schools during the late 1800s and early 1900s. The Minard School near Fairfield is a prime example of the once rural lifestyle, and a monument there memorializes the school and its dedicated teachers.

Jack Frostenson, majoring in Architecture, constructed the memorial complete with a triangular, shingled plywood roof shelter. Although Jack never went to the Minard School, his grandfather was a trustee, and his father, uncle, aunts, brother, sister, and cousins all attended. Jack's father also served on the schoolboard, and his mother and two aunts served as Minard teachers.

The monument today offers a touching dedication to the teachers who educated area children and lists the names of teachers who worked at Minard during the years of 1909 to 1948. The monument also includes the old school bell and pitcher pump. Visitors will also find bricks from the chimney placed in the walkway around the monument, while the school itself is visible to the southwest.

Section 4

CENTRAL AREA INCLUDING KETCHUM, SUN VALLEY, SALMON, ARCO, AND CHALLIS

V Mormon Reservoir
West of Fairfield off U.S. Hwy. 20

Nestled near the Camas Prairie just a few minutes from Fairfield, Mormon Reservoir is known as a sportsman's paradise. Geese and ducks frequent the area, while rainbow trout weighing up to five pounds are continuously reeled in at the reservoir's south end. Anglers must respect the reservoir's daily catch limit of two bags.

V Magic Reservoir
East of Fairfield off U.S. Hwy. 20

Magic Reservoir, created in 1910, is located in the heart of the Camas Prairie only a few miles east of Fairfield. The five-mile long reservoir is renowned for its five-pound rainbow trout with brown trout regularly weighing twelve pounds or more. During autumn, the area is a hunting hot-spot for upland game bird and waterfowl. The reservoir also boasts boat ramps, fishing lodges, and primitive camping areas.

V Soldier Mountain Ski Area
12 miles north of Fairfield on Soldier Creek Rd. 764-2526 or 764-2327.

An economic alternative to the nearby pricier Sun Valley Resort, Soldier Mountain Ski Area offers thirty-six groomed runs serviced by two double chairs, one rope tow, and one handle tow. The hill boasts a 1,400-foot maximum vertical drop, and a snowboarding park is available. In addition to traditional skiing, the mountain offers cat skiing, rentals, lessons, and a day lodge that serves breakfast, lunch, and dinner. Soldier Mountain is generally open December to April depending on snow conditions.

V Soldier Mountain Ranch Nordic Ski Trail
700 W. Fairfield N., Fairfield. 764-2506.

Soldier Mountain Ranch designs a winter wonderland for Nordic skiers each winter. The ranch regularly grooms its golf course to create approximately 5.5 miles of finely maintained cross-country trails. Trails range from beginner to advanced to accommodate skiers of all abilities, and a day lodge is available to all users. The ranch charges a $5 Nordic fee and is open for skiing Wednesday through Sunday from 9 AM to 5 PM.

V Fairfield Area Snowmobile Trails
Contact the Fairfield Ranger District at 764-3202.

Fairfield is quickly establishing itself as an Idaho must-see for snowmobilers. Centrally nestled between three snowmobiling park and trail access areas, the city of Fairfield oversees grooming for more than 200 miles of trails. New and expanded groomed trails are added each winter, and off-trail exploration opportunities are endless. Ranging in elevation from 5,000 to 10,000 feet, the trails stretch across the wide-open Camas Prairie to the Smokey Mountains and offer rides for beginners to experts. The free trail system is generally accessible from late November to April, and a warming hut is available at the Well Summit Family Area.

23 Limited Services

Corral
Pop. 15

Interestingly, this little village has been in six different counties during its existence. Today it lies within Camas County. Corral was named after the abundance of natural [livestock] corrals that white settlers discovered in the area and along Corral Creek.

Hill City
Pop. 30

A man named Mr. Nicklewaite founded this small community when he first learned that the Oregon Short Line Railroad was building a line through the area. The first name given to the town was Prairie, for Camas Prairie, but was later changed to Hill City in recognition of the Bennett Mountain Hills located nearby. Hill City became the railroad line's terminus in 1911 as it traveled northwest from Richland across the Camas Prairie. A post office was established a year later.

H Bannock War
Milepost 148.5 on U.S. Hwy. 20

Angered by encroachment of white men on Camas Prairie lands, which had been guaranteed to the Bannock Indians by treaty, Buffalo Horn's Band went to war May 30, 1878. The war started in June on the Camas Prairie and spread to central Oregon. The Indians were returning to their reservation at Fort Hall. Harried from the island, they soon lost the pursuing troops in rough country north of here. This was the last real battle of the war.

V Wilson Flat Trails
Contact the Fairfield Ranger District at 764-3202. From Fairfield, travel west on U.S. Hwy. 20 to the junction with Forest Road (FR) 134. Bear north on FR 134, continue 5 miles, cross over a dam, and proceed another 2 miles to the Wilson Flat Trailhead.

Situated near the Anderson Ranch Dam in the Boise National Forest, the Wilson Flat Trail system encompasses eleven miles of ATV loop trails. A variety of vegetation, including sagebrush, quaking aspens, and evergreen, line the canyon trails, and users will find outstanding vistas of the Anderson Ranch Reservoir and the South Fork of the Boise River.

V Fun Valley Snowmobile Trail
Contact the Fairfield Ranger District at 764-3202. Located between Fairfield and Mountain Home on U.S. Hwy. 20.

Appropriately named, the Fun Valley Snowmobile Trail provides fund and excitement for the whole family. Beginning at the Maclomson parking area, Fun Valley boasts several popular trails, including Trinity Lakes, Pfifer Creek, Pine, and Featherville. Idaho's Off-Road Motor Vehicle program partially manages the free area that is accessible from December through March.layl

SCENIC DRIVES

Lewis & Clark Expedition in Lemhi County
Retrace the Lewis & Clark Expedition Through Lemhi County • August 12 to September 3, 1805
Appointed by President Thomas Jefferson, Captains Meriwether Lewis and William Clark were charged with finding a navigable water route to the Pacific Coast. Departing Wood River, Illinois in May 1804, the expedition traveled for fifteen months to reach the headwaters of the Missouri River, then crossed the Continental Divide and entered the Lemhi Valley on August 12, 1805.

The Corps of Discovery faced many perils in this region. Stricken by limited provisions with winter fast approaching, the party transported mountains of canvas, wood, and iron gear. After paddling the length of the Missouri River, the treacherous current of the Salmon River and the steep, crumbly surrounding mountains proved to be formidable obstacles.

Lewis with three men led an Advance Party over Lemhi Pass and encountered the Lemhi Shoshoni Nation. Convincing the Shoshoni that the small party posed no threat to their well being, they agreed to accompany Lewis' party back over the pass and to assist the main party.

Clark led the Reconnaissance Party into the valley to explore the feasibility of navigating the Salmon River. Faced with the strong possibility of drowning should their flimsy canoes be swept into the rocks by the swift current, the party made a critical decision changing the course of the expedition and opted for a somewhat less hazardous, but equally difficult dry-land route.

Encamped in Montana, Lewis sorted supplies necessary for the Portage Party, then joined Clark's party. Winter now only weeks away, the Entire Expedition grew anxious to get to the Pacific Coast.

Imagine the hardships faced by these explorers as they trekked through the Lemhi and Salmon River Valleys, and uncover places where you can retrace Lewis and Clark's steps in areas where little has changed since they were here.

1) Sacajawea Memorial Camp - 0.2 mile, Motorway, (within Montana)
Headwaters of the Missouri River, Lewis writes in his journal August 12, "...Here I haulted...and rested myself, two miles below McNeal had exultingly stood with afoot on each side of this little rivulet and thanked his god that he had lived to bestride the mighty & heretofore deemed endless Missouri."

2) Lemhi Pass/Continental Divide - Mile 26.0, Motorway
The Advance Party were the first white men to cross Lemhi Pass (7,339'), a Shoshoni Indian hunting trail, on August 12, 1805.

3) First Taste of The Columbia River - Mile 27.5, Motorway
Lewis records their entry into Idaho "...I now descended the mountain about 3/4 of a mile which I found much steeper than on the opposite side, to a handsome bold running Creek of cold Clear water. here I first tasted the water of the great Columbia river..."

4) Lewis & Clark Trail Route - Mile 27.9, Motorway
Captain Lewis, leading the Advance Party of three men, passed through this area August 12. Captain Clark with 11 men, Sacajawea, and her husband Charbonneau, followed on August 19, 1805.

5) First Idaho Campsite - Trail Access at Mile 29.5, Motorway (Hike 0.75 Miles)
"...we found a sufficient quantity of dry willow brush for fuel, here we encamped for the night having traveled about 20 Miles." -Lewis, August 12, 1805

6) First View - Valley Floor - Trail Access at Mile 29.5, Motorway
On August 13, Lewis writes in his journal, "...a deep valley appeared to our left at the base of a high range of mountains which extended from S.E. to N.W. (Lemhi Range) having their sides better clad with pine timber than we had been accustomed to see the mountains and their tops were also partially covered with snow."

7) Clark campsite - Trail Access at Mile 29.5, Motorway
Captain Clark, with the Reconnaissance Party, headed for the Salmon River to make canoes. He camped on Pattee Creek on August 19, 1805.

8) Motorway Tour Kiosk - Mile 3.7, Motorway
This site welcomes you to Sacajawea's birthplace and serves as the jump-off point for the 39-mile loop road commemorating that expedition, this is the meeting place of two vastly different cultures which were to be forever changed.

9) Meeting of Two Cultures - Mile 4.1 - 0.2 miles on Alkali Flat Road
Lewis describes the historic and dramatic meeting of the two cultures for the first time as he was approaching their encampment near Kenney Creek. "...we had proceeded about four miles a wavy plain..." -Lewis, August 13, 1805

As Lewis' Advance Party traveled along the plain parallel to the river bottom he writes, "...we saw two women, a man and some dogs on an eminence immediately before us... two of them after a few minutes set down as if to wait our arrival we continued our usual pace...when we had arrived within half a mile of them I directed the party to halt and leaving my pack and rifle I took the flag which I unfurled and advanced singly toward them the women soon disappeared behind the hill, the man continued untill I arrived within a hundred yards of him and then likewise absconded." When Lewis surprised Shoshoni women later that day, he describes the encounter. "I now painted their tawny cheeks with some vermillion which with this nation is emblematic of peace." At a later meeting with about 60 warriors, he tells of the welcome, "...these men embraced me very affectionately...by puting their left arm over you wright sholder clasping your back, while they apply their left cheek to yours..."

10) Flag Unfurling Sign - Mile 115.8, State Hwy. 28, Tendoy
Upon reaching Lemhi Pass, 12 miles east of here, Lewis unfurled the American flag for the first time west of the Rockies on August 13, 1805. Sparked by Lewis and Clark crossing the Continental Divide, westward expansion brought a great influx of explorers, missionaries, miners, and settlers and with them great changes for those people already here.

11) Upper Village - Mile 120.5, State Hwy. 28, Look Northeast
August 13, Lewis and his advanced party arrived at this site after their dramatic meeting with the Shoshoni. Escorted by Chief Cameahwait and about 60 warriors, Lewis writes, "...on our arrival at their encampment on the river...at the distance of 4 Ms. from where we had first met them they introduced us to a londge made of willow brush and an old leather lodge which had been prepared for our reception by the young men..."

12) Upper Village II - Mile 120.2, State Hwy. 28, Look North
August 20, Clark and the Reconnaissance Party reached this village. Sergeant Gass, an expedition member, chronicles "We...travelled to a village of the Indians on the bank...At this place there are about 25 lodges made of willow bushes. They are the poorest and most miserable nation I ever beheld; having scarcely anything to subsist on, except berries and a few fish... They have a great many fine horses, and nothing more; and on account of these (the horses) they are much harassed by other nations." Gass continues, "Here we procured a guide, (Old Toby) and left our interpreters to go on with the natives, and assist Captain Lewis and his party to bring on the baggage..."

13) Wayside Sign - Mile 120.0, State Hwy. 28
Stone monument commemorating the Lewis and Clark Expedition.

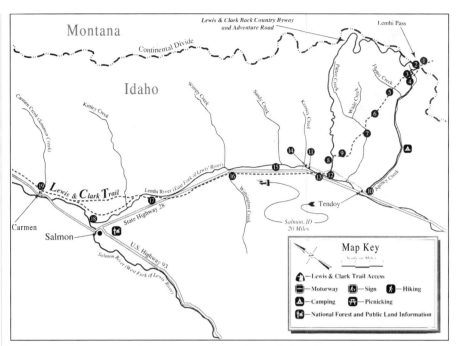

14) Sacajawea Monument - Mile 120.5, State Hwy. 28, North 0.5 Miles
Metal plaque celebrating the birthplace of Sacajawea, the Shoshoni woman who accompanied Lewis and Clark on their expedition.

15) Famed Interpreter - Mile 122.5, State Hwy. 28
Sacajawea returned to her homeland in the Lemhi Valley in 1805 as a member of the Lewis and Clark party. She was reunited with her family after being abducted by an Assiniboine war party and served as liason between her people and the expedition.

16) Withington Creek Camp - MP 125.9, State Hwy. 28
Clark with an Indian guide crossed over the Lemhi River and camped at Withington Creek. Sergeant Gass recalls "...Captain Clarke proceeded... about 8 miles and encamped on a fine spring, five of the Indians came and stayed with us during the night."

17) Fish Weir Village - Mile 131.4, State Highway 28
Site of a fish weir across the Lemhi River where the Shoshoni were able to trap enough Salmon for their subsistence and provide the expedition with as much broiled and dried salmon as they could eat, as well as dried chokecherries. Clark stopped here the 21st and writes, "...Those Indians are mild in their disposition appear Sincere in their friendship, puntial, and decided kind with what they have, to Spare ...The women are held more Sacred...and appear to have an equal Shere in all Conversation, ...their boeys & Girls are also admited to Speak except in Councils, the women doe all the drugery except fishing and takeing care of the horses, which the men apr. to take upon themselves."

18) Forks of Louis's River - Mile 306.0, U.S. Hwy. 93
Later at Tower Bluffs Clark reflects, "...I shall injustice to Capt. Lewis who was the first white man ever on this fork of the Columbia Call this Louis's river." (How do you spell Lewis? Clark apparently forgets.) His description continues, "The Westerley fork of the Columbia River (the Salmon River) is double the Size of the Easterley fork (Lemhi River) & below those forks the river is 100 yards wide, it is verry rapid & Sholey water

Clear but little timber." Clark goes on, "the forks of this river is famous as a gig fishery and is much resorted by the Natives."

19) Sammon Creek - Mile 309.9, U.S. Hwy. 93
Clark in his August 21, 1805 journal entry describes Sammon Creek (now known as Carmen Creek), "...Passed a large Creek which fall in on the right Side 6 miles below the forks a road passed up this Creek & to the Missouri."
Sergeant Gass adds, "In this branch we shot a salmon about 6 pounds weight."

20) The Bluff - Mile 315.1, U.S. Highway 93
On August 21, Clark and party first reached the Salmon River and camped near this spot by the bluff near the mouth of Tower Creek. "...This Clift is of a redish brown Colour, the rocks which fall from it is a dark flint tinged with that Colour. Some Gullies of white Sand Stone and Sand fine & white as Snow..."

21) Tower Creek/Pirimids-Mile 315.7, U.S. Hwy. 93
On August 31 the Expedition travelled up Tower Creek. Clark wrote, "...We proceeded on the road on which I had deceded as far as the 1st run below & left the road...& Encamped in Some old lodjes at the place the road leaves the Creek and ascends the high Country...passed remarkable rock resembling pirimids on the Left side."

22) Four Mountain Spur Crossing - Mile 319.1, U.S. Hwy. 93
Encountering rugged terrain, Lewis serves as scribe for Clark's account of the ordeal: "we set out early and passed...the points of four mountains which were high steep and rocky. the mountains are so steep that it is almost incredible to mention that horses had passed them. our road in many places lay over the sharp fragments of rocks which had fall from the mountains and lay in confused heaps for miles together, yet not withstanding our horsed traveled barefoot over them as fast as we could..." Notice the mountain spurs to the north and south.

23) Fourth Of July Creek - Mile 321.0, U.S. Hwy. 93
Looking south, you can see the descent from the mountain spur is an easy route compared to the northern spur. Faced with the proposition of swimming the river, the Reconnaissance Party climbed out of the canyon again over the difficult

WATERFALLS

Napias Creek Falls
Take U.S. Highway 93; merge onto Williams Creek Road #021 (5 miles south of Salmon) and follow for 21.6 miles
Contained in the Salmon National Forest's Salmon/Cobalt Ranger District, Napias Creek Falls cascades 70 feet and provides roadside views. Reflecting the area's 1866 gold rush history in its name, Napias Creek Falls means "money" in Shoshoni.

Fountain Creek Falls
Take U.S. Highway 93; exit west at North Fork onto Salmon River Road; drive westward 40.7 miles (the falls are located near Cache Bar Camp)
Descending in tiers 35 to 50 feet, Fountain Creek tumbles off a canyon wall to form this cataract within the Salmon National Forest. Fountain Creek Falls is accessible to motorists and sits at an elevation of 3,200 feet with a small watershed.

North Fork Falls
Take Scenic Route 75 north of Ketchum until reaching the recreation area headquarters in approximately 8 miles; here, merge north (right) onto North Fork Road #146; visitors are advised to check stream levels from the East Fork Big Wood River as it flows across the road in 3.5 miles; if the road is passable, proceed 1.5 miles and park at the trailhead for the North Fork Trail #115
Descending in segments as the North Fork Big Wood River divides, North Fork Falls is located within the Sawtooth National Recreation Area. Although grizzly bears inhabit the Sawtooth Mountains, hikers should not be deterred from visiting this cataract's 50 to 75 foot plummet. To begin, hike along Trail #115 until reaching Trail #128. Here, turn left (northwest) and follow the moderately difficult Trail #128 for 4 miles. The trail ascends the canyon, providing visitors with views of the falls on the canyon floor.

Lady Face Falls and Bridal Veil Falls
Take Scenic Route 21 5 miles northwest of Stanley; at the Stanley Lake Road #455, turn left and proceed 3.5 miles to Inlet Camp; locate the Stanley Lake Creek Trail #640 near the campground's Area B and park at the trailhead
Located within the Sawtooth Mountains of the Sawtooth National Recreation Area, both Lady Face Falls and Bridal Veil Falls require visitors to take a moderate to difficult day hike. However, both offer unique scenery surrounded by wilderness. To access the 6,680-foot elevation of Lady Face Falls, hike along Stanley Lake Trail for 2.6 miles. Although the first 2 miles is fairly effortless, the ascent steepens as you continue to hike. In another 0.5 mile, locate a sign facing the opposite direction pointing to the 50 to 75 foot plunge of Lady Face Falls. Follow the ridge path 0.1-mile to find a rim view of this waterfall as it descends into a basin below.

For those wishing to take a more difficult hike, continue on Stanley Lake Trail #640 past Lady Face Falls for 1.2 miles. Locate a sign marking Bridal Veil Falls where you will find a distant view of the falls' 120 to 160 foot tiered cascade from Hanson Lakes.

Goat Falls
Drive along Scenic Route 21 2.3 miles west of Stanley; merge onto Iron Creek Road #619 and continue 6 miles to a parking area near the Alpine Lake/Sawtooth Lake Trail #640
Found at an elevation of 8,100 feet within the Sawtooth Mountains, Goat Falls is rumored to offer the most breathtaking scenery of all waterfalls within the Sawtooth National Recreation Area. Goat Falls plummets 250 to 300 feet down a mountainside and broadens near the end of its descent. Distant views of the waterfall are possible along Scenic Route 21, but visitors can gain up-close access by taking a fairly difficult day hike. At the trailhead, hike along this trail for 1 mile and then proceed east (left) at the Alpine Trail #528 junction. Continue another moderately difficult 2.5 miles to reach the falls' viewing area.

Goat Creek Falls, Fern Falls, and Smith Falls
Access both falls by taking Scenic Route 21, exiting at the Grandjean Camp road; proceed along this gravel road 8 miles and park at the South Fork Trailhead
Cascading in a small series of steps, these waterfalls are located on the western side of the Sawtooth Wilderness area in the Sawtooth National Recreation Area. All three cataracts require visitors to take difficult hikes, and a pair of strong hiking boots is recommended at all times.

Goat Creek Falls is situated at an elevation of 5,260 feet and descends 50 feet into the wilderness. To begin, wind along the South Fork Payette River while hiking on South Fork Trail #452 for 1.3 miles. At the junction for Baron Creek Trail #101, remain on Trail #452 and hike 1.2 miles further to Goat Creek. Climb upstream to view this fall's medium watershed. To reach Fern Falls' 6,380-foot elevation, visitors must be ready for a difficult hike and an overnight stay in the wilderness. For those with no physical limitations, continue hiking past Goat Creek Falls for 7.5 miles along South Fork Trail #452. With a large watershed, Fern Falls descends 30 feet in a tier from the South Fork Payette River. To reach Smith Falls, proceed along Trail #452 past Fern Falls. In approximately 1 mile, backpackers will reach Elk Lake. Continue another 3.5 miles to access Smith Falls directly past the South Fork Payette River trail crossing. At this point, visitors are 14.5 miles from the trailhead.

Tohobit Creek Falls, Warbonnet Falls, and Baron Creek Falls
To reach the trailheads for all three falls, drive along Scenic Route 21 and turn off at the gravel access road for Grandjean Camp; proceed 8 miles to a parking area at the foot of the trailhead and begin ascending South Fork Trail #452
This triplet of waterfalls within the Sawtooth Wilderness of the Sawtooth National Recreation Area offers outstanding scenery for those visitors wishing to take a difficult hike where camping overnight is recommended. After hiking 1.2 miles, turn left onto Baron Creek Trail #101 and continue 7 miles. Tohobit Creek Falls is the first visible cataract. Maintaining considerable contact with a bedrock surface, Tohobit Creek Falls descends into the Baron Creek Valley sculpted during the Ice Age. Look across the canyon from the trail to view this waterfall.

To reach the 7,120 foot elevation of Warbonnet Falls, continue hiking along Baron Creek Trail #101 1 mile past Tohobit Creek Falls. Gaze cross-canyon from the trail to view an unnamed stream form Warbonnet Falls as it plummets into a valley below.

Baron Creek Falls may offer the best scenery of all three cataracts in this area. At an elevation of 7,500 feet, Baron Creek tumbles 50 feet in multiple threads across glacial rock fragments. Taking Baron Creek Trail #101, hike 1 mile past Warbonnet Falls to reach a viewing area for this waterfall. At this point, backpackers are approximately 10.2 miles from the trailhead, and an overnight stay is highly suggested near this cataract or further up the trail near Baron Lakes.

Dagger Falls, Velvet Falls, Tappen Falls, Veil Falls, and Forge Creek Falls
Rafters and kayakers can locate Dagger Falls 20 miles northwest of Stanley, ID; from Scenic Route 21, turn onto Forest Road #579 and drive approximately 10 miles; at the junction for Forest Road #568, bear right and head 13 miles to the launch ramp located at the base of Dagger Falls; visitors should note that access is easiest from early June through early September
This set of cataracts is designed for water enthusiasts and is recommended only for experienced kayakers and rafters or visitors on a guided whitewater trip. Found along the Middle Fork Salmon River, also dubbed "The River of No Return," these falls possess Class III – V rapids. For those ready for adventure, however, the river and various falls provide visitors with awe-inspiring scenery.

Dagger Falls is situated on Boundary Creek at an elevation of 5,800 feet. With several cascades, Dagger Falls also includes a fish ladder built to assist migrating salmon. Velvet Falls tumbles downstream five and one-half miles from Dagger Falls. The deceptively large cataract spans most of the Middle Fork Salmon River and is most easily accessed by raft. However, it is rumored that Velvet Falls can be located on land by hiking along a rough trail. Tappen Falls waits for river enthusiasts nearly 50 miles downstream of Velvet Falls. Located in the Frank Church River of No Return Wilderness, Tappen Falls is characterized by a string of four Class III rapids that tosses visitors along the river for approximately 1 mile. Continuing further into the Frank Church River of No Return Wilderness, locate Veil Falls near the 80-mile mark of raft trips beginning at Dagger Falls. After running Veil Rapids, park your boat on the shoreline and hike to Veil Falls. This cataract, running along Waterfall Creek at the union of two canyons, tumbles nearly 1,000 feet. Forge Creek Falls occurs further downstream, but topographic maps indicate that this cataract is inaccessible.

Salmon Falls and Mallard Creek Falls
For interested rafters, take U.S. Highway 93, exiting west at North Fork and merging westward onto Salmon River Road; in approximately 18 miles, reach Shoup, ID and continue an additional 22.2 miles to Cache Bar Camp; proceed 4 miles to the road's end at Corn Creek Camp
Experienced water enthusiasts will ride past massive boulders on white-capped waves before reaching Salmon Falls on the North Fork Salmon River. Novice boaters are urged to avoid this cataract as the waterfall's rapids are rated Class

V on the international six-point rating scale. After reaching Corn Creek Camp, begin rafting and reach Salmon Falls in 1.9 miles. Mallard Creek Falls also lies within the Salmon National Forest. However, topographic maps illustrate that this cataract is unreachable.

The following Idaho waterfalls are also located in this section with limited directions access available:

Upper Goat Greek Falls and Scenic Creek Falls
Upper Goat Creek Falls, located in the same general area as Smith Falls in the Sawtooth National Recreation Area, is not accessible according to topographic maps. Scenic Creek Falls is located in another area of the Sawtooth National Recreation Area. Maps suggest that an unnamed trail is found in the same vicinity as this cataract, but access may be limited.

Trail Creek Falls and Boulder Falls
Informally named by locals of Blaine County, Trail Creek Falls tumbles along Trail Creek in south central Idaho. Topographic maps imply that no trail access to the cataract is available. Boulder Falls, located in the same general vicinity inside the Sawtooth National Recreation Area, also offers hopeful sightseers no known road or trail access.

Devlin Falls
Take U.S. Highway 93 5 miles south of Salmon, ID and merge onto Williams Creek Road #021; drive along Williams Creek Road for 25 miles and continue past Leesburg
Devlin Falls offers adventurous visitors a glimpse of 1860's gold rush history. Located along Napais Creek in Lemhi County, Devlin Falls is found near the historic townsite of Leesburg (now a small mining outpost) that was once home to 7,000 hopeful gold seekers. Access to Devlin Falls beyond this point is uncertain, but four-wheel drive is strongly recommended in the area.

East Pass Creek Falls
The small cascade of East Pass Creek Falls is situated within the Salmon-Challis National Forest in Custer County. No motorized vehicles are allowed in the area. To reach the cataract, follow various wild game trails along East Pass Creek Trail #188 for 2 miles. Topographic maps imply that the cataract falls adjacent to the trail.

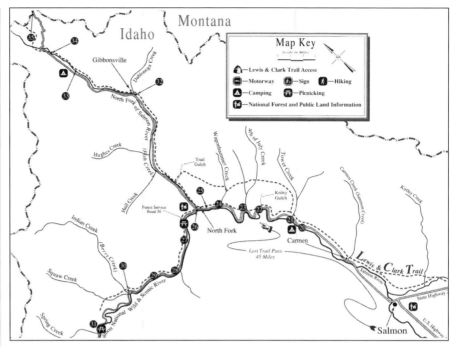

route you can see. Clark writes in his journal August 22, 1805, "...it is incrediable to describe the rocks in maney places loose & sliped from those mountains and is a (Solid) bed of rugid loose white and dark brown loose rock for miles."

24) Wagonhammer Springs - Mile 324.4, U.S. Hwy. 93
The trail Lewis and Clark took can be reached by walking approximately two miles up Wagonhammer Creek to the mouth of Thompson Gulch; follow marked trail to left. The trail is marked from that point to its return to the North Fork of the Salmon River at Trail Gulch, a distance of approximately six miles. You can hike a portion of the trail that remains virtually as it was when traveled by the expedition. This day hike is best in cooler weather.

25) Salmon River Reconnaissance Sign - Mile 326.2, U.S. Highway 93
Hoping for a navigable route to the Pacific, Clark explored the first few miles of the rugged Salmon River Canyon below here (North Fork) late in August. His small advance party camped near this location.

26) Fish Creek Village - Mile 326.4, U.S. Hwy. 93
Fish Creek, now known as the North Fork of the Salmon River, was the site of a Shoshoni village, which is described by Clark in his journal for August 22, 1805. "...Several families of Indians were encamped and had Several Scaffolds of fish & buries drying we allarmed them verry much as they knew nothing of a white man being in their Countrey, and at the time we approached their lodges which was in a thick place of bushes-my guiedes were behind.- They offered every thing they possessed (which was verry littl) to us, Some run off and hid in the bushes... I gave a fiew Small articles to those fritened people which added verry much to their pasification…"

27) Dreadful Narrows - Mile 3.6, Forest Road 30 - Deadwater Picnic Area
August 23, Sergeant Gass writes in his journal, "We proceeded down the river through dreadful narrows, (starts about 1 1/2 miles upstream from this point) where the rocks were in some places breast high, and no path or trail of any kind..."

28) Sore Horse Feet Camp - Mile 6.0, Forest Rd. 30
Clark writes in his journal, "...I deturmined to delay the party here with my guide and three men proceed on down to examine if the river continued bad or was practiable..." Sergeant Gass writes August 24, 1805, "...The river at this place is so confined by the mountains that it is not more than 20 yards wide, and very rapid. The mountains on the side are not less than 1000 feet high and very steep. There are a few pines growing on them. We caught some small fish to-day, and our hunters killed 5 prairie fowls. These were all we had to subsist on. At 1 o'clock Captain Clarke and his party returned after having been down the river about 12 miles..."
Lewis recalls Clark's journey, "...at the distance of four miles he arrived at the river and the rocks were here so steep and juted into the river such

manner that there was no other alternative but passing through the river, this he attempted with success tho' water was so deep for a short distance as to swim the horses and was very rapid; he continued his rout one mile along the edge of the river under this steep Clift to a little bottom…

29) Injured Leg Canyon - Mile 7.3, Forest Road 30
August 23, 1805. Clark writes in his journal, "...The River from the place I left my party to this Creek is almost one continued rapid... the passage of either with Canoes is entirely impossable, as the water is Confined between hugh Rocks & the Current beeting from one against another...at one of those rapids the mountains Close So Clost as to prevent a possibility of a portage with great labour...the others may be passed by takeing every thing over Slipery rocks, and the Smaller ones Passed by letting down the Canoes empty with Cords, as running them would certainly be productive of the loss of Some Canoes..." While returning to camp, Captain Clark fell from a rock and injured one of his legs.

30) Berry Creek - Mile 10.8, Forest Road 30
Lewis' journal reflects Clark's journey; August 23, 1805, "...a plain indian road led up this (Indian) creek which the guide informed him (Clark) led to a large river that ran to the North, and was frequented by another nation who occasionally visited this river for the purpose of taking fish...Cap. C... caught some smallfish, on which, with the addition of some berries, they dined...after dinner Capt. C. continued his rout down the river and at 1/2 a mile pased another creek (Squaw Creek)...leaving the creek on the wright he passed over a ridge, and at the distance of a mile arrived at the river where it passes through a well timbered bottom of about eighty acres of land..."

31) Final Observation of the River Canyon - Mile 16.5, Forest Road 30
August 23, Clark recalls, "...passed over a gap in the Mounts. from the top of which I could See the hollers of the river for 20 miles to a verry high Mountain on the left, at which place my guide made Signs that the bad part...of the river Comsd. and much worst than any I Saw..."

Lewis, in his journal, reviews why Clark decided to abandon his pursuit of the river route "...after the river reached this mountain it continued it's rout to the North between high and perpendicular rocks, roling foaming and beating against innumerable rocks which crouded it's channel; that then it penetrated the mountain through a narrow gap leaving a perpendicular rock on either side as high as the top of the mountain which he beheld. that the river here making a bend they could not see through the mountain, and as it was impossible to decend the river or clamber over that vast mountain covered with eternal snow, neither himself (Toby) no', any of his nation had ever been lower in this direction..."

From this point, one can see the ridge (about 1 mile northeast), where Clark was standing when he determined it was truly an impassable canyon.

32) Gibbonsville - Mile 337.2, U.S. Highway 93
Clark writes, September 2, 1805, "...Crossed a large fork from the right and one from the left, and at 8 mile left the roade on which we were pursuing and which leads over to the Missouri (Dahlonega Creek); and proseeded up a West fork...thro' thickets in which we were obliged to Cut a road, over rockey hill Sides where our horses were in pitial danger of Slipping to Ther certain destruction..."

33) Deep Creek - Mile 341.3, U.S. Highway 93
September 2, Lewis and Clark proceeded with much difficulty up the North Fork. Some authorities believe this may have been the most difficult terrain encountered by the expedition. They camped on the west side of the river in this vicinity.

34) Lewis and Clark/Last Ascent - Mile 345.5, U.S. Highway 93
Seeking a route through Idaho's mountain barrier, the Entire Expedition left the canyon and climbed a high ridge reaching the Bitterroot Valley on September 4. Without a trail, Toby, their Shoshoni guide, led them along a difficult ridgetop divide over high peaks, which are visible to the north.

35) Lost Trail Pass - Mile 351.1, U.S. Highway 93
The Lewis and Clark expedition likely lost the trail to this pass. They camped two miles west of here the night of September 3.

From here, the Lewis and Clark Expedition proceeded down the Bitterroot River Valley, back into Idaho and finally down the Columbia River. They reached the Pacific Ocean November, 1805.

Forever Changed
Findings from the Lewis and Clark Expedition were instrumental to westward expansion. Adventurers and scientists, Lewis and Clark recorded detailed descriptions of the plant, animal, geographic, and cultural elements of their trip.

Hoping to find a navigable route down the Salmon River, Clark was forced to retrace his steps opting for a safer, land-based route after viewing the "River of No Return." Although not "entirely impassable", the Salmon River to this day provides adventure to modern-day explorers.

Reprinted from Idaho Department of Transportation brochure

Sacajawea Historic Byway
Sacajawea, an "Agaidika" Shoshone woman born around 1788, is known around the world as a trusted and valuable member of the famed Lewis and Clark Corps of Discovery. A lesser-known fact, however, is her historical tie to Idaho's Lemhi Valley where she was born and raised until the age of twelve. Captured by the Arikira Indians and

forced to live among them in the Mandan Villages of North Dakota, Sacajawea would not see her home again until becoming part of the Corps of Discovery in 1805. It was during this expedition that she would help Lewis and Clark find the Salmon River and revisit her people.

This passage through the high country of eastern Idaho offers a wealth of engaging stories, many of them considered historical legacies of Idaho and beyond. Found here are fossils of the extinct North American (or Pliestocene) lion, Native American rock art, the compelling stories of the Lemhi-Shoshone people, the Lewis and Clark expedition's passage through Sacajawea's homeland, the flight of the Nez Perce, the Reverend Samuel Parker, Fort Lemhi, the legacy of Chief Tendoy, stage routes and rail lines that served the mining boom of the late 1800s, and much more. Come discover for yourself what makes Sacajawea Historic Byway such a legacy.

The byway begins at the intersection of Interstate 15 and Idaho 33 at Exit 143, follows Idaho 33 about 12 miles west to its junction with Idaho 28 northwest for 120 miles to Salmon, Idaho. Idaho 33 is a straight and flat road. Speed is limited through the towns of Terreton and Mud Lake. Idaho 28 is mostly straight, with some hills as you gradually make your way over Gilmore Summit, a low mountain pass at 7,186 feet. Watch for icy conditions and snowdrifts in winter. Both are two-lane roads, with areas for passing. The scenic byway can be seen year round. Summer months afford easier travel, while spectacular autumn colors are best viewed late September through October. Travelers should allow at least 2.5 hours for this 132-mile trip.

Reprinted from Idaho Department of Transportation brochure

Salmon River Scenic Byway
The northern end of the Salmon River Scenic Byway begins on the Montana border at the Lost Trail Pass (elevation 6,995 feet). Lewis and Clark came this way in 1805, and the spectacular view from this vantage point has changed little since that famous exploration of the West two centuries ago. The route follows the Salmon River – also called the River of No Return – through Salmon-Challis National Forest through the historic city of Salmon. The river and its forks serve as important natural pathways into Idaho's rugged backcountry. The deer, elk, and moose that often graze along the hills and meadows that line this road provide a glimpse of the wild country beyond.

Along the way, the town of Challis and the Land of the Yankee Fork Historic Area are just two points of interest, the latter being among Idaho's most famous mining areas. And as you head southwest along Idaho 75 toward Stanley, you'll begin to see glimpses of the majestic Sawtooth Mountains ahead before beholding their full splendor as you drop into town.

The byway begins at the Montana state line south on U.S. 93 to Challis, then west to Stanley on Idaho 75. The byway is a two-lane road with no passing lanes and some 25-mph curves. Best weather for travel is April to November, although access to the backcountry is best from July to October. Travelers should allow at least 3.5 hours for this 161.7-mile trip.

Reprinted from Idaho Department of Transportation brochure

Sawtooth Scenic Byway
The Sawtooth Scenic Byway has the distinction of being the 100th National Forest Scenic Byway. Beginning in Shoshone, the southern leg of the

byway features the new Black Magic Canyon geological attraction. The route then rolls north through fertile agricultural land to the resort towns of Hailey, Ketchum, and Sun Valley.

From there, the road carves its way through the Boulder Mountains to Galena Pass, showcasing the ridge of the Sawtooth Mountains. Beyond, the rocks and woodlands of the rugged Sawtooth National Recreation Area are packed with rivers, streams, and 300 alpine lakes, providing top-notch venues for a variety of year-round activities. Wildlife watchers should stay alert; the 756,000-acre recreational area is home to many species of wildlife, including pronghorn antelope, deer, elk, bear, and wolves.

The northern tip of the byway terminates in Stanley, where the Sawtooth meets the Ponderosa Pine and Salmon River Scenic Byways. So no matter which way you drive in or out, you're in for a treat.

The byway follows Idaho 75 north to Stanley from Shoshone. This is a two-lane road with some passing lanes. The 15-mile section over Galena Summit is winding with 5 to 6 percent grades. Winter weather can be severe. Check conditions before traveling. Travelers should allow at least 3 hours for this 115.7-mile trip.

Reprinted from Idaho Department of Transportation brochure

Lewis and Clark National Backcountry Byway and Adventure Road
This is the place where the discovery of the Northwest began. The stands of fir and pine trees hugging the skyline, the high mountain meadows, and the rolling brown hills look much the same today as when Meriwether Lewis and William Clark journeyed to the crest of Lemhi Pass late in the summer of 1805.

It's easy to imagine the presence of those early-day explorers as you travel the Lewis and Clark Backcountry Byway and Adventure Road. You'll see the place where the expedition unfurled the flag of the United States for the first time west of the Rocky Mountains, laying claim to the Pacific Northwest for the young, expanding country.

At the top of Lemhi Pass is the Sacajawea Memorial, a place to learn more of this remarkable woman who served as a guide and interpreter for Lewis and Clark. It is also believed she was born in Lemhi Valley.

The route also follows portions of the Lewis and Clark National Historic Trail and provides access to where the explorers reached the headwaters of the Missouri River. Not all the sights are tied to history. You'll be treated to spectacular vistas of the river valleys below – the Salmon and the Lemhi – as your vehicle climbs more than 3,000 feet up to the Continental Divide.

Wildlife abounds. Pattee Creek, far from the valley floor, attracts many animals, particularly elk and deer. In spring, when the water is high and noisy, it's possible to surprise these animals as they feed upon new growth or sip water from the roily creek.

Nature has left its mark in the area too. Forest fires through the years have left behind varying ages and sizes of trees in some areas. In places, lodgepole pines have been thinned to promote healthier, faster-growing trees for the future. Along the way, you'll also see rangeland and watershed management projects and improvements.

The Lewis and Clark Backcountry Byway and Adventure Road offers a mix of the northern Continental Divide – history, scenery, wildlife, and other natural wonders. If you visit east-central Idaho, it's a place you don't want to miss.

The Lewis and Clark Backcountry Byway is a cooperative effort of the Bureau of Land Management, the U.S. Forest Service, Lemhi County, and the Salmon Valley Chamber of Commerce. The byway is located in Lemhi County, about 20 miles south of Salmon, Idaho. It can be reached by turning east from State Highway 28 at the Tendoy intersection. The roads are single lane, with occasional pullouts for passing. They are a gravel surface which can be driven safely in an automobile. Grades in some areas exceed 5 percent. Roads are maintained by the county and the U.S. Forest Service. Snow usually closes the roads from November until June. The route is groomed in the winter months and is used heavily by snowmobile enthusiasts. The byway is 39 miles long and takes about a half-day drive.

Reprinted from U.S. Forest Service and Bureau of Land Management brochure

Valley Road Scenic Drive

Winding fourteen miles through the rugged land of Idaho's high country, the Valley Road scenic drive follows Pole Creek Road off State Highway 75. The dirt route represents the original major route used to traverse the upper eastern portion of the Sawtooth Valley. The historic road requires about one hour to drive, and users are urged to check road conditions prior to undertaking the route.

Trail Creek Canyon Scenic Drive

Winding east through a scenic valley, the Sun Valley Road proceeds up to the 7,896-foot Trail Creek Summit where magnificent views are afforded. Also known as Trail Creek, the route continues towards Idaho's highest peak, Mt. Borah, before ending near the small community of Mackay.

Historically, wagons used the Trail Creek Canyon route to haul gold ore from regional mines to Ketchum. Today, traces of this history are long gone, but the landscape retains much of the same pristine splendor as witnessed by 1880s travelers. The route is closed during winter, and all travelers are advised to contact the Forest Service for road conditions.

Sleeping Deer Backcountry Road

Delving deep into the Frank Church-River of No Return Wilderness region, Sleeping Deer Road provides sweeping views of the wilderness atop a high ridgeline separating Twin Peaks and Sleeping Deer Mountain. The twenty-five mile route leads to several trailheads providing access to the wilderness, and several small alpine lakes dot the landscape. In addition, the offshoot Twin Peaks Road leads travelers to the Rocky Mountain West's second tallest manned fire tower. The road is not recommended for sedans, and all users should contact the Forest Service for latest road conditions prior to departure.

Morgan Creek Backcountry Road

The Morgan Creek Backcountry Road provides a scenic detour into the mountains and forests surrounding Challis. Winding up babbling Morgan Creek, the road crosses a divide before descending Panther Creek. West of Shoup, the route joins the Salmon River Road leading travelers back to U.S. Highway 93. Cars, RV's, and any other towing vehicles are dissuaded from taking this route, and all users are encouraged to contact the Forest Service for the latest road conditions prior to departure.

HIKES

For information on additional are trails, please contact the Forest Service Ranger Districts listed at the back of this section.

Boulder and White Cloud Mountains Area

Special Considerations in this Area: Hikers must pay a Sawtooth National Recreation Area trailhead fee.

North Fork of the Big Wood River
Distance: 10.6 miles roundtrip
Climb: moderate
Difficulty: moderate
Usage: moderate
Location: Drive north from downtown Ketchum on State Highway 75 to the Sawtooth National Recreation Area (SNRA). Directly after passing the entrance sign, bear right and drive past the SNRA headquarters. Continue up the North Fork Canyon 5.1 miles to the road's end at the trailhead.

Traversing over eight major avalanche runs, lush wildflower meadows, and up a canyon, this trail leads hikers past a small waterfall, and with some route-finding skills, to the 10,250-foot Ibex Pass. From the trailhead, proceed along the right trail to its end at the trip's 4-mile mark. From here, a faint trail over rugged terrain leads to Ibex Pass and views of the surrounding Boulder Mountains. Best months for hiking are late-July through August.

Optional Hikes: After hiking 1.7 miles, hikers may opt to take the West Pass Trail. The West Pass Trail bears right and can be located at the far side of the meadow occurring right after sighting the waterfall. West Pass Trail is a difficult hike, climbing 2,900 feet in 2 miles to the 10,040-foot West Pass.

West Fork, North Fork of the Big Wood River
Distance: 6 miles roundtrip
Climb: moderate
Difficulty: moderate
Usage: moderate
Location: Drive north from downtown Ketchum on State Highway 75 to the Sawtooth National Recreation Area (SNRA). Directly after passing the entrance sign, bear right and drive past the SNRA headquarters. Continue up the North Fork Canyon 5.1 miles to the road's end at the trailhead.

This trail winds through dense old-growth forests into mountain meadows and avalanche areas containing numerous waterfalls. From the trailhead, hike along the left trail and at the 1-mile mark, reach the Amber Gulch Trail Junction where many hikers opt to take a side trip to Amber Lakes. On the main trail, reach an avalanche created meadow at the 2-mile mark. Continue hiking on a faint trail at the meadow's right side that climbs up into a canyon full of waterfalls and wildlife. At the trail's end in the rugged terrain, hikers should be aware that several mountain lions are known to inhabit the area. Best months for hiking are late June through September

Boulder Chain Lakes
Distance: 20 miles roundtrip
Climb: moderate
Difficulty: difficult
Usage: heavy
Location: Drive south of Challis on US Highway 93 to the junction with State Highway 75. Merge onto Highway 75 and continue approximately 16 miles south before turning left onto the East Fork of the Salmon Road. Drive 17 miles to the right turn on Forest Road (FR) 667 (Livingston Mill Road) and pro-

ceed 5 miles to the Livingston Mill Trailhead.

This trek is one of Idaho's most popular backpacking trails and for good reason. Hikers are greeted with lush forests, trout filled lakes that have also become popular swimming holes, and magnificent ridge views of the surrounding mountains. After hiking on an old jeep trail for 1 mile, hikers will reach the Big Baldy Junction and should proceed on the left fork. Following several switchbacks, the trail arrives at Red Ridge at the 5-mile mark and continues downhill to Frog Lake and Willow Lake. At the 7.25-mile mark (immediately past Willow Lake's outlet), hikers will reach another trail junction and should follow the right fork leading to the Boulder Chain Lakes and eventually up to Windy Devil Pass. Best months for hiking are mid-July through August.

Boundary Creek and Casino Lakes
Distance: 7.4 miles roundtrip
Climb: steep
Difficulty: difficult
Usage: moderate
Location: From Ketchum, drive 55 miles north on State Highway 75 to the marked Boundary Creek Trail Road. Turn on this road and proceed 1 mile to the trailhead.

Beginning in an open area of forest, this trail climbs steeply to the top of Boundary Creek Canyon, offering hikers outstanding views of the Mount Heyburn region of the Sawtooth Mountains rising in the west. After ascending the first 2.3 miles, hikers will reach a trail junction but should keep right. The trail winds through a thick forest, past Boundary Creek's headwaters, and up and over Peak 9,475 before dropping into the Casino Lakes' basin. Best months for hiking are July through September.

Optional Hikes: Before dropping into the middle of the three Casino Lakes, hikers reach a three-way trail junction. While the left fork takes hikers to the middle Casino Lake, the middle trail climbs to Garland Lakes and Rough Lake. The longest optional hike begins at the right fork. This trail leads to the upper Garland Lakes and Martin Creek, eventually ending at the Warm Springs meadow.

East Pass Creek
Distance: 19 miles roundtrip
Climb: moderate
Difficulty: moderate
Usage: moderate
Location: From Ketchum, drive east to Trail Creek Summit. After driving 8 miles beyond the summit down Summit Creek, exit onto Forest Road (FR) 444 (North Fork of the Big Lost River Road and drive 10.8 miles to the junction with FR 477. Follow FR 477 1 mile to Trail 050's beginning at Hunter Creek Trailhead.

Hikers will climb to Hunter Creek Summit before dropping down into East Pass Creek Canyon where views of Sheep Mountain and a large waterfall can be found. Many hikers also report seeing several elk in the area. After climbing to the top of Hunter Creek Summit, hikers should ignore the ridge trail and instead drop down into East Pass Creek Canyon. This trail leads to a grassy meadow, and at the 5.5-mile mark, hikers will view East Pass Creek falls cascading off a rocky ledge. Keeping right at all further trail junctions, the trail fades out at the 9.5-mile mark as it nears a gorge. Best month for hiking is July.

Optional Hikes: Hikers may take three optional trips leaving from the main East Pass Creek

Trail. The first option is to hike along the ridgeline immediately following Hunter Creek Summit. After arriving at the pass, hikers should proceed 0.7 miles along the right trail to Point 9,923 where panoramic views of the Boulder Mountains are found. Hikers can also opt to take the Bowery Creek Trail leaving to the left at the 7.7-mile mark. This trail leads down Bowery Creek with a view of Castle Peak rising in the distance before hikers reach the East Fork of the Salmon River. The final option is much more difficult and requires a strenuous climb as well as knowledge of topographic map reading. For this option, hikers should proceed past the gorge and ascend steeply to Lake 9,436 and its neighboring ridgeline. Here, hikers will view the summits of Bowery Peak and Sheep Mountain, the White Cloud Mountains, and the peaks of the Lost River Mountains.

Fourth of July Creek to Born Lakes
Distance: 8 miles roundtrip
Climb: moderate
Difficulty: moderate
Usage: heavy
Location: 15 miles south of Stanley, exit off State Highway 75 onto a gravel road leading to the White Cloud Mountains and the trailhead in 11 miles. The trail leaves to the east of the trailhead.

Although the beginning of the trail is open to motorcycles, hikers still have access to beautiful forests, meadows, subalpine lakes, and spectacular views of the granite White Cloud Mountains looming on the horizon. Climbing 1.4 miles, hikers will reach a trail junction and should proceed 100 yards along the right fork. This trail leads to Fourth of July Lake and a vista of Patterson Peak. Upon viewing the scenery, return to the trail junction and walk along the left Born Lakes Trail. The trail climbs to a ridgetop, switchbacks down into Ants Basin, and ends at Born Lakes. Best months for hiking are mid-July through early September.

Optional Hikes: At Fourth of July Lake, proceed along the trail's right fork to reach Washington Lake in 1 mile.

High Ridge Trail
Distance: 6.4 miles roundtrip
Climb: steep
Difficulty: moderately difficult
Usage: light
Location: Drive east from Ketchum on the road to Sun Valley and up Trail Creek Canyon. Proceed 0.5 miles past Trail Creek Summit, then turn left onto Park Creek Road. Proceed on this dirt road 1 mile before turning left on a side road leading to the trailhead above Trail Creek.

Climbing steeply through thick forests out onto an open flat, this trail winds up Cold Creek Canyon to Basin Gulch before topping out at the 9,450 foot Rock Roll Point. From the point, hikers have incredible vistas of the Pioneer Mountains rising to the southwest and Trail Creek Gorge. Best months for hiking are mid-July to late September, as hikers must ford Trail Creek 0.1 miles after the hike's start.

Craters of the Moon National Monument and Wilderness Area
Special Considerations in this Area: Hikers must pay a vehicle entrance fee as well as possess a backcountry permit for overnight trips. Hikers should also bring plenty of water, sunscreen, insect repellant, and flashlights for exploring caves (if desired). Magnetic compasses do not work in the area due to the lava rock's high iron content, and hikers are urged to stay close to

the trail as the area's massive landscape can be confusing. In addition, the rugged area is known for tearing apart boots, so hikers should plan on wearing backpacking boots with durable tread.

Echo Crater
Distance: 10 miles roundtrip
Climb: moderate
Difficulty: difficult
Usage: light
Location: Drive 18 miles southwest of Arco on US Highway 20/26 to the Craters of the Moon National Monument. Following the loop road, turn onto Tree Molds Road to locate the Tree Molds Trailhead.

Traversing across buttes and craters, hikers will wander over a colorful, twisted lava landscape to the Great Rift while enduring desert like conditions. From the trailhead, follow the trail 0.25 miles to the junction with Wilderness Trail. Bear right along Wilderness Trail and utilize cairns to travel between Big Cinder and Half Cone Buttes. At the 3-mile mark, stay to the right at a trail junction while crossing Trench Mortar Flat and proceed to Coyote Butte. Here, travel 0.75 miles northeast to Echo Crater, paralleling the Great Rift to the left. Proceed 1 mile southeast from Echo Crater to reach the large lava cone known as Watchman at the 4.5-mile mark. Staying along the Great Rift to avoid the jagged lava flows off-trail, travel 0.5 miles to the Sentinel's northwest side. Here, the trail begins its loop back to the trailhead. Best months for hiking are late May to early June and late fall due to extremely hot temperatures during peak summer months.

Frank Church-River of No Return Wilderness Area
Blue Bunch Mountain
Distance: 8 miles roundtrip
Climb: moderate
Difficulty: moderately difficult
Usage: moderate
Location: Merge off State Highway 21 onto a gravel road a few miles east of Banner Summit. Proceed on this all-weather road for 12 miles until reaching a sign and side road leading to Fir Creek Campground. Follow the side road, but stay to the left at the fork and continue to the road's end at Bear Valley Creek. Locate the trailhead at the beginning of Bear Valley Canyon where a pack bridge crosses over Bear Valley Creek.

Situated at the headwaters of the Middle Fork of the Salmon River, Blue Bunch Mountain's summit offers views of Poker, Bruce, and Ayers Meadows, as well as Cape Horn Mountain rising to the south. To reach the summit, cross Bear Valley Creek and bear left on the trail. Hike upstream and after 2 miles, reach a good water source at Cy Springs. Although the trail is difficult to find near the springs, continue walking another 0.5 mile to the ridge top where the trail can be found again. To reach the mountain summit and panoramic views of the surrounding area, proceed 1.5 more miles. Caution should be used, however, while walking along the ridge top as summer thunderstorms can be severe. Best months for hiking are mid-July through August.

Optional Hikes: At the trailhead, proceed right on the trail leading down the scenic Bear Valley Creek. This trail is quite difficult as it requires hikers to ford the creek in several places. The trail eventually leads to the beginning of the Middle Fork of the Salmon River at the convergence of Marsh Creek at Big Hole. Best month for hiking is

late August.

Cape Horn Mountain
Distance: 7 miles roundtrip
Climb: steep
Difficulty: difficult
Usage: moderate
Location: Merge off State Highway 21 onto a gravel road a few miles east of Banner Summit. Drive to Cape Horn Summit and park on the road's left side. Locate the Trail 024 Trailhead under the trees at Cape Horn Summit. Cross the road to take the trail leading to the northeast.

As the most southerly point in the Salmon River Mountain Range, the frequently scaled Cape Horn Mountain provides an outstanding vista of the Frank Church-River of No Return Wilderness and the nearby Sawtooth Mountains. As the trail begins, hikers will pass through a burned area from a 1990s wildfire. Although this part of the hike is not scenic, the trail quickly climbs into tree-lined, wildflower meadows. After climbing 1.5 miles, hikers will reach the mountain's shoulder. Continue hiking 1.3 miles to the summit of Cape Horn and follow this gentle trail along a mountain crest to overlook Bruce, Ayers, and Poker Meadows. At the trip's 3.5-mile mark, the trail steeply descends to Lola Creek, so most hikers opt to turn around and backtrack to the trailhead. Best months for hiking are mid-July to mid-August. Hikers should pack plenty of water to reach the summit as water resources are limited.

Optional Hikes: Instead of turning around at the 3.5 mile mark, hike down from the crest along Lola Creek into a canyon containing several ponds and four lakes. Hikers can proceed as far as Marsh Creek where Lola Creek Campground is situated.

Lightning Creek
Distance: 21 miles roundtrip
Climb: steep
Difficulty: difficult
Usage: moderate
Location: From Stanley, drive 13 miles east on State Highway 75 and exit at Sunbeam. Proceed north on a paved, two-lane road (which turns to gravel in 3 miles) up the Yankee Fork of the Salmon River. Reach the ghost town of Bonanza 7.5 miles north of Sunbeam, and bear left on Forest Road (FR) 074. Drive past the Forest Service Guard Station, and at the fork in the road, follow the road leading to "Boot Hill Cemetery." Drive downhill one mile to the West Yankee Fork Trailhead to locate the gated trail.

Meandering along creeks through narrow canyons and tree-lined meadows into some of Idaho's most rugged country, this trail requires hikers to ford several streams before reaching the final destination at Lightning Lake. To begin, hike 2.5 miles along West Yankee Fork Trail and merge onto Lightning Creek Trail. This trail switchbacks up Lightning Creek Canyon with several stream crossings, and hikers are advised to use caution as the trail winds along an edge of the canyon slope. After hiking 4.3 miles on the Lightning Creek Trail, visitors will reach the first of four fords of Lightning Creek. Once past these fords, hikers will gain views of the area's craggy mountains and continue climbing to a meadow. Past this meadow, the trail becomes faint in places as the terrain becomes more rugged. At the 6.8-mile mark along Lightning Creek Trail, hikers cross over a precipitous tributary before ascending the last, but very steep, 1.2 miles to the cirque containing Lightning Lake. Best months for hiking are July through mid-September. Hikers should bring wading shoes as well as rope for hanging food away from bears in the area.

Optional Hikes: The steep tributary 1.2 miles before Lightning Lake provides a cross-country hike where backpackers can ascend to waterfalls, meadows, and two alpine lakes. To reach the area, climb 300 feet along the ridge directly east from the tributary. Next, proceed over to the creek and cross it right above a scenic waterfall. Hikers will locate a trail leading up two meadows to an unnamed pass marked with a white bark pine. Angling westward down from the pass, hikers will locate two deep and rarely visited lakes.

Reflection Lake
Distance: 26 miles roundtrip
Climb: moderate
Difficulty: moderate
Usage: light
Location: At Salmon, proceed south on US Highway 93 5 miles before merging right onto Forest Road (FR) 021 (Williams Creek Road). Continue 12 miles to the junction with FR 055 (Panther Creek Road and turn left. Drive 10.5 miles up FR 055 to the junction with FR 112 (Porphyry Creek Road). Proceed 6 miles along FR 112 to a four-way junction where visitors should merge right onto FR 113. Follow FR 113 8 miles to FR 114, which leads 2.5 miles to the trailhead at Crags Campground.

Surrounded by rugged mountain scenery and wildlife that includes deer, elk, goats, and bighorn sheep, hikers will climb to numerous alpine lakes renowned for their beauty and ample fishing opportunities. From the trailhead, start near Golden Trout Lake and climb along a ridgeline past Cathedral Rock before reaching the trail junction for Clear Creek and Waterfall Trails at the 4.5-mile mark. Continue to the left and reach another trail junction at the 6.5-mile mark. Proceed left and follow the sign to the shallow, but scenic Welcome Lake where another trail junction directs the way to Reflection Lake. The trail continues to switchback down a tree-lined ridge to eight different lakes. At mile 12, hikers will reach the cutthroat and rainbow trout filled Reflection Lake. One mile past Reflection Lake lies Buck Lake, Doe Lake, and Fawn Lake, all of which are great fishing spots. Best month for hiking is August due to decreased mosquitoes and snow pack.

Ship Island Lake
Distance: 22 miles roundtrip
Climb: steep
Difficulty: very difficult
Usage: moderate
Location: At Salmon, proceed south on US Highway 93 5 miles before merging right onto Forest Road (FR) 021 (Williams Creek Road). Continue 12 miles to the junction with FR 055 (Panther Creek Road and turn left. Drive 10.5 miles up FR 055 to the junction with FR 112 (Porphyry Creek Road). Proceed 6 miles along FR 112 to a four-way junction where visitors should merge right onto FR 113. Follow FR 113 8 miles to FR 114, which leads 2.5 miles to the trailhead at Crags Campground.

Granite spires, knobs, and monoliths along this trail are breathtaking as the route climbs through forests, over narrow ridges in some of Idaho's most rugged country, and into the awe-inspiring basin cradling Ship Island Lake. The hike is very demanding and caution should be used along the ridges if thunderstorms threaten the area. Beginning at the trailhead near Golden Trout Lake, climb to a trail junction at the 2 mile mark and

proceed along the middle (northwestern) trail to the ridgeline. At the 3.5-mile mark, hikers can opt to take a 0.3-mile side hike to the rainbow trout filled Cathedral Lake. On the main trail, continue another mile to the Waterfalls Canyon Trail junction that descends into Wilson Canyon. Hikers will reach a fork in the trail at the 6.5-mile point and should take the right fork leading to Wilson Creek's headwaters near an alpine forest. Follow this trail to Wilson Lake and ignore topographic maps, which falsely illustrate the trail's location. Proceed along Harbor Lake Trail to Fishfin Pass at the 8-mile mark. This pass' switchbacks are extremely narrow and should not be attempted if horses are on the trail as there is not enough room to safely pass one another. After crossing over the pass, hikers will go by Gentian Lake and climb into Ship Island basin holding Airplane Lake and Ship Island Lake. Having hiked 3 miles from the pass, backpackers will reach the east side of the large Ship Island Lake surrounded by towering 10,000-foot peaks. Along the lake's east side, backpackers can opt to hike down a faint, rocky trail to the lake's outlet and glimpse down the trailless, granite walls forming Ship Island Creek Canyon. Best month for hiking is August.

Sleeping Deer Mountain and West Fork Lakes
Distance: 11 miles roundtrip
Climb: moderate
Difficulty: moderate
Usage: light
Location: From Challis' main street, bear north (right) onto Challis Creek county road and proceed 8 miles to a right turn on Forest Road (FR) 086 (Bear Creek Road). Drive past a few vacation homes, then up to a ridgeline that leads to the Sleeping Deer Trailhead at the road's end. The road leading to the trailhead is suitable for trucks and slow-moving sedans, but not appropriate for RV's and horse trailers.

Situated at an elevation of 9,881 feet, Sleeping Deer is one of the tallest mountains in the Frank Church-River of No Return Wilderness Area, but is by no means the only attraction this hike offers. Winding up and down over passes and into mountain basins, this trail traverses the wilderness and leads to several rarely used lakes. After hiking just 0.75 miles from the trailhead with continuous views of Sleeping Deer Mountain rising in the distance, backpackers will reach a trail junction and should take the right trail. Climb down seven switchbacks to an intersection at Pole Creek. Taking the left trail, proceed to the Pole Creek and Cache Creek divide. Hikers should keep their eyes on the weather as severe lightning storms are frequent in the area. After crossing the pass, descend to the four Cache Creek Lakes situated near the trail. Directly past the third lake, locate a trail junction on the right leading to Woodtick Summit. At the 8,863-foot summit, take the right fork in the trail leading to a grassy pass between Woodtick Creek and the West Fork of Camas Creek. At the divide, locate another trail junction and take the middle fork leading down to the three West Fork Lakes. The first of the West Fork Lakes is the largest and is the only lake known to hold any fish. Best months for visiting are mid-July to mid-September.

Soldier Lakes-Patrol Ridge Loop
Distance: 16.5 mile loop
Climb: moderate
Difficulty: moderate
Usage: heavy
Location: From Stanley, drive 18.6 miles northwest on State Highway 21 before merging north (left) onto a

gravel road. Almost immediately after this turn, bear right onto a different gravel road. Cross over Marsh Creek, and at the fork in the road, stay to the left and proceed to Vanity Summit. After crossing the summit and reaching a junction for Float Creek Road, proceed on Float Creek Road and follow the signed junctions leading to Josephus Lake Trailhead.

Crossing terrain ranging from heavy timber to alpine areas with views of rugged peaks, this trail begins and ends at the scenic Josephus Lake and passes by large basins containing several fishable lakes. Beginning above lower Josephus Lake, the trail rambles past natural springs through thick forests before reaching Helldiver Lake in 2 miles. 0.5 miles past Helldiver, hikers will reach the Float Creek and Soldier Creek divide. A trail junction occurs at the 3-mile mark, and hikers should follow the left Solider Lakes Trail that leads to the head of Soldier Creek Canyon. After reaching the first two Solider Lakes, take a left at the trail junction leading to the precipitous Patrol Ridge. This trail gradually climbs the steep wildflower covered ridge, offering panoramic views of Soldier Lakes, Cutthroat Lakes, and the headwaters of the Middle Fork of the Salmon River. At the 7 mile mark, Patrol Ridge trail reaches its highest point at 9,000 feet before dropping down to a saddle at the 8 mile mark where hikers should proceed eastward off Patrol Ridge back to the trailhead along the Muskeg Creek Trail. The trail winds through forest and meadows to reach a small waterfall flowing into Cutthroat Lake. 0.5 miles above Cutthroat, there is a trail junction. Hikers should proceed along the Cutthroat Trail leading to the junction at Colonel Lake, Staff Sargent Lake, and Sargent Lake. From here, proceed back past Helldiver Lake to the trailhead. Best months for hiking are July to mid-September.

Optional Hikes: At the Patrol Ridge divide that connects to Muskeg Creek Trail, hikers may opt to continue along the ridge trail to its end at the lookout on Big Soldier Mountain. This 3 mile roundtrip side hike offers views of the entire southern portion of the Frank Church-River of No Return Wilderness Area.

Stoddard Lake
Distance: 22.5 miles roundtrip
Climb: very steep
Difficulty: very difficult
Usage: light
Location: From Salmon, drive 11 miles north along US Highway 93 to North Fork. Exiting the highway, merge west (left) on Salmon River Road leading to Shoup in 19 miles. Here, follow this paved road as it turns to gravel and drive 21 miles to the mouth of the Middle Fork of the Salmon River. Directly past this is the Middle Fork Trailhead, but proceed 0.5 mile to the Stoddard Pack Bridge trailhead.

For backpackers even in excellent condition, the trail to Stoddard Lake is an extreme physical challenge as it climbs out of one of America's deepest canyons (Salmon River Canyon) along numerous switchbacks, high mountain ridges, and over deadfall with limited water sources. Those who are able to make the trek, however, are rewarded with breathtaking views of the Salmon River Canyon and the rugged Bighorn Crags as well as great cutthroat fishing at Stoddard Lake. After crossing the trailhead's pack bridge, backpackers will immediately begin climbing along twelve switchbacks and over 3,000 feet to the 4-mile mark at Color Creek. Continuing 0.25 miles beyond Color Creek, take the right, unmarked side trail leading to Nolan Mountain. This deteriorating trail switchbacks steeply to the summit of Nolan Mountain where it levels off and follows the ridgeline west toward Twin Peaks. The trail is faint at places and eventually fades completely at a saddle near Twin Peaks. Here, hikers should ascend the saddle and proceed to climb to the top of the first Twin Peaks' summit at 9,108 feet. From this point, drop down to a saddle and climb to the second peak at 9,258 feet. At this peak, drop 0.25 miles straight west to an outfitter trail. This trail is not illustrated on area maps, but it leads to a camp on Stoddard Lake's southwestern edge. An additional 1 mile descent down 700 feet of switchbacks leads to the lake. Several trails from the lake lead hikers deep into the backcountry containing Papoose Lake, Cottonwood Lake, Basin Lake, Black Lake, and Chamberlain Basin. Best months for hiking are mid-July to early September. Backpackers should be comfortable with rock scrambling and route finding along this hike.

Upper Vanity Lakes
Distance: 2.2 miles roundtrip
Climb: gentle
Difficulty: easy to moderate in places
Usage: light
Location: From Stanley, drive 18.6 miles northwest on State Highway 21 before merging north (left) onto a gravel road. Almost immediately after this turn, bear right onto a different gravel road. Cross over Marsh Creek, and at the fork in the road, stay to the left and proceed to Vanity Summit. Park at Vanity Summit to locate the unmarked trailhead leading to the trailless subalpine lakes.

Backpackers with a topographic map and knowledge of a compass can easily undertake this short day hike to four wilderness lakes that drain into Vanity Creek. From Vanity Summit, locate the broad ridge and begin hiking east by southeast, reaching a meadow and creek in 0.25 miles. Following the creek, reach the first and largest lake at the 0.5-mile mark. Continue along a game trail 0.25 miles further to the second and third lakes divided by a 30-foot ridge. From the second lake's south side, climb 0.3 miles south to the fourth lake. Best months for hiking are July through September.

West Yankee Fork-Crimson Lake
Distance: 17 miles roundtrip
Climb: moderate
Difficulty: moderate
Usage: moderate
Location: From Stanley, drive 13 miles east on State Highway 75 and exit at Sunbeam. Proceed north on a paved, two-lane road (which turns to gravel in 3 miles) up the Yankee Fork of the Salmon River. 7.5 miles north of Sunbeam, reach the ghost town of Bonanza and bear left on Forest Road (FR) 074. Drive past the Forest Service Guard Station, and at the fork in the road, follow the road leading to "Boot Hill Cemetery." Drive downhill one mile to the West Yankee Fork Trailhead to locate the gated trail.

Hiking through lush West Fork Canyon through occasional meadows and up to Crimson Lake, backpackers are surrounded with rugged, colorful peaks as well as an occasional mountain goat. Beginning at the gated trail, proceed across a gravel pit and locate West Fork Trail 155 on the west side. Follow Trail 155 through conifers and meadows, passing by Deadwood Creek Trail (leaving to the left) and Lightning Creek Trail (leaving to the

right) before turning right on Cabin Creek Trail 156. Crossing over Cabin Creek and through avalanche debris, avoid any side trails leaving to the left. Instead, stay to the right, and at the 6.8-mile mark, climb left up Crimson Lake Trail 202. This trail takes hikers across rocky terrain as it climbs 1.7 more miles to the large, deep Crimson Lake situated amid crimson rocks. The lake is known as one of the prettiest alpine lakes in the Frank Church Wilderness, and it also possesses a large population of cutthroat trout. Best months for hiking are mid-July through mid-September. Backpackers should bring wading shoes for some creek crossings, as well as rope to hang food away from bears.

Ketchum/Sun Valley Area

Bald Mountain Trail
Distance: 9 miles roundtrip
Climb: steep
Difficulty: moderately difficult
Usage: heavy
Location: From downtown Ketchum, drive west to the trailhead at the bottom of the River Run chair lift.

Popular among area locals, Trail #201 ascends to the top of Sun Valley's primary peak. The Bald Mountain Trail climbs 3,331 feet and ends at a fire tower. Best months for hiking are June through September.

Shadyside Trail
Distance: 3 miles roundtrip
Climb: gentle
Difficulty: easy
Location: From Ketchum, travel on State Highway 75 before exiting onto Adams Gulch Road. Travel 0.75 miles to locate Trail #177A at the Adams Gulch Trailhead.

Shadyside Trail #177A provides families with easy access to mountain scenery on a gentle trek. Best months for hiking are June through September.

Adams Gulch Trail
Distance: 14 mile loop
Climb: steep
Difficulty: difficult
Usage: moderate
Location: From Ketchum, travel on State Highway 75 before exiting onto Adams Gulch Road. Travel 0.75 miles to locate Trail #177 at the Adams Gulch Trailhead.

A loop trail beginning on Trail #177 and intersecting with Trail #142, this hike through mountain scenery is also a popular destination for mountain bikers. Best months for hiking are June through September.

Trail Creek Trail
Distance: 3 miles roundtrip
Climb: moderate
Difficulty: moderately easy
Location: From Sun Valley Village, travel 2 miles east up Trail Creek Road to locate the trailhead at Trail Creek Cabin.

Trail Creek Trail #305 parallels Trail Creek on a hike suitable for an afternoon excursion in the scenic area. Best months for hiking are June through September.

Aspen Loop Trail
Distance: 1.75 mile loop
Climb: gentle
Difficulty: easy
Location: From Sun Valley Village, travel 2 miles east up Trail Creek Road to locate the trailhead at Trail Creek Cabin.

Meandering under a canopy of aspen and evergreen trees, Trail #119A is strictly limited to foot-traffic and is a perfect option for a family hike. Best months for hiking are June through September.

Corral Creek Trail
Distance: 7 miles roundtrip
Climb: moderate
Difficulty: moderate
Location: From Sun Valley Village, travel 2 miles east up Trail Creek Road to locate the trailhead at Trail Creek Cabin.

An aspen and evergreen forest surrounds Trail #119B as it climbs through the scenic Sun Valley. Hikers should expect to encounter mountain bikers on this trail. Best months for hiking are June through September.

Pioneer Cabin Trail
Distance: 8.5 mile loop
Climb: steep
Difficulty: difficult
Usage: heavy
Location: From Sun Valley Village, travel east up Trail Creek Road. 1 mile northeast of Boundary Campground, merge onto Corral Creek Road to locate the trailhead for Pioneer Cabin Trail #122.

For those hikers ready for a long day in the sun, this trail ascends to an old ski hut constructed by the Union Pacific Railroad in 1937. Still in use, the cabin's 9,400-foot elevation provides panoramic views of the Pioneer Range. Although beginning on Trail #122, hikers should make the return loop on Long Gulch Trail #123. Best months for hiking are mid-June through September.

Lemhi Mountains Area

Bell Mountain Canyon Loop
Distance: 5 miles roundtrip
Climb: gradual
Difficulty: easy
Usage: light
Location: From Salmon, head south on State Highway 28. After crossing Gilmore Summit, proceed south 10.3 miles before exiting on a dirt road marked "Charcoal Kilns Historical Site, 6 miles." Follow this road 4.8 miles before turning left on another dirt road. Proceed 0.4 miles to another junction and stay right. After entering the Targhee National Forest, proceed downhill on the right fork to locate the informal trailhead.

Trailing through open wildflower meadows, this trek takes hikers through a canyon to two mountain passes affording views of 11,612 foot Bell Mountain, the Lemhi Mountains' second highest peak. From the trailhead, begin climbing uphill at the canyon's mouth. At the 1-mile mark, hikers will reach a fork in Bell Mountain Canyon. Taking either fork, walk 0.5 miles to an open pass. For additional mountain views, proceed 0.5 miles further to a second pass situated at 8,800 feet. Best months for hiking are mid-June to mid-July, but the trail is accessible from early June through October.

Optional Hikes: From the second pass, hikers can create their own trail through the forest to reach an upper canyon at the base of Bell Mountain.

Big Creek-Big Timber Creek Loop
Distance: 38 miles roundtrip
Climb: steep
Difficulty: difficult
Usage: light
Location: After locating Howe on State Highway 33, exit north (right) onto a county road leading through

Little Lost River Valley to Summit Reservoir. Approximately 57 miles north of Howe, bear left onto a dirt road marked "Big Creek Trail" and proceed 3.5 miles to the North Fork Trail at the Big Creek Camp Trailhead.

Ascending up narrow canyons, over three mountain divides, across high meadows, and through forests of aspen and conifer trees, this trail provides hikers with views of several mountains, including Yellow Peak, Flatiron Mountain, Big Creek Peak, Bell Mountain, and Diamond Peak. After fording several small tributaries, hikers will reach a trail junction at the 6.8-mile mark and should proceed to the right up Park Fork of Big Creek. At the trek's 9.9-mile mark, proceed south (right) at the trail junction and climb to Yellow Pass. From the pass, hike down to Cabin Creek and a large meadow at the 16.4-mile mark where hikers should proceed on Trail 127 (Cabin Creek Trail) up to Cabin Creek Pass. At Cabin Creek Pass, proceed right on Snowbank Trail for 7 miles, dropping off the ridge to Redrock Creek. At the 28-mile mark, hikers will reach a four-way junction. Proceed on the South Fork of Big Creek Trail leading over a divide, down into South Fork of Big Creek Canyon, and across the South Fork of Big Creek back to the trailhead. Best months for hiking are July through September.

Bear Valley Lakes
Distance: 11 miles roundtrip
Climb: moderate
Difficulty: moderate
Usage: moderate
Location: Drive 26 miles south of Salmon on State Highway 28 before bearing right (west) onto a marked county road leading up Hayden Creek. Proceeding 3.5 miles, turn left at the Basin Creek intersection and drive to the Salmon-Challis National Forest boundary. Directly after reaching this boundary, turn right on Forest Road (FR) 009 and continue to its end at the Bear Valley Lake Trailhead. Locate Bear Valley Trail 100 yards east of the trailhead.

Flanked by conifer trees and 600 to 900 foot jagged cliffs, the largest Bear Valley Lake is nestled at an elevation of 9,135 feet in a cirque at Bear Valley Creek's beginning. After starting out in an open area, the trail leads hikers through a forest and to a trail junction at the 2.5-mile mark. Proceed on the right trail up Bear Valley to reach another obvious trail junction at the 4-mile mark. Bear left on the Bear Valley Lakes Trail, and at the 4.5-mile mark, continue left at another trail junction to reach Bear Valley Lake at the 5.5-mile mark. Best months for hiking are July to late September.

Optional Hikes: At the 4.5 mile mark, hikers can turn right at the trail junction to reach the first of the Upper Bear Valley Lakes in approximately 1 mile. From here, hikers can opt to climb an additional mile to reach the highest Upper Bear Valley Lake where a vista of Lem Peak is also found.

Buck Lakes
Distance: 9 miles roundtrip
Climb: moderate
Difficulty: moderate
Usage: light
Location: Drive 26 miles south of Salmon on State Highway 28 before bearing right (west) onto a marked county road leading up Hayden Creek. Proceeding 3.5 miles, turn left at the Basin Creek intersection and drive to the Salmon-Challis National Forest boundary. Directly after reaching this boundary, turn right on

Forest Road (FR) 009 and continue to its end at the Bear Valley Lake Trailhead. Locate Bear Valley Trail 100 yards east of the trailhead.

Although the Buck Lakes Trail is not illustrated on topographic maps, hikers who follow Trail 081 will find the mountain scenery from the lakes worth the trip. Beginning on Bear Valley Creek Trail, hike 2.5 miles to the Buck Lakes Trail (Trail 081) junction and proceed right. After crossing Bear Valley Creek and ascending through a forest, hikers will reach the first of Buck Lakes approximately 1 mile from the trail junction. The trail quickly climbs up the mountainside to the largest of Buck Lakes situated at an elevation of 8,474 feet. From here, hike 0.5 miles cross-country to reach another Buck Lake set amidst the timber. Best months for hiking are July to late September.

Optional Hikes: For those in excellent condition, a hike to the highest Buck Lake offers outstanding views of Lem Peak. From the third Buck Lake, scramble cross-country across the rocky terrain up to Lake 9,456. Limited camping is available at this lake.

Bunting Canyon
Distance: 8 miles roundtrip
Climb: steep
Difficulty: difficult
Usage: light
Location: From Howe, drive 23.5 miles north on a paved county road leading up Little Lost River Valley before bearing right at a gravel pit. Proceeding on the dirt road leading to the right, drive up the bumpy road that becomes increasingly worse. Upon reaching a meadow, park at the first bridge crossing Badger Creek and locate the informal trailhead.

Limestone and dolomite mountains rising 11,500 feet line this trail as it twists intermittently through fir and aspen trees to the top of Bunting Canyon. After crossing the old bridge at the trailhead, proceed 0.5 miles to a fork in the trail. Following the right fork leading up Bunting Canyon, pass by a switchback road at the 1 mile mark leading to old mining ruins. At the 2-mile mark, Bunting Canyon angles southward and the trail appears to end near Bunting Creek's source. However, hikers can proceed onward, following a trail that fades in and out on the canyon's right side leading to the rugged head of Bunting Canyon. Best months for hiking are late June and mid-September due to cooler temperatures, scenery, and limited cattle grazing in the area.

Middle Canyon
Distance: 4 miles roundtrip
Climb: moderate
Difficulty: easy
Usage: light
Location: Drive 2.5 miles east on State Highway 22-33 from Howe before bearing north (left) on County Road 1300 West. Proceed 4.1 miles (passing the junction with County Road 3800 North) and turn left on County Road 3900 North. Travel 100 yards, bearing right at the first road junction. Drive along this canal road 1.5 miles to a right turn leading up Middle Canyon. Follow this rough road to its end near a steep incline and the informal trailhead.

Natural arches, hollowed-out limestone, and a narrow deep canyon possessing a variety of plants and trees await hikers on this trail leading up waterless Middle Canyon. Although the trail ascends steeply for the first 200 feet, it quickly levels out into a canyon receiving varying amounts of sunlight. As a result, the south facing slopes are covered with sagebrush, while shady areas are

characterized with moss, ferns, and old growth fir trees. The trail fades at the 2-mile mark near an abandoned sawmill. Best month for hiking is June, but the trail is accessible from mid-April through mid-November.

Optional Hikes: At the trail's end, hikers can opt to rock scramble up Saddle Mountain, but should be prepared to face sharp limestone rocks and zero water accessibility.

Mill Creek Lake and Firebox Summit
Distance: 10.5 miles roundtrip
Climb: steep
Difficulty: moderately difficult
Usage: moderate
Location: From Howe, drive 36 miles north up the Little Lost River Valley on a county road before heading right up Sawmill Canyon. Cross over Mill Creek and locate a dirt road leading to the east (right) approximately 100 yards past the Mill Creek Bridge. Drive 1.2 miles on this dirt road to the developed trailhead near Mill Creek where a "National Recreation Trail" sign clearly marks the route.

This trail climbs through a small canyon, past old-growth Douglas fir trees, and across landslides before leading to the rocky surroundings of Mill Creek Lake and the beautiful meadows and forests found on the way to Firebox Summit. On the well-marked trail, climb 1,200 feet in 2.3 miles to reach Mill Creek Lake, a popular spot for catching large cutthroat trout. From the lake, continue up the right side of Mill Creek Canyon 0.5 miles to a meadow. The trail fades in this meadow, so proceed into the trees lining the meadow's right side where the trail reappears and tree blazes help mark the path. Upon reaching the top of the meadow, locate Mill Creek's farthest left tributary as the trail crosses this stream and proceeds left into the forest. The trail is clearly marked as it climbs to Firebox Meadows and bears right through a small forest up to Firebox Summit. From this peak, hikers will have panoramic views of the Lemhi Mountain Range spanning the horizon. Best months for hiking are July and August.

Nez Perce Lake
Distance: 5.6 miles roundtrip
Climb: steep
Difficulty: moderate
Usage: light
Location: From Leadore, drive 6 miles south on State Highway 28 before bearing right on a Bureau of Land Management road leading to Timber Creek and Cold Springs. On this gravel road, drive 1 mile to an intersection and keep left. In another 2.8 miles, turn right and proceed past Purcell Spring. At the following intersection, bear right again and head into the Salmon National Forest. 7.5 miles from Leadore, locate the informal trailhead at Nez Perce Spring. A 4-wheel drive vehicle is highly recommended in reaching the trailhead.

Closed to all motorized vehicles, this trail climbs to a cirque of Sheephorn Peak cradling Nez Perce Lake at an altitude of 8,840 feet. With rocky shores, Nez Perce Lake is known for its solitude and Arctic grayling stocked waters, as well as for the many elk, deer, and mountain goats occupying the area. While the hike follows an old road the first 0.5 miles, the road soon ends and the well-marked Nez Perce Trail begins. Crossing over tributaries of Nez Perce Creek and switchbacking up a mountain ridge, hikers arrive at the uncrowded Nez Perce Lake at the 2.8-mile mark. Best months for hiking are July to late September.

South Creek Canyon

Distance: 7 miles roundtrip
Climb: moderate
Difficulty: moderately easy
Usage: moderate
Location: From Howe, drive 7.5 miles north on a county road up Little Lost River Valley. At South Creek Road, turn right and travel 2.5 miles to a road junction. Bearing left on a dirt road, proceed 1 mile to the obvious trail leaving immediately at the informal trailhead.

Passing through a canyon that includes both desert conditions as well as areas of riparian forest, this trail winds near South Creek (the only stream flowing off Saddle Mountain). Climbing past colorful cliffs, hikers reach a fork leading up a side canyon at the 2.5-mile mark. Continuing up the main South Creek Canyon, visitors will pass an old sod-roofed cabin, cross boggy areas, and end at a meadow filled with natural springs. Both the canyon and meadow are known to house several deer, elk, bears, mountain lions, and coyotes. Best months for hiking are mid-June to early July.

Optional Hikes: For a loop hike, continue up a draw on the meadow's north side leading down Camp Creek Canyon. From the canyon floor, follow game trails and abandoned mining roads leading southward back to the trailhead. This hike is steep and moderately difficult, and the best month for hiking is late June.

Lost River Range Area

Bear Creek Lake

Distance: 5 miles roundtrip
Climb: moderate
Difficulty: moderate
Usage: light
Location: 8 miles south of Mackay at an area called Leslie, merge off US Highway 93 onto a gravel road. Travel north 9.5 miles, then bear left on Bear Creek Road. Keeping left at all further road junctions, locate the trailhead in 1.2 miles

Winding up Bear Canyon, this trail leads hikers to Bear Creek Lake and offers stunning views of unnamed jagged peaks rising nearly 11,200 feet in Idaho's skyline. From the trailhead, proceed 0.7 miles along Bear Creek to the Methodist Gulch and Bear Creek forks. Disregarding the left, unmaintained trail, proceed along the main trail another 0.5 miles to a junction with Wet Creek. Staying to the left, continue hiking uphill to the shallow waters and lakeshore of Bear Creek Lake. Best months for hiking are late June to October. Caution should be used in the area after heavy rainstorms due to extremely muddy conditions that make it challenging to safely reach the trailhead.

Merriam Lake

Distance: 4 miles roundtrip
Climb: steep
Difficulty: moderate
Usage: heavy
Location: Drive south on US Highway 93 from Salmon over Willow Creek Summit and bear left on May-Patterson Road. Proceed past the picnic area and Doublespring Pass, turning right at Horseheaven Pass. Continue 7 miles to a fork in the road and proceed to the right. In approximately 1 mile, reach a four-way junction and drive straight, following Mahogany Creek. In 0.1 miles, bear left and drive uphill past a corral to a road fork. Taking the right fork, proceed 3 miles to the signed trailhead beginning on the West Fork of the Pahsimeroi's north (right) bank. A high clearance, 4-wheel drive vehicle is necessary.

Mount Idaho (Idaho's seventh tallest peak at 12,065 feet) and other peaks rising more than 11,000 feet frame this hike's destination, Merriam Lake. Situated in a cirque at 9,600 feet, the scenic Merriam Lake is a popular destination for fly-fishermen. At the 0.2-mile mark, hikers encounter a trail junction and should keep right, proceeding along Merriam Lake Trail. The well-maintained trail climbs through meadows and forests before switchbacking across quartzite boulders to Merriam Lake's shore. Best months for hiking are mid-July to late September.

Optional Hikes: After locating Merriam Lake's inlet stream, hike upstream to a small alpine lake set at 10,220 feet. Along the way, hikers will view several waterfalls as well as vibrant wildflowers. Although the lake contains no fish, many hikers find the mountain scenery makes the trek worthwhile. Another possibility is to hike northwest from the lake up to a mountain ridge. The ridge offers tremendous views of Leatherman Peak in the distance as well as an opportunity to search for fossils.

Mill Creek to Sheep Pen Basin

Distance: 7.2 miles roundtrip
Climb: moderate
Difficulty: moderate
Usage: light
Location: Drive south on US Highway 93 from Salmon and bear left on the May-Patterson Road. From the small town of May, proceed 1.5 miles south on a paved county road before bearing right on Hooper Lane. Drive to Hooper Lane's end and then turn left. After proceeding 1.5 miles, turn right on a marked dirt road leading to Grouse Creek and Meadow Creek. Follow this dirt road 2.9 miles to a Y fork, and then proceed left. After crossing Mill Creek, turn left and head up Mill Creek Canyon on a grassy road leading to the undeveloped trailhead above Mill Creek's mouth.

Along this trail, hikers will walk across grassy hillsides and thick fir forests before reaching the bubbling source of Mill Creek and the square mile rock glacier known as Sheep Pen Basin. Hikers will walk along game trails and wind through Mill Creek Canyon to reach the base of Sheep Pen Basin in 3.6 miles. From this slow-moving glacier, hikers have incredible vistas of the limestone Grouse Creek Peak and surrounding mountains. Best months for hiking are mid-June to mid-July.

Mount Borah

Distance: 7 miles round trip
Climb: very steep
Difficulty: very difficult
Usage: light
Location: On US Highway 93 between Challis and MacKay, exit east onto Birch Springs-Borah Access Road between mileposts 129 and 130. Drive 4 miles to the trailhead.
Special Considerations: There is no water available on this approximately 12-hour hike, so plan accordingly.

This trail leading to Mount Borah's summit (Idaho's tallest peak) at an elevation of 12,662 feet is designed for advanced hikers in peak physical condition who are unafraid of steep ridges, vertical drop-offs, and rock scrambling. Hikers should also be prepared to cross snowfields and use an ice axe and crampons if necessary. After leaving the trailhead, reach Knob 8,714 at the 0.9-mile mark. The trail becomes obvious here as it steadily climbs above the timberline to its end at 11,600 feet. At this point, hikers should look for rock cairns leading to Chicken-out Ridge at the 2.75 mile mark. Use caution on this knife-edge ridge as a long fall awaits on both sides of the exposure.

Walking along this ridge, drop down into a snowy slope, and then climb to a flat region between the summit and another spur. From here, rock scramble the last 0.5 mile to the summit, staying near the ridgeline to avoid the most precarious rocks. At the summit, hikers are rewarded with views of Idaho's tallest peaks surging 12,000 feet into the atmosphere. Best month for hiking is August, but caution should be used at all times as thunderstorms along this hike could prove fatal.

Ramshorn Canyon

Distance: 3 miles roundtrip
Climb: moderate
Difficulty: moderate
Usage: light
Location: At Darlington, exit off US Highway 93 and drive 2.9 miles east on a gravel road before turning onto a gated dirt road near Hill Road. Proceed on this dirt road 3.9 miles to the informal trailhead at the road's end.

Wandering amidst sagebrush, dry meadows, limestone cliffs, and rock ledges, this trail ends at a grassy bench where hikers can view rocky Ramshorn Canyon's west side. Beginning on an ATV road, the road soon turns into a well-developed trail leading across a rockslide and small meadow before it fades at the 1.5-mile mark. Best month for hiking is June when temperatures are still cool, but access is available from May through October.

Optional Hikes: Where the trail ends, hikers can opt for an additional 1.5-mile cross-country hike. At the grassy bench, head east up the canyon's right side to a ridge view of Ramshorn Canyon, King Mountain, and Cedarville Canyon. This option extends the hike to 6 miles roundtrip, and no water is available in the canyon, so plan accordingly.

Mount Bennett Hills Area

Burnt Willow Canyon

Distance: 3 miles roundtrip
Climb: moderate
Difficulty: moderate
Usage: light
Location: East of Fairfield, merge south off State Highway 20 onto State Highway 46. Drive 14 miles and then bear right onto a Bureau of Land Management road. Continue 2.8 miles and then turn left onto another dirt road. Proceed 0.75 miles to a parking area and hike the remaining distance to the trailhead at Burnt Willow Canyon.

The Burnt Willow Canyon trail offers magnificent scenery of strangely shaped basalt and volcanic ash boulders as well as vibrant wildflowers during late spring. Proceed down the shallow canyon that widens at the 1-mile mark. Here, most of the volcanic boulders disappear, and willow trees line the trail to its end in approximately 0.5 miles. Although Burnt Willow Canyon continues, hikers will have to create their own trail to continue down the canyon. Best months for hiking are mid-May to mid-June when temperatures are cool and the wildflowers are most scenic.

Optional Hikes: Instead of turning around at the trail's end, hikers can climb cross-country up the canyon's right side to a plateau separating Burnt Willow Canyon and Black Canyon.

Gooding City of Rocks/Fourmile Creek

Distance: 2.5 miles roundtrip
Climb: gentle
Difficulty: easy
Usage: moderate
Location: East of Fairfield, merge south off State Highway 20 onto Sate Highway 46. Drive 14 miles

and then bear right onto a Bureau of Land Management road. Continue on this well-maintained dirt road past the junction leading to Burnt Willow Canyon. After traveling several miles, bear left at the signed junction leading to the City of Rocks. Park near the whited-out sign to locate the informal trailhead. A 4-wheel drive vehicle is recommended in accessing this trailhead.

Lichen covered volcanic rock formations, wildflowers, and streamside meadows characterize this easy stroll. Heading eastward from the trailhead sign, descend down the meadowy Fourmile Creek Canyon to reach numerous picnic and camping spots amid the boulders in 1.25 miles. Best months for hiking are mid-May to mid-June.

Gooding City of Rocks/Coyote Creek Loop
Distance: 7.3-mile loop
Climb: gentle
Difficulty: difficult (due to lack of defined trail)
Usage: light
Location: East of Fairfield, merge south off State Highway 20 onto Sate Highway 46. Drive 14 miles and then bear right onto a Bureau of Land Management road. Continue on this well-maintained dirt road past the junction leading to Burnt Willow Canyon. After traveling several miles, bear left at the signed junction leading to the City of Rocks. Park near the whited-out sign to locate the informal trailhead. A 4-wheel drive vehicle is recommended in accessing this trailhead.

Situated amidst natural arches, large volcanic rock formations, and a scenic canyon, this loop trail is not physically demanding, but does require excellent map-reading skills as the trail fades in and out. Head south by southwest from the sign into a shallow canyon. At the 2-mile mark, the canyon narrows, then suddenly widens as hikers head up Coyote Creek. The canyon narrows significantly at the 3.7 and 5.5 mile marks. To get around the second narrow spot, climb 40 feet up the canyon's left wall and proceed to Coyote Springs at the 7-mile mark. From Coyote Springs, proceed along the canyon's right fork back to the parking area. Best months for hiking are mid-May to mid-June, and hikers should watch for rattlesnakes in the area.

Pioneer Mountains Area
East Fork of the Big Wood River
Distance: 4.6 miles roundtrip
Climb: moderate
Difficulty: difficult
Usage: heavy
Location: 5.5 miles north of Hailey, exit off State Highway 75 onto East Fork of the Big Wood River Road. Proceed 6 miles on this paved road to a junction and stay to the right. Continuing 1 mile, reach a Y intersection and keep left. Follow this bumpy road past Federal Gulch to the East Fork Trailhead, keeping left at all subsequent road junctions. The trailhead is unmaintained with no water available, and the road does require 4-wheel drive with high clearance.

White granite and reddish brown metamorphic peaks line this trail that begins in a landslide area, then climbs into a meadow and eventually up to Johnstone Pass. While the first 1.8 miles of the hike are moderately difficult and offer views of the Little Matterhorn Peak and an impressive waterfall, the hike from the base of Johnstone Pass is extremely difficult. Visitors should be prepared to rock scramble on all fours to reach the 10,002 Johnstone Pass at the 2.3 mile mark. Best months for hiking are July to mid-September.

Optional Hikes: 0.5 miles before reaching the East Fork Trailhead, locate Trail 174 at the Iron Mine Trailhead. This 8-mile roundtrip out and back hike climbs up and over PK Pass at an elevation of 9,450 feet before dropping down to the Little Wood River. This trail is rated difficult due to the trail's rapid elevation gain and loss. Best months for hiking are July to mid-September.

Fall Creek
Distance: 14 miles roundtrip
Climb: moderate
Difficulty: difficult
Usage: moderate
Location: From Ketchum, proceed eastward past Sun Valley up to Trail Creek Summit. Proceed to Copper Basin Road and turn right. Drive 2.5 miles on this road before exiting right on Wildhorse Creek Road. Continue 3.5 miles and merge onto Fall Creek Road to locate the Fall Creek Falls Trailhead in 0.3 miles.

Several waterfalls, wildlife ranging from mountain goats to wolves, and glaciated mountain peaks rising 12,000 feet are just some of the highlights on this trek through rugged Fall Creek Canyon to the headwaters of Fall Creek. Though the hike begins on a jeep trail, it is now closed to vehicles. Climbing moderately on this trail, hikers will reach a trail junction at the 3-mile mark. However, instead of following the trail marker sign, hikers should proceed on the left trail through a thick forest past several waterfalls. At the trip's 4.2-mile mark, the trail becomes faint. Hikers should follow the trail maintained mostly by wildlife and walk through bogs, meadows, and rockslides to reach Fall Creek's head at the 7-mile mark. Best months for hiking are August to mid-September.

Left Fork of Fall Creek
Distance: 12 miles roundtrip
Climb: moderate
Difficulty: moderate
Usage: light
Location: From Ketchum, proceed eastward past Sun Valley up to Trail Creek Summit. Proceed to Copper Basin Road and turn right. Drive 2.5 miles on this road before exiting right on Wildhorse Creek Road. Continue 3.5 miles and merge onto Fall Creek Road to locate the Fall Creek Falls Trailhead in 0.3 miles.

Situated amid the granite peaks of the Pioneer Mountains, the Left Fork of Fall Creek trail winds through volcanic rock hills covered with aspen trees and wildflowers with a variety of wildlife populating the area. Starting out on an old jeep trail, hike 1.8 miles up Fall Creek Canyon and locate the faint Left Fork Trail right after fording Left Fork Creek. The trail switchbacks up a hanging valley, and in several places, the trail is located next to a steep ledge where caution should be used. Hikers should continue up into the Left Fork Valley, ending where the rocky base of Pyramid Peak joins the sunny meadow. Best months for hiking are July to mid-September.

Right Fork of Fall Creek
Distance: 10 miles roundtrip
Climb: steep
Difficulty: moderately difficult
Usage: heavy
Location: From Ketchum, proceed eastward past Sun Valley up to Trail Creek Summit. Proceed to Copper Basin Road and turn right. Drive 2.5 miles on this road before exiting right on Wildhorse Creek Road. Continue 3.5 miles and merge onto Fall Creek Road to locate the Fall Creek Falls Trailhead in 0.3 miles.

Set in a hanging valley off Fall Creek, this trail winds through forests, meadows, and rugged igneous and sedimentary rocks before ending at the popular trout-fishing spot, Moose Lake. Beginning on an old jeep trail, hike 3 miles and bear right at the Right Fork Trail junction. Proceed along the most heavily used trail (ignoring faint side trails) and switchback up to the cirque containing Moose Lake. Visitors can opt to hike up to a smaller lake situated in the rocky peaks directly above Moose Lake, but the best angling can be found in the heavily trout populated waters of Moose Lake. Best months for hiking are July to mid-September.

Fall Creek to Surprise Valley
Distance: 12.6 miles roundtrip
Climb: steep
Difficulty: difficult
Usage: moderate
Location: From Ketchum, proceed eastward past Sun Valley up to Trail Creek Summit. Proceed to Copper Basin Road and turn right. Drive 2.5 miles on this road before exiting right on Wildhorse Creek Road. Continue 3.5 miles and merge onto Fall Creek Road to locate the Fall Creek Falls Trailhead in 0.3 miles.

This trail ascends steeply up boulder-covered slopes, through thick forests, and across scenic meadows before arriving at two alpine lakes with spectacular mountain views. Beginning on an old jeep trail, hike 3.3 miles up Fall Creek Canyon (staying to the left at the junction with Right Fork Trail) to the Surprise Valley Trail leaving to the left. Follow the faint trail 1.5 miles to reach a large pond situated 1,000 feet above Fall Creek. Staying 50 yards to the right of this pond's inlet, hike an additional 1.5 miles to reach Standhope Peak framing a deep, alpine lake. Best months for hiking are July to mid-September.

Hyndman Creek
Distance: 8 miles roundtrip
Climb: easy for the first 3 miles; very steep the last mile
Difficulty: moderate
Usage: moderate
Location: 5.5 miles north of Hailey, merge off State Highway 75 onto East Fork of the Big Wood River Road. Proceed 6 miles before bearing left on Hyndman Creek Road. Continue past the Bear/Parker Trailhead and Johnstone Creek Trailhead to reach Trail 166 at Hyndman Creek Trailhead in 4.4 miles. A Sawtooth National Recreation Area fee is required at the trailhead.

Climbing through aspen groves, vibrant wildflower fields, and past several rocky avalanche chutes, this trail ends in a meadow with 360-degree views of impressive mountain peaks. Leaving to the right at the trailhead, the trail follows an old road and does not begin steeply climbing until the 3-mile mark. After reaching an outfitter camp, hikers should stay to the right and climb 900 feet to the trail's end in 0.5 miles. This spring-filled meadow offers stunning views of Hyndman Peak, Old Hyndman Peak, Cobb Peak, Duncan Peak, and Duncan Ridge. Best months for hiking are July to mid-September.

Optional Hikes: At the trek's 2.5-mile mark, locate an old mining road leaving to the left. This trail wanders up Hyndman Creek, ending at the base of Old Hyndman Peak and the Big Basin Lakes. This hike is rated moderate and receives little usage. Best months for hiking are July to mid-September.

Iron Bog and Fishpole Lakes
Distance: 5 miles roundtrip
Climb: moderate
Difficulty: easy
Usage: heavy
Location: From Arco, drive 10.5 miles north on US Highway 93 before exiting onto Antelope Creek Road.

Proceed past Iron Bog Campground and bear left onto Forest Road (FR) 220 to locate the trailhead in approximately 1 mile.

Surrounded by scenic peaks, open meadows, and wildflowers, Iron Bog and Fishpole Lakes have been described as two of Idaho's prettiest alpine settings. Possessing tremendous fishing potential, the lake area is also populated with mule deer, coyotes, elk, and pronghorn antelope. Beginning on the right side of the trailhead, hikers will reach Iron Bog Lake's 9,067-foot elevation in 2.3 miles. The hike to Fishpole Lake begins at Iron Bog Lake's outlet. After locating a trail near the lake's outlet stream, ascend 450 feet to a cirque containing Fishpole Lake as well as three other small lakes. Best months for hiking are late June through September.

Summit Creek
Distance: 7 miles roundtrip
Climb: moderate
Difficulty: moderate
Usage: heavy
Location: From Ketchum, drive 12 miles east to Trail Creek Summit's crest to locate the trailhead on the summit's south side. An obvious trail leads to the left across Summit Creek.

This trail takes hikers through meadows, forests, and up a canyon full of avalanche debris while offering views of the Boulder Mountains to the north. After hiking 2 miles and arriving at a large wildflower meadow, visitors should proceed left at the meadow's end to climb up to a 9,500-foot pass. From the pass, hikers have views of Devil's Bedstead West rising before them. Best months for hiking are July through September.

Sawtooth Mountains Area
Special Considerations in this Area: Hikers must possess a free wilderness permit found at the trailhead and pay a Sawtooth National Recreation Area (SNRA) fee at the trailhead. For groups larger than eight, a special SNRA wilderness permit must be obtained from the SNRA headquarters. In addition, no campfires are allowed in the area and pets must be leashed through Labor Day.

Alpine Creek
Distance: 6 miles roundtrip
Climb: gentle
Difficulty: easy
Usage: heavy
Location: At Ketchum, drive 40 miles north on State Highway 75 and merge onto Alturas Lake Road. Continue past Alturas Lake as the paved road soon turns into gravel. Proceed 1.5 miles on this gravel road to locate the Alpine Creek/Alturas Creek Trailhead.

Hikers are rewarded with outstanding scenery of the Sawtooth Mountains while climbing through wildflower meadows, thick forests, and potentially up to area alpine lakes. Beginning in a level forested area, the trail soon climbs up to a granite shelf where views of the glacier formed Alpine Creek Canyon are found. Continue along the same trail to its end in 3 miles beside Alpine Creek in a dense forest. Many hikers opt to continue forward 0.6 miles in the trailless area to reach a large lake. Best months for hiking are July through September.

Optional Hikes: At the trailhead, hike along the Alturas Creek trail which winds through a large valley between the Sawtooth and Smoky Mountain Ranges.

Iron Creek to Sawtooth Lake
Distance: 10 miles roundtrip
Climb: moderate
Difficulty: moderate
Usage: heavy
Location: Drive on State Highway 21 2.6 miles northwestward from Stanley and merge onto Iron Creek Road. Continue 3.2 miles on this gravel road to the trailhead at Iron Creek Transfer Camp.

As the largest lake in the Sawtooth Mountain Range, Sawtooth Lake is also by far one of the most scenic. Generations of photographers have captured the lake on film, and its beauty makes it a popular destination for hikers of all ages. Beginning at the trailhead, proceed 1.2 miles and bear right onto Alpine Way Trail. In just 0.5 miles, turn left on the trail leading to Sawtooth Lake. Climbing along switchbacks under a canopy of Douglas fir trees, hikers will ford Iron Creek at the 3-mile mark. After 2 more miles, hikers will reach the overlook point of Sawtooth Lake reflecting the 10,190-foot Mount Regan in its waters. Best months for hiking are late July through August.

Optional Hikes: From the overlook point of Sawtooth Lake, hikers can proceed 1 mile along the trail's right fork that climbs to McGowan Pass and the impressive McGowan Lakes. Hikers can also opt to take the left fork southward to a small lake just beyond Sawtooth Lake and continue descending steeply past three additional lakes into the North Fork of Baron Creek. For a short side hike, backpackers may opt to travel to Alpine Lake. 1 mile after fording Iron Creek, locate a faint side trail leading to Alpine Lake. The lake is framed with subalpine fir and offers a view of Alpine Peak to the south.

Toxaway-Pettit Loop
Distance: 17.5 mile loop
Climb: moderately steep
Difficulty: difficult
Usage: heavy
Location: Drive 45 miles north of Ketchum on State Highway 75 and merge onto Pettit Lake Road. Proceed 2 miles to a T intersection, and then turn to the right. After reaching the next fork, bear left and continue 0.5 miles to the well-developed trailhead.

This trek takes hikers past all the features that have made the Sawtooth Mountains a celebrated wilderness area. Backpackers will pass jagged mountain peaks and granite cliffs, boulders, alpine lakes, avalanche sites, wildflower meadows, dense lodgepole forests, numerous cascades, and trickling mountain streams. From the trailhead, hike 0.1 miles to a trail junction and merge onto the right fork leading to Yellow Belly Creek. After switchbacking up and down the canyon of Yellow Belly Creek, passing McDonald Lake, and viewing a small waterfall tumbling next to the trail, hikers will reach another junction at the 6.5-mile mark. Staying to the left, pass Bowknot Lake and climb up to the fishable waters of Toxaway Lake. Several hikers report catching brook trout up to a foot long in this lake. Hiking around Toxaway Lake, switchback up the steep canyon leading to Snowyside Pass at the trek's 9.3-mile mark. Locate a notch at the pass and hike down a steep rock wall leading to the sapphire Twin Lakes. Here, proceed east over a saddle, pass Alice Lake, and head down to a bridge crossing of Pettit Lake Creek. After switchbacking along the canyon wall under jagged cliffs, hikers will reach Pettit Lake at the 16.4-mile mark with McDonald Peak rising in the distance. Proceed along the trail 1.1 miles back to the trailhead. Best months for hiking are August to mid-September.

Optional Hikes: At the 7.8 mile mark at Toxaway Lake, hikers can locate a trail on the lake's north side leading over the 9,400-foot Sand Mountain Pass to the scenic Vernon, Edna, and Virginia Lakes.

Norton Lakes
Distance: 4 miles roundtrip
Climb: gentle
Difficulty: easy
Usage: heavy
Location: Travel 15.5 miles on State Highway 75 north of Ketchum and exit west towards the Smoky Mountains on Forest Road (FR) 162 (Baker Creek Road). Follow FR 162 partway up to a spur in the road and locate the trailhead for Trail #135.

Forest Service officials recommend this trek to novice hikers interested in glimpsing some of the Smoky Mountains' majestic scenery without having to exert tremendous effort. Best months for hiking are July through September.

Horton Peak Lookout
Distance: 8 miles roundtrip
Climb: steep
Difficulty: difficult
Usage: moderate
Location: At the south end of Sawtooth Valley, drive on Forest Road (FR) 194 (Valley Road). Exit onto FR 459 to locate the Horton Peak Trailhead.

Gaining 2,700 vertical feet, this trail ends at the historic Horton Peak Lookout. Hikers will have a sweeping vista of the entire Sawtooth National Recreation Area. Best months for hiking are July through September.

Smoky Mountains Area
Special Considerations in this Area: Hikers must pay a Sawtooth National Recreation Area trailhead fee.

Baker Lake
Distance: 2.5 miles roundtrip
Climb: steep
Difficulty: moderate
Usage: moderate
Location: From Ketchum, drive 15.5 miles north on State Highway 75 into the Sawtooth National Recreation Area (SNRA). Bear left onto Baker Creek Road and proceed 9.5 miles to its end at the well-developed trailhead.

This short hike through wildflower meadows climbs 900 feet in just 1.5 miles to the scenic Baker Lake situated under the Smoky Mountains' crest. Shortly after starting out, hikers will ford a small tributary of Baker Creek that crosses over the trail. Beyond this point, the trail climbs under a few Douglas fir trees up to the divide between Baker Creek and an area canyon. Upon reaching the lake, many visitors opt to fish for 7 to 12 inch trout, but Baker Lake is restricted to catch and release fishing only. Best months for hiking are July through September.

Prairie Creek Loop
Distance: 10 mile loop
Climb: moderate
Difficulty: moderate
Usage: heavy
Location: From downtown Ketchum, drive 18.9 miles north on State Highway 75 into the Sawtooth National Recreation Area (SNRA). Bear left onto Forest Road (FR) 179 (Prairie Creek Road) and proceed 2.6 miles to the Prairie Lakes Trailhead.

Crossing through several meadows and some lodgepole forests, this trail leads hikers to Miner Lake and Prairie Lakes set amidst scenic mountain scenery. Immediately after leaving the trailhead on Trail 133, hikers will ford the West Fork of Prairie Creek rushing over the trail. After doing this, climb to the trek's 2.2 mile mark and take the left trail junction leading up to Miner Lake. At the 3.5-mile mark, backpackers will reach the bottom of Miner Lake cirque, and at the 4.1 mile mark is a trail junction leading to Prairie Lakes. Upon reaching and exploring the Prairie Lakes area at the 5.5-mile mark, hike straight down the canyon 4.5 miles back to the trailhead. Best months for hiking are July through September.

Optional Hikes: At Miner Lake's eastern side, follow a trail that steeply switchbacks up to a pass near Norton Peak, then drops quickly to both the upper and lower Norton Lakes. This side hike is rated difficult due to rapid elevation gain and loss.

West Fork of Prairie Creek

Distance: 3.6 miles roundtrip
Climb: gentle
Difficulty: easy
Usage: moderate
Location: From downtown Ketchum, drive 18.9 miles north on State Highway 75 into the Sawtooth National Recreation Area (SNRA). Bear left onto Forest Road (FR) 179 (Prairie Creek Road) and proceed 2.6 miles to the Prairie Lakes Trailhead.

This trail, winding near West Prairie Creek, gently climbs into a canyon covered with wildflowers, a few Douglas fir trees not crushed during the frequent winter avalanches, and rockslides before reaching a grassy meadow. On Trail 134, head northwest into the mouth of West Prairie Creek, crossing West Prairie Creek and heading up the forested canyon. At the 0.6-mile mark, hikers will begin climbing up a rockslide leading to a meadow in 0.7 miles. Hikers can opt to walk out into the meadow where the trail ends. However, many visitors choose to scramble up game trails here that lead further up the canyon past a few gurgling springs and more wildflowers.

INFORMATION PLEASE

All Idaho area codes are 208

Road Information

ID Road & Weather Conditions	
	888-432-7623 or local 884-7000
Idaho State Police	736-3090

Tourism Information

Idaho Travel Council 800-VISIT-ID outside Idaho
334-2470 in Idaho
www.visitid.org

Visit Sun Valley
800-234-0599 or 866-305-0408
www.visitsunvalley.com

Airports

Arco	527-3261
Hailey	788-4956
Howe	767-3455
Mackay	588-2274

Government Offices

Idaho Bureau of Reclamation	334-1466
www.usbr.gov	
Idaho Department of Commerce	
(800) 847-4843 or 334-2470	
www.visitid.org or http://cl.idaho.gov/	
Idaho Department of Fish and Game	
(800) ASK-FISH or 334-3700	
http://fishandgame.idaho.gov	
Idaho Department of Parks and Recreation	
334-4199	
www.idahoparks.org	
State BLM Office	373-3889 or 373-4000
www.id.blm.gov	

Bureau of Land Management Challis Field Office	
	879-4181
Bureau of Land Management Salmon Field Office	
	756-5400
Craters of the Moon National Monument	
	527-3257
Salmon-Challis National Forest	756-5100
Sawtooth National Recreation Area	727-5000
Sawtooth Wilderness Area	727-5013

Hospitals

Lost Rivers Medical Center • Arco	527-8206
St Lukes Wood River Medical Center	
Ketchum	727-8800
Steele Memorial Hospital • Salmon	756-8980

Golf Courses

Challis Golf Course • Challis	879-5440
Cottonwood Golf Course • Fairfield	764-3016
Soldier Mountain Ranch • Fairfield	764-2506
Bigwood Golf Club • Ketchum	726-4024
Cotton Wood Links • MacKay	588-3394
River park Golf Course • Mackay	588-2296
Salmon Golf Course • Salmon	756-4734
Elkhorn Golf Club • Sun Valley	622-4511
Sun Valley Golf• Sun Valley	622-2251

Bed & Breakfasts

Greyhouse Inn B&B • Salmon	756-3968
100 Acre Wood Resort and B&B	
North Fork	865-2165
Knob Hill Inn • Ketchum	726-80105
Indian Creek Guest Ranch	
North Fork	394-2126
Cross Canyon Country Inn • Salmon	756-2778

Guest Ranches & Resorts

Geertson Creek Trail Rides	
Salmon	756-2463
Sunbeam Village Resort • Stanley	838-2211
Syringa Lodge • Salmon	756-4424
Twin Peaks Ranch • Salmon	894-2290
Mountain Village Resort • Stanley	774-3661
Idaho Rocky Mountain Ranch	
Stanley	774-3544
Cowboy Trails Ranch Vacation	
Carey	280-0576
Jevne Ranch • Carey	246-9751
Cabin at the Riverranch • Challis	879-2788
Challis Hot Springs • Challis	879-4442
May Family Ranch • Clayton	838-2407
Soldier Mountain Ranch & Resort	
Fairfield	764-2506
Bald Mountain Lodge • Ketchum	726-4776
Galena Lodge • Ketchum	726-4010
Resorts West • Ketchum	726-5900
Sun Valley Resort, Pete Lane's Mountain Sports	
Ketchum	622-2276
Warm Springs Ranch • Ketchum	726-2609
Wild Horse Creek Ranch • Mackay	588-2575
Arctic Creek Lodge • North Fork	865-2372
Cummings Lake Lodge • North Fork	865-2424
River's Fork Inn & RV Park	
North Fork	865-2301
Cross Canyon Country Inn & Elk Ranch	
Salmon	756-2779
Elk Bend Sports Lodge • Salmon	894-2455
Middle Fork Lodge • Salmon	333-0783
Ram's Head Lodge • Salmon	394-2122
Royal Gorge Resort • Salmon	876-4130
Salmon River Lodge • Salmon	756-6622
Williams Lake Lodge • Salmon	756-2007
West Shore Lodge • Shoshone	487-3636
Indian Creek Guest Ranch • Shoup	394-2126
Diamond D Ranch • Stanley	336-9772
Mystic Saddle Ranch • Stanley	774-3591
Redfish Lake Lodge • Stanley	774-3536
Salmon River Lodge • Stanley	774-3422

Sulphur Creek Ranch • Stanley	377-1188
Sun Valley Lodge and Inn • Stanley	622-4111
Torrey's Resort & RV Park • Stanley	838-2313
Triangle C Ranch Log Cabins	
Stanley	774-2266
Yankee Fork Resort • Stanley	838-2662
Elkhorn Resort • Sun Valley	622-4511
Premier Resorts Sun Valley	
Sun Valley	727-4000
Sun Valley Resort • Sun Valley	622-4111
Tamarack Lodge • Sun Valley	726-3344

Vacation Homes & Cabins

Salmon River Cabins & Motel	
Stanley	774-3566
Riverside Motel & Sawtooth Rentals	
Stanley	774-3409

Forest Service Cabins

Salmon-Challis National Forest
North Basin A-Frame Cabin
1 mi. NE of Watson Peak 756-5100
Cap: 6 Nightly Fee: $20 Available: Year Round
Snow machine access in winter. Wood stove, outdoor privy. 1 ø hr. drive from Salmon

Peel Tree A-Frame Cabin
32 mi. SW of Salmon 756-5100
Cap: 6 Nightly Fee: $20 Available: Year Round
Snow machine access in winter. Wood stove, outdoor privy.

Williams Creek Summit A-Frame Cabin
17 mi. S of Salmon 756-5100
Cap: 6 Nightly Fee: $20 Available: Year Round
Snow machines access in winter. Wood stove, outdoor privy.

Iron Lake A-Frame Cabin
37 mi. SW of Salmon 756-5100
Cap: 6 Nightly Fee: $20 Available: 10/1-5/1
Snow machine access in winter. Wood stove, outdoor privy. Usually used by campground host in summer.

Cabin Creek
8 mi. SW of Cobalt Ranger Station 756-5100
Cap: 6 Nightly Fee: $20 Available: Year Round
2 mile hike from Rd. 105. Snow machine access in winter. Wood stove.

Sheephorn Lookout
Approx. 40 mi. SW of Salmon 756-5100
Cap: 2-3 Nightly Fee: $20 Available: Year Round
Lights provided by solar panel. Heat/mattresses provided, small wood stove. Propane refrigerator, range/oven. No water. Outdoor privy. Snowmobile access in winter.

Wallace Lake A-Frame Cabin
Hwy. 93 N, take Stormy Peak Rd. At summit, take Ridge Rd. #020 and turn at Wallace Lake turnoff 756-5100
Cap: 2-3 Nightly Fee: $20 Available: Year Round
Primarily used to house campground host during summer months.

Cape Horn Guard Station
Stanley Basin, 16 mi. NW of Stanley 838-3300
Cap: 8 Nightly Fee: $25 Available: 12/1-4/30
Wood stove for heat, backup cooking, outhouse, electric cook stove and lights unless power is out. Pack in water and/or melt snow. Access during winter is a 2-mi. ski or 4-mi. snowmobile run from parking areas on State Hwy. 21. Recommend calling for update on conditions.

Car Rental

Budget Car & Truck Rental • Bellevue	788-3660
Avis • Hailey	788-2382
Budget • Hailey	788-3660

Hertz • Hailey	788-4548
Sutton & Sons Auto • Hailey	788-2225
SUV Auto-Rentals • Hailey	788-9110
You Save Auto Rental • Hailey	788-3224
Clean Machine Auto • Salmon	756-8777
Salmon River Motors Inc • Salmon	756-4211
Express Car Rental • Sun Valley	622-5700
Thrifty • Sun Valley	622-2077

Outfitters & Guides

F=Fishing H=Hunting R=River Guides
E=Horseback Rides G=General Guide Services

Id Outfitters & Guides Association		
		800-49-IDAHO
Outfitters & Guides Licensing Board		327-7380
Richie Outfitters	FHEG	756-3231
Mile High Outfitters, Inc	FFHR	879-4500
Salmon River Scenic Run	FR	879-2249
100 Acre Wood Resort	FHERG	865-2165
Geertson Creek Trail Rides	EG	756-2463
Idaho Adventures	FRG	756-2986
Twin Peaks Ranch, Inc	FHERG	894-2290
Idaho Rocky Mountain Ranch		
	FHERG	774-3544
Sawtooth Fishing Guides	F	774-8768
Super Outfitter Adventures of Sun Valley		
	FHE	788-7731
Valley Ranch Outfitters		774-3470
Bighorn Outfitters	FHE	756-3992
American Adrenaline Co,	FHR	879-4700
Horse Creek Outfitters, Inc	FHR	879-5400
White Cloud Outfitters	FHERG	879-4574
Wild Idaho Outfitters and Guides	FH	382-6256

Wilderness Outfitters	FHEG	879-2203
High Country Outfitters	FHE	764-3104
Keating Outfitters	FHE	865-2252
Middle Fork River Tours	FHERG	788-6545
Sun Valley Trekking Company	RG	788-1966
Venture Outfitters	FEG	788-5049
Lost River Outfitters	FH	726-1706
Middle Fork Wilderness Outfitters, Inc		
	FHR	726-5999
Silver Creek Outfitters	FR	726-5282
Continental Divide	H	865-2665
Horse Mountain Outfitters	FHEG	394-2213
Indian Creek Guest Ranch, LLC		
	FHERG	394-2126
Salmon River Tours Co. Inc	FH	865-2375
Stub Creek Inc	R	865-2474
Aggipah River Trips	FHER	756-4167
Castle Creek Outfitters	FHG	756-2548
Eagle Eye Outfitters	HER	756-8111
Flying Resort Ranches	FHE	756-6259
Happy Hollow Vacation	FHERG	756-3954
Kookaburra	FHER	756-4386
Quartet Circle A Outfitters	HE	894-2451
Rawhide Outfitters	FHERG	756-4276
Rendezvous Sports	RG	756-4495
Saddle Springs Outfitters	HE	756-1881
Salmon River Lodge	FHERG	756-3033
Silver Cloud Expeditions, Inc	FHERG	756-6215
Warren River Expeditions, Inc	FHR	756-6387
Yellow Jacket River Guides	R	380-5525
Stanley Potts Outfitter	FH	394-2135
Galena State Stop Outfitters		726-1735

Middle Fork River Expeditions, Inc		
	FHR	774-3659
Mystic Saddle Ranch	FHEG	774-3591
Sawtooth Mountain Guides	FHG	774-3324
Triangle C Ranch	FR	634-4787
Bill Mason Outfitters	F	622-9305
Far and Away Adventures	R	726-2288
Sun Valley Horseman's Center	E	622-2391

Cross-Country Ski Centers

North Valley Trails • Hailey	726-4010
Galena Lodge • Ketchum	726-4010
Sun Valley • Sun Valley	622-2001

Downhill Ski Areas

Soldier Mountain • Fairfield	764-2300
Sun Valley • Ketchum	622-2001
Lost Trail Powder Mountain	
North Fork	821-3211

Snowmobile Rentals

100 Acre Wood Resort	
Northfork/Salmon	865-2165
Mountain Village Resort • Stanley	774-3661

Bike Rentals

Kelly Sport • Ketchum	**726-8503**
Sun Summit Ski & Cycle • Ketchum	**726-0707**
Pete Lane's Mountain Sports	
Sun Valley	**622-2279**
Pete Lane's Mountain Sports - River Run Bike Shop • Sun Valley	**622-6144**

NOTES:

352   *Ultimate* Idaho Atlas and Travel Encyclopedia

Campground Quick Reference

Campground Name				Phone
Public/Commercial	Unit Price	#Spaces	Max. Length	Seasons
Directions				
Amenities/Activities				

Arco

Landing Zone RV Park — 527-8513/877-563-0663
C $15-20   60   All Year
S. of Arco on County Rd. .25 mi.
Dump Station, Hookups, Mini-Mart, Pets OK, Playground, Pull-thru Sites, Reservations, Showers

Mountain View RV Park - Arco — 527-3707
C $19-23   34   45' Summer, Fall, Spring
Hwy. 20, .75 mi. W. of Arco
Dump Station, Hookups, Modem Hookups, Laundry

Craters of the Moon Natl. Monument & Preserve — 527-3257
P $10   52   35' Summer, Fall, Spring
Hwy. 93, 18 mi. SW of Arco
Drinking Water, Pull-thru Sites, Vault Toilets, Handicap Access

Garden Creek — 756-5400
P   None   May-October
43 miles NW of Arco on Hwy 93, then 15 miles W on Trail Creek Rd
Developed Campground, Handicap Accessible Restrooms, Fishing, Hiking/Backpacking, Wildlife Viewing

Bellevue

Riverside RV Park — 788-2020
C   38   All Year
403 Broadford Rd
Cable TV Hookups, Drinking Water, Dump Station, Hookups, Pets OK, Pull-thru Sites, Reservations, Showers

Riverside RV Park & Campground — 788-2020
C $24-475   38   40'   All Year
Hwy. 75, W. on Broadford Rd.
Cable TV Hookups, Drinking Water, Dump Station, Fire Rings, Hookups, Pets OK, Pull-thru Sites, Reservations, Showers, Tenters Welcome, Laundry

Copper Creek — 622-5371
P   None   5   May-October
25 miles east of Bellevue on Muldoon Canyon Rd, then N on FR 134
Primitive Camping, Restrooms, Fishing, Hiking/Backpacking, Picnicking

Challis

Challis Valley RV Park — 879-2393
C $19-22   65   All Year
Hwy. 93 at Ram's Horn
Cable TV Hookups, Dump Station, Hookups, Limited Access, Pets OK, Pull-thru Sites, Showers, Tenters Welcome, Handicap Access

Challis Hot Springs — 634-0700
C $18-23   30   All Year
4.5 mi. off Hwy. 93
Credit Cards OK, Dump Station, Hookups, Hot Springs, Pets OK, Reservations, Swimming Pool, Waterfront

Bayhorse Lake — 838-2201
P $5   6   21'   All Year
2 mi. S. on Hwy. 93, 7 mi. S. on Hwy. 75, 8 mi. W. on Forest Rd. 051
Drinking Water, Pets OK, Vault Toilets

East Fork — 879-6200
P $5   7   25'   All Year
18 mi. SW on Hwy. 93, then Hwy. 75
Drinking Water, Fire Rings, Pets OK, Pull-thru Sites, Tenters Welcome, Vault Toilets, Waterfront, Handicap Access

Mill Creek — 879-4100
P $4   8   35'   Summer, Fall
4.5 mi. W. on Garden Creek Rd., 11 mi. W. on Mill Creek Rd. 070
Drinking Water, Hookups, Pets OK, Reservations, Vault Toilets

---

Spring Gulch — 756-5400
P   30'   Summer, Fall
10 mi. N. on Hwy. 93
Drinking Water, Swimming Pool, Vault Toilets

Cottonwood — 879-6200
P $6   14   30'   All Year
Hwy. 93, 15 mi. N. of Challis
Drinking Water, Dump Station, Fire Rings, Pets OK, Pull-thru Sites, Tenters Welcome, Vault Toilets, Waterfront

Bayhorse — 879-6200
P $5   11   28'   Summer, Fall, Spring
8 mi. S. of Challis on Hwy. 93
Drinking Water, Fire Rings, Pets OK, Tenters Welcome, Vault Toilets

Mosquito Flat Reservoir — 879-4100
P   9   32'   Summer, Fall
15 mi. W. Forest Rd. 080, Challis Creek Rd.
Drinking Water, Pets OK, Vault Toilets

Herd Lake — 756-5400
P   None   Undeveloped   May-October
18 miles SW of Challis on Hwys. 93 and 75, then 16 miles SE on FR 120 and Herd Creek Rd
Primitive Camping, Restrooms, Fishing, Hiking/Backpacking, Horseback Riding, Hunting, Picnicking, Wildlife Viewing

Morse Creek — 879-4321
P   None   3   June-September
17 miles N of Challis on Hwy 93, then 10 miles SE on Farm to Market Rd, then 6 miles E on FR 094
Developed Campground, Restrooms, Biking, Fishing, Hiking/Backpacking, Horseback Riding, Hunting, Picnicking

Deadman Hole — 756-5400
P   None   Undeveloped   May-October
13 miles S of Challis on Hwys. 93 and 75
Primitive Camping, Drinking Water, Restrooms, Cultural/Historic Site, Fishing, Hiking/Backpacking, Picnicking

Boulder White Clouds Trailhead — 756-5400
P   Yes   May-October
18 miles SW of Challis on Hwys 93 and 75, then 18 miles S on FR 120
Developed Campground, Handicap Accessible Restrooms, Non-Motorized Boating, Fishing, Hiking/Backpacking, Picnicking, Wildlife Viewing

Mill Creek Campground West — 879-4321
P $5 Single.; $30-$40/Grp.   15   June-September
13 miles W of Challis on FR 070
Developed Campground, Group Camping, Drinking Water, Restrooms, RV Sites, Cultural-Historic Sites, Biking, Fishing, Hiking/Backpacking, Off Highway Vehicles, Picnicking, Scenic Driving

Mahoney Creek — 879-4100
P   None   2   July-September
26 miles from Challis on FR 086
Primitive Camping, Restrooms, Biking, Hiking/Backpacking, Horseback Riding, Picnicking, Scenic Driving

Sleeping Deer — 879-4101
P   None   Undeveloped   July-September
37 miles from Challis on FR 086
Primitive Camping, Restrooms, Biking, Hiking/Backpacking, Horseback Riding, Picnicking, Scenic Driving

Clayton

May Family Ranch — 838-2407
C   6   All Year
4 mi. W. of Clayton, N. at M. P. 219.5, go .5 mi.
Handicap Access

Campground Quick Reference - continued

Campground Name Public/Commercial	Unit Price	#Spaces	Max. Length	Phone Seasons
Directions				
Amenities/Activities				

Old Sawmill Station — 838-2400
C $18-22.5 40 All Year
Clayton area
Credit Cards OK, Drinking Water, Dump Station, Hookups, Mini-Mart, Pets OK, Pull-thru Sites, Showers, Tenters Welcome, Laundry

Bonanza — 838-2201
P 35' Summer, Fall
14.9 mi. NE on Hwy. 75, 8 mi. N. on Forest Rd. 013 (Yankee Fork), .25 mi. W. on Forest Rd. 074
Drinking Water, Pets OK, Reservations, Vault Toilets

Holman Creek — 727-5000/800-260-5970
P $8 10 22' Summer, Fall
7 mi. W. of Clayton on Hwy. 75
Drinking Water, Fire Rings, Pets OK, Tenters Welcome, Vault Toilets

Cobalt

Crags — 756-5200
P $4 24 16' Summer, Fall
9 mi. SW on Forest Rd. 60055, 7 mi. NW on Forest Rd. 112, 13 mi. N. on Forest Rd. 113, 2 mi. N. on Forest Rd. 114
Drinking Water, Fire Rings, Pets OK, Tenters Welcome, Vault Toilets

Yellowjacket Lake — 756-5200
P 7 22' Summer, Fall
9 mi. S. on Forest Rd. 60055, 7 mi. W. on Forest Rd. 60112, 16 mi. N. on Forest Rd. 60113
Drinking Water, Fire Rings, Pets OK, Tenters Welcome, Vault Toilets, Waterfront

Yellowjacket Lake — 756-5100
P Yes 7 July-September
9 miles S of Cobalt on FR 055, then 7 miles W on FR 112, and 16 miles N on FR 113
Developed Campground, Drinking Water, Restrooms, Biking, Fishing, Hiking/Backpacking, Hunting, Off Highway Vehicles, Picnicking

Middlefork Peak — 756-5100
P None Undeveloped July-September
9 miles S of Cobalt on FR 055, then 24 miles W on FR 112
Primitive Camping, Drinking Water, Restrooms, Biking, Hiking/Backpacking, Horseback Riding, Hunting, Picnicking, Scenic Driving

Fairfield

Soldier Creek RV Park — 764-3904
C 11 All Year
10 mi. N. of Fairfield at Soldier Creek Rd.
Drinking Water, Dump Station, Hookups, Pets OK, Reservations, Tenters Welcome, Vault Toilets

Iron Mountain RV Park — 764-2577
C $19-21 15 40' All Year
Hwy. 20, .25 mi. W. of Fairfield
Credit Cards OK, Drinking Water, Dump Station, Hookups, Pets OK, Showers, Laundry

Canyon Transfer Camp — 764-3202
P 26' Summer
26 mi. N. on Forest Rds. 094 & 227, past Big Smoky Guard Station
Drinking Water, Dump Station, Pets OK, Tenters Welcome, Vault Toilets

Gibbonsville

Broken Arrow — 865-2241
C $15 12 Summer, Fall, Spring
33 mi. N. of Salmon
Handicap Access

Gimlet

Sawmill — 622-5371
P None 3 May-October
E of Gimlet on FR 118
Primitive Camping, Restrooms, Fishing, Hiking/Backpacking, Horseback Riding

Hailey

Federal Gulch — 727-3200
P 9 22' Summer, Fall
6.1 mi. N. on Hwy 75, 11.5 mi. E. on Forest Rd. 70118
Drinking Water, Vault Toilets

Wolftone — 622-5371
P None 3 May-October
3 miles N of Hailey on Hwy. 75, then 7.5 miles W on FR 097
Primitive Camping, Restrooms, Biking, Fishing, Hiking/Backpacking, Horseback Riding, Picnicking, Water Sports

Bridge — 622-5371
P None 3 May-October
3 miles N of Hailey on Hwy. 75, then 9 miles W on FR 097
Primitive Camping, Restrooms, Biking, Fishing, Hiking/Backpacking, Horseback Riding, Picnicking

Ketchum

Boulder View — 727-5000/800-260-5970
P $10-18 10 22' Summer, Fall
15.5 mi. N. on Hwy. 75, 1 mi. on Forest Rd. 040
Drinking Water, Fire Rings, Hot Springs, Pets OK, Reservations, Swimming Pool, Tenters Welcome, Vault Toilets

Caribou — 727-5000/800-260-5970
P $8 7 22' Summer, Fall
7 mi. N. on Hwy 75, 3 mi. N.E on Forest Rd. 146
Fire Rings, Pets OK, Tenters Welcome, Vault Toilets

Murdock — 727-5000/800-260-5970
P $10 11 22' Summer, Fall
7 mi. N. on Hwy. 75, 1 mi. NE. on Forest Rd. 146
Drinking Water, Fire Rings, Pets OK, Tenters Welcome, Vault Toilets

North Fork - Sun Valley — 727-5000/800-260-5970
P $10-18 29 45' Summer, Fall
8.1 mi. N. on Hwy. 75
Drinking Water, Fire Rings, Pets OK, Reservations, Tenters Welcome, Vault Toilets

Cottonwood — 622-5371
P None 1 May-October
6 miles W of Ketchum on FR 227
Primitive Campground, Fishing, Picnicking, Water Sports

Leadore

Lema's Store & RV Park — 768-2647
C $10 10 All Year
Hwy. 28
Dump Station, Hookups, Mini-Mart, Pets OK, Pull-thru Sites, Reservations, Showers

Big Eight Mile — 768-2500
P 8 24' Summer, Fall
6.7 mi. W. on Cty. Rd., 1.5 mi. SW on Cty. Rd., 5 mi. SW on Forest Rd. 60096
Drinking Water, Vault Toilets

McFarland — 756-5400
P 28' Summer, Fall
10 mi. NW on Hwy. 28
Drinking Water, Handicap Access

Meadow Lake — 768-2500
P $5 17 16' Summer
16.8 mi. SE on Hwy. 28, 1.9 mi. W. on Cty. Rd., 3.9 mi. SW on Forest Rd. 60002
Drinking Water, Fire Rings, Pets OK, Pull-thru Sites, Tenters Welcome, Vault Toilets, Waterfront

Smokey Cubs — 756-5400
P $5 8 28' Summer, Fall
3 mi. E. on Hwy. 29
Drinking Water, Pets OK, Vault Toilets, Handicap Access

Section 4

Campground Quick Reference - continued

Campground Name Public/Commercial	Unit Price	#Spaces	Max. Length	Phone Seasons
Directions				
Amenities/Activities				

Lemhi

Bear Valley

P	None	2		768-2500 June-September

11 miles SW of Lemhi on Hayden Creek Rd and Bear Valley Creek Rd
Developed Campground, Drinking Water, Handicap Accessible Restrooms, RV Sites, Biking, Fishing, Hiking/Backpacking, Horseback Riding, Hunting, Picnicking, Wildlife Viewing

Mackay

Wagon Wheel Motel & RV Park

C	$6-70	18		588-3331 All Year

Hwy. 93
Handicap Access

River Park Golf Course & Campground

C	$15	26	30'	588-2296 Summer, Fall, Spring

Hwy. 93, turn SW 6 blks. on Capital Ave.
Cable TV Hookups, Drinking Water, Hookups, Modem Hookups, Pets OK, Pull-thru Sites, Reservations, Showers, Handicap Access

Cottonwood Links Golf Course & RV Park

C	$5-14	32		588-3394 All Year

Hwy. 93, 17 mi. N. of Arco, M P 100
Business Center, Credit Cards OK, Drinking Water, Dump Station, Fire Rings, Hookups, LP Gas, Mini-Mart, Modem Hookups, Pets OK, Playground, Pull-thru Sites, Reservations, Showers, Tenters Welcome, Handicap Access

White Knob Motel & RV Park

C	$38	21	38'	588-2622/800-314-2622 All Year

Hwy. 93, 2 mi. S. of Mackay
Camping Cabins, Credit Cards OK, Drinking Water, Dump Station, Hookups, LP Gas, Modem Hookups, Pets OK, Playground, Pull-thru Sites, Showers, Swimming Pool, Tenters Welcome, Laundry

Iron Bog

P	$5	21	32'	588-3400 Summer, Fall

10 mi. SE on Hwy. 93, 15 mi. SW on Hwy. 7, 2 mi. SW on Forest Rd. 137
Drinking Water, Pets OK, Vault Toilets

Mackay Reservoir

P	$6	38	40'	879-6200 All Year

Hwy. 93, 6 mi. NW of Mackay
Drinking Water, Dump Station, Fire Rings, Pets OK, Pull-thru Sites, Tenters Welcome, Vault Toilets, Handicap Access

Phi Kappa

P	$5	21	32'	588-3400 Summer, Fall

15 mi. NE on Trail Creek Rd.
Drinking Water, Pets OK, Vault Toilets

Star Hope

P	$5	21	32'	588-3400 Summer, Fall

16 mi. NW on Hwy. 93, 17 mi. SW on Trail Creek Rd. 208, 20 mi. SE on Forest Rd. 135, 9 mi. SW on Copper Basin Loop Rd. 138
Drinking Water, Pets OK, Vault Toilets, Handicap Access

Summit Creek

P		12	30'	879-6200 Summer, Fall, Spring

7 mi. S. on Hwy. 93, 28 mi. on Pass Creek Rd. 122, 9.5 mi. N. on Sawmill Canyon Rd. 101
Vault Toilets

Timber Creek

P	$5	12	32'	588-3400 Summer, Fall

7 mi. S. on Hwy. 93, 28 mi. on Pass Creek Rd. 122, 13 mi. N. on Sawmill Canyon Rd. 101
Pets OK, Vault Toilets

Wildhorse

P	$5	13	32'	588-3400 Summer, Fall

16 mi. NW on Hwy. 93, 17 mi. SW on Trail Creek Rd. 208, 3 mi. S. on Forest Rd. 135; 6 mi. on Forest Rd. 136
Drinking Water, Pets OK, Vault Toilets

Mill Creek Campground East

P	None		Undeveloped	588-2224 June-September

7 miles S of Mackay on Hwy. 93, then 28 miles NE on FR 122, and 10 miles N on FR 101
Primitive Camping, Restrooms, Biking, Fishing, Hiking/Backpacking, Horseback Riding, Hunting

North Fork

Cummings Lake Lodge

C	$15	12		865-2424 Summer, Fall, Spring

3 mi. N. of North Fork, W. up Hull Creek 3 mi.
Dump Station, Hookups, Pets OK, Playground, Waterfront

Corn Creek

P	$5	12	22'	865-2700 Summer, Fall, Spring

40 mi. W. on Forest Rd. 60030
Boating Facilities, Drinking Water, Fire Rings, Pets OK, Tenters Welcome, Vault Toilets, Waterfront

Twin Creek

P	$5	46	32'	865-2700 Summer, Fall

5 mi. NW on Hwy. 93, .5 mi. NW on Forest Rd. 449
Drinking Water, Fire Rings, Pets OK, Tenters Welcome, Vault Toilets

Ebenezer Bar Campground

P	$5	14	32'	865-2700 Summer, Fall

34.4 mi. W. on Salmon River Rd. 050
Drinking Water, Fire Rings, Pets OK, Pull-thru Sites, Tenters Welcome, Vault Toilets, Waterfront

Spring Creek - North Fork

P	$5	5	32'	865-2700 Summer, Fall

17.7 mi. W. on Salmon River Rd. 030
Boating Facilities, Drinking Water, Fire Rings, Pets OK, Tenters Welcome, Vault Toilets, Waterfront

Horse Creek Hot Springs

P	None	9		865-2700 June-October

14 miles W of North Fork on FR 030, then 8 miles N on FR 038, then 14 miles NW on FR 044 and FR 065
Developed Campground, Restrooms, RV Sites, Fishing, Hiking/Backpacking, Hunting, Picnicking

Deep Creek

P	None	3		756-5100 June-September

24 miles W of North Fork on FR 030, then 18 miles S on FR 055
Developed Campground, Drinking Water, Restrooms, RV Sites, Fishing, Hiking/Backpacking, Hunting

Picabo

High-Five Campground

P			60'	678-0461 Summer, Fall, Spring

15 mi. NW of Carey
Pets OK, Pull-thru Sites, Vault Toilets, Waterfront

Little Wood Campground

P		21	30'	678-0461 Summer, Fall, Spring

11 mi. NW of Carey
Drinking Water, Pets OK, Pull-thru Sites, Tenters Welcome, Vault Toilets, Waterfront, Handicap Access

Silver Creek

P	None		Undeveloped	886-2206 May-October

S of Picabo on the Picabo Cutoff Rd
Primitive Camping, Restrooms, Fishing, Hiking/Backpacking, Picnicking, Wildlife Viewing

Silver Creek South Recreation Site

P	None		Updeveloped	886-2206 May-October

S of Picabo on the Picabo Cutoff Rd
Primitive Camping, Restrooms, Fishing, Hiking/Backpacking, Picnicking, Wildlife Viewing

Section 4

CENTRAL AREA
INCLUDING KETCHUM, SUN VALLEY, SALMON, ARCO, AND CHALLIS

Campground Quick Reference - continued

Salmon

North Fork Motel & Campground   865-2412
C $11-15   30   45'   All Year
Hwy. 93, 21 mi. N. of Salmon
Credit Cards OK, Drinking Water, Hookups, LP Gas, Mini-Mart, Pets OK, Pull-thru Sites, Reservations, Showers, Tenters Welcome, Waterfront, Laundry

Wagonhammer Campground   865-2477
C $14-19   53   45'   Summer, Fall, Spring
Hwy. 93, 18 mi. N. of Salmon
Business Center, Credit Cards OK, Drinking Water, Dump Station, Fire Rings, Game Room, Hookups, Mini-Mart, Modem Hookups, Pets OK, Pull-thru Sites, Reservations, Showers, Tenters Welcome, Waterfront, Laundry, Handicap Access

Century II Campground   756-2063
C $15-18   25   80'   All Year
Hwy. 93, .25 mi. from downtown, next to Wagon West Motel
Drinking Water, Dump Station, Hookups, Modem Hookups, Pets OK, Playground, Pull-thru Sites, Reservations, Showers, Tenters Welcome, Waterfront, Laundry, Handicap Access

Heald's Haven RV & Campground   756-3929
C $12-15.5   20   Summer, Fall, Spring
Hwy. 93, 12 mi. S. of Salmon, near MP 293, 22 Heald Haven Dr.
Drinking Water, Dump Station, Fire Rings, Hookups, Pets OK, Pull-thru Sites, Reservations, Showers, Tenters Welcome

Salmon Hot Springs   756-4449/877-482-6569
C $4-24   48   All Year
Hwy. 93, 4 mi. S. of Salmon, 506 Main St.
Cable TV Hookups, Handicap Access

Salmon Meadows Campground & RV Park   756-2640
C $10-18   70   All Year
4 blks. N. of Main St. along the Salmon River
Cable TV Hookups, Dump Station, Hookups, Pets OK, Playground, Pull-thru Sites, Reservations, Showers, Tenters Welcome, Handicap Access

Salmon River RV Park, Campground & Country Store   894-4549
C $20   20   All Year
Hwy. 93, 22 mi. S. of Salmon
Boating Facilities, Drinking Water, Dump Station, Hookups, Hot Springs, LP Gas, Mini-Mart, Pets OK, Pull-thru Sites, Showers, Laundry, Handicap Access

River's Fork Lodge & RV Park 865-2301
C $24   8   All Year
21 mi. N. of Salmon on Hwy. 93 N.
Boating Facilities, Credit Cards OK, Drinking Water, Modem Hookups, Pets OK, Waterfront, WiFi

Royal Gorge Resort   876-4130
C $12-24   10   All Year
Hwy 93, 38 mi. S. of Salmon
Dump Station, Hookups, Playground, Showers, Waterfront

Cougar Point   756-5200
P $4   12   22'   Summer, Fall
5 mi. S. on Hwy. 93, 12 mi. W. on Forest Rd. 60021
Drinking Water, Fire Rings, Pets OK, Tenters Welcome, Vault Toilets

Iron Lake   756-5200
P $4   8   16'   Summer, Fall
5 mi. S. on Hwy. 93, 20 mi. W. on Forest Rd. 60021, 21 mi. S. on Forest Rd. 60020
Camping Cabins, Drinking Water, Fire Rings, Pets OK, Tenters Welcome, Vault Toilets

Morgan Bar   756-5400
P $5   8   28'   Summer, Fall
3.2 mi. N. on Hwy. 93, left on Diamond Creek Rd. 1.5 mi.
Drinking Water, Swimming Pool, Vault Toilets, Handicap Access

Shoup Bridge   756-5400
P $5   5   28'   Summer, Fall
5 mi. S. on Hwy. 93
Drinking Water, Tenters Welcome, Vault Toilets, Waterfront, Handicap Access

Wallace Lake   756-5200
P   12   16'   Summer, Fall
3.2 mi. N. on Hwy. 93. 14 mi. NW on Forest Rd. 60023, 4 mi. S. on Forest Rd. 60020
Camping Cabins, Drinking Water, Fire Rings, Pets OK, Tenters Welcome, Vault Toilets

Williams Lake   756-5400
P   28'   Summer, Fall
Hwy. 93, 5 mi. S. of Salmon, cross Shoup Bridge, follow signs 7 mi. Some steep gravel road.
Drinking Water, Swimming Pool, Tenters Welcome, Vault Toilets

Tower Rock   756-5400
P   Summer, Fall
11 mi. N. on Hwy. 93
Drinking Water, Pull-thru Sites, Swimming Pool, Tenters Welcome, Vault Toilets, Waterfront, Handicap Access

McDonald Flat   756-5100
P   None   6   May-September
24 miles W of Salmon on FR 030 and S on FR 055
Developed Campground, Restrooms, Biking, Fishing, Hiking/Backpacking, Hunting, Off Highway Vehicles, Scenic Driving, Wildlife Viewing

Stanley

Sunbeam Village   838-2211
C $15-28   12   All Year
Hwy. 75, 12 mi. NE of Stanley

Torrey's Resort & RV Park   838-2313/888-838-2313
C $22   20   All Year
Hwy. 75, 21 mi. E. of Stanley
Credit Cards OK, Hookups, Mini-Mart, Pets OK, Pull-thru Sites, Reservations, Showers, Tenters Welcome, Waterfront, Laundry

Elk Mountain RV Resort   774-2202
C $22   27   Summer, Fall, Spring
Hwy. 21, 4 mi. W. of Stanley
Hookups, Pets OK, Reservations, Showers

Camp Stanley   774-3591/888-722-5432
C   20   Summer, Fall

Alturas Inlet   727-5000/800-260-5970
P $10-18   28   32'   Summer, Fall
10 mi. S. on H'wy75, 5 mi. SW on Forest Rd. 205
Drinking Water, Fire Rings, Pets OK, Reservations, Tenters Welcome, Vault Toilets, Waterfront

Basin Creek   727-5000/800-260-5970
P $11-22   15   22'   Summer, Fall
8.9 mi. E. on Hwy. 75
Drinking Water, Fire Rings, Pets OK, Tenters Welcome, Vault Toilets

Beaver Creek - Stanley   838-2201
P $5   10   32'   Summer, Fall
17 mi. NW on Hwy. 21; 3 mi. N. Yankee Beaver Creek Rd. 008
Drinking Water, Pets OK, Pull-thru Sites, Vault Toilets

Blind Creek   838-2201
P $5   4   32'   Summer, Fall
14.9 mi. NE on Hwy. 75, 1 mi. N. Yankee Fork Rd. 013
Drinking Water, Pets OK, Vault Toilets

Boundary Creek   879-4101
P $5   4   22'   Summer, Fall
20 mi. NW on Hwy 21, 11 mi. W. on Fir Creek Rd. 198, 13 mi. N. on Boundary Creek Rd. 668
Drinking Water, Pets OK, Vault Toilets

Chemeketan 727-5000/800-260-5970
P   Summer, Fall
16 mi. S. on Hwy. 75; 4.5 mi. S. on Forest Rd. 215
Fire Rings, Pets OK, Reservations, Tenters Welcome, Vault Toilets

Campground Quick Reference - continued

Campground Name Public/Commercial	Unit Price	#Spaces	Max. Length	Phone Seasons
Directions				
Amenities/Activities				

Chinook Bay   727-5000/800-260-5970
P   13   22'   Summer, Fall
5 mi. S. on Hwy. 75, .5 mi. SW on Forest Rd. 214
Drinking Water, Fire Rings, Pets OK, Tenters Welcome, Vault Toilets, Waterfront

Custer #1   838-2201
P   6   32'   Summer, Fall
14.9 mi. E. on Hwy. 75,8 mi. N. on Forest Rd. 013,3 mi. NE on Forest Rd. 070
Drinking Water, Pets OK, Vault Toilets

Dagger Falls #1   879-4101
P $5   10   22'   Summer, Fall
20 mi. NW on Hwy. 21, 11 mi. W. Fir Creek Rd. 198, 13 mi. N. on Boundary Creek Rd. 668
Pets OK, Vault Toilets

Flat Rock - Stanley   838-2201
P $5   9   32'   Summer
14.9 mi. NE on Hwy. 75, 2 mi. N. on Forest Rd. 013
Drinking Water, Vault Toilets

Glacier View   727-5000/800-260-5970
P $13-26   65   32'   Summer, Fall
5 mi. S. on Hwy. 75, 2.4 mi. SW on Forest Rd. 70214
Drinking Water, Dump Station, Fire Rings, Pets OK, Playground, Reservations, Tenters Welcome

Iron Creek   727-5000/800-260-5970
P $11-22   9   22'   Summer, Fall
2 mi. W. on Hwy. 21, 4 mi. S. on Forest Rd. 019
Drinking Water, Vault Toilets

Lakeview   727-5000/800-260-5970
P $11-22   6   22'   Summer, Fall
2 mi. W. on Hwy. 21, 2.5 mi. W. on Forest Rd. 455
Drinking Water, Fire Rings, Pets OK, Reservations, Tenters Welcome, Vault Toilets, Waterfront

Lola Creek   838-2201
P $5   27   16'   Summer, Fall
17 mi. NW on Hwy. 21; 1 mi. NW on Forest Rd. 083
Drinking Water, Pets OK, Vault Toilets

Lower O'Brien   727-5000/800-260-5970
P $11-22   10   22'   Summer, Fall
15 mi. E. on Hwy. 75; .5 mi. S. on Forest Rd. 454, Robinson Bar Road
Drinking Water, Fire Rings, Limited Access, Pets OK, Tenters Welcome, Vault Toilets, Waterfront

Mormon Bend   727-5000/800-260-5970
P $11-22   12   22'   Summer, Fall
7 mi. E. on Hwy. 75
Drinking Water, Fire Rings, Pets OK, Reservations, Tenters Welcome, Vault Toilets, Waterfront

Mountain View Campground   727-5000/800-260-5970
P $13-26   7   22'   Summer, Fall
5 mi. S. on Hwy. 75, .5 mi. SW on Forest Rd. 70214
Drinking Water, Fire Rings, Pets OK, Tenters Welcome, Vault Toilets, Waterfront

Mt. Heyburn   727-5000/800-260-5970
P $13-26   20   22'   Summer, Fall
5 mi. S. on Hwy. 75, 3.1 mi. S. on Forest Rd. 70214
Drinking Water, Dump Station, Fire Rings, Pets OK, Reservations, Tenters Welcome, Vault Toilets, Waterfront

North Shore Alturas Lake   727-5000/800-260-5970
P $10-18   15   32'   Summer, Fall
10 mi. S. on Hwy. 75, 3.7 mi. SW on Alturas Lake Rd. (Forest Rd. 205)
Drinking Water, Fire Rings, Pets OK, Reservations, Swimming Pool, Tenters Welcome, Vault Toilets, Waterfront

Outlet - Stanley   727-5000/800-260-5970
P $13-26   19   32'   Summer, Fall
5 mi. S. on Hwy. 75, 2.4 mi. SW on Forest Rd. 70214
Drinking Water, Dump Station, Fire Rings, Pets OK, Reservations, Tenters Welcome, Vault Toilets, Waterfront

Point   727-5000/800-260-5970
P $13-26   8   Summer, Fall
5 mi. S. on Hwy. 75, 2.6 mi. SW on Forest Rd. 70214
Drinking Water, Fire Rings, Pets OK, Reservations, Swimming Pool, Tenters Welcome, Vault Toilets, Waterfront

Pole Flat   838-2201
P $5   10   32'   Summer, Fall
14.9 mi. NE on Hwy. 75, 3 mi. N. on Forest Rd. 013
Drinking Water, Pets OK, Vault Toilets

Riverside - Stanley   727-5000/800-260-5970
P $11   18   22'   Summer, Fall
6.8 mi. E. on Hwy. 75
Drinking Water, Fire Rings, Pets OK, Reservations, Tenters Welcome, Vault Toilets, Waterfront

Salmon River   727-5000/800-260-5970
P $11-22   30   32'   Summer, Fall
4 mi. E. on Hwy. 75
Drinking Water, Fire Rings, Pets OK, Reservations, Tenters Welcome, Vault Toilets, Waterfront

Smokey Bear at Alturas Lake   727-5000/800-260-5970
P $10-18   12   16'   Summer, Fall
10 mi. S. on Hwy. 75, 3.4 mi. SW on Alturas Lake Rd.(Forest Rd. 205)
Drinking Water, Fire Rings, Pets OK, Reservations, Swimming Pool, Tenters Welcome, Vault Toilets

Sockeye   727-5000/800-260-5970
P $13-26   23   22'   Summer, Fall
5 mi. S on Forest Rd. 75, 3.2 mi. S. on Forest Rd. 70214
Drinking Water, Dump Station, Fire Rings, Pets OK, Reservations, Tenters Welcome, Vault Toilets, Waterfront

Stanley Lake Inlet   727-5000/800-260-5970
P $11-22   14   22'   Summer, Fall
2 mi. W. on Hwy. 21, 6.5 mi. W. on Forest Rd. 455
Drinking Water, Fire Rings, Pets OK, Reservations, Tenters Welcome, Vault Toilets, Waterfront

Sunny Gulch   727-5000/800-260-5970
P $11-22   45   22'   Summer, Fall
3.2 mi. S. on Hwy. 75
Drinking Water, Dump Station, Fire Rings, Pets OK, Reservations, Tenters Welcome, Vault Toilets, Waterfront

Upper O'Brien   727-5000/800-260-5970
P $11-22   9   22'   Summer, Fall
E 15 mi. on Hwy. 75, 2 mi. E. on Forest Rd. 454, Robinson Bar road
Drinking Water, Fire Rings, Limited Access, Pets OK, Tenters Welcome, Vault Toilets, Waterfront

Trap Creek Campground   727-5000/800-260-5970
P $11-35   3   30'   Summer
Hwy. 21, W. 15 mi.
Drinking Water, Fire Rings, Pets OK, Reservations, Tenters Welcome, Vault Toilets

Elk Creek Campground   727-5000/800-260-5970
P $11-35   Summer, Fall
8 mi. W. of Stanley on H'wy 21
Drinking Water, Fire Rings, Pets OK, Reservations, Tenters Welcome, Vault Toilets

Stanley Lake   727-5000/800-260-5970
P $11-22   19   22'   Summer, Fall
2 mi. W. on Hwy. 21, 6.5 mi. W. on Forest Rd. 455
Drinking Water, Fire Rings, Pets OK, Tenters Welcome, Vault Toilets, Waterfront

Sheep Trail Group Site   727-5000800-260-5970
P $11-35   4   30'   Summer, Fall
Hwy. 21, 9 mi. W. of Stanley
Drinking Water, Fire Rings, Pets OK, Reservations, Tenters Welcome, Vault Toilets

Campground Quick Reference - continued

Eightmile

P	None	2		838-3300
				July-September

15 miles E of Stanley, then 8 miles N on FR 013, and 6.5 miles NE on FR 070

Developed Campground, Restrooms, RV Sites, Biking, Hiking/Backpacking, Picnicking, Scenic Driving

Josephus Lake

P	None	3		879-4101
				July-September

17 miles N of Stanley on Hwy. 21, then 18 miles N on FR 008

Primitive Camping, Handicap Accessible Restrooms, Non-Motorized Boating, Fishing, Hiking/Backpacking, Picnicking, Scenic Driving, Water Sports

Banner Creek

P	None	3		838-3300
				July-September

20 miles E of Stanley on Hwy. 21

Developed Campground, Restrooms, Fishing, Hiking/Backpacking, Picnicking, Scenic Driving, Wildlife Viewing

Sun Valley

Smiley Creek Lodge

C		25		774-3547
				Summer, Winter

37 mi. N. of Sun Valley

Credit Cards OK, Dump Station, Hookups, Mini-Mart, Modem Hookups, Playground, Pull-thru Sites, Showers, Laundry

The Meadows RV Park

C	$15-27	45		726-5445
				All Year

3 mi. S. of Ketchum, 7.5 mi. N. of Hailey

Cable TV Hookups, Credit Cards OK, Dump Station, Hookups, Pets OK, Pull-thru Sites, Showers, Tenters Welcome, Laundry, Handicap Access

Baker Creek

P			32'	727-5000/800-260-5970
				Summer, Fall

15 mi. N. on Hwy. 75, 1 mi. on Forest Rd. 040

Drinking Water, Vault Toilets

Easley

P	$10-18	10	22'	727-5000/800-260-5970
				Summer, Fall

14.5 mi. N. on Hwy. 75

Drinking Water, Fire Rings, Hot Springs, Pets OK, Reservations, Swimming Pool, Tenters Welcome, Vault Toilets

Park Creek - Sun Valley

P	$5	12	32'	588-3400
				Summer, Fall

12 mi. NE of Sun Valley on Trail Creek Rd.

Drinking Water, Pets OK, Vault Toilets

Wood River Campground 727-5000/800-260-5970

P				
				Summer

N. of Ketchum

Drinking Water, Dump Station, Vault Toilets

Sunbeam

Phillips Creek

P	None	2		879-4101
				July-September

31 miles N of Sunbeam on FR 112 and FR 007 (High Clearance Vehicles are Recommended)

Primitive Camping, Restrooms, Fishing, Hiking/Backpacking, Horseback Riding

Tin Cup

P	None	13		879-4101
				July-September

31 miles N of Sunbeam on FR 112 and FR 007 (High Clearance Vehicles are Recommended)

Developed Campground, Restrooms, Fishing, Hiking/Backpacking, Horseback Riding, Picnicking

Tendoy

Agency Creek

P	None	4		756-5400
				June-September

4 miles E of Tendoy on the Lewis and Clark Backcountry Byway

Primitive Camping, Restrooms, Cultural/Historic Sites, Biking, Fishing, Hiking/Backpacking, Horseback Riding, Hunting, Off Highway Vehicles, Picnicking, Scenic Driving, Wildlife Viewing

NOTES:

Dining Quick Reference

Price Range refers to the average cost of a meal per person: ($) $1-$6, ($$) $7-$11, ($$$) $12-up. Cocktails: "Yes" indicates full bar; Beer (B)/Wine (W), Service: Breakfast (B), Brunch (BR), Lunch (L), Dinner (D). Businesses in bold print will have additional information under the appropriate map locator number in the body of this section.

MAP NO.	RESTAURANT	TYPE CUISINE	PRICE RANGE	CHILD MENU	COCKTAILS BEER WINE	MEALS SERVED	CREDIT CARDS ACCEPTED
1	Lewis & Clark Cafe 2648 Hwy 93 N, North Fork, 865-2440	American	$-$$	N	B W	L/D	M V
2	The Ranch Hwy 93 N, Carmen, 756-6210	American	$$	Y	Yes	D	No
3	**Bertram's Brewery & Restaurant** 101 S Andrews St, Salmon, 756-3391	American/Fine Dining	$$	Y	B W	L/D	Major
3	**The Shady Nook Restaurant** 501 Hwy 93 N, Salmon, 756-4182	Fine Dining	$$$	Y	Yes	D	Major
3	Burger King 1110 Main St, Salmon, 756-4132	Fast Food	$	Y	N	L/D	M V
3	Burnt Bun 901 Mulkey St, Salmon, 756-2062	Family	$	Y	N	L/D	M V
3	China Garden 507 Main St, Salmon, 756-1011	Asian	$	N	N	L/D	Major
3	Last Chance Pizza 611 Lena St, Salmon, 756-4559	Pizza	$	N	N	L/D	No
3	Pierce Pancake & Steak 720 Union Ave, Salmon, 756-8727	Steakhouse	$-$$	Y	N	B/L/D	Major
3	Salmon River Coffee Shop 606 Main St, Salmon, 756-3521	Coffee/American	$$	Y	N	B/L/D	M V
3	Subway Sandwiches & Salads 910 Main St, Salmon, 756-6929	Fast Food	$	N	N	L/D	Major
3	Taco Grande/Subway 910 Main St, Salmon, 756-6929	Fast Food	$	N	N	L/D	M V
6	Sagebrush Cafe & Bar 301 S Railroad St, Leadore, 768-2606	American	$-$$	Y	B W	B/L/D	No
7	Mayford Cafe & Bar One Main St, May, 876-4496	American	$-$$	Y	B W	B/L/D	No
8	Antonio's 5th & Main St, Challis, 879-2210	Pizza/Italian	$-$$	Y	B W	L/D	Major
8	Cafe.com 430 Main, Challis, 879-2891	Pizza/American	$	N	N	L/D	M V
8	Elk Horn Bar & Grill Salmon River Campground,, Challis, 894-4549	American	$	N	Yes	L/D	Major
8	The Village Inn US Hwy 93, Challis, 879-2239	American	$	Y	B W	L/D	Major
9	Amy Lou's Steakhouse 503 W Custer St, Mackay, 588-9903	Steakhouse	$$	N	Yes	B/L/D	No
9	Miner Diner 125 S Main, Mackay, 588-3303	Family	$	Y	N	B/L	M V
11	Arco Village Club 659 W Grand Ave, Arco, 527-3002	Tavern/American	$	N	N	L/D	No
11	Carroll's Travel Plaza-truck stop Hwy 20-26, Arco, 527-3504	Family	$	Y	N	L/D	Major
11	Deli Sandwich Shop 119 N Idaho Ave, Arco, 527-3757	Deli	$	N	N	L/D	M V
11	Grandpa's Southern Bar-B-Q 434 W Grand Ave, Arco, 527-3362	American	$$	N	N	L/D	Major
11	Lost River Drive In 520 W Grand Ave, Arco, 527-3158	American	$	N	N	L/D	No
11	Mello-Dee Club And Steak House 175 Sunset Dr, Arco, 527-3125	Steakhouse	$$-$$$	Y	B W	L/D	Major
11	Number Hill Grill 238 S Front St, Arco, 527-8224	Family	$$	Y	N	L/D	No
11	Pickle's Place 440 S Front St, Arco, 527-9944	American	$$	Y	B W	L/D	M V
12	Rendezvous At The Sinks 3509 Lost River Hwy, Howe, 767-3816	American	$$-$$$	N	Yes	L/D	M V
15	**Mountain Village Resort** Hwys 21 & 75, Stanley, 774-3661	American	$$	Y	Yes	B/L/D	Major

Dining Quick Reference-Continued - continued

Price Range refers to the average cost of a meal per person: ($) $1-$6, ($$) $7-$11, ($$$) $12-up. Cocktails: "Yes" indicates full bar; Beer (B)/Wine (W), Service: Breakfast (B), Brunch (BR), Lunch (L), Dinner (D). Businesses in bold print will have additional information under the appropriate map locator number in the body of this section.

MAP NO.	RESTAURANT	TYPE CUISINE	PRICE RANGE	CHILD MENU	COCKTAILS BEER WINE	MEALS SERVED	CREDIT CARDS ACCEPTED
15	**Sunbeam Village Resort** 100 Yankee Fork Rd, Stanley, 838-2211	American	$-$$	Y	B W	B/L/D	M V
15	Kasino Club Bar & Restaurant Ace Of Diamonds St, Stanley, 774-3516	Tavern/American	$$	N	Yes	D	M V
17	Bald Mountain Pizza & Pasta Sun Valley Village, Sun Valley, 622-2143	Pizza/Italian	$$	N	N	L/D	Major
17	Lodge Dining Room SV Landing, Sun Valley, 622-2150	Fine Dining	$$$	N	B W	D	Major
17	Lookout Restaurant Top Of Baldy, Sun Valley, 622-6261	Fine Dining	$$$	N	B W	D	Major
17	Treat Haus Sun Valley, Sun Valley, 622-4089	Fine Dining	$$-$$$	N	B	L/D	Major
18	**Chandler's Restaurant & Baci Italian Cafe** 200 S Main, Ketchum, 726-1776	Fine Dining	$$$	N	B W	D	M V
18	**Cristina's Restaurant** 540 E 2nd St, Ketchum, 726-4499	European	$$	N	B W	B/BR/L	Major
18	**Ketchum Grill** 520 E Ave, Ketchum, 726-4660	Fine Dining	$$	Y	B W	D	Major
18	**Perry's Restaurant** 131 W 4th St, Ketchum, 726-7703	Deli	$$	Y	B W	B/L	M V
18	Apple's Bar & Grill 205 Picabo St Dr, Ketchum, 726-7067	American	$	N	Yes	L	No
18	Burger Grill 371 N Main St, Ketchum, 726-7733	American	$	N	B W	L/D	No
18	Fish On Wheels 891 Warm Springs Rd, Ketchum, 726-0852	Seafood	$-$$	N	N	L	No
18	Johnny G's Sub Shack 371 N Washington Ave, Ketchum, 725-7827	American	$	N	N	L	No
18	KB's Burritos 200 6th St E, Ketchum, 726-2232	Mexican	$	N	N	L/D	M V
18	Lefty's Bar & Grill 213 E 6th St, Ketchum, 726-2744	American	$	Y	B W	L/D	Major
18	Restaurant Esta 180 S Main St, Ketchum, 726-1668	Deli/Grill	$-$$	Y	B W	B/L	Major
18	Sawtooth Club Restaurant & Bar 231 N Main St, Ketchum, 726-5233	Steak/Seafood	$$-$$$	Y	Yes	D	Major
18	Shanghai Palace 531 N Main St, Ketchum, 726-2688	Asian	$$	N	B W	L/D	M V
18	Smoky Mountain Pizza & Pasta 200 Sun Valley Rd, Ketchum, 622-5625	Pizza	$-$$	N	N	L/D	M V
18	The China Pepper 620 Sun Valley Rd E, Ketchum, 726-0959	Asian	$-$$	N	N	L/D	M V
19	**CK's Real Food** 320 S Main St, Hailey, 788-1223	American	$$-$$$	Y	B W	D	Major
19	**The Red Elephant Restaurant & Saloon** 107 S Main St, Hailey, 788-6047	Steakhouse	$$-$$$	Y	Yes	D	M V
19	A Taste Of Thai 106 N Main St, Hailey, 578-2488	Asian	$$	N	B W	L/D	Major
19	Atkinson's Market 93 E Croy St, Hailey, 788-2294	Bakery/Grocery	$	N	N	B/L/D	Major
19	Chi-Chi's Cafe 721 N Main St, Hailey, 788-4646	Coffee/Deli	$-$$	Y	B W	B/L	M V
19	DaVinci's 17 W Bullion St, Hailey, 788-7699	Italian	$$-$$$	N	B W	D	Major
19	Domino's Pizza 16 E Bullion St, Hailey, 578-2100	Pizza	$-$$	N	N	L/D	M V
19	El Pacifico 16 W Croy St, Hailey, 578-9859	Mexican	$	N	N	L/D	Major
19	Hailey Hotel Bar & Grill 201 S Main St, Hailey, 788-3140	American	$$	N	Yes	D	Major

Dining Quick Reference-Continued - continued

Price Range refers to the average cost of a meal per person: ($) $1-$6, ($$) $7-$11, ($$$) $12-up. Cocktails: "Yes" indicates full bar; Beer (B)/Wine (W), Service: Breakfast (B), Brunch (BR), Lunch (L), Dinner (D). Businesses in bold print will have additional information under the appropriate map locator number in the body of this section.

MAP NO.	RESTAURANT	TYPE CUISINE	PRICE RANGE	CHILD MENU	COCKTAILS BEER WINE	MEALS SERVED	CREDIT CARDS ACCEPTED
19	Lago Azul 14 W Croy St, Hailey, 578-1700	Mexican	$$	Y	B	L/D	Major
19	McDonald's 720 N Main St, Hailey, 788-5986	Fast Food	$	Y	N	B/L/D	Major
19	Miramar Mexican Restaurant 401 S Main St, Hailey, 788-4060	Mexican	$-$$	N	B W	B/L/D	Major
19	Sakura Japanese Steak House 11706 Hwy 75 N, Hailey, 788-9730	Asian	$$-$$$	N	B W	D	Major
19	Shorty's 126 S Main St, Hailey, 578-1293	Family	$	Y	N	B/L	Major
19	Smokey Mountain Pizza 200 S Main St, Hailey, 578-0667	Pizza	$-$$	Y	B W	L/D	Major
19	Snow Bunny Drive-In 801 S Main St, Hailey, 788-6464	Family	$	Y	N	L/D	Major
19	Subway 600 N Main St, Hailey, 578-0650	Fast Food	$-$$	N	N	L/D	Major
19	Sun Valley Brewing Company 202 N Main St, Hailey, 788-0805	Tavern/American	$-$$	Y	Yes	L/D	Major
19	The Wicked Spud 305 N Main St, Hailey, 788-0009	American	$	Y	B W	L/D	M V
19	Wiseguy Pizza Pie 315 S Main St, Hailey, 788-8688	Pizza	$-$$	N	B W	L/D	Major
20	Full Moon Steak House 118 S Main St, Bellevue, 788-5912	Steakhouse	$$-$$$	Y	B W	L/D	Major
20	Gannett Country Club Cafe 789 Gannett Picabo Rd, Bellevue, 788-9066	American	$$	Y	B W	L/D	Major
20	Jesse's Country Grill 401 N Main St, Bellevue, 788-9002	American	$	Y	B W	B/L	Major
20	Phoenix Bar & Grill 110 S Main St, Bellevue, 788-9405	American	$$	N	B W	L/D	Major
20	South Valley Pizzeria 108 Elm St, Bellevue, 788-1456	Pizza	$	N	N	L/D	M V
20	Taqueria Al Pastor 1 321 S Main St, Bellevue, 578-2300	Mexican	$$	N	B W	L/D	Major
20	Wood River Valley Market 757 N Main St, Bellevue, 788-7788	American	$	N	N	L/D	M V
22	Breezie's Outlaws Bar & Grill Main St, Fairfield, 764-3812	American	$	N	Yes	L/D	Major
22	Jim Dandy's Pizza 505 N Soldier Rd, Fairfield, 764-2030	Pizza	$	N	N	L/D	Major
22	Sandwiched Inn Deli 507 Soldier Rd, Fairfield, 764-2100	Deli	$	N	N	L/D	Major
22	Soldier Creek Brewing Company 509 Soldier Rd, Fairfield, 764-2739	Tavern/American	$	N	N	L	No
22	The Prairie Kitchen 109 E Hwy 20, Fairfield, 764-2257	Family	$$	Y	N	B/L/D	Major
22	Wrangler Drive-In 105 W Hwy 20, Fairfield, 764-2580	Family	$	Y	N	L/D	M V

NOTES:

Motel Quick Reference

Price Range: ($) Under $40 ; ($$) $40-$60; ($$$) $60-$80, ($$$$) Over $80. Pets [check with the motel for specific policies] (P), Dining (D), Lounge (L), Disabled Access (DA), Full Breakfast (FB), Cont. Breakfast (CB), Indoor Pool (IP), Outdoor Pool (OP), Hot Tub (HT), Sauna (S), Refrigerator (R), Microwave (M) (Microwave and Refrigerator indicated only if in majority of rooms), Kitchenette (K). All Idaho area codes are 208.

MAP No.	HOTEL	NUMBER ROOMS	PRICE RANGE	BREAKFAST	POOL/ HOT TUB SAUNA	NON SMOKE ROOMS	OTHER AMENITIES	CREDIT CARDS
1	**100 Acre Wood Resort and B&B** 2356 Hwy 93 N, North Fork, 865-2165	9	$$$/$$$$	FB	HT	Yes		M/V
1	Broken Arrow Camp & Restaurant 3230 Hwy 93 N, Gibbonsville, 865-2241							
1	North Fork Resort & RV Park 2046 Hwy 93 N, North Fork, 865-2412	7	$$			No	P/D/K	Major
1	Arctic Creek Lodge North Fork, 865-2372							
3	**Greyhouse Inn B&B** 1115 Hwy 93 S, Salmon, 756-3968	9	$$$$	FB	HT	Yes	K	M/V
3	**Syringa Lodge** 13 Gott Lane, Salmon, 756-4424	6	$$$	Yes		Yes	P/DA	Major
3	Motel Deluxe 112 S Church, Salmon, 756-2231	24	$$/$$$			Yes	P/DA/R/M/K	Major
3	Stagecoach Inn Motel 201 Hwy 93 N, Salmon, 756-2919	100	$$$	CB	OP	Yes	DA	Major
3	Suncrest Motel 705 S Challis St, Salmon, 756-2294	21	$$			Yes	P/K	M/V
3	Super 8 104 Courthouse Dr, Salmon, 756-8880	30	$$/$$$	FB		Yes	DA	Major
3	Wagon's West Motel 503 Hwy 93 N, Salmon, 756-4281	55	$$$		HT	Yes	P/DA/K	Major
6	Leadore Inn 401 S Railroad St, Leadore, 768-2237	4	$			Yes	P/K	M/V
8	**Holiday Lodge Motel** Hwy 93 N, HC 63, Box 1667, Challis, 879-2259	11	$$			Yes	P/R/M	M/V/A
8	Corner Cottage Inn HC 63, Challis, 879-2788							
8	Creekside Inn 648 North Ave, Challis, 879-5608							
8	Challis Motor Lodge & Lounge Hwy 93 & Main St, Challis, 879-2251	19	$$		IP/OP	Yes	D	Major
8	Northgate Inn Hwy 93 N, HC 63, Box 1665, Challis, 879-2490	55	$	CB		Yes	P/DA/K	Major
8	The Village Inn Hwy 93, Challis, 879-2239	50	$$			Yes	P/D/K	Major
9	Bear Bottom Inn 412 W Spruce St, Mackay, 588-2483	5	$$			Yes	DA	M/V
9	Wagon Wheel Motel & RV Park 809 W Custer, Mackay, 588-3331	16	$$$			Yes	P/DA	M/V
9	White Knob Motel & RV Park 4243 US Hwy 93, Mackay, 588-2622	6	$		OP	Yes	P/D/K	Major
11	Arco Inn 540 W Grand Ave, Arco, 527-3100	12	$$			Yes	P/DA/R/M	Major
11	D-K Motel 316 S Front St, Arco, 527-8282	25	$$			Yes	R/M	
11	Lazy A Motel 318 W Grand Ave, Arco, 527-8263	20	$/$$			Yes	P/DA/K	M/V
11	Lost River Motel 405 Highway Dr, Arco, 527-3600	14	$$				P/K	M/V
15	**Idaho Rocky Mountain Ranch** Hwy 75, HC 64, Box 9934, Stanley, 774-3544	21	$$$$	FB	OP	Yes		M/V
15	**Mountain Village Resort** Hwys 21 & 75, Stanley, 774-3661	60	$$$		HT	Yes	P/D/L/K	Major
15	**Riverside Motel & Sawtooth Rentals** 13 River Rd, Hwy 75, Stanley, 774-3409	14	$$$/$$$$			Yes	R/M/K	Major
15	**Salmon River Cabins & Motel and Jerry's Country Store** 19055 Hwy 75, HC 67, Box 300, Stanley, 774-3566	24	$$$			Yes	R/M/K	Major
15	**Sunbeam Village Resort** 100 Yankee Fork Rd, Stanley, 838-2211	11	$$$/$$$$			Yes	D/L/R/M/K	M/V

Motel Quick Reference - continued

Price Range: ($) Under $40 ; ($$) $40-$60; ($$$) $60-$80, ($$$$) Over $80. Pets [check with the motel for specific policies] (P), Dining (D), Lounge (L), Disabled Access (DA), Full Breakfast (FB), Cont. Breakfast (CB), Indoor Pool (IP), Outdoor Pool (OP), Hot Tub (HT), Sauna (S), Refrigerator (R), Microwave (M) (Microwave and Refrigerator indicated only if in majority of rooms), Kitchenette (K). All Idaho area codes are 208.

MAP No.	HOTEL	NUMBER ROOMS	PRICE RANGE	BREAKFAST	POOL/ HOT TUB SAUNA	NON SMOKE ROOMS	OTHER AMENITIES	CREDIT CARDS
15	**Valley Creek Motel & RV Park** 62 Eva Falls Ave, Stanley, 774-3606	7	$$$$			Yes	DA/R/M/K	Major
15	Danner's Log Cabin Motel 31 Eva Falls Ave, Stanley, 774-3539	9	$$$/$$$$			Yes	P/DA/K	Major
15	Meadow Creek Inn & Spa Jct Hwy 21 & 75, Stanley, 774-3611	6	$$$$			Yes	R	M/V/A
15	Stanley High Country Inn Ace of Diamonds St, Stanley, 774-7000	15	$$$$		HT	Yes	DA/K	Major
18	**Best Western Kentwood Lodge** 180 S Main St, Ketchum, 726-4114	57	$$$$		IP	Yes	D/DA/R/M/K	Major
18	**Clarion Inn of Sun Valley** 600 N Main St, Ketchum 83340, Sun Valley, 726-5900	58	$$$$		OP/HT	Yes	DA/R/M	Major
18	Knob Hill Inn & Restaurant 960 N Main St, Ketchum, 726-8010	26	$$$$	FB	IP	Yes	DA	Major
18	Best Western Tyrolean Lodge 260 Cottonwood, Ketchum, 726-5336	56	$$$$	CB	OP	Yes	P	Major
18	Christophe Condominium Hotel 351 2nd Ave S, Ketchum, 726-5601	30	$$$$		OP/HT	Yes	DA/K	Major
18	Lift Tower Lodge 703 S Main St, Ketchum, 726-5163	14	$$$/$$$$	CB	HT	Yes	DA/R	Major
18	Smiley Creek Lodge HC 64, Box 9102, Ketchum, 774-3547	5	$$$		S	Yes	P/D	Major
18	Habitat 2000 601 Leadville Ave, ketchum, 726-8584							
18	Alpine Estates 200 River St E, Ketchum, 720-4958							
18	Bald Mountain Lodge 100 Picabo St, Ketchum, 276-4776	30	$$$/$$$$			Yes	R/M	Major
19	Airport Inn 820 4th Ave S, Hailey, 788-2477	29	$$$$	CB	HT	Yes	P/DA/R/M/K	Major
19	Hailey Hotel 201 S Main St, Hailey, 788-3140	7	$					M/V
19	Hitchrack Motel 619 S Main St, Hailey, 788-1696	8	$$$				P/K	Major
19	Wood River Inn 603 N Main St, Hailey, 578-0600	57	$$$$	FB	IP/HT	Yes	P/DA/R/M/K	Major
20	**Bell Mountain Inn** 1241 S Main St, Bellevue, 788-0700	4	$$$			Yes	DA/R/M/K	Major
20	High Country Motel & Cabins 756 S Main St, Bellevue, 788-2050	20	$$$/$$$$			Yes	P/DA/R/M/K	Major
22	Prairie Inn 113 E Hwy 20, Fairfield, 764-2247	18	$$$/$$$$			Yes	DA	M/V

NOTES:

Searching for that perfect western gift or decorative item? Don't miss the huge selection of quality-crafted items at the Gift Corral. A full selection of their signature products are available online, including handmade bath and body products, Moose Drool novelty items, whimsical bear and moose figurines, stuffed animals, wood carvings, Christmas ornaments reflecting the Western spirit, clothing, antler art, handcrafted jewelry, gourmet foods, Montana Silversmiths items, household décor items ranging from lamps to rustic furniture to picture frames, and much, much more!

GIFT CORRAL

FINE GIFTS AND ACCESSORIES

WWW.GIFTCORRAL.COM

Big Sky Carvers Moosetivity II
Pair this set with Moosetivity I for an awesome Christmas display. Western artist Phyllis Driscoll designed this set of resin figurines for Big Sky Carvers. The full set makes a wonderful moose gift. Drummer Boy: 2-1/2" long, 3-1/4" wide, 3-3/4" tall. Shepherd: 3-1/4" long, 3" wide, 5-1/4" tall. King: 5" long, 2-1/2" wide, 4-3/4" tall. Item # GC35676

Montana Silversmiths Elmer Paper Towel Holder
Western artist Phyllis Driscoll created this handsome horse piece for Montana Silversmiths. This paper towel holder makes an impressive horse gift. 17" tall, 10" wide. Item # GC36212

The Huckleberry People Moose Grub Beer Bread Mix
Add one bottle of beer, knead, and bake. Huckleberry People, a Montana company known for its dry mixes, candy bars and cordials, made this delicious bread mix. Add the Moose Grub Huckleberry BBQ Sauce for an amazing food gift. 16 ounces. Item # GC29492

Search these items and hundreds more at...

WWW.GIFTCORRAL.COM

Huckleberry Haven Huckleberry Lip Balm Huckleberry People, a Montana company known for its dry mixes, candy bars and cordials, created this SPF 15 lip balm. Add the Huck Hand Cream for a great bath and body gift. Item # GC19654

SECTION 5

SOUTH-CENTRAL AREA

INCLUDING TWIN FALLS, JEROME, BURLEY, AND CITY OF ROCKS

The towering boulders at the City of Rocks are a favorite destination for rock climbers, while crystal clear nights draw stargazers to the area.

1

T Bliss Reservoir
Contact the Idaho Parks and Recreation Dept. at 334-4199. At Exit 137, merge northwest off I-84 onto King Hill Rd. Proceed 7 miles, and bear south onto Idaho Power Rd. Continue 2 miles to the reservoir.

A great place to fish, picnic, or just relax, Bliss Reservoir also features docks for convenient boat and water-skiing access. The 254 acres of water at Bliss Reservoir provides anglers with an opportunity to catch rainbow trout, largemouth bass, bluegill, and sunfish.

2 *Food, Lodging*

Bliss
Pop. 275

Bliss was first founded in 1878 when David and Lydia Bliss sold their Denver and Boise ranches and moved to south-central Idaho with their three young children. Before long, the Oregon Short Line Railroad arrived and constructed livestock pens and a loading chute to draw sheepmen and cattle ranchers from the surrounding region. As the site continued to grow into an agricultural hub, Ben Mullins decided to survey and plat out a townsite in the 1890s. Mullins collected a fee from all the settlers who had already constructed build-

ings in the area, and Bliss entered the history of Idaho as an official community.

During Bliss' early years, long winters created fuel scarcities. Desperately needing to heat their homes and protect their families, several Bliss men came up with an ingenious plan. Trains loaded with coal frequently passed through town each night. Noting this fact, men would take turns hopping the east-bound train at King Hill. As the train surged towards the hill's crest, the stowaway would throw off large chunks of coal to the grade below. The next morning, the man would return with his wife and children to retrieve the stolen coal and carry it back to Bliss for winter provisions. Today, little trace is left of this heritage of hardship, and Bliss is most recognized for its location on the Thousand Springs Scenic Byway.

T Teater's Knoll
Near Bliss

Visitors who take the road less traveled near Bliss are rewarded with views of an architectural masterpiece. Heading directly south from downtown Bliss on the Old Bliss Road, travelers will pass by a private home designed by Frank Lloyd Wright. The residence, known as Teater's Knoll, represents the only Wright masterpiece in the entire state.

Situated atop a tree-covered knoll overlooking the Snake River, Teater's Knoll was home to the late landscape artist, Archie Teater. The artist loved south-central Idaho and desired a home as magnificent as the surrounding landscape. Hiring

Wright as his architect, Teater ended up with a 1,900 square foot home displaying an open floor plan that utilized 60 and 120 degree angles. The home was completed in 1957 much to the dismay of local architects and building inspectors and retains its original stone walls and interior oak and fir accents.

When Teater died in 1978, the home was sold and remains a private residence. The house is listed on the National Register of Historic Places.

M Bliss Chamber of Commerce
PO Box 102, Bliss. 352-1140.

3 *Food, Lodging*

Gooding
Pop. 3,228

First named To-po-nis, a Shoshone Indian word translated into English as "black cherries" or "trading post," Gooding was established in 1883 as a railroad stop for the Union Pacific Railroad. The name was changed in 1896 after Frank Gooding, a prominent landowner, sheep farmer, and founder of the town. Frank later served as town mayor and Idaho governor, and acted as a U.S. Senator from 1921 until his death in 1928.

T Gooding Country Club
1951 U.S. Hwy. 26, Gooding. 934-9977.

A member of the Pacific Northwest Golf Association, the Gooding Country Club was established in 1940. The par-35 public course spans 2,943 yards and offers two sets of tees for playing nine or eighteen holes. Weekday green fees are $12 for nine holes and $15 for 18 holes, while weekend green fees are $15 and $19 respectively for nine and eighteen holes.

TV Thorn Creek Reservoir
North of Gooding. Contact the Idaho Department of Fish and Game – Magic Valley Office at 324-4350. From Gooding, drive 25 miles north on State Hwy. 46. Bear east off the highway at the marked reservoir turnoff.

Surrounded by Great Basin desert conditions, sagebrush, grasslands, and rolling hills, Thorn Creek Reservoir provides a variety of recreational opportunities. The reservoir is open to non-motorized boats and is known to harbor a thriving trout population. The free area is also home to camping, antelope and deer hunting, and bird-watching.

TV Little City of Rocks
14 miles north of Gooding off State Hwy. 46. Contact the BLM – Shoshone Field Office at 732-7200.

Not to be confused with the world-famous City of Rocks outside Almo, Little City of Rocks offers

Gooding	Jan	Feb	March	April	May	June	July	Aug	Sep	Oct	Nov	Dec	Annual
Average Max. Temperature (F)	33.9	41.0	50.3	62.1	70.8	79.9	89.9	88.2	79.0	65.7	48.1	37.6	62.2
Average Min. Temperature (F)	18.4	22.1	27.9	35.1	42.1	49.2	56.2	54.0	46.3	36.9	26.5	21.4	36.4
Average Total Precipitation (in.)	1.45	0.84	0.91	0.61	1.00	0.70	0.18	0.23	0.50	0.51	0.99	1.44	9.36
Average Total Snowfall (in.)	10.2	5.0	1.7	0.1	0.1	0.0	0.0	0.0	0.0	0.0	2.1	6.9	26.2
Average Snow Depth (in.)	3	3	1	0	0	0	0	0	0	0	0	1	1

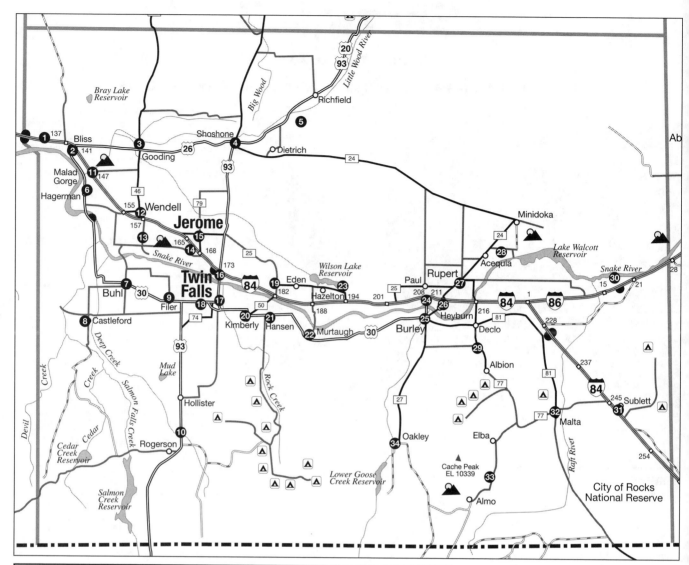

Legend

00 Locator number (matches numeric listing in section)

A Campsite

State Park

Rest stop

Interstate

U.S. Hwy.

State Hwy.

County Road

Gravel/unpaved road

---

access to hoodoo formations carved with thousands of years of erosion. The free site features relatively tall spires and impressive mushroom-capped formations ideal for beginning rock-climbing adventures. All sightseers and recreationists are encouraged to bring along plenty of water as the site often experiences extreme summer heat.

TV Gooding City of Rocks
18 miles north of Gooding off State Hwy. 46. Contact the BLM – Shoshone Field Office at 732-7200.

Situated nine miles off the main highway at the end of a dirt road, Gooding City of Rocks is an isolated, impressive area of basalt and rhyolite formations rising from the desert floor. Although not as tall as their counterparts at nearby Little City of

Rocks, the lichen-covered Gooding City of Rocks does offer outstanding views of the Snake River Plain as well as glimpses of area history. Indian petroglyphs have been found at the 20,000-acre site, and deer, black bear, chukars, range cattle, golden eagles, prairie falcons, great horned owls, and red-tailed hawks will occasionally make an appearance to scope out area sightseers. The free area is open year-round, and all visitors are encouraged to bring plenty of water due to extreme summer heat.

V Gooding County Snow Park
20 miles north of Gooding. Contact the BLM-Shoshone Field Office at 732-7200.

Situated at the Gooding-Camas County line, Gooding County Snow Park offers both locals and

visitors 150 square miles of snowmobiling options. The trails, which are always free and open during daylight hours, traverse both BLM and private land.

V Dog Creek Reservoir
North of Gooding on State Hwy. 46. Contact the BLM – Shoshone Field Office at 732-7200.

Dog Creek Reservoir spans just sixty acres but is a popular summer angling destination. The reservoir is stocked annually with thousands of catfish, and anglers may also catch yellow perch and rainbow trout. Boating is allowed, and a newly constructed handicap access is available at the dam.

M Gooding Chamber of Commerce
308 5th Ave. W., Gooding. 934-4402.
http://goodingidaho.net;
chamberinfo@goodingidaho.net

4 Food

Shoshone
Pop. 1,398

The Oregon Short Line Railroad established a post office in Shoshone as survey crews mapped out routes in 1883. When construction ensued for nearby Twin Falls, Shoshone served the area residents and crews with supplies. In its early days, the town was recognized as one of the roughest and wildest places in Idaho. Numerous arrests occured every day, with prisoners forced into tightly guarded holes in the ground (no jail was available)! Fights broke out on the street every hour, lot jumpers were the norm, bad whiskey flowed freely, and gunshots were fired no matter the time of day. The scene was further complemented by numerous gambling halls and plenty of brothels filled with enterprising women.

Shoshone has come a long ways since its inception, but the Wild West days and roots of its past are still evident amidst the town's numerous historical buildings.

H Shoshone Historic District
Milepost 72.9 on U.S. Hwy. 93

South-central Idaho's rail center since 1882 when trains reached here, Shoshone has a historic district of unusual interest.

Branch rail lines to the Wood River and Camas Prairie served distant farmers and miners, while a stage line to Shoshone Falls accommodated wealthy tourists who visited Idaho's foremost 19th-century attraction. Vast sheep grazing lands made this a major early center for Basque herders. Use of lava rock for building construction gives Shoshone a distinctive historic character.

T Shoshone Indian Ice Caves
North of Shoshone on State Hwy. 75.
886-2058.

As their name suggests, the Shoshone Indian Ice Caves were first known to ancient Native American tribes who roamed over south-central Idaho. These bands of Native Americans, who referred to the cave as "The Cave of Mystery," strongly believed that the cave was inhabited with evil spirits who swallowed up their Princess of Light and Fertility, Edahow. Despite possessing such a negative connotation, the caves were regularly home to Native American spring religious ceremonies.

In the 1880s, ten-year-old, Alfa Kinsey, stumbled upon the historic Native American site and became the first white person to see the geological wonder. Upon founding, the cave's chambers were completely logged with ice so that passage through the cave was impossible. As word of the discovery spread, curious pioneers traveled to the cave and used the sight as a year-round source of ice and refrigeration. The ice was so popular, in fact, that the town of Shoshone became famous for selling the region's first ice-cold beer! By 1900, however, the once steady ice enterprise had cooled, and by 1910, the ice began to melt just enough to let visitors inside the cave's lower chambers.

In the 1930s, a government committee under the Hoover Administration developed the site as the Shoshone Ice Caves Educational Project. The project gathered acclaim, and several visitors took advantage of a summer guide service that led throughout the cave's chambers. However, since the cave was left unattended for nearly eight

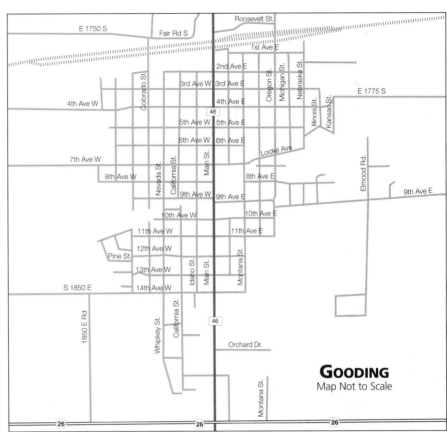

GOODING
Map Not to Scale

months each year, vandalism was frequent. The most severe vandalism occured in the mid 1930s when three CCC members took it upon themselves to create new entrances and pathways leading throughout the caves. As a result of their careless endeavor, the ice in the cave melted, and the government abandoned the project in 1939. The caves remained dormant until 1954 when Russell Robinson arrived in the area with his family. Robinson spent years restoring the caves' icy conditions with his air current experimentations, and his tireless efforts helped Shoshone Indian Ice Caves garner its designation as a National Historic Site.

Today, the large lava caves feature year-round ice floors and a fairly constant fifty degree Fahrenheit temperature. Cave guides are available and offer forty-minute tours through the unique volcanic tubes, explaining the caves' geology and history. Prehistoric animal fossils excavated in the caves are on display, and an on-site museum features gems, minerals, and Indian artifacts. Tours are available daily from May through September with reservations required for large groups. Ticket prices are $6 for adults, $5.50 for seniors and children 5-14, and $3.75 for children 4 and under. Groups are eligible for special discounted rates.

T Sculptured Canyon
Contact the BLM – Shoshone Field Office at 732-7200. Located near Shoshone Ice Caves at the point where State Hwy. 75 crosses the Big Wood River.

Sculptured Canyon treats Hwy. 75 travelers to unusual rock formations and geological wonders. The formations were carved at the hands of the Big Wood River and ages of erosion, and the area is open year-round free of charge. Although the Boise United Mining Corporation petitioned to remove many of the rocks in hopes of marketing

them as unique decorating and landscaping options, the courts nullified the mining claim. BLM has suggested developing the site, but no plans have been carried out to date.

T Historic McFall Hotel
230 N. Rail St W., Shoshone. Contact the Shoshone Chamber of Commerce at 886-2030.

In the wild and rowdy days of the Shoshone community, the McFall Hotel stood out as a more pretentious, well-mannered venue. The hotel, skillfully crafted out of the area's lightweight lava rock, was completed in 1896 and drew several prominent figures to its guest list. Ernest Hemingway, Teddy Roosevelt, and three other American presidents stayed at McFall during its glory days.

Several other buildings in Shoshone reflect the area's lava rock heritage dating back to the late 1800s, including the Hotel Shoshone, the W.H. Baugh Building, the Nebraska Bar, and the Doncaster Building.

TV Little Wood River
Northeast of Shoshone. Contact the Idaho Department of Fish and Game – Magic Valley Office at 324-4350.

Originating on the southern flank of the Pioneer Mountains, the Little Wood River flows south across the lava rock and sagebrush flats of south-central Idaho. Along its path, the world-famous Silver Creek joins in before the Little Wood dumps into its big brother, the Big Wood River. The Little Wood is most often recognized for its lava rock bottom and deep pools harboring trophy rainbow and brown trout.

Fishing well in June and again in late summer and fall, the Little Wood River has turned out brown trout up to twenty-six inches long. Anglers report that grasshopper and nymph flies are most appropriate and note that summer trout fishing

THE TRIALS AND TRIBULATIONS OF DESERT FARMING

Under the Desert Land General Revised Act of 1891, the U.S. Government opened up this stretch of Idaho to homesteaders, providing each settler with 320 acres of land with the understanding that at least one-eighth of the land would be cultivated within three years. Although the desert conditions did not look promising, hundreds of settlers jumped at the opportunity for free land and headed to south-central Idaho. Between 1912 and 1930, more than 325 claims were filed in the area.

Due to the recently passed Reclamation Project, settlers at the time believed that canals would soon appear in the region to aid them in fulfilling the General Revised Act's requirements. Until then, the confident workers vowed to dry-farm the area until the nearby Minidoka Irrigation Project was expanded. Eagerly anticipating the lush green farms they knew would eventually appear, the homesteaders planted Turkey Red wheat. Although the first couple years boasted promising crops, the success was short-lived. Plagues of wind and dust storms, coyotes, rattlesnakes, jackrabbits, squirrels, woodticks, and late frosts coupled with the area's driest recorded years in history resulted in an area depression. When the promised water from the Minidoka Irrigation Project failed to arrive, many of the eager homesteaders abandoned their claims in pursuit of more fertile land and dreams.

Finally, in 1946, deep wells and electric pumps with underground pipes turned the desert wasteland into a farmable area. Today, little trace is left of the first homesteaders' painstaking work and agricultural troubles.

generally tapers off around noon when both air and water temperatures are warm.

Featuring several miles of shoreline, the Little Wood River offers anglers a secluded fishing hole. Prior to fishing the Little Wood, anglers should familiarize themselves with the river's catch and release areas as well as catch limits on some portions of the river.

V Mammoth Cave and T-Maze Caves
6 miles north of Shoshone on State Hwy. 75. Contact the BLM – Shoshone Field Office at 732-7200.

The undeveloped Mammoth Cave is located just west of the highway on Bureau of Land Management acreage. The first one-quarter-mile-long lava tube was discovered in 1902 and was developed during the 1950s into an available government defense shelter and emergency supply center. Today, self-guided tours are available, and serious and experienced cave explorers have access to over a dozen unaltered lava tubes.

Nearby, the even more isolated T-Maze Caves are appropriate for expert cave explorers. This cave system features fourteen different lava tubes, including the longest "cave" currently mapped in all of Idaho. Contact the Bureau of Land Management Shoshone Field Office for more information and detailed maps.

M Shoshone Chamber of Commerce
PO Box 575, Shoshone. 886-2030.

5 *Food*

Dietrich
Pop. 150

Dietrich began as a railroad construction camp for the Oregon Short Line railroad. A post office was opened in 1906, and the town was named for Judge Frank S. Dietrich of Boise.

Richfield
Pop. 412

This small community began as part of the irrigation project pursued by the Idaho Irrigation Company. The company's 1907 construction of Magic Dam greatly contributed to the area's initial settlement. Upon the dam's completion, lots were provided to settlers under the Carey Act, and the town boomed as an agricultural center from 1924 to 1940.

Initially, Richfield was known as Alberta after Alberta Strunk, the first child born in the new town. However, when the New York based White and Company purchased the area irrigation project, business officals changed the name to entice prospective settlers with the implication that the area was covered with rich farmland.

6 *Food, Lodging*

Hagerman
Pop. 656

This small town and surrounding valley began as a Shoshone Indian fishing spot and later served as an important Oregon Trail stage station. Located near the Snake River's Lower Salmon Falls, the site was historically renowned for its large population of migrating salmon. When Stanley Hegeman and his partner Jack Hess arrived in the area, they applied for a post office under the name Hess. However, when the post office denied the name because too many other American cities were entitled Hess, the men reapplied for the name Hegeman. The post office accepted the suggestion, but in the process misspelled the name. Although the abundant fish populations certainly attracted residents to the area initially, the high quality fishing nature of Hagerman ended with the 1947 construction of an Idaho Power Company dam.

H Thousand Springs
Milepost 186.9 on U.S. Hwy. 30

A long series of lava flows buried old river channels in this area and created a multitude of famous springs here.

Over thousands of years, volcanic activity created a vast valley and plain, slowly forcing the Snake River southward in a great curve. Successive river channels were filled with spongy lava and became underground reservoirs and conduits. The Lost River and part of

the Snake River from near Rexburg slowly flow through them. Torrents from these buried channels now burst forth from this canyon wall.

H Fossil Beds
Milepost 175.7 on U.S. Hwy. 30

Fossil bones of zebras, beaver, otter, pelicans and other water birds are found in sediments left from a 3.4 million-year-old pond on the bluff across the Snake River.

Lava flows, pouring out over the plains on this side, met and dammed up sedimentary deposits washed in on the other side, making lakes and swamps. Here the river divides these two important geologic settings, formed at a time when the climate was wetter and the plains were tree-dotted grasslands where zebra-like horses used to graze.

H Salmon Falls
Milepost 184.5 on U.S. Hwy. 30 at the Hagerman Rest Area

In 1812, Joseph Miller found 100 lodges of Indians spearing thousands of salmon each afternoon at a cascade below here. Each summer, they dried a year's supply.

After 1842, they also traded salmon to Oregon Trail emigrants. John C. Fremont marveled at Salmon Falls' 18-foot vertical drop, adjacent to "a sheet of foaming water…divided and broken into cataracts" by islands that "give it much picturesque beauty and make it one of those places that the traveler turns again and again to fix in his memory."

H Payne's Ferry
Milepost 190.4 on U.S. Hwy. 30

A scow powered by oarsmen let Oregon Trail wagons cross the Snake River here from 1852 to 1870.

Then overland stage service from Boise to a rail terminal in Kelton, Utah, was moved to this crossing, and M.E. Payne installed a large (14-by-60-foot) new cable ferry that used river current for power. After stage service was shifted to a more direct route at Glenns Ferry in 1879, this boat handled mostly local traffic until 1910, when it broke away and sank three miles below here.

H Fishing Falls
Milepost 190.4 on U.S. Hwy. 30

When John C. Fremont came this way mapping emigrant roads in 1843, he found an important Indian village at Fishing Falls (Kanaka Rapids) about four miles above here.

He reported that native salmon spearers there were "unusually gay…fond of laughter; and in apparent good nature and merry character… entirely different from the Indians we had been accustomed to see." As the Snake River's highest salmon cascades, Fishing Falls was included on many early Western maps.

T Rose Creek Winery
226 E. Ave. N., Hagerman. 837-4413. In Hagerman, proceed along the Thousand Springs Scenic Route to the Hagerman Fossil Beds Visitors Center. Bear east on Reed St. and drive three blocks to locate the winery on E. Ave.

Established in 1984, Rose Creek Winery's owners work closely with small vineyards across Idaho to create high quality wines. Situated in the scenic Hagerman Valley, the winery is known for its production of oak-aged Chardonnay, light-bodied red wines, several varieties of Johannisberg Riesling, and a blush blend known as Rose Creek Mist. The winery is open daily during the summer from 11:30 AM to 5:30 PM and Wednesday through Sunday in the winter from 11:30 AM to 5:30 PM.

T Hagerman Valley Historical Society Museum

100 S. State St., Hagerman. 837-6288.

Situated in the historic Hagerman State Bank, the Hagerman Valley Historical Society Museum is home to numerous photos of the Hagerman Valley from past to present. Visitors will also find a full-size replica of a fossilized Hagerman horse. The museum is free of charge and is open from 1 PM to 4 PM Wednesday through Sunday from April to October.

T Hagerman Fossil Beds National Monument

Near Hagerman. 837-4793.

History of the Hagerman Area

Native American peoples now called the Shoshone-Bannock and Shoshone-Paiute tribes have lived in the Hagerman Valley for some 12,000 years. They caught and dried salmon, steelhead trout, whitefish, and other fish, including sturgeon weighing 1,500 pounds or more. They dug camas-lily and other roots for food and harvested various seeds, fruits, and other plants. They hunted mostly small game but also mountain sheep, elk, and deer.

Pristine segments of the Oregon Trail are located in the southern portion of the monument. The Snake River Plain was a difficult stretch for emigrants struggling to make their way west. Intense summer heat, dust, wind, and lack of water made the crossing of this sagebrush plain an ordeal. The Hagerman Valley was one of the few places where the Snake River Canyon was accessible and where emigrants could trade for fish with Native Americans. Another 700 miles of arduous travel lay ahead.

The 1862 Idaho gold rush brought an increase in both freight and stage traffic on the Oregon Trail. Trains of freight wagons hauling up to five tons each brought in goods to supply short-lived Army camps, mines, and developing towns. A few ranchers settled here after that. Farming in the valley began in 1879, with alfalfa growing by John Bell. In 1882, the Oregon Short Line railroad arrived north of the valley, and farming settlement increased. Farming continues today with sugar beets and potatoes as major crops.

Bounded on the east by basalt cliffs formed from past lava flows, the valley boasts many springs. Their water exits the ground at a consistent temperature ideal for raising trout commercially. Because the springs also keep the river from freezing in winter, some migrating waterfowl spend the winter here.

Visiting the National Monument

A temporary visitor center offers information and fossil displays across from Hagerman High School along U.S. Hwy. 30 in town (221 N. State Street) from 9 a.m. to 5 PM daily in summer. At other times call ahead, (208) 837-4793, for hours of operation. Schedules of educational programs are listed in The Fossil Record newsletter. For more information write to: Superintendent, Hagerman Fossil Beds National Monument, P0. Box 570, Hagerman, ID 83332.

For an easy view of the monument, drive south from Hagerman on Hwy. 30 past the road to Wendell and take the next right turn (0.25 mile), marked "Sportsman's Access." Follow the signs to the Bell Rapids boat dock on the Snake River for fishing, water sports, or viewing birds along the scenic shoreline. The 4,281-acre monument, across the river, includes seven miles of shoreline.

On Monument Land

To reach wheelchair accessible overlooks, continue south on Hwy. 30 and cross the Snake River. Turn right on Bell Rapids road and continue 2.8 miles. The parking lot is on the right, one tenth of a mile after you enter the monument. The boardwalk with wayside exhibits provides a commanding view of the fossil beds and Snake River and is a good place to watch waterfowl. Another exhibit is across the road along with a hiker's trailhead. Farther along this road, white stakes mark the historic Oregon Trail. Additional trails and wayside exhibits are at the top of this grade on the left.

At points along the road there are nice views of the Snake River, Hagerman Valley, and the slopes exposing the fossil beds. You should return along this same road. Before driving this or any other road in the monument, please check at the visitor center for complete directions, important safety warnings, and private property restrictions. Other improvements for visitor enjoyment are in planning stages.

Regulations and Safety

Do not move or take any fossil, rock, or plant. All plants and animals are protected by law, even rattlesnakes and scorpions and other noxious insects. Beware and give them room. Most areas are closed to public use. Check with a ranger before venturing out.

If you see a fossil, please do not pick it up; report its location to a ranger so important information can be gathered. Many fossils are fragile and must be protected by trained experts before they can be moved safely.

What the Scientists Found Here

No other fossil beds preserve such varied land and aquatic species from the time period called the Pliocene Epoch. More than 180 animal species of both vertebrates and invertebrates and 35 plant species have been found in hundreds of individual fossil sites. Eight species are found nowhere else, and 43 were found here first. The Hagerman Horse, Equus simplicidens, exemplifies the quality of fossils. From these fossil beds have come both complete and partial skeletons of this zebra-like ancestor of today's horse.

In 1929, paleontologists from the Smithsonian Institution in Washington, D.C., made the first scientific excavations at Hagerman Fossil Beds. A local rancher, Elmer Cook, had shown the fossil beds to a government geologist, Dr. Harold Stearns. The Smithsonian finds led to more expeditions in the 1930s. Its National Museum of Natural History excavated 120 horse skulls and 20 complete skeletons from an area now called the Horse Quarry. The Smithsonian exchanged some of these Hagerman Horse skeletons with other museums. This has resulted in their display around the world. Additional scientific expeditions have been conducted over the years by other museums, universities, and the National Park Service. More than 200 published scientific papers now focus on the Hagerman fossil species.

Clues in the Landscape

The 600-foot-high bluffs rising above the Snake River and comprising the Hagerman Fossil Beds reveal the environment at the end of the Pliocene Epoch. Grassy plains dotted with ponds and forest

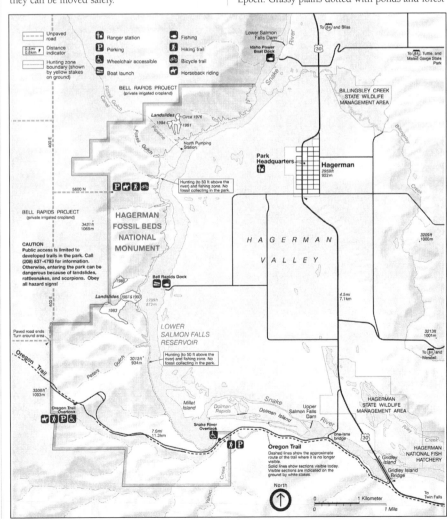

Malad Gorge from Interstate 84

stands then received over twice today's 10 inches of yearly precipitation. Mastodons, sabretooth cats, beavers, muskrats, otters, camels, antelope, deer, ground sloths, hyena-like dogs, and fish, frogs, snakes, and waterfowl lived here. The sediment layers from river level to bluff tops span some 550,000 years: from 3.7 million years old at river level to 3.15 million years old atop the bluff. These layers were deposited when rivers flowing into ancient Lake Idaho flooded the countryside. The much later Bonneville Flood, 15,000 years ago, carved the high bluffs, exposing the layers and fossils. This flood also deposited fields of so-called melon gravel - lava boulders ranging in size from a compact car to watermelons - from today's river level to gravel bars 225 feet higher.

The sediments in the bluffs include river sands, thin shale layers deposited in ponds, clay flood deposits, and occasional volcanic deposits such as ash and basalt. It is the radioactive elements such as potassium 40 in the volcanic ashes that allowed scientists to determine the age of the fossils by measuring the rate at which one radioactive element breaks down into another.

Adapt, Migrate, or Become Extinct

As significant environmental change happens, most plants and animals will have three options: adapt, migrate, or become extinct. The ancient ecosystem of Hagerman's fossil plants and animals shows each response as this region changed from a wetter grassland savanna to the drier high-desert conditions here today.

Adapted: Fossils of beaver and muskrat and many birds are similar or ancestral to today's species. Migrated: Llamas migrated to South America, while camels and horses crossed the Bering Land Bridge into Eurasia. Extinct: Ground sloths went extinct. So did mastodons and other large herbivores. As their primary prey disappeared, sabretooth cats and hyena-like dogs also became extinct.

Hagerman Fossil Beds is one of the few sites that preserves the necessary variety and quantity of fossil evidence to study past climates and ancient ecosystems. Fossil studies also add to contemporary research on biodiversity, wetlands ecology, and evolutionary patterns.

Reprinted from a National Park Service/U.S. Department of the Interior brochure

⊤ Hagerman National Fish Hatchery

South of Hagerman on State Fish Hatchery Rd.
837-4896.

Overview

The Hagerman National Fish Hatchery began operation in 1933, with a capacity of 800,000 fish. In 1983, the U.S. Army Corps of Engineers rebuilt and expanded the facilities as part of the Lower Snake River Compensation Plan – to offset losses caused by dams on the lower Snake River.

Since the constant 59-degree fresh water is gravity-fed to more than 60 rearing tanks and 102 raceways, the Hagerman National Fish Hatchery becomes one of the most cost-efficient mitigation hatcheries in the northwest. Fresh water flows through these rearing units at 25,000 gallons per minute.

The Hagerman National Fish Hatchery produces more than 1.5 million steelhead each year. The steelhead's life on the hatchery is completed each spring in April when it is transported to Idaho's Salmon River drainage.

There it will be released to commence its arduous and hazardous journey to the Pacific Ocean. Hatchery loss over the past five years has averaged only 23 percent, as compared to an estimated 97 percent loss of fish in the wild.

With the increasing man-made and environmental pressures existing on America's wild rivers today, facilities such as this are becoming increasingly essential to the steelheads very survival – operated by men dedicated to the preservation of a species, working to assist the struggle for new life.

For New Life

It begins somewhere in the Pacific Ocean, 12 months prior to the appearance of new life. A female steelhead, weighing 15-18 pounds, sleek and healthy from feeding on the rich ocean life, begins to produce the 2,500-4,000 eggs (roe) that she will carry back to the spawning grounds of her own origin. She undertakes the 8-month journey with single-minded purpose – to reproduce, to lay her eggs, and give new life. If she arrives at her chosen spawning grounds hundreds of miles inland, her mission – and her life cycle, is nearly complete.

Every step of the reproduction process is critical. The gravel streambed she has selected, for example, must be clean with water flowing through it, not just over it. Her freshly laid eggs must have sufficient oxygen. With a few powerful strokes of her tail fin, she rakes the streambed, preparing a shallow nest (redd) for her roe.

Once deposited in the redd she has just dug, the eggs must be fertilized by a male within 5-10 minutes. Longer delays mean the eggs will swell with water, preventing fertilization.

Even more critical is the life span of the sperm laid over the eggs by the male. Swimming at random, the sperm must contact an egg's tiny opening (micropyle) within 30-60 seconds or her eggs will not be fertilized.

But having done her part, she will cover the fertilized eggs with gravel for security during their incubation. Under increasingly complex and difficult environmental conditions, fewer than 50 percent of the female steelhead's roe will be fertilized.

That same steelhead, if taken from the wild and handled under hatchery-controlled conditions, will yield a 95 percent fertility count – a real justification for the hatchery you are visiting!

Life Begins

Whether in the wild or under hatchery conditions, the now-fertilized egg immediately begins dividing and developing. Depending on water temperature, cells can divide as often as every 20 minutes.

The egg next enters a 3-14 day "closed period." The embryo grows from a flat disc of cells to a recognizable body form. During this time, the egg and its new life are extremely fragile. Poor water flow, fungus growth, and predation all take a severe toll in the wild.

The Eye-Up Stage

At the end of the closed period, the steelhead egg enters the "eyed" stage. Having completed the delicate process of forming the spine and central nervous system, the retinal pigment of the eye now becomes highly visible through the egg's shell.

At this time, the egg becomes much more tolerable of rough handling. If necessary, hatcheries can ship eggs at this stage of development. Next the embryo, now 22 days after fertilization, releases an enzyme which softens the eggshell in preparation for hatching. The embryo finally breaks out of the shell, becoming what we call a sac fry.

Once free from the egg, the tiny steelhead lies helpless on the bottom, feeding off the highly nutritious protein and fat stored in its yolk sac. Its gills are active and the sac fry begins to respire – but it still can't swim.

At this stage, the steelhead sustains its greatest losses in the wild – primarily due to predation and slow growth due to water temperatures. Under hatchery conditions, the delicate sac fry stage can be reduced from a month or so to 10-15 days. Predation is totally eliminated, resulting in greatly increased rates of survival.

The Fry – A Tenuous Beginning

Emerging from its sac fry stage, the steelhead fry becomes a self-sufficient fresh water creature, capable of feeding and swimming. Still, the fry in the wild is literally swimming for its life. Some two to three years after hatching, the small fresh-water steelhead begins to undergo complex hormonal changes in preparation for its migration to the ocean.

Two vital elements must be present. First, the steelhead's size must be right, ideally 7-8 inches. Equally important is an increasing day length, which is nature's signal telling him to stop resisting the river's current.

On this day, "smoltification" begins. The young fish change color from dark green to the light silver of adulthood as they await the next stage of their amazing life cycle.

If all the factors aren't right, they will remain fresh water fish for life, becoming resident trout. But if they are fortunate and nature cooperates, they will begin a 2-3 month journey downstream to the ocean. Continuing to undergo biological changes as they migrate, the young steelhead face the most difficult and dangerous period of their lives.

In the wild, growth to ideal size can take as long as three years before smoltification and migration begin. Under hatchery conditions, the growth and biological changes are accelerated, bringing the steelhead to smolt size in 12 months.

Reprinted from Idaho Fish and Game and U.S. Army Corps of Engineers brochure

T Silgar's Thousand Springs Resort
U.S. Hwy. 30 near Hagerman. 837-4987.

Set amidst scenic views of the Snake River and Thousand Springs area, Silgar's Thousand Springs Resort features an indoor, hot spring fed pool along with private Jacuzzi baths. Tent and RV camping is available on-site, and the hot springs are open year-round Tuesday through Sunday. A small admission fee is charged.

T Priestly Pneumatic Water Lift
Located approximately 50 yards north of the Thousand Springs Power Company near U.S. Hwy. 30 south of Hagerman. Contact the Hagerman Valley Chamber of Commerce at 837-9131.

When the ingenious William Priestly arrived in the Hagerman Valley, he decided to invent a means of irrigating his land located on a bench 270 above the Snake River. Although Priestly first tried to dig a well, the basalt layer running underneath his land's topsoil returned futile results.

Noting the rapid flow of the nearby Thousand Springs, Priestly dreamed up an idea of a hydraulic ram efficiently powered by compressed air that would shoot water up from Thousand Springs onto his land. Priestly set to work, and within no time, a ten-foot high water tank and yards of pipe were riveted to the canyon wall. After the pipe's mouth was aligned to the largest spring, Priestly's invention carried the water to the reservoir tank and through a series of shorter pipes. In the end, the pneumatic water lift featured seventy-five p.s.i. and successfully carried water to Priestly's land.

In 1894, a Boise irrigation project engineer noted Priestly's invention, and the idea likely would have been an instant success. However, the rapid development of dams, reservoirs, and canal systems in south-central Idaho quickly outpaced the efficiency of Priestly's design. In 1972, the invention's remains were added to the National Register of Historic Places, and the large steel tank and a few pipes are still visible today.

TV Hagerman Wildlife Management Area/Hagerman State Fish Hatchery
Contact the Hagerman State Fish Hatchery at 837-4892 or the ID Dept. of Fish and Game at 324-4359. Take Hwy. 30 south of Hagerman for 2 miles; then follow the signs to the preserve and hatchery.

The Hagerman Wildlife Management Area preserves 880 acres of wetlands and riparian areas as wildlife habitat. The area remains ice-free year round thanks to its spring-fed waters, making it a haven for thousands of ducks and geese as well as peregrine falcons, ospreys, golden and bald eagles, and many upland game birds. The area is also home to larger animals, such as muskrats, beavers, porcupines, and mule deer. The Idaho Department of Fish and Game manages the area, which offers upland game and big game hunting as well as trapping and fishing.

The Hagerman State Fish Hatchery is located within the wildlife management area and raises millions of trout annually, including half of the rainbow trout yearly stocked in Idaho. Six miles of walking trails loop past numerous ponds and lakes open to anglers. All visitors should first check with the Idaho Department of Fish and Game for seasons and possible closures.

TV Blue Heart Springs
Near Hagerman. Contact the Hagerman Valley Chamber of Commerce at 837-9131.

Nestled in an area abundantly populated with waterfowl and wildlife, Blue Heart Springs is one of the Hagerman Valley's best-kept secrets. The crystal clear Blue Heart Springs rises deep within the Snake River bed and emerges as an inviting pool of blue water. The scenic springs are best viewed on a scuba diving excursion, and both rental equipment and guided tours are available in the Hagerman Valley.

TV Billingsley Creek State Park and Wildlife Management Area
0.5 miles northeast of Hagerman on U.S. Hwy. 30. Contact the Idaho Department of Fish and Game at 334-3700.

Operated under the direction of the Idaho Department of Fish and Game, the 284-acre Billingsley Creek State Park and Wildlife Management Area provides a secure waterfowl habitat as well as opportunities for hunting, fishing, trapping, wildlife observation, and photography. Anglers can try their hand at catching both rainbow and brown trout on the 1.25-mile stretch of Billingsley Creek that flows through the preserve, while hunters have access to both ducks and deer. Populated with a variety of upland game, waterfowl, and mule deer, the site is open year-round with no established visiting hours. As a newly added attraction, a blues festival is held amid the park's scenic setting each summer. Campfires and camping are expressly prohibited at all times.

V Lower Salmon Falls Park/Idaho Power Park
On Hwy. 30 between Bliss and Hagerman. Contact the Hagerman Chamber of Commerce at 837-9131.

Popular with anglers and water skiers, these parks are located on ten acres of scenic wooded land and offer easy access to the Lower Salmon Falls Reservoir. Aside from water sports, the reservoir has excellent trout fishing in the winter and bass fishing in the summer.

V Snake River Recreation – Hagerman & Bell Rapids
U.S. Hwy. 30 near Hagerman. Contact the BLM – Shoshone Field Office at 732-7200.

The Snake River twists its way through the Hagerman Valley, providing residents and visitors with plenty of recreational opportunities. Bell Rapids is a favorite angling destination, while drift boat trips and guided tours are popular day excursions. For the more adventurous, some Snake River sections around Hagerman boast challenging Class III rapids. The river is accessible year-round free of charge.

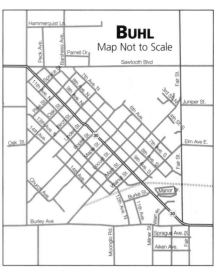

BUHL
Map Not to Scale

M Hagerman Valley Chamber of Commerce
221 N. State St., Hagerman. 837-9131.
www.hagerman-idchamber.org

7 *Food, Lodging*

Buhl
Pop. 3,985

Buhl was founded as part of the Twin Falls South Side irrigation project in 1905 and named for one of the founders, Frank H. Buhl. Although Frank originally came to the area in 1901 in hopes of purchasing a mining property, he soon discovered the property of his interest had been sold. Seeking opportunity, he investigated the possibility of developing an irrigation system. He and a gentleman named Peter Kimberly formed a corporation and completed their project. Buhl was platted in 1905, and lots sold for $1,750 each.

In 1928, Jack and Selma Tingey came up from Utah and began the area's first trout farm on the Snake River. Today, the trout farm produces over twenty-five million pounds of trout each year and is a proud employer of local residents. Buhl is also recognized as an agricultural center, and the famous Green Giant vegetable brand operates a factory in the heart of Buhl.

T Clear Lake Country Club
403 Clear Lakes Rd., Buhl. 543-4849.

The Clear Lake Country Club is nestled in the scenic Snake River Canyon and was established in 1987. Using the hilly, natural terrain to provide character, the 18-hole course is rated a par 72 and features challenging, small greens. The lush blue grass fairways often become home to an abundant variety of wildlife, and the Snake River creates water hazards on nearly one-third of the holes. Green fees for the 5,905-yard course are approximately $25, and it is open year-round Tuesday through Sunday. For fly-fishermen, the club offers a 15 acre spring fed lake and the winding Snake River. A $10 fishing fee is charged but no license is needed.

T Clear Springs Trout Farm Visitor Center
643-3416 Directly east of Buhl, turn off U.S. Hwy. 30 onto Clear Lakes Rd.. After crossing the Snake River, follow the signs to the Clear Springs Trout Farm Visitor Center.

One of the world's largest commercial trout farms, Clear Springs Trout Farm Visitor Center offers self-

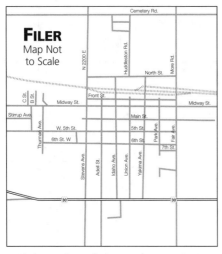

FILER
Map Not to Scale

guided tours that include an underwater viewing room beneath the rainbow trout and sturgeon ponds. The center is open daily from 9:00 AM to 5:30 PM with picnic areas available.

T Banbury Hot Springs
10 miles northwest of Buhl off U.S. Hwy. 30. 543-4098.

With a seventy-year history, Banbury Hot Springs is situated alongside the Snake River and offers an array of recreation for the entire family. The outdoor swimming pool features crystal clear water, a slide, and diving board, and hot baths and Jacuzzis are also available. In addition, the springs feature a picnic area and a convenient boat-launching ramp. The springs are open Memorial Day through Labor Day, and a small admission fee is charged.

T Miracle Hot Springs
In Buhl on the west side of U.S. Hwy. 30. 543-6002.

Offering two outdoor pools and nineteen private hot tubs, Miracle Hot Springs is open year-round for soaking and tent and RV camping. Operating hours are Monday through Saturday from 8 AM to 11 PM, and a small admission fee is charged.

T Melon Valley
Near Buhl

The Melon Valley twists its way around U.S. Highway 30 near Buhl and is recognized as one of the most scenic areas in the broader Hagerman Valley. The basin area was formed when the catastrophic Bonneville flood and subsequent lava flows reshaped the Snake River Plain 12,000 to 15,000 years ago. Today, the beautiful valley is filled with natural springs, streams, and abundant wildlife.

T Buhl's Historic Buildings
Downtown Buhl. Contact the Buhl Chamber of Commerce at 543-6682.

Although Buhl's townsite was platted in 1905, it took several years for new buildings to arrive in town. Some of Buhl's most historically important buildings remain standing as a testimony to the town's glory days.

Buhl City Hall
Southwest side of Broadway
Located near the town's entrance, the Buhl City Hall was built between 1919 and 1920 at a cost of $40,000. The Mission-style building originally housed the community's fire department and city offices, as well as restrooms, dressing rooms, and a waiting lounge for farm families visiting town.

Ramona Theater
1 block south of the Buhl City Hall on Broadway
Constructed in Buhl's founding years, the Ramona

Theater was refurbished in 1928 with a $70,000 price tag. The Spanish-Moorish style theater, named in a contest, honors the heroine in a Helen Hunt Jackson novel. Today, the once popular theater houses a restaurant.

United Methodist Church
1/2 block northeast of Broadway on Maple St.
The United Methodist Church may well boast the longest construction period in all of Buhl. Due to the agricultural depression and a shortage of finances, the church construction that began in 1920 was not completed until 1929.

TV Bordewick Sportsman's Access Area
Near Buhl. Contact the Buhl Chamber of Commerce at 543-6682.

South-central Idaho boasts several Snake River sportsman's access points. Few, however, rival the splendor of the Bordewick Area near Buhl. The access area is known for housing several large waterfowl species, including great blue herons, white pelicans, and Canadian geese. In addition, the Bordewick stretch of the Snake River offers excellent fishing opportunities, wading fun for children, and several primitive camping and picnicking areas.

M Buhl Chamber of Commerce
716 E. U.S. Hwy 30, Buhl. 543-6682.
www.buhlidaho.us/chamber-commerce/index.htm

8

Castleford
Pop. 277

Castleford draws its name from a crossing on the Salmon Falls Creek surrounded by a canyon lined with basalt formations. Pioneers journeying west used the crossing in 1849, and the site later became a famous crossing point on the Kelton-Dalles stage route. Today, the town is recognized as home to nearby Balanced Rock.

T Salmon Falls Creek Canyon
South of Castleford. Contact the Buhl Chamber of Commerce at 543-6682. From the intersection of 3300 N and 1000 E Rds. near Castleford, drive east to 1050 E Rd. Bear right. and continue to the canyon rim.

Home to the world-famous Balanced Rock, Salmon Falls Creek Canyon also houses breathtaking scenery amid an isolated landscape. The canyon rim, composed of basalt and rhyolite, descends more than 600 feet in a deep gorge to Salmon Falls Creek rushing below. The rim offers

MAGIC VALLEY

Ever wonder why south-central Idaho is frequently referred to as the Magic Valley? The nickname dates back to 1894 when Congress passed the Carey Act. The act entitled individuals to vast western desert acreage if they agreed to irrigate and cultivate the land. Eyeing the Snake River, a small group of agricultural and business enthusiasts developed plans to divert water from the massive river into a 2,600-mile canal network. The plan worked like magic, and the once arid land was magically transformed into a prosperous farming oasis. Today, the Magic Valley produces most of Idaho's sugar beets, and is also known for its high yields of potatoes, beans, peas, and barley.

spectacular views and solitude for hikers and anglers as well as frequent visits from hundreds of raptors circling above. The area is prone to landslides, so those considering hiking down to the creek should use extreme caution.

T Balanced Rock
South of Buhl. Contact the BLM-Shoshone Field Office at 732-7200. After following the highway signs leading from Buhl to Castleford, drive six miles northwest to the site.

The world-famous, mushroom shaped Balanced Rock rises high against the northern skyline in south-central Idaho. Carved by wind throughout the ages, Balanced Rock stands over 200 feet tall, weighs nearly forty tons, boasts a diameter of forty-eight feet, and rests haphazardly on a three foot by seventeen inch rocky pedestal. With growing concern mounting about the rock's stability, county lawyers ordered the rock and pedestal to be reinforced with concrete. The site is open year-round free of charge.

TV Balanced Rock State Park
South of Buhl. Contact the BLM – Shoshone Field Office at 732-7200. After following the highway signs leading from Buhl to Castleford, drive six miles northwest.

With Balanced Rock silhouetted against the horizon, Balanced Rock Park offers year-round recreation amid Mother Nature's unique basalt rock formations. The park is ideal for picnicking and is a popular rock-climbing destination for both beginners and advanced adventurers seeking to climb the area's stunning hoodoos. Situated alongside Salmon Falls Creek, the park also offers visitors a semi-natural Jacuzzi on the river's north side as hot spring water is pumped out of a pipe. Weather permitting, the free park is open year-round.

9 *Food*

Filer
Pop. 1.620

Filer was established in 1903 at the end of the Oregon Short Line Railroad, and is named after Walter Filer, general manager of the Twin Falls Canal Company. Initially, there were two small towns lying close together, Eldridge and Filer. The two eventually merged into one, and a post office was established in 1907.

ANNUAL EVENTS

Thousand Springs Festival
An annual arts festival is held at Thousand Springs Preserve on Ritter Island over a weekend in late September. Activities include a juried outdoor art show, live music, food and drink, antique dairy farm tours, hiking, huge raffle prizes, and free horse and wagon rides.

Annual Basque Picnic & Summerfest
Idaho is recognized for its dense Basque population, a heritage that is celebrated each July in Gooding at the annual Basque Picnic. The event includes a special church service and follows with a barbeque featuring traditional Basque foods. Dishes include lamb chops, Basque rice, beans, salad, bread, and chorizo. After eating, picnic attendees can take part in or watch a variety of activities, including games, children's foot races, adult weight carrying contests, an auction, and Basque dancing.

Coupled with the Basque Picnic is Gooding's Summerfest. The weekend event includes a street fair, antique cars, arts and crafts, and several food vendors.

Arts in the Park & Fiddles Jamboree
Every July, the Shoshone City Park fills with excitement at the annual Arts in the Park and Fiddlers' Jamboree. Art vendors and craft booths await, while the Mannie Shaw Fiddlers' Jamboree serves up some of the best fiddling around. The show is named after late Fairfield resident and fiddler, Mannie Shaw, and has a thirty-year history.

Arts on Tour
In association with the College of Southern Idaho, Twin Falls is host to an impressive live performance line-up each year. Past performances have included *The Nutcracker*, selections from Broadway, the New Shanghai Circus, and much more. Call for tickets and a complete schedule of events.

Buhl Sagebrush Days
Before the Magic Valley experienced the wonders of irrigation, the region was covered with sagebrush. The community of Buhl honors that history every Fourth of July weekend with Sagebrush Days. The three-day event features a craft fair, tennis tournament, fun run, youth fishing derby, bull riding, fish fry, mountain men, a Kiwanis breakfast, antique auto show, parade, firehose competition, and a magnificent fireworks display.

Hagerman Fossil Days
Hagerman Fossil Days arrives at Hagerman City Park at the dawn of summer each year, beckoning visitors with two days of old-fashioned family fun. The event includes live entertainment, dancing, craft and food vendors, children's games, and a parade.

Hispanic Fiesta
Idaho's Hispanic heritage is honored with the annual Hispanic Fiesta held each summer. Hosted in the Twin Falls City Park, the event features lively dancing, singing, and authentic Mexican food.

Idaho Regatta
Burley's population swells to twice its size each June with the annual Idaho Regatta. The three-day event features ninety of America's finest flat-bottom boats racing down the spectacular Snake River. Powerboat fans from far and wide attend the event where some boats reach speeds in excess of 200 miles per hour.

Jazz in the Canyon
Held early each summer, Jazz in the Canyon is a must-see Twin Falls' event. The weekend showcases both national and regional jazz entertainers performing in some of the community's most peaceful settings. Concerts are staged at the Kimberly Nurseries' garden, Centennial Park, and in the Snake River canyon. Advance tickets are strongly recommended.

Children's Art in the Park
Twin Falls is committed to exposing children to the arts, and the one-day Children's Art in the Park event is aimed at accomplishing this goal. The annual event includes short educational classes on visual and performing arts for youth ages pre-kindergarten through junior high.

Magic Valley Air Show
Twin Falls' bi-annual Magic Valley Air Show features flying fun for the whole family. The one-day event includes a veterans' pavilion filled with war memorabilia, a working replica of the Wright Brothers' invention, airplane stunts, and parachuters.

Magic Valley Dairy Days
The Magic Valley is known for its dairy farms, and this longstanding agricultural legacy is the focus of Magic Valley Dairy Days. The two-day summer event features a parade, art and crafts vendors, food booths, live entertainment, a Snake River Community Players melodrama, and of course, plenty of free ice cream.

Mini-Cassia Craft Fair
Held annually in Rupert during autumn, the Mini-Cassia Craft Fair draws onlookers from the local area as well as from more distant Idaho communities. The one-day event showcases over 100 craft booths featuring a variety of craftsmen and materials.

Nascar Weekly Racing Series
Spring and summer welcomes Twin Falls residents and visitors with the sound of zooming cars whirling down the raceway. The Nascar Weekly Racing Series is a popular weekend event held April through September at the Magic Valley Speedway near the Twin Falls Airport. Advance tickets are recommended.

Oktoberfest
The old-world tradition of Oktoberfest provides two days of lively entertainment and dancing in historic Old Town Twin Falls at the beginning of October. The event features traditional German food, beer, and of course, lots of polka dancing!

Pioneer Days
Idaho was founded upon the enduring spirit of pioneers, and their numerous sacrifices have not been forgotten. During the summer in Oakley, residents gather to remember their ancestors at the annual Pioneer Days. The three-day event includes chuckwagon breakfasts, Dutch oven cook-offs, Pony Express Rides and a rodeo, three-on-three basketball tournaments, a 10K run, one-mile kids' fun run, dancing, "old-fashioned" pioneer games, a parade and musical, pioneer program, and a huge fireworks display.

Snake River Arts Festival
The Snake River Arts Festival in Heyburn is a two-day family oriented event held each September. The festival includes numerous artistic displays featuring pottery, paintings, and sculptures. In addition, the event features music, entertainment, food booths, and children's activities.

Twin Falls County Fair & Magic Valley Stampede
Held during the end of August and beginning of September, the Twin Falls County Fair and Magic Valley Stampede includes a carnival, demolition derby, draft horse show, petting zoo, agricultural exhibits, antique tractor display and pull, a Miss Rodeo Idaho contest, a PRCA rodeo, and a country music concert.

Western Days
Grab your partner and saddle up for a truly western festival at Twin Falls' Western Days. The family-oriented three-day event showcases music, an arts and crafts show, a variety of food booths, a mock gunfight, community barbeques, chili cook-offs, a carnival, and a western dance.

Gooding County Fair & Rodeo
The Gooding County Fair and Rodeo brings a western flair to this small community each August. Held at the local fairgrounds, the fair features traditional fare complete with the state's Miss Teen Rodeo Idaho contest.

Jerome Live History Days
Jerome Live History Days is an annual event that has been celebrating the pioneer life and spirit for more than twenty consecutive years. Each year, a new pioneer theme is chosen for the weekend event, and crowds gather to witness the many interesting demonstrations and displays. Past activities have included horse-drawn wagon rides, antique tractor pulling, spinning, quilt making, blacksmithing, cornhusk doll making, and cooking and cleaning demonstrations. In addition, the event often features historical memorabilia, including antique guns, mountain man tools and apparel, and pioneer buildings dating back nearly 100 years.

Cassia County Fair & Rodeo
The Cassia County Fair and Rodeo serves up old-fashioned western fun each August. The six-day event includes a variety of food vendors, agricultural and home exhibits, carnival rides, and of course, a traditional rodeo.

Spudman Triathlon
Although it may possess a funny name, the Spudman Triathlon is no laughing matter. The July event has developed into a long-standing community tradition and has garnered the national spotlight several times. ESPN occasionally broadcasts coverage of the event, and *Triathlete* magazine dubs the triathlon an event that no serious athlete should miss. Evidently, the rumor is out about the Spudman as more than 300 athletes from across the U.S. annually compete in the event.

T Twin Falls County Historical Society and Museum
21337 A U.S. Hwy. 30 (3 miles west of downtown), Filer. 734-5547 or 423-5907.

The Magic Valley's early days are captured in the Twin Falls County Historical Society and Museum. Situated inside a restored pioneer schoolhouse, the museum offers both residents and tourists a glimpse into what life was like for the area's first settlers. Displays include antique farm machinery, intricate lacework, household utensils, vintage clothing, old report cards, and other miscellaneous artifacts illustrating how life was lived during the late 1800s and early 1900s. The museum is open from 10 AM to 5 PM Tuesday through Saturday from May through September, and 10 AM to 5 PM Wednesday through Saturday from October through April. Admission is free, but donations are always accepted.

T Basque Music Archives Filer Public Library,
Filer. 543-4690.

South-central Idaho is home to a large population of individuals with Basque heritage, and this cultural identity has been preserved in the Filer Public Library. The library possesses America's first Basque Music Archives, and the public is free to access the collection by contacting the library's archives' director.

T Magic Valley Steelhead Hatchery
7 miles northwest of Filer. 326-3230. From Twin Falls, proceed south on U.S. Hwy. 93 to Pole Line Rd. Bear west and continue 10 miles to Rd. 2000E. Turning right on 2000E, follow this road as it travels down a gravel grade to the hatchery.

Operating with a purpose of producing and sustaining steelhead trout runs in the Salmon River, the Magic Valley Steelhead Hatchery raises approximately two million smolts annually for a total of 450,000 pounds of fish each year. The hatchery features an incubation room with twenty rearing containers, thirty-two outdoor fish raceways, and two large settling ponds. Once the incubation and growing process is complete, hatchery officials release the offspring into several different Salmon River drainages.

The hatchery is open year-round, and visitors may access the site daily from 8 AM to 4 PM. Guided group tours are available upon advance reservation.

10 Food

Hollister
Pop. 237

This small community draws its name from Twin Falls Land and Investment Company supporter, H. L. Hollister. Hollister, who was also a promoter of the Salmon Irrigation Company, helped plot the townsite in 1909, and a post office operated under his name from 1910 to 1965.

Rogerson
Pop. 65

Formerly called Deep Creek Meadows by the first settlers in 1880, Rogerson was later named Terminal City because it served as the railroad line terminus in 1909. When a postal application was completed in 1910, the town selected Rogerson as its title. The name recognizes pioneer settler, Robert Rogerson, who became a prominent livestock rancher and assisted in platting the town site on his property. The town quickly became the center of the region's livestock economy, with cattle driven from hundreds of miles away to the Rogerson stockyards and railroad dock. Today, the quiet community serves the numerous anglers headed for Salmon Falls or Cedar Creek as well as the many tourists passing through on their way to Nevada's casinos.

H Salmon Dam
Milepost 11.2 on U.S. Hwy. 93

Constructed in 1910 about eight miles west of here, the Salmon Dam was a spectacular early irrigation structure.

Two hundred twenty feet high, it blocks a narrow lava gorge of Salmon Falls Creek. Intended to create a large reservoir to irrigate desert lands north of here, it was only a partial success. Porous lava canyon walls let water escape around it and lack of rainfall in Nevada's desert above here provided less than enough moisture for this reservoir. It did not fill up until 1984.

T Idaho Heritage Museum
2390 U.S. Hwy. 93, Hollister. 655-4444.

Housed inside a 7,000 square foot building, the Idaho Heritage Museum is home to one of the largest collections of Native American artifacts and mounted wildlife in the western U.S. Among the numerous exhibits are an antique gun collection, arrowheads, lance points, bone needles and awls, and a 15,000-year-old Bison skull. Visitors will also find displays of stuffed wolves, beavers, badgers, bobcats, bears, coyotes, deer, elk, mountain lions, ducks, pheasants, and moose. The museum is open from 10 AM to 4 PM daily from March to December.

T Nat-Soo-Pah Hot Springs
3 miles east of downtown Hollister on U.S. Hwy. 93. 655-4337.

Meaning "magic mineral water" in the Shoshone language, Nat-Soo-Pah has long been visited by weary travelers and those seeking peace and relaxation. Native Americans used the site for hundreds of years prior to its commercial establishment in 1926. Visitors will find a large, spring-fed swimming pool, water slide, diving boards, hot soaking pool, camping sites, and picnic areas complete with barbecue grills and horseshoe pits. The hot springs are open daily May through Labor Day, and a small admission fee is charged.

T Murphy Hot Springs/Desert Hot Springs
42 miles southwest of Rogerson near the Idaho/Nevada border. 857-2233.

Cradled amid Bruneau Desert Flats within a small gorge carved out by two forks of the Jarbidge River, Murphy Hot Springs' roots extend back to the 19th century. Native Americans first used the springs, believing that the natural mineral water possessed healing powers unrivaled by any other western hot spring. In 1885, Kittie Wilkins decided to turn the magical spot into a commercial destination. Using her father's squatter's land claim, Kittie established "Kittie's Hot Hole" with the pure artesian water that flows naturally hot out of the desert into the river below. Kittie enjoyed great success in her business venture, and in the early 1900s, sold the springs to Patrick Murphy. Murphy renamed the springs after himself and further developed the area, adding in more hot pools, rustic cabins, and a changing area.

Throughout the years, the hot springs has changed hands several times. However, the springs remain just as remote and rustic as their early days. Today, the name Murphy Hot Springs has been applied to the village of ten to thirty residents who live in the area year-round, while the springs themselves have been renamed Desert Hot Springs. Visitors to the area will enjoy a 104 degree Fahrenheit outdoor pool and a peaceful desert atmosphere. A small admission fee is charged, and the springs are open year-round.

TV Salmon Falls Creek Reservoir & Dam
8 miles west of Rogerson on Three Creek Rd. Contact the BLM – Shoshone Field Office at 732-7200.

Salmon Falls Creek Reservoir is the long awaited result of the nearby Salmon Falls Dam. Although the dam was completed in 1910, the area's low rainfall amounts and abundant porous lava rock prevented the reservoir from reaching its intended capacity until 1984. Today, the fourteen-mile long reservoir irrigates over 125,000 acres of land and is recognized as Idaho's premier walleye fishery. Another eight species of fish may also be caught here, all of which often produce trophy catches. Reservoir and dam amenities include five recreation sites, a boat ramp, primitive and fee camping, picnic sites, and a recreational vehicle dump station. The reservoir is accessible year-round.

V South Hills Snowmobile Trail
Southeast of Twin Falls. Contact the Twin Falls Ranger District at 737-3200.

The South Hills Snowmobile Trail, tucked inside the Sawtooth National Forest, offers snowmobilers access to stunning mountain views. The free trail is open during daylight hours, and trail maps are available from the Twin Falls Ranger District.

V South Hills Hiking and Mountain Biking
South of Twin Falls. Contact the Twin Falls Ranger District at 737-3200.

Although the mountains south of Twin Falls don't pierce the sky like their northerly Sawtooth neighbors, the terrain still attracts a variety of recreationists and offers its own style of outdoor adventure.

Speckled with desert canyons and grass covered meadows intermingled with cottonwood, pine, and aspen groves, the terrain offers outstanding views in all directions. Mountain biking trails in the South Hills are often quite challenging, and wildlife is a common sight. The Third Fork and Harrington Fork are the two most popular trails, both of which are rated moderate to difficult.

For hikers, the South Hills are covered with miles of winding paths leading to glorious destinations. For beginner to advanced hikers, a trail awaits. Fee camping is available in established sites along Rock Creek, but primitive camping is also allowed.

Interested recreationists should contact the Twin Falls Ranger District for further South Hills information and detailed trail/area maps.

11

T Malad Gorge State Park
I-84 Hagerman Exit 147 near Tuttle. Contact the ID Parks and Recreation Dept. at 334-4199.

Carved by the Malad River in the Hagerman Valley, the 250 foot deep Malad Gorge is the focal point of the 652-acre Malad Gorge State Park. The park's features include hiking trails, picnic shelters, interpretive viewpoints, and a three and a half mile scenic loop. From the 150-foot high footbridge spanning the gorge, visitors can appreciate a wonderful view of a sixty-foot waterfall that plunges the Malad River into a roiling basin known as "Devil's Washbowl." Park hours are 7:00 AM to 4:30 PM during the week and 8:00 AM to 6:00 PM on weekends. Contact the park regarding guided tours.

12 *Food, Lodging*

Wendell
Pop. 2,338

Once referred to as the "Hub City of the Magic Valley," Wendell was established in 1907 with the help of W. H. Kuhn. Kuhn and American Water Works out of Pittsburgh became major financiers of the North Side Irrigation Project during the development of the Twin Falls area. After selecting a town site and helping sell commercial lots, Kuhn christened the new settlement after his son, Wendell. A post office was established in 1908, and with the development of a Union Pacific Railroad line, the town began to grow.

T Ritter Island
Thousand Springs Preserve. 536-6797 or 536-5748.

The seventy-acre Ritter Island was once home to Millie Miller, the original owner of the preserve property that is now home to the Nature Conservancy's offices. The island is located in the middle of the Thousand Springs Preserve and features both walking trails and an early 1900s dairy farm, barn and now home to a museum. Ritter Island is open to the public during the summer on Fridays and Mondays from 9 AM to 5 PM and Saturdays and Sundays from 12 PM to 7 PM. During the winter, call ahead as hours are irregular.

T Earl M. Hardy Box Canyon Springs Nature Preserve
Between Wendell and Malad Gorge State Park. Contact Malad Gorge Park Rangers at 837-4505. At Wendell, merge off I-84 at Exit 155. Proceed 3.2 miles to 1500 E. Rd. and then bear south for 4.5 miles to a parking area.

The 350-acre Earl M. Hardy Box Canyon Springs Nature Preserve protects North America's eleventh largest natural spring. Pumping 180,00 gallons of water per minute into the Snake River, the crystal clear spring along with a twenty-foot waterfall and the scenic canyon are currently under the management of the Nature Conservancy and the State of Idaho. Eventually, Idaho officials hope to develop a state park here, offering increased access to area hiking, fishing, and biking. For now, the site is open year-round with limited hours, and a small admission fee is required.

TV Thousand Springs Preserve
837-9131. Merge off I-84 at Exit 155. After exiting, bear right and drive 3 miles, turning left onto 1500 E. for 2.5 miles. At 3200 S., turn right and proceed 2 miles to a sign for the preserve. Bear right at the sign followed by a quick right and more signs leading to a parking area.

Thousand Springs Preserve covers a 400-acre area bordering the Snake River in Hagerman Valley and is managed by the Nature Conservancy. Basalt cliffs edge this area of quiet bottomlands and spring fed creeks that is also home to cascading falls gushing out of canyon walls. Although a sanctuary for some endangered aquatic species, the preserve is open for fishing, hiking, birding, and waterfowl and upland hunting. Public boat ramps on the river's south side make this area a favorite water-skiing destination, and free tours of the springs are available year-round. Visitors should call in advance for operating hours.

13

T Niagara Springs Wildlife Management Area
324-4359 Take I-84 to Exit 157, and travel 7 miles south. Take a sharp left turn, and follow the road down into the canyon and the management area entrance.

Located between the Snake River and high lava rock canyon walls, the 957-acre Niagara Springs Wildlife Management Area offers opportunities for hiking, wildlife viewing, fishing, waterfowl hunting, upland and big game hunting, bicycling, and horseback riding. Aside from the natural sights, the wildlife management area is also home to a 1900s residence constructed from lava rocks that is listed on the National Register of Historic Places.

TV Niagara Springs and Crystal Springs State Parks
536-5522 or 837-4505. Coming from Wendell, cross the Snake River on Clear Lakes Rd. Bear right onto the Bob Barton Hwy., and continue past four intersections (1600 E, 1700 E. 1800 E. and 1900 E). Turn right onto Rex Leland Hwy. (1950 E.), and follow the road down to the river and the park. The gravel road into the canyon is narrow and not recommended for trailers or motor homes.

A National Natural Landmark, Niagara Springs State Park is located in a 350-foot deep canyon where icy blue spring water dives down the canyon walls. Composed of two sections, Niagra Springs State Park features picnicking and camping at the Emerson Pugmire Memorial Recreation Area and year-round fishing at Crystal Springs Lake. Located just a few miles up the road, Crystal Springs State Park features a steelhead hatchery as well as a wildlife area. Amenities at both parks include restrooms, picnic shelters, and picnic tables. A $2 car entry fee is required as well as a $7 overnight fee if visitors choose to camp. The park gates are open from 7:30 AM to 4 PM Monday through Thursday and all day on the weekends.

14 *Food, Lodging*

Jerome
Pop. 7,780

When sagebrush still ruled the land in 1907, this small town was platted by Jerome Kuhn (of Pittsburgh), I.B. Perrine, and S.B. Milner. These three men were influential in establishing the North Side Twin Falls Canal Project and subsequently created this community in 1908. It was incorporated in 1909 and later became the county seat (1919). Some residents and historians claim the town was named for Jerome Hill, grandfather of Jerome Kuhn. Regardless, this small town serves the surrounding farmers who raise sugar beets, beans, hay, wheat, and potatoes.

L Best Western Sawtooth Inn and Suites
2653 South Lincoln at I-84 Exit 168 in Jerome. 324-9200.

The Best Western Sawtooth Inn and Suites is conveniently located at I-84 exit 168. The Western themed décor of the Inn is accented with a river rock fireplace and stained glass windows in the large, spacious lobby. All suites have microwaves and refrigerators. There is a Bridal Suite with log furniture and Jacuzzi. The Kid Suite has bunk beds. The check in desk is open 24 hours, as is the indoor swimming pool. All guests enjoy a complimentary continental breakfast. Pets are welcome with a deposit. The Inn is close to Sun Valley, Craters of the Moon, Snake River, Shoshone Falls, Hagerman area, Balanced Rock, Jackpot, and local restaurants and shopping.

15 *Food, Lodging*

T Wilson Butte Cave
East of Jerome off State Hwy. 25. Contact the Jerome Chamber of Commerce at 324-2711. From Jerome, travel 12.7 miles southeast on State Hwy. 25. Bear north at the signed road, drive past the Minidoka Internment Center, and continue to a 4-way stop intersection. Bear west on the gravel road and drive 6.3 miles to a BLM directional sign. Follow the sign's directions to the cave.

Located in the secluded land outside Jerome, Wilson Butte Cave is actually a lava blister that formed when gas expanded within a cooling lava flow. The cave formed thousands of years ago, and archaeological evidence suggests that Shoshone Native Americans were in the area as early as 1300 A.D.

Twin Falls													
	Jan	Feb	March	April	May	June	July	Aug	Sep	Oct	Nov	Dec	Annual
Average Max. Temperature (F)	37.2	43.9	50.3	60.4	70.1	78.6	88.7	86.5	77.3	65.1	50.6	40.1	62.4
Average Min. Temperature (F)	18.6	23.1	26.4	33.4	41.7	48.8	54.8	52.1	43.3	34.0	26.9	21.2	35.4
Average Total Precipitation (in.)	1.06	0.75	0.84	0.81	1.13	0.88	0.20	0.41	0.54	0.69	0.93	1.11	9.36
Average Total Snowfall (in.)	6.3	3.4	2.9	0.8	0.8	0.0	0.0	0.0	0.1	0.4	1.3	5.4	21.5
Average Snow Depth (in.)	1	0	0	0	0	0	0	0	0	0	0	0	0

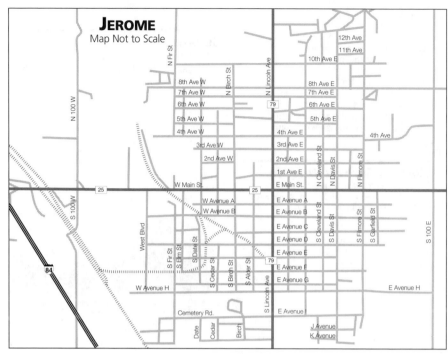

JEROME
Map Not to Scale

During the 1958 doctoral dissertation study of Ruth Grahn, the cave was determined to possess five major deposits of rock and sand. The bottom layer, which is also the oldest, yielded bones of two now extinct camel species and one extinct horse. While the middle layer contained the bones of more modern bison, the top layers were most impressive as archaeologists found a moccasin, pottery, arrowshafts, and arrowheads. Utilizing radiocarbon dating of the artifacts and bones, scientists concluded that the cave's lower and middle strata date back nearly 15,000 years.

Due to the researchers' significant finds and in-depth archaeological study, Wilson Butte Cave is now used as a reference point for archaeologists in studying the Indian cultures of the Plateau, Great Basin, and Plains regions.

The cave is easily accessible, but only experienced cave explorers should attempt to descend inside. For additional information, contact the BLM – Burley District at 678-5514.

T Jerome County Historical Museum
220 North Lincoln, Jerome. 324-5641.

This region's interesting past is captured in the Jerome County Historical Museum. Visitors will learn about the Hunt Japanese Relocation Center, the Minidoka Internment, county history, and irrigation projects under the Carey Act from the museum's informative displays. The museum also features a reading and research room and is open from 1 PM to 4:30 PM Tuesday through Saturday year-round.

T 93 Golf Ranch LLC
4 miles north of I-84 on U.S. Hwy. 93, Jerome. 324-9693.

Situated near Jerome, this 18-hole course is rated a par 72. The course is open daily from 7 AM to dusk and features four tee boxes. Green fees are $20.

M Jerome Chamber of Commerce
1731 S. Lincoln Ave., Suite A, Jerome. 324-2711. www.visitjerome.com; chamber@visitjerome.com

16 Food, Lodging

Twin Falls
Pop. 34,469

Serving as county seat for Twin Falls County, this community was founded in 1903 by I. B. Perrine. An Indiana born-Idaho settler, Perrine successfully developed an irrigated orchard near the Snake River Canyon just west of what would become Twin Falls. Drawing upon this idea, Perrine joined forces with several prominent businessmen from around the country to promote construction of a dam over the Snake River east of town. Doing so would provide reliable irrigation to the desert area and make it a livable place where an agricultural lifestyle would thrive. After enlisting more supporters and forming the Twin Falls Investment Company, Perrine's idea was endorsed with construction on the Milner Dam beginning in 1903. In 1904, the company platted the new town site of Twin Falls, and with the help of the 1894 Carey Act, 160-acre homesteads were offered at just $25 an acre. Settlers (mostly Midwestern businessmen and farmers) flocked to the area, and since the town grew so quickly, it was nicknamed "Magic City." In 1905, the town that was once a desert was officially incorporated as part of the state.

Named after the cataract flowing over the gorge of the Snake River, the city of Twin Falls attracts numerous tourists interested in the area waterfalls. The rushing rapids of Twin Falls were the site of Evel Knievel's failed attempt to cross the 1,500-foot gap in 1974. Local legend also relates several tales of both triumphant and unsuccessful individuals attempting to ride the 212-foot plunge of the nearby renowned Shoshone Falls.

Today, visitors will find that the town's founding agricultural legacy continues. Sugar beets, alfalfa, and potatoes are all important area crops, and cattle ranchers and dairy farmers have found the area ideal for business. The city's industry and more urban amenities combine with the farming lifestyle to offer a rich cultural heritage.

H Shoshone Falls
Milepost 50, Southbound on U.S. Hwy. 93, at Perrine Scenic Overlook

Four miles east of here, the Snake River thunders 210 feet over a rocky ledge higher than famous Niagra.

Indians, trappers, and travelers all knew the "Great Shoshonie." Now the waters upstream have been harnessed for irrigation and power, and in the dry summer months the rocks can be seen. The foaming river and the sheer walls of the canyon combine with the paths and shady lawns of the park and picnic area to make it one of Idaho's most spectacular scenes. At Shoshone Falls, a natural textbook of earth's forces lies open for you.

H College of Southern Idaho
Milepost 50, Southbound on U.S. Hwy. 93, at Perrine Scenic Overlook

In 1964, Twin Falls County voters established a community college, and Jerome County soon voted to join their college district.

Started in 1965 as part of a state and national effort to expand local educational opportunities, College of Southern Idaho arts, science, and vocational-technical programs also provide related community services for this area. In 1968, a modern campus was occupied a mile west of here, with a civic auditorium and a museum facility incorporated into that site.

H Emigrant Road
Milepost 51.5, Northbound on U.S. Hwy. 93

More than a century ago, fur trappers and emigrants followed an old Indian trail that crossed here on its way to Oregon.

Hudson's Bay Company traders preferred this route between Fort Hall and Fort Boise, but early emigrant wagons had to travel a road south of the Snake River until ferries and road improvements let wagons come this way. Shoshone Falls – known until 1849 as Canadian Falls to British and French trappers – was a spectacular attraction along this road.

T Buzz Langdon Visitors Center
3591 Blue Lakes Blvd. North, Twin Falls. 733-9458.

In 1974, Evil Knieval made the Snake River Canyon outside Twin Falls an instant attraction with his famous attempt to jump the Snake River. Visitors can see this historic site, learn more about Idaho, and locate unique Idaho memorabilia in

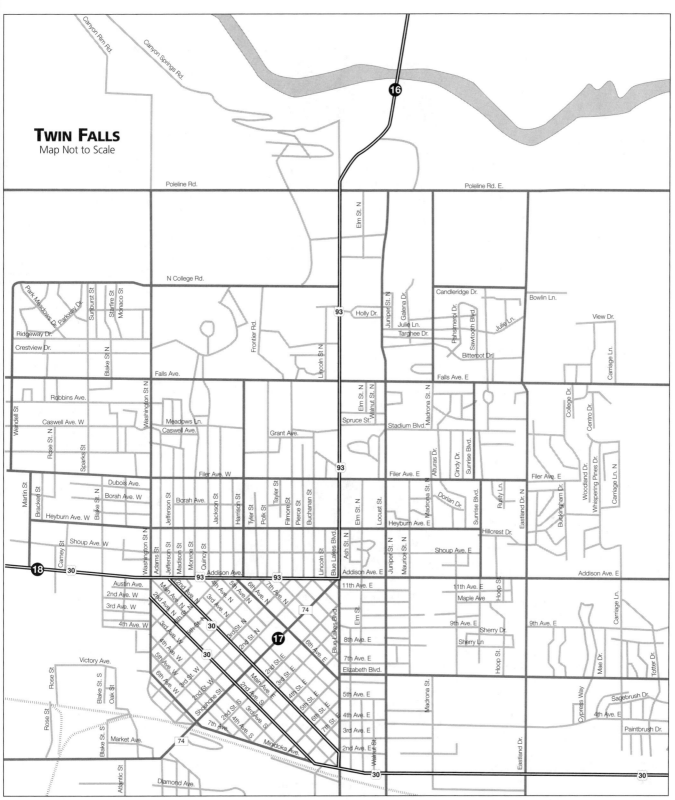

TWIN FALLS
Map Not to Scale

the Buzz Langdon Visitors Center. Call for additional information regarding the center's operating hours. Admission is free.

T Herrett Center for Arts and Science, College of Southern Idaho,
315 Falls Ave. W., Twin Falls. 732-6655.

Founded by Norman and Lillie Herrett, the Herrett Center for Arts and Science strives to educate elementary and secondary students, college scholars, and adults. The museum is dedicated to

preserving and presenting the world's history, with a particular emphasis on archaeology and the prehistoric American continent. Also inside is the Jean King Gallery of Contemporary Art and the Faulkner Planetarium, Idaho's largest planetarium. The center is open 1 PM to 9 PM Tuesday through Saturday from Memorial Day to Labor Day. During the remainder of the year, operating hours are 9:30 AM to 9:00 PM Tuesday and Friday, 9:30 AM to 4:30 PM Wednesday and Thursday, and 1 PM to 9 PM on Saturdays. Admission is free, but donations are accepted.

T Snake River Canyon
South-central Idaho surrounding Twin Falls. Contact the Twin Falls Chamber of Commerce at 733-3974.

Rising in an alpine lake in Yellowstone National Park, the Snake River curls 1,000 miles across Idaho on its journey to join the Columbia River in Washington State. In south central Idaho, the Snake River winds through a 105-mile canyon carved millions of years ago in the wake of volcanic activity and the historic Lake Bonneville flood.

The canyon extends more than 600 feet deep in places, and interesting geologic formations line the canyon walls. In addition to holding the imprints of Native American dwellers and early white pioneers, the canyon also holds vast recreational possibilities. Due to the region's warm microclimate, the canyon is accessible year-round and provides plenty of opportunities for the fishing or whitewater rafting enthusiast.

T Trout Mania
Snake River Canyon outside Twin Falls. Contact the Idaho Department of Game and Fish at 334-3700.

Like much of the rest of the state, south-central Idaho is known for its abundant trout populations. In fact, the state has so many trout that it ranks #1 in trout production across the entire U.S.. Numerous trout farms and state and federal hatcheries ensure repeatedly high numbers of trout in the state's lakes and reservoirs. Idaho also ships out several of its trout for use in restaurants across the country.

In south-central Idaho, the Snake River Canyon provides visitors with trout angling experiences at Oster Lakes, Anderson Ponds, West Bass Ponds, Riley Creek, and Billingsly Creek.

T College of Southern Idaho
315 Falls Ave., Twin Falls. 733-9554.

In 1960, the Twin Falls Chamber of Commerce established a junior college committee to discuss the possibility of founding a new community college that would serve both Magic Valley residents as well as students from other states. After actively pursuing and receiving financial support, the committee was instrumental in establishing the College of Southern Idaho in Twin Falls in 1965.

Since its inception, the college has grown steadily and is now one of the fastest growing institutions of higher learning in Idaho. The comprehensive college offers seventy-five academic programs leading to an Associate of Arts or Science degree as well as forty-four applied science degrees in a variety of technical programs. Today, the college maintains an average enrollment of 7,000 students, serving both American and foreign students.

T Millennium Sculpture
City Park on Shoshone St., Twin Falls. Contact the Twin Falls Chamber of Commerce at 733-3974.

In addition to numerous outdoor recreation opportunities, Twin Falls City Park is home to the famous "Millennium Sculpture." Nationally known Cambridge, Massachusetts' artist, Ted Clausen, joined forces with Twin Falls' bronze sculptor, Danny Edwards, to create this masterpiece. The sculpture depicts the strenuous lifestyle of the area's first farmers who helped establish the Magic Valley as one of America's most fertile agricultural areas.

TV Dierkes Lake & Shoshone Falls Park
Off Exit 173 in Twin Falls. Contact the Twin Falls Chamber of Commerce at 733-3974. Proceed on Blue Lakes Blvd. to Falls Ave. Drive 3 miles east, and bear north on E. 3300 Rd. Continue 2 miles to the parking area.

Nestled east of Shoshone Falls in a lush park setting, Dierkes Lake is a visitor's guide to outdoor adventure within the city. Hiking trails and rock-climbing routes surround the lake, and angling, swimming, and waterskiing are summer favorites. Lifeguards watch over the swimming areas during summer, and the park and lake are open from 7 AM to 9 PM daily.

TV Perrine Memorial Bridge & Snake River Rim Recreation Area
I-84 near Twin Falls Exit 173. Contact the Twin Falls Chamber of Commerce at 733-3974.

Distinguished as the American West's longest span bridge, the Perrine Memorial Bridge is situated outside Twin Falls and offers panoramic views of the Snake River Canyon. I. B. Perrine, a pioneer man who promoted the Twin Falls area and initiated regional irrigation projects, serves as the bridge's namesake. The 1,500 foot long bridge towers 486 feet above the winding river, and a pedestrian walkway on the bridge's southwest side is available to interested sightseers.

The area is also home to the Snake River Rim Recreation Area. On the canyon rim's south side, visitors can view the dirt launch site of Evel Knievel's ill-fated attempt to jump the canyon. Mountain biking and hiking trails wander in and out of the desert scrubland, and the area is accessible year-round.

TV Twin Falls Park
East of Twin Falls. Contact the Twin Falls Parks and Recreation Department at 736-2265. Proceed east on Falls Ave., driving past the marked turnoff for Shoshone Falls. At 3500 East Rd., bear left and continue to the park.

Logically named after its positioning next to the rushing rapids of Twin Falls, Twin Falls Park is the city's premier picnic destination. In addition to a boat ramp and dock that provides water skiers and anglers with easy access to Twin Falls Reservoir, the park features ten acres of tree-lined, manicured lawns. The park also provides access to trails meandering next to the Snake River below the waterfalls.

TV Frontier Park
Across from the College of Southern Idaho on Frontier Rd., Twin Falls. Contact the Twin Falls Parks and Recreation Department at 736-2265.

Twin Falls' Frontier Park is ideal for fitness enthusiasts. The landscaped park features several baseball diamonds, lighted tennis courts, and a 2.1-mile fitness trail tailored to walkers and joggers.

TV Cascade Park
Stadium Blvd., Twin Falls. Contact the Twin Falls Parks and Recreation Department at 736-2265.

Cascade Park provides an idyllic setting for a relaxing summer picnic. The park's large grassy area is spotted with picnic tables, and a play-

ground area and tennis courts provide additional recreational opportunities.

V Snake River Recreation – Twin Falls
Twin Falls. Contact the BLM – Burley Field Office at 677-6641.

A large area of public land surrounding Twin Falls and the Snake River offers easy access to year-round recreation. Conveniently located, the land offers a plethora of opportunities for four-wheeling, hiking, hunting, horseback riding, and whitewater rafting. For those with no experience, area outfitters offer several different trips catering to customers' needs and skill levels.

V Devil's Corral and Vineyard Lake
East of Perrine Bridge near the Snake River Rim Recreation Area, Twin Falls. Contact the Twin Falls Parks and Recreation Department at 736-2265.

Twin Falls' Snake River Rim Recreation Area offers numerous sightseeing and adventure opportunities, including rock-climbing in and around the rim. Trails lead to the verdant gorge known as Devil's Corral. Those who take the time to travel to the area are rewarded with two small lakes tucked inside the canyon as well as a cave filled with ancient Indian pictographs. Directly east of Devil's Corral is Vineyard Lake, which boasts two small waterfalls. Contact the Twin Falls Parks and Recreation Department for specific directions and area maps.

M Twin Falls Area Chamber of Commerce
858 Blue Lakes Blvd. N, Twin Falls. 733-3974 or (800) 255-8946. www.twinfallschamber.com; info@twinfallschamber.com

17 Food, Lodging

T Hegy's South Hills Winery
3099 E. 3400 N., Twin Falls. 734-6369. Exit off I-84 into Twin Falls and drive 4 miles south of Kimberly Rd. on Eastland Dr.

As one of Idaho's smallest wineries, Hegy's South Hills Winery has a capacity of only 1,800 gallons. Frank and Crystal Hegy and their two children own and operate the winery, and great pride is taken in their wine production. Renowned for using an antique Italian grape press in crafting their Chardonnay, Riesling, Chenin Blanc, Pinot Noir and Lemberger wines, the Hegy's add another special touch by hand bottling and corking each wine. The winery also specializes in custom bottle labels for special events such as weddings, anniversaries, and birthdays. Call them for more information and/or to schedule a visit.

T Canyon Springs Golf Course
199 Canyon Springs Rd., Twin Falls. 734-7609. www.canyonspringsgolf.com

Situated on the south side of the majestic Snake River Canyon, the Canyon Springs Golf Course features 6,205 yards providing a challenge to players of all skill levels. The course is rated a par-72 and is open year-round due to Twin Falls' unique microclimate. A practice facility, driving ranges, and PGA instruction are available, and green fees range from $20 to $29 for 18 holes.

T City Park
Shoshone St. between 4th and 6th Blvd., Twin Falls. Contact the Twin Falls Parks and Recreation Department at 736-2265.

City Park, situated in the heart of Old Town Twin Falls, was established in 1904 under the direction of founding community members. Today, the park still serves as a community center for annual events, including the Art in the Park festival and free municipal band concerts held every summer on Thursday nights.

T Magic Valley Mural
South of downtown Twin Falls at the Magic Valley Regional Airport. Contact the Twin Falls Chamber of Commerce at 733-3974.

Nationally acclaimed local artist, Gary Stone, leant his talent and helped beautify Twin Falls' Magic Valley Regional Airport. Stone created an impressive forty-two foot tall woodcut and acrylic paint mural depicting a historical timeline of transportation from the early 19th century to the present.

T Twin Falls Historical Tour
Downtown Twin Falls. Contact the Twin Falls Area Chamber of Commerce at 733-3974.

As the land around Twin Falls blossomed with irrigated green crops, hundreds of buildings sprouted in what had once been considered an uninhabitable desert. Today, a few of these notable buildings remain as a testament to the prosperity and hope that irrigation companies brought to the once fledgling Twin Falls settlement.

St. Edward's Catholic Church
Northeast corner of City Park
Displaying a Renaissance Revival architectural style, the St. Edward's Catholic Church was built in 1920 and 1921. Constructed at a cost of $60,000, the church's distinguishing features are its twin seventy-five-foot towers, stained glass windows, and a magnificently ornate interior.

Public Library
Southeast corner of City Park
Combining a $22,000 Public Works Administration grant and a $27,000 bond issue, Twin Falls received a public library in 1939. In addition to a remarkable variety of texts, the library boasts hundreds of prints and over 2,000 valuable glass negatives from photographer Clarence E. Bisbee. Owner of a popular photography studio, the talented Bisbee recorded the history of Magic Valley changes and progress from 1904 to 1934.

Methodist Church
Southwest corner of City Park
Twin Falls' Methodist Church opened for services in 1909. As the region continued to attract new residents, the church sanctuary overflowed and required construction of a new addition. In 1916, the brown Tudor Gothic style sandstone addition was completed, overshadowing the original church's dark brick exterior.

First Christian Church
Northwest corner of City Park
With the expertise of a regionally renowned Portland architect, the First Christian Church was completed in 1929. The brick church showcases a neoclassical design.

Justamere Inn
Second St. N.
Constructed out of concrete, the Justamere Inn first hosted guests in 1910. The hotel featured thirty-three guest rooms, a large dining area, and a red tile roof. The inn enjoyed a successful history before its conversion into an office building in 1979. Today, the building retains its status as one of the most impressive representatives of Mission style architecture in all of southern Idaho.

TV Harmon Park
Between Locust and Elizabeth Blvd., Twin Falls. Contact the Twin Falls Parks and Recreation Department at 736-2265.

Host to community baseball games, Harmon Park is known for its sports-oriented atmosphere. The park features several baseball diamonds, and a skateboard park opened during summer 2001. In addition, the park features playground equipment and picnic shelters.

TV Centennial Waterfront Park
South of downtown Twin Falls. Contact the Twin Falls Area Chamber of Commerce at 255-8946. From Twin Falls, take Fillmore Street west to Canyon Springs Rd. Follow Canyon Springs Rd. to the riverfront.

Away from the bustle of town, Centennial Waterfront Park offers an area for picnicking, boating, fishing, and hiking with beautiful scenic views. The park also includes a dock and boat ramp as well as picnic shelters and two covered pavilions available for reservation. Boat tours are offered during summer, and the park is closed in the winter.

18 *Food, Lodging*

19 *Food, Lodging*

Eden
Pop. 411

Eden was founded in 1905, with most homesteaders arriving in 1907 when a Union Pacific Railroad line was completed through the region. The town draws its name from the area's highly renowned fertile soil, and many settlers believed the beautiful valley surrounding town was representative of how the biblical Garden of Eden looked.

H Prehistoric Man
Milepost 14.8 on State Hwy. 25

Archaeological excavations show human occupation of the Snake River plain for more than 10,000 years.

Early men left weapons and other gear in a cave in a nearby butte. Bones show that they hunted game that is now extinct – camels, ancient horses, and ground sloths. In succeeding thousands of years the climate grew extremely dry, much drier than it is today. Still later, it became less arid again. Through all these changes, man succeeded in adapting and remained here.

H Hunt
Milepost 14.8 on State Hwy. 25

Excluded from their West Coast homes by military authorities, more than 9,000 Japanese Americans occupied Hunt relocation camps four miles north of here between 1942 and 1945.

Until they could resettle in other places, they lived in wartime tarpaper barracks in a dusty desert, where they helped meet a local farm labor crisis, planting and harvesting crops. Finally, a 1945 Supreme Court decision held that United States citizens no longer could be confined that way, and their camp became Idaho's largest ghost town.

T Minidoka Internment National Monument
Near Jerome. Contact nearby Hagerman Fossil Beds National Monument at 837-4793. From Eden, bear east onto State Hwy. 25, and drive 9.5 miles to Hunt Rd. Travel 2.2 miles east on Hunt Rd. to the site.

When the Japanese bombed Pearl Harbor on December 7, 1941, suspicion and hostility quickly rose against people of Japanese descent residing in the U.S.. Despite the fact that Japanese Americans had made hundreds of contributions to the state of Idaho and the first Idaho resident to sign up under the Selective Service Act was of Japanese descent, Japanese Americans faced discrimination everywhere they turned.

The situation only g[...]
19, 1942 when President [...]
signed Executive Order 90[...]
cation of more than 110,000 [...]
and Japanese resident aliens li[...]
coast. Although these individual[...]
ing wrong, they were discriminate[...]
their ancestry and were herded int[...]
camps established across the wester[...]

One of these ten camps was locate[...]
and governor at the time, Chase Clark,[...]
pleased with the plans. He was an extrem[...]
bigot who believed the Japanese were no [...]
than rats and denied that Japanese America[...]
any constitutional rights. Under the order of [...]
Roosevelt's decree and with Clark's approval, t[...]
Morrison-Knudsen Company began constructing[...]
the camp on June 5, 1942. Just two months later,[...]
the camp opened on 950 acres of land of a 34,000-acre reserve near present day Eden. Housing more than 9,400 evacuees from Oregon, Washington, and Alaska, the camp became the eighth-largest Idaho city and was dubbed "Hunt" by the postal service.

Nestled in a high desert area dominated by cinder cones, sagebrush, and other desert vegetation, the Minidoka Relocation Center featured five miles of barbed wire fencing and eight watchtowers. Prisoners were frequently told they would be shot if they came anywhere within four feet of the fence. Roll call was part of daily life, and mail censorship of both outgoing and incoming letters was standard.

Despite inflicting humiliating living conditions where residents were forced into tarpaper barracks, the U.S. government did attempt to give internees basic life necessities. Each of the thirty-five separate residential blocks included a mess hall, laundry house, bath/shower house, and a recreation hall. Serving all of the residential blocks were four general stores, two dry-goods stores, two barber shops and one beauty shop, two mail order stores, two dry cleaning stores, two watch repair shops, two radio repair stores, two elementary schools and one high school, a civic center, two fire stations, a health clinic and hospital, and a check cashing service.

Although nearly 800 young intern men were either forced or elected to serve in the U.S. Army, many of the other camp residents labored on camp and area farms, tending to both fields and livestock. During their freetime, the internees constructed a gym, nine baseball diamonds, and a swimming pool. In the winter, ice-skating was a popular pastime.

In August 1945, after the atomic bomb was dropped on Hiroshima, Roosevelt's order was rescinded. Evacuees all over the west were given $25 and a train ticket to Portland. The last family to leave the Minidoka Internment Center departed in October 1945, and the camp was officially closed on October 28th that same year. For those who traveled to Portland, many were greeted with no place to go and had difficulty finding both housing and jobs. Nearly 3,000 of the Minidoka evacuees stayed in Idaho for at least some time, but only 1,000 actually became permanent residents. As for the abandoned camp, the land was eventually divided into small farms, and only six acres of the original site remain as public land.

Today, the camp's remains include the standing basalt and concrete walls of a guardhouse and waiting room. The waiting room also retains its large stone fireplace. In 2001, the camp was authorized as a new National Monument site, which will further be developed in years to come.

...new worse on February
...Franklin Roosevelt
...6 authorizing the relo-
...ng on the west
...Japanese Americans
...had done noth-
...against due to
...one of ten
...U.S.
...in Idaho,
...was quite
...rely vocal
...etter
...s had

...ighboring mining
...finding riches along
...ers created Waterburg as
...in 1872. Waterburg's fate is
...but it is speculated that the camp
...short-lived as other placer camps in
...e area.

Springtown
0.5 mile below Hansen Bridge on State Hwy.
Springtown sprang up near Idaho's Snake River in 1870. A popular destination for Chinese prospectors, the placer mining camp was short lived. By 1876, Springtown was abandoned.

20 *Food*

Kimberly
Pop. 2,614

This town owes its name to Peter Kimberly, a Pennsylvania financer of the Twin Falls South Side irrigation project. Kimberly was founded in 1906 and prospered as the center of a rich agricultural area. The small town even boasted Idaho's first electric flour mill and alfalfa mill. The community retains its distinction as an agricultural hub in south-central Idaho.

H Hansen Bridge
Milepost 3.9 on State Hwy. 50 outside Twin Falls

Until 1919, when a high suspension bridge was completed here, this 16-mile long river gorge could only be crossed in a rowboat.

With 14 cables, each more than 900 feet long, a $100,000 suspension bridge was wide enough to accommodate two lanes of farm wagons or early cars that had begun to gain popularity then. From its deck, nearly 400 feet above the Snake River, travelers had a spectacular view that can still be seen from its replacement, built in 1966.

T Pleasant Valley Golf Course
3504 East 3195 North, Kimberly. 423-5800.
Located 5 miles south of town.

Designed by Lee Beam, the Pleasant Valley Golf Course opened in 1997 and recently expanded the course to a complete 18 holes. Situated near Rock Creek Canyon, this scenic course offers outstanding views of the South Hills and is nestled in a fairly flat valley. The 3,291-yard course features several water hazards and is rated at a par -69. The course is open daily 7:30 AM to dusk from March 1 to October 31 with tee times accepted up to one month in advance. Green fees are $13 on weekdays and $15 on weekends and holidays with special junior and senior rates available.

T Hansen Bridge
4.4 miles north of Kimberly on State Hwy. 50

Rising 350 feet above the Snake River and spanning 762 feet, the Hansen Bridge marks a historic pioneer crossing point. Before the first $100,000 suspension bridge was opened here on July 4, 1919, ...elers were forced to cross the river via a ferry ...Shoshone Falls.

...to safety issues with the suspension ...he present concrete span was constructed ...with a $1.4 million price tag. The bridge ...med after early residents, John and Lawrence ...ansen. John served as a reputable merchant and judge while Lawrence was a respected stockman who served from 1917-1918 in the Idaho Legislature.

The bridge features outstanding views of the snake river threading its way below, and a view area is available at the bridge's southern end on the highway's west side.

21 *Food*

Hansen
Pop. 970

Named for John F. Hansen, a pioneer merchant, businessman, and public official, this townsite was laid out in 1907, two years after welcoming postal services.

H Rock Creek Station
Milepost 227.3 on U.S. Hwy. 30

An 1864 overland stage station at Rock Creek, five miles south and a mile west of here, offered a desert oasis for 40 years before irrigated farming transformed this area.

James Bascom's 1865 store and Herman Stricker's 1900 mansion have been preserved there as reminders of pioneer life in an isolate outpost. In addition to freight wagons and Oregon Trail emigrants, miners and ranchers came from many miles to get their supplies there.

H Caldron Linn
Milepost 233.9 on U.S. Hwy. 30

In 1811, the Hunt party likened the terrific torrent of the Snake River three miles east of here to a boiling caldron, adding the old Scottish word "linn," meaning a waterfall.

They had lost a man and a canoe in a roaring chute upstream. Finding worse water ahead, they abandoned river travel. Next year, another explorer said of Caldron Linn, "Its terrific appearance beggars all description." Almost undisturbed by later farming, it survives as an exceptional natural spectacle.

T Stricker Ranch and Rock Creek State Station
5 miles south of Hansen (slightly west of County Rd. G3). 423-4000.

James Bascom established the log Rock Creek Station in 1865 as the first Oregon Trail trading post west of Fort Hall near present-day Pocatello. Out of necessity, the post became a popular campground for its location next to Rock Creek, the first water the travelers encountered after a twenty-mile jaunt away from the Snake River. As the site's popularity continued to increase, Ben Halliday dedicated Rock Creek in 1869 as a stop on his stage line that made three weekly trips between Utah and Boise.

In 1875, Herman Stricker and a partner purchased the Rock Creek transportation hub for $5,300. Herman's wife, Lucy, helped the couple scratch out a living on the extensive Snake River Plain. They established a home here, continued to operate the general store as a supply post, and

added a saloon, dance hall, post office, and polling place. When the Strickers' original home burnt down in 1899, Lucy had a more "modern" home built to ring in the 20th century.

Today, the log store/trading post is the oldest building in the county and was added to the National Register of Historic Places in 1979. The homesite is also available for viewing, while two sod-roofed underground cellars remember their past as a dry cellar for supplies and a wet cellar for storing the saloon's treasured liquor and beer. The free site is open daily from 8 AM to 8 PM year-round, and donations are appreciated.

T Pike Mountain Scenic Overlook
From Hansen, drive south to the Magic Mountain Ski Resort. Take the marked turnoff at the ski area's south end, and continue on the graded dirt road to the overlook.

Situated at an elevation of 7,708 feet, the summit of Pike Mountain displays panoramic views of the surrounding region. The scenic overlook offers visitors a breathtaking vista of the entire Magic Valley and the popular South Hills while asphalt pathways provide convenient wheelchair access. The overlook features a large parking area and is accessible by vehicle during summer or by cross-country skis during winter.

T Shoshone Wildlife Pond
From the Magic Mountain Ski Resort south of Hansen, proceed west on Forest Rd. 500. Contact the Idaho Department of Fish and Game at 334-3700.

Located between Magic Mountain and the small community of Rogerson on a scenic, dirt forest road, Shoshone Wildlife Pond provides a protected habitat for area wildlife. Numerous waterfowl species annually use the 27-acre enclosure and pond as a secure nesting site. The pond is open for wildlife viewing free of charge when road conditions allow.

TV Rock Creek Canyon-Magic Mountain Scenic Area
16 miles south of Hansen on County Rd. G3.
Contact the Twin Falls Ranger District at 737-3200.

Not only is south-central Idaho's Rock Creek area historical, but it is also breathtakingly scenic. On its journey to the Magic Mountain Ski Area, the paved road enters the Sawtooth National Forest and a basalt gorge lined with cottonwoods, juniper, lodgepole, quaking aspen, and subalpine fir. The scenic area boasts fishing in nearby Rock Creek while the Harrington Fork Picnic Area provides picnic tables, grills, and easily accessible restroom facilities. Harrington Fork also provides paved pathways for handicap access and serves as the trailhead for more than forty miles of South Hills hiking and mountain biking trails. The scenic area is accessible year-round.

V Wahlstrom Hollow Nordic Ski Trail
10 miles south of Hansen on Rock Creek Rd.
Contact the Twin Falls Ranger District at 737-3200.

Situated near the top of Rock Creek Canyon in south-central Idaho, Wahlstrom Hollow Nordic Ski Trail provides nearly four miles of groomed winter fun. The snow-covered desert landscape trail is free and appropriate for advanced skiers.

V Penstemon Nordic Ski Trail
10 miles south of Hansen on Rock Creek Rd.
Contact the Burley Ranger District at 678-0430.

The desert Rock Creek Canyon and Penstemon Nordic Ski Trail provide a striking winter landscape for Nordic skiers to get away from it all.

Covering just over eleven miles of territory, the trail is periodically groomed by the High Desert Nordic Club and requires intermediate skiing abilities. The trail is free to the public and open during daylight hours.

V Rock Creek Canyon Nordic Ski Trail
10 miles south of Hansen on Rock Creek Rd. Contact the Burley Ranger District at 678-0430.

Under the management of the High Desert Nordic Club, the Rock Creek Canyon Nordic Ski Trail winds a short four and one-half miles through scenic Rock Creek Canyon. The intermediate trail is groomed periodically, and is open daily free of charge. For skiers' convenience, restrooms and a warming hut are available on-site.

V Magic Mountain Ski and Summer Resort
South of Hansen on Rock Creek Rd. (County Rd. G3). 423-6221 or (800) 255-8946.

Opened in 1938 and spanning 280 acres, the small Magic Mountain Ski Area offers terrain for both skiers and snowboarders. Offering twenty runs and a maximum vertical of 700 feet, the resort offers runs from beginner to expert. The resort receives an average 180 inches of snow annually, and two surface lifts and a double chair lift service the area. The ski season generally lasts about seventy days, and a day lodge, equipment rentals, and family lift rates are available.

V Diamondfield Jack Snowplay Area
South of Hansen. Contact the Twin Falls Ranger District at 737-3200. From Hansen, bear south on Rock Creek Rd., and drive 28 miles to the area.

Covering over 200 square miles of Sawtooth National Forest and Bureau of Land Management lands, the Diamondfield Jack Snowplay Area offers hundreds of groomed, marked trails and is named after historic "range rider," Jackson Lee Davis. The area is nestled in the foothills and mountains surrounding the Snake River Valley and is a noisy snowmobiling scene each winter. Despite its seasonal name, Diamondfield is also popular during the summer for motorcycle and ATV riders. The area is open during daylight hours free of charge, and a warming hut and restrooms are available on-site.

V Eagle Nature Trail
South of Hansen on County Rd. G3 between the Pettit and Diamondfield Jack Campgrounds.

Winding underneath a shaded canopy of subalpine fir, aspen trees, and lodgepole pine, the Eagle Nature Trail makes an easy loop from the Pettit Campground to the Diamondfield Jack Campground and Trailhead. The 2.6-mile trail is nestled in the heart of the picturesque Rock Creek Canyon.

22 *Food*

Murtaugh
Pop. 139

After gold was discovered along the Snake River in 1869, Drytown, as the area was originally called, was located on this townsite. Jack Fuller homesteaded along Dry Creek to the south of the site, and Henry Shodde, a cattle rancher, settled above Starrhs Ferry. The settlement between the two homesteads was later named for Mark Murtaugh, the assistant superintendent of the Twin Falls Canal Co., who was head of construction on the South Side Irrigation Project.

Murtaugh Lake lies three miles southeast of town and provides area recreation. The town's current economy revolves around farming but still retains evidence of its roots as a railroad town. The old railroad depot, built in 1908, stands in town. Upon the closure of the rail line, the building has served as a car repair garage, general store, and a bar and grill.

H Milner Dam
Milepost 250.1 on U.S. Hwy. 30

When completed in 1904, Milner Dam raised the Snake River 38 feet to divert water into major north and south canals.

A gravity system unmatched in size in national reclamation development, this project irrigates 360,000 acres of land. Twin Falls, Jerome, and a half-dozen other communities suddenly sprang up in a desert plain watered by 160 miles of main canals. Located on lava channels formed by two rock islands, Milner Dam's three segments (462, 404, and 280 feet in length) were built by four locally powered electric cranes that were an engineering marvel of that time.

H Starrh's Ferry
Milepost 253.5 on U.S. Hwy. 30

In 1880, George Starrh, a Snake River placer miner, started a ferry across the Snake River one mile north of here.

From 1880-2, freighters hauling supplies for a mining rush to Wood River used Starrh's ferry (powered by river current when stiff winds were not blowing too hard), and local traffic lasted until Milner Reservoir flooded out summer operations after 1904. But a small town with a post office (1909-12) remained there for more than a decade. During that time, nearby bridges replaced Starrh's ferry.

T Dry Town
Present site of Murtaugh in Twin Falls County

Before the present community of Murtaugh was settled, Dry Town was a placer mining camp situated at the same location. Established on the mouth of Dry Creek in 1870, Dry Town included four saloons, a dance hall, two general stores, three restaurants, and a blacksmith shop to serve miners' needs.

T Caldron Linn Canyon
2 miles north of Murtaugh near the Snake River. Contact the BLM – Shoshone Field Office at 732-7200.

Tumbling furiously near the Oregon Trail, Caldron Linn is the point where the mighty Snake River is squeezed through a rocky passage less than 40 feet wide. As a result of this compression, the river rages and bubbles in resemblance to a witch's caldron. Early settlers nicknamed the hazardous waterfall "Devil's Scuttle Hole," and several people have drowned here attempting to navigate the raging waters. The most famous expedition to try its hand at the mighty waters was the 1811 Wilson Price Hunt Party. Employed by John Jacob Astor's Pacific Fur Company, the expedition capsized several times here and was forced to continue their journey on foot after losing one of the party's members. Today, the undeveloped site survives as a natural example of the power of southern Idaho's most famous river.

TV Milner Dam, Reservoir, and Historic Recreation Area
Between Murtaugh and Burley on U.S. Hwy. 30. Contact the BLM – Shoshone Field Office at 732-7200.

Completed in 1905, the Milner Dam was one of the first dams constructed on the Snake River to make farming possible in the high desert lands

comprising south-central Idaho. The dam created an irrigation system for over 360,000 acres of farmland, and as a result, settlers decided to stay in the region.

In addition to creating a huge economic and employment benefit, the Milner Dam paved the way for year-round area recreation. The Milner Reservoir is a popular area for boating, water-skiing, and fishing, and its waters are annually stocked with thousands of six to eight inch catfish. The 2,055-acre site includes boat ramps, docks, picnic tables with fire pits, vault toilets, and several free, undeveloped campsites along the reservoir's southern bank. The recreation area also preserves miles of Oregon Trail ruts, and a small outdoor interpretive center provides detailed information about the ruts and the settlers' westward journey.

The recreation area is open year-round during daylight hours and does require a small admission fee.

TV Murtaugh Lake, Dean's Cove, and Lake Park
2 miles south of Murtaugh off U.S. Hwy. 30.

Murtaugh Lake, in contrast to the rapids of the nearby Snake River, is a placid place situated in the middle of the hot desert landscape. The lake is a popular retreat for boaters, water-skiers, and anglers, and visitors are frequently treated to pelican sightings.

The tree-lined Dean's Cove is situated on the lake's western shore. The grassy area is home to shady picnic sites, a few boat docks, and camping. Also located on the western shore, the larger Lake Park features expansive grassy fields, boat docks and ramps, picnic tables and shelters, and a baseball field. The lake and recreation areas are accessible year-round.

V Snake River Recreation – Murtaugh
Outside Murtaugh. Contact the BLM – Burley Field Office at 677-6641. From Twin Falls, drive 3 miles south on 3500 E to the junction with Alternate U.S. Hwy. 30. Continue south on this highway, following it as it curves east for 12 miles. At Murtaugh, bear left (north) for 1 mile, turning right at the second road. Continue another 1 mile, turn left, and continue down to the river.

Murtaugh may boast a small population, but it claims rights to some of the largest rapids on the Snake River in south central Idaho. Featuring Class III and IV rapids, the thirteen river miles surrounding Murtaugh offer a challenge to both intermediate and advanced kayakers and rafters. Cliffs and spectacular canyon scenery tower overhead.

23

Hazelton
Pop. 687

Hazelton was first settled in 1905 and was named after Hazel Barlow, the daughter of Joe Barlow, the village's founder. A line of the Union Pacific Railroad arrived in 1907, increasing the town's popularity soon after.

TV Wilson Lake Reservoir
North of Hazelton off State Hwy. 25. Contact the Idaho Department of Fish and Game – Magic Valley District at 324-4350.

Spanning 600 acres in south-central Idaho, Wilson Lake Reservoir is a popular year-round recreational destination. Anglers are particularly enchanted with the reservoir, which offers both

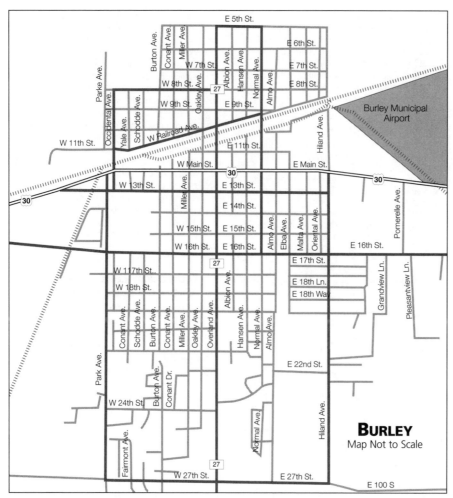

E 5th St.

Burley Municipal Airport

BURLEY
Map Not to Scale

TV Burley City Park
E. Main and Normal Sts, Burley. Contact the Mini-Cassia Chamber of Commerce at 679-4793.

Perched on the edge of the Snake River, Burley offers visitors several river access points. The 2.5-acre City Park is a particularly popular site, featuring a boat ramp and docks. In addition, the park boasts three picnic shelters and playground equipment and frequently host community events.

TV North Freedom Park
Burley. Contact the Burley City Parks and Recreation Department at 878-2256.

Burley's North Freedom Park is just one of many town sites offering convenient access to Snake River recreation. Park features include a soccer field, picnic shelters, and a boat ramp and docks for jet skiers, water skiers, and anglers.

TV Lex Kunau Park
Burley. Contact the Burley City Parks and Recreation Department at 878-2256.

Spanning 1.8 acres, Lex Kunau Park provides Burley residents and visitors with easy Snake River access. The park's boat dock and ramp are ideally situated for anglers and water skiers, while the large playground and five picnic shelters provide the setting for a fun family outing.

TV Riverfront Park
Burley. Contact the Burley City Parks and Recreation Department at 878-2256.

As its name implies, the three-acre Riverfront Park lies adjacent to the Snake River in the heart of Burley. The park features a boat ramp, boat docks, and an expansive picnic shelter.

TV Scholer Park
Near Burley. Contact the Burley City Parks and Recreation Department at 878-2256.

Characterized by its quiet atmosphere, Scholer Park provides a relaxing getaway for anglers. The park is also home to a well-maintained picnic area.

V Burley Area and Howell Canyon Snowmobile Trails
Near Burley. Contact the Burley Ranger District at 678-0430.

As with many other snowmobiling areas in south-central Idaho, Cassia County's countryside near Burley is lined with 120 groomed miles of snowmobiling trails. The region boasts some of south-central Idaho's highest snowfall totals and is recognized for its outstanding views of the Snake River Plain. The area has several access points, with Howell Canyon and North Heglar Canyon representing the most popular trailheads. Trail maps and specific area information are available from the Burley Ranger District.

V Snake River Recreation – Burley
State Hwy. 30 near Burley. Contact the BLM – Burley Field Office at 677-6641.

With its ideal location on the river's edge, Burley provides access to year-round recreation on the Snake River. Nearly twenty miles of the Snake River's most popular south-central Idaho shoreline is best reached from Burley, and the community takes advantage of its location. Boaters may access the river from ramps at Riverfront Park and North Freedom Park, and waterskiing, windsurfing, and fishing are all the rage during summer months.

V Emerald Lake
Near Burley. Contact the Burley City Parks and Recreation Department at 878-2256.

Located just outside Burley, Emerald Lake is a favorite local fishing hole. The scenic area is annu-

summer fun as well as ice-fishing. A boat ramp adds convenience in accessing the waters known to harbor some of Idaho's largest perch. In fact, the state record Perch was caught here in 1976 and measured in at 15.5 inches and nearly 3 pounds. The reservoir is free and open during daylight hours.

24 *Food & Lodging*

25 *Food, Lodging*

Burley
Pop. 9,316

Referred to locally as "Big River Country," Burley lies near the intersection of five pioneer trails: the Oregon Trail, California Trial, Salt Lake City-Oregon Trail, Salt Lake City-California Trail, and the Hudspeth Cutoff. The community was established in 1904, and David Burley originally named the site, "Commerce." Mr. Burley served as an agent for the Oregon Short Line Railroad, and the town's name was later changed in honor of him and his significant contributions to the local potato industry's growth and success. The community has served as the Cassia County seat since 1918, and together with Rupert, is recognized as Mini-Cassia Country.

T Ponderosa Golf Course
320 Minidoka Ave., Burley. 678-5730.

Established in 1930 with an Ernest Schneiter design, the Ponderosa Golf Course is one of the oldest courses in Idaho. The 9-hole course is rated a par-27, and a nearby lake creates water hazards

on three of the holes. This course is perfect for beginner golfers wishing to polish up their strokes or for the experienced golfer simply wanting to play a short game. The course is open daily from March 1 to October 31, and green fees are reasonably priced under $20.

T Burley Municipal Golf Course
131 State Hwy. 81, Burley. 678-9807.

William P. Bell designed the Burley Municipal Golf Course, and in 1928, it opened for business. Nestled next to the Snake River, the 18-hole, par 72 course covers 6,437 yards. Challenging greens and a well-maintained driving range cater to golfers of all skill levels. Players should call three days in advance to schedule a tee time. Green fees are $17.50 on weekdays and $18.50 on weekends, and the course is open from March 1 through November 1.

T Cassia County Historical Society Museum
Corner of E. Main St. and Highland Ave., Burley. 678-7172.

The Cassia County Historical Society Museum features numerous artifacts and interesting exhibits including replicas of a pioneer cabin, general store, schoolhouse, barbershop, doctor's office, photo studio, saloon, and a sheepherder's wagon. In addition, the museum displays collections of fossils, saddles, guns, dolls, sewing machines, historic regional photos, and relics from the area's sheep, mining, fur, and railroad industries. The museum is open 10 AM to 5 PM Tuesday through Saturday from April 1 to November 1 or by appointment.

ally stocked with channel catfish, and rainbow trout are rumored to occasionally surface. The lake is also open to non-motorized boating and swimming, and a picnic area lies near the lakeshore.

S Recollections, Inc., Home Decor & Unique Gifts
1214 Oakley Ave, Burley. 878-2554

26 Food, Lodging

T Heyburn
Pop. 2,899

Platted in 1903 as "Riverton" during the initial stages of the Minidoka reclamation project, Heyburn's current name is a reflection of U.S. Senator Weldon Brinton Heyburn (1903-1912), who lived and worked in the area during the 1890's. It is assumed that the post office chose the name when it was established in 1892; however, Bureau of Reclamation records indicate it named the town in 1905. In addition to its notoriety associated with Senatory Heyburn, this town also serves as the birthplace of Donald Crabtree, a renowned archaeologist who researched stone tool technology.

M Mini-Cassia Chamber of Commerce
1117 7th St., Heyburn. 679-4793.
www.minicassiachamber.org; VisitorInfo@pmt.org

27 Food, Lodging

Rupert
Pop. 5,645

When the construction of the Minidoka Dam was underway in 1905, the U.S. Bureau of Reclamation developed this town as a model city and placed a beautiful town square right in the middle. The city's name has two potential and widely disputed origins. Some say the town honors an early reclamation engineer. Other historians and local residents argue that the town's name honors one of the region's early mail carriers. Today, John Henry Rupert's family line believes he was that famous postman. Either way, the town caught on and boasted a large enough population to eventually be named the seat of Minidoka County.

Paul
Pop. 998

The U.S. Bureau of Reclamation platted this town site in 1905 as a Union Pacific Railroad station. The farming community honors reclamation engineer, C. H. Paul, and the post office was built in 1913.

T Minidoka County Museum
99 E. Baseline, Rupert. 436-0336.

In 1913, Rupert acquired its claim to fame by building the world's first all electric building. Today, historical information and photos about this building are just one of the many exhibits visitors can expect to find at the Minidoka County Museum. With an emphasis on regional history, the museum's exhibits include numerous historical photos, the town's 1906 railroad depot and

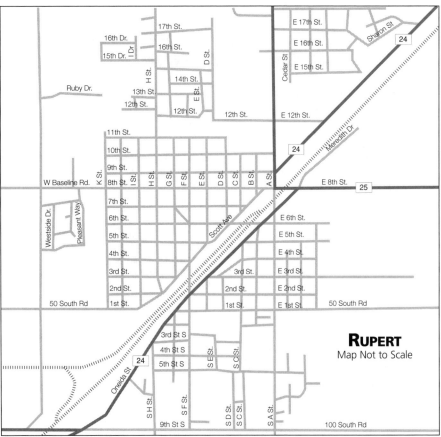

RUPERT
Map Not to Scale

caboose, wooden wheeled carts used by the town's first firefighters, a 1900s marble soda fountain including the original syrups and supplies, a 220 volt permanent wave machine, a restored sheep wagon, and horse drawn farming equipment. For those interested in the internment of Japanese Americans during World War II, the museum also offers an informative display about Idaho's Hunt Camp. Under the operation of the Minidoka County Historical Society, the museum is open from 1 PM to 5 PM Monday through Saturday year-round. Admission is free, but donations are gladly accepted.

TV Wapi Flow Area and Recreation
Northeast of Rupert on State Hwy. 24. Contact the BLM – Burley Office at 678-5514.

Although some individuals may believe the barren desert surrounding Rupert has little to offer in the way of recreation, the area actually boasts one of the state's most unique landscapes. 2,100 years ago, the Wapi Lava Flow slowly oozed its way out of Pillar Butte, covering the surrounding landscape in a hot molten mass that eventually cooled into cracks, deep gorges, and twisted landforms. Today, the desolate area is a haven for lava lovers and rock hounds interested in escaping the crowds and discovering some of Idaho's most interesting terrain.

As a result of the Wapi Flow, several unique sites were formed that are now open to experi-

enced explorers. The Baker Caves, discovered in 1985, encompass three individual caves formed from lava tubes. Archaeologists found evidence of human inhabitants there dating back nearly 1,000 years, including the bones of seventeen bison, stone pipes, and reed arrow shafts. Bear Trap Cave is also an interesting site of exploration, featuring a gaping hole in the ground as its entrance.

The Wood Road Kapuka showcases a small area of vegetation surrounded entirely by a barren lava flow. A craterlike hole known as Higgins Blow-Out is situated in a nearby butte.

All of these areas are isolated, and visitors should use extreme caution while exploring the lava backcountry. For additional information and directions, contact the Bureau of Land Management Office in Burley.

28

Acequia
Pop. 144

As part of the 1906 Minidoka project, the U.S. Bureau of Reclamation platted Acequia near Lake Walcott Reservoir. Situated near the confluence of several major canals, the town appropriately draws its name after the Spanish word meaning "canal" or "irrigation ditch."

Burley	Jan	Feb	March	April	May	June	July	Aug	Sep	Oct	Nov	Dec	Annual
Average Max. Temperature (F)	35.7	41.9	50.6	59.9	68.9	78.1	87.3	86.1	76.1	63.8	47.8	37.6	61.2
Average Min. Temperature (F)	18.2	22.6	27.7	33.6	41.4	48.2	54.1	51.8	43.3	34.1	26.1	19.9	35.1
Average Total Precipitation (in.)	1.16	0.79	0.91	0.96	1.22	0.86	0.35	0.48	0.56	0.61	0.94	1.05	9.89
Average Total Snowfall (in.)	6.9	3.8	2.5	1.2	0.2	0.0	0.0	0.0	0.0	0.2	2.4	5.8	23.0
Average Snow Depth (in.)	2	1	0	0	0	0	0	0	0	0	0	1	0

DIAMONDFIELD JACK:
A CASE STUDY IN IDAHO PIONEER JUSTICE

Between 1875 and 1885, Cassia County in south-central Idaho was recognized as the state's prime cattle grazing area with its abundantly lush rangeland. But due to hard winters and overgrazing, the landscape changed drastically by 1890, and sheepherders began moving in. While cattle need tall grasses in order to feed, sheep can graze on land that has already fed cattle and is depleted. However, when sheep graze an area first, they leave nothing behind for the cattle.

When sheepherders began moving to the area, cattle ranchers and longtime residents of Cassia County instantly became territorial and were furious at the invasion of these rangeland competitors. Needing to compromise, area sheepherders and cattle ranchers came to a "gentleman's agreement." The groups agreed that cattle ranchers would stay to the west of Deadline Ridge, while sheepherders would occupy the ridge's eastern side, including the areas of Oakley, Albion, and the Raft River Valley. For a period of time, this agreement operated without issue. When more sheepmen moved to Idaho, though, the agreement began to crumble as sheep started crossing over the ridge. In retaliation, the area's largest cattle dynasty, Sparks-Harrell Cattle Company, decided to take matters into its own hands and hire a range rider.

In 1895, at the same time the range conflict was in full swing, Jackson Lee Davis arrived in Albion. After being born and raised in Virginia, Davis moved westward in search of "get rich quick" mining claims, a pursuit that earned him his nickname, "Diamondfield Jack." Although no one knew anything about the new stranger's past at the time, Sparks and Harrell were more than happy to hire the tough looking 25-year-old as their new range rider.

Jack took a quick liking to his new job, using intimidation to keep sheepherders off his employer's cattle ranch. The young range rider patrolled Deadline Ridge, getting into several fights with sheepherders and handing out warnings to anyone breaking the "gentleman's agreement." On one occasion, however, Jack's encounter with a band of sheepherders turned violent. After wounding a man and further elevating Idaho's range war, Jack traveled to Nevada to wait out the ensuing storm of conflict.

In February 1896, Jack returned to Idaho

and continued his employment for Sparks-Harrell. By this time, Jack had earned a reputation throughout the region as one of the most vicious range riders around. It was no surprise, then, that when two young sheepherders were found dead on February 17, the public pointed blame at Jack and his fellow range rider, Fred Gleason. As the Albion sheriff investigated the scene, Gleason fled to Montana and Jack headed south to Arizona.

Three months later, a warrant was issued for the men's arrest and both were eventually extradited to Idaho where they sat in the Albion jail waiting their respective trials. While the murdered sheepmen's families and friends hired reputable William Borah as their counsel, Sparks firmly believed in Jack's innocence and was not about to let his prized range rider be proven guilty. Thus, Sparks hired James Hawley, a man known as the American West's best criminal lawyer with an extensive history handling murder trials.

The sensational range war trial began in Albion in April 1897. Although the public was convinced of Jack's guiltiness, the case would not prove itself clear-cut or simple. While Gleason was acquitted of the crime that same month, Jack was convicted of first-degree murder completely on circumstantial evidence and public opinion. Although the prosecution believed that Jack's scheduled hanging date of June 4, 1897 was set in stone, Sparks and Hawley had another plan in mind.

Jack's first execution date was postponed to a later date upon his lawyer's appeal to the Idaho Supreme Court. Although the lower court's order was upheld, Hawley fired back with another round of appeals. His case was further bolstered in October 1898 when Jim Bower, the general manager of the Spark's ranch, appeared before the state's pardon board and confessed to the crime. Bower stated that he and partner Jeff Gray encountered the sheepherders, and when an argument broke out, Gray shot the pair in self-defense. The two men were tried and acquitted based on the self-defense theory, so Hawley knew that Jack must then be freed.

But Idaho's pioneer justice system was not always logical, and the U.S. Supreme Court refused to rule in favor of the young range rider who was now quite obviously innocent. A new hanging date was set for sunset on July 3, 1901,

and Jack's last hope rested with the State Board of Pardons. On the morning of July 3, two of Jack's allies rode to Minidoka to receive a telegraph from the board. Much to Jack's friends' delight, the board reduced Jack's death sentence to life imprisonment in the Idaho Territorial Prison. His allies sped back to Albion with the news and arrived with just three hours to spare.

Throughout his stay in the Albion prison, Jack had managed to change many individuals' prior perceptions of him. The sheriff viewed Jack as a model prisoner, and parents often took their children to the jail to visit this inmate now known as a kind-hearted, polite man. It was no surprise, then, that when the Albion sheriff received the news, he was overjoyed and treated Jack to a decadent dinner. As Jack prepared to leave Albion, he was showered with gifts.

After Jack had spent eighteen months at the penitentiary, Sparks and several of Jack's closest friends gathered enough proof of the range rider's innocence to eventually convince the Board of Pardons to release Jack. Finally, on December 18, 1902, Jack's ordeal came to an end, and he walked away from the prison as a free man. Upon his release, Jack immediately went and had a drink with his indomitable lawyer, who by then had been elected Boise, Idaho's mayor. Jack's famous lawyer eventually went on to become Idaho's governor, while Sparks left his cattle ranch in Idaho and was elected governor of Nevada.

As for Jack, he was determined to put merit behind his nickname, "Diamondfield." After traveling to Tonapah, Nevada, Jack discovered several profitable mining claims and formed the Diamondfield Triangle Gold Mining Company, worth an estimated one million dollars at its peak. Jack never forgot those who saved him from death, and he gave away shares of his wealthy company to the men who had ridden from Minidoka with the telegraph that spared him from his scheduled hanging.

Jack, however, was not fiscally responsible, and he eventually exhausted the riches of his once famous company. Jack spent his last few years wandering from California to Montana, destitute and begging for mining claims. Idaho's most famous range rider died at the age of seventy-nine in Nevada, a mere shadow of his former fame and wealth.

Minidoka
Pop. 129

Union Pacific Railroad officials established this site as a siding and named it in 1884. The definition of Minidoka, an Indian term, cannot be decided upon. While some claim it means "broad expanse," because the Snake River's broadest part runs through this area, others say the term means "well" or "spring." The latter, however, doesn't seem logical as there was no area water source until 1946. A post office was established in 1883, and the town holds the distinction as the first permanent white settlement in Idaho's Minidoka County.

H Minidoka Dam
Milepost 10.6 on State Hwy. 24

An important pioneer federal reclamation dam and power plant provides water and electricity for farms and cities nearby.

Constructed five miles east of here between 1904 and 1906 at a cost of $675,000, Minidoka Dam diverts water into canals 86 feet above the Snake River. In order to reach still higher farms south of Burley, a $413,000 power plant was completed in 1913. Local irrigation districts have repaid costs of this project. This early federal power program led to national Rural Electrification Administration services.

T Minidoka Dam and Power Plant
Near Acequia off State Hwy. 24. Contact the Mini-Cassia Chamber of Commerce at 679-4793.

Constructed between 1904 and 1906, the earth-filled Minidoka Dam measures eighty-six feet high and nearly one mile long. The dam represents the first Reclamation Service project in Idaho and gave way to the establishment of the Pacific Northwest's first hydroelectric power plant.

Since hydroelectricity was cheap and readily available, the Minidoka Power Plant was built between 1908 and 1909 at the dam. The power plant granted Minidoka area farmers access to electricity long before other rural areas around the country, and the company has continued to expand. Today, the Minidoka Power Plant is capable of producing well over 10,000 kilowatts per hour. Due to the dam and power plant's historic and engineering significance, both were added to the National Register of Historic Places in 1974. Powerhouse tours are available daily during the summer.

T Lake Walcott State Park
11 miles northeast of Rupert off State Hwy. 24. 436-1258.

Overview

Nestled at the northwest end of the Bureau of Reclamation's Lake Walcott Project, Lake Walcott State Park is known for its outstanding fishing. Campers and picnickers enjoy the acres of grass beneath groves of stately hardwoods. Lake Walcott is home to Idaho's largest cottonwood tree. Paved trails connect restrooms, group shelters, an interpretive kiosk, and boat launch with a modern campground. Many trails along the lake are universally accessible.

You don't have to go far to enjoy the many attractions at or near Lake Walcott State Park. Wildlife abounds within the park or along the lake shoreline. Mule deer, coyotes, and songbirds are close by. One hundred fifty species of waterfowl, shore birds, and upland game birds make their homes in the area.

While at Lake Walcott State Park, visit the historic Minidoka Power Plant. With the construction of Minidoka Dam in 1904 came irrigation water for the surrounding Snake River Plain, and the first hydroelectric power plant on the Columbia River System. You may tour the power plant by contacting the Bureau of Reclamation personnel at 959 East Minidoka Dam Road in Rupert.

History

On August 20, 1989, ground breaking ceremonies were held at Lake Walcott establishing a 22-acre park. The park opened on July 3, 1990, and coincided with Idaho's Centennial Celebration. With cooperation of local citizens, chambers of commerce, and federal and state agencies, the park became a reality. In 1996, the Idaho Legislature authorized the Idaho Park and Recreation Board to enter into an agreement with the Bureau of Reclamation for the operation of facilities at Lake Walcott, making it a state park.

Walcott Park was designed with the Idaho traveler in mind. A quiet place on the edge of a vast lava field in Idaho's high desert, it is a great spot for a traveler to rest enroute to other locations, or stop for a day or two to visit the surrounding attractions.

Activities

Enjoy the park's 18-hole disk golf course. The course is the only one of its kind nearby and is utilized for tournament play.

Often called an oasis in the desert, Lake Walcott State Park is a favorite destination for family reunions.

The Minidoka National Wildlife Refuge offers some of the best birding in southern Idaho. The refuge extends upstream approximately 25 miles from the Minidoka Dam along both shores of the Snake River and includes all of Lake Walcott. It encompasses 20,699 acres, over half of which is open water with small marsh areas.

Reprinted from Idaho Department of Parks and Recreation brochure

T Minidoka National Wildlife Refuge
12 miles northeast of Rupert. 436-3589.

The Minidoka National Wildlife Refuge was established in 1909 and encompasses all of Lake Walcott in its twenty-five mile extension along the Snake River. Covering 20,721 acres, the preserve provides a summer refuge for molting waterfowl each summer and a safe habitat for both resident and migrating birds. Nearly 250,000 ducks and geese pass through the area each fall, and whistling swans, snowy egrets, great blue herons, bald eagles, mallards, ospreys, loons, pelicans, grebes, and tundra swans are also frequently sighted throughout the year. The area is open year-round free of charge for wildlife viewing with refuge office hours of 7 AM to 4:30 PM Monday through Friday.

29 *Food, Lodging*

Albion
Pop. 262

Founded in 1868 as "Marsh Basin" and renamed Albion in 1879 when its name was drawn out of a cowboy hat, this small community served as a logging headquarters for timber harvested in the adjacent Albion Mountains. In the same year that it received its new name, Albion acquired postal services and was designated seat of Cassia County, a distinction it held until 1919. Meaning "white," "white land," or "mountain land," Albion is most famous for the 1897 event where Diamondfield Jack Davis was jailed, tried, and convicted for the murder of two sheepmen. Years later, Davis was finally found innocent , but Albion retained notoriety regarding the incident.

Declo
Pop. 338

Declo began as a Mormon settlement in the late 1870s. In 1884 the rail line between Salt Lake City and Boise arrived, and the town experienced a slight influx of growth and prosperity. A post office was established in 1917 and the town was named "Marshfield." That name was later rejected because it was too long, and Declo was formed from the Dethles and Cloughly family names, prominent area settlers.

H Diamondfield Jack
Milepost 18.4 on State Hwy. 77 at Albion Public Square

J.L. Davis – Diamondfield Jack – spent most of six years in the Cassia County Jail while the courts and pardon board were trying to figure out what to do with him.

By far the best known of the gunmen who fought in Idaho's sheep and cattle wars, he was tried here for shooting two sheepherders in 1896. After he was convicted, other cattlemen confessed to the crime. Twice he narrowly escaped hanging, before the pardon board turned him loose late in 1902 after deciding he wasn't guilty after all.

T Albion Normal School
West side of State Hwy. 77 at the north end of downtown Albion.

In 1892, Cassia County residents decided to provide the region with a two-year teacher's curriculum. After receiving support from several local residents and J.E. Miller's donation of five acres of land, the county financed the construction of the two-story, three room Albion State Normal School. Just four years later, the state of Idaho gave the school $37,500 for additional acreage and the completion of the main classroom building.

Originally providing a two-year program, the Albion Normal School expanded its offering to a four year program in 1947 and renamed the facility "Southern Idaho College of Education." Over 3,000 young ladies and GI Bill veterans received an education here during the school's operation from 1893 to 1951. In March 1951, however, the popular program came to an end. The state decided that the school offered the same program as the nearby university in Pocatello, and funding was cut.

For six years, the buildings stood empty while the state maintained the grounds at a cost of $10,000 per year. In 1957, the Church of Christ decided to open its own school on the abandoned campus. Boasting $190,000 in new repairs, the site opened as the two-year Magic Christian College with a first-year enrollment of 117 students. The school, however, never reached its intended enrollment, and in 1967, the school closed and transferred its campus to a Baker, Oregon airbase.

Upon the college's closure, the Albion community purchased the deserted campus from the state for just $10. Today, the forty-four acre site stands empty amid rows of gigantic cottonwoods. With permission from Albion City Maintenance, visitors can stroll through the peaceful site and admire the historical buildings. The city still hopes to attract some organization or school wishing to relocate or establish services in this small south-central Idaho town.

TV Lake Cleveland
South of Albion in Howell Canyon off State Hwy. 77. Contact the Sawtooth National Forest at 737-3200. South of Albion, turn up Howell Canyon and drive past Pomerelle Ski Area and Thompson Flat Campground. A short distance past the campground, bear right at the road's fork, and descend to the lake.

Formed through glacial activity, the Sawtooth National Forest's Lake Cleveland is cradled within a cirque. Steep granite walls flank the scenic lake

Continued on page 388

AGAIDUKA: ANCIENT FISHERMEN OF SOUTHERN IDAHO

Prehistoric people in southern Idaho relied on many plants, animals, and fish for their survival. The technology used in ancient times to harvest, prepare, and store fish from southern Idaho waters is described. The story about the techniques and importance of fishing is based on archaeological and ethnographic research, early historic records, and legends passed on by ancient people.

Where Rivers Gouged Canyons into Solid Basalt
The main geological feature of southern Idaho is the Snake River Plain. This broad, high-desert plain is wedged between the Columbia Plateau to the north and the Great Basin to the south. It was formed as massive sheets of basalt flowed from sources to the north and south.

Constant erosion and a spectacular ice-age flood carved deep canyons into this basalt. These canyons now drain water from the Rocky Mountain region.

Through the largest of these canyons flows the Snake River, called Biavahuna (be-a-va-hun-u) by the Shoshoni Indians. The Snake River begins in western Wyoming and eventually joins the Columbia River in Washington. As it flows through the southern and western portions of the state, it is joined by several major creeks, streams, and rivers. In places, the Snake River flows slowly through a wide, meandering channel. Occasionally it is funneled into narrow crevices with powerful rapids and spectacular waterfalls. The highest of these is Shoshone Falls at 210 feet.

A Wealth of Native Fishes
The waters of the Snake River were home to many species of native fresh water fish like trout, sturgeon, suckers, and whitefish. From identifiable bones in archaeological sites, as well as oral tradition, it is known that most species were harvested. Most early explorers, emigrants, and ethnographers did not record the details of how these native fish were collected, prepared, stored, and eaten. The ancient names for many of the species are unknown.

Migrations from the Pacific
The Snake River was also used seasonally by ocean-going salmon that needed the fresh water for spawning grounds. Migrations of these fish, known as runs, were restricted to the western half of the Snake River because passage further upstream was blocked by Shoshone Falls. However, some species were able to migrate into north-central Idaho through the Salmon River.

Oral tradition and early written records indicate that three major salmon runs occurred each year. Steelhead trout made their first run in March or April. In May or June, the summer Chinook salmon entered southern Idaho. Late spring also saw the migrations of Sockeye, or Redfish, many of which reached Payette and Redfish Lakes in central Idaho. From September through November the Chinook salmon made a

fall run. The largest of these migrations were the Chinook runs. These important fish lost much of their weight during their long journey from the ocean. By the time they reached Idaho's waters, they averaged from 8 to 20 pounds, the largest weighed 50 pounds. After spawning, the salmon (not the steelhead) died, leaving their emaciated and battered bodies along the riverbanks providing food for other wildlife.

In most years, salmon were plentiful. Some years, because of low water, they failed to run into the Snake River Basin of southern Idaho. The quantity and quality varied from year to year as well as in the different runs. How long ago these runs first started is not known. However, through time the runs diminished in size and frequency. Today, the Snake River Basin salmon runs are nearly extinct.

The Archaeological Evidence
Archaeologists generally agree that humans first entered Idaho sometime prior to 12,000 years ago. This ancient past of Idaho has been divided into three general time periods – the Paleo-Indian, Archaic, and Historic.

The earliest is called the Paleo-Indian period. It lasted from 12,000 to 7,000 years ago. Paleo-Indians were immigrants from eastern Asia who crossed into North America in pursuit of now extinct ice age mammals such as mammoth, camels, giant bison, and ground sloth. Evidence of these first Idahoans can be found in beautifully worked stone weapons called Clovis points such as those found at the Simon Site near Fairfield. Further evidence was found deep inside Wilson Butte Cave, north of Eden. There, an ancient fire hearth containing burnt bones of extinct bison and camel, and stone tools, was dated at 10,500 years old. Around this time, Clovis points gave way to the smaller Folsom points. These are found across the southern part of the state and were used to hunt bison.

Around 7,000 years ago, a climatic change and other factors caused the mass extinctions of the large animals that had previously roamed across southern Idaho. A new lifestyle began to emerge marking the end of the Paleo-Indian period. The "Archaic Period," from 7,000 to 300 years ago, saw more diverse food procurement activities. Hunting, fishing, and gathering provided the food, and new techniques and tools enabled a more intense use of Idaho's natural resources. During this time period, many new inventions appeared in archeological sites, such as the atlatl (spearthrower), basketry, fiber cordage, and seed grinders. Near the end of the Archaic period, pottery and the bow and arrow appeared.

Although many archaeological sites in southern Idaho have been excavated, few have revealed notable evidence of fishing. Spears, nets, hooks, baskets, and drying racks were usually made of wood, bone, and fibrous materials which easily decay. Skeletal remains of most fishes are small and delicate and are seldom preserved. Backbones (vertebrae) and scales are sometimes preserved in sufficient quantity and condition to allow identification of species and dating of the remains.

Fish remains have been dated from nine archaeological sites. Some are nearly 7,000 years old. These include Schellbach Cave, Kanaka Rapids, 10-GG-273, 10-GG-278, 10-GG-1, 10-TF-352, Three Island Crossing, and the Clover Creek Site, all on the Snake River, Nahas Cave in the Owyhee Uplands, and Dry Creek Rockshelter in the Boise Foothills. A few

bits and pieces of fish line, netting, bone barbs, and hooks have also been recovered. An important exception to this scarcity of fishing gear was found in Schellbach Cave, near Swan Falls Dam, where harpoon points, net sinkers, a fish-hook, and fish line were found. In addition, stone fences which served as part of large fish traps still can be seen in the Snake River below Hagerman Valley.

The final period in Idaho prehistory is marked by the introduction of the horse and influx of Euro-American people from 300 to 100 years ago. The previous 7,000 years of prehistory, which saw little cultural change, came to an abrupt end as influences from a new culture spread rapidly across the West. Trappers, explorers, missionaries, ranchers, farmers, and soldiers brought many changes. Trade goods, firearms, new varieties of food, and textiles were embraced by the native inhabitants. Disease, starvation, and reservations changed traditional lifeways. The construction of dams brought an end to the migratory runs and to salmon fishing on the Snake River.

They Called Themselves
Because our archeological evidence identifies people by artifact type, not by name, scholars do not agree on the origin and identity of Idaho's ancient people. Several theories have been proposed including one which suggests that the Shoshonean people came to Idaho only within the last few thousand years, replacing other Great Basin people who came here earlier. Another theory suggests that there has been little cultural change in the last 10,000 years and the Shoshoni were the first and only inhabitants. In the first written accounts, it was reported that the Indians in the Snake River Basin referred to themselves by several different names although they spoke the same language. The names used by each group referred to the major food collecting activity practiced in their "home" territory. Thus, if in the homeland they hunted rabbits, they called themselves Rabbit Eaters or Kumaduka. If they hunted mountain sheep, they were Mountain Sheep Eaters or Tukuduka. Ground Hog eaters were Yahanduka. Those who ate salmon were the Salmon Eaters of Agaiduka. Together, they called themselves Neme or people. The name Shoshoni was given to them by the whites.

A Round of Seasons
The Indians who lived in southern Idaho spent much of each year on the move from one food resource to another. Each season brought forth varieties of nuts, seeds, roots, and berries. Wildlife was the food of choice during certain seasons. The seasonal movement from one food resource to another is called the "seasonal round." In southern Idaho, this strategy was elaborate and required people to move from low elevations in the cooler months to higher elevations in the spring and summer. The seasonal runs of migratory fish were an important influence on this movement of people. They collected camas on the Camas Prairie when it was ready, and fish from the Snake River when they were abundant.

Early Contacts
When explorers and trappers first entered southern Idaho, they met many native people. Some adventurers took the time to record their colorful observations and experiences. Some descriptions appear to be accurate, while others

are fanciful or derogatory. Surviving documents describe many facets of daily life of the native peoples. From early eyewitness accounts recorded in journals, and scientific studies by ethnographers, it appears that many Shoshoni of western Idaho spent much of the year near streams where salmon could be taken. Several writers indicate that fishing was an important subsistence activity.

On the Snake River, probably in the section between Shoshone Falls and Salmon Falls, the Astoria party saw a number of dwellings which, in October 1811,

"were very comfortable; each had its pile of wormwood at the door for fuel, and within was the abundance of salmon, some fresh, but the greater part cured…About their dwellings were immense quantities of the heads and skins of salmon, the best part of which had been cured, and hidden in the ground. Along this part of the river, the shores were "lined with dead salmon." There were signs of buffalo having been there, but a long time before."

On August 25, they saw about 100 lodges of Shoshoni fishing at Salmon Falls. On the northern side of the river below Salmon Falls they

"passed several camps of Shoshonies, from some of whom they procured salmon, but in general they were too wretchedly poor to furnish anything."

At Salmon Falls, in August 25, 1812, the Astoria party

"saw Shoshonies busily engaged killing and drying fish. The salmon begin to leap shortly after sunrise. At this time, the Indians swim to the center of the falls, where some station themselves on rocks, and others stand to their waists in the water, all armed with spears (harpoons), with which they assail the salmon as they attempt to leap, or fall back exhausted…Mr. Miller, in the course of his wanderings, had been at these falls, and had seen several thousand salmon taken in the course of one afternoon."

At the same falls, Fremont, 1842, observed that in the spring the salmon were so abundant,

"that they merely throw in their spears at random, certain of bringing out a fish."

The Indians were paddling about in

"boats made of rushes."

In 1842, Fremont mentioned no camps above Salmon Falls, but saw several at the falls and below it.

"We now very frequently saw Indians, who were strung along the river at every little rapid where fish are to be caught."

He described the Shoshoni at Salmon Falls as

"poor" and "but slightly provided with winter clothing; there is but little game to furnish skins for the purpose; and of a little animal which seemed to be most numerous, it required twenty skins to make a covering to the knees…(the Indians) grow fat and become poor with the salmon…" and lived in "semicircular huts made of willow, thatched over with straw and open to the sunny south."

How Fish Were Taken

The frequent movement of small groups of people across the countryside did not allow much opportunity for social interaction. However, fishing was one activity that did.

Many families would gather at good fishing sites, some cooperating in constructing dams and weirs, others fished alone with spears, hooks, and other devices. Others would assist in the drying of the catch for winter use.

Fishing places were not "private property" as we understand it today. Ownership of fishing places was based upon use. In effect, the fishing place was owned because it was used by a group. Fishing rights were shared as long as permission was granted from the current user. In fact, people were encouraged to visit good places. When a dam or weir was built, four or five families cooperated in its construction under the direction of a person with the necessary knowledge. The director was called kuwadangkhani (ku-wa-da-ngk-ha-ni).

"The kuwadangkhani was considered to be the owner of the dam. He took the responsibility of visiting the dam to remove the fish from the basket traps and of distributing them among the people who had assisted him. For his trouble, he kept the greater share of the catch. Dams and weirs were rebuilt each year. If the director died, any other competent person took charge."

"Construction of fish weirs involved several families. Weirs were built on the Lemhi River and other tributaries but not in the Salmon River. Usually three or four families cooperated. Other persons sometimes stole the catch or even parts of the weir, but nothing was done about it. For construction of more ambitious weirs, especially in the Lemhi River, about 20 families cooperated, erecting their tepees on the bank at each end of it. A man was stationed at each end of the weir to watch for the fish while the people danced. When the fish came he requested a number of men to go along the weir and help him remove the fish. They strung the fish on willows and carried them to shore, distributing them among the families…"

Fishing Devices

Many ingenious artifacts and techniques were developed to harvest fish from southern Idaho waters. Individuals fished with nets, traps, baskets, hooks and line, and harpoons of many varieties. Most fishing implements were made of bone or wood and were assembled using fiber cordage, sinew, and resinous glues (made from pine pitch) and sealants.

The most important fishing implement was the harpoon. They ranged in size from seven to 14 feet in length and had detachable, composite points attached to the shaft by loose cords. The shaft was often a single pole with a serviceberry or greasewood foreshaft and prongs.

"The fish-spear is a beautiful adaptation of an idea to a purpose. The head of it…is of bone, to which a small strong line is attached near the middle, connecting it with the shaft, about two feet from the point. Somewhat toward the forward end of this head, there is a small hole, which enters it ranging acutely toward the point of the head; it is quite shallow. In this hole the front end of the shaft is placed. This head is about two and a half inches long, the shaft about ten feet, and of light willow. When a

salmon or sturgeon is struck, the head is at once detached by the withdrawal of the shaft, and being constrained by the string, which still connects it with the operator, turns its position to one crosswise of its direction while entering. If the fish is strong, the staff is relinquished, and operates as a buoy to obtain the fish when he has tired down by struggling." – Alexander Wyeth, along the Snake River, 1851

Dip nets were made from willow rods bent into circular hoops about three feet in diameter. Cone-shaped nets hung from the hoops. With these, fishermen, sometimes standing on wooden scaffolds, scooped fish from small streams. Similar nets with two handles were used in rapids to catch fish.

"A scoop net without handles was held by a man wading in a small stream; other persons drove the fish to him. This net had a willow rim and cord made of a red-bark plant." – Alexander Ross, Lemhi River, 1855

Lifting nets consisted of two long poles fastened together with a rectangular section of netting gathered at one end. These worked somewhat like a purse, with the fisherman manipulating the poles to open and close the bag.

Seine nets were made from nettle or wild flax. The net was about 8 feet wide and 10-15 feet long. Net sinkers were made from river cobbles with a shallow groove pecked around the middle or smooth round cobbles wrapped with rushes and bound at both ends. Net floats kept the net in a vertical position in the water.

Seine nets were used for fishing on a large scale. On the Snake River near Fort Hall in 1811, the Astoria party observed a

"seine neatly made with meshes in the ordinary manner, of the fibers of wild flax or nettle."

Similar nets on the Lemhi River were 8-10 feet square, had stone weights, and were held by ropes at the corners by four swimmers or men on balsa rafts. Some seine nets were as much as 50-60 feet long and 15 feet wide. These larger nets had a vertical pole guide at each end, 10 wooden floats tied to their upper edges, and grooved stone sinkers tied to their lower edges. The floats were about four feet long and several inches in diameter.

Weirs were made of willow poles planted vertically in the streambed, or stone fences. The simplest weirs were straight or angled fences to stop the movement of fish. More complex weirs could involve multiple fences, raceways, and traps of many forms.

"I have not observed that the Indians often attempt fishing in the 'big river,' where it is wide and deep; they generally prefer the slues, creeks, etc. Across these, a net of closely woven willows is stretched, placed vertically, and extending from the bottom to several feet above the surface. A number of Indians enter the water about a hundred yards above the net, and walking closely, drive the fish in a body against the wicker work. Here they frequently become entangled, and are always checked; the spear is then used dexterously, and they are thrown out, one by one, upon the shore." – John Townsend, Ontario, Oregon, 1855

Baited hooks were frequently used in southern Idaho. The most common form was a small, bi-pointed piece of bone tied in the center to a length of line. A more elaborate variety involved two barbs which twisted in a cross-wise position when swallowed. Bone hooks which resembled modern hooks were also used. Single hooks were employed although it was common to use multiples with as many as several dozen hooks attached to a single line.

Storing, Cooking, & Preserving Fish
Fish were prepared by first being butchered using sharp stone flakes or stone knives with handles made of wood or bone. Two different butchery techniques were used. In the first, the head, tails, fins, and organs were removed and some of them eaten almost immediately. Eggs or roe were considered a delicacy and eaten raw much like caviar today. The body was cut into three sections – first lengthwise, then the lower sides were removed, but the body was split in half lengthwise.

Fish were then air dried, boiled in clay pots, baked in earthen pits, or smoked. Air drying was most common and smoking was the least common form of preparation. Prepared fish were eaten fresh or ground into a flour, then stored in bags made of fish skins. The meat was also combined with vertebrae, roe, and berries or other vegetable material then pulverized into a paste, formed into small cakes, and sun-dried into pemmican. Pemican could be stored for a long time. Cooked or dried fish were eaten fresh or stored for use later in the year. Dried fish were bundled with cord into bales.

Looking Into a Cloudy Past
The evidence presented above indicates that fishing was a major activity in the seasonal search for food for Idaho's Native Americans. Not all anthropologists agree on this issue. Recently, some scholars have reexamined the evidence and suggested that although fishing was important, the unpredictability of the runs and questionable nutritional value of the resource would have made fish a less attractive part of the seasonal round than is often assumed. These scholars ask why little archaeological evidence of fishing has been found, and why so few tales even mention fishing activities.

Critics argue that many of the sites which could have provided evidence have been destroyed by modern development or vandalism. They also contend that while the evidence of fishing is sparse, this may be due to poor preservation of the remains.

Reprinted from a Bureau of Land Management brochure

on three sides, and the 8,300-foot elevation lends itself to an alluring alpine atmosphere. The lake offers rainbow trout fishing and is heavily used by campers during the summer.

TV Sawtooth National Forest
South of Albion. Contact the Minidoka Ranger District in Burley at 678-0430.

Nestled in the heart of central Idaho, the Sawtooth National Forest was established on May 29, 1905 under the presidential order of Theodore Roosevelt. The forest spans 1,947,520 acres and contains archaeological and historical sites reflecting human habitation for over 10,000 years.

Spanning the territory south of Burley and Albion, the Sawtooth National Forest in south-central Idaho is governed by the Minidoka Ranger District. Recreational pursuits in this portion of the forest include cross-country skiing, snowmobiling, camping, hiking, backpacking, mountain biking, motorcycle/ATV riding, fishing, and horseback riding. The Sawtooth National Forest also encompasses several acres in north central Idaho that are managed under the Fairfield Ranger District, the Ketchum Ranger District, and the Sawtooth National Recreation Area. Contact the Minidoka Ranger District in Burley for more specific information and maps of the south central Sawtooth National Forest acreage.

V Pomerelle Ski Resort Nordic Ski Trails
Contact the Pomerelle Ski Resort in Albion at 673-5599. At Declo, bear south on State Hwy. 77, drive through Albion, and turn right onto Howell Canyon Rd. Proceed 5 miles to the resort.

In addition to offering downhill skiing, Pomerelle Ski Resort is known for its eight miles of groomed beginner and intermediate Nordic ski trails. Forest service trails surround the resort with the most popular traversing Connor Flat and Mount Harrison. All skiers are requested to check in at the Pomerelle ticket office prior to leaving as the area is not patrolled. The free trails are groomed sporadically and are open daily from 9 AM to 4 PM.

V Pomerelle Ski Resort
Near Albion. 673-5599. From Declo, bear south on State Hwy. 77, driving past Albion. At Howell Canyon Rd., turn right and proceed 5 miles to the resort.

Pomerelle Ski Resort, perched at an elevation of 8,000 feet, offers plenty of fluffy powder and terrain to satisfy skiers and snowboarders of all abilities. Nestled in the Sawtooth National Forest, Pomerelle receives a walloping 500 inches of annual snow and is generally the first Idaho ski resort to open and the last to close for the season.

The family-oriented resort features twenty-four groomed runs with a maximum vertical of 1,000 feet. A triple chair, double chair, and rope tow service the area, and a half-pipe caters to snowboarders. Night skiing, equipment rentals, and lessons are all available.

V Mt. Harrison Recreation Site
Southeast of Albion. Contact the Burley Ranger District at 678-0430. At Declo, turn south onto State Hwy. 77, continue past Albion, and turn right at Howell Canyon Rd..

Contained within the Sawtooth National Forest, Mt. Harrison rises to an elevation of 9,200 feet and provides access to year-round recreation. During warm weather, the area is inundated with hang gliders, and international hang gliding gatherings occasionally meet here. During winter, the area is turned into a snowmobiling mecca with miles of groomed trails and access to backcountry powder. No recreation fee is required to access Mt. Harrison.

V Howell Canyon Recreation Area
Immediately south of Albion off State Hwy. 77. Contact the Sawtooth National Forest at 737-3200.

The Howell Canyon Recreation Area is cradled indside the Sawtooth National Forest and is one of south-central Idaho's most popular recreation sites. The area boasts year-round outdoor adventures for campers, anglers, horseback riders, backpackers, skiers, and snowmobilers. Visitors to the area,

however, should expect company. Not only do sports enthusiasts heavily use the area, but the canyon is also home to a plethora of wildlife.

30

H Emigrant Trails
Milepost 18.4, Eastbound on I-86 at the Coldwater Hill Rest Area

Early California and Oregon Trail ruts, left by thousands of emigrant wagons as they ascended this bluff, are still visible below this viewpoint.

In 1859, F.W. Lander's wagon road builders dug an improved grade that shows more clearly. California traffic, for which Lander constructed a better road, diverged from this Snake River route to Oregon just beyond Raft River, six miles west of here. When they got up this grade, emigrants were thankful that they had passed 20 miles of bad road and that a less demanding trail lay ahead.

T Horse Butte
I-86 Eastbound, directly after the split of Interstates 86 and 84.

Rising ominously to the south of I-86, Horse Butte is a steep slope that was formed from natural faulting and erosion. Geologists consider the golden butte relatively young in the overall formation of south-central Idaho's landscape.

T Mountains Galore
I-86 Eastbound, east of the I-86 and 84 Junction

As travelers drive eastbound on I-86, several mountain ranges dot the horizon. The Raft River Mountains, which are actually located in Utah, parallel the interstate and appear as a long, low mountain range. Next, the Black Pine Range becomes visible, rising in the shape of a classic pyramid. Furthest east, the relatively low Sublett Range begins to the south in Utah and spans north towards the interstate.

T Snake River Plain
I-86 east of the I-84 junction to Pocatello

As I-86 carves its way north to Pocatello, it crosses over the Snake River Plain's southern edge. The plain is actually a basalt rock bed comprised of several ancient lava flows. The compressed layers extend thousands of feet deep and measure sixty miles wide by 300 miles long.

31

T Sublett
Located near I-84 on Warm Creek,

Sublett dates back to the mid 19th century. Ranchers first arrived in the area in 1865, and in 1877, Mormon settlers began homesteading in the area. The tiny village serves as the historic Oregon Trail junction with the Sublett Cutoff Route that many pioneers traversed on their journey to Oregon. A post office operated in the area from 1880 until approximately 1936.

32 *Food*

Malta
Pop. 177

Sara Condit, a teacher from Iowa who settled in the area, named the settlement of Malta because she liked the sound of the name. It is in honor of the island of Malta in the Mediterranean Sea. The settlement was originally founded in 1890 and served as a trade center for the surrounding livestock ranches. In 1912, a man named T.E.

Anderson installed a pump along the Raft River eight miles north of Malta. By doing so, he proved to the locals that water could be obtained underground from the river and used to irrigate their land. A post office was established here in 1883.

H Hudspeth's Cutoff
Milepost 2.8 on State Hwy. 77

This shortcut to the California gold fields, followed by most of the 49ers, came out of the hills to the east and joined the old California Trail just about here.

Opened by "Messers, Hudspeth, & Myers, of the Jackson County Missouri Company," who reached here on July 24, 1849, this new route was mistakenly thought to save nearly 100 miles over the old way along the Snake River to the north. From here, the 49ers struck southwest for California and golden riches.

H Idahome
Milepost 7.8 on State Hwy. 81

After wheat crops flourished in this dry farm area, Idahome sprang up here in 1916 as a railroad terminal. Irrigation projects boosted its economy.

When wheat farms disappeared and highway traffic replaced rail service here, Idahome became a ghost town. Its grain elevators, lumberyards, stores, airport, oil company, school, newspaper, and people are only past memories. An elevator and a few building foundations mark its site.

T Coe Creek Picnic Area
North of Connor Junction on State Hwy. 77. Contact the BLM Burley District at 678-5514. From Hwy. 77, bear right at the picnic area's signed turnoff. Continue 3 miles on a twisting dirt road to the site.

Under the operation of the Bureau of Land Management, the Coe Creek Picnic Area sits beside a seasonal spring in the Cotterel Mountains. The secluded site is nestled near a large aspen grove, but the area's overgrowth blocks any significant views of the surrounding area. However, picnickers are rewarded with views of the Albion Valley, Mt. Harrison, and Cache Peak on the journey back to State Hwy. 77. Due to the road's steep incline and windy nature, only small passenger cars and trucks are recommended to visit this site.

TV Raft River Valley
Paralleling State Hwy. 81 near Malta

The Raft River Valley is perhaps one of the most significant areas in south-central Idaho's pioneer and trapping history. In the early 1800s, famous trappers such as Peter Skene Ogden, John Work, and Milton Sublette frequently traveled through the area on trapping expeditions and loathed the swift, muddy Raft River that they were forced to cross. The river's rapids wreaked havoc on otherwise safe excursions, and the Raft River Valley was known for its fierce Blackfeet Indians.

Despite the trappers' unfortunate experiences with the Raft River Valley, trail makers and early pioneers snubbed the cautionary tales and used the Raft River Valley extensively on their migration west. The Oregon Trail crossed the mouth of the Raft River near its junction with the Snake, the California Trail paralleled the river's west bank, Hudspeth's Cutoff forced pioneers to ford the raging river, and a fourth rarely used route required travelers passing north of Salt Lake City to brave the notorious area. Today, little evidence remains of the Raft River Valley's turbulent past, with most current activity related to angling.

Fishing enthusiasts will find that the Raft River and the area's other major drainages of Goose Creek, Rock Creek, and Salmon Falls Creek support fair to excellent fisheries. Wild trout are abundant in some smaller streams, and rainbow, cutthroat, brook, and brown trout are known to reside in the waters. In addition, the drainage's game fish population draws upon the alpine Independence Lakes and Lake Cleveland.

V McClendon Spring Recreation Site
East of Connor Junction on State Hwy. 77 near Malta

Situated at the end of a gravel road amid a scenic, shaded grove of cottonwoods, McClendon Spring Recreation Site features a seasonal spring surrounded by views of the Black Pine Mountains. California Trail pioneers camped here on their journey west, and today's visitors will find several similarly primitive campsites scattered amongst the old-growth trees.

33

Almo
Pop. 40

Although the first settlers arrived here in 1877, it wasn't until 1881 that Almo acquired a post office and status as an official Idaho community. During its early years, Almo served as an important stage-stop on the Kelton-to-Boise route. Today, the hustle and bustle of the transportation industry has long left Almo behind, but the town remains viable as a supply center for the thousands of tourists and recreationists that visit the nearby City of Rocks each year.

While the history of Almo's contributions to Idaho are clear-cut, the origin of its name is widely disputed. A monument erected by the Sons and Daughters of Idaho Pioneers. It states, "…for those who lost their lives in a most horrible Indian massacre in 1861", and continues, "…of 300 emigrants, only five escaped." The details of such an event are lost in history, but other accounts of Shosone Indian run-ins with the locals claim no more than eight emigrants were killed in or near Almo between 1860-1862. Some believe that this folkore tale evoked feelings of the Alamo Battle in Texas, and the name was gradually mispronounced over the years. Others explain that the word Almo means "cottonwood tree" in Spanish, which logically relates to Almo's location on a cottonwood lined creek bank. All anyone knows for sure is that the name was applied to the neighboring creek and hot springs long before the town received its postal designation.

T Albion Mountains
West of Elba and Albion on State Hwy. 77

Cradled between the Idaho/Utah border and the Snake River Plain, the Albion Mountain Range represents Idaho's highest range south of the Snake River. The mountains rise jaggedly against the sky for thirty-one miles, and the high-alpine scenery suggests that glaciers carved the mountains thousands of years ago. Two of the range's highest peaks, Cache Peak at 10,339 feet and Mt. Harrison at 9,265 feet, host well-preserved cirques and moraines.

In addition to housing a wide range of recreational pursuits, the mountains hold an extensive history of Native American habitation. Based upon archaeologists' studies and findings, the first white men to discover the mountains were 1840s California Trail travelers. For more information about recreational pursuits in the Albion Range, contact the Burley Forest Service Ranger District at 678-0430.

T Pioneer Memorial
Downtown Almo

In 1938, the Sons and Daughters of Idaho erected a pioneer monument in remembrance of their hearty ancestors. The memorial commemorates the legendary deaths of 300 emigrants in an 1861 Indian massacre where only five white settlers were supposedly lucky enough to escape.

Although the monument touches the hearts of all who see it, many historians dispute the supposed massacre and simply stack the story up to pioneer folklore. Skirmishes between settlers and Native Americans were frequent in the region between 1860 and 1862. However, only six violent encounters were recorded, and no more than eight whites were killed during the entire two years.

TV City of Rocks National Reserve
4 miles west of of Almo. Contact the City of Rocks National Reserve Headquarters at 3035 Elba-Almo Rd., Almo. 824-5519.

Like A Dismantled City
"We encamped at the city of the rocks, a noted place from the granite rocks rising abruptly out of the ground," wrote James Wilkins in 1849. "They are in a romantic valley clustered together, which gives them the appearance of a city." Wilkins was among the first wagon travelers to fix the name City of Rocks to what looked like "a dismantled, rock-built city of the Stone Age."

Malta													
	Jan	Feb	March	April	May	June	July	Aug	Sep	Oct	Nov	Dec	Annual
Average Max. Temperature (F)	37.0	42.8	51.7	61.0	69.6	79.1	88.9	87.9	77.6	65.1	48.1	37.7	62.2
Average Min. Temperature (F)	16.8	20.7	26.2	31.5	37.9	43.7	49.8	48.1	40.0	31.5	24.1	16.5	32.2
Average Total Precipitation (in.)	0.72	0.58	0.86	1.09	1.64	1.23	0.93	0.89	0.84	0.72	0.76	0.74	11.01
Average Total Snowfall (in.)	4.1	1.7	1.6	0.7	0.4	0.0	0.0	0.0	0.0	0.1	1.5	3.1	13.1
Average Snow Depth (in.)	2	1	0	0	0	0	0	0	0	0	1	2	1

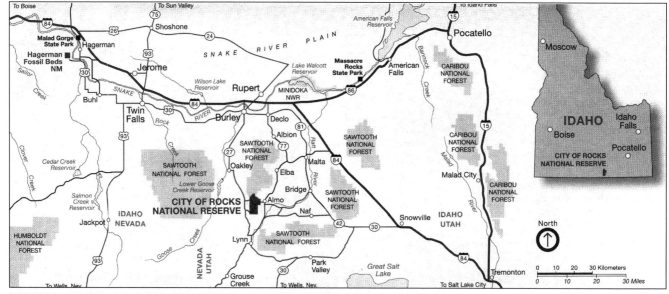

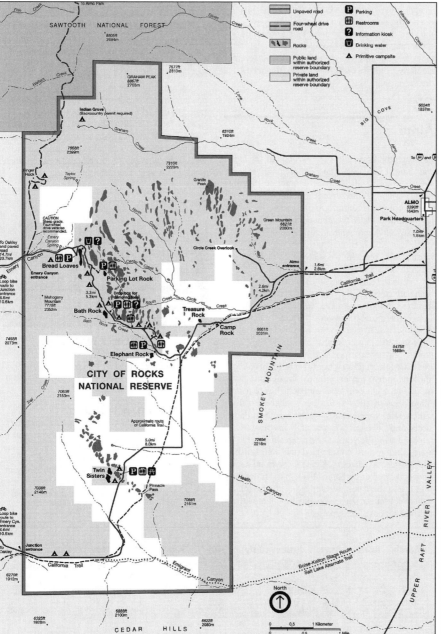

California Trail pioneers were leaving civilization, as they knew it in the East for new lives in the West. Some wrote their names in axle grease on rock faces, and their signatures can be seen today. No doubt thirsty on this northern edge of the Great Basin Desert, one emigrant saw the distant rocks in August like "water thrown up into the air from numerous artificial hydrants." Beginning in 1843, City of Rocks was a landmark for emigrants on the California Trail and Salt Lake Alternate Trail and later on freight routes and the Kelton, Utah to Boise, Idaho stage route. The area's historical and geological values, scenery, and opportunities for recreation led to its designation as City of Rocks National Reserve in 1988.

This unit of the National Park System is managed cooperatively by the National Park Service and Idaho Department of Parks and Recreation, who invite you to enjoy the wonders of the City of Rocks.

Nature and Culture Comingled

Shoshone-Bannock Indians hunted in the City of Rocks area and gathered nuts of the pinyon pine trees. The return of horses to the Americas in the 16th century and swelling European immigration disrupted the Shoshone-Bannock homelands and way of life. Indians grew to resent the intruders but could do little to stop them. Most emigrants on the California Trail saw no Indians, but some of their journals record smoke signals rising from high hills and the surrounding mountains. Peter Skene Ogden and his Snake River brigade of beaver trappers were the first non-Indians to note the City of Rocks, in 1826. Having few beaver, the area was ignored until growing summer streams of wagons flowed through starting in 1843.

Early emigrant groups were guided by experienced mountain men such as Joseph B. Chiles and Joseph A. Walker. Later wagon parties followed the trails themselves, perhaps with the help of diary accounts of previous emigrants. City of Rocks marked both progress west for the emigrants and, for their loaded wagons, a mountain passage over nearby Granite Pass. By 1846, emigrants headed for Oregon's Willamette Valley also used this route as part of the Applegate Trail. In 1848, the Mormon Battalion opened the trail from Granite Pass via Emigrant Canyon to Salt Lake. In 1852, some 52,000 people passed through City of Rocks on the way to California goldfields. When the trails opened in the 1840s, Granite Pass was in Mexico and less than a mile from Oregon Territory, which included the City of Rocks. After

CITY OF ROCKS WILDLIFE CHECKLIST

Wildlife at City of Rocks

At first glance, City of Rocks would appear to be a tough place for wildlife to survive. Diverse habitats at various elevations lead to an area bursting with wildlife. It goes without saying that animals at City of Rocks are equipped with special adaptations to survive extreme conditions. During summer, most fauna are active at night, thereby escaping the often hot, dry days. Winter forces wildlife to migrate to better environments or to hibernate. To see as many different types as possible, include the following habitats in your search: pinyon-juniper-mahogany forest, aspen-riparian areas, sagebrush flats, and spruce-fir-pine forest above 7,000 feet.

Rare and unusual sightings by visitors are important to reserve resource managers. Report any unusual wildlife sightings at the visitor center or write to: City of Rocks National Reserve, P.O. Box 169, Almo, ID 83312, (208) 824-5519.

Wildlife Encounters

During your visit, you will most likely encounter wildlife in their native habitat. The most common wildlife experienced by visitors include: Mule Deer, Mountain Cottontail, Blacktail jackrabbit, Whitetail Jackrabbit, Least Chipmunk, and Golden-mantled Ground Squirrel.

Species Highlights:

* *Mountain Lion (Felis concolor)*
With sightings documented from Canada to Argentina, the Mountain Lion (also known as Puma, Cougar, and Panther) is the most widely distributed feline in North America. Although as many as three individual lions include City of Rocks in their home range, the chance of actually seeing one is unlikely, but evidence of their existence is readily available. Tracks and scat are the most common clues to lion activity. Tracks are round with 4 distinct toe pads. No claw marks should be evident, as claws are retracted while walking. The size of the foreprint can range from 3-4" and the hindprint should be slightly smaller. Scat can range in shape and size from masses to irregular cylinders to pellets and frequently contains traces of hair and bone scraps. Sometimes covered by earth, scat is often left partially exposed as a form of territorial scent marking.

Strong, silent, solitary and territorial all accurately describe this elusive cat. Hunting by day or night, a male can cover up to 25 miles searching for prey. Lions preferably feed on large mammals such as mule deer. Lions also feed on coyotes, porcupines, mice, marmots, hares, raccoons, birds, and even grasshoppers.

Isolated incidents of mountain lions attacking humans have been documented in areas outside of City of Rocks (one documented attack in Idaho). Even when lions are encountered, they rarely pose a threat. In fact, most prefer to avoid human contact.

While hiking in lion country, always be aware of your surroundings and hike with a companion. In the event you observe a lion, don't run but instead make yourself appear larger and more aggressive. Make eye contact, raise your arms, and wave them slowly above your head while speaking in a slow, loud, firm voice. Fight back if attacked. When lions do attack, they target the head or neck, so try to remain standing and face the attacking animal. Use rocks, sticks, jackets, camping gear, or anything else available to fend off the attack. Lions are often easily discouraged by aggressive behavior.

* *Pygmy Rabbit (Brachylagus idahoensis)*
This Federally Endangered Species, with an average weight of less than 12 ounces, is the smallest rabbit in North America. The pygmy rabbit inhabits sagebrush flats common to City of Rocks. Many rabbits use burrows left behind from other animals or live outside of burrows. The pygmy is the only rabbit that is responsible for digging its own burrow system. Grazing on many grasses in spring and summer constitutes 40% of its diet. The rest of their diet is made up of sagebrush leaves. In winter, sagebrush is practically all it eats.

This rabbit's population has been on the decline for some time now. A captive-breeding program is active in several states, including Idaho, in hopes of increasing populations and reintroducing them into the wild. Loss of habitat (due to agricultural conversion) has been the major factor affecting the population. City of Rocks National Reserve provides important habitat for sustaining this species. Please report any Pygmy Rabbit sightings at the visitor center.

Wildlife Checklist
* Reptiles and Lizards
Skinks and Lizards

- Longnose Leopard Lizard
- Common Sagebrush Lizard
- Pygmy Short-horned Lizard
- Desert Horned Lizard
- Western Fence Lizard
- Tiger Whiptail Western Skink

Snakes

- Terrestrial Garter Snake
- Gopher Snake
- Western Rattlesnake
- Striped Whipsnake
- Rubber Boa
- Eastern Yellow- bellied Racer

Frogs and Toads

- Boreal Chorus Frog

* Mammals
Bats

- Big Brown Bat
- Hoary Bat
- Fringed Myotis
- Little Brown Myotis
- Long-eared Myotis
- Small-footed Myotis
- Silver-haired Bat
- Spotted Bat
- Townsend's Big-eared Bat
- Western Pipistrelle

Rabbits and Hares

- Mountain Cottontail
- Pygmy Rabbit
- Whitetail Jackrabbit
- Blacktail Jackrabbit

Squirrels and Chipmunks

- Belding's Ground Squirrel
- Cliff Chipmunk
- Golden-mantled Ground Squirrel
- Least Chipmunk
- Richardson's Ground Squirrel
- Townsend's Ground Squirrel

Large Rodents and Armored Mammals

- Beaver
- Muskrat
- Raccoon
- Yellow- bellied Marmot
- Porcupine

Weasels, Skunks, and Their Kin

- Badger
- Long-tailed Weasel
- Short -tailed Weasel
- Spotted Skunk
- Striped Skunk
- Mink

Cats, Foxes and Coyotes

- Bobcat
- Mountain Lion
- Coyote
- Red Fox

Mice, Rats, Voles, Shrews and Gophers

- Canyon Mouse
- Deer Mouse
- Western Jumping Mouse
- Western Harvest Mouse
- Great Basin Pocket Mouse
- Northern Grasshopper Mouse
- Bushy-tailed Woodrat
- Desert Woodrat
- Ord Kangaroo Rat
- Long-tailed Vole
- Mountain Vole
- Sagebrush Vole
- Vagrant Shrew
- Water Shrew
- Merriam Shrew
- Northern Pocket Gopher

Hoofed Mammals

- Elk *
- Mule Deer
- Pronghorn*
- Bighorn Sheep*
*Species documented near reserve boundaries.

Section 5

1850 the area became part of Utah Territory, but the 1872 Idaho-Utah boundary survey placed City of Rocks in Idaho Territory. With completion of the transcontinental railroad in 1869, the overland wagon routes began to pass into history. Wagons saw continued use instead on regional supply routes that spread out from the railroad lines. John Halley's stage route connected the railroad at Kelton, Utah, with Idaho's mining hub of Boise and supplied the early economic development of Idaho, which won statehood in 1890. The Kelton stage route passed through City of Rocks, with a stage station set up near the junction of the old California Trail and the Salt Lake Alternate.

Settlers began to homestead the City of Rocks area in the late 1800s. Dryland farming declined here during the drought years of the 1920s and 1930s, but ranching survived. Livestock grazing began with early wagon use of the area in the mid-1800s and continues today.

Geology

More like mother and daughter than siblings, the Twin Sisters of City of Rocks are made up of different rocks. The difference helps explain how the City of Rocks landscape came to be. The darker sister is made of rock in a formation that geologists call the Green River Complex. It is 2.5 billion years old and is some of the oldest rock in the Lower 48 states. The lighter sister is made of rock in a far younger formation that geologists call the Almo Pluton. It is 25 million years old.

Both formations began as molten matter in the Earth's crust. Eventually the Almo Pluton was thrust up through the Green River Complex, while both formations still lay beneath the Earth's surface and other layers of rock. As time passed, the overlying rocks and the formations beneath them cracked. Along the cracks and fissures erosion took place more rapidly and exposed the rocks of the Almo Pluton and Green River Complex.

The exposed rocks were then shaped by the forces of erosion. In weathering, the tops of rocks are dissolved by rainwater, and minerals, such as iron oxide, are redeposited to form crust-like caps. These caps are more resistant to weathering than the underlying rock, and this causes the formation of spires and pinnacles. When the caps erode, the inner rock can be molded by erosion into the many caves, arches, bathtubs, and hollow boulders seen at City of Rocks. On the sides of spires water seeps into cracks and frost wedging occurs. When the water freezes, it expands and can crack great slabs off the rock. This process already has removed some of the layers of rock bearing 150-year-old signatures left by the pioneers.

Today, many people see animals, faces, or buildings in the shapes of these rock formations. Only your imagination limits what you see in the City of Rocks.

Recreation in the Pioneers' Path

City of Rocks offers scenic walks near the historic California Trail and opportunities for wildlife watching, photography, world-class technical rock climbing, and picnicking and camping where children can frolic beneath the rock formations.

At City of Rocks the range of elevations in a compact area combines with other factors to create varied patterns of vegetation and wildlife habitat. At high elevations the forests are of lodgepole pine, limber pine, and Douglas fir. Middle elevation forests are of quaking aspen, mountain mahogany, and cottonwood. Sagebrush, pinyon pines, and juniper dominate lower elevations. The Reserve boasts Idaho's tallest pinyon pines, at more than 55 feet. The trees' nuts provide important proteins and fats for wildlife. Spring and summer displays of wildflowers can be spectacular. More than 450 plant species have been recorded in the Reserve.

Buffalo once roamed here, but now elk and mule deer are the largest mammals. The deer are hunted by mountain lions, and coyotes scavenge deer carcasses. Other mammals include badgers, bobcats, porcupines, ground squirrels, and bats. The Reserve is part of Idaho's Minidoka Bird Refuge. Just a few of the birds here are eagles, falcons, vultures, hawks, hummingbirds, jays, sparrows, doves, and Idaho's state bird, the mountain bluebird. The only poisonous snakes found in the Reserve are rattlesnakes, at lower elevations. Other reptiles include the sand lizard, watersnake, blowsnake, and rubber boa. All plants and animals are protected by law; do not disturb them.

Rock Climbing

City of Rocks rivals Yosemite National Park as a western favorite for North American technical rock climbers. International climbers come to the Reserve to climb on Rabbit Rock, Morning Glory Spire, and Bread Loaves. The degree-of-difficulty scale for rock climbing here runs from least difficult at 5.0 to 5.10, most difficult. City of Rocks contains a great number and variety of 5.10 climbs. Do not climb unless you have training and experience. Serious accidents can occur when rock scrambling. All climbers should stop at Reserve headquarters for regulations and current conditions.

Hiking and Camping

City of Rocks offers easy landscapes for hiking among the very rocks that stirred the imaginations of emigrants. Always carry water on longer hikes and watch the weather. Park elevations range from about 5,500 feet to 8,867 feet on top of Graham Peak. If you have physical limitations, check with your physician before exerting yourself. Hiking opportunities abound, but please stay on designated trails.

Camping is permitted only in designated primitive sites. Please use only a marked campsite and the established fire grill or grate. Cutting of trees and shrubs and the removal of vegetation are prohibited. Use a camp stove. Camping fees and regulations are enforced. There are no developed campground hookups. Backcountry use permits are required for all overnight use of the backcountry. They are available at Reserve headquarters in Almo.

Hunting

Much of the Reserve is private land and discharging or shooting firearms in part of the Reserve is prohibited. Where hunting is allowed, seasons and bag limits are regulated by the Idaho Fish and Game Department. A hunting license and game tag must be with the hunter at all times. Before hunting, contact the Idaho Fish and Game Department for information on types of hunts, location maps, seasons, and current regulations.

Visitor Information

For more information contact: City of Rocks National Reserve, PO. Box 169, Almo, ID 83312-0169; 208-8245519; or visit us at on the web at www.nps.gov/ciro. Reserve headquarters is located in a historic building in Almo. Stop at headquarters for current information on weather, road conditions, camping, climbing, and any restrictions that may be in effect.

Weather

City of Rocks National Reserve lies in southern Idaho on the northern edge of the Great Basin, but its streams flow into the Snake River Drainage. Outdoor recreation can be pleasant from April through October. Summers are generally dry: the 10 to 15 inches of annual precipitation fall mostly in winter and spring. Summer temperatures range wildly: the temperatures can approach freezing in July and August, but midday summer temperatures can hit 100° F. Those months also see afternoon thundershowers. Take precautions also for the very intense sunshine at high elevations.

Services and Facilities

Meals, overnight lodging, gasoline, and groceries are available in nearby communities. Reserve facilities are primitive, but restrooms are located throughout. Potable water is available at the hand pump well at the summit of Emery Canyon Rd., less than a mile above Bath Rock. This water is for drinking purposes; please help us keep the water source safe for all. Any other water in the Reserve should be treated properly for drinking - by boiling, chemicals, or adequate filtration - before use. In case of an accident or emergency, contact the Reserve headquarters or dial 911. Food supplies, pay phones, and gasoline are available at Almo and Oakley.

Drive Safely

The Reserve speed limit is 35 m.p.h. except where posted otherwise. Be wary of blind and sharp corners on the gravel roads. Drive defensively: you may come upon mountain bikers, hikers, or cattle drives using Reserve roads in spring and fall. Generally the person herding the cows will make a corridor through the herd and escort you through.

Getting Here

From Boise and the west take I-84 to the Declo exit south to Idaho Route 77 to Albion, Elba, and Almo. From Pocatello and Idaho Falls, take Interstates 86 and 84 to the Declo exit south to Almo. From Salt Lake City take I-84 to north of Snowville and Utah Routes 30 and 42, or keep going north on 1-84 to the exit for Sublette and then head west toward Malta, Elba, and Almo. There is a seasonal route through Oakley via Route 27.

Reprinted from National Park Service/U.S. Department of the Interior/Idaho Department of Parks and Recreation brochure

TV Jim Sage Mountains

East of Elba near the City of Rocks. Contact the Burley Ranger District at 678-0430. From Albion, drive south on State Hwy. 77, turning onto Conant and Ward Sheep Ranch Rd. Follow this road for mountain access.

The Jim Sage Mountains, although not officially designated as a wilderness, are just as isolated as more famous Idaho wilderness areas. Comprised of mainly quartz latite volcanic rocks, the mountains are part of the Western Basin and Range ecosystem and vary in elevation from less than 5,000 feet to over 8,000 feet. Red Rock Mountain represents the mountain's center point at 6,382 feet, and most of the range is located on Bureau of Land Management acreage.

Although one normally does not associate mountains with desert conditions, the Jim Sage Range experiences extreme weather patterns. The mountains generally receive less than twelve inches of precipitation annually, and temperatures often exceed ninety degrees Fahrenheit in July. Despite such harsh weather patterns, the mountains offer plenty of seclusion for recreationists interested in hunting, hiking, prospecting, and birding.

While the lower mountain elevations are usually accessible year-round, the higher elevations are frequently inaccessible from the end of December through mid-May. The range is completely undeveloped, so visitors are encouraged to share their travel plans with others prior to departing for the mountains. No access fees are charged, and the Burley Ranger District can provide more information about area trails, wildlife, and weather conditions.

Idaho Trivia

Idaho's City of Rocks is so remote that little, if any, light pollution masks the starry skies above. As a result, the park boasts some of the lowest light pollution statistics in the entire U.S. and draws amateur astronomers from across the world.

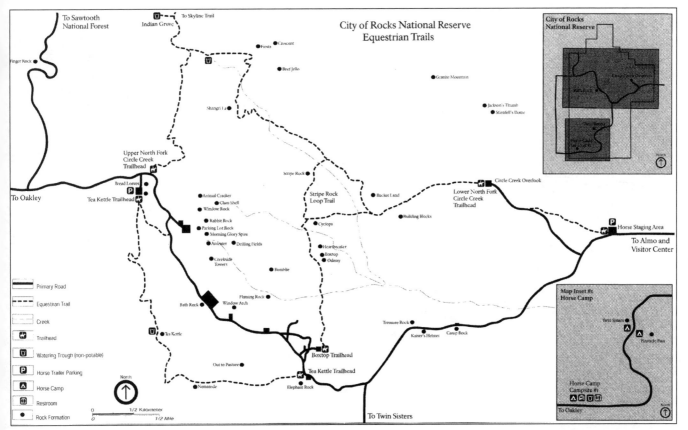

City of Rocks National Reserve
Equestrian Trails

V City of Rocks Equestrian Trails

Contact the City of Rocks National Reserve Headquarters in Almo at 824-5519.

General Information

Horses and other stock are a part of the history and culture at City of Rocks. Over 12 miles of equestrian trails lead to many of the most scenic areas of the reserve. Many sections of trail pass through areas with highly erosional soils. Help protect City of Rocks by staying on marked trails, packing out what you pack in, and by leaving natural features as you found them for others to enjoy. Many of the trails are rocky and traverse steep terrain. High country trails are covered by snow until the middle of May. Check with a ranger or visitor center personnel prior to entering the backcountry for latest conditions. Stock users share trails with hikers and bikers. Horses have the right of way with other users yielding to them.

Horse Camping, Water, & Staging Area

Camping with stock is welcome within the reserve. One improved group horse campsite (site #1) is available for use. The site includes a water trough, corral, and restroom. The site can accommodate up to 25 people and 5 horses. Reservations can be made up to eleven months in advance for this site at the park's visitor center or by calling (208) 824-5519.

Water for horses is provided through spring fed troughs that are located on the North Fork Circle Creek Trail, Tea Kettle Trail, and at Indian Grove. Please see map for exact locations of watering troughs.

A primitive horse staging area is located near the east entrance of the reserve. This area provides adequate space for horse trailer parking and allows direct access to North Fork Circle Creek Trail. Parking at Boxtop Trailhead and Circle Creek

Overlook cannot accommodate horse trailers. Please see map for location of staging area.

From June to September, cattle grazing is permitted in some areas. Be prepared to encounter livestock and be courteous of permittee operations. Leave gates as you find them.

Suggested Routes

Half Day - Tea Kettle Loop - 5 miles
Tea Kettle Trail is located on the west side of the reserve. Highlights include: two overlooks of the inner city and access to Private Idaho and Nematode. Trailheads are located at Bread Loaves and Elephant Rock. Suggested Route: Enter trail at Breadloaves. Descend southeast on Tea Kettle Trail, and exit trail at Elephant Rock. Connect into reserve road and ride northwest to campsite 62; follow trail back to the Bread Loaves.

Half Day Stripe Rock Loop – 5 miles
Stripe Rock Loop begins on the east side of the reserve. Highlights include: views of Steinfell's Dome, Circle Creek Overlook, access to Building Blocks, Bucket Land, Stripe Rock, and Cyclops. Suggested Route: Enter trail at Horse Staging Area. Travel northwest on access trail and road to Circle Creek Overlook. Join North Fork Circle Creek Trail, complete Stripe Rock Loop, and travel back to staging area.

Full Day - Trail System Loop – 12 miles
Experience all that City of Rocks has to offer on a full day ride, from sagebrush flats to high aspen groves with pinyon juniper forest found in-between. Suggested Route: Enter trail at Horse Staging Area. Travel northwest on access trail and road to Circle Creek overlook. Join North Fork Circle Creek Trail and follow trail to Indian Grove. From Indian Grove travel to Bread Loaves, join Tea Kettle Trail and follow to Elephant Rock. Take reserve road to Boxtop Trailhead. Follow Boxtop Trail to join back with North Fork Circle Creek Trail. Follow trail to Circle Creek Overlook and back to staging area.

Reprinted from a National Park Service brochure

V City of Rocks Snowmobile Trail

2 miles west of Almo in the City of Rocks National Reserve. 824-5519.

The 14,300-acre City of Rocks was established in 1988 as a national reserve. Featuring granite spires and home to world-class rock-climbing, the City of Rocks also features several hiking trails. Weather-permitting during winter, these trails are groomed for snowmobiling. All interested snowmobilers should contact the reserve headquarters prior to riding.

V City of Rocks Hiking Trails

Contact the City of Rocks National Reserve Headquarters in Almo at 824-5519.

Hiking at City of Rocks

To venture into the City of Rocks is to enter a world of slowly changing granite surrounded by high desert flora and fauna. Access to all parts of the reserve is found through 30 miles of trail. Many sections of trail pass through sensitive habitat. Help conserve City of Rocks by only using official trails and by leaving natural features as you found them for others to enjoy. Many of the trails are rocky and traverse steep terrain. Mountain trails are covered by snow until the middle of May. Check with a ranger or visitor center personnel prior to entering the backcountry for latest conditions.

Safety and Backcountry Regulations

• Be prepared for rapid weather changes; bring rain gear and extra clothing.
• Tell someone where you are going and when you expect to return.
• Backcountry sanitation: to prevent contamination of waterways, bury human waste in a hole 6-8 inches deep at least 200 feet from water. Pack out toilet paper and sanitary waste. Do not bury them.

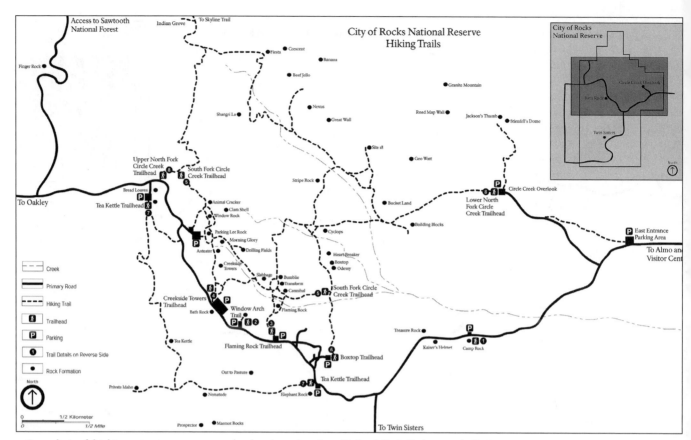

City of Rocks National Reserve
Hiking Trails

City of Rocks
National Reserve

Legend:
- Creek
- Primary Road
- Hiking Trail
- Trailhead
- Parking
- Trail Details on Reverse Side
- Rock Formation

North

0   1/2 Kilometer
0   1/2 Mile

- Carry plenty of drinking water.
- Horses have the right-of-way. Step off the trail and remain quiet while horses pass.
- Dogs must be leashed.
- Respect wildlife: observe and photograph from a safe distance. Do not approach or feed animals.
- Pack out what you pack in.
- Hike on established trails to prevent erosion.

Day Hikes
Trail distances indicate one-way lengths unless stated as a loop trail.

1) Camp Rock Trail: 300 Feet, Easy
The short walk around Camp Rock leads to many emigrant signatures left by California bound pioneers. As early as 1843, City of Rocks was a well-known landmark for emigrants on the California Trail. These travelers left their signatures in axle grease as a record of their 2000-mile journey.

2) Window Arch Trail: 300 Feet, Easy
Located behind campsite #44, this short walk leads to the impressive Window Arch which spans over 20 feet. Windows, bathtubs, and caves in the reserve are sculpted through erosion. This trail also offers one of the better vantage points for viewing various rock formations in the city.

3) Flaming Rock Trail: 1/2-Mile Loop, Moderate
Popular with many climbers, this trail provides access into the inner city. Located behind campsite #39, this short loop can also be used to access South Fork Circle Creek Trail.

4) Creekside Towers Trail: 1/2-Mile, Easy
This short walk provides direct access to the inner city and many popular spires. Interesting geologic sculptures are found adjacent to the trail. Spring brings a beautiful cascade of water draining into Circle Creek visible from several areas. This trail can also be used to access the Stairways Trail (additional 1/2 mile), which can be used to make

a loop in conjunction with South Fork Circle Creek Trail.

5) South Fork Circle Creek Trail: 1.5 Miles, Moderate
This trail serves as a main street through the inner city rock formations. The woodlands around the creek are home to many species of birds including Townsend's Solitaire, Yellow Warbler, Western Tanager, and Bullock's Oriole. Circle Creek also provides a habitat for types of wildflowers and plants not found in other parts of the reserve.

6) Boxtop Trail: 1.75 Miles, Moderate
From the start of this trail, hikers are provided with several unobstructed panoramic views of Circle Creek Basin. Bouldering is also popular on several formations along the trail. This trail accesses Bumblie Wall Trail (additional 3/4 mile), which can be used to create a loop.

7) Tea Kettle Trail: 2.5 Miles, Moderate
This trail is especially interesting for its variety. Whether you start at Elephant Rock or Bread Loaves, the trail passes through various ecosystems including aspen groves, pinon-juniper forests, and sagebrush flats. Wildlife such as mule deer and yellow-bellied marmots can be seen along the trail.

8) North Fork Circle Creek Trail: 5 Miles, Strenuous
Solitude is at a premium as you travel along North Fork of Circle Creek. From sagebrush flats to high country aspen groves, this trail takes you deep into the "city." Lost Horizons Arch, the largest erosional window in the reserve, and a portion of Shangri La highlight the hike as well as provides access to Indian Grove Trail (additional 2 miles) and several panoramic vistas.

Reprinted from National Park Service brochure

34

Oakley
Pop. 668

Mormons from Tooele, Utah, settled here between 1878 and 1880 and proceeded to raise alfalfa, wheat, and barley. The town, originally called Goose Creek Crossing, was renamed after local stage station operator, Thomas Oakley. With the construction of the Oakley Dam in 1911 came an interest from the Idaho Southern Short Line Railroad. Soon, the railroad was contracted to haul cement and timbers to aid in the construction process. Upon the dam's completion, farmers and ranchers turned the railroad into an important shipping and receiving line for livestock.

Although the town arose with vigor upon great hopes, the population began to diminish starting in 1918. Irrigated land was scarce, and a 1923 fire desecrated the majority of the town's business district. 1927 brought additional hardship to the area when the long-operating Vipoint Silver Mine closed. Subsequently, more residents fled the area.

Today, the small community's economy is dependent upon the several rock quarries operating nearby. The Idaho quartzite mined outside

Oakley is shipped all over the nation and world. Visitors should also note that the entire town is listed on the National Register of Historic Places!

H City of Rocks

Milepost 0.8 on State Hwy. 27 near Oakley

A vast display of towering granite rocks (16 miles southeast of here) attracted emigrants who were on their way to California.

A gold rush visitor, July 14, 1849, reported that "you can imagine among those massive piles, church domes, spires, pyramids…with a little fancying you can see (anything) from the Capitol at Washington to a lowly thatched cottage." Emigrants who never had seen anything like that before were impressed by so many "rocks of the most singular shapes." City of Rocks is a National Historic Landmark as well as a National Natural Landmark.

T Daughters of Utah Pioneer Museum

105 W Main St., Oakley. 862-3626.

Cassia County's history is documented in the Daughters of Utah Pioneer Museum. Housed in the old Worthington Hotel, the museum displays information related to early settlers, pioneer artifacts, guides to pioneer maps and trails, an original covered wagon, and models of an old general store and barbershop. The museum is open 2 PM to 5 PM on Saturday and Sunday during the summer with free admission.

T Oakley Warm Springs

5 miles southwest of Oakley. 862-3372.

The rustic Oakley Warm Springs welcomes visitors with several relaxing mineral hot spring choices. Patrons can relax in an outdoor pool, two indoor pools, and a few private tubs. The site is open sporadically throughout the year with more regular hours during summer. A small admission fee is charged.

T Historic Oakley Tour

Contact the Mini-Cassia Chamber of Commerce at 333-3408.

Although Oakley maintains a rural, small-town atmosphere, its landscape lives large with history. In fact, the community has such deep roots that the entire town has been designated a National Historic District. The buildings include both commercial and residential sites and all are easily located within walking and driving distance from the center of downtown.

Oakley Co-op

Southeast corner of Main & Center Sts.
Constructed from local stone in 1883, the Oakley Co-op building is the oldest structure still standing on Main Street.

Oakley Bank

Immediately east of the Co-op
The quartzite building situated directly east of the Oakley Co-op served as the community's first bank. The building's exterior is recognized throughout the region for its wonderful display of colored stone quarried locally.

Daughters of Utah Pioneers Museum

Northeast corner of Main St. & Blaine Ave.
The building that now houses the community's museum and hall of relics was once one of the finest places to spend the night in Oakley. The building was originally constructed as the Worthington Hotel.

SHOSHONE FALLS DAREDEVILS

As Shoshone Falls plunges a mighty 212 feet over rocky ledges into the Snake River Canyon below, visitors can't help but fear for the life of anyone who even dreams of diving along with the raging cataract. Idaho's most famous waterfall, however, has attracted hundreds of daredevils who have attempted this exact feat for a thrill of a lifetime. While several have tragically never risen to the surface again, a few have been lucky enough to walk away from the ordeal.

Harry Wilson
Everybody always knew Harry Wilson had a wild spirit, but few thought the half-Cherokee man would ever attempt a stunt that could spell his possible death. In March 1905, however, Wilson proved skeptics wrong when he calmly removed his clothing and jumped over the falls into a whirlpool below. Although Wilson's knee hit a rock during his descent, he suffered no serious injuries and calmly swam to a rock and waited for stunned on-lookers to toss down his clothing. His stunt received regional acclaim and was featured in the March 4, 1905 edition of the Twin Falls Daily News.

Al Faussett
Monroe, Washington lumberjack, Al Faussett, was a daredevil from the day he was born and ended up in the Pacific Northwest in 1926 following a paid offer to run the 275 foot long Sunset Falls in a canoe. Faussett couldn't pass up the challenge. Crafting his own canoe from a spruce log sheeted in metal, Fausset announced his plans to the region and decided to charge a $1.00 admission fee for every spectator. A crowd of more than 3,000 assembled to watch as Faussett accomplished the tumble unscathed and started his new career.

After fine-tuning his skills over the next three years, Faussett was ready to challenge Niagara Falls. When traveling expenses prohibited his plan, Faussett decided to take on the even higher Shoshone Falls. Signing a contract with the Twin Falls American Legion for half the proceeds raised from the event, Faussett took to the falls on July 28, 1929.

5,000 spectators flocked to the Snake River Rim while the American Electric Company provided radio music and dynamite explosions to further enhance the exciting ambience. At exactly 5:00 PM, Faussett slid himself into his inner-tube lined, football shaped canoe and plunged down the waterfall. After his descent, Faussett emerged from his craft, smiling at the crowds with only the slight injury of a broken right hand. For accomplishing this feat, Faussett received $733.

Tom Rauckhorst
Most people who hear the name "Tom Rauckhorst" do not respond with the same enthusiasm and reverence that is given to his preceding daredevil waterfall jumpers. Most, in fact, believe that the twenty-one year old lacked all common sense. Regardless, he is the third notorious Shoshone Falls jumper who lived to tell his own tale.

On a 1974 road trip from Ohio to Oregon to see a friend, Rauckhorst landed in Twin Falls on a whim to witness Evel Knevil's famous rocket launch across Shoshone Falls. Visiting the waterfall one day before Knevil's scheduled jump, Rauckhorst decided to have an adventure of his own. Without knowing the waterfall's depth or height, Tom relied on a few past high diving experiences as he dove off the cataract's south shoulder.

Upon striking the water, Tom lost consciousness. When he finally resurfaced, the handful of spectators who had witnessed his miraculous jump and survival raced him to the hospital. As battle wounds from his stunt, Tom crushed three vertebrae and was forced to wear a back brace for the next several months.

Jail Cell

Behind the City Park
Although several towns boast historic jails, few boast the history of holding notorious inmates. Oakley's jail cell once housed Diamondfield Jack Davis. Davis worked as a range rider during the late 1800s. After sparking a dispute with a sheepherder, Davis was later suspected of murder.

Farmers Bank

Southwest corner of Main St. & Blaine Ave.
Oakley's Farmers Bank was completed in 1910 and has maintained its historic location ever since. The brick building is accented with an ornate stone façade.

Union Pacific Depot

Near the railroad tracks at Main Sts west end
When the Idaho Southern Railroad began carrying supplies to labors working on the Oakley dam in the early 1900s, the Oregon Short Line decided to give the independent railroad a run for its money. The Oregon Short Line established a depot at this site and operated a line from Burley to Oakley for nearly forty years. Today, the building is home to a quartzite supply showroom with occasional visits from the Union Pacific freight line.

Judge Benjamin Howell Residence

202 N. Blaine Ave.
Built in 1909 in the Queen Anne style, the late Judge Benjamin Howell's mansion is the most frequently photographed building in town. The residence features a turret, balcony, and wraparound porch with decorative trim. The home is now a private residence that is rarely open to the public.

Howell Opera House

Blaine Ave.
The Howell Opera House was constructed in 1904 and provided early Oakley residents with a range of entertainment. In the 1980s, the opera house was remodeled to once again serve Oakley residents and visitors.

Jacob Dayley House

106 Poplar Ave.
The Jacob Dayley House was built in 1898 and bears the handcrafted marks of its builder. Chisel marks from Joseph Beck, a mason's apprentice, can still be found in the home's reddish gray stone walls. Beck emigrated from Germany to America as a stowaway at the young age of fourteen. When he arrived in the U.S., he made his way by rail to Idaho, and an Oakley family eventually adopted him. Beck helped build many of Oakley's finely crafted homes.

Continued on page 397

WATERFALLS

Shoshone Falls

At the city of Twin Falls, take Falls Avenue east 2 miles to the Shoshone Falls Park junction; turn at this junction and drive 2 more miles to reach the cataract.

Situated at an elevation of 3,200 feet in the Snake River Canyon East, Shoshone Falls is recognized as the most famous waterfall in Idaho. In addition, Shoshone Falls' large watershed and magnitude have placed the cataract in first place for the top ten waterfalls in the Pacific Northwest. With a width of more than 1,000 feet and a 212-foot descent, Shoshone Falls provides visitors with picture-worthy scenery and a bit of Native American history. During pioneer times, the Shoshoni Indian Quish-in-demi related the following story to J.S. Harrington regarding the cataract's tragic past. This tale is taken from the 1937 Federal Writers' Project publication of *Idaho: A Guide in Words and Pictures:*

"In the gloomy gorge above the falls there was, long ago, the trysting place of a deep-chested Shoshoni [warrior] and the slender wild girl whom he loved. Their last meeting was here on a pile of rocks which overlooked the plunging waters. He went away to scalp with deft incisions and then to lift the shaggy mane of white men with a triumphant shout; and she came daily to stand by the thundering avalanche and remember him. That he would return unharmed she did not, with the ageless resourcefulness of women, ever allow herself to doubt. But time passed, and the moons that came and ripened were many, and she still came nightly to stand on the brink and watch the changeless journeying of the water. And it was here that she stood one black night above the roar of the flood when a warrior stepped out of shadow and whispered to her and then disappeared. As quiet as the flat stone under her feet, she stood for a long while, looking down into the vault where the waters boiled up like seething white hills to fill the sky with dazzling curtains and roll away in convulsed tides. For an hour she gazed down there 200 feet to a mad pouring motion and sound into a black graveyard of the dead. And then, slowly, she lifted her arms above her, listed her head to the fullest curve of her throat, and stood tiptoe for a moment, poised and beautiful, and then dived in a long swift arc against the falling white background…And the river at this point and since that hour has never been the same."

Visitors should be advised that spring offers the best views of the cataract before summer crop irrigation consumes much of the Snake River.

Twin Falls

At the city of Twin Falls, drive east 5 miles on Falls Avenue; pass the Shoshone Falls junction and bear north (left) onto a marked access road for the falls; visitors will reach the falls and a nearby picnic area in approximately 1 mile.

Twin Falls is situated at an elevation of 3,400 feet along the basaltic-layered rocks of the Snake River Canyon East. Descending in segments as the Snake River divides, only one portion of this cataract is allowed to fall. While a dam blocks the larger section of Twin Falls, the smaller segment still descends. During the early spring months, this segment plunges 125 feet

with a large watershed. By summer, however, the flow is significantly reduced as a dam upstream draws water off the river for crop irrigation.

Bridal Veil Falls

At the city of Twin Falls, drive east along Falls Avenue 2 miles to the junction for Shoshone Falls Park; turn at the junction and proceed 2 miles to the falls.

The springs of Dierkes Lake feed the 25 to 40 foot plunge of Bridal Veil Falls in the Snake River Canyon East. Situated at an elevation of 3,200 feet, Bridal Veil Falls offers visitors easy access in the same vicinity as other reputable Idaho waterfalls.

Perrine Coulee Falls

Drive north on U.S. Highway 93 from Twin Falls; directly after Pole Line Road, bear west on Canyon Springs Road for 0.7 mile

Perrine Coulee Falls loses contact with its bedrock surface as it plunges 197 awe-inspiring feet in the Snake River Canyon West. Situated at an elevation of 3,500 feet, this cataract is fed by agricultural activities in the area and provides visitors with easy vehicle access.

Auger Falls

Proceed north of the city Twin Falls on U.S. Highway 93; at Golf Course Road, bear west and drive to a subdivision area in 5 miles for a semi-obstructed view; for up-close vantages, turn off U.S. Highway 93 at Canyon Springs Road and continue 5 miles west

Occurring along the Snake River, Auger Falls drops 25 to 50 feet over a rocky surface. Although the north rim of Snake River Canyon West used to provide outstanding vistas, public views are decreasing as more housing developments arise in the area.

Upper Salmon Falls

Take U.S. Highway 30 3.2 miles south of Hagerman; bear west (right) at the sign for Upper Salmon Falls; continue 1.5 miles to the power plant

Upper Salmon Falls divides into four segments along the Snake River as each section drops 15 to 25 feet. At an elevation of 2,880 feet, Upper Salmon Falls is easily accessible. For an up-close vantage, park at the road's east end and follow an unmarked footbridge across the Snake River to a small island. Continue down the cement path to the falls. Visitors are urged to use caution while viewing the falls as Idaho Power may at times flood the walkways with no liability for any accidents.

Lower Salmon Falls

U.S. Highway 30 south; approximately 6.8 miles south of I-84's exit to Gooding-Hagerman and 1.5 miles north of Hagerman, exit off U.S. Highway 30 at the Lower Salmon Power Plant entrance; continue 0.7 mile and look beyond the power plant's substation to locate the waterfall on the far side of the Snake River

Lower Salmon Falls is easily accessible and viewable for visitors of all ages. Descending as a wide band from a section of the Snake River, the cataract plunges 10 to 15 feet with a large watershed.

Falls of Thousand Springs

U.S. Highway 30/Thousand Springs Scenic Route (15 to 16 miles northwest of Buhl)

Falling in multiple threads as the Snake River diverges, Falls of Thousand Springs includes

eight major cataracts and several smaller waterfalls descending in ranges from 40 to 100 feet. Located next to a one-mile stretch of the Snake River Canyon's north edge, the springs significantly increase the river's volume.

Falls of Banbury Springs

U.S. Highway 30/Thousand Springs Scenic Route; continue 4 miles south past Falls of Thousand Springs and exit U.S. Highway 30 at the Banbury Hot Springs Resort access road; continue 1.5 miles

The Falls of Banbury Springs is located in the same general vicinity of Falls of Thousand Springs. However, gazing across the Snake River at the Falls of Thousand Springs access point provides limited views of this cataract's 30 to 80 foot descent. For up-close views, proceed to Banbury Hot Springs Resort.

Devils Washboard Falls

From U.S. Highway 30, take Clear Lakes Road to the Buhl County Club (approximately 7 miles north of Buhl and 12 miles south of Wendell)

Devils Washboard Falls is located near the Clear Lakes Trout Company, one of the world's largest trout farms. The cataract's spring-fed 15 to 30 foot plummet is impressive at times, but visitors should be warned that a nearby power company occasionally diverts some of the waterfall's flow from Clear Lakes.

Pillar Falls

Drive to Twin Falls, ID; from here, proceed north 1 mile on U.S. Highway 93, exiting east onto the dirt Golf Course Road; drive 0.9 mile and park your vehicle

Descending at an elevation of 3,200 feet, Pillar Falls drops along the Snake River amid 30 to 70 foot basaltic rock towers. With 10 to 20 feet cascades, this cataract's location is famous for Evel Knievel's 1970's attempt to jump the Snake River canyon on a rocket-cycle. After parking, hike 0.3 mile through abandoned dump areas to the Snake River Canyon ledge. Caution is advised in this area as the canyon rim occurs suddenly and is unfenced. Sightseers will find Pillar Falls descending directly below and a distant view of Shoshone Falls upstream.

The following Idaho waterfalls are also located in this section with limited directions/access available:

Little Drops Falls and Big Drops Falls

Located near Scenic Route 75 a few miles north of Shoshone, ID, both Little Drops Falls and Big Drops Falls are contained in the basaltic rock layers of the Snake River Canyon West on Milner Gooding Canal. While Little Drops falls is found next to a recreation area, Big Drops Falls is located adjacent to a dirt road. Both are shown on topographic maps in connection with historic lava beds.

Sinking Canyon Falls

Sinking Canyon Falls tumbles along an unnamed seasonal stream into Salmon Falls Creek Canyon in the Snake River Aquifer northeast of Hagerman, ID. This cataract may be located on private property, but topographic maps suggest that visitors can access a cross-canyon view during late spring and early summer.

Ross Falls and Phantom Falls

The Snake River Canyon East near Twin Falls, ID is home to Ross Falls and Phantom Falls. Found in the Geographic Names Information System,

Ross Falls occurs along Fourth Fork Rock Creek past the Magic Mountain Ski Area. Topographic maps show the cataract plummeting next to a gravel road. Access to Phantom Falls is more uncertain. The falls are along Fall Creek approximately 1.5 miles from the nearest road. Visitors interested in viewing the waterfall will likely need to create their own trail.

Marcus Funk Residence
Center Street just south of Poplar St.

Although there is speculation as to the accuracy of this story, local legend insists that this home was at one time intended to house one husband and three wives. Marcus Funk, a known Mormon polygamist with three wives, purportedly planned this three-story house as a means of accommodating one wife per floor. However, the legend remains a legend as Funk sold the house before ever moving in.

Center Street
3 blocks south of the Marcus Funk Residence

Situated at a bend on the street's south side, this brick house was built in 1912. The bungalow-style home took advantage of Oakley's three brick-yards as it features walls that are three bricks thick.

Cutler Worthington House
Worthington Ave.

In 1905, the impressive Cutler Worthington house was finished, complete with a center tower and two balconies. While the home's first story is built entirely out of stone, the second story utilizes frame construction.

Oakley Cemetery
Church St.

Oakley's cemetery is most notable for its striking white tombstones handcrafted in the 1800s and early 1900s. The locally quarried stone was found too soft for commercial use, so it was fashioned into headstones. While the cemetery houses the remains of many Oakley pioneers, the most interesting gravesite is that of Gobo Fango who died on February 10, 1886 at the age of thirty.

Gobo Fango, a black boy born in Africa, was orphaned young. Learning of the boy's plight, an LDS family smuggled the boy to Layton, Utah where they raised and educated him. As he grew older, Fango moved to the Oakley Basin where he and partner, Walt Matthews, leased a band of sheep.

Although the men had been highly successful, February 10, 1886 changed Fango's life forever and the men's fortune with sheep. While out tending the sheep alone, Fango was shot in the stomach. After plugging the wound with sage, Fango dragged himself back to Matthews' house where he died a few short hours later.

T Oakley City Park
Main St., Oakley.

The Oakley City Park serves as the community center for recreation and social gatherings. The park features an expansive shady lawn complete with a playground, picnic tables, and outdoor swimming pool. In addition, the park hosts annual community events, including a traditional Easter egg hunt held each Spring.

T Oakley Dam
Near Oakley

When the U.S. Government approved the Reclamation Act, the Kuhn brothers from Pittsburgh decided to capitalize on the interests of south-central Idaho settlers. In exchange for the settlers' water rights, the brothers gave away water contracts in the Twin Falls Oakley Land and Water Project. The plan was intended to irrigate 43,000 acres, and construction on the Oakley Dam near Goose Creek began in 1911. Just two years later, however, the company that financed $1.3 million in building bonds went bankrupt, and area residents were forced to complete the project with their own funds. The settlers reduced the project's irrigation capability to 21,000 acres and displayed their pioneer spirit in finishing the earthen dam on their own. Today, the dam feeds East Canal, which runs across Oakley's Main Street.

TV Lower Goose Creek Reservoir
7 miles southwest of Oakley. Contact the BLM – Burley District at 678-5514.

Lower Goose Creek Reservoir was established in the early 1900s upon the completion of the Oakley Dam. The reservoir is a popular summer attraction, drawing anglers, picnickers, and boaters to its shores. The reservoir, boasting healthy populations of both rainbow and cutthroat trout, is accessible year-round during daylight hours.

SCENIC DRIVES

Thousand Springs Scenic Byway
From the Snake River Plain Aquifer, an abundance of natural springs gush from the steep canyon walls and cascade into the river below. In fact, the aquifer creeps through an area of several thousand square miles under southern Idaho's porous volcanic rock before emerging from the springs in the cliffs of the Snake River Canyon.

This pure, clean, oxygenated water maintains a constant temperature of 58 degrees F., ideal conditions for trout. The hatcheries located along the 30-mile stretch of the Snake River in the Hagerman Valley raise about 70 percent of the trout produced in the United States.

Today, hydroelectric and irrigation projects divert some of the water. So while you won't see literally a "thousand springs" along the route, it is nevertheless an impressive sight.

In Twin Falls guided boat tours are available that take visitors to see Shoshone Falls. Passengers get close enough to feel the spray on their faces. At 212 feet, it is 52 feet higher than Niagara Falls. Boat tours and dinner cruises are available in the Hagerman area allowing visitors to get up close and personal with some of the Thousand Springs along a beautiful stretch of the Snake River.

The byway begins at Interstate 84 near Bliss and follows U.S. 30 southeast through Twin Falls to Idaho 50, then north on Idaho 50 to I-84. The byway also traverses U.S. 93 from Twin Falls north to I-84. The byway can be seen year round, and the Hagerman Valley is known for its very mild winters. The best time to see Shoshone Falls and Twin Falls is in early spring. Travelers should allow at least 1.5 hours for this 67.8-mile trip.

Reprinted from Idaho Department of Transportation brochure

City of Rocks Backcountry Byway
Forming a 49-mile necklace around the Albion Mountain Range, the City of Rocks Backcountry Byway traces a rural landscape steeped in history and geological significance.

Beginning in Albion on Idaho 77, the byway traverses the outskirts of the Pomerelle Ski Area and Lake Cleveland Recreation Area as it heads south.

At the base of the by[...] jewel, the City of Rocks [...] more than 700 challeng[...] National Park and mak[...] technical rock climbers [...] outcroppings – some m[...] old – soar above alpine [...] tree stands, offering a [...] opportunities; a visitor [...] tion of the Reserve and [...]

Heading north, the [...] in historic Oakley; the entire town, in fact, is [...] the National Register of Historic Places and features the state's largest concentration of old stone and wood-framed buildings.

The route begins along Idaho 77 at Albion south to the Connor Creek Junction, and continues south through Elba and Almo and the scenic City of Rocks National Reserve. From the Reserve, the route follows Birch Creek to the City of Oakley and the Oakley Historic District where it joins Idaho 27. It is a paved secondary highway from Albion to Connor Creek Junction. Connor Creek to Almo is a narrow winding paved road, and from Almo to Oakley the road is graveled until it joins Idaho 27 at Oakley. The best weather to travel is April to November. Call (208) 824-5519 for road conditions. Travelers should allow at least 1.5 hours for this 49-mile trip.

Reprinted from Idaho Department of Transportation brochure

HIKES

For information on additional area trails, please contact the Forest Service Ranger Districts listed at the back of this section.

Albion Range Area
Independence Lakes
Distance: 4.4 miles roundtrip
Climb: moderate
Difficulty: moderate
Usage: moderate
Location: From Burley, drive 20 miles south on State Highway 27 to Oakley's Main Street. Bear left onto 2000 South and follow the county road 11 miles to Elba Pass. At the pass, proceed on the right fork and drive to another road junction in 1 mile. Follow the right fork to Potholes Junction and bear left. Travel along this road to its end at Dry Creek and the Independence Lakes Trailhead. After parking, enter the gated picnic area, cross Dry Creek, and proceed through the picnic area to the trail.

Set amidst granite boulders and white quartzite, four subalpine lakes await hikers on this trail as well as magnificent views of the Jim Sage Mountains, Elba Basin, and Mount Harrison sprawling in the distance. The trail begins gently climbing through forests and wildflower meadows to a trail junction at the 1.2-mile mark. Ignoring the Ranger Trail, keep right to climb towards the lakes. The first lake, set in a cirque directly below Independence Peak, is reached at the 2-mile mark. While this lake is home to a few small fish, the second and much larger lake is renowned for its sizeable trout. From the first lake, hike 0.2 miles further to the second lake. The maintained trail ends at this point, but hikers can scramble over boulders to reach the shallow, clear blue waters of the two upper lakes. Best months for hiking are mid-July through August.

Optional Hikes: At the first lake, climb up the steep cirque wall to the top of Mount Independence situated at 9,950 feet. At the summit, hikers are rewarded with views of southern

CLOSE CALL

[In] 1882, merchants hungry for business and wealth established a ferry across the Snake River just 200 yards shy of the Shoshone Falls' drop. Although the ferry certainly offered travelers a convenient way to cross the river during a time when bridges were non-existent, the journey came with a price. Travelers far and wide worried about the ferry's close proximity to the falls and couldn't help but ask the question, "What if?" The "what if" eventually occurred in 1907. With five individuals on-board, the ferry cable broke and left passengers on the verge of death. Due to the smart thinking of one passenger who hurled the cable around a nearby beam, the passengers were tugged back to shore after the longest and scariest thirty-minute wait of their lives.

Idaho's mountains and valleys, the Silent City of Rocks National Reserve, and Utah's Raft River Range. This hike is difficult, and best months for hiking are late July through August.

Silent City of Rocks
Distance: Numerous short hikes and loops ranging up to 1.5 miles long
Climb: gentle to moderate in places
Difficulty: easy to moderate
Usage: heavy
Location: At Malta, exit off Interstate 84 and merge onto State Highway 77. Bearing left at Conner Junction, proceed to Almo. Drive south out of town 4.6 miles and turn right at the junction. Continue 1.3 miles to several trails leaving from Bath Rock on the road's left side.

Strangely shaped granite formations characterize this unique area, as well as several small meadows, aspen trees, and prickly pear cactus. Hikers can choose from a variety of short hiking trails leading through huge boulders that have become popular rock climbing spots. Best months for hiking are late May through September.

Malad Gorge State Park
South Rim to Woody's Cove
Distance: 4 miles roundtrip
Climb: gentle
Difficulty: moderate (due to precipitous ledges)
Usage: heavy
Location: Merge south off Interstate 84 at Exit 147 and enter Malad Gorge State Park. Upon entering, stay to the right at the junction and proceed 0.25 miles to the informal trailhead at a historic stone house.

With overviews of Malad Gorge plus scenic waterfalls and springs, this unfenced trail travels precariously close to the canyon's steep south rim and is not recommended for children. Beginning west of the historic stone house, the trail ends at the Hagerman Valley with an optional 0.25 cross-country mile hike to Woody's Cove. Best months for hiking are March through May and September through November due to desert conditions.

Malad Gorge Trail to Devil's Washbowl
Distance: 4 miles roundtrip
Climb: gentle
Difficulty: easy
Usage: heavy
Location: Merge south off Interstate 84 at Exit 147 and enter Malad Gorge State Park.

This trail leads hikers to awe-inspiring views overlooking the 250-foot deep canyon. After crossing over a footbridge above the gorge, hike along the fenced canyon rim. The trail ends at a cascade plunging 60 feet into the Devil's Washbowl.

South Hills Area
Eagle Loop
Distance: 2.5 mile loop
Climb: gentle
Difficulty: easy
Usage: moderate
Location: From south Twin Falls, bear left on Kimberly Road and travel 5 miles to Kimberly. Merge onto U.S. Highway 30 here and proceed to Rock Creek Road. Drive 28 miles south on Rock Creek Road to the Eagle Loop Trailhead just past the Rock Creek Ranger Station and Magic Mountain Ski Area.

Wandering gently through open forests with a variety of birds chirping along the way, this trail and its numerous resting benches is perfect for families with small children. Beginning next to Rock Creek Road, continue uphill at the 0.75-mile mark and proceed to a rocky ridge with views of Trapper Peak. Keep to the right at all times and drop back into the forest. At the trail junction, proceed on the middle route through thick aspen trees back to the trailhead. Best months for hiking are May, June, and September.

Third Fork Rock Creek-Wahlstrom Hollow Loop
Distance: 9 mile loop
Climb: moderate
Difficulty: moderate
Usage: moderate
Location: From south Twin Falls, bear left on Kimberly Road and travel 5 miles to Kimberly. Merge onto U.S. Highway 30 here and proceed to Rock Creek Road. Drive 23 miles to the Third Fork Trailhead located on the road's east (left) side. The trailhead is poorly marked and simply reads "trailers."

Hikers will pass through a variety of landscapes, including volcanic rock formations and cliffs, sagebrush, subalpine fir, and aspen trees. From the trailhead, cross over the Third Fork Bridge and hike 4 miles to the A.H. Creek Trail junction. Proceed northwest (right) at this junction up to Wahlstrom Hollow Pass. At the pass, ignore roads leaving to the left and right, and continue walking north-northwest to descend to a few beaver ponds. Follow the trail as it drops down near a stream, through a narrow canyon, and back to the trailhead. Best months for hiking are May, June, and September. Caution should be used at all times as bull snakes and rattlesnakes populate the area.

INFORMATION PLEASE

All Idaho area codes are 208

Road Information

ID Road & Weather Conditions
888-432-7623 or local 884-7000
Idaho State Police   736-3090

Tourism Information

Idaho Travel Council 800-VISIT-ID outside Idaho
334-2470 in Idaho
www.visitid.org
South Central Idaho Tourism & Recreation
Development Association   800-255-8946
732-5569
www.visitsouthidaho.com

Airports

Buhl	543-2192
Jerome	324-9980
Twin Falls	733-5215

Government Offices

Idaho Bureau of Reclamation	334-1466
	www.usbr.gov
Idaho Department of Commerce	
	(800) 847-4843 or 334-2470
	www.visitid.org or http://cl.idaho.gov/
Idaho Department of Fish and Game	
	(800) ASK-FISH or 334-3700
	http://fishandgame.idaho.gov
Idaho Department of Parks and Recreation	
	334-4199
	www.idahoparks.org
State BLM Office	373-3889 or 373-4000
	www.id.blm.gov
Bureau of Land Management Burley Field Office	
	677-6641
Bureau of Land Management Shoshone Field Office	886-2206
City of Rocks National Reserve	824-5519
Hagerman Fossil Beds National Monument	
	837-4793
Sawtooth National Forest	737-3200

Hospitals

Cassia Regional Medical Center Burley	677-6401
Gooding County Memorial Hospital Gooding	934-4433
Saint Benedicts Family Medical Center Jerome	324-4301
Minidoka Memorial Hospital • Rupert	436-0481
Magic Valley Regional Medical Center Twin Falls	737-2000

Golf Courses

Clear Lake Country Club • Buhl	543-4849
Burley City Golf Course • Burley	878-9807
Ponderosa Golf Course • Burley	679-5730
Gooding Golf Course • Gooding	934-9977
93 Golf Ranch • Jerome	324-9693
Pleasant Valley Golf Course Kimberly	423-5800
Canyon Springs Golf Course Twin Falls	734-7609
Twin Falls Golf • Twin Falls	733-3326

Bed & Breakfasts

Mountain Manor • Albion	673-6642
Magic Valley Country Charm B&B Twin Falls	326-7236

Guest Ranches & Resorts

Kilgore Adventures Lodge White Bird	839-2255
White Bird Summit Lodge White Bird	983-1802

Idaho Trivia

Almo may be up and coming in serving the needs of hardcore rock climbers headed to the nearby City of Rocks, but the town still preserves the past. Tracy's Merc, which was established in 1894, has forsaken modern gadgets to ring up customer purchases with a National cash register dating back to the late 1800s/early 1900s.

Winchester Lake Lodge
Winschester   924-6430

Car Rental

Enterprise • Burley   678-6841
Keith's Kleen KARS • Burley   678-1178
I-84 Xpress Rent A Car • Jerome 324-7570
Kim Hansen • Rupert   436-9001
Alamo • Twin Falls   733-3646
Avis • Twin Falls   733-5527
Budget • Twin Falls   735-6666
Budget Car & Truck Rental
Twin Falls   734-4067
Enterprise • Twin Falls   736-6281
Hertz • Twin Falls   733-2668

Latham Motors Inc • Twin Falls   733-5776
Mueller Auto • Twin Falls   736-3325
National • Twin Falls   733-3646
National Car Rental • Twin Falls   733-4830

Outfitters & Guides

F=Fishing H=Hunting R=River Guides
E=Horseback Rides G=General Guide Services

Id Outfitters & Guides Association
                             800-49-IDAHO
Outfitters & Guides Licensing Board   327-7380
Snake River Canyon Tours   R 934-8245
Thousand Springs Tours   R 837-4822
Pioneer Mountain Outfitters FHEG 324-7171

War Eagle Outfitter & Guides   FHE 645-2455
Hamilton Outfitters   FHEG 436-4251
Idaho Guide Service, Inc   FHRTG 734-4998
Pioneer Mountain Outfitters   H 734-3679

Downhill Ski Areas

Pomerelle • Albion   673-5599
Magic Mountain Ski & Summer Resort
Twin Falls   423-6221

NOTES:

Campground Quick Reference

Campground Name				Phone
Public/Commercial	Unit Price	#Spaces	Max. Length	Seasons
Directions				
Amenities/Activities				

Albion

Bennett Springs
P   678-0430   Summer, Fall
5.5 mi. SE on Hwy. 77, 4.9 mi. SW on Forest Rd. 549
Vault Toilets

Lake Cleveland
P $5   7   20'   678-0430   Summer, Fall
5.5 mi. SE on Hwy. 77, 10 mi. W. on Forest Rd. 549
Drinking Water, Fire Rings, Vault Toilets

Sublett
P   7   22'   678-0430   Summer, Fall
20.6 mi. E. on Forest Rd. 568
Drinking Water, Vault Toilets

Thompson Flat
P $5   16   22'   678-0430   Summer, Fall, Spring, Please Call
5.5 mi. SE on Hwy. 77, 8 mi. W. on Forest Rd. 549
Drinking Water, Fire Rings, Vault Toilets

Almo

City of Rocks National Reserve
P $7   78   824-5519   Summer, Fall, Spring
3 mi. SW of Almo on Cty. Rd.
Credit Cards OK, Drinking Water, Reservations, Tenters Welcome, Vault Toilets

Buhl

Banbury Hot Springs
C $10-25   40   543-4098   All Year
10 mi. W. on Hwy. 30, 1.5 mi. E. on Banbury Rd.
Drinking Water, Dump Station, Hookups, Hot Springs, Pets OK, Reservations, Showers, Swimming Pool, Tenters Welcome

Miracle Hot Springs
C $10-20   13   543-6002   All Year
Hwy. 30, halfway between Hagerman and Buhl
Hookups, Hot Springs, Pets OK, Pull-thru Sites, Reservations, Swimming Pool, Yurts/Teepees, Tenters Welcome, Handicap Access

Declo

Village of Trees - RV Park at Travel Stop 216
C $28-29   87   654-2133   All Year
I-84, exit 216
Boating Facilities, Cable TV Hookups, Credit Cards OK, Fire Rings, Hookups, LP Gas, Mini-Mart, Modem Hookups, Pets OK, Playground, Pull-thru Sites, Showers, Swimming Pool, Tenters Welcome, Waterfront, Work-Out Room

Filer

Curry Trailer Park
C $15   16   733-3961   All Year
3 mi. W. of Magic Valley Hospital, 21323 Hwy. 30
Hookups, Pets OK, Reservations, Showers

Twin Falls County Fairgrounds RV Park
C $12   159   326-4396   All Year
Hwy. 30, 7.5 mi. W. of Twin Falls

Hagerman

Sportsman's River Resort
C $16-40   10   837-6364   All Year
Hwy. 30, 5 mi. S. of Hagerman, 5 Gilhooley Ln.
Credit Cards OK, Drinking Water, Hookups, Reservations, Showers, Waterfront

High Adventure River Tours, RV Park & Store   837-9005/800-286-4123
C $8-26   26   Any'   All Year
I-84, exit 147, next to Malad Gorge State Park
Credit Cards OK, Drinking Water, Dump Station, Hookups, Mini-Mart, Modem Hookups, Pets OK, Playground, Pull-thru Sites, Reservations, Showers, Tenters Welcome, Laundry, Handicap Access

Sligar's Thousand Springs Resort
C $13-20   60   837-4987   All Year
18734 Hwy. 30
Boating Facilities, Drinking Water, Game Room, Hookups, Hot Springs, Pets OK, Playground, Pull-thru Sites, Reservations, Showers, Swimming Pool, Tenters Welcome, Waterfront, Handicap Access

Hagerman RV Village   837-4906/800-707-4906
C $15-35   60   75'   All Year
I-84, exit 141, 8 mi. E. on Hwy. 30, right side of road
Credit Cards OK, Drinking Water, Hookups, Mini-Mart, Modem Hookups, Pets OK, Playground, Pull-thru Sites, Reservations, Showers, Work-Out Room

Hansen

Diamondfield Jack
P $4   7   35'   678-0430   All Year
28 mi. S. on Cty. Rd. G3
Drinking Water, Fire Rings, Vault Toilets

Upper Penstemon
P $5   9   24'   737-3200   Summer, Fall
24.1 mi. S. on Cty. Rd. G3
Drinking Water, Fire Rings, Vault Toilets

Porcupine Springs
P $8-12   15   32'   737-3200   Summer, Fall
31 mi. S. on Cty. Rd. G3
Drinking Water, Fire Rings, Vault Toilets

Schipper
P   Yes   6   678-0430   April-October
16 miles S of Hansen on Rock Creek Rd/County Rd G3
Developed Campground, Drinking Water, Restrooms, RV Sites, Fishing, Picnicking

Steer Basin
P   Yes   5   678-0439   May-October
20 miles S of Hansen on Rock Creek Rd/County Rd G3
Developed Campground, Drinking Water, Handicap Accessible Restrooms, RV Sites, Biking, Fishing, Hiking/Backpacking, Horseback Riding, Off Highway Vehicles, Picnicking

Lower Penstemon
P   Yes   10; 2 Group Sites   678-0439   Year-Round
27 miles S of Hansen on Rock Creek Rd/County Rd G3
Developed Campground, Group Camping, Drinking Water, Restrooms, RV Sites, Biking, Caving, Fishing, Hiking/Backpacking, Horseback Riding, Picnicking, Winter Sports

Upper Penstemon
P   Yes   6   678-0439   June-September
27 miles S of Hansen on Rock Creek Rd/County Rd G3
Developed Campground, Handicap Accessible Drinking Water, Handicap Accessible Restrooms, Handicap Accessible RV Sites, Fishing, Picnicking, Winter Sports

Hazelton

R&E Greenwood
C $5-15   20   829-5735   All Year
I-84, exit 194
Credit Cards OK, Drinking Water, Dump Station, Hookups, Limited Access, Mini-Mart, Modem Hookups, Showers, Tenters Welcome

Heyburn

Country RV Village - Good Sam Park
C $23   31   70'   436-3652   All Year
Off Interstate 84
Credit Cards OK, Hookups, Modem Hookups, Playground, Pull-thru Sites, Reservations, Showers, Tenters Welcome, Laundry, Handicap Access

Heyburn City RV Park
P $21-23   29   40'   677-8610   Summer, Fall, Spring
I-84, exit 211, 2 mi. S. at the Snake River
Dump Station, Hookups, Pets OK, Pull-thru Sites, Reservations, Showers

Section 5

Campground Quick Reference - continued

Campground Name Public/Commercial	Unit Price	#Spaces	Max. Length	Phone Seasons
Directions				
Amenities/Activities				

Jerome

Big Trees RV Park   324-8265
C $12-15   25   All Year
Downtown
Hookups, Pets OK, Pull-thru Sites, Reservations, Showers, Laundry

Malta

McClenden Springs   677-6641
P   5   Summer, Fall, Spring
3 miles north on Hwy 81, then 2.5 miles west and south on Conner Creek Road.
Pets OK, Vault Toilets

Howell Canyon   678-0430
P   None   2   Year-Round
11 miles NW of Malta on Hwy. 77, then 5 miles W on FR 549
Primitive Camping, Restrooms, Fishing, Picnicking, Scenic Driving, Winter Sports

McClendon Spring   524-7500
P   None   Undeveloped   Year-Round
3 miles N of Malta on Hwy. 81, then 2.5 miles SW on Connor Creek Rd
Primitive Camping, Restrooms, Biking, Fishing, Hiking/Backpacking, Hunting, Off Highway Vehicles, Picnicking

Oakley

Oakley City RV Park   862-3313
P $5-10   11   Summer, Fall, Spring
Go through main intersection, 1.5 blocks, on left
Drinking Water, Dump Station, Hookups, Pets OK, Pull-thru Sites, Reservations, Showers, Tenters Welcome, Handicap Access

Bostetter   678-0430
P   18   16'   Summer
19.7 mi. W. on Forest Rd. 70500
Drinking Water, Tenters Welcome, Vault Toilets

Father and Son   678-0430
P   12'   Summer, Fall
21 miles west of Oakley, ID , Forest Rd 500
Drinking Water, Fire Rings, Tenters Welcome, Vault Toilets

Rogerson

Lud Drexler Park   677-6641
P $5   20   25'   Summer, Fall
22 mi. S. of Twin Falls near Salmon Falls Dam
Drinking Water, Dump Station, Pets OK, Vault Toilets

Rupert

Lake Walcott State Park   436-1258
P $12-16   22   35'   Summer
13 mi. NE of Rupert
Camping Cabins, Credit Cards OK, Drinking Water, Dump Station, Pets OK, Pull-thru Sites, Showers, Tenters Welcome, Waterfront

Shoshone

Burren West Resort   487-2571
C $10-20   45   Summer, Fall, Spring
18 mi. N. of Shoshone, Hwy 75, turn at W. Magic Reservoir sign
Waterfront

Sublett

Mill Flat   678-0430
P   Yes   6   June-October
Exit 228, 8.5 miles E on Yale Road, then 16 miles E on Haigler Canyon Rd
Developed Campground, Drinking Water, Restrooms, Biking, Fishing, Hiking/Backpacking, Off Highway Vehicles, Picnicking

Twin Falls

Twin Falls-Jerome KOA   324-4169/800-562-4169
C $19-30   70   45'   Summer, Fall, Spring
I-84, exit 173 N., 1 mi., 5431 Hwy. 93
Cable TV Hookups, Camping Cabins, Credit Cards OK, Drinking Water, Dump Station, Game Room, Hookups, LP Gas, Mini-Mart, Modem Hookups, Pets OK, Playground, Pull-thru Sites, Reservations, Showers, Swimming Pool, Tenters Welcome, Work-Out Room, Laundry, Handicap Access

Anderson Camp   825-9800/888-480-9400
C $18-55   120   All Year
I-84, exit 182, turn N., right on Tipperary Rd., proceed past two RV sales businesses. Turn left at the Sinclair Station
Business Center, Camping Cabins, Credit Cards OK, Drinking Water, Dump Station, Fire Rings, Game Room, Hookups, Hot Springs, LP Gas, Mini-Mart, Modem Hookups, Pets OK, Playground, Pull-thru Sites, Reservations, Showers, Swimming Pool, Tenters Welcome, Laundry

Blue Lakes RV Park   734-5782
C $16   37   All Year
Hwy. 93, 4.5 mi. S. of I-84
Cable TV Hookups, Hookups, Pets OK, Pull-thru Sites, Reservations, Showers, Handicap Access

Nat-Soo-Pah Hot Springs & RV Park   655-4337
C $12   75   Summer, Fall, Spring
16 mi. S. of Twin Falls on Blue Lakes Blvd., 2738 E. 2400 N.
Dump Station, Hookups, Hot Springs, Pets OK, Pull-thru Sites, Reservations, Showers, Swimming Pool, Tenters Welcome

Oregon Trail Campground & Family Fun Center   733-0853/800-733-0853
C $18-20   49   45'   All Year
I-84, exit 173 (Blue Lakes Blvd.), S. to Hwy. 30 (Kimberly Rd.), left (E.) about 1.5 mi.
Cable TV Hookups, Credit Cards OK, Drinking Water, Game Room, Hookups, Pets OK, Playground, Pull-thru Sites, Reservations, Showers, Tenters Welcome, Laundry, Handicap Access

South 93 RV Park   326-5092
C $17-20   35   70'   Summer, Fall, Spring
.5 mi. S. of Hwy. 30/93 junction on 93 S., 2404 Jordan Ln.
Cable TV Hookups, Credit Cards OK, Drinking Water, Dump Station, Hookups, LP Gas, Modem Hookups, Pets OK, Pull-thru Sites, Reservations, Showers, Tenters Welcome

Creekside Court   733-8841
C $17   35   35'   All Year
146 Addison Ave. W.
Credit Cards OK, Hookups, Pets OK

Pettit   737-3200
P $5   9   22'   Summer, Fall
27 mi. S. on Cty. Rd. G3
Drinking Water, Vault Toilets

Bear Gulch   678-0439
P   None   10   June-September
27 miles S of Twin Falls on Hwy 93, then 8 miles E on Foothill Rd, then 9 miles N on FR 500 and FR 513
Developed Campground, Handicap Accessible Drinking Water, Handicap Accessible Restrooms, Handicap Accessible RV Sites, Fishing, Hiking/Backpacking, Picnicking, Wildlife Viewing

Wendell

Intermountain Motor Homes & RV Park   536-2301
C $14-18   25   40'   All Year
I-84, exit 155 or 157
Drinking Water, Dump Station, Hookups, LP Gas, Modem Hookups, Pets OK, Pull-thru Sites, Reservations, Showers, Laundry, Handicap Access

Dining Quick Reference

Price Range refers to the average cost of a meal per person: ($) $1-$6, ($$) $7-$11, ($$$) $12-up. Cocktails: "Yes" indicates full bar; Beer (B)/Wine (W), Service: Breakfast (B), Brunch (BR), Lunch (L), Dinner (D). Businesses in bold print will have additional information under the appropriate map locator number in the body of this section.

MAP NO.	RESTAURANT	TYPE CUISINE	PRICE RANGE	CHILD MENU	COCKTAILS BEER WINE	MEALS SERVED	CREDIT CARDS ACCEPTED
2	Oxbow Cafe 199 E US Hwy 30, Bliss, 352-4250	Family	$$	Y	N	L/D	Major
2	Skinny Pig 700 Hwy 30, Bliss, 352-4356	Pizza	$	Y	N	L/D	M V
2	Ziggy's Express 745 Hwy 30, Bliss, 352-1070	American	$	N	N	L/D	M V
3	Coyote Joe's 426 Main St, Gooding, 934-9584	American	$	N	N	L/D	No
3	Dairy Queen 701 Main St, Gooding, 934-8127	Fast Food	$	N	N	L/D	No
3	El Commodore 127 3 Ave E, Gooding, 934-5852	Mexican	$	N	N	L/D	M V
3	Lincoln Inn Cafe 413 Main St, Gooding, 934-4423	American	$	N	Yes	B/L/D	Major
3	Rowdy's Pub & Grill 227 Main St, Gooding, 934-8003	American	$	N	Yes	L	M V
3	Woodriver Inn 530 Main St, Gooding, 934-4059	American	$-$$	Y	Yes	L/D	Major
4	Manhattan Cafe 133 S Rail St W, Shoshone, 886-2142	Family	$-$$	Y	N	B/L/D	Major
4	Shoshone Snack Bar 415 S Greenwood, Shoshone, 886-2294	American	$	N	N	B/L	No
4	Wyant's Taco Bell 805 S Greenwood, Shoshone, 886-2574	Fast Food	$	N	N	L/D	M V
5	New China Town 222 N Rail St W, Dietrich, 886-7169	Asian	$$	N	N	D	Major
6	Larry & Mary's Cafe 141 N State, Hagerman, 837-6475	American	$$	Y	B W	B/L/D	M V
6	Papa Kelsey 460 S State, Hagerman, 837-6680	Pizza	$	Y	N	L/D	M V
7	Grandstands 1003 Main, Buhl, 543-8064	American	$$	N	N	L/D	M V
7	Home Town Cookin' 1000 Burley Ave, Buhl, 543-2252	American	$-$$	Y	B W	L/D	M V
7	Jackson's Kountry Korner 1101 Broadway Ave N, Buhl, 543-6570	American	$-$$	Y	B W	L/D	M V
7	La Plaza 1206 Main St, Buhl, 543-8600	Mexican	$$	Y	N	L/D	Major
7	Subway 713 E US Hwy 30, Buhl, 543-2138	Fast Food	$	N	N	L/D	M V
7	Taco Maker Jake's Over the Top 715 Hwy 30, Buhl, 543-9169	Mexican	$	N	N	L/D	M V
7	Tacos El Korita 1051 Warren Ave, Buhl, 543-9954	Mexican	$	N	N	L/D	M V
9	Cedar Lanes 405 Hwy 30, Filer, 326-5902	Pizza/American	$	Y	B	B/L/D	Major
10	Boda's Bar 2695 Hwy 93, Hollister, 655-4350	Tavern	$	N	Yes	L/D	No
12	El Tapatio 88 S Idaho St, Wendell, 536-5584	Mexican	$-$$	N	N	L/D	M V
12	Farmhouse Restaurant 1955 B Frontage Rd S, Wendell, 536-6688	Steakhouse	$$-$$$	Y	N	B/L/D	Major
12	Wendell Snack Bar 319 S Idaho St, Wendell, 536-2118	Family	$	Y	N	B/L/D	No
14	Domino's Pizza 1976 S Lincoln, Jerome, 644-1300	Pizza	$	N	N	L/D	M V
14	McDonald's 2611 S Lincoln Ave, Jerome, 324-5505	Fast Food	$	Y	N	B/L/D	M V
14	Sonic Drive In 2700 S Lincoln Ave, Jerome, 324-7733	Fast Food	$	N	N	L/D	No

Dining Quick Reference - continued

Price Range refers to the average cost of a meal per person: ($) $1-$6, ($$) $7-$11, ($$$) $12-up. Cocktails: "Yes" indicates full bar; Beer (B)/Wine (W), Service: Breakfast (B), Brunch (BR), Lunch (L), Dinner (D). Businesses in bold print will have additional information under the appropriate map locator number in the body of this section.

MAP NO.	RESTAURANT	TYPE CUISINE	PRICE RANGE	CHILD MENU	COCKTAILS BEER WINE	MEALS SERVED	CREDIT CARDS ACCEPTED
15	China Village 123 S Alder, Jerome, 324-8777	Asian	$-$$	Y	B W	B/L/D	Major
15	Dino's Burger & Brew 402 DC Cir, Jerome, 324-6591	American	$-$$	Y	B W	L/D	No
15	El Sombrero Restaurant 143 W Main St, Jerome, 324-7238	Mexican	$	Y	Yes	B/L/D	Major
15	Idaho Pizza Company 220 W Main St, Jerome, 324-8858	Pizza	$	N	N	L/D	No
15	Dairy Queen 501 S Lincoln Ave, Jerome, 324-2500	Fast Food	$	N	N	L/D	No
15	Papa Kelsey's Pizza & Subs 222 S Lincoln Ave, Jerome, 324-7032	Pizza	$	N	N	L/D	Major
15	Sale Yard Cafes 313 3rd Ave W, Jerome, 324-6487	American	$	N	N	B/L	No
15	Sheppard's Drive In 306 S Lincoln Ave, Jerome, 324-4400	Family	$	Y	N	L/D	No
15	Taco Time 1100 S Lincoln Ave, Jerome, 324-2337	Fast Food	$	N	N	L/D	M V
15	The Double A Cafe 200 1st Ave W, Jerome, 324-2311	American	$-$$	N	N	B/L/D	M V
16	9 Beans & A Burrito 799 Cheney Dr Ste C, Twin Falls, 736-3773	Mexican	$-$$	N	B W	B/L/D	No
16	A Taste Of Thai 837 Pole Line Rd, Twin Falls, 735-8333	Asian	$$	N	N	L/D	No
16	Applebee's Neighborhood Grill & Bar 1587 Blue Lakes Blvd, Twin Falls, 735-0230	American	$$	Y	Yes	L/D	Major
16	Arby's 424 Blue Lakes Blvd N, Twin Falls, 734-8775	Fast Food	$	Y	N	L/D	Major
16	Arctic Circle 680 Blue Lakes Blvd N, Twin Falls, 733-3476	Fast Food	$	Y	N	L/D	Major
16	Chicago Connection Pizza 778 Falls Ave, Twin Falls, 733-7733	Pizza	$-$$	N	N	L/D	Major
16	Chili's Grill & Bar 1880 Blue Lakes Blvd N, Twin Falls, 734-1167	American	$$	Y	Yes	L/D	Major
16	Dairy Queen 805 Blue Lakes Blvd N, Twin Falls, 733-6557	Fast Food	$	N	N	L/D	No
16	Eduardo & Maria's Mexican Restaurant 1824 Blue Lakes Blvd, Twin Falls, 733-6695	Mexican	$-$$	N	N	L/D	Major
16	Golden Corral 1823 Blue Lakes Blvd N, Twin Falls, 735-1820	American	$$-$$$	N	N	B/L/D	M V
16	Idaho Joes 598 Blue Lakes Blvd N, Twin Falls, 734-9403	American/Steak/Seafood	$$	Y	B W	B/L/D	M V
16	Jaker's 1598 Blue Lakes Blvd N, Twin Falls, 733-8400	Steakhouse	$$	Y	Yes	L/D	Major
16	Johnny Carino's Italian Restaurant 1921 Blue Lakes Blvd N, Twin Falls, 734-4833	Italian	$$	Y	Yes	L/D	Major
16	Lotus House 1485 Poleline Rd, Twin Falls, 736-8988	Asian	$$	N	N	L/D	Major
16	Mandarin House 735 Blue Lakes Blvd N, Twin Falls, 734-6578	Asian	$$	N	N	L/D	Major
16	McDonald's 305 Blue Lakes Blvd N, Twin Falls, 734-5588	Fast Food	$	Y	N	B/L/D	Major
16	McDonald's 1485 Pole Line Rd E 204, Twin Falls, 736-0500	Fast Food	$	Y	N	B/L/D	Major
16	Montana Steak House 1826 Canyon Crescent, Twin Falls, 734-7476	Steakhouse	$$$	Y	Yes	B/L/D	Major
16	New China Buffet 570 Blue Lakes Blvd N, Twin Falls, 735-1225	Asian	$-$$	N	N	L/D	M V
16	New York Burrito 1239 Pole Line Rd E, Twin Falls, 733-9055	Mexican	$-$$	N	N	L/D	No

Dining Quick Reference - continued

Price Range refers to the average cost of a meal per person: ($) $1-$6, ($$) $7-$11, ($$$) $12-up. Cocktails: "Yes" indicates full bar; Beer (B)/Wine (W), Service: Breakfast (B), Brunch (BR), Lunch (L), Dinner (D). Businesses in bold print will have additional information under the appropriate map locator number in the body of this section.

MAP NO.	RESTAURANT	TYPE CUISINE	PRICE RANGE	CHILD MENU	COCKTAILS BEER WINE	MEALS SERVED	CREDIT CARDS ACCEPTED
16	Outback Steakhouse 1965 Blue Lakes Blvd N, Twin Falls, 733-4585	Steakhouse	$$	Y	B W	L/D	Major
16	Papa John's Pizza 960 Blue Lakes Blvd N, Twin Falls, 736-3333	Pizza	$	N	N	L/D	M V
16	Papa Kelsey's Pizza & Subs 637 Blue Lakes Blvd N, Twin Falls, 733-9484	Pizza	$	N	N	L/D	M V
16	Papa Murphy's Take 'N' Bake Pizza 562 Blue Lakes Blvd N, Twin Falls, 734-2977	Pizza	$$	N	N	L/D	Major
16	Peking Restaurant 824 Blue Lakes Blvd N, Twin Falls, 733-4813	Asian	$$	N	N	L/D	Major
16	Perkins Family Restaurant 1564 Blue Lakes Blvd N, Twin Falls, 736-8417	Family	$-$$	Y	N	B/L/D	Major
16	Pizza Hut 1099 Blue Lakes Blvd N, Twin Falls, 734-9063	Pizza	$	N	N	L/D	M V
16	Quizno's Subs 1111 Blue Lakes Blvd, Twin Falls, 737-0100	Fast Food	$	N	N	L/D	M V
16	Senor Caesars 645 Filer Ave, Twin Falls, 733-9716	Italian/Mexican	$$	Y	Yes	L/D	M V
16	Shari's Restaurant 1601 Blue Lakes Blvd N, Twin Falls, 734-2110	Family	$$	Y	N	L/D	Major
16	Sizzler 705 Blue Lakes Blvd N, Twin Falls, 733-8650	Family	$$	Y	N	L/D	Major
16	Skipper's Seafood'N Chowder House 334 Blue Lakes Blvd N, Twin Falls, 733-6977	Seafood	$$	Y	N	L/D	Major
16	Sonic Drive In 431 Blue Lakes Blvd N, Twin Falls, 736-8888	Fast Food	$	Y	N	L/D	M V
16	The Happy Burrito 772 Falls Ave, Twin Falls, 733-9323	Mexican	$	Y	N	L/D	M V
16	Wendy's Old Fashioned Hamburgers 818 Blue Lakes Blvd N, Twin Falls, 734-8255	Fast Food	$	Y	N	L/D	M V
17	Buffalo Cafe 218 4th Ave W, Twin Falls, 734-0271	American/Italian/Coffee	$$	Y	N	B/L	M V
17	Burger Stop 1335 Addison Ave E, Twin Falls, 734-0427	Family	$-$$	Y	N	B/L/D	No
17	Crowley's Soda Fountain & Gen Store 144 Main Ave S, Twin Falls, 733-1041	Family	$	Y	N	L	Major
17	Depot Grill 545 Shoshone S, Twin Falls, 733-0710	American	$-$$	N	N	B/L/D	Major
17	Dunken's Draught House 102 Main Ave N, Twin Falls, 733-8114	American	$-$$	N	B.W	L/D	Major
17	Frosty Mug Drive Inn 151 Blue Lakes Blvd, Twin Falls, 734-2958	Family	$	Y	N	L/D	M V
17	Gertie's Brick Oven Cookery 602 2nd Ave S, Twin Falls, 736-9110	Pizza/American	$-$$	N	B W	L/D	Major
17	Ground Round 2128 Kimberly Rd, Twin Falls, 736-6783	American/Tavern	$$-$$$	Y	Yes	B/L/D	Major
17	Happy Landing Restaurant 524 Airport Loop, Twin Falls, 736-3710	American	$-$$	Y	Yes	B/L/D	M V
17	Idaho Pizza Company 1839 Kimberly Rd, Twin Falls, 734-2778	Pizza	$$	Y	B	L/D	M V
17	Kelly's Breakfast & Lunch 110 Main Ave N, Twin Falls, 733-0466	Family	$	Y	N	B/L	M V
17	La Casita Mexican Restaurant 111 S Park Ave W, Twin Falls, 734-7974	Mexican	$-$$	Y	B W	L/D	Major
17	Little Caesars Pizza 820 Blue Lakes Blvd, Twin Falls, 733-7756	Pizza	$	N	N	L/D	Major
17	Loong Hing Restaurant 1719 Kimberly Rd, Twin Falls, 736-2882	Asian	$-$$	N	N	L/D	Major
17	Metropolis Bakery Cafe 125 Main Ave E, Twin Falls, 734-4457	Bakery/Café	$	Y	N	B/L	Major

Ultimate Idaho Atlas and Travel Encyclopedia

Dining Quick Reference - continued

Price Range refers to the average cost of a meal per person: ($) $1-$6, ($$) $7-$11, ($$$) $12-up. Cocktails: "Yes" indicates full bar; Beer (B)/Wine (W), Service: Breakfast (B), Brunch (BR), Lunch (L), Dinner (D). Businesses in bold print will have additional information under the appropriate map locator number in the body of this section.

MAP NO.	RESTAURANT	TYPE CUISINE	PRICE RANGE	CHILD MENU	COCKTAILS BEER WINE	MEALS SERVED	CREDIT CARDS ACCEPTED
17	Mister Burger 151 Blue Lakes Blvd, Twin Falls, 734-2958	American	$	N	N	B/L/D	Major
17	Norm's Cafe 803 Main Ave W, Twin Falls, 733-9735	Family	$$	Y	N	B/L/D	Major
17	Pizza Hut 1733 Addison Ave E, Twin Falls, 734-6170	Pizza	$	N	N	L/D	M V
17	Prasai's Thai Cuisine 428 2nd Ave E, Twin Falls, 733-2222	Asian	$$	N	N	L/D	M V
17	Pressbox Sports Bar 1749 Kimberly Rd, Twin Falls, 736-2427	American	$-$$	N	Yes	L	No
17	Shake Out 1186 Kimberly Rd, Twin Falls, 734-0300	American/Milkshakes	$	N	N	L/D	No
17	Sonic Drive In 2392 Addison Ave E, Twin Falls, 735-8080	Fast Food	$	Y	N	L/D	M V
17	Taco John's 1879 Addison Ave E, Twin Falls, 734-7280	Fast Food	$	Y	N	L/D	M V
17	Woody's Sports Bar and Grill 213 5th Ave S, Twin Falls, 732-0077	American	$	N	Yes	L/D	Major
17	Yoyo Cafe 1703 Addison Ave E, Twin Falls, 732-0044	Fine Dining	$$$	N	B W	L/D	M V
18	Addison West Restaurant 348 Addison Ave W, Twin Falls, 734-6722	Family	$-$$	Y	N	B/L/D	Major
18	Dairy Queen 379 Addison Ave W, Twin Falls, 734-8787	Fast Food	$	N	N	L/D	No
18	McDonald's 110 Addison Ave W, Twin Falls, 733-0088	Fast Food	$	Y	N	B/L/D	Major
18	Taco Bell Express 659 Addison Ave W, Twin Falls, 733-4476	Fast Food	$	Y	N	L/D	M V
18	West Addison 66 240 Addison Ave W, Twin Falls, 733-3427	Family	$	Y	N	L/D	Major
19	Russ' Market & Grill 115 W Wilson, Eden, 825-5933	American	$	Y	B W	B/L/D	Major
19	Traveler's Oasis Truck Plaza 1017 S 1150 E, Eden, 825-4147	American	$	Y	B W	B/L/D	Major
20	Fiesta Ole 144 Main S, Kimberly, 423-4333	Mexican	$	N	N	L/D	No
20	Maxie's Pizza & Pasta 626 Main N, Kimberly, 423-5880	Pizza/Italian	$-$$	Y	B	L/D	Major
21	Foothill Cafe 498 US Hwy 30 W, Hansen, 366-2536	American	$-$$	N	B W	B/L/D	Major
22	Sidewinders Bar & Grill 109 W Archer, Murtaugh, 432-5657	American	$	N	Yes	L/D	Major
24	Aguila Con El Taco 123 W 5th N, Burley, 679-1840	Mexican	$	N	N	L/D	No
24	Arby's 594 N Overland Ave, Burley, 678-8426	Fast Food	$	N	N	L/D	Major
24	Best Western Burley Inn & Convention Center 800 N Overland Ave, Burley, 678-3501	Family	$-$$	Y	N	B/L/D	Major
24	Burger King 114 W 5th N, Burley, 678-7779	Fast Food	$	Y	N	L/D	M V
24	Burgers Etc. 700 Overland Ave, Burley, 678-4189	American	$	N	N	L/D	No
24	China First 901 Overland Ave, Burley, 678-9399	Asian	$$	N	N	L/D	MV
24	George K's East Restaurant & Anchor Lounge 325 E 3rd N, Burley, 679-9173	American	$	Y	B W	L/D	Major
24	Guadalajara Mexican Restaurant 262 Overland Ave, Burley, 678-8695	Mexican	$$	N	N	L/D	Major
24	J B's Big Boy Family Restaurants 136 E 5th N, Burley, 678-0803	Family	$-$$	Y	N	B/L/D	Major

Dining Quick Reference - continued

Price Range refers to the average cost of a meal per person: ($) $1-$6, ($$) $7-$11, ($$$) $12-up. Cocktails: "Yes" indicates full bar; Beer (B)/Wine (W), Service: Breakfast (B), Brunch (BR), Lunch (L), Dinner (D). Businesses in bold print will have additional information under the appropriate map locator number in the body of this section.

MAP NO.	RESTAURANT	TYPE CUISINE	PRICE RANGE	CHILD MENU	COCKTAILS BEER WINE	MEALS SERVED	CREDIT CARDS ACCEPTED
24	Jack in the Box 491 Overland Ave, Burley, 678-3399	Fast Food	$	Y	N	L/D	No
24	McDonald's 415 Riverview Dr, Burley, 677-2230	Fast Food	$	Y	N	B/L/D	Major
24	McDonald's 394 N Overland Ave, Burley, 678-2230	Fast Food	$	Y	N	B/L/D	Major
24	Perkins Restaurant & Bakery 800 N Overland Ave, Burley, 678-1304	Family	$-$$	Y	N	B/L/D	Major
24	Subway 702 N Overland Ave, Burley, 677-2721	Fast Food	$-$$	Y	N	L/D	M V
25	A C Drive-In 601 E Main, Burley, 678-0141	Family	$	Y	N	L/D	No
25	Angela's Mexican Food 1198 E Main St, Burley, 678-9913	Mexican	$$	N	B	L/D	No
25	Charlie's Cafe 615 E Main, Burley, 678-0112	Family	$	Y	N	L/D	M V
25	China First 1242 Overland Ave, Burley, 678-7937	Asian	$$	N	N	L/D	M V
25	Dairy Queen 2200 Overland Ave, Burley, 678-9505	Fast Food	$	N	N	L/D	No
25	Domino's Pizza 2205 Overland Ave, Burley, 678-4993	Pizza	$-$$	N	N	L/D	M V
25	Edith's Cafe 144 E Hwy 81, Burley, 878-2248	Family	$	Y	N	B/L/D	Major
25	El Mercadito 407 E Main St, Burley, 878-0599	Mexican	$	N	B W	L/D	Major
25	Lee Chop Stick Restaurant 2126 Overland Ave, Burley, 678-2003	Asian	$-$$	N	N	L/D	M V
25	Little Caesars 2271 Overland Ave, Burley, 678-1223	Pizza	$	N	N	L/D	Major
25	Main Street Burger 333 W Main, Burley, 678-3020	Family	$	Y	N	B/L/D	Major
25	Michoacana II 1250 Overland Ave, Burley, 678-8288	Mexican	$$	N	N	L/D	Major
25	Nelson's Cafe & Pilot's Lounge 125 W Main, Burley, 678-7171	American	$	N	Yes	B/L/D	No
25	Papa Kelsey's Pizza & Subs 1061 Overland Ave, Burley, 678-5030	Pizza	$	Y	N	L/D	M V
25	Pizza Hut 2570 Overland Ave, Burley, 678-7867	Pizza	$-$$	Y	N	L/D	Major
25	Polo's Cafe 1255 Overland Ave, Burley, 878-7656	Family	$-$$	Y	N	B/L/D	M V
25	Price's Cafe 2444 Overland Ave, Burley, 878-5149	American	$-$$	N	N	B/L/D	Major
25	Shon Hing 109 E Main, Burley, 678-4950	Asian	$$	N	N	L/D	Major
25	Subway 2205 Overland Ave, Burley, 678-4225	Fast Food	$-$$	Y	N	L/D	M V
26	A&W Restaurant 326 S Hwy 24, Heyburn, 436-2929	Fast Food	$	Y	N	B/L/D	Major
26	Hub Plaza 332 S 600 W, Heyburn, 679-2122	American	$	N	N	B/L/D	Major
26	Taco Jalisco #2 1613 J St, Heyburn, 679-8226	Mexican	$	N	N	L/D	No
27	El Zaguan 210 Ellis St, Paul, 438-4444	Mexican	$	N	N	L/D	M V
27	Burgers Etc. 124 S Onea St, Rupert, 436-0600	Family	$-$$	Y	N	L/D	Major
27	Cathy's Kitchen 530 E St, Rupert, 436-0354	Family	$-$$	Y	N	B/L/D	Major

Dining Quick Reference - continued

Price Range refers to the average cost of a meal per person: ($) $1-$6, ($$) $7-$11, ($$$) $12-up. Cocktails: "Yes" indicates full bar; Beer (B)/Wine (W), Service: Breakfast (B), Brunch (BR), Lunch (L), Dinner (D). Businesses in bold print will have additional information under the appropriate map locator number in the body of this section.

MAP NO.	RESTAURANT	TYPE CUISINE	PRICE RANGE	CHILD MENU	COCKTAILS BEER WINE	MEALS SERVED	CREDIT CARDS ACCEPTED
27	China City Restaurant 5th & Scott Ave, Rupert, 436-8339	Asian	$	N	N	L/D	M V
27	Doc's Pizza 514 6th St, Rupert, 436-3300	Pizza	$	N	N	L/D	No
27	Drift Inn 545 F St, Rupert, 436-1300	Fine Dining	$$-$$$	Y	B W	L/D	Major
27	Figaro's Italian Kitchen 167 E 100 S, Rupert, 677-9999	Italian	$-$$	Y	N	L/D	M V
27	Loncheria El Veinte 1200 N Meridian, Rupert, 532-4821	Mexican	$-$$	N	N	L/D	No
27	Pizza Hut 302 Onea, Rupert, 436-1188	Pizza	$	N	N	L/D	M V
27	Playa Azul 531 5th, Rupert, 436-6713	Mexican	$$	N	N	L/D	M V
27	Subway 608 S Onea, Rupert, 436-0777	Fast Food	$	N	N	L/D	M V
27	Wayside 325 S 325 W, Rupert, 436-4800	American	$-$$	Y	B W	B/L/D	Major
29	Albion Cafe 228 W N St, Albion, 673-5404	American	$$	Y	Yes	L/D	Major
29	Sage Mountain Grill 251 W N St, Albion, 673-6696	American	$-$$	Y	Yes	L/D	Major
29	Blimpie 216 I 84, Declo, 654-2133	Fast Food	$	Y	N	L	Major
29	Jake's Over The Top 250 N Hwy 77, Declo, 654-9891	Family	$	Y	N	L	Major
29	Travel Stop #216 850 E 260 N, Declo, 654-2133	Family	$	Y	N	L	Major
32	Desert Dog Cafe/Saloon 190 S Main, Malta, 645-2258	American	$	N	Yes	L/D	Major

Motel Quick Reference

Price Range: ($) Under $40 ; ($$) $40-$60; ($$$) $60-$80, ($$$$) Over $80. Pets [check with the motel for specific policies] (P), Dining (D), Lounge (L), Disabled Access (DA), Full Breakfast (FB), Cont. Breakfast (CB), Indoor Pool (IP), Outdoor Pool (OP), Hot Tub (HT), Sauna (S), Refrigerator (R), Microwave (M) (Microwave and Refrigerator indicated only if in majority of rooms), Kitchenette (K). All Idaho area codes are 208.

MAP No.	HOTEL	NUMBER ROOMS	PRICE RANGE	BREAKFAST	POOL/ HOT TUB SAUNA	NON SMOKE ROOMS	OTHER AMENITIES	CREDIT CARDS
2	Amber Inn 17286 Hwy 30, Bliss, 352-1115	30	$/$$			Yes	P/D/DA	Major
2	Y-Inn Motel 260 Hwy 30, Bliss, 352-4451		$				P/D	Major
3	Cottage Inn 1331 S Main St, Gooding, 934-4055	16	$$			Yes	P/R/M/K	Major
6	Hagerman Valley Inn Frog's Landing Complex, Hagerman, 837-6196	16	$$			Yes	P/DA	Major
7	Oregon Trail Motel 510 S Broadway, Buhl, 543-8814	17	$$				P/DA	Major
7	Siesta Motel 629 Broadway, Buhl, 543-6427	12	$$				K	Major
12	Hub City Inn 115 S Idaho St, Wendell, 536-2326	10	$					
14	**Best Western Sawtooth** 2653 S Lincoln, Jerome, 324-9200	67	$$$$	CB	IP		P/D	Major
14	Crest Motel 2983 S Lincoln, Jerome, 324-2670	18	$$			Yes	P	M/V
15	Days Inn 1200 Centennial Spur, Jerome, 324-6400	73	$$$/$$$$	CB	HT/S	Yes	P/DA/K	Major

MAP No.	HOTEL	NUMBER ROOMS	PRICE RANGE	BREAKFAST	POOL/ HOT TUB SAUNA	NON SMOKE ROOMS	OTHER AMENITIES	CREDIT CARDS
15	Holiday Motel 401 W Main, Jerome, 324-2361	23	$/$$				P	Major
15	Towles Motel 261 E Main St, Jerome, 324-3267	14	$$			Yes	P	Major
16	Red Lion Hotel Canyon Springs 1357 N Blue Lakes Blvd, Twin Falls, 734-5000	112	$$$/$$$$		OP	Yes	P/DA/K	Major
16	Shilo Inn 1586 N Blue Lakes Blvd, Twin Falls, 733-7545	128	$$$$	FB	IP/HT/S	Yes	P/DA/R/M/K	Major
16	AmeriTel Inns 1377 N Blue Lakes Blvd, Twin Falls, 736-8000	118	$$$$	CB	IP	Yes	DA/R/M/K	Major
16	Weston Inn 952 N Blue Lakes Blvd, Twin Falls, 733-6095	25	$$	CB		Yes	P/DA/R/M	Major
16	Super 8 Motel - Twin Falls 1260 N Blue Lakes Blvd, Twin Falls, 734-5801	94	$$/$$$	CB		Yes	P/DA	Major
16	Holiday Inn Express 1910 Fillmore, Twin Falls, 732-6001	59	$$$$	CB	HT	Yes	R/M	Major
16	Comfort Inn 1893 Canyon Springs Rd, Twin Falls, 734-7494	52	$$$/$$$$	CB	IP	Yes	P/DA/M	Major
16	Motel 6 1472 N Blue Lakes Blvd, Twin Falls, 734-3993	132	$/$$		OP	Yes	DA	Major
16	Hampton Inn 1658 Fillmore St N, Twin Falls, 734-2233	75	$$$$	CB	IP/HT	Yes	P/DA/R/M	Major
17	Super 7 320 Main Ave S, Twin Falls, 733-8780	25	$$	CB	OP	Yes	P/DA/R/M	Major
17	Capri Motel 1341 Kimberly Rd, Twin Falls, 733-6452	23	$/$$			Yes	K	Major
17	Old Towne Lodge 248 2nd Ave W, Twin Falls, 733-5630	39	$				K	Major
17	Twin Falls Motel 2152 Kimberly Rd, Twin Falls, 733-8620	8	$$				P	Major
18	Branding Iron Motel 450 Addison Ave W, Twin Falls, 733-1438	10	$			Yes	R/M	
18	Holiday Motel 615 Addison Ave W, Twin Falls, 733-4330	18	$			Yes	P/R/M	Major
18	Best Western Apollo Motor Inn 296 Addison Ave W, Twin Falls, 733-2010	50	$$$	CB	OP	Yes	P/D/DA	Major
18	Dunes and Sands Motel 401 Addison Ave W, Twin Falls, 733-9141		$$$			Yes		Major
18	El Rancho 380 W Addison Ave, Twin Falls, 733-4021	14	$					M/V
18	Monterey Motor Inn 433 W Addison Ave, Twin Falls, 733-5151	28	$$		OP	Yes		Major
19	Amber Inn 1132 E 1000 S, Eden, 825-5200	25	$$			Yes	P	Major
24	Best Western Burley Inn & Convention Center 800 N Overland Ave, Burley, 678-3501	126	$$$	CB	OP	Yes	P/D/L/DA	
24	Budget Motel 900 N Overland, Burley, 678-2200	139	$$		OP	Yes	P/DA	Major
25	Evergreen Motel 635 W Main, Burley, 677-2769	13	$				DA	
25	Lampliter Motel 304 E Main, Burley, 678-0031	16	$				P	M/V
25	Parish Motel 721 E Main St, Burley, 678-5505	15	$$				DA/K	M/V
25	Powers Motel 703 E Main St, Burley, 878-5521	23					DA/K	M/V
25	East Park Motel 507 E Main, Burley, 678-2241							
26	Super 8 336 S 600 W, Heyburn, 678-7000	68	$$$	CB	IP	Yes	P/DA	Major
26	Tops Motel 310 S Hwy 24, Heyburn, 436-4724	16	$			Yes	P/D	Major
27	Flamingo Lodge Motel 406 E 8th St, Rupert, 436-4321	15	$/$$			Yes	DA/K	Major
29	Marsh Creek Inn 386 S Main St, Albion, 673-6259	12	$$	CB	HT	Yes	R	Major

SECTION 6

NORTHEAST AREA

INCLUDING IDAHO FALLS, ST. ANTHONY, REXBURG, AND TETON VALLEY

Extinct volcano vents created the St. Anthony Sand Dunes. Shoshone and Bannock Indian spirits supposedly haunt the area.

1

Kilgore
Pop. 30

Kilgore was settled as an agricultural community in 1885 and remained nameless for the first few months of its existence. In 1887, the town finally named itself after General James Kilgore, a gentleman who actively and bravely participated in the 1877 Nez Perce War events. A post office operated here from 1892 to 1965.

Spencer
Pop. 38

The Utah and Northern Railroad arrived here in 1879, bringing with it the birth of this town. The community draws its name from Hiram H. Spencer, a merchant and shipper who lived in the area during the line's construction. Although the town never attracted a large population, it has garnered national attention for its opals. In 1948, deer hunters stumbled upon a large deposit of the precious stones, which are formed underground in still pools of water. Layers of microscopic silica spheres reflect light in such a way to produce the gem's radiant rainbow colors. The Spencer Opal Mine offers tourists a chance to dig for their own opals.

H Beaver Canyon
Exit 180 on I-15 east of the interchange on road to Spencer

After Montana's gold rushes began in 1862, thousands of miners came past here, and a Beaver Canyon stage station was built here.

Freighters and travelers on stage lines from Salt Lake to Montana stopped at this station until Utah and Northern Railway service reached here in 1879. Large ranches also were supplied here until 1897, when they decided to move their Beaver Canyon town to a better site at Spencer.

T Spencer Opal Mines
Spencer. 374-5476.

The opal mine office is located in Spencer on Main Street's north end. Directions to the mine are available at the company office.

Few people realize how opals are formed or mined, but at the Spencer Opal Mines, visitors have the chance to learn about opals and potentially discover their own precious stone. Geologically, opals are hydrothermally deposited in successive layers in hollow geodes when a hot springs dries up.

While it is suspected that opals have hidden underneath Spencer's surface for hundreds of years, the first discovery of opals did not occur until 1948 when two lost deer hunters from nearby Rexburg happened upon the precious gem. This innocent discovery created the largest opal mine in the world and a major attraction in Spencer. Visitors can opt to purchase a permit and dig for their own opals, but they must provide their own tools and safety equipment. The mine is open daily from 8 AM to 8 PM Memorial Day to Labor Day.

T Camas Meadows Battle Sites
From Spencer, travel 18 miles northeast on the gravel road to Kilgore.

During the 1877 Nez Perce War with the U.S. Army, eastern Idaho was the site of many famous battles. These historic spots near Kilgore off I-15 are still visible.

Site 1 – Late evening of August 19, 1877
At 4:00 AM, Chiefs Looking Glass, Toohoolhollzote, and Ollokot rounded up twenty-eight warriors and sent them to General Oliver Howard's camp near Camas and Spring Creeks. The warriors' mission was to capture the cavalry horses, but when they arrived at the Army camp, pandemonium

broke loose. Instead of capturing the horses, the Indians accidentally stole away with the company's mules. With the Army in hot pursuit, fighting broke out. Few casualties were reported except that of an Army bugler.

To visit the site, drive four miles south from Kilgore to Idmon. Continue south one mile on Red Road, and then bear east one-half mile across Camas Creek. The battle site is situated in the flat valley between Camas and Spring Creeks. To visit the bugler's grave, proceed one-half mile across Spring Creek, and bear north one-half mile. The marked grave is found on the road's right side in a fenced area.

Site 2 – Morning of August 20, 1877
After the late evening/early morning encounter between the Native Americans and Army, Captain Randolph Norwood and the Second Calvary pursued the fleeing Indians. A four-hour battle ensued resulting in several casualties.

To visit the site, proceed approximately six miles east from Kilgore on A2 Clarks County Road. At the grouping of ranch buildings, bear right, and follow the dirt road to a lava rock formation. The battle took place in this area, and pits from flying bullets can still be found in the lava rock.

T Spencer Rock House
374-5359. In Spencer, drive under the I-15 overpass, bear right, and proceed downhill past the local bar & grill.

The Spencer Rock House has been unique since its 1919 origination. Charles Hardy was the builder and first owner of the craftsman-style home and was dismayed when he discovered a natural spring running through his basement. Despite Hardy's attempts to plug the spring, the water kept trickling in. Today, the current owners let the spring run naturally through this property listed on the National Register of Historic Places.

In addition to the spring, the home retains many of its original characteristics including 42-inch thick walls, toggle light switches, a footbath in the bathroom, and a small sleeping porch. Visitors are welcome to explore the home free of charge, but advance arrangements are requested.

2

T U.S. Sheep Experiment Station
Merge off I-15 at Exit 172, and proceed 2 miles east to the site.

The U.S. Department of Agriculture established the U.S. Sheep Experiment Station near Dubois in 1916. Operated in coordination with the Idaho Agricultural Station, the site investigates crossbreeding, nutrition, disease control, wool preparation, and range improvement. Sheep species used include approximately 6,000 Targhee, Columbia, Polypay, Rambouillet, and Finn Crossbred breeds. The site includes several office, laboratory, animal, and equipment buildings used in the elaborate research. Tours are available, but visitors should make advance arrangements.

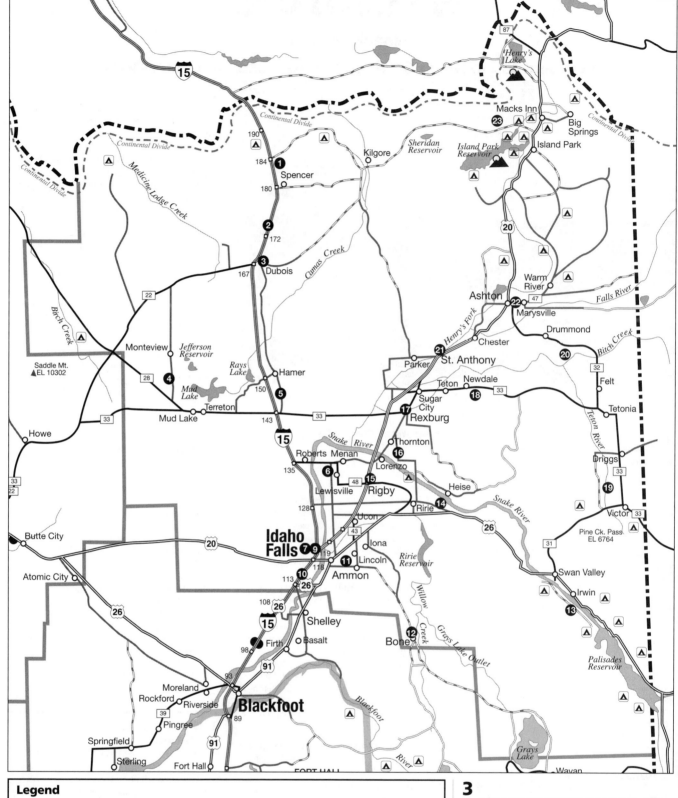

Legend

00 Locator number (matches numeric listing in section)

⬛ State Park

State Hwy.

⬛ Campsite

Rest stop

County Road

Interstate

Gravel/unpaved road

U.S. Hwy.

3

Dubois
Pop. 420

When settlers arrived in this area in the 1880s, the town was named after one of them, Fred Thomas Dubois. Fred was a U.S. Marshall who later became Idaho's Senator. The post office was established in 1892 and the settlement grew with the onset of successful farming that lasted from 1910-1920. After the farming boom fizzled, many of the residents, left town and most buildings were leveled. Today, the quiet town is best known for boasting a large grazing region.

H Nez Perce War
Milepost 167 on I-15 at the Dubois Rest Area

When General O. O. Howard tried to get more than 600 Nez Perce Indians to settle on a North Idaho reservation in 1877, he ran into a lot of trouble here.

On their way to Yellowstone Park, Chief Joseph's Nez Perce people reached Hole in the Rock Station (four miles north of here) on August 16, and shut down stage service to Montana. Howard's cavalry and volunteers followed only a day behind until August 20, when an Indian force made off with more than 100 Army mules. That raid halted military pursuit and forced Howard to continue his Nez Perce campaign for six more weeks.

T Heritage Hall Museum
1 block off Main St., Dubois.

The Heritage Hall Museum is housed within a Gothic Revival mission church and preserves the mission's history and artifacts. The museum is open from 2 PM to 5 PM on Fridays during the summer. Appointments can be made for private viewing during the rest of the year.

4 Lodging

Monteview
Pop. 10

The post office was established here in 1915. The town's first postmaster, Mabel E. Ellis, adopted the present name because of the settlement's panoramic view of the distant Gilmore Mountains. The area originated as and continues to be a farm and ranching region.

Mud Lake
Pop. 270

Mud Lake was formed along the shores of the lake bearing the same name. Cattlemen devised the moniker after the lake, which had a tendency to nearly dry up every year and provide cattle with only muddy water during late summer.

Terreton

Situated just two miles from the watering hole, Mud Lake, the tiny village of Terreton draws its name from Marshal M. Terry. Terry founded the community, became the area's first storeowner, and established a post office in 1920.

H Prehistoric Man
Milepost 44.3 on State Hwy. 28

Archaeological research has traced human occupation of this valley back more than 10,000 years.

The first men here found the valley forested. As the climate became drier, other mountain dwellers – known to archaeologists as people of the Bitterroot culture – settled here, perhaps about 8,000 years ago. These forerunners of the modern northern Shoshoni Indians lived in family bands and hunted big game, such as bison and mountain sheep.

T Mud Lake Historical Society
City Building, Mud Lake. 663-4376.

The Mud Lake Historical Society is dedicated to preserving the region's history. Visitors can browse through research archives highlighting important events in the area's development. The museum is open from 2 PM to 4 PM on the first and third Thursday of each month, and 2 PM to 4 PM on the second Monday with other times available by appointment.

T Birch Creek Massacre Site
On State Hwy. 28, 13.5 miles northwest of the State Hwy.s 28 and 22 junction.

In 1877, U.S. Army troops and Nez Perce Indians were not the only tragic casualties of the Nez Perce War. On August 15, the Nez Perce tribes of Chiefs Looking Glass, Joseph, and White Bird were fleeing from General Oliver Howard and traveling southeast towards Montana through Idaho's Birch Creek Valley. Much to their surprise, they happened upon a group of white travelers.

A group of eight wagons carrying three teamsters, a herder, two miners, and two Chinese laborers were peacefully enjoying their lunch when the Native Americans surprised them. Although eager to resume their journey to Salmon and deliver merchandise to Colonel George Shoup, the men graciously shared their lunch with the Indians. When the Indians discovered that the men were carrying barrels of whiskey, the encounter turned hostile. The Indians demanded that the men share the whiskey, and a raucous scene ensued. Sent to gather firewood, the Chinese laborers ran away, and the herder was able to slip back into the sagebrush. Unfortunately, the other five travelers were caught in a bloody battle where they lost their lives.

Fearing the worst for their counterparts, the Chinese fled to Salmon and contacted Colonel Shoup. Along with a group of volunteers and a band of Shoshone Indians, Shoup visited the tragic lunch spot and confirmed the Chinese men's fears – the wagons had been looted and burned and the five souls not lucky enough to escape had been killed. One week later, volunteers found the herder fearing for his life and hiding in the mountains.

Upon finding the bodies, Colonel Shoup and his men buried the remains on-site. Months later, the bodies were excavated and reburied in the Salmon cemetery. However, a marble marker identifies the massacre site along with the three teamster's names. The two miners are anonymously remembered as their names are still unknown to this day.

T Bison and Veratic Rockshelters
15.5 miles northwest of the junction of State Hwy.s 28 and 22; the site is located east of State Hwy. 28.

Idaho State University archaeology faculty excavations have revealed that Idaho's Birch Creek Valley has the most extensive history of buffalo hunting in all of North America. Funded through National Science Foundation grants, a team of archaeologists studied the area from 1959 to 1972 and discovered the Bison and Veratic Rockshelters. Radiocarbon dating and artifacts found in the shelters indicate that Northern Shoshone Native Americans continuously inhabited the shelters for 11,000 years. The last group to occupy the shelters was the Lemhi Shoshone from 1250 to 1850 A.D.

TV Mud Lake Wildlife Management Area
3 miles north of Mud Lake and Terreton. 663-4664. Merge off I-15 at Exit 143, and proceed to Mud Lake. At Mud Lake, turn onto County Rd. 1800 E. and drive to County Rd 1800 N. Bear west here and proceed 0.2 miles to County Rd. 1775 E. Turn north, and continue to 1900 N. Bear west here, and follow this road to the wildlife area.

Mud Lake Wildlife Manzgement Area was established in 1940 to preserve and improve waterfowl

nesting habitat. Starting out with just 607 acres, the management area has expanded to its present span of 8,853 acres thanks to subsequent land acquisitions. The area revolves around the 7,000-acre Mud Lake and its surrounding wetlands habitat. This lake measuring five miles deep is home to numerous waterfowl and mammals. Nearly 50,000 snow geese pass through the area in March and April, and the lake is populated with trumpeter swans and several species of ducks. Overhead, two species of hawks circle the skies and gaze down upon mule deer, white-tailed deer, and pronghorn antelope.

Visitors can gaze at the array of wildlife from the Kaster Overlook Tower situated on Mud Lake's north shore. To reach the overlook from the area's headquarters, travel two miles northwest along the main road to the first intersection. Bear right here and proceed one-quarter mile to another road junction. Turning right, proceed approximately two miles to the overlook. The entire management area is free and open year-round for camping, fishing, hunting, boating, and wildlife viewing.

V Sinks Drainages
Named after their characteristic sinking disappearance into the Snake River Plain Aquifer, the Sinks Drainages include the Big Lost and Little Lost Rivers as well as Beaver, Birch, Camas, and Medicine Lodge Creeks. Despite extensive habitat damage resulting from overgrazing and natural flooding, the drainages still maintain steady populations of small rainbow trout. Mountain whitefish are present only in the Big Lost River, and a few minor tributaries in the drainage area support native bull, cutthroat, and brook trout.

5 Food, Lodging

Hamer
Pop. 12

Easterners, who were later followed by Mormons, founded Hamer. The town draws its name from Illinois native, Colonel Thomas R. Hamer. Hamer moved to Idaho in 1893, later served as an Idaho legislator, and served in Congress from 1909 to 1911. The area's earliest Mormon settlers were responsible for establishing an artesian well irrigation system and successfully developed the local grain and hay industry.

H Market Lake
Milepost 142 on I-15 Southbound

The flat, irrigated fields that stretch to the next interchange used to be a great Indian and trappers' hunting ground in an old lake that came and went.

In historic times, Market Lake was formed during the great Snake River flood of 1853. When a new railroad grade blocked the overflow channel leading from the river, the lake disappeared for a time after 1887. Later, irrigation seepage restored the lake, and now the level is regulated for farming and a wildlife refuge.

H Menan Buttes
Milepost 70.3 on State Hwy. 33

Two cones of glassy lava are located directly south of here. The largest rises 800 feet above the surrounding plain.

Hot molten lava, erupting from great depth, met cold surface water in the west flood plain of the Snake River. The northern butte, in fact, formed in the channel of the Henry's Fork,

All Idaho Area Codes are 208

Section 6

Lewisville
Pop. 467

Lewisville was originally founded as a Mormon settlement. It is situated in Jefferson County.

Menan
Pop. 707

Founded as a Mormon settlement in 1879, this community was called Poole's Island, Heals Island, Cedar Butte, and Platt before finally arriving at its present moniker. Menan's current name was given in 1885 when the post office was established and is allegedly a Shoshoni Indian term meaning "island," or "many waters." The town itself lies amidst various bends in the Snake River, which would deem the name appropriate. The town continues to serve as a supply center for the surrounding agricultural area.

Roberts
Pop. 647

This small town is located on the southern end of a lake and waterfowl habitat area created during an 1863 Snake River flood. Prior to the site's development, Native Americans frequented the land, and Captain Bonneville's 1833 exploration party camped here while pursuing the area's abundant game.

A couple years after the lake's formation, Brigham Young led 142 of his followers here on his journey to Fort Lemhi. Young temporarily named the location Lava Lake. Market Lake was the next name applied, although few historians agree on the exact meaning behind the name. Some state the name was given because hunters and trappers "went to market" here for both necessity and livelihood. Others claim the name is derived from geese and ducks that were slaughtered and then sold here.

Regardless, the name didn't take hold. When the Union Pacific Railroad arrived in 1898 and the town was incorporated in 1910, officials changed the town's name to Roberts in recognition of Railroad Superintendent, H.A. Roberts.

T Menan Buttes
North of Menan on Twin Buttes Rd. Contact the Palisades Ranger District at 523-1412.

Menan Buttes are a National Natural Landmark and are recognized as two of the world's largest basaltic tuff cones. Formed during the late Pleistocene Era, the tuffs are made of volcanic glass formed from the sudden chilling of volcanic magma. Some geographers speculate that the buttes were formed from the interaction of magma with the ancient water source of the present day Snake River.

The North and South Buttes are nearly identical in shape and size. The crater at North Menan Butte measures 3,000 feet in diameter, and its cone rises nearly 800 feet. From the cone's top, visitors have access to panoramic views of the Snake River Valley and the winding Henry's Fork of the Snake River.

which was forced further east. Suddenly chilled into small particles of volcanic glass, the lava exploded in a great spray of steam and solid fragments that built up into windblown cones around large summit craters a half-mile long and 200 to 400 feet deep.

TV Camas National Wildlife Refuge
2150 E. 2350 N., Hamer. 662-5423. At Hamer, merge off I-15 and drive east through town to the frontage road. Bear north onto the frontage road, and proceed three miles. Following the highway signs, turn west, and continue two miles to the refuge headquarters.

The Camas National Wildlife Refuge spans 10,578 acres of lakes, ponds, creeks, marshlands, grasslands, sagebrush uplands, and meadows, and is one of America's 500 national wildlife refuges.

Known for its beautiful landscape, the refuge is home to a significant range of birds and mammals and is a wildlife enthusiast's dream come true. During spring and fall migration, almost 100,000 ducks have been spotted here, and nearly 180 species of birds continually frequent the refuge. Endangered and rare species such as trumpeter swans, bald eagles, and peregrine falcons are protected here. In addition, mammal sightings reported in the area include white-tailed deer, mule deer, pronghorn antelope, moose, elk, beavers, coyotes, and cottontail rabbits.

The refuge is open for wildlife viewing year-round, and recreationists can pursue off-road hiking, skiing, and snowshoeing from July 16 to February 28 each year. The free refuge opens 30 minutes prior to sunrise and closes 30 minutes after sunset.

Idaho Falls													
	Jan	Feb	March	April	May	June	July	Aug	Sep	Oct	Nov	Dec	Annual
Average Max. Temperature (F)	30.2	37.0	47.2	58.3	68.5	77.6	86.7	85.6	75.2	61.6	43.8	32.1	58.7
Average Min. Temperature (F)	13.0	17.6	24.6	31.8	39.7	46.7	52.3	50.2	41.7	32.2	23.4	14.5	32.3
Average Total Precipitation (in.)	1.03	0.93	0.99	1.12	1.62	1.28	0.56	0.75	0.85	0.94	0.99	1.04	12.11
Average Total Snowfall (in.)	8.2	5.3	3.1	0.9	0.4	0.0	0.0	0.0	0.0	0.5	3.2	7.1	28.7
Average Snow Depth (in.)	3	2	0	0	0	0	0	0	0	0	0	2	1

TV Market Lake Wildlife Management Area

20 miles north of Idaho Falls near Roberts. 228-3131. Taking Exit 135, merge off I-15 at Roberts, and proceed to County Rd. 2880 E. Bearing north onto this road, continue 0.5 miles through Roberts to a fork in the road. Turn right onto County Rd. 800 and follow to the wildlife area.

Located 4,780 feet above sea level, the Market Lake Wildlife Management Area sprawls across 5,000 acres. The area covers sandhills interspersed with igneous rock ledges and encompasses four distinct habitats: marsh/wetland meadow, desert uplands, Snake River riparian, and cropland. Due to the widely varying vegetation in each habitat, a diverse selection of wildlife populates the management area, while the lake supports yellow perch, bullhead trout, and Utah chubs. The area is free and open year-round for wildlife viewing, camping, fishing, hunting, and boating. Individuals should call the area headquarters for any seasonal restrictions on recreational activities prior to visiting.

7 *Food, Lodging*

Idaho Falls
Pop. 50,730

The first residents of this area were Shoshone-Bannock and Northern Paiute Indians. White settlers began arriving in the early 1860s when Harry Rickets constructed and operated a ferry across the Snake River. At the same time, James M. "Matt" Taylor was a hand for Ben Halliday's Overland Stage line between Salt Lake City and Virginia City, Montana. As Taylor was riding his horse one afternoon along the Snake River, he noticed a river section that was narrower than most places. Taylor concluded a bridge could be constructed there, and he rode to Montana to find supporters. After rallying the support of Ed Morgan and Bill Bartlett, Taylor began building his bridge. They worked during the winter of 1865, which allowed them access across the ice to work on both sides of the river. A sixty-foot long Queen-truss style bridge was their accomplishment.

Taylor's toll bridge was an instant success, and he and his partners took in nearly $3,000 each month in tolls. The miners and other settlers who landed on the east embankment of the river adopted the names of Taylor's Ferry, Taylor's Bridge, and Anderson's Bridge for the small town. In 1872, rumors of a forthcoming rail line persuaded Taylor to sell his bridge to the Anderson brothers. When the line did arrive, railroad officials renamed the town Eagle Rock. Some suggest the name is a reflection of the nearby Eagle Rock ferry, while others claim the name was chosen after a large rock resting in the middle of the river where bald eagles were known to nest. In either case, the railroad built its own bridge over the river just 150 feet downstream from Taylor's bridge, and the Andersons gave away 104 acres in Eagle Rock for

use as a railroad administrative site. The site's presence boosted the town's population to 670 in 1882. Times would soon change, though.

The railroad moved its headquarters to Pocatello just five years later. In addition, the gold in the mines was running out, and Eagle Rock's population began to dwindle. Realizing the undeveloped potential resting in the small community, Chicago developers convinced the townsfolk to change the name to Idaho Falls in 1891, despite no actual falls being located on the river at that time. In 1911, the city justified its name with the construction of a diversion dam and power plant that created a twenty-foot waterfall. This event helped ensure the future of Idaho Falls, and the area was developed into an agricultural center. Incorporated in 1900, Idaho Falls has boasted postal services since 1866 and was at one time the third largest city in the state.

H Taylor's Bridge
Exit 118 on I-15 Idaho Falls Business Loop

A landmark toll bridge spanned the Snake River at this rocky site in 1865, replacing the Eagle Rock Ferry, nine miles upstream.

James Madison Taylor (a relative of Presidents Madison and Taylor and a founder of Denver, Colorado) settled here in 1864 to develop an improved route for his freight line from Salt Lake to Montana's new gold mines. After his bridge was built, telegraph service reached here, July 16, 1866, and Eagle Rock (as Idaho Falls was known until 1890) became a regional transportation center. A railroad bridge was built adjacent to Taylor's Bridge in 1879.

H Eagle Rock Ferry
Exit 118 on I-15 Idaho Falls Business Loop

On June 20, 1863, Bill Hickman started a ferry nine miles up the Snake River for thousands of gold hunters headed for mines that now are in Montana.

Named for an eagle that had a nest on a rock here, his ferry flourished for two years. In 1864, J. Matt Taylor took it over and got an Idaho franchise to run it until he built a bridge here. Miners from Soda Springs and freighters from Salt Lake City all used Eagle Rock Ferry during Montana's gold rush.

H Elephant Hunters
Milepost 291.4 on U.S. Hwy. 20

Early day big game hunters, who occupied lava caves around here more than 12,000 years ago, had a diet that included elephants, camels, and giant bison.

When a gradual change to a warmer, drier climate made local grasslands into more desert, the elephant herds left for cooler plains farther north. But 8,000 years ago, bison still were available for hunting. Indians continued to hunt buffalo on these plains until 1840. Then they had to go to Montana for their hunting trips.

T Willard Arts Center & Colonial Theater
450 A St., Idaho Falls. 522-0471. www.idahofallsarts.org

The Willard Arts Center provides residents and tourists of Idaho Falls with a vast array of cultural enrichment experiences. Operated under the direction of the Idaho Falls Arts Council, the Willard Arts Center features three art galleries, three classrooms for arts appreciation/education, and a conference room. The center showcases touring exhibits as well as local artists, and features

the works of both adults and children. Past exhibitions have included ceramics, textiles, glass, photography, paintings, and bronze sculptures. Exhibits rotate every two to three months.

Also inside the Willard Arts Center is the popular Colonial Theater. Seating up to 970 individuals, the theater hosts a diverse display of entertainment throughout the year. Symphonies, local choirs, bluegrass and country musicians, and string quartets are joined by Broadway musicals, comedy troupes, and cultural and historical presentations. Famous performers and speakers continually frequent the theater, and past guests have included Ray Charles and Charleton Heston. Advance tickets are recommended for the range of shows presented here.

T Eagle Rock Art Museum and Education Center
300 S. Capital Ave., Idaho Falls. 524-7777. www.eaglerockartmuseum.org

After ten years of planning, the Eagle Rock Art Museum and Education Center in conjunction with the city of Idaho Falls opened its doors on October 19, 2002. Overlooking the Snake River, Eagle Rock is the newest museum in Idaho with a mission to culturally enrich the lives of residents and visitors. With the assistance of the Eagle Rock Art Guild, Eagle Rock strives to collect, preserve, and display Idaho artists' varied works of art. In addition, Eagle Rock offers community education classes for both young and old. The museum is open from 6 PM to 9 PM on Mondays, 10 AM to 4 PM Wednesday through Saturday, and 1 PM to 4 PM on Sundays. Admission is free.

In association with the museum, Eagle Rock Art Guild offers an annual summer sidewalk art show. Artists from around the Rocky Mountain Region are featured, and works include pottery, paintings, and jewelry. The event also features a variety of food vendors and live entertainment.

T The KNOW Place
Next to the Downtown Development Corporation, Idaho Falls. Contact the Idaho Falls Chamber of Commerce at 523-1010 or (800) 634-3246.

This interesting science museum helps kids learn and have fun at the same time. The KNOW Place offers several hands-on science exhibits sure to entertain and intrigue kids of all ages. The museum is open year-round by appointment.

T Museum of Idaho
200 N. Eastern Ave. (at the corner of Elm and Eastern), Idaho Falls. 522-1400.

Originally known as the Bonneville Museum and housed within a historic Andrew Carnegie endowed building, this museum has undergone a recent facelift. After adding 20,000 square feet to the original building, the new museum opened in February 2003 under its new name, the Museum of Idaho. As one of Idaho's largest museums, the facility presents the natural and cultural history of Idaho and the Rocky Mountain region. The Museum of Idaho features several permanent exhibits as well as numerous rotating displays and is proud to now offer educational programs. The museum is open Monday through Saturday from 10 AM to 8 PM and is operated by the Bonneville County Historical Society.

T Walking Tour of Idaho Falls' Historic Downtown

Contact the Idaho Falls Downtown Development Corporation for more information. 535-0399.

Robert Anderson and Matt Taylor laid the foundations for Idaho Falls when they opened the area's first trading post in 1865. Although the settlement was initially a crossroads on the way to other Western destinations, settlers eventually began to see opportunity in this frontier place. By the mid 1880s, an early business district was growing that would later swell to encompass present day Broadway Ave.. Although none of the original buildings from the 1880s boom remain, several prominent buildings erected between 1894 and 1940 stand as a testament to this town's long legacy. The buildings represented on this historic downtown tour reflect different architectural and construction styles and the growth of Idaho Falls.

Rocky Mountain Bell Telephone Company Building
246 W. Broadway
Built in 1910 by the Rocky Mountain Bell Company, this Renaissance Revival style building was used as the town's telegraph office until the late 1920s. Upon its closure, the Idaho Falls' Catholic Church purchased the building, renamed it Faber Hall, and used it as a church parish hall for several years. In 1953, the building changed hands again. A local carpenter's union purchased the building as a meeting hall, at which time the building received its current nickname "Labor Temple." Today, the building is used as a private residence.

Shane Building
381 Shoup Ave.
This building features a Renaissance Revival design embellished with terra cotta accents. Constructed in 1915, the building's first floor was home to a grocery store, furniture store, and a women's clothing store.

Montgomery Ward Building
504 Shoup Ave.
During the 1920s and early 1930s, Idaho architects favored a Renaissance Revival style with Art Deco accents. This building constructed in 1928 was used as the Montgomery Ward and Company Department Store and is an excellent example of this design style. Amazingly, the building has never been significantly remodeled in its near eighty years of existence.

Idaho Falls City Building
308 Constitution Way
Lionel E. Fisher designed this building in a Beaux Arts architectural style. This design is rare in the architectural styles favored throughout much of Idaho, but its stately appearance is fitting for the building's intended use as a city hall. Constructed in 1929 and 1930, the building's exterior remains unaltered and the interior lobby tiles are original.

Underwood Hotel
347 Constitution Way
This elaborate Renaissance Revival style building was erected in 1918 for one of Idaho Falls' earliest woman entrepreneurs, Jennie Underwood. Bearing her name, the building served as a hotel primarily for Oregon Shortline Railroad passengers awaiting their own departure or the arrival of a loved one.

Bonneville Hotel
410 Constitution Way
The Idaho Falls Community Hotel Corporation along with 421 local citizens constructed this Italian Renaissance building in 1926 and 1927. Created to bring a convention facility and premier hotel to Idaho Falls, the building cost $335,000. Upon its completion, the Bonneville Hotel included a ballroom, two elaborate dining rooms, a sample room, and a large central lobby to accommodate all the needs of its first-class guests.

Hotel Idaho
482 Constitution Way
Despite skepticism from his critics, F.C. Hansen went ahead and built the Hotel Idaho amid a neighborhood of vacant land and single-family homes. Upon its completion in 1917, the building not only housed a hotel, but also a business college and auto dealership. The Hotel Idaho's doors were open for business until 1979. Today, the building is home to several different offices.

Bonneville County Courthouse
605 N. Capital
Constructed immediately after World War I using concrete with a brick veneer, the Bonneville County Courthouse represents a simple, classic design. Charles Aitken and Lionel E. Fisher designed the building whose interior includes elegant marble stairs and wainscot, stained glass skylights, and mosaic floor tiles.

Former Idaho Falls Federal Building
591 N. Park Ave.
Philadelphia native, James A. Wetmore, designed the city post office in 1914 in a Georgian Revival style. At a cost of $86,199, the post office was completed in 1916. The U.S. Postal Service occupied the building until 1986, and throughout the years, the building was shared with the U.S. Geological Survey, the Civil Service Investigator, the Defensive Service Investigator, and the U.S. Department of Agriculture News. Upon the postal service's move, private investors purchased the building and remodeled the interior into its current use as various company offices.

Kress Building
541 Park Ave.
Between 1930 and 1932, this building was constructed for the S. H. Kress and Company. The building features a unique use of terra cotta and remains relatively unaltered from its original state.

I.O.O.F. Building
393 Park Ave.
Although Idaho Falls was still a fairly small settlement in the late 1880s and early 1890s, it did feature a thriving I.O.O.F. chapter. As the group continued to grow, the organization needed a new meeting place to accommodate all of its members. In 1909, this building was erected for that purpose, and it features the city's only remaining example of a Romanesque Revival architectural style. When it was first constructed, the building also housed a movie theater, funeral parlor, and grocery store. Today, the building retains its intended purpose as an I.O.O.F. lodge.

Farmers and Merchants Bank Building
346 Park Ave.
This building features a simplified version of the Renaissance Revival architectural style popular in Idaho Falls during World War I. Although the building now features a brick veneer, the building's early years were simply characterized with red and white sandstone. The building was constructed as the Farmers and Merchant Bank. The bank later shared the building with a drug store and a candy/tobacco store.

Hasbrouck Building
362 Park Ave.
At the turn of the twentieth century, stone buildings dominated the architectural style of Idaho Falls' business district. This building best represents this design principle, and construction on the basement and first floor began in 1895. Nebraska native and attorney, Herman J. Hasbrouck, used the original building for the Idaho law practice he began in 1890. In 1905, the second story was added, and Hasbrouck remained in the building until 1915.

The Colonial Theater
466 A St.
At a building cost of $175,000, the Colonial Investment Company completed the Colonial Theater in 1919. Owned at the time by some of Idaho Falls' most prominent residents, the building was hailed as Idaho's finest theater. Today, the Renaissance Revival style theater continues to be a popular city venue, and it retains its original terra cotta façade.

Former Idaho Falls Public Library
Elm Ave. & N. Eastern Ave.
With $15,000 in financial assistance from the Andrew Carnegie Corporation, Idaho Falls completed its first public library in 1916. The library's completion was due in great part to the Village Improvement Society, a group of wealthy Idaho Falls women who strove to improve the appearance of Idaho Falls and expand local attractions. From 1938 to 1940, a new Art Deco entrance was added to the library. Today, the former library is home to the Bonneville County Museum.

T Ridge Ave. Historic District Walking Tour

Idaho Falls. For more information, contact the City of Idaho Falls Planning and Building at 529-1276.

Before 1890, most residential building in Idaho Falls was restricted to the south of Broadway Ave. near the railroad and the Snake River. As the town's population began to swell, though, new residents flocked to the Ridge Ave. District, and the Idaho Register documented this building boom in 1896.

The first residents of Ridge Ave. came from all occupational backgrounds, from railroad workers to renowned lawyers. The style of houses they chose were just as diverse. This district provides exceptional examples of changing architectural styles. From modest Queen Anne's to Craftsman and Prairie styles, the houses have been lovingly cared for throughout the years and retain their distinctive features. This walking tour explores the history of sixty-five of Ridge Ave.'s 101 historical buildings.

313 N. Water Ave.
Stonemason, Isreal Vadboncoeur, built this home in 1896 and 1897 for Oregon Short Line Railroad stationmaster, George Changnon. The home was one of the first residences built east of the railroad, and its Craftsman style porch was added twenty years later. When Changon sold his home, it became a community mortuary.

327 N. Water Ave.
This simple Queen Anne style house was built between 1903 and 1905 and was home to Dr. G. W. Cleary. The home's porch still features original spindlework supports.

343 N. Water Ave.
Ralph A. Louis was an influential man who served as Idaho Falls' mayor from 1917 to 1919 and again from 1921 to 1927. This Queen Anne home was one of his first residences in the community.

344 N. Water Ave.
During the early twentieth century, Richard and Sadie Barry occupied this Queen Anne home. The

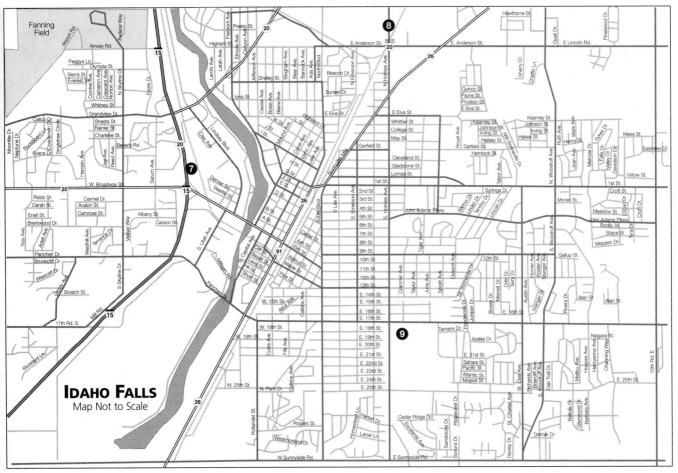

Idaho Falls
Map Not to Scale

house is unique as it features an inset porch, a steeply pitched roof, and an arched opening.

387 N. Water Ave.
Coltman Lumber Company owner, Edward P. Coltman, built this home in sometime prior to 1903. Coltman served as Idaho Falls' mayor from 1904 to 1907 and again from 1909 to 1910. His home was unusual for its time as it included eight dormers and a pyramidal shaped roof.

400 N. Eastern Ave.
Owner of the Idaho Café, W. Jay Brown was the first resident of this classical Queen Anne style home. The building is constructed out of cement blocks, a popular residential building material commonly used at the turn of the century. The building was originally to be used as a boarding house, but became a single-family dwelling instead.

422 N. Eastern Ave.
W. Jay Brown built this home as a rental for early business owners and railroad workers who were contributing to Idaho Falls' population growth. The house features an expansive front porch and gables.

468 N. Eastern Ave.
The exact building date of this home is uncertain, but it is speculated that construction was completed sometime between 1911 and 1921. The Craftsman style home is modest and features multi-paned windows and square wood supports.

156 Poplar
William P. Dawe built this simple Queen Anne home as a rental for the town's first workers. The cottage features spindlework on its full front porch.

491 N. Water
Idaho Falls' City Clerk, William P. Dawe, was one of the first occupants of this wood-sided home. The residence also features a small portico.

477 N. Water Ave.
This home is unique in the Ridge Ave. District due to its full porch and frieze accented with spindle-work supports. Dr. T. M. Bridges built this home prior to 1903 and was its first occupant. Bridges enjoyed a successful medical career in Idaho Falls along with his associate, Dr. Franklin LaRue.

478 N. Water Ave.
This home was built in 1903 as a residence for early settler, Ellen Moen. The small brick house features a gable with fishscale shingles, and the upstairs was originally accessed strictly through an exterior stairwell.

461 N. Water Ave.
This home features corner boards and fishscale shingled gables. The home was built sometime prior to 1910, and the first resident was F. H. Hollister.

460 N. Water Ave.
Thomas and Mary Wilson built this basalt stone home as a boardinghouse for local workers. The two-story home was constructed sometime in the early 1900s.

440 N. Water Ave.
This simple Queen Anne building was erected prior to 1903. Among its first occupants were the Charles W. Mulhall Real Estate, Loans, and Insurance business.

408 N. Water Ave.
Leslie B. Murphy, partner of the Clay and Murphy automobile dealership, had this home built in the early 1900s. The home features unique rounded

windows, fishscale shingled gables, and corner boards.

409 N. Water Ave.
Originally from Illinois, teamster Marquis L. McKee built this home in the late 1890s. It represents one of the first homes constructed east of the railroad and features a Queen Anne inspired design with a steeply pitched roof. McKee later built his famed "McKee Flats" behind his house that served as apartments for generations of Idaho Falls' workers.

233-241 Cedar St.
Leslie B. Murphy built this Craftsman duplex between 1915 and 1921. The duplex retains its original sense of style accented with concrete piers, wood railings, and cross-gabled porches.

255 Cedar St.
In approximately 1915, Henry Scarborough built this Craftsman style one-story bungalow. The home features multi-paned windows and a front porch supported with wooden piers.

406 N. Ridge Ave.
Wilford D. Huffaker was a prominent community figure in Idaho Falls' fledgling years. Huffaker served as Bonneville County Commissioners' Chairman and was president of the Iona Mercantile Company. His gabled Queen Anne home is embellished with spindlework detailing and fishscale shingles.

460 N. Ridge Ave.
Barzilla W. Clark enjoyed a life in the Idaho spotlight. He served as the Thousand Springs Land and Irrigation Company's manager and vice-president and also acted as Idaho Falls' mayor from 1913 to 1915 and 1927 to 1936. In 1936, Clark

won a two-year term as Idaho governor. During his residence in Idaho Falls, Clark occupied this brick bungalow featuring a unique curved railing.

482-486 N. Ridge Ave.
Idaho Falls' postmaster, Mr. Coltman, built this one and one-half story duplex around 1915. It reflects the building trends of the era as it features wood shingles, clapboard siding, brick piers with wood supports, and large overhanging eaves. The home still features its original doors.

498 N. Ridge Ave.
Before Mr. Coltman assumed his title as community postmaster, he was employed with the Western Land Company prior to 1903. This Queen Anne home represents Coltman's first building project, and the house features a gabled roof, clapboard siding, and fishscale shingles.

485 N. Ridge Ave.
The Louis A. Haley residence represents the popular bungalow style of the early 1900s. Erected in 1907, the home features numerous windows, exposed rafters, and overhanging eaves. One of Idaho Falls' first travel agents was the original occupant.

495 N. Ridge Ave.
This Craftsman style home retains much of its original character, including exposed rafters and overhanging eaves. The home was built around 1915 and was first occupied by a manager of the Western Machinery and Equipment Company.

520 N. Ridge Ave.
Known as the George Apartments, this Prairie style building was constructed around 1917 and quickly became known as the finest apartment building in the entire Northwest. Building costs

were estimated at $75,000, and the apartments remain adorned with multi-paned windows, terra cotta pendants, white stone trim, and interior marble wainscoting.

527 N. Ridge Ave.
Mary McCann enjoyed a prosperous career as the town corsetiere who helped Idaho Falls' women stay up to date in shape and style. Her brick Tudor Revival home was constructed sometime prior to 1926, and the house features multi-paned windows and an arched opening over the front door.

543 N. Ridge Ave.
Previously a judge in Saginaw, Michigan, Otto E. McCutcheon moved westward and became the attorney for the Great Western Canal Company. During his residence at this large two-story home, McCutcheon played an integral part in formulating Idaho's early irrigation regulations.

557 N. Ridge Ave.
Early Idaho Falls' mayor (1903-1904), Alvin T. Shane, became the first resident of this home in approximately 1911. The home features an upper gable extension and halve-timbered accents.

573 N. Ridge Ave.
This home featuring overhanging, bracketed eaves and stout wood porch supports represents another example of Idaho Falls' love of the Craftsman design. Charles C. Wilson served as Idaho Falls' assistant postmaster and was the home's first occupant.

344 Poplar Street
This home represents the third residence that Wilbert J. Coltman constructed in the Ridge District. To this date, the home retains its classical design and accents.

798 S. Boulevard
Outgrowing his existing practice, Dr. H.D. Spencer moved his hospital to this building in 1921 and continued practicing until 1941. At that time, the Franciscan Sisters of Perpetual Order Adoration purchased the building and turned it into the Sacred Heart Hospital. In 1949, the Order moved their hospital to a different location, at which time Dr. W.R. Abbott acquired the building and started the Idaho Falls Clinic.

425 Ash Street
This stately Colonial Revival home was built for D.F. and Gladys Richards in 1939. D.F. Richards became president of the Bowen Curley's American National Bank and also served as director of the San Francisco Federal Reserve Board. The home is embellished with Doric columns supporting a small portico at the entrance.

309 N. Placer Ave.
Herman J. Hasbrouck, a native Nebraska attorney who practiced law in Idaho Falls from 1890 to 1915, built this Colonial Revival home in 1907. Hasbrouck played an important role in the town's development and later served a two-year term in the Idaho Senate.

363 N. Placer Ave.
Constructed around 1931, this residence features Tudor styling and is one of the newest homes in the Ridge Ave. District. Geological Survey District Engineer, Lynn Crandall, first occupied this home featuring steep gabled roofs and half-timbered siding.

383 N. Placer Ave.
Although the original front porch has been removed, this Queen Anne style home still retains its original wood siding, wood accents, and fish-

scale shingles. The first occupant was Albert W. Rates who served as co-owner of Vogel and Rates Meats.

391 N. Placer Ave.
Local painter, George H. Warner, built this Queen Anne home in the early 1900s. He also built a paint shop behind the home that has since been remodeled into another home.

390 N. Ridge Ave.
This home features another impressive example of the Colonial Revival design popular in the 1930s and 1940s. Emery Owens constructed this home adorned with clapboard siding, multi-pane windows, and Doric columns.

370 N. Ridge Ave.
The Prairie style design of this home is associated with Frank Lloyd Wright and was developed by a firm of Chicago architects. The Prairie style design was short-lived in Idaho Falls' popularity, but the home has been well-preserved and retains its casement windows, lineal brick pattern, and overhanging eaves. The residence was built in 1917 and was first home to William Luxton, early Idaho Falls' entrepreneur and partner of Luxton Brothers Meats.

371 N. Ridge Ave.
Gilbert G. Wright built this stylish Queen Anne home in 1909. The residence is adorned with numerous classical detailings, including Ionic columns and modillions. Wright was a successful Idaho Falls' business owner, managing the Consolidated Wagon and Machine Company as well as the Idaho Falls Milling Company.

353 N. Ridge Ave.
Idaho Falls' lawyer, Oscar A. Johannsen, built this Queen Anne home between 1905 and 1911. The residence is unique as it features distinctive shingled porch supports.

345 N. Ridge Ave.
Orley K. Wilbur, vice-president of Farmers and Merchants Bank, constructed this home around 1914. The impressive brick bungalow features a stone foundation, lintels, and watertable.

340 N. Ridge Ave.
Charles A. Merriman built this unusual home sometime prior to 1903. Styled in a Queen Anne design, the home features classic accents on the window below the gable. Renowned president of the Holz Cigar and Tobacco Company, Clifford Holz, later occupied the home.

312 N. Ridge Ave.
This home is actually the second residence to occupy this site. Although little is known about the original house, the current Colonial Revival structure was built around 1920 and was occupied by mercantile owner, Eugene Wright. The home features unusual tapered wood columns and front shed dormers.

288 N. Ridge Ave.
This house features a combination of Queen Anne and Craftsman style details and was built around 1903. Frank and Minnie Hitt were the first occupants of the home. Mrs. Hitt was one of the first settlers in the Idaho Falls' area, and she started working at the Anderson Brothers Bank at age seventeen when Idaho Falls was still known as "Eagle Rock."

262 N. Ridge Ave.
Attorney Harrison Linger constructed this Craftsman inspired home between 1905 and 1911. The multi-paned windows characterizing Craftsman architecture are unusually small in this home.

325 Elm St.
Pennsylvania native, J.C. Fulton, designed the Neo-Classical Revival style First Presbyterian Church. The church was completed in 1920 and was added in 1978 to the National Register of Historic Places.

310 Elm St.
Around 1901, State Bank cashier Clinton G. Peck built this home. The residence is modeled in a Queen Anne design and features an elaborate spindlework porch.

346 Elm St.
Architect John W. Dill built this home between 1911 and 1921. The residence is distinctively Craftsman inspired with its decorative rafters, overhanging eaves, large porch supports, and a curved railing.

197 N. Placer Ave.
The Craftsman style home was popular in Idaho Falls for a period of several years. Frank Sheppard built this home in 1908 with a front gabled porch supported by large stone piers.

173 N. Placer Ave.
Blacksmith Robert Keddie's widow, Flora Keddie, was this home's first occupant. The brick bungalow features a distinctive false balcony on the top floor.

135 N. Placer Ave.
Edward Rowles was a prominent downtown businessman who was president of a company specializing in men's clothing. With his successes, Rowles built this impressive Colonial Revival home complete with sun porch, columns, multi-pane windows, and a gabled portico.

101 N. Placer Ave.
This unique Queen Anne features large columns dominating the architectural design. Dr. Fuller lived here in the early 1900s and established the Fuller and Soderquist Hospital in his home. In 1917, Dr. H.D. Spencer bought the Fuller's home/hospital. Both Dr. Fuller's wife and Dr. Spencer's wife noted great entertaining difficulties in leading guests through the second floor surgery unit to the third floor guest facilities.

315 Walnut St.
Harness maker, P.B. VanBlaricom, built this home between 1896 and 1897. The basalt foundation home is another one of the earliest homes built in the Ridge Ave. District east of the railroad.

151 N. Ridge Ave.
Sundberg and Sundberg designed this brick building built by Reed Construction Company from Pocatello. Construction on the O.E. Bell Junior High School began in 1928, and the first wing held classes in 1930. A north addition was added between 1935 and 1937, at which time cold winter winds whisked through the school's hallways and nearly froze out teachers and students.

258 Walnut St.
Utilizing his financial success as manager of the Great Western Canal and Improvement Company, A.D. Morrison built this stone home in 1896. The home features a Colonial Revival inspired design complete with Paladin windows and an inset porch. Morrison later sold the home to Claude C. Campbell, president of Anderson Brothers Bank.

290 Walnut St.
Nils Hoff, owner of Nils Hoff Grain and Coal Company, had this home built around 1900. The home once included several side porches that have since collapsed or been enclosed. However, the front window with entablature is original.

101 S. Ridge Ave.
O.J. Ellis was the first occupant of this Queen Anne home built between 1905 and 1911. The exterior siding has been replaced throughout the years, but the home's original design and massing remain the same.

188 S. Ridge Ave.
Carl Nation served as manager of the Sanitary Cash Grocery Company. With his earnings, Nation bought this Colonial Revival home and became its first occupant. The home features multi-pane windows, a portico, and carved Doric columns typical of this architectural style.

190 S. Ridge Ave.
Guy Smith served as one of Idaho Falls' earliest reputable dentists. He and his wife, Ethyl, built this Mission Revival home in 1917. The residence features an arched porch opening with overhanging eaves and numerous windows.

185 S. Ridge Ave.
For early residents, Geo. M. Scott and Sons was the place to go for stationary and correspondence. Owner Rollin C. Scott turned his profits into an impressive brick Tudor Revival style home.

288 Maple Street
Kate and Bowen Curley were members of Idaho Falls' elite society. While Bowen served as the American National Bank President and also as town mayor for two two-year terms, Kate was president of the women's Village Improvement Society, a group of wealthy women interested in improving the appearance of early Idaho Falls. Their home is a rare example of a Shingle design and features stone and basalt walls with wood shingles.

240 S. Ridge Ave.
Kate and Bowen Curley's daughter, Ethyl Smith, built this Colonial Revival home in the early 1920s.

270 S. Ridge Ave.
C. Fred Chandler was the first occupant of this Queen Anne home built between 1903 and 1905. The home features dormer fanlights and an unusual cut-away bay window.

284 S. Ridge Ave.
Holden and Eckhardt were well-respected attorneys in Idaho Falls' early days. Capitalizing on his success, Arthur Holden built this home between 1903 and 1905. The bungalow features a hipped roof and wood shingle exterior.

309 S. Ridge Ave.
This classical Queen Anne was built around 1903 for Louis A. Hartert. Hartert was co-owner of Johannsen and Hartert Real Estate and Loans.

291 S. Ridge Ave.
Built in 1916, this Colonial Revival home is embellished with a column-supported portico, a fanlight over the door, and beveled wood siding. The home was built for L.O. Naylor who managed the N.O. Taylor Studebaker Motor Cars Company.

257 S. Ridge Ave.
This home was originally built as a one and one-half story boardinghouse and private residence in 1901. In 1915, a framed addition was joined to the stone structure. D.B. Bybee, owner of the Idaho Saloon, was the first resident, while Addison V. Scott and his wife were the second occupants. Mrs. Scott was Idaho's first female justice of the peace.

225 S. Ridge Ave.
This classic Queen Anne was built around 1903 for Bertha Anderson. City school superintendent, Benjamin R. Crandall, later occupied the home with its classical detailings.

205 S. Ridge Ave.

A smaller home once occupied this lot, but in 1918, Louis and Phoebe Hartert built the existing Prairie style home. The residence features numerous windows and large porch supports. Hartert served as president of his own real estate, insurance, and loan company.

237 N. Water Ave.

In 1916-1917, the Tudor-Gothic style Trinity Methodist Church was constructed. A stone Celtic cross accents the gable, and stained glass windows adorn the front, celestory, and aisle windows. In the 1970s, the building was added to the National Register of Historic Places.

N. Eastern Ave. and Elm

Formerly home to the Idaho Falls Public Library, this Neo-Classical building was completed in 1916. The building was added to the National Register of Historic Places in 1984, and today, it is home to the Bonneville County Museum.

T Rotary International Peace Park
Snake River Greenbelt west of Broadway Bridge, Idaho Falls. Contact Idaho Falls Parks and Recreation Division at 529-1480.

Located alongside the city's greenbelt near the Snake River, the Rotary International Peace Park symbolizes peaceful relationships with individuals around the world. Park highlights include granite lanterns that were given to Idaho Falls' residents by their sister city, Tokai-Mura, Japan.

T Wilson Rawls Memorial Statue
457 Broadway, Idaho Falls.

Situated on the front lawn of the Idaho Falls Public Library is a statue entitled, "Dreams Can Come True," a memorial to writer W. Wilson Rawls. Rawls lived in Idaho Falls from 1958 to 1975 in a small house on 11th Street. Although he had always dreamed of becoming a writer who would inspire others to read and write, Rawls nearly gave up on his dream. But with the encouragement of his wife, Sophie, Rawls wrote his acclaimed *Where the Red Fern Grows*. With editing help from his wife, Rawls' children's classic was published in 1961.

To commemorate Rawls' accomplishments and his persistence in fulfilling his dream, a life-size statue was created depicting the story's main character (Billy Coleman) and his two dogs. Funded by donations from across the U.S. and a grant from the Idaho Commission on the Arts and National Endowment for the Arts, the statue was created by Idaho Falls artist, Marilyn Hansen. The mission of the statue is to inspire children to dream ambitious dreams and to encourage adults to support the pursuit of those dreams.

T Idaho Falls Temple
1000 Memorial Dr., Idaho Falls. 523-4504.

Constructed on land donated by the Idaho Falls Chamber of Commerce that overlooks the Snake River, the Idaho Falls Temple of the Church of Jesus Christ of Latter-Day Saints was completed after five years of hard labor. Plans for the temple were discussed as early as 1918, but the cornerstone was not laid until October 19, 1940. Although the project was only projected to take a couple of years to complete, World War II claimed many workers and created a shortage of building materials. Finally, on September 23, 1945, the temple was ready for dedication, and Church President George Albert Smith traveled from Salt Lake City to participate. It was not until 1983 that the Angel Moroni statue was placed on top of the white stone temple.

Although the temple itself is not open to the general public, a visitor's center in front of the temple is open daily from 9 AM to 9 PM. Here, non-Mormons have the opportunity to learn about one of Idaho's most prevalent religions. The center provides artwork, guided tours of the grounds, special exhibits, and video presentations free of charge.

T Snake River Fur Trader Monument
Intersection of Memorial Dr. and B St., Idaho Falls.

Idaho Falls' history is dotted with the lives of hearty pioneers, including several trappers and traders. To commemorate the town's past, renowned Idaho Falls artist, Roy Reynolds, was awarded a grant in 2001 to create the "Snake River Fur Trader" monument. The bronze statue measures eight feet tall and is one of the many highlights along the Snake River Greenbelt.

T Taylor's Crossing
South of the Broadway Bridge, Idaho Falls.

Early Idaho Falls settler, James "Matt" Taylor was an entrepreneur with a keen business mind. After obtaining a bridge and ferry franchise from the Idaho Territorial Legislature, Taylor hired the Oneida Road, Bridge, and Ferry Company in 1865 to create a bridge near the Eagle Rock settlement (Idaho Falls). This bridge dubbed "Taylor's Crossing" proved highly successful, allowing both pioneers and freight to cross the Snake River with ease. Taylor's contribution to Idaho Falls' development is honored with a full-scale replica of the area's first bridge.

T Idaho Falls Symphony
498 A St., Idaho Falls. 529-1080.

Nearly sixty volunteer and paid musicians from Idaho Falls and the surrounding region recreate the world's great music classics in their annual performances. The group was founded in 1949 when student and adult musicians came together to rehearse a community presentation of Handel's "Messiah." The result was legendary, and today, the community group performs five to six concerts between November and May. In addition, the associated Idaho Falls Symphony Chorale features an eighty-member choir that performs a series of chamber music concerts. For tickets and a schedule of events, contact the Idaho Falls Arts Council at (208) 522-0471.

T Idaho Falls Opera Theater
241 Cliff, Idaho Falls. 522-0875.

One of Idaho Falls largest cultural attractions is its Opera Theater. Drawing upon the talents of local musicians, actors, and technicians of all ages, the theater presents opera and other musical productions. Two full-stage shows are produced each year, and the theater also sponsors an annual professional Broadway touring show. Through their productions, the Opera Theater hopes to cultivate an interest in and appreciation of opera. Contact the Idaho Falls Arts Council at (208) 522-0471 for a complete schedule of events.

T Actor's Repertory Theatre of Idaho
257 W. Broadway, Idaho Falls. 522-8450. www.artidaho.org

For nearly twenty years, the Actor's Repertory Theatre of Idaho has been entertaining Idaho Falls' residents and visitors. Talented thespians from the surrounding region present a range of productions varying from light comedies to tearjerkers to inspiring dramas. No matter what genre of play is presented, however, it is skillfully portrayed to the highest quality. Past presentations have included *The Laramie Project*, *The Woman in Black*, *True West*, *Barefoot in the Park*, and *Sordid Lives*. Performed inside the remodeled 1800s Eleanor Hotel, all shows include a full dinner, and advance tickets are required.

T Stillwater Mansion
387 N. Water Ave., Idaho Falls. 524-4473.

In Idaho Falls' early days, a gentleman named Stillwater served as town mayor for several years. This prominent man built his famous Stillwater Mansion sometime prior to 1903, and to this day, it has been lovingly maintained. Featuring a Victorian ambience, the mansion is now open for historic tours. In addition, the site is known for hosting excellent Victorian Teas and Garden Teas for upscale social gatherings. Visitors are asked to call ahead and schedule a private tour.

T Russet Lions Noise Park
West of Idaho Falls. 523-6329 or 525-3850.

Established in 1972, the 400-acre Russet Lions Noise Park showcases a variety of motorized races. The city-owned facility features Moto-X races, modified stock car races, street stock, pure stock, mini stock, and hornet races, plus go kart races. The park is open during the summer season, and interested patrons should call in advance for race tickets.

TV Hell's Half Acre Lava Walk
Traveling west of Idaho Falls on Hwy. 20, look for mile marker 287 (about 20 miles west of Idaho Falls). Continue 0.3 miles until you see the "Lava Trail" sign. Turn south onto the gravel road, and continue 1/4 mile to the trailhead. You will find a picnic shelter, fire ring, and portable toilet in the parking area.

Geology of the Area

The Hell's Half Acre Lava Flows are within the Snake River Plain. The Snake River Plain is an expansive crescent-shaped depression 50 to 70 miles wide and 350 miles long that stretches across southern Idaho. This Plain is composed of lava flows formed over the last 15 million years that originated from volcanic vents and fissures.

The Snake River used to flow across the northern portion of the Snake River Plain, but now flows along the southern margin of the Plain. The river was pushed there by successive lava flows. Hell's Half Acre flows over about 222 square miles or 162,000 acres. Sixty-six thousand acres are within a Wilderness Study Area (WSA).

The Hell's Half Acre flows came from a vent that is located along a rift. This rift parallels the 62 mile long Great Rift that goes through Craters of the Moon National Monument. A rift zone is a line of weakness in the earth's crust associated with volcanism. The main vent for the Hell's Half Acre flow is 95 to 200 feet wide and 730 feet long. The highest point is 5,350 feet, whereas the lowest point is 4,600 feet. The vent has 13 pit craters where lava flowed out and then receded.

The last flow from the main vent occurred 2000 years ago. The older flows near Hwy. 20 are estimated to be 4,100 years old and came from an eruptive center about 3.5 miles in diameter. These older flows were covered by more recent flows from the main vent.

A Closer Look at the Lava Landscape

Hiking across the lava is a unique experience. Lava rock is extremely sharp, glassy, and fragmented with open cracks, lava tubes, and caves. The most prevalent landscape consists of A'a (ah-ah) and Pahoehoe (pa-hoy-hoy) lava flows. Pahoehoe lava is more fluid than A'a. It's outer surface cooled faster than the interior causing a 'ropey' appearance. The less fluid A'a formed leaving rough, irregular mounds. The areas of soil and vegetation not covered by lava are called 'kipuka,' a Hawaiian word meaning 'window in the lava.'

A variety of plants and wildflowers contrast the black and gray lava flows. In the spring and early summer, numerous wildflowers, such as Evening Primrose, Indian Paintbrush, wild onions, penstemon, geraniums, and Prickly Pear Cactus, color the landscape. Also coloring the landscape are ferns growing in deep cracks and a variety of desert vegetation. The spectrum ranges from tiny mosses and lichens to juniper trees hundreds of years old. Other native species include sagebrush, rabbit brush, bitterbrush, blue bunch wheatgrass, and needle-and-thread grass.

Wildlife roaming the lava flows include mule deer, antelope, sage grouse, bobcats, coyotes, foxes, and occasionally snakes. Soaring above the flows are red-tailed hawks, prairie falcons, and golden eagles.

Lava Walks in Hells Half Acre

The Bureau of Land Management, Bonneville County, and the Idaho Alpine Club along with numerous other people have cooperated to open this area for lava hiking. Hiking in lava fields is unique because of the rough terrain, unusual scenery, and the contorted landscape. Since this is a Wilderness Study Area (WSA), permanent trails have not been developed. The unimproved hiking routes are marked with poles.

Blue top poles mark a route around a short educational loop, which is a good introduction to lava hiking. The 1/2-mile loop takes about 1/2 hour to walk. On this loop note the pressure ridges, deep cracks with ferns at the bottom, and moss on the rocks.

Red top poles mark a 4 1/2-mile route to the main vent or source of the Hells Half Acre lava flow. A round trip to the vent will take a full day and should only be undertaken after adequate preparation has been made. Water is essential and boots with good soles are advisable. Estimated time to hike to the vent is 2 to 3 1/2 hours one-way.

Reprinted from Bureau of Land Management and Idaho Alpine Club brochure

TV Snake River Greenbelt Idaho Falls

Ducks and Canadian geese join the list of enthusiastic patrons who utilize the scenic twenty-nine acre greenbelt park spanning both sides of the lazy Snake River. The most heavily used stretch begins near the Broadway bridge and ends at the Hwy. 20 bridge. Hikers, joggers, and bicyclists frequent this popular 2.3-mile loop as well as the rest of the trail. In the winter, the greenbelt becomes a trail system for cross-country skiers and snowshoe lovers. Spectacular views of the town's waterfall greet greenbelt users.

FL Motel West & Hometown Kitchen Restaurant
1540 W. Broadway, Idaho Falls. 522-1112 or (800) 582-1063. www.motelwestidaho.com

Great Grandpa's West is gone into the history books forever, but the hospitality of the west lives on at Motel West. Each clean, comfortable, non-smoking room features color cable TV with HBO, free local calls, and queen size beds. Refrigerators, microwaves, and suites with jetted tubs are also available. After relaxing in the heated indoor pool and hot tub, head to the Hometown Kitchen Restaurant conveniently located on-site. The restaurant features homemade goodies including soups, breads, and pies. Breakfast, lunch, and dinner specials change daily with prime rib offered every Friday night. Restaurant hours are 6:30 AM to 9 PM Monday through Friday and 6:30 AM to 4 PM on Saturdays. Stay with the friendly staff at Motel West. They guarantee a pleasant experience where all your needs are met.

L Fairfield Inn & Suites
1293 W. Broadway, Idaho Falls. 552-7378. www.marriott.com/idafi

Fairfield Inn & Suites offers more than just a hotel but an experience like none other. Ranked as one of the top 25 hotels in both service and quality, the Fairfield Inn caters to vacationers and business travelers with its indoor swimming pool, spa, and comfortable rooms. The quiet, well-lit rooms are equipped with free high speed and wireless Internet, coffeemakers, hairdryers, irons, alarm clocks, individual climate control and air-conditioning, cable TV, in-room movies, CD players, bathtubs with spray jets, and down/feather and foam pillows ensuring a peaceful night's sleep. Cribs and rollaway beds are also available. In the morning, wake up to a complimentary breakfast and your free copy of the local paper and USA Today. On your next trip, enjoy the friendly, comfortable atmosphere at Fairfield Inn & Suites by Marriott.

S Jimmy's All Seasons Angler
275 A. St., Idaho Falls. 524-7160. www.JimmysFlyShop.com

Jimmy's All Seasons Angler has been serving those who enjoy the waters surrounding Idaho Falls since 1979. They offer a full selection of fly fishing supplies and huge selection of fly tying materials. They carry Sage fly rods, Winston fly rods, Columbia clothing, Simms waders, and Orvis tackle. They are also a Rio dealer and Cortland Pro Shop. The shop is an excellent source for regional fishing books and maps. You can also pick up your fishing license for Idaho or Yellowstone Park. Be sure and check with the professionals at Jimmy's for up to date information on area waters. Conveniently located near area lodging.

M Idaho Falls Chamber of Commerce
630 W. Broadway, Idaho Falls. 523-1010 or (800) 634-3246. www.idahofallschamber.com; info@idahofallschamber.com

8 *Food, Lodging*

T Pinecrest Municipal Golf Course
701 E. Elva St, Idaho Falls. 529-1485.

Pinecrest Municipal Golf Course is often referred to as Idaho Falls' most challenging round of golf. Established in 1934 under the design of W. H. Tucker, the 18-hole course covers 6,394 yards and is rated a par-70. The course is situated in the city's center, and players will encounter tight

ANNUAL EVENTS

American Dog Derby

Ashton's American Dog Derby held each winter is rumored to be the oldest dog sled race in the lower forty-eight states. The event dates back to 1917, and during the 1920s and 1930s, nearly 15,000 spectators arrived each year from Idaho and neighboring states to witness the annual derby. Although the race was suspended during World War II and for periods during the 1960s, 1970s, and 1980s, it was revived with enthusiasm in the early 1990s. Today, the weekend event draws large crowds of people cheering on their favorite dog sled driver in 60-mile and 100-mile races. In addition, the event features ice sculpting and a variety of food and craft vendors.

Free Fishermen's Breakfast

Idaho has long been known for its population of avid fishermen and trout-filled streams and rivers. So, when fishing season opens, it's essential that every angler head for the water with a satisfied stomach. St. Anthony annually honors these recreationists and celebrates the start of the fishing season with a free pancake feed held at Clyde Keefer Memorial Park.

Teton Valley Summer Festival

The Teton Valley Summer Festival in Driggs has been an annual celebration for nearly twenty-five years. The weeklong festival attracts locals and visitors and features hot air balloon rides, fireworks, arts and crafts, street fairs, parades, old time fiddlers' contests, barbeques, golf tournaments, and bike races.

Snake River Settlers' Festival & 4th of July Celebration

For years, Idaho Falls has celebrated the Snake River Settlers' Festival and Independence Day in grand style. The day starts out with a large parade and also features baseball games and other "old-fashioned" games and activities at Tautphaus Park. The activities wrap up with one of the largest fireworks displays west of the Mississippi. Showcased over the Snake River, the display is professionally choreographed and set to music, and it annually attracts an average of 100,000 spectators.

Idaho International Folk Dance Festival

Since its inception in 1986, the goal of the Idaho International Folk Dance Festival in Rexburg has been to promote cultural exchange between Idaho and countries across the world. Growing in leaps and bounds since its debut, this world-renowned festival has been rated as one of North America's top 100 events by the American Business Association. Up to 300 dancers perform annually, and an average of ten different countries are represented each summer. Previous dance teams have traveled from Africa, Asia, Europe, South America, North America, and island areas across the world. The festival includes opening ceremonies, a parade, street festivals, cultural classes, dance classes, a rodeo, and three full nights of spectacular dance performances.

Grand Targhee Bluegrass Festival

Music fans can enjoy a summer weekend of toe-tapping fun at the annual Grand Targhee Bluegrass Festival. Situated at an elevation of 8,000 feet and surrounded by the stunning peaks of the Teton Mountains, the festival headlines some of the country's greatest bluegrass talent on an outdoor stage. The three-day festival features both famous and local talent, music jams, contests, free workshops, great food, arts and crafts, games, and optional on-site camping. As the popularity of bluegrass music continues to grow, so does the acclaim of this beloved festival. Advance tickets are highly recommended.

War Bonnet Round Up

World champion cowboys ride, rope, and test their skills at eastern Idaho's oldest annual rodeo. Originating in 1921, the War Bonnet Round Up is a Mountain West PRCA event and is sponsored by the Bonneville County American Legion post.

Mountain Brewers Beer Fest

Idaho Falls' Sandy Downs Race Track is home to the annual Mountain Brewers Beer Fest. A tradition that started in 1994, the festival is now acclaimed across the U.S. and features more than 300 beers from over 80 different intermountain west breweries. The non-profit North American Brewers Association sponsors the event featuring beer tasting, food vendors, and live entertainment. The event serves as a pre-festival for the North American Beer Competition.

Mountain Men Rendezvous Celebration

Every year in August, Driggs honors the mountain men, trappers, and traders who first called Teton Basin home. The area's lively past is captured at the two-day Mountain Men Rendezvous Celebration. Several local residents dress in trapper or Indian clothes to take part in the weekend festivities. Annual events include the Mr. Pierre Tall Tale Contest and the 13-mile John Colter Indian Escape Dash Marathon.

Along the River

Performed amidst the scenic beauty lining the Snake River, the Idaho Falls "Along the River" concert series is an annual summer tradition loved by residents and visitors alike. From June through August, the Idaho Falls Arts Council sponsors midday one-hour music performances. These free outdoor shows take place once a week and are located on the Snake River Greenbelt between D and E Streets.

Alive After Five

During the summer, Idaho Falls residents and tourists have the opportunity to unwind after a long day of work or sightseeing at the "Alive After Five" concert series. The normal hustle of daily business dies down one evening each week and is replaced with live music and an array of food vendors. The annual event is free.

The Great Snake River Duck Race

Although real wildlife abounds in the Idaho Falls area and along the Snake River, one day each August is devoted to children's favorite yellow rubber duckies. Sponsored by the Idaho Falls Rotary Club, the event draws locals and visitors alike who line the waterfront to watch as hundreds of yellow duckies race down the river. Each duck is assigned a number, and top finishers secure large prizes.

greens, numerous sand traps, and several large pine trees. Green fees are $17.50 on weekdays and $18.50 on weekends with tee times available two days in advance. The course is closed during the winter.

T Idaho Vietnam Memorial
Science Center Dr. (off Fremont Ave.), Idaho Falls. Contact Idaho Falls Parks and Recreation Division at 529-1480.

The Idaho Vietnam Memorial is located inside the seventy-five acre Lewis A. Freeman Memorial Park. Situated atop a quiet and serene hill overlooking the Snake River, the stainless-steel, inverted V sculpture commemorates the lives of Idaho men and women who died while fighting in the Vietnam War. Each fatality and the names of those missing in action are engraved on the sculpture that was dedicated in 1990.

T Idaho Falls Family History Center
750 W. Elva, Idaho Falls. 524-5291.

Visitors have the opportunity to discover the past and honor their heritage at the Idaho Falls Family History Center. A multiregional facility, the center houses a warehouse of ancestral information in its library and research center and is connected to the world's largest family history center. In addition, the free facility offers family history workshops to encourage individuals to learn about and trace their genealogy. The center is open Monday and Saturday from 9 AM to 5 PM and Tuesday through Friday from 9 AM to 9 PM.

T Idaho Falls Padres
Corner of Bannock and W. Elva, Idaho Falls. 522-8363.

During the summer, Idaho Falls has another entertainment option to add to the list of recreational choices. The Minor League Idaho Falls Padres bats out a season of summer fun and action in the city's historic McDermott Field located in Highland Park at the corner of Bannock and West Elva. The team is part of the Pioneer League, which includes teams from as far north as Canada, and the Padres have enjoyed several winning seasons. The Padres are associated with sister team, the San Diego Padres, which helps move players from the Minor Leagues to the Major Leagues.

T Kate Curley Park
Emerson and Higbee Ave.s, Idaho Falls. 529-1480.

Idaho Falls' first settlers were not only interested in establishing a business community, but also a scenic town with recreation opportunities available to locals and passerby. As local groups and pioneers acquired land and beautified the area with trees and flowers, the Idaho Falls Village Improvement Society decided to join the action. Utilizing back county taxes, the women's group purchased the current city lot and began making plans for park development. To help pay for the plans, the ladies raised potatoes on the land for several years and saved every profit from the sales. In 1903, though, tragedy struck the group. Kate Curley, a prominent leader of the Village Improvement Society, died from cancer, and work momentarily stopped. But Kate's husband, Bowen, wanted to leave a legacy for his wife. As a town banker, Bowen carried forth the project and enlisted the help of Charles and Maude Shattuck to design the park layout and its placement of trees. The ladies' vision was finally completed, and in 1918, the City of Idaho Falls purchased the park from the society. Today, the park is a popular picnicking area due to its old-growth shade trees. Several community events, such as the annual Easter Egg Hunt, are also held here throughout the year.

F Teton Grille Restaurant
County Line Rd., Exit 318 on Hwy. 20, just 10 minutes north of Idaho Falls. 522-3444.

The Teton Grille Restaurant opened in 2003 offering casual dining in a traditional log cabin atmosphere. Since 1980, Executive Chef, Robert L. Martin, has received numerous awards and certifications. Now home in his new Teton Grille Restaurant, Martin's skills are exemplified in a variety of tasty fare. Full lunch and dinner menu items include appetizers, rainbow trout, buffalo, salmon, chicken, beef, Idaho potatoes, and specialty desserts. Featuring a summer dining patio, the 120-seat restaurant is open Monday through Saturday, and take-out lunch and dinner orders are available during the week. In addition to standard dining facilities, the restaurant includes banquet facilities and expertise to make any event a success. Discover Idaho's Teton Grille Restaurant today. It's a special place where Idaho flavors are infused with Idaho charm.

9 Food, Lodging

T Sage Lakes Golf Course
100 E. 65th N., Idaho Falls. 528-5535.

Sage Lakes Municipal Golf Course is the newest playing field in Idaho Falls. Opened in 1993, the 6,566-yard course features 18 holes and is rated a par-70. The course features several water traps, and tee times can be scheduled two days in advance. Green fees are $16.65 on weekdays and $18.70 on weekends. The course is closed during the winter.

T Sand Creek Municipal Golf Course
5200 S. Hackman Rd. (off E. 65th St.), Idaho Falls. 529-1115.

William Bell designed this 6,770-yard course in 1978, and it has become extremely popular with local residents. Rated at a par-72, the 18 hole course traverses a flat, open layout, and golfers are presented with several water traps. At times, wind can become a playing factor on this course. Green fees are $15.50 on weekdays and $16.50 on weekends. The course is closed during the winter.

T Walking Tour of Historic Churches in Idaho Falls
Contact the City of Idaho Falls Planning and Building for more information. 529-1276.

Idaho Falls has a long legacy of religious following. In 1896, despite the town's small size, Idaho Falls had more churches than any other similarly sized community in the state. Just four years later, Lutheran, Presbyterian, Catholic, Methodist, Baptist, Swedish Mission, and Mormon congregations served this town of 1,200. These first

churches have since eroded in time, but their larger, more substantial replacements have become engrained in the community. The doors are always open, and visitors are invited to explore this aspect of Idaho Falls' diverse history.

Trinity United Methodist Church
237 North Water Ave.
Around 1884, approximately fifty years after the first Methodist missionary arrived in Idaho Territory, the First Methodist Episcopal Church was established in Idaho Falls. Reverend E.B. Elder from Blackfoot journey to Idaho Falls once a month to service the congregation. As church membership swelled, a new church was needed to accommodate the congregation's growing needs. The corner lot at the present site was purchased for that purpose in 1886 at a cost of $285. Despite criticism for the church's construction far outside the established settlement, work continued and the church's foundation was laid in 1895.

Twenty years later, contractor Dan Sweeney agreed to build the present Tudor Gothic style church for $47,000. Dedicated in 1917, the church's stone walls were quarried near Heise, and the stained glass windows originated in West Virginia. In 1948, the church's education wing was added with stone taken from the original quarry. The church is listed on the National Register of Historic Places.

First Presbyterian Church
325 Elm St.
Idaho Falls' Presbyterian Church was organized in 1891, and just one year later, the congregation had a church located on the corner of Shoup Ave. and A Street. This first church cost $1,600 and was led by Charles Ramsays, S.C. Wishard, and eight other charter members.

In 1917, Reverend Arthur Richards assumed responsibility for the congregation, and he immediately purchased a lot to build a larger church. The old church was sold with the profit used as a down payment for the new church. Just three years later, this Greek Classic style church designed by Pennsylvania architect, J.C. Fulton, was complete. Total building cost was $90,000. The church windows are dedicated to the memory of World War I soldiers and other prominent church members, while the entry columns represent the largest stone columns ever quarried in Boise. The church is listed on the National Register of Historic Places.

Cornerstone Assembly of God (Formerly 3rd Ward LDS Church)
187 East 13th St.
As an influx of believers from the Church of Jesus Christ of Latter Day Saints (LDS) settled in Idaho Falls, in 1927 the church was forced to add a 3rd and 4th ward to accommodate its growing congregation. A new church site was selected at the corner of 13th Street and Lee Ave., and Aubrey O. Andelin was selected as the new church's bishop.

The church draws its design from sister chapels in Utah and neighboring Rexburg, and the LDS Church agreed to pay 65% of the building costs with ward members contributing the remaining 35%. As the Depression hit, though, the ward had difficulty in securing all of the necessary monies, resulting in a nine-year construction process. Finally, in June 1937, the new ward was completed at a cost of $152,000, and the LDS Church President held a dedication ceremony.

The 3rd Ward of the LDS Church utilized the building until 1981, at which time it became a counseling/community center. The Cornerstone

Assembly of God Church purchased the building in 1994, and it is listed on the National Register of Historic Places.

Holy Rosary Church
149 9th St.
The Catholic Church is one of the oldest congregations in Idaho Falls. In 1891, church members decided that an official church building was necessary. After raising money at County Fair concessions, the first church was constructed in 1895-96 at the corner of Eastern and Maple Ave.s. Today, a local bar stands at the original church's site.

In 1947, Boise architects Hummel, Hummel, and Jones designed the present English Gothic style church. The church included an attached rectory and was built by the Arrington Construction Company for $180,000. Easter Sunday, 1949, marked the first service held in the new church. The interior features a 22-foot high marble altar and a one-ton life sized crucifix made from Portuguese onyx. Trappist Monks from Layayette, Oregon hand-made the forty-eight oak pews, and the stained glass windows on the church's south side were constructed in Austria. Upon the church's completion, a bell was purchased for the bell tower. However, upon its first tolling, the great vibrations cracked the tower and the bell was put to rest. In 1977, the Mark Stevens Memorial Carillon replaced the unused bell. The church is listed on the National Register of Historic Places.

St. John Lutheran Church
290 7th St.
Reverend E.P. Meyer was one of the first Lutheran missionaries to arrive in Idaho in the early 20th century. After his departure, Reverend William Jaeger was assigned to the Idaho Falls area, and he established a Lutheran congregation in 1913. Until a parsonage was built in 1922, church members gathered on alternate Sundays at the old Swedish Lutheran Church. Finally, in 1950, the congregation received its long-awaited church. After two years of construction costing nearly $85,000, the Tudor Gothic style building was completed and dedicated. Congregation members donated the stained glass windows. The church was remodeled just ten years later in 1961.

9th Ward LDS Church (Formerly 5th Ward)
395 2nd St.
On August 23rd, 1936, the 5th Ward LDS Church was established under the leadership of Bishop William Grant Ovard. Greatly desiring a building of their own, ward members generously donated money to a building fund, and a lot was purchased later that year. H. M. Sundberg designed the Art Deco style church, and in 1937, Brigham Madsen began his building contract and broke ground in 1937. With the help of church volunteers, the recreating room was complete in 1939, and the chapel received its first use in 1942. Total building costs were approximately $50,900.

As church membership grew, so did the building. The building is now home to the 9th Ward of the LDS Church, and a 2,900 square foot addition was added in 1994.

Salvation Army Church (Formerly 4th Ward LDS Church)
605 N. Blvd.
On January 1, 1928, James Laird was appointed Bishop of the newly formed 4th Ward LDS Church. In 1935, a building lot was obtained, and Sundberg and Sundberg were hired to design a Tudor style church. Just one year later, ground was broken, and 4th Ward members were respon-

sible for much of the building labor. These members also raised 40% of the total $45,000 building cost. In 1937, LDS Church President Heber Grant dedicated the building.

In 1958, a 7,000 square foot east wing was added, and in 1984, the interior was remodeled. The building serviced the 4th and 10th Wards of the LDS Church, and in 1993, the building was sold to the Salvation Army.

T Tautphaus Park
Adjacent to Rollandet St. in Idaho Falls. Contact the Parks and Recreation Division at 529-1480.

Idaho Falls is known for the numerous city parks dotting the landscape, and Tautphaus Park is one of the most beloved and oldest parks in town. Acres of grass, old-growth shade trees, and landscaped flowerbeds beckon residents and visitors alike to spend a leisurely afternoon relaxing in the park.

Tautphaus Park is named after early residents, Charles and Sarah Tautphaus. In 1995, the Bonneville County Historical Society erected a historical marker at the park in remembrance of this couple's community contribution. The inscription on the marker reads as follows:

In commemoration of Charles and Sarah Tautphaus, who developed this area from sagebrush to a park for all to enjoy. Charles C. Tautphaus, of German ancestry, and Sarah Kane, from Ireland, were both immigrants to America. They met in California, where they married and had five daughters. The family traveled by covered wagon to Butte City, Montana, where they were successful at mining, freighting, and farming. In 1884, they purchased two sections of government land in Eagle Rock (Idaho Falls). Using primitive equipment, they transformed the desert into a farm that included a wooded hillside, poplar-lined drives, an apple orchard, and a six-acre lake with a waterfall. The lake, where the sunken baseball diamond now exists, was a center of social activity, with picnicking, boating, and swimming in the summer and ice-skating in the winter. To irrigate his land and that of others, Charles helped form the Idaho Canal Company in 1889 and designed a 30-miles canal from the Snake River to the Blackfoot River. For several years, this park was owned by the Reno family and called "Reno Park." It was purchased by the city in 1935 and named Tautphaus Park in 1943 to honor its original developer. Charles (1841-1906) and Sarah (1840-1917) are buried in the cemetery next to their beloved park in a plot marked by a large stone cross. We give thanks to these early settlers who, in fulfilling their own dreams, also improved the lives of their fellow citizens and future generations.

Inside this historical park are baseball fields, tennis courts, a fountain, playground, indoor ice rink, and a small amusement park called "Funland" that offers historic ferris wheel rides and a hometown carnival atmosphere.

T Tautphaus Park Zoo
2725 Carnival Way, Idaho Falls. 528-5552. www.idahofallszoo.org

Situated within Tautphaus Park is the popular Tautphaus Park Zoo. Accredited by the American Zoo and Aquarium Association, the zoo houses and protects more than 250 different animals from six continents, some of which are listed on the endangered species list. Natural habitats are recreated for each animal, and highlights include viewing snow leopards, kangaroos, penguins, otters, cotton top tamarins, and red ruffed lemurs. In the

Children's Zoo, kids and adults have the opportunity to pet bunnies and feed the flocks swimming in a special duck pond. Zoo hours are as follows: Memorial Day to Labor Day – Monday 9 AM to 8 PM, Tuesday through Sunday 9 AM to 5 PM; May and September – daily from 9 AM to 4 PM; April and October – 9 AM to 4 PM; November through March – closed for the season. Admission fees are $4 for adults ages 13+, $2 for youth ages 4-12, $2.50 for seniors ages 62+, and free to those 3 and under.

T Sandy Downs
6855 S. 15th St. E. (near St. Clair Ave. and E. 65th St. S.), Idaho Falls. 529-2276 or 529-1479.

Sandy Downs is a historical events center showcasing a variety of entertainment throughout the year. Circuses, three major rodeos, livestock programs, quarter horse racing, and chariot racing are just some of the events hosted here annually. A list of events is available at the center or by calling the Idaho Falls Chamber of Commerce at (208) 523-1010.

T Idaho Falls Aquatic Center
149 S. 7th, Idaho Falls. 529-1111.

The Idaho Falls Aquatic Center is a popular venue during all seasons of the year. The indoor facility features an Olympic size, Z-shaped pool holding 285,000 gallons of water just waiting to be splashed in and enjoyed. In addition, two whirlpool spas, a redwood outdoor deck, a summer outdoor wading pool, and an indoor observation deck are available.

T Idaho Falls Civic Auditorium
501 S. Holmes, Idaho Falls. 529-1396.

Recognized as one of the finest performing arts facilities in the Intermountain West, the Idaho Falls Civic Auditorium is the showplace for a variety of entertainment in the upper Snake River Valley. In 1949, a city bond was passed, and construction on the new auditorium was completed in 1952. Since then, the 1,892-seat facility has hosted opera, symphony, ballet, dance, conferences, and Broadway musicals. Renowned performers have included such icons as Louis Armstrong, Johnny Cash, and the San Francisco Opera. For a complete monthly schedule of events, contact the auditorium or the Snake River Territory Convention and Visitors Bureau at (208) 523-1010.

L Yellowstone Motel
2460 S. Yellowstone, Idaho Falls. 529-9738

Conveniently located on the way to Yellowstone National Park, Yellowstone Motel accommodates people of all ages and abilities with its ground floor design. Choose between smoking or non-smoking rooms, each including comfortable beds, 25" TV with remote and cable, refrigerator, microwave, coffee maker, and free local calls. Kitchenette units are also available, and guest laundry services are on-site. Featuring a pet

friendly environment where guests are charged a minimal extra $5 fee, the hotel prides itself on low nightly rates and discounted weekly and extended stay rates. On your next trip to Idaho Falls or Yellowstone, experience the friendly atmosphere of Yellowstone Motel where clean, quality rooms offered at an affordable price are a standard amenity.

M Help-U-Sell
1220 E. 17th St., Idaho Falls. 525-2525. www2.helpusell.com/idahofalls

Help-U-Sell prides itself on saving buyers and sellers thousands of dollars with a proven marketing system and menu of services. Maintaining a standard fee-for-service approach, Help-U-Sell charges customers only for the services they desire and not the traditional 6% all-inclusive fee. On average, Help U-Sell sellers enjoy a nearly 72% success rate, compared to just 63% with traditional real estate agencies. And buyers benefit too. Help-U-Sell offers experienced buyer specialists and 24/7 price and listing updates. With the motto "whatever it takes," the company also offers moving services. Using a company trailer, Help-U-Sell offers the convenience and affordability you need to quickly settle into the home of your dreams. So why pay for services you don't need? Call Help-U-Sell today to see results tomorrow.

M RE/MAX Homestead Realty
1301 E. 17th St, Idaho Falls. 529-5600 or (800) 729-5601. www.djskinner.com

RE/MAX Homestead Realty and professionally certified realtor, D. J. Skinner, specialize in purchases and sales of single-family residences and income properties. Frequently receiving rave reviews, the office prides itself on going the extra mile to ensure excellent customer service to individuals residing in Idaho Falls, Rigby, Shelley, Ammon, Iona, Ucon, Rexburg, and Menan. New to town? D.J. is happy to help you discover your new community, its schools, and other area amenities. So whether you need to sell your home or are just settling in and looking for your dream house, contact D.J. at RE/MAX Homestead Realty. With her assistance, you will gain the consumer knowledge you need in making informed decisions about one of your most precious investments.

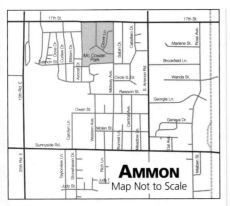

AMMON
Map Not to Scale

10 Food

T Gem Lake Marina
5 miles southwest of Idaho Falls On U.S. Hwy. 91, head southwest from Idaho Falls towards Shelley. Approximately 2 miles south of Idaho Falls, bear right (west) near the Fanning Memorial Society. Proceed 3 more miles to the marina.

Gem Lake Marina is located on the Snake River and is a popular recreational destination during late spring and summer. A boat launch area provides easy access for waterskiing, jet-skiing, and windsurfing. Anglers report excellent trout fishing in the area, and picnic gazebos provide covered shelter for a fun family outing.

11 Food

Ammon
Pop. 6,187

Now a suburb of Idaho Falls, the city of Ammon dates back to the arrival of Mormon pioneers during the 1890s. The town was originally a sprawl from nearby Iona, but when settlers applied for a post office in 1898, a separate community was formed. The town draws its name from a Mormon apostle featured in *The Book of Mormon*.

Iona
Pop. 1,201

Located just seven miles from Idaho Falls, Iona is an agricultural community that Mormon colonizers founded in 1884. The area was originally known as Sands Creek, but when Mormons arrived in the area, they renamed it after a small town in Israel. The term means "beautiful." The community's post office has operated since 1892.

Ucon
Pop. 943

Homesteaded in 1885 by Mormons, this town was originally dubbed "Willow Creek" after its plotting near this stream's banks. The name was changed to "Elba" a few years later, but when residents applied for a post office, they learned another Idaho town carried the same name. After looking through a list of the postal service's recommended town names, residents voted to call their settlement "Ucon." Ucon remained a relatively tiny village until the arrival of the railroad. In 1904, when the community learned a rail route was to be built seven miles west of town, residents packed their bags and moved the town near the railroad. This decision significantly aided the town's growth, and Ucon remains an agricultural hub and shipping point.

T Iona's Historic Places
Rockwood Ave. and Second St., Iona.

Settled in 1883, the small community of Iona retains some of its original buildings and architecture. On the corner of Rockwood Ave. and Second Street is the Iona Ward House. Constructed in 1888 and enlarged just six years later, the sandstone building has served as the community's school, social hall, and art gallery. Directly behind the Ward House is a Victorian brick home. Charles Rockwood, one of the town's first Mormon bishops, built the well-maintained home in 1905. Across the street from these buildings on Second Street is the town's original general store. Named the Sand Creek Store, the building was erected in 1897.

12

T Bone
With the first homesteaders arriving in 1905, the village of Bone is situated on Canyon Creek. The town was named after early pioneer, Orion G. Bone, and received postal services from 1917 to 1950.

13 Food, Lodging

Irwin
Pop. 157

This tiny town is reportedly named after Joseph B. Irwin, an 1888 settler and lucky Snake River prospector who located some of the area's best claims. The community post office was constructed in 1897.

Swan Valley
Pop. 213

Nestled in the scenic Swan Valley between the Caribou, Big Hole, and Snake River Mountain Ranges, the town of Swan Valley sits at the head of Rainey Creek. The town was plotted in 1886 and was named after the whistling swans populating the area.

T Palisades Dam
7 miles southeast of Irwin on U.S. Hwy. 26.

Situated near the picturesque Idaho/Wyoming border, Palisades Dam retains the 16,100-acre Palisades Reservoir. Construction for the dam was approved in 1941, but building did not commence until ten years later. Finally, in 1957, Palisades Dam was completed at a total production cost of $76 million. At the time, the 270-foot wall was the largest earthen dam ever constructed by the Bureau of Reclamation. Today, visitors are offered outstanding views of the dam, spillway, and reservoir from a nearby overlook area.

TV South Fork of the Snake River
Begins at Palisades Dam 7 miles southeast of Irwin and flows sixty-four miles to its convergence with Henry's Fork of the Snake River north of Idaho Falls at Meenan.

Flowing forth from Palisades Dam is the famous South Fork of the Snake River. Regarded as North America's premier river for dry-fly angling, the South Fork flows sixty-four miles through lush cottonwood valleys and rocky canyon walls and is home to mountain whitefish and trophy cutthroat, rainbow, hybrid, and brown trout. More than 4,000 fish crowd each mile of the river, and the South Fork has been rated as the best wild-trout fishery in the lower forty-eight states. In addition, a variety of wildlife surrounds the river resulting in one of Idaho's most unique ecosystems. Herons, Canadian geese, and bald eagles frequently circle above.

Besides fishing and wildlife viewing, the South Fork of the Snake River provides a host of other recreational activities. Hikers and equestrians populate the nearby backcountry, and float trips, kayaking, and canoeing provide excellent opportunities to see the river in its entirety. Thirty-nine islands scattered across the river's path provide perfect camping areas for an overnight river trip. For more information, contact the Idaho Falls Bureau of Land Management Office at (208) 524-7500.

TV Palisades Reservoir
Bureau of Reclamation, St. Anthony. 542-5800. Located on U.S. Hwy. 26 south of Swan Valley and Irwin.

Palisades Reservoir is formed by Palisades Dam, which is a major feature on the Palisades Project. Recreation on this twenty-five square mile (16,100-acre) reservoir with seventy miles of limited access shoreline is administered by the Caribou-Targhee National Forest. The reservoir is located in scenic southeast Idaho and west-central Wyoming, east of Idaho Falls. Palisades' fish species include cutthroat and brown trout, kokanee, and mackinaw. The fishing season is year-round, but fluctuations in the reservoir level during the summer months result in inconsistent fishing. Spring, fall, and winter ice fishing are most productive. The site offers restrooms, boat ramps, and campgrounds.

14 Food, Lodging

Ririe
Pop. 545

Ririe wasn't founded until 1915, and its post office arrived one year later. It was named for David Ririe, a Mormon settler who helped the Oregon Short Line Railroad secure rights to pass through local farmland. The railroad, in turn, honored him by naming the station and town after him. When the Latter Day Saints established the regional ward, it also adopted David's name, and the community legend became the ward's first bishop.

Heise
Pop. 84

This area has long been home to passerby, with Native Americans and early trappers first using the site for its relaxing and supposedly curative powers. When German immigrant, Richard C. Heise, heard the tales of healing waters, he went to the area to investigate in 1894. Heise liked the area so much that he homesteaded on the land and spent his entire life trying to develop the springs into a popular resort destination. After Richard's death, his daughter, Bertha Gavin, continued his work, and the construction of modern roads to the site further increased the area's popularity.

T Ririe Reservoir and Blacktail Park
226 Meadow Creek Rd. east of Idaho Falls (south of Ririe). Contact Bonneville County Parks and Recreation at 538-7285 or 538-5548.

During the period from 1970 to 1977, workers labored on the creation of Ririe Dam. As a result, Ririe Reservoir was formed and has since provided years of enjoyment to tourists and southeastern Idaho residents. Although the 1,560-acre reservoir was technically formed to help with flood control and irrigation, it offers a prime summer recreational area. Fishing, boating, camping, waterskiing, and picnicking are popular at the site.

On the south end of Ririe Reservoir is Blacktail Park where an additional boat dock is available. Rock formations created by eons of wind and rain surround the grassy park.

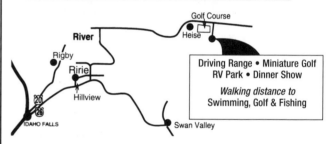

T Heise Hot Springs Golf
5116 E. Heise Rd., Ririe. 538-7327.

Mother Nature designed this executive 9-hole course situated near the South Fork of the Snake River. Nestled below towering cliffs lined with sagebrush and cedar, the course offers players continual scenery as resident deer peer at the action. The course is open from May 1 to October 1 and is rated a par 29. Green fees are a mere $7.50 for 9 holes and $14.00 for 18 holes.

T Heise/Kelly Recreation Area
5116 Heise Rd. in Ririe. 538-7963

TFLC Mountain River Ranch
98 N. 5050 E. at Heise-Kelly Canyon, Ririe. 538-7337. www.mountainriverranch.com

Nestled on the banks of the Snake River, Mountain River Ranch is eastern Idaho's authentic link to the old west. During the summer, take a scenic horse drawn wagon ride, visit the recreated 1890s Rock Bottom Springs frontier town, fish in the stocked trout pond, camp in the shaded RV Park/Campground, and catch some old fashioned western entertainment at the Meadow Muffin Dinner Theater. Summer fare includes BBQ steak and chicken, potato salad, beans, corn, sourdough bread, and dessert, while the winter menu features prime rib or Cornish hen, baked potatoes, salad, ciabatta, and dessert. Winter also brings holiday cheer, festive lights, and songs on frosty sleigh rides. Open year-round with rooms for rent, the friendly ranch and its staff encourage guests to make prior reservations for this fun western experience.

TVLFC Heise Hot Springs & Heise Expeditions
5116 Heise Rd., Ririe. 538-7312 or 538-7327. www.srv.net/~heise/heise.html

Nestled in the heart of the world's finest cutthroat trout fishing, family-owned Heise Hot Springs has blended history with modern recreation since 1896. Summer visitors can soak in 82 or 92 degree filtered freshwater pools and plunge down the 350-foot water slide while winter soakers can stay warm in the 105-degree natural hot springs. Poolside decks and a snack bar round out this entertaining environment. Uninterested in swimming? Heise Expeditions provides guided fishing expeditions on the Snake River, golf, and games. For overnight guests, the original log hotel, a modern two-bedroom cabin, and an RV Park and Campground service every patron's unique needs. With its host of activities and promise of excellence, Heise Hot Springs provides the whole family with a memorable experience.

TC 7N Ranch
5156 E. Heise Rd. at Heise-Kelly Canyon in Ririe. 538-5097.

Cradled between the Rocky Mountains and the South Fork of the Snake River, 7N Ranch Resort offers a relaxed atmosphere and recreation for both young and old. With moose and deer as your spectators, test your skills on the world-class driving range featuring all natural turf or travel down memory lane at the unique Old Farm Miniature Golf Course. For overnight guests, 7N Ranch Resort provides a meticulously maintained campground with a commitment to no overcrowding. RV's will find plenty of first class amenities in the pull-thru spaces, and the newly added "Red round roofed barn" assures each guest has plenty of room. Strategically located near several other area attractions, the 7N Ranch Resort is a great setting for both large group events and personal Rocky Mountain vacations.

V Kelly Canyon Winter Park
Hwy 26 at Heise-Kelly Canyon Recreation Area, Ririe. 538-6251. www.skikelly.com

Opened in 1957 in the Targhee National Forest, the family-friendly Kelly Canyon Winter Park averages 200 inches of powder annually and offers recreation for all ages. Take a lesson from a certified instructor or immediately start your day on the slopes. Encompassing 740 acres of both groomed and natural terrain, the area boasts 4 lifts, 26 runs for both expert and developing skiers, and a maximum vertical of 1,000 feet. Snowboarders are welcome on all runs as well as in the new terrain park, and the area offers lighted night skiing on major runs most nights of the week. For non-skiers, a newly constructed 600-foot tubing park is quickly becoming a family favorite. Lift tickets are reasonably priced to accommodate entire families, and the ski area is open Tuesday through Sunday.

V Kelly Canyon Nordic Skiing and Mountain Biking
Palisades Ranger District, Ririe. 523-1412. Drive 1 mile past Ririe on U.S. Hwy. 26 to a signed turn-off. Follow Kelly Canyon Road past the ski area to locate the trails system.

Continuing past Kelly Canyon Ski Area, over twenty miles of trails wind through the Targhee National Forest and offer scenic terrain to Nordic skiers of all abilities. While some of the trails are groomed, many others are simply marked. Trails include such favorites as the one-mile Tyro Loop for beginners and the Hawley Gulch Loop and Kelly Mountain Trail for advanced skiers. During the summer, these cross-country paths provide sweeping vistas of the Snake River Valley and become popular mountain biking destinations for both residents and tourists.

V Willow Creek Drainage
Running through southeastern Idaho, Willow Creek and its tributaries flow over a hundred miles and are dependent upon Ririe Reservoir. The reservoir boasts populations of stocked hatchery rainbow trout and kokanee salmon, while smallmouth bass, and cutthroat, brown, and lake trout have also been introduced. From Ririe Reservoir, Willow Creek continues its journey, winding through narrow canyons and supporting wild cutthroat trout. In addition to Ririe Reservoir, Willow Creek drainages include Grays Lake near the Caribou Mountains, Meadow Creek, and Tex Creek.

L Cutthroat Inn Bed & Breakfast
Hwy 26 to Heise Rd. at Heise-Kelly Canyon Recreational Area, Ririe. 538-7963. www.cutthroatinn.com

The beautiful Rocky Mountain foothills and world famous South Fork of the Snake River provide a relaxing backdrop for the Cutthroat Inn Bed & Breakfast. Start your day with a hearty, home-cooked breakfast before sampling the area's recreational opportunities. For anglers, practice your

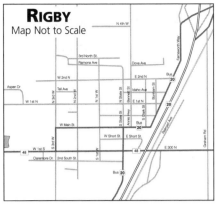

RIGBY
Map Not to Scale

fly-fishing techniques on the inn's private pond or book a guided fly-fishing trip. In the evening, unwind at an old-fashioned melodrama dinner theater before retiring in your country lodging style accommodations. The inn's cabins include two rough-pine queen size beds, private bathrooms, microwaves, refrigerators, and wildlife viewing opportunities right outside your front porch. So plan your getaway today! Group rates and weekday specials are available with a summer schedule from May 1 through October 31 and a winter schedule from November 1 through March 28.

15 *Food, Lodging*

Rigby
Pop. 2,998

Mormons from Utah's Cache Valley settled this area between 1883 and 1884. Their first order of business was to establish a canal system since water was scarce. For $20, the believers also purchased the town site and constructed a church in hopes of luring in more settlers. A few years later, controversy arose between the old settlers and new pioneers as townsite and homesteading laws began to be blatantly ignored. As a result, the townspeople re-purchased the town site for $250 and dictated strict property laws. At that time, the settlement was named after William Rigby, a Latter Day Saints church leader who helped establish and develop the community's growth. Today, the community retains its Mormon roots and was once home to television inventor, Philo T. Farnsworth.

T Jefferson County Historical Society and Farnsworth TV Pioneer Museum
118 W. 1st St. S., Rigby, 745-8423.

Rigby's most famous one-time resident receives the spotlight in this community museum. At age 11, Philo T. Farnsworth moved to Rigby and became intrigued with various electrical motors on his uncle's farm. Utilizing his interest in electrons, Farnsworth developed his idea of the cathode ray tube at age 14 and by the time he was 22, Farnsworth had created the first television. Today, the museum showcases the accomplishments of

RIGBY'S CLAIM TO FAME: THE INVENTION OF TELEVISION

Philo Farnsworth is perhaps Rigby's most famous inhabitant from the past. Moving from Utah to a Rigby area farm when he was twelve, Farnsworth loved to tinker with mechanical and electrical devices. He maintained all of the farm's mechanical equipment, and eventually created an electric motor for the family washing machine.

Farnsworth attended school in Rigby where he was admitted into senior level chemistry classes. While there, he read an article about television experiments, and with encouragement from his teacher, developed a hypothesis about how to produce an electrical counterpart of an optical image.

While still in high school, Farnsworth moved with his family to Provo, Utah, where he studied at Brigham Young University and took advanced courses in electronics. At just 19 years old, Farnsworth met two California businessmen and moved to Los Angeles where he established a scientific lab in his apartment. When he received financial backing from San Francisco bankers, Farnsworth applied for patents on his cathode-ray tube. By 1934, Farnsworth's cathode-ray tube landed him an agreement with London's Baird Television. Soon, viewers all over the world were watching television images, and NBC transmitted the first American TV program at the World Fair. Farnsworth led a brilliant life as a scientist, patenting more than 300 ideas related to TV and electronics, and is known for paving the way to modern television's success.

Farnsworth and his 125 patents, including some of his earliest inventions. In addition, visitors will find several historical photos of the region and displays about Native Americans and wildlife. The museum is open from 1 PM to 5 PM Tuesday through Saturday.

T Jefferson Hills Golf and Recreation Center
4074 E. 500 N., Rigby. 745-6492.

Mature cottonwoods, willows, and pine trees line the narrow fairways of this 5,883-yard, par 70 course. Built in 1970, this 18-hole course meanders near the Snake River, so water hazards come into play on several holes and present a challenge to players of all ability. The course opens daily at 7 AM from March 1 to October 31. Weekday green fees are $12 for 9 holes and $16 for 18 holes with weekend rates just $1 more.

TV Jefferson County Lake
490 N. 4000 E. St., Rigby. 745-7756.
12 miles south of Rexburg immediately off the N. Rigby exit.

From April 1 to October 1, Jefferson County Lake is a popular attraction for both residents and passerby. The scenic recreation area includes picnic shelters, camping, swimming, a children's play area, and bike trails encircling the entire lake. There is a $2 motor vehicle entrance fee at the site.

L Blue Heron Inn
4175 E. Menan Lorenzo Hwy. in Rigby. 745-9922 or toll free at 866-745-9922
www.idahoblueheron.com

The Blue Heron Inn is conveniently located on U.S. Hwy. 20, gateway to Yellowstone National Park, just 18 miles north of Idaho Falls. The Inn overlooks the scenic South Fork of the Snake River. Every room has a river view and is uniquely decorated with handmade quilts and hand-crafted log furniture. Amenities include fireplaces, jetted tubs, private balconies, and luxurious linens. The entire first floor of the Inn is wheelchair accessible. The Great Room is a restful setting with a large river rock fireplace and cathedral ceilings. Readers will enjoy the library nook on the second floor. Mornings begin with a full Western-style breakfast and in the early evening guests enjoy appetizers and complimentary wine, beer, or soft drinks.

L The BlackSmith Inn
227 N. 3900 E. in Rigby. 745-6208 or toll free at 888-745-6208. www.blacksmithinn.com

The BlackSmith Inn is a contemporary round "Eagle's Nest" home, cedar sided to give a unique western flavor. Each room features a mural depicting their western heritage, with locally made quilts and artwork by local artists adding to the western atmosphere. Each room includes a queen size bed, private bath, and TV/VCR. Massage therapy is available by appointment. The decks and surrounding patios are perfect for enjoying pleasant evenings. They are 95 miles from West Yellowstone and 20 minutes from Idaho Falls and I-15. The innkeepers are Registered Nurses and enjoy meeting and getting acquainted with guests. They raise and show Tennessee Walking horses. Horse boarding is available for guests.

M Rigby-Jefferson County Chamber of Commerce
PO Box 327, Rigby. 745-8701.
http://rigby.govoffice.com

16

Lorenzo
Pop. 100

In 1880, settlers began arriving here. Lorenzo Snow, once president of the Church of Jesus Christ of Latterday Saints, serves as the town's namesake. In 1900, development of an Oregon Short Line Railroad Bridge across the Snake River spurred area growth, and a post office was established in 1901.

Thornton
Pop. 150

Originally named Texas Siding, this community was established in 1887. The expansion of the railroad line across the South Fork of the Snake River and into Madison County was a turning point in the town's history. Equipped with a reliable transportation source, the town grew and it became an important freight stop. When the town acquired a post office in 1904, the community name was changed to Thornton in honor of the first postmaster.

T Twin Bridges Park
Archer Rd./Hwy. between Lorenzo, Thornton, and Rexburg. 356-3662.

Thirty-one acres of wild land on the South Fork of the Snake River is home to the Twin Bridges Park. Surrounded by trees, the area features a boat dock for easy river access, fishing, picnicking, and camping. Wildlife viewing is also popular in the area, and deer, moose, bears, and mountain lions are frequently sighted. The free area is open year-round.

17 *Food, Lodging*

Rexburg
Pop. 17,257

Mormon leader, Thomas Ricks, migrated north from Logan, Utah in 1882 at the direction of Mormon Church president, John Taylor. The townsite was platted one year later, and the Italian root of Ricks' name was adopted as the community title at the direction of Cache Valley Church Stake President, William Preston. Although only thirteen settlers joined Ricks initially, the town swelled to over 875 people by May of 1884.

The town's earliest residents were highly successful farmers, and thousands of acres were planted with a variety of crops. In 1888, the Latter Day Saints' Rick College (now BYU-Idaho) was established and named after the community founder. Today, this conservative town recognized for its religiously minded population still economically relies upon the agricultural industry.

H Ricks College
Milepost 334.5 on State Hwy. 33 at BYU-Idaho Campus

Ricks College commenced as a Church of Jesus Christ of Latter-day Saints stake academy in 1888. Ricks was first known as Bannock Stake Academy, then Remont Stake Academy, Smith Academy, and Ricks Academy before becoming Ricks College in 1918. The name memorializes Thomas E. Ricks, founder of Rexburg in 1883. Today Ricks College (BYU-Idaho), includes a modern campus surrounding the historic 1903 Jacob Spori building.

H Beaver Dick
Milepost 73.3 on State Hwy. 33 at Beaver Dick Park

This park is named for "Beaver Dick," a mountain man of late fur trade days who lived in this locality until 1899.

He was born in England, and his real name was Richard Leigh. He came west as a trapper, but the real fur trade was already over. So he married a Shoshoni woman and stayed here-abouts. A popular early outfitter and guide, he served the famous Hayden surveying party in 1872. Leigh Lake in Grand Teton National Park is named for him, and Jenny Lake for his first wife. A picturesque character, he was widely known and liked.

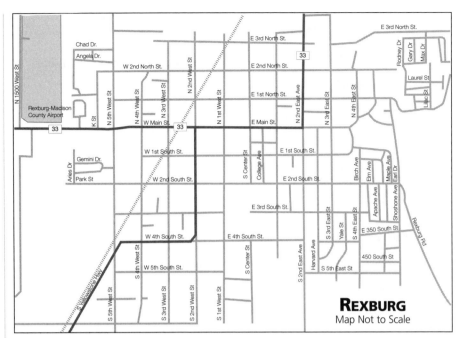

REXBURG
Map Not to Scale

T Teton Lakes Golf Course

1014 N. 2000 West, Rexburg. 359-3036. Located north of Rexburg on Hibbard Parkway Road

The majestic Grand Tetons form the backdrop for this 6,397-yard course situated near the Teton River. Opened in 1979 with a Billy Casper design, the 18-hole championship course is surrounded by lakes, canals, and rivers. This course is rated a par-71 and features mounded greens, shade trees, shrubs, and plenty of sand traps and water hazards. While the front 9 holes are fairly flat and expansive, the back 9 feature tighter fairways and increased hazards. With its diverse layout, this course is suitable for players of all skill levels. Tee times can be scheduled two days in advance, and the course opens daily at 7 AM from March 1 to October 31. Green fees are $10 for 9 holes and $15.50 for 18 holes.

T Rexburg Municipal Golf Course

26 S. Airport Rd., Rexburg. 359-3037.

This city-owned course was built in 1954 and is the second oldest course in eastern Idaho. Featuring 9 holes at par 35, the 3,100-yard course is easy to walk and is a great place for beginners to hone their skills. During late spring and summer, a nearby canal creates a unique water hazard. Tee times are rarely required, and the course is open daily until 11 PM March 15 to October 15. Green fees for 9 holes are $8 for adults and $4.50 for junior players. A round of 18 holes is $12 for adults and $6.50 for juniors.

T Upper Snake River Valley Historical Museum

51 N. Center, Rexburg. 356-9101.

Frequently dubbed the Teton Flood Museum, the Upper Snake River Valley Historical Museum is housed within Rexburg's 1911 old Mormon Tabernacle building. The Italianate-style church was added to the National Register of Historic Places in 1972, and in 1978, the church was sold to the city of Rexburg. The museum opened just four years later, and it continues to display numerous interesting exhibits. Visitors will find pioneer relics from homesteading days, an opal/agate collection, a North American animal head collection, and memorabilia from both World War I and II. In addition, many visitors are fascinated with the exhibits concerning the 1976 Teton Dam collapse and subsequent disastrous flood. Several artifacts, films, and photos of this event are available, and optional tours to the actual flood site are offered. The museum is open 9 AM to 4 PM Monday through Saturday from June through August, and 10 AM to 3 PM Monday through Friday during September through May. Admission is $1 for adults and $.50 for youth ages 12 and under.

T Porter Park

250 W. 2nd S., Rexburg. 359-3020.

Porter Park is nestled in the heart of downtown Rexburg and commemorates the life of Arthur Porter, Jr. The park features several old-growth shade trees, picnic and barbeque areas, tennis, basketball, and volleyball courts, an extensive children's playground, and a large waterslide and swimming pool. The waterslide is open daily during the summer from 12 PM to 6:30 PM.

T BYU-Idaho

525 S. Center St., Rexburg. 496-2411.
www.byui.edu

During the late 1800s, members of the Church of Jesus Christ of Latter Day Saints were under attack from the general population, and access to educational opportunities was limited. In response, the church-owned Bannock Stake Academy was established on November 12, 1888 to provide Rexburg with a grade school and high school. In 1901, grammar education was dropped, and the school was renamed Ricks Academy in honor of Thomas Ricks, a prominent Mormon leader.

As the need for advanced education increased, Ricks Academy began offering college courses. In 1923, the junior college became known as Ricks College, and in 1949, four-year degrees began being offered. But just five years later, the LDS Church President reverted the college back to its junior status. Finally, after fifty plus years of offering strictly associate's degrees, Ricks College was granted the four-year status for which it had longed. On August 10, 2001, Ricks College was rechristened Brigham Young University-Idaho, and several new programs and buildings were added to the campus.

Despite the LDS Church's attempts to give the school to Idaho for a period of nearly twenty years during the early 1900s, the state senate never approved the plans. Thus, the school remains part of the church educational system founded over a century ago while serving nearly 11,000 under-graduate students.

T BYU-Idaho Gardens

BYU-Idaho Campus, Rexburg. 496-1150.

Landscape Horticulture students attending BYU-Idaho use these demonstration gardens as a unique laboratory and study area. The public gardens feature numerous trees and shrubs, as well as 750 varieties of annuals and 200 different perennials. This gardener's dream plot is open year-round until dusk free of charge. In addition to the gardens, the area features beautiful walkways, covered picnic grounds, a pond, and volleyball area.

T Idaho Centennial Carousel

250 W. 2nd S., Rexburg. 359-3020.

Situated inside Porter Park, the Idaho Centennial Carousel is one of Rexburg's crown jewels. The carousel represents Idaho's only antique wooden carousel, and it is one of just 170 wooden carousels still remaining in the US.

The carousel has an extensive history dating back to its 1926 origination in New York at the Spillman Engineering Company. In its early days, the carousel was used as a traveling carnival machine. In 1947, the carousel was retired to Salt Lake City's Liberty Park, but it was soon moved to a park in Odgen, Utah and advertised for sale.

Rexburg	Jan	Feb	March	April	May	June	July	Aug	Sep	Oct	Nov	Dec	Annual
Average Max. Temperature (F)	29.3	33.5	46.3	57.4	66.0	74.8	83.6	84.3	74.0	60.3	41.4	30.4	56.8
Average Min. Temperature (F)	10.4	14.2	23.6	30.7	38.6	44.9	49.3	47.2	38.6	29.7	20.1	11.4	29.9
Average Total Precipitation (in.)	1.07	1.05	1.02	1.12	1.88	1.38	0.93	0.71	0.81	1.07	1.10	1.02	13.16
Average Total Snowfall (in.)	13.1	11.0	4.0	2.2	0.5	0.0	0.0	0.0	0.1	1.0	7.6	15.9	55.5
Average Snow Depth (in.)	9	8	4	0	0	0	0	0	0	0	1	6	2

Section 6

REMEMBERING CAPTAIN BONNEVILLE

Spanning 1,897 square miles and bordering Wyoming, Bonneville County was officially established in southeastern Idaho on February 7, 1911. Home to nearly 90,000 residents, the county memorializes the life and times of Captain Benjamin Louis Eulalie de Bonneville.

Bonneville was born in France in April 1796 to a wealthy Parisian family. After continuing struggles under Napoleon's rule, the family immigrated to America in 1803 where young Bonneville became passionate about the U.S. military. In 1813 at the young age of eighteen, Bonneville received an appointment to the U.S. Military Academy at West Point. He thrived in the disciplined environment, graduated in just two years, and became a military officer serving tours across the US.

While based in Missouri, Bonneville became fascinated with newspaper accounts of western exploration. He longed to travel west, so he petitioned General Alexander Macomb for a leave of absence. Under the strict guideline that Bonneville would collect valuable information about the west's topography and Native American inhabitants, Macomb granted the young officer's request. John Astor provided funding for Bonneville's expedition, and in May 1832, the party left Missouri. After wintering near present day Green River, Wyoming, Bonneville and his party explored Idaho's Snake River region during early 1833. He continued west, eventually exploring the Columbia River Valley. On his return east, Bonneville camped on the banks of Idaho's Portneuf River and wintered with the Shoshone Indians on Idaho's Upper Bear River in 1834.

After his western expedition, Bonneville continued to serve in the U.S. Army and participated in the Civil War. He eventually retired in Arkansas and died in 1878. Today, his name is memorialized with an Idaho County and an ancient lake that flooded southeastern Idaho and changed the state's landscape.

Learning of the carousel, Rexburg residents raised $5,500, bought the carousel, and had it set up in time for the town's 1952 4th of July celebration. In 1954, residents again raised money in the carousel's honor and constructed a protective dome over the structure. For over twenty years, the carousel provided summer days of fun to local residents and tourists. When the neighboring Teton Dam broke in 1976, however, the subsequent flood severely damaged the carousel and destroyed many of its horses. The carousel remained in ruin until 1988 when skilled craftsmen decided to restore the antique back to working order. The carousel was completed just in time to celebrate Idaho's 1990 Centennial.

Today, the renowned carousel features twenty-six of the original horses, twelve newly carved horses, and a brand new band organ run on paper rolls to provide the old-fashioned sounds one would expect to hear at an early 1900s carnival.

Although an antique, the carousel is open for rides Monday through Saturday from 12 PM to 6:30 PM during the summer.

T Rexburg Tabernacle Civic Center
51 N. Center, Rexburg. 356-5700.

In 1911, the Fremont Stake LDS Tabernacle was established to serve the needs of a growing Church of Jesus Christ of Latter Day Saints membership. In 1976, the building suffered major damage in the Teton Flood, at which time the LDS Church sold the tabernacle to the City of Rexburg. After extensive renovation, the building was added to the National Register of Historic Places and is currently used as a civic center and museum. The auditorium seats 1,000 people and provides numerous musical and educational performances throughout the year. Contact the Rexburg Chamber of Commerce for a schedule of events.

T Smith Park
E. Main & 3rd S. Streets; Rexburg. 359-3020.

Rexburg's Smith Park is one of the community's favorite recreation areas and cradles part of the area's history. In 1883, the Rexburg townsite was surveyed, and what was known as Block 36 at the time is now home to the grassy park. In 1954, the LDS Church transferred the lot to the city, and it was subsequently named Smith Park after city mayor, J. Fred Smith. The park's lush shrubbery and trees surround tennis courts, a gazebo, picnic and barbeque areas, playground equipment, and a historic steam engine. The antique engine was placed in the park in 1962 after its retirement from dry farming on the Rexburg Bench area. The park is open year-round until 11 PM.

T Beaver Dick Park
On State Hwy. 33, proceed 14 miles due east from the intersection of I-15 and State Hwy. 33. The site is located approximately five miles west of Rexburg on the road's south side.

During the early 1800s, an Englishman now known as Beaver Dick Leigh immigrated to America with hopes of becoming a renowned western trapper. Setting off to fulfill his dream, Leigh traveled through Utah, Idaho, and Wyoming before marrying an Indian woman named Jenny. Together, the couple had five children, and Leigh's trapping success earned him and his wife a lasting legacy in Grand Teton National Park. The park's Leigh and Jenny Lakes are named after the couple.

Despite many happy years together, tragedy struck the family. After a family hunting trip to Montana in 1876, Jenny became sick and the family returned to their home near this site west of Rexburg. Eventually, every member of the family came down with smallpox – only Beaver Dick survived the outbreak. Griefstricken, he buried his family near their home on the banks of Henry's Fork of the Snake River. The graves from this pioneering Western family are still visible. Beaver Dick eventually remarried and lived until 1899. He is buried near his second home in Newdale, Idaho.

Today, the Madison County Parks and Recreation Department administers Beaver Dick Park. This free, twelve-acre preserve located on the banks of the Henry's Fork of the Snake River includes boating and a boat dock, picnic areas, fishing, and a children's playground. The site is open daily year-round.

M Rexburg Chamber of Commerce
420 W. 4th S., Rexburg. 356-5700 or 888-INFO-880. www.rexcc.com; info@rexcc.com

18

Newdale
Pop. 358

Newdale was founded and established in 1916. One year later, the railroad laid tracks through town and christened the town after its location in a dale-like landscape.

Teton
Pop. 569

Located directly south of St. Anthony in Fremont County, Teton was settled in the mid 1800s and welcomed postal services in 1885. Named after Wyoming's Teton Peaks rising in the distance, the town is most widely recognized as one of many communities involved in the devastating 1976 Teton Dam break.

Sugar City
Pop. 1,242

Pioneers arrived in this area northeast of Rexburg on the Teton River as early as 1883, but the town's history really began when several Salt Lake City, Utah businessmen formed the Sugar City Townsite Company in 1903. Traveling to the homesteaded region, these men purchased 320 acres from the homesteaders and began building a sugar beet factory and workers' residences at the newly laid-out town. In 1904, the $1 million factory was up and running, and it took less than a year for it to become the largest sugar beet factory in the US. The industry continued to prosper, and by 1933, the Sugar City Townsite Company had a record year with production at 43 million pounds of sugar. Unfortunately, the Sugar Act limited farmers' acreage, and a dwindling labor supply forced the company to close its doors in 1942. Despite this set-back and a devastating 1976 flood from the Teton Dam, Sugar City has survived, and its post office has operated continuously since 1904.

H Fort Henry
Milepost 338.7 on State Hwy. 33 at Sugar City's Heritage Park

In 1810, Andrew Henry and a party of trappers from St. Louis established a winter outpost about six miles west of here.

Driven from their upper Missouri beaver camp by hostile Blackfeet Indians, they expanded their operation from United States territory into Oregon – a land with only a few British posts at that time. They built cabins and wintered here in deep snow. Game was scarce, and they had little to eat except horses. So they abandoned this area, and Henry took only 40 packs of beaver pelts – a thin catch – back to St. Louis after a season's work.

H Teton Flood
Milepost 110 on State Hwy. 33

When the Teton Dam suddenly washed away, June 4, 1976, a large reservoir of water (280 feet deep) was dumped on farms and towns below.

Houses floated away, and cropland was ruined as water surged into the Snake River and American Falls Reservoir, which finally controlled the flood. Church, government, and disaster relief agencies responded effectively, but 14 lives were lost, and hundreds of millions of dollars in damage resulted from that unforgettable calamity. All that remains of Teton Dam still can be seen from a viewpoint two miles north of here.

T Teton Dam Site
Drive 3.25 miles east from Newdale on State Hwy. 33. Bear north at the paved road marked "Teton Dam Site", and proceed 1 mile to the overlook area.

Known as one of the most ill-conceived dams in U.S. history, eastern Idaho's Teton Dam was controversial from the start. In 1948, the Fremont Madison Irrigation District petitioned the U.S. Bureau of Reclamation to construct a dam on the Teton River in hopes of gaining more water rights for their agricultural needs. Despite opposition from the Environmental Protection Agency, the Idaho Fish and Game Department, the Idaho Conservation League, and the Bureau of Sports Fisheries, Congress approved the dam in 1964.

Sent to survey the dam site, the U.S. Army Corp of Engineers determined that the project was not economically justifiable. The dam would not provide any great benefits for irrigation, hydropower, or flood-control. In addition, the selected site was composed of highly permeable, volcanic rocks that would not provide a stable foundation for the project. Regardless of recommendations against the Teton Dam, the Bureau of Reclamation persisted with their claims that a dam would provide numerous benefits to area residents at a low cost.

Under the direction of Morrison-Knudsen Company and Peter Kiewit Son's Company, construction began in 1972. With 500 men working three shifts around the clock, the dam was finally completed in spring 1976. Measuring 3,050 feet long, 1,600 feet wide, and 305 feet high, the dam held back the waters of the newly forming Teton Reservoir for a short period of time.

On June 5, 1976, problems began arising with the Bureau's pride project. With the reservoir now nearly full, workers reported two leaks in the dam at 8:30 AM. At 10:00 AM, another leak was discovered, and bulldozer crews were sent to patch the leaks. Despite the crew's efforts, the leaks continued to grow as the porous volcanic rock below the dam allowed reservoir water to easily slip through. Realizing the gravity of the situation, the Fremont and Madison County sheriff's office began issuing evacuation warnings, and at 11:52 AM, catastrophe struck.

As the dam burst open, eighty billion gallons of water spilled south, wreaking havoc in all directions. Roaring through the agricultural valleys, the community of Wilford was the first hit. 150 homes were destroyed and six people drowned as the river headed for the neighboring communities. At 1:00 PM, Sugar City was hit, at 2:30 PM came Rexburg, and then Idaho Falls, Shelley, and Blackfoot were affected. Three days later when the flood finally subsided at the American Falls Reservoir, the damage was incomprehensible. The dam that would supposedly provide so many benefits to Idaho's people instead became a costly mistake. Lives were lost, fertile topsoil was stripped, 25,000 people were temporarily displaced from their homes, 18,000 head of livestock were missing, and total damages amounted to over $800 million.

Today, little sign is left of the controversial dam and the damage it created. Visitors will find an abandoned engineering lab, a parking lot, and a few Bureau of Reclamation signs stating what benefits were lost as a result of the dam's failure. Owing up to the disaster, the Bureau of Reclamation now must have a team of non-government engineers review any major dam proposal.

TV Green Canyon Hot Springs
Newdale. 458-4454. Take State Hwy. 33 to milepost 116. Here, turn onto Canyon Creek Rd. and proceed 4 miles to the hot springs.

Green Canyon Hot Springs provides year-round recreation fun in a relaxing atmosphere. Boasting hot springs at a temperature of 118 degrees, Green Canyon features an indoor and outdoor pool. The area surrounding the hot springs is popular for camping, picnicking, huckleberry picking, mountain biking, and hunting. Green Canyon is open 10 AM to 10 PM Monday through Saturday from April 1 to September 30. From October through March, the site is open from 10 AM to 10 PM on weekends.

19 Food, Lodging

Driggs
Pop. 1,100

When Mormon homesteaders arrived here in 1888, there were few other settlers in this area. More Mormons ventured up from Utah soon after, and the town of Driggs was formed. As there were so many Driggses who signed the petition for a post office, the department decided to name the town after them. This was done in 1894, but the town itself was not incorporated until 1909.

In the early 1830s, trade gatherings between the Indians, trappers, and mountain men were held just one mile south of Driggs. Known by locals for years as "The Cultural Hub of the Teton Basin," Driggs is a blur of activity that offers supplies to those visiting the Tetons and Big Hole Mountains.

Tetonia
Pop. 247

Tetonia is situated on the northern end of the Teton Valley and draws its name from Wyoming's Teton Mountain Range rising in the distance. Settlers first began arriving in the area in 1881, and in 1910, the town was incorporated. However, much of the town's growth is due to the 1912 arrival of the Union Pacific Railroad. As the railroad passed through town, more business opportunities emerged, and a post office has continuously operated in the town since 1913.

Victor
Pop. 840

As Mormon emigrants migrated to the Teton Valley and settled the Driggs area, the Saints at Driggs advised later settlers to proceed south and settle the land near the Teton Pass. Following the Saints' order, several homesteaders moved to the area in 1899 and established a colony. With the LDS Church governing the community, the site became known as "Raymond" after Mormon Bishop David Raymond Sinclair. In 1901, the federal government finally incorporated the site, and the small colony grew into a town. Just a few years later, the town's name was changed to honor George Victor Sherwood. A courageous man, Sherwood continued to deliver mail from Victor to Jackson, Wyoming despite a hostile scare from Bannock Indians during the settlement's formative years.

While Victor's economy relied heavily upon a limestone quarry that operated from 1926 to 1970, the area now serves several alfalfa/hay ranches. Victor has also become a popular stopping point for tourists visiting Yellowstone National Park and the Grand Tetons.

Alta
Pop. 400

Although Alta is officially located in Wyoming, the only way to reach the mountain town is through Driggs, Idaho. The settlement, nestled in the grandeur of Wyoming's Teton Mountains, arose between 1888 and 1890 with the arrival of Mormon pioneers. The town draws its name from the Spanish word meaning "high," and is today recognized as home to the Grand Targhee Ski and Summer Resort.

H John Colter
Milepost 136.5 on State Hwy. 33

John Colter discovered this valley in 1808 while exploring the Yellowstone and upper Snake country in search of beaver.

Setting out by himself with his gun and a 30-pound pack, he tried to get the Indians to join in his trapping business. On the way here from a Yellowstone post 240 miles to the northeast, he came upon Colter's Hell – some hot springs near Cody, Wyoming. On his way back, he explored Yellowstone Park. In the spring of 1810, after several perilous escapes from the Blackfeet, he returned to Missouri, lucky to get back alive.

H Teton Range
Milepost 136.5 on State Hwy. 33

Flanked by rock formations more than 2.5 billion years old, these three granite peaks rose up in less than nine million years. Very new as mountains go, they still are rising.

Hinged at the base of the ridge before you, a block of rock 40 miles long broke along a fault line, where the rock tipped up to become the top of the ridge. During the past 250,000 years, extensive glacial ice sculpted these spectacular peaks from the hard, resistant granite.

H Pierre's Hole
Milepost 143.9 on State Hwy. 33

Teton Valley was known originally as Pierre's Hole. Rich in beaver, it was a favorite stomping ground for British and American fur traders and trappers between 1819-40.

"Old Pierre" Tevanitagon, an Iroquois Indian fur trapper for the Hudson's bay Company, gave his name to this beaver-rich valley. Pierre's Hole was the scene of the annual rendezvous of mountain men and suppliers – The Great Rocky Mountain Fair – in 1832. That wild party ended in a free-for-all battle with the Gros Ventre Indians, which the trappers and their Indian friends won. The valley was permanently settled in 1882.

T Targhee Village Golf Course
Stateline Rd. at Golf Course Rd., Driggs. 354-8577. Located 5 miles east of Driggs near Alta, Wyoming

Wide fairways lined with small trees greet golfers on this 6,238-yard course. Built in 1986, the 9-hole course is rated a par-70 and is framed by gorgeous views of the Grand Teton Mountains. Although water comes into play on several holes, the course is suitable for players of all ability. Tee times can be scheduled seven days in advance if so desired, but as all locals know, this course favors a more relaxed attitude where there's no dress code and mismatched clubs are the norm. The course is open daily from April 15 to October 31 with green fees at $14 for 9 holes and $22 for 18 holes.

A Scenic Journey Through the Bridger-Teton, Caribou, and Targhee National Forests

Three National Forests spread across a diverse ecosystem in southeastern Idaho and western Wyoming: the Bridger-Teton, Caribou, and Targhee. These forests are rich in natural wonders ranging from grasslands to dense stands of timber, lush canyons, pristine wild lands, clear lakes and wild rivers, alpine meadows, caves, craggy ridges, and towering mountain peaks. Within the three forests' boundaries are 6 million acres of America's public lands.

The Bridger-Teton, Caribou, and Targhee National Forests are surrounded by a neighborhood filled with wondrous diversity. Rugged plains, high deserts, and pastoral low country fringe national and state parks and monuments, wildlife refuges, sand dunes, lava flows, waterways, and a menu of National Natural Landmarks administered by the Bureau of Land Management. Everyone is welcomed as they journey through this Idaho/Wyoming neighborhood and partake in the feast of outdoor adventures.

Sagas of Bygone Days
Long before humans left their mark upon the land, wind and water shaped the face of the forests. Geological monoliths rose from the valley floors where erosion exposed ridges and peaks of hard naked stone. Crystal lakes collected water on the mountaintops to feed the rivers and streams below. Fertile soil encouraged trees and other vegetation to flourish in canyons and valleys while animals filled the forests with new life. Today, the National Forests in southeastern Idaho and western Wyoming are rich in nature's heritage.

A history of human influence is apparent on these National Forests. Explorers, trappers, mountain men, miners, and farmers followed in the footsteps of Native Americans who occupied the land for centuries. Pioneers seeking a new life in the West left evidence of their journey along the Oregon Trail. The sagas of this cultural heritage are preserved in ancient campsites, grave markers, abandoned mines, and historic structures.

Startling Spring
Nothing is more beautiful than spring in the western forests. It is heralded by rushing rivers, lush green grasses, budding trees, brilliant sunshine, and clean, crisp air. Animals emerge from their winter shelter and give birth to their young. It is time to begin fishing, hiking to the snowline, wandering the grasslands, and driving the Scenic Byways. Visitors may choose to ride horseback, spend a day in nature with their camera, float down a rushing river, or take a leisurely hike. Spring is a sensitive time for forest ecosystems. Visitors can protect these natural wonders by recreating with thoughtfulness and care. If the roads and trails are muddy or wet, leave the area and come back another day.

Stupendous Summer
Summer in southeastern Idaho and western Wyoming offers a myriad of outdoor delights to forest visitors. This is the busiest time of year on the Bridger-Teton, Caribou, and Targhee National Forests as trails, campgrounds, picnic areas, lodges, and resorts receive extensive use. Caving, "ATVing," rock climbing, mountain biking, and whitewater rafting are popular activities for the robust adventurer. Other visitors enjoy photography, watching the abundant wildlife, camping, and hiking. If professional assistance is needed, a list of outfitters and guides is available from Forest offices. Using the land safely and with respect ensures there will be recreation opportunities in the future.

Sizzling Scenery
Autumn nights bring freezing temperatures and spectacular fall colors to the National Forests and Grasslands in southeastern Idaho and western Wyoming. A breathtaking array of incandescent red, gold, and orange leaves contrast with the yellow grasses and luminous green pines reflected in crystal blue lake waters. There are fewer visitors on weekdays, but hunters, hikers, and other adventurers actively use campgrounds and trails on the fall weekends.

Snowy Splendor
Snow and ice turns the Bridger-Teton, Caribou, and Targhee National Forests into a virtual winter wonderland. Downhill and cross-country skiers, snowboarders, sledders, snowmobile and snowshoe enthusiasts can indulge in their favorite "cool experience" in the versatile terrain of the forests. Visitors need the proper clothing and equipment for cold, changeable weather to keep themselves safe, dry, and warm. Check avalanche conditions before venturing into the backcountry.

Big Springs National Recreation Water Trail
A leisurely float on the Big Springs National Recreation Water Trail gives visitors a chance to watch for abundant wildlife such as Canada geese, trumpeter swans, sandhill cranes, muskrats, moose, and kokanee salmon. Beautiful rainbow trout live year-round in the 52-degree springs at the headwaters of Henry's Fork.

Curlew National Grassland
Humans and animals have shared the grassy plains and perennial streams of the Curlew National Grassland for more than 2,000 years. Prehistoric sites reveal the history of aboriginal people who feasted on bison and other game, and took their fill of fresh water from the springs. Later, ranchers and homesteaders used the Grassland for farming and cattle grazing. Today, the unique values of the Curlew National Grassland are recognized and conserved. It is a literal outdoor classroom featuring precious water, valuable minerals, wildlife, native plants, cultural sites, wildlife, and quiet serenity.

Guidelines and More Information
Remember "Safety First" as you will be visiting the homes of wild animals living in the National Forests. Prior to your visit, learn about the resident wildlife and how to conduct yourself in their territory. Awareness is the key to your personal safety. Never approach wild animals – give them plenty of space.

For more information, contact the following agencies:

Bridger-Teton National Forest: (307) 739-5500
Jackson Hole Visitor Center:
  www.fs.fed.us/jhgyvc
Caribou National Forest: (208) 624-3151
National Forest Campground Reservation System:
  1-877-444-6777
Bureau of Land Management:
  Idaho Falls (208) 524-7559;
  Kemmerer, Wyoming (307) 828-4500;
  Pinedale, Wyoming (307) 367-5300
Idaho Department of Parks and Recreation:
  (208) 334-4199
Idaho Falls Visitor Center: (208) 523-3278
Idaho Division of Tourism: (208) 334-2470
Backcountry Avalanche Hotline:
  (307) 733-2664
SE Idaho Avalanche Hotline: (208) 239-7650

Reprinted from U.S. Forest Service (Intermountain Region) brochure

---

T The Links at Teton Peaks
127 N. 400 W., Tetonia. 456-2372. Located 4 miles west of Driggs

The Links at Teton Peaks is the only recognized Scottish style links course in Idaho. Opened in 2001 under the design of Bob Wilson, this course is extremely challenging. From the first of its 18 holes, the course tests the ability of even the most advanced player. As a result, a plaque in the clubhouse recognizes the few who have earned a score under 85. The course is open daily during spring and summer, and green fees are $19 for 9 holes and $25 for 18 holes.

T Teton River Basin
North of Driggs.

During the early 19th century, the lush Teton River Basin was known as "Pierre's Hole" and was a mountain man and fur trading hub. The valley drew its original name from Iroquois trapper, Pierre Tevanitagon, who frequented the area until his 1827 Montana death at the hands of the Blackfeet. In addition to Pierre, European and American trappers visited the basin, and Nez Perce, Flathead, and Gros Ventre Indians settled in the region. Although the fur trade started out on friendly terms, friction between trading parties and the Native Americans soon became a daily part of life. Skirmishes were common with only minor injuries resulting, but this trend soon ended. In 1832, a major battle broke out at a rendezvous, and nearly fifty Native American and white men, women, and children were killed with several others seriously wounded.

Despite its bloody beginnings, the Teton River Basin has quieted down and retains its lush landscape. Cradled between the forested peaks of the Grand Teton Mountains to the east and the Big Hole Mountains to the west, this rural mountain valley includes fertile farmland, pastures, and open ranges. It has often been nicknamed "The Tetons' Quiet Side."

T Pierre's Playhouse
27 N. Main, Victor. 787-2249.

Genteel heroines, handsome heroes, and lurking villains wait around every corner at Pierre's Playhouse. Originally built as the community's first movie theater in the late 1940s, the facility now hosts the Teton Players and welcomes nearly 9,000 spectators each summer. The Teton Players, an organization comprised of local volunteers, performs classic melodramas throughout the summer months in a spirit of promoting fun. Audience members are encouraged to participate, and booing and hissing at the villain is required. Advance reservations for the productions are highly recommended.

T Spud Drive-In
231 S. Hwy. 33, Driggs. 354-2727.
www.spuddrivein.com

The Grand Teton Mountains form the backdrop for one of America's few remaining historical entertainment venues. The Spud Drive-In was built in 1953 and has been playing to generations of movie lovers ever since. The theater was added to the National Register of Historic Places in June 2003 and is open on summer weekends. Look for "Old Murphy", the red truck with the giant spud sitting out front.

T Teton Mountain Range
Borders eastern horizon from Tetonia to Victor on State Hwy. 33.

Surrounded by mountains more than 2.5 billion years old, the Teton Mountain Range rose up along a faultline less than 9 million years ago. Ancient glaciers sculpted the granite, pegmatite, schist, and gneiss peaks, but it wasn't until 1820 that they received a name. A dazzling sight to behold, the peaks appeared to a group of French-Canadian trappers as "Les Trois Tetons" meaning "the three breasts." Today, the three peaks are known as the Grand (13,770 feet), the Middle, and the South Teton.

T Teton Pass
State Hwy. 33 near the Idaho/Wyoming border outside Victor

Situated at an elevation of 8,429 feet, Teton Pass offers breathtaking views into Wyoming's Jackson Hole valley and is steeped in history. John Colter was the first white man to cross the pass. In 1808, Colter used an Indian hunting trail to cross from Wyoming into Idaho. Just three years later, trapper Wilson Price Hunt led his expedition across the same route.

When mining became big business in the West, mining companies decided to build a primi-

A FLY FISHING PARADISE

Bruce Staples

Eastern Idaho hosts three world-class fisheries: the Henry's Fork, Henry's Lake, and the South Fork reach of the Snake River. These are only a few high quality trout waters available in this area on Yellowstone Park's doorstep.

Henry's Fork
The Henry's Fork has a hundred-year reputation because of the fabulous rainbow trout fishery in the Box Canyon-Last Chance-Harriman State Park (formerly Railroad Ranch) reach and in the river above Island Park Reservoir. Now emerging is the fact that an equivalent quality rainbow trout fishery exists in the Pinehaven-Hatchery Ford-Cardiac Canyon reach. Below, the superb rainbow-brown trout fishery from Bear Gulch downstream to below St. Anthony also vouches for how good the cold-water fishery habitat of this river is.

Over ninety miles of river are on the table here. Throughout are individuals ranging to double figure poundage. Presenting streamer patterns late and early in the season, giant stonefly imitations and caddis and mayfly imitations in season are the most effective means of encountering these individuals. The famous aquatic insect emergences of the Box Canyon–Harriman reach are mostly duplicated in the lower river. Throughout this length float fishing abounds and plenty of opportunities for walk-in fishing exist.

Further, if efforts of the Nature Conservancy to acquire a maintenance flow from Henry's Lake to their Flat Ranch Preserve succeed, six miles of walk-in meadow stream will be added to the Henry's Fork's array of high quality reaches.

South Fork Reach of the Snake River
This seventy-mile reach from Palisades Dam downstream to the Henry's Fork confluence rivals Montana's Bighorn River below Yellowtail Dam in popularity. Its high season begins with trout responding to the giant and golden stonefly emergences in late June, enters a great pale morning dun emergence, on to an early autumn blue winged olive emergence, and commences with the autumn brown trout run. Until the early 1960s, the South Fork was a cutthroat trout fishery. Now, it hosts Idaho's densest brown trout population. It also produced the state record brown trout. Browns in excess of twenty inches are common, and presenting streamer patterns throughout the season results in trophies. Rainbows are becoming numerous with many individuals exceeding the twenty-inch mark. A good population of cutthroat trout rounds out the South Fork's trout roster.

Famed as a drift boat destination, the South Fork and its major tributaries, Palisades and Pine Creeks, offer a huge variety of walk-in destinations. The best selection is off the fourteen mile long South Fork Road above Heise and along the south side of the river from Swan Valley Bridge upstream to Palisades Dam. On the lower river, the Twin Bridges area and around the Heise Bridge also offer opportunities.

Upland Rivers
If the Big Lost, Blackfoot, Fall, Teton, and Portneuf Rivers were placed in any other part of the country, they would become stars. Add to these the Salt River tributaries, Robinson Creek, Bitch Creek, Warm River and many others.

Media attention for the South Fork and the Henry's Fork has kept all these waters almost a secret. In many ways, they offer quality experiences not easily found on more heralded waters. Don't be fooled by their smaller size because many host trophy trout that rival the South and Henry's fork residents in size! Here are a few particulars. There are seven miles of public accessible meadow stream on the Blackfoot River Wildlife Management area. The late June giant stonefly emergence in Fall River's canyon has become a destination event. You can experience rainbows and cutthroat responding to Teton River's great pale morning dun and terrestrial emergences in a distractingly beautiful setting. Big Lost River's midseason crane fly and late season midge and blue winged olive emergences activate rainbows ranging to over two feet long.

Stillwaters
From Henry's Lake in the north to Treasureton Reservoir in the south, eastern Idaho hosts a matchless array of stillwater fisheries. Island Park Reservoir, Springfield Reservoir, Twenty-four mile Reservoir, Daniels Reservoir and the Harriman Fish Pond would also be top quality trout fisheries anywhere. Similar fishery quality exists in thirty or so remaining waters ranging from high mountain lakes to irrigation reservoirs because most have histories of producing trophy trout, whether cutthroat, rainbows, brookies or browns. Simulating superb midge emergences in season is the most effective way of fishing these waters, but seasonal dragonfly and damselfly, speckled dun emergences, or presenting leech and baitfish imitations are productive approaches.

Much more information is available. You can acquire it, strategy help, quality products, guide recommendations, licenses for Idaho and Yellowstone National Park, and enroll in classes in all fly fishing facets at:

Jimmy's All Seasons Angler
275 A Street
Idaho Falls, ID 83402
Phone: 208-522-9242
E-mail: jimmys@ida.net
Website:www.jimmysflyshop.com

St. Anthony	Jan	Feb	March	April	May	June	July	Aug	Sep	Oct	Nov	Dec	Annual
Average Max. Temperature (F)	28.7	33.7	42.6	55.5	66.2	74.2	83.3	82.4	72.6	60.2	42.1	30.6	56.0
Average Min. Temperature (F)	8.3	11.3	18.7	27.6	35.5	42.0	46.8	45.1	37.1	28.4	19.6	9.9	27.5
Average Total Precipitation (in.)	1.39	1.01	1.07	1.20	1.80	1.61	0.79	0.78	0.90	0.99	1.25	1.43	14.22
Average Total Snowfall (in.)	12.8	8.7	3.2	0.9	0.1	0.1	0.0	0.0	0.0	0.4	4.1	12.2	42.5
Average Snow Depth (in.)	10	10	4	0	0	0	0	0	0	0	1	5	2

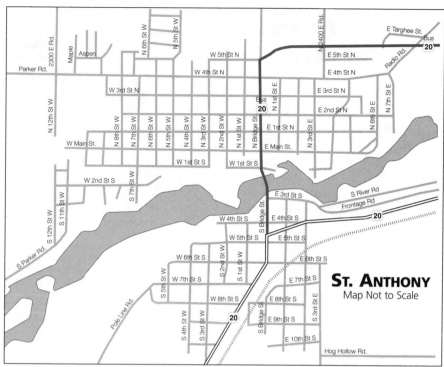

ST. ANTHONY
Map Not to Scale

tive road leading into Jackson Hole. In the early 1900s, the Dunn Mining Company carved a windy road through the granite mountains. Just a few years later, the U.S. Forest Service decided to build its own road. Between 1913 and 1917, young forest service crews used horses and plenty of manpower to create a more user-friendly road. Cars first used the road in 1913.

Today, these old roads have been nearly forgotten, but the individuals who created them helped open the west to further expansion. While these original roads no longer exist, the current highway does parallel the historic routes in many places.

V Grand Targhee Ski and Summer Resort

(800) 827-4433. In Driggs, proceed through town. Bear left at the traffic light near Key Bank onto Ski Hill Rd. Continue approximately 6 blocks to a fork in the road. Turn left here, following Ski Hill Rd. through Alta, Wyoming to its end at the resort.

Officially located in Wyoming, Grand Targhee Ski and Summer Resort is only accessible from Idaho. This full-service resort nestled in the western slope of the majestic Teton Mountains is known as a powder paradise. Receiving an average of 500 inches of snow annually, Grand Targhee has been dubbed as one of the best family resorts in the West with the finest powder in North America.

The resort includes 2,000 acres of lift terrain with an additional 1,000 acres strictly reserved for snowcat powder skiing. The lift acreage includes 64 wide-groomed runs, a 2,200-foot vertical drop, one rope tow, one quad chair, one double chair, and one high-speed quad chairlift. Unsurpassed scenery awaits those ready for a day of snowcat powder skiing. For those uninterested in a down-hill adventure, several Nordic trails are available.

The resort is open daily during ski season from 9 AM to 4 PM. Full-day lift tickets are $53 for adults 15 and older, $33 for youth ages 6-14, and free to those under 5 who are accompanied by a paying adult. Half-day adult lift tickets are $38. In addition, multi-day value rates are available as well as reasonably priced season passes.

V Teton River Drainage

The Teton River flows off the Grand Tetons' western slopes and is responsible for draining 890 square miles before merging with the Henrys Fork of the Snake River outside St. Anthony. While a flat valley floor and sandhill cranes characterize the river's upper portion, the lower portion winds through tight canyons. Both sections, however, provide excellent fishing opportunities to both novice and expert anglers in one of Idaho's most serene settings. The drainage supports populations of wild cut-throat trout, wild and hatchery released rainbow trout, brook trout, hybrids, and mountain white-fish. At one time, the Idaho Department of Fish and Game released over 7,500 rainbow trout annually into the Teton River. Today, the Teton River is open for fishing Memorial Day through November 30th.

S Bergmeyer Manufacturing Co., Inc.

229 N. Hwy. 33, Driggs. 354-2000 or 800-348-3356 www.bergmeyermfg.com

The Bergmeyer Manufacturing furniture showroom and warehouse is located approximately two miles north of Hwy. 33 in the scenic Teton Valley. Award winning architect, Mori Bergmeyer, and his knowledgeable staff design and craft custom furniture with a variety of finishes for the discriminating interior designer. Specializing in accommodating all decor types, the staff utilizes the most advanced machinery along with art metal, log, and custom shops to fill the demand for unique furnishings. These finely crafted pieces are built on-site, and many are on display to the public. The

showroom is open Monday through Friday from 8:30 AM to 5 PM where visitors will find the company's regular Farmhouse furniture line along with occasional overruns of custom designs.

M Driggs - Teton Valley Chamber of Commerce

75 N. Main St., Driggs. 354-2500. www.tetonvalleychamber.com; tvcc@tetonvalleychamber.com

20

Drummond
Pop. 15

This tiny town was named after a construction engineer who worked on the railroad in 1911 as the line was built from Ashton to Driggs.

Felt
Pop. 35

John Felt and his brother first settled this area in 1889. They claimed land near Badger Creek, and within no time, other homesteaders began arriving. By 1911, most of the land in the area was taken, and a townsite was dedicated. The Post Office arrived in 1913.

21 Food, Lodging

St. Anthony
Pop. 3,342

In 1887, Charles H. Moon homesteaded and built a bridge and general store in this location. He became the first postmaster a year later and named the town because he noted a resemblance between the nearby Henry's Fork waterfall and the Mississippi River's St. Anthony Falls in Minnesota. The community's location on Henry's Fork of the Snake River provides excellent fly-fishing opportunities, while the St. Anthony Sand Dunes has long been a local draw.

Parker
Pop. 319

This small community was originally called Garden Grove and is said to be named after Wyman Parker, an early Mormon Bishop, and Isaac Parker, the town's postmaster in 1900. Others claim that the "Parker" in the name is drawn from Adelbert Parker who served as post-master of the nearby Egin community in 1880. Nonetheless, when Garden Grove became the larger of the two settlements, Garden Grove residents relocated a few miles away from Egin and established a post office under the name Parker.

Egin

Located just seven miles west of St. Anthony, Egin is the oldest permanent settlement in Fremont County and was established by Mormon settlers in 1879. In 1810, when Andrew Henry wintered in the area, he built a temporary post consisting of a few log houses. This small town was formerly called Greenville but that changed in 1880 with the arrival of the first post office. The term Egin comes from the Shoshone word "ech-unt," meaning "cold."

T Sandbar Swimming Area
St. Anthony. Contact the St. Anthony Chamber of Commerce at 624-4870.

St. Anthony's Sandbar Swimming Area is an easily accessible summer recreation zone. Sandy shores provide perfect opportunities to construct elaborate sandcastles, while a playground area and roped-off swimming area on the Henry's Fork of the Snake River offer hours of entertainment. The free area is open daily during the summer from 9 AM to 5 PM, and a lifeguard is always on duty.

T Fremont County Golf Course
674 N. Golf Course Rd., St. Anthony. 624-7074.

The Fremont County Golf Course is a 9-hole public course that has operated since 1967. Designed by Marvin J. Aslett, the 3,000-yard course features several out-of-bounds stakes and a few undulating bent grass greens. Rated a par-36, the course is open April 1 to October 1. Daily green fees are $8.40 for 9 holes and $13.65 for 18 holes. Tee times are only accepted for weekends and holidays.

T Sand Creek Wildlife Management Area
17 miles north of St. Anthony at the end of Sand Creek Rd.

The Sand Creek Wildlife Management Area is part of the larger Sands Habitat Management Area and is situated at the foot of the Island Park caldera. The area was established to provide a wintering ground for elk, moose, and mule deer that summer in Island Park and nearby Yellowstone National Park. Since the area's establishment, sandhill cranes and trumpeter swans have also occasionally been spotted. The free site is open year-round for wildlife viewing, hiking, camping, and fishing.

T Clyde Keefer Memorial Park
Downtown St. Anthony. Contact the St. Anthony Chamber of Commerce at 624-4870.

Clyde Keefer Memorial Park offers a relaxing atmosphere in downtown St. Anthony. The park is equipped with a large playground area, barbeque facilities, and covered picnic areas, and also offers fishing access ideal for beginning anglers.

T Henry's Fork Greenway
Downtown St. Anthony. Contact the St. Anthony Chamber of Commerce at 624-4870.

Known as the place where nature and people meet, the Henry's Fork Greenway was recently completed through the efforts of St. Anthony volunteers. The one-mile trail winds next to the Henry's Fork of the Snake River and provides an easy walk with beautiful views. Wildlife, including moose, coyotes, foxes, and several bird species, populate the area, and fishing is an ever-popular

ST. ANTHONY SAND DUNES

Geology & History
The St. Anthony Sand Dunes is an unusual area 35 miles long and 5 miles wide. Beautiful dunes, white rolling hills of sand (most 200-300 feet above the valley floor), were formed when quartz sand, carried from the nearby Snake River and ancient lake shorelines, was deposited by prevailing winds among the Juniper Hills. These hills are extinct volcano vents that once poured molten lava onto the Snake River plain.

A local Indian legend about the formation of the sand dunes says that this area was the site of fierce, bloody battles between the Bannock and Shoshone Indians and the Blackfoot tribes, at war over hunting grounds. One day as the sun was sinking, flooding the west with a brilliant afterglow, 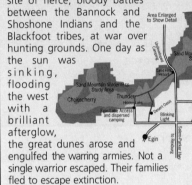 the great dunes arose and engulfed the warring armies. Not a single warrior escaped. Their families fled to escape extinction.

Each evening as the sun sets, the spirits of the warriors are said to chant and moan the tortured cry of the vanquished. Maybe it's just the wind, but with the discovery of arrowheads and other Indian artifacts, you might find yourself wondering just how much of the story is legend.

Facilities
Facilities include a gravel access road, a 60 car parking area, an unloading ramp, and restrooms. A small informal camping area is also available near the parking area. If you enjoy tent camping you are in luck! It is allowed just about anywhere on the dunes when access is gained by foot or off road vehicles. And, if after a day of playing in the sand you'd just love a hot shower and comfy bed, we have lots of great lodging alternatives available in Rexburg. (For more information on camping and lodging alternatives refer to Local Business Information.)

Recreation
In the summer, sandrails and off-road vehicle enthusiasts from all over come to ride the dunes. Though the sand gets hot, the temperature rarely tops 90 degrees. With small rolling hills in the east suitable for youngsters and beginning ATVers, and challenging hills in the west, mountains of sand up to 600 feet high, there's sure to be a dune for everyone.

If off-road vehicles aren't your thing, there's fun to be had hiking, horseback riding, sandboarding, hunting, primitive camping, and cooling off in the warm shallow waters of Hidden Lake.

In the winter, the sand dunes transform with the cold and snow to a popular winter playground that lures cross country skiers, snowboarders, and snowmobilers. It's also a great place to take the kids tubing and sledding. But bundle up! It's cold out there!

Rules & Regulations
The St. Anthony Sand Dunes are part of the Sand Mountain Wilderness Study Area managed by the BLM. This area provides critical winter range for deer, elk, antelope, and moose. Recreation use off of the open sand or designated trails can result in the destruction of vegetation and other features of the landscape. To protect this area, the following rules apply:

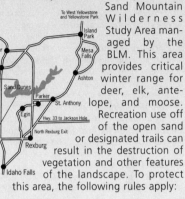

- Stay on the open sand. Protect the vegetation.

- Follow designated trails. Unless a route is specifically signed OPEN, it is closed.

- Use only plastic beverage containers; glass containers are prohibited.

- Make sure off road vehicles are equipped with a 6-foot long whip antenna with a red or orange flag.

- Motorized vehicles yield the right of way to those on foot or horseback.

- Pack out trash.

- Drive only ATVs, motorcycles, and dune rails beyond parking area.

- Idaho residents must display a valid state ORV sticker on their motorcycle or ATV. Out-of-state ATs must have a valid registration sicker if one is required in their home state.

- No open campfires are allowed inside the WSA (Wilderness Study Area) except in the designated Red Road Open Sand Campfire Area.

- The burning of pallets, treated wood, or non-wood materials is prohibited in any campfire area.

- Quiet hours within the Egin Lake Access Site and the Red Road Recreation Area are from 11 PM to 7 AM.

Reprinted from Idaho Travel Council brochure

sport along the path. In addition, informational signs along the trail educate users about the vegetation and wildlife in the surrounding region. The greenway is open year-round free of charge.

T Fort Henry Historic Site
Contact the St. Anthony Chamber of Commerce at 624-4870. In St. Anthony, locate the Fourth St N. Extension Rd. Proceed 3 miles south across the extension road, cross the Henry's Fork of the Snake River, and locate the site monument on the road's east side.

Situated next to the Henry's Fork of the Snake River, Fort Henry represents the first American fur trading post established west of the Rocky Mountains. Former Pennsylvania lead miner and partner of the St. Louis Missouri Fur Company, Andrew Henry was dispatched to present day Idaho on a trapping expedition in 1809. Although Henry looked forward to the excursion as a western adventure, he and his party of 400 men experienced great hardship. Blackfoot Indians attacked the group several times on the eastern side of the Rockies, so Henry was anxious to establish winter camp on the mountain's western side. After discovering a beautiful lake near present day Island Park in July 1810, the men proceeded several miles downstream and built a fort consisting of numerous log buildings where they would winter until early 1811.

The men, however, were inadequately prepared for the severe winter season. By the end of winter, the group was forced to slaughter and eat its own horses to survive. When spring arrived, Henry broke his group into three smaller parties. He traveled to the Mandan villages to visit Manuel Lisa and then returned home to Missouri where he remained sporadically involved in the fur trade until 1824.

In 1937, a local Boy Scout troop erected a monument near the fort site honoring Henry and his men. The actual fort stood approximately 1,700 feet west of this monument. His legacy is also remembered in the naming of Henry's Lake State Park near Island Park and the Henry's Fork of the Snake River.

LM Colonial Rose Tearoom and Bed & Breakfast
411 N. Bridge, St. Anthony. 624-3530.

Would you like some tea and crumpets? If so, then discover the Colonial Rose Tearoom and Bed & Breakfast located within walking distance of downtown St. Anthony. Nestled inside a historic 1906 home, the tearoom offers custom teas, low teas, and high teas in a cozy Victorian atmosphere. For overnight guests, the Bed & Breakfast provides two uniquely decorated bedrooms with a shared bath, beautiful area views, and scrumptious breakfasts including egg and bacon quiche, sourdough hotcakes, and homemade raspberry and huckleberry preserves. Whether you're planning a special gathering or staying overnight in St. Anthony, the Colonial Rose Tearoom and Bed & Breakfast offers something for both young and

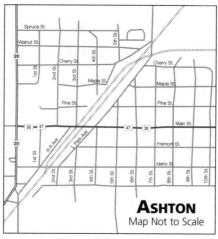

ASHTON
Map Not to Scale

old. The doors are always open with a cup of warm tea inviting you to stay awhile and feel at home.

M St. Anthony Chamber of Commerce
420 N. Bridge St. Ste C., St. Anthony. 624-4870. www.stanthonychamber.com; sachamber@fretel.com

22 Food, Lodging

Chester
Pop. 100

Utah pioneers founded Chester in the late 1880s. Originally known as Fall River because of its proximity to that water source, the town's name was changed in 1894 under Post Office Department orders.

Ashton
Pop. 1,129

Founded in February 1906 with the arrival of the Oregon Shortline Railroad, Ashton draws its name from the railroad's chief construction engineer, William Ashton. William and his son settled in the area after the OSL shifted its tracks two miles west of Marysville to avoid the high priced right-of-way in that area. A month after the railroad arrived, the town was incorporated.

The town's original railroad economy has long since shifted to agriculture. Recognized as the world's largest seed-potato producing region, Ashton's economy is dependent upon potatoes. In fact, every fall the school kids are released for a two to ten week period where they spend time helping their family and neighbors harvest the area's average 11,000 planted acres of potatoes. Canola, peas, hay, wheat, and barley are also raised in the area fields.

Marysville
Pop. 200

Mary Lucinda Baker was one of the first women to settle here, along with Mary Dorcheus, Mary Patlow, Mary Spratling, and Mary Smith. They were all part of the Mormon ward organized and established here in 1893, and the town's name is therefore plural in honor of all of them. Mary Baker later served as the town's first postmaster. The nearby Falls River was used as the source for a canal that continues to irrigate the farmland surrounding Marysville to the north and south.

Warm River
Pop. 10

Situated near the swiftly flowing Warm River from which it received its name, this tiny village operated a post office from 1907 to 1924. Today, it is known as Idaho's smallest incorporated city.

H The Three Tetons
Milepost 362.7 on U.S. Hwy. 20

The giant peaks to the southeast were a famous early Western landmark known to fur hunters and mountain men.

Perhaps as early as 1819, French-speaking trappers were calling them the Trois Tetons – the three breasts. More prosaic English-speaking mountain men named them the Pilot Knobs, but the romantic French name stuck. This is one of the finest views of the peaks from the west, the side from which they were seen by the men who named them.

T Aspen Acres Golf Course
4179 E. 1100 N., Ashton. 652-3524 or (800) 845-2374. Eight miles southeast of Ashton

An old farm and aspen groves provide the backdrop for this 18-hole, executive length course. Measuring 2,992 yards, Aspen Acres is a par-60 course offering scenic views of the neighboring Teton Mountains, bird watching, and wildlife encounters. While the course is suitable for beginners, it also offers plenty of challenges to the experienced player. The course is open daily from daylight to dusk. Green fees for 18-holes are $11 for adults, $7.75 for teens, and $5.25 for juniors.

T Hess Heritage Museum
3417 E. 1200 St., Ashton. 652-7353.

On this restored 250 acre pioneer farm, visitors will find an old home, carriage house, social hall, village square, school, blacksmith shop, and park. The museum is open from mid-April to mid-October by appointment only.

T Mesa Falls Recreation Area
North of Warm River on State Hwy. 47/Mesa Falls Scenic Byway

Recreation Area & Scenic Byway
The Mesa Falls Recreation Area, beginning at Bear Gulch, follows the Mesa Falls Scenic Byway and includes Upper and Lower Mesa Falls and Grandview Campground. It ends at the junction with Hwy. 20 near Harriman State Park. The entry fee at Upper Mesa Falls is also good for Harriman Park (save your stub). A pathway and boardwalk leads from the Inn right to the brink of the falls. The upper part of this walkway is universally accessible. The visitor center and gift shop at Upper Mesa Falls will be open seven days a week from Memorial Day to Labor Day.

Approximately 1.3 million years ago, a huge volcanic eruption created an ash layer hundreds of feet deep. The ash layer was compressed into rock known as Mesa Falls Tuff. Later eruptions filled the area with basalt lava flows. For 500,000 years the Henry's Fork of the Snake River has been carving the canyon seen today. The Mesa Falls Tuff forms the ledge that the falls cascade over. Upper Mesa Falls is 114 feet high.

American Indians used the upper Snake River Valley for centuries before the arrival of Europeans. Small and large game, fish, berries, lodgepole pine, and other resources of the Mesa Falls area were harvested seasonally.

Mesa Power Company built Big Falls Inn between 1912 and 1914, probably to be an office. A dam and power generation plant were planned but never built. Instead the area became a tourist attraction and the Inn became a stage stop and hotel for travelers going to Yellowstone National Park. Montana Power purchased the area in 1936. In later years, the Inn was used as a restaurant, dance hall, and scout camp. The Forest Service acquired the property in 1986 through a land exchange.

Work on restoring the Inn began in 1997. The Idaho State Department of Parks and Recreation and the U.S. Forest Service became partners in managing the site. Over the next three years, the Inn was restored to historic standards and is now listed in the National Register of Historic Places.

One mile south of Upper Mesa Falls is the Grandview Overlook of Lower Mesa Falls. Lower Mesa Falls is 65 feet high. The Civilian Conservation Corps (CCC) built the rock and mortar overlook in the 1930s. Grandview Campground is adjacent to the overlook.

The Mesa Falls Scenic Byway begins in Ashton, Idaho and winds through farmland, forest, logged over areas, and open meadows. The roadway was recently rebuilt and resurfaced.

A seasonal progression of wildflowers blankets the ground in the Mesa Falls Recreation Area. Look for glacier lilies, spring beauties, and heartleaf arnica in the early spring, camas and mules ears a littler later, and lupine, asters, and Indian paintbrush in mid-summer.

Please be safe during your visit to Mesa Falls and stay on the walkways at all times. Special group tours of the site are available throughout the summer and can be arranged by calling the Ashton/Island Park Ranger Station at (208) 652-7442, Harriman State Park at (208) 558-7368, or inquire inside Big Falls Inn.

The History of the Big Falls Inn
John Henry Hendricks and his wife, Clara Wahlen, homesteaded 160 acres in the Mesa Falls area in 1901. He paid $1.25 per acre. They built a cabin 200 feet from the Upper Falls and lived in it with their four small children. Hendricks was hoping to one-day harness the power of the upper falls to bring electricity to Marysville, Idaho.

To make ends meet, he drove a stagecoach in Yellowstone in the summers. He worked in sawmills and ran a trap line in the winter. Clara worried about her children – the steep cliffs and fast water of the isolated homestead were dangerous. She couldn't wait to move. Hendricks made final proof on the claim on January 26, 1903 before

Thomas Elliott, United States Commissioner in St. Anthony. Hendricks then immediately sold the property to Elliott, although the patent had not yet been received. It is interesting to note that U.S. Commissioners couldn't file for homestead property.

Elliott and a group of other businessmen formed the Snake River Electric Light and Power Company. Hendricks received cash and stock as payment for the land. Both parties later disputed the exact amount of both. When Hendricks received patent on the property on November 25, 1904, he signed it over to other wealthy members of the company then voted a $1000 assessment per member to begin development of the site. Hendricks and others of modest means were thus effectively removed from the company.

The proceedings did not pass unnoticed, and by 1905, the Government Land Office was investigating. Supervisor Homer Fenn of the Targhee National Forest stated in a letter to the Chief Forester in February 1907 that Elliott had admitted that he earlier gave $200 to Hendricks to file on the property, but as there were not witnesses to that statement there was not a "suitable case for cancellation of the claim and sale."

Though the mission of the Snake River Electric Light and Power Company was to produce electricity, they never succeeded. In 1912, for unknown reasons Elliott and the Snake River Electric Light and Power Company began a series of sales of the property. The land changed hands three times, although the board members (all associated with Montana Power) remained the same.

A power dam or penstock was never built, but shortly after 1913 a log building – Big Falls Inn – was erected at the present site. Mesa Power Company (one of the many names given to this Montana power subsidiary) records show expenditures of $14,000 for building materials and labor between 1913 and 1916. The layout of the building is far more suited to an office space or company retreat center than to a lodge with paying visitors. This fact suggests the company did not initially intend to use the building as an inn at all. Perhaps the increase in tourist traffic along the highway to Yellowstone National Park impressed them and they decided to take advantage of it. The road to the park at that time was grueling and Big Falls Inn would be a good halfway point.

Operation of the Big Falls Inn continued into the 1930s. The long time caretaker, Charlie Causey, was famed for his hospitality, especially his cooking, gambling, and homemade spirits. Big Falls Inn is mentioned in the Administrative Plan for the Targhee Forest in 1924. Supervisor Stoddard noted that though the road from the highway to the Inn was in poor condition a cooperative agreement had been made with the Ashton Commercial Club to help with maintenance on the road.

The improvement of the old Yellowstone Hwy. was already taking its toll on hotel finances. Better road conditions on the old highway brought more and more people pushing straight through to Yellowstone. The hotel had evidently closed down by 1932, as it receives no mention in the final

Administrative Plan for the Hwy. Uses of the area that year.

In December of 1935, Mesa Power Company sold the property to Idaho Transmission Company. This firm had numerous holdings in Idaho, and it appeared that a power dam might become a reality. The deepening Depression seems to have claimed the company as it sold not just the Mesa Falls property, but also all of its holdings to Montana Power in May 1936.

Though closed for some time, the hotel was apparently in fair condition as Montana Power used it as a company resort and hunting lodge for executives and employees. Tom Williams of Sunlight Development Company (a subsidiary of Montana Power) verified this. Even this Montana Power Company use of the hotel diminished. The Edginton family of Island Park and St. Anthony ran Big Falls Inn as a restaurant and dance hall in the late forties. It was mostly open in the summers. The Boy Scouts, under the leadership of Cat Thompson used it in the late fifties and sixties. The Fremont County Police Officers Association leased the Inn for $1 per year as a retreat and meeting facility in 1974-75. Use feasibility was studied during the late 1950s in hope of finally utilizing the site. By then, however, cost was not the only consideration. Increasing environmental restriction made any future development of the site doubtful.

The Forest Service had long been interested in obtaining the property. It had been listed as a desired acquisition from the early 1950s. Though not recorded, it is believed that talks with Montana Power began soon after their decision to not develop the site.

In 1986, a meeting between the Forest Service and Montana Power resulted in a proposed exchange of the Mesa Falls property for lands in the Lolo National Forest in Montana. This proposal failed because of the Forest Service Policy against exchanges involving properties in different states.

The solution to the stalemate was somewhat complicated but satisfied all parties. Targhee National Forest deeded to Montana Power developed special use areas at Mack's Inn, Pond's Lodge, and portions of the summer home areas at Flat Rock, Buffalo, and North Fork, all in Island Park. Montana Power subsequently sold the properties to the various tenants. The Targhee received in return the Upper Mesa Falls property and additional cash. The final exchange took place on December 18, 1986.

The walkways were built in 1992, as was the new road that accesses the site and the vault toilets. In partnership with the Idaho State Department of Parks and Recreation, Big Falls Inn underwent a complete renovation during the years 1997-2001. It was restored to its historic splendor, and is now on the Register of Historic Places. The Mesa Falls Scenic Byway was also transformed. Eleven million dollars worth of improvement to the road made the old, pothole filled route one of the best roads in Idaho. Continuing renovations will add additional parking, picnicking, and pathways. A visitor center, gift shop, and museum now fill the old Big Falls Inn with new life.

Reprinted from U.S. Forest Service and Idaho State Parks and Recreation brochures

T Ashton State Fish Hatchery
1 mile south of Ashton. 652-3579. 1 mile south of Ashton, bear right onto the marked county road. Travel 1 mile west on this road to reach the hatchery.

The Ashton State Fish Hatchery dates back to 1920 and has been responsible for producing fish

planted in the Upper Snake River Valley region. The hatchery serves as a specialty station that raises nine species of trout and salmon. Catchable size fish measuring eight to ten inches as well as fry and fingerling are managed throughout the year and released at the appropriate time. The hatchery is open for touring, but arrangements should be made ahead of time.

TV Ashton Reservoir
North of Ashton. Contact the Ashton Chamber of Commerce at 652-3987.

Ashton Reservoir lies on the Henry's Fork of the Snake River and spans 400 acres. Just as the Henry's Fork is renowned for its quality trout fishing, Ashton Reservoir is also a high-quality fishing area. The reservoir is stocked annually to ensure good fishing throughout the season. In addition, the reservoir provides recreation opportunities for water skiers and canoeists. Ashton Reservoir features picnicking and restroom facilities, as well as a public boat dock and ramp, all free of charge.

TV Horseshoe Lake
Ashton. Contact the Ashton Ranger District at 652-7442.

Tucked inside the Targhee-Caribou National Forest off of Cave Falls Road is Idaho's scenic Horseshoe Lake. From here, visitors have outstanding vistas of the Grand Teton Mountains and great fishing opportunities. The Idaho Fish and Game Department stocks Horseshoe Lake each spring as soon as the snow and ice melts. Anglers should note that power driven watercraft are not permitted on the lake, but canoes, rowboats, and rafts are always welcome. Visitors also have quick access to Yellowstone National Park via several trails that begin at the Horseshoe Lake Campground.

V Bear Gulch/Mesa Falls Cross-Country Ski Trails
7 miles northeast of Ashton on Mesa Falls Forest Hwy. 47. Contact the Idaho Department of Parks and Recreation at 334-4180.

Recommended for intermediate and advanced skiers only, the Bear Gulch/Mesa Falls trail system is nine miles long and is groomed only periodically when weather conditions permit. The trail begins near the area snowmobile trail and winds steeply up to the Lower and Upper Mesa Falls. Here, the trail diverges from the snowmobile track and follows the Bear Gulch rim back to the trailhead. The area is part of Idaho's Park N' Ski system, and permits are required. Permits may be obtained at the nearest Ranger Station and fees are as follows: $25 annual permit (good at all Idaho Park N' Ski areas), $7.50 3-day permit, and $2 day use permit.

V Fall River Ridge Cross-Country Ski Trails
10 miles east of Ashton on Cave Falls Rd. Contact the Idaho Department of Parks and Recreation at 334-4180.

Approximately seven miles of periodically groomed trails comprise the Fall River Ridge ski area. Rolling hills, meadows, and groves of lodgepole pines and aspen trees greet users along the various loop trails. These trails are best suited to beginner and intermediate Nordic skiers. The area is part of Idaho's Park N' Ski system, and permits are required. Permits may be obtained at the nearest Ranger Station and fees are as follows: $25 annual permit (good at all Idaho Park N' Ski areas), $7.50 3-day permit, and $2 day use permit.

V Falls River Ridge Cross-Country Ski Trails
10 miles east of Ashton on North Cave Falls Rd. Contact the Idaho Department of Parks and Recreation at 334-4180.

The Falls River Ridge cross-country ski trails wind between open and forested landscapes, and a variety of wildlife inhabits the area. The seven miles of trails are designed for beginner and intermediate skiers, and some of the trails are shared with snowmobilers. The area is part of Idaho's Park N' Ski system, and permits are required. Permits may be obtained at the nearest Ranger Station and fees are as follows: $25 annual permit (good at all Idaho Park N' Ski areas), $7.50 3-day permit, and $2 day use permit.

M Ashton Chamber of Commerce
64 N. 10, Ashton. 652-3987.

23 *Food, Lodging*

Island Park
Pop. 215

Island Park Village is said to have been named for the neighboring islands of timber located on the high sagebrush plains. Incorporated in the late 1940s as a Swiss colony, Island Park owes its founding to the Arangee Company. Spanning thirty-five miles along U.S. Hwy. 20, Island Park includes several lodges and inns that house the many recreational enthusiasts who travel to the area. Besides camping, hiking, and world-class fishing, 600 miles of groomed snowmobiling trails await visitors to the area's giant caldera landscape.

Macks Inn
William H. Mack founded this resort town in 1921, and a post office was established here in 1923. The town honors the long legacy of its founding father. Mack, nicknamed "Doc" immi-

grated from Germany to America at age 12 and worked with his uncle in two San Francisco bakeries. After learning the English language, Mack married and enrolled in medical school. With years of studying, Mack earned his optometry degree, and he moved his family to Rexburg to open an optometry store. Although Mack's business was highly successful, he soon realized that he was more passionate about the outdoors. He applied for and accepted a position as a regional game warden and was assigned to the Island Park area. While there, Mack and his family developed a small resort area that would eventually bear his name.

H Volcanic Calders
Milepost 368.9 on U.S. Hwy. 20

Some two million years ago, massive eruptions of hot rock boiled for 60 miles from this high rim through Yellowstone Park.

An exceptionally large crater remained when that lava surface collapsed. Another smaller caldera followed north of here about 1.3 million years ago. Yellowstone's geysers and hot springs continue to spout as remnants of those volcanic displays formed as underground rock gradually moved westward across a tremendous source of interior heat.

H Caldera Lookout
Milepost 376.3 on U.S. Hwy. 20

High on Island Park Caldera's west rim, a 72-foot-high Forest Service lookout tower affords an excellent view of this large volcanic feature.

No other steel tower has been preserved in this part of Idaho. When it was erected in 1936, lookouts were essential for fire detection in all of this region's forests. This one still is used in times of especially severe fire hazard, but planes now are responsible for regular fire patrol. Forest Service road 80120 ascends to the Bishop Mountain Lookout at an elevation of 7,810 feet.

H Harriman State Park
Milepost 378 on U.S. Hwy. 20

Started in 1902 as a large cattle ranch, Railroad Ranch soon became a summer retreat for wealthy Easterners and eventually Idaho's largest state park.

Railroad magnate and diplomat W. Averell Harriman and his brother Roland donated the ranch to Idaho in 1977, thus preserving the area's remarkable wildlife, and prompting development of a professionally managed state parks' system.

H Harriman Wildlife Refuge
Milepost 382 on U.S. Hwy. 20

Henry's Fork meanders through a 16,000-acre wildlife refuge that retains diverse habitats for many kinds of birds and animals.

Lodgepole pine forests and open meadows provide many opportunities to enjoy wildlife here, and fly fishing still is allowed in this region of scenic beauty. Moose, deer, and elk find plenty of food and shelter, while eagles, hawks, and owls thrive in open hunting grounds. Access is through Harriman State Park.

H Pierre J. DeSmet
Milepost 400.7 on U.S. Hwy. 20

Roman Catholic missionary services began in Idaho on Sunday, July 10, 1840, in Teton Valley, followed by a Mass held near here at Henry's Lake, July 23.

Pierre J. DeSmet, a Belgian Jesuit leader, accompanied a Pend d'Oreille-Flathead band on their way northwest to their homeland. Climbing a mountain here along streams "descending from dizzy heights, leaping from rock to rock with a deafening noise," he invoked divine thanks for his successful tour into Idaho and Montana.

H Sawtell's Ranch
Milepost 5.1 on State Hwy. 87

In 1868, Gilman Sawtell started a dude ranch and Henry's Lake fishery that did much to develop this natural resort area.

Sawtell did everything from supplying swans for New York's Central Park zoo to building a network of roads for tourist access to Yellowstone National Park. His commercial fishery served Montana mining markets. His pioneer Henrys Lake ranch was a major attraction here for a decade before rail service brought more settlers to this area.

T Island Park Village Golf Course
Hist County Rd. 66, Island Park. 558-7550.

Scenery surrounds golfers on this 9-hole, par 35 course that was established in 1970. Spanning 2,668 yards, the course is slightly hilly with lakes coming into play at least three times. The course is open daily from May 1 to October 15 with reasonable green fees under $20. During the winter, the course becomes a popular groomed snowmobiling area.

T Targhee Pass
U.S. Hwy. 20 near the Idaho/Montana border. Contact the Targhee National Forest at 624-3151.

Situated at 7,072 feet, Targhee Pass and the surrounding forest draws its name from legendary Bannock Indian Chief, Tahgee. Tahgee served as head chief over all the Bannock tribes and strove to maintain peace between whites and Native Americans. In 1863, Tahgee met with the Utah governor and just four years later, met with Idaho's governor. Despite other tribe's conflicts with the white government during the 1860s, Tahgee kept his tribe at peace. A friend to both whites and Indians, Tahgee died in 1871.

Targhee Pass not only marks the stateline between Idaho and Montana but also reflects the region's early history. In peaceful times, the Shoshone Indians used the pass to cross over to the Musselshell and Yellowstone Rivers during annual buffalo hunts. But the pass was not always a place of peace. During the Nez Perce War of 1877, Chief Joseph led his tribe across the pass in retreat from the U.S. Army. Although Lieutenant George Bacon was supposed to guard the area, he

abandoned his post assuming that the tribe had already crossed and made it safely to Jackson Hole. He was wrong at the time, however. In Bacon's absence, the tribe escaped, once again eluding and infuriating General Oliver Howard.

T Mount Sawtelle
In Island Park, merge off U.S. Hwy. 20 onto the gravel Sawtell Peak Rd. The road is located approximately 13 miles southeast of Yellowstone National Park's west entrance.

The 9,902-foot summit of Mount Sawtelle provides visitors with an incredible vista of Idaho, Montana, Wyoming, and Yellowstone National Park and is easily accessible by car during the summer. Surrounded by knee-high wildflowers, the flat plateau on top of Mount Sawtelle captures views of Henry's Lake, Island Park Reservoir, and formidable mountain ranges rising in all directions. Mount Sawtelle is named after Gilman Sawtell who arrived in the area in 1868. He established a ranch and became Island Park's first resident but later moved when the mosquitos and horseflies ran his horse ranching business into the ground .

T Mack's Inn Dinner Theater
Mack's Inn. 558-7871.

Located in the heart of Island Park's 35-mile "main street," the Mack's Inn Dinner Theater provides a touch of culture amid the endless area recreational opportunities. The theater performers present live music and melodramas daily from Memorial Day to Labor Day, and reservations are highly recommended.

T Henry's Lake Fish Hatchery
Island Park. 558-7202. Take State Hwy. 87 at its junction with U.S. Hwy. 20 and proceed 3.5 miles northwest. The hatchery is located on the road's left side.

The Henry's Lake Hatchery began as a privately owned facility prior to Idaho State acquiring the hatchery. Operated for more than 75 years by the state, the facility is the oldest continuously running hatchery in the state. The facility is strictly an egg-taking station featuring a fish ladder and spawn house. Every March and April, fish return to the spawning ladder, and the subsequent eggs are then collected and raised. Upon collection, the eggs are sent to the Mackay Fish Hatchery where fish are bred and stocked back in the Henry's Lake region. The hatchery is open March through October, and tours are provided during spawning season. In addition, a small public fishing area is available Memorial Day weekend through September, and an on-site interpretive center is planned.

T Henry's Flats Conservation Area
Island Park. Contact The Nature Conservancy at 788-2203. Located on U.S. Hwy. 20 in Island Park across from Aspen Ridge.

Managed by the Idaho Nature Conservancy, the Henry's Flats Conservation Area coexists along with the conservancy's working cattle ranch, Flat Ranch. The free site offers a visitor's center and observation area and is open daily from 9 AM to 5 PM Memorial Day through Labor Day.

GHOST TOWNS

Ora
Previously referred to as Sand Creek and Arcadia, the first post office of 1890 wanted to name the town Ola, after the first postmaster, Ola N. Kerr. Since there was already an Ola, Idaho, the name was changed.

Birch Creek
Near the Clark-Butte County line
Idaho's Clark County has never been known to contain vast mineral deposits, but when a copper boom hit the state during the 1880s, Birch Creek was born. Named after the numerous birch trees dotting the landscape, Birch Creek produced large quantities of copper for a few years. A post office was opened in the area in the late 1880s, but when the copper vein was exhausted, the post office closed and most miners moved in search of better prospects. Today, the few remaining individuals in the area are predominantly cattle and sheep ranchers.

T Island Park Caldera
Island Park

Geologists identified Island Park's Caldera in 1939, and it is now considered the world's largest caldera. The caldera formed nearly two million years ago when a huge volcano erupted and blew rhyolite (acid rock) over a 6,000-square-mile surface. An eighteen by twenty-three mile diameter crater formed. The crater later collapsed 1,200 feet and formed the caldera. Today, the caldera's edge is bounded on one side by Upper and Lower Mesa Falls and is covered with pine trees and meadows.

TV Big Springs & Johnny Sack Cabin
From Mack's Inn or Island Park Village, exit off U.S. Hwy. 20, and follow Forest Rd. (FR) 059 (Big Springs Loop Rd.) to the springs. 588-7755.

Dumping over 120 million gallons of water per day into the Henry's Fork of the Snake River, Big Springs serves as the headwaters for the Henry's Fork and is one of America's forty largest natural springs. Consistently clear and holding a steady temperature of 52 degrees, Big Springs provides the perfect spawning ground for a variety of fish. Huge rainbow, cutthroat, and brook trout populate

Island Park													
	Jan	Feb	March	April	May	June	July	Aug	Sep	Oct	Nov	Dec	Annual
Average Max. Temperature (F)	30.4	32.5	42.0	54.1	63.7	73.8	83.7	82.7	72.1	58.9	41.3	31.3	55.5
Average Min. Temperature (F)	8.9	10.2	19.2	26.5	34.2	39.8	44.7	44.0	36.0	26.6	18.4	9.1	26.5
Average Total Precipitation (in.)	1.11	1.14	1.34	1.28	2.29	1.35	1.25	1.28	1.25	1.24	1.15	1.06	15.76
Average Total Snowfall (in.)	11.1	8.6	7.6	3.1	0.5	0.1	0.0	0.0	0.0	1.1	5.8	10.4	48.2
Average Snow Depth (in.)	9	9	4	0	0	0	0	0	0	0	1	5	2

HELPFUL HINTS FOR SAFELY VIEWING AND PHOTOGRAPHING WILDLIFE IN THE YELLOWSTONE REGION

A wide variety of wildlife abundantly populates the Montana, Wyoming, and Idaho region surrounding Yellowstone National Park. Although these animals are intriguing and invite curiosity, all wildlife needs its space just like human beings. To safely and responsibly enjoy wildlife near the road or in the backcountry, follow these helpful hints.

What Is A Safe Observing Distance?
Although animals in and around Yellowstone National Park may appear or act tame, they are not. Humans should remain at least 100 yards away from wildlife at all times, and longer distances are recommended for viewing bears and bison. Humans put wildlife in jeopardy when safe observation distances are not maintained. In situations like this, animals risk losing their footing on cliffs, being separated from their offspring, being hit by traffic, and abandoning food sources – all of which greatly reduce these animals' chances of survival in their natural environment.

Observation Guidelines – On the Road and In the Backcountry
Remember the following guidelines the next time you're viewing wildlife:
- You are responsible for your own safety!
- Never follow, surround, or surprise a wild animal as it may feel threatened and charge. If an animal approaches you, back away slowly to provide it with more space.
- Do not make loud noises in an attempt to gain the attention of a wild animal. Instead, quietly view the animal from established observation areas.
- Avoid direct eye contact with bears as they view this as a direct challenge.
- Safely view wildlife with binoculars, spotting scopes, and telephoto lenses.

- While photographing animals, use an appropriate lens and always maintain your distance. Never attempt to coax an animal to a different location, and never ask anyone to pose with a wild animal no matter how tame it appears. Serious injuries can result from such activities!
- If you encounter a wild animal while hiking, back away slowly. Remain alert at all times to your surroundings and any potential dangers, and always carry bear spray in the Yellowstone region. If you encounter an aggressive mountain lion, be prepared to fight back.
- If you encounter a wild animal while driving, stop and remain in the car and observe/photograph wildlife from inside. Do not drive towards the animal as large animals have been known to seriously damage vehicles when they feel threatened. Keep children inside and educate them on the dangers that wildlife can pose when proper safety techniques are not followed. Also, watch for other animals in the area.
- Never lure animals to your car with food. This not only poses a threat to you, but also conditions the animal to approach humans and the road area. As the saying goes, "A fed bear is a dead bear." This statement, however, applies to all wildlife.
- Never stop in the middle of the road to observe or photograph wildlife. Instead, pull off into the shoulder or stop in an established parking area.

Be prepared for the wildlife that you may encounter during your visit to the Yellowstone region. For more information, contact the Center for Wildlife Information at www.bebearaware.org or the National Park Service.

---

the waters, as well as coho and kokanee salmon and mountain whitefish. Blue herons, muskrat, geese, and moose help keep the fish company. Although many fishermen are tempted to sample these clear blue waters, fishing is strictly prohibited.

Amid the wildlife and scenery is a one-mile interpretive trail leading to the historic Johnny Sack cabin. Built by a German immigrant in the 1930s, the cabin reflects the talents and creativity of Johnny Sack who developed a nearby waterwheel to provide his cabin with water and electricity.

One of the most popular attractions in the Big Springs area is the Big Springs National Recreation Water Trail. Located approximately 0.75 miles from the springs, this water trail is populated with recreationists during the summer time. The two to four hour float trip provides rafters and canoeists with incredible forest scenes, glimpses of wildlife, and mountain vistas.

TV Island Park Reservoir
558-7755.

Surrounded by lodgepole pine trees in the Targhee National Forest, the 8,400-acre Island Park Reservoir was formed when the Island Park Dam plugged the Henry's Fork of the Snake River in

1938. Today, the large reservoir is home to a variety of recreational pursuits. Fishermen love the trout and salmon infested waters year-round, and boating, water skiing, and camping are also popular pastimes. Free boat ramps and docks can be found at Island Park, Lakeside Lodge, McCrea Bridge Campground, Mill Creek, West End, and Buttermilk Campground. Visitors can also opt to drive across the dam for panoramic views of Box Canyon and the Centennial Mountains.

TV Harriman State Park
3489 E. Hwy. 20, Island Park. 558-7368. Located 18 miles north of Ashton near Island Park on U.S. Hwy. 20/191.

Harriman State Park is located inside a wildlife reserve providing sanctuary to a plethora of birds and mammals found within the greater Yellowstone ecosystem. The area originated in 1902 as the private "Railroad Ranch" for the Harrimans of the Union Pacific Railroad and their associates, the Guggenheims. After meticulously maintaining the ranch for 75 years, the Harriman family donated the property to Idaho State in 1977 under the agreement that the acreage would be used to protect wildlife. Complying with the Harrimans' wishes, Idaho State opened Harriman

State Park in 1982 at the center of a 16,000-acre wildlife refuge. Today, the region is known for harboring a large population of trumpeter swans, sandhill cranes, muskrat, elk, and beaver.

In addition to protecting wildlife, Harriman State Park provides numerous recreational opportunities and spectacular views of the Grand Teton Mountains. During the summer, twenty-one miles of hiking, horseback riding, and mountain biking trails await visitors in the wildflower dotted sage meadows. Anglers also frequent the area in search of trophy trout as the Henry's Fork of the Snake River cuts through nine miles of the park. On summer weekends, visitors can opt to take a guided tour of twenty-seven well-preserved buildings dating back to Railroad Ranch's early days, while the winter season ushers in cross-country skiing along groomed trails. No camping is allowed within the park, but cabin lodging for group retreats is available. A $4 motorized vehicle entrance fee is required to enter the park.

TV Henry's Lake State Park
3917 E. 5100 N., Island Park. 558-7532 or 652-7442. Located 15 miles west of Yellowstone National Park's west gate off U.S. Hwy. 20/191.

Established in 1965 and encompassing 586 acres in the Caribou-Targhee National Forest, Henry's Lake State Park is named after Major Andrew Henry, the first European-American to explore the beauty of the Island Park area and Henry's Fork of the Snake River. Since Henry's stop here in 1810, the area has been visited by a range of historical figures. Famous mountain man, Jim Bridger, stayed here along with other trappers and Flathead Indians in 1835, and the Nez Perce Indians stopped briefly in the area during their evasion from General O.O. Howard in the 1877 Nez Perce War. Today, the area continues to attract a host of visitors throughout the year, and an annual Fort Henry Mountain Man Rendezvous honors the area's traditional past.

The park's most noted feature is Henry's Lake cradled within a high mountain bowl along the Continental Divide at an elevation of 6,470 feet. Lush meadows and eight towering 10,000-foot Sawtooth Mountain peaks surround the lake. Found within the lake and nearby streams are trophy rainbow and cutthroat trout, as well as mountain whitefish. A modern fish cleaning station located near the lake's boat ramp awaits anglers and their catch of the day. Besides great fishing opportunities, Henry's Lake State Park also offers swimming in designated areas, a 3-mile self-guided interpretive trail, camping areas, boating, and picnicking. The park is open from the Thursday prior to Memorial Day through October 31 depending on the weather. Access to the park requires a $4 motorized vehicle entrance fee.

TV The Continental Divide in Idaho
Idaho/Montana Border. Contact the Continental Divide Trail Alliance at (888) 909-CDTA.

Excluding Antarctica, every continent in the world features a Continental Divide. In North America, this natural parting follows the backbone of the

Rocky Mountains from Mexico to Alberta, Canada. This line divides the flow of water between the Pacific and Atlantic Oceans. All rain/snow melt and rivers to the east of the divide drain into the Atlantic, while water on the divide's western ridge flows to the Pacific.

After traveling through Wyoming, the Continental Divide arrives on the Idaho/Montana border, traveling near Henry's Lake State Park and Dubois. Idaho's Centennial and Beaverhead Mountains form the backdrop for the Continental Divide as it passes through the state, and the area is characterized with diverse conifer forests of lodgepole pines, Douglas fir, subalpine fir, and Engelmann spruce.

This area of Idaho is also home to a portion of the 3,100-mile Continental Divide National Scenic Trail. Established by Congress in 1978, the trail winds through some of North America's most scenic backcountry while staying within five miles of the divide at all times. Interested users should contact the Continental Divide Trail Alliance for specific information and travel considerations.

TVF Meadow Vue Ranch

3636 Red Rock Rd., Henry's Lake at Island Park. 558-7411. www.meadowvueranch.com

Experience the west at the working Meadow Vue Ranch. Overlooking Henry's Lake and just minutes from Yellowstone Park, the secluded ranch offers numerous summer recreational activities beginning Memorial Day weekend. View wildlife, and take a guided scenic trail ride along the Continental Divide. Want a unique dinner experience? Make reservations for the Wednesday, Friday, and Saturday night live entertainment found at the Old West Bar-b-Que and Rodeo from mid-June to mid-August. For boys and girls ages nine through eighteen, the summer program provides the opportunity to live on a working ranch while learning rodeo skills, self-confidence, and personal responsibility under the supervision of veteran ranch workers. No matter what you're looking for, Meadow Vue Ranch provides an ideal venue for family vacations, reunions, company parties, and outdoor enthusiasts.

V Howard Springs

U.S. Hwy. 20 near the Idaho/Montana border and Targhee Pass. Contact the Targhee National Forest at 624-3151.

Located on the east side of the highway, Howard Springs provides a pretty day-use picnic stop amidst the scenery of Targhee National Forest. The site remembers the legacy of General Oliver Howard who passed through the area in 1877 on his chase of the elusive Nez Perce Indians.

V Brimstone/Buffalo River Cross-Country Ski Trails

Trailhead and parking area are located at the Island Park Ranger Station on U.S. Hwy. 20. Contact the Idaho Department of Parks and Recreation at 334-4180.

Spanning eleven miles, the Brimstone/Buffalo River trails are regularly groomed and offer a variety of terrain to suit cross-country skiers of all abilities. From gentle grades to downhill slopes through tree groves, each trail offers scenic views of the Island Park area. Highlights include vistas of Island Park Reservoir, Box Canyon, and the Buffalo River. The trails are groomed on a weekly basis (except Thurmon Ridge), and frequent sightings of moose are common. Trails in the Brimstone/Buffalo River area include Buffalo River Interpretive Ski Trail, Moose Loop, Eagle Trail, Thurmon Ridge, Boggy Springs Loop, Antelope Park Loop, and the Brimstone Connector Trail. The area is part of Idaho's Park N' Ski system, and permits are required. Permits may be obtained at the Ranger Station and fees are as follows: $25 annual permit (good at all Idaho Park N' Ski areas), $7.50 3-day permit, and $2 day use permit.

V Buffalo River

Mack's Inn. Contact the Idaho Department of Parks and Recreation at 334-4180. From Mack's Inn, proceed on the Big Springs Loop and continue on Forest Rds 082, 292, and 1219.

The Buffalo River is just one of many tributaries in the Island Park area that eventually flows into the Henry's Fork of the Snake River. Spring fed and maintaining a consistent temperature of fifty-two degrees, the Buffalo River provides perfect spawning grounds for rainbow trout. Besides angling opportunities, the river provides an easy float trip for recreationists of all skill levels.

V Henrys Fork of the Snake River and Major Tributaries

Before it joins with the acclaimed South Fork of the Snake River, the Henrys Fork winds through southeastern Idaho and provides a critical rainbow trout habitat and fishery. The drainage supports fluctuating populations of wild rainbow, cutthroat, and brown trout, and hatchery fish are added to some river sections where stocking is permitted.

The Henrys Fork supports several important and major tributaries. Island Park Reservoir features rainbow trout and kokanee salmon, and Henry's Lake affords native cutthroat. While the Warm River is characterized as an ideal trout-spawning region, Fall River serves as the largest tributary and contains a substantial wild rainbow trout fishery. Other tributaries in the Henrys Fork drainage include the Teton River and Buffalo River.

Nearby, the thirty-five acre Roberts Gravel Pond produces pumpkinseed, channel catfish, yellow perch, and rainbow and bullhead trout.

FL The Pines at Historic Phillips Lodge & The Lodgepole Grill

3907 Phillips Loop Rd., Island Park. 558-0192 or 888-455-9384. www.pinesislandpark.com

Nestled in the shadow of the Rocky Mountains, The Pines at Island Park offers Idaho's finest luxury cabin resort lodging in the solitude of the Targhee National Forest. Each 1,500+ square foot cabin features log furnishings and four luxurious queen size beds in two main level private sleeping areas and a semi-private loft. While here, grab a delicious bite to eat at The Lodgepole Grill, and then cozy up to your cabin's fireplace or enjoy a soak in the hot tub. Cabin amenities include two baths, full kitchen, washer/dryer, satellite TV, fine linens, private deck, hot tub, and grill. For more privacy, reserve the master suite loft at an additional charge. Accommodating up to eight people, the cabins at The Pines leave little left to decide except where to play.

M Island Park Chamber of Commerce

3416 N. Hwy. 20, Island Park. 558-7755. www.islandparkchamber.org; ipchamber@yahoo.com

SCENIC DRIVES

Fort Henry Historic Byway

See the first white settlement marked by the Fort Henry Monument, from which this byway gets its name. A new monument now replaces the old one at the original site. The old monument relocated in an adjoining field can be viewed from the original site. This route trails along BLM land, desert and mountain ranges where herds of deer and elk, as well as Sharp Tail and Sage Grouse can be seen as you journey along the Red Road.

This byway crosses camas Creek, connects to County Road A-2 in Clark County at the "Y." Sand Hill Cranes are early spring visitors in the Camas Meadows. Luscious mountain streams are enticing for fisherman, hikers, bikers and campers. Beautiful fields of wildflowers include seasonal Camas which can be seen throughout the Caribou-Targhee National Forest and flat lands.

The heritage of Clark and Fremont Counties is very unique and full of early history of mountain men, Indians, including Camas Meadows Battle Grounds, Nez Perce Trails, miners, stagecoach liners and early day ranching.

This scenic byway begins at North Rexburg U.S. 20 Exit, onto Salem Highway, to St. Anthony Sand Dunes on Red Road and on to A-2 Road Junction. Continue on A-2 north, then east to Island Park and U.S. 20. This is a two-lane road with no mountain passes. North Rexburg exit to A-2 in Clark County to Kilgore Store exit is paved. The only gravel road includes eleven miles from Kilgore to the Fremont County line, and is then paved to U.S. 20. The byway can be seen from mid-April to mid-November. In winter, roads become snowmobile trails. Travelers should allow at least 2 hours for this 81-mile trip.

Reprinted from Idaho Department of Transportation rochure

Lost Gold Trails Loop

The Lost Gold Trails Loop ventures off the Fort Henry Historic Byway at the "Y" Junction onto County Road A-2. The loop then travels southwest along the desert-lava rolling hill terrain where cattle and wild game peacefully share spring and fall months grazing. Crossing the railroad, which originated the town of "Dry Creek," now Dubois, and traveling west through town over I-15 overpass on Idaho 22, you connect with Old Highway 91. Turn north on Old Highway 91 and head to Spencer, passing near the U.S. Sheep Experiment Station. This early-day Gold Trail closely follows Beaver Creek towards the Montana gold mines. At Spencer the Gold Trail of yesterday becomes the Opal Trails of today and passes several high grade Opal Shops within the original Wood Live Stock town site. Leaving Spencer, the trail heads east to Idmon. This early day Nez Perce Trail has spurs off of its main roadway to private opal mines, Caribou-Targhee Forest fishing and primitive camping areas, and an old cemetery, connecting again to the Fort Henry Historic Byway at the old Idmon town site.

This is a two-lane road with no mountain passes. "Y" on A-2 to Dubois and Old Highway 91 Dubois to Spencer is paved. Spencer/Idmon is 3 miles paved and 11 miles of gravel. The road from Dubois to Spencer is open year round. Highway A-2 "Y" to Dubois and Spencer/Idmon road are closed through winter. Closed roads in winter become snowmobile trails. Travelers should allow at least 1.5 hours for this 47.8-mile trip.

Reprinted from Idaho Department of Transportation brochure

Mesa Falls Scenic Byway

The Mesa Falls Scenic Byway begins where the Teton Scenic Byway reaches it northern end in Ashton, at the junction of U.S. 20 and Idaho 47. From there, the route travels through the town of Warm River toward its main attractions: the Upper and Lower Mesa Falls.

The Mesa Falls are the only major falls in Idaho not used for irrigation or hydroelectric projects, and as such maintain a look and feel of nature undisturbed. At 110 feet and 85 feet, respectively, the Upper and Lower Mesa falls offer equally spectacular views in a beautiful forest setting. Both falls can be viewed in full, with the area surrounding the upper waterfall enhanced with paths and viewing areas that make it easily accessible to all. Though only about an hour's driving time, the Mesa Falls Scenic Byway is often a half-day's journey, with travelers mesmerized by the spectacular display in the midst of a truly backcountry setting. In addition, the historic Mesa Falls Lodge has been restored to its original splendor and is now open seasonally for visitor information.

This scenic byway begins at the southern end of Idaho 47 in Ashton, northeast 12.4 miles to the old Bear Gulch Ski Area site, then northwest along Forest Service Route 294 to the northern end at U.S. 20. Idaho 47 is a two-lane road. Forest Service Route 294 is closed in winter and becomes a Forest Service snowmobile route. If you have a snowmobile or cross-country skis, winter is the time to see the byway; if you don't, there is no access. Spring through fall is great by car. Travelers should allow at least 1 hour for the 28.7-mile trip.

Reprinted from Idaho Department of Transportation brochure

Teton Scenic Byway

The jagged teeth of the Teton Mountain Range are actually in Wyoming, but Idahoans prefer "the quiet side" on the western slopes, along the Teton Scenic Byway.

At nearly 10 million years young, the Tetons are the newest mountains in the Rockies. In fact, they continue to grow today at the snail-like pace of about an inch every hundred years. In fact, the largest peak on the range, Grand Teton, now stands at 13,772 feet.

Beginning at Swan Valley, this byway travels east on Idaho 31 through beautiful Pine Creek Pass to the town of Victor, and then north on Idaho 33 along the western side of the Teton Range. The mountains sharply contrast with the rolling agricultural fields to the north and west. In the towns of the Teton Valley, Victor, Driggs, and Tetonia, travelers can enjoy small town hospitality, internationally famous resorts and festival events held throughout the year.

North of Tetonia, the byway turns west on Idaho 32, offering glimpses of the Henry's Fork and Teton River Valleys toward the town of Ashton, where the Mesa Falls Scenic Byway begins.

Pine Creek Pass is a two-lane roadway with no passing lanes. It has 6-percent grades, some 35-mph curves, and often has a snow floor in winter. Idaho 33 is a two-lane roadway with ample passing opportunities. The byway can be seen year-round, but fall foliage is spectacular as are the wildflowers of late spring. Travelers should allow at least 2.5 hours for this 68.9-mile trip.

Reprinted from Idaho Department of Transportation brochure

Big Hole Mountains Tour

Winding north 21 miles from Swan Valley to Victor, State Highway 31 takes individuals on a scenic drive through the Big Hole Mountains and Targhee National Forest. The route ascends past aspen and fir trees to Pine Creek Pass at an elevation of 6,764 feet. From there, meadows and forests are interspersed as drivers descend into the Teton Basin and are greeted with views of the Grand Teton Mountains.

Hikes

For information on additional area trails, please contact the Forest Service Ranger Districts listed at the back of this section.

Big Hole, Snake River, and Caribou Mountains Area

Black Canyon to Big Burns
Distance: 10.5 mile near loop
Climb: moderate
Difficulty: moderate
Usage: moderate
Location: Traveling east on U.S. Highway 26 from Idaho Falls, proceed 11 miles past the junction with State Highway 43 and bear left (north) onto the Kelly Canyon Recreation Area Road. Proceed on this road 2 miles to a Y intersection and turn right on County Road 100 North. After crossing the South Fork of the Snake River, bear right on Heise Road and continue 2 miles to another fork in the road. Follow the right gravel road (which turns into Forest Road 206) 16.1 miles to the Black Canyon Trailhead.

This trail winds through rugged mountains and over ten creek crossings amidst beautiful forests comprised of chokecherry and wild rose bushes, as well as Douglas fir, spruce, juniper, cottonwood, aspen, and oak trees. Wildlife is abundant in the area as well, and it is not unusual to see moose, elk, bighorn sheep, and bald eagles. Beginning on a trail that is open to ATVs, mountain bikes, horses, and hikers, make several creek crossings until reaching the 2.2-mile mark where the trail begins climbing up a forested canyon. At the 4-mile mark, hikers will reach the Black Canyon/Little Burns Divide and should proceed left down the ridge 1 mile to a trail junction. Proceed left down the scenic Little Burns Canyon and cross Big Burns Creek to reach the Big Burns Trailhead 3 miles from the convergence of Big Burns and Little Burns Creeks. Walk along the Forest Road to reach the parking area at Black Canyon Trailhead. Best months for hiking are late June through September.

Big Elk Creek
Distance: 13 miles roundtrip
Climb: gentle
Difficulty: easy
Usage: heavy
Location: Drive southeast of Idaho Falls on U.S. Highway 26 through Swan Valley. 14 miles south of Swan Valley, exit onto a marked road leading to Big Elk Creek and proceed 2.5 miles to the trailhead.

Scenery abounds on this trail as hikers wander in

and out of the Snake River Range's patchy forests past numerous avalanche chutes. Walking through the wide Big Elk Creek Canyon, hikers will pass side routes leading to Dry Canyon at the 2.5-mile mark and Hells Hole Canyon at 3.4 miles. At this point, the trail narrows through the limestone cliffs and a waterfall can be viewed as hikers cross over into Wyoming at the 4.5-mile mark. Crossing over Big Elk Creek, hikers reach the turnaround destination at 6.5 miles near this creek's union with the Siddoway Fork of Big Elk Creek. Best months for hiking are late July through September.

Optional Hikes: Hikers can wander up the Siddoway Fork Canyon on Trail 167, which provides access to both the Austin Canyon meadows (Trail 105) as well as to the mountain ridge located between Swan Valley, Idaho and Jackson, Wyoming.

A second option is to proceed past the convergence of Big Elk Creek and the Siddoway Fork and locate Trail 125. This trail climbs up into Dry Canyon and over to the scenic Garden Canyon.

Indian Creek Loop
Distance: 18 mile near loop
Climb: steep
Difficulty: difficult
Usage: moderate
Location: On U.S. Highway 26, drive 73 miles southeast of Idaho Falls through Swan Valley beside Palisades Reservoir. Nearing Indian Creek, drop down to a canyon mouth and merge east onto a gravel road. Proceed 2 miles to a fork in the road and bear left on Forest Road (FR) 282 leading to Trail 122 at the undeveloped North Fork Indian Creek Trailhead.

Rugged canyon walls lined with waterfalls, wildflower meadows, alpine lakes, and impressive unnamed peaks rising sharply against the sky are just some of the many sights awaiting hikers on this trail situated near the Idaho/Wyoming state border. Starting out on an ATV trail, proceed across North Indian Creek and ignore all faint trails leaving to the sides of Trail 122. After hiking 7.2 miles to the North Indian Creek Basin, locate a faint trail leaving to the right marked "Big Basin 1.5; Lake Basin 2.5; So Fk. Indian Cr. 3.5." Now on Trail 099, hikers will ascend steeply to the 9,500-foot North Indian Pass located at the trek's 9.4-mile mark. Continuing over the pass and down to a pond, stay on Trail 099 and climb to Lake Basin. Shortly after reaching Lake Basin, hikers will find a trail junction near South Indian Creek's head. Proceed down into South Indian Creek on Trail 045 past Cabin Creek, Deadhorse Canyon, and Oat Canyon. From Oat Canyon, the trail winds gently downhill 2.5 miles to the South Fork Indian Creek Trailhead where hikers should walk along the road back to the North Fork Trailhead's parking area. Best months for hiking are August to early September.

Little Elk Creek
Distance: 8 miles roundtrip
Climb: steep
Difficulty: difficult
Usage: moderate
Location: On U.S. Highway 26, drive southeast of Idaho Falls through Swan Valley to the Palisades Dam. Continue 2.5 miles past the dam and bear left (east) onto Little Elk Creek Road. Follow this road approximately 1 mile to the trailhead and locate the trail leaving to the right.

This trail climbs through the highest portion of the Snake River Mountains, offering hikers incredible views of Mount Baird, Palisades Peak, and Little Palisades Peak, as well as several other unnamed peaks rising more than 9,000 feet. Although the first mile of the trek gently meanders through a forest, hikers should expect the trail to become significantly steeper. At the 1-mile mark, hikers pass Conglomerate Canyon and begin winding up another canyon through scenic cliffs. After making several switchbacks, hikers finally reach a high saddle at 9,200 feet at the 4-mile mark where panoramic views of the surrounding area are found. Best months for hiking are mid-July to mid-September.

Optional Hikes: From the high saddle, hikers can take a cross-country hike east across the basins below and then climb to a narrow ridgeline. This ridge provides hikers with access to Mount Baird's summit.

Palisades Creek
Distance: 13 miles roundtrip
Climb: gentle
Difficulty: easy
Usage: heavy
Location: On U.S. Highway 26, drive 52 miles east from Idaho Falls through Swan Valley and Irwin. At the small town of Palisades, bear left onto the gravel Forest Road (FR) 255 (Palisades Creek Road). Proceed 1.8 miles to Palisades Campground and park on the road's left side just before the Palisades Creek bridge crossing. Locate the Palisades Creek Trail 084 at the campground's eastern end.

A forest canopy shades hikers as they wander through the rugged walls of Palisades Canyon up to Lower and Upper Palisades Lakes. Following Palisades Creek, hikers will arrive at Lower Palisades Lake in 4 miles. The area has a few good camping spots and is known to harbor several moose. To reach Upper Palisades Lake, continue on Trail 084 0.6 miles past Chicken Springs Canyon. From here, cross over Palisades Creek and continue up Waterfalls Canyon Trail to locate Upper Palisades Lake at the 6.5-mile mark. This fertile lake is known for its dense population of cutthroat trout. Best months for hiking are early June to mid-October.

Optional Hikes: Bypass the trail leading to Upper Palisades Lake and continue up Palisades Creek Trail 084. This hike is difficult as the trail is faint in most places and it fords Palisades Creek twenty-two times. The third and final option is to proceed up Chicken Springs Canyon at the trip's 5.4-mile mark. Hikers will reach the canyon springs 0.75 miles from the trail junction. While this canyon is very scenic, it is also very steep.

Rainey Creek
Distance: 13 mile loop
Climb: moderate
Difficulty: moderate
Usage: moderate
Location: On U.S. Highway 26, drive 1 mile south from the town of Swan Valley, bearing east (left) onto a county road directly before the Church of Jesus Christ of Latter Day Saints. Proceed 5 miles to the well-developed trailhead.

The trail leading through Rainey Creek Canyon is scenic and offers a wide variety of landscapes. From dense forests of conifers, aspens, and berry bushes to rockslides, overhanging cliffs, and creek crossings, this trail offers something for every hiker. Beginning on an abandoned road, ascend up the north slope of Rainey Creek canyon and ford Rainey Creek. At the 2.25-mile mark, proceed on South Fork Rainey Creek Trail through a rocky canyon past Dry Elk Canyon. Upon reaching a trail fork, proceed left and climb up and over a summit down to the North Fork of Rainey Creek Trailhead. At this 8-mile mark, locate the

North Fork trail leaving at the trailhead's downstream end. The trail winds through a lush canyon bottom and past a scenic rockslide area before winding back to the first trailhead. Best months for hiking are mid-July through September.

Trail Creek
Distance: 10 miles roundtrip
Climb: gentle
Difficulty: moderate
Usage: moderate
Location: Follow State Highway 34 to its end near Freedom, Wyoming, and then follow the Stateline Road north 2 miles to Jackknife Road. At the 4-way stop, bear left and head into the Caribou National Forest. Proceed on this road to the undeveloped Trail Creek Trailhead.

Wildlife is abundant on this trail that winds near Trail Creek up to the 7,090-foot Trail Creek and Taylor Creek Divide. From this ridge, hikers have vistas of Bald Mountain as well as the scenic Taylor Creek Canyon. Following the trail from its start above Jackknife Creek, hike to a trail fork at the 0.8-mile mark. Proceed along the right fork up Trail Creek as it winds through meadows and a patchy forest. Throughout the hike, Trail Creek Trail fades in and out with game trails becoming the most obvious routes. Hikers should remember to always keep right of Trail Creek in such instances. At the 3-mile mark, the main trail fades, but hikers should ignore the game trail and continue right up the canyon. As hikers near their destination, an unnamed fork appears in the trail. Taking the trail's left fork, stay to the creek's right and follow the metal signs attached to trees signaling the correct route to the pass. Best months for hiking are mid-June to mid-October.

Waterfall Canyon/Palisades Lakes
Distance: 24 miles roundtrip
Climb: moderate
Difficulty: moderate
Usage: heavy
Location: On U.S. Highway 26, drive 52 miles east from Idaho Falls through Swan Valley and Irwin. At the small town of Palisades, bear left onto the gravel Forest Road (FR) 255 (Palisades Creek Road). Proceed 1.8 miles to Palisades Campground and park on the road's left side just before the Palisades Creek bridge crossing. Locate the Palisades Creek Trail 084 at the campground's eastern end.

Hikers will pass two alpine lakes on this scenic trail that winds near the Snake River Range's highest peaks through meadows and canyons lined with waterfalls and wildflowers. From the trailhead, proceed through a forested canyon bottom past Lower Palisades Lake and Chicken Springs Canyon to a trail junction at the 6-mile mark. Crossing over Palisades Creek, merge onto Waterfall Canyon Trail and hike to the 7.5-mile mark at the upper end of Upper Palisades Lake. 0.25 miles above this inlet, keep right at the trail junction and cross the creek. At the next trail junction near the creek, stay right again and begin ascending up the glacier-carved Waterfall Canyon. At the 9.8-mile mark, hikers will reach the scenic Waterfall Meadow where a 920-foot cataract tumbles down the canyon's east wall. Early in the season, this meadow is lined with waterfalls. From the meadow, make a creek crossing and proceed right up a cirque, past a gorge, and into a small basin where the trail forks. Bear right at this fork and follow the trail to a large basin. Here, hikes should return 12 miles back to the trailhead on the same route or follow one of the optional hikes detailed below. Best months for hiking are July and August with the best waterfall views available in early July.

Optional Hikes: From the trek's trail junction at the 12-mile mark, hikers can make an optional loop hike back to Upper Palisades Lake. Proceeding east along Waterfall Canyon's ridge, climb over Peak 9,630 and follow the scenic Dry Canyon Trail back to the lake.

Another loop takes hikers back to Lower Palisades Lake. At the trail junction, proceed on the Sheep Creek-Lake Canyon Trail to a high divide where grand views of Wyoming's Teton Mountains can be found. At the divide, drop northwest down onto the Lake Canyon Trail. This scenic trail is faint in places as it passes through meadows and forests, but hikers will likely be rewarded in sighting several mountain goats roaming the canyon's cliffs.

Driggs/Victor Area
South Darby Canyon Trail
Distance: 5.4 miles roundtrip
Climb: moderate
Difficulty: moderate
Usage: moderate
Location: Travel 3 miles south from Driggs on State Highway 33 and bear east on Forest Road (FR) 012 (Darby Canyon Road). Follow this road 8 miles to the trailhead for South Darby Trail 033.

Meandering along the South Fork of Darby Creek into Wyoming's Jedediah Smith Wilderness Area, this trail offers a vast array of beautiful scenery. Hiking on the west slope of the Teton Mountains, hikers will walk through forests and wildflower meadows and pass tumbling waterfalls. At the 2.7-mile mark, hikers will reach their destination at the 10,966-foot Mount Bannon and its Wind and Ice Cave. Best months for hiking are July and August.

Alaska Basin
Distance: 15.4 miles roundtrip
Climb: moderate
Difficulty: moderate
Usage: heavy
Location: From Driggs, travel east to Alta, Wyoming and locate the road leading to the ski resort. Taking the right fork, proceed up Teton Canyon to locate the trailhead for Trail 027.

Hikers will climb up into the wild and scenic Teton Mountains, surrounded often times by 10,000- to 12,000-foot peaks. At the 7.7-mile mark, Trail 027 levels out at the alpine Alaska Basin. The basin is home to several scenic alpine lakes. Best months for hiking are July and August.

Moose Creek
Climb: moderate
Difficulty: moderate
Usage: moderate
Location: From Victor, travel southeast on State Highway 33. Immediately before reaching the Mike Harris Campground, exit east onto Forest Road (FR) 276. Locate the trailhead for Moose Creek Trail 038 in 1.5 miles.

A waterfall and several alpine lakes are this trek's highlights as the trail wanders next to Moose Creek up into Wyoming's Teton Mountains. Best months for hiking are July through September.

Patterson Creek
Climb: moderate
Difficulty: moderate
Usage: moderate
Location: From Victor, drive west out of town on Cedron Road. This road travels several miles and then heads north. When the road bears north, continue 1 mile to locate the trailhead for Patterson Creek Trail 054 on the road's left side.

Located in the Big Hole Mountains, this trail winds along Patterson Creek and over Mahogany Ridge before ending at Red Mountain. Red Mountain's 8,715-foot summit offers hikers outstanding views of Wyoming's Teton Mountain Range rising in the distance as well as Idaho's Teton Valley lying below. Best months for hiking are July through September.

Great Divide Area

Aldous and Hancock Lakes
Distance: 5 miles roundtrip
Climb: moderate
Difficulty: moderate
Usage: moderate
Location: Merge off Interstate 15 at Dubois and proceed east on County Road A2. Travel 27 miles to a fork in the road and bear north towards Kilgore. At Kilgore, turn left at the T intersection and continue 0.3 miles to a right turn leading across Camas Meadows. From this turn, drive 4.2 miles to a road junction and keep right as the road becomes Forest Road (FR) 026. At the junction with FR 026 and FR 027, bear right on FR 027 and proceed 6 miles to the Ching Creek Trailhead and the trail leading north.

This well-maintained trail wanders in and out of thick forests and small meadows on the climb to Aldous and Hancock Lakes. Constantly passing by a variety of wildflowers, hikers will reach Aldous Lake at the 1.5-mile mark. Situated at 7,340 feet and surrounded by trees, Aldous Lake has become a popular fishing destination. Continuing northeast around Aldous Lake, climb steeply 1 mile to Hancock Lake. This lake sits in a bowl formed in an old landslide. Today, the lake is surrounded by old trees, and above the lake, hikers can view the Centennial Mountains and Continental Divide ridge. Best months for hiking are mid-June through mid-Septemer.

Salamander Lake Loop
Distance: 9 mile loop
Climb: moderate
Difficulty: moderate
Usage: moderate
Location: Exiting off Interstate 15 at Dubois, merge onto County Road A2 at the eastern edge of town. Proceed 27 miles and bear north (left) towards Kilgore. Continuing through Kilgore, turn left at the T intersection and drive to the road junction of Forest Roads (FR) 026 and 02. Bearing left on FR 026, drive 0.75 miles and turn right on FR 029 (Cottonwood Creek Road). Locate the undeveloped trailhead in approximately 2 miles.

A variety of wildflowers surround hikers on this loop trail winding through meadows to Salamander Lake near the Continental Divide. Starting out on Trail Creek Trail, keep right at the junction for Lake Creek Trail and continue to another junction at the 1.5-mile mark. Stay to the right and follow the trail as it crosses Trail Creek, climbs up to wildflower meadows, and descends to Salamander Lake at the 4.2-mile mark. Hiking along the lake's south (left) shore, locate a trail junction and proceed along the right "Lake Creek" fork across the Salamander Creek Bridge. At the bridge, utilize tree blazes to locate the trail heading into the forest and to a ridge. This ridge offers spectacular views into Montana. At the 4.8-mile mark, walk past the sign indicating the Divide Trail and follow the blazed trees to another large meadow. As the trail continues to climb up and down ridges, hikers will eventually reach another trail junction near the Salamander Creek crossing. Follow the well-used trail on the left over Salamander Creek Bridge leading back to the

trailhead in 1.5 miles. Best months for hiking are mid-June to mid-October.

Optional Hikes: At the junction located at the 1.5-mile mark, hikers can veer left and head to Salamander Lake along this route. Although this trail cuts the trip's length by 1.25 miles, the scenery is not as breathtaking along this route. Another option is to leave the main trail at the 4.8-mile mark and head at an angle between 45 and 90 degrees up to the Continental Divide Trail. Hikers will reach the Divide about 1,000 feet up from the main trail and can continue hiking in either direction along the divide for views of the meadows below.

Sawtell Peak – Rock Creek Basin
Distance: 8 miles roundtrip
Climb: moderate
Difficulty: moderate
Usage: moderate
Location: Travel 85 miles north of Idaho Falls along U.S. Highway 20 and turn onto the marked Forest Road (FR) 024 (Sawtell Peak Road). Proceed 12 miles to the trailhead located at a small turnout in the road.

Traveling on or near the Continental Divide throughout the entire trek, hikers will access incredible views of the Teton and Centennial Mountains while overlooking Idaho, Montana, and Wyoming. Starting out on an old road, hikers will pass by numerous wildflower fields and view the 9,866-foot Sawtell Peak rising in the distance. After crossing over a rocky avalanche area, the trail begins descending and reaches Rock Creek Basin at the 4-mile mark. The area is filled with a variety of rock types and colors as well as wildlife. Moose, elk, and deer commonly frequent the area, and grizzly bear sightings are rising. Best months for hiking are mid-July through September.

Targhee Creek
Distance: 12.4 miles roundtrip
Climb: moderate
Difficulty: moderate
Usage: moderate
Location: On U.S. Highway 20, drive north past Ashton into Island Park and across Henrys Lake Flat. Ignoring the junction with State Highway 287, proceed 2.2 miles and bear left onto the dirt road marked "Targhee Creek Trail." Locate the trailhead in approximately 1 mile.

Fine views of Targhee Peak and Bald Peak await hikers on this trek leading through a canyon lined with forests and limestone cliffs, past alpine meadows, and up to several scenic alpine lakes. Starting out gently from the trailhead, hikers should keep going straight at the 0.8-mile trail junction with Dry Fork and cross Targhee Creek at the 2.3-mile mark. Climbing upwards, reach another crossing of Targhee Creek at the 3.2-mile mark and begin heading up the canyon through a thick forest. At the 4.2-mile mark, hikers will reach a small meadow where a waterfall can be found, and the 4.7-mile mark brings hikers to a third and final crossing of Targhee Creek. After hiking a total of 6 miles, hikers should bear right (east) on Watkins Creek Trail to locate numerous alpine lakes housed within the Targhee Basin. Passing by the first unnamed lake situated to the right of the trail, locate the seasonal Clark Lake at the 6.2-mile mark. Best months for hiking are July and August. Bear safety precautions should be taken at all times as grizzly bears heavily populate the area.

Optional Hikes: Continuing cross-country, hikers can access four scenic lakes situated above Clark Lake. Adventurous hikers can also opt to climb any of the numerous mountainsides lining

Targhee Basin. From the top of these peaks, hikers will be able to view Yellowstone National Park and the Teton, Gravelly, and Centennial Mountains.

A second optional hike allows hikers to make a loop. At the trip's 6-mile mark, hikers should bear left on Targhee Creek Trail at the Continental Divide Trail junction. This trail leads down to Dry Fork Trail, which then loops back to the Targhee Creek Trail 0.8 miles from the trailhead.

Webber Creek
Distance: 18 miles roundtrip
Climb: moderate
Difficulty: moderate
Usage: moderate
Location: At Dubois, merge off Interstate 15 onto State Highway 22 and drive 6 miles west before bearing right (north) onto a county road. Continue 22.5 miles up this road and turn onto Forest Road (FR) 196 (Webber Creek Road). Locate Trail 111 leaving upstream at the Webber Creek Trailhead in approximately 5 miles.

The jagged Italian peaks frame this hike near the Continental Divide as hikers climb through Webber Creek Canyon up to alpine lakes hidden between rugged mountain ridges of Idaho and Montana. Beginning in a narrow, forested canyon, climb 4 miles to a trail junction with the South Fork of Webber Creek. Ignoring this junction, continue up the North Fork trail as views of the glacial Webber Peak and Scott Peak line the horizon. At 7.1 miles, merge left onto Trail 034 and quickly reach the first lake in just 0.6 miles. Continue another 0.6 miles to reach the second lake and 1.3 miles to reach the upper lake situated at an elevation of 9,560 feet. Limestone cliffs line this trail, and the rugged canyon wall to the right of Trail 034 is the Continental Divide. Best months for hiking are July to October. Bear safety precautions should be taken as grizzly bears are known to inhabit the area.

Harriman State Park Area

Ranch Loop
Distance: 1 mile loop
Climb: gentle
Difficulty: easy
Usage: moderate
Location: On U.S. Highway 20, drive north from Idaho Falls to Harriman State Park to locate the trailhead.

This gentle walk takes hikers back to earlier days with a historic tour of several Railroad Ranch buildings in the area. Best months for hiking are July through September.

Ridge Loop
Distance: 5.5 mile loop
Climb: moderate
Difficulty: moderate
Usage: moderate
Location: On U.S. Highway 20, drive north from Idaho Falls to Harriman State Park to locate the trailhead.

Climbing 400 feet, this trail takes hikers through several forests to the top of a mountain ridge. From the crest, hikers are rewarded with an incredible vista of the Teton Mountains. Best months for hiking are July through September.

Island Park Area

Coffee Pot Rapids Trail
Distance: 5 miles roundtrip
Climb: gentle
Difficulty: easy
Usage: moderate
Location: From Island Park, travel 6 miles north to the Upper Coffeepot Campground in Targhee National Forest to locate the trailhead.

This gentle trail winds next to Henry's Fork of the Snake River. While the trail begins near placid waters, the trek takes hikers to a scenic river area full of raging rapids. Best months for hiking are July through September.

Box Canyon Trail
Distance: 6 miles roundtrip
Climb: gentle
Difficulty: easy
Usage: moderate
Location: From Island Park, travel to the Box Canyon Campground and locate the trailhead for Box Canyon Trail.

This trail is a fly-fisherman's dream, providing access to the trout-filled waters of Henry's Fork of the Snake River. Beginning at the campground, the trail wanders south along Box Canyon's rim for 3 miles, bringing hikers to the river after passing through a colorful wildflower landscape. Best months for hiking are June through September.

Union Pacific Railroad Bed
Distance: variable
Climb: gentle
Difficulty: easy
Usage: heavy
Location: Exit off U.S. Highway 20 3 miles south of Island Park and merge onto the signed Forest Road (FR) 291 (Chick Creek Road). Proceed 4 miles to a parking area at the trailhead.

When Union Pacific abandoned this old railroad bed, the area was turned into a popular recreation area east of Island Park. Running north to south, the trail is open to hikers, mountain bikers, and motorized vehicles. Best months for hiking are June through September.

Lemhi Mountains Area
Rocky Canyon
Distance: 10 miles roundtrip
Climb: moderate
Difficulty: moderate
Usage: moderate
Location: On State Highway 28, drive west through the town of Mud Lake and bear right at the highway junction heading towards Lone Pine. 7 miles north of Lone Pine bear left onto a dirt/gravel road and drive approximately 2 miles. Turn right on the side road and drive 1.5 miles to a fork in the road. Proceed left towards Rocky Canyon and park at the informal trailhead where the road ends on a steep hill.

Antelope, elk, deer, bighorn sheep, mountain goats, black bears, and mountain lions are all common sights on this trek taking hikers through a meadow canyon amid semiarid mountain peaks. After climbing over the steep hill at the trailhead, descend down to a spring in Rocky Canyon and proceed upcanyon following a trail next to a small brook. At the 2.3-mile mark, the trail passes through a narrow, rocky stretch before reaching a large meadow and canyon fork at the 4.8-mile mark. Best months for hiking are late June to mid-July, but the trail is accessible from early June through October in most years.

Optional Hikes: From the meadow, hikers can opt to hike up the left or right fork of Rocky Canyon. While the right fork leads to scenic views of the surrounding area from a small meadow, the left fork takes hikers up into a tree-lined meadow.

Ririe/Heise Area
Cress Creek Nature Trail
Distance: variable
Climb: steep
Difficulty: moderate
Usage: moderate

Location: From Ririe, drive on U.S. Highway 26 towards Heise Hot Springs and Kelly Canyon. Immediately after crossing the Snake River, bear left and proceed to the Bureau of Land Management's parking area for the Cress Creek Nature Trail.

A perfect trek for a weekend picnic, this trail follows the crystal clear waters of Cress Creek. Winding up hillsides covered with both sagebrush and juniper, the hike terminates at a ridge view overlooking the Snake River and Big Southern Butte. Best months for hiking are June through August.

INFORMATION PLEASE

All Idaho area codes are 208

Road Information

ID Road & Weather Conditions
888-432-7623 or local 884-7000
Idaho State Police   736-3090

Tourism Information

Idaho Travel Council 800-VISIT-ID outside Idaho
334-2470 in Idaho
www.visitid.org
Eastern Idaho Yellowstone Teton Territory
800-634-3246
356-5700
www.yellowstoneteton.org/

Airports

Driggs   354-3100
Idaho Falls   612-8221
Rexburg   356-9960
St. Anthony   624-9901

Government Offices

Idaho Bureau of Reclamation   334-1466
www.usbr.gov
Idaho Department of Commerce
(800) 847-4843 or 334-2470
www.visitid.org or http://cl.idaho.gov/
Idaho Department of Fish and Game
(800) ASK-FISH or 334-3700
http://fishandgame.idaho.gov
Idaho Department of Parks and Recreation
334-4199
www.idahoparks.org
State BLM Office   373-3889 or 373-4000
www.id.blm.gov
Bureau of Land Management Idaho Falls Field
Office   524-7500
Caribou-Targhee National Forest   624-3151

Hospitals

Teton Valley Hospital • Driggs   354-2383
Eastern Idaho Regional Medical Center
Idaho Falls   529-6111
Madison Memorial Hospital • Rexburg 356-3691

Golf Courses

7N Ranch Resort • Ririe   538-5097
Heise Hot Springs • Ririe   538-7327
American Falls • American Falls   226-5827
American Falls Golf Club
American Falls   226-5827
Aspen Acres Golf • Ashton   652-3524
Timberline Golf • Ashton   652-3219
Links at Teton Peaks • Driggs   456-2374
Targhee Village Golf • Driggs   354-8577
Idaho Falls Golf • Idaho Falls   529-1115
Pinecrest Golf Course • Idaho Falls 529-1485
Sage Lake Golf • Idaho Falls   528-5535

Sandcreek Golf • Idaho Falls   529-1115
Island Park Village Resort
Island Park   558-7550
Rexburg City - Golf Courses • Rexburg 359-3037
Teton Lake Golf Course • Rexburg   359-3036
Cedar Park Golf Course • Rigby   745-0103
Jefferson Hills Golf • Rigby   745-6492
Fremont County - Golf Course
Saint Anthony   624-7074
Links at Teton Peaks • Tetonia   456-2374

Bed & Breakfasts

BlackSmith Inn • Rigby   745-6208
Cutthroat Inn B&B • Ririe   538-7963
Blue Heron Inn • Rigby   745-9922
Colonial Rose Tearoom and B&B
St. Anthony   624-3530
Jessenis B&B • Ashton   652-3356
Locanda di Fiori (Inn of Flowers)
Drigg   456-0909
Grand Valley Lodging • Driggs   354-8890
Hamer House B&B • St Anthony   624-3530
Kasper's Kountryside Inn Bed & Breakfast
Victor   787-2726

Guest Ranches & Resorts

Meadow Vue Ranch
Island Park [Mack's Inn]   558-7411
7N Ranch • Ririe   538-5097
The Pines at Historic Phillips Lodge &
The Lodgepole Grill • Island Park   558-0192
Mountain River Ranch • Ririe   538-7337
Grand Targhee Ski & Summer Resort
Alta   353-2300 x 1311
Squirrel Creek Elk Ranch • Ashton   652-3972
Dry Ridge Outfitters & Guest Ranch
Driggs   354-2284
Grove Creek Lodge • Driggs   354-8881
Intermountain Lodge • Driggs   354-8153
Teton Teepee Lodge • Driggs   353-8176
Teton Valley Lodge • Driggs   354-2386
Jacob's Island Park Ranch • Hamer   662-5567
Hyde Outfitters & Last Chance Lodge
Idaho Falls   558-7068
Aspen Lodge • Island Park   558-7407
Eagle Ridge Ranch • Island Park   558-0900
Elk Creek Ranch • Island Park   558-7404
Henry's Fork Lodge • Island Park   558-7953
Island Park Village Resort & Golf Course
Island Park   558-7502
Lakeside Lodge & Resort • Island Park 558-7147
Mack's Inn Resort & Family Restaurant
Island Park   558-7272
Pond's Lodge • Island Park   558-7221
Sawtelle Mountain Resort & RV Park
Island Park   558-9366
Staley Springs Lodge • Island Park   558-7471
TroutHunter Riverfront Lodge, Fly Shop and Bar
& Grill • Island Park   558-9900
Wild Rose Ranch • Island Park   558-7201
McGarry Ranches • Rexburg   410-299-1995
Sheffield Park Ranch • Rexburg   356-4182
Granite Creek Guest Ranch • Ririe   538-7140
Heise Canyon Ski Resort • Ririe   538-6251
Hideaway B&B Guest Ranch
Rockford   666-8846
Sandhills Resort • St. Anthony   624-4127
Hansen-Silver Guest Ranch
Swan Valley   483-2305
Teton Mountain View Lodge • Tetonia 456-2741
Teton Ranch • Tetonia   456-2010
Teton Ridge Ranch ª Tetonia   456-2650
Bagley's Teton Mountain Ranch
Victor   787-9005
Moose Creek Ranch • Victor   787-2284
Teton Springs Resort • Victor   787-8008

Vacation Homes & Cabins

Powder Valley Townhouses • Driggs	354-8881
Rainbow Realty • Island Park	558-7116
Chapin Cabins • Victor	787-1922
Oxbow Property Management LLC Victor	787-2871

Forest Service Cabins

Caribou-Targhee National Forest

Bishop Mountain
27 mi. NW of Ashton 652-7442
Cap: 4 Nightly Fee: $25, limit 6 nights, $30 for first night Available: Year Round
Snow machine access in winter. One room, wood cook stove, 2 bunk bed sets. No water, no lights. Outdoor privy. Parents adv. Not to bring children under 12 years of age.

Squirrel Meadows Guard Station
23 mi. E of Ashton 652-7442
Cap: 6 Nightly Fee: $35, max. 8 nights, $40 for first night Available: Year Round
Access by snow machines or skiing in winter. 2 rooms, wood heat/cook stove, 3 bunk bed sets, outside hand pump for water. No lights. Outdoor privy.

Warm River Hatchery
24 mi. E/NE of Ashton 652-7442
Cap: 10 Nightly Fee: $45, max. 20 nights, $50 for first night Available: Year Round
Access by snow machines or skiing in winter. 2 bedrooms, 6 bunk bed sets, wood cook stove, wood furnace. No lights. Outdoor privy. River

water only.

Car Rental

Dollar • Driggs	354-3100
Driggs Airport/Teton Aviation Center Driggs	354-3100
Alamo • Idaho Falls	522-0340
American Carriage RV & Marine Idaho Falls	529-5535
Avis • Idaho Falls	529-4225
Budget • Idaho Falls	522-8800
Dodge Authorized Dealer Idaho Falls	522-2610
Enterprise • Idaho Falls	523-8111
Hertz • Idaho Falls	529-3101
Leasing Service Inc • Idaho Falls	522-2610
National • Idaho Falls	522-5276
Overland West • Idaho Falls	529-3101
Ron Sayer Dodge • Idaho Falls	522-2610
Thrifty • Idaho Falls	227-0444
Enterprise • Rexburg	356-8889
Practical • Rexburg	356-9018
Smith Ford Mercury Inc • Rexburg	356-3636
Stones Town & Country Motors Rexburg	356-9366

Outfitters & Guides

F=Fishing H=Hunting R=River Guides
E=Horseback Rides G=General Guide Services

Id Outfitters & Guides Association	800-49-IDAHO
Outfitters & Guides Licensing Board	327-7380

Ski Kelly Canyon • Rigby	538-6261
Grand Targhee • Driggs	353-2300

Cross-Country Ski Centers

Teton Ridge Ranch • Tetonia	456-2650

Downhill Ski Areas

Grand Targhee • Driggs	353-2300
Ski Kelly Canyon • Rigby	538-6261

Snowmobile Rentals

The Pines • Island Park	**888-455-9384**
Robson Outfitters • Felt	456-2805
Aspen Lodge • Island Park	558-7407
High Country Snowmobile Tours Island Park	558-9572
Island Park Rentals • Island Park	558-0112
Island Park Reservations Island Park	558-9675
Lakeside Lodge • Island Park	558-7147
Landon Lodge • Island Park	521-7448
Winchester Lodge • Island Park	888-762-9057
Elkins Resort • Nordman	443-2432
Yellowstone Teton Terrritory Rexburg	656-0654
Goosewing Ranch • St. Anthony	624-1499
Rendezvous Snowmobile Rental Tetonia	456-2805
Teton Springs Resort • Victor	787-8008

NOTES:

Campground Quick Reference

Ashton

Squirrel Creek Elk Ranch, Inc. — 652-3972
C $75-105 16 All Year
12 mi. E. of Ashton on Reclamation-Flagg Ranch Rd.

Aspen Acres Golf Club & RV Park — 652-3524/800-845-2374
C $15-25 40 Summer, Fall, Spring
9 mi. SE-of Ashton

Jessen's RV, B & B, Cottages & Tents — 652-3356/800-747-3356
C 22 All Year
Hwy. 20, 1.5 mi. S. of Ashton

Timberline RV Park — 652-3219
C $15 25 35' All Year
E. of Ashton on Cave Falls Rd.
Hookups, Playground, Pull-thru Sites, Showers, Tenters Welcome

Buttercup — 382-6544
P $7-22 28 32' Summer, Fall, Spring
22.4 mi. N. of Cascade, W. side of Cascade Reservoir
Credit Cards OK, Drinking Water, Pets OK, Tenters Welcome, Vault Toilets, Handicap Access

Cave Falls — 558-7301
P $8 16 24' Summer
6 mi. E. on Hwy 47, 5.5 mi. NE on Cave Falls Rd., 11 mi. NE on Forest Rd. 582
Drinking Water, Pets OK, Pull-thru Sites, Tenters Welcome, Vault Toilets

Pole Bridge — 558-7301
P 10 22' Summer, Fall
12 mi. NE on Hwy. 47, 5 mi. N. on Forest Rd. 150
Fire Rings, Pets OK, Tenters Welcome, Vault Toilets

Riverside - Ashton — 558-7301
P $8-10 57 34' Summer, Fall
16.5 mi. N. on Hwy. 20, 1 mi. SE on Forest Rd. 304
Credit Cards OK, Drinking Water, Fire Rings, Pets OK, Pull-thru Sites, Reservations, Tenters Welcome, Vault Toilets, Waterfront, Handicap Access

Warm River — 558-7301
P $7-120 17 24' Summer, Fall
10 mi. NE on Hwy. 47
Drinking Water, Fire Rings, Pets OK, Reservations, Tenters Welcome, Vault Toilets, Waterfront, Handicap Access

West End — 558-7301
P 19 22' Summer, Fall
18 mi. N. on Hwy. 20, 15 mi. NW on Forest Rd. 167
Fire Rings, Tenters Welcome, Vault Toilets

Grandview — 652-7442
P None 5 June 1-September 30
14 miles N of Ashton on Hwy. 47
Developed Campground, Restrooms, RV Sites, Scenic Driving, Winter Sports

Driggs

Reunion Flat Group Area — 354-2312
P $10-20 3 Summer, Fall
6 mi. NE on Cty. Rd. 009, 3 mi. E. on Forest Rd. 009
Drinking Water, Pets OK, Reservations, Vault Toilets, Waterfront, Handicap Access

Dubois

Kilgore General Store — 778-5334
C $10 2 All Year
26 mi. E. of Dubois, 31 mi. W. of Island Park
Hookups, Mini-Mart, Showers

Scoggins Inc. — 374-5453
C $16.20 9 All Year
I-15, exit 167
Credit Cards OK, Drinking Water, Game Room, Hookups, LP Gas, Mini-Mart, Pets OK, Pull-thru Sites, Reservations, Showers, Tenters Welcome, Handicap Access

Stoddard Wagon Wheel Court — 374-5330
C $10 3 All Year
Main St., S. on Thomas St. to 4th St., behind City/County Annex Bldg.
Dump Station, Hookups

Steel Creek Group Area — 374-5422
P 22' Summer, Fall, Spring
3.5 mi. N. on Hwy. 15, 17 mi. SE on Forest Rd. 006, 1.2 mi. W. on Forest Rd. 478
Drinking Water, Reservations, Vault Toilets

Stoddard Creek — 374-5422
P $6-12 24 32' Summer, Fall, Spring
16 mi. N. on Hwy. 15, 1 mi. NW on Forest Rd. 80003
Drinking Water, Fire Rings, Pull-thru Sites, Tenters Welcome, Vault Toilets

Webber Creek — 374-5422
P None 4 June 15-September 15
30 miles NW of Dubois on Hwy. 22 and FR 196
Developed Campground, Restrooms, RV Sites, Fishing, Hiking/Backpacking, Horseback Riding

Idaho Falls

ARM'S Shady Rest RV Park — 524-0010
C $12-20 30 40' All Year
N. Idaho Falls area, .25 mi. N. of Anderson/Lincoln
Drinking Water, Dump Station, Hookups, Pets OK, Pull-thru Sites, Reservations, Showers, Tenters Welcome, Laundry

Sunnyside Acres Park — 523-8403
C $22.30 25 All Year
Exit 119 or 113 off Hwy. 20 to W.Sunnyside Rd.
Dump Station, Hookups, Pets OK, Showers, Laundry

Idaho Falls KOA — 523-3362/800-562-7644
C $24-32 130 All Year
I-15, exit 118 to Utah Blvd., turn left, continue to campground
Credit Cards OK, Dump Station, Hookups, LP Gas, Mini-Mart, Modem Hookups, Pets OK, Playground, Pull-thru Sites, Reservations, Showers, Swimming Pool, Tenters Welcome

Irwin

McCoy Creek — 523-1412
P $8/night 19 June 1-September 15
S of Irwin on Hwy. 26/89, then 7 miles N on FR 087
Developed Campground, Primitive Camping, Drinking Water, Restrooms, RV Sites, Boat Ramp, Biking, Motorized and Non-Motorized Boating, Fishing, Hiking/Backpacking, Horseback Riding, Hunting, Picnicking, Scenic Driving, Water Sports, Wildlife Viewing

Alpine — 523-1412
P $8/single; $16/double 33 May 25-September 15
S of Irwin on Hwy. 26/89 near the ID/WY Border
Developed Campground, Group Camping, Drinking Water, Restrooms, RV Sites, Biking, Fishing, Hiking/Backpacking, Horseback Riding, Picnicking, Scenic Driving, Water Sports, Winter Sports

Island Park

Robins Roost Chevron & Grocery Store — 558-7440
C $15 10 60' Summer, Fall, Spring
Hwy. 20, N. end of Big Springs Rd.
Credit Cards OK, Hookups, LP Gas, Mini-Mart, Reservations, Showers

Mack's Inn Resort — 558-7272
C $10-115 73 All Year
Hwy. 20, N. of Island Park
Credit Cards OK, Dump Station, LP Gas, Mini-Mart, Pets OK, Playground, Reservations, Showers, Laundry

RedRock RV & Camping Park — 558-7442/800-473-3762
C $16-21 54 65' Summer, Fall
Hwy. 20, M P 398, W. on Red Rock Rd. 5 mi.
Camping Cabins, Credit Cards OK, Drinking Water, Dump Station, Fire Rings, Hookups, Mini-Mart, Modem Hookups, Pets OK, Playground, Pull-thru Sites, Reservations, Showers, Tenters Welcome, Laundry, Handicap Access

Campground Quick Reference - continued

Campground Name				Phone
Public/Commercial	Unit Price	#Spaces	Max. Length	Seasons
Directions				
Amenities/Activities				

Valley View RV Park, Campground & Laundromat 558-7443/888-558-7443
| C | $17-24 | 53 | 50' | All Year |

Near Henrys Lake, 13.5 mi. S. of West Yellowstone, near airport
Drinking Water, Hookups, LP Gas, Modem Hookups, Pets OK, Pull-thru Sites, Reservations, Showers, Tenters Welcome, Laundry

Pond's Lodge 558-7221/888-731-5153
| C | $10.50 | 50 | | All Year |

Hookups, Mini-Mart, Pets OK, Waterfront, Handicap Access

Wild Rose Ranch 558-7201
| C | $18-25 | 60 | 45' | All Year |

Hwy. 87, N. shore of Henrys Lake
Credit Cards OK, Dump Station, Hookups, Modem Hookups, Pets OK, Pull-thru Sites, Waterfront, Work-Out Room, Laundry

Sawtelle Mountain Resort 558-9366/866-558-9366
| C | $21.50 | 60 | | All Year |

Hwy. 20 between M P 394 & 395 at Sawtelle Peak Rd.

Enchanted Forest RV & Campground 558-9675
| C | $10-14 | 14 | | All Year |

6 mi. W. of Hwy. 20 on Yale-Kilgore Rd.
Handicap Access

Buffalo Run Campground 558-7112/888-797-3434
| C | $15 | 42 | | All Year |

3402 N. Hwy. 20

Lazy Trout Lodge & Cafe 558-7407/877-529-9432
| C | $18 | 8 | | All Year |

Hwy. 20, M P 397

Staley Springs Lodge 558-7471
| P | $49-175 | 44 | | All Year |

Camping Cabins, Credit Cards OK, Dump Station, Hookups, Mini-Mart, Pets OK, Showers, Waterfront

Big Springs - Island Park 558-7301
| P | $10 | 15 | 32' | Summer, Fall |

4.5 mi. E. of Macks Inn on Forest Rd. 059
Drinking Water, Fire Rings, Pets OK, Pull-thru Sites, Tenters Welcome, Vault Toilets

Box Canyon 558-7301
| P | $10 | 19 | 32' | Summer, Fall |

7 mi. S. of Mack's Inn on Hwy. 20, .3 mi. SW on Hwy. 134, .9 mi. NW on Forest Rd. 284
Drinking Water, Fire Rings, Pets OK, Tenters Welcome, Vault Toilets

Buffalo 558-7301
| P | $10-120 | 127 | 34' | Summer, Fall |

5.5 mi. S. of Mack's Inn on Hwy. 20
Drinking Water, Fire Rings, Pets OK, Pull-thru Sites, Reservations, Tenters Welcome, Vault Toilets

Buttermilk 558-7301
| P | $10-100 | 54 | 32' | Summer, Fall |

Hwy. 20, 3.5 mi. S. of Mack's Inn, 2.2 mi. NW on Hwy. 030, 4 mi. SW on Forest Rd. 334
Drinking Water, Fire Rings, Pets OK, Pull-thru Sites, Reservations, Vault Toilets

Flat Rock - Island Park 558-7301
| P | $10-30 | 40 | 32' | Summer |

Across from Mack's Inn
Drinking Water, Fire Rings, Pets OK, Reservations, Tenters Welcome, Vault Toilets

Henrys Lake State Park 558-7532
| P | $9-16 | 45 | 40' | Summer, Fall |

45 mi. N. of Ashton on Hwy. 20, M P 401, 15 mi. S. of W. Yellowstone
Credit Cards OK, Drinking Water, Dump Station, Hookups, Reservations, Showers, Tenters Welcome, Vault Toilets, Waterfront

McCrea Bridge 558-7301
| P | $10-20 | 25 | 32' | Summer, Fall |

3.5 mi. S. of Mack's Inn on Hwy. 20, 2.2 mi. NW on Cty. Rd. 030
Drinking Water, Fire Rings, Pets OK, Reservations, Vault Toilets

Upper Coffee Pot 558-7301
| P | $10-30 | 15 | 32' | Summer, Fall |

.5 mi. S. of Mack's Inn on Hwy. 20, 2 mi. SW on Forest Rd. 130
Drinking Water, Fire Rings, Pets OK, Reservations, Tenters Welcome, Vault Toilets, Waterfront

Mud Lake

Haven Motel & Trailer Park 663-4821
| C | $12 | 13 | | All Year |

Hwy. 33
Credit Cards OK, Dump Station, Hookups, Pets OK, Reservations

Birch Creek 524-7500
| P | | 16 | 25' | Summer, Fall |

25 mi. NW of Mud Lake on Hwy. 28
Vault Toilets

Palisades

Palisades RV Park & Cabins 483-4485
| C | $16 | 14 | | Summer |

Hwy. 26, M P 385
Credit Cards OK, Drinking Water, Dump Station, Hookups, Pets OK, Playground, Reservations, Showers, Tenters Welcome, Waterfront

Big Elk Creek 523-1412
| P | | 21 | 22' | Summer, Fall |

5.4 mi. SE on Hwy. 26, 1.4 mi. NE on Forest Rd. 262
Drinking Water, Fire Rings, Reservations, Vault Toilets

Blowout 523-1412
| P | $7 | 19 | 32' | Summer, Fall |

9 mi. SE on Hwy. 26
Boating Facilities, Drinking Water, Fire Rings, Reservations, Vault Toilets

Calamity 523-1412
| P | | 41 | 32' | Summer, Fall |

2.6 mi. S. on Hwy. 26, 1.1 mi. SW on Forest Rd. 058
Boating Facilities, Drinking Water, Fire Rings, Reservations, Vault Toilets

Palisades Creek 523-1412
| P | | 8 | 22' | Summer, Fall |

2 mi. NE on Forest Rd. 255
Drinking Water, Fire Rings, Vault Toilets

Rexburg

Rainbow Lake & Campground 356-3681
| C | $16-20 | 60 | | All Year |

S. Rexburg exit, .25 mi. W., then S. 1.25 mi.
Credit Cards OK, Drinking Water, Dump Station, Hookups, Playground, Pull-thru Sites, Showers, Handicap Access

Thompson's RV Park 356-6210
| C | $15 | 9 | | All Year |

Hwy. 191, 4 mi. S. of Rexburg
Hookups, Showers

Sheffield RV Park 356-4182
| C | $14-17 | 25 | | All Year |

Hwy. 20, N. of Idaho Falls, right after M. P. 328 at Shell Sta. to stop sign. From Rexburg go south on Hwy 20 for 4 miles, just after M.P. 329. Turn left at Shell Sta. To Stop sign- follow sign 5362 S. Hwy 191
Camping Cabins, Credit Cards OK, Drinking Water, Dump Station, Fire Rings, Hookups, Modem Hookups, Pets OK, Pull-thru Sites, Reservations, Showers, Tenters Welcome, Waterfront, Laundry, Handicap Access

Section 6

Campground Quick Reference - continued

Campground Name Public/Commercial	Unit Price	#Spaces	Max. Length	Phone Seasons
Directions				
Amenities/Activities				

Rigby

Jefferson Lake RV Campground — 745-7756
C — All Year

Ririe

7N Ranch — 538-5097
C | $12-19 | 28 | | All Year
Hwy. 26, 21 mi. from Idaho Falls
Handicap Access

Heise Hot Springs — 538-7453
C | | 14 | | All Year
Hwy. 26, 3 mi. NE of Ririe, 5116 Heise Rd.
Hookups, Mini-Mart, Reservations, Showers, Swimming Pool, Handicap Access

Mountain River Ranch RV Park & Campground — 538-7337
C | $12-20 | 27 | | All Year
18 mi. NE of Idaho Falls off Hwy. 26
Camping Cabins, Drinking Water, Dump Station, Hookups, Pets OK, Reservations, Showers, Tenters Welcome, Handicap Access

Kelly's Island — 524-7500
P | | | 40' | Summer, Fall
2 mi. E. of Heise on access road N. of river
Drinking Water, Pets OK, Pull-thru Sites, Tenters Welcome, Vault Toilets, Waterfront, Handicap Access

Table Rock — 524-7500
P | | 9 | 22' | Summer, Fall, Spring
12 mi. SE on Hwy. 26; 1.5 mi. SE on Forest Rd. 218; 1.3 mi. SE on Forest Rd. 217
Drinking Water, Reservations, Vault Toilets

Juniper Park — 678-0461
P | $9-16 | 49 | 42' | Summer, Fall, Spring
15 mi. SE of Idaho Falls, 1 mi. S. on Hwy. 26
Drinking Water, Dump Station, Hookups, Pets OK, Pull-thru Sites, Reservations, Showers, Tenters Welcome, Vault Toilets

Spencer

Spencer Stage Station — 374-5242
C | $12 | 14 | | All Year

Hookups, Pets OK, Showers

Spencer Opal Mines — 374-5476
C | $10-15 | 12 | | Summer, Fall, Spring
N. end of Main St.
Dump Station, Hookups, Mini-Mart, Pets OK, Pull-thru Sites, Reservations, Showers, Tenters Welcome

St. Anthony

Fenton's RV & Camping — 624-7854
C | $8-20 | 14 | 40' | Summer, Fall
Hwy. 20 to Relay Station Restaurant, then E. 500 yds.
Drinking Water, Hookups, Pets OK, Playground, Pull-thru Sites, Reservations, Showers, Tenters Welcome

Notes:

Sandhills Resort Inc. — 624-4127
C | $19-24 | 110 | | Summer, Fall, Spring
4 mi. W., 3 mi. N. of St. Anthony, 865 Redroad
Credit Cards OK, Drinking Water, Dump Station, Hookups, Mini-Mart, Modem Hookups, Pets OK, Playground, Pull-thru Sites, Reservations, Showers, Tenters Welcome, Laundry

Swan Valley

Falls — 523-1412
P | $8 | 23 | 24' | Summer, Fall
4 mi. W. on Hwy. 26, 2.3 mi. S. on Forest Rd. 076
Drinking Water, Fire Rings, Reservations, Vault Toilets

Falls Group Area — 523-1412
P | | | 22' | Summer, Fall
4 mi. W. on Hwy. 26, 2.6 mi. S. on Forest Rd. 076
Drinking Water, Fire Rings, Reservations, Vault Toilets

Riverside Park — 523-1412
P | | 24 | | Summer, Fall
Hwy. 26, just below Palisades dam
Drinking Water, Dump Station, Fire Rings, Hookups, Pull-thru Sites, Vault Toilets

Teton Valley

Teton Valley Campground — 787-2647/877-787-3036
C | $23-42 | 75 | | All Year
Hwy. 31, 1 mi. W. of Victor, 128 Hwy. 31
Credit Cards OK, Drinking Water, Dump Station, Hookups, Pets OK, Playground, Pull-thru Sites, Reservations, Showers, Swimming Pool, Tenters Welcome

Pine Creek — 354-2312
P | $6-12 | 11 | 30' | Summer, Fall
6.5 mi. W. on Hwy. 31
Drinking Water, Pets OK, Pull-thru Sites, Vault Toilets, Handicap Access

Teton Canyon — 354-2312
P | $8-16 | 20 | 24' | Summer
6 mi. NE on Cty. Rd. 009, 4.5 mi. E. on Forest Rd. 009
Drinking Water, Pets OK, Pull-thru Sites, Reservations, Vault Toilets, Handicap Access

Trail Creek - Teton Valley — 354-2312
P | $8-16 | 11 | 20' | Summer, Fall
6 mi. SE of Victor on Hwy. 33
Drinking Water, Pets OK, Pull-thru Sites, Vault Toilets

Victor

Mike Harris — 354-2312
P | $6-12 | 11 | 30' | Summer, Fall
4 mi. SE on Hwy. 33
Drinking Water, Pets OK, Pull-thru Sites, Vault Toilets, Handicap Access

Dining Quick Reference

Price Range refers to the average cost of a meal per person: ($) $1-$6, ($$) $7-$11, ($$$) $12-up. Cocktails: "Yes" indicates full bar; Beer (B)/Wine (W), Service: Breakfast (B), Brunch (BR), Lunch (L), Dinner (D). Businesses in bold print will have additional information under the appropriate map locator number in the body of this section.

MAP NO.	RESTAURANT	TYPE CUISINE	PRICE RANGE	CHILD MENU	COCKTAILS BEER WINE	MEALS SERVED	CREDIT CARDS ACCEPTED
5	Corner Bar & Cafe	American	$	N	Yes	L	No
	2099 N Old Butte Hwy, Hamer, 662-5253						
6	Amy's Place	Family	$-$$	Y	N	B/L/D	V
	Exit 135, Roberts, 228-2692						
7	**Motel West & Hometown Kitchen Restaurant**	Family	$$	Y	N	B/L/D	Major
	1540 W Broadway, Idaho Falls, 552-1112						
7	A&W Family Restaurant	Fast Food	$	Y	N	L/D	M V
	Idaho Falls, 524-3713						
7	Applebee's Neighborhood Grill & Bar	American	$$	Y	Yes	L/D	Major
	635 N Utah Ave, Idaho Falls, 528-8985						
7	Arby's	Fast Food	$	Y	N	L/D	Major
	1547 W Broadway, Idaho Falls, 542-6066						
7	Arctic Circle	Fast Food	$	Y	N	L/D	M V
	805 W Broadway, Idaho Falls, 522-6611						
7	Burger King	Fast Food	$	Y	N	L/D	M V
	1463 W Broadway, Idaho Falls, 522-8120						
7	Dairy Queen	Fast Food	$	N	N	L/D	No
	1507 W Broadway, Idaho Falls, 522-9877						
7	Denny's Restaurant	Family	$-$$	Y	N	B/L/D	Major
	950 Lindsay Blvd, Idaho Falls, 528-9210						
7	Domino's Pizza	Pizza	$-$$	N	N	L/D	M V
	945 W Broadway, Idaho Falls, 523-7530						
7	George's Place	Family	$-$$	Y	N	B/L/D	No
	950 Park Ave, Idaho Falls, 525-2571						
7	Grandpas Southern Bar B Que	American	$$	Y	N	L/D	Major
	1855 W Broadway, Idaho Falls, 522-1890						
7	Happy's Chinese Restaurant	Asian	$$	N	N	L/D	Major
	549 Park Ave, Idaho Falls, 522-2091						
7	Hometown Kitchen	Family	$-$$	Y	N	B/L/D	Major
	1540 W Broadway, Idaho Falls, 542-0950						
7	Hong Kong Restaurant	Asian	$$	N	N	L/D	Major
	1570 W Broadway, Idaho Falls, 522-9914						
7	Hyde Outfitters & Last Chance Lodge	Fine Dining	$$-$$$	N	B W	B/L/D	Major
	1520 Pancheri Dr, Idaho Falls, 558-7068						
7	J B's Family Restaurant	Family	$-$$	Y	N	B/L/D	Major
	1331 W Broadway, Idaho Falls, 522-4224						
7	Jack In The Box	Fast Food	$	Y	N	L/D	M V
	1458 W Broadway, Idaho Falls, 552-2613						
7	Kathryn's Restaurant	American	$-$$	Y	B W	B/L	Major
	2140 N Skyline Dr Ste 6, Idaho Falls, 523-5969						
7	Los Panchos	Mexican	$-$$	N	N	L/D	M V
	486 F St, Idaho Falls, 524-8331						
7	McDonald's	Fast Food	$	Y	N	B/L/D	Major
	1485 W Broadway, Idaho Falls, 522-1621						
7	O'Brady's Restaurant	Family	$$	Y	N	B/L/D	M V
	1438 W Broadway, Idaho Falls, 523-2132						
7	Outback Steakhouse	Steakhouse	$$	Y	B W	L/D	Major
	970 Lindsay Blvd, Idaho Falls, 523-9301						
7	Papa Murphy's Take 'n' Bake	Pizza	$$	N	N	L/D	M V
	1857 W Broadway St, Idaho Falls, 528-9800						
7	Pizza Hut	Pizza	$	N	N	L/D	Major
	1970 W Broadway, Idaho Falls, 523-7411						
7	Pizza Hut	Pizza	$	N	N	L/D	Major
	2250 E 17th, Idaho Falls, 524-1211						
7	Quizno's Subs	Fast Food	$	N	N	L/D	M V
	620 W Broadway, Idaho Falls, 552-7011						
7	Red Lion Hotel On the Falls	Fine Dining	$$-$$$	Y	Yes	L/D	Major
	475 River Parkway, Idaho Falls, 523-8000						
7	Subway	Fast Food	$	N	N	L/D	M V
	1595 W Broadway, Idaho Falls, 523-9162						

Dining Quick Reference - continued

Price Range refers to the average cost of a meal per person: ($) $1-$6, ($$) $7-$11, ($$$) $12-up. Cocktails: "Yes" indicates full bar; Beer (B)/Wine (W), Service: Breakfast (B), Brunch (BR), Lunch (L), Dinner (D). Businesses in bold print will have additional information under the appropriate map locator number in the body of this section.

MAP NO.	RESTAURANT	TYPE CUISINE	PRICE RANGE	CHILD MENU	COCKTAILS BEER WINE	MEALS SERVED	CREDIT CARDS ACCEPTED
7	The Frosty Gator 298 D St, Idaho Falls, 529-3334	American/Tavern	$	N	N	L/D	No
7	The Sports Page 1505 W Broadway, Idaho Falls, 529-4445	American	$	N	B W	L	No
7	Wendy's 1275 W Broadway, Idaho Falls, 542-5322	Fast Food	$	Y	N	L/D	M V
7	Westbank Restaurant & Lounge 475 River Parkway, Idaho Falls, 523-8000	American	$-$$	Y	Yes	B/L/D	Major
7	Yummy's 480 Park Ave, Idaho Falls, 529-9804	American	$	N	N	L/D	No
8	**Teton Grille Restaurant** Exit 318 Hwy 20, Idaho Falls, 522-3444	Fine Dining	$$$	Y	B W	L/D	Major
8	A Little Bit Of Mexico 465 E Anderson, Idaho Falls, 528-8185	Mexican	$-$$	Y	B W	L/D	Major
8	Albertos Restaurant 1855 N Yellowstone Hwy, Idaho Falls, 542-0391	Mexican	$-$$	Y	N	B/L/D	Major
8	Burger King 1750 N Yellowstone Hwy, Idaho Falls, 529-4725	Fast Food	$	Y	N	L/D	M V
8	DB's Steak & Brew House 216 1st St, Idaho Falls, 529-4070	Steakhouse	$$-$$$	Y	B W	L/D	Major
8	First St Saloon 285 1st St, Idaho Falls, 525-9917	American	$	N	B W	L/D	M V
8	Godfather's Pizza 1680 E 1st, Idaho Falls, 529-0553	Pizza	$	Y	N	L/D	M V
8	Great Wall Restaurant 201 1st St, Idaho Falls, 524-5188	Asian	$	Y	N	L/D	Major
8	Hardy's Pub & Grill 2626 N Yellowstone Hwy, Idaho Falls, 525-9705	American	$	N	B W	L	M V
8	Los Betos Mexican Food 1739 N Yellowstone Hwy, Idaho Falls, 552-2650	Mexican	$-$$	N	N	L/D	Major
8	McDonald's 1575 Northgate Mile, Idaho Falls, 524-2757	Fast Food	$	Y	N	B/L/D	Major
8	Mitchell's Restaurant 615 E Iona Rd, Idaho Falls, 525-8834	Family	$$	Y	N	B/L/D	Major
8	Morenita's 450 Whittier, Idaho Falls, 522-9319	Mexican	$-$$	N	N	L/D	M V
8	Peppertree Restaurant 888 N Holmes Ave, Idaho Falls, 524-6226	Family	$$	Y	N	L/D	Major
8	Pinecrest Diner 1471 Northgate Mile, Idaho Falls, 524-4133	American	$-$$	Y	B W	B/L/D	Major
8	Pizza Hut 725 E Anderson, Idaho Falls, 524-2727	Pizza	$	N	N	L/D	Major
8	Pockets Inc 905 E Lincoln Rd, Idaho Falls, 525-9962	Tavern	$	N	Yes	L/D	Major
8	Puerto Vallarta Mexican Restaurant 1480 Fremont Ave, Idaho Falls, 523-0437	Mexican	$$	N	N	L/D	Major
8	Sage Lakes Cafe 100 E 65th N, Idaho Falls, 535-0414	American	$	N	B W	B/L/D	No
8	Taco John's 930 Northgate Mile, Idaho Falls, 529-3081	Fast Food	$	N	N	L/D	M V
8	Teton Grille 3 N 3800 E, Idaho Falls, 522-3444	Regional/Casual Fine Dining	$$	Y	B W	L/D	Major
8	Thai Kitchen 775 N Yellowstone Hwy, Idaho Falls, 523-0255	Asian	$	N	N	L/D	Major
8	The Crimson Teahouse 301 Poulson, Idaho Falls, 522-2829	Teahouse/Fine Dining	$$	N	N	L	No
8	Wendy's Old Fashioned Hamburgers 1333 Northgate Mile, Idaho Falls, 522-5322	Fast Food	$	Y	N	L/D	M V
8	Wrangler Roast Beef 645 N Holmes Ave, Idaho Falls, 523-8838	Steakhouse	$-$$	Y	N	L/D	M V

Dining Quick Reference - continued

Price Range refers to the average cost of a meal per person: ($) $1-$6, ($$) $7-$11, ($$$) $12-up. Cocktails: "Yes" indicates full bar; Beer (B)/Wine (W), Service: Breakfast (B), Brunch (BR), Lunch (L), Dinner (D). Businesses in bold print will have additional information under the appropriate map locator number in the body of this section.

All Idaho Area Codes are 208

Section 6

MAP NO.	RESTAURANT	TYPE CUISINE	PRICE RANGE	CHILD MENU	COCKTAILS BEER WINE	MEALS SERVED	CREDIT CARDS ACCEPTED
8	Wright Brothers Travel Center 615 E Iona Rd, Idaho Falls, 524-3012	Family	$-$$	Y	N	L/D	Major
9	Arby's 2130 E 17th, Idaho Falls, 524-2521	Fast Food	$	Y	N	L/D	Major
9	Baskin-Robbins 1253 E 17th, Idaho Falls, 524-3131	Fast Food	$	N	N	L	M V
9	Burger King 2325 E 17th, Idaho Falls, 525-8820	Fast Food	$	Y	N	L/D	M V
9	Canton Restaurant 2173 E 17th, Idaho Falls, 523-3448	Asian	$$	N	N	L/D	No
9	China Super Buffet 888 E 17th, Idaho Falls, 528-0747	Asian	$	N	B W	L/D	Major
9	Chinese Garden Restaurant 1646 E 17th, Idaho Falls, 522-6300	Asian	$-$$	N	N	L/D	Major
9	Chuck-A-Rama Buffet 999 S 25th E, Idaho Falls, 524-5511	Family	$$	Y	N	L/D	Major
9	Cold Stone Creamery 2019 S 25th E, Idaho Falls, 522-3347	American	$	N	N	L/D	M V
9	Dairy Queen 1562 E 17th St, Idaho Falls, 524-3251	Fast Food	$	N	N	L/D	No
9	Ever Green China Buffet 2223 E 17th St, Idaho Falls, 524-0999	Asian	$$	N	N	L/D	M V
9	Fanatics Sports Grill 2040 Channing Wy, Idaho Falls, 529-5022	American	$	N	B W	L/D	Major
9	Fazolis Restaurant 3003 S 25th E, Idaho Falls, 523-4030	Italian	$$	Y	B W	L/D	Major
9	Garcia's Mexican Restaurant 2180 E 17th, Idaho Falls, 522-2000	Mexican	$-$$	Y	N	L/D	M V
9	International House of Pancakes 2463 S 25th E, Idaho Falls, 524-0885	Family	$-$$	Y	N	B/L/D	Major
9	Jack In The Box 424 S Woodruff Ave, Idaho Falls, 528-9489	Fast Food	$	N	N	L/D	M V
9	JJ North's Country Buffet 2450 E 17th, Idaho Falls, 529-0181	Family	$-$$	Y	N	L/D	Major
9	Kentucky Fried Chicken 900 E 17th, Idaho Falls, 523-3270	Fast Food	$-$$	Y	N	L/D	Major
9	Leo's Place Restaurants 155 S Holmes Ave, Idaho Falls, 529-5090	Pizza	$$	N	N	L/D	M V
9	Little Caesars Pizza 2075 E 17th St, Idaho Falls, 525-2646	Pizza	$	N	N	L/D	Major
9	McDonald's 1201 S 25th E, Idaho Falls, 522-6245	Fast Food	$	Y	N	B/L/D	Major
9	McDonald's 650 E 17th, Idaho Falls, 529-4608	Fast Food	$	Y	N	B/L/D	Major
9	Mongolian Grill 2153 E 17th, Idaho Falls, 524-7768	Asian	$-$$	N	N	L/D	M V
9	Mornitas #4 3390 S Yellowstone Hwy, Idaho Falls, 523-3990	Mexican	$-$$	N	N	L/D	M V
9	Papa Johns Pizza 555 S Woodruff Ave, Idaho Falls, 522-7272	Pizza	$$	N	N	L/D	M V
9	Papa Murphy's Take 'n' Bake 1600 E 17th St, Idaho Falls, 523-7200	Pizza	$$	N	N	L/D	M V
9	Papa Tom's Pizza 1830 S Woodruff Ave, Idaho Falls, 523-6800	Pizza	$	N	N	L/D	M V
9	Plum Loco 235 Cliff, Idaho Falls, 524-3663	Mexican	$-$$	N	N	B/L/D	M V
9	Puerto Vallarta Mexican Restaurant #2 1902 Jennie Lee Dr, Idaho Falls, 529-3267	Mexican	$$	N	N	L/D	Major
9	Quizno's Subs 2001 S 25th E, Idaho Falls, 528-8577	Fast Food	$	N	N	L/D	M V

Ultimate Idaho Atlas and Travel Encyclopedia

Dining Quick Reference - continued

Price Range refers to the average cost of a meal per person: ($) $1-$6, ($$) $7-$11, ($$$) $12-up. Cocktails: "Yes" indicates full bar; Beer (B)/Wine (W), Service: Breakfast (B), Brunch (BR), Lunch (L), Dinner (D). Businesses in bold print will have additional information under the appropriate map locator number in the body of this section.

MAP NO.	RESTAURANT	TYPE CUISINE	PRICE RANGE	CHILD MENU	COCKTAILS BEER WINE	MEALS SERVED	CREDIT CARDS ACCEPTED
9	Sandcreek Cafe 5200 S 25th E, Idaho Falls, 524-8302	American	$	N	B	B/L/D	No
9	Sol Rio 2635 S 25th E, Idaho Falls, 557-0321	Mexican	$$	N	N	L/D	M V
9	Sonic Drive-In 2785 E 17th, Idaho Falls, 528-7662	Fast Food	$	Y	N	L/D	M V
9	Subway 2300 E 17th , Idaho Falls, 528-7827	Fast Food	$	N	N	L/D	M V
9	Subway 995 E 17th, Idaho Falls, 528-0812	Fast Food	$	N	N	L/D	M V
9	Subway 316 S Woodruff Ave, Idaho Falls, 522-0662	Fast Food	$	N	N	L/D	M V
9	Subway 2220 Channing Way, Idaho Falls, 552-6582	Fast Food	$	N	N	L/D	M V
9	Sunset Strips 2300 E 17th, Idaho Falls, 552-4650	American	$-$$	N	N	L/D	Major
9	Taco Bell 2740 S 25th E, Idaho Falls, 552-3102	Fast Food	$	N	N	L/D	M V
9	Taco Bell 1000 E 17th, Idaho Falls, 522-8951	Fast Food	$	N	N	L/D	M V
9	Texas Roadhouse 2535 S 25 E, Idaho Falls, 542-9988	American	$$-$$$	N	B W	L/D	Major
9	The Sandwich Tree 500 W 17th, Idaho Falls, 529-5875	American/Deli	$	N	N	L	M V
9	Wendy's Old Fashioned Hamburgers 830 E 17th, Idaho Falls, 524-2291	Fast Food	$	Y	N	L/D	M V
9	Winger's Diner 2770 S 25th E, Idaho Falls, 552-5312	American	$-$$	Y	B	L/D	Major
9	Yen Ching Express 2647 S 25th E, Idaho Falls, 552-3000	Asian	$	N	N	L/D	M V
10	Dad's 113 Travel Center 6485 S Overland Dr, Idaho Falls, 552-0113	Family	$-$$	Y	N	B/L/D	Major
10	Frontier Pies Of Idaho 6485 S Overland Dr, Idaho Falls, 528-6300	Family	$-$$	Y	N	B/L/D	Major
11	Chuck-A-Rama Buffet 999 S 25th E, Ammon, 524-5511	American	$$	N	N	L/D	M V
11	Fazolis Resteraunt 3003 S 25th E, Ammon, 523-4030	Italian	$$	Y	B W	L/D	Major
11	Firehouse Grill 2891 S 25th E, Ammon, 524-1740	American	$$	Y	Yes	L/D	Major
11	Ground Round Grill & Bar 2891 S 25th E, Ammon, 524-1740	American	$$	Y	Yes	L/D	Major
11	International House of Pancakes 2463 S 25th E, Ammon, 524-0885	Family	$	Y	N	B/L/D	Major
11	Johnny Carino's Italian Kitchen 2833 S 25th E, Ammon, 523-4411	Italian	$$	Y	B W	L/D	Major
11	McDonald's 1875 S 25th E, Ammon, 542-6246	Fast Food	$	Y	N	B/L/D	Major
11	Pickerman Soup & Sandwich 2523 E Sunnyside Rd, Ammon, 522-0808	American/Deli	$	N	N	L/D	Major
11	Quizno's Classic Subs 2001 S 25th E, Ammon, 528-8577	Fast Food	$-$$	Y	N	L/D	M V
11	Sonic Drive-In Inc 2785 E 17th St, Ammon, 528-7662	Fast Food	$	Y	N	L/D	No
11	Texas Roadhouse 2535 S 25th E, Ammon, 542-9988	American	$$-$$$	Y	Yes	L/D	Major
11	Typhoon's Teriyaki Grill 2035 S 25th E, Ammon, 529-2695	Asian	$	N	N	L/D	M V
11	Yen Ching Express 2647 S 25th E, Ammon, 552-3000	Asian	$	N	N	L/D	M V

Dining Quick Reference - continued

Price Range refers to the average cost of a meal per person: ($) $1-$6, ($$) $7-$11, ($$$) $12-up. Cocktails: "Yes" indicates full bar; Beer (B)/Wine (W), Service: Breakfast (B), Brunch (BR), Lunch (L), Dinner (D). Businesses in bold print will have additional information under the appropriate map locator number in the body of this section.

All Idaho Area Codes are 208

Section 6

MAP NO.	RESTAURANT	TYPE CUISINE	PRICE RANGE	CHILD MENU	COCKTAILS BEER WINE	MEALS SERVED	CREDIT CARDS ACCEPTED
11	McDonald's 1875 S 25th E, Ammon/Idaho Falls, 542-6246	Fast Food	$	Y	N	B/L/D	Major
11	Ez Mart Convenience Store 5182 E Owens Ave, Iona, 529-4576	American	$	N	B W	L	M V
13	Opal Mountain Cafe Main St, Dubois, 374-5504	Family	$	Y	N	B/L/D	M V
13	Angus Restaurant 2986 Swan Valley Hwy, Irwin, 483-2666	Steakhouse	$-$$$	Y	N	B/L/D	Major
13	SouthFork Lodge 40 Conant Valley Loop, Swan Valley, 483-2112	Fine Dining	$$$	Y	B W	D	Major
14	**Mountain River Ranch-Meadow Muffin Theater** 98 N 5050 E at Heise-Kelly Canyon, Ririe, 538-7337	American/Fine Dining	$$-$$$	N	N	D	Major
15	Arctic Circle 241 S State St, Rigby, 745-6111	Fast Food	$	Y	N	L/D	M V
15	Bandos Mexican Restaurant 142 E Main St, Rigby, 745-9370	Mexican	$	N	N	L/D	M V
15	Subway 290 S State St, Rigby, 745-8762	Fast Food	$	N	B W	L	No
15	Fiesta Ole' 182 S State St, Rigby, 745-8060	Mexican	$	N	N	L/D	No
15	La Pizzeria 185 W Main St, Rigby, 745-8529	Pizza	$	N	N	L/D	No
15	Me & Stan's 100 W Main St, Rigby, 745-6999	Family	$-$$	Y	N	B/L/D	Major
15	Papa Kelsey's Pizza & Subs 160 E Main St, Rigby, 745-0010	Pizza	$	N	N	L/D	M V
15	Subway 200 S State St, Rigby, 745-0540	Fast Food	$	N	N	L/D	M V
17	Arby's 478 N 2nd E, Rexburg, 359-1345	Fast Food	$	Y	N	L/D	Major
17	Burger King 1130 University Blvd, Rexburg, 356-5128	Fast Food	$	Y	N	L/D	M V
17	Craigos Sourdough Pizza 120 Viking Dr, Rexburg, 359-1123	Pizza	$	N	N	L/D	M V
17	Fong's Restaurant 26 E Main St, Rexburg, 359-2566	Asian	$	N	N	L/D	Major
17	Frontier Pies Of Rexburg 460 W 4th S, Rexburg, 356-3600	Family	$-$$	Y	N	B/L/D	Major
17	Jack In The Box 461 N 2nd E, Rexburg, 656-9284	Fast Food	$	Y	N	L/D	No
17	JB's Big Boy Family Restaurants 150 W Main St, Rexburg, 356-7722	Family	$-$$	Y	N	B/L/D	Major
17	Kentucky Fried Chicken 568 N 2nd E, Rexburg, 356-7374	Fast Food	$-$$	Y	N	L/D	Major
17	Little Caesar's Pizza 26 W 1st S, Rexburg, 359-0071	Pizza	$	N	N	L/D	M V
17	McDonald's 175 Valley River Dr, Rexburg, 356-0060	Fast Food	$	Y	N	B/L/D	Major
17	Pizza Hut 163 W Main St, Rexburg, 356-7811	Fast Food	$	N	N	L/D	Major
17	Quizno's Subs 485 N 2nd E, Rexburg, 656-9477	Fast Food	$	N	N	L/D	M V
17	R & B Drive In 115 S 2nd W, Rexburg, 356-5545	American	$	N	N	L/D	M V
17	Ramirez Mexican Food 27 W Main, Rexburg, 359-8114	Mexican	$	N	N	L/D	Major
17	Subway 80 E Main St, Rexburg, 356-8234	Fast Food	$	N	N	L/D	M V
17	Taco Bell 22 W Main St, Rexburg, 656-0220	Fast Food	$	N	N	L/D	M V

Dining Quick Reference - continued

Price Range refers to the average cost of a meal per person: ($) $1-$6, ($$) $7-$11, ($$$) $12-up. Cocktails: "Yes" indicates full bar; Beer (B)/Wine (W), Service: Breakfast (B), Brunch (BR), Lunch (L), Dinner (D). Businesses in bold print will have additional information under the appropriate map locator number in the body of this section.

MAP NO.	RESTAURANT	TYPE CUISINE	PRICE RANGE	CHILD MENU	COCKTAILS BEER WINE	MEALS SERVED	CREDIT CARDS ACCEPTED
17	Taco Time 274 S 2nd W, Rexburg, 356-9005	Fast Food	$	N	N	L/D	M V
19	Burger King 195 N Main St, Driggs, 354-3185	Fast Food	$	Y	N	L/D	M V
19	Trails End Cafe 110 N Main St, Tetonia, 456-2202	American	$	N	B W	B/L/D	Major
19	Pierre's Dutch Oven 27 N Main St, Victor, 787-2971	American	$$-$$$	N	N	D	Major
21	Big J's Burgers & Pizza 245 N Bridge, St Anthony, 624-3969	American	$	N	N	L/D	No
21	Chiz'cougar Cave 246 N 2nd W, St Anthony, 624-7633	American	$$	N	N	L/D	No
21	Jill's Place 310 Bridge, St Anthony, 624-4499	Family	$-$$	Y	N	B/L/D	Major
21	Relay Station 593 N 2600 E, St Anthony, 624-4640	American	$$	Y	B W	B/L/D	Major
21	Subway 247 S Bridge, St Anthony, 624-4089	Fast Food	$	N	N	L/D	M V
22	Annie's Bakery & Pizzaria 514 Main, Ashton, 652-7641	Bakery/Pizza	$	N	N	L/D	M V
22	Big Juds Country Diner 1370 Hwy 20, Ashton, 652-7806	American	$	N	N	L/D	Major
22	Dave's IGA 108 S Hwy 20, Ashton, 652-7771	Deli/Grocery	$	N	N	L	Major
22	Frostop Drive-In 26 N Hwy 20, Ashton, 652-7762	American	$	N	N	L/D	M V
22	Imperial Club 504 Main, Ashton, 652-7782	American	$$	N	B W	L/D	Major
22	Trails Inn Restaurant 213 Main, Ashton, 652-9918	Steak/American	$$	Y	N	L/D	No
23	**Meadow Vue Ranch** 3636 Red Rock Rd, Island Park, 558-7411	American	$$-$$$	N	N	D	Major
23	**The Lodgepole Grill** 3907 Phillips Rd, Island Park, 558-0192	Steaks/Ribs/Pasta	$$-$$$	Y	Yes	L/D	Major
23	Henry's Fork Landing At Macks Inn N Hwy 20, Island Park, 558-7672	Family	$$	Y	N	B/L/D	Major
23	Island Park Restaurant/Saloon 4153 N Big Springs Rd, Island Park, 558-7281	American/Tavern	$$-$$$	N	Yes	L/D	Major
23	Phillips Lodge 3907 Phillips Loop Rd, Island Park, 558-9379	Fine Dining	$$-$$$	Y	Yes	L/D	Major
23	Pond's Lodge Ponds, Island Park, 558-7221	Fine Dining	$$-$$$	Y	Yes	B/L/D	M V
23	Shotgun General Store Yale Kilgore Rd, Island Park, 558-7090	American	$	N	B	L	Major
23	Subway 4141 Sawtelle Peak Rd, Island Park, 558-9884	Fast Food	$	N	N	L/D	M V

Section 6

NOTES:

Motel Quick Reference

Price Range: ($) Under $40 ; ($$) $40-$60; ($$$) $60-$80, ($$$$) Over $80. Pets [check with the motel for specific policies] (P), Dining (D), Lounge (L), Disabled Access (DA), Full Breakfast (FB), Cont. Breakfast (CB), Indoor Pool (IP), Outdoor Pool (OP), Hot Tub (HT), Sauna (S), Refrigerator (R), Microwave (M) (Microwave and Refrigerator indicated only if in majority of rooms), Kitchenette (K). All Idaho area codes are 208.

MAP NO.	MOTEL	NUMBER ROOMS	PRICE RANGE	BREAKFAST	POOL/ HOT TUB SAUNA	NON SMOKE ROOMS	OTHER AMENITIES	CREDIT CARDS
4	B-K's Motel 1073 E 1500 N, Mud Lake, 663-4578	5	$$					
4	Haven Motel 1079 E 1500 N, Mud Lake,	7	$$			Yes	P	M/V
5	Super 8 Motel - Pocatello 1330 Bench Rd, Pocatello, 234-0888	80	$$$	CB		Yes	P/DA	Major
7	**Fairfield Inn & Suites** 1293 W Broadway, Idaho Falls, 552-7378	81	$$$	CB	IP	Yes	DA/R/M	Major
7	**Motel West & Hometown Kitchen Restaurant** 1540 W Broadway, Idaho Falls, 522-1112	80	$$	CB	IP/HT	Yes	P/R/M	Major
7	Best Western Driftwood Inn 575 River Parkway, Idaho Falls, 523-2242	74	$$/$$$/$$$$	CB	OP	Yes	P/D/L/DA/R/M/K	Major
7	National 9 Executive Inn 850 Lindsay Blvd, Idaho Falls, 523-6260	130	$$		OP/HT/S	Yes	P/D/L/DA	Major
7	Red Lion Hotel On the Falls 475 River Parkway, Idaho Falls, 208-523-8000	138	$$$/$$$$		OP/HT/S	Yes	P/D/L	Major
7	Best Western Cottontree Inn 900 Lindsay Blvd, Idaho Falls, 523-6000	93	$$$/$$$$	CB	IP	Yes	D	Major
7	Days Inn 700 Lindsay Blvd, Idaho Falls, 523-8900	97	$$/$$$	CB	OP	Yes		Major
7	Shilo Inn Suites Hotel 780 Lindsay Blvd, Idaho Falls, 523-0088	161	$$$$		HT/S	Yes	P/DA	
7	Super 8 705 Lindsay Blvd, Idaho Falls, 522-8880	90	$$/$$$	CB	HT/S	Yes	DA	Major
7	Le Ritz Hotels & Suites 720 Lindsay Blvd, Idaho Falls, 528-0880	125	$$$/$$$$	CB	IP/S	Yes	P/DA/R/M	Major
7	Comfort Inn 195 S Colorado, Idaho Falls, 528-2804	56	$$$	CB	IP/HT	Yes	P/DA/R/M	Major
7	GuestHouse Inn & Suites 850 Lindsay Blvd, Idaho Falls, 523-6260	130	$$$		OP	Yes	P/D/L	Major
7	Towne Lodge 255 East St, Idaho Falls, 523-2960	40	$$			Yes		Major
7	AmeriTel Inn 645 Lindsay Blvd, Idaho Falls, 523-1400	126	$$$$	CB	IP	Yes	DA/R/M/K	Major
7	Motel 6 1448 W Broadway, Idaho Falls, 522-0112	48	$$		OP	Yes	P/DA/R/M	Major
7	Ramada Inn & Convention Center 133 W Burnside Ave, Pocatello, 237-0020	116	$$$		OP		P/D/L/DA/R/M	Major
7	Ross Hotel 343 Constitution Way, Idaho Falls, 525-9958	21	$$$/$$$$			Yes	L	M/V
8	Best Value Pinecrest Inn 888 N Holmes, Idaho Falls, 523-5993	72	$$$		OP	Yes	P/L/DA/R	Major
8	Quality Inn 807 N 5th Ave, Idaho Falls, 523-6260	62	$$$		IP/HT	Yes	P/D/L/DA	Major
9	**Yellowstone Motel** 2460 S Yellowstone, Idaho Falls, 529-9738	18	$			Yes	P/R/M/K	M/V/D
9	Evergreen Gables Motel 3130 S Yellowstone, Idaho Falls, 522-5410	33	$			Yes	P/R/M/K	M/V
9	Hampton Inn 2500 Channing Way, Idaho Falls, 529-9800	63	$$$$		IP	Yes	DA	Major
9	Holiday Inn Express 2270 Channing Way, Idaho Falls, 542-9800	101	$$$	CB	IP	Yes	DA/R/M	Major
13	South Fork Lodge 40 Conant Valley Loop, Swan Valley, 877-347-4735	19	$$$$		HT	Yes	D/DA	Major
14	**Cutthroat Inn B&B** Heise Rd, Ririe, 538-7963	18 individuals	$$$$	FB		Yes	R/M	Major
14	**Heise Hot Springs** 5116 Heise Rd, Ririe, 538-7312		$$-$$$		OP	Yes	D/L	Major
15	**Blue Heron Inn** 4175 E Menan Lorenzo Hwy, Rigby, 745-9922	7	$$$$	FB		Yes	DA	Major

454

Motel Quick Reference - continued

Price Range: ($) Under $40 ; ($$) $40-$60; ($$$) $60-$80, ($$$$) Over $80. Pets [check with the motel for specific policies] (P), Dining (D), Lounge (L), Disabled Access (DA), Full Breakfast (FB), Cont. Breakfast (CB), Indoor Pool (IP), Outdoor Pool (OP), Hot Tub (HT), Sauna (S), Refrigerator (R), Microwave (M) (Microwave and Refrigerator indicated only if in majority of rooms), Kitchenette (K). All Idaho area codes are 208.

MAP NO.	MOTEL	NUMBER ROOMS	PRICE RANGE	BREAKFAST	POOL/ HOT TUB SAUNA	NON SMOKE ROOMS	OTHER AMENITIES	CREDIT CARDS
15	**The BlackSmith Inn** 227 N 3900 E, Rigby, 745-6208	6	$$$$	FB	HT	Yes	D	M/V/D
15	South Fork Inn Motel 425 Farnsworth Way, Rigby, 745-8700	39	$$			Yes	P/DA	Major
17	Super 8 214 W Main St, Rexburg, 356-8888	41	$$	CB		Yes	R/M	Major
17	Best Western Cottontree Inn 450 W 4th S, Rexburg, 356-4646	97	$$$$	CB	IP	Yes	P/D/DA	Major
17	Days Inn 271 S 2nd W, Rexburg, 356-9222	43	$$$	CB	OP	Yes	P	Major
17	Comfort Inn 885 W Main St, Rexburg, 359-1311	52	$$$/$$$$	CB	IP	Yes	P/DA	Major
19	Pines Motel Guest Haus 105 S Main St, Driggs, 208-354-2774	7	$$		HT	Yes	P/R/M	Major
19	Trails End Motel 10 N Main, Victor, 787-2973	7	$$			Yes		Major
19	Best Western Teton West 476 N Main St, Driggs, 354-2363	40	$$$	CB	IP/HT	Yes	P/D	
19	Super 8 Teton West Motel 133 State Hwy 33, Driggs, 354-8888	46	$$/$$$	CB	IP/HT	Yes	DA/R/M	Major
19	Timberline Motel 38 W Center St, Victor, 787-2772	22	$$			Yes	K	Major
21	**Colonial Rose Tearoom and B&B** 411 N Bridge, St. Anthony, 624-3530	2	$$$$	FB		Yes		Major
21	Best Western Henry's Fork 115 S Bridge St, St. Anthony, 624-3711	30	$$$		HT	Yes	P/DA	Major
22	Ashton Super 8 Motel 1370 Hwy 20 N, Ashton, 652-3699	38	$$	CB		Yes	P/DA	Major
22	Four Seasons Motel 112 Main St, Ashton, 652-7769	12	$$			Yes	DA	M/V
22	Log Cabin Motel 1001 Main St, Ashton, 652-3956	10	$$			Yes	P/DA	Major
22	Rankin Motel 120 S Hwy 20, Ashton, 652-3570	12	$$			Yes	P/DA	Major
23	**The Pines at Historic Phillips Lodge & The Lodgepole Grill** 3907 Phillips Loop Rd, Island Park, 558-0192	24	$$$$		HT	Yes	D/L/R/M/K	Major
23	A-Bar Motel & Supper Club 3333 Hwy 20, Island Park, 558-7358	8	$$/$$$				P/D/L	Major
23	Mack's Inn Resort & Family Restaurant Island Park, 208-558-7272	65	$$$			Yes	P/D/DA/K	Major
23	TroutHunter Riverfront Lodge, Fly Shop and Bar & Grill 3327 N Hwy 20, Island Park, 558-9900	11	$$$$		HT	Yes	P/D/L/DA	Major
23	Henry's Fork Lodge HC 65, Box 600, Island Park, 558-7953							
23	Meadow Vue Ranch 3636 Red Rock Rd, Island Park [Mack's Inn], 558-7411							
23	Angler's Lodge 3363 Old Hwy 191, Island Park, 558-9555	15	$$$/$$$$			Yes	P/D/DA/K	Major

NOTES:

**J.S. Drake Originals
Wolf Toilet Paper Holder**
Made of heavy gauge metal, triple-coated with copper and sealed with a urethane topcoat, this delightful piece is durable. Complete a fun bathroom look by adding the wolf towel bar and single hook. An American artist known for his wolf, bear and deer switch plates, J.S. Drake created this piece. 10" tall, 6-1/2" long. Item # GC31163

Montana Silversmiths Elmer Paper Towel Holder Western artist Phyllis Driscoll created this handsome horse piece for Montana ilversmiths. This paper towel holder makes an impressive horse gift. 17" tall, 10" wide. Item # GC36212

*S*earching for that perfect western gift or decorative item? Don't miss the huge selection of quality-crafted items at the Gift Corral. A full selection of their signature products are available online, including handmade bath and body products, Moose Drool novelty items, whimsical bear and moose figurines, stuffed animals, wood carvings, Christmas ornaments reflecting the Western spirit, clothing, antler art, handcrafted jewelry, gourmet foods, Montana Silversmiths items, household décor items ranging from lamps to rustic furniture to picture frames, and much, much more!

GIFT CORRAL

FINE GIFTS AND ACCESSORIES

WWW.GIFTCORRAL.COM

Big Sky Brewing Co. Long Sleeve Moose Drool Script T-Shirt
Lightweight, stylish, and comfortable, this 100% cotton white long sleeve beer t-shirt proudly sports the Moose Drool logo across the chest. Great for Skiing, Mountain Biking, Sleeping, or watching TV at your friends house. Show your love of the brown ale with this awesome beer t-shirt. Item # GC26036

Big Sky Carvers Last Glance — Whitetail Deer Sculpture Montana artist Dick Idol designed this serialized and numbered cold cast bronze piece for Big Sky Carvers. Made of a bronze and resin mixture, this sculpture makes a great wildlife gift. 17" long, 5" wide, 15-3/4" tall. Item # GC39472

Big Sky Carvers Moosetivity II
Pair this set with Moosetivity I for an awesome Christmas display. Western artist Phyllis Driscoll designed this set of resin figurines for Big Sky Carvers. The full set makes a wonderful moose gift. Drummer Boy: 2-1/2" long, 3-1/4" wide, 3-3/4" tall. Shepherd: 3-1/4" long, 3" wide, 5-1/4" tall. King: 5" long, 2-1/2" wide, 4-3/4" tall. Item # GC35676

Search these items and hundreds more at…

WWW.GIFTCORRAL.COM

SECTION 7

SOUTHEAST CORNER

INCLUDING POCATELLO, BLACKFOOT, AMERICAN FALLS, AND BEAR LAKE VALLEY

The Snake River meanders through Section 7 past Blackfoot, Chubbuck, and Pocatello.

1 *Food, Lodging*

Shelley
Pop. 3,813

Migrating north from American Fork, Utah, John F. Shelley became the town's founding resident in 1884. He was soon joined by a string of other Mormon believers, and within no time, Shelley was serving as the community's Mormon bishop, first postmaster, and first businessman. When the Union Pacific Railroad set up shop, railroad officials honored the founding father's contributions by christening the town with his name.

Since its founding days, Shelley has relied upon the agricultural industry for sustenance. Although potatoes now represent the area's primary crop, the planting and harvesting of sugar beets initiated the area's farming boom.

Basalt
Pop. 419

Basalt was founded in 1885 as a Mormon settlement and was originally known as Cedar Point. When railroad services reached the area in 1889, railroad officials renamed the community Monroe, which was then changed to Basalt in 1903. The present name reflects the area's landscape of basalt rock formations lining the Snake River.

Firth
Pop. 408

Swedish emigrants who were Momon colonizers settled this area in 1885. Lorenzo J. Firth, an English emigrant, and William Dye swayed the

decision to place the railroad station at Firth's location in 1890. Lorenzo Firth donated some of his land on which to place the station house and water tank. As a result, railroad officials dubbed the growing town after him in 1903, and a post office arrived just two years later.

Lincoln
Pop. 300

This small town was appropriately named after President Abraham Lincoln, under whose administration the Idaho Territory was established.

H Lava Formations
Milepost 101.3 on I-15 at the North Blackfoot Rest Area

Molten rock, forced upward for 30 to 50 miles through fissures in the earth, has cooled into hard lava found here.

Continued pressure from below has made great cracks in the contorted surface. This lava solidified only a few thousand years ago, and not very much soil covers it yet. But vegetation is getting a start and unless new flows intervene, windblown soils will cover these rock layers. The surface here will then look the same as the surrounding plains, which also are layers of lava and windblown soils.

T Potato Cellars
Milepost 98 on I-15. Contact the Southeast Idaho Pioneer Country Travel Council at (888) 201-1063.

Idaho's Bingham County is known throughout America as the top potato-producing region in the country, and the local landscape confirms this

agricultural lifestyle. Dotting the interstate and state highways are miles of farmland and potato storage units. One of the most interesting storage facilities reflects potato-farming history and is found at I-15's milepost 98. Early Idaho potato producers created triangle-shaped buildings with peaked sod roofs as an efficient and cost-effective means of storing the state's famous crop. To the right is a rounded, more modern storage facility. While the newer buildings are slowly growing in popularity over the sod-roof structures, the historical storage facilities remain efficient and are still used in some parts of the county to handle the many tons of potatoes produced each year.

T Tex Creek Wildlife Management Area
20 miles southeast of Idaho Falls on U.S. Hwy. 26. Contact the Southeastern Idaho Pioneer Country Travel Council at (888) 201-1063.

Developed in the 1990s, the Tex Creek Wildlife Management Area provides visitors with year-round wildlife viewing opportunities. The large area is home to songbirds and upland birds during the spring and summer, and moose, deer, elk, sage grouse, sharp-tailed grouse, and bald eagles are regular residents of the site.

M Shelley Chamber of Commerce
101 S. Emerson Ave., Shelley. 357-3390.

2 *Food, Lodging*

Blackfoot
Pop. 10,419

Drawing its name from its placement at the confluence of the Snake and Blackfoot Rivers, the community of Blackfoot was founded in 1879. In its infancy, the community first served as an important stage station and then shifted in importance as a Union Pacific Railroad station. Today, Blackfoot revolves around an agricultural lifestyle and maintains the impressive distinction as the world's largest potato producing region. Naturally, the town is referred to as the "Potato Capital of the World." Blackfoot is also recognized as Idaho's top grain producer.

T Blackfoot Community Players
Blackfoot. 785-5344.

The non-profit Blackfoot Community Players was organized in 1977 and has been entertaining southeastern Idaho ever since. Relying on volunteers, the troupe presents several productions each year. Past performances have included musicals, dramas, dance, and old-fashioned melodramas. The group is also committed to providing youth education and arts advocacy. Average ticket prices are $7, and interested individuals should call for an upcoming schedule of events.

Blackfoot	Jan	Feb	March	April	May	June	July	Aug	Sep	Oct	Nov	Dec	Annual
Average Max. Temperature (F)		31.5	37.9	48.4	59.6	69.5	78.3	86.9	85.8	76.0	62.7	45.5	33.4	59.6
Average Min. Temperature (F)		14.5	18.8	25.5	32.1	40.0	46.6	52.4	50.3	42.3	32.7	24.1	16.1	32.9
Average Total Precipitation (in.)		0.91	0.81	0.88	0.97	1.25	1.02	0.47	0.48	0.68	0.72	0.89	0.93	10.00
Average Total Snowfall (in.)		6.7	4.0	2.1	0.9	0.0	0.0	0.0	0.0	0.0	0.6	2.3	6.4	23.1
Average Snow Depth (in.)		2	2	0	0	0	0	0	0	0	0	0	1	0

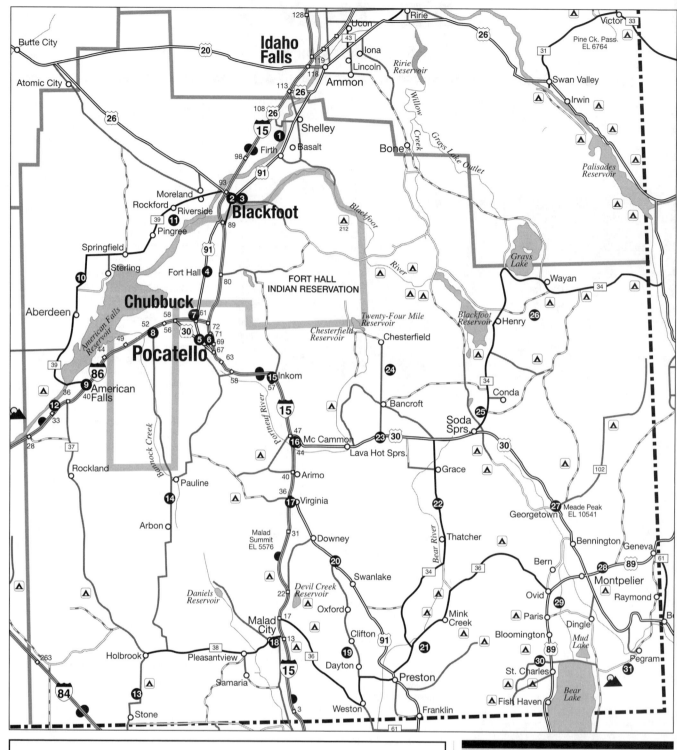

Butte City
Atomic City
20
26
26
15
108
26
128
Ucon
43
119
Iona
118
Lincoln
113
26
Idaho Falls
Ammon
Ririe
Ririe Reservoir
Willow Creek
Grays Lake Outlet
Victor
33
Pine Ck. Pass EL 6764
31
Swan Valley
Irwin
Palisades Reservoir
Shelley
98
Firth
91
Basalt
93
Moreland
Rockford
Riverside
39
11
Pingree
Blackfoot
89
Bone
212
Blackfoot
River
Grays Lake
Wayan
34
Springfield
Sterling
91
10
Fort Hall
4
80
FORT HALL INDIAN RESERVATION
Twenty-Four Mile Reservoir
Chesterfield Reservoir
Chesterfield
Blackfoot Reservoir
26
Henry
Aberdeen
Chubbuck
58
52
49
44
56
7
61
72
71
69
67
63
30
8
5
6
Pocatello
American Falls Reservoir
86
9
40
American Falls
36
12
33
28
37
24
34
Conda
25
Soda Sprs.
30
30
102
Rockland
Bannock Creek
Pauline
Portneuf River
15
57
58
Inkom
47
16
44
Mc Cammon
Lava Hot Sprs.
23
30
Grace
22
Bear River
27
Meade Peak EL 10541
Georgetown
Bennington
Geneva
61
Arbon
40
Arimo
36
17
Virginia
Malad Summit EL 5576
31
Downey
20
Swanlake
34
36
Thatcher
Bern
Mink Creek
Ovid
Paris
29
Bloomington
Dingle
Mud Lake
28
89
Montpelier
Raymond
B
Daniels Reservoir
Devil Creek Reservoir
22
Oxford
Clifton
91
19
Dayton
21
Preston
89
30
St. Charles
31
Bear Lake
Pegram
Malad City
17
18
13
36
15
Holbrook
263
38
Pleasantview
Samaria
Weston
Franklin
61
Fish Haven
84
13
Stone
3

Legend

00 Locator number (matches numeric listing in section)

🅰 Campsite

🏔 State Park

🛏 Rest stop

═══ Interstate

═══ U.S. Hwy.

━━━ State Hwy.

━━━ County Road

┅┅ Gravel/unpaved road

Idaho Trivia

The original Fort Hall treaty was signed in 1868, but the U.S. Congress spent the next few decades making amendments to the original agreement. On June 5, 1900, Congress approved the Pocatello Cession Agreement. This amendment forced the Bannock-Shoshone Indians to sell 150,000 acres of their land located at the southern end of the Fort Hall Indian Reservation. In ratifying this agreement, Congress obtained possession of the Lava Hot Springs area and opened the region to further white settlement.

SHELLEY
Map not to scale.

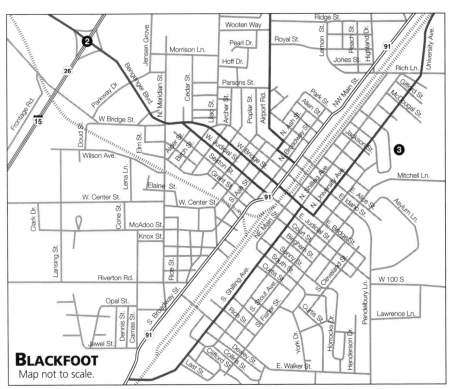

BLACKFOOT
Map not to scale.

TV Jensen Grove

Blackfoot. Contact the Southeast Idaho Pioneer Country Travel Council at (888) 201-1063. Merge east off I-15 at exit 93. Turn at the first left and continue to the park.

Blackfoot is known as one of Idaho's "City of Trees," and Jensen Grove provides visitors with plenty of shade under its stands of old-growth cottonwood trees. The 55-acre recreation site is Blackfoot's largest and most popular park featuring picnic areas, a playground and a 20-acre lake. Jensen Grove Lake provides hours of waterskiing and swimming fun, and a two-mile greenbelt path around the lake connects the community with the Snake River. Jensen Grove is open daily year-round.

3 Food, Lodging

T Historic Tour of Blackfoot

Contact the Blackfoot Chamber of Commerce at 785-0510.

Blackfoot's historical district features a myriad of architectural styles reflecting the town's influx of settlers and expansion. Many of these well-maintained buildings were constructed during the nineteenth century or at the dawn of the 1900s.

120 S. Shilling Ave.

Situated on a northeast corner, this two-story, semi-circular building was constructed between 1920 and 1921 at a cost of $78,000. The building was originally used as an LDS Tabernacle and could seat 1,000 people on the main floor while holding an additional 500 in the balconies. While the exterior features intricately designed brickwork and oval stained glass windows, the interior utilizes maple accents. In 1959, the Blackfoot LDS Stake converted the main floor into offices, and in 1980, sold the building to Bingham County as a community center.

72 N. Shilling Ave.

St. Paul's Episcopal Church is one of the oldest religious institutions in Blackfoot. The building has been used continuously since 1890.

Idaho Trivia

In 1885, Idaho Territorial Legislature passed $20,000 in bonds to create the state's first mental health hospital. The asylum, established in Blackfoot, abolished the need for patients to be sent to Oregon and ensured that family members would be able to visit admitted clients.

Corner of N. Shilling Ave. and East Idaho

A prominent Blackfoot businessman built this lava rock home in 1905 as a personal residence. During its 100-year history, the home has served as a community social center, an American Legion Home, and now as the Bingham County Historical Museum.

Across the street and northwest from the Bingham County Historical Museum

Dolf Johnson built this rustic stone house for his new bride in 1893. The home features a turret and two dormers and also once included exterior gingerbread accents. After Johnson was forced to foreclose on the property, the building was utilized as a hotel before being converted back into a private residence.

N. Main St.

Located on the east side of North Main Street, the Oregon Short Line Depot was constructed in 1913 at a cost of $27,000. Today, the depot serves the Union Pacific.

T Idaho's World Potato Expo

130 NW Main St., Blackfoot. 785-2187.

The famed Idaho spud enjoyed by millions of individuals every year receives a large dose of admiration and praise in Idaho's World Potato Expo Museum. Designed to celebrate the potato and its many uses, the museum displays interesting anecdotes about potato history, growth, and harvesting, as well as the social, economic, educational, scientific, and artistic contributions of the Idaho potato. Among the numerous exhibits, visitors will locate a tribute to Mr. Potato Head, the world's largest potato chip, and the world's largest Styrofoam potato. During the summer, the gift shop features signature potato fudge, potato ice cream, and potato cookies. Call for additional details regarding museum hours.

T Blackfoot Municipal Golf Course

3115 Teeples Dr., Blackfoot. 785-9960.

Golf Digest has rated the Blackfoot Municipal Golf Course as one of Idaho's best public courses. Spanning 6,722 yards, the 18-hole course is rated a par-72. While the front nine presents players

with difficult, narrow play, the back nine is much more open and therefore easier. Water hazards challenge players on half the course, and it is open Tuesday through Sunday from March 1 to October 31. Green fees start at $15.75.

T Bingham County Historical Museum

190 N. Shilling, Blackfoot. 785-8065.

Housed in a restored 1905 Southern style mansion, the Bingham County Historical Museum is dedicated to preserving the region's history. Exhibits include Native American artifacts, period clothing and furnishings, World War II uniforms, and numerous historical photos. The museum is open 1 PM to 5 PM Wednesday through Friday from May to October. Admission is free.

T Historic Nuart Theater

195 N. Broadway, Blackfoot. 785-5344.

The historic Nuart Theater is a cinema treasure that opened in 1930 at a cost of $100,000. Built by Paul Demordaunt, the theater features an Art Deco facade with white terra cotta cornices. Inside, the modern architectural style features hand-painted terra cotta friezes and ornamental plaster. Later, Demordaunt opened a small chain of Idaho movie theaters along with business partner, Hugh Drennen. Demordaunt's first theater, the Nuart, was added to the National Register of Historic Places in 1978. It is now home to the Blackfoot Community Players and hosts several theatrical events throughout the year.

TV Wolverine Canyon

Drive 9 miles north of Blackfoot on U.S. Hwy. 91, bearing right onto Wolverine Canyon Rd. Contact the Blackfoot Chamber of Commerce at 785-0510.

Nestled on the western slope of the fifty-mile long Blackfoot Mountain Range, Wolverine Canyon is a scenic area providing breathtaking views and recreational opportunities year-round. The canyon is a popular destination for hiking, whitewater rafting, camping, fishing, cross-country skiing, and snowmobiling and is open to the public free of charge.

TV Blackfoot River
East of Blackfoot. Contact the Palisades Ranger District at 523-1412.

The Blackfoot River, named after the Blackfoot Indians who once populated this Idaho region, is formed by the joining of Slug and Lane Creeks near the Caribou-Targhee National Forest in Caribou County. After traversing through desert canyons and past the Blackfoot Mountain Range along a ninety-five mile course, the river empties into the much larger Snake River. The river provides excellent whitewater rafting and kayaking, and wildlife viewing is especially popular on the river's course near Blackfoot.

When the Blackfoot River is combined with its tributaries, the drainage area covers 734 total surface acres and winds nearly 350 miles. The drainage, which includes Blackfoot Reservoir, supports mountain whitefish and hatchery-raised rainbow trout. In addition, the river serves as a corridor for wild cutthroat trout each spring as they ascend to area tributaries for spawning in late May and June.

M Blackfoot Chamber and Visitor Center
130 NW Main, Blackfoot. 7785-0510. www.blackfootchamber.org; chamber@blackfootchamber.org.

4

Fort Hall
Pop. 600

Nathaniel Wyeth built the original Fort Hall in 1834 primarily to store $3,000 worth of merchandise that Thomas Fitzpatrick and Milton Sublette were intending to purchase at the area's annual fur trapper rendezvous. The two men ultimately refused the product, and Wyeth then decided to sell the merchandise from his fort to the Indians. With him, Wyeth brought over sixty other settlers, and together they erected Old Fort Hall in the form of a stockade, surrounded by a ten-foot wall. Wyeth named the fort in honor of his top New England financier, Henry Hall. Eventually, Fort Hall's existence as a trade center combined with nearby Fort Boise to end the annual rendezvous between the Indians and traders. This was due to the forts' permanent nature and ability to offer year-round trade to everyone.

The Hudson Bay Company, which operated Fort Boise, purchased Fort Hall from Wyeth in 1836 and continued its trading operations until 1856. Oregon Trail pioneers frequented both forts from 1843 to 1855, but Fort Hall was forced to close in 1856. Today, the site is located in the middle of tribal land and is marked with a National Historic Landmark. A full-size replica of Fort Hall stands in Pocatello's Ross Park.

In 1870, a military post was established about forty miles away on Lincoln Creek. This fort became the second Fort Hall, but eventually it too was abandoned and its name was given to the headquarters of the Fort Hall Indian Reservation that President Andrew Johnson established in 1867 for the Shoshone-Bannock Indians. The town of Fort Hall now serves as the tribal headquarters.

T Shoshone-Bannock Tribal Museum
Directly west of I-15 off Exit 80 on Gay Mine Rd., Fort Hall. 237-9791.

Located on the Fort Hall Indian Reservation, the Shoshone-Bannock Tribal Museum offers many interesting displays. Reopened in 1993, the museum evokes tribal pride while showcasing numer-

ous black and white photos and informational exhibits depicting how the Shoshone and Bannock tribes settled the area around eastern Idaho. The museum also features books, posters, and authentic arts and crafts made by tribal members. Operating hours are 10 AM to 6 PM daily April through October and 10 AM to 5 PM daily November through March. Admission is $2 for adults, $1 for senior citizens, and $.50 for youth ages 6-18. Special group and school tour rates are available by arrangement.

T Fort Hall Indian Reservation
Fort Hall Reservation was opened in 1869 and originally encompassed 1.8 million acres. Formed under the 1868 Treaty of Fort Bridger, the reservation measured twenty-five miles wide and seventy-five miles long. Under the terms of the treaty, the Government encouraged the Indians to farm the land and agreed to furnish annuities, farm implements, food, irrigation, and instruction. Aid, however, was never furnished, leading to extreme hardship. Some of the Indian agents fulfilled their responsibilities well while others shirked their duties. In addition, although some of the Native Americans desired to learn the craft of farming as a means of becoming self-sufficient, others were simply uninterested. Due to the government's broken promises and some Native Americans' unwillingness to farm, many Indians were forced to leave the reservation in search of food. The only relief provided under the treaty was that the Shoshone-Bannock Indians were allowed to visit the camas lily grounds near Fairfield and harvest the bulbs during summer. These bulbs provided the tribe with supplemental food for just a short time period, though. When a Washington, D.C. official misnamed Camas Prairie as Kansas Prairie, white farmers in Idaho took advantage of the mistake. These early Idaho homesteaders trespassed on the Indians' much-needed food source, providing their cattle and hogs with a rich grazing land. As a result of such careless actions, many Shoshone and Bannock Indians starved, felt mistreated, and ultimately engaged in the 1878 Bannock War. The war lasted three months and claimed the lives of many men, including Buffalo Horn and Chief Egan.

When General George Cook visited Fort Hall to determine the war's cause, he sympathized with the tribe and determined the lack of proper food sources was to blame for the battle. He adamantly declared that Native Americans could not be expected to stay on a reservation when the American government did not fulfill the treaty promises and deprived tribe members of every means of living. After General Cook's visit, reservation life gradually improved. In 1898, however, the two tribes were forced to surrender 418,000 acres of their land to the government for a meager payment of $600,000 in an effort to support the tribe's growing needs. Much to the dismay of the tribes, the land was opened up for homesteading just two years later.

In 1934, a turning point was reached when the Shoshone-Bannock tribes established the Fort Hall Business Council to represent the tribe. Two agreements, in 1947 and 1960, allowed the tribes to mine the Gay mine phosphate deposits. Gay mine is located on the reservation, about thirty miles northeast of Pocatello. This mine annually produces more than two million tons of ore and provides essential tribal income. In 1972, the Fort Hall Business Council accepted a $9.3 million settlement for loss of aboriginal lands. Today, the Reservation consists of 525,000 acres and is home to thousands of Shoshone-Bannock tribal members.

T The Historic Buildings of Fort Hall Indian Reservation
The Fort Hall Indian Reservation opened in 1869, and some of the site's earliest buildings can still be found.

Bannock St.
Located near the Fort Hall Agency, the Tribal Court Building located on the street's west side was originally the quartermaster building. The stone structure was built in 1896.

Yakima St.
Located on the corner of Yakima Street one block off of Pima Street is an old frame building constructed in 1893. The building was the original superintendent's quarters, and the reservation physician lived next door.

Mission Rd.
Built in 1904, the Good Shepherd Episcopal Mission is situated 0.6 miles from the Fort Hall Agency entrance. The Methodist Episcopal Church was given charge of educating the Shoshone-Bannock people in the 1870s, but it failed to take responsibility for any mission until the early 1900s. At that time, the church applied for a Congressional grant of 160 acres on reservation land, and the brick Gothic Revival Church was built. In 1967, 140 acres of this land was returned to the tribe with the mission church remaining in use.

Next door to the church is a large wooden building. This structure served as the area's boarding school.

T Wah'-Muza Archaeology Site
Fort Hall Indian Reservation north of Pocatello. 237-9791.

In 1985 and 1986, Dr. Richard Holmer and a team of other Idaho State University archaeologists discovered a link to the past on the Fort Hall Indian Reservation. Meaning "cedar point" in Shoshone, Wah'-Muza represents 2,000 years of Native American habitation. The site includes three house floors, a large debris hill, and numerous fire hearths. Using radiocarbon dating, the latest fire hearth dated is approximately 1850 AD. Artifacts from the four distinct periods of occupation include stone tools, pottery fragments, musketballs, cartridges, glass, horse harnesses, and buttons from U.S. military uniforms. Visitors are allowed access to the site but must first schedule a private tour with a tribal guide.

M Shoshone Bannock Indian Tribe Information
PO Box 368, Fort Hall. 237-8433 or (800) 806-9229. www.sho-ban.com

5 Food, Lodging

Pocatello
Pop. 51, 466

"Po-ca-ta-ro" (meaning unknown) was Chief of about three hundred northwestern Shoshone Indians. After being arrested twice for harrassing Oregon Trail pioneers, Po-ca-ta-ro signed the Treaty of Box Elder in 1863 and moved to the Fort Hall reservation. Upon his 1884 death, he was placed in a spring now buried under the American Falls reservoir.

Named after this historical chief, Pocatello began as a railroad station house in 1864. The government had secured forty acres from the Shoshone-Bannock tribes, but by 1866, the U.S. government decided it needed 1,600 more acres to accommodate the herds of migrating settlers who decided to plant roots in the area. Finally, in 1887, the Native Americans agreed to sell the requested land for $8.00 per acre. Although the

SHOSHONE BANNOCK TRIBES/GAMING ENTERPRISE

Celebrating the Traditions of Eastern Idaho's Shoshone-Bannock Tribes

In eastern Idaho, along Interstates 15 and 86, lies the 544,000-acre Fort Hall Indian Reservation. The reservation, situated at the crossroads of the Oregon Trail, encompasses a small part of the land that the Shoshone and Bannock Indians have roamed for several thousand years.

Before recorded history, the Shoshone and Bannock originally roamed areas now included in the states of Wyoming, Utah, Nevada, and Idaho. In their search for food, they hunted, gathered, and fished for salmon. The introduction of horses in the early 1700s allowed some groups to travel great distances in pursuit of buffalo.

The tribes' roaming heritage and access to open lands, however, was threatened by the arrival of white explorers. The first white men to explore the west were the trappers and explorers. Sacajawea, a Lemhi Shoshone woman, led Lewis and Clark through the west to the Pacific Ocean.

As more settlers poured westward in search of new frontiers and dreams, the Shoshone-Bannock Indians tribal lands were significantly altered. Like other Native Americans, the Shoshone-Bannocks were forced onto a reservation. A Presidential Executive Order established a 1.8 million acre reservation in 1867 that was confirmed one year later in the Fort Bridger Treaty of 1868. A supposed survey error reduced the reservation's size to 1.2 million acres in 1872, and other encroachments reduced the reservation to its present size.

Ruts of the historic Oregon Trail lead past the obscure monument of the original Fort Hall founded in 1834 by Nathaniel Wyeth. In later years, Fort Hall became an important supply and rest stop for the seemingly endless flow of settlers to the west.

Today, the Tribes on the Fort Hall Reservation are organized as a sovereign government that provides many services to Tribal members and non-Indians. Revenues are gained from such avenues as agriculture, business enterprises, tourism, and gaming industries. Visitors passing through the area are encouraged to stop by the many Tribal Enterprise businesses that celebrate the future while honoring the traditions of the Shoshone-Bannock tribes.

Shoshone Bannock Tribal Enterprises

A Mecca for travelers in eastern Idaho, the Shoshone-Bannock Tribal Enterprise businesses welcome tourists and locals alike. Owned by the Tribes, eight different businesses employ many Tribal members and provide a range of products, from staples to fine art to entertainment. The enterprises operate at two locations: on I-15 at Exit 80 and I-86 at Exit 56. Since the Shoshone Bannock Tribal members are the owners as well as a large part of the work force, the enterprise profits also contribute to the growth and improvement of the reservation.

Trading Post Full-Service Grocery

Opened in April 1978, the Trading Post Grocery store at Exit 80 was the first tribal business established. Featuring 10,000 square feet of selling space, the full-service supermarket provides employment for over twenty-five Tribal members. On-site, a butcher shop provides fresh cut meats while a bakery, deli, ice cream counter, and produce department provide quick snacks for the busy traveler and nutritious ingredients for a home-cooked meal. On occasion, the grocery store even features prime buffalo meat from the tribe's own herd.

The Trading Post Grocery Store is also the proud carrier of Idaho's largest tobacco selection including cigarettes, cigars, chewing tobacco, and imported tobacco. All are Reservation priced, making the selection the region's lowest priced. The store is open 7 AM to 10 PM Monday through Saturday and 8 AM to 9 PM on Sunday.

Oregon Trail Restaurant

The Oregon Trail Restaurant is situated off Interstate 15 Exit 80 and provides a unique and authentic dining experience. Every meal is made to order, and menu specialties include buffalo steaks, buffalo burgers, buffalo stew, Indian tacos, and traditional Indian fry bread. The restaurant also carries standard fare with a full breakfast, lunch, and dinner menu.

Shoshone Bannock Gaming

Southeastern Idaho's newest fun spot is the 1,000-seat Shoshone-Bannock Gaming Facility. Located off Interstate 15 at Exit 80, the business represents the region's premier gaming facility and includes fun and excitement for everyone.

High Stakes Bingo is available on Tuesday, Friday, Saturday, and Sunday, with all games featuring the chance for high Bingo payouts. In addition to electronic bingo machines, the gaming facility also operates two "mega Bingo" games via satellite from Tulsa, Oklahoma on weekends.

For those disinterested in Bingo, a large casino room contains over 350 video gaming machines. The casino is open seven days a week, and large progressive jackpots lead to payouts ranging from $62.50 to $1 million.

Trading Post Clothes Horse

The Shoshone-Bannock Tribes are considered producers of the world's finest handcrafted beadwork. Selections of the tribes' work are on display in the nation's Smithsonian Museum, while local tribal artisans proudly display their beadwork, leather crafts, and quillwork at the Trading Post Clothes Horse.

Situated off I-15 at Exit 80, the Clothes Horse is the retail outlet and division center for the worldwide distribution of the Tribes' crafts. Opened in June 1981, the store carries a complete line of authentic Native American beaded moccasins, purses, bolo ties, belt buckles, hat bands, and jewelry. In addition, they also carry traditional brain-tanned and smoked leather goods, porcupine quill work, contemporary and traditional Indian art work, books, Pendleton clothing, and western style shirts and jeans.

For those unable to visit the outlet store, the Clothes Horse is available online. Just like the products offered in-house, the online store specializes in selling the handiwork created by Fort Hall artisans.

Travel Plaza Fuel & Convenience Store

The Travel Plaza Fuel Stop is a favorite of travelers and truckers with its new, modernized facility opened in spring 2001. Conveniently located immediately off I-15's Exit 80, the store offers competitive prices along with fifteen pull through islands for diesel. Turns are easy and the parking lots are spacious for truckers or travelers with trailers or recreational vehicles.

Inside, the facility features standard convenience store amenities, along with a lounge, shower facilities, a restaurant, and Reservation priced tobacco products.

Shoshone-Bannock Tribal Museum

The Shoshone-Bannock Tribal Museum at Exit 80 both preserves the traditions of the tribes and shares the tradition with visitors. Exhibits are designed to illustrate the lifestyle of the tribes, while the museum gift shop features tribal arts and crafts.

Bannock Peak Fuel & Convenience Store

The Bannock Peak Fuel Stop and Convenience Store is available to serve travelers on I-86. The business features easy on and off access to the interstate with competitive gas and diesel prices.

Inside the 2,400 square foot convenience store is a hot deli and a complete line of Reservation priced tobacco products. The store is open November to March from 6 AM to 10 PM and March through October from 6 AM to midnight. With the latest in fuel pump technology, travelers with major credit cards can fill up throughout the night.

Sho-Ban News

The Sho-Ban News, the official Tribal newspaper, is published every Friday and is available at all Tribal outlets and other businesses in eastern Idaho. Originally created to keep tribal members up to date on reservation news, the paper has expanded to be nationally regarded as a definitive source of information for and about all Native Americans. The paper is now distributed in almost every state and in several foreign countries.

Paving the Road to the Future

With its many Tribal Enterprises, Fort Hall's Shoshone-Bannock Tribes have discovered a means of preserving their heritage and ensuring economic success for future generations. Each enterprise represents a thread winding the tribal members together, and the legacy created by this sovereign government will continue to leave a lasting impression on both locals and travelers alike.

Mashed, baked, fried, twice-baked, shredded, roasted, spiced, and unspiced – no matter how they're prepared, potatoes have become one of the most loved and frequently served foods in the world. Although Americans most often associate the potato with Idaho, and rightly so for the state is the nation's market leader, potatoes have a long agricultural history dating back to South America's Andean Mountains.

Harsh weather conditions prevented Indians in Peru from harvesting wheat or corn, so 4,000 years ago, the first potato was grown and became a favorite of Mochia, Symara, Chimu, and Inca cultures. These tribes did not stop with the basic white potato, though. More than 200 varieties of potatoes were developed over the course of several years, and as a result, the tribes began worshipping a "Potato God" who ensured successful crops each year.

The potato remained strictly in South America until the 1500s when Spanish conquerors arrived in South America and looted the native settlements. Among other things stolen, the Spaniards carried away pounds of potatoes and took them back to their homelands. The curious food, however, was looked upon as unhealthy, unsanitary, primal, and "un-Christian," so it received little acceptance. But when rumors spread that the strange new food actually possessed aphrodisiac and medicinal qualities, the potato's popularity spread and gained status as a delicacy.

Nearly a century after its first European introduction, most European countries excluding France accepted the potato as a diet staple, and Ireland found the crop quite suitable to the soil and growing season. Germany's King William encouraged his subjects to grow the hearty food, and even distributed potatoes in his country by royal decree. It was not until the 1700s that France caught up with the potato craze. When Marie Antoinette paraded through France wearing a potato blossom crown, the vegetable became an instant hit. Germany's King Frederick the Great enjoyed potatoes so much that he planted potatoes in his Berlin Pleasure Garden in the late 1700s.

By this time, the potato had also arrived in the American colonies. In 1621, Bermuda Governor, Captain Nathaniel Butler, sent two large chests of potatoes to Jamestown, Virginia Governor, Francis Wyatt. Irish and Scottish immigrants to the New Hampshire area in the early 1700s reinforced the potato's popularity, and in no time, crops were popping up all over North America. Finally, in 1837, the potato arrived in Idaho. Early missionaries, Henry Harmon and Eliza Spalding, planted and harvested the first crop at the Lapwai Mission with the help of Nez Perce Native Americans. Since then, the potato has been an Idaho agricultural mainstay significantly contributing to the nation's potato production.

Following are some interesting facts about the potato and its industry in Idaho:

- Potatoes are produced in every U.S. state and in 125 countries across the world.
- Potatoes are about 80% water and 20% solid.
- Idaho grows more potatoes than any other U.S. agricultural region. Fall harvesting in Idaho alone yields 30% of total U.S. production – approximately 13.8 billion pounds! Astonishing as that sounds, Idaho annually only harvests about 60% of the planted crops.

- Southeastern Idaho's Bingham County produces as many potatoes as the entire state of Maine.
- Idaho grows 27 billion potatoes each year – enough for 120 potatoes for each U.S. resident.
- Idaho potato production contributes 32.8% of southeastern Idaho's economy, 27.4% of the southcentral Idaho's economy, and 6.8% of southwestern Idaho's economy. In sum, potatoes yield $2.5 billion of the state's gross product.
- The average American eats 142 pounds of potatoes each year, the equivalent of nearly 365 potatoes per person! Germans, on the other hand, consume nearly 220 pounds per person.
- Thomas Jefferson first introduced french fries to the U.S. when he served them at a Whitehouse dinner. John Adams reportedly scoffed at Jefferson, suggesting he was putting on airs by offering such frivolous foods.
- Today, Americans consume more than 4 million tons of french fries each year
- 2/3 of all potatoes harvested in the U.S. are used for production of french fries, hash-browns, tater-tots, and other processed potato products.
- Potato chips were invented at Moon's Lake Hotel in Saratoga, New York when the hotel chef responded to a regular customer's complaints about soggy french fries. The chef sliced a potato into thin wafers, fried them to a crisp, and then salted them. Although he expected the customer to be dissatisfied, the chef's "Crispy Salt Potatoes" were an instant hit.
- According to the Guinness Book of World Records, the largest potato ever grown was 18 pounds and 4 ounces. Thomas Seddal of Chester, England, grew the massive potato in 1795.
- Residents and physicians in Ireland still consider the potato a powerful aphrodisiac.
- In October 1995, the potato became the first vegetable grown in space.

---

post office was established in 1883, the village wasn't officially platted until 1889. Through the years, the town continued to grow and expand its boundaries into reservation land. In 1898, the Shoshone-Bannock tribes reluctantly sold 418,000 acres on the south end of their reservation for a measly $600,000.

The Utah and Northern railroad, which came up from Salt Lake City and Franklin, came through Pocatello in 1879. They continued to extend the line to Butte, Montana, but in order to do so, had to cross seventy miles of Indian reservation land. Although the tracks were completed by 1881, a legal right-of-way over the reservation was not obtained until 1886 when the Native Americans were compensated with $6,000. On its path to Oregon, the Union Pacific railroad laid its track westward through town in 1884.

On June 17, 1902, the "Day of the Run," the reservation land opened up to settlement, and Pocatello's roots firmly took hold. During a public auction, the land within five miles of town was sold to homesteaders in forty-acre tracts. Pocatello soon became the American West's largest railroad hub, bringing with it an ever-expanding population. By 1920, the community boasted over 15,000 residents, and more than 4,500 railroad cars poured through town daily during World War II.

Today, the area is still a railroad center but has also garnered attention as home to Idaho State University. The university boosts the area's cultural amenities, and Pocatello continues to boast historically phenomenal sunsets.

T Highland Golf Course

201 Von Elm Ln. (near Bench Rd.), Pocatello. 237-9922.

George Von Elm designed this 18-hole course that opened in 1962. Featuring hilly terrain and fairways lined with pine trees and Russian Olives, the course spans 6,512 yards and includes just one small water hazard. Due to its rolling landscape, carts are highly recommended. The par 72 course opens daily at 6 AM from March 1 to October 31, and green fees are $16 on weekdays and $17 on weekends.

L Red Lion Hotel Pocatello

1555 Pocatello Creek Rd. (1-15 at Exit 71), Pocatello. 233-2200 or (800) RED-LION. www.redlion.com/pocatello or www.westcoasthotels.com

Conveniently located near several area attractions, Red Lion Hotel Pocatello can accommodate all your travel needs. All guest rooms feature in-room coffee, hairdryers, irons/ironing boards, cable TV, dataports, and free high speed wireless Internet and local calls, with King rooms including microwaves and refrigerators. In your free time, work up a sweat in the fitness center, relax in the indoor swimming pool and hot tub, dine in the on-site Pantry Café' Restaurant, or enjoy sports and entertainment in the PorterHouse Pub. Complimentary airport shuttles and parking are standard, while same day dry cleaning, guest laundry, room service, corporate/vacation packages, and a 13,000 square foot meeting and banquet space add the finishing touch. On your next business or leisure trip, expect royal treatment while staying in the heart of town.

L Super 8 Motel

1330 Bench Rd., Pocatello. 234-0888 or (866) 378-7378. www.super8.com

Conveniently situated off I-15, Pocatello's Super 8 Motel is AAA approved. Rooms include queen and king size beds, cable TV, and free local calls, voicemail, and high-speed wireless Internet. Lounge in the queen rooms' recliners, enjoy the king rooms'

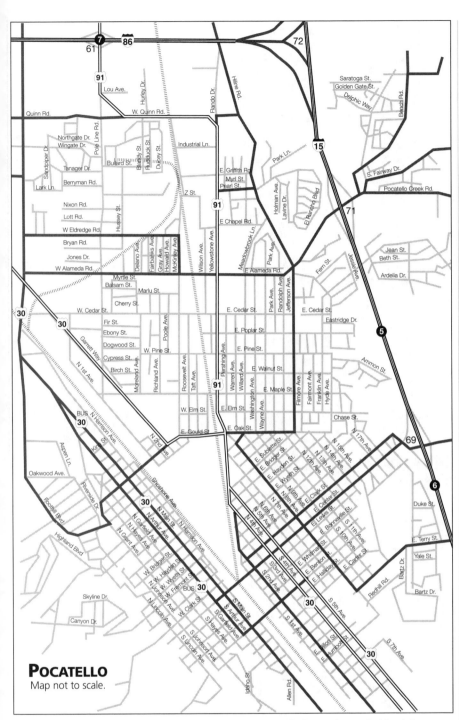

POCATELLO
Map not to scale.

microwaves and mini-fridges, or opt for a whirlpool suite. Children 12 and under stay free, and pets are welcome for a small fee. To meet every guest's needs, the motel also offers a 24-hour front desk, complimentary continental breakfast, laundry facilities, fax and copy service, handicapped rooms, an elevator, non-smoking available in all room types, and large vehicle parking. Featuring a prime location, Pocatello's Super 8 Motel provides walking access to nine different sitdown and fast food restaurants with the city's numerous attractions just minutes away.

6 *Food, Lodging*

H Idaho State University
Exit 67 at the I-15 Pocatello Business Loop

This great institution began here on September 22, 1902, with 4 teachers and 40 students.

Originally the Academy of Idaho, it became Idaho Technical Institute in 1915, the Southern Branch of the University of Idaho in 1927, and Idaho State College in 1947. Its development of professional and graduate programs and its continued growth in stature led to its designation as a university in 1963.

T Standrod Mansion
648 N. Garfield, Pocatello. Contact the Pocatello Convention and Visitors Bureau at 233-7333.

Drew W. Standrod was one of Pocatello's most successful working professionals, and the elaborate home built for him and his family reflects his wealth. Born in Kentucky and an accomplished student of law, Standrod moved to Idaho and was elected district attorney in 1886 on the Independent Anti-Mormon political ticket. In 1889, he served in the Idaho Constitutional

Convention, and just one year later, was elected judge of the Fifth Judicial District. Holding this position for nine years, Standrod was also a prominent investor in Idaho businesses. He held interests in eleven different banks, and served as a bank president in the late 1890s.

Built as a monument to reflect his wealth and community prominence, the Standrod Mansion was designed by San Francisco architect, Marcus Grundfor, in a French Renaissance style. The home was palatial at the time of its construction between 1899 and 1901, featuring twelve rooms spread across 3,252 square feet. The mansion features gray and pink sandstone blocks quarried from the nearby McCammon community, long wooden verandahs accented with turned balusters, rounded corner towers, and a lacy cast-iron fence ornamenting the roofline. The interior is characterized with oak accents, tile, and imported

tions. In response, Idaho State Senator, Theodore F. Turner, introduced a bill to the Idaho State Legislature in 1901 calling for establishment of the Academy of Idaho if land could be located. Despite bitter battles over the proposed school, the Academy opened its doors in the fall of 1902 complete with electric lights, steam heat, and the latest furnishings. On the first day, only three students enrolled, but as soon as the men's dormitory was added in 1903 and a women's dormitory was completed in 1906, enrollment increased. During its first years, 80% of the Academy's students were from Pocatello, and students enrolled in predominantly high school level and vocational courses rather than standard college fare. As Pocatello's population grew and the Academy's academic reputation soared, the school was promoted to junior college status in 1915 and renamed Idaho Technical Institute. In 1927, the school was designated as the Southern Branch of the University of Idaho, was then given independent four-year status in 1947 as Idaho State College, and finally became Idaho State University in 1963. Today, the 790-acre campus is home to nearly 12,000 students and offers an extensive array of undergraduate and graduate programs.

T Holt Arena
550 Memorial Dr., Pocatello. 282-2831.

Located on the campus of Idaho State University, Holt Arena is eastern Idaho's largest public facility. The building is named after Milton W. Holt, Idaho State University Athletics Director in the late 1960s who suggested the idea of building an enclosed football stadium. Despite harsh criticism, a building plan was approved, and the arena was completed in September 1970 at a total cost of $2.8 billion. The arena became the first covered stadium in Idaho, as well as the first enclosed football stadium constructed on a college campus. Encompassing 194,400 square feet, the arena not only hosts college and high school sporting events, but also famous entertainers, rodeos, monster truck events, religious conferences, Bolshoi Ballet performances, and trade shows. Contact the arena for a complete schedule of events.

T Idaho State Arboretum
Located on the Idaho State University campus, Pocatello. Contact the Idaho Museum of Natural History at 282-3168.

The Idaho State Arboretum features a guided walking tour of the numerous trees and shrubs dotting Idaho State University's campus. Featuring 51 different labeled botanical species, the arboretum tour includes detailed information about each plant. Idaho's state flower, the syringa, is always a fragrant favorite. Tour brochures are available at the Idaho Museum of Natural History information desk.

T Idaho State Civic Symphony
Idaho State University Goranson Hall, Pocatello. 234-1587. www.thesymphony.us

On a mission to enhance the cultural environment of southeastern Idaho, the Idaho State Civic Symphony was established in the early 1900s and

French marble. In addition, a coal furnace supplied the home with a central heating system and was wired with electricity, making it the first residence in Pocatello equipped with electric lights.

As with other old buildings, folklore surrounds the Standrod Mansion. Despite his wealth and access to fine medical treatments, Standrod was unable to save his beloved daughter, Elvira Standrod. Suffering from a mysterious illness, Elvira died in the mansion at age sixteen. She reportedly haunts the home's left corner tower and balcony.

After years of neglect, the City of Pocatello purchased the mansion in 1974 and restored it to its original splendor. The mansion now houses a furniture store, but it is open to curious visitors interested in viewing one of the state's most impressive homes built at the turn of the twentieth century.

T Riverside Golf Course
3500 Bannock Hwy., Pocatello. 232-9515.

The 18-hole, par-72 Riverside Golf Course is known for accommodating golfers of all abilities. While the older front nine features tight fairways clogged with elm and pine trees, the back nine designed by Pete Hiskey is relatively flat and open. The course has been open since 1961 and has developed a reputation as a great target course. Green fees are $16 on weekdays and $17 on weekends, and the course is open daily from March 1 to October 31.

T Idaho State University
921 S. 8th Ave., Pocatello. 282-0211. www.isu.edu

In early Idaho, access to sound schooling opportunities was limited, and residents began worrying about the educational training of young generais the state's oldest orchestra. Since its inception, the orchestra has created a tradition of music excellence respected throughout the Intermountain West region. The non-profit orchestra features 60 to 65 members and presents four annual classical concerts and one POPS concert. Season tickets are available as well as one-time only performance tickets. Reservations are highly recommended.

T Fort Hall Replica
Upper Ross Park on Alvord Loop, Pocatello. 234-1795.

On the Oregon Trail in the early 1800s, Fort Hall was an extremely important trading post where pioneers, fur trappers, and Native Americans all gathered together. Historically situated north of Pocatello on the Fort Hall Indian Reservation, today's replica at Ross Park provides visitors with a glimpse into early 19th century life. Visitors will find extensive Native American displays, exhibits detailing the fort's history, and a blacksmith and carpentry shop. Upon request, visitors can also view a videotape about Fort Hall's history. The replica is open 10 AM to 6 PM daily from Memorial Day to Labor Day, 10 AM to 2 PM daily the rest of September, and 10 AM to 2 PM Tuesday through Saturday from April to Memorial Day. Admission is $2.50 for adults, $1.75 for youth ages 12-18, and $1 for seniors over 60 and children ages 6-11. The fee includes entrance to the replica as well as the Bannock County Historical Museum.

T Bannock County Historical Museum
3000 Alvord Loop, Pocatello. 233-0434.

Numerous exhibits outline Pocatello's and Bannock County's history with an emphasis on railroad contributions and area Native Americans. The museum is open daily Memorial Day through Labor Day and Tuesday through Saturday the rest of the year.

T Idaho Museum of Natural History
S. 5th Ave. at E. Dillon St., Pocatello. 282-3168. http://imnh.isu.edu

The Idaho Museum of Natural History is on a mission to preserve, interpret, and display some of the most important objects and events in the state's natural history. Through well-maintained exhibits and educational classes, the museum staff hopes to provide both residents and tourists with an understanding and appreciation of Idaho's rich cultural and natural heritage. Numerous displays can be found on topics such as anthropology, botany, geology, paleontology, and zoology, and the museum offers both permanent and rotating collections. The museum is open from 4 PM to 8 PM on Monday's Family Night, 10 AM to 5 PM Tuesday through Friday, and 12 PM to 5 PM on Saturdays. Admission is $5 for adults, $4 for seniors, $3 for students with a valid ID, $2 for youth ages 4-11, and free for children under 4.

T Pocatello Art Center
444 N. Main, Pocatello. 232-0970. www.Pocatelloartctr.org

The Pocatello Art Center has provided the community with a center for visual arts for more than forty years. A non-profit organization, the center features a well-maintained gallery where art students have the opportunity to hang their works beside those of professional artists. Displays are changed monthly, and a variety of mediums are presented. In addition, the center features art classes for children and adults, and frequently held workshops feature nationally known artists. The gallery is open to the public free of charge from 10 AM to 4:30 PM Tuesday through Friday and 10 AM to 2 PM on Saturdays. Special group tours are available by appointment.

T Simplot Square
Corner of Arthur Ave. and Center St., Pocatello. Contact the Pocatello Convention and Visitor Bureau at (877) 922-7659.

Dedicated to the City of Pocatello in March 1989, Simplot Square is situated on the site of the historic Bannock Hotel built in the late 1800s. J.R. Simplot acquired the hotel in the 1970s, but ten years later, decided to tear it down and donate the land to the city for use as a park in the center of Oldtown Pocatello. Today, Simplot Square features a fountain of dancing salmon, twelve teaching plaques relating the region's history and geography, and fragrant flower gardens. During the summer, the square is the site for concerts in the park and other local entertainment venues.

T Memorial Park
Johnson St. directly north of Fremont St., Pocatello. Contact the Pocatello Convention and Visitor Bureau at (877) 922-7659.

Pocatello's original powerhouse is displayed at the community Memorial Park. In addition, a local group of volunteers created a meditation garden and amphitheater along the Portneuf River, making the park one of the most peaceful spots in town.

T Pioneer Park
Corner of N. Arthur Ave. and Benton Sts., Pocatello. Contact the Pocatello Convention and Visitor Bureau at (877) 922-7659.

Once home to the Union Pacific Railroad line, this area was refurbished and converted into a town park. Through the combined efforts of local Latter Day Saints Church members, Pioneer Park was finished and dedicated on July 24, 1997 in celebration of Mormon settlers. Visitors will find granite murals in the park depicting the 1847 pilgrimage of these pioneers from the Midwest to Idaho Territory and the Salt Lake Valley.

T Ifft-Trappers Park
N. Ave. and Benton St., Pocatello. Contact the Pocatello Convention and Visitor Bureau at (877) 922-7659.

Pocatello's Ifft-Trappers Park is not only a recreational site, but also an educational forum. A dry riverbed is strewn with basalt boulders deposited thousands of years ago in the Lake Bonneville Flood. In addition, a large bronze sculpture and fountain created by Idaho artist, Doug Warnock, is complete with lighting, making this park an enjoyable place during both daylight and evening hours.

T Sarah Bandes Rose Garden
Pocatello. Contact the Pocatello Convention and Visitor Bureau at (877) 922-7659. From Benton St. W., proceed south on S. Grant Ave. to the park.

The Sarah Bandes Rose Garden donated by Joan Downing is situated alongside the newly constructed Portneuf Greenway. Volunteers from the Pocatello Regional Medical Center completed the garden in 1996, and the neighboring babbling Lower City Creek adds to the area's peaceful ambience.

T Edson Fichter Nature Area
1 mile south of Pocatello. Contact the Pocatello Convention and Visitor Bureau at (877) 922-7659. Proceed on S. Bannock Hwy. to the nature area's designated parking located on Cheyenne Ave.

Once an unkempt area of brush and bramble, the 43-acre Edson Fichter Nature Area is now one of the city's finest places to enjoy a peaceful day outdoors. The riparian area draws its name from a late Idaho State University professor and is now under management from the Idaho Fish and Game Department. Featuring a variety of vegetation along the Portneuf River front, the area is populated with songbirds, geese, and waterfowl and provides a look at an interesting parcel of land. Only one percent of the Idaho landscape is characterized as riparian, making this marshy place extraordinarily unique. An interpretive nature trail provides educational signs about wildlife, plants, and the environment, and a barrier free fishing pier and river swimming offers hours of recreational fun. The area is open year-round.

T Rotary Rose Garden
Corner of S. 4th and S. 5th Aves, Pocatello. Contact the Pocatello Convention and Visitor Bureau at (877) 922-7659.

Maintained through volunteer time donated by the Pocatello Rotary Club, the Rotary Rose Garden is a summer city favorite. The garden features 2,500 tenderly cared for rose bushes, providing a sweet smelling spot for an outdoor picnic or gathering.

Pocatello	Jan	Feb	March	April	May	June	July	Aug	Sep	Oct	Nov	Dec	Annual
Average Max. Temperature (F)		32.4	38.3	47.4	58.2	68.2	77.5	88.3	86.8	75.8	62.5	45.2	35.0	59.6
Average Min. Temperature (F)		15.0	19.8	26.2	32.9	40.4	46.9	53.2	51.6	42.8	33.6	24.8	17.6	33.8
Average Total Precipitation (in.)		1.09	0.93	1.11	1.10	1.32	1.03	0.53	0.61	0.79	0.86	1.05	1.05	11.47
Average Total Snowfall (in.)		9.3	6.6	5.4	3.5	0.4	0.0	0.0	0.0	0.0	1.8	4.6	8.7	40.4
Average Snow Depth (in.)		2	1	0	0	0	0	0	0	0	0	0	1	0

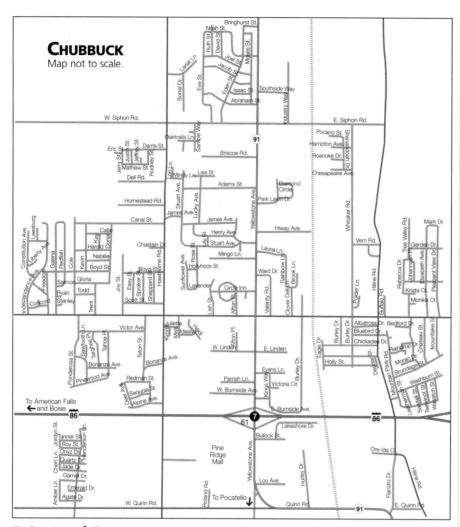

CHUBBUCK
Map not to scale.

T Portneuf Greenway

Downtown Pocatello. Contact the Portneuf
Greenway Foundation at 234-4929.
www.pgfweb.com

Established under the direction of the non-profit
Portneuf Greenway Foundation, Pocatello's
Portneuf Greenway began in 1990 as a cooperative
effort between the city and the National Park
Service. Seven years later, construction on the
project was finally underway with a mission to
restore the natural areas along the Portneuf River
while providing a community recreational
resource. Today the greenway provides thirteen
miles of paved pathways ideal for bicyclists, hikers,
walkers, joggers, and rollerbladers. The greenway
is also the site for the annual Greenway Fun Run,
Riverfest, and the Recycle Regatta. Through the
coming years, the foundation hopes to add interpretive signs along the greenway educating users
about local history and the natural environment.

T AMI Kirkham Trail

Located between S. Second Ave. and Upper Ross
Park, Pocatello. Contact the Portneuf Greenway
Foundation at 234-4929.

This newly completed two mile paved trail commemorates the monetary and labor donations of
the Kirkham Family and American Microsystems
Incorporated. The trail meanders across an ancient
lava flow, through basalt rock formations, and
next to desert plants while providing scenic views
of the Portneuf Gap.

T Ross Park

Located between Second and Fifth Aves, Pocatello.
Contact the Pocatello Convention and Visitors
Bureau at (877) 922-7659.

Pocatello's largest park, Ross Park, provides a
range of recreational opportunities for both residents and visitors. Grassy and shaded picnic areas
await visitors along with a large playground, baseball fields, horseshoe pits, and volleyball courts.
For those seeking a more active day, rock climbing
is also popular in the area. Natural lava rock walls
formed thousands of years ago provide more than
seventy-five recorded climbing routes of varying
difficulty. Opened in 1999, the park's aquatic center
provides summer tubing on the man-made "Lazy
River," waterslides, water volleyball, a jungle gym,
and lap pools. In addition, wildlife is occasionally
reported at the park, making the area one of the
most diverse attractions in Pocatello.

T Pocatello Zoo

2900 S. 2nd Ave., Pocatello. 234-6196.
www.pocatellozoo.org

The Pocatello Zoo encompasses eighteen acres of
natural Rocky Mountain landscapes and specializes
in preserving wildlife native to North America's
Intermountain West region. Featuring mammals,
birds, and reptiles and amphibians, the zoo provides
rare opportunities to view some of the west's most
wild species while also striving to educate its visitors. In addition to the larger displays, the zoo features a children's barnyard animal petting area.
Operating hours are 9 AM to 5 PM daily from
April 1 to June 15, 10 AM to 6 PM daily from

June 16 to Labor Day, and 10 AM to 4 PM post
Labor Day through October 31. In October, the
zoo is only open on weekends.

T Portneuf Gap

Located at Pocatello's southern entrance. Contact
the Pocatello Convention and Visitor Bureau at
(877) 922-7659.

Marking the southern entrance into the Pocatello
cityscape, the Portneuf Gap was created when the
flow of the ancient Bear River carved a niche
through the rocky walls nearly one million years
ago. Following an east-west faultline in the
Bannock Range, the canyon opens up into the
Portneuf Valley. This valley was shaped approximately 600,000 years ago during a volcanic eruption near present day Bancroft, Idaho.

T Justice Park

12 miles south of Pocatello. Contact the Westside
Ranger District at 236-7500. From Pocatello, pro-
ceed south on the Bannock Hwy. Bear east at
Forest Road 001, and continue to the park.

Located near scenic Scout Mountain in southeastern Idaho, Justice Park offers picnicking, short
nature trails, an archery range, and an amphitheater. The site is open during the summer and early
fall.

T Oldtown Pocatello Historic Tour

Downtown Pocatello. Contact the Pocatello
Convention and Visitors Bureau at 233-7333 for a
walking tour brochure.

Established as a stagestop in 1864, Pocatello soon
became known as the "Gate City" to the West.
With the arrival of the Oregon Short Line
Railroad, new residents and visitors flocked to the
area resulting in a building boom. Oldtown
Pocatello captures this golden age of growth and
preserves the area's diverse architectural history.

Mountain View Cemetery
S. Fifth Ave.
Several of Pocatello's pioneering residents can be
found in the town's Mountain View Cemetery,
including James Brady. Serving as Idaho's governor
from 1909-1910 and as a U.S. Senator from 1913-
1918, Brady was one of Idaho's first prominent
political figures. His ashes were once buried in the
cemetery's Gothic stone crypt, but due to increasing vandalism to the stained glass windows, his
ashes were moved outside. The mausoleum is one
of the most elegant in Idaho, and visitors who
scope out the interior will discover a small alcove
and memorial.

554 S. Fifth Ave.
John Hood was an established and respected businessman across Idaho and Utah. He successfully
opened and operated a chain of Golden Rule
stores and resided in this Colonial Revival home.
The Idaho State University Alumni Association has
occupied the residence since 1977.

President's House
Northwest corner of E. Whitman St.
Nicknamed the "Xavier Serval house," this three-
story home was completed in 1917. Featuring
round-roof dormers, the home has provided residence for Idaho State University's presidents since
1951.

506 N. Garfield St.
This home features one of Pocatello's most unique
architectural designs. Local dance hall owner and
skilled mason, Mr. Nichols constructed the home
in the 1930s. Building the exterior from cinder
bricks made in Wyoming, Nichols finished the

---

interior with an impressive rock fireplace and jagged stucco details.

St. Joseph's Catholic Church
435 N. Hayes
Since its founding, Pocatello has offered residents a wide array of churches and religious choices. The St. Joseph's Catholic Church was built in 1897 and retains its original sheeted copper steeple.

First Congregational Church
W. Lander St.
Stone was a popular building material in the early twentieth century, and the First Congregational Church reflects this architectural style. The church dates back to 1904 and recently celebrated 100 years of worship in this building.

Trinity Episcopal Church
248 N. Arthur Ave.
This architectural delight is one of Pocatello's oldest standing churches. The church was constructed between 1897 and 1899 and represents the state's first stone Episcopal Church. The exterior rock was quarried on Ross Fork in the Fort Hall reservation, and the stained glass windows were imported from Ireland. Oak furnishings and embossed tin ceiling panels round out the interior's impressive details.

Old Carnegie Library
100 N. Garfield and W. Center St.
Once home to the Pocatello Library and now serving as headquarters for the Bannock County Historical Museum, this building was erected in 1907. Featuring pressed bricks with sandstone trim accents, the building was designed to resemble a Palladian villa.

Kinney House
441 S. Garfield
Along with the transportation industries, agriculture was an economic mainstay in Pocatello's founding days. A well-respected and highly successful sheep rancher constructed this impressive home in 1900.

Old Oregon Short Line/Union Pacific Railroad Depot
E. end of W. Bonneville St.
Once the largest rail hub west of the Mississippi, Pocatello was outfitted with a resplendent depot. Completed in 1915 at a cost of $325,000, former President William Taft was present for the dedication of the three-story depot.

Yellowstone Hotel
230 W. Bonneville St.
Located across the street from the train depot in the heart of Oldtown Pocatello is the four-story Yellowstone Hotel. Featuring wine-colored bricks and ornate terra-cotta trim, the hotel was built in 1916 as a premier lodging facility for train passengers.

V Mink Creek Cross-Country Ski Trails
15 miles south of Pocatello on the Bannock Hwy. Contact the Idaho Department of Parks and Recreation at 334-4180.

The Mink Creek cross-country ski trails are ideal for the practiced beginner and intermediate

Nordic skier. Covering approximately fifteen miles, five different trails wind through heavily timbered draws. Only five miles of the trails are regularly groomed due to funding restrictions. The area is part of Idaho's Park N' Ski system, and permits are required. Permits may be obtained at the nearest Ranger Station, and fees are as follows: $25 annual permit (good at all Idaho Park N' Ski areas), $7.50 3-day permit, and $2 day use permit.

V Bartz Field Cross Country Ski Trails
Near Reed Gym on the Idaho State University Campus, Pocatello. Contact the Pocatello Convention and Visitor Bureau at (877) 922-7659.

Bartz Field provides easy access to cross-country skiing anytime during the winter months. The rolling terrain is popular with beginners and those honing their basic skills. The free area is lit at night for user safety and convenience.

V Crystal Summit Cross-Country Ski Area
From Pocatello, proceed south on Bannock Hwy., continuing two miles past the S. Fork of Mink Creek. Contact the Idaho Department of Parks and Recreation at 334-4180.

Crystal Summit divides Idaho's Arbon Valley and Mink Creek and represents the Bannock Hwy.'s highest point. It also represents one of Idaho's most popular Nordic skiing areas. Crystal Summit offers trail skiing, backcountry skiing, telemarking, ridge tours, and excellent vistas of Scout and Long Tom Mountains. The area is not recommended for beginners as the trails wind across a variety of terrain. The area is part of Idaho's Park N' Ski system, and permits are required. Permits may be obtained at the nearest Ranger Station and fees are as follows: $25 annual permit (good at all Idaho Park N' Ski areas), $7.50 3-day permit, and $2 day use permit.

V Blackrock Canyon Cross-Country Ski Area
From Pocatello, drive 8 miles south on 5th St. (Old Hwy. 30). At Blackrock Canyon Road, bear left and park at the road's end. Contact the Pocatello Convention and Visitor Bureau at (877) 922-7659.

Although not maintained by the Idaho Department of Parks and Recreation, Blackrock Canyon still provides fine access to cross-country skiing. Winding along the Blackrock Canyon Road, the trail is fairly easy the first two miles but progressively requires more advanced skills. For those continuing up the ridge overlooking Inkom, extreme caution should be used as the area is known for dangerous avalanches. This ski area is free, but users are asked to leave all pets at home.

M Pocatello Convention & Visitors Bureau
2695 5th Ave., Pocatello. 233-7333 or (877) 922-7659. www.pocatellocvb.com

M Pocatello Chamber of Commerce
343 W. Center St., Pocatello. 233-1525. www.pocatelloidaho.com

7 *Food, Lodging*

Chubbuck
Pop. 9,700

Chubbuck, situated directly north of Pocatello, possesses its own status as an incorporated city but has since been enveloped by Pocatello's metropolitan area sprawl.

8 *Food*

T FMC Factory
4 miles west of Pocatello on I-86

The FMC plant is the world's largest elemental-phosphorous factory. The company was formed in 1883 and produces various solid and liquid fertilizer products.

9 *Food, Lodging*

American Falls
Pop. 4,111

"American Falls," located on the Snake River, were named for a party of American trappers whose boat was carried off by the river and plummeted over the falls. Only one man survived to tell of their journey. An attraction for early travelers, pioneers on the Oregon Trail (which passed just north of the present town) would hear the falls and investigate the origin. Emigrants described the falls as, "…a grand site", and, "truly magnificent."

As for the city for American Falls, a virtual Atlantis exists beneath the irrigation waters of American Falls Reservoir. In 1880 the city's first permanent settlement consisted of just a few houses and cabins built on the Snake River's west side. The Oregon Short Line Railroad chugged through town in 1883, and the city assumed a leadership role as the trading center for cattle ranches in this territory along the Snake River. In 1888, the town was moved to the east side of the river to a location now considered the "original townsite." In 1925, the city's landscape changed dramatically when the American Falls Dam was built in order to provide electricity to the city. In the building process, the falls were eliminated and the entire town was forced to move one-half mile east to higher ground. Not long after its 1925 re-establishment in its present location, the original American Falls townsite was flooded in the creation of the American Falls Reservoir. "Atlantis", as though it were, appears when the water level drops during the hot summer months, revealing the roofs of buildings and other evidence of the old 19th century townsite.

H American Falls
Milepost 3.1 on State Hwy. 39 at the U.S. Bureau of Reclamation Information Center

More than two decades before the American Falls Dam was built, water power was generated in a series of plants at American Falls.

Starting with an island plant to serve Pocatello in 1902, this superlative site was used soon after as long transmission lines were developed. As new kinds of turbines and generators were invented, they were installed here. Rare examples of old technology still are preserved in these landmark plants.

American Falls	Jan	Feb	March	April	May	June	July	Aug	Sep	Oct	Nov	Dec	Annual
Average Max. Temperature (F)	32.8	38.5	48.1	59.2	68.5	77.9	87.2	86.2	76.2	62.8	45.7	35.0	59.8
Average Min. Temperature (F)	16.5	20.6	27.0	33.9	41.4	48.1	54.2	52.9	44.5	35.2	26.8	19.4	35.1
Average Total Precipitation (in.)	1.04	0.85	1.04	1.10	1.47	0.94	0.51	0.59	0.72	0.80	1.03	0.99	11.08
Average Total Snowfall (in.)	9.2	5.3	3.1	1.3	0.4	0.0	0.0	0.0	0.0	1.3	2.7	7.2	30.3
Average Snow Depth (in.)	3	2	0	0	0	0	0	0	0	0	0	1	1

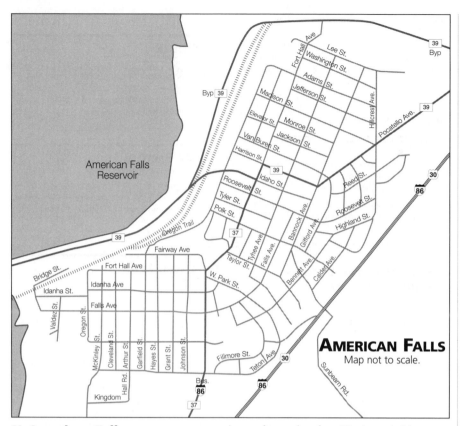

AMERICAN FALLS
Map not to scale.

across Idaho creating the mighty Snake River Plain. Today, it is a uniquely functioning ecosystem that is rich in cultural, historical, natural, and recreational resources.

So what is the Great Rift? Scientifically, the Great Rift is a 635 square mile geological phenomenon that makes up the earth's "plumbing system," a pathway that drove molten magma to the surface. It is a series of fissures, spatter cones, and lava tubes represented by 60 different lava flows and over 25 volcanic events. It is the geological sector within the Snake River Plain that most vividly symbolizes the intense forces of nature that makes South Central Idaho a unique and wondrous place of diversity and adventure.

The fissure extends over 65 miles and is recognized as the largest and most recent rift system in the lower 48 states. The only other similar geological area in the world is a rift found in Africa.

Partially reprinted from a South-Central Idaho Tourism and Recreation Brochure

TV American Falls Dam, Reservoir, and Snake River Tributaries

American Falls. Contact the Southeast Idaho Pioneer Country Travel Council. (888) 201-1063. Traveling on Fort Hall Ave. in downtown American Falls, bear west onto Idaho St., and proceed on State Hwy. 39 to the dam.

American Falls has seen a succession of dam building projects since its origination in the late 1800s. In 1925, the first dam was built, consequently flooding the original townsite and forcing residents to rebuild on higher ground. Just two years later, the Bureau of Reclamation ordered construction of a reinforced dam. At a cost of $3 million and the loss of the waterfalls after which the town had been named, the new dam provided irrigation storage for the area. Although the dam functioned properly for nearly five decades, fifty years of weathering reduced the dam's efficiency. In 1976, plans were drawn to build a new dam immediately downstream from the old dam site. With two years of labor and a $23 million building price, the dam was completed in 1978. The new dam, which created Idaho's second largest reservoir, measures 2,900 feet long and eighty-six feet high.

At full capacity, American Falls Reservoir contains 56,000 acres of water and provides more than 100 miles of shoreline. The reservoir was created primarily for irrigation water storage, electric power, and flood control protection, but it has also become one of the most popular recreation areas in the state, especially for windsurfing. Since 1981, Idaho Power has annually stocked the waters with 8,000 pounds of rainbow trout, forming one of the best fisheries in the entire state. In addition to recreation opportunities, visitors can learn more about the dam and reservoir's history at an on-site informational center. Located on the dam's north side, the center is open May through October and displays exhibits and historical photographs pertaining to the dam's construction and reservoir.

H American Falls

Exits 36 & 40 on I-86, American Falls Business Loop at American Falls Park

The town is named for the nearby falls of the Snake River, a famous landmark for fur trappers and early Western travelers.

The Oregon Trail passed close to the falls, which had been named in contrast to Canadian Falls – now known as Shoshone Falls – 95 miles downstream. The town of American Falls was founded when the railroad came in 1882 and served a ranching area. An important power dam was built in 1902. When the present large irrigation dam was built in 1925-27, the town had to be moved out of the reservoir area.

T American Falls Golf Club

610 N. Oregon Trail, American Falls. 226-5827.

Lush greens, expansive fairways, and hilly terrain characterize the American Falls Golf Club. Popular among locals, the 9-hole course covers 4,689 yards, is rated at par 66, and possesses no water hazards. The course is open March 1 to November 1, and daily green fees are $20 or less.

T American Falls State Fish Hatchery

2974 S. Hatchery Rd., American Falls. 226-2015. Merge off I-86 at Exit 40, and proceed on State Hwy. 39. After crossing American Falls Dam, bear left, and then take another immediate left. Continue 1 mile to the hatchery.

The American Falls State Fish Hatchery is a modern production facility that raises primarily rainbow trout placed in southeastern and northern Idaho. The hatchery features twenty outdoor raceways and a large nursery and incubation building. With drop-in hours from dawn to dusk, the hatchery also features guided tours from 7:30 AM to 4 PM. Reservations are suggested for the guided tours. A self-guided nature trail is also available on-site and

can take anywhere from 30 minutes to 2 hours to complete based on the route selected. The fish hatchery is open 365 days a year.

T City Park

American Falls. Contact the American Falls Chamber of Commerce at 226-7214.

City Park, the largest park in American Falls, is situated on seven acres central to the community's business district. The park includes an Oregon Trail Memorial, picnic areas, and a large playground while also playing host to the area's numerous community events.

T Trenner Park

American Falls. Contact the American Falls Chamber of Commerce at 226-7214.

Trenner Park is one of American Falls' most historic parks. Constructed in 1933, the park is maintained as a public recreation area under the management of Idaho Power. The park is situated on the site of the town's old powerhouse and provides gorgeous views of the area. Park features include picnic shelters and an easily accessible fishing dock.

T Great Rift Country

Northeast of American Falls. Contact the BLM - Burley Field Office at 677-6641. Take Exit 40 off I-86 and proceed northeast on State Hwy. 39.

Great Rift Country is a diverse and incomparable regional landmass that was originally shaped by the dynamic forces of tumultuous volcanic activity. It is a place where hardy people created imaginative ways to survive and prosper for over 10,000 years, and a surreal landscape from which an astonishing variety of plants and wildlife sought nourishment and sustenance. This 30,000 square mile expanse is a world-class geological phenomenon high-lighted by twisted lava formations, level basalt plains, rich volcanic soils, deep canyons, and spectacular waterfalls. For the past 15 million years, a "volcanic hot spot" deep within the earth slowly migrated

Ultimate Idaho Atlas and Travel Encyclopedia

In addition to American Falls Reservoir's first-class fishery, Clear Creek and Spring Creek are located nearby. These Class 1 fisheries contain rainbow trout, brown trout, cutthroat trout, and mountain whitefish. Other reservoirs in the area drawing upon the Snake River include Springfield Reservoir, McTucker Ponds, and Rose Pond. Encompassing 66 acres, Springfield Reservoir is similar to its American Falls counterpart, boasting stocked hatchery-raised rainbow trout. McTucker Ponds may not cover as much area as Springfield, but the eight small gravel pits do support rainbow trout, largemouth bass, channel catfish, and bluegill. Directly north of Blackfoot, Rose Pond residents include largemouth bass, bluegill, and rainbow trout.

TV Willow Bay Recreation Area
2830 Marina Rd., American Falls. 226-2688.

Located on American Falls Reservoir, Willow Bay Recreation Area encompasses 128 acres of outdoor fun. The site provides swimming beaches, year-round fishing, boating access, picnic areas, camping, baseball fields, bike paths, and horseshoe pits to accommodate everyone's personal preferences.

TV Snake River Vista
Downstream from the American Falls Dam. Contact the American Falls Chamber of Commerce at 226-7214. Traveling on Fort Hall Ave. in downtown American Falls, bear west onto Idaho St. and proceed on State Hwy. 39 to the dam. After crossing the dam, immediately bear left and continue 5 miles to the site.

The Bureau of Land Management oversees the Snake River Vista Recreation Area. Situated on the river's north side, the site provides easy water access for boating and fishing as well as limited primitive camping areas.

M American Falls Chamber of Commerce
239 Idaho St., American Falls. 226-7214. www.americanfallschamber.org; info@americanfallschamber.org

10 Food, Lodging

Aberdeen
Pop. 1,840

Named after Aberdeen, Scotland, this small community was established by American Falls Canal and Power Company stockholders in 1906. The town, which is nestled near the west banks of American Falls Reservoir, began receiving postal services in 1907.

Springfield
Pop. 100

Historians speculate that the first Mormon emigrant settlers most probably named this small community after Springfield, Illinois. Located in a rich agricultural area, this community once served as a railroad stop. Its post office was established in 1905.

Sterling
Pop. 70

Sterling arrived on the Idaho map as Mormon settlers moved to the area in 1910. Noting that the area had exceptional soil, early settler Thomas L. Jones dubbed the new town Sterling because he believed the town had great potential to prosper agriculturally and economically. Although the town did survive and a post office was established in 1911, Sterling never thrived and remains a tiny farming community to this day.

T Hazard Creek Golf Course
419 East Bingham St., Aberdeen. 397-5308.

Hazard Creek Golf Course opened in 1983 and is known for its casual atmosphere where a dress code is not enforced. Golfers can play nine holes or opt for an additional set of tees to play eighteen holes. Spanning 5,707 yards, the eighteen-hole course is rated a par-70 and water comes into play on 14 of the holes. The course is designed for intermediate to advanced players as the elevated small greens are challenging. Green fees are $14 for 18 holes and $9 for 9 holes on weekdays, while weekend rates are $15 for 18 holes and $11 for nine holes. The course is open March 1 to November 1.

T King's Bowl
Approximately 30 miles northwest of American Falls. Contact the American Falls Chamber of Commerce at 226-7214. From American Falls, follow State Hwy. 39, passing American Falls Dam and continuing 5 miles. Bear west at a sign for "Crystal Ice Cave," and proceed 28.2 miles.

King's Bowl stands directly over the main fracture of the 169,000-acre Great Rift Natural Landmark. In this land of unusual geologic formations, Kings Bowl is a 150-foot deep crater measuring 100 feet wide. The crater was formed in a prehistoric volcano explosion, and rocks from the blast can still be found west of the crater.

T Crystal Ice Cave
Approximately 30 miles northwest of American Falls. Contact the American Falls Chamber of Commerce at 226-7214. From American Falls, follow State Hwy. 39, passing American Falls Dam and continuing 5 miles. Bear west at a sign for "Crystal Ice Cave," and proceed 28.2 miles.

Formed over 2,000 years ago as part of Idaho's Great Rift system, Crystal Ice Cave was discovered as early as 1929, but a detailed report of the cave was not produced until 1956. The cave is situated in a dormant volcano 160 feet below the lava beds of the Columbia Plateau and features a frozen river, frozen waterfall, and numerous other interesting ice formations. The cave was also the discovery site of a new beetle species in 1961. Today, visitors can view the crystal ice formations and three distinct lava flows along a one-eighth mile walking path. The Bureau of Land Management oversees the site, and visitors can access the cave May through September.

T Sterling Wildlife Management Area
2 miles east of Aberdeen on State Hwy. 39. Contact the Southeastern Idaho Pioneer Country Travel Council at (888) 201-1063.

Located near the shores of American Falls Reservoir, the Sterling Wildlife Management Area is open year-round, providing numerous wildlife viewing opportunities. The free area features song birds, birds of prey, shore birds, marine birds, upland birds, marsh birds, waterfowl, and sandhill cranes. The area is also home to the annual youth pheasant-hunting clinic.

V Sportsman Bay
Near Aberdeen north of American Falls on State Hwy. 39. Contact the Southeast Idaho Pioneer Country Travel Council at (888) 201-1063.

Sportsman Bay provides access to some of southeastern Idaho's finest rainbow trout fishing. Complete with a boat launch area, Sportsman Bay is located on the American Falls Reservoir.

M Aberdeen Chamber of Commerce
PO Box 276, Aberdeen. 397-5200.

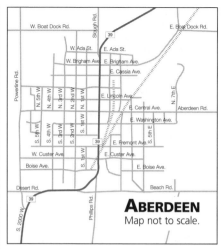

ABERDEEN
Map not to scale.

11 Food

Moreland
Pop. 300

Originally named Keever, John England suggested a new name of Moreland because he found more land available here for homesteading than anywhere else he had previously traveled. Local residents accepted his suggestion, and the post office adopted the town name when it established services in 1916.

Pingree
Pop. 100

Named after Salt Lake City financier and platter, John Pingree, this town was developed as a primarily Mormon settlement. The post office operated here from 1909 to 1930.

Riverside
2 miles west of Blackfoot in Bingham County

Established on the right hand side of the Snake River, early Mormon settlers christened their new community Riverside after its location. The settlement was officially named in 1885, but a post office existed in the area as early as 1879 and operated until 1905. Today, the historic site has become a bedroom community of Blackfoot.

Rockford
Rockford is located in a rural area of Idaho's Bingham County and is nestled just minutes away from the neighboring towns of Riverside and Pingree.

12

Rockland
Pop. 316

Named for nearby Rock Creek and the area's rocky landscape, Rockland was settled in 1876. Mormon settlers who arrived in 1879 are credited with providing the town its name, and postal services were established shortly thereafter in 1886.

H Oregon Trail
Milepost 30.4, Westbound on I-86 at Massacre Rocks Rest Area Picnic Loop

You have just crossed a small canyon that Oregon Trail emigrants regarded as their most dangerous exposure to Indian hostility.

After 1854, they had good reason to be alarmed. Wagon traffic had ruined important traditional Indian trails. Thousands of oxen, horses, sheep, and cattle had overgrazed a broad zone along their trail, leading to Indian resentment. Worse yet, a few emigrants had shot enough

Indians to provoke a great deal of bitterness. On August 9, 1862, Pocatello's Shoshoni band resisted further wagon traffic here, trapping a small emigrant party in a deep gully. An unusually fine stretch of wagon tracks leading to that site can be reached by a marked trail from here.

T Indian Springs Resort
3249 Indian Spring Rd. 226-2174. On State Hwy. 37, located 1.5 miles south of I-86 at Exit 36

A 90-degree underground natural spring bubbles to the surface in the peaceful rural setting surrounding Indian Springs Resort. Every four-five hours, 285,000 gallons of fresh water circulate through the Olympic sized pool, ensuring the cleanliness of the facility. Indian Springs also features a picnic area, horseshoes, volleyball, and family entertainment center. The site is open daily during the summer.

T Massacre Rocks State Park
Near Exit 28 on I-86. 548-2672.

The Story Behind Massacre Rocks
The name "Massacre Rocks" was probably coined during the 1920s, after an Indian skirmish with two pioneer immigrant trains on August 9, 1862. The word "Massacre" is perhaps harsh and somewhat misleading; but the name, along with historical information, helps us to understand the significance of this period in history.

The following is a reconstruction of the happenings of August 9, 1862. Immigrant traffic on the Oregon Trail was well established by 1862. Most wagon trains were fairly small with only ten to fifteen wagons and a following of extra stock. There were many trains, usually only a few miles apart.

On August 9, 1862 in sequential order from Massacre Rocks back to American Falls were the following trains: The Smart Train was nearest the Massacre Rocks; then came the Adams Train, and the Kennedy Train. The Wilson Train was the next train and closest to American Falls. On this day, the first two of the small trains were attacked. The Smart Train was attacked first at a location about a half-mile east of Massacre Rocks. Whether or not the Indians planned to hit the second wagon train, we will never know. It is likely they came upon it on their way back to their camp.

In any case, the Adams Train skirmish was the next event of the day. During the two attacks, five white men were killed. The next morning, Sunday, August 10, Captain Kennedy and 35 men started in pursuit of the Indians to recover their stolen property. They came upon the Indian camp just south of the present Indian Springs Natatorium location. They fought for about three miles as Captain Kennedy and his men tried to retreat. Two more white men were killed, several wounded, and two presumed dead. This brought the total number of white men killed to nine (including

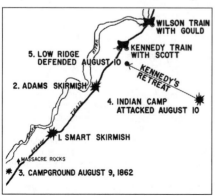

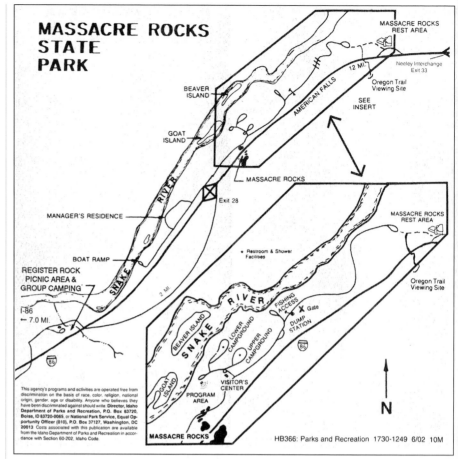

MASSACRE ROCKS STATE PARK

This agency's programs and activities are operated free from discrimination on the basis of race, color, religion, national origin, gender, age or disability. Anyone who believes they have been discriminated against should write: Director, Idaho Department of Parks and Recreation, P.O. Box 83720, Boise, ID 83720-0065, or National Park Service, Equal Opportunity Officer (010), P.O. Box 37127, Washington, DC 20013. Costs associated with this publication are available from the Idaho Department of Parks and Recreation in accordance with Section 60-202, Idaho Code.

HB366: Parks and Recreation 1730-1249 6/02 10M

those thought to be dead). Five of the men believed to be buried in the Massacre Rocks area are: A. J. Hunter and Masemo Lepi of the Smart Train; George Adams, Charles Bulwinkel, and George Shepherd of the Adams Train.

On August 11, one of the missing men was found at the place of the first skirmish, but farther down the trail lying near a large rock. This man apparently was fishing during the attack on the Smart Train.

Finally, the wounded daughter of Captain Adams died the evening of August 11 and was buried the next morning, thus bringing the total number of immigrants killed to ten.

Reprinted from a "Friends of Massacre Rocks" brochure

Register Rock
Oregon Trail pioneers used this area as a rest stop for many years. Many travelers' names and dates are inscribed on the large rock, which is protected by a weather shelter. A scenic picnic area surrounds the rock, creating an attractive and historical stopover for the modern traveler.

Geology
The park is rich in geological history. Volcanic evidence is everywhere. The Devil's Gate Pass is all that remains of an extinct volcano. The prehistoric Bonneville Flood shaped the landscape of the area, rolling and polishing the huge boulders found throughout the park. The flood was caused when eroding waters broke through Red Rock Pass near the Idaho/Utah border to the south 14,500 years ago. Lake Bonneville, which covered much of what is today the state of Utah, surged through the pass and along the channel of the Snake River in a few short months. The flow was four times that of the Amazon River for a few weeks.

Plants and Animals
Massacre Rocks State Park is a favorite for bird watchers. Over 200 species of birds have been sighted in the park. Whistling swans, bald eagles, pelicans, and blue herons are commonly seen. Mammals include the cottontail, jackrabbit, coyote, muskrat, and beaver. The high desert environment produces about 300 species of plants in the park. The dominant species are sagebrush, Utah juniper, rabbit brush, and cactus.

Facilities
- 990 acres
- 43-unit campground with water and electrical hookups and two sleeping cabins
- Restrooms with hot showers
- Picnic area with horseshoe pits
- Summer campfire programs nightly

- Visitor center
- 12 Kilometers of hiking trails with maps available, including interpretive hikes and geology exhibit trails
- Self-guided nature trail
- Access to Oregon Trail ruts
- Fishing
- Boat launching area
- Winter camping available

Fees
There is a fee for camping, a motorized vehicle entrance fee, and a reservation fee.

Reprinted from Idaho State Parks and Recreation brochure

T Register Rock
Near Exit 28 at Massacre Rocks State Park, 3592 N. Park Ln., American Falls. 548-2672.

Located ten miles west of American Falls, Register Rock records the names and dates of many Oregon Trail pioneers' passage to the west. The twenty foot tall lava boulder was a popular camping spot for 1800s travelers and is now a historical monument. The Idaho Department of Parks and Recreation administers the site, and all visitors are reminded to respect the rock's historical significance and refrain from leaving any marks.

T Devil's Garden
Massacre Rocks State Park, 3592 N. Park Ln., American Falls. 548-2672.

Situated in the park's upper campground loop, Devil's Garden represents a volcanic oddity. A fenced, fifty square foot plot contains numerous pinnacles measuring six inches tall and four inches in diameter. Two theories have been proposed to explain the phenomena. Some geologists theorize that the rounded pinnacles are the result of air bubbles that formed as lava solidified after a volcanic eruption. The second theory states that escaping gas and silica bonded with volcanic ash in the area. As the ash was melded together, hardened spires formed around each vent hole.

TV Pipeline Recreation Area
Downstream from the American Falls Dam. Contact the American Falls Chamber of Commerce at 226-7214. Merge off I-86 at exit 36, and proceed west to the area.

Located along the mighty Snake River's south side, Pipeline Recreation Area is an appropriate destination for those interested in a less crowded fishing site and primitive camping. The well-marked site administered by the Bureau of Land Management draws its name from an area pipeline that crosses the river.

13

Holbrook
Pop. 50

Originally settled and established by Mormons, Holbrook retains its heritage as a wheat-growing community. It was named for Heber Holbrook, the first town bishop, when the post office was established in 1901.

Samaria
Pop. 135

Welsh Mormon immigrants first settled here in 1868 and named their settlement after a district in Palestine. Shortly after arriving, the pioneers built irrigation canals to raise sheep and cattle and grow wheat and hay. Flour and saw mills were also established, and the population surged over 800 in 1890. A post office operated from 1881 to

Idaho Trivia
In 1866, J.J. Hansen arrived at Idaho's Register Rock with his family. Just seven years old at the time, Hansen carved an Indian's head into the lava boulder. At age 54 and as a professional sculptor, Hansen returned to the rock in 1913 and carved his name and date again. His handiwork, among hundreds of other pioneer signatures, is still evident at the rock.

1983, and the town residents have long been recognized throughout the area for their good samaritan ways.

Stone
Pop. 10

Situated on Deep Creek bordering the Utah-Idaho state line, this tiny community of Mormon settlers was named after a well-respected lawyer in Malad City. A post office has operated in the area since 1910.

H Lake Bonneville
Milepost 269 on Interstate 84 at the Juniper Rest Area

Twenty thousand years ago, this land was underwater. Not far to the north, you can see the old shore of Lake Bonneville.

Formed in a basin from which no river reached the ocean, this became the largest lake in North America. Finally, the lake rose enough to overflow into the Snake River. Then, after the climate got drier and the great basin of Utah and Nevada became mostly a desert, the lake receded. Salt Lake and two other remnants are all that are left of this old 20,000-square mile lake.

T Curlew National Grasslands
One mile northwest of Holbrook on State Hwy. 37. Contact the Southeast Idaho Pioneer Country Travel Council at (888) 201-1063.

The Curlew National Grasslands is a demonstration site of how land can be reclaimed and restored to a natural cycle after agricultural mistreatment. Encompassing more than 47,000 acres, the grassland is administered under the Caribou National Forest as a multiple use land area. Livestock grazing from April 15 to November 15 is allowed, and watershed management, wildlife preservation and viewing, and recreation use are also emphasized. At Sweeten Pond, waterfowl and shore birds abound, and the annual spring courtship dances between the sharptail and sage grouse are a must-see for bird lovers. Nearby Stone Reservoir is a popular site for boating, waterskiing, swimming, and fishing for rainbow trout, bass, and crappie. The grasslands area is open year-round free of charge.

V Pleasantview Reservoir
North of Pleasantview on Sand Ridge Rd. Contact the Idaho Department of Game and Fish at 334-3700.

Two different lakes and forty-seven acres of highly fishable waters await anglers at Pleasantview Reservoir. Largemouth bass, bluegill, rainbow trout, and tiger muskies can be caught year-round. Private property surrounds the reservoir, so anglers should be courteous and aware of any area travel/fishing restrictions.

V Stone Reservoir
South of Holbrook. Contact the Idaho Department of Game and Fish at 334-3700.

Early residents began building Stone Reservoir in 1907, and the area continues to be a popular recreation site. Encompassing 250 acres, the reservoir is located in the Curlew National Grassland and measures three miles long and one-quarter mile wide. Stone Reservoir is drawn from the Malad River system, and rainbow trout, largemouth bass, yellow perch, and black crappie populate the water. Motorized boats are allowed on the reservoir, making water-skiing a favorite recreational past-time in the area. The reservoir is open year-round free of charge and also features picnic shelters, camping areas, fire pits, and a boat ramp.

LEGEND OF THE RUMBLING SAMARIA MOUNTAINS

Every year, a low rumbling emerges from the Samaria Mountains south of Samaria as winter creeps away and spring pokes out its head. This rumbling has created quite a stir, resulting in a series of mystical and geological explanations.

When Native Americans roamed these lands, they believed the mountains were home to sacred Indian spirits. The Washakie Indians in particular theorized that the rumblings were simply the conversations between the mountain spirits. Humans, then, were allowed to hear the rumblings as proof of the spirit world.

Geologists, however, propose a much more scientific reason for the rumbling. They agree that since the rumbling occurs at regular periods of time in only one particular season, it is unlikely that any seismic or volcanic activity is taking place underneath the surface. Instead, experts have hypothesized that water running deep beneath the mountain's walls causes the "talking," while still many others believe temperature plays a major role in the event. Geologists speculate that warming spring temperatures force air to expand in the mountain's numerous underground caverns, resulting in a rumbling from the rushing air.

No matter what its cause, this annual spring awakening continues to draw intrigue from locals, tourists, and the wildlife population.

14

Arbon
Pop. 10

Situated in Arbon Valley, this village sprang to life in the late 1890s with farming activity. The town was named in 1897 out of respect to the area's oldest settler, Joseph N. Arbon, and a post office was opened just one year later.

Pauline
38 miles southeast of American Falls in Power County

Situated at the junction of Arbon Valley Hwy. and Crystal-Pocatello Road, Pauline was established in 1890. The town was first christened "Meadow" after the many meadows covering the surrounding landscape. Early settler and Mormon bishop, Kornwalles, changed the town's name to Pauline in honor of his mother, and a post office operated in the town from 1911 until 1920.

15 Food

Inkom
Pop. 738

Inkom was settled in 1895 and mapped out in 1914. Today, it is part of Pocatello's metro area and is home to the state's only cement producer. Lime is also mined in the area. The post office was established here in 1903, and the town is reportedly named after the Indian term Ink-um, which means "come ahead."

H Idaho's First Railroad
Milepost 59.1 on I-15 at Inkom Rest Area

Through this canyon once puffed the wood-burning locomotives of the narrow-gauge Utah Northern Railway.

Construction, undertaken by a Mormon co-op, came northward from a junction with the transcontinental line, but stopped in 1874 at Franklin on the Utah-Idaho border. Jay Gould, famous financier of the Union Pacific, took over in 1877. Trains were passing here the next summer, and the rails reached Montana in 1880. New life for eastern Idaho followed the shrieking whistles of those little Northern trains.

V Pebble Creek Ski Area
3340 E. Green Canyon Rd., Inkom. 775-4452 or (877) 524-SNOW www.pebblecreekskiarea.com

Pebble Creek Ski Area is situated inside Idaho's Caribou National Forest and is known for non-existent lift lines and Western hospitality dating back to 1949. Nestled on top of Mount Bonneville, the ski area originated with a U.S. Forest Service report compiled in 1937. The report found that Mount Bonneville's eastern slopes possessed ideal skiing terrain. Although local adventurists trudged up the unimproved roads to sample the hillside, the area was not commercially developed until 1949. Ski pioneer Paul Hill created Skyline Ski Area on the mountain's western slope and established two tow-ropes and a small warming hut. The area was primitive, however, and ungroomed slopes and a bumpy ride up the tow-ropes awaited skiers. In 1957, the area changed management, and in 1968, the current ski lodge was constructed. As the ski area continued to change hands, more amenities were added and dreams of expanding to Mount Bonneville's eastern slopes began to materialize. The current name was added in the late 1970s,

and emphasis on expansion and guest services became the owners' primary goal.

Today, Pebble Creek Ski Area receives an average of 250 inches of snow annually and features 1,100 acres of skiable terrain with a maximum vertical of 2,200 feet. Two triple chairs and one double chair wait to whisk skiers and snowboarders to the varying levels of terrain. The fifty-four runs are rated 12% beginner, 35% intermediate, and 53% advanced. Rentals and ski and snowboarding instruction are available on-site, and a season pass provides discounted rates at other Idaho ski resorts. Daily lift tickets are $30 for adults full-day and $20 for half-day passes, while youth ages 6-12 can ski a full day for $17 and a half-day for $10. Pebble Creek is open Friday through Sunday during the early and late seasons. From December through February, the area is open daily from 9:30 AM to 4 PM, and in March and April, business hours are 9:30 AM to 4:30 PM Wednesday through Sunday. Night skiing is available January to early March on Friday and Saturday evenings until 9:30 PM.

V Inman Canyon Cross-Country Ski Area
From Inkom, proceed 2 miles up Rapid Creek Rd. before bearing right on Inman Rd. The parking area is located at the end of the road's plowed stretch.

The primary Nordic route in the Inman region winds gently along Inman Creek. This 2.5-mile trail is relatively easy, but skiers are encouraged to rise early as snowmobiles also use the route. While many skiers turn around at the 2.5-mile route, an optional tour can be taken up the South Fork of Inman Creek. The heavily timbered South Fork trail requires advanced skills but offers a more secluded atmosphere than the main route. The area is part of Idaho's Park N' Ski system, and permits are required. Permits may be obtained at the nearest Ranger Station and fees are as follows:

$25 annual permit (good at all Idaho Park N' Ski areas), $7.50 3-day permit, and $2 day use permit.

16 Food

McCammon
Pop. 805

In 1873, the U.S. Congress gave John W. Young, son of Brigham Young, the right-of-way to build the Utah and Northern Railroad in Idaho Territory. The line's intended path was through the Bear River Valley to Soda Springs, up the Snake River Valley, and eventually across Montana. Despite Young's plan, it wasn't until 1882 that the government finally ratified an agreement between the Shoshone and Bannock Indians, J.H. McCammon, and several railroad officials that allowed the intended line to cross reservation lands. The eventual placement of this railroad served as motivation for settlement of southeastern Idaho. Many small towns, including McCammon, sprang up near the tracks. The town's post office was established in 1883 and adopted the name of J.H. McCammon, who was instrumental in finally bringing Young's railroad line to fruition.

T Indian Rocks
Near McCammon at I-15 Exit 47.

Once an official state park spanning 3,500 acres, Indian Rocks is now simply a scenic stopping point for those interested in up-close views of sagebrush, juniper, and ancient lava rock.

17

Arimo
Pop. 348

Located just five miles south of McCammon, Arimo dates back to the 1870s Mormon settlement of Oneida. When the railroad rolled through town, a railroad official renamed the town Arimo after a historical Indian chief. A post office operated in the area from 1878 through 1926.

Virginia
Pop. 50

Homesteaders arrived in the area as early as 1885 and christened their tiny settlement Thatcher. The town soon began to attract Mormon emigrants, and in 1912, an official LDS ward was founded. At that time, the Mormon settlers renamed the area North Cambridge, and a post office was established. In later years, the town's name changed again to its current identity after Mormon converts from Virginia settled in the community.

18 Food, Lodging

Malad City
Pop. 2,158

French trappers who experienced a bout of food poisoning after eating beaver meat named this area and nearby river in the 1830s. "Malade" means "sick" in French. Although trappers led by John C. Fremont passed through the area in 1843, it wasn't until 1856 that the area was officially settled. At the encouragement of Brigham Young, several Utah members of the Church of Jesus Christ of Latter Day Saints migrated to the region. They were greeted with fields of grass, streams, and wild game.

Despite such ideal agricultural and ranching conditions, the town didn't boom until 1864. Henry Peck arrived about that time and was influential in developing the area for hay production. As the town's first chamber of commerce president,

IN SEARCH OF THE MYSTERIOUS IRON DOOR: TREASURE SEEKERS ABOUND IN MALAD CITY

Tales of lost gold and buried treasure excite both young and old as visions of the Old West come back to life in far-fetched folklore. But in Malad City, legends of buried treasure refuse to die, continuing to be a focus of both residents and area visitors.

Back in the early days of Idaho and Montana Territory, a stagecoach ran from Malad City north to Montana, and robberies were frequent. One significant outlaw group of three bandits was particularly successful and decided to hide their loot in the hills surrounding Malad City. After finding a heavy iron vault door in a Utah town destroyed by fire, the bandits bought the door and returned to the Malad Valley hills in search of a cave. The plan – stash the loot in the cave and secure the treasure inside with the heavy iron door.

The plan worked well for a while as the desperados continued their successful stagecoach heists, accumulating mass quantities of gold. But eventually the trio had a major disagreement over their partnership, resulting in a serious gunfight that left all three wounded in the cave. After the battle was over, the most conniving member of the group escaped and

locked his accomplices inside. Crawling to a nearby ranch to summon a doctor's help, the outlaw knew he would die before a doctor arrived. In desperation, the bandit gave up the tale of the iron door but died before telling the rancher the cave's location.

From that moment on, the search was on for the buried treasure. Supposedly area rancher, Glipsy Waldron, found the door during a severe storm but was unable to find it again when he returned in fairer weather. More recently, miner Leo D. Williams and a Utah doctor found what looked like an abandoned mine shaft. Believing they would find an iron door fallen to the bottom of the shaft, the two men dug inside and actually discovered remains of two humans. The two were sure that the bones were that of the famous outlaws, and the doctor agreed to take the bones to a Utah university for identification. But in between their find and planned destination, the bones were lost and the doctor mysteriously died.

Since then, treasure seekers of all ages have combed the hills surrounding Malad City, but to no avail. The treasure remains hidden, and the legend of the iron door continues.

ANNUAL EVENTS

Massacre Rocks Rendezvous

The lively fur trading past comes alive at the annual Massacre Rocks Rendezvous. Held each June, the event features re-enactments of the mountain man lifestyle, Teepee Village, Trader's Row, black powder shoots, and knife throwing contests. Nearly 2,000 people attend the event every summer for a live look into Idaho's history.

Sagebrush Arts Festival

Hosted on the campus of Idaho State University, the Sagebrush Arts Festival is a community favorite held annually during autumn. The Pocatello Art Center sponsors the two-day affair where arts and crafts booths are available for children, live entertainment is presented throughout the entirety of the event, and select art pieces are on sale at reasonable prices.

The Famous Preston Night Rodeo

Preston offers residents and tourists a chance to experience Idaho's oldest night rodeo. The PRCA event is held each summer and draws national attention. In addition to the rodeo, the three-day event includes citywide sidewalk sales, a craft and antique fair, children's festival, live entertainment, a parade, and an old-fashioned Wild West Shoot-Out.

Festival of Lights

Every year in Preston, the weekend following Thanksgiving is filled with the Christmas spirit as residents and visitors gather to celebrate the Festival of Lights. Two days of shopping, bed racing, musicals, theater, live entertainment, parades, children's activities, and fireworks cumulate with the lighting of the town's festively decorated downtown. The lights remain brightly lit until the New Year, and the festival is recognized as one of Idaho's best holiday light displays.

Dodge National Circuit Finals Rodeo & Cowboy Ski Classic

Pocatello's Frontier Rodeo Association dates back to 1942 and has consistently provided rodeo events annually for the last 57 years. In 1987, the Association gained the national limelight with the establishment of the Dodge National Circuit Finals Rodeo. A PRCA event ranking as America's second-largest point-earning rodeo, the national competition features two champions from each of twelve rodeo circuits across the nation vying for fame and prizes. Advance tickets for the event are highly recommended.

In conjunction with the rodeo is the Cowboy Ski Classic held each year at the Pebble Creek Ski Area. Riding a saddle attached to a barrel with skis bolted to it, contestants zoom downhill and try to remain on their saddle while traversing turns and humps in the slopes. The lighthearted event draws hundreds of spectators each year.

Geyser Days

Every summer, residents of Soda Springs gather to celebrate the natural springs and geyser for which the town has historically gained fame. The weeklong event includes community potlucks, truck mud bog races, live entertainment, and park dances.

Shoshone-Bannock Indian Festival

Held annually for more than forty years, the Shoshone-Bannock Indian Festival is a renowned event drawing nearly 50,000 spectators each year from places as distant as Europe and Japan. The four-day celebration of Shoshone-Bannock tribal culture features a parade, clowns, powwows, dancing, live entertainment, a rodeo, and nearly 100 arts and crafts booths. In addition, visitors can sample original Native American cuisine at the event's various food booths.

Eastern Idaho State Fair

Ranked as one of the top five agricultural fairs in the U.S., the Eastern Idaho State Fair is an eight-day event with deep roots. The fair began in 1902 as an opportunity for students, housewives, farmers/ranchers, and businessmen to gather and trade valuable information. During World War II, the fair was shut down to support the war effort, and in autumn 1944, the fairgrounds became home to 500 Italian prisoners of war sent to Idaho to harvest sugar beets and potatoes. Fair activities resumed after the war ended, and new events have been added throughout the years.

Today, the fair features pari-mutuel horse racing, rodeos, thrilling carnival rides, recipe contests, 2,000 farm animals, agricultural, artistic, and culinary exhibits, big-name nightly entertainment, and two small entertainment stages.

Bear Lake Raspberry Festival

The lush region surrounding Bear Lake is ideal for growing raspberries, and the area's abundant crop is celebrated each summer during a weeklong festival in Idaho and Utah. The festival features an arts and crafts fair, rodeo, raspberry recipe cook-offs, the Miss Berry Princess contest, street dances, nightly fireworks, and local entertainment venues.

Bannock County Bluegrass Festival

Held annually in Pocatello, the Bannock County Bluegrass Festival provides a weekend of guitar pickin', toe-tappin', hand-clapping fun with a variety of bluegrass and bluegrass gospel music. The festival continues to attract more visitors each year, so advance arrangements are highly suggested.

American Falls Founders Day

American Falls celebrates its town's founding settlers in a community event filled with Western spirit. Held one day each summer, the festival includes a pancake feed, parade, children's games, an old-fashioned community barbeque in the park, western music, live entertainment, and an outdoor dance.

Heritage Festival

Held annually each summer in Ross Park, the Pocatello Heritage Festival honors its pioneer roots. The weekend event includes pioneer activities and arts and crafts booths.

Butch Cassidy Days

Montpelier remembers its most famous historic event with the annual Butch Cassidy Days. The two-day event features a reenacted shootout, a community dinner, bed races, parade, free pancake feed, and fireworks.

---

he encouraged construction and growth in the valley. Malad served as the center for southeastern Idaho's first prosperous farming enterprises and was an important commercial center between Salt Lake and Butte, Montana. The town continued to prosper when the Union Pacific Railroad built a line to Malad from Brigham City, Utah in 1906. A post office has operated here since 1865.

T Oneida County Pioneer Museum

27 Bannock St., Malad City. 766-4847.

The history and antiques of southeastern Idaho are preserved in the Oneida County Pioneer Museum. Opened in 1992, the museum is housed in a 1914 building first used as a community drug store and later as a state liquor store, ice cream shop, dentist's office, and apartment building. The historic pressed-tin ceiling is just one of the many artifacts visitors will find inside. A famed display derived from local legend encourages treasure seekers to search the town's surrounding hills for a cave with an iron door supposedly home to a pile of riches. The museum is open 1 PM to 5 PM Tuesday through Saturday year-round with free admission.

T Gateway Southeast Idaho Visitor Center

7 miles north of the Idaho/Utah border on I-15. 766-4788.

For those entering Idaho from Utah, the Gateway Southeast Idaho Visitor Center provides a wealth of information about the state. Located at the Cherry Creek Rest Area and thus often referred to as the Cherry Creek Visitor Center, the site is supplied with a variety of informational brochures highlighting the region's numerous attractions.

T Evans Co-Op Mercantile

25 N. Main St., Malad City. Contact the Southeastern Idaho Pioneer Country Travel Council at (888) 201-1063.

The Evans Co-Op Mercantile has been a landmark since Malad City's founding and represents Idaho's first department store. From the late 1860s through the 1880s, a national anti-Mormon campaign broke out across the U.S. In response, Mormon bishops across the west were encouraged to organize cooperative stores to help Latter Day Saints residing in Idaho and Utah Territory with local production and purchasing. The Malad bishop accepted the suggestion and organized the Malad Cooperative, a strictly Mormon store associated with Brigham Young's United Order of Enoch. Prominent Mormon businessman, David Evans, decided to reorganize the cooperative in 1882 but was leery about tying the store too closely with the Mormon Church.

As a result, Evans erected a new building over the original bishop's cooperative and paved the way for more department stores to strike up business in Idaho. In addition to the general store, Evans' building also housed a bowling alley, meeting room, dance hall, and state bank.

T Iron Door Playhouse

59 N. Main St., Malad City. 766-4705.

The Iron Door Playhouse is home to several fine performances presented by the Malad Valley

MALAD CEMETERY'S MOST UNIQUE RESIDENT

Tales of pioneer days run rampant in southeastern Idaho, but one of the most interesting stories lies inside the gates of the Malad Cemetery. In 1878, early resident and farmer, Ben Waldron, lost one of his legs in an unfortunate threshing accident. Not knowing exactly what to do with his dismembered leg, Waldron proposed that the limb be given a proper burial at the local cemetery. Local officials agreed to the plan, and shortly thereafter, Waldron's leg was buried on the cemetery's east side complete with a headstone.

But problems soon arose after the leg's burial. Waldron complained of continuous pain in the remaining portion of his leg, insisting that his buried limb was resting in a twisted position and subsequently causing him discomfort. Despite harsh skepticism, the leg was exhumed and was indeed found buried in an awkward position. After straightening out the leg and reburying it, Waldron's pain mysteriously disappeared.

Waldron's leg can still be found on the cemetery's east side marked with a headstone featuring the initials "B.W.," a carved picture of a leg, and the date of the accident. Waldron himself lived until 1914 and is buried far away from his leg on the cemetery's west side.

Theater Guild. The non-profit guild was established in 1991 and features numerous theatrical and musical productions throughout the year. Average ticket prices are $7, and reservations are highly suggested for all performances.

V Daniels Reservoir
18 miles northwest of Malad City on Bannock Street. Contact the Idaho Department of Game and Fish at 334-3700.

The Malad Valley, dotted with reservoirs, is an angler's dream. At 375 acre Daniels Reservoir, the waters are filled with trophy sized Bonneville cutthroat and rainbow trout. Anglers may only use artificial flies or lures, and only one barbless hook is permitted per lure. In addition, the reservoir offers a boat dock, a few camping sites, and excellent bird-watching opportunities.

V Devil Creek Reservoir
7 miles north of Malad City. Contact the Idaho Department of Game and Fish at 334-3700.

This 142 surface acre lake is annually stocked with rainbow trout and features a growing population of kokanee salmon. Fed by a mountain stream, the reservoir is equipped with a concrete boat launch as well as a developed campground.

V St. Johns Reservoir
3 miles northwest of Malad City. Contact the Idaho Department of Game and Fish at 334-3700.

This forty-eight acre lake is a favorite local destination and is often described as a beginning angler's dream. Rainbow trout, bass, bluegill, and perch proliferate the waters. The only restriction is that bass between twelve and sixteen inches cannot be harvested.

V Crowthers Reservoir
Northern outskirts of Malad City. Contact the Idaho Department of Game and Fish at 334-3700.

Measuring 33 acres, Crowthers Reservoir is a favorite children's fishing spot and ensures an easy catch. The waters are annually stocked with rainbow trout, and largemouth bass and bluegill are also known to populate the reservoir.

V Deep Creek Reservoir
4.4 miles south of the I-15 and State Hwy. 36 interchange near Malad City. Contact the Idaho Department of Game and Fish at 334-3700.

Deep Creek Reservoir is home to a plentiful supply of rainbow trout, native cutthroat trout, and largemouth bass. In addition, the reservoir is fed by runoff so kokanee salmon are also sometimes present. Boats are allowed on the reservoir, and a boat ramp and dock provides easy access to this year-round angling destination.

V Malad River Drainage
Recognized for its high silt content and warm water temperatures, the Malad River drainage area includes several small streams and covers eighty-six surface acres over a total watercourse spanning eighty-three miles. From 1987 to 1992, a severe drought in the Magic Valley region significantly depleted the drainage's warm water fish populations. In response, the Idaho Department of Fish and Game began stocking channel catfish in lower stretches of the Malad River. The river was subsequently are opened to year-round angling in 1994.

In addition to the rivers and streams comprising the Malad River drainage, several stocked reservoirs can be found in the area. Daniels, Devils Creek, Deep Creek, and St. John's Reservoirs are all annually stocked with rainbow trout. Nearby, Stone Reservoir is also stocked with an abundance of rainbows, but it is capable of sustaining populations of wild crappie and largemouth bass naturally.

M Malad Chamber of Commerce
59 Bannock St., Malad City. 766-9230.
www.maladidaho.org

19

Banida
Pop. 85

Upon its early twentieth century founding near Bannock and Oneida Counties, Banida was noted for its abundant fertile soil and was logically named, Richfield. The name didn't stick for long, though, and the town voted in 1908 to combine the Bannock and Oneida county names into the new community name "Banida." Four years later, postal services were obtained.

Clifton
Pop. 213

Mormons who originally settled in nearby Franklin migrated to this site between 1864 and 1865. The town was platted in 1869, and early resident, John Saut, named the area after cliffs surrounding the rocky area.

Dayton
Pop. 444

This small town has quite a name history. It was first called Franklin Meadows because the original settlers arrived from Franklin. Five Mile Creek was its second name because it was located five miles from Weston and five miles from Clifton. Next, it was called Chadville, after Joseph Chadwick. The name Dayton was finally given to the town in

recognition of Bishop William B. Preston because he always visited the town during daylight hours. Opened in 1912, the community's post office discontinued services in 1931.

Oxford
Pop. 53

Early trappers and hunters named this area for the oxen tracks they found at the ford in a nearby stream. The town subsequently draws its name from Oxford Creek, and Mormons initially settled this southeastern Idaho village.

Weston
Pop. 425

Located just five miles north of the Utah/Idaho border, Weston was established in 1865 as the second Mormon settlement in the state. Migrating from Utah, fifteen families crossed the icy Bear River and soon realized their new village was the only settlement west of Franklin. Thus, early pioneer Ezra T. Benson dubbed the site "West Town." The name was later shortened to Weston, and the town acquired postal services in 1873. Near the community is historical Weston Canyon. Findings from a 1969-1970 digging have led several archeologists to conclude that big game hunters inhabited the area over 7,000 years ago.

T Weston Canyon Prehistoric Rock Shelter
Near Weston on Weston Canyon Rd. Contact the Southeast Idaho Pioneer Country Travel Council at (888) 201-1063.

Nearly 7,000 years ago, prehistoric big game and mountain sheep hunters are believed to have inhabited this Idaho region. Excavated by Idaho State University archaeologists in 1969 and 1970, a primitive rock shelter left behind by these early inhabitants can be found approximately four miles down the Weston Canyon Road. The find was significant as it represented a shift in living styles from other inhabitants speculated to have once occupied the area. This site at the southern mouth of Weston Canyon was added to the National Register of Historic Places in 1974.

T Standing Rock
On State Hwy. 36 near Weston. Contact the Southeast Idaho Pioneer Country Travel Council at (888) 201-1063.

As State Hwy. 36 passes Weston Reservoir and narrows into the granite lined Weston Canyon, a huge granite tower called Standing Rock is visible. On August 29, 1843, John C. Fremont and his party of explorers discovered the rock and christened it with its present name. Geologists agree that at some unknown time, the rock fell from its original positioning on the steep canyon wall and landed near the present-day road.

V Weston Reservoir
Midway between Malad City and Weston on State Hwy. 36. Contact the Idaho Department of Game and Fish at 334-3700.

Stocked annually, this 112-acre reservoir offers anglers access to yellow perch, largemouth bass, and rainbow trout. Motorized boats are not

Idaho Trivia

Malad City is not only one of Idaho's oldest communities, but it also boasts the state's oldest continuously running weekly newspaper. *The Idaho Enterprise* has been recording the region's events since its first publication on June 6, 1879.

JESSIE JAMES STRIKES MALAD CITY

After recovering from a gun battle wound in Missouri, Jessie James left the south and headed to Idaho Territory. He arrived in Malad City in the mid 1860s under the pseudonym, William Cole. Although James had been engaged to a Southern belle for nearly nine years, he abandoned any thought of the woman when he met Susan Palmer Debuque. Susan was a widow with four children with whom James fell madly in love. After a short engagement, the couple was married on May 30, 1869. Still posing as the upstanding William Cole, James bought into his wife's family farm business. He labored for a year, watched as Susan gave birth to their daughter, Alice, and then promptly left his wife and Idaho behind after only one year of marriage.

allowed on the water, but float tubes are acceptable. Open year-round, the reservoir is an extremely popular ice-fishing destination.

20 *Food*

Downey
Pop. 613

The Union Pacific RR came through this area in 1894 and thus started the settlement of Downey. In 1910, the settlement gained in popularity when an irrigation canal brought water in from the Portneuf River. The town itself was named after an official on the UPRR, and the post office was established in 1894. Farming and ranching currently drive the economy. In addition, Downey is recognized for sporting the state's first Pony Express line and for establishing Southeastern Idaho's first stagecoach stop.

Swanlake
Pop. 135

Mormon homesteaders settled this village in the 1870s, and a post office arrived to serve the residents' needs in 1880. The town draws its name from the nearby Swan Lake.

H Red Rock Pass
Milepost 30.2 on U.S. Hwy. 91

You are standing in the outlet of ancient Lake Bonneville. It was a vast prehistoric inland sea, of which Salt Lake is a modern remnant.

Covering over 20,000 square miles when it overflowed here about 14,500 years ago, its winding shoreline would have stretched from here to New Orleans if it were straightened out. This pass was deepened considerably when Lake Bonneville began to flow into the Snake River. For a time, a torrent several times larger than the Amazon was discharged here. Finally, with a hotter, drier climate that slowly emerged about 8,000 years ago, Lake Bonneville gradually disappeared.

T Downata Hot Springs
25901 Downata Rd., Downey. 897-5736. 3 miles south of Downey. www.downatahotsprings.com

A 2,000-acre farm and quiet, country atmosphere surrounds visitors at Downata Hot Springs. The area was once known as "Marshall's Springs," and commercial use of the natural springs dates back to 1907. When Alexander Marshall purchased the estate, he created the first pool featuring rock sides and a mud bottom. The site became so popular with local residents that church officials from the Church of Jesus Christ of Latter Day Saints frequently used the pool for member baptisms. In 1929, a full-scale resort was built that included thirty gas lanterns used to light the pool area in the evening. Throughout the years, numerous owners have acquired Downata, all leaving their own mark.

Today, Downata features a large naturally heated pool, a water playground, two hydro-tube slides, and a hot tub. While the nearby rock-bottomed spring is naturally 109 degrees, cool water is pumped in to make the pool and hot tub comfortable for soaking. Downata is open daily from Memorial Day through Labor Day with limited winter hours.

T Red Rock Pass
5 miles south of Downey on U.S. Hwy. 91. Contact the Southeast Idaho Pioneer Country Travel Council at (888) 201-1063.

Nearly 15,000 years ago, Red Rock Pass served as the site of a natural rock dam for the prehistoric Lake Bonneville. A highly active volcanic region at the time, lava flows near present-day Pocatello suddenly diverted the Bear River into Lake Bonneville. The large influx of water from the river caused Lake Bonneville to overflow the dam's 300-foot banks and eventually crushed the dam with the weight of the steady flow. As a result of the dam's collapse, the narrow dolomite and limestone gap known as Red Rock Pass was created.

T Lake Bonneville Flood
Original site at Red Rock Pass 5 miles south of Downey on U.S. Hwy. 91. Contact the Southeast Idaho Pioneer Country Travel Council at (888) 201-1063.

Thousands of years ago, 20,000 acres of southern Idaho, eastern Nevada, and Utah were covered with prehistoric Lake Bonneville. After lava flows and an influx of water forced the lake over its natural rock dam now known as Red Rock Pass, a wave of destruction hit today's southeastern Idaho. More than 1,000 cubic miles of water raged through the dam at an average flow of sixteen miles per hour. Discharging more water than three times the average flow of the Amazon River (the world's largest river), the Bonneville Flood lasted nearly eight weeks with residual effects up to a year. Ranking as the world's second largest known flood, a wall of water reaching 400 feet tall washed over today's Portneuf Meadows, Marsh Valley, and Pocatello. As a result, the Snake River channel was formed along with several subsidiaries and hanging valleys lining the Snake River's rim. Today, all that is left of Lake Bonneville is Utah's Great Salt Lake.

PRESTON

Map not to scale.

T Downey City Park
Downtown Downey. Contact the Southeast Idaho Pioneer Country Travel Council at (888) 201-1063.

The Downey City Park is a favorite relaxation spot for both locals and travelers. The park features several picnic tables and pavilions, baseball fields, tennis and basketball courts, and a large playground. In addition, a historic pioneer cabin is situated on-site to provide individuals with a visual reminder of the region's founding settlers. William Jackson and Cyrus Coffin constructed the small cabin sometime prior to 1866, and it became the first residence built in the Marsh Valley. Eventually, Abigail Coffin purchased the cabin, and along with her three sons, used the cabin to provide the area's first school and general store.

T Woodland Memorial Park
Downtown Downey. Contact the Downey Chamber of Commerce at 897-5033.

Woodland Memorial Park commemorates the life and sacrifice of Daniel Platt Woodland. Woodland died on July 16, 1964 and remains the community's only police officer killed in the line of duty. The park features covered picnic shelters, tables, large shade trees, fire pits, and a winter ice skating pond.

M Downey Area Chamber of Commerce
S. Main St., Downey. 897-5033.
www.downeyidaho.com

21 *Food, Lodging*

Preston
Pop. 4,682

William Head originally founded this town in 1866 because of its location along the freight road from Corinne, Utah, to Helena, Montana. When the Utah Northern Railroad chugged into town in 1878, it brought with it a steady stream of settlers. Originally called Worm Creek, the name was changed in 1881 to honor prominent Mormon settler, William B. Preston. The name change helped lure more people to the area, and the town site was surveyed in 1888. Finally, in 1913, the town incorporated while at the same time becoming the seat of Franklin County.

Preston	Jan	Feb	March	April	May	June	July	Aug	Sep	Oct	Nov	Dec	Annual	
Average Max. Temperature (F)		31.1	36.6	48.7	58.2	68.5	77.7	87.3	86.6	75.5	61.8	44.8	32.7	59.1
Average Min. Temperature (F)		12.8	15.7	24.7	31.6	39.2	45.3	51.3	50.5	41.4	31.7	23.4	14.0	31.8
Average Total Precipitation (in.)		1.27	1.22	1.34	1.41	2.03	1.40	0.86	1.01	1.40	1.63	1.29	1.55	16.42
Average Total Snowfall (in.)		11.1	8.5	4.1	1.6	0.1	0.0	0.0	0.0	0.0	0.9	3.1	13.1	42.6
Average Snow Depth (in.)		3	3	0	0	0	0	0	0	0	0	0	3	1

Section 7

IDAHO'S MILITARY HEROES

During World War II, hundreds of Idaho men joined American forces in serving their country. As a result, the U.S. awarded four Congressional Medals of Honor to Idaho servicemen. Out of the entire state, young men from Preston received two of the medals. One was awarded for heroism in an attack on a Philippines pillbox, while the other was granted for outstanding defense of a New Guinea beach that prevented a Japanese landing and subsequent invasion.

The area continued to grow as a regional agricultural center and currently produces bountiful crops of corn, beans, hay, and a variety of grains. Preston also gained the national spotlight when it recently became the filming site for the comedic high school tale of "Napoleon Dynamite."

Mink Creek
Pop. 50

In late 1871, Janus Keller and his sons built a log cabin along nearby Strawberry Creek. Mr. Keller left his two sons, ages twelve and fourteen, at the cabin alone while he went sixty miles away to the rest of the family in Utah. While the younger son grew impatient for his father's return and hiked back to Utah, the older boy wintered at the cabin alone and took care of the family hay and cattle business. The entire family arrived the following spring with provisions, and the settlement of Mink Creek arose directly south of Keller's residence in 1873. A predominantly Mormon community upon its founding, Mink Creek at one time boasted a population of 500 residents. However, the town's population has continually declined, and Mink Creek students have been bused to nearby Preston since 1965. The town reportedly draws its name from an area creek, which drew its name from the plethora of mink that was trapped there during the mountain man era.

Franklin
Pop. 641

In the spring of 1860, thirteen Mormon men and some of their families arrived in present-day Franklin. Although the colonizers believed they were in Cache County, Utah, and the town was incorporated as a Utah village in 1868, an 1872 survey revealed that Franklin was in fact not part of Utah at all. Unbeknownst to them at the time, the first settlers had actually founded Idaho's very first permanent white community. It was named after Franklin Richards, a prominent Mormon apostle.

Franklin grew rapidly between 1873 and 1878 when the Utah Northern Railroad established the community as the end of the northern line running from Ogden, Utah. A pit sawmill and later a steam-powered mill was important in providing continous building materials to the city, wooden railroad ties for the railroad, and thousands of board feet of wood used in constructing Salt Lake City's ZCMI building. The area's flour mill provided local residents with a necessary cooking staple and played an integral role in allowing residents to trade surplus flour for Native American buckskins.

As a result of its founding date, Franklin enjoyed several Idaho firsts. The community received the state's first railroad line and first telegraph connection, as well as the first telephone

service. Today, Idaho's first town has preserved several of its original buildings and pioneer relics while standing as a mecca of Mormon history.

H Old Delta Sediments
Milepost 12.9 on State Hwy. 34

Diverted into this valley by lava flows, the Bear River deposited a huge, mostly red clay delta here where it entered a vast inland sea that covered much of Utah.

About 14,500 years ago, its shoreline suddenly went down about 80 feet following an enormous discharge into the Snake River. From then on, it gradually receded to become the Salt Lake. Bear River then had to cut through and erode its old delta, forming the steep sides and gullies you see here today.

H Hatch House
Milepost 1.4 on U.S. Hwy. 91 in the Franklin Historic District; East on Main St. 1 1/2 blocks

In 1874, Bishop L.H. Hatch built a mansion that has been preserved as a fine example of pioneer Idaho architecture.

Idaho's only railroad, serving Montana's thriving mining camps, reached here that year during a time of depression between gold rushes. At the time, Franklin was Idaho's largest city. Two years later, rail construction resumed, and freighters moved on. But Hatch's elegant house remains as a reminder of a bygone era.

H Idaho's Oldest Town
Milepost 1.4 on U.S. Hwy. 91 at Franklin

Franklin was settled April 14, 1860, by Mormon pioneers. The free local museum exhibits a large collection of tools and relics of pioneer days.

The founding of Franklin was part of a well-organized plan of Mormon expansion. Church authorities sent the colonists under Thomas Smart from Provo, Utah. Men of many trades were included in order to make the community self-sufficient. From 1874-77, Franklin was the busy terminus of the Utah Northern Railroad, where freight for the Montana mines was reloaded for the long wagon haul north.

H Bear River Battle
Milepost 13.2 on U.S. Hwy. 91

Very few Indians survived an attack here when the California volunteers trapped and wiped out the Cache Valley Shoshoni.

Friction between the whites and these Indians, who had suffered from too many years of close contact with fur hunters, led P.E. Connor to set out from Salt Lake on a cold winter campaign. The Shoshoni had a strong position along Battle Creek Canyon just north of here. With a loss of about 400, they met the greatest Indian disaster in the entire West, January 29, 1863.

H Utah Northern Railway
Milepost 13.2 on U.S. Hwy. 91

Directly west of this highway, an old 1878 railway grade is still visible, although trains have not used it since 1890.

Jay Gould – a nationally prominent financier and Union Pacific owner – extended Utah Northern service north from Franklin to Montana by 1880. A narrow-gauge line until 1887, it helped build up Cache Valley and accounted for many new Idaho cities and towns farther north. But small, wood-burning locomotives had a hard time ascending this hill. After a more direct route four miles west of here was completed, service north of Preston was abandoned on this grade.

T Little Mountain
Northwest of Franklin

Rising one mile into the Idaho sky, Little Mountain was known to the region's first settlers as Lookout Mountain. Fearing attacks from neighboring Native American villages, pioneers employed professionally trained military scouts to keep watch from the mountaintop for any imminent threat.

T Preston Golf and Country Club
1215 N. 800 E., Preston. 852-2408.

Surrounded by views of the Wasatch Mountains and Wellsville and Malad Ranges, golfers at the Preston Golf and Country Club can play a round on this 18-hole course opened in 1965. The par-72 course is situated on fairly flat terrain, allowing an easy walk for players of all ages. Covering 6,550 yards, the course features fairways lined with both old growth and newly planted trees. The course is open daily March 15 to October 31, and green fees are $11 on weekdays and $15 on weekends.

T The Battle of Bear River Site
Drive on U.S. Hwy. 91 3 miles northwest of Preston to locate a historical marker on the highway's east side; bear west onto the gravel road across from the sign, and proceed 300 yards to a branch in the road; taking the right fork, drive 0.3 miles up the Battle Creek ravine to locate this almost forgotten site.

Tales of fierce encounters between white men and Native Americans spread like wildfire across the American West and became great subjects of interest to U.S. politicians and the military. Although Native Americans did wreak havoc against numerous wagon trains traveling west on the Oregon Trail, white settlers were not blameless. As more and more pioneers arrived in the newly established western territories, the Native Americans felt increasingly threatened as their lands were encroached upon and their resources began to dwindle. At the same time, some unprincipled white men further marred the settlers' reputations. Instances of horse thievery, murder, and rape against their women outraged the Native Americans, and frequency of attacks against the newly established white communities rapidly began to rise.

In the 1850s, Mormon emigrants from Utah began drifting north and established new settlements in southeastern Idaho Territory. Frightened by horror stories of Native American conflict with previous white pioneers, this new wave of settlers decided to follow Brigham Young's advice. Instead of warring with the Indians and hoarding food and supplies, Young encouraged his followers to be generous and kind, supplying the Indians with whatever goods they needed. But as more and more settlers arrived and winter fell, resources dwindled and the Native Americans were the first deprived of assistance. Young's policy soon failed, and murders and robberies against the white settlers began occurring in the mid 1850s and continued into the 1860s.

Learning of the continual skirmishes in Idaho and Utah Territory, General-in-Chief H.W. Halleck sent Colonel Patrick Connor of California to establish Fort Douglas in Salt Lake City for the pioneers' protection. Connor arrived in October 1862 and instantly had a vendetta against the Native Americans. In December, Shoshone-Bannock Indians ambushed a party of miners near Bear River, killing one. Upon hearing of the incident, Connor immediately began planning a counter attack. His campaign would become the deadliest military massacre of Native Americans in U.S. history.

Under the command of Colonel Connor, Major McGarry, and Captain Hoyt, infantry and cavalry from Fort Douglas began marching toward Battle Creek and Bear River on the night of January 28, 1863 and waited until dawn on January 29 to wage their attack. After being taunted by a small party of Shoshone Indians and losing fourteen cavalry in the first assault, Connor had his men regroup and ordered McGarry to flank the Indian position on Battle Creek. Connor's strategy worked, and despite the Native Americans' desperate attempts to defend themselves, the battle was gruesome. After four hours of fighting, Colonel Connor had lost twenty-two men. Despite repeated attempts to surrender, the Shoshone pleas were ignored and an estimated 300 to 400 Shoshone men, women, and children were slaughtered. As if the massacre was not enough, the military also burned seventy tepees, seized 175 horses, and left the few surviving women and children to fend for themselves.

As a result of the massacre, Connor was promoted to the rank of brigadier-general, and the spirit of the Native American people began to crumble. In the summer of 1863, federal peace treaties with five Shoshone tribes were signed at Camp Connor in Idaho and in Tooele Valley, Utah, and the Indians were forced onto reservations.

T Idaho Pioneer Association
Main St., Franklin. 646-2437.

Hailed as the first permanent settlement in Idaho, Franklin is home to a wealth of history dating back to its 1860 founding. Amid the many historic buildings, a log cabin structure constructed in 1937 is home to the Idaho Pioneer Association. The building was designated as the community's Relic Hall, and it displays several artifacts from pioneer days. In addition, Mormon history buffs can find a picture of the Illinois jail where Joseph Smith was murdered, as well as photographs of Franklin's founding pioneer men and women. The free museum is open 10 AM to 12 PM and 1 PM to 5 PM Monday through Friday from May to September.

T Riverdale Resort Hot Springs
Route 2, Preston. 852-0266. From Preston, travel north on U.S. Hwy. 91. At the junction with State Hwy. 36, bear right and proceed 5 miles to the springs. www.riverdaleresort.com

Riverdale Resort Hot Springs is located just six miles north of Preston near the banks of Idaho's famous Bear River. In addition to excellent hunting

and fishing opportunities, the area abounds with natural hot springs. At Riverdale, visitors will find five natural hot springs pools and a junior Olympic size pool filled with naturally warm water. The pool also features the Riverdale Rattler and Python Panic hydro-tube slides as well as a children's area. The hot springs are open year-round from 11 AM to 10 PM daily.

T Worm Creek Opera House
70 S. State St., Preston. 852-0088.

Named after a creek that flows through Preston, the historical Worm Creek Opera House was restored and reopened nearly thirty years ago. The opera house features Northern Cache Valley Theater Guild productions during the summer, including melodramas, plays, and movies. During the winter, community activities, school productions, and special theater guild performances are provided. Reservations are recommended for all events.

T Franklin's Historical Building Tour
Downtown Franklin. Contact the Southeast Idaho Pioneer Country Travel Council at (888) 201-1063.

Distinguished as Idaho's first town of white settlers, Franklin is filled with history dating back to 1860 and several historical buildings left behind by the town's earliest residents. The following buildings have all played an important role in Franklin's long history.

Corner of E. Main and First St. E.
Leland Scarborough and his family were among the many pioneers who flocked to Franklin during the late 19th century for its progressive amenities. As Idaho's first town, Franklin also enjoyed many other firsts, including the state's first telegraph wire, telephone service, and railroad line. Scarborough and his family built this home in 1890.

Relic Hall
Located one-half block from First St. E.
This log-cabin style building was constructed in 1937 and has always been used to preserve Franklin's history and the legacy of the founding pioneer families.

Museum
Adjacent to the Relic Hall one-half block from First St. E.
This two-story stone building dates back to 1895 and was the new site for a growing cooperative general store. Organized by Bishop Lorenzo Hatch in 1868, the Franklin Cooperative Mercantile Institution outgrew its original building and moved to this location in the late 1890s. The store not only provided residents with general goods, but also served as the community tithing house. The Bishop theorized that residents would be more likely to meet their religious offertory duties if they could tithe at the same time they completed their personal shopping. The Franklin Cooperative Mercantile Institution served as one of the first branches of the Mormon owned department store, ZCMI. Today, the building houses a collection of pioneer antiques.

Hatch House
127 E. Main
Lorenzo Hill Hatch was appointed the town's second Mormon bishop in 1863 in succession of Preston Thomas. He also served as Franklin's first mayor and was the first Mormon to serve in Idaho's territorial legislature. To accommodate one of Franklin's most important citizens, his three wives, and their twenty-four children, the two-story

house was constructed in 1872 out of locally quarried sandstone. The Greek Revival style home was the town's largest residence when it was built, and Hatch's descendants occupied the house until the 1940s. While the first floor interior has been extensively changed with the yellow brick addition completed in 1910, the second story is relatively unmodified from its original state. In 1979, the Idaho State Historical Society acquired the house, and there are high hopes that the Hatch House will one day be restored and open to the public for tours.

First City Building
Across the street from the Hatch House on E. Main
This small brick building dates back to 1910. Set on a stone foundation, the square structure served as Franklin's public meeting hall with a jail in the basement.

T Oneida Stake Academy
Corner of East Oneida and First East Sts., Preston. Contact the Southeast Idaho Pioneer Country Travel Council at (888) 201-1063.

In response to the 1885 anti-Mormon Idaho Test Oath barring Church of Jesus Christ of Latter Day Saints followers from participating on Idaho school boards, Salt Lake City LDS Church authorities declared that Mormons should create their own school system. Complying with this decree and wishing to provide residents with better educational opportunities, early members of the Preston community raised $46,000 to build the Oneida Stake Academy. Architect Don Carlos drew up plans for the Romanesque Revival style building, and construction was completed from 1889 to 1894 under the direction of German immigrant and stonemason, John Nuffer.

During its early years, the Academy required principals and teachers to be upstanding members of the LDS Church. In 1908, sports were added to the school's offerings, and in 1927, the Church sold the Academy to the city for use as the public Preston High School. The facility was used as a school through the early 1990s and has been listed on the National Register of Historic Places. Historians estimate that the Oneida Stake Academy is the oldest of thirty-five such Mormon educational academies in Canada, Mexico, Arizona, Wyoming, Idaho, and Utah. In 2003, the Academy was moved to its new location in Benson Park, and plans are in place to restore the building into a community center.

T The Shoshone Trail
Near Preston. Contact the Southeast Idaho Pioneer Country Travel Council at (888) 201-1063. From Preston, drive 3 miles south on U.S. Hwy. 91. Turn onto County Rd. 406 (Cub River Rd.) and continue 12 miles before turning onto Willow Flat Rd.

Long before white settlers arrived in Idaho, the Shoshone Indians called the scenic territory home. In both hunting and traveling expeditions, the Shoshone Indians used this historic trail to traverse the Wasatch Mountain Range separating the Cache and Bear Lake Valleys. When Mormon settlers arrived in Idaho, the trail was used as a mail route between the two regions. Today, a commemorative marker located near Thomas Spring on Willow Flat Road highlights the trail's history.

T Historic Cowley Home
100 S. 100 East St., Preston. Contact the Southeast Idaho Pioneer Country Travel Council at (888) 201-1063.

Matthias Foss Cowley was one of the first Mormon settlers in Franklin County and quickly emerged as a community religious leader. Cowley's

Ezra Taft Benson Home and Gravesite

Franklin area farmers founded the now nearly non-existent agricultural community of Whitney in the late 1860s. The small town, however, produced a recognizable leader. Ezra Taft Benson was born and raised in Whitney before being appointed Secretary of Agriculture in President Eisenhower's Administration. Benson's leadership career continued as he acted as President of the Church of Jesus Christ of Latter Day Saints from 1985 to 1994. His boyhood home is still visible at 2003 East 800 South Street, and he is buried in the nearby community cemetery.

wife, Abbie Hyde, gave birth to Matthew Cowley in 1897 in the family home. This stone residence still stands in downtown Preston and honors the lives of both father and son who served as Apostles in the LDS Church.

T Emigration Canyon
6 miles north of Mink Creek on State Hwy. 36.

Emigration Canyon winds through the Cache National Forest and was named after the large groups of Mormon settlers who rushed to Idaho during the mid 1800s. When Brigham Young, leader of the Church of Jesus Christ of Latter Day Saints, escorted Mormon followers through the area in 1847, he reportedly declared Emigration Canyon and the surrounding area as the region where the Mormon religion would be spread. A monument in the canyon marks the spot where Young made his declaration. In the 1860s, pioneers used the canyon to travel from Franklin, Idaho to the Bear Lake Valley. The area was so heavily used in early days that building a railroad route leading through Emigration Canyon from Idaho to Utah was seriously considered.

Today, traffic has quieted and Emigration Canyon is now a popular recreational destination. Mountain marathons, hiking, and cross-country skiing are all popular area pastimes.

TV Oneida Narrows Reservoir
At the junction of State Hwy.s 34 and 36, proceed on State Hwy. 36 approximately 3 miles. Turn on Oneida Narrows-Bear River Rd., and continue to the reservoir. Contact the Upper Snake River District BLM Office at 478-6340.

Situated in southeastern Idaho and originally created for energy purposes, Oneida Narrows Reservoir covers 515 acres. While trout fishing is especially popular in the region, this reservoir has never possessed a healthy trout population. As a result, the reservoir has been stocked with walleye since 1976. This annual stock has created an ever-increasing population of sizeable walleye. Anglers also report catching yellow perch. In addition to fishing, the site is host to motorboating, jet-skiing, waterskiing, and camping.

TV Willow Flats
15 miles east of Preston. Contact the Southeastern Idaho Pioneer Country Travel Council at (888) 201-1063.

Nestled beside the spring-fed Cub River in the Caribou-Targhee National Forest, Willow Flats offers a peaceful atmosphere amid beautiful scenery. Dominated by a landscape of willows, pines, and cottonwood trees, the hills surrounding Willow Flats provide a colorful spectrum of wildflowers during the early summer months. The area is also a popular picnicking and fishing site open year-round.

V Condie Reservoir
North of Preston on State Hwy. 34. Contact the Idaho Department of Game and Fish at 334-3700. From Preston, drive north of the State Hwy. 34 and 36 Junctions. Bear west on Winder Reservoir Rd., and locate Condie directly north of Winder Reservoir.

Since 1990, Condie Reservoir has been developed for trophy largemouth bass. While it is likely that anglers will catch a bass over twenty inches, regulations mandate the release of all bass under twenty inches. The reservoir is also full of bluegills, yellow perch, and hatchery rainbow trout, and fishing is available year-round.

V Glendale Reservoir
North of Preston. Contact the Idaho Department of Fish and Game at (800) 232-4703. From Preston, drive north on State Hwy. 34, bearing east at the Sportsman's Access Rd. Continue 4 miles to the reservoir.

With willow-enclosed banks, Glendale Reservoir is best suited for boat fishers. Although small, the reservoir reports the highest bass catch rates in the region with bass here growing one to two inches per year. The waters also support a large population of bluegill, rainbow trout, and stocked adult white crappie. The area is open year-round to anglers and wildlife viewers free of charge, the only restriction being that all bass less than sixteen inches must be released.

V Foster Reservoir
Near Preston. Contact the Idaho Department of Game and Fish at 334-3700.

Fairly small in size, Foster Reservoir is an ideal destination for anglers and canoe enthusiasts. The reservoir is closed to motorboats, but float tubes, canoes, and kayaks are allowed on the peaceful waters. Every spring and fall, the lake is stocked with rainbow trout. Other present fish species include largemouth bass and bluegill perch. The reservoir is open year-round for fishing.

M Preston Chamber of Commerce
49 N. State St.- A, Preston. 852-2703. www.prestonidaho.org

22 *Food, Lodging*

Grace
Pop. 973

The original name given to this small community was Riverside, but after that was rejected by the Post Office Department in 1894, it was named Grace, for the wife of D.W. Standrod, a government agent residing in Blackfoot. The first settlers to arrive in Grace Valley faced a difficult task in terms of gaining water rights in the valley. They had to figure out a way to get the Bear River water from the west side of the valley to the east side. Their first attempt, in 1895, utilized wooden flumes. This worked well in the summer months, but heavy winter snows demolished them. The wooden flumes were thus only a temporary solution, and the residents knew the only permanent solution to perfect their water rights would be to dig a tunnel through a problematic lava-rock hill and run an aqueduct through it. The Morrison-Knudsen Corporation was hired, and two brothers started digging the tunnel, one starting from each side of the hill. After meeting in the middle, the aqueduct finally became a reality in 1917. A steel pipeline now transports the water four miles from Grace Dam to a Black Canyon power plant located on the Bear River.

Thatcher
Pop. 50

John B. Thatcher, a prominent Mormon bishop who later served as an Idaho senator, serves as this town's namesake. Settled on the Bear River in 1870, this Mormon community waited thirty years before acquiring postal services in 1900.

H Range Wars
Milepost 31.4 on State Hwy. 34

Armed cattle ranchers delayed farm settlement here for six years before a permanent farm community was organized in 1872.

This kind of conflict occurred in widely scattered Western areas when farm crops displaced range land. Families of early farm pioneers still occupy holdings here that are well over a century old, although many of them finally shifted from planting crops to raising cattle after winning their battle against early stock herders.

T Central Links Golf Course
1750 Gibson Ln., Grace. 425-3233. www.centrallinksgolf.com

Located in the Caribou Highlands of Idaho's Gem Valley, the Central Links Golf Course offers golfers a secluded atmosphere surrounded by farmland and lava rock formations. Family operated since its origination in 1996, this course draws its name from the original community name, "Central." The 9-hole course is continually expanding and offers target golf that is enjoyable to players of all experience levels. The course is open daily from April 1 to October 15 with reasonably priced green fees.

T Maple Grove Hot Springs
11386 N. Oneida Narrows Rd., Thatcher. 851-1137. www.maplegrovehotsprings.com

Maple Grove Hot Springs, nestled beside the Bear River in the scenic Oneida Narrows Canyon, has a long and varied history. Native Americans discovered these pools in the 1800s and used them for ceremonial and recreational purposes. In 1910, the Charles Hopkins family arrived in Idaho, staking their claim near the pools and turning the hot springs into a commercial area. The business venture was highly successful, and the pools became known as Hopkins Hot Springs. Utilizing their profit, the Hopkins built a wood-sided swimming pool that, although updated, is still in use today. They also were responsible for the creation of an additional pool. Since European Americans refused to soak with Native Americans, the Hopkins constructed the second pool to segregate their clientele and keep all customers happy.

In 1921, the Hopkins sold the claim to the Jepsen family who in turn sold the site in 1945 to the Kershaws. The Kershaw family lovingly cared for the springs, christening them with their current name. However, when the Kershaws were forced to sell the springs, the area suffered. A succession of owners and the end of commercialized service in 1975 brought significant vandalism and neglect that would cause Maple Grove Hot Springs to lay in ruins for several years. When the current owners acquired the property, the area was restored, and the springs were reopened to the public in 2003.

Maple Grove Hot Springs features three natural, therapeutic hot pools boasting different temperatures. Fresh water continually flows in and out of the pools to keep it natural, and the pools are also cleaned frequently throughout the month. Maple Grove Hot Springs is open year-round from 10 AM to 10 PM daily.

T Niter Ice Cave
From Grace, travel south on State Hwy. 34. The well-signed cave is located approximately 3 miles from Grace off the main highway Contact the Southeast Idaho Pioneer Country Travel Council at (888) 201-1063.

In June 1898, early pioneer John A. Dalton homesteaded 160 acres of land southwest of present day Grace. Much to his surprise and delight, Dalton discovered the famous Niter Cave on his property. Created from a collapsed basalt lava tube that once flowed thousands of years ago, the cave stretches 3/8 of a mile beneath the surface. After locating the cave and realizing its refrigeration potential, Dalton constructed a ladder used to enter the cave's food refrigeration area. This historic entry point, nicknamed "window," was situated 650 feet east of the cave's present day main opening. The highway. covers the "window" today.

Although the cave has not been commercially developed, the site is well-marked and easily accessible during spring, summer, and fall. Not only does the cave provide visitors with a glimpse of Idaho history, but it also offers an interesting look at Idaho's geological landscape.

T Last Chance Dam
North of Grace. Contact the Southeast Idaho Pioneer Country Travel Council at (888) 201-1063. From Grace, drive north on the Pioneer Historic Byway. At Last Chance Ln., bear east and proceed to the dam.

Early settlers in Grace faced innumerable problems in securing continuous water flow and irrigation to the community. After several failed efforts, the community gave it "one last chance" and succeeded. A dam was created to back up the Bear River, and flumes were used to carry the water from the dam site to the settlement. Today, this 100 year old log dam built by the town's first pioneers is still used as an integral part of securing Grace's waterflow.

T Gem Valley Performing Arts Center
654 S. Main St., Grace. 425-3731 or 425-3785.

Recently constructed near Grace High School, the Gem Valley Performing Arts Center can accommodate up to 520 individuals and is sponsored by the non-profit Gem Valley Performing Arts Committee. The center's goal is to bring national entertainment to Gem Valley, increase appreciation of the arts, and provide a stage where local talent can perform and be recognized. The center features a variety of performances year-round including comedy, theater, ballet, musicals, and vaudeville. Nationally ranked musical groups from all genres frequently play to a packed house. Ticket prices vary according to event, and advance tickets are recommended.

T Grace Fish Hatchery
390 Hatchery Rd., Grace. 427-6364. On State Hwy. 34, travel 7 miles south of Grace through Niter. At Fish Hatchery Rd., bear left, and follow the brown signs leading to the hatchery.

Operating since 1946, the Grace Fish Hatchery raises rainbow trout, lake trout, three different species of cutthroat trout, and splake. A freshwater spring supplies the facility with its water. The hatchery includes sixteen indoor vats used for incubating fish eggs, sixteen small raceways, four medium raceways, and six larger raceways used for catchable sized fish. The hatchery is open daily

from 7 AM to 7 PM, and guided tours are available upon request. In addition, the facility features a shaded picnic area and access to excellent fishing on nearby Whiskey Creek.

T The Legacy of State Hwy. 34
Southeastern Idaho's State Hwy. 34 runs 33 miles through Hay Valley and is characterized by its farming heritage. The road features more large wooden barns than any other stretch of Idaho highway of similar length.

TV Black Canyon
Approximately 1 mile west of Grace. Contact the Southeast Idaho Pioneer Country Travel Council at (888) 201-1063.

Twisting and turning through Grace Valley, the rapid waters of the Bear River not diverted for irrigation have carved out the impressive Black Canyon. Beginning narrowly at 100 feet deep, Black Canyon expands downstream into a large gorge measuring nearly 1,000 feet deep. Cutting through solid lava rock, the canyon waters are nationally recognized as one of the most difficult kayak runs in America. In addition, a set of deep pools and gentle terraces near the Sportman's Access Area on River Road makes the canyon a popular fishing destination.

V Bear River Drainage
Nestled in southeastern Idaho near the Utah border, the Bear River and its tributaries wind nearly 525 miles. Main tributaries in the Bear River drainage include the Malad and Cub Rivers in addition to Bloomington, Eight Mile, Georgetown, Mink, Montpelier, Paris, and St. Charles Creeks. Another major tributary, Thomas Fork, is highly regarded for its unique population of Bonneville cutthroat trout. Most of the other tributaries feature wild brook, brown, and cutthroat trout that are capable of self-sustenance.

Although standard irrigation practices have significantly decreased fish populations in this drainage area as a whole, a few irrigation reservoirs support largemouth bass, yellow perch, and bluegill. The largest reservoir in the drainage is Bear Lake, which encompasses 32,000 acres in the southeastern corner of Idaho.

M Grace and Gem Valley Chamber of Commerce
PO Box 214, Grace. 425-3912.
www.graceidaho.com; info@graceidaho.com

23 Lodging

Lava Hot Springs
Pop. 521

Long before whites arrived in southern Idaho, Shoshone and Bannock Indians soaked in these warm waters located along the Portneuf River. Considering the water a gift of the Great Spirit, the tribes created a truce and used the area as a neutral gathering spot.

Eventually, the Hudspeth Cutoff along the Oregon Trail passed by, and the springs became a

popular resting point along the trail. When whites began to actually settle the area in the 1880s, they christened the fledgling town Dempsey in honor of an Irish-born trapper who frequently camped in the area before migrating to Montana Territory. At that time, the area technically still belonged to the Bannock-Shoshone Indian tribes. But when the U.S. government discovered that the area was quickly gaining popularity as a potential white Idaho community, 183 acres of land was purchased and ceded from the reservation, including the natural hot springs.

In 1911, Englishman John Hall platted out Lava Hot Springs, and the town was incorporated in 1915. Area recreation began immediately, and a log structure was constructed over a portion of the hot springs. As the site became more frequently used and more settlers were attracted to the area, mud baths and indoor-outdoor swimming pools were added and enclosed in the State Natatorium. In addition to the forty-five by ninety foot indoor pool, the elaborate building also contained sixty-two dressing rooms and a three-sided balcony capable of holding 300 spectators.

Since its official establishment, the community has catered to tourists and locals alike with its small-town resort atmosphere. With more than 20,000 people reportedly visiting the site in 1924, word spread about the area. The town and its natural relaxation properties continue to lure record numbers of visitors each year.

H Lava Hot Springs
Milepost 371.2 on U.S. Hwy. 30

Long before white men discovered these springs, September 9, 1812, Indians gathered here to use the free hot water.

Except where they found hot springs, prehistoric Indians had a hard time getting hot water. They wove water-tight baskets into which they put heated rocks. Here they had plenty of hot water for baths and for processing hides without going to all the work of heating baskets. This was one of their major campgrounds, especially in the winter. After 1868, when they began to stay mostly on the Fort Hall Indian Reservation, this spot lost its importance as a winter camp.

T Thunder Canyon Golf Course
9898 E. Merrick Rd., Lava Hot Springs. 776-5048.
www.golflava.com

Located 2 miles south of Lava Hot Springs Mountain views and farmland surround this scenic, rural course established in 1964. Spanning 3,177 yards, this 9-hole par 35 course features large greens constructed on rolling hills. A creek and two canals create water hazards throughout much of the course. In 1998, the course was completely rerouted and now includes up to four sets of tees per hole. The course is open daily from April 15 to October 15 with green fees reasonably priced at $15.

T South Bannock County Historical Center and Museum
110 E. Main St., Lava Hot Springs. 776-5254.

The South Bannock County Historical Center and Museum is committed to preserving and presenting local heritage in southern Idaho. The informative rotating exhibits focus on regional history, including the history of small communities such as Swan Lake, Virginia, and McCammon. The permanent "Trails, Trappers, Trains, and Travelers" exhibit explores how Shoshone and Bannock Indians, mountain men and the fur trade, 1800s wagon trains, the railroad, and tourists shaped South

Bannock County into what it is today. The museum is open 12 PM to 5 PM daily with free admission.

T Lava Hot Springs
431 E. Main St., Lava Hot Springs. 776-5221 or (800) 423-8597. www.lavahotsprings.com

"Poha-Ba," meaning 'land of healing waters' was the first term given to the natural warm pools found at Lava Hot Springs. Utilized by Shoshone-Bannock Indians, the hot springs were historically peaceful grounds shared with all in neutrality as a place of ceremonial worship and recreation. The hot springs were originally part of the Fort Hall Reservation, but in the late 1800s, the U.S. government amended this treaty and purchased 178 acres of land including the springs. In 1902, a federal act granted the springs to Idaho State and its people for public use, and in 1911, the Idaho Legislature approved $500 in funding to develop the area. Seven years later, a state natatorium was constructed, and the springs' long legacy of public use began.

With water that geologists say has maintained a consistent temperature of 110 degrees for 50 million years, these hot pools are both sulfur and odor free. Several pools are situated in a hollow near the Portneuf River, combining relaxation with beautiful scenery. The area is open year round except Thanksgiving and Christmas.

T Lava Hot Springs Historical Walking Tour
Downtown Lava Hot Springs. Contact the Lava Hot Springs Chamber of Commerce at 776-5500.

With a pioneer history dating back to the 1880s, Lava Hot Springs features numerous buildings capturing the area's rich heritage. Although the community is primarily known as a resort town, these buildings are well-preserved and add historical depth to the famous community.

Lava Hot Springs' First House
One block south of Center St. on Elm St.
John Hall, English immigrant and community founder, built the town's first home in 1910 in a log cabin style. Now covered with stucco, the small home is located behind the Royal Hotel.

Whitestone Hotel
Main St. and E. Second Ave.
Featuring a Renaissance revival architectural design, the Whitestone Hotel was constructed by the Maranoni brothers using locally quarried sandstone. The hotel opened on July 4th, 1919 and featured a ballroom, cabaret, theater, elaborate rooms, and free mineral baths. The hotel and theater closed in the 1960s.

Riverside Inn
E. Second Ave.
This L-shaped, Georgian revival hotel faces the Portneuf River and opened in 1914. William Godfrey, a local rancher, filed a claim to use the area's naturally hot water and opened the hotel to cater to tourists' intrigue with local mineral hot springs. Today, the hotel has been restored, and four mineral hot tubs are still available onsite.

Historic State Natatorium
Located near the Portneuf River Footbridge
In 1920, the State Natatorium was constructed in Lava Hot Springs and operated until the more modern complex was established in 1968, At the height of its popularity, the natatorium featured mud baths and indoor-outdoor hot springs swimming pools drawing residents and visitors from miles around. Although not open to the public, the structure retains its original features, including the roof supported by massive wooden beams.

V Chesterfield Reservoir
Near Chesterfield. In Bancroft, cross the railroad tracks at the Bancroft Post Office, and proceed 11 miles on Chesterfield Rd. to historical Chesterfield. The reservoir is located nearby. Contact the Idaho Department of Game and Fish at 334-3700.

Also commonly referred to as Portneuf Reservoir, Chesterfield Reservoir encompasses 1,600 acres and is a popular local fishery. Open year-round and complete with two boat ramps, the waters are known for hatchery raised rainbow, cutthroat, brown, and hybrid trout species.

TV Portneuf River
Southeastern Idaho. Contact the Southeastern Idaho Pioneer Country Travel Council at (888) 201-1063.

Commemorating the life of a mountain man trapper murdered by Native Americans along its banks in the 1800s, the Portneuf River originates near the Chesterfield Reservoir on the Fort Hall Indian Reservation. From there, the river cuts through the sixty-mile Portneuf Mountain Range and ends at the American Falls Reservoir. Filled with a mixture of hatchery and wild rainbow trout, brown trout, and cutthroat trout, the river and its tributaries cover 297 miles and provide a popular angling destination. Major tributaries and reservoirs in the Portneuf drainage include Dempsey, Mink, Marsh, Pebble, Rapid, and Toponce Creeks and Chesterfield, Twenty-Four Mile, Hawkins, and Wiregrass Reservoirs. Although the river section stretching from Pocatello to Marsh Creek receives little use due to nearly non-existent trout populations, the remaining river sections are frequently visited year-round.

In addition to angling, the Portneuf River and its tributaries support kayaking and wildlife viewing.

TL Lava Hot Springs Inn & Spa
94 E. Portneuf Ave., Lava Hot Springs. 776-5830 or (800) 527-5830. www.lavahotspringsinn.com

Whether you're looking for a romantic getaway, a healthful retreat, or a soul-soothing afternoon, come to Lava Hot Springs Inn and Spa. Situated near the Portneuf River, this European style inn was crafted in the 1920s as a hospital. Today, the facility features three buildings and five free-flowing hot mineral water outdoor pools open to the general public. Unwind in the eighty foot long Therapy Pool, soak beside the Portneuf River in the hot River Pool, relax to the sound of fountains in the Aztec Pool, or take an icy dip in the Cold Plunge Pool. Overnight guests can select from a variety of lodging styles including Jacuzzi suites. Pets are allowed for an extra $10, and all lodging includes admission to the mineral pools and a full breakfast buffet.

V Portneuf River Tubing
Downtown Lava Hot Springs. Contact the Southeast Idaho Pioneer Country Travel Council at (888) 201-1063.

Tubing the Portneuf River in southeastern Idaho is big business and a popular family activity during

the summer months. The one-mile run across the shallow river begins on the eastern edge of town and takes approximately ten to fifteen minutes to complete. At the end of the run, tubers can either walk back to the starting point or take a community shuttle to the launch area. Several companies rent both personal and group tubes for the activity with average rental prices starting at $3 per hour.

M Lava Realty Services
56 E. Main, Lava Hot Springs. 776-5941. www.lavarealty.com

Picture yourself owning your dream house or a vacation home in one of America's most appealing hot springs recreational areas. With the help of Lava Realty Services, your dreams can become a reality. Situated amidst clean air and foothill mountain treasures, Lava Realty Services is the only real estate office operating in Lava Hot Springs. Idaho native and broker, Janice Poole, has been in the real estate business since 1974 and takes great pride in offering unique real estate opportunities. Lava Realty Services is actively involved with the Chamber of Commerce and the local senior center, and her familiarity with the area lends the expertise you need in finding the perfect property. Coordinating with other area realty offices, Lava Realty Services strives to meet every customer's distinctive tastes and needs.

M Lava Hot Springs Chamber of Commerce
110 E. Main St., Lava Hot Springs. 776-5500. www.lavahotsprings.org; findout@lavahotsprings.org

24

Bancroft
Pop. 382

Originating in 1885 under the name "Squaw," this small community was established with the arrival of a band of Arkansas farmers. The town was renamed in 1905 after Oregon Short Line Railroad Vice President, William H. Bancroft. Bancroft retains its heritage as a farming community.

H Hudspeth's Cutoff
Milepost 376.2 on U.S. Hwy. 30

Here, at a landmark called Sheep Rock, Hudspeth's Cutoff left the Oregon Trail and struck straight west to California.

Stampeding 49'ers would try anything to save miles and time in their rush for California gold. Earlier emigrant wagons headed northwest to Fort Hall, but on July 19, 1849, Benoni Hudspeth and John Myers led their party west along an old Indian trail they had checked out across rough country in 1848. Their difficult cut-off immediately became popular, though it saved only about 25 miles and two days' travel.

H Chesterfield
Milepost 378.8 on U.S. Hwy. 30

Farmhouses and pioneer buildings of an old Mormon community have been preserved at Chesterfield, 16 miles north of here.

Located in 1879 by a Mormon bishop, Chesterfield offered a good opportunity to farmers from Utah, which then was becoming overcrowded. Within two years, a group of settlers helped construct a nearby railroad that made their town grow to more than 400 people. Chesterfield thrived for more than a generation before new trends in farming and transportation led to its decline.

T Chesterfield
In Bancroft, cross the railroad tracks at the Bancroft Post Office, and proceed 11 miles on Chesterfield Road to the historical site. 648-7177 or 648-7395. www.chesterfieldfoundation.org

Situated in the Portneuf Valley, Chesterfield was an early Mormon settlement established by Chester Call and his nephew, Christian Nelson, in 1879. In search of rich grazing land for his horses, Call found the Chesterfield area ideal and moved from Bountiful, Utah to establish a homestead. Soon, Call had convinced twelve other families from Bountiful to join him in hopes of creating a new Mormon outpost in Idaho Territory.

Named after its founder, Chesterfield was laid out over thirty-five ten-acre blocks. In 1884, Chesterfield's LDS Ward was officially recognized and residents numbered nearly 400. During its heyday, nearly 80% of the residents were direct lineal descendants of Chester Call and his forefather, Cyril Call (1785-1873) or married to a descendant. The rest of the population was comprised of friends Call knew before moving to the area.

Although the town thrived for over two decades, events during the early 1900s painted a dismal future for Chesterfield. The Carey Land Act, World War I, and the Great Depression were disastrous for Chesterfield, and the town was abandoned in search of better prospects. Today, the entire site is listed on the National Register of Historic Places. Twenty-seven original structures, all but two of which were constructed before 1910, showcase a variety of architectural and building styles. The site is open for tours during the summer months.

V Twenty-four Mile Creek Reservoir
In Bancroft, cross the railroad tracks at the Bancroft Post Office, and proceed 11 miles on Chesterfield Road to historical Chesterfield. The reservoir is located nearby. Contact the Idaho Department of Game and Fish at 334-3700.

Measuring forty-four acres and open to anglers year-round, Twenty-four Mile Creek Reservoir was

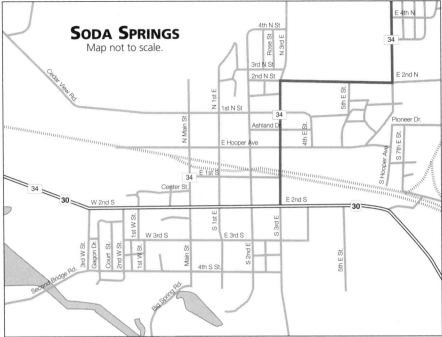

SODA SPRINGS
Map not to scale.

established for trophy trout fishing. Rainbow, cutthroat, and brook trout populate the waters with average fish lengths measuring fifteen to nineteen inches. Anglers must be aware that only artificial flies and lures and one barbless hook are allowed.

25 Food, Lodging

Soda Springs
Pop. 3,381

Soda Springs was named after the area's numerous bubbling springs and the unique soda deposit rock formations surrounding the region. John C. Fremont and a man named Wyeth initially called the location Beer Springs in 1832 after a spring that contained naturally carbonated salt water. In fact, some parched Oregon Trail pioneers who stopped here to rest actually believed some of the springs tasted like beer! Despite the town's early moniker, the name was changed to its present title sometime before the community's appearance on an 1859 territorial map.

Today, the Alexander Reservoir unfortunately covers many of the springs for which the area first became noted. The original town site, which began as Camp Connor in 1863, is also covered. The fort was home to Colonel Patrick Connor and

the soldiers who led the notorious Bear River Massacre, as well as 160 followers involved in the Morrisite Rebellion. The Morrisites followed their leader Joseph Morris, who shared revelations with Brigham Young regarding theological error. The Mormon religion rebuked Morris, and thereafter he and his 160 followers left town. They first went to General Patrick Connor's Camp Douglas in 1862, then on to Soda Springs, near Camp Connor, in 1863.

Although an area post office opened in 1865, the town didn't really take hold until Brigham Young and an associate purchased enough acreage to accommodate twelve families in the town's present site. When these families moved north from Utah and the Oregon Short Line Railroad arrived, the present townsite sprung to life. Today, the area is still known for its bubbling springs, as well as its vast amounts of phosphate ore.

Conda
Pop. 200

The Anaconda Copper Company founded Conda as a model industrial town in 1920. The town served as a home base for employees of the company's nearby phosphate mine. The name was a derivative of the company itself, and the company built about seventy houses, a church, school, and store to lure people to the town's isolated location. Since 1959, the J.R. Simplot Company has owned and operated the phosphate mine at Conda. The open-pit mine is about thirteen miles long. After the ore is harvested, upgraded, and calcined, it is shipped to Simplot's Pocatello fertilizer company.

H Bear River Lava
Milepost 399.9 on U.S. Hwy. 30 at the Soda Point Power Plant

Until about 28,000 years ago, the Bear River used to flow northwest from here through the Portneuf Canyon into the Snake River.

Lava eruptions blocked that route, diverting the Bear River south into what is now Salt Lake. At that time, a large inland sea – known as Lake Bonneville – covered much of Utah. Additional water from the Bear River helped it overflow into the Snake River before a change in climate dried it up about 8,000 years ago.

THE MORRISITE WAR OF 1862

Soda Springs owes its founding to

religious turmoil in Utah Territory and an ensuing series of tragic events that challenged individuals' faith and resulted in a number of deaths, imprisonment, and displacement. At the heart of this bitter moment in history are the Mormon Church and a man named Joseph Morris. As turning points in both Utah and Idaho's religious landscapes, these events remain a hotbed of controversy.

The Man Known as Praying Joe

Joseph Morris, nicknamed "Praying Joe" for his continuous search of solace through prayer, was born in 1824 in England and was converted to the Church of Jesus Christ of Latter Day Saints at age twenty-three. Shortly thereafter, Joseph married his first wife, Mary Thorpe, and both decided to immigrate to America's Utah Territory where the Mormon religion was flourishing. After spending time in Missouri, the Morris' arrived in Salt Lake City in autumn 1853. Although things went smoothly for the couple upon first arrival, it wasn't long before Joseph's troubles began. At the urging of the ward bishop, Mary left Joseph, taking their child and the family's belongings. Remarried in 1855, Joseph's second wife divorced him within six months. Leaving Salt Lake City behind, Joseph moved to Provo, Utah during the spring of 1857 and married Elizabeth Jones. Enthused with Utah's religious awakening, Joseph became a passionate teacher, determined to make others aware of the evils he saw in the Utah Territory. Joseph's newfound career marked the beginning of his long demise and conflict with church authority.

The Conflict Begins

Joseph never learned to accept the early Mormon doctrine of polygamy, and in his new teaching role, Joseph began relaying his conviction that polygamy was simply the church's means of sanctioning adultery. Within weeks, Joseph was stripped of his teaching title, the local bishop and ward members abandoned their friendships with him, and yet another wife left him. Turning to his habitual practice of prayer, Joseph began receiving revelations in 1857 indicating that he was to become a church prophet. Inspired, Joseph began writing letters to Church President Brigham Young, requesting that a dual church presidency be split between them. His letters were never answered.

Drifting from Provo across Utah Territory, Joseph continued to experience revelations, and by 1860, he was positive that the Mormon Church's leadership was under the influence of Satan. Subsequently, Joseph began writing letters to Brigham Young, advising him that he was

wandering off-course from correct theological doctrine. At the same time, Joseph began sharing his revelations along his travels to Slaterville, Utah, and a small group of followers joined him. After successfully converting the ward bishop in Warm Springs, Utah, the group settled in Slaterville and the new faith began to spread.

Church officials in Salt Lake City quickly learned of this faction, and in a February 11, 1861 meeting in Slaterville, Morris and seventeen of his followers were excommunicated from the church after stating their convictions. These excommunications were exactly what Morris needed to start his new church.

The Founding of the Morrisites

Joseph Morris officially organized his new church on April 6, 1861 on a foundation of a few Mormon beliefs and a set of new principles revealed to him throughout his revelations. Among the Morrisites' beliefs were a firm conviction that the second coming of Christ was near, a rejection of polygamy and racism, a belief in reincarnation, rejection of personal property as all things belonged to God, and a priesthood that was open to both men and women. With these beliefs and his fervent speeches, Joseph's appeal and his church's following grew quickly. Within months, his congregation included a thousand members, even though the Morrisites faced continuous threats from Mormon followers in the area.

Settling down in the Kingston Fort near the mouth of Weber Canyon, Joseph ordered that an eighteen-inch thick wall be constructed six feet high around the entirety of the community. Joseph's plan never fully materialized, however, as the Morrisites were at the center of constant attacks. The community's stock was frequently stolen, threats were made against the town's food supply, and some visitors even attended Morrisite worship services with guns and knives poised for attack. After one particular incident in March 1862, the Morrisite community declared themselves immune from civil law and authority, and from that moment on, continued to reject any civil notices from outside individuals.

Uprisings Among the Morrisite Followers

In addition to outside attacks, Joseph was also plagued with a growing number of dissidents inside his community. Many of the original followers began questioning Joseph's authority after his visions of doomsday never materialized, and there was a growing dissatisfaction about property doctrines. When three followers attempted to escape the commune, they were quickly caught and imprisoned in the community. To handle both outsider and insider uprisings, Joseph established an army on May 16, 1862.

When the imprisoned men's wives appealed to authorities to intervene, Justice John Kinney sent a decree to Joseph declaring his actions ille-

gal. Morris promptly disregarded this document. In response, Justice Kinney ordered Robert T. Burton, deputy territorial marshal, to lead an armed group of men to Kingston Fort to confront the issue. Leaving Salt Lake City on June 12, 1862, Burton arrived at the fort with approximately one thousand armed men at his side the following day. Although Burton expected that Joseph would surrender after this impressive show of force, Joseph instead called his followers to worship. Growing impatient, Burton ordered the first cannonball fired. The siege was on.

The Morrisite Tragedy

As cannonballs crashed into the church and several of the members were injured or killed, Joseph ordered the rest of his followers home where they were to protect themselves as best as possible. Joseph's community was significantly outnumbered. His poorly equipped army consisted of only 150 men, and only a handful of the other residents owned guns. After three dreary days of waiting out the enemy, the Morrisites raised their flag of surrender on June 15, 1862 to avoid any further confrontation with the approaching riflemen. Noticing the flag, deputy marshal Burton rode into the fort. Although Joseph's followers agreed to surrender, Joseph would not. Upon Burton's demands, Joseph adamantly refused time and again, and a scene of chaos soon enveloped the town. As the gunfire quieted, Joseph and three others lay dead, along with several others who were wounded. On June 16, Burton and his men marched ninety Morrisite prisoners back to Salt Lake City where they were sentenced from five to fifteen years in jail. Brigham Young reputedly rejoiced at the outcome, stating that the Morrisites were akin to Satan and could never reenter the Mormon Church.

After territorial governor Stephen S. Hardy pardoned the prisoners, the displaced Morrisites found refuge in Utah's Camp Douglas under the direction of General Patrick Connor. Realizing the gravity of the situation and sympathizing with their plight, Connor took 160 members of the Morrisite faith with him and his troops to Idaho Territory. In May 1863, Connor and the Morrisites arrived in present day Soda Springs. Under the protection of soldiers stationed at Camp Connor, the dissidents from the Mormon Church established the community of Morristown in honor of their fallen leader. The community thrived for two years, but after seasons of meager crops, the abandonment of Camp Connor, and the arrival of Mormons in the new community of Soda Springs, many of Morristown's residents moved. Despite their tragic history, the Morrisites were responsible for the initial founding of economic and agricultural activity in Soda Springs, and several Morrisite graves can still be found in the Soda Springs cemetery.

Soda Springs	Jan	Feb	March	April	May	June	July	Aug	Sep	Oct	Nov	Dec	Annual	
Average Max. Temperature (F)		30.4	32.5	42.0	54.1	63.7	73.8	83.7	82.7	72.1	58.9	41.3	31.3	55.5
Average Min. Temperature (F)		8.9	10.2	19.2	26.5	34.2	39.8	44.7	44.0	36.0	26.6	18.4	9.1	26.5
Average Total Precipitation (in.)		1.11	1.14	1.34	1.28	2.29	1.35	1.25	1.28	1.25	1.24	1.15	1.06	15.76
Average Total Snowfall (in.)		11.1	8.6	7.6	3.1	0.5	0.1	0.0	0.0	0.0	1.1	5.8	10.4	48.2
Average Snow Depth (in.)		9	9	4	0	0	0	0	0	0	0	1	5	2

H John Bidwell
Milepost 399.9 on U.S. Hwy. 30 at the Soda Point Power Plant

In 1840, John Bidwell began to assemble emigrants from Missouri to open a road to California, and a year later he set out with a party of 69 Pacific Coast pioneers.

When they reached here, August 12, 1841, half of his group decided to go northwest to Oregon instead. His California crew turned south down the Bear River to try a terrible route west of Salt Lake. So, Joseph R. Chiles returned east in 1849 to find a practical California Trail across Idaho through Fort Hall and Granite Pass.

H Soda Springs
Milepost 403.8 on U.S. Hwy. 30 at Corrigan Park

In this area is a group of springs famous to Oregon Trail travelers, most of whom stopped to try the "acid taste and effervescing gasses" of the waters.

Earlier fur traders, often less elegantly, called the place "Beer Springs" after one spring whose water tasted "like lager beer...only flat." Another, Steamboat Springs, made sounds "exactly resembling… a high pressure steam engine." Both springs are now drowned in the modern reservoir, but others still can be tasted.

H Camp Connor
Milepost 403.8 on U.S. Hwy. 30

Colonel P.E. Connor set up the old town of Soda Springs, now mostly flooded, and an adjacent Army post near here May 20, 1863.

The gold rush to Idaho had greatly increased traffic on the Oregon Trail, and the post was needed to protect travelers from the Indians. Along with his troops, Connor brought 160 settlers from Utah, and the town they founded became the Oneida County seat from 1864-66. It soon declined, but in 1870, Brigham Young visited here and established the present townsite just east of the earlier location.

H Hooper Spring
Milepost 405.2 on U.S. Hwy. 30

Free, clear, sparkling soda water still is available in beautiful Soda Springs City Park, located two miles from here.

The prime attraction for more than 160 years, soda water from these springs was marketed nationally after rail service reached this resort area in 1882. W.H. Hooper, Salt Lake City's leading banker and president of Zion's Cooperative Mercantile Institution, had his summer home here. He did much to found and promote Soda Springs and its soda water industry while serving as Utah's delegate to Congress.

T Thomas Corrigan Park
Corner of Main St. and First Street South, Soda Springs. Contact the Southeast Idaho Pioneer Country Travel Council at (888) 201-1063.

Corrigan Park is one of the most popular recreational parks in Soda Springs that also preserves the community's heritage. Featuring normal park amenities such as tennis and basketball courts, the park also includes two historic locomotive engines. The first engine, nicknamed "Dinky Engine," was used in the construction of Alexander Reservoir. When the reservoir water began filling up the site, the Dinky Engine was trapped and left abandoned at the reservoir floor. In 1977, the reservoir was drained, at which time the historic locomotive was recovered. After being restored to its original condition, the engine was donated to the city and placed in Corrigan Park.

The second historical locomotive on display is known as the "Galloping Goose." During the region's mining boom, the Galloping Goose carried miners and ore from Soda Springs to nearby Conda. When the mines were closed, the Galloping Goose was retired.

T The Oregon Trail in Caribou County - A Complete Tour of the Area's Historical Attractions
Soda Springs

Early pioneers on the Oregon Trail in southeastern Idaho closely followed the present location of U.S. Hwy. 30 to Sheep Rock Point (now also known as Soda Point). The area is lined with historic points, and well-worn ruts from pioneers' covered wagons still dot the landscape. While visiting the Soda Springs area, explore the geographical and historical sites experienced by Oregon Trail emigrants that also influenced the development of Idaho's Caribou County.

Sulphur Springs
While traversing the Oregon Trail, emigrants discovered several notable springs along the way. The first of these springs is known as Sulphur Springs. With a distinct rotten egg odor, the springs were a famous stopping point of curiosity along the trail. Although area droughts often prevented any water from bubbling out of the surface, the odor was always present around the yellow sulphur beaches surrounding the springs. Many emigrants in the mid 1800s speculated about how to make a profit off the extensive sulphur piles, but it was not until the late 1800s that a business plan originated. Under the direction of Charlie Lewis and Charles Henry, a sulphur mine operated in the area with little demand for the product. In 1918, great plans were made to help out with the wartime need for sulphur. As a result, the Idaho Sulphur Company was established and a new mine was set to open in 1919. However, with the signing of the war armistice, the plans for a great sulphur mine never materialized.

To reach the springs, drive four miles east of Soda Springs on U.S. Hwy. 30 to Sulphur Canyon Road. Proceed one mile northeast to the first junction on Sulphur Canyon Road. The main spring is situated approximately 50 yards east of the junction between the road's forks.

Pyramid Spring
The entire Soda Springs area was akin to a geologic novelty for nearly all Oregon Trail pioneers and early Idaho trappers. Diaries and early letters from emigrants address the strange white soda mounds and "chalklike" rocks representing pioneers' first glimpses of this Idaho community and its bubbling springs. Many also reported that the formations sounded hollow when they walked over them. Although many of these soda cones have been weathered down or graded away, a few mounds remain testifying to the emigrants' observations. Pyramid Spring, now site of the town's famous geyser, is characterized with a soda mound and other unusual mineral formations serving as a conversation piece for Oregon Trail pioneers.

Visit Pyramid Spring in the town of Soda Springs. At the intersection of 2nd South and Main Streets, bear north, and locate the mound behind Enders Hotel.

Brigham Young Cabin
The Soda Springs area was not only a popular stopping point for Oregon Trail travelers, but also a hotbed of Morrisite (an off-shoot of the Church of Jesus Christ of Latter Day Saints) and Mormon

religious beliefs. In 1870, members of the Mormon Church in the nearby community of Paris learned that church founder, Brigham Young, was planning a trip to Soda Springs. In response, fifty men loaded with building materials headed to Soda Springs and constructed an eighteen by twenty-two foot log cabin for Young. The cabin was luxurious by 19th century standards and included a solid wood floor, glass windows framed with calico curtains, and a shingled roof. Upon his arrival, Young used the cabin as his home and a religious center while developing the new Upper Town of Soda Springs. The cabin became the first home in Soda Springs and it stood until 1944 when it was accidentally destroyed in an attempt to move it. Today, logs from the home line the driveways of the Brigham Young Lodge, and a historical marker records the original site of the cabin's location.

Visit the original site of the first cabin in Soda Springs on the south side of U.S. Hwy. 30 between 1st and 2nd East Streets in front of the Brigham Young Lodge.

Wagon Box Grave
Many Oregon Trail emigrants lived in fear of hostile encounters with Native Americans along their long journey, and one unlucky group of pioneers met with an untimely fate near Soda Springs. After camping overnight near Little Spring Creek (near the present southwest corner of First West and Fourth East Streets), one man's horses had strayed away. Urging the other members of the wagon train to continue on, this man and his family stayed behind to locate the missing horses before catching up with the rest of their party. Unfortunately, the family never rejoined their fellow Oregon Trail emigrants.

The following day, trappers George Goodhart, Bill Wilburn, and John Taung noticed the lone wagon with no evidence of activity near the site. Deciding to investigate, the three discovered the man, his wife, and their five children brutally murdered inside. George Goodhart rode ahead to the next wagon train of emigrants. Learning that these pioneers were part of the same wagon train as the dead family, Goodhart delivered the news, and several of the emigrants returned with him to the site. Without any lumber but desiring a proper burial, the trappers and pioneers decided to bury the family in their own wagon box. This common grave was the first grave in what is now called the Soda Springs Fairview Cemetery. The grave is marked with a historical monument.

To visit the grave, drive on U.S. Hwy. 30 in Soda Springs and bear north onto First West Street. The cemetery entrance is located at the end of the first bock at the corner of Center and First West Streets. From the entrance, the grave is 200 feet straight ahead. It is situated 40 feet from the road's right side and is bordered by two spruce trees.

Ninety Percent Spring
Just as the Soda Springs area was renowned to Oregon Trail pioneers for its strong sulphuric odor, many natural springs in the region also became famous for their excellent water quality. One particularly exceptional spring was discovered sometime in late 1864. According to one emigrant letter, the spring was accidentally found by Morrisite settlers, and for some unknown reason was dubbed "Ninety Percent Spring."

Learning of the excellent spring, Utah distillery operator and wholesale liquor dealer, Fred. J. Kiesel, decided to forge a new business venture. With help from his Montana partner, W.J. Clark, Kiesel established a water bottling plant at the

GHOST TOWNS

Caribou City
40 miles north of Soda Springs
Originally called Iowa Bar and Iowa City, Caribou City received its current moniker when early settlers decided to honor of one of the first settlers. In 1869, Jesse "Cariboo" Fairchild arrived in Idaho after prospecting for gold near Canada's Caribou Range in 1860. When he discovered placer gold, the settlement of Caribou City arose, and a gold rush to the area soon followed. With more than 1,500 residents, Caribou City was extensively mined and deep gouges can still be found in the surrounding hillsides. As with many other early mining settlements, Caribou City burned to the ground in 1885 and was never rebuilt.

Bonanza Bar
Power County
In 1878, miners established the mining camp of Bonanza Bar on the Snake River. Unfortunately, miners never met with much luck at the settlement as no practical method could be found to recover the fine gold from the area's black sand. By 1881, miners gave up their pursuits at Bonanza Bar, and the camp was abandoned.

Keenan City
25 miles north of Soda Springs in Caribou County
Situated at the convergence of Barnes Creek and City Creek, Keenan City was established in 1870 as a placer mining camp. The settlement quickly grew, and by 1871, more than 500 Caucasian miners called Keenan City home. On top of this population was a Chinese settlement established on the outskirts of town where more than 400 Chinese immigrants and their families resided. Evidence still remains testifying to extensive placer mining along Barnes Creek, and several log cabins can still be found near the old townsite.

spring's site. Filling bottles with spring water and then charging them with gas from nearby Mammoth Spring, the Natural Mineral Water Company opened its doors on May 17, 1887. The plant proved highly successful, and bottled water was shipped all across the world. The water claimed first prize at the Chicago World's Fair in 1893, stole first prize at the Paris World's Fair, and helped the small community of Soda Springs gain international recognition.

To visit the famous spring, drive north onto Main Street from U.S. Hwy. 30. After crossing the railroad tracks, turn onto North Main and at the first stop sign, bear left onto First North Street. Follow this street as it becomes Cedar View Road 1.8 miles to the spring. Although the spring is no longer highly active, it can be located 90 feet before the road's end. It is marked with a concrete spillway and informative sign.

Camp Connor
Irish immigrant, Patrick Edward Connor arrived in America and promptly enlisted in the U.S. Army at the tender age of nineteen. After serving in the Mexican-American War, Connor was promoted in rank and settled in California. When the California governor called for military volunteers, Connor eagerly arose to the occasion and was named Colonel. As a fierce supporter of the Union and hoping to see more wartime action, Connor petitioned General H.W. Halleck for permission to travel east and fight the Confederates during the Civil War. Much to his displeasure, Colonel Connor's request was denied. Instead, Connor was ordered to Salt Lake City, Utah to help control Indian uprisings and the growing Mormon population.

While stationed in Utah, Connor commanded territories in Nevada, Idaho, and Utah, and planned the deadly 1863 Bear River attack against the Shoshone-Bannock Indians. Connor was immediately commissioned as a general after this attack and decided to use his rank to establish other posts in the area. In May 1863, Connor and his infantry arrived in Idaho Territory near Soda Springs and established Camp Connor. The fort was one of the first military posts in Idaho and was organized to help protect pioneers on the Oregon Trail. From its arrival in 1863 to its abandonment in 1865, Camp Connor was home to more than 300 soldiers.

Camp Connor also served as an important fort in establishing peace with area Native Americans. After Connor's deadly campaign against the Shoshone-Bannock tribe at Bear River, a peace treaty was drawn up demanding the end of hostile attacks against white pioneer emigrants. With the aid of Governor Doty (superintendent of Indian affairs), a peace treaty was signed in October 1863 at Camp Connor. Upon this historical signing, Connor assured his supervisors that the Oregon Trail could now be safely traveled without fear of thievery, molestation, or murder. This treaty was a turning point for all emigrants migrating west.

Although the exact location of Camp Connor is unknown, historical documents and testimonies from trappers suggest that the site was situated southeast of Soda Springs near the present day Caribou Memorial Hospital.

Visit the historical site that shaped southeastern Idaho by merging south off Hwy. 30/34 onto 3rd East Street in Soda Springs. Travel one-half block before turning right into the LDS Church parking lot. The approximate location of the camp can be viewed from the parking lot's west end.

Morrisite Settlement
While many pioneers on the Oregon Trail simply passed through Idaho territory and enjoyed natural spring water and refreshing hot springs along the way, the area was home to a large population of Utah emigrants at the center of a major religious conflict.

After receiving divine visions, LDS Church member Joseph Morris separated from the church and established a new religious communal at Utah's Kingdom Fort along the Weber River in 1862. Along with his followers, Morris stood his ground as a fierce battle ensued between the Mormons and Morrisites. Although Morris lost his life and several of his followers were taken to Salt Lake City as prisoners, the territorial governor pardoned the individuals. Upon their pardon, the scorned men and women drifted to General Connor's Camp Douglas in Utah. Searching for a better life and needing the protection of Connor's infantry, 160 Morrisite followers accompanied Connor and his troops to Idaho territory to establish Camp Connor. After arriving in May 1863, the Mormon dissidents established Morristown on the Bear River's north side near present day Soda Springs.

Morristown thrived for two years under the protection of Connor's troops. However, when Camp Connor was abandoned and Mormon emigrants began arriving in the area, the settlement began to lose its population. A new Mormon settlement was established northeast of Morristown, and the original community became known as "Lower Town." Today, Alexander Reservoir's waters partially cover the Morristown settlement, but in dry years, a few of the town's stone foundations can be seen.

View the first settlement at Soda Springs by exiting south off Hwy. 30/34 onto 3rd East Street in Soda Springs. Travel one-half block before turning right into the LDS Church parking lot. The approximate site of Morristown can be found in the lowland area west of the LDS Church and the Caribou County Memorial Hospital.

First Marriage in Soda Springs
When Morristown was established in the early 1860s, Neils Anderson and Mary Chistofferson were among the first residents. Although Mary's face was permanently disfigured after being shot at the battle between Morrisites and Mormons at Utah's Kingston Fort Weber, she was still as beautiful as ever to Neils. On July 30, 1863, Justice of the Peace, Lieutenant Shoemaker, united Neils and Mary in marriage. Married near a rock outcropping that still stands on their descendants' land, Neils and Mary enjoyed a long life together. Not only were Neils and Mary the first couple married at Camp Connor/Morristown, but they also bore the first child born in Morristown, Abraham C. Anderson.

Today, Neils' and Mary's grave can be found at the Fairview Cemetery. After much dissatisfaction with both the Mormon and Morrisite beliefs, Neils became known as the Idaho father of anti-Mormonism, and he and his wife's beliefs are recounted on their headstone.

Visit the site of the first marriage in Soda Springs by driving south on 3rd East Street. Proceed past the Caribou County Hospital to the street's end, bear right, and drive to the Bear River Bridge. Parking here, gaze to the northeast and view the rock outcropping that served as the ceremony and reception site for Neils and Mary.

Sheep Rock and Hudspeth's Cutoff
The great granite stone rising several hundred feet above the Bear River was an important and recognizable point for pioneers on the Oregon Trail. Early travelers named the area Sheep Rock after the numerous mountain sheep found populating the area. Serving as a junction point along the Oregon-California Trail, emigrants were presented with three routes. The first route was known as the Bidwell-Bartleson Trail. This route headed south across the deserts of Utah and was used in 1841 by the earliest group of emigrants. After word spread that the trail was incredibly difficult, the route was abandoned. The next option to take was the main trail leading northwest to Fort Hall around the area's mountain ranges. The final and newest option was the direct route leading west across the mountains known as Hudspeth's Cutoff.

Growing weary of the established route leading to Fort Hall, Benoni M. Hudspeth, captain of a wagon train destined for California, and the train's guide, John Myers, decided to forge a new route across the west on July 19, 1849. Both men had traveled the area before on previous guiding expeditions, and the 132-mile trail dropped twenty-five miles from the original route. With the wagon train's permission, Hudspeth and Myers led seventy wagons and 250 people that fateful July day on what would become the Hudspeth Cutoff. Although the route was difficult, it became the favored route after 1849 for those emigrants headed to California. Foliage abounded for both the emigrants and their animals along the Cutoff, which made it a favorable option compared to the over-used route leading to Fort Hall.

Head 5 miles west of Soda Springs on Hwy. 30/34 to view Sheep Rock. Stunning views can be found from the Alexander Dam located 0.5 miles from the State of Idaho Transportation Road Maintenance Compound. To view Hudspeth's Cutoff, drive 6 miles west of Soda Springs. At the junction of Hwy.s 30 and 34, bear north for approximately 100 yards. Here, turn right on an old highway and park at the pavement's end. Walking towards the railroad tracks, note the Oregon-California Trail Association white markers pointing out the route of Hudspeth's Cutoff.

Volcanic Craters

Amid the sulphuric springs, refreshing spring water, and strange soda mounds, Oregon Trail emigrants also found volcanic crater sites in the Soda Springs area. Diaries from numerous pioneers and fur trappers note two craters, prominent features from Hudsperth's Cutoff. Pioneers described the craters as approximately ten feet deep, lined with sagebrush, grass, and layers of cooled lava.

To visit the craters, drive west of Soda Springs 5 miles along Hwy. 30/34 to the Oregon Trail Road. Bear north (right), cross the railroad tracks, and proceed along the left road that crosses a canal. Park at the rock outcropping and walk 120 yards to an overlook. Tremendous views of both volcanic craters can be found here.

Steamboat Springs and Beer Springs

Steamboat Springs was by far the most famous spring along the route of Oregon Trail emigrants, and many even traveled out of their way to view the famed site. Gushing three feet into the air, the hot Steamboat geyser could be heard gurgling under the surface long before its regular eruptions. Today, the spring lies forty feet below Alexander Reservoir's waters. On a calm day, though, visitors can still see the active Steamboat Springs bubbling on the reservoir's surface.

Named by the area's early fur trappers, Beer Springs had a reputation for inciting joviality and an intoxicated atmosphere. Although varying reports place the springs in different locations, Beer Springs was a favorite among Oregon Trail pioneers who let their imaginations run wild at the site. Today, all that is known is that Beer Springs rests under the waters of Alexander Reservoir.

Visit these famous stopping points by traveling west on U.S. Hwy. 30. At the country club, bear south on a gravel road and proceed 0.4 miles to an overlook of Alexander Reservoir near a picnic pavilion.

T **Monsanto Chemical Company Slag Pour**

2.5 miles northeast of Soda Springs. Contact the Southeast Idaho Pioneer Country Travel Council at (888) 201-1063.

For those who have never witnessed a major industrial site, Soda Springs offers a glimpse at the

During the years of westward expansion, Oregon Trail pioneers delighted at the naturally carbonated water found at Hooper Spring. Today visitors can find the same water under this gazebo in Soda Springs.

Monsanto Chemical Company slag pour. Headquartered in Missouri, the company's Soda Springs branch was established in 1951 and is housed in a multi-million dollar plant. The company strip-mines phosphate ore in the region and then uses the product to manufacture detergents, fertilizer, herbicides, and water treatments.

After it is mined, the phosphate is heated to 1,400 degrees Celsius. Using as much electricity per day as a community the size of Kansas City, the plant separates the elemental phosphorous from the slag. The red-hot slag is then hauled to a perimeter of the plant where a man-made "lava flow" occurs when the slag is dumped. This slag pour happens approximately five times each hour of every hour of every day. While no facility tours are offered, interested visitors can view the slag pour from the roadside.

T **Oregon Trail Country Club Golf Course**

2525 Hwy. 30, Soda Springs. 547-2204.

The Oregon Trail Country Club Golf Course not only offers a traditional round of golf, but also a glimpse into the past. This 9-hole, par-36 course features wide open fairways, as well as Oregon Trail wagon ruts winding between holes one, eight, and nine. Mountain views dominate the landscape, and nearby Alexander Reservoir creates water hazards on four of the nine holes. Built in 1964, the course is open from March 1 to October 1 with green fees starting at $10.

T **Hooper Spring**

Downtown Soda Springs. Contact the Southeast Idaho Pioneer Country Travel Council at (888) 201-1063. From Main St., drive three blocks on First S. St. before bearing north on Third E. St. Continue 1.5 miles, and at the Y in the road, proceed to the west to reach the spring in 0.5 miles.

Sheltered underneath a gazebo and surrounded by a community park, Hooper Spring is one of the region's natural springs that led to the naming of this community. During the years of westward expansion, Oregon Trail pioneers delighted in the naturally carbonated water, and encampments surrounding Hooper Spring abounded between 1840 and 1860. The spring's popularity continues as locals and tourists alike flock to the gazebo for

free water samples. While some find the water's taste repulsive, many others swear the soda water cures arthritis and other chronic medical conditions.

T **Octagon Spring Park**

Downtown Soda Springs. Contact the Southeast Idaho Pioneer Country Travel Council at (888) 201-1063.

The natural springs dotting the Soda Springs landscape were important stopping points for Oregon Trail travelers. Searching for a moment of peace and restoration, the various springs provided ideal camping spots and also sparked a sense of curiosity among the pioneers. At Octagon Spring, the travelers were intent on protecting the area for future generations. In response, a group of unknown pioneers erected a wooden gazebo to shelter and mark the spring's location. In 1995, the shelter was renovated but retains much of its original character.

T **Sheep Rock Point**

5 miles west of Soda Springs on Hwy. 30/34. Contact the Southeast Idaho Pioneer Country Travel Council at (888) 201-1063.

Rising several hundred feet above the Bear River, the massive granite stone dubbed "Sheep Rock Point" was an important trail marker for pioneers heading west on the Oregon Trail. Named after the numerous mountain sheep inhabiting the area, Sheep Rock Point acts as the region's historical, geological, and geographical crossroads. Lifted off the valley floor during ancient volcanic eruptions, Sheep Rock Point served as the junction for the Oregon-California Trails. In later years, Sheep Rock Point and the surrounding area also welcomed the first line of the Oregon Shortline Railroad on its path to the Northwest.

T **Natural Area**

Immediately west of Soda Springs on U.S. Hwy. 30. Contact the Southeast Idaho Pioneer Country Travel Council at (888) 201-1063.

In this unusual geographical gap, local weather patterns and fierce winter winds have established a cool microclimate resulting in vegetation normally found only at much higher elevations. Most notable are the groves of limber pines that usually survive at altitudes exceeding 9,000 feet.

THE IDAHO TEST OATH OF 1885

During the late 1800s, fierce campaigns against Mormons and their belief system were waged all across America and the Idaho territorial government upheld extremely prejudiced laws. Growing increasingly tired of practicing Mormon polygamists establishing residences within the territory's borders, Idaho politicians enacted the Anti-Mormon Test Oath on February 3, 1885.

The Anti-Mormon Test Oath required all citizens to swear contempt and lack of support for any organization teaching plural marriage. Thus, every Mormon was prohibited from voting whether or not he was a practicing polygamist. In addition, Mormons were not allowed to hold any political or public office and could not serve on juries. Despite some Mormons' attempts to reject their ideology and convert to a new religion accepted in the territory, the law also encompassed all former Latter Day Saints. As a result of the new law, the Latter Day Saints developed their own school system to ensure a fair education to young believers.

Mormon polygamy and concern for how Latter Day Saints' beliefs might affect America's political and domestic standards was such a sweeping issue that Idaho's 1888 Republican platform was "Stamping out the Wickedness of Polygamy." Four years later, suspicion of Mormons was on the decline, and Idaho Republicans begrudgingly agreed to allow Mormon believers into its party.

In 1895, the Idaho Test Oath was repealed in the name of fairness and justice. However, it was not until 1982 that Idaho voters finally amended the state constitution to remove all anti-Mormon sentiments and language.

T Soda Springs Geyser
1 block north of U.S. Hwy. 30 on Main St., Soda Springs. Contact the Southeast Idaho Pioneer Country Travel Council at (888) 201-1063.

Located in the city center, Soda Springs' famous geyser was actually discovered by accident. In 1937, a drilling crew searching for hot water to fill a proposed community pool accidentally hit a chamber of carbon dioxide and geothermal water. As a result of pressure being released, the subsequent geyser thrust into the air and had to be capped. Once the geyser was capped at its now maximum height of 150 feet, it was put on an hourly eruption timer. More predictable than Yellowstone National Park's Old Faithful, the Soda Springs geyser comes to life on the hour of every hour each day and is the world's only captive geyser. Visitors can gain up-close views of the geyser featured on "Ripley's Believe It or Not" via walking paths surrounding the area.

T Formation Springs Preserve
Soda Springs. Contact the Southeast Idaho Pioneer Country Travel Council at (888) 201-1063. From Soda Springs, travel north on State Hwy. 34 to Trail Canyon Rd. Turn right and proceed to the well-marked preserve.

Nestled at the base of the scenic Aspen Mountains, the Formation Springs area was developed by the Nature Conservancy to protect the wooded wetland, its clear cold springs, and an increasing winter waterfowl population. Terraced pools characterize the area, and the water's high calcium carbonate content has created a unique geological landscape. Visitors can explore the preserve via numerous trails, one of which leads to the impressive Formation Cave. The cave meanders underground for 500 feet and features a ten-foot-tall entrance. The free site is open year-round.

T Enders Hotel
76 Main St., Soda Springs.

Added to the National Register of Historic Places in 1993, the 100 plus year old Enders Hotel in Soda Springs serves not only today's patrons, but guests from the past. From footsteps marching around on the second floor when no other human is in the building to full pots of boiling water careening off the kitchen stoves, the hotel is plagued with unexplainable events. The spooky atmosphere and continuous mysterious occurrences have landed the hotel on the list of the "Top Ten Most Haunted Hotels in the U.S."

TV Alexander Dam and Reservoir
2 miles west of Soda Springs on U.S. Hwy. 30. Contact the Southeast Idaho Pioneer Country Travel Council at (888) 201-1063.

Built in 1923 and 1924 under the direction of the Utah Power and Light Company, the Alexander Dam and Reservoir are often referred to as Soda Point Reservoir. In the region's early days, Oregon Trail pioneers used Steamboat Springs and Beer Springs as popular landmarks on their journey west. However, when the dam was constructed, the springs were flooded and now lie buried beneath the reservoir's surface. With scenic views of the neighboring Aspen Mountain Range, the reservoir also features an abundant wildlife population. Sandhill cranes, waterfowl, and marine and marsh birds flock to the area year-round, and trumpeter swans are frequently spotted in the winter.

TV Oregon Trail Public Park and Marina
2 miles west of Soda Springs on U.S. Hwy. 30 at Alexander Reservoir. Contact the Southeast Idaho Pioneer Country Travel Council at (888) 201-1063.

The Oregon Trail Public Park and Marina offers both recreation and a piece of history. Located on the shores of Alexander Reservoir, the park features wagon ruts left by early Oregon Trail pioneers, as well as a boat ramp, dock, playground, and picnic areas. The free site is open daily from 8 AM to 10 PM spring through fall.

V Trail Canyon Ski Area
12 miles northeast of Soda Springs on Trail Canyon Rd. Contact the Soda Springs Chamber of Commerce at 547-4964. From Soda Springs, travel north on State Hwy. 34, exiting at Trail Canyon Rd.

No longer maintained as a state Park N' Ski Area, Trail Canyon offers ungroomed trails and beautiful scenery along five loop trails with a maximum length of ten miles. The area is suitable for skiers of all abilities.

M Soda Springs Chamber of Commerce
9 W. 2nd St., Soda Springs. 547-4964. www.sodachamber.com; sodacoc@sodachamber.com

26

Wayan
Wayan honors the memory of early residents, Wayne and Ann Nevils. The couple were among the first permanent settlers during the 1890s and used their home to house the area's first post office. Located near Grays Lake and Blackfoot Reservoir, the town acquired postal services in 1894 and retains its quiet country atmosphere.

Henry
Resting in the shadow of Henry Mountain, the community of Henry is located near Blackfoot Reservoir and dates back to the 1880s. The first settlers named their town, "Omega," and the U.S. Postal Department accepted this name when postal services were granted. However, residents changed the name in 1885 to commemorate Henry Schmidt, one of the area's first settlers and an important business owner.

H John Grey
Milepost 93.7 on State Hwy. 34

John Grey discovered this valley in 1818 or 1819 while hunting beaver for Donald Mackenzie's North West Company trappers.

An Iroquois leader, also known as Ignace Hatchioraquasha, he also explored Grey's River nearby in Wyoming. Aside from his trapping skills, he was noted for his unusual aptitude in fighting grizzly bears. After trapping in this country for 20 years, he retired with his Iroquois band in 1836 to help found Kansas City, Missouri.

H Cariboo Mountain
Milepost 93.7 on State Hwy. 34

Rising to an elevation of more than 6,800 feet, Cariboo Mountain – visible north of here – has two of Idaho's highest gold camps.

Jesse "Cariboo Jack" Fairchild discovered gold high on Cariboo Mountain in August 1870, and a mining rush from Utah followed in September. Production continued for two decades before the gold ran out, with millions of dollars worth of gravels yielding mineral values during that long period of successful mining. But Cariboo Jack was killed by a bear there in 1884.

T Grays Lake National Wildlife Refuge
74 Grays Lake Rd., Wayan. 574-2755. Travel north on State Hwy. 34 from Soda Springs. After driving approximately 33 miles, turn at the refuge marker and continue 2 miles west of Wayan.

Grays Lake National Wildlife Refuge provides an 18,330-acre marshy wildlife sanctuary at the foot of the Caribou Mountains. The area boasts the largest sandhill cranes nesting population in the world and is home to a variety of other migratory waterfowl. Canadian geese have been observed as well as a flock of endangered whooping cranes. After wintering in New Mexico, these birds return to Grays Lake for the spring and summer. The refuge provides opportunities for wildlife observation, photography, and waterfowl hunting free of charge.

TV Caribou National Forest
Southeastern Idaho. Contact the Caribou National Forest Headquarters at 624-3151.

Established in 1907 by President Theodore Roosevelt, the Caribou National Forest draws its name from 1870 gold miner, Jesse "Cariboo Jack" Fairchild. The forest encompasses 1,000,000 acres, and the U.S. Forest Service oversees a variety of multiple uses. Recreationally, the forest provides a mecca of activities, including cross-country skiing, snowmobiling, four-wheeling, mountain biking, backpacking, horseback riding, camping, hunting, and fishing. In addition, sheep and cattle are allowed to graze the area under special permits, and limited mining and timber harvesting is strictly controlled.

V Blackfoot Reservoir

25 miles northeast of Soda Springs on State Hwy. 34 near Henry. Contact the Idaho Department of Game and Fish at 334-3700.

Covering 18,000 acres, Blackfoot Reservoir is situated on the Blackfoot River in Idaho's Caribou County. The reservoir was created primarily for agricultural purposes but has expanded into a popular recreational destination. Windsurfing is a growing attraction, and boat ramps provide convenient access year-round. Anglers will find both rainbow and cutthroat trout, but all wild cutthroat trout must be released in coordination with local and state recovery efforts of the species. All hatchery trout are open for taking and are marked with a clipped adipose fin. Bird-watching fans also frequent the area as the high elevation boasts songbirds, upland and marsh birds, waterfowl, birds of prey, and sandhill cranes. The reservoir is open to the public free of charge, and a few campsites are dispersed throughout the area.

27

Bennington
Pop. 160

Bennington rests along the Bear Lake-Caribou Scenic Byway and was established by Mormon believers in 1864. The area's first presiding elder, Evan M. Greene, named the small community after Brigham Young's hometown of Bennington, Vermont.

Georgetown
Pop. 538

In 1870, Brigham Young urged a band of Mormon followers to establish a community between Soda Springs and Montpelier. The colonizers followed his orders and named their settlement Twin Lakes. When Young visited the town three years later with George Q. Cannon, he declared the name unfit and requested that the residents rename their community in honor of his traveling companion. The residents obeyed Young's wishes, renaming their community Georgetown just in time to receive postal services in 1873. Cannon later became a delegate to the Utah Congress.

T Georgetown Relief Society Hall
161 3rd Northwest St., Georgetown.

Settled in 1870, Georgetown still reflects its founding fathers' Mormon heritage. This legacy is readily apparent in the historic Georgetown Relief Society Hall. Constructed shortly after the community's settlement, the building is now over 125 years old. The hall was the first public building in Georgetown and served as the community's first LDS Chapel, a school, and a Daughters of Utah Pioneers meeting hall. The building was added to the National Register of Historic Places in 1998 and is open daily to the public at no charge.

T Georgetown Summit Wildlife Management Area
On State Hwy. 30 near Georgetown. Contact the Idaho Department of Game and Fish at 334-3700.

The Georgetown Summit Wildlife Management Area was created in 1992 with the coordinated efforts of the Elk Foundation and the Idaho Department of Fish and Game. The region is a critical wildlife area, and the rolling, grassy habitat provides a winter range for large populations of moose and elk. During the summer and fall, the area is home to large herds of mule deer. The area is open to wildlife watchers free of charge, but all other recreational activities are prohibited in an effort to protect the wildlife and its habitat.

V Meade Peak

East of Georgetown on Georgetown Canyon Rd. Contact the Idaho Department of Parks and Recreation at 334-4180.

Soaring 9,957 feet into the air, Meade Peak is southeastern Idaho's highest point. Contained within the Caribou National Forest, Meade Peak is a popular early spring destination for backcountry skiers and snowboarders.

28 Food, Lodging

Montpelier
Pop. 2,785

Brigham Young named Montpelier for the capital of Vermont, his home state. Relocating from the Bear Valley's west side, sixteen Mormon families moved to this town site in 1864. A ferry was immediately erected across the Bear River, and within a year, the number of families in town had doubled.

When the Oregon Short Line railroad arrived in 1882, Montpelier became an important shipping point for the local valleys. Stockyards and a railroad maintenance shop where built to accommodate these industries. There was conflict over "outsiders" doing business in town, however, and people began referring to the community as "Mormon uptown," and "Gentile downtown." Washington Street connected the two districts. This religious conflict continued for twenty years until the highway was rerouted westerly on Washington Street, and the uptown businesses were compelled to move downtown. The post office was established in 1873, and by 1900, the town boasted a population of 1,400 people, making it Bear Lake Valley's largest settlement. Although other regional Mormon towns delcared that Montpelier housed second-class citizens, the slur did not slow the town's growth, and Montpelier has maintained a fairly stable population.

Geneva
Pop. 30

Cattle ranchers first settled Geneva in 1878. Mormon colonizers, mostly from Switzerland, joined them in 1879 and established dairy farms. Twenty years went by before settler Henry Touvscher finally gave the settlement a name. He chose Geneva in honor of his hometown in Geneva, Switzerland. The post office was established in 1898.

H Bank Robbers
Milepost 25.5 on U.S. Hwy. 89 in downtown Montpelier

On August 13, 1896, Butch Cassidy and his infamous Wild Bunch of gunmen invaded Montpelier's banks and scooped up more than $16,500 in gold, silver, and currency.

Leaving a surprised cashier and his terrified customers, they calmly rode away. A deputy sheriff who borrowed a bicycle to pursue them up Montpelier Canyon was quickly outdistanced. Cassidy never was caught, but Bob Meeks was imprisoned until 1912 for helping in Montpelier's great bank robbery.

T Montpelier Historic District Tour
Downtown Montpelier. Contact the Bear Lake Valley Convention and Visitor Bureau at (800) 448-2327.

Established in 1864, Montpelier retains a handful of historic buildings relevant to the community's legacy.

One home worth visiting in Montpelier is a three-story Queen Anne-style mansion John Bagley built for his wife in 1890. Bagley was an

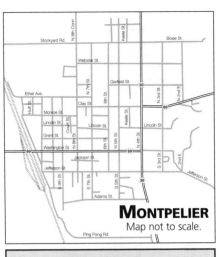

MONTPELIER
Map not to scale.

LUTHER BURBANK'S LEGACY

Luther Burbank, one of Idaho's earliest settlers, is one of the individuals most responsible for creating Idaho's famed potatoes. A potato farmer, Burbank noticed in 1872 that one of his Early Rose potato varieties had produced an unusual seedpod. Saving twenty-three seeds, Burbank planted the seeds along with his normal Early Rose crop. When harvest arrived, Burbank was pleased to discover that the unique seed variety actually produced larger, higher quality potatoes than the Early Rose variety.

Burbank sought to profit off his discovery and offered the potato variety to a Massachusetts grower. Slighted $350 from his original asking price, Burbank accepted $150 for his product and moved from Idaho to California. While there, Burbank introduced his potato variety and by 1906, more than six million bushels of his famous potato were grown on the West Coast. Although he experimented with other hybrids, Burbank never found a more successful potato.

Today's russet Burbank features a modified skin developed by Colorado resident, Lon Sweet. The skin is resistant to blight, and the potato itself is still an Idaho potato farmer's favorite.

important LDS elder in the town's early years and also served as state attorney general from 1903 to 1904. Although impressively beautiful, the mansion reportedly holds a mysterious story of a mother and daughter's suicide.

430 Clay St.
Constructed in 1895, this building represents Montpelier Stake Center's first LDS tithing center. Tithing was extremely important in the town's fledgling days. Latter Day Saints church members were expected to give one-tenth of their income and donate one-tenth of their time and labor to the church. Today, the Daughters of Utah Pioneers organization has restored the building into a community relic hall.

Washington St.
Montpelier's City Hall was completed in 1918 and features a neo-classical revival design. Constructed

Section 7

THE OUTLAW WEST ARRIVES IN MONTPELIER: A RECOUNTING OF THE 1896 MONTPELIER BANK ROBBERY

As one of the largest settlements in Bear Lake Valley in the late 1800s, Montpelier established southeastern Idaho's first bank in April 1891. The Bank of Montpelier acquired the first state charter and opened its doors under the direction of G. C. Gray. Bank operations went off without a hitch for five years, but plots were brewing in outlaw minds.

Learning of the prosperous bank, Wild Bunch gang members Robert Leroy Parker (alias Butch Cassidy), William McGinnis (alias Elza Lay), and Bob Meeks formulated a plan. The trio agreed to rob the bank, using the stolen money to post bail for partner and friend, Matt Warner, who was waiting trial in an Ogden, Utah jail on a murder charge.

On August 13, 1896, the men casually rode into town and slammed a few shots at the local saloon. Just prior to bank closing time, the trio hitched their horses across from the bank. Meeks tended the horses and held responsibility for a successful escape while Cassidy and Lay carried out the plan inside. As the two approached the building, owner G. C. Gray was standing outside conversing with his friend, Ed Hoover. Much to the gentlemen's surprise, Cassidy and Lay ordered them inside and the robbery began. Teller A. N. Mackintosh and a young female stenographer were forced to press their faces against the wall while Lay carefully laid out an impressive array of guns and sighted them on the bank personnel. Meanwhile, Cassidy swiftly emptied the bank's money into his gunny sac and exited the building without a word. After Cassidy calmly mounted his horse and slowly rode down the street, Lay left the bank and his scared victims and rode with Meeks up Montpelier Canyon in pursuit of Cassidy. Before the outlaws left, though, teller Mackintosh was able to get a good look at the third man (Meeks) waiting outside. His mental note later came in handy in Meeks' incarceration and conviction.

Immediately after the trio left, chaos broke

out in the bank. Town Deputy, Fred Cruikshank, responded to the alarm. Initially unable to find his horse, Cruikshank chased the outlaws on his bike. Moments later, he was given a horse and joined by Attorney Bagley and Sheriff Jefferson Davis. For nearly a week, these men chased the Wild Bunch but to no avail. The trio escaped into Montpelier Canyon, and the money was forever lost. Meeks was arrested weeks later for his connection to the robbery, but Cassidy and Lay remained at large.

Upon his arrest, Meeks went to trial and was sentenced to thirty-five years in Boise's Idaho State Penitentiary. However, Meeks' outlaw spirit could not be crushed. After his first escape, Meeks was promptly found and returned to prison. His second escape cost him one of his legs after he received a gunshot wound from one of his pursuers. Officials determined that Meeks was an inappropriate inmate at the prison and would best be served at Idaho's insane asylum located in Blackfoot. Meeks' pattern of escaping continued here. Unlike his other attempts, this time he was successful. After making it to his brother's ranch in Fort Bridger, Wyoming, the local sheriff decided to let Meeks stay and left the convicted outlaw in peace.

Several rumors surround the historical event. While some report that the trio stole away with $7,100 in currency, gold, and silver, other historians estimate the loss at nearly $16,500. Bank teller at the time, A. N. Mackintosh, had his own theory about the cause of the robbery. A superstitious man, Mackintosh surmised that the event was correlated to the "unlucky number 13." Coincidentally, the robbery occurred at 3:13 PM after the 13th deposit of the day was made for $13 on the 13th day of August. Today, the legendary event remains part of town folklore. The robbery still surfaces in everyday conversations, and the robbery is periodically reenacted. Interested spectators can still view the historic bank building that now services a small local business.

out of buff brick from the Ogden, Utah Pressed Brick and Tile Company, the building features a unique portico with pairs of ornamental Tuscan columns. City Hall is the oldest building in the Montpelier historic district.

Washington and Sixth Sts.
Completed at a cost of $50,000 in 1918 and designed by a Salt Lake City architectural firm, the Montpelier LDS tabernacle features a classical motif. Utilizing a semi-circular structure, the tabernacle is constructed out of red bricks and features impressive arched entries. The building represents the town's largest auditorium.

Washington St.
In 1937, the Public Works Administration set out to construct a new educational facility for the Montpelier School District. Constructed out of mountain red variegated tapestry brick, the school is accented with heavily ornate terra cotta trim. Originally used as the community high school, the building is now home to Montpelier Middle School.

T Montpelier Municipal Golf Course
210 Boise St., Montpelier. 847-1981.

The Montpelier Municipal Golf Course offers players open fairways on fairly flat terrain. The 9-hole course is meticulously well-maintained and features just one water hazard coming into play on a single hole. With 3,172 yards of play, the course is rated a par 36 and is open from April 15 to October 15. Green fees for 9 holes are $9, while 18 holes are just $16.

T National Oregon/California Trail Center and Bear Lake Rails and Trails Museum
320 N. 4th St., Montpelier. 847-3800.

The National Oregon/California Trail Center and Bear Lake Rails and Trails Museum is one of the newest museums to arrive in Idaho. On the first floor, visitors experience interactive exhibits describing pioneer life on the journey west, and

living history exhibits can also frequently be seen. Downstairs, visitors will travel back into regional history with displays highlighting topics such as Bear Lake Valley, area Native Americans, and the famous 1827 Bear Lake Rendezvous. The center is open daily during the summer with a small admission fee.

T Montpelier Canyon and Geneva Summit
East of Montpelier on U.S. Hwy. 89.

U.S. Hwy. 89 winds up Montpelier Canyon to the 6,922-foot Geneva Summit before crossing over the Idaho/Wyoming border. In 1896, Montpelier Canyon served as the escape route for Butch Cassidy and his Wild Bunch after they successfully robbed the Montpelier Bank. Today, the canyon is known for its unstable rock strata, fossil formations, and abundant mineral deposits.

T Bear Lake Hot Springs
N. Beach State Rd., Montpelier. 945-4545.

Situated near the beautiful shores of Bear Lake, these hot springs emerge at 118 degrees. The piping hot water is then cooled as it is pumped from the mountains to the surface. By the time it reaches the hot tubs at Bear Lake Hot Springs, the water is just the right temperature for a relaxing soak. Bear Lake Hot Springs is open daily from 10 AM to 10 PM Mother's Day to Labor Day.

TV Montpelier Reservoir & Rearing Pond
North of Hwy. 89 between Montpelier and Geneva. Contact the Bear Lake Convention and Visitor Bureau at 945-3333 or (800) 448-BEAR.

Montpelier Reservoir is situated in the Caribou National Forest at an elevation of 6,517 feet. The man-made reservoir containing 3,850 acre-feet of water is impounded with an 82-foot high earthen dam. Although no motorized boats are allowed in the area, Montpelier Reservoir is still a popular fishing destination. Bonneville cutthroat trout, rainbow trout, kokanee, and yellow perch populate the water, and float tubing is a growing attraction at the reservoir. Below the Montpelier Reservoir Dam is the Montpelier Rearing Pond, which provides ample fishing opportunities and easy access for beginners, children, and the disabled.

M Greater Bear Lake Valley Chamber of Commerce
322 N. 4th St., Montpelier. 847-0067 or (800) 448-BEAR. www.bearlakechamber.og

29 *Food*

Dingle
Pop. 100

Originally called Dingle Bell after the ringing bell located around the neck of lead sheep, this small town originated as a Mormon settlement in the 1870s. It was then called Cottonwood because of all the trees in the area. Finally, after much controversy, the name Dingle stuck for good in 1881. The Post Office was established in 1890.

Ovid
Pop. 145

Settled primarily by Scandinavian Mormons in 1864, Ovid was the first town in Bear Lake Valley to establish a curfew. Children had to be off the streets by 9:00 PM and unescorted women were to be locked inside by 10:00 PM Ovid may have been named for Ovid, New York, but some say it was named after the poet, Ovid.

Paris
Pop. 576

Although it is often assumed that Paris draws its name from the famous French city, the town is actually named after Frederick Perrs who platted the townsite. Recognized as Bear Lake Valley's first Mormon settlement, the community was organized at the command of Brigham Young. Charles Coulson Rich led thirty Mormon families from Utah to the area in 1863. Upon arriving in present day Idaho (although the travelers actually believed they were still in Utah), Shoshone Chief Washakie permitted the emigrants to settle peacefully in the valley's northern end with the understanding that the pioneers would give the Native Americans a portion of the crops grown in the area. The settlers agreed but later violated the terms.

The town was platted with forty-yard wide streets, suitable city lots, and buildings situated for convenience and permanence. One cabin that housed a couple through the first winter still stands on Main Street's west side! Several hundred more families arrived from England and the East coast in 1864, and within no time, a flour mill and a planing and shingling mill was humming with activity. A post office was established in 1873, and in 1882, a small church-operated telephone company was formed. It provided service to St. Charles and Bloomington. Interestingly, the system was predominantly used not as a standard means of communication, but as a warning system to area polygamists who received frequent harrassment from federal officials. Electricity arrived in 1902 thanks to the Electric Light Company.

Today, Paris maintains its stance as a predominantly Mormon community. Several notable historic buildings are scattered throughout town.

Bern
Pop. 50

In 1880, John Kuntz and his family of eight sons and two daughters, along with George Alleman and Alleman's children and grandchildren, migrated to southeastern Idaho and established a new Mormon settlement. Possessing Swiss roots, these first settlers christened their town after Bern, Switzerland, and a post office operated in the area from 1901 to 1927.

H Paris
Milepost 15.8 on U.S. Hwy. 89 at Old Tabernacle

This pioneer Idaho town was founded September 26, 1863, when a wagon train brought more than 30 families of Mormon colonizers.

More pioneers soon followed, some living in huts of quaking aspen and others building log cabins for the mild first winter. Next spring, 700 more people arrived in the valley. The second winter was terrible, but the settlers persevered. They thought they were in Utah until an 1872 boundary survey showed this was part of Idaho. When Bear Lake County was created in 1875, Paris became the county seat.

H Paris Tabernacle
Milepost 15.8 on U.S. Hwy. 89 at Old Tabernacle

Designed by one of Brigham Young's sons, this imposing Romanesque tabernacle was built between 1884 and 1889 by skilled local craftsmen.

Swiss stonemasons cut and carved red sandstone that horse and ox teams hauled from a canyon 18 miles away. In winter, sledloads of rock were pulled over ice across Bear Lake. Shingles and other lumber came from nearby forests. After a century of use, this unaltered monument remains as a reminder of pioneer achievement.

"PEG LEG" SMITH: IDAHO'S MOST NOTORIOUS MOUNTAIN MAN

In the 1800s era of trapping and trading, hundreds of adventurous men surged westward. Leaving behind all the comforts of home, these individuals were often the bravest and fiercest men of their time. Self-sufficient and living off the land, these men embodied the early pioneer spirit and set the stage for westward migration. While Jim Bridger and Jedediah Smith evoke recognizable images of bold mountain men, early southeastern Idaho Territory had its claim to western fame with the notorious frontiersman, "Peg Leg" Smith.

Peg Leg's Early Days
"Peg Leg" Smith was born as Thomas Long Smith in 1801 in Kentucky. From boyhood, Smith was known as an adventurous, resourceful child, so it came as no surprise that he dreamed of heading west and leaving the civilized east behind. In the early 1820s, Smith noticed an ad from a Western newspaper calling for hunters in the Rocky Mountains at an annual salary of $200. He immediately responded and thus began his life as a wandering mountain man.

Peg Leg Heads West and Acquires His Nickname
Upon answering the employment ad, Smith traveled south to the Colorado River and trapped for furs up into the Colorado Desert. As he charged west, Smith was recognized among his friends and other trappers as the bravest man alive. This bravery paid off after an 1827 bloody skirmish with Crow Warriors. Despite fighting fiercely, Smith was shot in one of his legs, leaving the bones below his knee shattered. When Smith's friends carried him off the battlefield, they were sure that the wound was fatal. Smith's fighting spirit willed him to live, though, and he decided the only way to survive was to amputate the shattered leg.

Squeamish at the thought, Smith's friends refused to partake in the procedure, so Smith undertook the operation himself. Between bouts of nausea, fainting, and swearing at his friends, Smith painfully sawed off his own leg with the camp's butcher knife and then wrapped the stump in a dirty shirt. As luck would have it, Smith's leg became infected and swollen, but Smith persevered. During his long recovery, Smith carved himself a wooden leg, and from that moment on, became known as "Peg Leg."

Post Recovery Years
After fully healing from his wound and teaching himself how to walk with his wooden leg, Peg Leg and a comrade headed for California in search of gold. Upon his arrival in Los Angeles, Peg Leg immediately sought out the nearest saloon and proceeded to get drunk. It wasn't long before Peg Leg was spinning yarns about his mountain man adventures and calling for fights with other saloon patrons. Using his wooden leg as his weapon of choice, Peg Leg wound up in jail for disorderly conduct. After his release, local residents chased Peg Leg out of town, at which time he stole a handful of horses as revenge.

Shortly thereafter, Peg Leg decided that stealing horses could become a lucrative business while providing him with the thrill and risk-taking lifestyle he loved. Numerous raids later, Peg Leg had a herd so large that he needed a removed place where he could tend the horses

and sell them to Native Americans or white passerby. Leaving California and the southwest behind, Peg Leg headed east with his three wives, a few friends, and 1,500 horses.

Peg Leg Arrives in Idaho Territory
In 1842, Peg Leg arrived in Idaho's Bear Lake Valley and became the first permanent white settler in the region. He quickly went to work developing his plot of land and constructed what became known as "Fort Smith" south of Montpelier near present day Dingle. Unbeknownst to Peg Leg at the time, he had chosen an ideal supply location for Oregon Trail pioneers. In 1848 and 1849, a flood of Oregon Trail immigrants passed through Idaho Territory, and Peg Leg capitalized on their desperate needs and the lack of other supply stations in Idaho. He purposely charged steep prices to the needy pioneers, watered down the whiskey, and marked up his flour 1,000%. Despite such schemes, the pioneers paid Peg Leg what he asked and spread the word that he offered the finest horses along the trail. The once adventurous mountain man had successfully turned himself into Idaho's greediest, most deceptive entrepreneur of the day.

Conflict Arises Over Peg Leg's Character and Fort Smith
Settled near the Green River in Wyoming Territory was one of Peg Leg's most famous mountain man acquaintances, Jim Bridger. Despite similar beginnings in the trapping and trading industry, Peg Leg and Bridger were now archrivals. Long before Smith's arrival in Idaho, Bridger established the legitimate Fort Bridger along the Oregon Trail in Green River. He was known for offering fair prices to pioneers, and he attempted to steer travelers away from the swindling Peg Leg and Fort Smith. Outraged at Bridger, Peg Leg sent men eastward to divert wagon trains away from Fort Bridger and onto a path that would lead to Fort Smith. Due to Peg Leg's actions, Bridger began losing customers and eventually went out of business.

Jim Bridger was not the only one aware of Peg Leg's scheming character. Mormon leader, Brigham Young, was wary of the man and built a ferry over the Green River to carry pioneers and prospective religious converts away from the infamous outpost. Young then attempted to purchase Fort Smith from Peg Leg in 1848 with the intention of turning it into a religious post for the Church of Jesus Christ of Latter Day Saints. Peg Leg stubbornly refused and carried about his conniving business manner.

Peg Leg Wanders Again
Eventually, traffic on the Oregon Trail decreased, and activity at Fort Smith died down. In response, Peg Leg left Idaho Territory in 1850 and returned to California. But his restless soul was not content, and by 1855, Peg Leg was residing again in the Bear Lake Valley. Just two years later, Peg Leg left Idaho Territory for good. Over the course of the next ten years, Peg Leg lived as a nomad and made a living off trapping, traveling, and fighting. Despite his earlier business success in Idaho, Peg Leg died penniless and alone in 1866. Although he was a notorious swindler and liar, he is still remembered as a fierce mountain man who carried the pioneering spirit of the west with him until he died.

THE CACHE VALLEY: PAST AND PRESENT

Straddling the Idaho/Utah border and measuring twenty miles wide by fifty miles long, the Cache Valley has been a popular gathering place across centuries and cultures. The valley was formed in the ancient flood of Lake Bonneville and the landscape continues to change as new waves of settlers leave their imprint on an area nicknamed the west's green oasis.

The Valley's First Residents
The area was first home to Shoshone, Blackfoot, and Ute Indians who inhabited the area for nearly 5,000 years. Often referred to as "the house of the great spirit," the valley and its wild nature were ideal for the nomadic hunting and gathering lifestyle of the Native Americans.

During the era of the Shoshone people, the valley was lined with bushes and trees, and the abundant willows growing along area streams and rivers provided the valley with its first official name, Willow Valley. However, due to fires that the Native Americans purposely set to drive buffalo herds toward them, the valley's landscape has dramatically changed since it's first use thousands of years ago.

Mountain Men Arrive
When the Rocky Mountain Fur Trading Company opened up for business, thousands of young and adventurous men left their established lives behind and headed west. In an era where fur-trapping, trading, and rendezvous reigned, the Cache Valley became one of the most treasured gathering places. Rendezvous were held annually, and the valley's current name reflects its mountain man past. In French, "cache" means to hide or store one's treasures. Due to physical restraints of carrying beaver pelts with them on all their travels, the mountain men created an ingenious system. In between rendezvous, the men would dig a hole in the ground or in a mountainside and "cache" the pelts. Since the area provided innumerable hiding spots, it soon became known as "Cache Valley." The area's most famous visitor, Jim Bridger, is reported to have stored nearly $150,000 worth of pelts in the Cache Valley before moving on to new adventures.

White Settlements Arise
Despite random residences established by a few rogue mountain men, the Cache Valley remained relatively uninhabited by white settlers until the mid 1800s. As the Church of Jesus Christ of Latter Day Saints moved west, so did thousands of its followers. The Cache Valley quickly became dotted with Mormon settlements in both Idaho and Utah, and it wasn't long before the area's mountain man past became a faint memory and a new era was ushered in.

The Cache Valley Today
Over its longstanding history, the Cache Valley has been transformed into an important agricultural and tourist area. The beautiful landscape and surrounding mountains make the valley a desirable place to live and recreate. Today, 80% of the Cache Valley's inhabitants call Utah home, while 20% reside in the more rural Idaho communities.

father, Rich constructed five identical three-room log cabins, which he and his wives occupied until the late 1870s. Upon the death of one of his wives in 1879, Rich replaced the log homes with four adobe brick houses. These structures, although now covered with modern siding, represent the oldest brick buildings in the community.

Main St. adjacent to the Paris Tabernacle
Although no longer in existence, the site of one of Paris' most controversial buildings can still be found neighboring the Paris Tabernacle. In 1913, residents constructed a large octagonal shaped dance hall. The impressive building represented the finest architecture of the day, and visitors to the site marveled at the hall's interior. Inside, four-inch wide boards joined in octagonal patterns and supported beneath by springs comprised the floor. This distinctive design allowed the floor to "bounce" with the dance rhythms. Despite the building's uniqueness, Latter Day Saints authorities ordered the dance hall be demolished in 1979 because it "distracted from the Tabernacle." Although locals at the time strongly objected to the demolition of this incredible building, church officials received their wish and the building was torn down to put the spotlight back on the Paris Tabernacle.

Northeast corner of Center and Main Sts.
Truman O. Angell, architect who designed the Salt Lake City Mormon Temple and Brigham Young's Salt Lake City home, was hired in the early 1800s to draw up plans for a new courthouse that would serve the Bear Lake Valley's growing population. Upon the plan's completion and with two years of hard labor, the Revival inspired Bear Lake County Courthouse was completed at a cost of $8,100 in 1885. The two-story building originally boasted just forty-six square feet, but later additions have expanded the facility. In addition, the original building's roof included a "widow's walk." During the anti-polygamy raids of the late 1880s, the roof walkway was utilized as a community lookout station to scan for prowling raiders.

58 Center St.
Featuring an octagonal corner porch, this two-story Queen Anne home was built in 1890. J. R. Shepherd, early resident and one of Paris' first business owners, built the house and resided here while operating the Paris Mercantile Company.

T Paris Pioneer Museum
20 S. Main St., Paris.

The history of Idaho's second oldest town is captured with several pioneer relics displayed at the Paris Pioneer Museum. Established in 1989 in the town's old city hall, the museum includes collections of antiques that the first Mormon settlers brought with them in 1863 as well as photographs of servicemen and women from World Wars I and II. In addition, the museum now offers a historic homes tour guiding visitors to several of Paris' historic buildings. The museum is open from 9:30 AM to 5:30 PM daily Memorial Day to Labor Day. For additional information, contact the Bear Lake Visitors Bureau at (208) 945-2333.

T Paris Tabernacle Historical Site
109 S. Main St., Paris. 945-2072.

Perhaps one of Paris' most notable landmarks, the Paris Tabernacle Historical Site is well worth visiting. Now listed on the National Register of Historic Places, the Paris Tabernacle has a rich heritage rooted in the community's early days. Designed by Joseph Young, the Gothic style church was constructed by the town's first Mormon settlers over the course of five years. Residents quarried red sandstone from eastern Bear Lake nearly eighteen miles away to build the church's exterior, and a former shipbuilder handcrafted the interior with pine from nearby forests. To the astonishment of visitors today, all of the interior woodwork is held together with the original handmade square nails. After a significant amount of time and labor, residents finally completed the tabernacle in 1889. The tabernacle, which served Mormons within a fifty-mile radius, became the first Church of Jesus Christ of Latter Day Saints stake center outside of Utah. Today, visitors can marvel at this architectural beauty on a guided tour. The site is open from 9:30 AM to 5:30 PM daily Memorial Day to Labor Day. Admission is free.

T Charles C. Rich Memorial
109 S. Main St., Paris.

Charles Coulson Rich, an Illinois teacher who gave up his position to travel to Missouri and learn about Mormonism, is memorialized in the Paris Tabernacle. Upon being baptized into the LDS Church, Rich moved with his wives and children to Salt Lake City whereupon Brigham Young dispatched him to settle the Bear Lake Valley. Rich arrived in Paris in 1863, helped settle the new community, and served as president of the Bear Lake Stake Center until 1869.

T Paris' Historic Buildings
Downtown Paris. Contact the Bear Lake Convention & Visitor Bureau at (800) 448-2327.

Originating in 1863, Paris still boasts some of the original buildings and construction sites that early Mormon pioneers and their descendents erected upon following Charles C. Rich to the Bear Lake Valley.

S. First W. St.
When Charles C. Rich arrived in Paris, five of his six wives accompanied him along with several of Rich's fifty-one children (the sixth wife remained in Salt Lake City). As a dutiful husband and

T Bear Lake National Wildlife Refuge
7 miles southwest of Montpelier on the north shore of Bear Lake. 847-1757. From Montpelier, drive 3 miles west on U.S. Hwy. 89. At the junction with Bear Lake County Airport Rd., head south and proceed 4 miles to the refuge's north entrance.

Bear Lake National Wildlife Refuge spans 17,600 acres of public land and was established in 1968. Including marshes, open water, and grasslands, the area is situated at an elevation of 5,900 feet and preserves natural habitats for birds and other wildlife. Although herons, sandhill cranes, snowy egrets, terns, rails, bitterns, grebes, avocets, and pelicans are known to frequent the area, the refuge is best known for possessing one of the largest nesting grounds of Great Basin Canadian Geese and harboring America's largest white-faced ibis nesting population. Walking trails in the refuge provide visitors with excellent vantages of the wildlife and refuge topography. In addition to wildlife viewing and photography, the area also boasts opportunities for hiking, canoeing, boating, bike touring, fishing, cross-country skiing, snowshoeing, and upland and waterfowl hunting. The refuge is open daily year-round free of charge.

T Paris Ice Cave

From Paris, travel west up Paris Canyon Rd to a fork in the road. Bearing left, proceed approximately 5 miles up the gravel road to the cave's entrance.

Located in the mountains west of Bear Lake Valley, Paris Ice Cave is located at the bottom of a doline at the top of Paris Canyon. Runoff from melting snow in nearby Paris Flats runs down the doline into the cave. The continual presence of water has caused the gray limestone to sink, thereby causing the rock ceiling of the cave's outer chamber to collapse and exposing the room to the sky. This fifty-foot deep chamber is only a short distance from the cave's entrance. From this chamber, visitors can opt to follow another passage to an inner chamber approximately 100 feet above.

Although the cave is not developed, a well-established path leads visitors to the outer and inner chamber with ease. Due to the cave's high elevation, it is extremely cold. Sightseers are strongly encouraged to wear warm clothes and appropriate footwear and bring flashlights or lamps. The cave is usually dried out by mid-July and is then accessible to the public free of charge.

30

Bloomington
Pop. 251

Bloomington was originally a Mormon settlement platted in 1864 by Charles Rich and his eldest son, Joseph. The men first laid out the site in ten-acre parcels, later dividing each parcel into ten equal lot sizes. The lots were then assigned during a community meeting, and five-acre farms were distributed at the same time. The town sprouted with activity, and new settlers arrived every day to construct permanent residences. By the late 1860s, the town produced such a bountiful harvest that Rich named his town site Bloomington. However, it wasn't until 1910 that Idaho recognized the area as an official community.

Fish Haven
Pop. 100

This tiny resort community's roots date back to a Shoshone Indian summer campsite. Fish such as brown trout, lake trout, perch, and carp were abundant in Fish Haven Creek and nearby Bear Lake, making it an ideal location for finding food. New species of whitefish were discovered in this lake in 1915 and both still inhabit its waters. Unfortunately, the Utah cutthroat (aka. bluenose trout) found in 1912 is now extinct.

Legend states that in the 1800s, two Mormon pioneers pulled 1,800 pounds of fish from the nearby stream in one day. From 1900 to 1925, Fish Haven was the site of a commercial fishing operation. In 1925, however, both Idaho and Utah outlawed commercial fishing on Bear Lake, and the town shifted its attention to the tourism market. The local post office has operated since 1873.

St. Charles
Pop. 156

In 1864, settlers from Soda Springs trickled down to this area and began a new community. They planted a commercial garden on a site surveyed by

Joseph Rich and built homes out of quaking aspen. The town was named for Charles Rich, Mormon apostle and leader of the Bear Lake Valley's Mormon colonization. The town is best known as the birthplace of Mount Rushmore sculptor, Gutzon Borglum.

H Bear Lake
Milepost 2.2 on U.S. Hwy. 89

Discovered in 1812 by trappers returning home from Astoria, Oregon, this valley and its large lake soon became an important fur trade center.

Donald Mackenzie, Jim Bridger, and a host of famous beaver hunters operated here. Two major summer frolics and trade fairs brought plenty of excitement to Bear Lake in 1827 and 1828. Helping local Indians repel Blackfoot invaders, those trappers never forgot their wild festivals here.

H British Settlers
Milepost 13 on U.S. Hwy. 89

Most early Bear Lake settlers came from Britain. Ann Elizabeth Walmsley Palmer was the first woman convert to the LDS Church in Europe.

Born in Preston, England, August 24, 1806, she was baptized July 30, 1837. An invalid, she was carried into the water, but walked out unaided. After coming to Nauvoo, Illinois, in 1842, she drove an ox team to Utah in 1849 and settled there in 1863. She died here November 2, 1890. Through faith she gained the strength to overcome trials and to achieve triumphs.

T Bear Lake Valley's Oldest Tree

West of Bloomington on Forest Road (FR) 409. From Bloomington's city center, head west towards Cache National Forest up Bloomington Canyon on FR 409. Travel 8.4 miles to a fork in the road and bear right. Proceed 0.4 miles to the tree site.

Prior to 1992, Bear Lake Valley boasted the region's largest Engelmann Spruce tree. Measuring seventy-five inches in diameter and 107 feet high, the gigantic spruce was 448 years old. After years of drought, the tree was weakened and blew down in a rare microburst storm in 1992. Today, the tree's carcass remains in its place as a testimony to the spruce's long growing history.

T Bear Lake West Golf Course
155 U.S. Hwy. 89, Fish Haven. 945-2744. Travel south of Fish Haven on U.S. Hwy. 89

Situated in Idaho on the west side of Bear Lake, the Bear Lake West Golf Course provides golfers with a challenging 9-hole, par-33 round of play. Scenic vistas of the lake and surrounding mountains greet golfers at every bend in the course, and players are challenged with water hazards and sand traps on many of the holes. Green fees start at $12, and the course is open April through October.

T Gutzon Borglum Monument
St. Charles. Contact the Bear Lake Convention & Visitor Bureau at (800) 448-2327.

Located on the grounds of the St. Charles' church, this monument commemorates the birthplace of famous American sculptor, Gutzon Borglum. Borglum was born on March 25, 1867 to the second wife of a Danish Mormon who practiced plural marriage. Borglum resided in St. Charles during his first year of life before moving with his family to California. During his childhood, Borglum became intrigued with his father's woodworking, and some suggest this is where his love of sculpting originated. He later perfected his craft in Paris and went on to create South Dakota's Mount Rushmore and nearly 170 other statues and monuments. Today, St. Charles' residents have preserved the

BEAR LAKE: A ONE OF A KIND FISHERY

Southeastern Idaho and northern Utah's Bear Lake features a unique ecosystem containing five fish species natural only to the lake. Since their discovery, some of these fish have been planted successfully in other reservoirs, but only Bear Lake supports the natural and original habitat for these fish.

The Bonneville Cisco is perhaps the most widely discussed of the five original species. Generally growing no longer than seven inches and weighing no more than a mere two ounces, the Bonneville Cisco has been nicknamed "the Bear Lake sardine." The species begins reproducing at age three, and a six-inch female can produce an annual 2,500 eggs for spawning each January and February along the lake's eastern shores. Schools of these planktivores always swim in a counter-clockwise circular motion, and an estimated nine million Cisco populate the lake. Standard fishing gear is usually inefficient in catching these small fish, so anglers typically wade into the lake with dip-nets. Anglers are only allowed thirty of these fish at one time.

The Bonneville Whitefish has earned a reputation for its delicate white meat. With large mouths, this species can grow up to twenty-one inches long and weigh nearly five pounds. The Bonneville Whitefish spawns during early winter in water averaging two to ten feet deep.

The Bear Lake Whitefish grows to a maximum of ten inches long with average sizes reported at six inches. The species features large mouths and spawns in mid-February in water more than thirty feet deep. Early area settlers once harvested the Bear Lake Whitefish and sold them commercially at fish markets. Since then, commercial fishing on Bear Lake has been banned.

Bear Lake Sculpin are generally characterized as a bullhead species and are important prey for rainbow trout, lake trout, cutthroat trout, and whitefish. Baby blue eyes characterize these fish that grow no more than three inches long. After spawning in April, the Sculpin move to waters measuring 175 feet deep. They are listed as a sensitive species, and since their discovery, have been planted in the Flaming Gorge Reservoir located on the Wyoming/Utah border.

The last endemic species present is the Bear Lake Cutthroat. Feeding on other fish, the species features deep orange pelvic fins and a sparsely spotted upper body with few or no spots on the head. They also lack a brightly colored jaw slash. The fish average just two pounds and seventeen inches long, but a record cutthroat measured in at eighteen pounds. This species spawns from mid-April through the end of June, and fishing for the native trout is popular both on and offshore.

THE BEAR LAKE MONSTER: TRUTH OR FICTION?

It lurks under the surface with beady, red eyes. A mysterious creature ready to lash out from the turquoise waters at any moment. Have you seen it? Do you believe in it?

Those questions have plagued Bear Lake Valley residents and tourists since the first account of the Bear Lake Monster circulated in the early 1860s. Local Native Americans warned the first settlers of a horrific creature occupying the seemingly placid lake. With great detail, the Indians related how two braves had been swallowed alive while swimming. They were no match for the large-mouthed, slimy green serpent that could swim more than a mile per minute with its eighteen-inch legs. As a result, the Native Americans gave up recreating in their favorite swimming hole and urged the new arrivals to do the same.

Forewarned, the new residents settled into the valley with a certain sense of unease. Before long, accounts of the Bear Lake Monster poured in. Some claimed that the creature was a speedy alligator, a descendant of ancient dinosaurs who never went extinct, or a deformed walrus missing its tusks. No matter what the monster looked like, it became the focus of the community and published reports poured throughout town in 1868.

Akin to Scotland's Loch Ness Monster and Montana's Flathead Lake creature, accounts of the creature suddenly disappeared, turning the monster into a mythical figure. But in the 1990s, the creature reappeared, and a surge of new curiosity has enveloped the area ever since.

Skeptics say the monster is merely a tourist ploy to attract spectators to the area, but what do you think? Is it really possible that Bear Lake's beautiful serene waters could harbor such a dangerous monster? Truth or fiction? It's up to you to decide.

cabin in which he was born and erected a monument in honor of the town's most famous resident.

T Minnetonka Cave
945-2407. From St. Charles, drive 9 miles up St. Charles Canyon on the paved Forest Rd. (FR) 412.

In 1907, an early resident of St. Charles luckily happened upon the spectacular Minnetonka Cave while grouse hunting in the Caribou National Forest. Although amazing, his discovery went relatively unheeded until the U.S. Forest Service stepped in years later to prevent vandalism to the cave. Upon building a trail to the cave and pouring steps twisting throughout the cave's unique formations, Minnetonka was opened to the public in 1947 and became one of only a handful of federally funded show caves in the world.

Today, Minnetonka is the largest commercially developed limestone cave in the U.S. Nine rooms full of stalactites, stalagmites, banded travertine, and caverns await visitors on the ninety-minute, half-mile tour that traverses up and down over nearly 450 steps. The most popular formations

include the Seven Dwarfs, Devil's Office, and the Bride (appropriately named after its lacy appearance). Visitors are highly encouraged to wear sturdy shoes, and jackets are recommended as the cave maintains a continuous 40-degree farenheit temperature. Minnetonka Cave is open June through Labor Day, and guided tours are available every half hour from 10 AM to 5:30 PM.

T Wasatch-Cache National Forest
Southeastern Idaho. Contact the Caribou National Forest Service at 624-3151.

The Wasatch-Cache National Forest honors the legacy of the region's first settlers. Shoshone and Ute Indians who lived in the area referred to the land as "wasatch," meaning "low place in high mountains." The term "cache," meaning "to hide," honors the legacy of area fur trappers who explored here in the 1800s.

As more and more pioneers moved west, the forested area in present-day Idaho and Utah quickly became the site of major resource damage. By the early 1900s, unrestricted logging, uncontrolled fires, and overgrazing had turned the once beautiful land into a disaster area that regularly polluted water supplies. As a result, the Wasatch National Forest was established in 1906 with the Cache National Forest created in 1907 to protect the environment. In coordination with the Civilian Conservation Corp, the Forest Service redeveloped the land, and in 1973, the Cache National Forest was split at the Idaho/Utah State line.

Now administered under the Caribou National Forest Service, Idaho's portion of the Cache National Forest provides a host of outdoor recreation opportunities. Year-round activities include mountain biking, hiking, horseback riding, fishing, picnicking, skiing, and snowshoeing.

T Bear Lake Valley
U.S. Hwy. 89. Contact the Southeast Idaho Pioneer Country Travel Council at (888) 201-1063.

Northwestern trappers and traders under the leadership of Donald McKenzie christened this area Bear Lake Valley in the early 1800s. It stretches along Bear Lake's shores and was once a hub of mountain man activity.

TV Bear Lake State Park
Bear Lake Park Office: 320 N. 4th, Montpelier. 847-1045. The park is located on Bear Lake's north shore 20 miles south of Montpelier on U.S. Hwy. 89.

Unlike most Idaho state parks offering an array of recreational activities, Bear Lake State Park's main attraction is the lake itself. Encompassing fifty-two acres, the park primarily draws anglers and swimmers. A volleyball court is available, and snowmobiling is popular in the winter. On the north shore, the park provides a day-use beach and boat launch, and the eastern shore boasts a small campground. Picnic tables and a group shelter are also available, and the park is open daily year-round. A $4 motorized vehicle entrance fee is required.

TV Bear Lake
On U.S. Hwy. 89 straddling the Idaho/Utah border

Nicknamed the "Caribbean of the Rockies," Bear Lake was first discovered by white trappers in 1812 on a return trip from Oregon. It has since played a key role in the area's history. Once used as the site for mountain men rendezvous, the lake is now a prime recreational destination. Its intense turquoise blue water, due to dissolved limestone particles, measures twenty miles long by seven miles wide and is surrounded by white sandy beaches. While the lake is home to the angler's favorite rainbow and cutthroat trout, its waters also boast the rare Bonneville cisco found nowhere else on Earth. A specially designed fish ladder on the lake's north end helps fish migrate up Charles Creek to nearby spawning grounds.

31

Pegram
Situated on the Bear River banks near Bear Lake, this tiny village was founded upon the Oregon Short Line Railroad route. The community was established in approximately 1883 and draws its name from a railroad engineer. A post office operated in the area from 1901 to 1940.

Border
The quiet village of Border sprang to life on the Idaho/Wyoming stateline during the late 1900s. Neighboring the Bear River, the town boasted postal services for just eight short years between 1892 and 1900.

Raymond
Raymond's roots as an agricultural community extend back to 1873 and a band of Mormon colonizers who moved from nearby Montpelier. The town was originally named Thomas Fork, but the title was later changed to honor Grandison Raymond, the area's first permanent settler.

H Smith's Trading Post
Milepost 440.1 on U.S. Hwy. 30

In 1848, Pegleg Smith started a trading post on the Oregon Trail at Big Timber on the Bear River about a mile northwest of here.

Some travelers called it Fort Smith, though it had only four log cabins and some Indian lodges. Packing a plow and tools from Salt Lake City, Smith (a mountain man who had to amputate his own leg 20 years before) tried unsuccessfully to raise crops. But he did a big business when the California gold rush of 1849 brought thousands past here. The 49ers reported that he had many horses and cattle and was making $100 a day.

H Big Hill
Milepost 441.7 on U.S. Hwy. 30

On their way west to Oregon and California, emigrant wagons often crossed high ridges in order to avoid gullies and canyons.

When he came here in 1843, Theodore Talbot noted that he "had to cross a very high hill, which is said to be the greatest impediment on the whole route from the United States (over 200 miles east of here) to Fort Hall (over 120 miles farther west). The ascent is very long and tedious, but the descent is still more abrupt and difficult." Many wagons had to be let down by ropes tied to trees that disappeared long ago.

H McAuley's Road
Milepost 441.7 on U.S. Hwy. 30

Coming west with Ezra Meeker in 1852, Thomas McAuley decided to build a road to let emigrants bypass Big Hill.

Worst of all Oregon Trail descents, Big Hill needed replacement. Eliza McAuley reported that her brother Tom "fished awhile, then took a ramble… and discovered a pass by which the mountain can be avoided by doing a little road building." With an emigrant crew, he opened a wagon toll road that followed current Hwy. 30. After 1852, no one maintained the new route and it fell into disuse.

H Thomas Fork
Milepost 454.5 on U.S. Hwy. 30

A bad ford gave trouble to wagon trains crossing this stream on the trail to California and Oregon in 1849.

In that year, gold-seeking 49ers developed a shortcut that crossed here. Then emigrants built two bridges here in 1850. But an enterprising toll collector came along and charged $1 per wagon, which was more than some could afford. Penniless emigrants, who had to make an eight-mile detour, cursed, while their richer companions comfortably clattered across both bridges.

SCENIC DRIVES

Oregon Trail-Bear Lake Scenic Byway
Bear Lake straddles the Idaho-Utah border and boasts sandy beaches, great water sports, fishing, boating, and the famous Bear Lake State Park. This byway follows Bear Lake north on US 89 to Montpelier, then north on US 30, where you leave the Cache National Forest and enter the Caribou National Forest.

The intersection of US 89 and US 30 at Montpelier is the site of the attractive National Oregon-California Trail Center dedicated to the history and scenic wonders of the 2,000-mile Oregon-California Trail, part of the largest voluntary migration ever. There, you can ride in computer-controlled covered wagons, journey nearby trails with experienced guides in period costume, and handle the tools and other artifacts used by the pioneers. There is also an expansive park and playground to stretch your legs, as well as a general store and gift shop to help you remember your visit.

There are 13 Oregon-California Trail sites identified in the Soda Springs area. These sites are documented in diaries of the emigrants, in military records, by early mountain men, and settlers. "Travel the Oregon Trail in Caribou County" brochure contains information and directions on each site. The Mormon ghost town of Chesterfield lies 25 miles northwest of Soda Springs and is located right on the Oregon-California Trail.

This scenic byway begins at the Utah state line and follows US 89 north to US 30, then north and west to Soda Springs, where it meets the Pioneer Historic Byway. This section of US 89 is a two-land road. It can receive heavy snowfall in winter. This section of US 30 is a two-lane road with passing lanes and one short, 5 to 6 percent grade

Idaho Trivia

Southeastern Idaho and the Bear Lake Valley extending into northeastern Utah claim some of America's highest ice cream consumption rates. Many theorize the statistic is directly related to the region's high Mormon population that denies itself other guilty pleasures such as coffee and alcohol.

THE IRON HORSE'S ARRIVAL: RAILROAD EXPANSION IN SOUTHEASTERN IDAHO

As line after line of railroads were built in Utah Territory, LDS Church leader Brigham Young decided to enter the profitable business associated with "the iron horse." In 1871, Young and several Mormon followers established the Utah Northern Railroad, intending to build a line from Ogden, UT to the Montana gold fields. Through cooperative efforts of LDS Church members, the line arrived in Franklin on May 2, 1874. This line represented the first railroad in Idaho Territory, and Franklin quickly grew into a site of major shipping and receiving transactions. Although a financial crisis later that year halted further building progress, construction began again in 1875 under the direction of the Utah and Northern Railway Company and proceeded towards Butte, Montana.

The advent of the railroad greatly influenced southeastern Idaho's landscape. Immigration to the area was made considerably easier, and a string of Mormon settlements sprouted near the line. From 1879 to 1889, numerous new settlements were formed, including Victor, Sugar City, Rigby, Rexburg, and Menan. The Utah Northern Railroad also helped spread the Mormon religion north from Utah into the fledgling territory. Although the original route is no longer utilized, the old grade of the historic line is readily visible in the state's southeastern corner. Near Preston, the grade can be seen to the west of U.S. Highway 91.

Shortly after the arrival of the Utah Northern Railroad, Union Pacific Railroad scouts were dispatched to the area to discover possible routes near the Oregon Trail. A route was chosen in 1881, and work began on the Oregon Short Line Railway. Running from Granger, Montana to Huntington, Oregon, the line passed through Montpelier and Pocatello in southern Idaho. Pocatello became the most important rail center west of the Mississippi, serving as the junction for the Utah and Northern Railway and newly constructed Oregon Short Line. The new line also aided the Snake River Valley's agricultural market. Although farmers once relied on slow wagon trains for necessary seeds and supplies, the railroad ensured quick and easy access to farm equipment and provided a means of shipping harvested crops.

The iron horse's arrival in Idaho created numerous economic and transportation opportunities for early settlers. Utilizing the railroad in the late 1800s, Idaho was steadily on its way to becoming a productive and prosperous part of the U.S.

at Georgetown Summit. The byway can be seen year-round, and travelers should allow at least 1 hour for this 54-mile trip.

Reprinted from Idaho Department of Transportation brochure

Pioneer Historic Byway
On this route, travelers can retrace some steps of Idaho's early pioneers and follow the historic path taken by early-day Yellowstone Park visitors. From Franklin, Idaho's oldest settlement, this byway heads north to Soda Springs and on to the Wyoming border. This route offers the shortest distance and time between Salt Lake City and Yellowstone Park.

Along the way you can see the remnants of the first grist mill in Idaho, one of the original Yellowstone Highway markers, the 100+ year old Mormon Oneida Academy, the site of the massacre at Bear River, Devil's Hand, the Niter Ice Cave, Last Chance canal, cinder cones from extinct volcanoes, a section of the Oregon-California Trail, and many other historical points of interest, documenting early settlement in this portion of Idaho.

Soda Springs offers numerous opportunities for visitors. Among a variety of historic attractions, the town features the world's only captive geyser, with a plume of almost 100 feet. In addition, the nearby Formation Springs Nature Conservancy Area contains a travertine-formed cave and excellent waterfowl and wildlife viewing.

This scenic byway begins at the Utah state line and follows US 91, then Idaho 34, north to US 30 and then east to Soda Springs where it meets the Oregon Trail-Bear Lake Scenic Byway. From there, north on Idaho 34 toward the Wyoming state line. US 91 is a two-land road with some passing lanes. Idaho 34 is a two-lane road with one moderately steep grade between Wayan and the Wyoming border. This is a heavy snowfall area with most winter travel being made on a snow floor. The section of Idaho 34 between Soda Springs and the Wyoming border may occasionally be closed in the winter. The byway can be seen year-round, and travelers should allow at least 2.5 hours for this 127-mile trip.

Reprinted from Idaho Department of Transportation brochure

Lower Blackfoot River Backcountry
Accessible during summer and early fall, the Lower Blackfoot River Backcountry Scenic Drive follows the Blackfoot River rim, offering unbeatable views of the canyon below. Steep canyon cliffs, aspen groves, and cottonwood trees line the entire drive, and a few pullouts provide optimal photo opportunities of the area. On the drive, visitors will also likely spot nesting golden eagles, prairie falcons, red-tailed hawks, great horned owls, and other raptor species. The route should only be attempted during daylight hours, and users are encouraged to contact the Palisades Ranger District for the latest road and weather information prior to departing.

HIKES

For information on additional area trails, please contact the Forest Service Ranger Districts listed at the back of this section.

Bannock Range Area
Corral Creek
Distance: 4 miles roundtrip
Climb: moderate
Difficulty: moderate
Usage: moderate
Location: From Pocatello, drive south on South Arthur Street as it becomes Bannock Highway and heads up Mink Creek Canyon. After reaching the signed boundary for the Caribou National Forest, proceed 4.1 miles

Section 7

WATERFALLS

Campground Falls

From the city edge of Lava Hot Springs, drive 0.3 mile east along U.S. Highway 30

Unofficially named Campground Falls due to its location within a private campground, this cataract is located at an elevation of 5,000 feet with a large watershed. Campground Falls drops 10 to 15 feet from the narrow Portneuf River into a pool below.

Lower Portneuf Falls

From Lava Hot Springs, Idaho, take U.S. Highway 30 west for 6 miles; park at an old jeep road and take an easy walk down to the Portneuf River

Lower Portneuf Falls tumbles 15 to 25 feet as the Portneuf River divides into two cataracts. At an elevation of 4,840 feet, one of the falls descends vertically as it loses contact with the bedrock surface. The other fall cascades along a series of rocky steps.

Falls along the Portneuf

From the city edge of Lava Hot Springs, drive 0.5 miles east along U.S. Highway 30, exiting onto Pebble Area Road. Continue north 2 miles to an unnamed loop in the road and park here; take a moderate walk on an undeveloped trail to the Portneuf River

North of Lava Hot Springs, ID, several small unofficially named waterfalls drop along the Portneuf River. Located along a 1-mile marshy stretch of the river, the falls require visitors to take a short but moderate walk on an undeveloped trail. Sightseers are urged to wear appropriate footwear.

The following Idaho waterfalls are also located in this section with limited directions/access available:

Houtz Creek Falls and The Falls (Auborn)

Found along Scenic Route 34 in southeastern Idaho, Houtz Creek Falls can be viewed from the road approximately 1 mile east of Pine Bar Campground. For the best vantages, visitors should be prepared to visit the cataract during the late spring and summer months. The Falls (Auborn) are located upstream from a fish hatchery.

to a road junction. Ignoring the junction, stay on Bannock Highway and locate the fenced trailhead parking area in approximately 50 yards.

Dogwood, aspens, willows, and chokecherry bushes partially shade hikers as this trail climbs beside a wildflower meadow and switchbacks up Corral Creek Canyon to the 6,490-foot summit of Corral Creek. Hikers begin with a gentle uphill climb, crossing over Corral Creek and reaching a natural spring. Although the creek and spring appear harmless, they actually contain high levels of arsenic and should not be used for drinking water (even with a filter). Continuing to climb, the trail provides views of Scout Mountain and other peaks in the Bannock Mountain Range before reaching its destination at the summit at the 2-mile mark. Best months for hiking are June and September due to cooler temperatures in the area.

Gibson Mountain Loop

Distance: 8 mile loop
Climb: moderate
Difficulty: moderate
Usage: moderate
Location: From Pocatello, drive south on South Arthur Street as it becomes Bannock Highway. 4.7 miles south of Pocatello's center and across the road from the country club, bear right (south) onto Gibson jack Road. Proceed 3.3 miles and locate the Gibson Jack Trail leaving straight from the trailhead.

This trail is thickly lined with foliage and wildflowers as it winds near Gibson Jack Creek and up a ridge to great views of Pocatello, the Pocatello and Portneuf Ranges, and Portneuf Gap. Climbing above Gibson Jack Creek, hikers will reach a trail junction at the 2-mile mark and should proceed left up the South Fork of Gibson Jack Creek. At approximately the 3.75-mile mark, veer left on the obvious trail leading up and over the densely forested Gibson Mountain. Stay to the left at all further forks as the trail climbs on the rocky ridge separating Gibson Jack Creek and Dry Creek and back down to the trailhead. Best months for hiking are June through September, with the best wildflower views found in early June.

Scout Mountain-East Fork of Mink Creek

Distance: 4 miles roundtrip
Climb: moderate
Difficulty: easy
Usage: heavy
Location: From Pocatello, drive south on South Arthur Street as it becomes Bannock Highway and heads up Mink Creek Canyon. After reaching the marked boundary for the Caribou National Forest, continue 1 mile and bear left onto the East Fork of Mink Creek-Scout Mountain Road for 6 miles. Turning right, drive past the picnic area to locate Trail 064 leaving from the East Fork of Mink Creek Trailhead.

A popular area for Pocatello residents, this trail climbs through forest up Scout Mountain's west slope, to a plateau area, and to an old beaver pond. Although the trail is scenic and worth the easy hike, hikers should expect company from mountain bikers, equestrians, and ATV users. Ignoring a trail leaving to the right at the 1-mile mark, proceed to the plateau area where views of Arbon Valley can be found. At the 1.75-mile mark, hikers will encounter another trail junction, but should disregard the trail leading east to Box Canyon. As the trail levels out, most hikers stop at the 2-mile mark beside an abandoned beaver bond. Best months for hiking are late June and September.

Optional Hikes: Hikers may opt to continue past the beaver pond 1 mile to the trail's junction with the Scout Mountain Top Road. From here, many hikers take the steep, 2-mile climb to the Scout Mountain's summit.

West Fork of Mink Creek

Distance: 6 miles roundtrip
Climb: gentle
Difficulty: easy
Usage: heavy
Location: From Pocatello, drive south on South Arthur Street as it becomes Bannock Highway and heads up Mink Creek Canyon. After reaching the marked boundary for the Caribou National Forest, proceed another 3.2 miles to the trailhead on the road's right side.

Heading up the West Fork of Mink Creek Canyon, this trail traverse between open, wildflower slopes and densely forested areas that provide a canopy of shade to hikers. A perfect hike for families, this scenic trail begins gently climbing from the trailhead, and after 0.5 miles a possible side hike trail is found. Disregard this faint trail and continue up the main trail 2.5 more miles to the headwaters of West Fork of Mink Creek. Beaver ponds characterize the area, and several hikers report moose sightings here. Best months for hiking are mid-April to mid-November.

Optional Hikes: At the 0.5-mile mark, proceed left on the faint trail that leads up Chimney Creek Canyon. This canyon is densely vegetated, and the 0.5-mile trail winds along a brook, passes a few beaver ponds, and ends at a natural spring.

Bear Lake Area

Bear Trail

Distance: 8.4 miles roundtrip
Climb: flat
Difficulty: easy
Usage: heavy
Location: From Bear Lake, locate the trail leaving at Harbor Village.

This gentle, paved trail is a perfect choice for families interested in a leisurely stroll amidst Bear Lake's beautiful scenery. The trail meanders 4.2 miles from Harbor Village to Ideal Beach. Best months for hiking are May through September.

Limber Pine Trail

Distance: 1 mile loop
Climb: flat
Difficulty: easy
Usage: heavy
Location: Near Bear Lake in Bear Lake State Park.

This gentle and popular stroll takes hikers to the famous 2,000-year-old limber pine tree still thriving in the park. Best months for hiking are May through September.

Great Western Trail

Distance: variable
Climb: moderate
Difficulty: moderate
Usage: moderate
Location: The trail passes through the Bear Lake area. Please contact local officials for more information.

The Bear Lake Valley is not only scenic, but it also claims a portion of the Great Western Trail. This extended trek that begins near the Arizona border passes through Bear Lake on its journey to Canada. Best months for hiking are June through August.

Bloomington Area

Bloomington Lake

Climb: gentle
Difficulty: easy
Usage: heavy
Location: From Bloomington, proceed west up Bloomington Canyon on Forest Road (FR) 409. Bear right at the fork in the road leading to the Bloomington Lake Trailhead.

This short trail in the wildflower meadows of Bloomington Canyon passes two popular fishing holes on the way to the spectacular Bloomington Lake. Set amidst towering granite peaks and waterfalls, this clear glacial lake is a must see. Best months for hiking are June through September.

Highline National Recreation Trail

Distance: 55 miles
Climb: moderate
Difficulty: moderate
Usage: heavy
Location: Drive south on US Highway 89 and exit onto Forest Road (FR) 411. Locate the trailhead at Beaver Creek Campground.

Hikers can choose to walk this entire trail or just a portion of it as it winds across the scenic ridge of the Bear River Mountains. However, hikers should expect company from equestrians, ATV users, as well as mountain bikers. The trail ends at the Soda Point Trailhead near the town of Grace on Highway 34. Best months for hiking are June through September.

Deep Creek Mountains Area

Deep Creek Crest

Distance: 4.4 miles roundtrip
Climb: moderate
Difficulty: difficult
Usage: light
Location: At Arbon Valley, merge off Interstate 86 at Exit 52 and follow Arbon Valley Road 24 miles to a road junction. Proceed straight at this junction on Arbon Valley Road. After 3 miles, bear right onto Knox Canyon Road heading toward the Deep Creek Mountains and locate the informal trailhead in 7 miles at the 7,330-foot pass. Park next to a dirt roadway on the pass' right side and locate the obvious trail marked "no motor vehicles" leading through the brush.

The Deep Creek Crest trail is ideal for hikers who enjoy solitude, cross country hikes, and route finding along mountain crests. Hikers will traverse over and around lichen covered limestone with spectacular views of Deep Creek Peak, Bannock Peak, and several other area peaks. Heading up the trail through the brush, the trail soon fades, so hikers should proceed toward Peak 7,814. In just 0.3 miles, this peak will be attained, and hikers should proceed east (right) around this peak. From here, hike north along a saddle to Peak 7,804 and drop down on the ridgeline, staying east of Peak 7,800 to reach Peak 7,855. At this point, bear northeast through sagebrush and wildflowers to this hike's 2.2-mile destination at Peak 7,580. Best months for hiking are June through September.

Optional Hikes: For adventurous hikers confident in their route finding skills, the Deep Creek Crest continues for approximately 8 more miles amid limestone cliffs and lichen covered boulders.

Gannett Hills Proposed Wilderness Area

Giraffe Creek Loop

Distance: 4.5 mile loop
Climb: moderate
Difficulty: moderate
Usage: moderate
Location: At Montpelier, proceed 7 miles east on US Highway 89 and exit onto Forest Road (FR) 111 (Crow Creek Road). Follow FR 111 13 miles to a road junction, and bear right onto FR 147. Continue 3.6 miles to the unmarked Boulevard Jeep Trail and turn right. Locate the trailhead in 1.8 miles next to a marked tree on the road's left (east) side. Hikers MUST have 4-wheel drive on the Boulevard Jeep Trail as the road is extremely rough.

Table Mountain greets hikers on the northern horizon and birds chirp continuously on this trail that winds through wildflowers and beaver ponds. Beginning at the marked tree, the well-groomed trail drops down into a valley of aspens and conifers and passes the first beaver pond at the 1-mile mark. Hikers will likely see moose and deer as the trail wanders past more beaver ponds to the 2.75-mile mark crossing of Giraffe Creek's left fork. Hikers will follow the creek for a short distance, climb uphill through a forested area, and reach a ridge where it is approximately 0.75 miles back to the trailhead. Best months for hiking are mid-June to late September.

Optional Hikes: Hikers can opt to follow the Giraffe Creek Trail all the way into Wyoming. However, the trail becomes much rougher and more difficult.

Lava Hot Springs Area

Petticoat Peak Trail

Distance: 4 miles roundtrip
Climb: steep
Difficulty: moderate
Usage: moderate
Location: Travel 4 miles northeast of Lava Hot Springs to locate the trailhead.

Climbing through the Fish Creek Range, hikers will end their hike at an 8,000-foot summit with panoramic views of the surrounding area. Best months for hiking are June to September.

Pocatello Area

City Creek Trail to Kinport Peak

Distance: variable
Climb: moderate
Difficulty: moderate
Usage: heavy
Location: In Pocatello, drive west on West Center Street to Lincoln Avenue. Bear left on Lincoln Avenue, and then turn right on City Creek Road to locate the trailhead.

Local hikers and mountain bikers as well as tourists have grown to love this popular trail in downtown Pocatello. While some opt to follow the trail for a short ways next to City Creek, the trail does lead to incredible area views from the pinnacle of 7,222-foot Kinport Peak. Best months for hiking are May through September.

Cherry Springs Nature Trail

Climb: gentle
Difficulty: easy
Usage: heavy
Location: From downtown Pocatello, drive south on Bannock Highway up Mink Creek Canyon. At the bottom of the hill, park at the turnout next to Cherry Springs Nature Area.

Hikers stroll next to a creek amidst beautiful and varied vegetation. Best months for hiking are May through September.

INFORMATION PLEASE

All Idaho area codes are 208

Road Information

ID Road & Weather Conditions
888-432-7623 or local 884-7000
Idaho State Police   736-3090

Tourism Information

Idaho Travel Council 800-VISIT-ID outside Idaho
                                        334-2470 in Idaho
www.visitid.org
Pioneer County Travel Council of Souther Idaho
888-201-1063
www.seidaho.org

Airports

Aberdeen	397-9910
Blackfoot	785-2727
Malad City	766-4835
Pocatello	234-6154
Soda Springs	547-9927

THE WILSON PRICE HUNT EXPEDITION

In the early 1800s, entrepreneur John Jacob Astor dispatched two separate parties west from New York City to establish a fur trading post on the Pacific Coast for his newly founded business, the Pacific Fur Company. While one group traveled by ship around the tip of South America, Wilson Price Hunt served as expedition leader for the "Overland Astorians." The group's initial journey from New York to Missouri was uneventful, but the rest of the trip would prove much more difficult.

Setting off from St. Louis in June 1810 armed with journals and maps from the Lewis and Clark Expedition, Hunt and his party abandoned river routes due to feared conflict with hostile Native Americans. Instead, the group forged their way through Wyoming's Bighorn Mountains, across the Grand Tetons, and finally arrived in eastern Idaho at the abandoned Fort Henry in October 1811. By this time, the group was weary. Several of Hunt's attempted shortcuts along the way had proven disastrous, forcing the group to survive on coyotes with little access to water. At the recommendation of his men, Hunt decided to try out a river route that would possibly decrease travel time to the Pacific Coast. After fashioning canoes from cottonwood trees and leaving their horses at the abandoned fort, the group set off down the Snake River. However, the eastern portion of the Snake River is deceptively calm, and when the men reached present day Murtaugh, disaster hit again. The peaceful river they had located in eastern Idaho had turned into impassable raging rapids causing the men to lose most of their supplies. Leaving behind the "Mad River" and now more ill-equipped than before, Hunt split his party into five small groups and ordered them to proceed on foot. These groups were plagued with sickness, disorientation, and hunger, and only thirty-five of the crew's fifty-nine original members made it to the final destination at Astoria, Oregon.

Although John Jacob Astor sold his fur company to a rival Canadian fur trapping company shortly after the Hunt party arrived in Oregon, the expedition's route was not forgotten. Thirty years later, Oregon Trail pioneers traversed across some of the same terrain. In addition, the Oregon Shortline Railroad later followed the party's route in eastern Idaho when it established a line and created a railroad station in Pocatello.

Government Offices

Idaho Bureau of Reclamation   334-1466
www.usbr.gov
Idaho Department of Commerce
          (800) 847-4843 or 334-2470
www.visitid.org or http://cl.idaho.gov/
Idaho Department of Fish and Game
          (800) ASK-FISH or 334-3700
http://fishandgame.idaho.gov
Idaho Department of Parks and Recreation
334-4199
www.idahoparks.org
State BLM Office   373-3889 or 373-4000
www.id.blm.gov

Bureau of Land Management Malad
Field Office | 766-4766
Bureau of Land Management Pocatello
Field Office | 478-6340
Caribou-Targhee National Forest | 624-3151

Hospitals

Harms Memorial Hospital
American Falls | 226-3200
Bingham Memorial Hospital
Blackfoot | 785-4100
Oneida County Hospital • Malad | 766-2231
Bear Lake Memorial • Montpelier | 847-1630
Portneuf Medical Center • Pocatello | 239-1000
Franklin County Medical Center
Preston | 852-0137
Caribou Memorial • Soda Springs | 547-3341

Golf Courses

Hazard Creek Golf Course
Aberdeen | 397-5308
Blackfoot Golf Course • Blackfoot | 785-9960
Bear Lake West • Fish Haven | 945-2744
Central Links Golf Course • Grace | 425-3233
Thunder Canyon Golf & Country Club
Lava Hot Springs | 776-5048
Montpelier Golf Course
Montpelier | 847-1981
Highland Golf Course • Pocatello | 237-9922
Riverside Golf Course • Pocatello | 232-9515
Preston Golf & Country Club
Preston | 852-2408
Krystal Lake • Shelley | 357-7329
Krystal Lake Golf Course • Shelley | 357-7329
Oregon Trail Country Club
Soda Springs | 547-2204

Bed & Breakfasts

Black Swan Inn • Pocatello | 233-3051

Guest Ranches & Resorts

Kelly Toponce Guest Ranch • Bancroft 648-7347
Pardners' Working Cattle Ranch
Bancroft | 648-0880
Andrus Working Guest Ranch
Lava Hot Springs | 776-5113

Elkhorn Guest Ranch • Montpelier | 640-3323
Riverdale Resort • Preston | 852-0266
Sheep Creek Guest Ranch
Soda Springs | 746-6276
Trail Creek Outfitters & Lodge & RV
Campground • Soda Springs | 547-3828
Coeur d'Alene Casino Resort Hotel
Worley | 686-0248

Forest Service Cabins

Caribou-Targhee National Forest
Eight Mile Guard Station
11 mi. SW of Soda Springs 847-0375
Cap: 6 Nightly Fee: $30 Available: Year Round
Beds/mattresses provided. Snow machine access in winter. Propane lights, heater, cook stove, wood stove. Bring potable water.

Clear Creek Guard Station
19 mi. NE of Montpelier 847-0375
Cap: 4 Nightly Fee: $20 Available: Year Round
Snow machine access in winter. Beds/mattresses provided. Equipped with propane lanterns, wood stove. Outhouse fac. Bring potable water.

Caribou Guard Station
45 mi. NE of Soda Springs 547-4356
Cap: 8 Nightly Fee: $30 Available: Year Round
Snow machine access in winter. Beds/mattresses provided. Propane lights, heater, cook stove.

Johnson Guard Station
20 mi. W of Afton 547-4356
Cap: 6 Nightly Fee: $30 Available: Year Round
Snow machine access in winter. Beds/mattresses provided. Propane lights, heater, cook stove.

Stump Creek Guard Station
14 mi. NW of Afton 547-4356
Cap: 4 Nightly Fee: $30 Available: Year Round
Snow machine access in winter. Beds/mattresses provided. Propane lights, heater, cook stove.

Cub River Guard Station
14 mi. SE of Preston 847-0375
Cap: 6 Nightly Fee: $30 Available: Year Round
Snow machine access in winter. Beds/mattresses provided. Propane lights, heater, cook stove, wood stove. Indoor plumbing. May-Oct. Outhouse only Nov.-Apr. Bring potable water during winter.

Car Rental

Avis • Pocatello | 232-3244
Budget • Pocatello | 233-0600
Budget Car & Truck Rental • Pocatello 234-7599
Enterprise • Pocatello | 232-1444
Hertz • Pocatello | 233-2970
Robert Allen Mercedes-Benz
Pocatello | 232-1062
Ted S Chry Ply Dodge • Pocatello | 232-3322
West Motor Company Inc • Preston | 852-1337

Outfitters & Guides

F=Fishing H=Hunting R=River Guides
E=Horseback Rides G=General Guide Services

Id Outfitters & Guides Association
800-49-IDAHO
Outfitters & Guides Licensing Board | 327-7380
Rudeen Ranches | HG 226-5591
HIgh Country Outfitters | FHE 684-5554
Outlaw Outfitters | FHEG 785-7001
Buffalo Ridge Outfitters | FHE 346-4274
White Water West, LLC | HFG 684-3121
Anderson Outfitting | FHER 237-6544
Premier Adventure Company | FHEG 238-3036
Bar H Bar Ranch, Inc | H 547-3082
Sheep Creek Guest Ranch | FHEG 540-1513
Trail Creek Outfitters | FEG 547-3828

Cross-Country Ski Centers

Pebble Creek Ski Area • Inkom | 775-4452

Downhill Ski Areas

Pebble Creek • Lava Hot Springs | 775-4452
Pebble Creek • Pocatello/Inkom | 775-4451

Snowmobile Rentals

Bear Lake CVB • Fish Haven | **945-3333**
Bear Lake Rental • St. Charles | 945-7368

Bike Rentals

Instant Replay Performance Sports
Pocatello | 233-6936
Mountain Mann Bicycles • Pocatello | 237-4139

NOTES:

Campground Quick Reference - continued

Campground Name				Phone
Public/Commercial	Unit Price	#Spaces	Max. Length	Seasons
Directions				
Amenities/Activities				

Aberdeen

Sportsman Park on American Falls Res. 678-0461
P $5 29 30' Summer
3 mi. from Aberdeen on Boat Dock Rd.
Drinking Water, Dump Station, Hookups, Playground, Reservations, Tenters Welcome, Vault Toilets, Waterfront, Handicap Access

American Falls

Indian Springs Resort 226-2174
C $12-18.5 125 Summer
Hwy. 37, 3 mi. W. of American Falls, 3249 Indian Springs Rd.
Dump Station, Hookups, Hot Springs, Pets OK, Pull-thru Sites, Reservations, Showers, Swimming Pool

Willow Bay Recreation Area 226-2688
C $11-16 24 All Year
I-86, exit 40, Hwy. 39, .5 mi., right on Marina Rd.
Credit Cards OK, Drinking Water, Dump Station, Hookups, Limited Access, LP Gas, Mini-Mart, Pets OK, Showers, Waterfront, Handicap Access

Massacre Rocks State Park 548-2672
P 43 55' Summer, Fall, Spring
10 mi. W. on I-86, exit 28
Credit Cards OK, Drinking Water, Dump Station, Hookups, Pull-thru Sites, Reservations, Showers, Vault Toilets

Pipeline 478-6340
P 5 17' Summer, Fall
2 mi. W. off Neeley Road
Pets OK, Vault Toilets, Waterfront

Seagull Bay Yacht Club 678-0461
P $10-15 45 Summer, Fall, Spring
I-86, Seagull Bay exit
Drinking Water, Dump Station, Hookups, Playground, Showers

Bear Lake

Bear Lake Hot Springs 945-4545
C All Year
7 mi. E. of St. Charles on N. Beach State Park Rd.
Mini-Mart, Pets OK, Pull-thru Sites, Showers, Waterfront, Handicap Access

Bear Lake State Park 847-1045
P $7-13 48 60' Summer, Fall, Spring
11 mi. E. of Paris on E. Beach Rd.
Credit Cards OK, Drinking Water, Dump Station, Hookups, Pets OK, Pull-thru Sites, Reservations, Tenters Welcome, Vault Toilets, Waterfront

Cloverleaf 847-0375
P $8-60 19 22' Summer, Fall
Hwy 89, 16 mi. S. of Montpelier, 7 mi. W. on Forest Rd. 512
Drinking Water

North Fork Overflow 847-0375
P 10 22' Summer, Fall
1.5 mi. N. of Montpelier on Hwy. 89, then W. approx. 8 mi.
Vault Toilets

Porcupine 847-0375
P $8-12 12 22' Summer, Fall
1.2 mi. N. on Hwy. 89 2.5 mi. W. on Hwy. 30012
Drinking Water, Pets OK, Handicap Access

Downey

Flag's West Truck Stop 897-5238
C 18 All Year
I-15, exit 31
Credit Cards OK, Drinking Water, Dump Station, Hookups, LP Gas, Mini-Mart, Pets OK, Pull-thru Sites, Reservations, Showers, Laundry, Handicap Access

Downata Hot Springs
Downata Hot Springs 897-5736
C $11-20 60 Summer
3.5 mi. S. of Downey
Credit Cards OK, Drinking Water, Hookups, Hot Springs, Pets OK, Playground, Reservations, Showers, Swimming Pool, Yurts/Teepees, Tenters Welcome, Laundry, Handicap Access

Hawkins Reservoir 478-6340
P 14 20' Summer, Fall
10 mi. W. along the Hawkins Reservoir Rd.
Pets OK, Tenters Welcome, Vault Toilets, Waterfront

Summit 547-4356
P 19' Summer, Fall
10 mi. SW on Cty. Rd. 80 N., 1.5 mi. W. on Cty. Rd., 1 mi. W. on Forest Rd. 41
Drinking Water, Pets OK, Pull-thru Sites, Reservations, Tenters Welcome, Vault Toilets

Cherry Creek 766-5900
P None 5 June-September
10 miles S of Downey on FR 047
Developed Campground, Drinking Water, Restrooms, RV Sites, Biking, Fishing, Hiking/Backpacking, Horseback Riding, Hunting, Off Highway Vehicles, Picnicking, Scenic Driving, Wildlife Viewing, Winter Sports

Georgetown

Summit View 847-0375
P $8-40 20 32' Summer, Fall
2.4 mi. E. of Georgetown on Cty. Rd. 102, 6 mi. N. on Forest Rd. 095
Drinking Water, Vault Toilets

Summit View 847-0375
P $8/sgle; $40/grp19; 3 Grp. Sites June-October
2.4 miles E of Georgetown on County Rd 102, then 6 miles N on FR 095
Developed Campground, Group Campground, Drinking Water, Restrooms, RV Sites, Biking, Fishing, Hiking/Backpacking, Hunting, Off Highway Vehicles, Picnicking, Wildlife Viewig

Grace

Central Links Golf Course & RV Park 425-3233
C $20 10 70' Summer, Fall, Spring
4 mi. S. on Anderson Road, off Hwy. 30, E. of Lava Hot Springs, M P 383
Credit Cards OK, Drinking Water, Hookups, Pets OK, Pull-thru Sites, Showers, Tenters Welcome

Lava Hot Springs

Cottonwood Family Campground 776-5295
C $19-27 83 Summer, Fall, Spring
Hwy. 30, .5 mi. past Olympic Pool
Credit Cards OK, Dump Station, Hookups, LP Gas, Mini-Mart, Pets OK, Playground, Pull-thru Sites, Reservations, Showers

Lava Spa Motel & RV Park 776-5589
C $18-27 15 All Year
On the Portneuf River across from hot springs

Mountain View Trailer Park Inc. 776-5611
C $22-29 80 36' Summer, Fall
300 Bristol Park Ln.
Hookups, LP Gas, Pets OK, Showers, Laundry

Smith's Trout Haven 776-5348/800-776-5348
C $10-13 50 Summer, Fall, Spring
1 mi. W. of town
Credit Cards OK, Drinking Water, Fire Rings, Game Room, Hookups, Pets OK, Playground, Pull-thru Sites, Reservations, Tenters Welcome

Rivers Edge RV Park 776-5209
C $10-22 87 All Year
Hookups, Mini-Mart, Pets OK, Playground, Showers

Lava Ranch Inn Motel & RV Camping 776-9917
C $20-100 9 All Year
1 mi. W. of Lava Hot Springs, 9611 Hwy. 30
Credit Cards OK, Drinking Water, Hookups, Pets OK, Playground, Reservations, Showers, Tenters Welcome, Waterfront, Handicap Access

Campground Quick Reference - continued

Aura Soma Lava

C $30   776-5800/800-757-1233   All Year
Main St. to 2nd E, N. to the River
Handicap Access

Big Springs - Lava Hot Springs

P $8   30   30'   236-7500   Summer, Fall
9 mi. N. of Lava Hot Springs on Bancroft Hwy., 8 mi. W. on Forest Rd. 036
Drinking Water, Reservations, Vault Toilets, Handicap Access

Malad City

Dry Canyon

P   None   3   766-5900   May 20-September 30
3.5 miles N of Mald City on I-15, then 17 miles E on Weston Hwy., then 6 miles W on FR 053
Primitive Camping, Restrooms, Biking, Hiking/Backpacking, Horseback Riding, Hunting, Off Highway Vehicles, Picnicking, Scenic Driving, Wildlife Viewing, Winter Sports

McCammon

McCammon RV Park Campground

C $15-19.95   50   80'   254-3630/866-254-3630   All Year
I-15, exit 47, Hwy. 30
Business Center, Credit Cards OK, Drinking Water, Dump Station, Hookups, Mini-Mart, Pets OK, Pull-thru Sites, Reservations, Showers, Tenters Welcome, Laundry, Handicap Access

Goodenough Creek

P   None   10   478-6340   June-October
From McCammon, bear 1 mile W over I-15 and take the S Fork. Travel 0.25 miles, turn right on Goodenough Creek Access Rd, and continue 2 miles.
Primitive Campground, Handicap Accessible Restrooms, Biking, Hiking/Backpacking, Off Highway Vehicles, Picnicking

Montpelier

Montpelier Creek KOA

C $16-35   50   847-0863/800-562-7576   Summer, Fall, Spring
Hwy. 89, 2 mi. E. of Montpelier
Camping Cabins, Credit Cards OK, Dump Station, Fire Rings, Game Room, Hookups, Mini-Mart, Modem Hookups, Pets OK, Playground, Pull-thru Sites, Reservations, Showers, Swimming Pool, Tenters Welcome, Laundry

Rendezvous Village RV Park

C $10-15   30   847-1100   Summer, Fall, Spring
.5 mi. N. of Hwy. 30/89 junction
Dump Station, Hookups, Modem Hookups, Pets OK, Pull-thru Sites, Reservations, Showers, Tenters Welcome

Montpelier Canyon

P $4   13   32'   847-0375   Summer, Fall
3.3 mi. E. on Hwy. 89
Drinking Water, Vault Toilets

Paris

Emigration

P $10-60   26   22'   847-0375   Summer, Fall
10.5 mi. W. on Hwy. 36
Drinking Water, Showers, Tenters Welcome, Handicap Access

Paris Springs

P $8-60   11   22'   847-0375   Summer, Fall
10 mi S. on Hwy. 89, W .4.5 mi. on Paris Canyon Rd.
Drinking Water, Vault Toilets

Pocatello

Cowboy RV Park

C $25.27   41   60'   232-4587   All Year
I-15, exit 67, 1 mi. N., right on Barton Rd.
Cable TV Hookups, Credit Cards OK, Drinking Water, Dump Station, Hookups, Modem Hookups, Pets OK, Playground, Pull-thru Sites, Reservations, Showers, Laundry, Handicap Access

Pocatello KOA

C $18-35   48   233-6851/800-562-9175   All Year
I-15, exit 71, 9815 W. Pocatello Creek Rd.
Camping Cabins, Credit Cards OK, Drinking Water, Dump Station, Fire Rings, Game Room, Hookups, LP Gas, Mini-Mart, Modem Hookups, Pets OK, Playground, Pull-thru Sites, Reservations, Showers, Tenters Welcome, Laundry, Handicap Access

Budget RV Park

C $19.20   24   237-0148   All Year
I-86, Chubbuck exit, N. on Yellowstone
Drinking Water, Dump Station, Hookups, Showers, Laundry, Handicap Access

Sullivan's Mobile Home & RV Park

C   237-3609   All Year
I-15, exit 67, 1 mi. into town on left
Dump Station, Hookups, Pets OK, Playground, Pull-thru Sites, Showers, Laundry

Scout Mountain

P $8   32   16'   236-7500   Summer, Fall, Spring
13 mi. S. on Cty. Rd. 38, 3.8 mi. SE on Forest Rd. 2000
Drinking Water, Pets OK, Pull-thru Sites, Reservations, Tenters Welcome, Vault Toilets

Preston

Riverside RV & Trailer Park

C $10-15   12   852-1569   All Year
3.5 mi. N. of Preston on the Bear River
Credit Cards OK, Drinking Water, Hookups, Pets OK, Playground, Tenters Welcome, Waterfront

Cub River Lodge and Guest Ranch

C $69-109   10   852-2124/866-400-2124   All Year
Head East off of Highway 91 between Preston and Franklin 8 1/2 miles up Cub river Canyon.
Credit Cards OK, Drinking Water, Dump Station, Fire Rings, Hookups, Hot Springs, Pets OK, Showers, Swimming Pool, Tenters Welcome

Albert Moser

P $8-16   9   20'   847-0375   Summer
3 mi. SE on Hwy. 91, less than 8 mi E. on Cub River Rd.
Drinking Water, Vault Toilets

Maple Grove Campground

P $5   12   17'   478-6340   Summer
5.5 mi. NE on Hwy 34, 3 mi. NE Hwy 36, 8 mi. N on Oneida Narrows Rd.
Pets OK, Vault Toilets, Waterfront

Redpoint

P   6   20'   766-5900   Summer, Fall
5.5 mi. NE on Hwy 34, 3 mi. NE Hwy 36, 4 mi. N. on Oneida Narrows Rd.
Tenters Welcome, Vault Toilets, Waterfront

Willow Flat

P $10-60   52   22'   847-0375   Summer, Fall
3 mi. SE on Hwy. 91, the 12 miles E. on Cub River Rd.
Drinking Water, Vault Toilets

Soda Springs

Cedar Bay Marina & RV Park

C $16   51   574-2208   All Year
Hwy. 34, 18 mi. N. of Soda Springs
Boating Facilities, Dump Station, Hookups, LP Gas, Pets OK, Reservations, Showers, Waterfront, Handicap Access

Lakeview Motel

C $29-50   12   547-4351   All Year
Hwy. 30, W. end of Soda Springs

Section 7

Campground Quick Reference - continued

Campground Name				Phone
Public/Commercial	Unit Price	#Spaces	Max. Length	Seasons
Directions				
Amenities/Activities				

Trail Motel & RV Park — 547-0240
C · · 17 · · All Year
Hwy. 30

Sheep Creek Guest Ranch — 540-1513/877-787-0301
C · $12-50 · 50 · · All Year
Lanes Creek Rd. (Diamond Creek Area)

Cutthroat Trout — 478-6340
P · · 5 · 15' · Summer, Fall
11 mi. N. on Hwy. 34, W. 4 mi. on China Cap Rd., NW on Government Dam Rd. 14 mi., N. 9 mi. on Corral Creek Rd. & Lincoln Creek Rd.
Vault Toilets, Waterfront

Diamond Creek — 547-4356
P · · 12 · · Summer, Fall
10.1 mi. N. on Hwy. 34, 11.4 mi. E. on Cty. Rd. 30C, 4.9 mi. NE on Forest Rd. 95, 12.5 mi. SE on Forest Rd. 102
Fire Rings, Tenters Welcome, Vault Toilets

Dike Lake — 478-6340
P · · 35 · 34' · Summer, Fall
11 mi. N. on Hwy. 34
Drinking Water, Vault Toilets, Waterfront

Eightmile Canyon — 547-4356
P · · 7 · 16' · Summer, Fall
13 mi. S. on Bailey Creek-Eightmile, then Forest Rd. 425
Drinking Water, Pets OK, Vault Toilets

Graves Creek — 478-6340
P · · 5 · 15' · Summer, Fall
14 mi. N. on Hwy 91, 10 mi. E. on Wolverine Creek Rd. for 13 mi., right on Trail Cr. Bridge Rd. 12 mi.
Vault Toilets, Waterfront

Mill Canyon — 547-4356
P · · 10 · 32' · Summer, Fall
10.1 mi. N. on Hwy. 34, 11.4 mi. E. on Blackfoot River Rd., 1.9 mi. E. on Forest Rd. 095, 6 mi. W. on Forest Rd. 099
Fire Rings, Pets OK, Pull-thru Sites, Tenters Welcome, Vault Toilets

Sage Hen Flats — 478-6340
P · · 5 · 15' · Summer, Fall
Hwy. 34, N. of Soda Springs 11 mi., W. 4 mi. on China Cap Rd., NW on Government Dam Rd. 14 mi., N. 8 mi. on Corral Creek Rd. & Lincoln Creek Rd.
Tenters Welcome, Vault Toilets, Waterfront

Pinebar — 547-4356
P · · 5 · 20' · Summer, Fall
45 NE of Soda Springs on Hwy. 34
Fire Rings, Pets OK, Tenters Welcome, Vault Toilets

Tincup — 547-4356
P · · 5 · 20' · Summer, Fall
Hwy. 34, 52 mi. NE of Soda Springs
Fire Rings, Pets OK, Pull-thru Sites, Vault Toilets

Gravel Creek — 547-4356
P · · 9 · 20' · Summer, Fall
31 mi. N. on Hwy. 34 to sign, then 5 mi. S.
Fire Rings, Pets OK, Pull-thru Sites, Tenters Welcome, Vault Toilets

Cold Springs — 847-0375
P · Yes · 3 · · June 1-September 31
12 miles S of Soda Springs on Bailey Creek/Eightmile Rd and FR 425
Developed Campground, Restrooms, Handicap Accessible RV Sites, Biking, Fishing, Hiking/Backpacking, Horseback Riding, Off Highway Vehicles, Picnicking, Scenic Driving, Wildlife Viewing

Morgans Bridge — 524-7500
P · None · 5 · · May-October
11 miles N of Soda Springs on Hwy. 34, then 4 miles W on China Cap Rd, then 14 miles NW on Government Dam Rd, then 14 miles N on Corral Creek Rd, Lincoln Creek Rd, and Trail Creek Rd
Primitive Camping, Restrooms, Non-Motorized Boating, Whitewater Rafting, Fishing, Picnicking, Water Sports

Trail Creek Bridge — 478-6340
P · None · 12 · · May-October
11 miles N of Soda Springs on Hwy. 34, then 4 miles W on China Cap Rd, then 14 miles NW on Government Dam Rd, then 20 miles N on Corral Creek Rd, Lincoln Creek Rd, and Trail Creek Rd
Primitive Camping, Restrooms, Whitewater Rafting, Fishing, Picnicking

St. Charles

Bear Lake North RV Park & Campground — 945-2941
C · $14-18 · 42 · · All Year
18 mi. S. of Montpelier on Hwy. 89
Credit Cards OK, Drinking Water, Dump Station, Hookups, Modem Hookups, Pets OK, Playground, Pull-thru Sites, Reservations, Showers, Tenters Welcome, Handicap Access

St. Charles Canyon Campground — 945-2407
C · · 40 · · Summer, Fall, Spring
17 mi. S. of Montpelier, 10 mi. W. of Bear Lake, 5 mi. up St. Charles Canyon
Drinking Water, Dump Station, Hookups, Pets OK, Pull-thru Sites, Reservations, Showers, Tenters Welcome, Vault Toilets

Thatcher

Maple Grove Hot Springs — 851-1137
C · $15 · 2 · · All Year
11386 N. Oneida Narrows Rd.
Boating Facilities, Camping Cabins, Credit Cards OK, Drinking Water, Fire Rings, Hot Springs, Pets OK, Reservations, Showers, Tenters Welcome, Waterfront

NOTES:

Dining Quick Reference - continued

Price Range refers to the average cost of a meal per person: ($) $1-$6, ($$) $7-$11, ($$$) $12-up. Cocktails: "Yes" indicates full bar; Beer (B)/Wine (W). Service: Breakfast (B), Brunch (BR), Lunch (L), Dinner (D). Businesses in bold print will have additional information under the appropriate map locator number in the body of this section.

MAP NO.	RESTAURANT	TYPE CUISINE	PRICE RANGE	CHILD MENU	COCKTAILS BEER WINE	MEALS SERVED	CREDIT CARDS ACCEPTED
1	Arctic Circle 606 S State St, Shelley, 357-7313	Fast Food	$	N	N	L/D	M V
1	China King 196 N State St, Shelley, 357-9973	Asian	$	N	N	L/D	Major
1	Madrigals Mexican Restaurant 190 S State St, Shelley, 357-5565	Mexican	$-$$	Y	B	B/L/D	M V
1	Mick's 398 S State St, Shelley, 357-9903	Family	$	Y	N	B/L/D	No
1	Mr Pizza 164 S State St, Shelley, 357-5560	Pizza	$	N	N	B/L/D	Major
1	Subway 532 N State St, Shelley, 357-5444	Fast Food	$	N	N	L/D	M V
1	The Taco Maker 498 S State St, Shelley, 357-2434	Mexican	$	N	N	L/D	No
1	Taqueria Alejandra 190 S State St, Shelley, 357-5565	Mexican	$	N	N	L/D	M V
2	Alder Inn 384 Alder St, Blackfoot, 785-2356	American	$-$$	N	B W	L/D	Major
2	Cowboy Heaven 50 N Spruce St, Blackfoot, 785-0155	Family	$	Y	N	L/D	M V
2	Domino's Pizza 798 W Judicial St, Blackfoot, 785-2535	Pizza	$-$$	N	N	L/D	M V
2	El Dorado 6 W Bridge St, Blackfoot, 785-6666	Mexican	$$	N	B W	L/D	M V
2	El Mirador 620 W Bridge St, Blackfoot, 785-1595	Mexican	$$	N	B W	L/D	M V
2	Hong's Take Out 977 Market St, Blackfoot, 782-1116	Asian	$-$$	N	N	L/D	Major
2	Kentucky Fried Chicken 845 W Bridge St, Blackfoot, 785-1776	Fast Food	$-$$	Y	N	L/D	Major
2	La Casita 80 Wooton Way, Blackfoot, 785-8998	Mexican	$-$$	N	N	L/D	M V
2	Little Ceasars Pizza 1355 Parkway Dr, Blackfoot, 785-0040	Pizza	$-$$	N	N	L/D	Major
2	McDonald's 1275 Parkway Dr, Blackfoot, 785-0810	Fast Food	$	Y	N	L/D	Major
2	Morenitas #3 1355 Parkway Dr 10, Blackfoot, 782-0647	Mexican	$$	N	N	L/D	M V
2	Papa Kelseys 590 Jensen Grove Dr, Blackfoot, 782-0444	Pizza	$	N	N	L/D	M/V
2	Papa Murphy's Take 'N' Bake Pizza 977 Market St, Blackfoot, 785-7272	Pizza	$$	N	N	L/D	M V
2	Pizza Hut 44 N 700 W, Blackfoot, 785-6330	Pizza	$$	N	N	L/D	M V
2	Subway Sandwiches 1350 Parkway Dr, Blackfoot, 785-1116	Fast Food	$	N	N	L/D	M V
2	Taco Bell 1475 Parkway Dr, Blackfoot, 785-2830	Fast Food	$	N	N	L/D	M V
2	Taco Time 895 W Sexton St, Blackfoot, 785-2262	Fast Food	$	N	N	L/D	M V
2	Wendy's Old Fashioned Hamburgers 1195 Parkway Dr, Blackfoot, 785-4111	Fast Food	$	N	N	L/D	M V
3	Arctic Circle 814 S Broadway St, Blackfoot, 785-2161	Fast Food	$	Y	N	L/D	M V
3	El Vaquero Restaurant 960 S Broadway St, Blackfoot, 782-1300	Mexican	$$	N	B W	L/D	Major
3	Hong Kong Restaurant 156 N Broadway St, Blackfoot, 785-7102	Asian	$	N	N	L/D	Major
3	Melina's Mexican Restaurant 321 NW Main St, Blackfoot, 785-3525	Mexican	$$	N	N	L/D	Major

Ultimate Idaho Atlas and Travel Encyclopedia

Section 7

Dining Quick Reference - continued

Price Range refers to the average cost of a meal per person: ($) $1-$6, ($$) $7-$11, ($$$) $12-up. Cocktails: "Yes" indicates full bar; Beer (B)/Wine (W), Service: Breakfast (B), Brunch (BR), Lunch (L), Dinner (D). Businesses in bold print will have additional information under the appropriate map locator number in the body of this section.

MAP NO.	RESTAURANT	TYPE CUISINE	PRICE RANGE	CHILD MENU	COCKTAILS BEER WINE	MEALS SERVED	CREDIT CARDS ACCEPTED
3	Mr Pizza 125 NW Main St, Blackfoot, 785-3785	Pizza	$	N	N	L/D	M V
5	Arby's 791 Yellowstone Ave, Pocatello, 233-3445	Fast Food	$	Y	N	L/D	Major
5	Arctic Circle 198 Yellowstone Ave, Pocatello, 232-0523	Fast Food	$	Y	N	L/D	M V
5	Bamboo Garden 1200 Yellowstone Ave, Pocatello, 238-2331	Asian	$	N	N	L/D	M V
5	Big Foot Pizza 168 Jefferson Ave, Pocatello, 233-1041	Pizza	$	N	N	L/D	M V
5	Chang Garden 1000 Pocatello Creek Rd, Pocatello, 234-1475	Asian	$	N	N	L/D	Major
5	Dairy Queen 978 Hiline Rd, Pocatello, 233-6015	Fast Food	$	N	N	L/D	No
5	Domino's Pizza 275 Yellowstone Ave, Pocatello, 232-4332	Pizza	$-$$	N	N	L/D	M V
5	El Herracero 123 Jefferson Ave, Pocatello, 233-6747	Mexican	$-$$	N	N	L/D	No
5	Golden Corral 800 Yellowstone Ave, Pocatello, 478-2057	American	$$-$$$	N	N	B/L/D	M V
5	Jeri's Jumbo's Cafe 3122 Poleline Rd, Pocatello, 237-2158	Family	$	Y	N	B/L	Major
5	Kentucky Fried Chicken 670 Yellowstone Ave, Pocatello, 233-1676	Fast Food	$-$$	Y	N	L/D	Major
5	Mandarin House 675 Yellowstone Ave, Pocatello, 233-6088	Asian	$-$$	N	N	L/D	Major
5	McDonald's 831 Yellowstone Ave, Pocatello, 233-3642	Fast Food	$	Y	N	B/L/D	Major
5	Papa Kelsey's 840 E Alameda Rd, Pocatello, 232-6931	Pizza	$	N	N	L/D	M V
5	Pier 49 San Francisco Sourdough Pizza 1000 Pocatello Creek Rd, Pocatello, 234-1414	Pizza	$	Y	N	L/D	Major
5	Pizza Hut 1151 Yellowstone Ave, Pocatello, 237-5211	Pizza	$	N	N	L/D	Major
5	Pocatello's Pizza Place 285 E Alameda Rd, Pocatello, 233-6066	Pizza	$	N	N	L/D	Major
5	Remo's Steak Seafood Pasta 160 W Cedar St, Pocatello, 233-1710	Steak & Seafood	$$-$$$	Y	N	D	Major
5	Sandbaggers Bar & Grill 296 Yellowstone Ave, Pocatello, 232-9595	American	$	N	Yes	L	M V
5	Sandpiper Restaurants East 1400 Bench Rd, Pocatello, 233-1000	American	$$	N	N	L/D	No
5	Shifters Cafe 3256 US Hwy 30, Pocatello, 232-9404	Family	$	Y	N	B/L/D	No
5	Skipper's Seafood 'N Chowder House 303 E Alameda Rd, Pocatello, 233-7751	Seafood	$$	Y	N	L/D	Major
5	Sonic Drive-in 710 Yellowstone Ave, Pocatello, 478-0134	Fast Food	$	N	N	L/D	M V
5	Subway 690 Yellowstone Ave, Pocatello, 234-0559	Fast Food	$	N	N	L/D	M V
5	Subway 1544 Pocatello Creek Rd, Pocatello, 233-2210	Fast Food	$	N	N	L/D	M V
5	Taco Bell 941 Yellowstone Ave, Pocatello, 233-9331	Fast Food	$	Y	N	L/D	M V
5	Taco Johns 249 Yellowstone Ave, Pocatello, 232-8370	Fast Food	$	Y	N	L/D	M V
5	Taco Time 1060 Yellowstone Ave, Pocatello, 233-8840	Fast Food	$	Y	N	L/D	M V
5	The Pressbox 1257 Yellowstone Ave, Pocatello, 237-9957	American	$	N	B W	B/L/D	Major

Dining Quick Reference - continued

Price Range refers to the average cost of a meal per person: ($) $1-$6, ($$) $7-$11, ($$$) $12-up. Cocktails: "Yes" indicates full bar; Beer (B)/Wine (W), Service: Breakfast (B), Brunch (BR), Lunch (L), Dinner (D). Businesses in bold print will have additional information under the appropriate map locator number in the body of this section.

MAP NO.	RESTAURANT	TYPE CUISINE	PRICE RANGE	CHILD MENU	COCKTAILS BEER WINE	MEALS SERVED	CREDIT CARDS ACCEPTED
5	Wendys Old Fashioned Hamburgers 929 Yellowstone Ave, Pocatello, 233-8383	Fast Food	$	Y	N	L/D	M V
5	Winger's Diner 696 Yellowstone Ave, Pocatello, 232-0420	American	$	Y	B	L/D	Major
6	5th St Bagelry 559 S 5th Ave, Pocatello, 235-1311	American	$	N	N	L	No
6	Blue Heeler 2735 Bannock Hwy, Pocatello, 232-8145	Tavern	$	N	B W	L/D	Major
6	Bourbonbarrel Bar 238 W Clark St, Pocatello, 232-9856	Tavern	$	N	Yes	L	No
6	Center Street Bar And Grill 542 E Center St, Pocatello, 232-9654	American	$	N	Yes	L	No
6	Chop Stick Cafe 228 S Main, Pocatello, 232-5782	Asian	$	N	N	L/D	Major
6	Grecian Key Restaurant 314 N Main, Pocatello, 235-3922	Greek	$$	Y	B W	L/D	Major
6	Jack In The Box 123 S 4th Ave, Pocatello, 478-8035	Fast Food	$	Y	N	L/D	No
6	Jimmy John's Gourmet Sandwich Shop 625 S 5th Ave, Pocatello, 478-1693	American	$	N	N	L/D	Major
6	Kowloon Express 408 S 4th Ave, Pocatello, 232-0622	Asian	$	N	N	L/D	Major
6	Little Caesar's Pizza 310 S 4th Ave, Pocatello, 232-3133	Pizza	$	N	N	L/D	Major
6	McDonald's 1011 S 5th Ave, Pocatello, 232-8268	Fast Food	$	Y	N	B/L/D	Major
6	Ming's Cafe 714 N 5th Ave, Pocatello, 232-3388	Asian	$	N	N	L/D	M V
6	New Hong Kong Restaurant 548 E Center St, Pocatello, 236-6637	Asian	$$	N	N	L/D	Major
6	Office Bar And Grill 251 E Center, Pocatello, 232-9816	American	$	N	Yes	L/D	Major
6	Papa John's Pizza 114 S 5th Ave, Pocatello, 232-7272	Pizza	$	N	N	L/D	M V
6	Pizza Hut 945 S 5th Ave, Pocatello, 234-0449	Pizza	$	N	N	L/D	Major
6	Poppa Paul's Cafe 2251 S 5th Ave, Pocatello, 233-4506	Coffee/Bakery/Deli	$-$$	Y	N	B/L/D	Major
6	Quizno's Subs 114 S 5th Ave, Pocatello, 478-4700	Fast Food	$	N	N	L/D	M V
6	Riggio's Pizza & Pasta 230 W Bonneville St, Pocatello, 233-4995	Pizza/Italian	$-$$	Y	N	L/D	Major
6	Roberto's Mexican Food 754 N Main St, Pocatello, 232-5643	Mexican	$-$$	N	N	L/D	M V
6	Ross Park Drive Inn 2340 S 2nd Ave, Pocatello, 233-3860	American	$	N	N	L/D	No
6	Sand Trap Bar & Grill 2720 Bannock Hwy, Pocatello, 232-9850	American	$	N	Yes	L	No
6	Shanghai Cafe 247 E Center St, Pocatello, 233-2036	Asian	$	N	N	L/D	Major
6	Southwest Stylin' Chicken 1836 S 3rd Ave, Pocatello, 234-0927	Family	$	Y	N	L/D	No
6	Subway 1301 S 5th Ave, Pocatello, 236-1622	Fast Food	$	N	N	L/D	M V
6	Taco Bell 1133 S 5th Ave, Pocatello, 232-3077	Fast Food	$	Y	N	L/D	M V
6	The Sand Trap Grill 2720 Bannock Hwy, Pocatello, 232-9424	American	$	N	B W	L/D	Major
6	Uncle Jim's Family Dining 1010 Pocatello Ave, Pocatello, 478-6937	American	$$	Y	B W	B/L/D	M V

All Idaho Area Codes are 208

Section 7

Dining Quick Reference - continued

Price Range refers to the average cost of a meal per person: ($) $1-$6, ($$) $7-$11, ($$$) $12-up. Cocktails: "Yes" indicates full bar; Beer (B)/Wine (W), Service: Breakfast (B), Brunch (BR), Lunch (L), Dinner (D). Businesses in bold print will have additional information under the appropriate map locator number in the body of this section.

MAP NO.	RESTAURANT	TYPE CUISINE	PRICE RANGE	CHILD MENU	COCKTAILS BEER WINE	MEALS SERVED	CREDIT CARDS ACCEPTED
7	Arctic Circle 4488 Yellowstone Ave, Chubbuck, 237-2650	Fast Food	$	Y	N	L/D	Major
7	Burger King 4508 Yellowstone Ave, Chubbuck, 237-3302	Fast Food	$	Y	N	B/L/D	Major
7	Denny's Restaurant 4310 Yellowstone Ave, Chubbuck, 238-1223	Family	$-$$	Y	N	B/L/D	Major
7	Fazolis Restaurant 4333 Yellowstone Ave, Chubbuck, 637-2900	Italian	$	Y	B W	L/D	Major
7	Geraldine's Bake Shoppe And Deli 246 E Chubbuck Rd Ste B, Chubbuck, 238-1909	Bakery/Deli	$	N	N	B/L	No
7	Johnny B Goode's 4564 Yellowstone Ave, Chubbuck, 237-6113	Family	$	Y	N	L/D	Major
7	Mama Inez Express 140 W Chubbuck Rd, Chubbuck, 237-1792	Mexican	$	N	N	L/D	M V
7	McDonald's 4260 Yellowstone Ave, Chubbuck, 237-2088	Fast Food	$	Y	N	B/L/D	Major
7	Pizza Hut 113 W Burnse Ave, Chubbuck, 237-1371	Pizza	$	N	N	L/D	Major
7	Subway 4544 Yellowstone Ave, Chubbuck, 237-5554	Fast Food	$	N	N	L/D	Major
7	Arctic Circle 4488 Yellowstone Ave, Pocatello, 237-2650	Fast Food	$	Y	N	L/D	M V
7	Leis Mongolian B-b-q 141 E Linden Ave, Pocatello, 238-7377	Asian	$$	N	N	L/D	Major
7	Me-N-Lous 4225 Yellowstone Ave, Pocatello, 237-2720	American	$$	Y	B W	B/L/D	M V
7	Pizza Hut 113 W Burnside Ave, Pocatello, 237-1371	Pizza	$	N	N	L/D	Major
7	Red Lobster 4105 Yellowstone Ave, Pocatello, 238-7700	Seafood	$$	Y	N	L/D	Major
8	Bannock Peak Truck Stop 1707 E County Rd, I-86 Exit 52, 232-9413	American	$	N	N	L	Major
9	China City 220 Harrison St, American Falls, 226-7038	Asian	$	N	N	L/D	M V
9	Fairview Inn & Catering 2998 Fairview Ln, American Falls, 226-2060	American	$	Y	B W	L/D	M V
9	Hilltop Truck Stop & Cafe Interstate 86, American Falls, 226-2697	Family	$	Y	N	L/D	Major
9	La Esperanza Panaderia Y & Restaurant 616 Fort Hall Ave, American Falls, 226-5822	Mexican	$	N	N	L/D	No
9	Pizza Hut 2840 Pocatello Ave, American Falls, 226-5707	Pizza	$	N	N	L/D	M V
9	R & B Drive In 277 Harrison St, American Falls, 226-2245	American	$	N	N	L/D	No
9	Silver Horse Shoe 572 Fort Hall Ave, American Falls, 226-9600	American/Tavern	$$	Y	B W	L/D	Major
9	Stardust Sports Bar 180 Harrison St, American Falls, 226-2855	American/Tavern	$$	N	Yes	L/D	Major
9	Tres Hermamos 2854 Pocatello Ave, American Falls, 226-2223	Mexican	$$	N	N	L/D	No
10	Country Kitchen 16 S Main, Aberdeen, 397-4980	Family	$	Y	N	L/D	Major
10	Jalisiense 14 N Main, Aberdeen, 397-3907	Mexican	$	N	B W	L/D	M V
10	The Pizzeria 27 E Central St, Aberdeen, 397-3018	Pizza	$	N	N	L/D	M V
10	Tiger Hut 386 N Main, Aberdeen, 397-3043	Family	$$	Y	N	L/D	No
11	Rockford Rows End Cafe 57 S 1200 W, Rockford, 684-4355	American	$$	N	N	L/D	Major

Dining Quick Reference - continued

Price Range refers to the average cost of a meal per person: ($) $1-$6, ($$) $7-$11, ($$$) $12-up. Cocktails: "Yes" indicates full bar; Beer (B)/Wine (W), Service: Breakfast (B), Brunch (BR), Lunch (L), Dinner (D). Businesses in bold print will have additional information under the appropriate map locator number in the body of this section.

All Idaho Area Codes are 208

Section 7

MAP NO.	RESTAURANT	TYPE CUISINE	PRICE RANGE	CHILD MENU	COCKTAILS BEER WINE	MEALS SERVED	CREDIT CARDS ACCEPTED
11	The Roadhouse 1501 W Hwy 39, Pingree, 684-9471	American/Tavern	$-$$	N	N	L/D	No
15	El Rancho Cafe 360 Hwy 30 E, Inkom, 775-4441	Mexican	$$	Y	Yes	B/L/D	Major
16	A&W/Taco Time 898 E Hwy 30, McCammon, 254-3838	Fast Food	$	Y	N	L/D	M V
16	Flying J Restaurant 115 Hwy 20, McCammon, 254-9110	American	$	N	N	B/L/D	Major
16	Riverwalk Cafe 4810 E US Hwy 30, McCammon, 776-5872	Family	$-$$	Y	N	L/D	M V
16	Subway 980 E US Hwy 30, McCammon, 254-9337	Fast Food	$	N	N	L/D	M V
16	Taco Time 898 E US Hwy 30, McCammon, 254-3838	Fast Food	$	N	N	L/D	M V
18	Burger King 295 E 50th S, Malad City, 766-5140	Fast Food	$	Y	N	L/D	M V
18	Dude Ranch Cafe 65 N Main, Malad City, 766-4327	Family	$-$$	Y	N	B/L/D	No
18	Me And Lou's Diner 75 S 300 E, Malad City, 766-2919	Family	$	Y	N	B/L/D	M V
18	Paula's Goodies & Sandwich Shop 226 E 50th S, Malad City, 766-5455	American	$	N	N	L/D	Major
18	Pizza Xtreme 93 Bannock St, Malad City, 766-2222	Pizza	$	N	N	L/D	No
18	Taco Time 226 E 50th S, Malad City, 766-8226	Fast Food	$	N	N	L/D	M V
18	Tillie's 331 S Main, Malad City, 766-2277	Family	$	Y	N	L/D	M V
20	Flags West Truck Stop I 15 Exit 31, Downey, 897-5238	Family	$	Y	N	B/L/D	Major
21	Arctic Circle 42 N State, Preston, 852-1248	Fast Food	$	N	N	L/D	M V
21	Big J Burgers 196 N State, Preston, 852-2800	Family	$-$$	Y	N	L/D	Major
21	Burger King 800 N State, Preston, 852-2170	Fast Food	$	Y	N	L/D	M V
21	Chester Fried Chicken - Kelly's Exxon 113 N State, Preston, 852-5900	Family	$-$$	Y	N	L/D	Major
21	Deer Cliff Inn Restaurant & Cabins 2016 N Deercliff Rd, Preston, 852-0643	Fine Dining	$$-$$$	Y	N	D	No
21	McDonald's 196 S State St, Preston, 852-9250	Fast Food	$	Y	N	B/L/D	Major
21	Mis Amores Mexican Restaurant 101 N State St, Preston, 852-7133	Mexican	$	N	N	L/D	M V
21	Polar Bear 145 S State St, Preston, 852-1802	Coffeehouse	$	Y	N	L/D	No
21	Subway 104 S State St, Preston, 852-2600	Fast Food	$	N	N	L/D	M V
21	Tattles Bar & Grille 790 W Onea St, Preston, 852-9156	American	$-$$	Y	B	B/L/D	V
22	Bergy's 4 N Main St, Grace, 425-9110	Family	$-$$	Y	N	L/D	Major
25	Arctic Circle 100 E 2nd S, Soda Springs, 547-3635	Fast Food	$	N	N	L/D	M V
25	Caribou Mountain Pizza And Grill 84 S Main St, Soda Springs, 547-4575	Pizza	$-$$	Y	N	B/L	M V
25	Crystal Cottage 30 W 2nd S, Soda Springs, 547-0072	Family	$	Y	N	L	M V
25	El Toro 651 W Hwy 30, Soda Springs, 547-4720	Mexican	$	N	N	L/D	No

Dining Quick Reference - continued

Price Range refers to the average cost of a meal per person: ($) $1-$6, ($$) $7-$11, ($$$) $12-up. Cocktails: "Yes" indicates full bar; Beer (B)/Wine (W), Service: Breakfast (B), Brunch (BR), Lunch (L), Dinner (D). Businesses in bold print will have additional information under the appropriate map locator number in the body of this section.

MAP NO.	RESTAURANT	TYPE CUISINE	PRICE RANGE	CHILD MENU	COCKTAILS BEER WINE	MEALS SERVED	CREDIT CARDS ACCEPTED
25	Subway 90 E 2nd S, Soda Springs, 547-4777	Fast Food	$	N	N	L/D	M V
28	Butch Cassy's Restaurant & Saloon 230 N 4th St, Montpelier, 847-3501	American	$-$$	N	B W	L/D	Major
28	Dan's Drive In 733 Washington St, Montpelier, 847-1963	Family	$	Y	N	L/D	M V
28	Dusty's Delites 818 Washington St, Montpelier, 847-0048	Deli/Dessert	$	N	N	L	No
28	El Rodeo 690 N 4th St, Montpelier, 847-0324	Mexican	$	Y	N	L/D	M V
28	Mandarin Cafe 453 S 4th St, Montpelier, 847-2088	Asian	$	N	N	L/D	Major
28	Pizza Alley 629 N 4th St, Montpelier, 847-2471	Pizza	$	N	N	L/D	M V
28	Ranch Hand Truck Stop 23200 US Hwy 30, Montpelier, 847-1180	American	$-$$	Y	B W	B/L/D	Major
28	Studebaker's Pizza 802 Washington, Montpelier, 847-3020	Pizza	$	N	N	L/D	M V
28	Subway 101 N 4th, Montpelier, 847-2353	Fast Food	$	N	N	L/D	M V
29	Paris Cafe Paris, 945-1100	American	$$	N	N	B/L/D	M V

Motel Quick Reference

Price Range: ($) Under $40 ; ($$) $40-$60; ($$$) $60-$80, ($$$$) Over $80. Pets [check with the motel for specific policies] (P), Dining (D), Lounge (L), Disabled Access (DA), Full Breakfast (FB), Cont. Breakfast (CB), Indoor Pool (IP), Outdoor Pool (OP), Hot Tub (HT), Sauna (S), Refrigerator (R), Microwave (M) (Microwave and Refrigerator indicated only if in majority of rooms), Kitchenette (K). All Idaho area codes are 208.

MAP No.	MOTEL	NUMBER ROOMS	PRICE RANGE	BREAKFAST	POOL/ HOT TUB SAUNA	NON SMOKE ROOMS	OTHER AMENITIES	CREDIT CARDS
1	Lakeview Motel & RV Lot 341 W 2nd S, Soda Springs, 547-4351	14				Yes	D/DA	Major
2	Super 8 1279 Parkway Dr, Blackfoot, 785-9333	61	$$/$$$	CB		Yes	P/DA/R/M	Major
2	Best Western Blackfoot Inn 750 Jensen Grove Dr, Blackfoot, 785-4144	60	$$$	CB	IP/HT	Yes	P/DA	Major
2	Weston Riverside Inn 1229 Parkway Dr, Blackfoot, 785-5000	80	$$/$$$/$$$$		OP	Yes	P	Major
3	Y Motel 1375 S Broadway, Blackfoot, 785-1550	23	$$			Yes	K	Major
3	Sunset Motel 1019 W Bridge St, Blackfoot, 785-0161							
5	**Red Lion Hotel** 1555 Pocatello Creek Rd, Pocatello, 233-2200	150	$$$		OP	Yes	P/D/L/DA	Major
5	**Super 8 Motel** 1330 Bench Rd, Pocatello, 234-0888	80	$$$	CB		Yes	P/DA	Major
5	AmeriTel Inns 1440 Bench Rd, Pocatello, 234-7500	148	$$$$	CB	IP/HT	Yes	DA/R/M/K	Major
5	Best Western CottonTree Inn 1415 Bench Rd, Pocatello, 237-7650	149	$$$	CB	IP/HT	Yes	P/DA/K	Major
5	Comfort Inn 1333 Bench Rd, Pocatello, 237-8155	52	$$$	CB	IP	Yes	P/DA/R/M	Major
5	Holiday Inn 1399 Bench Rd, Pocatello, 237-1400	205	$$$$	CB	IP/HT	Yes	P/DA/L/DA	Major
6	Black Swan Luxurious Theme Suites 746 E Center, Pocatello, 233-3051	14	$$$$	CB	HT	Yes	DA/R/M	Major
6	Econo Lodge 835 S 5th Ave, Pocatello, 233-0451	54	$$	CB		Yes	P/DA	Major

Motel Quick Reference - continued

Price Range: ($) Under $40 ; ($$) $40-$60; ($$$) $60-$80, ($$$$) Over $80. Pets [check with the motel for specific policies] (P), Dining (D), Lounge (L), Disabled Access (DA), Full Breakfast (FB), Cont. Breakfast (CB), Indoor Pool (IP), Outdoor Pool (OP), Hot Tub (HT), Sauna (S), Refrigerator (R), Microwave (M) (Microwave and Refrigerator indicated only if in majority of rooms), Kitchenette (K). All Idaho area codes are 208.

MAP No.	MOTEL	NUMBER ROOMS	PRICE RANGE	BREAKFAST	POOL/ HOT TUB SAUNA	NON SMOKE ROOMS	OTHER AMENITIES	CREDIT CARDS
6	Thunderbird Motel 1415 S 5th Ave, Pocatello, 232-6330	45	$$		OP	Yes	P/DA/R/M	Major
7	Motel 6 291 W Burnside Ave, Pocatello, 237-7880		$$		OP	Yes	P/R/M	
7	Pine Ridge Inn 4333 Yellowstone, Chubbuck, 237-3100	104	$$		OP/HT	Yes	P/D/DA/M/K	Major
9	American Motel 2814 S Pocatello, American Falls, 226-7271	10	$$			Yes	P/K	Major
9	Falls Motel 411 Lincoln, American Falls, 226-9658	10	$$			Yes	P	Major
10	Targhee Inn & RV 6805 W Overland, Idaho Falls, 523-1960	20	$$			Yes	P/DA	M/V/A
18	Village Inn Motel 50 S 300 E, Malad City, 766-4761	21	$$			Yes	P/R	Major
21	Plaza Motel 427 S Hwy 91, Preston, 852-2020	31	$$	CB			P/DA	Major
22	Black Canyon Motel 103 N Main St, Grace, 425-3497	49	$$$		OP	Yes	P/L/DA	Major
23	**Lava Hot Springs Inn & Spa** 94 E Portneuf Ave, Lava Hot Springs, 776-5830	27	$$$/$$$$	FB	OP/HT	Yes	P/DA/K	Major
23	Lava Spa Motel & RV Park 359 E Main St, Lava Hot Springs, 776-5589	22	$$/$$$			Yes	R/M	Major
23	Dempsey Creek Lodge 162 E Main St, Lava Hot Springs, 776-5000	3	$/$$			Yes	DA/R/M/K	Major
23	The Home Hotel & Tumbling Waters Motel 306 E Main St, Lava Hot Springs, 776-5507	38	$$		HT	Yes	DA/R/M/K	Major
23	Lava Ranch Inn Motel & Campground 9611 E Hwy 30, Lava Hot Springs, 776-9917	10	$$$			Yes	P/DA/K	Major
23	Riverside Inn & Hot Springs 255 E Portneuf Ave, Lava Hot Springs, 776-5504	17	$$$/$$$$	CB	HT	Yes	P	M/V
23	Oregon Trail Motel 196 E Main St, Lava Hot Springs, 776-5920	8	$$/$$$			Yes		M/V
25	JR Inn 179 W 2nd S, Soda Springs, 547-3366	43	$$			Yes	P	Major
25	Caribou Lodge & Motel 110 W 2nd S, Soda Springs, 547-3377	30	$$			Yes	P/K	Major
25	Trail Motel & Restaurant 213 E 200 S, Soda Springs, 547-0240	30	$/$$			Yes	P/D/R/M	M/V
25	Trail Creek Lodge 3367 Trail Canyon Rd, Soda Springs, 547-3828							
25	Enders Hotel 76 S Main St, Soda Springs, 547-4980	30		FB		Yes	D/DA	A
28	Best Western Clover Creek Inn 243 N 4th St, Montpelier, 847-1782	65		CB		Yes	P/D/R/M	Major
28	Budget Motel 240 N 4th St, Montpelier, 847-1273	24	$			Yes		Major
28	Fisher Inn 401 Boise, Montpelier, 847-1772	10	$$		OP	Yes	P/R/M	Major
28	Park Motel 745 Washington, Hwy 89, Montpelier, 847-1911	25				Yes		Major
28	Super 8 276 N 4th St, Montpelier, 847-8888	50	$$/$$$	CB		Yes	DA/R/M	Major
28	Three Sisters Motel 112 S 6th St, Montpelier, 847-2324	8	$$			Yes	P/K	

INDEX

Index

Index

Index

Ultimate Idaho Atlas and Travel Encyclopedia

Index

Index

Recommended Outdoor Guidebooks
Superior photography in these popular field guides by Dr. Dee Strickler makes wildflower identification quick and easy:

Favorite books about Yellowstone National Park

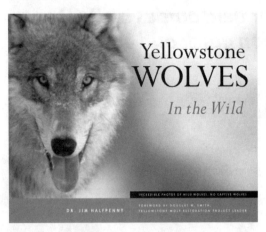

Yellowstone Wolves in the Wild
By Dr. James C. Halfpenny
Foreword: Dr. Douglas W. Smith, Yellowstone Wolf Project Leader
$19.95, ISBN 1-931832-26-9

An unprecedented portrait of individual wolves and wolf packs, and how wolves are changing the park's very nature.

"The book is breathtaking! For anyone who has traveled to Yellowstone in recent years and seen the wolves, this book is must reading." —NATIONAL WILDLIFE FEDERATION

"Captivating and thoroughly fascinating." —BIG SKY JOURNAL

"Photographically rich." —WASHINGTON POST

"Outstanding and very accurate. (Halfpenny) puts all the scientific research into common language. He filled in with personal observations. The stories really personalize what happened." — U.S. FISH AND WILDLIFE SERVICE

"A great collection of photographs and a compelling story."
—JACKSON HOLE NEWS

Yellowstone Bears in the Wild
By Dr. James C. Halfpenny
Foreword by Kerry Gunther, Bear Management Biologist
Photographs by Michael Francis
$29.95, ISBN 1-931832-79-X

From claws to cubs and fur to food, this book accurately describes the lives of grizzly and black bears in the Greater Yellowstone Ecosystem. This book features the newest discoveries about bear biology and ecology, skillfully enhanced with amazing personal stories. As a special bonus, the actual tracks of beloved Yellowstone Grizzly Bear Number 264 are imprinted on the front and back covers.

Watching Yellowstone and Grand Teton Wildlife

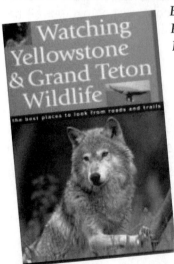

By Todd Wilkinson, Photos by Michael H. Francis
$12.95, ISBN 1-931832-27-7
Identifies the best viewing locations for 45 major species, including wolves and bears.

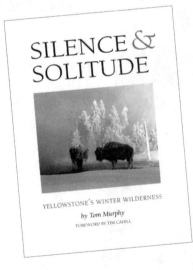

Silence & Solitude: Yellowstone's Winter Wilderness
By Tom Murphy
Foreword by Tim Cahill
$29.95
ISBN 1-931832-00-5

The highly acclaimed book about Yellowstone's longest season. Stunning photography and beautiful descriptions.

Riverbend Publishing • www.RiverbendPublishing.com • Toll-free 1-866-787-2363

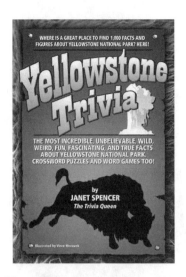

Yellowstone Trivia
By Janet Spencer, The Trivia Queen
  $9.95, ISBN 1-931832-70-6
Eye-popping, jaw-dropping, and heart-stopping facts, figures, and fun about Yellowstone National Park. Crossword puzzles and word games too!

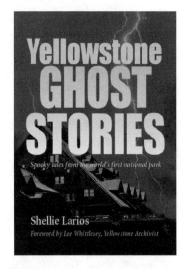

Yellowstone Ghost Stories
By Shellie Larios
Foreword by Lee Whittlesey,
Yellowstone Historian
  $9.95, ISBN 1-931832-71-4
Yellowstone National Park is haunted—or is it? Find out the spooky answers in this book. Read it late at night around your campfire— if you dare.

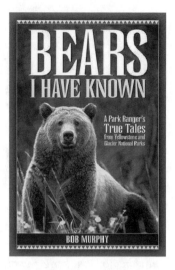

Bears I Have Known
By Bob Murphy
  $10.95, ISBN 1-931832-64-1
A former park ranger relates his most memorable experiences with bears. These first-hand stories are great entertainment and an inside look at early bear management in our national parks.

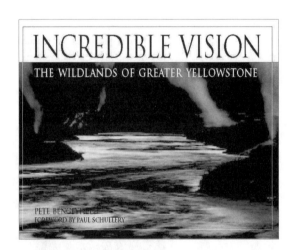

Incredible Vision: The Wildlands of Greater Yellowstone
By Pete Bengeyfield
Foreword by Paul Schullery
  $22.95, ISBN 1-931832-25-0
Exquisite color photos highlight a fascinating understanding of the forces that have shaped—and threatened—the Greater Yellowstone region.

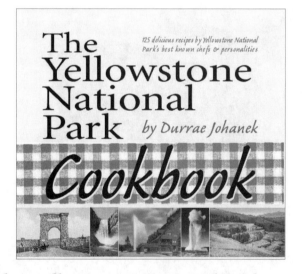

The Yellowstone National Park Cookbook
By Durrae Johanek
  $19.95, ISBN 1-931832-78-1
Great food, stories, and history make a memorable feast in this unique cookbook. More than a dozen park personalities share their favorite recipes while telling a little bit about their lives in the world's first national park.

Riverbend Publishing • www.RiverbendPublishing.com • Toll-free 1-866-787-2363

GIFT CORRAL

FINE GIFTS AND ACCESSORIES

WWW.GIFTCORRAL.COM

Searching for that perfect western gift or decorative item? Don't miss the huge selection of quality-crafted items at the Gift Corral. A full selection of their signature products are available online, including hand-made bath and body products, Moose Drool novelty items, whimsical bear and moose figurines, stuffed animals, wood carvings, Christmas ornaments reflecting the Western spirit, clothing, antler art, handcrafted jewelry, gourmet foods, Montana Silversmiths items, household décor items ranging from lamps to rustic furniture to picture frames, and much, much more!

J.S. Drake Originals Wolf Toilet Paper Holder
Made of heavy gauge metal, triple-coated with copper and sealed with a urethane topcoat, this delightful piece is durable. Complete a fun bathroom look by adding the wolf towel bar and single hook. An American artist known for his wolf, bear and deer switch plates, J.S. Drake created this piece. 10" tall, 6-1/2" long. Item # GC31163

Big Sky Carvers Last Glance — Whitetail Deer Sculpture
Montana artist Dick Idol designed this serialized and numbered cold cast bronze piece for Big Sky Carvers. Made of a bronze and resin mixture, this sculpture makes a great wildlife gift. 17" long, 5" wide, 15-3/4" tall. Item # GC39472

Huckleberry Haven 11-Ounce Huckleberry Jam Huckleberry Haven, a Western company known for its gourmet food, jams and candy, made this delicious jam. Pair this with their Huckleberry Honey for a wonderful food gift. Item # GC16561

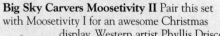

Big Sky Carvers Moosetivity II Pair this set with Moosetivity I for an awesome Christmas display. Western artist Phyllis Driscoll designed this set of resin figurines for Big Sky Carvers. The full set makes a wonderful moose gift. Drummer Boy: 2-1/2" long, 3-1/4" wide, 3-3/4" tall. Shepherd: 3-1/4" long, 3" wide, 5-1/4" tall. King: 5" long, 2-1/2" wide, 4-3/4" tall. Item # GC35676

Find these favorites and many more Western items at…

WWW.GIFTCORRAL.COM

**Mill Creek Studios
Unbearable —
Black Bear Block**
David Morales, an American artist, designed this alabaster and resin sculpture. Mill Creek Studios, a company known for its images of wolves, bears and deer, created this piece of wildlife art. One side of this sculpture features a black bear track. This piece makes a wonderful bear gift. Includes authenticity coin. 4" tall. Item # GC38081

**Montana
Silversmiths Elmer
Paper Towel Holder** Western artist Phyllis Driscoll created this handsome horse piece for Montana Silversmiths. This paper towel holder makes an impressive horse gift. 17" tall, 10" wide. Item # GC36212

Big Sky Brewing Co. Long Sleeve Moose Drool Script T-Shirt Lightweight, stylish, and comfortable, this 100% cotton white long sleeve beer t-shirt proudly sports the Moose Drool logo across the chest. Great for Skiing, Mountain Biking, Sleeping, or watching TV at your friends house. Show your love of the brown ale with this awesome beer t-shirt. Item # GC26036

Marcha Labs 9-Ounce Wool Wax Crème
Perfect for anyone from gardeners to construction workers, this lanolin-based lotion heals cracked skin and protects from dryness. The clean smell and fast absorption make this a great lotion for guys, too. This awesome cream comes from the Montana company Marcha Labs. Item # GC24066

**The Huckleberry People
Moose Grub
Beer Bread Mix**
Add one bottle of beer, knead, and bake. Huckleberry People, a Montana company known for its dry mixes, candy bars and cordials, made this delicious bread mix. Add the Moose Grub Huckleberry BBQ Sauce for an amazing food gift. 16 ounces. Item # GC29492

**Huckleberry Haven
Huckleberry Lip Balm**
Huckleberry People, a Montana company known for its dry mixes, candy bars and cordials, created this SPF 15 lip balm. Add the Huck Hand Cream for a great bath and body gift. Item # GC19654

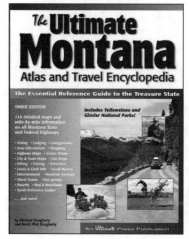